LEO BAECK INSTITUTE
YEAR BOOK

1993

Schutzjuden
oder

Staatsbürger?

von

einem jüdischen Staatsbürger.

> Es ist Arznei, nicht Gift, was
> ich Euch reiche.

The Centralverein deutscher Staatsbürger jüdischen Glaubens
was founded one hundred years ago

The brochure of 1893 by the writer and theatre director, Raphael Löwenfeld (1854–1910),
led to the formation of the defence organisation of German Jewry

LEO BAECK INSTITUTE

YEAR BOOK
1993

XXXVIII

SECKER & WARBURG · LONDON
PUBLISHED FOR THE INSTITUTE
LONDON · JERUSALEM · NEW YORK

FOUNDER EDITOR: ROBERT WELTSCH (1956–1978)
EDITOR EMERITUS: ARNOLD PAUCKER (1970–1992)

Editorial office: Leo Baeck Institute
4 Devonshire Street, London W1N 2BH

THE LEO BAECK INSTITUTE
was founded in 1955 for the study of the history and culture of German-speaking Central European Jewry

The Institute is named in honour of the man who was the last representative figure of German Jewry in Germany during the Nazi period

LEO BAECK INSTITUTE

JERUSALEM: 33 Bustanai Street
LONDON: 4 Devonshire Street, W1
NEW YORK: 129 East 73rd Street

© Leo Baeck Institute 1993
Published by Martin Secker & Warburg Limited
Michelin House, 81 Fulham Road, London SW3 6RB
ISBN 0 436 25552 9
Photoset by Wilmaset Limited, Birkenhead, Wirral
Printed in Great Britain by Clays Ltd, St Ives plc

J. A. S. Grenville
EDITOR

Julius Carlebach
ASSOCIATE EDITOR

Sylvia Gilchrist
ASSISTANT EDITOR

ADVISORY BOARD

Great Britain:	Marianne Calmann	London
	David Cesarani	London
	Ian Kershaw	Sheffield
	Jeremy Noakes	Exeter
	Peter Pulzer	Oxford
	Robert S. Wistrich	London
Germany:	Wolfgang Benz	Berlin
	Ursula Büttner	Hamburg
	Arno Herzig	Hamburg
	Stefi Jersch-Wenzel	Berlin
	Monika Richarz	Cologne
	Reinhard Rürup	Berlin
United States:	Christopher Browning	Tacoma
	Vicki Caron	Brown
	Peter Gay	Yale
	Marion Kaplan	New York
	Hillel J. Kieval	Washington
	Steven Lowenstein	Los Angeles
	Michael A. Meyer	Cincinnati
	Jehuda Reinharz	Brandeis
	Ismar Schorsch	New York
	David Sorkin	Madison
	Fritz Stern	New York
	Guy Stern	Wayne State
	Bernard Wasserstein	Brandeis
Israel:	Steven Aschheim	Jerusalem
	Avraham Barkai	Lehavoth Habashan
	Evyatar Friesel	Jerusalem
	Michael Graetz	Jerusalem
	Hagit Lavski	Jerusalem
	Robert Liberles	Beersheva
	Paul Mendes-Flohr	Jerusalem
	Chaim Schatzker	Haifa
	Shulamit Volkov	Tel-Aviv
	Moshe Zimmermann	Jerusalem

Contents

Preface by John Grenville and Julius Carlebach ix

I. GERMAN JEWS IN THE ERA OF EMANCIPATION

Marc Saperstein: War and Patriotism in Sermons to Central European Jews: 1756–1815 3
Franz Levi: The Jews of Sachsen-Meiningen and the Edict of 1811 .. 15
Christopher Clark: Missionary Politics. Protestant Missions to the Jews in Nineteenth-Century Prussia 33
Derek J. Penslar: Philanthropy, the "Social Question" and Jewish Identity in Imperial Germany 51
John M. Efron: Scientific Racism and the Mystique of Sephardic Racial Superiority 75

II. AUSTRIA, THE "JEWISH QUESTION" AND PERSECUTION

Helmut Gruber: Red Vienna and the "Jewish Question" 99
Michael Gehler: Murder on Command. The Anti-Jewish Pogrom in Innsbruck, 9th–10th November 1938 119

III. THE NATIONAL SOCIALIST YEARS: DIFFERENT ASPECTS

Rivka Elkin: The Survival of the Jewish Hospital in Berlin 1938–1945 157
Leonidas E. Hill: Walter Gyssling, the Centralverein and the Büro Wilhelmstraße, 1929–1933 193
Alan E. Steinweis: Hans Hinkel and German Jewry, 1933–1941 .. 209
Andrew Chandler: A Question of Fundamental Principles. The Church of England and the Jews of Germany 1933–1937 221
Hans Sode-Madsen: The Perfect Deception. The Danish Jews and Theresienstadt 1940–1945 263

IV. DISPLACED PERSONS AND EMIGRANTS

Ronald Webster: American Relief and Jews in Germany, 1945–1960. Diverging Perspectives 293
Yoav Gelber: The Historical Role of the Central European Immigration to Israel 323

V. SOURCES ON JEWISH HISTORY

JOSEPH M. DAVIS: The Cultural and Intellectual History of Ashkenazic Jews 1500–1750. A Selective Bibliography and Essay 343

ELISABETH BRACHMANN-TEUBNER: Sources for the History of the Jews from the Eighteenth Century to the Twentieth Century in the Archives of the Former DDR 391

BRUCE F. PAULEY: Bibliographical Essay: Recent Publications and Primary Sources on Austrian Antisemitism in the Nineteenth and Twentieth Centuries 409

VI. BIBLIOGRAPHY 425

VII. LIST OF CONTRIBUTORS 537

VIII. INDEX 541

Illustrations

Founding of the Centralverein	..	..	Frontispiece
Edict of 1811	..	..	..	..	between pp. 22–23
Innsbruck	..	..	..	..	..	between pp. 150–151
Jewish Hospital Berlin	..	..	..	between pp. 182–183
Jüdischer Kulturbund	..	..	..	between pp. 214–215
Theresienstadt	..	..	..	..	between pp. 278–279
Föhrenwald DP Camp	..	..	..	between pp. 310–311

Preface

The Year Book has been edited since 1956 by only two editors, Robert Weltsch and Arnold Paucker. For almost forty years their guiding hands provided continuity and raised the Year Book to an enviable standard of academic distinction and a world-wide reputation. During Arnold Paucker's 20-year editorship the Year Book also gained the accolade of support from the British Academy. They have been eventful years reflecting the multi-faceted history of German-speaking Jewry. In 1956, with the exception of Holocaust history, scholarship of the centuries of German-speaking Jewry and its vital role in Central European history was almost extinguished. It is in no small measure due to the first two editors and the international contributors of the Year Book – by no means only Jewish scholars – that the study of Central European Jewry and its impact on European history and the history overseas flourishes.

With the passage of time two new editors are now entrusted with the task of carrying on an unbroken tradition and they do so with some humility, conscious of the high standards that have been set. They will, in fact, be the last editors of the Year Book whose childhood was spent in National-Socialist Germany.

Perspectives change. One only has to recall the successive volumes of the Year Book to discover that under Arnold Paucker's editorship this has been fully reflected in the contributions of the last twenty years. They will continue to change.

It needs to be borne in mind that Year Book editors cannot, and should not, impose rigid editorial directives, but should be aware of, and reflect, ongoing scholarship so that the Year Book remains at the forefront of research. It has to rely on high quality contributions being submitted.

There will be some new departures. While the Year Book should continue to focus on German-speaking Jewry, the editors are keen to extend a comparative approach, so contributions may well be included which do not focus exclusively on German-speaking Jewry or "German" antisemitism.

The editors hope it will be possible to broaden even more the periods covered and to bring them into better balance, so as to cover the whole history of German-speaking Jewry from medieval to contemporary times. Despite the expense, the editors will retain the valuable Bibliography, although they are looking for separate financial support for it.

The most immediate departure has been the creation of a distinguished international board of advisers. The Year Book is the pre-eminent academic international English-language publication on German Jewry and attracts contributors from all over the world, including the Federal Republic of

Germany. The composition of the advisory board reflects this and is, consequently, large. The editors will be in regular touch with the "advisers" to help guide Year Book policy and to encourage young scholars and colleagues to submit articles.

A special note as regards Germany: the Year Book editors are making a specific effort to promote German-Jewish studies in the new *Bundesländer*.

The Year Book editors wish to reach a wide audience, not only specialists. They will continue, therefore, to pay regard to attractive and easily read presentation. As far as funds allow, the editors will also help to finance translations from languages other than English.

It will not be the custom of the editors to write obituaries unless there are exceptional reasons for doing so. With the death at the venerable age of 93 of Dr. Max Gruenewald, the Leo Baeck Institute's International President, German-speaking Jewry and the new democratic Germany have lost a link with the past and the present. When Max Gruenewald and Chancellor Helmut Kohl stood side by side to welcome the participants to the Berlin international conference of the Leo Baeck Institute in 1985, it personified a reconciliation, mutual respect and support for the living traditions of German-speaking Jewry. Dr. Gruenewald's long and fruitful life spanned several eras, as Rabbi of the Jewish community in Mannheim during the years of Weimar and National Socialism and as a member of the *Reichsvertretung* from 1933 to 1938. In 1939, at the invitation of the Jewish Theological Seminary, he emigrated to the United States and served as Rabbi of the Congregation "B'nai Israel" in Millburn, NJ, for over a quarter of a century. Among many honours and associations one of the most important was his election as President of the New York Leo Baeck Institute in 1955 and his International Presidency of the Leo Baeck Institute after 1974. As a leader of clear vision, of the highest ethical standards, he combined firmness with gentleness and a respect for individual opinions. The Institute's success over nearly four decades in maintaining the scholarly study of German-speaking Jewry during the barren years of the 1950s to its present flourishing state owes much to men like Dr. Gruenewald. His wise counsel and support leave a gap that cannot be readily filled.

During the past year the Leo Baeck Institute suffered a second grievous loss with the death of Dr. Hans Feld. His robust commonsense, good nature and sharp mind – to the age of 90 – made a vital contribution to the London Leo Baeck Institute which he served as honorary treasurer from 1977 until his death. The London Institute owes it to his good judgement that many a year of financial pressure was overcome, enabling the Institute to publish the Year Book regularly and engage in an ever-widening range of activities. His urbanity and humour contributed over the years to many enjoyable Executive meetings, even when dealing with difficult issues. Hans Feld also provided a link with Weimar Germany where he pioneered the journal *Film Kurier*. Emigrating to England he founded and edited *World Film News* and an association began with John Grierson and the British film industry. It gave him particular pleasure to be awarded the *Filmband in Gold* by the German government in 1982 and to be rediscovered by a younger generation of film-makers. The lasting impression Hans made on his many friends and colleagues was of a man who gave his unstinting help to the many causes he supported and each one, like the Leo Baeck Institute, felt that it was the main focus of his professional life. A man of immense charm, culture and experience, his contribution to the Leo Baeck Institute in London was second to none. But all of us knew that his amazing vitality was anchored in his happy and harmonious partnership with his wife Käthe. The London Board and Executive feel his loss deeply.

John Grenville *Julius Carlebach*

German Jews in the Era of Emancipation

War and Patriotism in Sermons to Central European Jews: 1756–1815

BY MARC SAPERSTEIN

It was a German-Jewish scholar, Leopold Zunz, who wrote the first systematic study of the history of Jewish preaching, published in 1832,[1] but little of his material from before the nineteenth century derived from Germany. The great tradition of Jewish preaching in the Middle Ages and early modern period was not Ashkenazic, but fundamentally Sephardic, and secondarily Italian. It was in the synagogues of the Iberian Peninsula, and later of the Sephardic Diaspora in Italy, Turkey, the land of Israel and the Netherlands, where the practice was established that a respected rabbi would deliver a sermon each Sabbath. It was the Sephardim who cultivated the sermon into an art form with a characteristic structure and a set of homiletical and rhetorical conventions.[2] Finally, it was primarily Jews from the Mediterranean basin and not from northern Europe who went to the trouble of writing the texts that enable us to know what they preached.

A late medieval German rabbi, Jacob ben Moses Halevi Moelln of Mainz, noted that unlike Jews in talmudic times, his contemporaries were "not accustomed to preaching".[3] Ashkenazic Jews established the custom that the rabbi would preach only twice a year – on the Sabbaths preceding Pesach and Yom Kippur – in addition perhaps to much more modest homiletical exercises on life-cycle events such as circumcisions,[4] weddings or funerals. And in many cases the content of these sermons was not the great theme of liberation and repentance, but rather an explication of the technical laws relating to the observance of these days or the even more technical talmudic disputes that bear upon them.

Nevertheless, it would be incorrect to dismiss Ashkenazic Jewry as barren of any significant homiletical creativity. It may be true that, unlike many of their Sephardic colleagues, most Ashkenazic rabbis did not view preaching as a major responsibility. But, particularly in Poland, there were some who did. Many communities of Poland and Central Europe appointed individuals responsible

---

[1] Leopold Zunz, *Die gottesdienstlichen Vorträge der Juden, historisch entwickelt*, Frankfurt a. Main ²1892; the Hebrew translation, *Ha-Derashot be-Yisra'el*, Jerusalem 1954, is supplemented with important additions by Hanokh Albeck.
[2] See Marc Saperstein, *Jewish Preaching 1200–1800*, New Haven 1989, pp. 63–77.
[3] Jacob ben Moses Halevi Moelln (MaHaRIL), *Hilkhot Hol ha-Mo'ed*, p. 25b (see Saperstein, *Jewish Preaching*, p. 27).
[4] Jacob Elbaum, 'Shalosh Derashot Ashkenaziyot Qedumot mi-Q[etav] Y[ad] Beit ha-Sefarim', *Kiryat Sefer*, 48 (1973), pp. 340–347, on sermons at circumcisions in the thirteenth century.

for delivering a sermon each Sabbath to the position called "Maggid". By the late eighteenth century, the title "Maggid" could be almost as prestigious as "Rabbi". In addition, itinerant preachers having no contract with a particular community would travel from town to town – and sometimes to the big cities – in the hope of being allowed to preach on a fee for service basis.

These men, some of whom were extremely talented, developed an Ashkenazic preaching tradition of considerable quality. Two elements in particular seem to have been cultivated with unique success in the popular preaching of Ashkenazic Jews. The first is the illustrative parable, or *mashal*. Now of course this rhetorical device goes back to the Bible and the rabbinic *aggadah*; it was used by medieval Jewish philosophers and Sephardic preachers throughout the centuries. But never before had it become the supple, flexible rhetorical tool that would both entertain the listeners and drive home a serious lesson in an unforgettable manner, as it had at the hands of a preacher like the Maggid of Dubno (Jacob Kranz).[5]

The second characteristic is humour. The reason is not clear, but in Sephardic preaching humour is rare while in Ashkenazic preaching it is common. Many sources confirm the listeners' delight in the humour they heard from the pulpit.[6] Some contemporaries were incensed; they considered this style of preaching indecorous. "It is their foolish way", wrote a seventeenth-century Polish critic about some of his colleagues, "to mix humorous content into their rebukes so that the entire audience bursts out laughing. There is hardly any difference between them and the comedians at wedding feasts."[7] Nevertheless the style continued, and the mode of witty, semi-facetious interpretations of biblical verses and well-known rabbinic statements acquired a technical name: the interpretation *be-derekh halatsah*. This is to be found everywhere: in the preaching of Central and of Eastern Europe, in the preaching of *Hasidim* and their opponents. Indeed, there are indications that the humorous comments were often removed when a preacher prepared his material for publication, suggesting that the humour in the average sermon was greater than that indicated in the written texts.[8]

Most of these generalisations are based on the popular preaching of the Yiddish-speaking *maggidim* in Poland. (When such individuals ventured into German synagogues, they were sometimes treated with a certain contempt because of what was regarded as their all but unintelligible "jargon".)[9] Does this mean that the established rabbis of the German-speaking communities in eighteenth-century Central Europe had neither interest nor talent in homiletical endeavours? Not at all. During this period, Prague became one of the most important centres of Jewish preaching in Europe. While German-speaking rabbis did not deliver sermons every week, some of them were widely known for

[5] On the controversy over the use of the *mashal* in preaching, see Saperstein, *Jewish Preaching*, pp. 100–103, 427.
[6] Haim Hillel Ben-Sasson, *Hagut ve-Hanhagah*, Jerusalem 1959, p. 45; Jacob Elbaum, *Petihut ve-Histagrut*, Jerusalem 1990, p. 244.
[7] The remark is quoted in Ben-Zion Dinur, *Be-Mifneh ha-Dorot*, Jerusalem 1955, p. 138.
[8] See the examples cited in Saperstein, *Jewish Preaching*, p. 23.
[9] See Benno Heinemann, *The Maggid of Dubno and His Parables*, New York 1967, p. 242, citing Abraham Flahm, *Shemen ha-Ma'or*.

their homiletical talent, originality and power. Moreover, in their sermons are new themes, bearing on some of the most significant transformations of modern Jewish life.

The background for this development is the Seven Years' War. In a dazzling re-alignment of European powers, Britain and Prussia were pitted against France, Austria and Russia, and patriotic sentiments welled up in all of these countries. Did the Jews share in these sentiments? This was, it should be noted, a generation before the beginning of the Emancipation. Juridically, Jews were not yet full and equal citizens of Britain or France; in the popular consciousness they were considered to be a foreign nation, living as guests of the host country, often speaking a different language from the vernacular of the majority, restricted by special legislation, precluded from living in many cities. The historic memory of expulsion remained powerful. Jews did not serve in the armed forces of any of the combatants. They had often lived on opposite sides of the battle lines between nations; so long as the actual fighting was far away, they do not seem in the past to have felt much personal psychological stake in its outcome. Would the Jews of the Austrian Empire now identify with the armies of the Empress Maria Theresa, who had prohibited them from living in Vienna and had expelled them from Prague only thirteen years before the outbreak of the war? Would the Jews of Prussia identify with the armies of Friedrich der Grosse, who prohibited most of them from living in Berlin and had limited their economic activities and imposed harsh tax burdens in the legislation of 1750?[10] Would they share the attitudes of their Christian neighbours towards the "enemy"?

A partial answer to these questions may be found by referring to a new kind of occasional sermon.[11] There had long been special occasions for preaching to supplement the sermons delivered on the Sabbath and holidays and at events such as circumcisions, marriages and funerals. There were also other occasions that directly affected the Jewish community: celebrations, for the dedication of a new synagogue, common deliverance from a danger or threat, appointment of a new rabbi, completion of a book, even the ceremonial visit of a notable dignitary to the synagogue; or summons to repentance and prayer because Jews were suffering or in serious danger, either in the community or far away. Now for the first time, Jews began to be included in public expressions of mourning and celebration for events concerning the nations in which they lived. A new occasion for Jewish preaching came into being: the synagogue service on a day ordained

---

[10]Cf. the discussion of the Jews in Prussia in Michael A. Meyer, *The Origins of the Modern Jew. Jewish Identity and European Culture in Germany 1749–1824*, Detroit 1967, pp. 23–25.

[11]There are, to be sure, methodological problems in using sermons as evidence for the attitudes and views of the community as a whole. In some cases, the points that a preacher chooses to emphasise in his sermons may be selected because he considers them to be a matter of contention and not part of a shared consensus. Nevertheless, unlike the writer of a book, who may represent no one other than himself, the preacher faces an audience that may react strongly and immediately to statements with which they disagree (see Saperstein, *Jewish Preaching*, pp. 54–57). We may assume, therefore, that views expressed in these sermons are not unrepresentative of those shared by many in the congregation. Particularly on public occasions, such as the ones described below, the preacher's role is to represent the congregation, not to convince it of views it rejects.

by the government for public prayer. What was actually said in these sermons is very significant.

In the Great Synagogue of the Ashkenazic community in London, a recent arrival from Germany, originally from Galicia, was Rabbi Hirschel Levin, known in England as Hart Lyon.[12] The manuscript collection of his sermons includes four delivered on special occasions connected with the Seven Years' War. The first was delivered near the beginning of the war, when British military reverses and severe economic hardship had produced a crisis in national morale. The central theme, appropriate for a day of national fasting, was the need for repentance. Levin emphasised the obligation of Jews to serve their King through prayer, conceding that Jews could make little contribution in actual military service. He evoked the economic pressures and political turmoil caused by the war, and reflected on its causes:

> "We see that sometimes kings quarrel with each other over matters that seem trivial, and eventually go to war for a reason no rational person could believe to be the actual cause of the fighting. The real reason, however, is known by the kings, about whom the wise king Solomon testified, *The mind of kings is unfathomable* (Proverbs XXV:3). They can foresee what will eventually develop from this trivial matter, and they therefore anticipate and go to war to prevent evil times."[13]

While the tone of this passage is open to different interpretations, the thrust is clearly that the sovereign must be trusted and supported even if the ordinary subject cannot understand all of his decisions.

A second sermon was delivered in a very different spirit; it was on a day "ordained by the King" as an occasion for public celebration following a military victory. Rabbi Levin raises a moral issue of relevance not only in its own day:

> "How can people rejoice at the destruction of their fellow human beings? Look how many thousands have died as a result of the great battles of our times. Many have been killed, many drowned in the sea, many kingdoms have been devastated, become desolate overnight, wholly consumed by terrors. Is this good in God's sight? If God did not want to destroy those pagan nations that lived in antiquity, that did not believe in God or His salvation at all . . . how much more is this true for the nations among whom we, the people of Israel, find refuge, who treat us with kindness and mercy, who are religious and act in accordance with the values of truth, justice and peace. God forbid that we should rejoice in their downfall! On the contrary, we should look out for their well-being, and pray for their peace."[14]

The nature of the occasion requires the preacher to provide a solution to his question that will justify the celebration: if one person is attacked by another and kills the aggressor in self-defence, it is appropriate to rejoice, not that someone has been killed, but that the endangered individual has escaped harm, and this is true also of conflicts between countries. We see here evidence of a new Jewish consciousness about the problems of warfare between nations that are founded on ethical and religious principles of conduct and were on the whole well-disposed to the Jewish people. The welfare of all these nations is a matter of concern to God. Yet nations may be aggressors, and the defeat of these nations

---

[12] On Levin see Saperstein, *Jewish Preaching*, pp. 347–358.
[13] *Ibid.*, p. 353.
[14] Hirschel Levin, "Derashot", Jewish Theological Seminary, New York, MS R 79 (Adler, 1248), fol. 23b.

can be a legitimate cause for rejoicing. Rarely before had the battles between Gentile nations become a matter of internal Jewish concern in a context devoid of any messianic speculation.

Hirschel Levin was not the only Jewish thinker to wrestle with the implications of the Seven Years' War. After the stunning Prussian victory over the Austrian forces at Leuthen (5th December 1757), Moses Mendelssohn wrote a sermon of thanksgiving that was delivered by Rabbi David Fraenkel in Berlin, published in German, then immediately translated into English and published in London.[15] The sermon is remarkable in that it gives virtually no indication that it was written and preached by Jews. Two rabbinic statements in the sermon are cited as they might have been by a knowledgeable Christian, not subjected to the detailed analysis such statements usually undergo at the hands of Jewish preachers. Particularly appropriate for the context is God's rebuke of the angels for singing praises while the Egyptians were drowning in the sea (B. Meg 10b). Throughout the discourse, this universalistic concern is combined with patriotic fervour.

Thus the sermon affirms that the proper form of thanksgiving for the victory of the Prussian army against the more numerous Austrian forces was to fulfil vows of benevolence for the relief of the poor, especially the widows and orphans of soldiers who gave their lives for their country. Furthermore, King Friedrich II presented a model worthy of emulation in his public expression of gratitude to God – a role played by King George II in the London sermons of Hirschel Levin. God is providentially responsible for the victory, but human beings are expected to do all they can to prepare the best possible military tactics and fight with bravery. Finally there is an affirmation that,

> "we are all children of the one living God. They who declare themselves our Enemies, are equally the work of his Hands, and love and fear him; and we should love them, were they not seduced by perverse Passions to disturb the Tranquility of our dear sovereign."

The publication of this sermon in German and English soon after its delivery shows that Jews wanted their Christian neighbours to be aware of the enlightened patriotic sentiments being expressed in the synagogues.

Needless to say, the Seven Years' War was perceived quite differently by those Jews living in the nations of the opposing coalition. At the outbreak of the hostilities (5th September 1756), Rabbi Ezekiel Landau composed a public prayer to be used with accompanying Psalms in all synagogues of the realm, appealing to God to grant the Empress Maria Theresa and the Austrian armies good fortune in the war. A few months later (22nd December 1756) Landau and the other leaders of Prague Jewry proclaimed a ban of anathema on any Jew who

---

[15]This sermon is mentioned in Meyer, *The Origins of the Modern Jew*, p. 24; Alexander Altmann, *Moses Mendelssohn. A Biographical Study*, Alabama 1973, p. 68. Both discuss the circumstances of the sermon but not its content, although Altmann identifies it as "the earliest known specimen of modern Jewish preaching in the German tongue". The German text is entitled *Dankpredigt über den grossen und herrlichen Sieg . . . bey Leuthen . . .* Berlin 1757; the English version is *A Thanksgiving Sermon for the victory [of Leuthen]*, London 1758. I have used the copy of the English text in Harvard's Houghton Library; I have not been able to consult the German text. On the Battle of Leuthen see Robert Asprey, *Frederick the Great*, New York 1986, pp. 475–481.

might harm "our most gracious Queen" in even the slightest manner by aiding the enemy as spies. The text of both the prayer and the proclamation was printed in German and distributed.[16] In June 1757, the Jews of Prague gathered in the *Altneuschul* to thank God for the Austrian defeat of the Prussian forces at Kollin, which thwarted Friedrich's attempt to capture Prague.[17] In a sermon delivered at the *Hochsynagoge* in 1766, Zerah Eidlitz recalled the trauma of those days: "We were in mortal danger when we were besieged by the Prussian king; we feared for our lives night and day, and they plundered and ravaged us."[18]

Thus we see that Jews on both sides of the war that convulsed Central Europe showed a keen interest in the fortunes of their side, both when it directly affected their own welfare, as in Prague, and when it did not, as in London and Berlin. In each case, it is the monarch who serves as the embodiment of aspirations, a symbol of goodness and piety, with which the Jews as well as their Christian neighbours can identify.

This is particularly surprising with regard to the Austrian Empress. Maria Theresa is widely known to historians as one of the most anti-Jewish monarchs of her age; her personal antipathy was well recognised by contemporaries. In addition to her role in the expulsion of the Jews from Prague, her government imposed confiscatory taxes on Jewish subjects, at one point considering an unprecedented levy on the etrogim necessary for the observance of Sukkot.

Yet, when the Empress fell ill in 1767, Rabbi Ezekiel Landau composed a prayer for her recovery and had it printed in German, together with calls for public fasting and another extravagant prayer of thanksgiving for her return to health.[19] And when she died in 1780, Landau eulogised her in a ceremonial gathering at the Meisl Synagogue in Prague (10th December 1780) in a sermon filled with professions of the most profound admiration and deep personal grief; praising her abilities as a ruler; her courage as a leader in war; her capacity to inspire the dedication and sacrifice of her soldiers; her commitment to social welfare programmes; even her Christian piety. This eulogy was a sincere expression of Landau's recognition that the monarch was more than the source of a particular policy towards the Jews and his appreciation of qualities that were widely admired throughout the realm. As we are told that Christian notables from the government and the army attended the service in the synagogue, we may assume that the eulogy was delivered in German. It was published soon after in Hebrew and in two German editions, one in German type, the other in Hebrew characters.[20]

---

[16]Otto Muneles, *Bibliographical Survey of Jewish Prague*, Prague 1952, p. 79, items 261 and 262; Yekuthiel Kemelhar, *Mofet ha-Dor*, Pietrokov 1934, pp. 30–35. Muneles states that it was a "Hebrew prayer", but Kemelhar makes it clear that the printed text was in German and that he had it translated into Hebrew for his book.

[17]Muneles, *op. cit.*, p. 80, item 266.

[18]Zerah Eidlitz, *Or La-Yesharim*, Prague 1785, p. 22d. A translation of the full passage is in Saperstein, *Jewish Preaching*, pp. 86–87 (the page reference cited there in note 18 should be corrected to 22c–d). On the Siege of Prague and the Battle of Kollin see Asprey, *Frederick the Great*, pp. 445–458; and Hans Delbrueck, *History of the Art of War*, 4 vols., Westport, CT 1985, vol. IV, pp. 340–344.

[19]Muneles, *op. cit.*, p. 83, item 282; Kemelhar, *op. cit.*, pp. 65–68.

[20]Landau, *Derush Hesped . . . 'al Mitat ha-Qaisarit Maria Theresa*, Prague 1780. See Marc Saperstein, 'In Praise of an Anti-Jewish Empress', *Shofar*, 6 (1987), pp. 20–25.

Sermons to Central European Jews

These sermons delivered in London, Berlin and Prague represent an important new phenomenon in Jewish life. They are all occasioned not by a holiday in the Jewish calendar, or by an occurrence that primarily affects the Jewish community, but by historical events in which Jews participate as part of the surrounding society. They all express a sense of personal loyalty to the political ruler of the realm in which the preacher and his listeners live, and an identification with the fate of the nation's armed forces, feelings that were shared with their Christian neighbours. In short, they point to the striking psychological transformation within major Jewish communities of Central and Western Europe preceding the emancipation that might be called an incipient patriotism.

But what about the attitude towards armies and war? Judaism is not a pacifist tradition. Jews of antiquity are known to have fought as bravely and as fiercely as any other people. This tradition was not abandoned in the Middle Ages. During the periods of the First Crusade, the Black Death, and, later, the Cossack uprising of 1648–1649, Jews armed themselves and attempted to defend their communities. But these were cases of Jews fighting for Jewish lives and possessions. On the whole, military activity was not a Jewish practice in the Middle Ages; Samuel the Nagid, who led the army of the eleventh-century Berber princedom of Granada in at least seventeen campaigns, was an anomaly. Medieval Jews may have read of ancient Jewish armies with nostalgia, and turned to arms as a last resort in times of immediate danger, but most of them did not have much use for the exploits or the values of contemporary Christian or Muslim armies, except insofar as they might figure in some eschatological scenario. Let us recall that the dominant tradition in illustrating both manuscript and printed Haggadahs was to depict the "wicked son" as a soldier.[21]

The prevalent outlook is expressed in *Sefer Hasidim*, that fascinating compilation of the superstitious beliefs, ethical ideals and spiritual aspirations of the German-Jewish Pietists in the High Middle Ages. "One should always think intelligently and reverently about how the ingenious ruses of the world can be honourably redeemed", we are told.

> "Look how a man takes his life in his hands to go into a place of danger for his own glory. For example, knights will enter the thick of battle, ready to sacrifice their lives for their glory, to avoid being shamed. Similarly, noble women who become pregnant from their adulterous affairs devise ingenious ruses so they will not be shamed. The same is true of thieves. If this is so for temporal glory, how much more ingenuity should be devoted to the glory of the Creator."[22]

In this passage, knights, together with adulterous women and thieves, serve as examples of human ingenuity and energy misdirected to the attainment of personal glory and the avoidance of personal shame. The lesson for the Jew is simple: if people have such devotion for a misguided purpose, it is inconceivable for you to slacken in your devotion to a religious end.

This theme was developed and transformed by Jonathan Eybeschuetz, the

---

[21]Yosef Hayim Yerushalmi, *Haggadah and History*, Philadelphia 1975. It is striking that the military exploits of Samuel the Nagid are not mentioned in Abraham ibn Daud's *Sefer ha-Kabbalah*, written c. 1161, a major source for our knowledge of his career.

[22]*Sefer Hasidim* (Parma MS), ed. by Jehuda Wistinetzki, Frankfurt a. Main 1924, §985, p. 242.

brilliant and controversial rabbi from Prague who served in the Alsatian community of Metz. This is what he said on 25th January 1745, in a sermon delivered upon hearing the news of the expulsion of the Jews from Prague.

> "There are many nobles and dukes among those who serve human kings. They pay no attention at all to ordinary desires. In times of war, they lie upon the ground, ignoring the furious torrents of hail or rain. Sometimes they sleep in villages that their servants' servants would not deign to live in. They go for days without bread, meat and wine. When the war begins, they stand at the head of their troops. They deny themselves sleep. Their garments are splattered with the blood of the fallen. Yet they pay no attention to all this. On the contrary, they long for it, knowing that in this way they will be praised in the royal palace and find favour in the sight of the king and the court."

Eybeschuetz goes on to draw the appropriate religious moral: "How can one not learn from this to annul every desire for the vanities of this world in order to serve the King of kings and find favour in His sight."[23]

The affinities with the *Sefer Hasidim* passage are clear, but there is also a world of difference. The eighteenth-century preacher devotes considerable rhetorical energy to his description of the king's officers. They are not dismissed with contempt as misguided fools, but depicted with what appears to be considerable admiration. A small, but crucial, change has been introduced: these soldiers are motivated not merely by a desire to avoid personal shame, but by love for their king. The discipline and devotion of the soldier fighting for his country has become a positive model for the Jew to emulate in the spiritual arena appropriate for the Jew.

This passage points in two directions. One is an increased use of military imagery to characterise Jewish spirituality: the Jew as God's soldier – in one extreme formulation, "God's Cossacks" – who musters all the self-discipline and unquestioning obedience of army life to fight the spiritual battle, against temptation within and the mystical realm of the *kelippot*("husks"), the forces of evil and impurity that Jewish mystics believed to be prevalent throughout the world in which we live. This became part of the rhetoric of the later *Musar* movement; we find it expressed in a powerful speech in Feierberg's classic *Le'An?* (Whither?).[24] But another direction is to a more positive evaluation of the actual armies, a tendency towards the glorification of military values expressed not in the spiritual domain but in training exercises and parades and the battlefield. There is some evidence that in the late eighteenth and early nineteenth century Jews in Central European countries began to feel these emotions as well.

Jewish leaders reacted with some ambivalence to this development. In a sermon of 1780, Eliezer Fleckeles, one of the leading rabbis and preachers of Prague, criticised the practice of Jews going on excursions during the month of *Elul* to observe military exercises of the army and cavalry, when they should have been preparing for the High Holy Days.[25] But in the same year, the Chief Rabbi,

---

[23] Jonathan Eyebeschuetz, *Ya'arot Devash*, Jerusalem 1968, vol. I, p. 50a.
[24] Rabbi Israel Meir Ha-Kohen, the "*Hafetz Hayyim*", is said to have referred to the rabbis and students of an East European *yeshivah* as "Gott's Kozak'n", a term he intended as a compliment. See Irving Greenberg, in *Sh'ma*, vol. 10, No. 187 (8th February 1980), p. 55; M.Z. Feierberg, *Whither? and Other Stories*, Philadelphia 1973, pp. 156–162. The phrase "Tsiv'os ha-Shem" (God's armies) has been extensively used in the rhetoric of Lubavitch, especially in literature intended for children.
[25] Eliezer Fleckeles, *Olat Hodesh*, Prague 1785, p. 73a.

Ezekiel Landau, eulogising the Empress Maria Theresa, spoke of the devotion she inspired within the Austrian armed forces: "In times of war, we saw that all her subjects actually risked their lives for her. Those in the army, from the highest officers to the lowly privates, stood their ground and fought her battle with all their might."[26] Here the bravery and self-sacrifice of soldiers is clearly presented as a value in its own right.

A few years later, Landau was confronted with a very different situation. As part of the process of improving the civil status of Jewish subjects and integrating them into the surrounding society, Emperor Joseph II had made the Jews in the Austrian Empire liable for military service, the first European ruler to do so. On 10th May 1789, Landau stood before 25 young Jews and their officers as they prepared to leave Prague for their basic training. His German address to these young men was recorded in Hebrew characters in *Hame'asef*, the Hebrew periodical of the Berlin Jewish Enlightenment.

Most of the speech is an appeal to the novice soldiers not to forget their religion or be ashamed of their Jewish identity, to continue to observe the obligations of prayer, Sabbath, and dietary laws even in their new circumstances. But the climax, delivered, we are told, with tears running down the speaker's cheeks, makes a rather different point.

> "Earn for yourselves and for our entire nation gratitude and honour, so that all will see that the Jewish people, persecuted until now, loves its sovereign and its government, and is ready, if necessary, to offer up their lives [for their sake]. It is my hope that through you – if you will behave honourably and loyally as is the duty of every subject – those remaining neck-chains that to some extent continue to oppress us will be removed."[27]

There is certainly ambivalence here, but this passage does not suggest that Landau viewed induction of Jews into the Emperor's army as an unmitigated calamity, as some writers have suggested. It certainly presents an obstacle and a challenge to Jewish observance, but it is also an opportunity to demonstrate the loyalty to the Emperor that many felt deeply.

Within a few months, Landau was preaching a thanksgiving sermon at a public gathering to celebrate the victory of Joseph II's Austrian army in their siege of Belgrade against the Ottoman Turks.[28] Landau vigorously affirms the high ethical standards of his sovereign and the justice not only of his cause but of his method of warfare. "Before he began this conflict, he gave warning to his enemies, as is known from his Manifesto. The Muslims were the aggressors in the war. If they did not commence against the Emperor himself, they began against

---

[26] Landau, *Derush Hesped*, p. 5b; Saperstein, 'In Praise', p. 21.

[27] *Hame'asef*, 5 (1789), p. 254. The full German text of the speech is given by Ruth Kestenberg-Gladstein, *Neuere Geschichte der Juden in den böhmischen Ländern. Erster Teil. Das Zeitalter der Aufklärung 1780–1830*, Tübingen 1969 (Schriftenreihe wissenschaftlicher Abhandlungen des Leo Baeck Instituts 18/1), pp. 70–72, as part of her discussion of the first conscription of Jewish soldiers. A very free and somewhat unreliable Hebrew translation is given by Aryeh Gelman, *Ha-Noda' bi-Yehudah u-Mishnato*, Jerusalem 1962, pp. 128–129.

[28] *Derush ha-Shevah ve-ha-Hoda'ah 'al Hatslahot Adonenu ha-Qaisar Yosef ha-Sheni Be-Lakhdo 'Ir ha-Betsurah Belgrad 'al Yedei Sar Tsava' ha-Mefursam Baron Landau*, Prague 1790. On the first page Landau gave exclusive rights to publish the sermon to Abraham Kish, a poor man, in the hope that he would make a profit from it.

his allies . . . Thus all that the Emperor and his officers did in this war was done justly."

The ethical qualities of the "field marshals and generals" are also emphasised. Finally, the most decisive proof of divine favour for the Austrian cause was that the city was taken without Austrian casualties. "As soon as the Field Marshal gave the signal and commenced firing a heavy bombardment, they immediately surrendered and sued for peace."[29] Although there was no blatant violation of the laws of nature, this was a miracle, a "hidden miracle" like many of those in the Bible, revealing God's providence.

Very similar themes, accompanied by even greater patriotic fervour, are revealed in the sermon delivered by Ezekiel Landau's son, Samuel, in the Meisl Synagogue in Prague on 7th July 1814.[30] It was a heady, exhilarating time. The Austrian Emperor Franz I had just returned to Vienna from Paris, following the occupation of the French capital by the European allies and the abdication of Napoleon; the stage was being set for the Congress of Vienna. Not surprisingly, the transformation of European politics is placed in an explicitly providential context:

> "We have seen the great victory and triumph of our sovereign king, the Emperor Franz, may His Majesty be exalted, whom God has chosen for this great work of liberation: to free kingdoms and states from their suffering.[31] We and all the inhabitants of Europe were distraught because of the chaos of war, subjugated by the power of the aggressor [Napoleon], forced to toil under a heavy yoke. Now by the enormous power of his heroic armies, he has prevailed, conquering the enemy, bestowing peace upon all the lands of Europe. God has delivered them through our sovereign, the Emperor Franz."

He cannot simply assert that victory proves God's favour, as Napoleon himself had been astoundingly successful on the battlefield. Landau therefore argues that the proof of God's providence lies in the noble qualities of the leaders of the anti-Napoleonic forces.

> "We have proof that this liberation is permanent, that cynical men will oppress us no more. For it was wrought through our sovereign, the pious and merciful ruler, who acts justly and charitably toward his servants, the subjects of his state. Furthermore, the kings who were his allies – the Emperor of Russia [Alexander I] and the King of Prussia [Friedrich Wilhelm III] – are all pious and act charitably and graciously . . ."

Most of the preacher's emphasis, however, is not on the ideals of liberation or peace, but on the decisive defeat of Napoleon's forces in the "Battle of the Nations" at Leipzig, some ten months earlier.

> "God has blessed our countrymen in that all of his generals are from our state – the Grand Duke Prince Schwarzenberg, through whom the victory was accomplished, for he was

---

[29]The victorious siege actually lasted from mid-September to 8th October 1789. See Karl Roider, *Austria's Eastern Question 1700–1790*, Princeton 1982, pp. 185–186. The war did indeed begin because of an Ottoman offensive against Russia, Austria's ally; cf. the discussion of the diplomatic background, *ibid.*, pp. 169–185.

[30]Ezekiel and Samuel Landau, *Ahavat Tsiyon*, Jerusalem 1966, sermon 11, p. 18a–b.

[31]The rhetoric of liberation played an important role as a rallying cry for the alliance forces. The order of the day sent out by the allied commander immediately before the Battle of Leipzig said, "Russians! Prussians! Austrians! You are fighting for one thing – the liberation of Europe, for the independence of your sons, for the immortality of your names." Antony Brett-James, *Europe Against Napoleon. The Leipzig Campaign, 1813*, London 1970, p. 114.

Sermons to Central European Jews 13

commander of all the armed forces, and he struck the enemy with a shattering blow and pursued him to the point of destruction. This liberation will certainly endure because the Duke, a military hero, Prince Schwarzenberg, is known to all for his noble qualities; he is outstanding in his virtues. Similarly the other generals – Prince Liechtenstein, Count Bubna, Count Nostitz, Count Klenau – and many other officers like them – are blessed by God.[32] We may rejoice that God has blessed some of our own sons – natives of Bohemia – to be worthy of being officers of our sovereign the Emperor."

In this sermon, there is no wrestling with the problem of rejoicing over the defeat of another army, as in the sermons of the Seven Years' War. There is no evident awareness that Jews were among the 60,000 French soldiers killed on the battlefield. The patriotic identification with the armies of the Austrian alliance, the sense of national pride in the glory redounding to Bohemia, the equating of the imperial cause, morality, and God's providential plan, is complete.

We see that Jews – or at least their "spiritual leaders" – were caught up in the military fever of these campaigns, and rabbis were not at all reluctant to show themselves knowledgeable about military affairs.[33] But the moralised militarism of Ezekiel Landau's praise to God for the fall of Belgrade or Samuel Landau's jubilation over the defeat of Napoleon should not be taken to express the only Jewish opinion. On a different ethical level altogether is Moses Mendelssohn's 'Friedenspredigt' (Sermon on Peace), delivered by Chief Rabbi Aaron Mosessohn at a thanksgiving service in Berlin on 12th March 1763, on the conclusion of the Seven Years' War. Rather than exulting in the achievements of military power – even military power justly and ethically employed – Mendelssohn caustically, with considerable rhetorical force, repudiates the notion that war can produce any virtues of value to civilisation. Appealing to recent experience, he evokes the devastating waste of war, which threatens the very foundations of humane culture, and expresses a genuine yearning for peace, the only true manifestation of God's purpose in creation.

"We have learned to understand that the 'vicious beasts' of human society cannot be more destructive than suspicion, hatred, jealousy, dissension, and their horrible consequence, war, with all of its barbarities. Days of sorrow are still present in our memory ... In war, the good have no pleasure, diligence receives no reward, the worthy no prize, the honest no satisfaction; religion groans, virtue goes into hiding, and – according to the talmudic statement the

---

[32]Prince Karl Philipp Schwarzenberg, commander of the army of Bohemia, became the supreme commander of the allied forces. On him and the other figures named in the Battle of Leipzig, see Gunther Rothenberg, *Napoleon's Great Adversaries. The Archduke Charles and the Austrian Army*, Bloomington 1981, pp. 178–185. The letter written by Schwarzenberg to his wife on the eve of the Battle of Leipzig does indeed reveal some rather impressive personal qualities; see Brett-James, *Europe Against Napoleon*, pp. 114–115.

[33]On the patriotism of Russian Jews during the War of 1812 see Simon Dubnow, *History of the Jews in Russia and Poland*, 3 vols., Philadelphia 1916, vol. I, pp. 355–359. On the patriotism of Prussian Jews, who volunteered to fight against Napoleon in 1813, see Meyer, *The Origins of the Modern Jew*, pp. 138–139. Further investigation of sermons will undoubtedly fill out the picture. Israel Meshulam Solomon's *A Sermon preached ... 13th of December 1776 ... for a general fast to pray for the success of His Majesty's Arms*, published in London 1777; and Solomon's Herschel's *Sermon preached ... success of His Majesty's Fleet under Lord Nelson, off Trafalgar*, published in London 1805, are important texts I have not been able to trace. These texts were ephemeral; printed, read and soon thrown away when they were no longer of current interest. Copies are extremely difficult to find. See Cecil Roth (ed.), *Magna Bibliotheca Anglo-Judaica. A Bibliographical Guide to Anglo-Jewish History*, London 1937, pp. 325, 437.

harshest curse of all – the young are arrogant towards the aged, as are the dissolute towards the honourable.

In war . . . cities are reduced to ashes, palaces demolished, all beneficent institutions destroyed, the laws trampled underfoot, the arts despised, and that which men have conceived and realised over a period of centuries for the betterment of their condition is quickly ruined . . . Fields are uprooted, crops are trodden down, and what does manage to grow is not enjoyed by the farmer, for the enemy consumes the fruit of his labours. That is why God, after having promised all forms of earthly happiness to those who walk in His precepts and keep His commandments, adds finally that blessing without which we cannot enjoy any other: 'I will grant peace in the land' (Leviticus XXVI:6). I will guide the hearts of those who have the power over war and peace to choose what is best."[34]

Perhaps that may serve as a message and a prayer appropriate for our times too.

---

[34] Moses Mendelssohn, *Gesammelte Schriften*, Leipzig 1845, vol. IV, pp. 407–415, passage from p. 409. The "vicious beasts" mentioned in the first sentence is Mendelssohn's allegorical understanding of the phrase in Leviticus XXVI:6. Cf. Altmann, *Moses Mendelssohn*, pp. 68–69, which focuses on some philosophical points in the sermon.

The Jews of Sachsen-Meiningen and the Edict of 1811

BY FRANZ LEVI

SETTLEMENTS

Some solitary gravestones in the town of Erfurt in the former county of Saxony-Prussia, are the only evidence for the existence of Jews in Thüringen during the ninth century. The prominent kabbalist Eleazar ben Jehuda ben Kalonymus of Worms lived there in the twelfth century.[1] After their expulsion in 1349, for centuries Jews were no longer tolerated in the town of Meiningen, the residence of the Dukes of Sachsen-Meiningen. Jews were accepted on land belonging to the nobility in the adjacent countryside from the fourteenth century onwards. A very small number of Jews were allowed to settle in Meiningen again at the beginning of the nineteenth century. This situation ended with their expulsion in October 1819.[2] Jews were deported for the last time in 1942.

In the year 1442 Jews had to leave Upper Bavaria; followed in 1450 by Lower Bavaria. The same process developed in the cities of the *Reich*, i.e. the cities directly subservient to the emperor; in 1440 Augsburg expelled its Jews; in 1499 Nürnberg followed; in 1519 the turn came for Regensburg's Jews. Pogroms were rife in the Archbishopric of Bamberg; Jews in 40 villages had to leave their homes. In 1561 they were driven out of the Archbishopric of Würzburg. Prior to that date, in 1422 and 1453, attempts had been made to expel them from the High-Diocese of Würzburg. Thereafter, from the year 1567 onwards, in principle, no Jew was allowed to live in Würzburg; the same applied to the Würzburg-owned territories of the Archbishopric in Sachsen-Meiningen.[3]

The re-settlement of Jews in Sachsen-Meiningen began again in the seventeenth century, documented by records such as the 'Judenschutz in Marisfeld' in 1679,[4] and the reference to Jews in the *Konsistorialreskript* of 6th May 1682,[5] prohibiting trading between Jews and Christians on Sundays. The largest Jewish community existed in Walldorf adjacent to Meiningen, next in size were the communities in Berkach, Gleicherwiesen, Dreissigacker, Bibra and Bauerbach, designated villages where Jews sometimes constituted nearly half – up to forty-

---

[1] *The Jewish Encyclopedia*, vol. III, New York 1916, p. 101.
[2] See Ulrich Heß, *Forschung zur Verfassungs- und Verwaltungsgeschichte des Herzogtums SCM* (Sachsen–Coburg–Meiningen), 1680–1829 (Ms 1954) in Thüringisches Staatsarchiv Meiningen.
[3] Heinrich Graetz, *Volksthümliche Geschichte der Juden*, Leipzig 1888, here English transl., New York 1891, pp. 388–390.
[4] Thüringisches Staatsarchiv (hereafter St. Arch.) Meiningen, Hildburghausen, 14.2.
[5] Heß, *op. cit.*

five per cent – of the population. For instance, in the village of Nordheim, settlement commenced some time prior to the year 1700 when the knights of the von Stein, permitted Jews to settle on their estate and thereafter in 1700 on their land in Berkach. The re-settlement from one place to another was said to be due to the Jews having "ridiculed Good Friday", a strange pretext when, in fact, they were re-settled only in the next village – two kilometres away.[6]

On 5th August 1710 a decree was issued by the Duke's administration in Meiningen for the village of Berkach. It read:

> ". . . because other landlords of Berkach had now accepted Jews, the mayor should not refuse to admit them [the Jews] in return for a payment of the protection levy . . ."

The Jews of Walldorf amalgamated in the year 1777 into a single community, although they were settled on lands belonging to three different knights, as well as that of the Bishops of Würzburg.

It is not clear where the Jews came from, because the evidence is circumstantial. The study of names provides the best available clue. Up to the year 1811 Jews were not required by law to be known by German names. They were distinguished in most cases by Hebrew names, sometimes by sons inverting their fathers' names (1803), using the forename as a surname or by adding to the forenames a surname, such as the place they had come from. The latter category is used here to assume their places of origin. A list from Berkach (1810) for example, contains the name "Pollack" suggesting descendancy from Poland. The tax assessment list for Walldorf of 1820[7] gives some indication, such as: Battenheimer (Battenheim near the Rote Gebirge), Lichtenstein (near Coburg, alternatively the principality), Ortweiler (Hessen), Lißner (Lissingen, Hessen), Holländer (Holland), Mannheimer (Mannheim), Schlesinger (Silesia), Rügheimer (Rügheim near Coburg), Nordheimer (Nordheim in the Grabfeld). As can be seen from this list there is no pattern, except pointers to an origin in central Germany from the Rheinland to Coburg, with two exceptions such as Holland and Silesia. There is only one Sephardic name in any of the tax lists (1803),[8] which clearly suggests an Ashkenasic dominance.

STATUS

At the end of the eighteenth century, and beginning of the nineteenth, Germany and the small *Länder*, such as the duchies of Saxony, were divided lands. Germany as a whole consisted of approximately 300 political units of which eight were ruled by electors; forty by archbishops or bishops; ninety-four by abbots, dukes, margraves, landgraves; fifty-one were ruled as free cities and the rest were ruled by imperial counts or knights.[9]

The imperial counts or knights, described as "reichsunmittelbare Ritter-

---

[6]Rörich, *Chronik von Berkach*, Church Archives, Berkach.
[7]St. Arch. Meiningen, In Alt, 42, 1401.
[8]St. Arch. Würzburg, Gebrechenamt Sig. Vii, W, No. 1606 I, II, III.
[9]A. Ramm, *Germany 1789–1919*, London 1967, pp. 1–16.

schaft" – were well organised and their name derived from their having no authority above themselves, except the Emperor. The system was designed to be balanced, so that the weakest might survive.[10] An imperial count or knight, who ruled his sometimes minute estate, was able to exercise his power as much as an Ecclesiastical Prince, or the Elector or the Archbishop of Würzburg or the Abbot of Kempten or the King of Prussia – they had their own courts and appointed judges. All these elevated persons were in theory on an equal footing as vassals of the Holy Empire. They all were empowered by the Emperor to offer "Schirm- und Schutzbriefe" (letters of protection).

The "reichsunmittelbare Ritterschaft" were officially in power until the year 1806. Their rights, such as the power to give "protection" in the form of a poll tax etc., remained with the landowners, now called "Mediatsherren", after the date of dissolution. The payment of a protection levy formed a primary income for the aristocrats and gentry. The Edict of 1811, as described later was intended to form the basis for the Ducal Authorities' interference with this privilege.

The issue of *Schirm- und Schutzbriefe* did not necessarily mean unrestricted life on the land of the knights or in the country at large. For instance, a Jew obtained a letter of protection which specifically said that he was afforded such protection for himself, his wife and his future children and permission was given to be housed in an abode, on condition that the Jew followed an honest trade. The Jew was then obliged to apply to the *Amt* to obtain permission to get married and to be issued with the necessary trading licence.[11]

"Schutzjuden" in the same village (Berkach) came under the administration of the *Churfürstliche Landesregierung* of Bavaria after Würzburg had been ceded to Bavaria in 1803 following the Treaty of Lunéville (1801). Yet they came under the protection of three different landlords: The *Churfürst* with his *Amt* in Mellrichstadt, the *Freiherr* von Steinchen's *Amt* in Nordheim and the *Kalbche Verwaltung* in Waltershausen.[12]

The Ducal Authorities in Sachsen-Meiningen treated the Jews in general as foreigners until 1811. They were not considered to be Ducal subjects. The status of the Jews settled under the protection of individual knights in the prescribed villages, prior to this date was unresolved. During the period of Bernhard I (seventeenth century) the attitude of the Ducal Government was dictated by religiously motivated intolerance towards the Jews. This changed marginally during the Enlightenment. During this period the Ducal Government eyed the Jews purely from the commercial viewpoint rather than from one of religion or race. In the reign of Charlotte Amalie (1763–1775), widow of Duke Anton Ulrich, a mandate was issued for the procurement of grain, in which Jews were pronounced to be profiteering usurers.

The Jews in Sachsen-Meiningen had concentrated primarily on the cattle trade. Consequently they played a prominent role in the Seven Years' War (1756–1763), preventing embarrassment to the government by acting as convenient middlemen in supplying the Army of Occupation. The supply of food to

[10]*Ibid.*
[11]St Arch. Meiningen, In Alt, 42, 1393, 5. März 1809.
[12]St. Arch. Würzburg, Gebrechenamt Sig. Vii, W, No. 1606, I, II, III.

foreign troops was, from 1760, completely in Jewish hands. In the fight against starvation in the *Land* during the years 1770 to 1772, the Jews were extremely active as wholesale suppliers of foodstuffs.[13]

Shortly after Duke Georg I came to power in 1782, for no specific reason, he drastically restricted trading by Jews. He declared all agreements with Jews to be null and void unless they had been countersigned by a village mayor or the *Amt*.[14] Jews were subjected to special taxes and levies. In the following centuries policies towards Jews were unfriendly. On 10th October 1794 a decree was issued prohibiting Jews to trade in skins. On 2nd October 1798 all Jewish traders had to provide securities to the *Amt*. On 8th November 1799, the restriction edict for the Jews issued in 1782 by Georg I was reissued with new enforcement laws to be executed by the common *Amt* at Römhild.[15]

Coming to power on 24th December 1803, Duchess Luise Eleonore, widow of Georg I, decreed on 20th September 1804 that all previous restrictions on Jews, imposed by Georg I, should be enforced. Even after the decree of 1811, which is referred to in detail in later parts of this paper, another order was issued on 27th December 1813, drawing attention to the prohibition of trading by Jews without specially written privileges and trading passports issued by the *Kammer*.

SIGNIFICANCE OF THE DECREE OF 1811

A specific decree regarding Jews was issued on 5th January 1811 by Luise Eleonore "verwittwete Herzogin zu Sachsen und geborne Fürstin zu Hohenlohe und Obervormünderin und Landesregentin".[16]

The decree declared that all Christian subjects of differing denominations were citizens with equal rights. The Jews were not yet entitled to be fully qualified subjects. The reason given was that they were "not adequately educated and would have to change their means of subsistence before they could aspire to such status". The decree gave Jews the right to an education comparable to that of their Christian neighbours. In one respect conditions differed in Sachsen-Meiningen from many other *Länder* in Germany, in that this decree gave nominal legal autonomy to the Jewish communities, even if the elected Jewish officers were without real authority. Their function was not quite comparable to that of their Christian counterparts, such as the village mayor. One community even sued the government, to enable one of its Jewish officials to hold the title "Syndicus". The case dragged on for years.

The decree was not issued in isolation, although it was distinctly geared to a very clearly defined area of Germany. Identical legal conditions prevailed in many other *Länder*, sometimes marginally more advanced and liberal, sometimes even more backward. The French Revolution of 1789 had brought a whiff of

---

[13] *Meininger Chronik*, I, p. 155.
[14] Heß, *op. cit.*, Bd. II.
[15] Landesarchiv (LA) Meiningen ZM, No. 261, "Patent, den Handel mit Juden betreffend, 1. März 1782".
[16] See illustrations between pp. 22–23.

liberty to the Jews of Europe. This promised liberty was soon revoked and followed by clamp-down legislation, by which means the so-called "Geist des aufgeklärten Absolutismus" could be imposed. (It was more *Absolutismus* than Enlightenment.) On the other hand the rulers, the Duchess and her *Geheimrats Collegio* used the instrument of the "Jews Edict of 1811" to stem the power structure of the *Mediatsherren* and the guilds, without this becoming too obvious.

The Edict was intended to exert pressure on the Jewish population to abandon trading, especially hawking, peddling and huckstering (*Schmusen*), to stop acting simply as agents, and to introduce them to artisan work, factory or agricultural labour. The insistence on re-education was intended to be a safety measure inasmuch as Jewish trading was considered to be detrimental to the farming community, to lead to ruin, and to involve cheating. The authorities did not understand that the Jewish cattle traders fulfilled the function of providing some measure of food distribution within the *Land* and in addition advanced money on cattle – a proceedure often abused by farmers who took money from all sides, paying off one Jew against the other.[17]

The Jewish religion was considered to be noxious and to create divisions within the population. To combat these characteristics, as perceived by the ruler and her advisers, education and training for a profession as prescribed by the Edict, would create conditions under which Jews would cease to be "Jews", i.e., become integrated into the population.[18]

One of the major objectives of the Government's *Erziehungsedikt*, as the Edict of 1811[19] or similar edicts are sometimes called, was the concept of *Bildung*, stated in the Edict to be a precondition for the awards of equal status as subjects to the Jews.

> "Wenn Wir daher vor der Hand annoch Bedenken tragen, Unsern jüdischen Unterthanen alle Rechte einzuräumen, welche den christlichen Bewohnern der hiesigen Lande, ohne Unterschied der Confession, zustehen . . . daß dieselben zu dem vollständigen Genuß der Staatsbürgerrechte noch nicht hinlänglich vorbereitet und geeignet sind, und daß sie sich, durch bessere Bildung und eine veränderte Nahrungsweise hierzu erst gehörig qualificieren müssen."[20]

In a contemporary context *Bildung* is only used in the connotation of improvement of the mind. This was also how the term was understood by the representatives of the Jewish communities. Not so the legislators who used the word in place of *Ausbildung*, i.e. training. The Jews argued that their *Bildung* was certainly not inferior to that of the Christians, that in the "*Königreich* Westphalen" Jews had no higher education, yet were given the same rights as their Christian compatriots.

---

[17]St. Arch. Meiningen, Nassfelder Amtsbericht, 9. Mai 1820, In Alt, 42, 1373, pp. 106/108.
[18]Jacob Jacobson, *Mitteilungen des Gesamtarchivs der deutschen Juden*, Jhrg. 6, Gutenberg 1926, pp. 54–73.
[19]Some of the material referred to in this paper was seen in 1926 by Jacobson. He refers to the Edict, the response and the *Ablehnung* (see note 21 below) of 1812, but not to the *ad hoc* document (see note 43) or any other document seen by the present author in the Staatsarchiv in Meiningen in 1990 and 1991. For all practical purposes the archives were closed to scholars for 65 years. Ulrich Heß, archivist and historian of the Town Council of Meiningen, *op. cit.*, makes a reference to the "*Edikt*" of 1811, which he had seen in a publication of 1898. Heß, however, was politically ostracised and was unable to publish.
[20]See the introduction to the *Edikt* reproduced in the illustrations between pp. 22–23.

> "... To some extent many of the Christian subjects are peasants, day labourers and common soldiers, etc., and certainly have no higher education than that possessed by Jews ..."[21]

This meaning of the word *Bildung* was not accepted by the *Vice-Kanzler*, Karl von Künßberg, in his *ad-hoc* document "*Votum*". If the exclusion of Jews *from becoming subjects*, as insisted on in the preamble to the Edict, was to be justified, he and his *Geheimrats Collegio* had to pretend that the word *Bildung* applied also to the training of soldiers or agricultural labourers, a training which the Jews did not undergo.

The *Vice-Kanzler* said:

> "... One also says, that one can educate oneself to a business or an occupation – to agriculture or to being a farmer, to being a soldier etc. And that is what is demanded of Jewry ..."

The deliberate ambiguity of language in the Edict was the result of different concepts of the word *Bildung* and *Kultur*, which are used in the same context by the "Herzl. oberv. Regierungsbericht" on 1st August 1810.[22] The Edict issued in 1811 reverts again to the word *Bildung*, most probably in order to support the argument.

The official rejection, *Ablehnung*, does not enter into this argument at all. Instead reference is made to equality of rights previously given to Jews in other countries, such as in France or in the *Rheinbundstaaten*. These rights had now been deferred, although promised for the future. The same unspecified promises were offered to the Jews in the Dukedom of Sachsen-Meiningen.

> "... While there is evidence that in the towns and cities it was a flowering period of German philosophy and literature: the age of Kant, of Schiller and Goethe, the years when the University of Königsberg, where Kant lectured, stood at the forefront of learning, and Jena was not far behind, yet there was much in German society that was distinctly old-fashioned, had even a medieval look ..."[23]

Paragraph 13 set out to regulate the funding of schools, while §20 opened the Christian schools and the teacher-training institutions to Jewish pupils. Whilst the former paragraph consisted of nebulous promises, the latter was a genuine attempt to attract Jewish pupils.

There is no evidence that Gentile villagers had a better standard of education than the Jews in their midst. The *Berkach Chronik*[24] describes the construction of a new synagogue and schoolhouse in 1847 to replace the old school, which must have existed since 1768 when the first teacher was recorded in Berkach. Up to 1808, the nomination of a teacher depended on the patronage of the *Herren* von Stein (the landlord). A document exists in the *Thüringisches Staatsarchiv*, Meiningen, which clearly demonstrates the resistance of the authorities to Jewish learning:

---

[21]The Jewish community produced a detailed protest (*Ablehnung*) signed by six names (hereafter Einwand), St. Arch. Meiningen, In Alt, 42, 1373, pp. 53–85.
[22]St. Arch. Meiningen, In Alt, 42, 1393, p. 36.
[23]Ramm, *op. cit.*, pp. 1–16.
[24]*Chronik von Berkach*, *op. cit.*

"... the high-handed, unauthorised erection of a Jewish school in Simmershausen by the Jew Isaak Levi 1767–1768".[25]

The *Berkach Chronik* lists the names of teachers in Berkach and their years of service, and shows that teachers were continuously employed at least from the year 1766 onwards, which coincides with the date of the inauguration of the school in Simmershausen. That some of these teachers were qualified rabbis is evidence that at times there were some standards of proficiency. It must be assumed that most of the education had a Hebrew or Jewish character. Some parts of it must have been of a general nature or with a German syllabus, otherwise it would have been rejected by the inspectors. In general the school was subordinate to the school inspectorate of Sachsen-Meiningen. Until 1850 the parish priest carried out the local inspection of the school.

Another observer was Judge G. Brunngräber of the "Freyherrlich Wolzogen" court of Bauerbach (1819), who stated that to teach Jewish children cost the Jews considerably more than it cost the peasants.[26] There were complaints by members of the Jewish community to the authorities about the poor qualifications of some of the teachers. Although these complaints were written slightly later than the time of the decree, i.e. in 1825 etc., the complaints sound convincing. ". . . Some of the teachers were in fact only Jewish butchers (*shochet*) with a smattering of Hebrew."[27] It was probably not far from the truth that the teachers' standards might often have been less than adequate. Teachers were sometimes not treated well by their Jewish communities. This was shown in a much later testimony by a teacher, Hermann Ehrlich, who, however, came to Berkach only in 1845.[28]

A very harsh report of 1819–1820 is contained within a statement made by a judge from Römhild who appears to be strongly biased and is a very critical observer. He does not seem to understand that he deals with people of a different culture. Nevertheless he is quoted here to convey the attitude of the intelligentsia during that period.

> "The improvement of Jews has to commence with the young people, and to this end the prime consideration is the engagement of better Jewish teachers. Most Jewish teachers are not worth their salt. They are not capable of teaching Jewish children their own mother tongue. Their religious instruction consists of teaching a smattering of a few prayers. They are not capable of teaching children to understand, because they do not understand anything themselves.
> Most of them speak German abysmally and cannot write it at all. When such a teacher attempts to write a German essay, everything is so jumbled that one is unable to make sense of it.
> However, the major problem with Jewish teachers is that they are also the ritual butchers. Whether they understand that particular trade properly is the first question they are asked. If they can prove proficiency in this respect then little is asked about their teaching ability. Complaints by the poorer population about neglect of their children are to no avail – they do not use the services of the ritual butcher very much. One can bet on it that the more affluent will support the teacher . . .
> It is a major disadvantage that Jewish teachers are also butchers."

[25] St. Arch. Meiningen, LR Hildburghausen, 14.8.
[26] St. Arch. Meiningen, In Alt, 42, 1373.
[27] St. Arch. Meiningen, In Alt, 42, 1401.
[28] Archives of the LBI New York, M.E. 419.

> Teaching must be regular and especially that of children. This is missing in the education of Jewish children. Even during a lesson a Jewish teacher is sent here or there as a *shochet*. Often he has to walk long distances; and may not come home for more than half or even a whole day. The children are only left with whatever hours the teacher has free from his duties as a butcher. As a result the children become disorderly, are not used to steady work and learn to be lazy.
>
> It is essential to create a better class of teachers, after which regular teaching hours have to be set and only before or after lessons may the teacher be called away to attend to the slaughter business. Hebrew and Jewish religion must be taught. So-called *Judendeutsch* is not to be taught at any time.
>
> In order to learn German and to write it properly and also to be educated in other matters Jewish children must be strongly urged to attend Christian schools. They should start there at the age of six, when other children are also sent to school. Going to school twice should be beneficial, and one hour a day should suffice to instil in Jewish children adequate knowledge of Hebrew and their religion. In this way Jewish children will get used to performing set tasks and learn to sit still, especially if in addition to their lessons they go to the spinning-mill and the girls learn knitting and sewing. Like Christian children they will continue with their education until the age of fourteen and fathers will be strictly forbidden to take them away to participate in trading and haggling.
>
> At an age when Christian boys decide on a particular profession, Jewish boys should do the same. For a Jewish boy to have such an opportunity, all craftsmen should be obliged to teach them. However, this may be achieved only when no-one is exempt from journeyman duties and nobody is permitted to become a master craftsman unless he undertakes to teach Jewish boys. Moreover, since the Jewish code of law ('*Policey*') is inherently prescriptive, which may cause inconveniences when a Christian teaches a Jewish child, his own teacher of religion should distinguish between current prescriptions and those laws resulting from specific conditions in the past; separating especially those regulations which were the result of teachings of rabbis and scholars . . ."[29]

Another aspect which had to be investigated in addition to *Bildung* was the *Nahrungsweise*, best translated by the phrase "means of livelihood". This, the second criterion mentioned in the preamble to the Ducal decree, demands that the Jews change their means of support to enable them to have equal rights with Christians bestowed on them.

It must be understood that the attitude of the administration, towards trading and hawking of wares, was sometimes still somewhat medieval. Jews had been excluded from owning agricultural land and property, so they had turned to money-lending, hawking, and cattle dealing, in order to meet the financial demands made on them. Even if a large number of Jews only just scraped a living in the Jewish designated villages, some managed to acquire considerable amounts of money, especially through the lending of capital.[30]

The document of 18th April 1820 "Nassfelder Amtsbericht", a report written by the Ducal Sachsen-Meiningen *Amt*, ostensibly posed the question, how much capital the running of large or small commercial enterprises would require. The real underlying question was, in fact, whether to grant privileges to wholesale traders only; and also the creation of monopolies and the raising of special taxes. The "Nassfelder Amtsbericht" continues:

> "They [the Jews] more or less control the cattle trade. Should they be restricted or hindered, it will be to the detriment of trade and life in our small country and leave a great gap. The necessary competition will be removed and will bring about a monopoly and privileges for the richer affluent cattle dealers only . . ."

[29] St. Arch. Meiningen, In Alt, 42, 1373.
[30] Christopher Daxelmüller, *Jüdische Kultur in Franken*, Würzburg 1988, p. 32.

Von Gottes Gnaden Wir Luise Eleonore,

verwittwete Herzogin zu Sachsen ꝛc., geborne Fürstin zu Hohenlohe ꝛc. ꝛc.

Obervormünderin und Landesregentin,

sind jederzeit von dem Wunsche belebt gewesen, Unsern getreuen Unterthanen, ohne Unterschied der Religion, die möglichste Gleichheit der Rechte zuzugestehen, und haben solches bey mehreren Veranlassungen bereits zu bethätigen gesucht.

Wenn Wir daher vor der Hand annoch Bedenken tragen, Unsern jüdischen Unterthanen alle die Rechte einzuräumen, welche den christlichen Bewohnern der hiesigen Lande, ohne Unterschied der Confession, zustehen: so ist dieses lediglich die Folge der, nach reiflicher Prüfung und Erwägung des jetzigen Zustandes der inländischen Juden erlangten Ueberzeugung, daß dieselben zu dem vollständigen Genuß der Staatsbürgerrechte noch nicht hinlänglich vorbereitet und geeignet sind, und daß sie sich, durch bessere Bildung und eine veränderte Nahrungsweise hierzu erst gehörig qualificiren müssen.

Wir betrachten es jedoch als eine Unserer vorzüglichsten Regentenpflichten, ihnen den Weg dazu zu bahnen und zu erleichtern, weshalb Wir die gegenwärtige Verordnung haben entwerfen lassen, wodurch zugleich die verschiedenen Verhältnisse, in welchen Unsere jüdischen Unterthanen stehen, nebst den ihnen eingeräumten Rechten und obliegenden Verbindlichkeiten genauer bestimmt werden sollen.

§. 1.

Als Landesunterthanen sind anzusehen,

1) die Juden, welche bey der Publication dieser Verordnung sich in den hiesigen Landen wirklich niedergelassen und Schutz erlangt haben.
2) die Kinder derselben, welche in einer rechtmäßigen Ehe erzeugt worden sind und erzeugt werden, und
3) diejenigen ausländischen Juden, welchen Wir die Einwanderungs-Erlaubniß ertheilen lassen. Dieses soll jedoch nur Ausnahms Weise und aus ganz besonders erheblichen Rück-

Rücksichten geschehen, wenn auch die sonst zur Aufnahme der Ausländer erforderlichen Bedingungen erfüllt werden könnten.

§. 2.

Die jüdischen Familien in den hiesigen Landen sollen, bis zu weiterer Verordnung, auf die jetzt vorhandene Anzahl derselben eingeschränkt bleiben. In dieser Hinsicht wird verordnet:

1) aus jeder Familie darf, in der Regel, nur ein Sohn die Familie durch Heirath fortsetzen.
2) die Wahl eines Sohns hierzu, unter mehreren gleich qualificirten Söhnen, bleibt dem Vater, in dessen Ermangelung der Mutter, und nach der Eltern Ableben der obrigkeitlichen Entscheidung, mit Zurathziehung der nächsten Verwandten, überlassen, wenn sich die Brüder selbst hierüber nicht vereinigen können.
3) die übrigen Söhne dürfen, ohne besondere Landesherrliche Erlaubniß, in den hiesigen Landen keine neuen Familien stiften. Diese Erlaubniß aber soll nur denjenigen werden, welche sich den Wissenschaften und Künsten widmen, Professionen oder Handwerker erlernen und Ackerbau oder Taglohn treiben, wenn sie sich über ihre erworbene Geschicklichkeit und Arbeitsfähigkeit legitimiren können.

§. 3.

Die Judenfamilien werden zwar noch zur Zeit, zur Niederlassung und wesentlichen Wohnung, nur an ihren bisherigen Wohnorten zugelassen, und daselbst als Schutzverwandte aufgenommen. Allein wenn es dereinst die fortschreitende Bildung der Juden und ihre Beschäftigung mit andern, ihnen selbst und dem Staate nützlicheren Nahrungszweigen unbedenklich, und mit Unsern Regentenpflichten vereinbar machen wird, deren weitere Ausbreitung zu gestatten, dann sollen ihnen, zur Niederlassung mit ihren Familien, mehrere Orte angewiesen werden.

Der bloße Aufenthalt, ohne wesentliche Wohnung, wird allen jüdischen Individuen, welche hiesige Unterthanen sind, an allen Orten verstattet, und die bisherigen Einschränkungen deshalb, sind als aufgehoben zu betrachten. Doch sollen die Hausir-, Schacher- und Schmus-Juden dieser Begnadigung nicht theilhaftig seyn, sondern in Ansehung derselben bewendet es lediglich bey der Einrichtung jedes Orts.

§. 4.

". . . It would be a pity if the success of negotiations concerning the intended improvement of the Jews' situation resulted in a new levy on the cattle trade, the only branch of the economy which is alive in our small country and which has penetrated and influenced the peasants' life through and through . . ."[31]

It can be seen that this attempt to restrict the trade to benefit a few Christian wholesalers, might be in part a case of cause and effect. Jews had concentrated in one specific sphere of activity – the cattle trade – and one small part of the economy was created, which was lively and produced benefits all round. The outcome was envy and resentment. Jewish cattle dealers acted, in fact, as bankers by extending credit to the farming community,[32] a role taken over much later by the communal agricultural banks, beginning in a very small way with F. W. Raiffeisen in 1848 in Germany.

The edict places strong emphasis on removing Jews from any form of trading, be it cattle dealing, horse dealing, hawking, "*schmusen*" and trading in haberdashery (*Schnittwaren*). Dealing in foodstuffs was prohibited except for bulk retailing and that only under special conditions.

Ulrich Heß signified attitudes for the time as follows:

". . . The conservatism which had spread widely during the government of Luise Eleonore had its roots to no small extent in the composition of the secret cabinet (*Geheimrats Collegio*). This composition in turn led to the conditions prevailing at the time of the take-over of government by Bernhard II in 1821, in that the Dukedom of Meiningen in many respects was the most backward of all the Saxony dukedoms."[33]

The events in October 1819 in the capital demonstrate how little the population wished to see an economic emancipation of the Jews after the Seven Years' War. At the time, Court Purveyor Romberg, a member of an affluent Jewish family of traders, intended to procure some houses with the agreement of the government. This led to a real uprising and to the election of a delegation of burghers, who were to defend the rights of the town against the government. In fact it resulted in the driving out of the few Jews who, in the meantime, had settled in Meiningen proper.

It was only the decree of 17th December 1822 which brought some gradual alleviation of the strictures against Jews. This continued until Jewish and Christian trade and industry was treated on an equal basis. The Meiningen decree of 16th June 1862, brought down the last barriers.

In §1 of the Edict, the status for Jews to be elevated to *Landesunterthanen* (i.e. subjects) was restricted to legitimate children only. Illegitimate children were excluded.

In §2 it was decreed that until further order Jewish families were restricted to their existing size. Only one son was permitted to continue the family by getting married. The selection of this particular son from among a number of equally qualified sons was reserved to the father; and in his absence given to the mother and after the death of the parents to the authorities, on consideration of the advice given by the nearest relatives if the brothers could not agree. The

---

[31] St. Arch. Meiningen, Nassfelder Amtsbericht, 6. Juli 1820, In Alt, 42, 1373.
[32] St. Arch. Meiningen, In Alt 42, 1401.
[33] Heß, *op. cit.*

remaining sons could not create new families without the permission of the Ducal Regent. However, there was a proviso that permission would be given to those who devoted their life to the sciences or the arts, acquired professions or became artisans or engaged in agriculture or labouring, provided they could prove their skill and ability to work.

Then §4 amplified the prohibition against Jews getting married. It said that from the date of this edict, no Jew who obtained his living as a peddler, hawker, agent or *Schmuser* would be permitted to create a family by marriage. Those Jews who were engaged in trading in merchandise had to provide evidence that they had the necessary assets for their selected branch of enterprise and were capable of keeping a trading book in German. Neither of these stipulations was required of Christian traders.

Both these rulings (§2 and §4) had devastating effects. Young women were forced to emigrate to seek husbands, and sometimes became pregnant without society being able to put pressure on "responsible partners" to get married. Illegitimate children could not become subjects (§1). Thus a substantial number of women had illegitimate children or, if at all, managed to marry late, as documented by birth certificates from the early 1830s onwards.[34] Their offspring were ostracised. It appears to have been quite common for young men to remain bachelors or to seek their luck abroad. Emigration to America was not cheap, but many young women banded together and sought their luck in the New World.[35]

Turning to direct observers of the conditions imposed by the legislation, the dignitaries of the six communities were of the opinion that the decree applied to Jewish sons who were too old to learn new trades, or professions. The penalty of having to remain unmarried was unwarranted. They had been excluded by regulations from becoming craftsmen and excluded from similar burgher's occupations. The law was effectively retrospective, whereas younger boys could prepare themselves suitably by apprenticeship.

The dignitaries said that they considered the Edict to be justified in applying to sons who were still able to learn another trade, but they questioned the justice and wisdom of the existing version of the decree. A proper explanation by the ducal administration would be appreciated, they said. Moreover, many fathers had daughters growing up who would be penalised and have no future. There was little chance for their daughters to be given in wedlock to indigenous men. With the decreed restrictions as to numbers of households, fathers would be unable to embrace a foreigner as a son-in-law. A much more lenient limitation on marriage would be restricted to Jewish sons who were still of an age appropriate to learning; which would serve the same purpose, without making so many families and individuals unhappy. Free enterprise was open to all Christian subjects. They could participate in all commercial activities without hindrance. Should not at least one trade be open to all Jewish individuals and not only to bachelors? In respect of the provisions contained in §4, the heads of the Jewish communities complained that the Ducal Police had issued patents for hawking to

[34] Jüdisches Museum, Frankfurt a. Main. Birth certificates of Berkach.
[35] Jacob Toury, 'Jewish Manual Labour and Emigration. Records from some Bavarian Districts (1830–1857)', in *LBI Year Book XVI* (1971), pp. 45–62, here p. 58.

foreign Christians and Jews alike against a small consideration, but now the Edict prohibited such activity to indigenous Jewish traders. They continue:

">. . . Until now, surely there was no case when a Christian who traded and intended to get married had ever been asked how much capital he possessed and how he intended to keep himself in future . . ."[36]

Jacob Toury[37] has pointed out the extraordinary concentration of Jews on *Mediatsherren* land under the Ducal House of Meiningen and the apparent autonomy during the years 1811 to 1856 as the result of the Jews' Edict of 1811:

> "The political intention is made clearer by the paragraph of the same law which declared the former Jewish 'Elders' (*Parnasse*) to be henceforth the heads and spokesmen of the now unified local communities: 'The functions of the village-mayor should be conferred upon them, insofar as the prevailing circumstances warrant it.'
> In other words, the Jews in some villages of Sachsen-Meiningen continued even after 1811 to form local political corporations quite separate from the village-communities, just as in the village of Aschenhausen in Sachsen-Weimar."

Toury's statements are based most probably on the patent of 1856. He assumed that the Jewish communities prior to that date had a degree of autonomy. This was only partially substantiated when a search was made through the collection of documents at the State Archives in Meiningen. It made little difference, because in the year 1849 an attempt was made to revoke the status of independent communities for Jews. As an introduction the following official notice was given:

> "In the execution of the basic rights of the German nation Jews cannot be permitted to maintain special civic communities, instead a stipulation is necessary whereby all the civic communities are to be amalgamated. The questions hereby arise, which ordinance has to be issued concerning communal assets and the entitlement of members of the communities, in such circumstances as may prevail. An order is given to the Ducal Administration to investigate the assets of those communities which formerly comprised specifically Jewish communities. To hear the heads of both [Jewish and Gentile] communities and attempt to reconcile the combining of joint assets and to submit files within a period of three weeks and to report conclusively on the subject."
> Meiningen, the 1st April 1849
> *Herzogliches Staatsministerium, Abtheilung des Inneren*
>
> R. Liebmann[38]

The law to dismantle the autonomy of the Jewish communities was issued in fact on 22nd May 1856. It took the Ducal State Ministry until 23rd April 1868 to process the act implementing it and to deal with the resulting appeals against the law. It was only after this that the State Parliament issued a new bill concerning the conditions of the Jews. This established that the Jews' Law of 1856 applied only to those Jewish communities which at the time of legislation (i.e. 1856) were within the confines of the designated localities where special Jewish communities existed.

It is emphasised that the creation of the autonomous community and the role

---

[36] Einwand, St. Arch. Meiningen. In Alt, 42, 1373, pp. 53–85.
[37] Jacob Toury, 'Types of Jewish Municipal Rights in German Townships. The Problems of Local Emancipation', in *LBI Year Book XXII* (1977), pp. 55–80, here pp. 66–67.
[38] St. Arch. Meiningen. Migration File resp. Bürgschaftsgesetz, 6. Juni 1844.

of the *Parnass* ("*Barnass*") is described in detail in §8 of the patent of 1811. It is also known that they were to be tax collectors with personal liability for the revenue. Yet in §14 any form of jurisdiction for the Rabbi and *Parnass* is withheld. There was to be a Chief Rabbi, stipulated by §7. The communities tried to resist §12 of the Edict which decreed that in spiritual as well as in marital matters, which normally would be dealt with by the clergy or the courts, Jews were subjugated to the Jewry Court in the first stage of appeal. This Jewry Court consisted of Christian clergymen with the Chief Rabbi as adviser. At the second stage of appeal, cases were to be submitted to the Consistory, which in all instances was to operate as the supreme authority.

Like all other stipulations in this Edict, supervision in any matter of the community or individual rested with the Christian authorities or Inspectorate; that is to say the Jewry Court, which consisted of Christian churchmen or *Consistorii*, was in fact a farce. It was the Chief Rabbi's right to be consulted, but that was all, while at the second stage of appeal no Jewish participation was to be provided in any form and thus was without Jewish authority.

The response of the representatives of the Jewish community makes light of this part of the Edict. It seems they were not very much concerned over this issue:

> ". . . their [the Jews'] spiritual affairs are now the concern of the Christian secular authorities or of the Ducal Consistory. Their wise advisers are as familiar as rabbis with the mosaic laws, thus they are able to decide . . ."[39]

This conciliatory response was dictated by a cool look at the cost involved: if the procedures mapped out by the authorities were to be followed they would cost money:

> ". . . If all the cases which are easy to deal with, by ban or school punishment, be delegated to a Jewry Court or to the *Amt* then this will cost as many Thaler as it costs now in Batzen. If it cannot be solved by the *Parnass*, this nonsense cannot be controlled at all. If jurisdiction and authority is not given to the rabbis and *Parnassim* then the question arises: Why do Christian mayors hold a variety of functions as adjudicators, judges of the peace, lower police functions, the right to assemble the community, publication of ordnances and orders, and to draw up contracts?"[40]

In other words, two aspects are being addressed. The first of them, and foremost in the mind of the community leaders, was the lack of authority given to their rabbis and *Parnassim*. An attempt was made to impose a cumbersome Christian authority to solve simple community problems. The second more disturbing circumstance was the imbalance of power between the role of the *Parnass* and his counterpart, the mayor or village headman. This shows all too clearly the bias held by the ducal authority.

The degree of contempt for Jews was shown in that a Ducal Higher Consistory (nominated president and vice president of the Chamber), who would issue rulings in a court of Jewry and the appeal court made disparaging remarks about the Jewish religion. This contempt comes to the foreground in an ignorant and arrogant document issued in 1825:

---

[39]Einwand, St. Arch. Meiningen, In Alt, 42, 1373, pp. 53–85.
[40]*Ibid.*

"... Praying to God in a language long extinct, hardly ever understood properly, and moreover in an unproductive idiom which leaves the spirit and heart cold, in a so-called divine service ..."[41]

There is a link between §§18, 19 and 4 in that they all deal with the regulations in regard to means of livelihood (*Nahrungsweise*).

In fact §18 decreed that in order to encourage different modes of livelihood for the Jews and in order to give them the opportunity to support themselves by other means, the ducal authority had decided that Jews should be permitted, as before, to own and acquire houses and property in their designated locality. They would also be permitted in the future to lease property, but only on condition that they themselves tilled the ground or had it done by Jewish dayworkers or Jewish servants. This paragraph further stipulated that Jews might develop factories and manufacturing enterprises for the employment of Jewish labour and that this would not only be permitted but even subsidised by the administration once success was assured.

Jews were to be permitted to learn the professions and craftsmanship of all kinds. All Christian masters were to be allowed to accept Jewish apprentices. Should these [Jewish] professionals and craftsmen be unable to find acceptance and admission by the guilds, then they could be assured that they would find a living as "free masters" in the trade they had learned. Premiums were to be paid to Christian masters to encourage them to accept Jewish apprentices. Incentives were also provided to promote apprentices from any Jewish family. Further, there was to be the award of dispensations from service in the armed forces, as well as the promotion of grants to Jewish farmhands and labourers.

The community representatives were not very happy with the proposals contained within §18, maintaining that Jewish apprentices, when accepted at all by Christian masters, were unfairly treated. This seems to be substantiated by the memorandum of Schwendler submitted to the privy council, in which he says:

"ad §18 c. It is common knowledge that the Jews who wish to learn a trade have to fight not only Christian prejudice, but also the attitudes of the guilds ..."[42]

In order to help the poorer classes to eke out their living in secure and mutually beneficial ways – instead of in their present highly deleterious pursuits of peddling, hawking and *Schmusen* – §19 proposed that woollen mills be financed from public funds. These were to be set up in each of the designated areas of Jewish residence to benefit the local cloth-making trade. To this end immediately after the publication of the Edict suitable persons were to be selected from the respective Jewish communities. Jews were to be taught appropriately in the local spinning mills to be managers of the proposed enterprise in due course.

The ducal administration was confident of obtaining from this measure the greatest possible benefit for poorer Jewish families, since this occupation was considered to be especially suitable for females, who till then could only scrape a living by knitting etc. However, the Jews rejected this suggestion:

[41]St. Arch. Meiningen, Herzogliche Sächsische Consistorial Akten, 'B' 110.
[42]St. Arch. Meiningen, Schwendler, 'Promemoria', In Alt, 42, 1393, pp. 13–16.

"... only then when Jews are entitled to live anywhere in the land, should they consider factory installations and manufacture."[43]

This benevolent piece of legislation was basically flawed from its inception. Nobody in the ducal administration had ever considered that in order to run spinning jennies or looms in the mills, power sources and industrial washing facilities were required. Yet, other than Walldorf on the river Werra, none of the Jewish designated localities was near to strong running water sources. There was a small brook with intermittent water supply near Bauerbach; Berkach had nothing but a common well in the centre of the village; Dreissigacker, in fact, seems to have been almost dry in some summers. Jewish village representatives commented on this and observed that not every location was suitable for the siting of a factory; villages even less so than towns. Villages where there was an endemic water shortage could not be considered suitable for factories.

The argument about water supply was swept aside by the President of the *Geheimrats Collegio*, according to the *ad hoc "Votum"*, as being a silly argument used by the Jews, harking persistently on this lack of water in Dreissigacker. The water shortage in all the villages was a bone of contention between the Christian and Jewish inhabitants. The latter were not entitled to the same ration of water from the wells, as conceded in the *"Votum"*.

"They [the Jews] complain in Dreissigacker concerning the restrictions on the use of the well, ad 1. [every Christian] has the use of the well for one hour while 5 or 6 Jews have to share the same period. But the farmer has to water his livestock too and that requires as much water as 4–6 Jews."[44]

The president of the privy council was on record as saying this. He might not have realised that Jews had to look after cattle as well. Normally they drove their cattle home, stabled and watered them before delivering them to the market. Jews had to pay a special tax (*Dorfgeld*) for the privilege of using the wells.[45] This entitled them normally to considerably less water, however, and then only after the cattle owned by Christian neighbours had been watered.

The taxes and levies Jews had to pay under the new regulations were covered in §15 of the decree. The first principle established was that Jews were to be put on a par with other subjects. Indigenous Jews would be taxed in future by an occupational income tax (*terminliche Nahrungssteuer*) at regular intervals, instead of by the Jewish trade tax (*Judengewerbsteuer*); which would cease to exist. Foreign Jews allowed to trade in the *Land* would have to pay taxes and levies as before. Property owned or acquired (by Jews) was to be taxed equally with that of Christians.

The decree stipulated that the poll tax charged by the *Mediatsherren* should remain their prerogative, except that there was to be a compulsory grading of the tax into four classes according to assets. Revisions of the poll tax were to be

---

[43]Einwand, St. Arch. Meiningen, In Alt, 42, 1373, pp. 53–85.
[44]*Vice-Kanzler* Karl Konstantin von Künßberg, *ad hoc "Votum"*, St. Arch. Meiningen, In Alt, 42, 1393, pp. 20–29. (Künßberg, born 18th July 1756, entered government at the age of 33, became *Vice-Kanzler* in 1802.)
[45]St. Arch. Meiningen, Herzogliche Sächsische Consistorial Akten, 'B' 110.

carried out annually by the courts of the *Mediatsherren* and there was to be official confirmation as to whether a Jew stayed in his class or was to be regraded. The same §16 also stated:

> "Apart from the poll tax, all personal levy has to cease unless it is also paid by Christian tenants or *Hintersassen*.
> Those who subsist by any other means than by trading, hawking or acting as agents shall make payments equal to those paid by Christians as *Schutzverwandte* . . ."

The Jewish representatives were apparently not favourably impressed because they responded:

> "As Your Ducal Highness has declared that the equal standing of the Jews in regard to other subjects in respect of the imposed levy is of highest concern, then the question arises: would not this equality also be fair and reasonable when it comes to the awarding of equal rights? It is not Jewish culture and subsistence which is a burden to Christians. They [the Jews] surely should also be able to attain the benefits and entitlement of total citizens' rights. Would Your Ducal Highness, therefore, at least, deign not to apportion harsher and greater levy [on the Jews] than is imposed on Christian subjects engaged in trade."[46]

The public servant Friedrich August Schwendler held[47] that the Jewish Trade Tax had been badly administered and this had led to malpractice. Jewish individuals of high income had paid less than Christian traders annually. Schwendler was well aware that Jews did not pay war contributions, nor enlisted for war service, nor paid rates on houses. But he disregarded all levies or poll taxes incumbent on Jews. The imposed levy should be collected in future by the *Parnassim*.

In order to impose Jewish Trade Tax on foreign traders, Westphalian practices should be followed (as advocated by Schwendler) and traders should obtain patents (trading licences) annually. Any future abolition of the Jewish Trade Tax for foreigners would be adequately compensated for by the occupational income tax (from the indigenous Jewish population), especially when the minute amount obtained from the Jewish Trade Tax and the trouble in obtaining it are taken into consideration. In 'Promemoria' Schwendler continued to gloss over the facts of diminishing returns to the *Mediatsherren* from the changes in the poll tax:

> "The proposed equal levelling of the poll tax everywhere will hardly produce a deficit for the *Gerichtsherren* [another name for *Mediatsherren*] and in its wake a loss for the Ducal Administration [who took a cut of the revenues from the *Mediatsherren*]. Should there be a reduction, there should not be any doubts concerning the rights of the country at large. The *Reichstritterschaftliche* vassals are basically entitled to a poll tax comparable to that which is obtained from the Christian *Schutzverwandte*. This right to give Jews protection and admission had been a prerogative of the Emperor and afterwards that of the Estates and not of the '*Landsaßen*'."[48]

The situation was bizarre in that it attempted to diminish the power of the "*reichsunmittelbare Ritterschaft*" through a fiscal manoeuvre, enshrined in a Jew Law. Although the *Herzogliche Kammer* participated in the proceeds from the poll

---

[46]Einwand, St. Arch. Meiningen, In Alt, 42, 1373, pp. 53–85.
[47]St. Arch. Meiningen, Schwendler 'Promemoria', in Alt, 42, 1393, pp. 13–16.
[48]*Ibid.*

tax obtained by the *Mediatsherren*, reduced returns therefrom were acceptable to the ducal administration, since the diminished returns were compensated for by the anticipated increase in revenue from the "occupational income tax" to which the *Reichsunmittelbaren*, were no party. The fight against the privileges of the *reichsunmittelbare Ritterschaft* had been won through the dissolution of the latter organisation in 1806. Privileges had to be returned to some degree only nine years later in 1815, when holders of these privileges were given more or less identical licence under the title of *Mediatsherren*. Even in 1811 the ducal administration ceded the right to levy poll tax to former members of the *reichsunmittelbare Ritterschaft*.

The ancient power and privilege of the guilds could also be curtailed under the guise of the "Jew Law". The Duchess had implied:

> "The Jews wish to be accepted everywhere as neighbours and master craftsmen . . . and thus all statutes and guilds would have to be abolished and this would cause well established rights of Christian subjects to come into conflict. This might also be a valid reason. The main cause, however, is the different life style and means of livelihood of the Jews . . ."[49]

The privileges of the guilds were a thorn in the flesh of the authorities. When discussing §18 attention was drawn to the proviso that should there be no agreement with the guilds to admit into their ranks professional Jewish masters, the Ducal Government would give the Jews permission to call themselves *Freymeister*. This proviso ran contrary to one of the basic stipulations of guild membership, the *conditio sine qua non*, of being Christian as a necessity for acceptance into the ranks of the guilds (a reference made in the official "Ablehnung" under §6).

A slightly different light on the same subject is provided by the *ad hoc "Votum"* document. Künßberg confirms the intention that Jews should be treated for the poll tax purposes in the same manner as Christians except for the poll tax (incumbent on Jews only) divided into four classes. Then, however, he continues, that whatever the Jews say on the subject is unimportant. "They do not want to pay poll tax any longer . . ." This does not concur with the *Einwand* response. Under §16 the representatives of the Jewish communities say:

> "Would it not be feasible to retain the poll tax as at present, without additional [taxes], when Jews already have to carry a heavier burden than Christians and yet do not obtain their rights."

No further light has been thrown by any other document on this difference of interpretation. Schwendler does not enter the argument. It appears that every landlord interpreted the Edict's four classes in another way, so that injustice in the application of the law was noted. The Duchess became involved and asked for clarification. Again *Vice-Kanzler* Künßberg points us to the Edict's true intent: curbing the power of the *Gerichtsherren*.

Schwendler suggests, that in order to prevent misapplication of the tax it should be the government's duty to stipulate a classification for each Jew individually and to advise all *Gerichtsherren* of how much they are allowed to

---

[49]St. Arch. Meiningen, *ad hoc "Votum"*, In Alt, 42, 1393, pp. 20–29.

charge in poll tax. For this purpose the Chancellor was to get hold of the appropriate lists of asset assessment for each Jew, normally prepared by the *Parnass* for the benefit of the *Gerichtsherren*. Thus another step in controlling the aristocracy and landowners is introduced. Lists of such a nature were in fact prepared in 1820.[50]

There is neither space nor time to describe in detail every sundry paragraph of the Edict. Worth repeating is §21 of the Edict, relevant as it is to a modern democratic state.

> "We charge all our faithful subjects to behave to each other – without regard to the difference of religious beliefs – in such a manner as it behoves law-abiding citizens and thus to fulfil duties which are incumbent on all religions. We especially renew herewith the ban that no member of any religion may mock or abuse another because of his adherence to a religion or its customs, under pain of severe punishment or Our serious displeasure."

The "Jews Edict of Sachsen-Meiningen of 1811", as it became known, had analogues in Bavaria, Franconia, in other parts of Saxony, in Baden, Swabia, Hesse etc. These documents had sometimes even identical phraseology, although the number of paragraphs differed. For instance:

> "§2. Until further orders are issued – the Jewish families within this county shall remain restricted to the present number.
> In general, only one son from each family may continue the family by getting married . . ."

The prohibition preventing the Jews growing in number in Bavaria found in the *Matrikel* Edict of Montgelas dated 1813 under §12 was an almost verbatim reflection of the one which was issued in Sachsen-Meiningen in 1811 except that the one in Bavaria had a rider declaring:

> "The number of Jewish families in designated villages, may not in general be increased. On the contrary, should it be too large it should be decreased gradually . . ."[51]

The identical language between various edicts issued in divers places is not coincidental. A major component of the decree of Sachsen-Meiningen was drafted by a professional administrator, Schwendler who was instructed to extract information on legislation in other duchies. Thus, he refers to the Ducal *Geheimrats Kollegium* report of 4th July 1809 and 20th January 1810 in his submission of a draft report dated 4th March 1810.[52] In this report, as justification for his recommendation, he also cited various documents: i.a. the French Emperor's Decree at previously held discussions in the years 1806, 1807 and 1808;[53] the "Fürstliche sogenannte Primatische 'Neue Stättigkeiten Schutzverordnung der Judenschaft zu Frankfurt' . . ."[54] The "Grossherzogliche

---

[50]St. Arch. Meiningen, Schwender, 'Promemoria', In Alt, 42, 1393, pp. 13–16.
[51]St. Arch, Meiningen, 'Tabellarische Uebersicht', In Alt, 42, 1393.
[52]St. Arch. Meiningen, Schwendler, 'Promemoria', In Alt, 42, 1393, pp. 13–16.
[53]See *Hallische Literaturzeitung* (1808), Nos. 239 and 240.
[54]For extracts of the 'Neue Stättigkeiten Schutzordnung der Judenschaft zu Frankfurt, deren Verfassung, Rechts und Verbindlichkeiten betr. del Paris den 30. Nov. 1807 und publicato Januar 1808', see *Rheinischer Bund*, vol. XIV, February 1808.

Badische Verordnung, die verschiedenen Stände im Grossherzogtum Baden betr.",[55] and a collection of unspecified documents held by Schwendler.

Although he drafted the Edict, it would be misleading to believe that Schwendler had a major influence in deciding its contents. The most active of all persons in drafting the text was the president of the *Geheimrats Collegio*, Künßberg. From his own account, under the title "*Votum*", he had close personal contact with the Duchess and reported on every attitude she had towards the decree.

The Duchess was Luise Eleonore, born on 11th August 1763, eldest daughter of *Fürst* Christian Albrecht Ludwig von Hohenlohe-Langenberg. She was married at the age of nineteen to Duke Georg I of Sachsen-Meiningen. On his death in December 1803 she took over as Regent and Guardian of her son, Bernhard Erich Freund (1803–1866). One of her daughters was Adelhaid, the later Queen Adelaide, married to William IV of England.

Another member of the inner cabinet was Christian Ferdinand von Könitz, born 7th March 1756 and educated at the University of Jena. He was an advocate for the feudal aristocracy and was said to have been a compassionate fighter for paternal attitudes towards the poorer population. No sign of such compassion can be noted from his attitude towards Jews.

Oberstallmeister Gottlieb Friedrich Hartmann von Erffa was born on 6th November 1761 and entered on a military career. Nominated by Georg I as a stablemaster, he became a member of the inner cabinet in 1792. He was active for the state in his mission to Poznań in 1806 to conclude a peace treaty with Napoleon, which ended in the duchy entering the *Rheinbund*.

Konsistorial Vize-Präsident Johann Ludwig Heim, born on 9th June 1741 in Solz, was the son of a parish priest and was the only member of the cabinet of humble origin. Through his position as a tutor to Georg I he became the Duke's friend in later years and thus was nominated to the inner cabinet. He had hardly any interest in politics unless they revolved around the church and education. His was one of the few voices against the stipulations of §2, although he must have abandoned his opposition since the decree of 1811 was unopposedly accepted in its entirety on 30th March 1810.

All the members of the *Herzogliche Geheimrats Collegio*, including the Duchess, took an active part in the drafting of the Edict of 1811. Their motives as well as their characters and their individual contributions in formulating the Edict have become very clear during study of the documents. One document most probably never designed for public scrutiny is the record entitled "*Votum*".[56] With equal clarity the life of the Jews in the villages has been revealed through the uniqueness of the evidence preserved in the *Einwand Ablehnung* and the testimony of the submission "Nassfelder Amtsbericht".

This essay serves to indicate the link between the two intentions of the Edict: the emancipation of the Jews and the opening of the doors to their German education; and the desire of the ducal authorities to curb the power of the *Mediatsherren* and the guilds.

[55] Printed in the *Rheinischer Bund*, vol. XXVIII.
[56] St. Arch. Meiningen, *ad hoc "Votum"*, In Alt, 42, 1393, pp. 20–29.

Missionary Politics
Protestant Missions to the Jews in Nineteenth-Century Prussia

BY CHRISTOPHER CLARK

On 25th January 1822, a group of men gathered at the Berlin residence of General Job von Witzleben to found the Berlin Society for the Promotion of Christianity among the Jews. Throughout the nineteenth century and indeed up until its closure by the *Gestapo* in 1941, the Berlin Society distributed conversionary texts in German, Yiddish and Hebrew to Jews throughout the eastern provinces of Prussia. It produced an annual report for its membership and published a number of missionary journals. The Society also sent out missionaries, mainly into the provinces of Poznań and Silesia, whose job it was to address Jews in the streets and inns of the Jewish quarters, and to stage missionary sermons in local Protestant churches which all truth-seeking children of Israel were cordially invited to attend. The missionaries sold or gave away edifying texts with titles like *Light at Eventide* and *The Lamb of Pesach*, in which, for example, it was argued that Christ was the true lamb of the Passover. In addition to all this, the Berlin Society was able, with financial assistance from the wealthy London Society for Promoting Christianity among the Jews (LSPCJ), to found a series of Jewish free schools in the Province of Poznań. The Berlin Society quickly became the hub of a network of auxiliary societies in the cities and towns of the eastern provinces. These "daughter societies" gathered donations from local missionary enthusiasts and supported the work of the itinerant agents of the Berlin Society. In 1845, a "sister society", which commanded a similar network of auxiliaries, was established in Cologne.

There are two reasons above all why the attitudes and ideology reflected in the journals, reports, records and correspondence of the Berlin Society for the Promotion of Christianity among the Jews and its various daughter-societies should be of particular interest to us. Firstly: no other body of texts can provide us with as sustained and considered an appraisal of the "Jewish Question" as it evolved in nineteenth-century Prussia. Secondly: the voices of the mission were not those of a fanatical and isolated coven of enthusiasts. Missionary work to Jews in nineteenth-century Prussia engaged the approval and support of some of the most powerful individuals in the kingdom. King Friedrich Wilhelm III pledged a yearly donation, which his successors continued to pay throughout the century, and personally informed the Society's president, Job von Witzleben, that the new foundation expressed his "innermost wishes".[1] Witzleben himself had been chief of the Military Cabinet, the king's personal correspondence bureau, since 1817 – an appointment which brought him into almost daily contact with the sovereign. Among the founding members of the mission committee were Court Chaplain Franz Theremin, the theologian and orientalist Friedrich August Tholuck, who was shortly to become the chief academic spokesman of theological anti-rationalism in Prussia, the Chargé d'Affaires of the Grand Duchy of Baden, and the British envoy in Berlin, Sir George Rose, a director of the LSPCJ. Another member of the committee was the former tutor of Crown Prince Friedrich Wilhelm (later Friedrich Wilhelm IV), Johann Peter Friedrich Ancillon, then a legation counsellor and later (from 1832) Prussian Minister of Foreign Affairs.

Throughout the 1830s, 1840s and 1850s, the Society continued to engage the interest and participation of a remarkable sample of Prussia's conservative Protestant elite. Among later members of the successive boards of directors which met to determine policy and to approve new publications were Ernst Hengstenberg, founder-editor of the conservative anti-rationalist *Evangelische Kirchenzeitung* and Friedrich Julius Stahl, the foremost theorist of the Christian State. Among the directors were several men – Adolf von Thadden, Ernst von Senfft-Pilsach and Leopold von Gerlach – who were close associates of the Crown Prince and followed him into power after his accession in 1840. When a *camarilla* formed around the King in 1848, it included Leopold von Gerlach and General Karl von der Gröben, both members of the Berlin Society. Two members (Stahl and Senfft-Pilsach) later went on to become leaders of the Conservative faction in the Prussian Diet. In other words, the Berlin Society was not the work of isolated and marginal true believers, but it cannot be said to have reflected the broad spectrum of Prussian church opinion. Indeed, with the exception of the missionaries themselves, who were generally theological aspirants looking for employment, clerical participation in missionary work to Jews remained at a conspicuously low level until the 1860s. But Berlin Society did represent the attitudes of a disproportionately powerful, if socially narrow, Christian constituency to the "Jewish Question" in Prussia.

The involvement of aristocrats, military personnel and senior bureaucrats in the Berlin mission, and the support it received from the highest state authorities are understandable if we consider two factors. In the late 1810s and the 1820s, it was not unusual for government officials at central and local level to recommend conversion as the best means of ensuring the seamless absorption of the Jews into the Prussian State. In 1816, for example, the Ministry of Finance made the following contribution to a debate within the Ministerial Council over the status of the Jews in Prussia: "The conversion of Jews to the Christian religion must be made easier and should entail the granting of all civil rights. However, as long as the Jew remains a Jew, he must not be permitted to take up a position in the

---

[1]Richard Bieling, *Die Juden vornehmlich 1822–1901* (with a supplement by K. Schaeffer for the period 1903–1912), Berlin 1913, p. 12.

state."[2] In a report of 1819, the district government of Arnsberg in the Rhineland affirmed that religion was the main hindrance to Jewish emancipation and recommended that the state introduce measures to encourage the Jews to convert to Christianity.[3] Such recommendations were typical of the conservative trend in government attitudes to emancipation after 1815, and their impact on Prussian Jewry was enhanced by the fact that Jews continued, after the "Edict of Emancipation" of March 1812, to be excluded by law from state and teaching offices. When the mathematician David Unger, who had been a citizen of Prussia since 1822, applied for a teaching position at the *Bauakademie* in 1824, he was advised by Friedrich Wilhelm that his application would be reconsidered "after his conversion to the Evangelical Church".[4] In the widely-discussed case of the Jewish lieutenant Meno Burg, who was due in 1830 to be promoted to the rank of captain, the King issued a Cabinet Order in which he expressed his assumption that Burg would have the sense to come to a recognition of the truth and redeeming power of the Christian faith and thus "clear away any obstacle to his promotion".[5] For Prussian Jews, conversion to Christianity continued to be, as Heine put it, "a ticket of admission into European society".

The second factor influencing the readiness of persons of elevated social status to patronise missionary activity was the movement of neo-Pietist religious revival known as the "Awakening". A variety of revivalist movements had gathered momentum among German artisans and peasants during the last decades of the eighteenth century. In the years following the end of the Napoleonic Wars, however, a distinctly patrician revivalism emerged in Berlin, in which noblemen, senior officials and military brass played a dominant role. This was the age of "perfumed Pietism", as Arnold Ruge called it in his *Hallische Jahrbücher*. It was not unusual during the 1820s for generals and aristocrats who spent their afternoons in staff headquarters or ministerial offices to pass their evenings with communal prayer and Bible-reading. Like the adherents of the "original" pietism of the late seventeenth and early eighteenth centuries, the "awakened" were relatively uninterested in institutional religion. Awakened Christians, as one of their number, Ludwig von Gerlach, was later to recall, were less interested in the church service than in "the private devotional meeting, the sermon in the house, the barn or the field, the *conventicle*. Here one could find a statement of faith which was more vigorous, more lively, more intimate, more in tune with a sense of brotherly community."[6] The religious zeal of the "awakened" expressed itself in enthusiasm for a missionary offensive against unbelief at home. The pious Anton

---

[2]Cited in *Juden in Preußen. Ein Kapitel deutscher Geschichte*, hrsg. vom Bildarchiv Preußischer Kulturbesitz, Dortmund 1981, pp. 161–162.

[3]Horst Fischer, *Judentum, Staat und Heer in Preußen im frühen 19. Jahrhundert. Zur Geschichte der staatlichen Judenpolitik*, Tübingen 1968 (Schriftenreihe wissenschaftlicher Abhandlungen des Leo Baeck Instituts 20), p. 95.

[4]Friedrich Wilhelm III, Cabinet Order of 14th June 1824, reproduced in *Juden in Preußen, op. cit.*, p. 195.

[5]Friedrich Wilhelm III, Cabinet Order of 6th December 1830, cited in Nathan Samter, *Judentaufen im neunzehnten Jahrhundert*, Berlin 1906, p. 19. Burg was, in fact, subsequently promoted to captain when it became impossible for him to remain in service without loss of honour.

[6]E. Ludwig von Gerlach, 'Das Königreich Gottes', in *Evangelische Kirchenzeitung*, 68 (1861), cols. 438–454, here cols. 438–439 (Gerlach's emphasis).

von Stolberg, for example, who participated in the conservative noble club life of post-war Berlin, made the following promise: "We shall become missionaries, not among the wild tribes in India and Africa, but among the heathens of the Fatherland."[7] The Jews were not "heathens", but it could be argued that in the absence of overseas colonies, they should be Prussia's first missionary priority. In his inaugural address to the Berlin Society Sir George Rose urged that those pious German Christians, who had hitherto been "excluded from that field of heathen-conversion to which only seafaring nations have direct access", should now look to "those millions of the old People of God who live amidst them or in their immediate vicinity".[8]

Yet, despite the powerful patronage enjoyed by the Jewish mission, and its pivotal position between the activist piety of the revivalist aristocrats in Berlin and the Christian statism of the Prussian government, the Berlin Society has received very little scholarly attention. The only two historical monographs to appear since 1945 on missionary activity amongst Jews in Germany stem from the Cologne theologian Paul Gerhard Aring.[9] But like the much more numerous nineteenth-century studies of the subject – those of Johannes de le Roi, Gustav Dalman and Richard Bieling deserve special mention[10] – Aring's work is dominated by theological perspectives. The work of those who write from within the church can offer a deep acquaintance with missionary theology and sometimes even the experience of missionary life which one would be very unlikely to find in the secular scholarship, but it is relatively uninterested in the political and cultural contexts of missionary work. The task of historicising missionary activity in ways which question the trans-historical and trans-political claims of missionary self-representation is by no means new, but it has not as yet been carried out in the field of the Jewish mission.

This analysis of missionary ideology in nineteenth-century Prussia will concentrate on two issues. Firstly: the response of the missionary societies to the phenomenon of Jewish Reform – the liturgical "modernisation" of German Judaism which originated in the eighteenth-century *Haskalah*. And secondly: the impact on missionary attitudes of the campaign for the legal emancipation of Jewry in Prussia. A consideration of these questions will in turn permit us to draw some connections between the ideology of Christian missionary activity and that of nineteenth-century German antisemitism. This article is not concerned with the phenomenon of conversion as such. Notwithstanding the unease and occasional hysteria of contemporaries, the rate of German-Jewish

---

[7] Anton von Stolberg, cited in J. Althausen, *Kirchliche Gesellschaften in Berlin, 1810–1830. Ein Beitrag zur Geschichte der Erweckungsbewegung und des Laienapostolats in den evangelischen Kirchen des 19. Jahrhunderts*, Ph.D. diss., University of Halle-Wittenberg 1965, p. 21.
[8] Bieling, *op. cit.*, p. 14.
[9] Paul Gerhard Aring, *Christliche Judenmission. Ihre Geschichte und Problematik dargestellt und untersucht am Beispiel des evangelischen Rheinlandes*, Neukirchen-Vluyn 1980; idem, *Christen und heute – und die Judenmission? Geschichte und Theologie protestantischer Judenmission in Deutschland, dargestellt und untersucht am Beispiel des Protestantismus im mittleren Deutschland*, Munich 1987.
[10] Johannes F.A. de le Roi, *Stefan Schulz. Ein Beitrag zum Verständnis der Juden nach ihrer Bedeutung für das Leben der Völker*, Gotha 1871; idem, *Die evangelische Christenheit und die Juden unter dem Gesichtspunkte der Mission betrachtet*, 3 vols., Karlsruhe–Leipzig 1884, 1891; Gustav Dalman, *Kurzgefaßtes Handbuch der Mission unter Israel*, Berlin 1893; Bieling, *op. cit.*

Protestant Missions to the Jews in Prussia

conversions to Christianity was at no time during the nineteenth century sufficient to challenge the existence or the identity of the Jewish communities. The annual rate of apostasy was probably substantially under one per cent. Missionary activity accounted in turn for only a very small fraction of total Jewish conversions. In other words, the numerical impact of the missions on the Jewish community was negligible. The missions could not and did not justify themselves by convert numbers. But, as I will show, there were other ways of defending the necessity of missionary work to Jews in nineteenth-century Prussia.

Even before the foundation of the Berlin Society in 1822, the response of neo-Pietist circles in Berlin to the Jewish Reform movement had been overwhelmingly positive. In 1820, the journal *Neueste Nachrichten*, which was read by awakened Protestants throughout Northern Germany, reported on the existence of a "beautiful synagogue" in Berlin, where a German liturgy had been installed to replace the "senseless blabbering of prayers in a language which most [of them] do not understand".[11] It referred, no doubt, to the religious services held by the layman Israel Jacobson in the spacious villa of the banker Jacob Herz Beer, father of the composer Giacomo Meyerbeer.[12] Jacobson had opened a Reform temple in Seesen in 1810 and subsequently promoted the cause of Reform as head of the Jewish Consistory in the Napoleonic Kingdom of Westphalia. After the collapse of Napoleonic power in 1814, he moved to Berlin, where his religious meetings quickly became the focus of a nascent Reform movement in Berlin. Awakened Christians welcomed the movement's emphasis on the pedagogical and ethical dimensions of religion and its rejection of the talmudic devotion which still characterised Orthodox Judaism. An article printed one year later in *Neueste Nachrichten* compared the Reform Jews favourably with their Orthodox counterparts. Whereas the latter were "mostly avaricious, superstitious and earthly-minded people", the Reformers were clearly in search of "more religious nourishment for their hearts than the cadaverous pomp (*Leichengepränge*) of the old ceremony could offer them".[13]

The Berlin Society was founded amidst pious rumours that the end of Judaism was at hand and its members believed that the Reform movement would play an important role in accelerating its decline. As Friedrich August Tholuck pointed out in the journal *Der Freund Israels* in 1825, there were two possible ways of looking at the phenomenon of Reform. One could either see it as a symptom of the alienation of the Jews from their own Old Testament belief, or one could see it as a sign of spiritual hunger among those who sought true belief, whose hearts had "warmed" to some extent, but who were not yet ready to convert to

---

[11] 'Juden in Deutschland', in *Neueste Nachrichten aus dem Reich Gottes*, 4 (1820), pp. 284–287, here p. 286.

[12] For a brief summary of the Reform movement in Berlin, see Albert H. Friedlander, 'Von Berlin in die Welt. Personen und Stationen der jüdischen Reformbewegung', in Andreas Nachama, Julius H. Schoeps and Edward van Voolen (eds.), *Jüdische Lebenswelten. Essays*, Frankfurt a. Main 1991, pp. 13–22.

[13] 'Das Christenthum unter den Juden', in *Neueste Nachrichten aus dem Reich Gottes*, 5 (1821), pp. 439–446, here p. 441.

Christianity. Tholuck endorsed the latter view. He saw Reform as a half-way-house for those whose spirituality was still "weak and lethargic" (*schwach und unlebendig*). It was incorrect, he pointed out, to confuse Reform with unbelief.[14]

In fact, Reform Jewish services had been forbidden in Berlin by royal order on 9th December 1823. The prohibition reflected the conservative spirit of the King's religious policy. Throughout the 1820s, Friedrich Wilhelm III did all he could to prevent the proliferation of potentially separatist groups within the recognised confessional communities. The committee of the Berlin Society disapproved of the King's measure against the Reformers. It was widely assumed in the Jewish community that the Society itself had been the instigator of the prohibition. "They should assure themselves", wrote Tholuck, "that not one step in that direction was taken by this society". Christians should not fear that the adherents of a Reformed, deistic Jewish religion would be harder to convert than those of the old talmudic Judaism. Tholuck observed that Reform rabbis were generally trained at "Christian universities" and argued that Christians ought to welcome every development which might increase the influence of the Christian environment upon the Jewish religion.[15]

The readiness of the missionaries to believe that Reform meant the end of Judaism was due in part to the widespread assumption that Reform represented little more than an assimilation to Protestant norms. But it also expressed a hope which had always played an important role in motivating missions to Jews. Throughout the eighteenth and the nineteenth centuries, missionaries in Prussia pointed to various passages of the Bible – among which Paul's Letter to the Romans was the most important – as scriptural authority for the millenarian expectation of a mass conversion of the Jews to Christianity. It was argued that the restoration of the Jews would herald the fall of Babylon and the entry of the heathens into the Christian fold. Mel Scult has already shown how important this belief was in the development of missionary activity and the campaign for Jewish emancipation in Britain.[16] One advantage of this millenarian scenario was that it provided the missions with a way of distracting attention from their poor performance in terms of convert numbers. It was not the trickle of converts each year that mattered, but the subterranean shifts which missionary propaganda was supposedly generating in the religious sentiment of the Jewish communities. When describing this process, the missions favoured the biblical metaphor of the *Sauerteig*, that little lump of leaven which, when added to the dough, ferments and alters the whole by progressive inward transformation.

But like Martin Luther, whose early hopes of a mass Jewish conversion to Christianity were also linked with millenarian anticipation, the missionaries were soon to be disappointed. The Jews failed to show signs of softening, and bitterness and disillusionment set in when it became clear that, far from heralding the end of Judaism, the Reform movement had in effect given it a new

---

[14]Friedrich August Tholuck, 'Über die neue Synagoge der sogenannten reformirten Juden', in *Der Freund Israels*, 2 (1825), pp. 41–83, here pp. 41–43.
[15]*Ibid.*, pp. 45–47.
[16]Mel Scult, *Millennial Expectations and Jewish Liberties. A Study of Efforts to Convert the Jews in Britain up to the mid-19th Century*, Leiden 1978.

lease of life. During the early years of the mission's existence, it was sometimes still possible for the missionaries to enter synagogues and preach to the Jews inside. In 1826, for example, one Jewish community in Prussian Poland permitted the missionary Friedrich Händes to preach, wearing a surplice, for two hours in the synagogue on the subject of "the revelations which God has prepared in the Old Covenant and fulfilled in the New".[17] In the following year, however, Händes and his companion, the convert missionary Johannes Ball received an unfriendly reception when they tried to enter a synagogue during Sukkot. Ball recorded the incident in his diary.

> "The festival dance had not yet begun. The children crowded around me in the entrance chamber. I bade them to go to their prayers and spoke to some of the old people. One of them said: 'The world stands on the children'. 'No', I said. 'It stands on *one* child and this child is the one of which Isaiah speaks: "Unto us a child is given" . . . namely, the King, Jesus of Nazareth, may his name be praised. If the world stood on your sinful children, it would have perished long ago.'"[18]

Because they had "mentioned the name of the Crucified One" in the entrance to the synagogue, Ball reported, the Jews became very angry and the missionaries were forced to withdraw. When they returned a short while later, they found themselves surrounded by a hostile crowd.

> "One of them stood before me with a clenched fist and screamed: a Christian would still be deserving of respect, but a convert like me was an abomination and an outrage. On all sides they cried: 'May the tongue rot which has spoken these lies.'"[19]

After a number of episodes in which missionaries – and not merely convert missionaries – were threatened by angry crowds of worshippers, the societies restricted themselves to "quiet housecalls" on individual Jews.[20] Although it continued to be possible for missionaries to enter synagogues in order to hear sermons, an active missionising role there was seen to be impracticable. In 1856, the Berlin Society adopted the practice of applying to the Jewish communal authorities for permission to preach in the synagogues, but permission was always refused.[21]

The attendance by Jews of the regular missionary sermons in Berlin and those given by intinerant missionaries on route was hardly more encouraging than the reception missionaries received in synagogues. Missionary sermons were often ambiguously titled in order to conceal their conversionary purpose, and they generally attracted good audiences for as long as they retained their novelty. In later years, the missionaries often had to cope with miserably small audiences. Missionary Teichler informed the Berlin committee in 1840 that it was his policy

---

[17] *Jahresbericht der Gesellschaft zur Beförderung des Christenthums unter den Juden zu Berlin* (hereafter *Jahresbericht der GBCJ*), 3 (1826).
[18] Most of the missionaries kept diaries which were later sent as reports to the committee in Berlin. This passage is cited in 'Nachrichten aus der Mission von Preußisch-Polen', in *Neueste Nachrichten aus dem Reich Gottes*, 11 (1827), pp.120–136, here pp. 128–129.
[19] *Ibid.*, p. 130.
[20] See 'Einleitung', in *Missionsblatt des Rheinisch-Westphälischen Vereins für Israel*, 1 (1845).
[21] *Jahresbericht der GBCJ*, 33 (1856), p. 12.

to start his sermons with an explicit reference to Christ's divinity, so as to get the message across before the Jews in the audience started leaving.[22]

Even the Jewish children in the free schools of Poznań seemed impervious to the hints and nudgings of their Christian teachers. 'The hearts of the little ones are less stubborn than ours", one of the teachers observed. But they were clearly not the clear sheets of paper awaiting inscription that the missionaries may have wished for. In 1831, Missionary Händes made the unpleasant discovery that Jewish children, far from being in an unsullied state of nature, displayed *in nuce* all the regrettable traits of their elders: "No-one who has not had to do with Jewish children can possibly have any idea of their depravity (*Verderbtheit*)", he reported to Berlin, "that is, how mighty the sin in them has grown because no struggle has been undertaken against it. I am getting to know them better and better and the more I do so, the more I am aware that I am far from knowing them through and through, and so it goes on."[23] The Berlin committee and its daughter and sister societies were agreed that the mission to the Jews was, as they put it, "*eine Thränensaat*," a "sowing of tears".[24]

The fact that the Jews failed to flock to the mission at a rate of more than around ten converts per year was certainly galling, but the situation was exacerbated by the missionaries' awareness, in the late 1820s and 1830s, that they were increasingly isolated within the Christian community. Although, as has been pointed out, the missions enjoyed influential patronage, they were hampered at the local level by provincial church authorities dominated by theological rationalists, jealous of their authority and suspicious of the meddlings of laypersons in what they regarded as church affairs. The problem was that the missionary and voluntarist culture of which the Berlin Society was typical had grown up out of the Prussian "Awakening": the public bearing and religiosity of the missionaries marked them out as anti-rationalist neo-Pietists who had come to spread the word among Christians as well as Jews. The predilection of the missionaries for conventicles and prayer groups aroused the suspicion of local church authorities. In May 1826, the consistory of the province of Prussia in Königsberg complained to the Ministry of Church, Health and Educational Affairs that while ministering to the Jews of the province, Missionary Händes of the Berlin Society had "gathered about him the inexperienced female youth of Neidenburg, so that after his departure a regular society for religious purposes had formed in the house of the dyer Oettinger". The consistory argued that the meetings in Oettinger's house constituted a "sect" in the "general sense of any separatist gathering". As a result of these meetings, the young women of Neidenburg had been "filled with fantasy", rendered "mentally confused and physically exhausted", and were "unfit for chores and numb to all appeals".[25] This complaint exemplifies the hostility which organised, non-ecclesiastical

---

[22]'Auszüge aus dem Tagebuch des Missionars und Predigtamts-Candidaten Teichler', in *Jahresbericht der GBCJ*, 18 (1841), pp. 10–25, here p. 24.

[23]Cited from Friedrich Händes's service diary, in *Königsberger Missionsblatt*, December 1831, p. 183.

[24]'Das Missionswerk an Israel ist eine Thränensaat!', in *Jahresbericht der GBCJ*, 21 (1844), p. 27.

[25]Royal Prussian Consistory to the *Kultusministerium*, Königsberg, 18th May 1826, in Geheimes Staatsarchiv Merseburg, Rep. 76 III, Sekt. 1, Abt. XIV, fols. 55–57.

religiosity could arouse among the still largely rationalist officials of the state church. In other words, the missionaries frequently faced the resistance and indifference not only of the Jewish communities, but also of the state church itself.

Another reason for the increasing ferocity of missionary attacks on the Reform movement was the appearance in the Jewish press of articles which questioned the integrity and efficacy of the missions. The creation in the 1830s and early 1840s of journals which took an interest in religious and secular issues affecting the Jewish communities testifies to the cultural and political vigour of a fast-growing Jewish middle class which was willing to mount a counter-offensive against missionary propaganda. Ludwig Philippson's *Allgemeine Zeitung des Judenthums*, for example, repeatedly cast doubt on the motives of converts from Judaism and the ability of baptism to effect a genuine transformation in the individual . Stories were published about Jewish boys "fished up" in coffee houses by "convert missionaries".[26] Julius Fürst's journal, *Der Orient*, frequently stressed the role of material rewards in the motivation of Jewish applicants for conversion. The credibility of such claims was bolstered by the fact that converts to Christianity who had the King of Prussia entered in the church records as their nominal "godfather" were offered a "baptismal gift" (*Pathengeschenk*) of ten ducats or thirty marks, a sum which did not fail to evoke uncomfortable New Testament associations in the minds of some contemporaries. The distribution of royal baptismal gifts to Jews had begun in the mid-1820s and it continued unabated through the 1830s. In October 1842, however, royal cabinet secretary Müller informed Johann Albrecht Eichhorn of the Ministry of Church, Health and Educational Affairs (*Kultusministerium*) that the King now had doubts about the practice It was Eichhorn's view that the royal *Pathengeschenk* should be abandoned. "In my view", he wrote to Müller on 30th October 1842, "only the really needy Jewish proselytes ought to be considered, and even with these, it seems inappropriate and could easily lead to sceptical judgements (*schiefe Urtheilen*) about the dignity and purity of this holy matter, if a close association is established between the act of baptism and a gift of money".[27] Friedrich Wilhelm accepted this view and announced in a Cabinet Order of January 1843 that the giving of money on the day of baptism was to be discontinued, although provisions were made for later assistance if this should prove necessary.[28] *Der Orient* responded by running an article which reported that prices for Jewish souls were falling fast and that the "share values of the conversion clubs had plummeted".[29] *Der Orient* consistently depicted the activity of the missionary

---

[26] For sceptical accounts of missionary activity, see, for example, 'Zeitungsnachrichten. Oesterreich', in *Allgemeine Zeitung des Judenthums*, 8 (29th July 1844), pp. 430–432; 'Stimmen in der christlichen Kirche', in *Allgemeine Zeitung des Judenthums*, 8 (18th November 1844), pp. 665–672.

[27] Minister Eichhorn to Privy Cabinet Secretary Dr. Müller, Berlin, 30th November 1842, in GeStA Merseburg, Geheimes Zivilkabinett, 2.2.1, Nr. 4544.

[28] Friedrich Wilhelm IV to Eichhorn, Berlin, 11th January 1843, in GeStA Merseburg, Geheimes Zivilkabinett, 2.2.1, Nr. 4544.

[29] *Der Orient*, 5 (1844), p. 229.

societies – for which it used the contemptuous term *Proselytenmacherei* – as a grotesque and morally distasteful speculation in souls.[30]

The missionary journals responded vigorously to these sallies. In 1845, Missionary Bellson's Berlin-based *Blätter für Israels Gegenwart und Zukunft* observed that the Jewish press and the Reform rabbis seemed recently to have acquired the need to "deal out stinging blows upon the missionaries" and to "shower them with the blunt spears of their irony".[31] In the same year, the missionary journal *Dibre Emeth* ran an article entitled: '*Der Orient* – a lying rag', in which it refuted charges which the latter had made against individual missionaries working in the Prussian provinces.[32] Indeed the witty and caustic reporting of the Jewish journals may have been the chief reason for the appearance of these two new missionary publications in 1845 – namely *Dibre Emeth* and *Blätter für Israels Gegenwart und Zukunft*. *Blätter*, in particular, openly avowed that its foremost aim was to "correct lying attacks against the church of Christ, ecclesiastical offices and missionary activity". The wounds sustained by the missions from these volleys may help to explain their repeated references to the poisonous influence of what they called the "Jewish press" or to the Jews as the "bearers of public opinion, who rule us as Jesuitism never could".[33] The journalistic skirmishes of the 1840s certainly help to explain the increasingly negative attitude of the missions to Jewish Reform. In 1845, *Blätter für Israels Gegenwart* announced that the very idea of Jewish Reform was an absurdity, since Judaism was incapable of being reformed without being destroyed in its essence. "For all the noise which has been made for decades" about Jewish Reform, the journal announced in the following year, the actual changes have been "external and superficial". The very things which hopeful Christians had once prized about Reform were now the proofs of its inadequacy. The missionary journals now argued that the wholesale adoption of Christian forms – organs, hymns, sermons – was incontrovertible testimony to the "emptiness and barrenness of the Jewish Reform-spirit".[34]

The conflation of Jewish Reform with "rationalism" and "unbelief" produced a further problem, familiar from the history of Christian-Jewish relations. If one insists that Judaism lacks religious content of any kind, what is one to make of the "Jewish community", or of those who call themselves "Jews"? The missionaries were unwilling to concede that modern Judaism might be founded upon a subjective adherence to certain religious principles. In denying that Reform Judaism was anything more than an assemblage of empty forms and prescriptions, they were reiterating a critique which German idealism had repeatedly made of unreformed Judaism, namely that it lacked the subjective dimension, the dimension of positive belief. Immanuel Kant, for example, maintained that

---

[30] See, for example, *Der Orient*, 3 (1842), p. 348; *ibid.*, 11 (1850), pp. 8, 84.

[31] 'Einige Worte an den Herrn Leopold Löw, Oberrabbiner zu Groß-Kanische in Ungarn', in *Blätter für Israels Gegenwart und Zukunft*, 1 (1845), pp. 64–75.

[32] 'Der Orient, ein Lügenblatt', in *Dibre Emeth, oder Stimmen der Wahrheit an Israeliten und Freunde Israels*, 1 (1845), pp. 56–63.

[33] 'Das Moderne Judenthum und dessen moderne Reformation', in *Blätter für Israels Gegenwart und Zukunft*, 1 (1845), pp. 7–22, here p. 21.

[34] 'Miscellen', in *Blätter für Israels Gegenwart und Zukunft*, 2 (1846), p. 223.

whereas Christianity constituted a "pure religious faith", Judaism had always consisted of "burdensome ceremonies" imposed from without by a "purely civil" code of law, in which "the inner essence of the moral disposition was not considered in the least".[35] In his early theological writings, Friedrich Hegel took a similar view. The Jewish service of God had been "ordered and compressed in dead formulas". As a result Judaism had failed to develop a true religious subjectivity: "Of spirit nothing remained, save obstinate pride in slavish obedience." Adherence to the Jewish religion meant the death of selfhood and the degradation of the individual to a "lifeless machine".[36] These critiques were directed, of course, against talmudic Judaism and may indeed have contributed to the Reform movement's rejection of Talmudism. But the central import of the missionary critique of Jewish Reform in the 1840s and 1850s was that the movement had failed to introduce an authentically positive element into Jewish religion. According to this view, the "modern Jew" had neither laws nor positive belief; his religion could not be defined as the subjective affirmation of faith, but only as the negation of Christianity. "What is the meaning of modern Judaism?" asked the Jewish-missionary journal *Jeschurun*. "What is its positive characteristic? . . . For the modern Jew in his freedom, there is no borderline, no obligation, no law. He and all of his kind are characterised solely by the negation of Christianity and of Christ himself."[37] An anonymous article printed in Hengstenberg's *Evangelische Kirchenzeitung* conveys an impression of the extremes to which this kind of critique could go:

> "The true Reform Jew is a thoroughly specific and peculiar being of a particular smell and taste. Even among the rodents, which gobble and beslaver everything and leave everywhere the traces of their gluttony, there is a variation in the degrees of their repulsiveness. The mouse, with its gnawing tooth, is not as odious as the caterpillar with its soft cold body and its countless legs, or the snail, which leaves behind its thick slime and always arouses disgust. Both are sometimes at large and eat up everything which is green, so that nothing remains but the bare stalks. Similarly, the Reform Jews gnaw away at everything which is still green in human life, at everything which warms the soul, which is beautiful, which is lofty and lovely: and if it were up to them, nothing would be left over but bones and brushwood."[38]

The Jewish negation of Christianity, as the missionary journal *Jeschurun* pointed out, did not always wear a "repellent cloak"; it clothed itself more often in "tolerant rationalist phrases".[39] It was the perceived association between Jewish Reform and the Christian rationalism which was gaining ground in the Prussian theological faculties in the 1830s and 1840s, that made the Reform movement seem so existentially threatening to the missions and their powerful

---

[35]Immanuel Kant, *Religion within the Limits of Reason Alone*, transl. by T. M. Greene, 2nd edn., La Salle, Ill. 1960, esp. pp. 74 and 116.

[36]Georg Wilhelm Friedrich Hegel, 'The Positivity of the Christian Religion', in *On Christianity*, transl. by T. M. Knox, Gloucester, Mass. 1970, Part 1: p. 68, Part 3: p. 178; idem, *Philosophie der Geschichte*, ed. by F. Brunstad, Leipzig 1961, pp. 285–286.

[37]'Zum Römerbrief. Die Nothwendigkeit des Judenthums', in *Jeschurun. Ein Monatsblatt für und über Israel im Verein mit Freunden Israels*, 1 (1859), pp. 37–46, here p. 41.

[38]'Fanny Lewald, oder das entleerte Judenthum', in *Evangelische Kirchenzeitung*, 80 (1865), cols. 945–952, here cols. 945–946. The second half of the article is in *Evangelische Kirchenzeitung*, 81 (1865), cols. 961–968.

[39]'Zum Römerbrief', *loc. cit.*, p. 41.

supporters. The motivating force behind the resistance of both Jews and Christians to the promptings of awakened Christianity, was, in the Berlin Society's view, the corrosive doctrine of rationalism, which was tantamount to unbelief. When an acrimonious public debate broke out in 1830 over the rationalist teachings of the theology faculty at the University of Halle, three members of the Berlin Society's committee (Friedrich Tholuck and Otto and Ludwig von Gerlach) were closely involved in the anti-rationalist agitation. In the rapidly escalating conflict between *Finsterlinge* and *Lichtfreunde*, the Berlin committee was clearly to be found in the former camp. The Berlin Society's increasingly sceptical responses to Jewish Reform must be seen against the background of this struggle between neo-Pietists or Orthodox fundamentalists and the neological "friends of light". In the 1820s it had still been possible to see the Reform movement as a Jewish version of the Protestant Reformation, but the events of the 1830s and 1840s suggested that the drift of Christians away from positive religion was a more appropriate analogy.

Nowhere was the alleged alliance between Reform Judaism and Christian liberalism more apparent to the missionaries than in the campaign for the legal emancipation of Jewry. It is well known that many Jewish liberals and radicals saw Jewish emancipation as part of a wider emancipatory process which would embrace the totality of German society. Conversely, a number of non-Jewish Prussian liberals were willing to include the emancipation of the Jews in their programmes for the liberalisation of Prussian society. This is certainly not to suggest that Jewish emancipationists and Christian liberals were in fact all united on the question of Jewish emancipation. No-one was more sensitive than Jewish emancipationists to the existence of the "false liberalism" espoused by men like Georg Herwegh, Franz von Dinglestedt, Arnold Ruge and Bruno Bauer, who, as "terrorists of freedom" saw the total disappearance of Judaism as the key to true emancipation.[40] The existence of widespread antisemitism and anti-Jewish prejudice in the liberal camp is well documented.[41] Nevertheless, for the opponents of both liberalism and modern Judaism, there was no shortage of evidence for a close connection between the two.

Until 3rd July 1869, when Jews throughout Prussia and the North German Confederations were granted full political emancipation, the missions consistently opposed the measure. Mission books and journals figured legal emancipation as the false reflection or travesty of conversion. The claims made for these two transformations by their respective adherents were indeed very similar. But the missions insisted on the fundamental difference between the merely legal freedoms furnished by emancipation and the true spiritual freedom promised by authentic conversion, between the shallow unity of mere citizenship, and the deeper *Wesenseinheit* or unity of essence of a people bound together by a common religious faith. Conversion and emancipation were seen as mutually negating – it

---

[40]*Zeitschrift für die religiösen Interessen des Judenthums*, 3 (1846), p. 389.
[41]See Helmut Berding, *Moderner Antisemitismus in Deutschland*, Frankfurt a. Main 1988, pp. 51–59; Reinhard Rürup, *Emanzipation und Antisemitismus. Studien zur "Judenfrage" der bürgerlichen Gesellschaft*, Göttingen 1975, p. 14.

was impossible to imagine them as complementary or parallel processes. It should be stressed that there was nothing inevitable or self-evident in this relationship between a missionary and an anti-emancipatory posture. The evangelical Lewis Way, who by his sizeable benefactions and personal support had made possible the establishment of a prosperous Jewish Mission in London, was a passionate supporter both of legal emancipation and of missionary activity among the Jews. Way and those members of the London Society who defended Jewish rights during discussion of the "Jew Bill" in the 1830s[42] are a reminder that the intransigence of Prussian missions on the emancipation question was more a result of their political provenance than of the Christian missionary imperative *per se*.

Thanks to the rank and influence of its most prominent members and sympathisers, the Berlin Society was able to participate directly in the efforts by conservative circles within or close to the government to prevent the legal emancipation of the Jews in Prussia. Until the eve of the 1848 Revolution, by contrast with the constitutional states of Southern and South-Western Germany, there was little public discussion of the emancipation question in Prussia. Debates were hardly necessary, since the government and the Provincial Diets of 1824–1828 were united in opposing the measure. But when the admission of Jews to teaching offices was debated at the First United Prussian Diet of 1847, one of its most vigorous opponents was Adolf von Thadden, a committee member of the Berlin mission and a leading figure in Christian revivalism in the province of Pomerania. During a long speech, von Thadden asked the assembly to imagine a Jewish professor explaining to his students the history of the Crusades. How would he present the figure of Godfrey de Bouillon, who refused to be named "King of Jerusalem" because he was unworthy of wearing a king's crown in the place where Christ had worn his crown of thorns? "If the Jew is neither a hypocrite nor a scoffer", von Thadden insisted, "*that* word will freeze on his lips!" His speech closed with a plea to all the deputies present that they should become missionaries. And in brackets, beneath the text, the transcripts report the response from the liberal benches: "Hilarity" (*Heiterkeit*).[43] General Ludwig Gustav von Thile, Privy State and Cabinet Minister, Minister of the Treasury, General of the Infantry and President of the Berlin Society for the Promotion of Christianity among the Jews, was able to offer the assembly more philosophical grounds for resisting Jewish emancipation. He argued that the "humanity-principle" (*Humanitätsprincip*) that underlay the liberal advocacy of emancipation could never alone constitute the foundation for the laws of the Prussian state because it did not defer to the principles of Christianity which that state ought to embody. As von Thile put it: "Christianity should not be constituted within the state, it should be above the state and should govern it."[44]

The view that the fundamentally Christian character of the Prussian state was the most significant obstacle to Jewish emancipation – a view shared by all of the

[42]Scult, *op. cit.*, p. 91.
[43]Forty-third session of the Three Estates, 17th June 1847, in *Der erste preußische vereinigte Landtag*, Berlin 1847, cols. 678–679.
[44]Thirty-first session of the Three Estates, 14th June 1847, *ibid.*, col. 467.

missionaries and the fundamentalist Christians of their milieu – found its most coherent expression in the works of a committee member of the Berlin Society, the conservative legal theorist Friedrich Julius Stahl. Born into a Jewish family in Bavaria, Stahl converted to Protestantism at the age of seventeen. Like so many of his colleagues on the Berlin committee, Stahl had come under the influence of Christian revivalism. During the late 1830s, he had attended the prayer and Bible-study groups of awakened Protestants in the city of Erlangen, where he taught at the university, before following a call to the University of Berlin in 1840. In a book called *Der christliche Staat*, Stahl argued that since the administrative structure of the state concerned itself with questions such as marriage, religion and public morality, its laws must express the "moral essence" (*das sittliche Wesen*) of the nation which had created it, and whose interests it represented. Since religion, in Stahl's view, was the foundation of all ethics, the state must be Christian in its essence. It would not, therefore, be possible to admit Jews and other non-Christians to political office without doing an injury to the principles upon which the state was founded. Failure to abide by this principle would lead, in Stahl's own formulation, to "the complete de-Christianisation of the state".[45]

During the middle decades of the nineteenth century, the missions to the Jews were redefining their role in Prussian society. The missionaries and their influential patrons felt themselves to be on the internal frontier of their own society. They were front-line fighters in the battle against unbelief in the Fatherland. Metaphors of struggle were invoked with increasing frequency. The role of the missions was no longer merely offensive, but defensive. To the missionaries, the Jews appeared to have allied themselves with the rationalism, liberalism and atheism of the non-Jewish environment. This alliance with what the missionary journals described as "the powers of unbelief" had enabled the Jews to make substantial inroads into the culture and constitution of the Prussian state. The Christian revivalist triumphalism of the early decades had vanished, and the millennial restoration of the Jews seemed further away than ever. In their moments of melodrama or melancholy, the missionaries could claim in their journals and reports that they were not merely the hope of Israel, but the last hope of Christianity itself.

As this defensive posture suggests, the attitude of the missionary societies to the Jewish Question resembled in some respects that of the antisemites who were to gain much political ground in late nineteenth-century Germany. The convergence of antisemitic views with those of some of the missionaries can be illustrated with a selection of examples. In a speech given at the Barmen *Kirchentag* in 1860 during a session devoted to the Jewish mission, a Pastor Schulze warned his listeners not to let the Jews out of sight,

> "for it is from them that so much ruin and misery have come over our people, and it is they who destroy the flower of your labour. Before, they had no honest profession, now they

[45] See esp. Friedrich Julius Stahl, *Der christliche Staat und sein Verhältniß zu Deismus und Judenthum. Eine durch die Verhandlungen des vereinigten Landtages hervorgerufene Abhandlung*, Berlin 1847, pp. 5, 7, 27, 31–33.

dominate whole fields of mercantile and social life . . . They have trapped many of our people in the net of capital and usury and bound them with the fetters of debt."[46]

In 1872, the missionary journal *Friedensbote* warned that the Jews sought the dissolution of German nationhood: "Let us not be deceived, the Jews want to wash away the national peculiarity, the historic rights and the special tasks of the nation, in order to transform the peoples into an undifferentiated mass."[47] In the same year, an article entitled 'Towards a Physiognomy of modern Judaism' by Pastor Dr Weber, which appeared in the Leipzig-based missionary journal *Saat auf Hoffnung* (Seed sown in hope), made the following claim: "First Jewry strove for tolerance, then for civic rights, today it proclaims as the goal of the history of mankind its own domination."[48] Many of the missionaries shared the antisemites' sense of urgency – the conviction that "German culture," which they understood to be an outgrowth of German Protestantism, was under threat. Some of them recognised that Christian society was in the midst of an endogenous crisis to which the Jews bore a merely incidental relation, but by suggesting that the Jews would know better than anyone else how to make use of this crisis for their own ends, they restored agency and centrality to the Jewish role in a Christian future. "They [the Jews] want life to become a source of manifold pleasures in the present", wrote the missionary Johannes de le Roi in a work on the eighteenth-century history of Jewish missions in Prussia. "In order to obtain this, they turn to the most influential powers of the present time, to the Great Powers of the modern world, they seek to take control of capital and of the press (*des öffentlichen Wortes*). For capital dominates outward life and provides it with the greatest well-being; the press dominates inward life and channels it in the desired direction."[49]

Despite the unmistakeable parallels – which are hardly surprising if one views the cultural pessimism of both missionaries and antisemites as unreflected reactions to the strains of rapid modernisation – the growth of an increasingly virulent antisemitism in Germany from the late 1860s and 1870s placed the missions in a very awkward position. The missionaries had no difficulty in rejecting the violent and often anti-Christian polemic which characterised much antisemitic propaganda of the 1870s and 1880s. Clearly no missionary could accept the arguments of a man like Wilhelm Marr, who asserted that Christianity must be regarded as "a disease of the consciousness". Literary reviews in the missionary journals attacked unhesitatingly the works of such antisemites as Otto Hentze, August Rohling, Otto Glagau, Joseph Rebbert and Jakob Ecker. The Leipzig editor of *Saat auf Hoffnung*, the Hebraist and student of Julius Fürst, Franz Delitzsch, became well-known for his public defence of the Jews against August Rohling's assertion that they required Christian blood for certain rituals. In a pamphlet entitled *Rohling's Talmud-Jew Elucidated* (1881), Delitzsch showed

---

[46]Pastor [?] Schulze, 'Zeugnisse des Barmer Kirchentags für die Mission unter Israel', in *Jeschurun*, 2 (1860), pp. 348–355, here p. 349.

[47]W. Gutschmidt, review of J.F.A. de le Roi, *Stefan Schulz*, in *Der Friedensbote*, January 1872, pp. 12–15, here p. 15.

[48]Dr. [?] Weber, 'Zur Physiognomie des modernen Judenthums', in *Saat auf Hoffnung*, 9 (1872), pp. 4–16, here p. 14.

[49]J.F.A. de le Roi, *op. cit.*, p. 194.

that Rohling's translations were faulty and that his material had been plagiarised from Eisenmenger's notorious *Entdecktes Judenthum*.[50] In Berlin, the editor of the missionary journal *Nathanael* and founder of the *Institutum judaicum* there in 1883, Hermann Strack, defended Jewish texts against the antisemitic charge that they contained unethical material. Strack attacked the antisemite Theodor Fritsch, and published texts refuting various false opinions about the Jews – the belief, for example, that they had to defile meat before selling it to Christians.[51] The reasons for these sallies against the antisemites are not hard to discern. The missionaries were well aware that public incitements to Jew-hatred were unlikely to promote sympathy for the work of the mission. They were "Friends of Israel" not merely by name, but also in their own sincerest estimation. Moreover, to accept the criterion of race as decisive would have been to deny the efficacy of baptism and hence, of conversion. The missionary journals frequently invoked, implicitly or explicitly, the notion of an unchanging Jewish ethnic identity, shaped by centuries of talmudic enslavement, but for them the moment of conversion remained – as it had been for early nineteenth-century Christian revivalism – a sacred mystery, the moment at which the old Adam made way for the new, at which the Jew could cease to be himself.

The sensitivity of the missionaries to the anti-Christian implications of racial antisemitism did not diminish their own pessimism regarding the declining role of Christianity as a system of values underpinning German society. They did not doubt that the end of Protestantism as a cultural force would mean the end of German nationhood. But whereas the racial antisemites metaphorised the prophesied victory of Judaism over Christianity as a process of biological dissolution, the missionaries borrowed their prognoses from the language of revelation and millenarian expectation. If it should succeed in bringing the transforming and revivifying power of baptism to bear against the "dead letter" of the Synagogue, then Christianity would be armed with new and formidable servants, for the Jews were not merely "a stiff-necked people with iron veins", but, in Johannes de le Roi's words, "a people which never rests until it has attained its final and uttermost goals, a people which is never content with anything half-done".[52] The suggestion that the Jews would become, in the event of their conversion, the foremost servants of Christianity was commonplace in late nineteenth-century missionary literature and it testifies to the endurance of chiliastic fantasies in the late nineteenth-century Protestant imagination. The *telos* towards which de le Roi and his colleagues were working was essentially that which Philipp Jakob Spener had projected in his *Pia Desideria*, the founding text of Pietism, in 1675. It was that final moment in which the restoration of the Jews would bring in its train the resolution of all the divisions and conflict within Christianity itself. But for Spener's utopian "hope for better times" (*die Hoffnung*

---

[50]S. Wagner, *Franz Delitzsch. Leben und Werk* (Beiträge zur evangelischen Theologie, vol. 80), Munich 1978, pp. 409–412.

[51]Hermann Strack, 'Geschichte und Wesen des Antisemitismus', in *Nathanael*, 25 (1909), pp. 99–120; review of Theodor Fritsch's *Handbuch der Judenfrage*, in *Nathanael*, 24 (1908), pp. 20–22; Hermann Strack, *Sind die Juden Verbrecher von Religionswegen?*, Leipzig 1893.

[52]J.F.A. de le Roi, *op. cit.*, p. 217.

besserer Zeiten), the missionaries of late nineteenth-century Germany substituted a darker, more pessimistic prognosis. In 1858, the Berlin committee announced in its annual report that "the conflicts between Judaism and Christianity are no longer a superficial matter; they have penetrated into the depths and the Judaism of our times is moving towards a struggle to the death".[53] In the annual report of 1860, they declared that the old struggle between the "Kingdom of the Lord" and the "Kingdom of this world" was about to culminate in a "final catastrophe (*Schlußkatastrophe*)".[54] That the Jews would play a decisive role in shaping the destiny of (German) Christianity was not in question, but there was now some doubt as to whether their influence would be benign. The most striking example of millenarian hope gone sour can be found in a biography of the eighteenth-century Jewish missionary Stefan Schulz written by his nineteenth-century colleague, Johannes de le Roi, in 1870. If the Germans should fail to defend themselves against the Jewish threat from within, de le Roi foresaw the following scenario:

> "[The Jews] will drag us into a thousand things before we have had time to collect our thoughts; they will goad us from sentence to sentence, from catch-cry to catch-cry, from constitutional amendment to constitutional amendment, from one breach in the bonds which unite the people with Christ . . . to another . . . Our people will lie like a man by the road whose veins have been cut open one by one. One last stab to the heart – and his life will be gone . . . The New Testament speaks of a final alliance which the All-destroying Ruler of this World and the highest Lord of Lies shall make with one another. Let us look at what it says, and let us look with eyes which ask after the goal towards which the competing forces of the historical present are leading. Should that moment come, we may find that we were acting like suicides when we failed to heed the warnings in our life."[55]

How can we explain the convergence of missionary attitudes in Prussia with those of late nineteenth-century antisemitism? I would argue that two factors deserve special mention. Firstly: Although the Berlin mission was part of a wave of voluntary, revivalist religious foundations in early nineteenth-century Prussia, it legitimised its work in terms of a state project, namely, the seamless absorption of the Jewish minority into a Christian state of Prussia. The mission societies conceived of their work within parameters which were entirely foreign to the culture of Christian voluntarism in Great Britain. The "statism" of the missionaries meant that they were reluctant to see themselves as participants in a pluralist competition for religious allegiance. So strong was their identification with the state, that they believed the failure of their own undertaking would entail the failure of the state itself. As the revivalist wave lost its momentum and the theological faculties became bastions of theological liberalism, the credibility of the missions' claim to speak for a homogeneous Christian community and the likelihood of a missionary success appeared to diminish. Missionary pessimism now embraced the state in its entirety, just as missionary optimism had held out the hope of a regeneration of the state through Christian revival.

Discussion of the relationship between Christian belief and antisemitism has been dominated by two alternative approaches to the problem.[56] The first sees

---

[53] *Jahresbericht der GBCJ*, 35 (1858), p. 15.
[54] *Ibid.*, 37 (1860), p. 1.
[55] J.F.A. de le Roi, *op. cit.*, pp. 269, 271.
[56] Cf. Hermann Greive, *Geschichte des modernen Antisemitismus in Deutschland*, Darmstadt 1983, pp. 5–9.

antisemitism as a consequence of the "failure" of Christianity. Antisemitism was possible either because people were not Christian enough, or it developed in the vacuum which secularisation left behind, becoming a kind of *Ersatzreligion* which usurped the explanatory and legitimating roles of Christianity. One consequence of this view is, of course, the exoneration of Christianity from any direct responsibility for the phenomenon of antisemitism. Adherents of this view point to the stridently anti-Christian content of much antisemitic ideology. The other view stresses the continuities between Christian Jew-hatred and antisemitism, arguing that the latter should not be seen as a distinct phenomenon arising in the wake of secularisation, but as the secularisation of the anti-Judaism implicit in Christian tradition. Adherents of this view point to the presence of believing Christians in the antisemitic camp. The two theses are clearly not mutually exclusive. The present study would appear to bear out the second. But the evidence considered suggests that it was not Christian anti-Judaism, but rather the philosemitic tradition of millennial hope, which linked the Christianity of the missionaries with the antisemitic world-view. In his essay on Philosemitism, Ernst Bloch remarked that "philosemitism implies an element of antisemitism which has been overcome but remains immanent".[57] More proverbially expressed: a philosemite is an antisemite who loves Jews. Missionary philosemitism and nineteenth-century antisemitism were animated by the same inner logic. Axiomatic to both was the assumption that the collective destiny of the Jews and that of the Christians were inseparably bound up. When the struggle against emancipation had been well and truly lost, the missions painted increasingly drastic pictures of the Christian future. Their vision of a Judæo-German future shock was the exact inversion of millenarian hope. The Jews were still going to usher in the end of days, but it seemed that they might do so in a purely secular sense.

---

[57]Ernst Bloch, 'Die sogenannte Judenfrage', in *idem*, *Literarische Aufsätze* (Gesamtausgabe, vol. 9), Frankfurt a. Main 1965, pp. 549–554, here p. 552: "Indem überhaupt von einer Judenfrage gesprochen wird, streift man antisemitische Fragestellung und setzt sie widerwillen fort. Ja selbst die betonte Liebesantwort auf diese Frage, der Philosemitismus, er impliziert selber so etwas wie ein überwundenes, doch immanentes Stück Antisemitismus."

Philanthropy, the "Social Question" and Jewish Identity in Imperial Germany

BY DEREK J. PENSLAR

The terms "the social question" and "the Jewish Question" enjoyed wide currency in nineteenth-century Europe. For antisemites, the two terms were consonant if not entirely synonymous.* Europe's social crises, the result of the spread of capitalist forms of production and industrialisation, were attributed to Jewish domination in banking, commerce and the stock exchange. In the German empire, unusually rapid industrialisation after the founding of the *Reich* in 1871, economic crises during the following decades and the growth of a massive labour movement made the "social question" particularly acute. One popular response to that question was to blame the *Reich*'s social woes on the Jews; this sentiment was best summed up by the journalist Otto Glagau's notorious statement of 1879 that "the social question is the Jewish question".[1]

It is an error, however, to understand the term "Jewish Question" entirely as a form of antisemitic discourse and to see its relation with broader social issues simply as a projection of popular resentment onto a helpless minority. Ever since the late eighteenth century, German-Jewish activists had displayed a tendency to internalise the Gentile critique of Jewish economic behaviour. The notion of Jewish socio-economic dysfunction was a staple of the Jewish Enlightenment, the *Haskalah*; the call for an occupational redistribution of the Jews from commerce to crafts and agriculture was part of the general programme for Jewish internal regeneration implemented by the German *Maskilim* and their successors up to the Revolution of 1848. Although efforts to train Jewish youth in crafts and agriculture waned in the following decades, the growth of political antisemitism in the 1880s caused German-Jewish activists, while denying antisemitic charges that Jews dominated the economy, to agree with their critics that there was a "Jewish social problem", caused by overcrowding in commerce and an influx of impoverished Jews from Eastern Europe. The result was a broad range of philanthropic activity designed to channel Jews into respectable, productive livelihoods, thereby reducing Jewish poverty and antisemitism alike. The practical benefits of this activity were at least equalled by the sense of Jewish solidarity which it instilled into its organisers. Moreover, the Jewish philanthro-

---

*This article is based on a paper presented at the Leo Baeck Institute, New York on 14th March 1991. Research for this article was supported by summer fellowships from the Leo Baeck Institute/ Deutscher Akademischer Austauschdienst and the National Endowment for the Humanities.

[1]Shulamit Volkov, 'Antisemitism as a Cultural Code. Reflections on the History and Historiography of Antisemitism in Imperial Germany', in *LBI Year Book XXIII* (1978), p. 40.

pic project engendered new forms of Jewish knowledge, manifested in the paradigm of Jewish social science, which, it was believed, would provide the theoretical underpinnings necessary for effective philanthropic praxis.

I

Although Imperial Germany is known to have pioneered modern social policy in the form of workers' insurance, state governments made little provision for the unemployed or unemployable. Traditionally, the churches and the communities were the pillars of philanthropic activity; in the second half of the nineteenth century, the church took on an increasingly visible role as an agent of social reform. In 1848, the Lutheran minister Johann Wichern founded the *Innere Mission*, a federation of Protestant charitable and educational institutions.[2] Under the Empire, Catholic as well as Protestant social work intensified, although an umbrella Catholic *Caritas* League was only established in 1897.[3] It may well be that, as the historian Thomas Nipperdey has argued, such ecclesiastical social activism was late in coming and largely conservative in its orientation.[4] One should not, however, lose sight of the churches' self-image, presented in a steady stream of literature, as the natural source of a solution to the social problem. Christ, the Catholic bishop Wilhelm Ketteler claimed in 1864, was the "saviour of the working class"; the academically orientated *Evangelisch-Sozialer Kongreß*, founded in 1890, produced what the historian Rüdiger vom Bruch has described as an "alignment of theology and political economy".[5] Moreover, whatever the actual effect of the churches' social work, the fact remains that social activism as such provided an important source of identity for Christians whose religious faith was crumbling and who defined themselves increasingly in terms of associational life.[6]

During the second half of the nineteenth century the reigning philosophy of philanthropy in Germany was one of corporate voluntarism. Ecclesiastical, communal and private philanthropies sought to work in concert in order to rationalise and centralise poor-relief. This rationalisation process took place outside the parameters of the state, which philanthropists did not see as a source of funding or guidance. Moreover, the principle goal of philanthropic action was the integration of the able-bodied poor into a market economy, not the establishment of elaborate programmes of social maintenance. The "Elberfeld system", developed in that Westphalian town in 1853 and later implemented in

---

[2]W. O. Shanahan, *German Protestants Face the Social Question*, South Bend, Ind. 1954, p. 81.
[3]Christoph Sachsse and Florian Tennstedt, *Geschichte der Armenfürsorge in Deutschland*, Stuttgart 1980, pp. 227–232.
[4]Thomas Nipperdey, *Religion im Umbruch, Deutschland 1870–1918*, Munich 1988.
[5]Rüdiger vom Bruch, 'Bürgerliche Sozialreform im deutschen Kaiserreich', in *idem* (ed.), *Weder Kommunismus noch Kapitalismus. Bürgerliche Sozialreform in Deutschland vom Vormärz bis zur Ära Adenauer*, Munich 1985, pp. 101, 109. Cf. E. I. Kouri, *Der deutsche Protestantismus und die soziale Frage 1870–1919*, Berlin 1984, pp. 104–111, 117–123.
[6]Nipperdey, *op. cit.*, pp. 24–31.

other communities, consolidated poor-relief into a single body. A staff of volunteers, each responsible for a small number of cases, closely supervised its charges in order to separate the able-bodied, employable poor from the invalid. For the former, the case-workers functioned as a labour exchange, finding work in the private sector, and only occasionally providing public-sector employment or long-term financial aid.[7] The same combination of economic liberalism, paternalism, and a yearning for efficiency characterised the *Deutscher Verein für Armenpflege und Wohltätigkeit* founded in 1880 as an attempt to co-ordinate charitable activity on the national level and to put an end to unreflective almsgiving, which was said to relieve only the symptoms of poverty, and not its causes.[8]

The tension between the striving for efficiency and rationalisation of charitable services, on the one hand, and the limitation of those services to the reintroduction of the needy into a capricious market economy, on the other, began at the *fin de siècle* to produce a new philanthropic paradigm. As in other European lands, the idea of welfare – a comprehensive body of preventive and social-maintenance programmes, including health services, subsidised housing, and child care – grew out of and subsumed older forms of philanthropy. In Germany, the terms *Soziale Fürsorge* and *Wohlfahrtspflege* gained currency, and the older *Wohltätigkeit* assumed a negative connotation, as it was associated with unplanned, piecemeal reformism. Social activists began to call for public direction of welfare, and social work began to shed its purely voluntarist quality and assume the status of a profession.[9]

The Jewish philanthropic ethos in Imperial Germany clearly bore the influence of its environment. Like their Christian counterparts, Jewish activists looked to the powers of organised religion to solve the social question. Editorials in the *Allgemeine Zeitung des Judentums* attest to this sentiment, be it in Ludwig Philippson's statement of 1867 that "the *social* question is the religious idea of our time", or Gustav Karpeles's proclamation in 1905 of the existence of a "social Judaism" akin to "social Christianity".[10] The general prescriptions offered by Jewish activists differed little from those coming from the churches and communities. One encounters the same assault against traditional charitable practices and the same striving for efficiency. For example, the Bohemian Rabbi Adolf Kurrein's pamphlet of 1890, *Die sociale Frage im Judenthume*, concludes a 60-page of survey of the history of Jewish social ideals and legislation with a bland call for social involvement by the well-to-do, honest labour from the poor, and rationalised philanthropy.[11] One also finds in Jewish philanthropic methods the same sort of evolution from a rationalised but purely reactive approach at the

---

[7]Sachsse and Tennstedt, *op. cit.*, pp. 214–222; Rolf Landwehr and Rüdiger Baron, *Geschichte der Sozialarbeit. Hauptlinien ihrer Entwicklung im 19. und 20. Jahrhundert*, Weinheim-Basel 1983, pp. 22–26.
[8]*Ibid.*, pp. 28–32, 145.
[9]*Ibid.*, pp. 40, 67, 148; Sachsse and Tennstedt, *op. cit.*, pp. 220–221.
[10]Ludwig Philippson, cited in Jacob Toury, *Die politischen Orientierungen der Juden in Deutschland. Von Jena bis Weimar*, Tübingen 1966 (Schriftenreihe wissenschaftlicher Abhandlungen des Leo Baeck Instituts 15), p. 161; Gustav Karpeles, editorial in the *Allgemeine Zeitung des Judentums*, vol. LXIX, No. 41 (13th October 1905).
[11]Adolf Kurrein, *Die sociale Frage im Judenthume*, Mülheim a. Rhein 1890.

beginning of the Empire to a more elaborate system of preventive social welfare after the turn of the century.[12]

The most important stimulus behind the development of Jewish social welfare in Imperial Germany was the flood, beginning at the end of the 1860s and intensifying in the 1880s and following decades, of itinerant, impoverished Jews from the East. The *Deutsch-Israelitischer Gemeindebund* (DIGB), formally established in 1872, considered the problem of care for the vagrant poor to be one of its principle concerns. Until the turn of the century, the DIGB's main contribution was the transmitting of information between communities, so that methods of itinerant poor-relief in one particular region could be implemented elsewhere.[13] For example, model proposals distributed by the DIGB in the early 1870s stipulated that the itinerant poor in a given locality be directed to a central office, certified, and given cash and/or a rail ticket, all in order to ensure a rapid departure from the area. All applicants were to be checked against "black lists" of inveterate *Schnorrers*; no aid was to be given to booksellers, self-professed *shalihim*, or Jews claiming, "out of 'pious' impulses", to be en route to Palestine.[14] From 1899, the DIGB began to seek a national policy on care for the itinerant poor; the result was the establishment in 1910 of the *Deutsche Zentralstelle für Jüdische Wanderarmenfürsorge*, consisting of representatives from major communities and several national and international Jewish organisations. The *Hilfsverein der deutschen Juden* made available its border stations, the *B'nai B'rith* its national network of labour exchanges.[15]

Relief for the vagrant poor primarily took the form of outdoor relief, that is, cash or compensation in kind. But after 1898, when a change in legal status allowed the DIGB to acquire property, its programmes of "indoor", or institutional, relief expanded greatly.[16] The most celebrated of these institutions was a workers' colony established at Weissensee near Berlin in 1902. The colony housed Jewish vagrants and ex-convicts for three-month stays, during which, according to DIGB literature, they received vocational training and acquired a

---

[12] See, for example, the comments of the *B'nai B'rith* activist Benjamin Auerbach, 'Die Aufgaben und Bestrebungen der Logen auf dem Gebiete der Wohlfahrtspflege und Fürsorgethätigkeit', in *Festschrift zur Feier des zwanzigjährigen Bestehens des U.O.B.B. Herausgegeben von der Gross-Loge für Deutschland. 20. März 1902. Redigiert von San.-Rath. Dr. Maretzki*, Berlin 1902, pp. 52, 69. See also Aharon Bornstein's important doctoral dissertation, which argues that the German-Jewish image of the Eastern Jewish immigrant changed over the period of the Second *Reich* from that of a shiftless vagabond to one of an unemployed labourer in need of social services: *From Beggars to Seekers of Work. Jewish Migratory Poor in Germany, 1869–1914* (in Hebrew), Ph.D. diss., Tel-Aviv University 1987.

[13] *Mitteilungen vom Deutsch-Israelitischen Gemeindebunde* (hereafter *Mitteilungen vom DIGB*), No. 1 (1873), pp. 3–4, 15–17; No. 2 (1875), pp. 27–43. For a general account of the DIGB, see Ismar Schorsch, *Jewish Reactions to German Anti-Semitism 1870–1914*, New York 1972.

[14] *Mitteilungen vom DIGB*, No. 2 (1875), pp. 28–31. Despite the anti-Orthodox tone of these pronouncements, Orthodox German Jews generally accepted the wisdom of closing their doors to the migrant poor and replacing traditional charity with centralised, rationalised philanthropy. Mordechai Breuer, *Jüdische Orthodoxie im deutschen Reich, 1871–1918. Die Sozialgeschichte einer religiösen Minderheit*, Frankfurt a. Main 1986, Veröffentlichung des Leo Baeck Instituts, pp. 210–211.

[15] *Mitteilungen vom DIGB*, No. 51 (1899), pp. 14–15; No. 75 (1910), pp. 1–2; No. 76 (1910), p. 19; No. 80 (1912), pp. 39–40.

[16] Schorsch, *op. cit.*, p. 156.

Philanthropy in Imperial Germany

taste for hard work and clean living. The colony's "regenerated" charges were then released, where they became productive members of society. Supporters of the colony touted it as the most efficient and effective form of philanthropy, superior to direct gifts from donor to donee.[17] The colony did, in fact, produce impressive results; by 1912 it had provided vocational training and job-placement services for some 5,000 individuals, approximately three-quarters of whom were from Galicia or Russia.[18]

The problem of the vagrant poor was not, of course, unique to the Jews. Under the Empire, freedom of movement and an easing of residency requirements for the receipt of communal charity promoted an explosion of internal migration. By 1914, some two million people had migrated from the Eastern provinces to Berlin, the Ruhr area, and Central Germany.[19] The DIGB's poor-relief commission was aware of the common elements shared by the Jewish and the general "social problem". The commission studied church and communal philanthropic practices, and called in a prominent Lutheran pastor for expert advice.[20] In 1899, the year that work on behalf of the Weissensee colony began, there were 28 interconfessional workhouses in Germany, similar to Weissensee in their general programme, though the former suffered the disadvantage of working with unskilled agricultural labourers, whereas the large number of Jewish craftsmen in Eastern Europe ensured that many of Weissensee's visitors had artisanal experience.[21]

Conversely, the DIGB's indoor relief activities were not limited to the itinerant poor. Between 1901 and 1908, the DIGB founded schools for wayward boys and girls and a home for retarded children. Expenditure on children's institutions climbed from RM 28,000 in 1907 to RM 91,000 in 1912.[22] And the DIGB's actions only represent a small part of the phenomenal growth of Jewish philanthropic institutions during the Wilhelminian period. The DIGB's statistical year book for 1889 records twenty Jewish hospitals and sanitoriums, ten retirement homes, and twenty-five orphanages in Germany. The 1913 volume lists, *inter alia*, 109 institutions for children, seventy-one hospitals and sanitoriums, fifty-six retirement homes, thirty-four institutions for women's education and twenty-two labour exchanges and workhouses.[23] These institutions, combined with the provisions for outdoor relief made by local poor commissions in

---

[17] *Mitteilungen vom DIGB*, No. 51 (1899), pp. 21–22; No. 58 (1902), pp. 91–94; No. 60 (1903), pp. 11–12; No. 80 (1912), p. 39. A detailed study of the Weissensee colony may be found in Aharon Bornstein, *To Reject or Accept? Solutions to the Problem of the Itinerant Jewish Poor in Germany, 1900* (in Hebrew), Spiegel Lectures in European Jewish History No. 8, ed. by Lloyd P. Gartner, Tel-Aviv 1988.

[18] *Mitteilungen vom DIGB*, No. 71 (1908), p. 19; No. 80 (1912), p. 39. There were also Jewish *Arbeitsstätten* in Cologne and Breslau. *Mitteilungen vom DIGB*, No. 78 (1911), p. 48.

[19] Bornstein, *From Beggars to Seekers of Work*, op. cit., pp. 10–34; Ulrich Herbert, *A History of Foreign Labor in Germany, 1880–1980*, Ann Arbor 1990, p. 73.

[20] *Mitteilungen vom DIGB*, No. 51 (1899), p. 20; see also the speech by Bernhard Kahn, General Secretary of the *Hilfsverein der deutschen Juden*, on German attempts to solve the problem of itinerant beggars, in *Mitteilungen vom DIGB*, No. 74 (1909), pp. 109–130.

[21] *Mitteilungen vom DIGB*, No. 51 (1899), p. 20; Bornstein, *To Reject or Accept?*, op. cit., pp. 12–13.

[22] *Mitteilungen vom DIGB*, No. 68 (1907), p. 13; No. 82 (1912), pp. 83–85.

[23] *Statistisches Jahrbuch des Deutsch-Israelitischen Gemeindebundes*, Berlin 1889, pp. 90–91; 1913, pp. 238–239.

virtually every German-Jewish community, formed an intricate philanthropic network which scholars have claimed to be denser and more generous than its non-Jewish counterparts.[24] Even if true, it is important to point out that no less a figure than Louis Maretzki (1843–1918), president of the German Grand Lodge of the *B'nai B'rith* between 1887 and 1897 and an indefatigable Jewish philanthropist, worked under the assumption that Jewish organisations trailed behind the churches in the development of modern social welfare.[25]

The pre-war development of Jewish social welfare in Germany would have been inconceivable without the *B'nai B'rith*. When first constituted in 1882, the *B'nai B'rith*'s lodges contented themselves with the promotion of good fellowship, solidarity and mutual aid among their brethren. Within a decade, however, a group of activists had started to push the Order away from its original philanthropic purview towards national social work. This group was led by Maretzki, who practised medicine in Berlin; other members included Benjamin Auerbach (1855–1940), a doctor from Köln, Julius Plotke (1857–1903), an attorney from Frankfurt a. Main, and Gustav Tuch (1834–1909), a journalist and long-time president of the Hamburg *B'nai B'rith* lodge.[26] The writings of these activists defined social work as the very essence of the Order.[27] Thanks to the *B'nai B'rith*'s social work, according to Maretzki, "the gap between the propertied and the propertyless, between the educated and the uneducated, is gradually filled in ... Delicate threads are spun from the low to the high, from the well-off to the poor. The spirit of the weary is elevated and strengthened, when they see that a feeling of community manifests itself in good will and humanity."[28]

In many communities, *B'nai B'rith* lodges took the lead in providing social services such as labour exchanges, workshops, kindergartens and holiday camps.[29] The Order's women's societies played an indispensable role in the development of these services, particularly those that directly affected women and children. This concentration resulted at least in part from the attitudes of the

[24] E.g., Giora Lotan, 'The Zentralwohlfahrtsstelle', in *LBI Year Book IV* (1959), pp. 185–207; Bornstein, *From Beggars to Seekers of Work, op. cit.*, chap. 6, *passim*; Stefi Jersch-Wenzel, 'Minderheiten in der bürgerlichen Gesellschaft. Juden in Amsterdam, Frankfurt und Posen', in Jürgen Kocka (ed.), *Bürgertum im 19. Jahrhundert. Deutschland im europäischen Vergleich*, 3 vols., Munich 1988, vol. II, pp. 404–405, note 22.

[25] Louis Maretzki, *Geschichte des Ordens Bnei Briss in Deutschland, 1822–1907*, Berlin 1907, pp. 182–183. Cf. the comments of a Dr. Rahmer, speaking at a DIGB *Gemeindetag*, that German Jews were behind their Christian neighbours in the development of a confessionally-based health-care system, *Mitteilungen vom DIGB*, No. 10 (1882), p. 31.

[26] On Maretzki, see Salomon Wininger, *Grosse Jüdische National-Bibliographie*, 7 vols., Czernowitz 1925–1936, vol. IV, p. 269. On Auerbach, see Siegfried Auerbach, *The Auerbach Family. The Descendants of Abraham Auerbach*, London 1957, p. 122. On Plotke, see his obituary in the *Allgemeine Zeitung des Judentums*, vol. LXVII, No. 41 (9th October 1903), pp. 484–485. On Tuch, see Wininger, *op. cit.*, vol. VI, p. 149.

[27] Maretzki, *Geschichte, op. cit.*, pp. 183–187. A similar development occurred simultaneously in the American *B'nai B'rith*. Leo Levi, the Order's president from 1899 to 1904, formalised and gave an ideological base to this turn. See Deborah Dash Moore, *B'nai B'rith and the Challenge of Ethnic Leadership*, Albany, N.Y. 1981, p. 64.

[28] Louis Maretzki, 'Die Leistungen des Ordens', in *Das Wesen und die Leistungen des Ordens U.O.B.B.*, Berlin 1911, p. 37.

[29] B. Auerbach, *loc. cit.*, pp. 59–63.

B'nai B'rith's male executives, who accorded women a vital but highly circumscribed role in the solution of the social problem.[30] Maretzki attributed to Jewish women vast nurturing powers; he saw women as the glue which binds families together and mends a shattered social order. It is the task of well-to-do women, he argued, to inculcate domestic skills into their poorer sisters and to provide them with household services after childbirth. Thereby, working women will take their rightful place in the home, and thanks to the interaction between women of different classes, "... oppressive reserve disappears, the icy crust of envy melts, trust develops between them, they approach one another without restraint. This does more to bridge the social chasm than all arguments, regulations, and [expressions of] sympathy."[31]

Despite this gushing praise, men in the *B'nai B'rith* leadership offered women only limited operational independence. The Order's philanthropic activities on behalf of women were often initiated by men, and men held the highest positions therein. A Dr. Silberstein founded the women's vocational school in Breslau in 1891, and a similar institution in Hamburg, founded in 1897, was directed by Gustav Tuch.[32] A group of Jewish men in Frankfurt a. Main founded the first association to train Jewish nurses; Adolf Mayer, a *B'nai B'rith* activist, established a national nurse-training programme under the Order's auspices in 1901. Notably, however, Mayer expected women to manage matters on the local level and to supervise the training process, just as the founder of the Breslau women's school entrusted fund-raising to a committee of female volunteers.[33] More importantly, we must note that the *B'nai B'rith* was not typical of German-Jewish philanthropy as a whole, for it has become clear from the research of Marion Kaplan that women not only staffed but often organised and managed philanthropy in Jewish communities.[34]

The question of the role of women reveals that the *B'nai B'rith* cannot be identified with German-Jewish philanthropy as a whole. None the less, the Order represented the vast majority of German Jews in one important aspect: it epitomised nineteenth-century "associational Judaism", that is, Jewish identity expressed through activity in sub- or extra-communal, voluntary social organisations. European historians have long emphasised the importance of associational life as the expression of a maturing bourgeois consciousness, and the Jewish historians David Sorkin and Henry Wassermann have applied this paradigm to

---

[30]For a full treatment of this issue, see Claudia Prestel, 'Weibliche Rollenzuweisung in jüdischen Organisationen. Das Beispiel des Bnei Briss', in *Bulletin des Leo Baeck Instituts*, No. 85 (1990), pp. 51–80.

[31]Louis Maretzki, 'Die Frauen und der Orden', in *Festschrift zur Feier . . . des U.O.B.B.*, *op. cit.*, p. 89.

[32]On Breslau, see *ibid.*, pp. 81–82. On Hamburg, see the *Satzungen der Israelitischen Haushaltungsschule in Hamburg*, Hamburg 1900, in Central Archives for the History of the Jewish People, Jerusalem (hereafter CAHJP), AHW/539.

[33]Maretzki, 'Die Frauen und der Orden', *loc. cit.*, pp. 81, 86–87.

[34]Marion Kaplan, 'Tradition and Translation. The Acculturation, Assimilation and Integration of Jewish Women in Imperial Germany', in *LBI Year Book XXVII* (1982), p. 23; idem, *The Jewish Feminist Movement in Germany. The Campaigns of the Jüdischer Frauenbund, 1904–1938*, Westport, Conn. 1979, pp. 154–156, 172–173 and *passim*; idem, *The Making of the Jewish Middle Class. Women, Family and Identity in Imperial Germany*, Oxford 1991, pp. 192–227.

German Jewry over the period 1780–1880.[35] The attraction of associational Judaism in the decades before the First World War is revealed by a study of Berlin Jewry carried out in 1909. It found that out of a population of 122,000, 20,141 belonged to at least one Jewish association, 1,090 to three associations, and 250 to six or more. (The last number points nicely to the existence of an activist elite, members of which grounded their Jewish identity in associational life.)[36] Throughout the nineteenth century, philanthropy had figured prominently among the activities of these associations, and towards the end of the century, their engagement with philanthropy deepened considerably. To be sure, in the Jewish case the adoption of the bourgeois association co-existed with the retention of traditional notions of the holy society (*Chevra Kadisha*). Associational Judaism represented in part a secularised expression of group solidarity, whereby, for example, involvement in a local hospital association created a sense of communal sympathy akin to that gained by practising the rabbinic commandments of ministering to the sick and dead. As mentioned above, such associational identity was common enough in Christian society, but it was of particular importance to the leaders of Germany's small Jewish minority. For Maretzki, only social work, salutary both for the empathy its practice instills into the agent and its healing effects on the social body, could revive the Jewish spirit.[37]

For some Jewish activists, however, philanthropic activity did not merely affirm Jewish identity but actually defined it. Just as the churches proclaimed that Christian ethics provided the answer to the social question, and interpreted Christian doctrine to support their views, so did Jews state that theirs was an inherently social-activist faith whose biblical and talmudic texts foreshadowed advanced policies of social welfare. The idea of a "Jewish mission" to embody rational religion in its purest form originated in the late eighteenth century; and during the decades before 1848, the mission assumed a specifically political connotation, calling upon Jews to fulfil their religious obligations by being exemplary citizens.[38] Under the Empire, Jewish activists expressly associated their creed with an imperative to resolve social tensions. Statements to this effect abounded in the periodical and pamphlet literature of the time; they shared a common apologetic structure, in which a historical narrative documented

[35]David Sorkin, *The Transformation of German Jewry, 1780–1840*, Oxford 1987, pp. 112–123; Henry Wassermann, *Jews, "Bürgertum" and "Bürgerliche Gesellschaft" in a Liberal Era (1840–1880)* (in Hebrew), Ph.D. diss., Hebrew University 1979, pp. 75–93.
[36]'Jüdische Wohlfahrtspflege in Berlin', in *Zeitschrift für Demographie und Statistik der Juden* (hereafter *ZDSJ*), V (1909), pp. 75–78.
[37]Maretzki, *Geschichte, op. cit.*, pp. 186–187. On the relationship between philanthropy and modern Jewish identity, see Moore, *op. cit.*; Phyllis Cohen Albert, 'Ethnicity and Jewish Solidarity in 19th-Century France', in Jehuda Reinharz and Daniel Swetschinski (eds.), *Mystics, Philosophers, and Politicians. Essays in Jewish Intellectual History in Honor of Alexander Altmann*, Durham, N.C. 1982, p. 266; Nancy L. Green, 'To Give and to Receive. Philanthropy and Collective Responsibility Among Jews in Paris, 1880–1914', in Peter Mandler (ed.), *The Uses of Charity. The Poor on Relief in the Nineteenth-Century Metropolis*, Philadelphia 1990, pp. 197–226; the works of Sorkin and Wassermann cited in note 35 above; and Marsha L. Rozenblit, *The Jews of Vienna, 1867–1914. Assimilation and Identity*, Albany 1983, pp. 148–150.
[38]Cf. Max Wiener, 'The Concept of Mission in Traditional and Modern Judaism', in *YIVO Annual of Jewish Social Science*, 2–3 (1947/1948), pp. 9–24; Sorkin, *op. cit.*, pp. 103–104.

manifestations of the Jewish social ethos through the ages. Ancient Israelite social legislation was the centrepiece of such apologetics, ostensibly for its function as a preventive against pauperisation. Rabbinic sources were combed for appropriate citations, and no speech on "social Judaism" could refrain from piously invoking Moses Maimonides's celebrated medieval compilation of talmudic dictums on charity.[39] In keeping with general trends of modern Jewish secularisation, Maimonides's statements about charity, which represent only the smallest fragment of his vast code of Jewish Law, were wrenched out of context and placed in the centre of a new form of Jewish identity based on social action.

So far this paper has indicated the many similarities between the Jewish philanthropic network in Imperial Germany and its Gentile counterparts. The DIGB and the *B'nai B'rith* merely followed patterns set earlier by German philanthropists by setting up workshops, labour exchanges for men and women, and home economics courses for women. Except for their clientele, Jewish institutions of indoor relief – hospitals, orphanages, sanitoriums, and the like – were not easily distinguishable from church-sponsored ones. Yet it is precisely the differences in clientele which point to significant structural differences between Jewish and non-Jewish philanthropy. Throughout the nineteenth century, as German Jews ostensibly gained equal juridical and political rights, the Jewish community remained a legal entity with taxation powers and considerable responsibilities, including the welfare of its members. The emancipation of Frankfurt Jewry in 1864 came with the expectation that the Jewish community would continue to educate and succour its poor and ill members. Although the 1869 Industrial Ordinance of the North German Confederation technically permitted German Jews and foreign Jews on German soil to receive aid from non-Jewish charities, these charities were not forthcoming. The 1909 statues of the Berlin *Armenkommission*, for example, explicitly required charities to send Jewish applicants to Jewish institutions.[40] Besides, itinerant Jews from Eastern Europe preferred Jewish to Gentile charities, partly out of fear of Gentile authority, and partly because Jewish charities provided higher levels of aid.[41]

The continuing distinctiveness of the Jewish community and the realisation that it alone would provide essential social services furnished Jewish activists with an identity based on the notion of common struggle against a hostile environment. The Jews have been left on their own, wrote Maretzki, to fight the "struggle for existence", which modern capitalism and urban life have engendered. Trying to keep the Jews' heads above the water, the *B'nai B'rith* strives "to equip our co-religionists physically, economically, spiritually and ethically so

---

[39]E.g. B. Auerbach, *op. cit.* and Kurrein, *op. cit.*; Friedrich Wachtel, *Das Judenthum und seine Aufgabe im neuen deutschen Reich*, Leipzig 1871. This "strong misreading" of Jewish social legislation was by no means limited to Germany. Ephraim Frisch's classic, *An Historical Survey of Jewish Philanthropy from the Earliest Times to the Nineteenth Century*, New York 1924, is a highly apologetic work which, among other things, presents the medieval *gabbai* as a prototype of the contemporary social worker (p. 118).

[40]Bornstein, *From Beggars to Seekers of Work, op. cit.*, pp. 181, 192–193, 222; Robert Liberles, 'Emancipation and the Structure of the Jewish Community in the Nineteenth Century', in *LBI Year Book XXXI* (1986), p. 63.

[41]Bornstein, *From Beggars to Seekers of Work, op. cit.*, pp. 194, 275–276. The case was similar, though not identical, in France. See Green, *loc. cit.*, pp. 197–198.

that a socially healthy ethnic body (*Volkskörper*) is mobilised, which will be capable of combating opposing powers, hostile influences, internal social ills and dangers which threaten human society . . ."[42] The military metaphors are obvious; of interest as well is the use of the term *Volkskörper*. I translate the word as "ethnic" and not "national" because there is nothing in Maretzki's thought to suggest that he was a Jewish nationalist in any conventionally understood sense of the term. But Maretzki undoubtedly conceived of the Jews as a separate entity within German society, an entity which required an independent social policy.[43]

And what were the hostile forces to which Maretzki so darkly referred? In part, they came from outside the Jewish community, from antisemites. But the dangers also came from within. The *B'nai B'rith* must correct "defects which have nested in our national body" through "internal Enlightenment".[44] Jewish welfare work, then, was more than the latest manifestation of the Jewish charitable tradition or the assertion of Jewish identity through social action. It was also a response to what was perceived as a very real problem, a uniquely Jewish variant of the "social problem" that so worried the citizens of Imperial Germany.

II

The aspect of the "Jewish social problem" most visible to German-Jewish philanthropists was the plight of Eastern European Jewry. The massive international relief operations of the *Hilfsverein* and the domestic activities of the DIGB and the *B'nai B'rith* were directed primarily towards the two million Jews who entered Germany from the East during the Second *Reich*. They did their utmost to expedite the movement of foreign Jews through the *Reich*, onto steamships and off to distant lands. For those Eastern European Jews who stayed in Germany (approximately 70,000 by 1910) the charitable agencies offered educational, vocational and job-placement services.[45] Although compassion and a sense of solidarity underlay the philanthropic enterprise, its language was often harsh and paternalistic. The DIGB's campaign against begging was based on the assumption that, until proven otherwise, all applicants for aid were *Schnorrer* who aspired to live indefinitely off communal largesse. *B'nai B'rith* literature described Eastern European Jews as wretched human material whose regeneration would require Herculean efforts and constant surveillance.[46]

As mentioned above, the DIGB leadership was aware that its efforts against begging by vagrants were part of a concerted German social policy towards

---

[42]Maretzki, 'Die Leistungen des Ordens', *loc. cit.*, p. 28; *idem, Geschichte, op. cit.*, p. 183.

[43]For applications of the concept of ethnicity to modern European Jewry, see Albert, 'Ethnicity and Jewish Solidarity', *loc. cit.*; and *idem*, 'L'intégration et la persistance de l'ethnicité chez les juifs dans la France moderne', in Pierre Birnbaum (ed.), *Histoire politique des juifs de France*, Paris 1990, pp. 221–243.

[44]Maretzki, 'Leistungen', *loc. cit.*, p. 20; also B. Auerbach, *loc. cit.*, p. 69.

[45]The best treatment of this subject is Jack Wertheimer, *Brothers and Strangers. East European Jews in Imperial Germany*, New York 1987.

[46]*Mitteilungen vom DIGB*, No. 2 (1875), pp. 28–31; B. Auerbach, *loc. cit.*, pp. 68–69.

internal migration as a whole. But in much Jewish philanthropic literature this context is missing. Instead, one sees that antisemitic obsessions with the Eastern Jew instilled into Jewish activists a tendency to see the problem of the poor, wandering Jew as *sui generis*. Jews eager to speed their immigrant brethren out of Germany did not did take into consideration Imperial Germany's need for foreign workers (over 732,000 in 1907). Internalising German hostility to Slavic peoples, Jews did not seek common ground with the hundreds of thousands of Poles, most of them German citizens, living in the *Reich*.[47] None the less, even if Jewish philanthropists exaggerated the uniqueness of the immigration, its vast size and the government's expectation that the Jewish community would handle it alone do support the philanthropists' self-image as the bearers of a unique burden.

The Jews' social problem was perceived as unique in a positive way as well. According to an article in the *Israelitische Wochenschrift* in 1873, the Jews had no revolutionary proletariat. There were poor masses, to be sure, but no threatening element that sought to destroy the "educated upper classes".[48] Throughout the Second *Reich*, Jewish philanthropists, unlike their Gentile counterparts, were not likely to express fear of their charges, or to describe their work as a way of diffusing revolutionary tensions. What Todd Endelman has written about the Jews of Georgian England applies to the Jews of Imperial Germany as well:

> "The Anglo-Jewish poor were not a potentially revolutionary class and were not viewed as such by the Anglo-Jewish elite. They were politically apathetic and hardly constituted a threat to the established order. The discipline the Jewish magnates sought to impose was designed to promote their own status rather than protect their property. The schools they established did not aim to keep the poor in their place, but proposed to do just the opposite: to remove the Jewish poor from London's streets and turn them into respectable artisans, clerks, and domestic servants, or possibly even better. Social mobility was a key objective, not the preservation of the socioeconomic status quo. For it was only through the *embourgeoisement* of the entire community – or so some believed – that their own integration into English society could be secured."[49]

This quotation is especially significant for an analysis of the relations between German Jews and those Eastern European Jews who settled in the *Reich*. Fear, not of social revolution from below, but of antisemitic reaction from all strata, motivated the Jews to tackle their social problem. The solution was to transform the newcomers into upright members of the German middle class, that is, to re-enact the metamorphosis that German Jewry itself had only recently completed.

Although German-Jewish philanthropists expended much of their energy on Jews in and from Eastern Europe, Jewish philanthropic discourse often failed to specify the provenance of its subjects, and instead depicted its subjects simply as "Jews in Germany". The DIGB's Weissensee workers' colony featured a largely

---

[47]By 1914, 400,000 Poles with German citizenship (*Inlandspolen*) were labouring in the Ruhr, and another 270,000 Poles with foreign citizenship were at work in Germany, mostly in agriculture in the Eastern provinces. Herbert, *op. cit.*, p. 54; see also, Bornstein, *From Beggars to Seekers of Work*, *op. cit.*, pp. 58–59.

[48]Toury, *Die politischen Orientierungen*, *op. cit.*, p. 169.

[49]Todd M. Endelman, *The Jews of Georgian England, 1714–1830. Tradition and Change in a Liberal Society*, Philadelphia 1979, pp. 246–247.

foreign clientele, but the colony's publicists did not make anything of this fact, and instead presented the institution as a source of aid for Jews on German soil.[50] Moreover, the scores of societies in Imperial Germany that promoted handicrafts and agriculture among Jewish youth did not, so far as can be seen from the sources, depict themselves as specifically serving Jews of Eastern European origin. If they targeted any group, most Jewish philanthropists addressed the poor as such. When the Central Committee of the DIGB met in March 1880 to prepare a circular urging member communities to promote handicrafts, the Dresden lawyer Emil Lehmann complained that the circular demeaned the merchant class and did not specify that only poor Jews were to undergo vocational training. The authors of the circular assured Lehmann that they were critical only of impoverished pedlars and hawkers; "the educated merchant", they said, "is entirely out of the picture".[51]

The 2,000-member *Verein zur Förderung der Bodenkultur unter den Juden Deutschlands* (VFB) and Ahlem, a Jewish agricultural school near Hannover, explicitly directed their efforts at German Jewry, claiming that incoming Eastern European Jews merely aggravated what a VFB report described as a pre-existing "Jewish social problem".[52] Nor did activists in these organisations limit their purview to the poor. In these and other organisations one finds a body of Jewish activists for whom the "Jewish social problem" afflicted German Jews no less than the masses to the East, and the bourgeois no less than the *Luftmensch*. Jewish philanthropic rhetoric was like a point on a Möbius strip, switching surfaces without rupture: Jews in the Pale of Settlement, transients and immigrants in Germany, the *Reich*'s own "Eastern" Jews from Poznań and finally Jews in Germany regardless of origin, became the subjects of a criticism which always had the potential to become a self-criticism.

Leaders of the DIGB, the *B'nai B'rith*, and other organisations responded to the antisemitic movement of 1879/1880 by indulging in trenchant economic self-criticism. Indictments of Jewish economic behaviour saturated the Jewish press and appeared in scores of pamphlets and philanthropic reports. Its producers were the activists we have mentioned so far and some two dozen others, the most significant of whom were Samuel Kristeller (1820–1900), Marcus Adler (1830–1904), Arthur Kahn (1850–1928) and Julius Moses (1868–1942). Despite their bulk, the arguments can be easily summarised, as they repeated themselves time and time again and were not distinguished by intellectual complexity. The Jews' occupational concentration in commerce and the professions was said to be both economically and psychically toxic. Commerce was overcrowded, hence overly competitive, offering little financial security and encouraging unethical business behaviour. The professions, the arguments continued, were no better; Germany

---

[50]Bornstein, *To Reject or Accept?, op. cit.*, p. 18.
[51]*Mitteilungen vom DIGB*, No. 8 (1880), pp. 63–64.
[52]*Jahresbericht des Vereins zur Förderung der Bodenkultur unter den Juden Deutschlands*, III (1901); V (1903); see also Eugen Katz, *Die Alexander und Fanny Simon'sche Stiftung zu Hannover. Ihre Ziele und ihre Arbeiten von 1907–1914*, Hannover 1914, pp. 5–6.

teemed with unemployed doctors, lawyers and scholars.[53] Clerical and other salaried middle-class occupations offered low pay, high expenses and boring work, and antisemitism in large enterprises kept Jews out of managerial positions. These purely economic criticisms virtually always overlapped with psychological and medical ones. Jews lacked manual dexterity and a sense of self-reliance. They were too highly strung; rates of suicide and mental illness were disproportionately high.[*] German Jewry was said to be overly acquisitive and materialistic; it suffered from unnatural hungers; it was "innerlich mammonisiert".[54]

These arguments were not the rantings of tortured, self-hating Jews like Walther Rathenau, Otto Weininger or the young Theodor Lessing.[55] Nor did they come from Jewish social critics with Zionist leanings, men like Arthur Ruppin or Felix Theilhaber.[56] Rather, they came from Jewish critics intensely committed to the Jewish community, and who expressed that commitment through labour to improve and strengthen German Jewry within the German Fatherland. These non-Zionist social critics worked within organisations such as the DIGB and the *B'nai B'rith*, organisations which Jehuda Reinharz has identified as the province of a "highly-acculturated, upper-class" elite.[57] Indeed, the *B'nai B'rith*'s high educational requirements and entrance fees assured that only members of the Jewish professional and mercantile elite would be admitted.[58] Maretzki and Kristeller, a learned but non-observant Jew who served as president of the DIGB between 1882 and 1896, are typical examples of the Jewish notables.[59]

Yet terms such as "notable" and "elite" do not capture the complexity and radical tendencies of the figures under analysis here. Marcus Adler was a wealthy factory-owner, but he had spent his youth as a mason and foreman, and his advocacy of Jewish vocational education was based on profound personal

---

[53]This critique co-existed with an earlier-developed view, itself an outgrowth of the concept of the Jewish mission, that Jewish over-representation in these occupations took advantage of Jewish particularity for the good of all society. See Moritz Lazarus, 'Was heißt National? (1880)', in Walter Böhlich (ed.), *Der Berliner Antisemitismusstreit*, Frankfurt a. Main 1965, p. 84; Emil Lehmann, *Gesammelte Schriften*, Berlin 1899, p. 292; Gustav Karpeles in the *Allgemeine Zeitung des Judentums*, vol. LXXII, No. 22 (29th May 1908), pp. 1–2. Significantly, though, Lazarus decried the Jews' lack of participation in agriculture, 'Was heißt National?', *loc. cit.*; idem, *Juden als Ackerbauern. Ein Beitrag zur Lösung der sozialen Frage der Juden in Galizien*, Lemberg 1885.
[*]For a detailed study on this see John M. Efron, 'The "Kaftanjude" and the "Kaffeehausjude": Two Models of Jewish Insanity. A Discussion of Causes and Cures among German-Jewish Psychiatrists', in *LBI Year Book XXXVII* (1992), pp. 169–188 – (Ed.).
[54]Arthur Kahn, 'Klassengeist und Titelnarrheit. Eine Betrachtung zum Tode August Bebels', in *Die Jüdische Presse*, Beilage to No. 36 (1913), pp. 371–372.
[55]On these figures, see Sander L. Gilman, *Jewish Self-Hatred. Anti-Semitism and the Hidden Language of the Jews*, Baltimore 1986.
[56]On Ruppin, see Derek J. Penslar, *Zionism and Technocracy. The Engineering of Jewish Settlement in Palestine*, Bloomington, Ind. 1991, pp. 80–91; on Theilhaber, see John M. Efron, *Defining the Jewish Race. The Self-Perceptions and Responses of Jewish Scientists to Scientific Racism in Europe, 1882–1933*, Ph.D. diss., Columbia University 1991, pp. 376–404.
[57]Jehuda Reinharz, *Fatherland or Promised Land. The Dilemma of the German Jew, 1893–1914*, Ann Arbor 1975, pp. 12, 28.
[58]Prestel, *loc. cit.*, p. 52.
[59]Schorsch, *op. cit.*, p. 35.

experience.[60] Arthur Kahn, a physician from Hessen, was a savage critic of Jewish economic behaviour, yet considered himself Orthodox and laboured tirelessly on behalf of consciousness-raising youth groups in the *B'nai B'rith*.[61] Perhaps the most fascinating figure is Julius Moses, a medical doctor best known as a Socialist *Reichstag* member and proponent of public health programmes under the Weimar Republic.[62] Before the First World War, however, Moses, who had a traditional Jewish upbringing in his native Poznań and edited an anthology of poems on Jewish themes, was intensely involved in Jewish politics and philanthropy. A political firebrand, Moses published the *General-Anzeiger für die gesamten Interessen des Judentums*, a Socialist-orientated newspaper which was unsparing in its criticism of the German Progressive Party and the *Centralverein* leadership for supporting it. As an activist in the Berlin *B'nai B'rith* lodge, Moses presented himself as the enemy of the Jewish *haute bourgeoisie* and champion of the Jewish artisan class.[63]

Adler, Kahn, Moses and others concurred that occupational restructuring was an essential remedy for Jewish economic dysfunction. The Jews were to adopt a more varied occupational profile; *viz*., they were to abandon commerce for manufacture and agriculture. As is well known, the idea of Jewish occupational restructuring (*Berufsumschichtung*) dated back to the Enlightenment; Jewish social critics were merely pouring old wine into new bottles. In the late eighteenth and early nineteenth century, numerous adherents of the *Haskalah* accepted the physiocratic view that the masses of Jewish pedlars were unproductive and must be guided towards manufacture and agriculture. Accordingly, after 1815, although economic developments in Germany promoted the gradual strengthening of a Jewish mercantile middle class, communal activists rushed into philanthropic activity aimed at training Jewish youth in handicrafts and farming.[64] Between 1848 and 1879, however, the notion that equal rights were conditional upon Jewish regeneration lost currency, and Jewish leaders felt more positive about trade and industry as sources of social mobility.[65] But with the

---

[60]On Adler, see the obituary in *Mitteilungen vom DIGB*, No. 63 (1904), pp. 3–8. His personal views emerge clearly in a lengthy pamphlet, *Chronik der Gesellschaft zur Vebreitung der Handwerke und des Ackerbaues unter den Juden im Preussischen Staate*, Berlin 1898.

[61]This combination of Orthodoxy and economic self-criticism was admittedly idiosyncratic; Orthodox Jews tended to look favourably upon commercial occupations, as they were thought to be more conducive to religious observance than others. Breuer, *op. cit.*, p. 199. For biographical information on Kahn, see the Arthur Kahn Papers, *Nachrufe* file, Leo Baeck Institute Archives, New York, AR-C 3100. Kahn was a prolific writer; his economic jeremiads include the pamphlets *Hin zur Scholle*, Berlin 1912; and *Der Weg zur wahren Emanzipation*, Berlin 1915.

[62]Unlike Kahn, Moses has received serious biographical attention: Daniel S. Nadav, *Julius Moses und die Politik der Sozialhygiene in Deutschland*, Gerlingen 1985.

[63]On Moses's political journalism, see Marjorie Lamberti, *Jewish Activism in Imperial Germany. The Struggle for Civil Equality*, New Haven–London 1978, pp. 35–37, 47, 75–76, 89–90, 94–95. For one of Moses's economic broadsides, see *Das Handwerk unter den Juden. Vortrag gehalten im Verein selbstständiger Handwerker jüdischen Glaubens*, Berlin 1902.

[64]Cf. B.D. Weinryb, *Der Kampf um die Berufsumschichtung*, Berlin 1936, pp. 14–33; Adolf Kober, 'Emancipation's Impact on the Education and Vocational Training of German Jewry', in *Jewish Social Studies*, XVI (1954), pp. 155–165; Sorkin, *op. cit.*, pp. 117–119.

[65]Jacob Toury, *Soziale und politische Geschichte der Juden in Deutschland 1847–1871. Zwischen Revolution, Reaktion und Emanzipation*, Düsseldorf 1977, p. 72.

appearance in the 1880s of political antisemitism, the Jewish leadership elite's crisis of economic identity reappeared, and with it the call for Jewish occupational restructuring.

This interest manifested itself in a flurry of philanthropic activity. The oldest extant society for Jewish vocational training, the Berlin-based *Gesellschaft zur Verbreitung der Handwerke und des Ackerbaues unter den Juden im Preussischen Staate*, experienced a sharp rise in membership after decades of stagnation.[66] A new crop of societies and trusts promoting Jewish vocational training sprang up; there were 31 such enterprises in 1889, 65 in 1898, and 129 in 1913. One of the most popular of these new societies began in Düsseldorf in 1880 with a handful of Jewish members; ten years later it boasted 1,464 members (both corporate and individual) from 185 communities throughout the Ruhr and the *Reich* as a whole.[67] Jews who were already working as artisans received aid from prosperous well-wishers. In 1911, Berlin's Jewish artisans' sick-fund listed, in addition to 201 working regular members, 50 life and over 300 extraordinary members, many of whom bore professional and honorific titles.[68] The subject of Jewish artisanal education was regularly discussed at the *B'nai B'rith*'s annual conferences, and both the national organisation and individual lodges contributed to vocational projects.[69] Most significantly, in 1882 the DIGB went beyond its established brief and added "encouraging educating youth in crafts, agriculture, and technical occupations" to its official list of responsibilities. Two years later the DIGB established a department which sponsored apprentices and publicised the virtues of crafts and agriculture.[70]

By and large, enthusiasts for Jewish vocational education in Germany limited their purview to crafts. Agriculture was considered too difficult, unrewarding and alien to Jewish urban sensibilities to be feasible. But one faction of Jewish philanthropy saw in agriculture alone the salvation of German Jewry. In 1884 Moritz Simon, a wealthy Hannover merchant, decided to establish a Jewish agricultural school. The result was the Ahlem school, founded in 1893. Four years later, Kahn, Gustav Tuch and his son Ernst founded the above-mentioned VFB in Berlin. The association sponsored agricultural education projects throughout the *Reich*, and collaborated with the Simon Foundation, set up after the philanthropist's death in 1905, in the establishment of a training farm near

---

[66] Adler, *op. cit.*, p. 8.
[67] *Statistisches Jahrbuch des Deutsch-Israelitischen Gemeindebundes*, Berlin 1889, pp. 90–91; 1898, pp. 153–154; 1913, pp. 238–239; *Bericht über die Wirksamkeit des Vereins zur Verbreitung und Förderung der Handwerke unter den Juden*, Düsseldorf 1890.
[68] *Namen-Verzeichnis der Mitglieder der Gesellschaft zur Unterstützung jüdischer Handwerker und Künstler in Krankheitsfällen*, Berlin 1911, CAHJP, TD114.
[69] B'nai B'rith, *Verhandlungen der Grosse-Loge für Deutschland VIII (1886–1902)* (1893) p. 345, 357, 406; (1894), pp. 418–419; (1895), pp. 475–476; (1897), pp. 569–570. See also the Düsseldorf *Verein*'s *Bericht* for 1887, p. 2; *Mitteilungen vom DIGB*, No. 32 (1892), pp. 6–7; Maretzki, *Geschichte, op. cit.*, pp. 232, 237; B. Auerbach, *loc. cit.*, p. 61.
[70] *Mitteilungen vom DIGB*, No. 24 (1889), p. 7.

Hannover in 1909.[71] These undertakings embodied the Jewish ideology of productivisation in its most extreme form. Their publications combined autarkic economic nationalism, *völkisch* romanticism, and profound self-criticism. They argued that a massive Jewish return to the soil would simultaneously provide a guaranteed livelihood, heal moral defects and strengthen the German economy in its struggle with the nations of the world.[72] Moreover, German-Jewish agrarians made the sentimental association between country life and spirituality that was so widespread among Wilhelminian German cultural critics. Ravaged by flight from the land, the *Dorfgemeinde* were seen as the bedrock of traditional Judaism, wherein piety and fertility were inextricably linked. One VFB enthusiast proposed that incoming Eastern European Jews be forcibly directed into the countryside where they could serve as spiritual ballast for the tottering rural Jewish communities.[73]

Such sentiments, when expressed by late-nineteenth-century Central European Jews, are normally associated with Zionist yearnings for an autonomous Jewish national economy and a regenerated Jewish culture. But German-Jewish agrarianism developed separately from and alongside the Zionist movement. The Jewish agrarians' attitude towards Zionism was complex. None was overtly sympathetic to Jewish nationalism, which contradicted the agrarians' goal of maximising Jewish integration into the Fatherland. On the other hand, on the operational level, a certain measure of collaboration existed between the World Zionist Organisation (WZO) and the agrarian groups. Most of the 214 gardeners trained at the Ahlem school by 1913 went to work in Central Europe or the USA, but eight wound up in Palestine.[74] Ruppin, director of the WZO's Palestine Office, corresponded frequently with the Ahlem school and similar German-Jewish philanthropies, although the correspondence suggests that the Zionists sought a closer relationship with these than the latter desired. None the less, the *Simon'sche Stiftung* did donate money to a number of Zionist enterprises in Palestine.[75]

Some of German Zionism's greatest luminaries encountered Germano-centric Jewish agrarianism either before or while professing Zionist sentiments. Max

---

[71]Secondary literature on these projects is scarce. See E. G. Lowenthal, 'The Ahlem Experiment', in *LBI Year Book XIV* (1969), pp. 165–181; Tamar Bermann, *Produktivierungsmythen und Antisemitismus*, Vienna 1973, pp. 57–59; and the connecting narrative passages in Friedrich Homeyer, *Beitrag zur Geschichte der Gartenbauschule Ahlem 1893–1979. Dokumentarische Bearbeitung*, Hannover 1980. Both the VFB and the Ahlem school published detailed annual reports, and the history of Ahlem is nicely summarised in E. Katz, *op. cit.*

[72]Gustav Tuch, *Referat betreffend Beteiligung deutscher Juden an heimischer Landwirtschaft, gehalten am 24. Oktober 1897*, Berlin 1902; idem, *Innere Kolonisation*, [no place] 1897; A. Kahn, *Hin zur Scholle, op. cit.*; A. M. Simon, *Sollen sich Juden in Deutschland dem Handwerk, der Gärtnerei, und der Landwirtschaft widmen?*, Berlin 1902; idem, *die Erziehung zur Bodenkultur und zum Handwerk. Eine Soziale Frage*, Berlin 1904; E. Katz, *op. cit.*

[73]'Verlierende Volkskraft', attached to the *Satzungen* of the VFB, Berlin 1898. See also A. Kahn, *Hin zur Scholle, op. cit.*, p. 19; and 'Zum Projekt einer jüdische Gartenstadt bei Berlin', undated flyer (probably 1914), in Central Zionist Archives (CZA), Jerusalem, A12/7.

[74]Verein ehemaliger Ahlemer, *21er Bericht*, Hannover 1913.

[75]E. Katz, *op. cit.*, pp. 31–32; Ahlem school to Arthur Ruppin, 5th March 1911, CZA, L2/21/V; Land- und Lehrgutgesellschaft, Hannover, to Otto Warburg, 24th March 1911, CZA, L2/21/II; general correspondence between Simon'sche Stiftung and Ruppin, CZA, L2/147 and 148.

Bodenheimer, founder of the German Zionist Federation and director of the WZO's Jewish National Fund, became familiar with international Jewish settlement operations while serving in 1895–1896 on the colonisation committee of Tuch's *Freie Israelitische Vereinigung*, a group of Hamburg Jews who met occasionally to discuss the Jews' sundry social and cultural problems.[76] Franz Oppenheimer, a utopian Socialist economist who began to agitate in 1903 on behalf of co-operative settlement in Palestine, was a member of the VFB's board of directors, as was the botanist Otto Warburg, who initiated the WZO's first colonisation ventures. In 1908, Warburg became the VFB's director. Finally, although Ruppin, the WZO's reigning technocrat up until the First World War, did not participate directly in any of the agrarian charities, his own conversion to Zionism was preceded by more than a decade of longing for a massive Jewish occupational restructuring within his native Germany.[77]

Like Zionists, the German-Jewish agrarians refused to consider their enterprise utopian or unfeasible. The Jewish agrarians provide an especially clear example of a tendency, running through all Jewish vocational projects, to present themselves as extending logical and successful German social policies to the Jewish minority. For the agrarians, popular German anti-urban sentiment, the Garden City movement, and state-sponsored colonisation projects in Prussian Poland seemed to justify their actions.[78] For Jewish crafts enthusiasts, two different sets of models presented themselves for use. First, there was Germany's network of compulsory industrial continuation schools (*Fortbildungsschule*), established by liberal social reformers seeking to preserve the artisan class and save labouring youth from the snares of Socialism.[79] Second, pedagogic reformers at the *fin de siècle* placed arts and crafts within the framework of universal primary education. The *Kunsterziehungsbewegung* championed the education of the "whole child", whose motor skills, creative powers and self-confidence would be heightened through exposure to the industrial arts.[80] The DIGB leadership discussed both these developments in detail.[81] The latter was especially important to the founders of a Jewish student workshop in Köln, which taught children to work with wood and *papier mâché* in order to promote "a harmonious

---

[76] See the correspondence between, *inter alia*, Bodenheimer, Tuch and Simon, in CZA, A15/II/5 and A15/II/8. On the *Vereinigung*, see its *Mitteilungen der Ausschüsse. Stenographischer Bericht*, Hamburg 1896.

[77] On these figures, see Penslar, *op. cit.*, chaps. 2–4, *passim*.

[78] On agrarian romantic settlement in Imperial Germany, see Klaus Bergmann, *Agrarromantik und Grossstadtsfeindschaft*, Meisenheim a. Glan 1970; and Wolfgang Krabbe, *Gesellschaftsveränderung durch Lebensreform*, Göttingen 1974. On internal colonisation, see William Hagen, *Germans, Poles, and Jews. The Nationality Conflict in the Prussian East, 1772–1914*, Chicago 1980, chap. 5. For references to the German environment by the Jewish agrarians, see Gustav Tuch, *Schulgarten*, Berlin 1898; idem, *Innere Kolonisation*, *op. cit.*, pp. 10–15; the 1906 report of the VFB, pp. 5–6; and its 1913 report, pp. 4–5.

[79] Ironically, these schools were often opposed by master artisans, who saw in them an encroachment on their authority. See Derek S. Linton, *"Who Has the Youth, Has the Future". The Campaign to Save Young Workers in Imperial Germany*, Cambridge 1991, pp. 69–97.

[80] Fritz Stern, *The Politics of Cultural Despair. A Study in the Rise of the Germanic Ideology*, Berkeley–Los Angeles 1961, pp. 172–174.

[81] *Mitteilungen vom DIGB*, No. 9 (1881), p. 55; No. 24 (1889), pp. 1–2, 6–7, 25–28; No. 33 (1892), pp. 17–19.

development of all the spiritual and bodily powers slumbering inside the child".[82]

The vocational societies and Jewish arts-and-crafts programmes accomplished little. The Düsseldorf society aided at most 100 apprentices yearly; its Berlin-based counterpart reached 845 young men between 1889 and 1898.[83] The few youths who turned to the societies received small subventions for room and board, a referral to a master willing to take Jewish apprentices and periodic supervision of their progress. The reason most often given for this small range of operations was a chronic lack of funds, about which the societies complained bitterly. The DIGB itself, despite the publicity which it lavished on vocational projects, spent far less on them than on religious education, institutions of indoor relief and cultural projects. From the beginning, the DIGB's involvement in vocational education had been more symbolic than substantive. Between 1884 and 1912, the DIGB's Handicrafts Department assisted all of 376 apprentices.[84] Vocational training was promoted by a fixed group of activists, and when, after the turn of the century, they began to die off or withdraw from the organisation, the DIGB's vocational activity ebbed, although its propaganda continued unabated.[85]

There is little doubt why such programmes remained unsuccessful. Throughout the nineteenth century German Jews remained in the commercial sector of the economy because it was familiar and promised substantial rewards. Neither handicrafts nor agriculture, both in decline throughout the period, were particularly enticing.[86] Philanthropists who laboured on behalf of Jewish vocational education complained constantly that the Jewish public had little respect for manual labour and that only mental defectives and other misfits were pushed into artisanal careers. Moreover, those few hardy souls who did try to make it in handicrafts aroused antisemitism in their Christian workmates. Indeed, already in the early 1880s, some DIGB activists opposing the vocational education drive pointed to these obstacles.[87] Even enthusiasts for vocational education acknowledged that a massive shift of Jews into crafts would only arouse antisemitism among the artisan class.[88]

One cannot help wondering, therefore, why the concept of occupational restructuring won so much support in Jewish philanthropic circles. The most obvious reason is that Jewish social critics internalised economic antisemitism. Respectable Jews engaged in self-criticism precisely because they wanted so dearly to be respected. Sometimes this desire for acceptance resulted in bizarre actions, such as Kattowitz Jewry's attempt in 1912 to import 6,000 Polish Jews

[82] *Mitteilungen vom DIGB*, No. 45 (1897), pp. 2–4; see also No. 24 (1889), pp. 25–28.
[83] Statistical data on the work of the Düsseldorf and other vocational societies were tabulated by Adler and printed in No. 24 (1889) and No. 45 (1897) of the *Mitteilungen vom DIGB*. For statistics on the Prussian society, see Adler, *op. cit.*, p. 57.
[84] *Mitteilungen vom DIGB*, No. 80 (1912), p. 36.
[85] *Mitteilungen vom DIGB*, No. 68 (1907), p. 3.
[86] Jacob Katz, *Out of the Ghetto. The Social Background of Jewish Emancipation, 1770–1870*, New York 1970, pp. 176–190; Wassermann, *op. cit.*, pp. 14–24, 193–242.
[87] *Mitteilungen vom DIGB*, No. 9 (1881), p. 54; No. 10 (1882), p. 36; No. 13 (1884), p. 14.
[88] Moses, *op. cit.*, p. 11; W. Pohlmann, *Die Juden und die körperliche Arbeit*, Berlin 1894, pp. 14–15.

into Silesia, put them to work in the mines, and prove thereby that Jews were capable of hard labour.[89] More often, projects that served genuinely useful goals were burdened with apologetic intentions. For example, between 1901 and 1911 the *B'nai B'rith* sponsored the training of over 200 nurses, who staffed Germany's growing network of Jewish hospitals. For Maretzki, what mattered most about this venture was that Jewish nurses would raise the image of Jews in Gentile eyes by countering the accusation that Jewish women were spoiled and indolent.[90]

A Jew did not, however, have to suffer from internalised antisemitism to accept wholeheartedly mainstream German social and economic ideologies, many of which were nostalgic for the pre-industrial order. Beginning in the 1870s, numerous studies by members of Germany's prestigious *Verein für Sozialpolitik* anxiously took the pulse of the country's master craftsmen, symbols of the pre-industrial order. In the Wilhelminian period, public policy sought to strengthen the artisanate through financial aid and the empowerment of the guilds.[91] Ironically, these guilds, bastions of political reaction and antisemitism, were cited by the DIGB as proof that the artisan sector was holding its own and that crafts rested on "goldener Boden".[92]

The Jewish economic self-critique, then, was not anomalous. Nor was it totally without substance. Self-employed Jewish merchants were but part of the vast pool of German shopkeepers who faced cut-throat competition from each other, department stores and consumer co-operatives.[93] As to the professions, Norbert Kampe has written that law and medicine in Imperial Germany were indeed overcrowded; the term "educated proletariat", which Jewish critics so readily applied to their own kind, enjoyed wide currency in the late 1800s.[94] And since Jews found access to the civil service and academia extremely difficult, the plight of the Jewish educated proletariat was especially acute. Finally, although many craftsmen lost their livelihood during the economic crises of the 1870s and 1880s, others actually profited from the new economic order. Industrialisation created a greater, not smaller, need for butchers and bakers, and bourgeois affluence sustained demand for hand-made furniture and other luxury crafts. There was also considerable (albeit exaggerated) hope that machinery could be introduced to the small workshop in order to bring down production time and costs.[95]

Aware of these developments in handicrafts, Jewish philanthropists routinely claimed that vocational training sought to create technically advanced Jewish artisans whose product would be assured of a market. Jewish agrarians also displayed a technophilic approach; it was assumed that agriculture would have

---

[89]Jacob Toury, 'Ostjüdische Handarbeiter in Deutschland vor 1914', in *Bulletin des Leo Baeck Instituts*, 6, Nos. 21–24 (1963), pp. 81–91.
[90]Maretzki, 'Die Leistungen des Ordens', *loc. cit.*, pp. 38–39; *idem*, 'Die Frauen und die Orden', *loc. cit.* pp. 86–87.
[91]Shulamit Volkov, *The Rise of Popular Antisemitism in Germany. The Urban Master Artisans, 1873–1896*, Princeton 1978, pp. 17, 197–203, 247–256, 296.
[92]*Mitteilungen vom DIGB*, No. 9 (1881), p. 55.
[93]Cf. Robert Gellately, *The Politics of Economic Despair*, London–Beverly Hills 1974.
[94]Norbert Kampe, 'Jews and Antisemitism in Universities in Imperial Germany', in *LBI Year Book* XXX (1985), pp. 357–394.
[95]Volkov, *op. cit.*, pp. 53–59.

little appeal to Jews were it not for recent technological advances that reduced the need for menial labour and increased yields.[96] Such arguments, combined with those raised above, suggest that the Jewish vocational training project was not quite as naive and unfeasible as historians have made it out to be. None the less, we must keep in mind that most Jewish artisans aided by vocational societies were traditional craftsmen, and there is no sign that their production techniques were any more advanced than those of non-Jews. Moreover, given the especially large number of tailors, cobblers and locksmiths churned out by these societies, it is hard to see how these artisans stood on the "goldener Boden" which Jewish philanthropists often attributed to handicrafts.[97] Finally, the most damning evidence for the unworkability of the Jewish vocational programme came from the thousands of Jewish artisans from Poznań and Silesia who migrated to the western portions of the *Reich* and who, once there, encountered significant problems trying to make a living. They met antisemitism from German craftsmen, who considered them a threat.[98] In addition, the Jewish artisans' relations with their own communities were tense. In Berlin and other cities, professional associations representing Jewish artisans waged a propaganda war against community leaders over the latter's alleged unwillingness to hire Jews for public works projects.[99] The artisans also accused Jewish consumers of being loath to patronise Jewish producers.

Clearly, then, the Jewish vocational project in Imperial Germany was fatally flawed. The project does, however, have great historical significance, not for its paltry accomplishments but as an expression of the sensibilities of a neglected but sizeable segment of the German-Jewish leadership elite. As mentioned above, for a certain type of Jewish activist, social work in and of itself both created and affirmed Jewish identity. The sense of crisis created by antisemitism and the plight of Eastern Jewry intensified this associational identity. More than anything else, however, it was the corrective enterprise itself, the project of Jewish socio-economic regeneration, that nourished the Jewish identity of the activists described here. It was not merely a case of collective action instilling a sense of *esprit de corps* into a group of actors. Rather, as Alphonse Blum, a leader of the *B'nai B'rith* in Baden and a proponent of occupational restructuring, explained:

---

[96]*Mitteilungen vom DIGB*, No. 12 (1884), pp. 14–15; Simon, *op. cit.*, p. 5; E. Katz, *op. cit.*, pp. 6–7.

[97] In 1896 these occupations accounted for 22 of the 41 apprentices supported by the DIGB's *Abteilung für Handwerk und technische Gewerbe*, 17 of the 35 graduates of the Düsseldorf *Verein*, 53 of the 144 apprentices in Beuthen and 19 of 44 in Kassel. Most of the rest were bakers, bookbinders, furriers, upholsterers and painters. *Mitteilungen vom DIGB*, No. 45 (1897), pp. 8–9, 13, 16, 20.

[98]Volkov, *op. cit.*, pp. 313–319. Cf. Robert S. Wistrich, *The Jews of Vienna in the Age of Franz Joseph*, Oxford–New York 1989, p. 67.

[99]Moses, *op. cit.*, pp. 17–18; *Zur Geschichte des "Vereins selbstständiger Handwerker jüdischen Glaubens" zu Berlin. Ein Gedenkblatt zum X. Stiftungsfeste am 2. Dezember 1905*, Berlin 1905; Louis Wolff, *Handwerk im Judentum. Entwicklung und Aufstieg. Aus den Reden und Schriften von Louis Wolff (1909–1934)*, Berlin 1935, pp. 35–41. Relations between Jewish artisans and the *Gemeinde* leadership were poor in Frankfurt a. Main and Kassel, as well as Berlin, but smooth in Hamburg, Köln and Hannover. Zentralverband selbstständiger jüdischer Handwerker Deutschlands, *III. Verbandstag. Köln 1913. Verhandlungsbericht*, Berlin 1913, pp. 31–35.

"Our task is the true and final emancipation of the Jews in the ethical and social realms . . . This goal becomes clearer and the prospects for its attainment more promising the more the awareness spreads that Jewry must be treated as a whole, because of its common social structure. The singular occupational and professional limitations, which held into the 1860s, have naturally separated us from the rest of society, and we appear today as a special social body."[100]

Jewish social critics perceived Jewry as a *volkswirtschaftlich* entity which had to act collectively, through communally-generated social policy, to solve its ostensibly unique economic problems. Paradoxically, then, the expression of belief in a "Jewish social problem" was not only an exercise in self-criticism, but also a confession of identity.

III

Feeling that the Jews in Germany lived in a state of socio-economic crisis, Jewish philanthropic activists searched for new forms of knowledge that could produce successful responses thereto. This new knowledge took the form of Jewish social science. The origin of Jewish social science is a vast topic, which awaits systematic study.[101] This article seeks merely to establish the intellectual and institutional link between the Jewish sociological project in *fin-de-siècle* Germany and the philanthropies that nutured it.

The earliest manifestation of Jewish social science was statistical inquiry. A rabbinical synod held in Augsburg in 1871 formed a commission to undertake statistical studies of the Jews in German-speaking lands. The DIGB started publishing a statistical year book in 1885, approximately the same time that Joseph Jacobs in England and Cyrus Adler in the United States began producing statistical studies of their respective communities.[102] Alfred Nossig, who founded a *Verein für Jüdische Statistik* in Berlin in 1902, claimed that statistical inquiry was both a purely scholarly enterprise and a source of practical information for Jewish communities to use in the construction of their social policies.[103] Nossig's statement merely reflected the common conception in *fin-de-siècle* Germany of social reform as praxis, *viz.*, purposeful action resting on solid theoretical underpinnings and accompanied by constant empirical investigation. The exhaustive statistical studies of the German *Verein für Sozialpolitik* and the journalistic publications of the two million-member *Gesellschaft für Soziale Reform* were not meant to be purely academic exercises, but rather the building blocks of a rational social policy.[104]

---

[100]Quoted in Maretzki, *Geschichte, op. cit.*, p. 183.

[101]The lack of research on this important subject has been noted by David Sorkin, 'Emancipation and Assimilation. Two Concepts and their Relation to German-Jewish History', in *LBI Year Book* XXXV (1990), p. 24, note; and Todd M. Endelman, 'The Legitimization of the Diaspora Experience in Recent Jewish Historiography', in *Modern Judaism*, vol. XI, No. 2 (1991), p. 206, note.

[102]Verein für jüdische Statistik (ed.), *Jüdische Statistik*, Berlin 1903, pp. 7–22.

[103]See Alfred Nossig's comments in the report from the *Hauptversammlung des Vereins für Statistik der Juden*, 2nd March 1910, reproduced in *ZDSJ*, VI, No. 5 (1910), unnumbered pages at end of issue.

[104]Vom Bruch, *op. cit.*, pp. 130–137.

Operating in this spirit, Maretzki claimed that Jewish social science was the handmaid of his programmes for social reform.[105] Sure enough, German Jewry's statistical enterprise depended heavily on the *B'nai B'rith* and other philanthropic organisations. The statistical association may have been Nossig's brainchild, but it was Maretzki who mobilised funds from various Jewish communities and organisations in order to bring it to life. Throughout the period before the First World War, Maretzki was the association's chairman, and its directional board included representatives of the *B'nai B'rith*, DIGB, *Hilfsverein*, *Alliance Israélite Universelle*, and *Centralverein*. The statistical association's working arm, the *Bureau für jüdische Demographie und Statistik*, received funding from these and other organisations to undertake statistical inquiries.[106] Before the statistical office began operations in 1904, the *B'nai B'rith* sponsored its own demographic and occupational investigations of the Jews of Hessen, Baden and Poznań. In these investigations, there was no clear dividing line between scholarship and social activism; the Baden study was prepared by Moses and Blum.[107]

When seen as a source of Jewish social policy, statistical data appeared as manifestations of Jewish particularism, and the statistical enterprise as an exercise in consciousness-raising. This sentiment was forcefully expressed in an article of 1911 by the economist Arthur Cohen, co-founder and director of Munich's *Verein für Statistik der Juden*:

> "We see a statistical organisation arise everywhere where states exist, where the state's life is felt, a living state flourishes, in every sociologically distinct people or portion of a people. Jewish statistics arose with the strengthening of Jewish self-consciousness. The Office for Jewish Statistics and the *Zeitschrift für Demographie und Statistik der Juden* are its aids. *Statistics are Jewish in that they restrict themselves to Jewish society and the numerical recording of those social data by which Jews are differentiated from the rest of the society.*"[108]

Cohen ends this article by reproducing, with underscoring, a comment on the manuscript by his mentor, the celebrated statistician Georg von Mayr: "Only peoples on the descent scorn statistics. Those on the ascent love them." And yet, despite the nationalist tone of these remarks, Cohen does not appear to have had a Zionist orientation or affiliation.[109] And although statements of this type appeared in the statistical office's publications, and Zionists like Ruppin and Theilhaber contributed heavily to them, the office itself, notes John Efron, "was never truly a Zionist organization".[110] None of the activists discussed in this essay was affiliated with the Zionist movement; Moses once attended a Zionist congress, but as an observer, not a delegate.[111] The economic ideology of the

---

[105]Maretzki, *Geschichte, op. cit.*, p. 187; idem, 'Die Leistungen des Ordens', *loc. cit.*, p. 51.

[106]See note 53; also the testimonial to Maretzki by Bruno Blau, in *ZDSJ*, IX, No. 1 (January 1913), pp. 1–2.

[107]Julius Moses, 'Statistische Erhebungen über die Berufswahl der jüdischen Jugend in Landgemeinden Badens', in *Jüdische Statistik, op. cit.*, pp. 202–208; Maretzki, *Geschichte, op. cit.*, pp. 245–250.

[108]Arthur Cohen, 'Georg von Mayr und die Statistik', in *ZDSJ*, VII, No. 3 (March 1911), pp. 33–36, emphasis in original.

[109]For biographical sketches of Cohen, see *Jüdisches Lexikon*, 5 vols., Berlin 1927–1930, vol I, p. 1418; and Wininger, *op. cit.*, vol. I, p. 561.

[110]Efron, *op. cit.*, p. 439.

[111]Nadav, *op. cit.*, pp. 130–131.

Jewish social critics strongly resembled Zionist thought, but the former worked within the framework of a Jewish *Volkskörper* which, despite its unique features and needs, would remain integrally attached to the German Fatherland.

CONCLUSION

For many Jewish activists in Imperial Germany, acculturation to the German environment, a process which historians normally associate with the adaptation of religious, social and political behavioural norms, involved an internalisation of German economic ideologies as well. As with other forms of acculturation, however, distinctively Jewish forms of self-presentation persisted. Popular mentalities were refracted through a Jewish ideological prism, which could magnify, distort or reduce as the case may be. In the case studied here, German economic anti-modernism amplified longstanding Jewish concerns about the Jews' peculiar economic profile, a profile criticised since the eighteenth century by Gentile and Jewish writers alike.

Jewish social science, the project of socio-economic reform which nourished it, and the network of Jewish philanthropies which supported the project all provided Jews in Imperial Germany with a non-religious and non-political form of Jewish identity. This phenomenon fits into the general observation, made in a number of recent works of Jewish historiography, that in the nineteenth century the Jews of Western and Central Europe, despite acculturation into their host societies, retained or developed a sense of ethnic self-awareness.[112] Philanthropic institutions, many of these studies have shown, figured prominently in Jewish associational life, which provided Jews with a sense of identity derived from collective action. In Imperial Germany, for many Jewish activists philanthropic activity in the form of social welfare became a pre-eminent vehicle of Jewish self-expression. Among the social programmes which they developed, vocational education stood out for its advocates' particularly clear articulation of a Jewish identity based on a sense of socio-economic crisis and the need for a comprehensive Jewish social policy.

---

[112]Wassermann, *op. cit.*; Albert, *loc. cit.*; Rozenblit, *op. cit.*; Shulamit Volkov, 'Jüdische Assimilation und jüdische Eigenart im Deutschen Kaiserreich. Ein Versuch', in *Geschichte und Gesellschaft*, 9 (1983), pp. 331–348; Liberles, *loc. cit.*; Sorkin, *op. cit.*; Michael Graetz, *Les juifs en France au XIXe Siècle. De la Révolution française à l'Alliance israélite universelle*, Paris 1989; Green, *loc. cit.*; Kaplan, *Making of the Jewish Middle Class, op. cit.*; and Jonathan Frankel and Steven Zipperstein (eds.), *Assimilation and Community. The Jews in Ninteenth-Century Europe*, Cambridge 1991.

Scientific Racism and the Mystique of Sephardic Racial Superiority

BY JOHN M. EFRON

Recent research in German-Jewish history has effectively demonstrated that nineteenth-century German-Jewish intellectuals, especially those practitioners of the scholarly study of Jewish history and literature, known as *Wissenschaft des Judentums*, concentrated on the cultural productions of Sephardic Jewry with a view to creating an acceptable paradigmatic model of Jewish assimilation, one which would most readily fulfil the immediate political and cultural requirements of German Jewry itself.[1]

Although the history of this enterprise is yet to be written in full, a preliminary contribution to the historiography on this subject has been made in a provocative article by Ismar Schorsch, entitled 'The Myth of Sephardic Supremacy'.[2] Loosened from the moorings of their Ashkenazic patrimony, according to Schorsch, emancipation saw German Jewry "cultivate a lively bias for the religious legacy of Sephardic Jewry . . . [This] enabled them to redefine their identity in a Jewish mode".[3] Correctly, Schorsch points out that: "As construed by Ashkenazic intellectuals, the Sephardic image facilitated a religious posture marked by cultural openness, philosophic thinking, and an appreciation for the aesthetic."[4] The "Sephardic mystique", Schorsch continues, could most clearly be detected in four discrete areas of Jewish life in nineteenth-century Germany – in liturgy, synagogue architecture, literature and scholarship. A fifth category, however, should be added, namely physical anthropology. It can be shown that a similar process of "Sephardic idealisation" took place within the contemporary biological sciences as well, and that although the cult of the Sephardic Jews was also celebrated by Gentiles, the non-European Jew became, especially for European-Jewish anthropologists, an example of the physically perfect Jew.

The motivation for this idealisation comes from *fin-de-siècle* European national-

---

[1] In fact, the allure of Iberian Jewish studies was so strong, that the relevance of the study of Spanish-Jewish history for German Jewry was not lost on historians in the twentieth century either. Although clearly motivated by different impulses from those which guided his predecessors, the distinguished German-Jewish scholar at the Hebrew University, Fritz (Yitzhak) Baer, poignantly noted in the 1940s: "History brought one of the most creative Jewish communities of the Diaspora into collaboration with one of the most gifted peoples of Christian Europe, the Spaniards. Far-reaching historical developments, affecting both groups, carried this association to dramatic heights and brought it to a tragic end." The veiled reference to contemporary German Jewry is clear. Yitzhak Baer, *A History of the Jews in Christian Spain*, vol. I, Philadelphia 1971, p. 2.
[2] Ismar Schorsch, 'The Myth of Sephardic Supremacy', in *LBI Year Book XXXIV* (1989), pp. 47–66.
[3] *Ibid.*, p. 47.
[4] *Ibid.*

ism, which bred a cult of virility and celebrated the culture of manliness. One manifestation of this was the stress placed on not just individual, but racial fitness, and the need for general racial improvement. One outgrowth of such sentiment was the propagation of the "racial myth" – a loose concept that was not open to empirical investigation, but which posited that certain races displayed features, both positive and negative, that were definitive of a particular race. Predictably, when one spoke of one's own race the features tended to the desirable and *vice versa* when the discussion turned to the racial qualities of another people. Depending on who was talking, the myths generally held that Germans were honest and fearless; Blacks, emotional and passionate; Asians, industrious; Jews, physically deformed, devious and intelligent. These were not just the quirky opinions of fringe dwellers on the European intellectual landscape. Rather, mainstream thinkers shared many of these prejudices and indeed descriptions such as these could be found in important European scientific textbooks and articles from the eighteenth century on.[5]

Swept up in this general atmosphere were European Jews who were also poised to give expression to their own nationalist movement. They, too, were engaged in the process of countering racial myths about themselves by the further creation of new racial myths. Sephardic Jews were the focus of this myth, providing Ashkenazic Jews with a counter model to the negatively stereotyped Jew. For Jewish commentators on the subject, the Sephardic Jew was not only a foil for the Ashkenazic Jew but was also conceived of as a model of impending Jewish racial rebirth.

While the bulk of the evidence presented here comes from the German *Kulturbereich*, it is not exclusively so. Race science was a world-wide phenomenon, and discussions about the racial qualities of the Jews were the focus of anthropological debates in the rest of Europe and the United States as well.

Physical anthropology or race science was, in the nineteenth and early twentieth centuries, central to the Western intellectual tradition.[6] The idea of race was one, if not the most important, of the categories of group self-definition at the time. Jewish race scientists, no less than their Gentile colleagues, eagerly took part in the scientific debates on biological "Otherness", primarily focusing on the heated debate about the "racial characteristics" of the Jews.[7] Of the many themes pursued in this literature, one that occurs with consistent frequency is the discussion over the "racial" differences between Sephardim and Ashkenazim.

Not only among Jewish anthropologists, but among non-Jewish as well, the aesthetic and intellectual dimensions of this ethnic split were debated. In sum, both groups of scientists perpetuated a myth of Sephardic racial superiority. They tended to inflate the image of the Sephardic Jew, seeing him as "beautiful", a model of racial nobility. Indeed, when the glowing anthropological descriptions of Sephardic Jews are compared to those of Ashkenazim, it can be seen that the Sephardi served as the equivalent of the Jewish "Aryan", a glorious figure,

---

[5]See Louis L. Snyder, *Race. A History of Modern Ethnic Theories*, New York 1939.
[6]George L. Mosse, *Toward the Final Solution. A History of European Racism*, Madison 1985, Introduction.
[7]For the history of this enterprise see my *Defining the Jewish Race. The Self-Perceptions and Responses of Jewish Scientists to Scientific Racism in Europe, 1882–1933*, Ph.D. dissertation, Columbia University 1991.

characterised by his nobility, breeding and poise. He was portrayed as the physical counterpoint to the ignoble Jew of Central and Eastern Europe.

In one sense, however, the discussions about Jewish racial types do differ according to whether the anthropology was being investigated by Jews or non-Jews. For the non-Jewish scientist, the Sephardic Jew, idealised, thanks to the comfortable distance provided by time and space, was proof that a noble, physically beautiful Jew had at one time been a historical reality.

For the Jewish anthropologist, the process was more complex. It also involved the idealisation of the physical appearance of the Sephardic Jew, but since almost all Jewish anthropologists were of Ashkenazic background, their comparative distinctions often involved no small amount of self-abnegation.[8] Comparative descriptions of the two groups were polemically charged and infused with general notions dating back to the Enlightenment concerning the relative beauty and ugliness of certain races.[9]

For Jewish race scientists, furthermore, unlike their earlier co-religionist historians who concentrated on the cultural achievements of Iberian Jewry, the paradoxical situation arose whereby the contemporary cultural level of Sephardic Jewry was regarded as clearly inferior to that of Jewish civilisation in either Eastern or Central Europe. For the late-nineteenth-century Jewish physical anthropologist, living at a time when rising nationalism and notions of racial superiority and inferiority permeated European culture in general, it was primarily the physical features of the Sephardim which could serve as a potentially liberating force from the accusations of Jewish racial degeneracy.[10] In addition to physical features, however, the apparent greater openness of intellectual inquiry among Sephardim was also juxtaposed with the more closed talmudic culture of the Ashkenazim. Consequently, many of the race scientists spoke as though the differing modes of thought of the two groups were transmissible mental characteristics.

One more point needs to be made concerning the role that the Sephardic Jew played in the anthropological discourse. The nationalistic and racially charged atmosphere of the late nineteenth century saw great emphasis placed on notions of racial "authenticity" and antiquity.[11] For many Jewish scientists, especially Zionists, the Sephardic Jew represented the *Urjude*, the original Jew, the Jew who could be authentically linked to both an ancient and glorious past, and by extension, could serve as a model for a future rejuvenated Jewry.

In the 1860s, under the influence of polygenism (the notion that the human races did not form a single species, but were the products of separate acts of creation), and the sway of rising nationalism, anthropology split people into myriad groups and types, eschewing the more static and uniform pictures it had

---

[8]The Jewish assumption of antisemitic discourse about Jews is discussed in Sander L. Gilman, *Jewish Self-Hatred. Anti-Semitism and the Hidden Language of the Jews*, Baltimore–London 1986.
[9]On the relationship of aesthetics to race science see Mosse, *Toward the Final Solution*, pp. 10–12.
[10]On European concepts of degeneration see J. Edward Chamberlain and Sander L. Gilman (eds.), *Degeneration. The Dark Side of Progress*, New York 1985.
[11]On this very phenomenon see the superb study by Léon Poliakov, *The Aryan Myth. A History of Racist and Nationalist Ideas in Europe*. New York 1977.

previously portrayed.[12] With this new development challenges were posed to one of the most sacred canons of anthropological theory – that of Jewish racial uniformity. Mainstream anthropology argued that the Jews were a Semitic race, which over the past two thousand years had, through intra-marriage and the pursuit and maintenance of a segregated existence, remained pure and essentially unchanged.[13]

Yet the absence of morphological homogeneity among the Jews was problematic. Focusing on head shape as an indicator of relative purity because the head was held to be the most consistent racial feature, scientists were at pains to explain how Jews, if they were Semites and a pure race, no longer resembled either ancient Semitic types or modern Arabs in craniometric dimensions.

Comparative craniometry (the measuring of skulls) was the defining methodology of modern race science. In 1844, the Swedish anatomist Andreas Retzius introduced the cranial index and this became the crucial measure of race.[14] Craniometric measurement of Jews from the last quarter of the nineteenth century indicated, it was maintained, the existence of at least two distinct "racial types" among them, the dolichocephalic and the brachycephalic; the former represented by the Sephardim and the latter by the Ashkenazim.

The most important, and earliest, discussion of the fact that the Jews seemed to display two distinct cranial types, round brachycephalic and long dolichocephalic, was that of the German naturalist and physician Carl Vogt (1817–1895). In 1864, Vogt published his celebrated *Lectures on Man* in which he made clear for the first time that not all Jews appeared alike and that there were two distinct, yet related, branches of Jewry. Invoking the authority of anonymous Jewish thinkers, Vogt noted that:

> "All Jewish scholars agree also that both types have existed from the remotest period, so that some reduce them to the multitude of people which accompanied the Jews on their departure from Egypt, and passed with them through the Red Sea . . . Thus the differences obtaining between Jews seem to result rather from original tribe peculiarities than from changes of localities. Another argument in favour of this view is, that the Jews of the Oriental type expelled from Portugal, who for several centuries have been settled in Holland, have preserved their peculiarities unaltered; whilst, on the other hand, in the East, the two Jewish types lived also for centuries side by side in the same climate and conditions, and preserved their respective characters."[15]

Vogt described the two great branches of Jews, the Ashkenazim and the Sephardim thus:

---

[12] In addition to nationalism, polygenesis as an explanation for human difference was given impetus by recent advances in geology, archaeology and paleontology. These three disciplines tended to expand science's concept of time, thus challenging biblical chronology and the idea that humans originated from a single pair. Nancy Stepan, *The Idea of Race in Science. Great Britain 1800–1960*, London 1982, p. 40.

[13] Numerous scientists, both Jewish and Gentile maintained this belief. One of the most representative expressions of this idea is to be found in Richard Andree, *Zur Volkskunde der Juden*, Bielefeld–Leipzig 1881, p. 24.

[14] To calculate the index, the most important measurement of the skull, anthropologists multiplied the width of the head by 100 and divided the product by the length. When a cephalic index measured above 80, it was regarded as brachycephalic; between 75 and 80, mesocephalic; and below 75, dolichocephalic.

[15] Carl Vogt, *Lectures on Man. His Place in Creation, and in the History of the Earth*, London 1864, p. 434.

"There exists chiefly in the North, in Russia and Poland, Germany and Bohemia, a tribe of Jews frequently with red hair, short beard, pug nose, small grey cunning eyes, massive trunk, round face and broad cheek bones, resembling many Sclavonian tribes of the North. In the East, on the contrary, and about the Mediterranean, as well as in Portugal and in Holland, we find the Semitic stock with long black hair and beard, large almond-shaped eyes with a melancholy expression, oval face and prominent nose; in short, that type represented in the portraits of Rembrandt."[16]

In distinguishing one group of Jews from another, Vogt's observations mark a clear change in the direction of German anthropology's previous discourse on the Jews.[17] No longer represented as an homogeneous mass, the Jews were now recognised as composed of two distinct racial elements. More than this, Vogt's descriptions betray his sense that the Ashkenazi is less than desirable in both a moral and a physical sense. After all, did he not possess a disproportionately ugly and deformed body, and did not the nature of his expression reveal a mendacious trickster ready to gain at the expense of others?[18] By contrast, the Sephardic Jew is portrayed as sensual, reflective and worthy of commemoration by one of Europe's greatest painters.

After Vogt, the view of the anthropological "splitters" held sway. This did not mean a complete consensus on this issue. For example, Vogt ascribed the East European Jewish type to the admixture of Slavic blood, while four years later, the anthropologist Friedrich Maurer, although concurring with Vogt that the Jews presented two racial types, claimed that the racial split was caused by the introduction of Turanian elements.[19] Turanian was the racial classification of people known to history as the *Khazars*. Some nineteenth-century scholars pointed to the *Khazar* conversion to Judaism in the seventh century as the time when the Jewish racial type ceased to be exclusively Semitic. From then on, said the race scientists, the Semitic Jews mixed with the Turkic *Khazars* to produce the unique Ashkenazic type.[20]

In 1877 the Austrian physician, Augustin Weisbach, published the findings of his craniometric examinations of nineteen Jewish males and concluded that:

"among the European Jews there are undoubtedly two cephalic types. One is dolichocephalic, with a narrow, long face, [and] on the whole a big nose and thin lips. [It is] almost always without exception beautiful, slender, though like most narrow-shouldered forms, it has an exquisitely long, narrow head and even a kind of prognathous face. [In addition, there is] a brachycephalic type, with a wide face, low, broad, small nose and thick lips."[21]

---

[16]Vogt, *Lectures*, p. 433.
[17]Efron, *Defining the Jewish Race*, pp. 1–44.
[18]For a discussion of modern images of the Jewish body, drawn heavily from literary representations, see Sander L. Gilman, *The Jews' Body*, New York–London 1991.
[19]Friedrich Maurer, 'Mitteilungen aus Bosnien', *Das Ausland*, No. 49 (1869), pp. 1161–1164; and No. 50 (1869), pp. 1183–1185.
[20]On the history of the *Khazar* conversion see Douglas Morton Dunlop, *The History of the Jewish Khazars*, Princeton 1954. The most extensive discussion of the conversion by a Jewish race scientist was that of Samuel Weissenberg. See his, 'Die südrussischen Juden. Eine anthropometrische Studie', *Archiv für Anthropologie*, vol. 23 (1895), esp. pp. 578–579.
[21]Augustin Weisbach, 'Körpermessungen verschiedener Menschenrassen', *Zeitschrift für Ethnologie*, vol. 9 (1877), pp. 212–214.

Put simply, there is a marked absence in Weisbach's description of Ashkenazim of adjectives such as exquisite, slender and beautiful. Instead, the Ashkenazi is a creature devoid of both aesthetic charm and worth.

The celebrated German geographer, Richard Andree, likewise divided the Jews into two racial types. Significantly, in describing the Sephardim, he used such adjectives as "fine", "noble" and "graceful". The Ashkenazic Jew, on the other hand, appeared "ignoble", and had a "large mouth, fleshy nose, deep furrows from the nose to the mouth, and often, curly hair".[22] Andree, it must be noted, was of the opinion that racial characteristics such as these were permanent and unchanging.

Andree's scientific agenda is clearly reflective of the political circumstances under which he worked. His study appeared in 1881, in the midst of massive Russian Jewish emigration from the East. That it is laden with ideological baggage becomes apparent when one takes into account the bulk of the book, which is an ethnographic survey of Jewish (mostly Ashkenazic) customs.

For example, when discussing the exotic nature of such rites and rituals, Andree's descriptions are based on his theoretical assumption that Jews who live in large, compact masses, as they do in Eastern Europe, are unable to shed their Jewishness, and thus remain on "a lower cultural level".[23] By contrast, German Jews, who accounted for a tiny percentage of the German population, had been able to modernise somewhat, precisely because they had not settled in great numbers.[24] Andree clearly feared that Ashkenazic immigrants were not only unassimilable, but that their presence in Germany would reverse the process of Jewish acculturation already underway in that country.[25]

For Andree, Sephardic Jews provided a stark contrast to this situation. Though like all Jews, they too were unable to assimilate completely because of their indelible racial characteristics, they had been able to integrate into the majority culture, and so had proven themselves historically, as far as Andree was concerned, to be a more desirable type of Jew.[26] For Andree, Ashkenazic Jews of neither German nor Russian origin could ever enjoy the success of the superior Jews of the Iberian Peninsula.

The higher cultural level of the Sephardim was often used by commentators to deny the Ashkenazic Jew any significant role in the development of what is commonly mislabelled, "Judeo-Christian" culture. Bernhard Blechmann's study of 1882 convinced him that present-day East European Jews were racially different from both their Semitic forefathers and their direct descendants, the Sephardim.[27] The implication in Blechmann's observations was that the modern East European Jew constituted an intellectual and aesthetic decline from the original noble type that had given the world pure monotheism.

Two other German anthropologists whose views were widely regarded by

[22]Andree, *Volkskunde*, p. 39.
[23]*Ibid.*, p. 130.
[24]*Ibid.*, p. 129.
[25]*Ibid.*, p. 261.
[26]*Ibid.*, pp. 54–55.
[27]Bernhard Blechmann, *Ein Beitrag zur Anthropologie der Juden*, Dorpat 1882, p. 59.

contemporaries, Ludwig Stieda, professor of anatomy at Dorpat and Julius Kollmann, professor of anatomy at Basel, both maintained on the basis of cranial measurements that the Jews were composed of two racial types, one of which, the brachycephalic Ashkenazic, was completely different from that of the original dolichocephalic Sephardic.[28] Kollmann's study, conducted in 1885 on twelve medieval skulls from the ancient Jewish cemetery in Basel, found that the skulls had an almost hyper-brachycephalic cranial index of 84.66.[29] For Kollmann, this was clear proof that the Jews were originally composed of two racially distinct types. He was unable to entertain any other explanation because of his unshakable belief in the permanency of racial characteristics and his belief in Jewish racial purity.[30] Just how such morphological divergences arose among the Jews, divergences which included hair, eye and skin colour, as well as widely differing bodily measurements, became the central debate in modern anthropological theories about the Jews.

The above examples indicate that a subtle political agenda impinged on the scientific practice of these anthropologists. The division and separate classification of the "Jewish race" into two separate "Jewish types" served to draw a distinction between contemporary Jews and ancient Israelites. In this way, the modern Jew of Central and Eastern Europe, a figure long vilified, was juxtaposed with, by being separated from, the more praiseworthy ancient Semite (read Sephardic Jew).

By doing this, modern anthropological theory incorporated and indeed inherited a form of traditional Christian antisemitism that expressed its hostility primarily towards rabbinic, rather than biblical Judaism.[31] And, despite the fact that certain intellectuals began to express a more tolerant attitude towards Jews beginning in the seventeenth century, much literature from the period also indicates that in the minds of many European writers, contemporary Jews (read Ashkenazim) were often seen as identical to savages; both being observed as enemies of civilised humanity.[32] Modern biological racism inherited this

[28] See Ludwig Stieda, 'Ein Beitrag zur Anthropologie der Juden', *Archiv für Anthropologie*, vol. 14 (1883), pp. 61–71.

[29] See Julius Kollmann, 'Schädel und Skeletreste aus einem Judenfriedhof des 13. und 14. Jahrhundert zu Basel', *Verhandlungen der naturforschenden Gesellschaft zu Basel*, vol. 7 (1885), pp. 648–656.

[30] Julius Kollmann, 'Die Rassenanatomie der Hand und die Persistenz der Rassenmerkmale', *Archiv für Anthropologie*, vol. 28 (1903), pp. 91–141.

[31] In fact, early reformers of Judaism in Germany sought to dissociate themselves from the political-national conception of Judaism as manifested in rabbinic Judaism by referring to themselves as Israelites instead of Jews. Gotthold Salomon (1784–1862), one of the first preachers at the new Hamburg Reform Temple opened in 1818, sought to universalise Judaism by invoking the ancients when he said, "The summons to be an Israelite is the summons to be a human being." The issue of changing nomenclature is an important one in modern Jewish history, going to the heart of oscillating modes of self-perception. On the ideological implications of the different names Jews used at varying times to refer to themselves, see Michael A. Meyer, *Response to Modernity. A History of the Reform Movement in Judaism*, New York–Oxford 1988, p. 30.

[32] On seventeenth-century expressions of tolerance towards Jews see Shmuel Ettinger, 'The Beginnings of the Change in the Attitude of European Society Towards the Jews', *Scripta Hierosolymitana*, vol. 7 (1961), pp. 193–219. On the conflation of Jews and savages and the view of anthropology in general towards Judaism see Howard Eilberg-Schwartz, *The Savage in Judaism. An Anthropology of Israelite Religion and Ancient Judaism*, Bloomington 1990, pp. 37–39.

antisemitic tradition and thus it is not surprising to see Jews divided into categories of ancient/good versus contemporary/bad.

In addition, another opinion was being subtly voiced here. The bulk of these anthropological reports were being issued at the time of both the rise of modern antisemitic mass political movements, and, as noted above, the massive westward migration of Jews from Eastern Europe.[33] A stock-in-trade accusation then hurled at the incoming Russian Jews was that they would do irreparable harm to the nations to which they came because they were a largely unassimilable group.

By way of contrast, Sephardic Jews, because they were conflated in the European mind with ancient Israelites who had enjoyed normal relations with other Near Eastern powers in antiquity, were long observed, by both Central European Jews and non-Jews, to be an example of an integrated and "normal" Jewish community *par excellence*.[34]

On the other hand, according to the view of hostile observers, the historical absence of ordinary political relations between Ashkenazim and Gentiles had been replaced by the attempt to cultivate strong cultural ties which had resulted in assimilation. In the minds of these men, this was especially true of German Jews. Racist antisemites employed a biological argument of Aryan-Semite incompatibility against assimilated German Jews, whose very integration, although long demanded, was now classed as a major threat to the German *Volk*.[35] This idea, that Jews sought to insinuate themselves culturally into the life of the host nations, became a focus of popular antisemitic, as well as scientific literature of the *fin de siècle*.[36] It should be noted that in this context, Ashkenazim were held to a different standard than Sephardim. While acculturated Spanish Jews were seen to "celebrate" Spanish culture, Central European Jews were held to "infiltrate" German culture.

It was Jewish scholars who actually contributed the lengthiest discussions to the debate on the anthropology of Sephardim and Ashkenazim. One of the very

---

[33]The literature on this subject is enormous. See for example, Peter Pulzer, *The Rise of Political Anti-Semitism in Germany and Austria*. 2nd rev. edn., London 1988; Paul W. Massing, *Rehearsal for Destruction: A Study of Political Anti-Semitism in Imperial Germany*, New York 1967; and on the impact of East European immigration on German policy during the *Kaiserreich*, Jack L. Wertheimer, *Unwelcome Strangers. East European Jews in Imperial Germany*, New York–Oxford 1987; see also Jack Wertheimer's essays on this topic in *LBI Year Book XXVI* (1981), *XXVII* (1982) and *XXVIII* (1983).

[34]Not all Europeans were happy about this. For example, so successful was the assimilation and integration of Jewish converts into the highest echelons of Iberian society, that legislation was passed in Spain and Portugal prohibiting *conversos* and their descendants from holding office or receiving privileges and honours. Known as the "*estatutos de limpieza de sangre*" ("statutes of purity of blood"), the statutes were perhaps one of the earliest manifestations of an antisemitic race law in history. See Yosef Hayim Yerushalmi, *Assimilation and Racial Anti-Semitism. The Iberian and the German Models*, Leo Baeck Memorial Lecture, No. 26 (1982). In fact, the statutes were not repealed until 1773 in Portugal and 1860 in Spain.

[35]For example, Julius Langbehn, *Rembrandt als Erzieher*, Leipzig 1909, p. 43.

[36]See for example, Karl Eugen Dühring, who commented that: "The Mosaic attempt to locate within the base of our people a Jewish component only makes the Jewish question a more burning issue. The diverse admixture of our modern cultures, or in other words, the sprinkling of racial-Jewry in the cracks and crevices of our national abode, must inevitably lead to a reaction . . ." Quoted in *The Jew in the Modern World*, ed. by Paul R. Mendes-Flohr and Jehuda Reinharz, Oxford 1980, pp. 273–274.

first to address the differences between the two Jewish types formally was the distinguished Oxford scholar and librarian at the Bodleian, Adolf Neubauer (1831–1907). In a paper delivered to the Royal Anthropological Institute in 1885, Neubauer offered his opinion on the causes of the seeming differences as well as the reasons for them.[37] On the basis of historical evidence which suggested wide-spread patterns of inter-marriage and proselytism, Neubauer argued against the notion of the purity of the Jewish race. In his opinion, only inter-marriage and climate could explain the existence of so many different appearances among the Jews in so many different countries, especially the Sephardic-Ashkenazic split.[38]

The bifurcation of Jews into a Sephardic and an Ashkenazic type was, for Neubauer, pointless. Having rejected the notion of Jewish racial purity as well as the idea that the morphology of Jews was biologically determined, he nevertheless described the two groups in the typical language of contemporary race science. There were: "First, those with a well-developed nose, black and striking eyes, and fine extremities – in one word, the noble race of the Sephardim, or the Spanish-Portuguese Jews; second, those who have a thickish nose, large mouth, and curled hair, features which are represented amongst the Ashkenazim, or the German-Polish Jews." Tellingly, Neubauer notes that the division of the two Jewish types:

> "... is only a revival of the old legend which existed for a long time amongst the Jews themselves in the middle ages, viz., that the noble Spanish race are descended from the tribe of Judah and the rougher German-Polish Jews from the tribe of Benjamin. This legend had such effect that intermarriage between the Spanish and German Jews was for a long time avoided."[39]

Late nineteenth-century discussions of the physical attributes of certain peoples were very often accompanied by highly subjective evaluations of the behavioural and cultural level of those groups under review. Neubauer's study does not constitute an exception to this normative mode of anthropological argumentation. His cultural descriptions of Sephardim and Ashkenazim clearly betray a preference for Sephardic customs. Moreover, his bias in favour of this group highlights his own belief that the Sephardic Jew represents a more noble type, one whose conduct in general, and whose mode of Jewish expression in particular, are clearly superior to that of the Jews of Central and Eastern Europe.

Neubauer's descriptions are worth quoting in full for they constitute one of the clearest expressions of a nineteenth-century Jewish scholar's opinions on this problem. A Hungarian-born Jew himself, Neubauer vilified the Jewish culture of the Ashkenazim when he wrote that:

---

[37] The paper was read in the author's absence.
[38] Adolf Neubauer, 'Notes on the Race-Types of the Jews', *Journal of the Royal Anthropological Institute of Great Britain and Ireland*, vol. 15 (1885), p. 19.
[39] Neubauer, *loc. cit.*, p. 19. Neubauer is actually referring to at least two celebrated English cases, the first in 1766, when the Sephardic community's leader, the *Mahamad*, declared that a Sephardi may not marry an Ashkenazi and that the Ashkenazi wife or widow of a Sephardi was not entitled to receive congregational charity (except in the case of illness). The second was the outright refusal of the London Sephardic community in 1772 to permit one Asser del Banco to marry a "Tudesca". *Jewish Chronicle*, June 28th 1901, p. viii.

"What is curious to notice is that the manners and habits of the so-called distinct tribes are also different, in accordance with the features, viz., the Spanish and Eastern Jews have a kind of refinement in speech and gesture, while the German-Polish Jews are rougher in both; and the Italian Jews lie again between the two. But this also must be attributed to the manners and speech of the nations amongst whom they lived, and with whom they are in daily contact. We shall go further; – there is even a difference in the literature of the mediaeval Jews of the two so-called tribes. The Spanish Jews are much more logical and clear in their casuistic compositions, and dislike scholastic discussions, whilst the contrary is the case with the German-Polish Jews, whose casuistry reaches the climax of logical mistakes, of scholastic torture, and absurd thinking. The Italians stand again between these two in this matter. Can this be attributed to a difference between the two tribes, or rather not to the character and tone of the nations amongst whom they lived?"[40]

Neubauer's descriptions are representative of a kind of scientific writing about race in the late nineteenth century that, even if not wedded to a belief in biological determinism, nevertheless employed the language of scientific racism. In this case, for example, Neubauer affirmed the existence of "national character". Insisting that it was not racially determined, but, rather, culturally conditioned, he made sweeping assessments about the two great branches of Jewry; assigning, for example, the qualities of logic and clarity to the Sephardim while denying the Ashkenazim those very characteristics.

It is important to note from this example, that Neubauer's criticism of Ashkenazic Jewry is in complete accord with a long line of scholars steeped in the tradition of *Wissenschaft des Judentums*, who explicitly criticised the talmudic-casuistic tradition of East European Jewry.[41] The description by Neubauer's contemporary, Heinrich Graetz, of the consequences of Talmud study in Poland accurately sums up the nineteenth-century Western Jewish view of this culture. It was his opinion that:

"[t]he cultivation of a single faculty, that of hair-splitting judgement, at the cost of the rest, narrowed the imagination, hence not a single literary product appeared in Poland deserving the name of poetry . . . A love of twisting, distorting, ingenious quibbling, and a foregone antipathy to what did not lie in their field of vision, constituted the character of the Polish Jews."[42]

Implicit in this criticism is that this mode of thinking is incompatible with the norms of modern critical scholarship, and that the "logic" of Sephardic Jewry, as well as its more highly developed aesthetic sensibilities, serve as the best Jewish

---

[40]Neubauer, *loc. cit.*, p. 20.

[41]Among sixteenth- and seventeenth-century critics of talmudic casuistry, the most well known are Jehuda Löw ben Bezalel of Prague (the MaHaRaL, 1525–1609), Rabbi Isaiah Halevi Horwitz (1565–1630), and Rabbi Yair Haim Bakhrakh (1638–1702). See David Sorkin, *The Transformation of German Jewry, 1780–1840*, New York–Oxford 1987, p. 50. For an eighteenth-century example, see the highly sarcastic and derisory description of talmudic disputation by the Polish-born Jewish philosopher Solomon Maimon (c.1753–1800), as recounted in his autobiography, partially reprinted in Mendes-Flohr and Reinharz (eds.), *op. cit.*, p. 215.

[42]Heinrich Graetz, *History of the Jews*, vol. 5, Philadelphia 1895, pp. 4–5. For a fuller discussion of early *Haskalah* attitudes towards the Talmud, see Moshe Pelli, 'The Attitude of the First Maskilim in Germany towards the Talmud', in *LBI Year Book XXVII* (1982), pp. 243–260.

model for contemporary Ashkenazic integration into modern European society.[43]

It would appear that a scholar such as Neubauer was a Lamarckian. When he discussed the distinguished literary legacy, especially poetry, of the Sephardim, he implied that their acquired clear thinking had been passed on to their descendants. Likewise, Ashkenazic Jewry could also acquire this inheritable characteristic, provided it was removed from the Polish *milieu* in which it lived.

Neubauer's fellow Anglo-Jewish scholar, Joseph Jacobs (1854–1916), the first Jewish physical anthropologist, was also a firm believer in the power of the environment to affect human behaviour.[44] Commenting on this latter point in the context of a discussion about the apparent craniometric differences between Sephardim and Ashkenazim, Jacobs wrote that "in races where progress depends upon brain rather than muscle the brain-box broadens out as a natural consequence". Jacobs explained himself in purely Lamarckian terms, noting that:

> "[t]he application of all this to the case of the Jews seems obvious. If they had been forced by persecution to become mainly blacksmiths, one would not have been surprised to find their biceps larger than those of other folk; and similarly, as they have been forced to live by the exercise of their brains, one should not be surprised to find the cubic capacity of their skulls larger than that of their neighbours."[45]

By this reasoning, Jacobs concluded that those Sephardic Jews and Gentiles still displaying dolichocephalism had simply not progressed as far as those Jews and other races, who had attained brachycephalism and thus intellectual preeminence. When he conducted his craniometric research on English Jewry in the early 1880s, Jacobs sought to prove that it was not race but environment that caused changes in skull shape. He found that the Sephardim of Britain (originally dolichocephalic) displayed greater brachycephalism than the Ashkenazic population because they had attained a higher level of intellectual achievement than the Ashkenazim.[46] This was based, of course, on their long residency in the British Isles. It was, therefore, only a matter of time before England's beneficial effect would begin to manifest itself among East European Jews and they too, would begin to show a broadening of the "brain-box". Anthropometry aside, it is important to note that, even for Jacobs, the Sephardic Jew of Britain became a model for Ashkenazic integration into English society.

---

[43]This view was even prevalent prior to the advent of either Jewish emancipation or *Wissenschaft des Judentums* in the nineteenth century. In the seventeenth century, Ashkenazic critics of *pilpul* (talmudic casuistry) pointed to Sephardic schools, especially those in Amsterdam, as exemplary models of what Jewish education should be. Sorkin, *op. cit.*, p. 51. For an eighteenth-century critique of German Jewry see Morris M. Faierstein, 'The Liebes Brief. A Critique of Jewish Society in Germany (1749)', in *LBI Year Book XXVII, op. cit.*, pp. 219–241. The author of the Yiddish language *Liebes Brief*, Isaac Wetzlar, makes clear that the practices of the Sephardim stand in stark contrast to those of the Ashkenazim and, moreover, should serve as a model for the latter group to emulate.

[44]On Jacobs as an anthropolgist and Jewish historian see Efron, *Defining the Jewish Race, op. cit.*, pp. 101–183.

[45]Joseph Jacobs, 'Are Jews Jews?', *Popular Science Monthly*, vol. 55 (May–October 1899), p. 507.

[46]See the entry, 'Craniometry', written by Maurice Fishberg and edited by Joseph Jacobs in *Jewish Encyclopaedia*, New York 1901–1905, vol. IV, p. 336.

Another point needs to be recognised and that is that Jacobs was responding to the then current Aryan racial theory that vaunted the cultural achievements of long-headed Indo-Europeans as being superior to those of other races.[47] For Jacobs, the distinguished, brachycephalic Sephardic community was not only proof of the speciousness of the Aryan theory, but confirmation of the assimilability and adaptability of all Jews.

In 1900, Jacobs emigrated to the United States in order to take up a position as revising editor of the great *Jewish Encyclopaedia* then in preparation. In addition to heading the encyclopaedia's departments of England and Anthropology, he contributed a staggering 450 entries on numerous subjects. Never before had such a reference work on the Jews paid so much attention to Jewish anthropology, both physical and cultural, nor had one focused so attentively on different Jewish "types" and the Jewish racial question.

Not surprisingly, the entry under 'Sephardim' in the encyclopaedia's eleventh volume is a perfect example of Ashkenazic scholarly lionising of the Sephardim. Its author was Meyer Kayserling (1829–1905), the German-born historian and rabbi of Budapest. Kayserling produced a very large corpus of work on many aspects of Jewish history, literature and religion, but is best known for his pioneering work on the history of Spanish Jewry and the Marranos. Kayserling wrote a two-volume history of Iberian Jewry, works on the poetry of the Sephardim, a biography of Manasseh ben Israel, a study of the Jewish role in Columbus's voyages of discovery, and a bibliography of Marrano literature. In addition, he published well over 500 scholarly articles on Sephardic Jewry and other aspects of Jewish history and literature.[48] This number includes the scores of entries he contributed on Spanish and Portuguese Jews to the *Jewish Encyclopaedia*.

Although he was not a scientist in the technical sense, Kayserling's article on 'Sephardim' is included here, because his language borrows heavily from the contemporary scientific (and at times antisemitic) discourse on the Jews as a race and, in addition, its subtext is clearly a polemic against Ashkenazic Jewry. Without even mentioning this latter group, Kayserling's adulation of the Sephardim saw him present them as ideal Jews in contra-distinction to the Jews of Central and Eastern Europe. Noting that *vis à vis* the Ashkenazim, the Sephardim "considered themselves a superior class, the nobility of Jewry", Kayserling went on to claim that:

> "[t]his sense of dignity which the Sephardim possessed manifested itself in their general deportment and in their scrupulous attention to dress. Even those among them whose station in life was low, as, for example, the carriers in Salonika, or the sellers of 'pan de España' in the streets of Smyrna, maintained the old Spanish 'grandezza' in spite of their poverty."[49]

So deeply ingrained were these characteristics, that they seemed to be impervious to changes of environment. It is clear from this description, that the noble bearing that seemed to mark the Jews of Spain was also portrayed by

---

[47]On the origins and development of the Aryan theory see Snyder, *op cit.*, pp. 58–89.
[48]Meyer Kayserling, *Biblioteca Española-Portugeza-Judaica*, New York ³1971.
[49]Meyer Kayserling, 'Sephardim' in *Jewish Encyclopaedia*, vol. XI, p. 197.

Kayserling to have been an inheritable trait, one that even withstood the debilitating effects of grinding poverty in both Greece and Turkey. Few, if any, authors prior to the First World War ever remarked on the nobility of penury-stricken Ashkenazic Jewry in the Pale of Settlement.[50] None the less, Sephardic Jews, because of their glorious past and the mystique that surrounded their present, remained exceptional in the minds of Jewish scholars.

As if to reinforce further the supposedly greater dignity of the Sephardim, Kayserling again took direct aim at the economic and occupational activities of the Ashkenazim without actually mentioning them. Nevertheless, the reference is abundantly clear when he notes that:

> "[t]he Sephardim never engaged in chaffering occupations nor in usury, and they did not mingle with the lower classes. With their social equals they associated freely, without regard to creed, and in the presence of their superiors they displayed neither shyness nor servility."[51]

This claim about the dignified behaviour of the Sephardim was often repeated, and it will appear again below in the discussion by America's most celebrated Jewish race scientist, Maurice Fishberg. But more than mere deportment, Spanish Jews, in stark contrast to the Ashkenazim, remained linguistically pure. Here, Kayserling was direct and voiced a banal, *maskilic* view of Yiddish, declaring that:

> "From Tangier to Salonica, from Smyrna to Belgrade, and from Vienna to Amsterdam and Hamburg, [the Sephardim] preserved not only the Spanish dignity, but the Spanish idiom also; and they preserved the latter with so much love and with so much tenacity that it has remained surprisingly pure up to the present day. It must be remembered that Judæo-Spanish, or Ladino, is in no wise as corrupt a language as is the Judæo-German."[52]

In combining categories such as race and language, Kayserling fell victim to the then contemporary misconceptions which associated the two with each other. In turn, the unspoken assumption surrounding his praise of Ladino because of its supposedly greater purity was that it extended to its speakers. In other words, like other Jewish and Gentile scholars of his day, Kayserling's praise of the language and Hebrew pronunciation of the Sephardim implied their greater racial purity. In an interesting and instructive footnote to this discussion, the *Jewish Encyclopaedia* has no corresponding article on the 'Ashkenazim'. This *lacuna* would further reinforce the proposition that the Sephardim were thought, by nineteenth-century Jewish scholars, to be of greater ethnological worth.[53]

That this was so should not be surprising. Since all the Jewish physical anthropologists writing on the Jews were European Ashkenazim, the Sephardim

---

[50] This situation was somewhat rectified with the development in Germany of the cult of the East European Jew from the time of the First World War. On this, see Steven Aschheim, *Brothers and Strangers. The East European Jew in German and German-Jewish Consciousness, 1800–1923*, Madison 1982; and also, more specifically, *idem*, 'Eastern Jews, German Jews and Germany's Ostpolitik in the First World War', in *LBI Year Book XXVIII* (1983), pp. 351–365.

[51] Kayserling, 'Sephardim', *loc. cit.*, p. 197.

[52] *Ibid.*, p. 197.

[53] To be sure, the *Encyclopaedia* is full of articles on all aspects and major personalities of Ashkenazic civilisation. Nevertheless, it is noteworthy that a single entry under 'Ashkenazim' was not regarded as a valid category for discussion.

represented, for them, the Jewish "Other". Jewish physical anthropology at the *fin de siècle* was a microcosm of race science in general, in that it too had its "superior" and "inferior" types.

While it may be an exaggeration to say that for the Ashkenazic race scientist, the Sephardic Jew was a kind of "noble savage", it is nevertheless reasonable to assert that the same process of distancing and sense of fascination that eighteenth-century Gentile observers adopted towards pre-industrial peoples, was to be met with among nineteenth-century Ashkenazic Jewish race scientists in their study of the Sephardim. When seen in this light, it is little wonder that encyclopaedia entries and travel acccounts primarily focused on what one author called the "exotic Jews".[54]

One of the pioneers of Jewish race science was the Russian-born Samuel Weissenberg (1867–1928). He was widely celebrated, with an international reputation which was founded upon the approximately 200 pioneering articles and several books he published on Jewish physical and cultural anthropology. Even in Russia, from where he had to make his way to Heidelberg University to study medicine because of the *numerus clausus*, Weissenberg's 1895 work on the physical anthropology of the Jews of Southern Russia was so enthusiastically received that he was awarded a gold medal by the Moscow Society for the Natural Sciences.[55]

Weissenberg's travels, his quest to find the Jewish *Urtypus*, were based upon his assumption that one branch of the descendants of the ancient Israelites, commonly but incorrectly known as the Sephardim, had maintained a certain level of racial purity and uniformity. These Jews would most likely be found either in, or within relatively close geographical proximity to, Palestine, and it is to those places that Weissenberg went upon being awarded a grant from the *Rudolf Virchow Stiftung* in 1908.[56] He saw the primary objective of his tour of the Near East as the gathering of anthropological data on the Sephardim, and the elucidation of the problematic anthropological split between them and the Ashkenazim.[57]

Weissenberg measured 175 Sephardic Jews from Constantinople and Jerusalem. So physically similar were the two groups of Near Eastern Jews that Weissenberg was prepared to regard them as "forming a uniform type". He described this group as being of medium height, mesocephalic, commonly having the "Semitic" nose, and brunette. After comparing the results with a sample of Ashkenazim from Southern Russia, with a view to ascertaining which group was nearer to the Semitic type, Weissenberg declared that "as the older authors have asserted, the *Spaniolen* have preserved themselves more purely to the Semitic type than the East European Jews".[58]

Thus, on the basis of anthropometric measurement, Weissenberg had con-

---

[54]See Esriel Carlebach, *Exotische Juden*, Berlin 1932.
[55]Salomon Wininger, *Grosse Jüdische National-Biographie*, vol. 6, Czernowitz 1936, p. 250.
[56]See the report of Weissenberg's journey, 'Bericht über den Stand der Rudolf Virchowstiftung für 1908', *Zeitschrift für Ethnologie*, vol. 40 (1908), p. 977.
[57]Samuel Weissenberg, 'Die Spaniolen. Eine anthropometrische Skizze', *Mitteilungen der Anthropologische Gesellschaft in Wien*, vol. 39 (1909), p. 227.
[58]*Ibid.*, p. 235.

firmed the anthropological split between Sephardim and Ashkenazim, and established that the former more closely corresponded to the original Jewish type. The overarching significance of such a finding is of crucial importance when looked at in the context of rising nationalism, and especially its Jewish variants, at the *fin de siècle*.

Although never wholeheartedly won over to the Zionist cause, Weissenberg was none the less the Elizavetgrad representative to the Seventh Zionist Congress in Basel in 1905. Despite his tepid support for the movement, he was greatly impelled by one of the major concerns for any late nineteenth-century nationalist group, including Zionism – the problem of establishing authenticity, originality and antiquity.[59]

For almost his entire career, Weissenberg was absorbed with the problem of tracing roots and beginnings. His enormous corpus of articles on cultural anthropology focused on establishing the ancient and unique nature of East European Jewish civilisation.[60] Similarly, his physical anthropology centred on identifying the original Jewish type, the Sephardi, and locating that type in his ancestral home – in and around Palestine. Moreover, his long standing affirmation of the cultural and racial rootedness of East European Jewry scientifically validated for him the correctness of Dubnowian "Diaspora Nationalism". Consequently, his was a selective Zionism, predicated upon the fact that it would be primarily efficacious for the *Urjuden*, the "Semitic" Jews (whose rich culture he all but ignored), rather than for East European Ashkenazim.[61]

Zionist authors on race also tended to see in Iberian Jewry an ideal type of Jew; one who was worldly, yet whose Jewish identity or "racial instinct", to use the language of the day, was intact. For example, in 1907, the physician and early settler in Palestine, Elias Auerbach, referred to this "feature" of Spanish Jews in his long discussion of the Jewish racial question.[62]

Influenced heavily by contemporary *völkisch* ideology, Auerbach spoke

---

[59]Mosse, *Toward the Final Solution, op. cit.*, pp. 35–50. On this phenomenon and its relation to German *völkisch* ideology, see idem, *The Crisis of German Ideology, Intellectual Origins of the Third Reich*, New York 1964.

[60]See for example, Samuel Weissenberg, 'Palästina in Brauch und Glauben der heutigen Juden', *Globus*, vol. XCII, No. 17 (1907), pp. 261–264; idem, 'Jüdische Kunst und jüdisches Kult- und Hausgerät', *Ost und West*, vol. III, No. 3 (1903), pp. 201–206; and idem, 'Jüdische Museen und jüdisches in Museen', *Mitteilungen der Gesellschaft für jüdische Volkskunde*, vol. III, N.F., No. 3 (1907), pp. 77–88.

[61]On the Jewish historian Simon Dubnow's concept of "Diaspora Nationalism", see his *Nationalism and History. Essays on Old and New Judaism*, New York 1970, esp. pp. 131–142. The idea that the goals of Zionism are of greater value for one group of Jews than another, is reminiscent of early German Zionism's belief that a national Jewish homeland in Palestine would primarily be for East European, and not West European, Jews.

[62]On Auerbach's life, see his autobiography, *Pionier der Verwirklichung. Ein Arzt aus Deutschland erzählt vom Beginn der zionistischen Bewegung und seiner Niederlassung in Palästina kurz nach der Jahrhundertwende*, Stuttgart 1969. Auerbach's most comprehensive treatment of the Jewish racial problem was his, 'Die jüdische Rassenfrage', *Archiv für Rassen- und Gesellschafts-Biologie*, vol. IV, No. 3 (1907), pp. 332–361.

vaguely about there being a particular Jewish survival instinct.[63] In switching the discussion to an analysis of large-scale inter-marriage in Germany, Auerbach juxtaposed medieval Jewish society in the Iberian Peninsula with that of his contemporary Germany and claimed that German Jews had, because of this inter-marriage, abandoned their racial instinct, losing the will to survive.[64] According to Auerbach, Spanish Jews provided an example of an acculturated Jewish community which still preserved intact its separatist identity, both cultural and racial, while German Jews had become assimilationists, destined to disappear and blend insensibly into the German nation.[65]

Other Zionist anthropologists could interpret different kinds of scientific observations about Sephardim to suit their political agendas. Even Jewish authors who rejected the notion that there existed any significant physical differences between Sephardim and Ashkenazim sometimes unconsciously lapsed into making qualitative assessments about the two groups. For example, the Polish-Jewish anthropologist, I. M. Judt, held that physically, Jews were the product of racial mixing in antiquity.[66] For him, the Jews had begun to "deviate from their original Semitic form at the time of the political independence of the twelve tribes".[67] Nevertheless, he maintained that, over the course of centuries, a single Jewish "type" formed and now all Jews were physiognomically uniform.[68]

Like others before him, Judt drew upon the extant archaeological evidence to help make his case. In his opinion, contemporary Jews often bore resemblances to those portraits of ancient Israelites appearing on the antique friezes and monuments of Egypt and Assyria.[69] For Judt, the pictorial evidence showed the close physiological relationship of the Jews with the various ancient peoples of the Near East. In fact, Judt sought to minimise the influence of both "the ghetto" and "European civilisation", noting that what they imparted to the Jews in either

[63]On the appropriation of *völkisch* ideology by Jews see George L. Mosse, *Germans and Jews. The Right, the Left, and the Search for a "Third Force" in Pre-Nazi Germany*, New York 1970, pp. 77–115.
[64]Other Zionist assessments of inter-marriage and the harm it brought to the "race" are Felix Theilhaber, *Der Untergang der deutschen Juden*, Berlin 1921, pp. 124–137; and Arthur Ruppin, *Die Juden der Gegenwart*, Berlin 1911, pp. 154–179.
[65]For Auerbach, one of the laudatory features of pre-modern Jewish society was that through *Halakhah*, or Jewish law, the Jews themselves instigated their own self-preservation based on a legal code characterised by its stringent proscriptions against inter-marriage. Auerbach, 'Die jüdische Rassenfrage', *loc. cit.*, p. 335.
[66]I. M. Judt, *Die Juden als Rasse. Eine Analyse aus dem Gebiete der Anthropologie*, Berlin 1903, p. 221.
[67]*Ibid.*, p. 142.
[68]*Ibid.*, p. 67.
[69]Judt maintained that even today some Jews atavistically displayed the same features as those Jews appearing on the *bas reliefs* of Lachish: "brown complexion, low forehead, curly hair, thick lips and prognathism". *Ibid.*, p. 141. This opinion was widespread and was supported in both the scientific and lay community. See for example J. C. Nott and G. R. Gliddon, *Types of Mankind: or Ethnological Researches*, Philadelphia 1854, pp. 111–141; and Joseph Jacobs who insisted on the consistency of the Jewish type and its "practical identity with the ordinary Semitic type", as evidenced by the representations of Jews on the Assyrian *bas relief* of the captive Jews of Lachish (701 B.C.E.) appearing before Sennacharib. Joseph Jacobs, *Jewish Statistics*, London 1891, p. xvii. For a layman's view see the comments of the Chief Rabbi of England, Hermann Adler, who in a response to a paper on the racial characteristics of the Jews, delivered by Joseph Jacobs to the Royal Anthropological Society of Great Britain in 1885, also said that the ancient pictorial evidence was worthy of attention in determining the persistency of the Jewish type. See *ibid.*, p. xxxiv.

a physical or intellectual sense was of secondary importance and that it was the ancient world which stamped the Jew as such. This was clear from the ancient monuments.[70]

Although Judt did not overtly tout the superiority of the Sephardic Jew, his observations are pertinent to this discussion because they reflect the larger implications of Jewish racial science. The point of using archaeological evidence was that it had the power to confirm a people's antiquity and, in the nationalistic atmosphere of the *fin de siècle*, antiquity meant legitimacy. More specifically, using the archaeological remains of the ancient Near East, arguing for the similarity of the physical representations of Jews with the portraits of ancient non-Jews, and maintaining that contemporary Jews appear exactly as they did two millennia before, was to assert on the one hand the assimilability of the ancient Jew, as well as the potency and authenticity of the Semitic Jewish "type". By extension, it was implied that these characteristics were passed on to his direct descendent, the Sephardic Jew. More than this, for Zionists such as Judt, the archaeological evidence tended to confirm the correctness of their political views. It seemed to affirm that, on the basis of physiognomic evidence, the rightful place of the Jew was back in Palestine, living among those whom he resembled, those with whom he was racially akin.

In 1920, the Berlin gynaecologist and science writer Fritz Kahn (1888–1968), published an important book on the racial qualities of the Jewish people entitled, *The Jews as a Race and Civilisation*.[71] Kahn, who wrote on topics as diverse as sexual hygiene and atom-theory, wrote this work in the wake of the First World War and its impact on the "Jewish Question". With a sense of great urgency, Kahn noted that his intention was to produce a "text and defence book" (*Lehr- und Wehrbuch*) in light of the highly charged antisemitic atmosphere in post-war Europe.[72]

In brief, this apologetic work of Kahn's sought to demonstrate the importance of both nature and nurture in the development of races. He took issue with other contemporary works that sought to deny the importance of "race" and at the same time with those which denied its centrality in favour of a wholly environmentally deterministic view.[73]

As for the Jews, Kahn objected to the oft-repeated notion that they constituted a pure race, dismissing it as an "a-historical fable". "The Jews were not", he wrote, "a race, but became one!" According to Kahn, by the year 1000 B.C.E., the Jews, under the leadership of David and Solomon, had become "consolidated into a single national unit", as a result of the mixture of three major Near Eastern

---

[70]Judt, *op. cit.*, pp. 220–221.
[71]Fritz Kahn, *Die Juden als Rasse und Kulturvolk*, Berlin 1921.
[72]*Ibid.*, p. 5.
[73]An example of a work which rejected "race" as a category was that of the philosopher Friedrich Hertz, *Rasse und Kultur. Eine kritische Untersuchung der Rassentheorien*, Leipzig 1915, esp. pp. 157–249 and 285–317. The book Kahn and other Jewish race scientists such as Joseph Jacobs and Ignatz Zollschan most strenuously objected to, because of its strict biological determinism and blatant antisemitism, was Houston Stewart Chamberlain's *Foundations of the Nineteenth Century*, 2 vols., New York 1977.

peoples – the Babylonians, the Bedouins and the Canaanites.[74] This point went to the heart of Kahn's theories about the development of the higher races. As he put it, "inbreeding and crossing must stand in a certain proportion to each other". This theory, and it does not differ that much from Judt's abovementioned views as they pertained to Jews, suggested that a short period of racial miscegenation, followed by a long period of intra-marriage as demanded by the prophet Ezra, was beneficial for the betterment and survival of the "race".[75] In Kahn's view, this was exactly how the Jews had progressed biologically and culturally.

After a long survey, which attempted to account for the various and differing types of Jews, such as Ethiopian, Yemenite, and Caucasian Mountain Jews, Kahn turned his attention to the Sephardic-Ashkenazic split. He was of the opinion that it was the infusion of "Slavic-Mongolian blood" which had led to the creation of the Ashkenazim. The Sephardim, on the other hand, were characterised by the very absence of these racial elements. What is of gravest importance for this discussion is Kahn's evaluation of this morphological divide. In his assessment, Kahn's concerns reflected all the contemporary issues relating to racial and ethnic authenticity and vitality. For him, "the Ashkenazic type is the richer, for it contains the Sephardic within it; it is the younger type, while the Sephardic is the older, more authentic one".[76] Kahn did not go on to elaborate. His primary concern was to write a book defending the Jews as a whole.[77] Nevertheless, his method, like that of his contemporary Ignatz Zollschan (1877–1948), was to refute the antisemitic claims about Jewish cultural worthlessness by stressing the antiquity, longevity and cultural contributions of the Jews and Judaism.[78] Just how indebted the Germans were to the Jews could be deduced, according to Kahn, from the fact that only with the translation of the Bible, did "the history of the German *Nationalkultur* begin".[79]

Either implicitly or explicitly, when Jewish race scientists invoked the grandeur of ancient Israel they were referring to non-Ashkenazic culture. In so doing, they echoed, to a great extent, the anti-Rabbinism of many antisemites and some of the more strident Jewish critics of East European and talmudic culture mentioned above.

Thus, as has been demonstrated, whenever Jewish physical anthropologists

---

[74]Kahn, *op. cit.*, p. 135.

[75]*Ibid.*, p. 19.

[76]The full sentence reads: "Der aschkenasische Typus ist der reichere; er trägt den sephardischen in sich; er ist der jüngere Typ, während der Sepharde der ältere, 'echtere' ist." *Ibid.*, p. 157.

[77]That he had to do so saddened him. As he wrote: "Ein Volk, dessen Volksbuch die Bibel ist, ist rassenwertig. Daß man über den Rassenwert eines solchen Volkes eine Verteidigungsschrift verfaßt, ist ein Verdammnisurteil für die Zeit, der man es muß, ist ein Armutszeugnis für die Kultur, die den Gedanken hieran in dem Hirne eines Menschen hat erwecken können." *Ibid.*, p. 169.

[78]Zollschan was a Zionist race scientist from Austria. His *Das Rassenproblem unter besonderer Berücksichtigung der theoretischen Grundlagen der jüdischen Rassenfrage*, Vienna–Leipzig 1912, went through four editions and was regarded in its day as the premier scientific text about the Jews as a race. In addition, a large part of the book was concerned with refuting the claims of the "Political-Anthropological" school of Ludwig Woltmann, by documenting the "Jewish contributions to civilisation". On Zollschan see Efron, *Defining the Jewish Race, op. cit.*, pp. 404–434.

[79]Kahn, *op. cit.*, p. 169.

wrote a scientific apologia, they either consciously or unconsciously elevated the status of the Sephardic Jew, thereby seeking to elevate the status of all Jews. Because of the need to lay claims to the antiquity of Jewish civilisation, the argument, in the minds of the scientists, would have carried no weight if it were inverted and the Ashkenazic Jew was held up as the paradigmatic representative of his race.

It was not only in Europe that the political and cultural exigencies of Jewish life led scientists and scholars to idealise the Sephardic Jew and tout the myth of his superiority. In the United States, the celebrated physician and physical anthropologist, Maurice Fishberg (1872–1934) also contributed to the debate. In addition to being Clinical Professor of Medicine at New York University and Bellevue Hospital Medical College, Fishberg was an anthropological consultant to the Bureau of Immigration.[80] It was in this latter capacity that he undertook two trips to Europe in 1905 and 1907, on behalf of a US Congressional Committee, to study the immigration problem.

Although deeply involved in Jewish communal life, and intellectually motivated by Jewish issues, Fishberg was none the less dedicated to the thorough Americanisation of immigrant Jews. And an examination of his anthropological work relating to Jewish racial types reveals that for Fishberg, it was the Sephardic Jew who offered the ideal model for Jewish acculturation. A comparison of his descriptions of both branches of Jews shows the powerful influence of the above-mentioned German dissatisfaction with Ashkenazic, and specifically East European culture.[81]

One of the cornerstones of scientific racism was its elevation of subjective notions of beauty and ugliness to legitimate scientific categories of classification. From the following description, it is clear that Fishberg delighted in the appearance of the Sephardic Jew, while Ashkenazic Jewry was distinguished by its less than desirable physical features. He noted that the Sephardim:

> "... have generally black or brown hair, occasionally red and rarely blonde; large black or brown eyes, seldom grey, and rarely blue. In addition to their dark complexion, they are short of stature and either dolichocephalic or mesocephalic. The face is oval, the forehead receding, the eyes almond-shaped with the outer extremity very pointed, while the dark eyebrows are very bushy at the inner end, where they tend to unite over the root of the nose. The traditional Semitic beauty, which in women often assumes an exquisite nobility, is generally found among these Jews, and when encountered among Jews in Eastern or Central Europe is always of this type. Indeed, it is hard to imagine a beautiful Jewess, who looks like a Jewess, presenting any other physical type. It appears that in addition to the delicacy and the striking symmetry of the features which are often met with, it is also the brilliant, radiant eyes which give these Sephardim their reputation for bewitching elegance and charm. The Spanish and Andalusian women are said by some to owe their charms to these beautiful eyes, which are alleged to have their origin in the small quantities of Semitic blood which flows in their veins."[82]

[80]The biographical data on Fishberg is to be found in the *Encyclopaedia Judaica*, vol. VI, Jerusalem 1971, cols. 1328–1329.

[81]Fishberg was very familiar with the German scene. Not only does his bibliography indicate that he was widely read in the area of Jewish history, much of it written by German-Jewish scholars, but he was also intimately familiar with contemporary European Jewish journals and newspapers. In addition, Fishberg published a number of articles in German scientific periodicals and his book, *The Jews as a Race*, appeared in a German edition in 1913 and enjoyed enormous success.

[82]Maurice Fishberg, *The Jews. A Study of Race and Environment*, New York 1911, pp. 108–110.

Fishberg's semi-erotic descriptions of Sephardic women reveal an attraction and fascination that seems to stem from the cultural and physiological distance that he as a Russian-born Jew felt from these people. Most telling in this picture of Jewish beauty he has drawn is that he denies the Ashkenazic Jew any inherent attractiveness, claiming that if an Ashkenazic female was ever to display beautiful features, then they had to be of Sephardic origin. In fact, the existence of Semitic characteristics, according to Fishberg, even lies at the root of Spanish female beauty.

The exotic and sensual Sephardi is juxtaposed with the coarse and physically unappealing Ashkenazi. For as Fishberg goes on to say:

> "The Jews of Germany, Russia, Poland, etc., known as the Ashkenasim, are generally of a type which differs much from the one just described. Their features are not as elegant, not as graceful as those of the Sephardim. Indeed, as has already been stated, most of the beautiful Jewesses, irrespective of the country in which they are encountered, are of the Sephardic type. A blond Jewess, no matter how charming she may be, is not in conformity with what one would expect a Jewess to look like . . . [The Ashkenazi] face is round, with prominent cheek bones, and the nose medium-sized, broad, with fleshy wings, often narrow and depressed at the root, appearing generally somewhat pear-shaped . . . The chin is heavy, the mouth large, and the lips thick, all of which give a rather heavy expression to the countenance."[83]

Fishberg was not content to draw a distinction between Ashkenazim and Sephardim purely on the basis of outward appearance. For this distinguished professor of medicine, there was also a clear difference to be observed in terms of comportment and behaviour. According to *fin-de-siècle* race science, these characteristics were believed to be inheritable. They fell largely under the rubric of "national character". Making reference to the differences between the two Jewish groups under consideration here, Fishberg said of the Sephardim that:

> "They are medium-sized, slender, narrow-shouldered, but graceful people, with a somewhat melancholy expression. Only very rarely is to be seen a Spanish Jew displaying a servile or cringing attitude in the presence of superiors, as is often to be seen among German and Polish Jews. The Sephardim are very proud, and their sense of dignity manifests itself even in their dress and deportment, to which they pay scrupulous attention. These traits, which they acquired while living for centuries among the Castilians, have been transmitted to their descendants of today. [In addition], they look down on their German co-religionists and consider them an inferior race."[84]

The exotic Sephardi clearly represented for Fishberg the model of an ideal Jew. Here were Jews who were physically beautiful and graceful. Their manner was especially commendable in that they displayed a dignified pride that bespoke a knowing self-confidence and a mature aesthetic sensibility.

Fishberg's critique of Ashkenazic Jewry was of an essentially traditional, *maskilic* variety. The Jew of Central or Eastern Europe was presented as a debased or degraded figure who only stood to benefit from emulating his Sephardic co-religionists. This is what places many of the Jewish race scientists like Fishberg in a long tradition of Ashkenazic self-criticism. To be sure, the discourse of the anthropologists, peppered with detailed anthropometric descriptions, differs markedly from that of their rabbinical predecessors of the sixteenth

---

[83] *Ibid.*, pp. 111–113.
[84] *Ibid.*, p. 110.

and seventeenth centuries, as well as subsequent Reformers of Judaism and representatives of *Wissenschaft des Judentums*. Nevertheless, for both groups, the objects of their criticism, the Ashkenazim, and those of their adulation, the Sephardim, are exactly the same. Ironically, it was because of his antiquity and his ancient rootedness, in addition to his perceived physical and mental superiority, that the Sephardic Jew represented for all of these critics, the noble Jew of the future.

In conclusion, it should be clear that in the scientific discourse about Jewish racial types at the *fin de siècle*, one can detect the construction of an elaborate racial myth – that of the superiority of the Sephardic Jew over the Ashkenazic. The incorporation of such a notion into the discussions about Jewish physical anthropology afforded Jewish scientists the possibility of refracting through the prism of their own historical experience, a variation on contemporary European myths of racial and national origin. The historian Léon Poliakov has noted that "every society claims a genealogy, a point of origin. There is no culture, however old, which has not in this manner provided itself with a spontaneous anthropology."[85] This is precisely what late-nineteenth-century Jewish scholars were doing when they elevated the Sephardic over the Ashkenazic Jew and thus found within Jewry a superior and, by extension, an inferior type.

Nineteenth-century physical anthropology, which was classificatory in nature, was, in fact, an elaborate system of ranking human groups. It should not surprise us then to find that when Jews practised race science (using the same methodology as their non-Jewish colleagues), that they, too, would rank the objects of their investigations, the Jews, on an arbitrary and ascending scale of perfection.

From at least the seventeenth century in Central Europe, Jews, who were on the cusp of modernity or at the very least desirous of modernising traditional aspects of Jewish life such as education, looked to Sephardic Jews as paragons of Jewish rationalism, creativity and, indeed, superior dignity. Initially, this was not merely a fantasy created by Ashkenazic scholars for Ashkenazim, but was carefully cultivated by the Sephardim themselves, particularly after their expulsion from the Iberian Peninsula at the end of the fifteenth century. An illustration of the cultural distance and superiority the Sephardim felt is made clear when one considers that in various European cities, such as Amsterdam, London and Hamburg, Sephardic community elders did their utmost to prevent the development of religious, social and intimate relations between Sephardim and Ashkenazim. All this was predicated on the desire to preserve a certain purity, even if such a notion was not fully articulated.

The sense of self-worth exhibited by the Sephardim themselves was first given impetus by the reference in the Book of the Prophet Obadiah (I:20) to a community of Jerusalem exiles living in Sepharad. Now the town of Sepharad was most likely Sardis, the capital of ancient Lydia, 60 miles from Turkey's West coast.[86] Known as Sardis in English and Sfard in Lydian and Persian, the city is erroneously identified as Spain by Jews because in Hebrew the name for Spain is

[85]Poliakov, *The Aryan Myth, op. cit.*, p. 3.
[86]*Encyclopaedia Judaica*, Jerusalem 1971, vol. XIV, col. 876.

Sepharad (as mentioned by Obadiah). Thus, with their antiquity established by Scripture (all the more so for their having been directly linked with the holy city of Jerusalem), the Sephardim had a heightened sense of their own self-worth and importance. These vague conceptions were made concrete by the magnificent civilisation they subsequently created for themselves in Spain.

Thus, the Ashkenazim of modern and early modern Europe accepted the myth of Sephardic superiority by glorifying the latter's antiquity and noble descent. However, they also expanded upon the myth in the nineteenth century, by holding up Sephardic civilisation and, as did the physical anthropologists, the Sephardim themselves, to a rather uncritical assessment and evaluation. All this was for the purpose of both finding a superior Jewish type (largely motivated by the need to rebut contemporary antisemitic charges of Jewish degeneracy) as well as providing a model for Ashkenazic Jews to emulate.

The counter-myth to the myth of Sephardic superiority was that of Ashkenazic inferiority. Jewish criticism of Ashkenazic culture and, indeed, pathology largely came from Ashkenazim. First from the traditional elite in the seventeenth and eighteenth centuries and then from nineteenth-century German-Jewish historians, who researched the Iberian Jewish past, because it was that community which seemed to them to display the noblest attributes of a community which led a thoroughly Jewish existence as well as one fully conversant and at home with secular culture. By drawing on this model, nineteenth-century Jewish scholars projected an ideal future for German Jewry. These same critics saw in the Ashkenazim an insular, parochial folk, portrayed not as worldly but really as country-bumpkins. Their knowledge was dismissed as "hair-splitting casuistry" (Graetz), while the Sephardim were held up as pillars of rational thought (Neubauer). The language of the Ashkenazim, Yiddish, was dismissed as jargon, yet Ladino, a mix of Spanish and Hebrew was celebrated as pure (Kayserling).

Finally, it is important to recognise that from dismissing the culture and behaviour of another group as inferior, it is but a short step to denigrating the physical attributes of that group. A complex system of aesthetic acceptability determined the work of the anthropologists I examined here. In short, the Sephardic Jew was portrayed as beautiful, the Ashkenazi as ugly (Fishberg). The impetus for this process came from two directions: the glorification of the Sephardic body as a mere extension of the cultural idealisation of the Sephardic Jew; and the very language and nature of modern scientific practice. There is an imperious quality in the language employed by the anthropologists. First, in the way the Ashkenazic race scientists were able to distance themselves from the object of their scorn, their fellow Ashkenazim, as if they were not Ashkenazim themselves. Second, in that as educated, European males, Jewish race scientists looked at the Sephardim as "far-away natives", swarthy, sensual and desirable.

For all these men, irrespective of their politics, or the communal positions they held, the promise of Jewish regeneration (and, for the Zionists, the salutary benefits to be accrued from the establishment of a Jewish national homeland) was predicated upon the revitalisation of the frail, Ashkenazic, ghetto Jew in the image of the mythically robust and "racially superior" Sephardi.

Austria, the "Jewish Question" and Persecution

Red Vienna and the "Jewish Question"

BY HELMUT GRUBER

In modern times the place of Jews in Vienna has been problematic and ambiguous. With the growth in size and importance of the Jewish community by the end of the nineteenth century, various forms of Judeophobia were forged into political antisemitism by Mayor Karl Lueger to provide a means of rallying the heterogeneous members and followers of his Christian Social Party. The racist undertones of this ideology are not likely to have escaped the bystander Adolf Hitler. The virulence and pervasiveness of antisemitism in this period also convinced Theodor Herzl that it could not be overcome by Jewish assimilation, that only the creation of a Jewish national state could save threatened Austrian Jewry. Nearly a half century later, the spontaneous brutality towards Jews by native Austrian Nazis and others during the first nine months after the *Anschluß* closed the circle of what ultimately became an epic tragedy. Even in recent times antisemitism, despite the relative absence of Jews, has resurfaced during the campaign leading to the election of Kurt Waldheim as President of the Second Austrian Republic and failed to produce an appropriate and decisive response.

These milestones in the history of Jews in Vienna during the past century have been well researched and recorded.[1] The same cannot be said for the brief period when Vienna was under the political control of the Socialist Party (from 1919 to 1934) and engaged in an ambitious experiment to create a working-class culture. What was the relationship between self-proclaimed "Red Vienna" and its substantial Jewish population? This essay will explore this question in various ways.

Judeophobia in a variety of forms had deep roots and was widespread in Austrian society. The Catholic Church clung to the imagery of Jews as Christ-killers. The Christian Social Party (*Christlich-Soziale Partei*) under Karl Lueger had fostered a populist antisemitism before the turn of the century, which was adopted by the Christian-Conservative camp in post-war Vienna.

From the beginning of the Republic it was apparent that the Conservative parties had decided to use antisemitism as a weapon not merely against Jews but principally against the Social Democratic Party (*Sozialdemokratische Arbeiterpartei*

---

[1] The literature on these periods and events is huge. I have found the following very useful: John W. Boyer, *Political Radicalism in Late Imperial Vienna*, Chicago 1981; Carl E. Schorske, *Fin-De-Siècle Vienna. Politics and Culture*, New York 1980; Alan Bullock, *Hitler. A Study in Tyranny*, New York 1964; Erika Weinzierl, *Zu wenig Gerechte. Österreicher und Judenverfolgung 1938–1945*, Vienna 1986; Anton Pelinka and Erika Weinzierl (eds.), *Das grosse Tabu. Österreichs Umgang mit seiner Vergangenheit*, Vienna 1987; Hans Safrian and Hans Witek (eds.), *Und keiner war dabei. Dokumente des alltäglichen Antisemitismus in Wien 1938*, Vienna 1988. See also Helmut Gruber, *Antisemitismus im Mediendiskurs. Die Affäre "Waldheim" in der Tagespresse*, Wiesbaden 1991.

[SDAP]). This meant that the Socialists' total programme – its Viennese municipal Socialism as well as attempts to create a working-class culture – was under constant attack by their Conservative opponents, who contrasted their own German-Christian-Aryan-*völkisch* qualities with the foreign, degenerate, godless, un-German attributes they assigned to the Socialists, for whom *Judensozi* was the epithet of choice.

As virtually nowhere else in Europe, the Catholic Church continued to play an extraordinary political and social role in the Austrian Republic.[2] In its conception of "Christ the king over all" it harked back to some golden age of ecclesiastical power, thereby rejecting the pluralistic republic and all attempts at reform and innovation in the secular realm which in any way might be construed to impinge on its present or past claims to supremacy.[3] The pastoral letters of the Austrian bishops read very much like ideological justifications for the Christian Social Party's fight against "Red Vienna". The Church's anathema against all it deemed "un-Christian" was directed at the Socialists; the form and tone were a thinly veiled Judeophobia. The bishops presented themselves as being above the battle, but in the Christian Socials' *Kulturkampf* against "Red Vienna" the Church was the real source of the "Catholic Action" groups which were repeatedly called upon to battle against the Jewish-Socialist anti-Christ.

How did the Socialist leaders react to the antisemitism directed against them and their social and cultural mission, especially since a large number of the most prominent and visible of them were assimilated Jews? Programmatically the Socialist Party rejected antisemitism. In practice it pursued a disastrous policy of fighting its opponents' antisemitism with a special brand of the same poison: the Christian-Conservative camp was accused of being financed by Jewish capitalists, of harbouring clandestine Jews within its own leadership, and of engaging in "Jewish practices". The Socialists never openly and forcefully challenged the Church as the fount of the attacks against their cultural experiment, as purveyor of the linkage "alien-Jewish-Socialist-bolshevik", and as the organisational base of the Christian Social Party.

Elsewhere I have attempted to demonstrate that the Socialist experiment in Vienna was the largest and most successful attempt by a Socialist party in interwar Europe to create a comprehensive proletarian counter-culture.[4] As such, Red Vienna served as a counter model to the bolsheviks' cultural project in Soviet Russia. Before turning to the subject of Socialists and Jews, it would be useful to set the stage – to given an overview of the commanding position of the SDAP in the city and province of Vienna and to highlight some of the aspects of

---

[2]The Catholic Church in Austria was among the most ultramontanist in Europe, receiving repeated papal commentaries on activities of the Christian-Conservative camp. See '"Aus christlicher Verantwortung am Schicksal der sozialistischen Bewegung teilnehme". Gespräch mit Otto Bauer, dem Vorsitzenden der Religiösen Sozialisten, über die Entwicklung zum 12. Februar 1934', in *Mitbestimmung* vol. XIII, No. 5 (1984), pp. 26–29. For the effusive Papal congratulations of Dollfuss, see *Wiener Diözesanblatt* (February 1932).

[3]See Ernst Hanisch, 'Der politische Katholizismus als ideologischer Träger des "Austrofaschismus"', in Emmerich Tálos and Wolfgang Neugebauer (eds.), *Austrofaschismus. Beiträge über Politik, Ökonomie und Kultur 1934–1938*, Vienna 1984, p. 57.

[4]See Helmut Gruber, *Red Vienna. Experiment in Working-Class Culture 1919–1934*, New York 1991.

the cultural programme the Socialists aspired to and were actually able to carry out.

Republican Austria with a population of 6.4 million, which emerged in November 1918, comprised the principal German-speaking enclave of the former multi-national empire of 52 million.[5] Considering Vienna's former standing as imperial capital and cultural metropolis of Central Europe, one might speak of two post-war Austrias: Vienna with 1.8 million aspiring to hold on to its *fin-de-siècle* reputation for modernism, and the alpine and agrarian provinces still on the threshold of the twentieth century. From the beginning this duality was apparent in the political constellation of the country. The Social Democratic Party dominated Vienna with majorities of 54 to 60 per cent, and a coalition of the Christian Social, Pan-German, and Peasant parties controlled the nation with majorities of never less than 57 per cent. In other words, the division into opposing camps with clearly marked terrains emerged early and remained the political pattern throughout the republican period. It prompted Otto Bauer, the undisputed leader of the Socialists to formulate a theory of "the balance of class forces" according to which the bourgeoisie and proletariat were in a sort of equipoise, which could only be broken by civil war and which made it impossible for either camp to govern without the tacit agreement of the other. Bauer's optimism failed the test of reality when Dollfuss suspended parliament in 1933 and outlawed the Social Democratic Party after the abortive workers' rising in February 1934.

Seen from the perspective of Vienna alone, Bauer's optimism may not have been so misplaced. At its high point Socialist Party membership stood at 440,000 and membership in the Socialist Free Trade Unions at 460,000, with a surprisingly large percentage of female and young workers in both. Moreover, a constitutional amendment in January 1921 formalised the city's status as both capital and province. This expanded political domain was of signal importance to the experiment in working-class culture which the Socialists had already begun with a series of municipal reforms. The Viennese "laboratory" was henceforth empowered to revise the local tax structure and raise new taxes, which were used in implementing not simply municipal Socialism but a broad array of cultural innovations as well. It is this conjunction of mass membership, electoral superiority, and independent financial power, as well as the absence of a Communist competitor for leadership of the working class (so strong in Germany and France, for instance), which encouraged the Socialist leaders to believe that Austro-Marxism, unlike other versions of Marxism, could fulfil the promised foretaste of the Socialist utopia in the present. When Otto Bauer spoke of "a revolution in the soul of man",[6] he implied much more than the elevation of oppressed and deprived proletarians through *Bildung* (civilising education) in order to make them conscious actors in the dialectical unfolding of history. His

---

[5]For the following, see Gruber, *op. cit.*; Charles A. Gulick, *Austria from Hapsburg to Hitler*, 2 vols., Berkeley 1948, Anson Rabinbach, *The Crisis of Austrian Socialism. From Red Vienna to Civil War 1927–1934*, Chicago 1983.

[6]Otto Bauer, *Die österreichische Revolution*, in Arbeitsgemeinschaft für die Geschichte der österreichischen Arbeiterbewegung (ed.), *Werkausgabe*, Vienna 1975–1979, vol. II, p. 742.

aphorism suggested as well a sea change in the behaviour and mentality of workers through invasions of their private and personal spheres leading to the creation of *neue Menschen* (a new proletariat).

What were the accomplishments of municipal Socialism that prompted the Socialists to advertise Vienna as the "Mecca" of social innovation? The centrepiece was the 64,000 apartments housing some 200,000 Viennese in over 300 projects of which the largest had the monumental quality of "peoples' palaces".[7] The latter were serviced by a host of communal facilities: mechanised laundries, bathhouses, kindergartens, playgrounds and swimming pools, medical and dental clinics, libraries and lecture halls, and young people's and mothers' consultation bureaus. An aggressive public health programme sought to combat tuberculosis and malnutrition by providing medical and dental check-ups and free lunches in the schools; numerous swimming pools for children were built throughout the city and summer camps were created to acquaint urban youth with nature and pure air. Venereal disease, which had become rampant in the immediate post-war years, was combated by a marriage consultation bureau through which prospective couples could assure themselves of the health of their intended partners. Even ugliness through physical deformity was to be dealt with in a municipal clinic providing cosmetic surgery.

The Public Welfare Office undertook to uplift the moral climate in Vienna by the creation of the *ordentliche Arbeiterfamilie* – a term connoting not only orderliness but also decency, respectability and discipline.[8] Strongly eugenic in orientation, the Welfare Office proceded in various ways to intervene in the lives of working-class families to ensure the children were raised properly.[9] After 1927, for instance, the municipality distributed free layettes to mothers of all newborn babies, allowing it to intervene in infant care. The Socialist city fathers were less forthcoming on the problems of birth control and abortion, for which they offered admonitions and restrictions rather than constructive assistance.

Attempts were made to reform the educational system by substituting student motivation and participation for the traditional methods of learning by rote and drill.[10] But the Socialists' greatest efforts were devoted to reducing the class bias in higher education, from which workers had been virtually excluded. The curriculum of secondary schools was revised so as to allow for late specialisation and thereby open up a wider array of choices for working-class youth. Free textbooks and other materials were provided for all students regardless of need.

[7] See Rainer Bauböck, *Wohnungspolitik im sozialdemokratischen Wien, 1919–1934*, Salzburg 1979; Maren Seliger, *Sozialdemokratie und Kommunalpolitik in Wien. Zu einigen Aspekten sozialdemokratischer Politik in der Vor- und Zwischenkriegszeit*, Vienna 1980; Felix Czeike, *Wirtschafts- und Sozialpolitik der Gemeinde Wien, 1919–1934*, Vienna 1959.
[8] For the origin and development of the concept of *"ordentliche Arbeiterfamilie"*, see Joseph Ehmer, 'Familie und Klasse. Zur Entstehung der Arbeiterfamilie in Wien', in Michael Mitterauer and Reinhard Sieder (eds.), *Historische Familienforschung*, Frankfurt a. Main 1982.
[9] For an interesting critique of the Viennese welfare programme that views it as a principal means of disciplining the workers, see Doris Beyer, 'Sexualität – Macht – Wohlfahrt. Zeitgemässe Erinnerungen an das "Rote Wien"', in *Zeit-Geschichte*, vol. XIV, Nos. 11/12 (August/September 1987).
[10] For an exceptionally well documented and analytical study of educational reform efforts, see Erik Adam, *Austromarxismus und Schulreform. Die Schul- und Bildungspolitik der österreichischen Sozialdemokratie in der Ersten Republik*, Vienna 1983.

But the traditional power of the Church in the schools was not broken. Though religious practice was abolished, priests remained in the schools to provide compulsory religious instruction for the Catholic majority, with instruction for other religions relegated to places away from the schools. Without a doubt the Catholic Church acted as a "fifth column" in the schools, undermining all of the Socialists' reform efforts in education and other areas.

Reforms in housing, health, social welfare and education merely formed the framework within which the Socialists hoped to create a particular political culture for Viennese workers. The Viennese Socialists were surely not the first to imagine that their party could fulfil all of the workers' needs from the cradle to the grave. But they went further than anyone else in the West in putting such aspirations into practice. What was their plan of action in transforming Viennese workers into self-aware, willing actors in their own liberation as *neue Menschen*? At its high point the Socialist Party directed more than forty cultural organisations with an aggregate of some 400,000 members.[11] The party sought to include and sponsor the most diverse interests through a network of cultural enterprises running the gamut from the popular workers' libraries; lecture bureaus; theatre, choral, art, film and radio societies; an association for sports and physical culture; and a department sponsoring mass festivals to the more esoteric clubs for chess players, animal lovers and Esperanto enthusiasts. The numerical success of some of these enterprises was remarkable: 6,500 lecture evenings in 1932 drew an audience of 160,000; book borrowing from the 53 public libraries reached 2.4 million in the same year;[12] 2 million theatre and concert tickets were distributed by the arts centre between 1922 and 1926; membership in sport clubs reached 110,000 in 1931; and a mass festival at that time drew an audience of 260,000 over four days.

Impressive as such an array of cultural organisations and number of participants may appear, they are deceptive. For reasons which cannot be pursued here, the great majority of Viennese workers experienced none, or few, of the benefits of municipal Socialism and party culture directly. At the same time the symbolic effect of the Socialists' experiment should not be overlooked, for the workers perceived a sea change in the daily life of Vienna where the mayor and most officials who counted were Socialists, where the fortress-like "Peoples' Palaces" (such as the kilometre-long art deco Karl-Marx-Hof) suggested proletarian power as well as a more decent form of habitation, and where the ensemble of Socialist initiatives signalled an entirely new dignity for the status of worker.[13] But the symbols, too, were deceptive. In the Austro-Marxists vision culture would play the role of a weapon in the armoury of the class struggle.

---

[11]Two very useful works dealing with the structure of Socialist Party culture are: Dieter Langewiesche, *Zur Freizeit des Arbeiters. Bildungsbestrebungen und Freizeitgestaltungen österreichischer Arbeiter im Kaiserreich und in der Ersten Republik*, Stuttgart 1979; Joseph Weidenholzer, *Auf dem Weg zum "Neuen Menschen". Bildungs- und Kulturarbeit der österreichischen Sozialdemokratie in der Ersten Republik*, Vienna 1981.

[12]For the magical powers the SDAP attributed to the printed word, see the perceptive study of Alfred Pfoser, *Literatur und Austromarxismus*, Vienna 1980.

[13]For discussions of the new symbolic role of the worker's body, see Dietmar Petzina (ed.), *Fahnen, Fäuste, Körper. Symbolik und Kultur der Arbeiterbewegung*, Essen 1986.

Increasingly, however, the cultural experiment in Vienna became a surrogate for political action in the national arena where the real exercise of power by the Catholic-Conservative camp was to sweep the cultural experiment from the stage of history.

Why was there a Jewish question or problem for the Socialist cultural experiment in Vienna? A quick look at the number, position in society and role as outsiders of the significant Jewish minority in German Austria should provide us with some clues to the reasons for and nature of the problem.

In 1923, 201,513 or 10.8% of Vienna's population was Jewish by religion. But Jews already constituted 8.6% of Viennese by 1910, making the vast majority during the First Republic second generation residents of the city.[14] The desire of Jews to integrate into German-Austrian society through acculturation and assimilation was widespread, expressed in the hope of shedding their Jewishness and identification as aliens by the Gentile world.[15] A minority of Nationalist/Zionist Jews sought either a Jewish homeland or recognition as a national minority in Austria. The latter aim was strangely consonant with Christian Social attempts to re-ghettoise the Jews as a subject nationality. Another minority converted to Christianity as a means of integration and of access to positions in the civil service and university barred to Jews. The majority belonged to the lower middle class engaged in various aspects of commerce; a minority of professionals belonged to the solid middle and upper middle class; isolated figures – Camillo Castiglioni or Louis Rothschild – were prominent bankers; a significant minority were white-collar workers; and few were blue-collar workers.[16]

The desire to assimilate, which was strong in most sectors of the Jewish community, expressed itself in the drive to attain *Bildung* – the acquisition of German culture through higher education leading to the liberal professions. With the road to integration into society barred by past and present antisemitism, assimilation took an essentially cultural form predicated on the hope that through *Bildung* a true acceptance into society could be attained in the future. It comes as no surprise, therefore, that Jews were prominent in most institutions of Viennese high culture and even predominant in some. A few examples of Jews in the cultural life of the city are listed as illustration:[17] some 60% of lawyers, 50%

---

[14] For the most detailed history of Vienna's Jewish community, see Harriet Freidenreich, *Jews in Vienna during the First Republic*, Bloomington, Ind. 1990.

[15] For an extensive treatment of the pattern of assimilation in Vienna's Jewish community, see Marsha L. Rozenblit, *The Jews of Vienna 1867–1914. Assimilation and Identity*, Albany 1983. Rozenblit's analysis of assimilation and identity is parochial. She tends to treat the Jewish minority as unique and fails to consider the common features of all minorities seeking to integrate into the social mainstream. How different, after all, was the experience of a Czech undergoing assimilation from that of a Jew at the time or from that of an African American in contemporary America? Is not negative consciousness (passing as German or white) common to all three?

[16] See Freidenreich, *op. cit*, p. 12; and John Bunzl, 'Arbeiterbewegung, "Judenfrage" und Antisemitismus. Am Beispiel des Wiener Bezirks Leopoldstadt', in Gerhard Botz *et al.* (eds.), *Bewegung und Klasse. Studien zur österreichischen Arbeitergeschichte*, Vienna 1978, p. 745. Jews predominated in the Trade Union for Employees in Vienna (p. 748).

[17] For the following, see Steven Beller, *Vienna and the Jews 1867–1938. A Cultural History*, Cambridge 1989, pp. 14–21, 32–39.

of physicians, and 50%–60% of journalists below the level of editor; up to one third of the students and nearly 40% of the teaching faculty (in all but the professorial ranks) at the university. Jews among the luminaries in Viennese cultural life included: the writers Stefan Zweig, Joseph Roth, Hermann Broch, Franz Werfel, Arthur Schnitzler; the philosopher Ludwig Wittgenstein; the composer Arnold Schönberg; the director Max Reinhardt; the economist Ludwig von Mises; more than half the members of the *Wiener Kreis*; the legal theorist Hans Kelsen; and the psychoanalysts Sigmund Freud and Alfred Adler.

This list of individuals could be greatly enlarged if one included those Jews who had formally become Christians or whose ancestors had done so. Would such an addition be justified considering that conversion was considered an *entrée* into the social mainstream? The particular nature of Viennese antisemitism, which demanded conversion but at the same time rejected the convert as still alien, and the uncertainty and insecurity it created in the mind of the convert, leads one to conclude that some aspect of Jewish identity remained as an atavistic residue in the make-up of the convert and his descendants. Gustav Mahler, who had converted to Catholicism in 1897 to attain the prestigious post of court opera director, later reflected: "I am rootless three times over: as a Bohemian among Austrians, as an Austrian among Germans, and as a Jew everywhere in the world. Everywhere I am regarded as an interloper, nowhere am I what people call 'desirable'."[18] Neither could the Conservative Catholic Hugo von Hofmannsthal ever completely free himself from the shadow of his Jewish great-grandfather Isaak Löw-Hofmann,[19] nor could Wittgenstein and Schönberg rest at peace with the conflict between their families' formal Protestantism and their Jewish ancestry in the poisonous atmosphere of antisemitism in the late twenties (Schönberg strongly asserted his Jewish origins).[20]

Identity was an inescapable problem for all Jews save, perhaps, the religious and Zionists. In the intellectual elite, from which the Jewish Socialist leaders were drawn, the tendency to deny Jewishness, to avoid any association with the Jewish community, and to exhibit a "negative consciousness" was very strong. Yet, despite all attempts at assimilation and even conversion Jews remained pariahs in Gentile society. No one has more poignantly described this dilemma than Arthur Schnitzler in his brilliant *roman à clef*, *Der Weg ins Freie*.[21] For educated assimilated Jews the Socialist Party, formally on record as a staunch opponent of antisemitism, promised the possibility of being accepted as

---

[18]Quoted *ibid.*, p. 207.
[19]See Hermann Broch, *Hugo von Hofmannsthal and His Time. The European Imagination 1860–1920*, transl. and ed. by Michael P. Steinberg, Chicago 1984, pp. 83–86, 102–105; Beller, *op. cit.*, pp. 12–13, 76–77.
[20]*Ibid.*, pp. 77, 229–230, 235–237; Allan Janik and Stephen Toulmin, *Wittgenstein's Vienna*, New York 1973, pp. 172–173.
[21]Frankfurt a. Main 1978. This *roman à clef* was first published in 1908. The large cast of Jewish characters make it clear that the road to assimilation and acceptance in the Gentile world is blocked. Even in politics, where, as a principal character puts it: the Jews have created the liberal and Pan-German movements in Austria and have been betrayed and reviled by them; and the same will happen with Socialism and Communism once they have established themselves (pp. 68–69).

comrades, of finding an outlet for their commitment to *Bildung* and Enlightenment, and of building a new world of true equality and justice.[22]

The fact that the Socialist Party was alone in opposing antisemitism explains why 80% of Viennese Jews voted for it and even helped to increase its majority in the districts where Jewish concentration was greatest.[23] That the party spoke for the workers who were also outsiders and struggled to provide a better future for all helps to explain why so may educated assimilated Jews entered its ranks. Indeed, the number of Jews in leading positions was truly remarkable: roughly 50% as compared to 10% in the *Sozialdemokratische Partei Deutschlands* (SPD). Both in the party and the Viennese municipal and provincial administration and the national parliament, Jews occupied the most visible positions, providing easy targets for antisemitic gutter politics. Nearly half of the party executive was Jewish, headed by Otto Bauer, who also led the Socialist delegation in the national parliament. The party secretary, Robert Danneberg, was also president of the provincial parliament. Jews, in the persons of Friedrich Austerlitz, Julius Braunthal, Otto Leichter and Oskar Pollak, dominated the party's publications and press. The party's cultural network was directed by David Joseph Bach and Otto Felix Kanitz and the *Republikanischer Schutzbund*, the party's paramilitary republican defence force, was under the command of Julius Deutsch. In the Municipal Council the most powerful departments of finance and health and social welfare were headed by Hugo Breitner and Julius Tandler.

A similarly strong representation of Jews could be found in the second echelon of party leaders, among the 1,200 paid party functionaries, and probably among the 21,500 unpaid party cadres (although no statistics for the latter have come to light). Only in the trade unions, where the leadership rose from the shop floor, was Jewish presence negligible. How should we interpret these illustrations? It would be all too easy to conclude that the number and visibility of Jews in the post-war Socialist Party's leading institutions and in the municipality spawned the antisemitism with which the Socialists were smeared by their Christian Social, Pan-German, and Nazi opponents, although Gentile Socialists in the outlawed party after 1934 and Gentile leaders of the party after 1945 came close to doing just that. But Austrian antisemitism had a far longer history. Judeophobia had been developed to a fine art and the epithet *Judensozi* was in use long before the party attained its mass base and Jews played such a pronounced and visible role.

The real question to be explored is: how did the Socialist Party respond to the antisemitism directed at it by its opponents? Did the party understand the social network from which antisemitism emanated and the role of the Catholic Church within it? How did the Jewish Socialist leaders respond to being their party's principle targets? To what extent was the party's rank and file affected both by

---

[22]But the party made it quite clear that to enter its ranks meant to abandon all aspects of a Jewish identity. The demand for assimilation was absolute. See Otto Bauer, 'Die Bedingungen der nationalen Assimilation', in *Der Kampf*, vol. V, No. 6 (1912), p. 261; and *idem, Die Nationalitätenfrage und die Sozialdemokratie*, Vienna 1924, pp. 371–373.

[23]See Walter B. Simon, 'The Jewish Vote in Austria', in *LBI Year Book XVI* (1971), p. 118; Freidenreich, *op. cit.*, p. 10.

antisemitism used to smear the party's programme and the leadership's defensive response?

The use of antisemitism as a political weapon directed at the Socialists dates back to the era of Karl Lueger, Mayor of Vienna and founder of the Christian Social Party, for whom the Jew – a "guest" in Christian-German Vienna who had abused his rights as temporary resident – was the convenient scapegoat used to attract and hold his diverse following.[24] He played on the "Red" fear prevalent in the bourgeoisie at the turn of the century, combining it with antisemitism to stigmatise Social Democracy in the formulation of the term *Judensozi*. Another pre-war legacy was the linking of Jews and Socialists with intellectuals in an appeal to popular philistinism and resentment. It was best expressed in the frequently quoted *bon mot* of the Christian Social deputy Hermann Bielohlawek that literature was "what one Jew copied from another".[25]

Antisemitism, particularly as an instrument directed at the Socialists, weathered the stormy transition from the collapsed monarchy to the new republic and became more aggressive with the appearance of the Socialist Party as a major contender in the political arena. The common refrain in early statements from the Christian-Conservative camp was that the Jews were both the problem of and danger to the Christian-German Austrian state. A few examples of these should render both the substance and flavour. The Christian Social Party manifesto of 1918 proclaimed: "The corruption and power mania of Jewish circles, evident in the new state, forces the Christian Social Party to call on the German-Austrian people for a most unrelenting defensive struggle against the Jewish peril."[26] It went on to recognise Jews as a nation to be segregated from the Gentile world and stripped of their influence within it. The Pan-German party programme of 1920 was equally vehement: "The party . . . is in favour of a campaign of enlightenment about the corrupting influence of the Jewish spirit and the racial anti-Semitism necessitated thereby. It will combat Jewish influence in all areas of public and private life."[27] It, too, recognised the Jews as a nation with the prescription that Jewish influence in public life be reduced. The political manifesto of the Agrarian League of 1923 pledged itself "to fight against the Jewish race as a subversive element in the nation".[28]

The clearest and sharpest warning about the present and long-range danger of Jews to a Christian Austria came from the prelate Ignaz Seipel, who became head of the Christian Social Party and Chancellor in 1922. In an analysis of the

---

[24] See John W. Boyer, 'Lueger and the Viennese Jews', in *LBI Year Book XXVI* (1981), pp. 131–132.
[25] Quoted in Pfoser, *Literatur und Austromarxismus, op. cit.*, p. 182.
[26] 'Das Programm der Christlichsozialen Partei, 1918', in Klaus Berchtold (ed.), *Österreichische Parteiprogramme 1868–1966*, Vienna 1967, p. 357. The party programme of 1926 continued the demand for the protection of a Christian-German nation against "the predominance of the subversive Jewish influence in intellectual and economic life". See 'Das Programm der Christlichsozialen Partei, 1926', in Albert Kaden and Anton Pelinka (eds.), *Die Grundsatzprogramme der österreichischen Parteien*, Vienna 1979, pp. 115–116.
[27] Quoted in Peter Pulzer, *The Rise of Political Antisemitism in Germany and Austria*, 2nd revised edn., London 1988, p. 309.
[28] 'Politische Leitsätze des Landbundes für Österreich, 1923', in Berchtold, *op. cit.*, p. 483.

"Jewish problem" he concluded that Jews were not Europeans.[29] Their difference was not merely a matter of their religion; they also constituted a class based on their merchant ethos.[30] Christians were, therefore, called upon to wage a class struggle against them. The danger of Jewish domination of national life was doubly grave, he argued, because the Socialist Party was under Jewish leadership. His solution to the problem was to recognise the Jews as a national minority whose influence could then be reduced through segregation.

Whereas Seipel couched his radical proposal for re-ghettoisation in somewhat moderate political terms (he was, after all, a former professor of theology), Leopold Kunschak, head of the *Christlich-sozialer Arbeiterverein* and the second most powerful figure in the Christian-Conservative camp, provided both the tone and substance of a more populist politics. His solution for the Jewish problem, which, in principle at least, did not meet with serious objections from Seipel, was an exceptional law to segregate Jews as a national minority including the following:[31] restriction to their own voting curia; exclusion from civil service positions and from teaching in the public schools; education only in their own schools; and immediate expulsion of all who had immigrated since 1914 and where that proved impossible, their internment in special camps. In attacking the Socialist leaders he drew a distinction between the small Aryan minority and the coterie of "academic Jewish closet bolsheviks", which dominated them.[32]

The foregoing represents only a very small sample of the antisemitic theorising in the Christian-Conservative camp. Its press, mainly the *Reichspost*, which bore the subtitle *Unabhängiges Tageblatt für das christliche Volk* and its afternoon edition *Wiener Stimmen*, formerly the *Spätnachmittagszeitung für Nichtjuden*, wallowed in the conception: "The Jew is guilty, whether in the form of Marxist, speculator, or immoralist."[33]

What we have here is the theory underlying the antisemitism used by the Christian-Conservative camp, which until 1934 was virtually indistinguishable from that of the Pan-Germans and Austrian Nazis. Before we look at the specific Socialist targets of this ideology and the tactics used to promote it, it seems necessary to clear the air as to whether or not we are dealing with varieties of antisemitism – some "benign" or "defensive" and others more repulsive – an issue which has clouded our understanding of its role in Viennese inter-war politics. It seems to me that the construction of an antisemitic typology with gradations from neutral to negative[34] overlooks both the specific historical

---

[29]Ignaz Seipel, 'Minoritätenschutz und Judenfrage nach dem christlichsozialen Programm', in *Volkswohl*, 10 (1919), pp. 49–54; *Die Reichspost*, 21st January 1919, p. 2.

[30]Here Seipel echoed the ideas of Werner Sombart in *Händler und Helden*, Munich 1915.

[31]See Anton Staudinger, 'Christlichsoziale Judenpolitik in der Gründungsphase der österreichischen Republik', in *Jahrbuch für Zeitgeschichte, 1978*, Wien 1979, pp. 36–48.

[32]*Ibid.*, p. 29.

[33]See Ulrich Weinzierl, 'Die Kultur der *Reichspost*', in Franz Kadrnoska (ed.), *Aufbruch und Untergang. Österreichische Kultur Zwischen 1918 und 1938*, Vienna 1981, pp. 329–331.

[34]For a clear example of such a typology, see Sigurd Paul Schleichl, 'The Contexts and Nuances of Anti-Jewish Language. Were all the "Antisemites" Antisemites?' in Ivar Oxaal, Michael Pollak and Gerhard Botz (eds.), *Jews, Antisemitism and Culture in Vienna*, London 1987, pp. 89–110. For a rejection of such typologies, see Jacques Le Rider, 'Réponses à Allan Janik', in *Austriaca. Cahiers Universitaires d'Information sur l'Autriche*, 14 (1983), pp. 192–193.

circumstances and the perception of the victims. A conjecture: Could any Viennese Jew cursed as a "Zurgrasster [alien] Saujud" distinguish the intention of his defamer – whether it was religious, cultural, political or racial? I believe that in his perception the epithet included all of these.

John Boyer avers that Lueger's antisemitism was cultural and not racial;[35] Klemens Klemperer argues that in contrast to the racists Seipel's antisemitism was defensive and ethical;[36] and Bruce Pauley judges Seipel's characterisation of the Jews as a nation to be benign because the Zionists made the same claim.[37] Boyer seems to be fixated on Lueger as manipulator without considering his impact on the popular prejudices to which he appealed. Nor does he consider that in the perception of Viennese Jews, given the climate of hate Lueger had created, it made little difference that the intention was cultural; it was antisemitism all the same – in which a racial component was present. Klemperer's claim is made possible by suppressing an important part of Seipel's speech of 1919 in which he called Jews a class to be combated by Christians.[38] The notion that Seipel's prejudice was somehow "ethical" because he "never allowed himself public antisemitic outbursts" overlooks that he left such vulgarity to henchmen such as Kunschak and the editorialists of the *Reichspost*.

The Zionists too emphasised the issue of Jewish nationality. But the implications of Seipel's conception were quite different. They conjured up a modern ghetto in which Jews would be second-class citizens and projected a German-Christian Austria in which assimilated Jews had no place. When Seipel asserted that Jews were not Europeans he was not talking about religion but about race. During the fifteen years of the Republic the various categories historians have devised for antisemitism – religious, cultural, political and racial – were blended into one undifferentiated mass both in theory and, as we shall see, in practice. The common and seemingly more polite epithets used for Jews by Christian Socials, Pan-Germans and Nazis were the same: parasites, speculators, blackmarketeers, aliens, pornographers, merchants, Asiatics, non-Aryans, degenerates.[39] In the arena of gutter politics the terms *Jud*, *Saujud* and *Judensozi* became synonymous.

From the beginning of the Republic the Socialists were under constant attack by the Christian-Conservative camp for attempting to carry out sweeping

[35]See Boyer, 'Lueger', *loc. cit.*, pp. 132–136. Freidenreich, *op. cit.*, p. 7, claims that Seipel "never openly adopted a racist version [of antisemitism]".
[36]Klemens von Klemperer, *Ignaz Seipel. Christian Statesman in a Time of Crisis*, Princeton 1972, p. 256.
[37]Bruce F. Pauley, 'Political Antisemitism in Interwar Austria', in Ivar Oxaal *et al.* (eds.), *op. cit.*, p. 159. He calls Christian Social antisemitism "old-fashioned and comparatively subtle cultural and religious" and "semi-religious, semi-racist, and basically defensive" (pp. 152, 165). He ignores Seipel's article 'Minoritätenschutz', *loc. cit.*, where Jews are classified not merely as a religion or nation but also as a class and as non-Europeans. Seipel's aim in recognising Jews as a nation was to reduce them to second-class citizens.
[38]Klemperer, *loc. cit.*, pp. 156–157.
[39]See Pauley, *loc. cit.*, p. 172. Pauley makes one other claim which must be challenged. He states that the Christian Social Party "preferred slogans and demagogy to antisemitic legislation" (p. 158). Pauley overlooks the fact that such legislation, as a constitutional issue, would have required a two-thirds majority, which the Socialist Party would have prevented. When the Minister of Education and the Rector of Vienna University conspired to introduce a *numerus clausus* for Jews in the university, the *Verfassungsgerichtshof* dismissed the measure.

reforms in the municipality and for their cultural experiment.[40] The battle was waged in every conceivable arena from the Municipal Council to the Provincial and National Parliaments in a mixture of legalistic wrangling and character assassination in which antisemitic attacks played a prominent role. But much of the Christian Social Party's attempt to maintain the *status quo* or to turn back the historical clock was conducted outside the institutional realm through smear campaigns in its press, through the mobilisation of Catholic Action groups and Catholic rallies addressed by such prominent churchmen as Cardinal Piffl. Everywhere, it was claimed, the pernicious hand of *Judensozi* could be seen striving to undermine and destroy the Christian-German social and moral order.

The following are just a few telling examples of the targets: in fulminating about the new housing and luxury taxes Councillor Breitner was characterised as a heinous Jewish sadist; the public housing programme was pictured as creating barracks for staging a future *coup d'état* and as a means of buying worker loyalty; the marriage consultation bureau was condemned as an intrusion into the sanctity of Christian marriage as was the municipal/provincial law allowing for the annulment of marriages; the Socialists' cautious position on abortion was branded an invitation to murder; educational reforms were denounced as subverting the position of the Catholic Church as moral preceptor and the Christian family as educator; medical examinations and sports in the schools were charged with destroying the Christian modesty of girls, as were the numerous swimming pools created by the municipality for failing to be segregated by sex;[41] the creation of a public crematorium was denounced as an insult to Catholic sacraments; the Socialist municipal administration's refusal to exercise censorship against Schnitzler's play *Der Reigen* or Lewis Milestone's film *All Quiet on the Western Front* (among many other examples) was fought with particular viciousness; and all aspects of the Socialist Party culture were condemned out of hand as means of deceiving the workers and leading them away from the path of a Christian-German social order. During the bitter struggle over the première of *Der Reigen* in 1921, Seipel charged that the moral sensibilities of the "the native Christian people" were gravely injured by the performance of "this dirty piece from the pen of a Jewish author" and accused the Socialists of defending speculators and whores.[42]

In this protracted *Kulturkampf* one did not have to read between the lines to discover the antisemitic *Leitmotif*. Leading Socialists were subjected to a constant barrage of antisemitic vituperation: Otto Bauer was harangued as "an arrogant

[40]See, for instance, Zyrill Fischer, *Sozialistische Erziehung*, Vienna 1926, with a foreword by Cardinal Piffl; Eduard Jehly, *Zehn Jahre rotes Wien*, Vienna 1930. It was published by the *Generalsekretariat der Christlichsozialen Partei Österreichs*.

[41]The Church laid down a list of Catholic principles on behaviour and morality (for girls and women), which was aimed both at municipal reforms and Socialist cultural organisations. See *Wiener Diözesanblatt* (July 1926), pp. 41–43; *St. Pöltner Diözesanblatt* (June 1926), pp. 50–51.

[42]See Alfred Pfoser, 'Der Wiener "Reigen"-Skandal. Sexusalangst als politisches Syndrom der Ersten Republik', in Helmut Konrad and Wolfgang Maderthaner (eds.), *Neuere Studien zur Arbeitergeschichte*, Vienna 1984, vol. III, p. 685. Karl Paumgarten, one of the *Reichspost*'s prominent editorialists asked why the Socialists should want to defend the rights of "drones and exploiters", the "lascivious thrills of Asiatics who have forced their way into our country". He concludes that the Socialist Party is once again engaged in its mission to protect the Jews. Quoted *ibid.*, pp. 686–688.

Czech Jew daring to speak in a German Parliament";[43] Hugo Breitner was confronted publicly by a prominent opponent with the view that "only when the head of this Asiatic rolls in the sand will victory be ours";[44] and when Robert Danneberg spoke as President of the Provincial Parliament he was greeted with howls of "*Saujud*".[45] With very rare exceptions these assaults went unanswered.[46] (One cannot fail but compare them to the courageous stand taken by Léon Blum in similar situations.)[47] Antisemitic slurs were directed at Gentile Socialist leaders as well. In 1923, when Karl Seitz became Mayor of Vienna, Christian Social publications spread the rumour that he was the illegitimate son of a Jew named Pollak. Henceforth Seitz was called "*Pollaksohn*" by the mud slingers.[48]

No doubt the repeated use of the word "Christian" in the above syllabus of Socialist errors will have been remarked. It is an important clue to the close relationship between the Christian Social Party and the Catholic Church. That tie is central to an understanding of the forces arrayed against Social Democracy and of the important political role played by antisemitism in the activities of that alliance. The Christian Social Party had nothing comparable to the dense network of organisations and institutions of the Socialists. Instead, it relied mainly on existing religious and lay organisations of the Church and drew its cadres at the local level from the priesthood.[49] But the Church provided the party with more than structures; it also served as an ideological *éminence grise* in providing the arguments and justifications for the moral terms in which the party cast its struggle against Social Democracy.

From the beginning of the Republic, the Austrian episcopate declared itself to be the moral guardian of a "Christian and German nation".[50] The bishops' pastoral letters issued during the next fifteen years made it quite clear that nothing in contemporary life was excluded from the moral supervision and control of the Church: marriage and intermarriage, burial, family planning, education, the arts and leisure time pursuits, to name but a few from a long

---

[43]See Leopold Spira, *Feindbild "Jud". 100 Jahre politischer Antisemitismus in Österreich*, Vienna 1981, p. 19. In another parliamentary debate Bauer was attacked as an arrogant Jew by a Christian Social deputy. *Ibid.*, p. 55.

[44]The attack was by Ernst Rüdiger Starhemberg, head of the *Heimwehr*. Reported in *Neue Freie Presse*, 5th October 1930.

[45]Spira, *op. cit.*, p. 67.

[46]In the controversy over building the municipal crematorium, the municipal councillor for social welfare Julius Tandler did stand his ground against antisemitic slurs, the bishops' proclamation of the excommunication of Catholics supporting cremation, and the threats of Chancellor Seipel. Vienna's right to build the crematorium was upheld by the constitutional court. See Karl Sablik, *Julius Tandler. Mediziner und Sozialreformer*, Vienna 1983, pp. 269–274.

[47]On at least two occasions, in 1923 and 1936, Blum responded to antisemitic slurs in the Chamber of Deputies by proudly acknowledging his identity as a Jew and Frenchman. See Joel Colton, *Léon Blum. Humanist in Politics*, Durham, N.C. 1987, p. 6. For a discussion of antisemitism and Socialism in France, see Pierre Birnbaum, *Un mythe politique. La République juive de Léon Blum à Pierre Mendès France*, Paris 1988, pp. 61–85.

[48]See Rudolf Spitzer, 'Karl Lueger und Karl Seitz', in *Archiv. Jahrbuch des Vereins der Geschichte der Arbeiterbewegung*, 6 (1990), p. 215.

[49]See Wolfgang Maderthaner, 'Kirche und Sozialdemokratie. Aspekte des Verhältnisses von politischem Klerikalismus und sozialistischer Arbeiterschaft bis zum Jahre 1938', in Konrad and Maderthaner (eds.), *Neuere Studien, op. cit.*, vol. III, p. 533.

[50]See *Wiener Diözesanblatt* (January 1919), pp. 1–3; *St. Pöltner Diözesenblatt* (January 1919), pp. 5–7.

catalogue. Strictures about these went hand in hand with admonitions to the communicant to "remember that you will have to answer to God for your membership of Social Democracy".[51] By 1930, as the political struggle became more confrontational and violent, pastoral messages demanded "every vote for a Catholic, truly Christian party, faithful to the Church".[52] Until then the Church's Judeophobia relied on inference and innuendo; blatant antisemitism could be left to the Christian Social Party. But with the growth of the Nazis the Christian Social Party was forced into a competition about who was the better antisemite. In a pastoral letter of 1933 Bishop Johannes Gföllner denounced degenerate Jewry as the apostle of Socialism and harbinger of bolshevism and called on every true Christian to break the influence of Jewry.[53] In closing, he invited the Nazis and other Aryans to adopt this "spiritual and ethical antisemitism" in their programme but to keep in mind that the Catholic Church was the strongest bulwark against Jewish atheism.

The foregoing analysis establishes clearly that antisemitism was a major weapon used by the Christian-Conservative camp and, it goes without saying, also of the Pan-Germans and Nazis, in their bitter struggle against the Viennese cultural experiment – and ultimately against the existence of the Socialist Party. How did the Socialists respond? How did they answer the smear campaign that their proud efforts in Vienna were the work of the Antichrist intent on destroying the Christian-German essence of the "native" population and that their party was in the grip of a coterie of non-European, non-Aryan, decadent immoralists determined to corrupt and exploit the Christian-German workers?

To a large extent the Socialists' response to the "Jewish Question" grew out of positions taken by pre-war German and Austrian Social Democracy. Then, Victor Adler, founder of the Austrian party had already warned about pulling the chestnuts out of the fire for either Jews or antisemites and advocated a neutral position.[54] But that this stance was disingenuous can be seen in Adler's acceptance of a resolution of the German SPD in 1893 which asserted that antisemitism, "despite its reactionary character ... ultimately acts in a revolutionary way", because the Socialist Party could make the masses stirred up by it understand that not just Jewish capitalists but all capitalists held them in

[51] *Wiener Diözesanblatt* (December 1925), p. 73.

[52] *St. Pöltner Diözesanblatt* (September 1930), p. 4. The faithful were instructed to be guided by the warnings and advice of their priests and the leaders of Catholic organisations (p. 3). But the episcopate threatened mass action as well. If the Catholic politicians failed to act in legal ways against "Socialist terrorism", "the people were justified in resorting to self-help". *Ibid.* (April 1922), p. 3.

[53] Cited in Anton Pelinka, 'Christlicher und rassischer Antisemitismus', in *Das Jüdische Echo. Zeitschrift für Kultur und Politik*, vol. XXXV, No. 1 (October 1986). Pelinka points out that in the conception of Gföllner the terms Aryan and Christian were practically synonymous, demonstrating how little difference there was between religious and racist antisemitism.

[54] See Victor Adler, 'Der Antisemitismus', in *Die Gleichheit*, 7th May 1887. But this proclaimed neutrality was only rhetorical. On another occasion "Adler spoke about 'Jewish' exploiters lording it over 'Aryan' workers, and criticized Lueger's party for always siding with the Jews'. See Robert S. Wistrich, 'An Austrian Variation on Socialist Anti-Semitism', in *Patterns of Prejudice*, vol. VIII, No. 4 (1974), p. 3. For the best discussion of Adler's alleged neutrality, see Jack Jacobs, *On Socialists and "the Jewish Question" after Marx*, New York 1992, pp. 98–104.

Red Vienna and the "Jewish Question"

thrall.[55] Despite the very different historical conditions of republican Austria (and one must add, in a very un-Marxist way) the Socialists clung to this formulation and even exaggerated it in a self-destructive way.

It was indeed a tragedy that the Viennese Socialists' main defence against the antisemitic onslaught was to fight fire with fire and even to outdo their enemies with antisemitic responses of their own.[56] Articles in the party's main newspaper, *Die Arbeiter-Zeitung*, as well as a series of pamphlets, played on the theme that the Christian Social and Pan-German government was the executive organ of the "bank Jews";[57] that the election campaigns of the Christian-Conservative camp were financed by Jewish industrialists; that the leadership of the opposition was itself riddled with Jews or converts from Judaism.[58] In response to Nazi gains in the elections of 1932, Otto Bauer sought to convince Christian Social voters that their party lacked the courage to be antisemitic because it took money from Jewish industrialists and gave away the people's wealth to Jewish banks.[59]

The step to mud-slinging was not far, as a few examples will illustrate: a Christian Social official was stigmatised for being a convert: "A few drops of holy water and out of the Polish Jewess emerges a Christian Social leader";[60] Seitz attacked Seipel in parliament in a parody of a Yiddish accent;[61] the *Arbeiter-Zeitung*, in an attempt at sarcasm, claimed to find the most typical Jewish nose in the antisemitic face of Chancellor Seipel.[62] Such foul representations were repeated in cartoons of Jewish stereotypes in the Socialist press of which one depicting an emblem combining a hooked nose and the Nazi swastika was truly pernicious.[63]

---

[55]See Pulzer, *op. cit.*, pp. 266, 268.

[56]See Jack Jacobs, 'Austrian Social Democracy and the Jewish Question in the First Republic', in Anson Rabinbach (ed.), *The Austrian Socialist Experiment. Social Democracy and Austromarxism, 1918–1934*, Boulder, Col. 1985, esp. pp. 158–160.

[57]'Die Zionisten für Seipel', in *Arbeiter-Zeitung*, 17th September 1922; 'Die Juden beim Seipel', *ibid.*, 3rd December 1922. Of a half dozen antisemitic pamphlets produced by the Socialist Party publishing house, two were particularly pernicious: Christoph Hinteregger, *Der Judenschwindel*, Vienna 1923 and Robert Danneberg, *Die Schiebergeschäfte der Regierungsparteien. Der Antisemitismus im Lichte der Tatsachen*, Vienna 1926. Both of these, as well as the others, linked Jewish capital, banks and the press with the Christian Social and Pan-German parties and "exposed" Jews in their service.

[58]*Arbeiter-Zeitung*, 4th April 1933.

[59]Otto Bauer, 'Der 24. April', in *Der Kampf*, vol. XXV, No. 5 (May 1932). Jacobs argues that Bauer was ambiguous about his Jewish identity because he paid dues to the Viennese Jewish community (*Israelitische Kultusgemeinde*) in 1920 and 1924. This evidence is too slight to sustain the point. Bauer's behaviour on the "Jewish Question" was no different from that of other assimilated Socialist leaders who had taken the legal step of being "without confession". See Jacobs, *Socialists and "the Jewish Question"*, *op. cit.*, pp. 104–114.

[60]*Arbeiter-Zeitung*, 21st March 1921.

[61]See George E. Berkley, *Vienna and Its Jews. The Tragedy of Success 1880s–1980s*, Cambridge, Mass. 1988, p. 160.

[62]There must have been an interloper in Seipel's family tree, the satire suggested, to account for such a Jewish nose in the middle of an antisemitic face. See 'Die antisemitische Judennase in der Rassenrubrik', in *Arbeiter-Zeitung*, 11th February 1923.

[63]'Das neue Wappen der Hackenkreuzler', in *Arbeiter-Zeitung*, 11th October 1925. This vile cartoon was no exception. During the election campaign of 1923 the SDAP produced posters of men with hooked noses wearing kaftans and captioned to make clear the relationship between Jewish bankers and the Christian Social and Pan-German parties.

One can only assume that the rationale behind the tactic of projecting stereotypes of the rich Jew, the Jewish banker, the Jewish capitalist, and the Jewish speculator was based on the historically mistaken notion that the followers of the opposition, by being made aware of their own party's dependence on Jewish capitalism, could be persuaded to support the Socialists who fought against capitalism of every stripe. It was an extremely naive assumption and very dangerous at the same time, for if what the Christian-Conservative camp said about the Socialists was true – that they were dominated by a Jewish cabal – and what the Socialists said about the Christian-Conservatives was true – that they were the mere instruments of Jewish capital – then what should loyal Socialist Party members and trade unionists think about the poisonous charges they encountered that "the Jew was guilty"?

At no time did the Socialist leaders respond to antisemitism and defend the Jews by detailing the considerable contribution Jewish intellectuals and artists made to the cultural life of Vienna or by proclaiming the leading role of Jews in carrying out municipal Socialism and the cultural experiment. The public, and even the workers, learned about the latter only from the diatribes of the antisemites. Nor did the party ever attempt to discuss the varied components which constituted antisemitism – religious, national, racial, cultural – for fear of being considered a "protective troop" or bodyguard of Jewry. Moreover, the party kept the Viennese Jewish community at arm's length while enjoying its overwhelming electoral support. The positive actions of the SPD in Weimar Germany on behalf of Jews and against antisemitism provide a stark contrast.[64] There the SPD publicly countered racist contentions about Jews with carefully reasoned arguments to expose the fallacies of antisemitism; it exposed antisemitic incidents in the army, the courts and the bureaucracy; it attacked the activities of Judeophobic Nationalist groups in its election campaigns; and it cooperated closely with various Jewish organisations. In all of these activities Jewish intellectuals in leading party positions were particularly visible.

The party also refused to confront the considerable power and political activity of the Catholic Church: the fact that it vigorously pursued electoral politics, that priests could hold public office and were salaried by the state, that it dominated mandatory religious education in the schools, that it was among the most ultramontanist in Europe, and that it was the fount of anti-Socialist ideology. It is ironic, to say the least, considering the power and role of the Catholic Church, that rich Jews became the main target of the Socialist leaders in fighting antisemitism. This was particularly true of Jewish Socialist leaders who, in the spirit of negative consciousness, hid behind the party's programmatic position "that religion was a private matter". But if the latter were true, if Austria really was a secular state, why did they accept the payment of the Catholic

---

[64]For the following, see Donald L. Niewyk, *Socialist, Anti-Semite, and Jew. German Social Democracy Confronts the Problem of Anti-Semitism 1918–1933*, Baton Rouge 1971, pp. 215–221; Hans-Helmuth Knütter, *Die Juden und die deutsche Linke in der Weimarer Republik 1918–1933*, Düsseldorf 1971, pp. 207–217.

clergy's salaries out of public funds and tolerate the Viennese municipality's distribution of free religious textbooks in the public schools?[65]

How can we explain the reluctance of the Socialists to engage the Catholic episcopate directly? To be sure, the majority of Viennese (79%) were nominal Catholics.[66] But some 160,000 Viennese Catholics (94% of them workers) left the Church formally during the republican period, and one must assume that many others simply lapsed without going through the legal process. Church attendance was about 10%, and the continued observance of some Christian holidays in working-class communities was atavistic-ritualistic rather than devotional.[67] It would seem, therefore, that the risk of alienating workers by challenging the Church as a reactionary and socially regressive institution was slight. Yet, the Socialist Party was not prepared to fight against the influence of the Church by asking workers or at least party members to leave it *en masse*.[68] Can the low profile of the Jewish Socialist leaders on the "Jewish Question" simply be explained as a desire not to burden the party with their Jewish identity?[69] But that was hardly a secret in view of their constant exposure to antisemitic attacks. Or – and this is an important conjecture – were they afraid that if their presence and prominence as Jews in the party received that considerable public exposure, which a courageous self-defence would entail, then the quiet antisemitic currents among both leaders and rank and file in their own party would become turbulent?

The latter possibility, the existence of an antisemitic undercurrent in the Socialist Party, has been the subject of much speculation and controversy.[70] Although the evidence for such a view is sparse and much of it inferential, the conclusion is not without foundation. There are reports of antisemitism within the *Sozialistischer Arbeiterjugend*[71] and in the party's economic enterprises[72] and there exists a dossier on the secret, last-minute negotiations in February 1934

[65] Hanisch, *loc. cit.*, p. 57.
[66] For the following, see Maderthaner, 'Kirche und Sozialdemokratie', *loc. cit.*, p. 556, note 43; Hanisch, *loc. cit.*, pp. 55–56; *Der Pionier. Mitteilungsblatt das Landesvereines Wien des "Freidenkerbund Österreichs"*, vol. IV, No. 9 (September 1929), pp. 5–6; and vol. VIII, No. 1 (January–February 1933), p. 101.
[67] See Eva Viethen, *Wiener Arbeiterinnen. Leben zwischen Familie, Lohnarbeit und politischen Engagement*, Ph.D. diss., University of Vienna 1984, pp. 192–201.
[68] See Gerhard Steger, *Rote Fahne Schwarzes Kreuz. Die Haltung der Sozialdemokratischen Arbeiterpartei Österreichs zur Religion, Christentum und Kirchen von Hainfeld bis 1934*, Vienna 1987, pp. 296–299.
[69] Reminiscent of party founder Victor Adler's privately expressed lament that he, as a born Jew (and despite his conversion to Protestantism), was a burden to the party. See Julius Braunthal, *Victor and Friedrich Adler. Zwei Generationen Arbeiterbewegung*, Vienna 1965, pp. 144–145.
[70] Helmut Konrad is the first among the new generation of historians of the Austrian working class to attempt to assess the degree of antisemitism in the Socialist Party's rank and file during the First Republic. He concludes, in a pilot study, that "anti-Semitism within the Austrian workers' movement was a phenomenon of the provinces . . ." The corollary argument advanced is that the cultural network in Vienna kept antisemitism at bay. The argument is inferential and hardly convincing. Clearly, empirical work on the party base in Vienna needs to be done. See 'Social Democracy's Drift towards Nazism before 1938', in F. Parkinson (ed.), *Conquering the Past. Austrian Nazism Yesterday and Today*, Detroit 1989, *passim* and esp. p. 115.
[71] See Friedrich Scheu, *Ein Band der Freundschaft. Schwarzwaldkreis und Entstehung der Vereinigung Sozialistischer Mittelschüler*, Vienna 1985, p. 190; Adolf Sturmthal, *Democracy Under Fire. Memoirs of a European Socialist*, Durham, N.C. 1989, p. 175.
[72] See Ernst Eppler, 'Du bist ein Jud . . .', in Ruth Beckermann (ed.), *Die Mazzesinsel. Juden in der Wiener Leopoldstadt 1918–1938*, Vienna 1984, p. 80.

between the Lower Austrian party leaders Oskar Helmer, Heinrich Schneidmadl, and Adolf Schärf and Chancellor Dollfuss offering "the resignation of Seitz, Bauer, and Deutsch from the party executive and the withdrawal of all Jewish party leaders" in exchange for maintaining the legal status of the party.[73]

With the outlawing of the party in 1934 and in the attempts to explain the party's defeat strong antisemitic strains appeared.[74] It is quite natural for younger leaders to blame the old guard for having allowed the party's power to wither away, but they were blamed as Jews and not as erring Socialists. Then, the often made claim, that the workers were fascinated with Jewish intellectuals who streamed into important party positions and grateful that they were prepared to throw in their lot with the downtrodden, was finally put to rest in an anti-intellectual upsurge of grass-roots resentment.[75] The best account of those immediate post-defeat months, when a new entirely Gentile party leadership was in the making, can be found in the personal history of Joseph Buttinger, a shining light of the party's younger generation and head of the underground party (*Revolutionäre Sozialisten*) from 1935 to 1938.[76] Though Buttinger cleverly tries to disguise his own views by putting them into the mouths of others, in assessing who had ruined the party and led it to defeat, who had abandoned the workers at the barricades, and who had used the party for professional advancement and material advantage, it becomes quite clear that Buttinger is speaking for himself. And the answer he gives to these rhetorical questions is that the Jews were guilty!

It is no secret that some of this resentment lingered on in the Gentile leadership that emerged after the Second World War. In the first message sent from party headquarters to former comrades, largely Jewish refugees, it was bluntly stated that "the return of Jews to Austria in great numbers would be viewed with a certain apprehension".[77] Though Vienna has become virtually a "city without Jews",[78] a high level of antisemitism lingers on among its population.[79] Alas, there is also recent evidence that, with respect to the "Jewish

---

[73] See Spitzer, *loc. cit.*, pp. 216–217.
[74] See the reminiscences of Manfred Ackermann and Emmerich Czermak in Spira, *op. cit.*, pp. 98–101.
[75] See Robert Schwarz, 'Antisemitism and Socialism in Austria 1918–1962', in Joseph Fraenkel (ed.), *The Jews in Austria*, London 1967, pp. 446–447, 450. John Bunzl traces the upsurge of antisemitic resentment after 1934 not only to anti-intellectualism but also to xenophobia and fear of competition among the workers. See 'Arbeiterbewegung und Antisemitismus in Österreich vor und nach dem Ersten Weltkrieg', in *Zeitgeschichte*, vol. IV, No. 5 (February 1977).
[76] Joseph Buttinger, *In the Twilight of Socialism. A History of the Revolutionary Socialists of Austria*, New York 1953, pp. 74–81, 91.
[77] See Julius Braunthal, *The Tragedy of Austria*, London 1948, p. 121.
[78] See the prophetic novel of Hugo Bettauer, *Die Stadt ohne Juden. Ein Roman von Übermorgen*, Vienna 1922, which describes the future expulsion of the Jews, but comes to a happier end than history was to provide.
[79] See Bernd T. Marin, 'Antisemitismus unter Arbeitern? Einige Daten und Thesen zum "Klassencharakter" des nachfaschistischen Antisemitismus', in Botz *et al.* (eds.), *Bewegung und Klasse, op. cit.* Marin cites a Viennese survey of antisemitic prejudices of 1977 in which the prevalence was: 20.1% high; 58.8% medium; 22.1% low (p. 772). *Idem*, 'Antisemitism Before and After the Holocaust. The Austrian Case', in Oxaal *et al.* (eds.), *op. cit.*, pp. 216–233, covers antisemitism in contemporary Austria up to the Waldheim campaign. Marin suggests here that antisemitic prejudice should be understood as a "cultural sedimentation of an earlier 'Austrian ideology'". Rather than enlightening, this seems to throw a veil over the subject.

Question" the contemporary Austrian Socialist Party has still refused to master its own past.[80]

If we look back on the failure of the Viennese experiment both in cultural and political terms, the Socialists' ability to address the "Jewish Question" or, more precisely, their perverse attempts to do so is symptomatic of their failure to confront their opponents in the political and cultural arena directly, openly and powerfully. The Austro-Marxist aphorism "against the idea of force, the force of ideas" signified an unwillingness to recognise that the Socialist Party was engaged in a struggle for power at all levels. In consistently shrinking from that reality or, as Bauer put it, "avoiding it at virtually any cost"[81] their Christian-Conservative opponents were given ideological advantages they were able to put to good use.

What should the Socialists have done about the linkage of Jews and their party by antisemites? They should have faced their enemies forthrightly by acknowledging the leading role played by Jewish Socialists in the transformation of the Viennese municipality, by pointing to the contributions of Jewish professionals, intellectuals and artists to the cultural life of Vienna, and by demonstrating the clear connection between the Christian-Conservative camp and the subversion by capitalists and the Catholic Church of the pluralistic republic. The latter, particularly, would have provoked the ultimate confrontation between the two camps earlier, but at the time when the outcome was not a foregone conclusion. It is doubtful whether such a confrontation would have taken the form of civil war, let us say in 1927, when all the working-class organisations were at their height (the *Schutzbund* had more than 100,000 members), before the working-class communities were demoralised by economic crisis and constant political retreats, and before the growth of the Nazi Party in Germany cast a long shadow over Austrian and international politics.

---

[80]In 1988 Jack Jacobs, an American political scientist, was commissioned to write a brief article aimed at the general reader on 'Austrian Social Democracy, Anti-Semitism, and the "Jewish Question"' for the catalogue of an extensive exhibition commemorating the one hundredth anniversary of the Socialist Party. The initial response of the editor, Helene Maimann, was favourable, and he received a cheque from the publisher for his contribution. Two months later Maimann rejected the piece on the grounds that the text was polemical, tendentious and not sufficiently multidimensional: it did not critically reveal that in the First Republic there were also Right-wing Jews and even Jewish Fascists. Jacob's article was finally published in the independent *Der Standard* and the Dutch *Vrij Nederland*. This was followed by self-justifications from Maimann in which she impugned the character and scholarly ability of Jacobs. It would appear that the initiative for censorship came from higher party echelons fearful of challenges to the heroising platitudes with which the party presents its past.

[81]See Norbert Leser, *Zwischen Bolschewismus und Reformismus. Der Austromarxismus als Theorie und Praxis*, Vienna 1968, pp. 397–398.

Most of all, a positive approach to the "Jewish Question" by the Socialist Party would have accorded it a sense of dignity, which the party's constant denials and even pseudo-antisemitic responses destroyed. That dignity was essential for the rank and file, bombarded by antisemitism from all sides and, one cannot help but suspect, infected by its poison. The Socialist Party's failure to deal with the "Jewish Question" in a constructive way remains an important example of its leadership's malaise in addressing the issue of power on which, ultimately, its cultural experiment depended.

Murder on Command
The Anti-Jewish Pogrom in Innsbruck
9th–10th November 1938

BY MICHAEL GEHLER

In Austria, the Year of Remembrance, 1988, was marked by wide-ranging debates, not only about the "Anschluß" but also about the "*Reichskristallnacht*"[1] fifty years earlier. This has provided further impetus to the research of an event that was a milestone in the persecution of the Polish, German and Austrian Jews on the eve of the Second World War.[*] Although, as Wolfgang Benz asserts, the November Pogrom of 1938 has been well documented, many questions remain unanswered.[2] Our understanding will be increased by local and regional studies, which, in turn, will raise new issues.[3]

In Innsbruck there were many unusual features. The evidence, from previously known as well as new sources, provokes the question especially: why here, where only a small number of Jews lived, the pogrom led by the SA and SS was so particularly brutal and contemptuous of common humanity? The pogrom

---

[1]Opinions about the origins of the term "*Reichskristallnacht*" vary. Contemporary Nazi sources, such as newspaper and SD reports, spoke of "*Aktionen*", "justifiable popular fury" and "understandable measures of retaliation". Cf. Arno Mayer, *Why Did the Heavens Not Darken? The Final "Solution" in History*, New York 1988, p. 169. See also Heinz Lauber, *Judenpogrom. "Reichskristallnacht" November 1938 in Großdeutschland. Daten, Fakten, Dokumente, Quellentexte, Thesen und Bewertungen*, Gerlingen–Bad Württemberg 1981, p. 41; Walter H. Pehle (ed.), *Der Judenpogrom 1938. Von der "Reichskristallnacht" zum Völkermord*, Frankfurt a. Main 1988, pp. 9–10; Wilfred Mairgünther, *Reichskristallnacht*, Kiel 1987; and Hermann Graml, *Reichskristallnacht. Antisemitismus und Judenverfolgung im Dritten Reich*, Munich 1988.
[*]This article was translated from the German by Norma von Ragenfeld-Feldman.
[2]See Ursula Homann, 'Warnsignal auf dem Weg zum Holocaust. Pogromnacht 1938. Leben und Verfolgung der Juden im Dritten Reich', *Das Parlament*, 44 (1988), pp. 14–15.
[3]See *Widerstand und Verfolgung in Tirol, 1934–1945. Eine Dokumentation*, publication of the Dokumentationsarchiv des österreichischen Widerstandes, 2 vols., Vienna–Munich 1984, vol. I, pp. 420–425, 448–462; Gretl Köfler, 'Die Austreibung der Juden aus Tirol im Jahr 1938', *Fenster*, 29 (1981), pp. 2926–2929; idem, 'Antisemitismus in Tirol, 1918–1945', *Gaismair Kalender* (1985), pp. 120–123; idem, 'Tirol und die Juden', in *Tirol und der Anschluß. Voraussetzungen, Entwicklungen, Rahmenbedingungen, 1918–1938*, Innsbrucker Forschungen zur Zeitgeschichte, vol. III, ed. by Thomas Albrich, Klaus Eisterer and Rolf Steininger, Innsbruck 1988, pp. 169–182; *Die Geschichte der Juden in Tirol von den Anfängen im Mittelalter bis in die neueste Zeit*, Special Issue 15–16 (1986) of *Sturzflüge*; Gad Hugo Sella, *Die Juden Tirols. Ihr Leben und Schicksal*, Tel-Aviv 1979; Andreas Maislinger, '"Die Verletzung wirkte sofort tödlich". Dokumentation über die blutrünstige November-Pogromnacht 1938 in Innsbruck', *Tribüne. Zeitschrift zum Verständnis des Judentums*, 107 (1988), pp. 151–158; Günter Fellner, 'Der Novemberpogrom 1938 in Westösterreich', *Mitteilungen der Gesellschaft für Salzburger Landeskunde*, 130 (1990), pp. 725–738.

was, in fact, only the penultimate step of a policy to "free" Germany and Austria of Jews.[4]

There is a close connection between the Austrian Nazi tactics against Jews (*Judenpolitik*) prior to 1938, which aimed at forcing them out of Austria, and the night of the pogrom. Already in the two decades following the First World War, the Jewish population of the Tyrol and Vorarlberg had decreased by one third; and between March and November 1938, it declined by another third to about 130 Jews.[5] But even that number was too high for the new rulers of Austria, and the Jews were to be induced to leave the country rapidly. Thus, for the Nazi agencies that viewed Jewish emigration as being too sluggish, the night of the pogrom came at an opportune moment; after abating in the autumn of 1938, the Jewish exodus gathered momentum again after the events of 9th–10th November.

Before the so-called "*Kristallnacht*", however, as the SS Security Service (*Sicherheitsdienst*, SD) carefully observed, there was a lack of interest on the part of the Jews in leaving the country, a condition they intended to remedy fast. In September 1938 SS-*Obersturmführer* Adolf Eichmann, chief of the Central Office for Jewish Emigration in Vienna, was asked by the SD District (*Unterabschnitt*) of the Tyrol to come to Innsbruck, for it had been noted "that the desire amongst the Jews to emigrate has increasingly weakened". The report added that, "a certain arrogance in the attitude of the Jews has become evident". In agreement with the SD and the Innsbruck *Gestapo* office, Eichmann summoned a number of Jews living in Innsbruck and ordered them "to submit an application to the passport office by 19th September 1938 with a request for a passport for the purpose of emigration". Eichmann also told them that their presence in the Tyrol as well as the German *Reich* was not desired and that they therefore were to make arrangements to emigrate as quickly as possible. Those Jews who still had not succeeded in securing admission to another country were given a time limit for leaving the Tyrol (wealthy Jews were given eight to fourteen days; the less well-off, four to eight weeks); and they would have to report to the *Israelitische Kultusgemeinde* in Vienna; their emigration would then be given further attention.

The Innsbruck meeting was attended by three representatives from the Innsbruck *Gestapo*: Commissar Werner Hilliges, Regional Inspector of Police (*Polizeirayonsinspektor*) Josef Mösinger, chief of the Jewish Office (*Judenreferat in der Gestapoleitstelle Innsbruck*) and *Kriminal-Assistenzanwärter* Ernst Rüdiger; two from the SD: Eichmann and SS-*Obersturmführer* Dr. Ernst Chlan; and from the Office for Aryanisation: engineer Hermann Duxneuner.[6] Among the Innsbruck Jews summoned by Eichmann were also those who were later murdered or severely

---

[4]Lauber, *Judenpogrom*, pp. 42–43; see also special number on antisemitism, *Österreichische Zeitschrift für Geschichtswissenschaft*, 3 (1992), pp. 421–599.
[5]Herbert Rosenkranz, *Verfolgung und Selbstbehauptung. Die Juden in Österreich 1938–1945*, Vienna–Munich 1978, p. 161.
[6]Innsbruck, Private Archive Edwin Tangl: SD Unterabschnitt, SS Untersturmführer Fast, to Gauleitung Tirol, 19th September 1938. This private archive was set up by Edwin Tangl a former resistance fighter, and is not open to the public. .

maltreated: Karl Bauer, Alfred Graubart and the engineer Richard Graubart.[7] At the time of this meeting, none of them could have imagined an imminent act of violence directed against Jews.

As is well known, however, following Herschel Grynszpan's assassination attempt on Ernst vom Rath (which was itself a consequence of the Nazi expulsion of Polish Jews from Germany),[8] violent excesses had already taken place in several small locations in Kurhessen and Magdeburg-Anhalt.[9] Vom Rath's death on 9th November,[10] providing Goebbels with an immediate goad for instigating violent antisemitism.

THE INNSBRUCK POGROM AND ITS VICTIMS

In the Nazi Party region (*Gau*) Tyrol-Vorarlberg, the pogrom centred on Innsbruck, the capital of the region (*Gauhauptstadt*). This has been documented and the identities of its Jewish victims have been established. A report about the events of the night from 9th to 10th November by the SS Region (*Oberabschnitt*) Danube concluded that the "operations" in Innsbruck were set in motion around 3.30 a.m. "without any warning whatever" and that "three Jews were killed" and "virtually all Jews were wounded".[11]

Who were the victims of these murders and the persons most affected? The chairman of the Jewish community, *Oberbaurat* Richard Berger, an engineer formerly with the Federal Railway, was apprehended at his home at Anich Str. 5 and taken to a place outside the city. There he was brutally beaten with fists and pistols and finally stoned to death. His corpse was thrown into the River Inn in order to erase all traces of the crime.[12]

Murder was also committed at Gänsbacher Str. 5, where the victims were the merchant and head of the Jewish trade organisation, Dr. Wilhelm Bauer, and the engineer Richard Graubart. Mrs. Graubart telephoned for the physician Dr. Luis Brenn in the early hours of 10th November. When the doctor arrived, Bauer

---

[7]*Ibid.*, Copy of List 1. For the accuracy of the list, see Landesgericht (LG) Innsbruck, Abteilung 10, 9th May 1947. Among the others summoned were the brothers Rudolf and Josef Brüll. See the interview with Ingeborg Brüll, tape in possession of the Innsbruck *Institut für Zeitgeschichte*.
[8]Lauber, *Judenpogrom*, pp. 54–58. See also Sybil Milton, 'The Expulsion of the Polish Jews from Germany, 1938', in *LBI Year Book XXIX* (1984), pp. 169–199.
[9]Lauber, *Judenpogrom*, p. 74.
[10]Wolfgang Benz, 'Der Rückfall in die Barbarei. Bericht über den Pogrom', in Pehle (ed.), *Der Judenpogrom 1938*, p. 25.
[11]Private Archive Edwin Tangl: SS Oberabschnitt Donau II 112, 'Erfahrungsbericht über die Aktionen gegen die Juden in der Zeit vom 9. bis 11. November 1938', 21st November 1938; copy also in LG Innsbruck, files Vr 1119/64/II.
[12]Volksgericht (VG) beim LG Innsbruck, Urteil gg. Walter Hopfgartner, Vg 10 Vr 744/50 (HV 215/50), 20th September 1950, pp. 1–7. See also Wolfgang Plat, 'Die Ermordung Richard Bergers', in *Voll Leben und voll Tod ist diese Erde. Bilder aus der Geschichte der jüdischen Österreicher, 1190–1945*, ed. by Wolfgang Plat, Vienna 1988, pp. 266–271. Also of importance is Hans Safrian and Hans Witek, *Und keiner war dabei. Dokumente des alltäglichen Antisemitismus in Wien 1938*, Vienna 1988, a basic study done for the 50th anniversary of the events in Austria of 1938; and Günter Fellner, 'Der Novemberpogrom 1938. Bemerkungen zur Forschung', *Zeitgeschichte*, 16 (November 1988), pp. 35–58.

still showed signs of life, and Dr. Brenn ordered his immediate transfer to the hospital. For both victims, however, all help came too late. Wilhelm Bauer died on the way to the hospital, and Richard Graubart was dead before the doctor arrived.[13]

The Nazi perpetrators also forced their way into the apartment on Anich Str. 5 and battered its residents, the *Oberbaurat* and engineer Josef Adler and his wife. Adler, an active member of the Innsbruck Zionists, was so severely manhandled that he became paralysed; his wife suffered a concussion. The couple's private physician, Dr. Köllensberger, ordered Adler transferred to a neurological clinic, where he died five weeks later.[14] He was the fourth murder victim during this night of the Innsbruck pogrom.

Karl Bauer, co-owner of the department store *Bauer & Schwarz* and head of the local *Bund jüdischer Frontsoldaten*, who lived at Gänsbacher Str. 4 was also assaulted in his apartment. Suffering severe injuries, he was taken to the hospital in the early hours of the morning.[15] The 57-year-old Bauer showed bruises and stab wounds to his face, for which he was treated as an outpatient until 26th February 1939. By cutting the telephone wires, Bauer's assailants had prevented rapid medical assistance from reaching him.[16] He survived another twenty years, but remained mentally incapacitated.[17]

In addition to the four murder victims, many other Jews were physically maltreated. The engineer Alfred Graubart, who lived at Haydnplatz 8, was physically attacked at about 3.30 a.m. Men demanded to be let in, proceeded to lock up his wife, and severely abused Graubart. There was no way to get medical help since the intruders had cut the telephone wires and locked up the house. Using cold compresses, Mrs. Graubart took care of her unconscious and heavily bleeding husband as best she could until Graubart, who had suffered facial injuries and a concussion, regained consciousness at around 6.30 a.m. Half an hour later the news reached Alfred Graubart that his brother Richard had been murdered.[18]

Altogether eighteen Jews were arrested. According to the SD, all of them "were persons fit for work". Almost all were injured, one of them even "quite severely". Among those taken into custody were a husband and wife named Popper, who, after their apartment had been wrecked, were thrown into the

---

[13]On Bauer, see Innsbruck, Archiv des Bundes der Opfer des politischen Freiheitskampfes in Tirol (hereafter BDO): Bericht des Sicherheitsdirektors für Tirol, Regierungspolizei, 7th September 1945. On Graubart, see VG beim LG Innsbruck, Vg 20 Vr 876/61, 20th March 1961: Margarete Graubart, Innsbruck, 'Bericht über die Vorgänge des 10. November 1938 im Haus Gänsbacherstraße 5', p. 117.

[14]VG beim LG Innsbruck, Vg 20 Vr 876/61, p. 119: Gertrude Adler to Israelitische Kultusgemeinde, 17th February 1961; interview with Josef Adler's son, the engineer Felix Adler, 1988, tape in the possession of the author.

[15]BDO: Memorandum of the Bundespolizeidirektion Innsbruck, Staatspolizeiliche Abteilung, 14th February 1946, pp. 1–3, concerning Haftbericht Alois Schintlholzer.

[16]VG beim LG Innsbruck, Beschluß der Ratskammer des LG Innsbruck, betr. Strafsache gg. Alois Schintlholzer, 10 Ns 2149/62, Vg 20 Vr 876/61, 16th May 1962, pp. 21–22.

[17]Maria-Luise Stainer, '"Wir werden den Juden schon eintunken!" Ein Beitrag zur Geschichte der Juden in Innsbruck, Vorarlbergs und des übrigen Tirol', *Sturzflüge*, 15–16 (1986), p. 30.

[18]VG beim LG Innsbruck, Vg 10 Vr 104/46, pp. 46–47: Testimony of Maria Graubart, 3rd July 1945.

River Sill; they saved themselves, however, by swimming to the banks of the river.[19]

During the night of the pogrom, virtually all homes "of Jews who had not yet emigrated [were] heavily damaged". As the SD stated laconically: "If some Jews suffered no damage in this operation (*Aktion*), then it is probably because they were overlooked." In two cases, as the SD also ascertained, the property of "Aryans" had been wrecked: in the first because the racial ancestry of the owner was unknown, and in the second because "the apartment had only recently come into Aryan hands".[20] Indeed, the houses of Innerebner and Mayr were attacked, as was later established, "and there, due to a mix-up, non-Jews were also affected".[21] Furthermore, the Jewish synagogue in the Straße der Sudetendeutschen (today Sillgasse) was forced open, and its furnishings were demolished.[22]

Altogether eighteen persons were physically attacked, and two stores were looted. Damage to property amounted to RM 200,000.[23] On 14th November 1938 SS-*Obersturmführer* Dr. Karl Gelb, chief of the SS District of the Tyrol, reported to the chief of SS Region Danube that "an operation [was] carried out only in the capital of the region, Innsbruck", because "the number of Jews living in the countryside of the Tyrol and Vorarlberg is extraordinarily low".[24] Only in Ehrwald was a guest house damaged to the amount of RM 300 because the owner's wife was Jewish.[25]

THE ROLE OF THE NAZI PARTY REGIONAL LEADER

Surviving documents permit a relatively clear reconstruction of the conduct of *Gauleiter* Franz Hofer at the time of the "*Kristallnacht*" in Innsbruck. Nevertheless, such men as Klaus Mahnert, at the time of the pogrom Nazi district leader (*Kreisleiter*) stationed at Kitzbühel, still think it is an "open question" as to who was "ultimately responsible" for the excesses. According to Mahnert, Hofer himself declared at the time, as well as after 1945, that he had left the 9th November anniversary celebration of the Hitler *Putsch* in Munich only after 1.00 a.m. on the 10th, "and thus arrived in Innsbruck only after everything was

---

[19]BDO: SD-Unterabschnitt Tirol (Fast) to SD-Führer des SS-Oberabschnittes Donau-Wien, 12th November 1938.
[20]*Ibid.*
[21]VG beim LG Innsbruck, Vg 10 Vr 104/46, pp. 48–55: Interrogation of Dr. Herbert Mannlicher, 24th Octobr 1945.
[22]BDO: Bericht des Sicherheitsdirektors für Tirol, Regierungspolizei, 7th September 1945, pp. 1–17. A commemorative stone, only placed there decades after 1945, could be found in place of the old synagogue. However, it was positioned in such a way that pedestrians could not easily see it. A new synagogue has now been built on the site. Also see note 147.
[23]*Widerstand und Verfolgung in Tirol*, vol. I, p. 424.
[24]Private Archive Edwin Tangl: SS Obersturmführer Gelb, SD-Unterabschnitt Tirol, to SD-Führer, SS-Oberabschnitt Donau, 14th November 1938.
[25]*Widerstand und Verfolgung in Tirol*, vol. I, p. 453: Chronik des Gendarmeriepostens Ehrwald, 13th November 1938.

over".²⁶ But the facts found in the relevant documents (reports from the SD District of the Tyrol, the SD chief of SS Region Danube, and the Supreme Party Court) do not support this version of the story in any way, indeed they clearly contradict it.

SS-*Untersturmführer* Gustav Fast, at the time acting as deputy for Gelb, who was away on official business, described in a report how he was asked to come to Hofer's office at 1.00 a.m. on the morning of 10th November. Upon arriving from Munich at around that time, Hofer met with SS-*Oberführer* Hanns von Feil; SA-*Brigadeführer* Vinzenz Waidacher; the chief of the *Ordnungs- und Sicherheitspolizei* in Innsbruck, SS-*Hauptsturmführer* Dr. Spann from the Innsbruck *Gestapo* office; SS-*Untersturmführer* Dr. Adolf Franzelin of the *Polizeidirektion*; Hermann Duxneuner, Plenipotentiary for Aryanisation; and Fast himself as the representative of the SD in the Tyrol. Hofer announced that, "in response to the cowardly Jewish assassination of our embassy counsellor vom Rath in Paris", it is necessary "also in the Tyrol" that in this night "the seething soul of the people (*kochende Volksseele*) rise against the Jews". But looting should be prevented and damage to "Aryan property" should be avoided. At the end of the "operation", the Jews "are to be taken into protective custody for their own security". This "seething soul of the people" was to have "full freedom of action" until 6.00 a.m. Until that time the police "should appear nowhere near the demonstrators".²⁷ At the meeting Dr. Spann received a teletype from Reinhard Heydrich in Munich containing the well-known directives on how the *Gestapo* and the SD were to respond to the pogrom.²⁸

Thus, Hofer not only knew of the incidents of the "*Kristallnacht*" in Innsbruck but was also implicated in them; that is, he took a leading role in issuing orders

[26]Klaus Mahnert, *Mildernde Umstände. Bericht über den Lebensabschnitt 1913–1945*, Innsbruck 1977, p. 90. This is an unpublished manuscript in my possession. In connection with *Gauleiter* Hofer's complicity, Mahnert also mentions that there had been long proceedings against Hofer by the German de-Nazification court. Hofer was allegedly acquitted on the basis of testimony given by his former driver, Fritz Popp, and the SS leader from Innsbruck, Eberhard Quirsfeld. Popp and Quirsfeld, both of them present at the Munich celebration, are said to have confirmed that together with Hofer they arrived in Innsbruck long after 1.00 a.m. and the events of the "*Kristallnacht*". But I would argue that witnesses who are less suspect than these two men would be more credible; it seems quite evident that they made statements to favour the accused. In 1945, while interned by the Allies at Dachau, Hofer declared that he had no personal knowledge of the events of the "*Reichskristallnacht*", but Mahnert conceded that this was said within a certain context and "at that time we were on the defensive". Interview with Klaus Mahnert, 1988, tape in my possession.

[27]Private Archive Edwin Tangl: Memorandum of SS Untersturmführer Fast, 12th November 1938. See also Herbert Rosenkranz, "*Reichskristallnacht*". *9. November 1938 in Österreich*, Vienna–Frankfurt–Zurich 1968, pp. 52–53; Erika Weinzierl, *Zu wenige Gerechte. Österreicher und Judenverfolgung, 1938–1945*, 2nd edn., Graz–Vienna–Cologne 1985, pp. 57–59. It was not Fast, however, as Weinzierl states, who was chief of the SD District Tyrol, but Dr. Karl Gelb. Furthermore, not Karl Bauer but Dr. Wilhelm Bauer was killed during the night of the pogrom. See Vienna, Dokumentationsarchiv des Österreichischen Widerstandes (hereafter DÖW), file 9333: Amtsgericht Köln, interrogation of Gustav Fast, 28th April 1964. Regarding Hofer's role, Fast stated that "from the time of Austria's incorporation to about 1941 I was a member of the SD District Innsbruck and worked on questions of organisation and personnel. In November 1938 I had the rank of SS-*Untersturmführer*. I was present at the meeting held on the night of 9th–10th November in the office of the *Gauleiter*... I was officially requested to attend the meeting, and the *Gauleiter* himself, that is, the accused, was present at the meeting. But I cannot today say when he arrived and whether he came from Munich."

[28]Weinzierl, *Zu wenige Gerechte*, p. 59.

for the pogrom. Furthermore, a report of the SD leader of SS Region Danube shows that in Innsbruck the SD and the *Gestapo*, as well as the police, the SS, SA and the Party, "were already informed of the forthcoming operations at around 1.00 a.m. on 10th November by *Gauleiter* Hofer, who had by then returned from Munich". According to this report, Hofer "had asked the various authorities who were to take part in the operation to meet at 1.00 a.m. in his office, where he announced the guidelines".[29] One of the SS men involved in the assault on Richard Berger later stated that

> "I only heard later, that is two or three days after the operation, that a meeting of the Nazi *Gauleiter* had taken place in Munich and that Hofer returned to Innsbruck that night supposedly to issue his instructions."[30]

To solve the question of Hofer's role during the night of the pogrom, it is necessary briefly to consider the Party celebration in Munich that he attended. Every year on 9th November, the Nazi Party commemorated the abortive Hitler *Putsch* of 1923 in the old town hall of Munich. The celebration always culminated in the social gathering, the *Kameradschaftsabend*, when the old Party veterans, the so-called *"Alte Kämpfer"*, congregated around their *Führer*. Around 9.00 p.m. Hitler received the news that vom Rath had succumbed to his injuries. Hitler left the meeting after a lengthy talk with Goebbels, and, at approximately 10.00 p.m., Goebbels announced the death of vom Rath and made his maliciously antisemitic speech culminating in an appeal for revenge and retaliation. The assembled *Gauleiter* and SA chiefs gained the impression from this speech that it was up to them to take action.

Goebbels achieved the intended result without issuing an express order for a pogrom. He stimulated the latent antisemitic mood in such a way that the Party chiefs thought they were expected to launch pogroms against the Jews. As was learned later from the investigations conducted by the *Parteigericht*, Goebbels had designed his speech to be the signal for the attack against the Jews and, with Hitler's knowledge and approval, had "ignited the fuse".[31] The Party leaders interpreted Goebbels's speech in the sense that, while organising the pogroms, the Party itself should not appear to the outside world as the actual instigator.

After the *Kameradschaftsabend* was cut short at about 10.30 p.m., the Nazi regional leaders contacted their headquarters and local offices from the town hall and instructed them more or less exactly as to the operations that were being planned.[32] The *Oberstes Parteigericht* (Supreme Party Court) later found that Hofer had also listened to Goebbels's speech and thus gained the impression that "this was to be quite a far-reaching operation against the Jews" so that – in

---

[29] Private Archive Edwin Tangl: 'Erfahrungsbericht', 21st November 1938.

[30] VG beim LG Innsbruck, Vg 10 Vr 2372/50, Bundespolizeidirektion Innsbruck, interrogation of Walter Hopfgartner, 1st April 1950.

[31] Benz, 'Der Rückfall in die Barbarei', pp. 18–19; Uwe Dietrich Adam, 'Wie spontan war der Pogrom?', in Pehle (ed.), *Der Judenpogrom 1938*, pp. 76–77. See also Hans Jürgen Döscher, 'Der Tod Ernst vom Raths und die Auslösung der Pogrome am 9. November 1938. Ein Nachwort zur "Reichskristallnacht"', *Geschichte in Wissenschaft und Unterricht*, 41 (1990), pp. 619–620, who has concluded that Hitler had received news of vom Rath's death prior to 9.00 p.m. and therefore staged his "surprise".

[32] Adam, 'Wie spontan war der Pogrom?', p. 77.

Hofer's own words – "Jewry will be done away with". Further, "still on the same night of 9th–10th November", Hofer issued instructions "to his subordinate chiefs in Innsbruck". On his arrival there, he declared "that the male Jews are to be given a good and proper beating". The impression he also got in Munich that "it would not matter that much whether one or the other Jew was killed" was reinforced by the *Gestapo* order "to protect the life and property of Aryans". The directives of the Ministry of Propaganda yet to follow had a similar effect on Hofer.[33] In short, the Nazi leader of the Tyrol not only received precise information about events in Innsbruck; he also played a leading role in issuing the order for a pogrom. In view of Hofer's prominent position, any other interpretation would be quite improbable. The 1947 arrest warrant for the fugitive Hofer is thus absolutely correct: "He is responsible for the execution of the Jewish pogrom of 9th November 1938, which he ordered to be implemented in agreement with the highest leadership of the *Reich*."[34]

THE PERPETRATORS AND THEIR CRIMES

During the night from 9th to 10th November, a swearing-in of the General SS took place throughout the *Reich*; at midnight *Reich* Leader SS Heinrich Himmler administered the oath via radio. In Innsbruck the SS formations of the entire battalion (*Sturmbann*) were sworn in at the so-called Adolf-Hitler-Platz, where they had taken up their positions. In the absence of SS-*Obersturmführer* Josef Pfefferkorn, the *de facto* leader of the battalion, SS-*Hauptsturmführer* Hans Aichinger was appointed to administer the oath and to notify SS-*Standartenführer* Erwin Fleiss, who then passed on the report to SS-*Oberführer* Hanns von Feil.[35]

After the ceremony the leaders of the various companies were ordered to report to von Feil, who informed them of the death of vom Rath, adding that a popular uprising could therefore be expected against the Jews living in Innsbruck and the SS would be called upon to maintain order. The companies were to hold themselves ready at their meeting places, while veteran SS men selected from the various companies were to prepare for immediate disposition. The latter were told to change into civilian clothing and go to the offices of the SS District, where they would receive further special instruction.[36] Around 2.30 a.m., the SS, having been supplied with lists of Jews by Plenipotentiary Duxneuner, set out systematically to violate Jews – their persons as well as their possessions.[37]

---

[33] Berlin Document Center (hereafter BDC): Beschluß des Sondersenats des Obersten Parteigerichts betreffend Einstellung des Verfahrens gegen SS-Hauptsturmführer Hans Aichinger und SS-Untersturmführer Walter Hopfgartner wegen Mordes an Richard Graubart, Wilhelm Bauer und Richard Berger, 9th February 1939.

[34] DÖW, file 9333; LG Innsbruck, 10 Vr 4944/47–3, Strafverfahren gg. Franz Hofer, order of arrest, 14th December 1947.

[35] BDO: Bericht des Sicherheitsdirektors für Tirol, Regierungspolizei, 7th September 1945, p. 9.

[36] Staatsanwaltschaft (StA) Innsbruck, Anklageschrift gg. Hans Aichinger und Gottfried Andreaus, St 8705/45, 16th August 1946, p. 98.

[37] *Widerstand und Verfolgung in Tirol*, vol. I, p. 451: Memorandum of SS Untersturmführer Fast, SD-Unterabschnitt Tirol, 12th November 1938.

Once the SS men had appeared in civilian clothing, they received an order from von Feil, in the presence of Fleiss, to proceed to Gänsbacher Str. 4 and 5. In retaliation for the murder of the German diplomat in Paris, they were to "kill (*umlegen*) with as little noise as possible" the male members of the Jewish families living there, that is, Karl Bauer, Dr. Wilhelm Bauer and engineer Richard Graubart. This group of SS men received further instructions from Fleiss on how to carry out the murders and thereafter left immediately. They were joined by other SS men assigned to participate in the pogrom, who had been assembled nearby. Thus, every one of the SS men detailed for the pogrom was informed about the plan either during the meeting or on the way to the scene of the crime.[38] The stenographic notes taken during questioning on 10th November of the murdered men's wives, Edith Bauer and Margarete Graubart, showed that the assault took place shortly before or at 3.00 a.m.[39]

The leader of the raid on Graubart and Bauer was SS-*Hauptsturmführer* Hans Aichinger. Other participants included *Obersturmführer* Rudolf Schwarz; SS-*Stabsscharführer* Benno Bisjak; SS-*Untersturmführer* Rudolf Exner; and the *Oberscharführer* Franz Dobringer, Gottfried Andreaus and Herbert Rendl. The following were strongly suspected of complicity: SS-*Obersturmführer* Alois Schintlholzer, SS-*Oberscharführer* Robert Huttig and Hans Müller, SS-*Scharführer* Walter Saurwein and SS member Ferdinand Kurz.[40]

The SS commando arrived as one unit at Gänsbacher Str. 5, whereupon Schintlholzer and his group separated and went to Gänsbacher Str. 4 to carry out their order to kill the merchant Karl Bauer. During the attack Bauer received severe injuries as he was punched many times and stabbed three times in the head. He survived only because the perpetrators thought him dead or, at least, that he would die from his wounds.[41] After 1945 Schintlholzer admitted after repeated questions that not only he but also his companions had beaten Bauer. One of them even used a coal shovel to hit the victim's head. Suffering a severe concussion and other injuries, Bauer was then taken to the hospital.[42] Concerning his orders, Schintlholzer commented:

> "I admit that at that time, during the *Kristallnacht*, together with other SS officers, I received instructions at the *Hochhaus* in Innsbruck from regional leader Feil to kill the Jews on Gänsbacher Str. silently. The order was given to us there after the general swearing-in ceremony of the Innsbruck SS . . . We had to appear dressed in civilian clothing. Altogether three Jews were to be murdered: Graubart, Dr. Bauer and the merchant Bauer. The killing commandos were led separately, that is, in three groups."[43]

It was thought probable that after leading the assault on Karl Bauer, Schintlholzer also participated in the murders at Gänsbacher Str. 5 (Richard Graubart

---

[38]StA Innsbruck, Anklage Aichinger und Andreaus, St 8705/45, 16th August 1946, pp. 98–99.

[39]VG beim LG Innsbruck, Vg 10 Vr 104/46, Testimonies of Edith Bauer and Grete Graubart, 10th November 1938.

[40]BDO: Bericht des Sicherheitsdirektors für Tirol, Regierungspolizei, 7th September 1945, pp. 10–12.

[41]StA Innsbruck, Anklage Aichinger und Andreaus, St 8705/45, 16th August 1946, p. 99; VG beim LG Innsbruck, Vg 10 Vr 2372/50, Interrogation of Walter Hopfgartner, 1st April 1950, p. 4.

[42]VG beim LG Innsbruck, Vg 20 Vr 876/61, Interrogation of Alois Schintlholzer, 7th November and 19th December 1961, pp. 16–19.

[43]*Ibid.*, Interrogation of Alois Schintlholzer, 21st April 1961, p. 7.

and Dr. Wilhelm Bauer). This, at any rate, can be gathered from the arrest warrant issued in 1957 by the District Court of Innsbruck.[44]

At the time of the Schintlholzer assault at number 4, Aichinger and his men forced their way into the villa at number 5 next door, occupied on the first floor by Dr. Wilhelm Bauer and his wife Edith, and on the second floor by the engineer Richard Graubart and his wife Grete. The SS intruders climbed over the fence into the garden, rang the bell, forced the caretaker who opened the door to disappear into his basement apartment, and then went to the second floor. There Graubart opened the door. They pushed him into his bedroom and, while ordering him to get dressed and go with them, they took him unawares and killed him. Graubart was evidently stabbed in the back with an SS dagger, for his corpse revealed an approximately three-centimetre-long wound that was inflicted by a double-edged weapon and must have led to his immediate death from the heavy loss of blood. The killers locked the wife and daughter of the victim in a room, from which they were released only much later.[45]

On the first floor, Wilhelm Bauer, awakened by the ringing of the bell and still scantily dressed, opened the door and was immediately seized by the SS men; they dragged him into the hall, stabbed him, and beat him with their pistols, while one of them kept his wife in the bedroom. She heard her husband cry out that he had been stabbed and needed a doctor, but her SS guard took the telephone out of her hand. After the raiders had left, she managed to call a physician who ordered Bauer to be taken to the hospital; as many of his vital organs had been punctured, Bauer died on the way.[46]

After participating in the assault on Richard Graubart and Wilhelm Bauer at Gänsbacher Str. 5, the truck driver Gottfried Andreaus went to the synagogue, which had already been destroyed by the SS. There he saw the SS officer Walter Linser standing on a scaffold and ripping the Star of David from the ceiling. Many of the damaged furnishings of the synagogue were scattered in the courtyard.[47]

Concerning the killings of Richard Graubart and Wilhelm Bauer, Aichinger testified after 1945 that Franz Dobringer and Benno Bisjak "were the real murderers in question".[48] As Graubart even knew Bisjak personally, he loudly beseeched Bisjak not to harm him. But, according to Aichinger, this was precisely the reason impelling Bisjak "to silence Graubart (*mundtot zu machen*)", while, as was corroborated by Gottfried Andreaus, Dobringer apparently inflicted on Dr. Wilhelm Bauer a lethal stab wound with an SS dagger.[49]

---

[44]*Ibid.*, Arrest order for Alois Schintlholzer, 13th December 1957, p. 7.

[45]StA Innsbruck, Anklage Aichinger und Andreaus, St 8705/45, 16th August 1946, pp. 99–100; *Tiroler Nachrichten*, 226 (16th October 1946), p. 2.

[46]StA Innsbruck, Anklage Aichinger und Andreaus, St 8705/45, 16th August 1946, pp. 100–101.

[47]VG beim LG Innsbruck, Vg 10 Vr 104/46, Interrogation of Gottfried Andreaus, 23rd August 1945, pp. 65–66.

[48]VG beim LG Innsbruck, Vg 10 Vr 104/46, Belastungsangaben concerning Franz Dobringer (case Vg 10 Vr 2372/50), 16th January 1951.

[49]VG beim LG Innsbruck, Vg 10 Vr 104/46, Interrogation of Hans Aichinger, 17th August 1945, p. 83; BDO: Bericht des Sicherheitsdirektors für Tirol, Regierungspolizei, 7th September 1945, p. 12.

Aichinger also identified the perpetrators who attacked Richard Berger as the SS men Walter Hopfgartner and Dr. Gerhard Lausegger, as well as two other men, named Meier and Weichert.[50] The lawyer Dr. Lausegger, who had been given the special commission "to do away" with Berger, was a member of the student corporation *Suevia*, commander of the SS student company (*Studentensturm*), and a former adjutant of Fleiss. His assault commando included, among others, the SS-*Untersturmführer* Robert Duy and Walter Hopfgartner; Duy, a student from St. Pölten, studied medicine at the University of Innsbruck. Their victim was the engineer Richard Berger, the long-term president of the local Zionist chapter, as well as chairman of the Jewish community in Innsbruck.

Berger was rudely awakened after midnight in his home on Anich Str. and, dressed only in pyjamas and a winter coat, was taken away by Lausegger's SS commando. Under the pretext of taking Berger to the *Gestapo*, the SS men drove towards Kranebitten, to the west of Innsbruck, in order to kill him there. One of the perpetrators, Hopfgartner, thus recalled the fatal journey:

> "We drove west through Anich Strasse, over the university bridge, in the direction of Kranebitten. During the trip, Berger asked where we were going, since this was not the way to the *Gestapo*. Berger, who, understandably, was somewhat nervous, was calmed down by the men in the back of the car, and there was no further discussion. We were probably still in the Kranebitter Allee or had just left the part of the city called Höttingerau, when suddenly Lausegger announced in a voice sufficiently loud so that all could hear him, that 'no firearms are to be used'. This upset Berger again and he asked what we wanted from him, but he was quietened down again . . . After Lausegger's statement, I realised immediately that Berger was to be killed."[51]

In fact, shortly thereafter the car stopped on a bend near the Inn, and the SS men dragged the protesting and struggling Berger out of the car and brutally battered him. They hammered at his head with their fists and pistols and struck him with stones until he no longer moved. They then threw him into the river and Duy, counter to instructions, fired several shots at him. As the *Gestapo* established later, Duy hit Berger in the back, but the victim must have been dead already.[52]

Though the SS played the major role in the Innsbruck pogrom, other Nazi Party organisations were also active. Already on the evening of 9th November several roll calls took place separately for the SS, SA and the *Nationalsozialistisches Kraftfahrer Korps* (NSKK); the roll for the SA and NSKK was called at the *Standartenheim* at Bürger Straße 10 in Innsbruck. Messengers had earlier told the participants to report dressed in civilian clothing. SA-*Brigadeführer* Vinzenz Waidacher probably instructed SA-*Standartenführer* Johann Mathoi to announce the death of vom Rath and inform the assembled groups that Supreme SA Command had ordered measures in retaliation against the Jews, which were to be carried out by the SS in co-operation with the SA. Calling on all the "participants in this operation" to give the Jews "a good hard" thrashing, Mathoi left it up to the men as to how they would satisfy their need for revenge. There

---

[50] VG beim LG Innsbruck, Vg 10 Vr 104/46, Interrogation of Hans Aichinger, 17th August 1945, p. 83.
[51] VG beim LG Innsbruck, Vg 10 Vr 2372/50, Interrogation of Walter Hopfgartner, 1st April 1950.
[52] VG beim LG Innsbruck, Vg 10 Vr 104/46, Interrogation of Gottfried Andreaus, 23rd August 1945, pp. 65–66; Sella, *Die Juden Tirols*, pp. 54–55.

was obviously a great desire for revenge because the question was raised whether killing the Jews was also permitted. In principle, Mathoi approved radical methods and stated explicitly that "these operations will be protected by the *Gestapo*".

Among those attending this roll call were Anton Haupt, Richard Dietrich and Alfred Gnesetti, all from Innsbruck and all members of SA-*Sturm* 5. Following the orders they received, they brutally assaulted Julie and Rudolf Brüll in their home at Anich Str. 7 and Mindel and Ephraim Dimand (Diamant) in their home at Adamgasse 9, inflicting some very serious injuries. After 1945 the defendants Haupt and Dietrich testified that the leader of their group had been SA-*Hauptscharführer* Rosenbaum, a master printer at the former Nazi regional publishing house, who was allegedly killed during the war. Gnesetti, however, named *Obersturmführer* Stanzl, a prisoner-of-war who at that time had not yet returned to Austria, as heading his group.[53]

Furthermore, according to investigations conducted after the war, *Obersturmführer* Dr. Theodor Tapavicza, Party member since 1933, who had been cofounder of the SA medical company (*Sanitätssturm*) in Innsbruck and a doctor in the Austrian Legion, also participated in the persecutions and the beatings, together with SA-*Scharführer* Max Adermann and Wilhelm Eder and SA-*Hauptscharführer* Dr. Hubert Stoiber. On the evening of 9th November, they were told by Mathoi and Waidacher "that the Jews living in Innsbruck were to be 'routed and beaten' in retaliation for the murder of Counsellor vom Rath by a Jew". The highest Party authorities then organised several squads of eight to ten SA men, who received slips of paper with the addresses of the Jews to be attacked. The SA squad led by Wilhelm Eder forced their way into the apartment of Dr. Eduard Fuchs in Museum Str., while the one led by Tapavicza raided the residences of Alfred Graubart and of Gottlieb and Jutta Fuchs in the Haydnplatz. Whether and from whom Dr. Eduard Fuchs suffered a broken nose could not be determined with certainty. At the preliminary hearings, Tapavicza stated that a few SA men, "primarily students, had [also] joined in the operation against the Jews". All of them had to be dressed as civilians in order to attract as little attention as possible for fear of a reaction from abroad.[54]

The incidents in Innsbruck did, in fact, interest foreign diplomatic representatives and created such a stir that even Nogaret, the French consul in Munich, heard about them. Already on 14th November, he was relatively well-informed about the events in the regional capital of the Tyrol and cabled the following message to the Quai d'Orsay:

> "I understand from reliable sources that on the night of 9th–10th November antisemitic demonstrations took place in Innsbruck. The participants, wearing civilian clothing, forced their way into the houses of Jews and smashed and destroyed the furnishings. There are a large number of victims of this aggression, many of whom had to be taken to the hospital.

---

[53] *Tiroler Tageszeitung*, 190 (1946); *Tiroler Neue Zeitung*, 161 (1946); *Volkszeitung*, 190 (1946).
[54] VG beim LG Innsbruck, Vg 10 Vr 651/46, 102, Beschluß des LG Innsbruck, 27th November 1946; Innsbruck, Universitätsarchiv, File Theodor Tapavicza: Prof. Herdltczka to Medizinisches Dekanat, 22nd October 1956.

Seven [sic] were killed; two were drowned in the river flowing through the city [sic].[55] The synagogue and Jewish stores have also been destroyed."[56]

In addition to minor inaccuracies, Nogaret's report also shows that it was not clearly recognised that this pogrom, decreed from above, had been systematically planned.

The secret report of 12th November from the SD District of the Tyrol to SD leader of SS Region Danube, according to which on the night of 9th–10th November "the people suddenly went into action against the Jews in Innsbruck",[57] demonstrates that even internally the Nazi authorities tried to fool themselves into thinking that the pogrom was initiated by the "people".

THE SOCIAL BACKGROUND OF THE PERPETRATORS

A closer look at the perpetrators who attacked Richard Graubart and Wilhelm Bauer shows that, without exception, all of them had been long-standing members of the Nazi Party and of the SS during the period it was illegal and that they had all been active in the vanguard of those waging the political fight for National Socialism in Austria. They were, above all, ideologically committed and fanatic followers of Hitler who had served long prison terms in the period of the Austrian corporate state (*Ständestaat*). The SS personnel records of the perpetrators contain evaluations for promotion that repeatedly describe them as "in every respect a true SS man, ready for action and very capable", one of "the most capable men", "a very diligent SS man who is always available when needed", "a valued veteran" (*verdienter Kämpfer*), an SS man "recommended for promotion on the basis of special achievements" or as "bearer of the *Reichsführers* dagger of honour, the death's head ring of the SS", and so on.[58]

Hans Aichinger, the leader of the squad that attacked Richard Graubart and Wilhelm Bauer, was the son of Innsbruck tavern owners, worked as a skiing instructor and in the tavern business, and became a particularly dedicated Nazi and active SS man in the period of illegality. Shortly before the Party was again legalised, Aichinger showed himself to be one of the most energetic SS lieutenants. Only a few days after the *Anschluß*, Aichinger was promoted from SS-*Untersturmführer* to *Hauptsturmführer* because of his special accomplishments during the period of illegality. The promotion brought him to the attention of prominent Nazis in Innsbruck, because one had to be particularly "outstanding"

---

[55]The writer probably referred to Mr. and Mrs. Popper.
[56]Paris, Ministère des Affaires Etrangères, Sèrie Z-Europe 1930–40, Allemagne, vol. 707, fol. 115: 'Télégramme à l'arrivée de M. Nogaret, Munich le 14 Novembre 1938 à 13 h. 25, Reçu le 14 h. 45'. Klaus Eisterer of Innsbruck has kindly directed my attention to this document, for which I thank him.
[57]BDO: SD-Unterabschnitt Tirol to SD Führer des SS-Oberabschnittes Donau-Wien, 12th November 1938.
[58]BDO: Report of the Bundespolizeidirektion Innsbruck, Staatspolizeiliche Abteilung, 3rd May 1946, pp. 18–25.

to miss out an officer rank in the SS. Thus, Aichinger was presented to Hitler when the *Führer* visited Innsbruck on 5th April 1938.[59]

Already during the so-called period of struggle (*Kampfzeit*), Aichinger had been "an especially reliable SS officer". As a member of the German Gymnastics Club (*Deutsche Turnerschaft*) (1929) and the Alpine Club (*Alpenverein*) (1930), he had long been familiar with the German *völkisch* ideology. Ideological conviction and economic reasons led Aichinger to join the Nazi Party on 5th May 1932. He believed that National Socialism "is really good for us Austrians and will help us get ahead economically". He joined the Party against parental wishes and while still a minor. In summer 1933 Aichinger joined the illegal SS, as did the majority of the young members of the *Deutsche Turnerschaft* (DT).[60] After he was promoted to SS-*Untersturmführer* during the time it was banned, Aichinger took command of the Innsbruck SS battalion, consisting at that time of three companies with about 40 to 50 men in each.[61]

Gottfried Andreaus, about whom more will be said below, later transformed himself from a convinced Nazi into an active member of the resistance. He also indicated idealistic motives for joining the Party:

> "I belonged to the Nazi Party from April 1933 because I truly believed that this idea would result in good for us Austrians."[62]

Von Feil, chief of the SS Region of the Tyrol, Vorarlberg and Salzburg, actually gave the command for the Innsbruck pogrom. The son of a tax official, he came from Upper Austria (Leonfelden-Linz). After completing his *Gymnasium* studies, he joined the Imperial Habsburg Infantry Regiment (*Kaiserlich-königliches-Schützenregiment*) in April 1915 as a one-year volunteer and served at the front after October 1915. Von Feil participated in the South Tyrolean attack against Italy, the Brussilov offensive in Eastern Galicia, and the battles at Isonzo. After what he considered a disappointing end to the war, von Feil attended the teachers' college in Linz, specialising in drawing, which he later taught at a secondary school. He joined the Nazi Party and the SS in 1932. At a meeting of officers in September 1932, he was promoted by Himmler himself to the rank of captain.

After the abortive July *Putsch* in 1934, von Feil escaped to Czechoslovakia and, together with his wife, moved to the *Reich* in 1935. Working full time for the SS, he lived in Munich, including the SS training camp at Dachau, and in Hamburg. On 21st March 1938, shortly after the *Anschluß*, von Feil assumed command of SS Region XXXVI in Innsbruck, and as SS-*Oberführer*, he gave the command for the murder of the Jews in Innsbruck. In February 1940 he reported for duty with the *Waffen* SS, holding the service rank of SS-*Sturmbannführer* and ultimately reached the rank of colonel. In Poland, Norway, and Italy, he served at the office

---

[59]BDO: Bericht des Sicherheitsdirektors für Tirol, Regierungspolizei, 12th October 1945, pp. 35–36.

[60]VG beim LG Innsbruck, Vg 10 Vr 104/46, Interrogation of Hans Aichinger, 17th August 1945, pp. 78–79; BDC, dossier Hans Aichinger: Race and Resettlement Questionnaire and handwritten Lebenslauf.

[61]StA Innsbruck, Anklage Aichinger und Andreaus, St 8705/45, 16th August 1946, p. 98.

[62]VG beim LG Innsbruck, Vg 10 Vr 104/46, Interrogation of Gottfried Andreaus, 21st August 1945, p. 60.

of the *Höheren SS- und Polizeiführer* (HSSPF). Shortly before the end of the war, von Feil fought in Berlin with the *Waffen* SS.[63]

Erwin Fleiss, also responsible for issuing the orders to kill, came from Innsbruck. He was the son of a senior administrator at the Chemical Institute of the University. Fleiss himself worked as office manager for a firm selling building materials. He had joined the SS already in 1931, had been awarded the *Blutorden*, and belonged to the Nazi Party before it was banned. During the period of illegality, Fleiss spent 42 days in custody and 210 days in the Wöllersdorf Camp. After the *Anschluß* he assumed full-time command of SS Regiment 87 with the rank of *Obersturmbannführer*. He led the regiment (*Standarte*) for over a year and in April 1938 entered the "*Reichstag* of Greater Germany". In 1942 Fleiss joined the armed forces, where he reached the rank of lieutenant.[64]

It was no accident that Dr. Gerhard Lausegger, the person selected to lead the squad that killed the chairman of the Jewish community, had been a member of the student corporations, the *Burschenschaften*. Student antisemitism in Austria, especially among the student corporations, had a long-standing tradition dating back to the years before 1918. It was particularly pronounced during the interwar period; at that time radical racial antisemites could be found especially among academics. Lausegger, a native of Klagenfurt who had been an active member of *Suevia* between 1934 and 1938, was one of those racial antisemites. He had been expelled from the *Gymnasium* in Carinthia and was later suspended for two semesters from the university. In 1936 he was kept in custody for three months and shortly before the *Anschluß* spent eight days arrested on remand. An SS officer during the "*Kampfzeit*", he also served as illegal leader of the *Nationalsozialistischer Deutscher Studentenbund* (NSDStB) and headed the federation of all duelling corporations at the University of Innsbruck. In his capacity as commander of the *Studentensturm*, he participated in the occupation of the *Landhaus* on the eve of 11th March 1938, that is, shortly before the arrival of the German troops.[65]

The close personal ties between the *Suevia*, whose members participated in the SA and SS companies already before 1938, and the SS leadership in the Tyrol continued after the *Anschluß*. Thus, the festive ceremony of the *Suevia* on 14th May 1938 included, next to the rector of the university, such prominent guests as von Feil. Lausegger was, of course, admired by his fellow corporation members long after 1945.[66]

Walter Hopfgartner, who participated in the fatal assault on Richard Berger, was the son of a butcher. From early youth on, he was a member of the Young Workers of Austria, the DT and the Alpine Club. From the Young Workers, a

---

[63]BDO: Bericht des Sicherheitsdirektors für Tirol, Regierungspolizei, 12th October 1945, pp. 37–39; BDC, dossier Hanns von Feil: Lebenslauf, 26th May 1940. See also Nikolaus von Preradovich, *Österreichs höhere SS-Führer*, Berg am See 1987, in part rather one-sided.

[64]BDC, dossier Erwin Fleiss: handwritten Lebenslauf, Innsbruck, 13th March 1941.

[65]Hans Schödl, *Geschichte der akademischen Burschenschaft "Suevia" zu Innsbruck. Nachtrag, 1928–1938*, Innsbruck 1938, p. 35. See also Michael Gehler, *Studenten und Politik. Der Kampf um die Vorherrschaft an der Universität Innsbruck, 1918–1938*, Innsbrucker Forschungen zur Zeitgeschichte, vol. VI, Innsbruck 1990, pp. 93–116, 407, 434, 456.

[66]Schödl, *Geschichte der Burschenschaft Suevia. Nachtrag, 1928–1938*, pp. 30, 40.

kind of predecessor to the Hitler Youth, he moved to the Hitler Youth itself and advanced from there to the SA. At the age of eighteen, he enrolled in the Nazi Party, and on 1st June 1931 he enlisted in the SS. During the period the Nazi Party was banned, Hopfgartner was one of the most active of its illegal members. Hopfgartner described his conversion to National Socialism and his Nazi career prior to the *Anschluß* as follows:

> "I joined the Nazi Party at a very early age, for reasons of idealism, because I believed that progress would be assured. I joined the Party in 1927, and still remember my membership number, 54,701; in this way I later received the decoration of the Nazi Party (Golden Party Insignia). I became a member of the SS already some time before the ban . . . In the period of illegality, I was a member of the SS terror squad and, at the same time, leader of the motorised unit of this squad. The squad consisted of seven or eight members."[67]

This SS terror squad, also called T Group, included the most reliable Nazis and planned assassination attempts against prominent politicians. It also played a considerable role in the *Putsch* operations in the Tyrol around 25th July 1934.[68]

Alois Schintlholzer from Innsbruck, the leader of the assault group against Karl Bauer, was a member of the DT and later a locally known boxer. Under the impact of the battle at the Höttinger meeting hall, he became a member of the Hitler Youth in June 1932 and a Party member in the same year. In December 1932 he joined the SA and in December 1933 transferred to the SS. After his arrest in July 1937, he spent five months on remand pending trial, becoming an even more determined Nazi. Known as a daredevil, Schintlholzer was very active during the *"Kampfzeit"*. During the war he served in the *Waffen* SS, where he advanced to the rank of major and commander of the alpine training camp at Predazzo.[69] In 1979 a Bologna court sentenced him to life imprisonment *in absentia*. According to the court, Schintlholzer was responsible for a retaliatory operation for a partisan attack on the village of Falcade in the province of Belluno. During his punitive raid of 22nd August 1944, the town of Caviola was burned down, and 40 civilians were killed.[70]

As can be seen from these brief résumés, the perpetrators were long-time members of the Party as well as the SS, always ready for action and capable of anything. Thus Aichinger and Hopfgartner, for example, were SS men who, according to their leaders, "were prepared to make any sacrifice for the movement, be it their possessions, be it their lives".[71]

---

[67] VG beim LG Innsbruck, Urteil gg. Walter Hopfgartner, Vg 10 Vr 744/50 (HV 215/50), 20th September 1950, p. 2; Vg 10 Vr 744/50 (HV 215/50), Bundespolizeidirektion, interrogation of Walter Hopfgartner, Innsbruck, 1st April 1950, p. 3; BDC, dossier Walter Hopfgartner: Race and Resettlement Questionnaire and handwritten Lebenslauf, Innsbruck, 8th April 1939.

[68] Harald Walser, 'Der Juli-Putsch 1934', in *Tirol und der Anschluß*, pp. 333–334, 339–344.

[69] VG beim LG Innsbruck, Case of Alois Schintlholzer, Vg 20 Vr 876/61 (HV 702/61); *Widerstand und Verfolgung in Tirol*, vol. I, pp. 461–462; BDC, dossier Alois Schintlholzer: Luis Schintlholzer's Race and Resettlement Questionnaire and handwritten Lebenslauf, n.d.; Predazzo [operational zone in the foot-hills of the Alps] to Schriftleitung des Schwarzen Korps, 6th January 1945.

[70] 'Fall "Schintlholzer" vor Militärgericht', *Tiroler Tageszeitung*, 267 (16th November 1988); 'Lebenslängliche Haft für Alois Schintlholzer', *ibid.*, 268 (17th November 1988); 'Prozeß in Verona gegen einen Innsbrucker Kriegsverbrecher', *Neue Tiroler Tageszeitung*, 266 (15th November 1988).

[71] BDC: Beschluß des Sondersenats des Obersten Parteigerichts betr. Einstellung des Verfahrens gegen SS-Hauptsturmführer Hans Aichinger und SS-Untersturmführer Walter Hopfgartner wegen Mordes an Richard Graubart, Wilhelm Bauer und Richard Berger, 9th February 1939.

NAZI REACTIONS TO THE POGROM

Could the SS men assigned to the assault groups have resisted the murder orders? It is significant that the perpetrators scarcely considered resistance at the time, and even after 1945 they saw it as an impossibility. It occurred to none of them to refuse to obey. From the perspective of those receiving the orders, the testimony of Gottfried Andreaus concerning motives at the time is not untypical:

> "For moral reasons alone, it was hardly feasible to exclude oneself from this affair. Frankly, I must say that the matter was managed in such a way that it was considered a special honour to have been assigned, that is chosen, to do this thing."[72]

Hopfgartner perceived it in a similar way:

> "In practice, it would have been impossible to refuse co-operation in this operation; a refusal would have immediately resulted in expulsion from the SS and I would have been removed from the position to which I was only recently appointed."[73]

Hopfgartner's statement implies that the psychological impact of the swearing-in ceremony, which immediately preceded the pogrom, where everyone pledged eternal loyalty to the Party, affected the behaviour of the perpetrators that night.

The anti-Jewish pogrom was a taboo subject in the inner circle of Nazis and among the perpetrators of the so-called "*Kristallnacht*". A blanket of silence covered the deeds. Looking back on that night, Gottfried Andreaus commented that "this subject was not discussed among us, and even later, therefore, I did not get to know any of the details".[74] Similarly, Aichinger said: "Afterwards the participants no longer talked about the operations in a coherent fashion."[75] Nevertheless, the fact that the Party had planned, ordered and later covered up these murders of Jews was well known among the inner circle of the Nazi movement.

The men assigned to the raiding squads treated their victims with a relentless harshness and brutality that, according to some, they even found surprising themselves. According to the testimony of Irmgard Stecher:

> "My husband had served for many years with the detective forces and in 1938, after the Nazis seized power, he was . . . transferred to the newly established *Gestapo* . . . Around 2.00 a.m. that night [10th November] he was picked up at the apartment by a man from the office . . . My husband had to get ready at once and drive away with him. When he returned home in the morning he seemed so 'shattered' that I knew he must have had a terrible experience. He looked very white, vomited and felt quite ill, and then he gradually recovered . . . When I asked what had happened he did not respond at all, and finally gave me a sort of answer by declaring that, if it were not for his family, he would escape to Switzerland. Later on I found out in the city, in a general way, that there had been pogroms against the Jews and secretly I

---

[72]VG beim LG Innsbruck, Vg 10 Vr 104/46, Interrogation of Gottfried Andreaus, 21st August 1945, pp. 61–62.
[73]VG beim LG Innsbruck, Vg 10 Vr 2372/50, Interrogation of Walter Hopfgartner, Innsbruck, 1st April 1950, p. 8.
[74]VG beim LG Innsbruck, Vg 10 Vr 104/46, Interrogation of Gottfried Andreaus, 21st August 1945, p. 64.
[75]BDO: Memorandum (concerning Hans Aichinger) of Sicherheitsdirektion für Tirol, Regierungspolizei, 12th September 1945, p. 94.

thought to myself that in some way he must have been officially connected with them . . . I did not press him further and soon the whole matter was forgotten bit by bit."[76]

But Stecher's conscience, she claimed, kept troubling him. In December 1941 he was detailed to the Soviet Union for a "political operation". Before he left, she continued, not expecting to return, he had confided specific details of the pogrom night and the names of the perpetrators to her. His very words, she added, were that "this terrible thing must not remain unpunished", and that at the proper time she was to pass on the information to the appropriate office.[77]

While personal experiences during the pogrom evoked repulsion and horror among bystanders, they also led, in some cases, to an inner rejection of National Socialism among the perpetrators. A case in point is Gottfried Andreaus. After his participation in the assaults, he experienced a "noticeable revulsion to the methods of violence and terror used by the *Gestapo*, the SS, etc.". An employee in the administration of the SS since April 1938, Andreaus persistently tried to leave his position. He finally succeeded in finding employment in the city administration and left the SS in March 1939. He subsequently resisted induction into the *Waffen* SS (Death's Head units) and instead managed to be drafted into the *Wehrmacht* in August 1939. Severely wounded in May 1940, he was transferred home to serve at the Military Motor Park in Innsbruck. Having shed his former ideological beliefs, Andreaus, together with Dr. Kurt Egerth and Franz Plattner, joined the resistance in July 1944. In 1945 Andreaus and Egerth captured the transmitting station of the Innsbruck radio as well as the armoury stored in the cellar of the Nazi Party regional headquarters, which, because the American forces had not yet reached the Tyrol, was still in Nazi hands. The arms were then distributed to the resistance.[78]

Only very few of those implicated in the "*Kristallnacht*" subsequently rejected Nazism, but many of them did feel uneasy. Hopfgartner testified during the Party Court proceedings that they had "a very queasy feeling" afterwards, "since we SS men do not particularly enjoy such operations". All of them had simply been following orders.[79] But while the pogrom could still evoke repulsion among the rank and file of the Nazi movement, it was viewed with satisfaction by the leadership. Von Feil, for example, declared himself "satisfied"[80] on hearing Aichinger's report on 10th November describing the assaults on Richard Graubart and Dr. Wilhelm Bauer.

As for the question of purely personal motives, it is quite evident that the perpetrators had few or no personal contacts with their Jewish fellow citizens, nor could they recall any untoward experiences with them. Only Hopfgartner, who in January and February 1938 had worked as a salesman at the Jewish

[76] BDO: Memorandum of the Sicherheitsdirektor für Tirol, Regierungspolizei, with statement by Irmgard Stecher, 13th August 1945, pp. 27–29.
[77] *Ibid*.
[78] VG beim LG Innsbruck, Vg 10 Vr 104/46 (HV 59/46), submissions by Gottfried Andreaus, 15th October 1946.
[79] BDC: Beschluß des Sondersenats des Obersten Parteigerichts betr. Einstellung des Verfahrens gegen SS-Hauptsturmführer Hans Aichinger und SS-Untersturmführer Walter Hopfgartner wegen Mordes an Richard Graubart, Wilhelm Bauer und Richard Berger, 9th February 1939.
[80] BDO: Bericht des Sicherheitsdirektors für Tirol, Regierungspolizei, 7th September 1945, p. 13.

textile firm Pasch, stated that he left his workplace because of "unsatisfactory working conditions",[81] but he maintained that this experience had not influenced his behaviour during the night of the pogrom. As the Supreme Party Court ascertained, there had been no personal differences between Hopfgartner and Richard Berger or between Aichinger and Richard Graubart or Dr. Wilhelm Bauer. Hopfgartner did not even know Richard Berger.[82]

THE ROLE OF THE AUTHORITIES

In a report on the pogrom, the SD office of SS Region Danube stated that the events occurred "almost everywhere even before the SD and the *Gestapo* had been informed about them". At about midnight the SD office was informed by signal "of the forthcoming operations" and thereupon immediately sent a cable to the *Gestapo* offices requesting that they pass this information to all districts.[83] Whatever role the various Nazi authorities played that night or however they interacted with each other, one thing seems certain: without the collaborative effort of the authorities, the "people's fury" (*Volkszorn*) could not have been staged.

As one detective later recalled, the chief of the police, SS-*Untersturmführer* Dr. Adolf Franzclin, issued an order in the late evening of 9th November that all incoming calls for help during the night were to be ignored.[84] Also, the deputy chief of the *Gestapo*, Werner Hilliges, clearly remembered that on the evening of 9th November he was alerted by a telex from the *Reichssicherheitshauptamt* (RSHA) in Berlin which had reached the *Gestapo* office. It stated:

> "The Party will initiate measures against Jews in retaliation for the murder of Counsellor Rath in Paris. These measures, which are to be expected during the course of the night, will be co-ordinated throughout the Reich."
>
> "In case Jewish property was burned, we were to prevent the fires from spreading elsewhere. But if excesses occurred, we should not interfere with the operations that had been ordered. I remained at the office and learned from the incoming police reports that Jews were being maltreated and that three Jews had been killed."[85]

Like the SS assault units, the members of the SD also had to wear civilian clothes and remain on alert at their offices. They were to support the security

---

[81]VG beim LG Innsbruck, Vg 10 Vr 2372/50, Interrogation of Walter Hopfgartner, Innsbruck, 1st April 1950, p. 2.
[82]BDC: Beschluß des Sondersenats des Obersten Parteigerichts betr. Einstellung des Verfahrens gegen SS-Hauptsturmführer Hans Aichinger und SS-Untersturmführer Walter Hopfgartner wegen Mordes an Richard Graubart, Wilhelm Bauer und Richard Berger, 9th February 1939.
[83]Private Archive Edwin Tangl: SD-Führer des SS-Oberabschnittes Donau (Polte) to Reichssicherheitshauptamt Berlin, 21st November 1938, with 'Erfahrungsbericht über die Aktionen gegen die Juden in der Zeit vom 9. bis 11. November 1938'.
[84]BDO: Bericht des Sicherheitsdirektors für Tirol, Regierungspolizei, 7th September 1945, pp. 3–4.
[85]VG beim LG Innsbruck, Vg 10 Vr 104/46, Interrogation of Werner Hilliges, 13th June 1946, pp. 71–72.

measures and take possession of assets belonging to the Jewish community.[86] The *Gestapo* had thus received clear instructions not to take any steps against the anticipated excesses that would have impeded the "operations" ordered from above. In this way all traces of the violence committed could be covered up, and none of the participants held responsible.[87] But it was not only the *Gestapo* who took care of this matter. As Hans Aichinger remembered, the SS men not already assigned were assembled at company headquarters, appropriately uniformed and prepared for action. Moving out from there, they systematically closed off the streets of the city in order to "protect" the Jews against the expected "fury" of the people. The manoeuvre had its desired effect. According to rumours circulating later in Innsbruck, it was none other than the SS which had demonstrated exemplary, that is, "very loyal", behaviour during the night of the pogrom against the Jews; indeed, "it was the SS itself which had provided protection". Furthermore, as city rumour had it, the NSKK was "the main participant" in the pogrom, and the SA was used only in second place.[88]

Such accounts, of course, turned the actual events upside down, for the killing operations were carried out, without exception, by SS men dressed in civilian clothing. A former administrative official of the *Gestapo* stated after 1945 that the entire *Gestapo* was supposedly assigned the job of "protecting the Jews who were going to be attacked. In reality the *Gestapo* were employed to secure and observe the Jewish residences that had been designated for the assaults. On the night of the pogrom, as he admitted, this administrative *Gestapo* official himself lingered (certainly not by pure accident) in the exclusive residential Innsbruck area Saggen, where Richard Graubart and Dr. Wilhelm Bauer lived. There interestingly, he observed the SS officers Aichinger, Schintlholzer and Fleiss, together with others, climbing over the fence of a villa and walking towards the city.[89]

Efforts to establish the facts of this case led to differences between the investigating police agencies and the *Gestapo*. Heading the homicide division of the *Kriminalpolizei* (*Kripo*), Dr. Herbert Mannlicher stated that on the morning of 10th November he received a request from the Chief of the Police, Dr. Franzelin, to "go to the scene of the crime and, with as little fuss as possible, remove the corpses". After his visit there, Mannlicher, who at this point did not know about the pogrom, informed Franzelin that without doubt the men there had been murdered; they had not, as Franzelin had told him before, committed suicide. Franzelin's behaviour led Mannlicher to conclude that the police chief knew about the murderous assaults.

After the bodies were taken to the Institute for Forensic Medicine, Mannlicher was called before the *Gestapo* chief, Dr. Wilhelm Harster, who took him to task "in an unusually brusque manner", asking "why there was so much commotion concerning these cases and why the bodies were not simply made to disappear

---

[86] Private Archive Edwin Tangl: Memorandum of SS-Untersturmführer Fast, 12th November 1938. The material confiscated from the Jewish community was subsequently taken to the office of the SD District.

[87] StA Innsbruck, Anklage Aichinger und Andreaus, St 8705/45, 16th August 1946, p. 101.

[88] VG beim LG Innsbruck, Vg 10 Vr 104/46, Interrogation of Hans Aichinger, 22nd August 1945, p. 92.

[89] BDO: Bericht des Sicherheitsdirektors für Tirol, Regierungspolizei, 12th October 1945, pp. 40–41.

The November Pogrom in Innsbruck

without further investigation". Harster immediately ordered that no autopsies be undertaken or completed, that the police secure and guard the bodies until further notice, and that all pictures and reports be submitted to the *Gestapo*. Harster, who subsequently served as *Höherer SS- und Polizeiführer* (HSSPF) in The Hague, also repeatedly told Mannlicher "that authentic material about this case must under no circumstances reach foreign countries".[90]

Complications arose again between the investigating police and the *Gestapo* when Richard Berger's body was being retrieved near Kranebitten. Shots were fired from the other side of the River Inn at the investigating police.[91] In this case, too, the *Kripo* could not properly conclude its investigation; the *Gestapo* ordered that the *Kripo* terminate official action on the killings immediately. From then on, all further inquiries were conducted by the *Gestapo* alone.[92] Finally, the police agencies were not notified uniformly of the "operations" planned for 9th–10th November. Only on the evening of 10th November did the *Kripo* office in Innsbruck learn the approximate nature of the pogrom that had been launched against the Jews throughout the *Reich* during the preceding night.[93]

Mannlicher submitted the police notes, reports and pictures to the *Gestapo*, but he retained a set of stenographic notes on the questioning by a detective of Grete Graubart, Edith Bauer and the caretaker, Karl Hosp. Leaving the police a short time later, Mannlicher handed those documents to another official who kept them at home until the end of the war and then submitted them to the agencies investigating the events of 9th–10th November 1938. The stenographic notes constitute the only contemporaneous evidence for the sequence of the criminal operations in the early morning hours; all other evidence – interrogations, testimonies and the files of the People's Court – stems from the post-war period.

The *Gestapo* prohibited autopsies of the bodies of Richard Graubart, Wilhelm Bauer and Richard Berger, and they were taken to Munich for cremation. As Mannlicher remembered, the post-mortem examinations attributed the deaths of the three men to suicide.[94] As a result of the orders issued by Harster, the investigation into the killings was discontinued on 10th November, and no criminal prosecution took place until 1945.[95]

Some time after the "*Kristallnacht*", the deputy chief of the *Gestapo*, Werner Hilliges, received a request from Berlin to uncover for the Nazi Party how the murders happened, ascertain the identity of the perpetrators and report his

---

[90] VG beim LG Innsbruck, Vg 10 Vr 104/46, Interrogation of Dr. Herbert Mannlicher, 24th October 1945, pp. 49–51; BDC, dossier Wilhelm Harster: Lebenslauf and Dienstlaufbahn; *Tiroler Nachrichten*, 226 (16th October 1946), p. 2.
[91] *Ibid.*
[92] BDO: Bericht des Sicherheitsdirektors für Tirol, Regierungspolizei, 7th September 1945, p. 4.
[93] VG beim LG Innsbruck, Vg 10 Vr 104/46, Testimony of Kriminal-Revier-Inspektor Wischatta, 24th July 1945, p. 34.
[94] StA Innsbruck, Anklage Aichinger und Andreaus, St 8705/45, 16th August 1946, p. 101; VG beim LG Innsbruck, Vg 10 Vr 104/46, Interrogation of Dr. Herbert Mannlicher, 24th October 1945, p. 53; 'Bestätigung des Stadtmagistrats Innsbruck vom 24. November 1938 aus dem Sterberegister, Nr. 12, Seite 45, des Rabbinates der Israelitischen Kultusgemeinde Innsbruck', document in private possession of Frederik Richard Benson; it states that Berger died on 10th November 1938 in Innsbruck "from a head wound", concluding that his death was not suicide.
[95] BDO: Bericht des Sicherheitsdirektors für Tirol, Regierungspolizei, 7th September 1945, pp. 4–6.

findings. Suspecting that it was SS men who committed the crimes, Hilliges summoned the leaders of the Innsbruck SS and commenced regular interrogations. He later testified that within the SS, Hanns von Feil ordered the killings and a group of SS-*Unter-* and *Obersturmführer* executed the order. Hilliges later described how the line of authority in the killing operation started with von Feil, the leader of the SS Region of the Tyrol, Vorarlberg and Salzburg, passed through Erwin Fleiss, the leader of the SS regiment of the Tyrol and Vorarlberg, and ended with Hans Aichinger, the leader of SS Battalion I/87, encompassing Innsbruck and about half of the Tyrol. According to Hilliges, it was not difficult to get the perpetrators to make a statement to him:

> "Since none of the men interrogated had to fear punishment, they all told the truth openly so that I got a fairly true picture of all events. Also the statements they made separately accorded with each other."

Hilliges sent his report, as ordered, to the RSHA, and "after considerable time had passed, he was instructed to take no action against the guilty men and to destroy the files".[96]

The judicial proceedings of the Nazi Party, which Göring initiated because of excesses and "race defilement" (in Linz the SA men had raped a Jewish woman) and which were also held *pro forma* for the region of the Tyrol and Vorarlberg, revealed the despicable character of the SS leaders who had issued the killing orders. Von Feil and Fleiss denied all responsibility. The result was a private dispute between them and Aichinger, who considered it irresponsible to disown the orders they had issued. According to Hilliges, Aichinger at first did not want to reveal the names of the men implicated in the assaults to the deputy chief of the *Gestapo*, but then apparently changed his mind. At any rate, the minutes based on Aichinger's interrogation concluded that Richard Graubart and Dr. Wilhelm Bauer were killed in "self-defence".[97] The proceedings of 9th February 1939 before the Supreme Party Court concerning the *"Kristallnacht"* in Innsbruck revealed that when he issued his orders, Hanns von Feil had used words that implied "that while carrying out the retaliatory measures the life of one Jew does not matter". Von Feil also told his men explicitly that nothing would happen to them, "no matter what the result of the operations".[98]

Based on the findings of the *Gestapo* and its own interrogations, the Supreme Party Court discontinued the proceedings against Aichinger and Hopfgartner. It concluded that the killing of Jews was motivated by the commitment to the ideals of National Socialism, and for this reason only minor penalties or no sentence at all should be imposed. In the case of Aichinger and Hopfgartner, who went scot-free – as did most of the perpetrators – the Supreme Party Court's decision read as follows:

---

[96] VG beim LG Innsbruck, Vg 10 Vr 104/46, Interrogation of Werner Hilliges, 13th June 1946, pp. 72–74.

[97] *Ibid.*, Interrogation of Hans Aichinger, 17th August 1945, pp. 78–83, and Werner Hilliges, 13th June 1946, pp. 72–73.

[98] BDC: Beschluß des Sondersenats des Obersten Parteigerichts betr. Einstellung des Verfahrens gegen SS-Hauptsturmführer Hans Aichinger und SS-Untersturmführer Walter Hopfgartner wegen Mordes an Richard Graubart, Wilhelm Bauer und Richard Berger, 9th February 1939.

"The men were utterly convinced that their deed served the *Führer* and the Party. Hence they have not been expelled from the Party. In the opinion of the Supreme Party Court, the ultimate purpose of these proceedings, and thus also the guideline for judging these cases, must be the aim to protect those Party members who, out of their upright National Socialist position as well as readiness for action, overstepped the mark. On the other hand, however, a line must be drawn between the Party and those persons who in despicable fashion have abused the racial struggle of the Party against Jewry for their own ends or, in addition, acted from criminal motives."[99]

Ultimately, however, the Supreme Party Court held that no such self-serving and base motives figured in the night of the Innsbruck pogrom, a view that obviously must be doubted today.

POPULAR REACTIONS TO THE "KRISTALLNACHT"

To what extent were the events of the pogrom publicly known? How did the people of Innsbruck react to them? These are important questions, particularly in view of the Nazi propaganda campaign that spoke of the "guilt of Judas", "the cowardly Jewish assassination", "the profound outrage of the German people", and of the "just, popular fury" that had unleashed itself that night. These views spread to a large part of the population and were reflected in popular opinion. In part, this defamation produced an attitude that considered the use of force against the Jews as an appropriate act of revenge. The report of 21st November 1938 from SS Region Danube confirmed this:

"In response to the official measures, the general population followed their natural instincts and therefore viewed these measures as a form of liberation; in contrast, the intellectual upper classes have for the most part displayed economic and emotional misgivings."[100]

The SD District of the Tyrol reported that "some parts of the population" believed that "the instigators were *agents provocateurs*"; some circles even argued that "the Communists were behind it all". At any rate, the SD also observed how liberal as well as clerical circles opposed, "as expected, the manner in which action" was taken. Because, according to the SD, specific details were "not yet known" to the public, there circulated "a lot of silly rumours". Among Party followers and devoted Nazis, the news "of these operations and the announcement of further laws [against Jews] was uniformly received with great satisfaction".[101]

On 11th November 1938 the evening edition of the *Innsbrucker Nachrichten*, since 2nd July 1938 the official paper of the Nazi Party region Tyrol-Vorarlberg,[102]

---

[99]Lauber, *Judenpogrom*, pp. 225–233.
[100]Private Archive Edwin Tangl: SD-Führer des SS-Oberabschnittes Donau (Polte) to Reichssicherheitshauptamt Berlin, 21st November 1938, with 'Erfahrungsbericht über die Aktionen gegen die Juden in der Zeit vom 9. bis 11. November 1938'.
[101]BDO: SD-Unterabschnitt Tirol (Fast) to SD-Führer des SS-Oberabschnittes Donau-Wien, 12th November 1938. See also Rosenkranz, *Reichskristallnacht*, pp. 52–53.
[102]Michael Gehler, 'Viel Sand im Getriebe. Medien und Propaganda im Gau Tirol-Vorarlberg nach dem "Anschluß"', in *Die veruntreute Wahrheit. Hitlers Propagandisten in Österreich "38"*, ed. by Wolfgang Duchkowitsch, Fritz Hausjell and Oliver Rathkolb, Vienna 1988, p. 428.

reported the destruction of the synagogue, but there was no news about the dead and wounded. The region's newspaper carried only the official version, issued by the Ministry of Propaganda, that the pogrom against the Jews had been a spontaneous outbreak of popular fury as a result of vom Rath's murder in Paris by the Jew Grynszpan. The newspaper also included the misleading information that it had been necessary for the authorities to protect the Jews.[103]

Among Nazis the rumour also circulated that in the main it was members of the NSKK who had been involved in the pogrom and were thus responsible for the murders, while the general SS had performed the task of protecting the Jews from "popular fury". As indicated above, this notion of the SS had not emerged without reason. Be that as it may, the post-war investigations into the "*Kristallnacht*" conducted by the Tyrolean Security Office in 1945 established that the major crimes, namely the murders, were without exception committed by the SS.[104] But at the time the people of Innsbruck probably received only limited information on the killings. Some facts, of course, were first known in the immediate vincinity of the crimes. The residence of one of the Jews slated for the assault was located in the house where the Italian consul lived, and he was furious that the perpetrators had climbed through the window of his wife's bedroom to get to the apartment of their victim. The SD report on this incident commented that the consul "immediately calmed down . . . after being told what the whole thing was about".[105] There was, of course, no way for the authorities to cover up the incidents of the pogrom. Had they tried, it would have made matters "only worse since the residents of the house [where Graubart lived] already knew – and it was being talked about in the neighbourhood – that murder squads had been operating there".[106]

How did non-Jews living in the immediate vicinity of the threatened Jews behave that night? Alois Riedl, the janitor of Gänsbacher Str. 4, was awakened by the wife of Karl Bauer. Evidently, as a post-war inquiry established, Riedl lacked the courage to help.[107] In contrast, Karl Hosp, the janitor of Gänsbacher Str. 5, wanted to get a doctor, but the SS men in the house and the *Gestapo* outside did not allow him to leave. His efforts were thus thwarted by force. Despite the violence, as Grete Graubart remembered, her husband was still alive when the ambulance picked him up.[108] On Haydnplatz 8, by contrast, Maria Graubart did not even call for help within the house:

[103]'Vergeltungsmaßnahmen im ganzen Reich – Gerechter Volkszorn gegen die Juden', *Innsbrucker Nachrichten*, 262 (11th November 1938); 'Die Synagogue in Innsbruck zertrümmert', *Neueste Zeitung*, 257 (11th November 1938); 'Hinaus mit den Juden', *ibid.*, 256 (10th November 1938).
[104]BDO: Bericht des Sicherheitsdirektors für Tirol, Regierungspolizei, 7th September 1945, p. 3.
[105]BDO: SD-Unterabschnitt Tirol (Fast) to SD-Führer des SS-Oberabschnittes Donau-Wien, 12th November 1938
[106]VG beim LG Innsbruck, Vg 10 Vr 104/46, Interrogation of Dr. Herbert Mannlicher, 24th October 1945, p. 50.
[107]BDO: Memorandum of the Bundespolizeidirektion Innsbruck, Staatspolizeiliche Abteilung, concerning arrest order for Alois Schintlholzer, 14th February 1946, pp. 1–3.
[108]VG beim LG Innsbruck, Vg 10 Vr 104/46, Testimonies of Grete Graubart and Karl Hosp, 10th November 1938.

The November Pogrom in Innsbruck

"Because we were in such an exposed position and, due to our circumstance, in such isolation, I could not call on the help of the other occupants of the house, and none of them came voluntarily."[109]

As mentioned above, the Jewish couple Popper were also surprised by the SS men who dragged them from their apartment and pushed them into the River Sill. Fortunately the water level was not very high, and after the SS departed, they climbed out of the river near a mill. But when they stopped there for assistance, the porter brusquely turned them away. Soaking wet, they had to walk through the whole town only to find their home turned upside down and wrecked. Shortly thereafter they were taken into custody.[110]

But there were some people who helped their Jewish fellow citizens and acted with courage even during the night of the pogrom. For instance, Luis Brenn, the doctor sent for by Grete Graubart, immediately called an ambulance and then went to the Graubart residence, where the *Gestapo* first tried to prevent him from entering. Firmly committed to his professional ethics, Brenn persisted and finally managed to see the injured man. He again showed civic courage (*Zivilcourage*) by notifying the authorities. When he encountered the passive attitude of the police, he understood very quickly that these savage killings had been organised, or at least covered up, at a higher level:

"I phoned the police and told them that I had been called to a certain Mr. Graubart on Gänsbacher Str. 5. I described the facts of the case and asked that a homicide investigation team be sent immediately, adding that I would wait until it arrived. To this the police official replied that it did not concern the police. I asked whether I had somehow misunderstood, and he said again that it was none of their business. Then I said: 'excuse me, but from my studies in forensic medicine I know that I have to inform the police immediately when called to a case that appears to involve a violent death'. Since he did not change his position, it dawned on me that this could not have been an act of revenge by one or more persons, but an organised operation."

The next day, however, Brenn insisted on seeing the chief of the *Gestapo* personally and expressed his displeasure at the way police officials had behaved:

"After I described my experiences of the previous night exactly, Dr. Harster replied that he was already informed of the matter and thanked me for my report. He added that at best I could compose a written report and personally hand it over . . . to the attorney general, Dr. Moser. After all this, I realised that the whole matter was a farce and that this report would end up in the waste-paper basket. Becoming increasingly disgusted with the proceedings, I did not submit the report."[111]

In the days following the pogrom, the operations against the Jews were increasingly talked about in the city so that most people could hardly avoid hearing about them. As the Supreme Party Court acknowledged, it was no secret to the large majority of the population as to who had initiated the whole operation:

---

[109] *Ibid.*, Testimony of Maria Graubart, 3rd July 1945.
[110] Carmela Flöck, a former resistance fighter, received this information on 10th November 1938 from an acquaintance. See radio programme on the "*Reichskristallnacht*" of ORF Radio Tyrol, November 1983, tape in my possession.
[111] VG beim LG Innsbruck, Vg 10 Vr 104/46, Testimony of Maria Graubart, 3rd July 1945.

"Whether we admit it or not, the public also knows, right down to the last man, that political operations like the one on 9th November are organised and carried out by the Party. When all of the synagogues burn down in one night, then this must have been organised somehow, and it can only have been done by the Party."[112]

As the SD had reported, not everyone in Innsbruck condoned the excesses. The rabbi, Dr. Elimelech S. Rimalt, told of people who, never having spoken to him before, now approached him, visited him in his apartment, or offered help to him on the street and, at the same time, did not hold back their criticism of what had happened.[113] To what extent large groups of people harboured such sentiments can hardly be ascertained today. The SD report mentioned above clearly shows that certain circles of the population were openly repelled by the pogrom. On the other hand, it seems certain that the large majority remained silent and returned to their daily business. The church, too, wrapped itself in silence.

Could the Jews have behaved differently? Did they have a chance to resist? After 1945 Maria Bliem, who had been the housekeeper of the Wilhelm Bauer home for many years, testified that, after the *Gestapo* forbade residential positions with Jewish families in 1938, she worked at the Bauer residence only during the day and at night returned to her own home in Hötting. Bliem's recollection of the happily married Bauer couple, who always treated the housekeeper as a member of the family, shows how unprepared the Innsbruck Jewish community was for the pogrom: "When I said good-bye to the Bauers on 9th November, that is, the evening before the persecution of the Jews . . . they were both quite unsuspecting."[114] Even at that late date, it was inconceivable to them that a pogrom against the Jews of Innsbruck could take place.

Jews had resisted antisemitic attacks by individuals under the old Austrian *Ständestaat*, and in rare cases even after the *Anschluß*, but they were basically helpless in the face of a deliberate anti-Jewish policy organised by the state. Even before 1938 the Austrian Jews were going through an inner crisis and a period of reorientation; the Jewish community was divided between assimilationists and Zionists and their conflicts soon broke into open hostilities. The threats coming from Austrian antisemitism and German Nazism did nothing to lessen those antagonisms. On the contrary, the attacks intensified the divisions since each side accused the other of providing the antisemites with grounds for their position.[115] Also, Nazi antisemitism was frequently underestimated. The Jews of Austria, at any rate, were neither a conspiratorial community nor a unified group capable of staging a vigorous defence in November 1938.

CONSEQUENCES OF THE POGROM

The night of the pogrom severely unsettled the Innsbruck Jewish community, which was already greatly diminished in numbers. The murders were an eye-

[112]Lauber, *Judenpogrom*, p. 155; Benz, 'Der Rückfall in die Barbarei', p. 33.
[113]Rosenkranz, *Verfolgung*, p. 161.
[114]VG beim LG Innsbruck, Vg 10 Vr 104/46, Testimony of Maria Bliem, 26th June 1946.
[115]Sylvia Maderegger, *Die Juden im österreichischen Ständestaat 1934–1938*, Veröffentlichungen des Historischen Instituts der Universität Salzburg, Vienna–Salzburg 1973, p. 266.

The November Pogrom in Innsbruck

opener to all who until then had not taken seriously the disquieted voices of the community. Jews had already been migrating from the Tyrol in the 1930s, increasingly as a result of events following the *Anschluß*; but after the appalling events of the *"Kristallnacht"* in Innsbruck, many more concluded that they must leave. An incomplete list concerning the whereabouts of Jewish families who had lived in Innsbruck until 1938 showed that from Innsbruck alone 26 Jews left the Tyrol already in November or December 1938, or as it was officially described, they "went to Vienna to cancel their registration as residents".[116]

Furthermore, the authorities themselves pushed more vigorously for the expulsion of Jews who were not willing to emigrate. In this sense the *"Kristallnacht"* doubtless accelerated expulsion policies. A report by SS-*Hauptsturmführer* Polte, the deputy SD chief in the SS Region Danube, made a similar point:

> "The protest operation will result in speedier emigration. The Jews will try to use their remaining wealth for the purpose of more rapid relocation. Therefore, as of 28th November 1938 the Central Office for Jewish Emigration (*Zentralstelle für jüdische Auswanderung*) will handle double the number of Jews wanting to leave, so that from this point on between 600 and 700 Jews per day will be forced to emigrate."[117]

On 10th November 1938 all the male Jews of Innsbruck were taken into "protective custody". After being told that they had to leave the city without delay, they were released.[118] As Polte ascertained, a total of about 8,000 Jews in Austria were taken into custody, and about 5,000 of them were sent to Dachau. Over 1,000 Jews whose visas for other countries had already been obtained, that is already processed by the *Zentralstelle für jüdische Auswanderung*, were arrested.[119]

After the pogrom the position of the Jews became virtually unbearable. Their already critical situation was exacerbated because shortly after the *"Kristallnacht"* the authorities intensified their anti-Jewish measures. Jews were prohibited from attending public cultural events, their crafts and retail trade permits were revoked, they had to leave all managerial positions, and they were not allowed to become members of co-operatives. Students of Jewish origin could no longer register at the university, and Jewish children could no longer attend the schools in Innsbruck.[120]

The Nazis evidently also had a practical political reason for killing Jews and confiscating their apartments. As Hilliges commented:

> "Since that time I assumed that the underlying reason for the operation in the villa belonging to the Graubarts was that the SS District urgently needed a good location for its headquarters

---

[116]Innsbruck, Archiv der Israelitischen Kultusgemeinde: Bundespolizeidirektion Innsbruck to Kultusgemeinde Innsbruck, 16th May 1961, concerning 'Auskünfte über den Verbleib jüdischer Familien, die bis 1938 in Innsbruck gelebt haben'.

[117]Private Archive Edwin Tangl: SD-Führer des SS-Oberabschnittes Donau (sig. Polte) to Reichssicherheitshauptamt Berlin, 21st November 1938, with 'Erfahrungsbericht über die Aktionen gegen die Juden in der Zeit vom 9. bis 11. November 1938'.

[118]Stainer, 'Wir werden den Juden schon eintunken!', p. 30.

[119]Private Archive Edwin Tangl: SD-Führer des SS-Oberabschnittes Donau (sig. Polte) to Reichssicherheitshauptamt Berlin, 21st November 1938, with 'Erfahrungsbericht über die Aktionen gegen die Juden in der Zeit vom 9. bis 11. November 1938'.

[120]*Widerstand und Verfolgung in Tirol*, vol. I, p. 424.

and hit on the idea of taking over the villa for this purpose. Aichinger was, therefore, probably very interested in this piece of property."[121]

With the November Pogrom, too, life in the Jewish community of Innsbruck came to a standstill. The Jewish community practically stopped its activities; the rabbi went to Vienna, and the board members had either been murdered or had emigrated. After 1938 the community continued a purely formal existence. Finally in March 1940, all local Austrian-Jewish communities, except for Vienna, were ordered to disband, and the one in Innsbruck was henceforth administered by the Viennese Jewish community.[122]

The Innsbruck *Gestapo* chief, Harster, established in May 1939 that during the night of 9th to 10th November the benches and the Torah Ark in the sanctuary of the synagogue had been smashed and thrown into the street. He claimed that: "With the agreement of the former chairman of the Jewish community, Julius Pasch", the shattered objects were "given to the janitor to be used as firewood". According to Harster, the house itself "suffered no significant damage". The former sanctuary, actually only a large hall, was used by the Hitler Youth as a storeroom.[123]

On 19th November 1938 the *Gestapo* demanded the emigration of all Jews still living in the Tyrol and Vorarlberg and, shortly thereafter, forbade residency to all Jews of Polish citizenship.[124] After the November Pogrom, the authorities intended to forbid residency to Jews throughout the whole of Austria if they did not possess a visa for another country. The final date for the departure of the Jews from the Tyrol was set for 15th March 1939; the orders of expulsion were issued by the district administrations (*Bezirkshauptmannschaften*).[125] But Harster's measures against the Jews vacillated between a scheduled emigration from Austria and transfer to Vienna. In his directives to the district administrators (*Landräte*), he repeatedly requested them to abstain from coercive measures, since experience had taught "that force was not necessary to get the Jews to leave the Tyrol". Nevertheless, until the beginning of December 1938, force had been used to expel 22 Polish and stateless Jews from the district and city of Innsbruck and from Bludenz. In January 1939 Harster also ordered the *Landräte* of the Tyrol and Vorarlberg to send, without the use of coercion, all Jews to Vienna so that, with one exception, only couples of mixed marriages were left in Innsbruck.[126]

Gauleiter Hofer's aim, however, to make the *Gau* of the Tyrol and Vorarlberg "*judenrein*" by the beginning of 1939 could not be accomplished. In the course of the war years, Jewish refugees from Eastern Austria, Germany and Eastern Europe appeared again and again, and the Tyrol offered them, partly against its will, the right of passage or a shelter for periods of time.[127] Jews were only

---

[121] VG beim LG Innsbruck, Vg 10 Vr 104/46, Interrogation of Werner Hilliges, 13th June 1946, p. 73.
[122] *Widerstand und Verfolgung in Tirol*, vol. I, p. 425.
[123] Archiv der Israelitischen Kultusgemeinde: Dr. Harster, Staatspolizeistelle Innsbruck, to Landeshauptmannschaft von Tirol, 12th May 1939. In December 1943 the synagogue was razed to the ground by Allied bombs.
[124] *Ibid.*, Chronologisches Verzeichnis der Kultusgemeinde.
[125] *Widerstand und Verfolgung in Tirol*, vol. I, pp. 423–424.
[126] Rosenkranz, *Verfolgung*, p. 161.
[127] *Widerstand und Verfolgung in Tirol*, vol. I, p. 425.

insufficiently – or not at all – recompensed after 1945 for the destruction, theft and confiscation of their property in November 1938.[128]

THE PERPETRATORS AFTER 1945

After the war the perpetrators of the November Pogroms who could be located were arrested, interrogated, and sentenced by the People's Court (*Volksgericht*). Their sentences were based on the Law Concerning War Crimes and Other National Socialist Offences (War Crimes Law) and on the Law Concerning the Prohibition of the Nazi Party (Prohibition Law). According to the former, anyone who had knowledge of a punishable action and did not prevent it was responsible for it. The sentence for murder or acting as an accessory to murder was capital punishment or, at a minimum, incarceration for life in a maximum security prison. The People's Court of the District Court (*Volksgericht beim Landesgericht*) in Innsbruck tried the perpetrators of the night of the pogrom who had been indicted by the state prosecutor (*Staatsanwalt*) of Innsbruck for the crime of mistreatment under the War Crimes Law or for the crime of high treason under the Prohibition Law.

Although no death sentences were pronounced, the *Volksgericht* initially attempted to impose just penalties. Many of those charged with very serious crimes received more than ten years in prison, their assets reverted to the state, and under Article 35 of the penal code they were locked up in a dark cell every November 10th. Nevertheless, at the end of the 1940s and the beginning of the 1950s, many were released from prison, after a pardon or on parole. Still, in the period after 1945, the court cannot be accused of being remiss in dealing with the perpetrators of the "*Kristallnacht*". In most cases it concluded that the deeds of the night of 9th–10th November had arisen out of a "particularly reprehensible sentiment" and must be described as "particularly base and in gross contradiction to the laws of humanity". The court also took into consideration as extenuating circumstances behaviour proving that after the November Pogrom the accused had turned away, inwardly and outwardly, from the goals and ideas of the Nazi Party and its organisations. However, not all of the accused had behaved in this fashion; the "extenuating circumstances" will be discussed below.[129]

Gottfried Andreaus played a key role in the post-war investigations of the surviving "*Kristallnacht*" perpetrators; he revealed the names of those involved in the killing squads. Similarly, Werner Hilliges, who, as mentioned before, had been in charge of questioning the SS men suspected of theft and rape during the

---

[128]Interview with Heinz Mayer, president of the *Bund der Opfer des politischen Freiheitskampfes* in Tyrol, 1988; tape in my possession. The Plansee works of Schwarzkopf in Reutte, which had been sold prior to *Anschluß*, were one exception.

[129]VG beim LG Innsbruck, Beschluß gg. Hans Aichinger und Gottfried Andreaus, Vg 10 Vr 104/46, 16th October 1946, pp. 106–116; *Tiroler Nachrichten*, 227 (17th October 1946), p. 2; see also Klaus Eisterer, 'Französische Besatzungspolitik. Tirol und Vorarlberg 1945/1946', *Innsbrucker Forschungen zur Zeitgeschichte*, vol. IX (1992), pp. 250–258.

"*Kristallnacht*", provided very detailed information on the perpetrators and on other matters pertaining to the case.

At the interrogations after 1945 by the authorities, as well as during proceedings in open court, many said they could not remember detailed events concerning the night of the pogrom and claimed they had forgotten the names of fellow perpetrators. They pushed the responsibility onto others, played down their own roles in the crimes, and frequently pointed to duress under orders. Hans Aichinger, for example, defended himself in this way:

> "It was decided that I take part in this thing, and to have openly refused would have resulted in the most serious measures against me, at least the concentration camp, for resisting an order."[130]

The reference to the concentration camp and similar penalties can be seen as an effort by Aichinger to exculpate himself and as a self-serving exaggeration of the then existing power relations. For an SS officer, refusal to partake in the pogrom would hardly have resulted in being sent to a concentration camp. It could, however, have meant a loss of "honour", which was very deeply felt, as well as expulsion from the SS. Aichinger did not have to reckon with more than that in the way of penalties, but expulsion apparently sufficed to prevent him from even considering an open rejection of the order.

The argument advanced by the accused Walter Hopfgartner that he was given "a task to test him" when chosen to participate in the night of the pogrom turned upside down the intention of the SS chiefs at that time, since they had specifically chosen already tried and proven SS men – those who had already gone through the "ordeal of fire" – to take on the killings.[131]

The accused also made a partial attempt to relativise their intentions or the intensity of their brutal methods against the Jews by claiming that they never intended to murder them. They just wanted to "beat them up". Alois Schintlholzer, for example, disclaimed having stabbed Karl Bauer, although he admitted to the order from above to commit murder. Denying that he had intended to kill, he did at least confess that he had severely injured his victim:

> "Without exchanging a word with Bauer, I beat him up. I hit him hard about the head two or three times . . . I did intend to hurt Bauer because I felt a distinct aversion against Jews, a feeling which, like everyone else, I was brought up with."[132]

Since the pogrom was assigned to the "most reliable" of the SS men, those who had already proven themselves during the period of illegality and could be trusted to carry out a homicide, the post-1945 investigating authorities found it difficult to believe "that the participants in such an operation were left in the dark concerning the purpose of their undertaking". The sequence of events and the brutality and ruthlessness with which the SS squads proceeded against their

---

[130] VG beim LG Innsbruck, Vg 10 Vr 104/46, Interrogation of Hans Aichinger, 17th August 1945, p. 82.
[131] VG beim LG Innsbruck, Vg 10 Vr 2372/50, Interrogation of Walter Hopfgartner, 1st April 1950, p. 8.
[132] VG beim LG Innsbruck, Vg 20 Vr 876/61, Interrogation of Alois Schintlholzer, 21st April 1961, p. 7.

victims demonstrate that they launched their assaults with the clear intention of murder. Moreover, the perpetrators performed their tasks in the shortest time possible, with dogged, unshrinking determination.[133]

Not all the perpetrators were tried for their crimes. Gerhard Lausegger, for example, was taken into custody by the British military authorities at Wolfsberg in Carinthia. There, as confirmed by the Austrian police at Innsbruck, Lausegger was questioned by Frederik R. Benson, the son of the murdered Richard Berger, who had changed his name in exile in Great Britain and returned to Austria as a member of the British Armed Forces. Lausegger was able to escape on 6th March 1947 at the railway station in Villach; he was never apprehended again. All traces of him seemed lost until his name appeared in the *Festschrift* of his fraternity *Suevia*, which "mourned the passing of several senior members", including Lausegger:

> "On 20th December 1966, Dr. Gerhard Lausegger died as the result of an industrial accident, far away from home in Argentina, where after the war and great personal misfortunes he had been able to establish himself again as an office manager."[134]

On 25th January 1967 a memorial service was held for the deceased at the *Suevia* clubhouse in Innsbruck. As recorded in a published history of the *Suevia*, "for the memorial service fifteen senior members had appeared, and it could be seen how greatly senior member Dr. Lausegger was respected by his fellow members".[135] In this historical self-portrayal, characteristic of student corporations and demonstrating in exemplary fashion the relationship of their members to the Nazi period, there is, of course, no mention of Lausegger's role during the night of the pogrom. Coming to grips with the past (*Vergangenheitsbewältigung*) was certainly no concern of the *Suevia*. Furthermore, as one of the squad leaders, Lausegger had tried to absolve himself from all responsibility by disappearing from Innsbruck soon after 10th November 1938. He was never subjected to the Party Court hearings.

After the war Lausegger warned Walter Hopfgartner not to return to Austria, since he, Lausegger, had incriminated him when questioned by Benson.[136] But Hopfgartner returned to the Tyrol, where he was arrested. Charged with high treason and with abuse and torture of other persons under Article 3 of the War Crimes Law, he was sentenced to three years in prison, and his property was forfeited, though the People's Court acquitted him of the murder charge. When the state prosecutor, Dr. Friedrich Nowakowski, petitioned for a revision, the Supreme Court accepted the petition, reversed the "not-guilty" verdict, and ordered a new trial by the People's Court. Hopfgartner was then convicted of

---

[133] StA Innsbruck, Anklage Aichinger und Andreaus, St 8705/45, 16th August 1946, p. 104.
[134] See *Widerstand und Verfolgung in Tirol*, vol. I, pp. 459–460: Testimony of Gerhard Lausegger, 2nd June 1946, concerning the murder of engineer Richard Berger, director of the Israelitische Kultusgemeinde Innsbruck; Sella, *Die Juden Tirols*, p. 56; and Hans Schödl, *Geschichte der akademischen Burschenschaft Suevia zu Innsbruck. Nachtrag 1958–1968*, Salzburg 1968, pp. 53–55.
[135] *Ibid.*
[136] VG beim LG Innsbruck, Urteil Walter Hopfgartner, Vg 10 Vr 744/50 (HV 215/50), 20th September 1950, p. 5; *Volkszeitung*, 219 (21st September 1950); interview with Frederik Richard Benson, 1992, tape in my possession.

murder and torture, and was sentenced to ten years in a maximum-security prison.[137]

The People's Court of Innsbruck imposed prison sentences ranging from six months to thirteen years on more than twenty Tyroleans who had participated in the crimes of the *Pogromnacht*. In August 1946 Anton Haupt received a six-year prison sentence, and Richard Dietrich and Alfred Gnesetti, three-year prison sentences, for assaulting the married couples Brüll and Dimand. In October 1946 Hans Aichinger was sentenced to thirteen years and Gottfried Andreaus to twelve years in a maximum-security prison for being accessories to the attack, that is, the murders of Karl and Wilhelm Bauer and Richard Graubart. Andreaus was pardoned in 1951. Aichinger was able to escape before being imprisoned, but gave himself up in 1959 and was pardoned in 1961. In November 1946 Heinrich Huber received five years in prison, Otto Mohr three years, Alfons Ullmann and Johann Schöpf two-and-a-half years, Georg Weintraut fifteen months, and Josef Girardi eighteen months, for severely assaulting Josef Adler and his family and Flora Bauer and her son; and for destroying the residences of Adler, Schwarz, Spindel and Bauer. For mistreating members of the families Schindler, Löwensohn, Schwarz, Schenkel, Meisel and Dimand, the court handed out the following sentences in 1947: Josef Ebner one-and-a-half years in prison, August Hörhager and Alois Hochrainer two years, Hans Ruedl fourteen months, Karl Handl twenty months, Hans Bayer fourteen months, Hermann Moser six months, Sepp Ramersdorfer fifteen months and Alois Seipt thirteen months in prison. In October 1947 Theodor Haller, who had pushed the Poppers into the River Sill, received a six-year prison sentence. A prominent boxer, Haller had also been one of the most reliable agents for the "illegal" Nazis before the *Anschluß*, while serving with the police in Innsbruck. In December 1947 Rudolf Schwarz was sentenced to eleven years in prison, and Robert Huttig to twelve years, for participating in the murders of Richard Graubart and Wilhelm Bauer. In August 1948 Johann Mathoi, who had destroyed the residences of Dubsky and Fuchs, received a three-and-a-half-year prison sentence. In November 1945 Robert Duy, who took part in the murder of Richard Berger, was arrested in Amsterdam and then taken into custody by the Soviet Union. Later he made his way via the German Democratic Republic to the Federal Republic of Germany, where he lived for quite some time after the war without being apprehended.[138]

Alois Schintlholzer, however, never had to stand trial for heading one of the murder squads. After testifying before the District Court in Innsbruck, he was held on remand for a year. His case was dropped in 1962,[139] a decision that, in retrospect, is questionable. By the 1960s, however, public interest in the November Pogrom had disappeared, and the courts did not consider it

[137] *Ibid.*; *Tiroler Nachrichten*, 6 (14th April 1951).
[138] See Gretl Köfler, '"Wir wollen sehen, ob das Kreuz oder der siebenarmige Leuchter siegt!". Antisemitismus in Nord- und Osttirol seit 1918', *Sturzflüge*, 15/16 (1986), pp. 93–94.
[139] VG beim LG Innsbruck, Beschluß der Ratskammer des LG Innsbruck, betr. Strafsache gegen Alois Schintlholzer, 10 Ns 2149/62, Vg 20 Vr 876/61, 16th May 1962; StA Innsbruck, St 2643/61, Files for the Untersuchungsrichter, 2nd March 1962.

Innsbruck after the Anschluß
Spring 1938

Josef Adler

Richard and Gretl Berger

opportune to inflict harsh penalties on the perpetrators. There is a marked contrast between the intensity with which the police, the state prosecutors and the courts had pursued this case in the immediate post-war years and the flagging interest during the period of the "Cold War". The "minor" perpetrators now frequently received clemency instead of justice.

Yet the claim that the Tyrolean courts did not deal harshly enough with the "*Kristallnacht*" criminals is not completely justified if based on the Schintlholzer case.[140] The People's Court in Innsbruck certainly cannot be accused of "laxity" in the years 1945–1948. The fact that this situation changed at the end of the 1940s and the beginning of the 1950s must be seen within the context of the growing East-West conflict. At that time, the People's Court increasingly adhered to the principle of extenuating circumstances and often placed "clemency before justice". In the trials of the "*Kristallnacht*" accused, it applied this principle extensively and imposed penalties within a prescribed framework of between ten and twenty years imprisonment. None the less, the court sometimes used dubious arguments to justify extenuating circumstances. Thus it accepted the contention of the "*Kristallnacht*" perpetrators that they had no alternative but to obey their orders.[141]

In the case of Walter Hopfgartner, the *Volksgericht* granted extenuating circumstances for the following reasons: Hopfgartner had made a complete and remorseful confession; he had a good reputation and no other convictions; he had taken care of his wife and child; his career had been predetermined by poor education and warped political training; the crime he committed had occurred "many years ago". The "Cold War" realities of 1950 were reflected in one of the extenuating circumstances cited by the court:

> "Furthermore, it has to be considered extenuating that the defendant [Hopfgartner], although a prominent Party member, did not remain at home as a Party bigwig, but served at the front, especially in the last year of the war. Also, on 9th May 1945 he became a prisoner of war in Russia, and as a special prisoner in the NKVD camps he experienced – as is known to the courts here – human degradation and horror."[142]

CONCLUSIONS

In March 1938 approximately 350–380 people of the Jewish faith lived in the Tyrol and Vorarlberg. According to estimates, about half of them were able to emigrate and thus escaped persecution, the Pogrom of 1938 and the Holocaust. After 8th May 1945 about fifteen Tyrolean Jews returned home from the concentration camps, and twenty from emigration.[143]

---

[140] Andreas Maislinger, '"Zurück zur Normalität". Zur Entnazifizierung in Tirol', in *Verdrängte Schuld, verfehlte Sühne. Entnazifizierung in Österreich*, ed. by Sebastian Meissl, Klaus Dieter Mulley and Oliver Rathkolb, Vienna 1986, pp. 344–346. For a view that diverges from Maislinger's, see Theodor Veiter, *Gesetz als Unrecht. Die österreichische Nationalsozialistengesetzgebung. Eine kritische Untersuchung, mit einem internationalen Rechtsvergleich*, Vienna 1949, p. 44.

[141] *Tiroler Nachrichten*, 227 (17th October 1946), p. 2.

[142] VG beim LG Innsbruck, Urteil Hopfgartner, Vg 10 Vr 744/50 (HV 215/50), 20th September 1950, p. 6.

[143] Archiv der Israelitischen Kultusgemeinde: Memorandum from Dr. med. Esther Fritsch and Reg. Rat Paul Reitzer, Kultusgemeinde, 8th August 1987.

In Innsbruck the anti-Jewish pogrom was not – as could be read in the *Reich* press – the spontaneous expression of "popular fury". Rather, as the People's Court established, it was "nothing other than well-organised and centrally directed operations . . . during which many Jews suffered inhuman maltreatment, were injured and even killed".[144] Thus, in Innsbruck as elsewhere, the pogrom would not have been possible without the Nazi Party and its organisations, especially the SS, and without the collusion of the authorities. For this reason one might call it a "Party pogrom".[145]

The pogrom itself was not planned long beforehand but had been organised during the night of the event; it was partly improvised and, without question, ordered from above. The commitment and the unequivocal obedience with which the commands were carried out provide the focus for an analysis of the pogrom in Innsbruck, which can be fully understood only within the context of traditional Austrian antisemitism. This antisemitism was also an important factor in the Tyrol. For in no other Austrian city, with the exception of Vienna, did the *"Reichskristallnacht"* proceed with such brutality and result in so much bloodshed.

There are several reasons for this development. First, the *Gau* of the Tyrol and Vorarlberg was administered by *Gauleiter* Franz Hofer, a politician known for his antisemitism, who never concealed his hatred of the Jews. Second, a social biography of the perpetrators shows that to a large extent they were "old Party veterans" – *Alte Kämpfer* – who had served in the period of illegality; in other words, they were fanatical and dedicated Nazis who were prepared to go to extremes. All of them were Austrians, and most of them Tyroleans; they committed this crime not only on command but also out of their own beliefs. Third, to anyone examining the background of the pogrom night in Innsbruck, it is evident that in the early morning hours of 10th November a clear order to murder was given to a group of SS dressed in civilian clothes. Hence, it must be pointed out that in the series of assaults throughout the *Reich*, Innsbruck presented a special case.

Gauleiter Hofer was obviously receptive to the appeal to base human instincts issued by Goebbels. With Hofer's knowledge and approval, the perpetrators unleashed vandalism, destruction and murder in Innsbruck. In Austria, as in the *Altreich*, the Pogrom served to intimidate the Jews and to put pressure on them to emigrate, and it became the prelude to the war-time mass murder in the East.

Even if the concept of *"Reichskristallnacht"* is inadequate, implying, in many respects, a positive connotation that is most unfortunate, it nevertheless seems to reveal, indirectly, an important historical fact. Those who experienced the events of November 1938 as passive witnesses or who later heard accounts about them, did not exhibit, by and large, a sense of dismay or sympathy. Either they refused

---

[144] VG beim LG Innsbruck, Urteil Hopfgartner, Vg 10 Vr 744/50 (HV 215/50), 20th September 1950, pp. 4–5.

[145] Lauber, *Judenpogrom*, p. 42; Wolfgang Scheffler, 'Ausgewählte Dokumente zur Geschichte des Novemberpogroms 1938', *Aus Politik und Zeitgeschichte. Beilage zur Wochenzeitung "Das Parlament"*, B 44 (4th November 1978), p. 6.

consciously to notice the atrocities of the *Pogromnacht*, or they minimised the persecution as a few broken windows.[146] There were no group protests against the antisemitic excesses and no wholesale condemnation of them afterwards. It is indeed incomprehensible that many people, even those who associated with Jews or worked for them, accepted the events without reaction or criticism.[147]

---

[146] Lauber, *Judenpogrom*, pp. 41–44.
[147] Interview with Heinz Mayer, 1988, tape in my possession; Günther Pallaver, 'Auch Schweigen macht schuldig', *Sturzflüge* 15/16 (1986), p. 4. It is quite astounding that on the occasion of the unveiling of a commemorative plaque on the site of the former Innsbruck synagogue in 1978, Mayor Alois Lugger and *Landeshauptmann* Eduard Wallnöfer managed to make speeches in which the words *Jew* and *synagogue* did not appear even once.

The National-Socialist Years: Different Aspects

The Survival of the Jewish Hospital in Berlin 1938–1945

BY RIVKA ELKIN

The survival of the Jewish Hospital in Berlin – as a Jewish hospital – in the fateful years for German Jewry, 1938–1945, is a puzzling phenomenon. The crucial question is clearly why the hospital was left intact throughout the period and, conversely, what interest the Germans had in letting it survive, particularly after Berlin was ostensibly emptied of its Jews.[*]

The private hospital of Berlin's Jewish community was established in its modern form in 1913, at 11a Exerzierstrasse, which subsequently became 2–4 Iranische Strasse.[1] The new facility superseded earlier structures, at 7 Oranienburger Strasse and at 14 Auguststrasse. Its true origins go back to the inception of the city's organised Jewish community in the early eighteenth century, and its development reflects both the central importance which the community ascribed to "caring for the sick" and the impact on the community of changes in the local surroundings. The hospital was originally located in the area where the central offices of the Jewish establishment developed. The institution built on Auguststrasse in 1861 was intended to fulfil new objectives arising from current needs, notably an increase in the number of patients.[2] As one of the first general hospitals in Berlin, and indeed as one of the largest hospitals of its type at the time, it served the German-Jewish population.[3] However, this facility, although considered ultra-modern, was unable to cope with the demand, and a new complex was built in the Wedding neighbourhood, relatively far from the community's centre. In time, the Auguststrasse site was occupied by out-patient clinics (in addition to those at the hospital itself), which continued to serve the Jewish population still residing in that area.[4] These ambulatory services constituted the medical institution's continuing link with the general public,

---

[*]The article is based on the author's M.A. thesis. *Das Krankenhaus der Jüdischen Gemeinde zu Berlin 1938–1945*, sponsored by Professor Israel Gutman, Institute of Contemporary Jewry, Hebrew University, Jerusalem 1989.
[1]Manfred Stürzbecher, 'Aus der Geschichte des Jüdischen Krankenhauses in Berlin', *Historia Hospitalium*, Sonderheft (1970), p. 65. The hospital's historical development is also described in Jessica Jacoby, 'Anfänge und Entwicklung der jüdischen Krankenpflege in Berlin', in Dagmar Hartung-von Doetinchem and Rolf Winau (eds.), *Zerstörte Fortschritte. Das Jüdische Krankenhaus in Berlin 1756–1861–1914–1989*, Berlin 1989, pp. 28–67.
[2]Stürzbecher, *loc. cit.*, p. 71.
[3]*Ibid.*, p. 65.
[4]*Führer durch die jüdische Gemeindeverwaltung und Wohlfahrtspflege in Deutschland 1932–1933*, hrsg. von Zentralwohlfahrtsstelle der Deutschen Juden, p. 47.

especially the needy among them, and lightened the hospital's load.[5] The hospital also served (until 1938) non-Jews, who were covered by health insurance funds.[6]

The hospital on Exerzierstrasse was a complex of seven buildings, with all the latest equipment. At first it had 270 beds – three times as many as on Auguststrasse – and this number gradually increased.[7] On its staff were top rank, internationally famous physicians, who also fulfilled functions in the medical community. The administration consisted of the physicians who headed the main departments.[8] In terms of both organisation and personnel, this administrative structure probably lasted at least until November 1938. The directors were Professor Hermann Strauss, head of the Internal Medicine Department,[9] Professor Paul Rosenstein, head of Urological Surgery,[10] and Dr. Karl Abel, head of the Gynaecological Department.[11] The National Socialists' accession to power in January 1933 brought structural and personnel changes in the hospital, and it found itself facing the same problems as Jewish hospitals in other large German cities such as Breslau, Cologne and Hamburg.[12] Jewish hospitals suffered financially, because of a decline in the number of patients who were referred to them by health insurance and welfare funds,[13] and because of the pressure put on the Aryan population to avoid Jewish hospitals. Immediately following the *Machtergreifung* only 180 of the Berlin hospital's 380 beds were occupied.[14] These developments also caused underemployment among the staff.

If in 1933 the hospital's activity was reduced and the medical staff found itself partially idle, 1938 saw the situation change.[15] The race laws that forced the hospital to admit only Jewish patients meant that all non-Jews officially ceased to use the institution and it filled up with Jews from the city, who had been turned away by general public hospitals, and with patients from Jewish hospitals in the provinces which had been forced to close. The new situation necessitated

[5]Stürzbecher, *loc. cit.*, pp. 82, 83. See also G. H. 'Das Jüdische Krankenhaus in der Persischen Strasse', *Gemeindeblatt*, 28th April 1935, p. 4.
[6]Stürzbecher, *loc. cit.*, p. 77; see also G.H., *loc. cit.*, *Gemeindeblatt*, 28th April 1935.
[7]Georg Herlitz and Bruno Kirschner (Hrsg.), *Jüdisches Lexikon*, Bd. I, Berlin 1927, p. 894.
[8]Jacob Jacobson, *Jüdisches Jahrbuch für Gross Berlin 1928*, Berlin 1928, pp. 304, 305.
[9]From 1912 Hermann Strauss also served as a professor in the *Charité* university hospital. See Ernst G. Lowenthal, *Juden in Preussen. Ein biographisches Verzeichnis*, Berlin 1982, p. 221.
[10]*Ibid.*, p. 191. Paul Rosenstein was until 1933 president of the Berlin Urological Society.
[11]See *ibid.*, p. 14.
[12]Mary Lindemann, *140 Jahre Israelitisches Krankenhaus in Hamburg. Vorgeschichte und Entwicklung*, Hamburg 1981, p. 61. The problems were set out in the concluding document of the meeting of directors of Jewish medical institutions in the cities, held on 12th June 1933.
[13]*Ibid.*, pp. 61, 63. On the pressure exerted by the health insurance funds see Siegfried Ostrowski, 'Vom Schicksal jüdischer Ärzte im Dritten Reich. Ein Augenbericht aus den Jahren 1933–1939', in *Bulletin des Leo Baeck Instituts*, 24 (1968), p. 320, note 2. On the fluctuation in the numbers of patients treated in the Jewish Hospital from its founding until 1938, see the graph in Stürzbecher, *loc. cit.*, p. 83. In this connection see also G.H., *loc. cit.*, in *Gemeindeblatt*, 28th April 1935, p. 4. Regarding the admittance to the Hospital of patients covered by the health insurance funds, see the order of late July 1933, cited in Joseph Walk (Hrsg.), *Das Sonderrecht für die Juden im NS-Staat. Eine Sammlung der gesetzlichen Massnahmen und Richtlinien – Inhalt und Bedeutung*, Heidelberg–Karlsruhe 1981, p. 44, No. 208.
[14]*Gemeindeblatt*, No. 7 (July 1933), p. 2.
[15]*Jüdisches Nachrichtenblatt*, 9th December 1938.

The Jewish Hospital in Berlin

changes in the hospital's structure, for which plans had already been made at the beginning of 1938,[16] and towards the end of the year some medical departments were expanded.[17] The high turnover in this period among the hospital staff, caused by emigration or by incarceration in concentration camps,[18] was a destabilising factor, both administratively and medically, and organisational changes became necessary. Jewish specialists, expelled from general hospitals on racial grounds, were employed by the hospital in wards which had previously been part of its out-patient clinics. Although, unlike other Jewish hospitals, the Berlin institution was relatively unaffected by the events of the *"Kristallnacht"*, their impact was felt indirectly, as victims of the pogrom sought treatment. It also admitted people released from the nearby Oranienburg and Sachsenhausen concentration camps who required medical attention.[19]

In late 1938 the general view was that the hospital would probably be left alone; a view based in part on the fact that thus far it had been untouched, even on the *"Kristallnacht"*.[20] The prevailing assumption of the hospital's invulnerability made it a magnet for the persecuted who sought a haven.[21] But this assumption was not borne out by future events.

Under the "Aryanisation" laws and decrees affecting medical institutions, the hospital became a Jewish hospital in the full sense of the word and with all that this implied during the National Socialist regime. Yet its fate differed from that of other Jewish hospitals in the Third *Reich*. Whereas Jewish medical institutions in other large cities were closed down or relocated, the Berlin hospital remained intact and in its same location until the Liberation. Indeed, attempts to close it were blocked by Eichmann's department in the *Reichssicherheitshauptamt* (RSHA). One could conjecture that the hospital, as a Jewish institution, would be utilised by the authorities in the pursuit of their anti-Jewish policy only as long as was felt necessary. Even so, this does not account for the fact that the hospital was not relocated. One must examine, too, to what degree the hospital became a "tool of the authorities" over time, and the continuity that was manifested in its activity as a Jewish hospital in terms of its patients, medical services, procedures and administrative staff. Is the fact that the hospital was left on its original site attributable, among other reasons, to power struggles among government authorities over control of Jewish property?

THE HOSPITAL AS A MEDICAL INSTITUTION OF THE BERLIN JEWISH COMMUNITY

The hospital was a private institution of the Berlin Jewish community, its buildings constructed by the community on land it owned, with the aid of funds

---

[16]Bauschein Nr. 1/826, Berlin 12/1/38; Nr. 1/862, Berlin 31/3/38, der Jüdischen Gemeinde Berlin, v. der Oberbürgermeister Baupolizei Wedding, Bezirksamt Wedding von Berlin, Abteilung Bau- und Wohnungswesen, Bau IV 111.
[17]Ostrowski, *loc. cit.*, pp. 344, 345.
[18]*Ibid.*, p. 349. See also Paul Rosenstein, *Narben bleiben zurück*, Munich 1954, p. 267.
[19]Ostrowski, *loc. cit.*, pp. 349–351.
[20]*Ibid.*, p. 342.
[21]*Ibid.* See also Rosenstein, *op. cit.*, p. 267.

donated by community members.[22] Legally and officially that ownership continued for a time even during the Nazi period until the hospital's forced sale. However, the erosion of the community's authority and influence over the hospital was discernible earlier, as the onset of the transports brought it under growing pressure. The relationship between the hospital and the community was reflected in statutes promulgated in 1909, covering method of appointments, budget and statutory powers.[23] The hospital's directors were answerable to the community's elected assembly, although economically the hospital was not absolutely dependent on the community as it was not fully financed by it. Among the resources at its disposal was the interest-bearing Hospital Jubilee Fund.[24]

The legal change that occurred in the status of the Jewish communities in 1938, and the establishment the following year of the *Reichsvereinigung der Juden in Deutschland* as the central organisation of the Jewish community, also affected the hospital's relationship with the Berlin community.[25] Administratively, the link between the community and the hospital was effectively severed, as the German-Jewish communities were, like other groups, brought under the authority of the *Reichsvereinigung*. Prior to this the hospital, as a private body of the Jewish community, had been answerable to the *Polizeipräsidium*. Under the new arrangement, the hospital was placed under the supervision of Section IV B 4 of the RSHA. At first this was done through the *Reichsvereinigung*, but direct supervision began in October 1942 with the appointment of Fritz Wöhrn, from Eichmann's department, as the hospital's inspector.[26] Changes were also evident in the organisational structure. Henceforth the hospital would be subordinate to the Jewish community through the latter's health services, and to the *Reichsvereinigung* through the relief and welfare programme.[27] Since some members of the Community Council also held senior posts in the *Reichsvereinigung*,[28] in practice the relationship with the community was maintained.[29]

However, as financial dependence was not the decisive factor in the hospital-community relationship, the community's influence may be found in the two

---

[22]Alexander Philipsborn, 'The Jewish Hospitals in Germany', in *LBI Year Book IV* (1959), p. 222.
[23]*Revisierte Statuten für das Krankenhaus der Jüdischen Gemeinde zu Berlin*, Berlin 1909.
[24]*Ibid.*, Paras. 25, 26. The "Medical Institution Jubilee Fund" was founded in 1803. See also Stürzbecher, *loc. cit.*, p. 67.
[25]The law of 28th March 1938 took effect on 31st March 1938, see Bruno Blau, *Das Ausnahmerecht für die Juden in Deutschland 1933–1945*, Düsseldorf 1965, pp. 41, 42, No. 148.
[26]Trial of War Criminals, Yad Vashem Archives (YVA), TR–10/1193, pp. 48, 49; Blau, *Das Ausnahmerecht*, *op. cit.*, p. 11. Hilde Kahan says that until June 1943 the orders from this office were transmitted to the hospital through the *Reichsvereinigung*. (Author's interview with Hilde Kahan, 2nd May 1988.)
[27]Robert Prochnik, 'Bericht über die Organisation und sonstige Verhältnisse der Jüdischen Bevölkerung in Berlin unter Berücksichtigung des gesamten Altreichs 18.8. 1941', YVA 08/108, p. 12.
[28]*Ibid.* The report notes the community's special status as the largest of Germany's Jewish communities and its senior place among them.
[29]In this connection the dual role played by Dr. Lustig as official-in-charge of health in the *Reichsvereinigung* and director of the Jewish community's health service was significant; see 'Reichsvereinigung der Juden in Deutschland Organisationsplan', in Otto Dov Kulka and Esriel Hildesheimer, *Documents on the History of the Central Organisation of Germany's Jews in the Third Reich* (forthcoming).

The Jewish Hospital in Berlin 161

other areas already mentioned: appointments and statutory powers. In at least one case during this period (October 1942) it was noted that the hospital director was appointed without the statutory consultation with the Community Council. (This topic is discussed more extensively below.)

The change from community to national institution was primarily the result of the admission of patients from the entire *Reich* following the closure of Jewish hospitals.[30] It also bears stressing that from the summer of 1941 the hospital served 43 per cent of all the Jews in the *Reich*, who had flocked to Berlin, and whose numbers rose steadily throughout the period.[31] This is reflected in the financial allocations in the Berlin community's budget for that year.[32] At the same time, the hospital did not lose its legal status as an institution of the Berlin Jewish community, even in the eyes of the authorities. In one meeting with the *Gestapo*, the assurance was given that the Jewish Hospital in Berlin would continue to belong to the community despite the order to admit patients from all over the *Reich*.[33] That pledge could be made even though preparations to purchase the hospital were already underway. The hospital's enforced sale was meant to sever the still-existing link between the hospital and the community. Purchase of the grounds by the *Akademie für Jugendmedizin*,[34] was meant to serve the future needs of the *Akademie* and bring about the complete evacuation of the Jewish Hospital. The documentary evidence shows that although the process of the coerced sale largely followed the pattern involved in the transfer of similar properties from the *Reichsvereinigung* to *Reich* medical projects,[35] the final outcome was in this case different, as ultimately the "purchase" was not effected. Transfer of ownership required the consent of Eichmann's department in the RSHA. Everything – the permit for the community to continue using the premises, the date of evacuation and the transfer of the property – depended on the order of this department. The documents show that on 1st September 1942 the

---

[30] Hilde Kahan, *Chronik Deutscher Juden 1939–1945*, YVA 08/145, p. 10; Hermann Pineas, 'Unsere Schicksale seit dem 30. Januar 1933', in Monika Richarz (ed.), *Jüdisches Leben in Deutschland*, Bd. 3, *Selbstzeugnisse zur Sozialgeschichte 1918–1945*, Stuttgart 1982, Veröffentlichung des Leo Baeck Instituts, p. 432; *Jüdisches Nachrichtenblatt*, 31st December 1942, p. 1; (anonymous), 'The Jewish Hospital in Berlin 1943–1945', Wiener Library Tel-Aviv (WLT), P IIIa No. 202, p. 2.

[31] About 43 per cent of the entire Jewish population of the *Altreich*, referring to 167,245 people on 30th June 1941, as against 32 per cent of 500,000 in 1933. See Prochnik, 'Bericht', *loc. cit.*, p. 2.

[32] Jüdische Kultusvereinigung zu Berlin, Rechnungslegung 1941, WLT, W 1b/JUD.

[33] Rücksprache bei der Gestapo, Staatspolizeileitstelle Berlin, Aktennotiz, 7.10.1942, from Kulka and Hildesheimer, *Documents, op. cit.*

[34] The Academy for Youth Medicine was formed as a legally registered association for the purposes of promoting this branch of medicine and training a professional staff. Its heads were the chief of the *Reich*'s health services, Dr. Leonardo Conti, and the head of the Nazi Party's Youth Leadership and leader of *Reich* Youth, Artur Axmann. The director was Dr. Liebenow, the physician of the *Hitlerjugend*. The board members were medical personnel, senior officials and the heads of the *Hitlerjugend*. See Protokoll der konstituirenden Sitzung des Vereins "Akademie für Jugendmedizin", Berlin, 10.12.1942, Bundesarchiv (BA) Koblenz, R-18/3228.

[35] H. G. Adler, *Der verwaltete Mensch. Studien zur Deportation der Juden aus Deutschland*, Tübingen 1974, p. 643. See there regarding the *Heilanstalt der Rothschild'schen Stiftung* in Nordrach/Baden, which was requisitioned for the needs of the *Lebensborn*.

representatives of the *Gemeinde* and of the *Reichsvereinigung* were informed of the intent to purchase, and formal steps were taken towards executing the transaction.[36] The enforced sale took place on 30th November 1942, shortly after the founding of the *Akademie für Jugendmedizin*, and the property was ceded by the community on 23rd January 1943, i.e. before its liquidation.[37] One must assume, then, that the transaction was geared to serve the RSHA's interest to prevent the *Finanzamt* from seizing the property at a future date.[38] This conjecture is further backed up by the fact that the purchase could not be effected and the institution continued to function as a Jewish hospital, under the management of Walter Lustig, as head of the *Reichsvereinigung*, even though transfer of ownership had been legally executed (on 17th May 1944).[39] In other words, the body that was delaying the process (Section IV B 4) maintained throughout that the facility was required for Jewish patients.[40] The Jewish Hospital was not evacuated despite the Academy's plans to establish on the site a hospital for children and the young. Furthermore, the evacuation order was not given even when the bombing of Berlin intensified, and conditions justified the carrying out of the plan; the more so as the number of Jewish patients declined drastically owing to the deportations. Even the excuse offered by the association – that the purchase was not effected because of the damage sustained by the buildings in the heavy bombings – can be attributed to the obstacles that Eichmann's department created.[41] The protracted delay shows that the interest that Section IV B 4 had in the Jewish Hospital's continued existence took priority over the *Reich*'s ideologically orientated medical project. There is reason to think that the delay in handing over the property was caused basically by the RSHA's desire to keep the property for itself, which was possible as long as it was in the possession of a

[36]Aktennotiz, 1.9.1942, p. 1; Aktennotiz, 28.9.1942, p. 1; Protokoll Nr. 19 der Vorstandssitzung am 28.9.1942, p. 2, in Kulka and Hildesheimer, *Documents, op. cit.* The *Gestapo* was represented in the talks by Franz Wilhelm Prüfer, *Kriminalobersekretär*, in the Berlin police. Dr. Lustig's presence at the meeting of 28th September 1942 attests to the scale of his involvement in hospital-related matters. This meeting noted the Berlin municipality's intention to forgo purchase of the property, to ensure the purchase at a later date, when the property would no longer be in the Jewish community's use. See *ibid.*, Aktennotiz, 20.4.1942.

[37]Bezirksamt Wedding, Abtl. f. Finanzwesen Amt f. Kriegsschaden und Besatzungstoken, an d. Magistrat v. Gross Berlin Kammerei, Berlin 30.6.1947, p. 2, Landesarchiv (LA) Berlin, Rep 12 Nr. 317.

[38]For more on this see Esriel Hildesheimer, *The Central Organisation of German Jews in the Years 1933–1945. Its Legal and Political Status and its Position in the Jewish Community*, Ph.D. diss., Hebrew University Jerusalem 1982, p. 234. In the case under discussion, the hospital was sold after the date mentioned above, but remained available for use by the *Reichsvereinigung*.

[39]Bezirksamt Wedding, Abtl. f. Finanzwesen Amt f. Kriegsschaden und Besatzungstoken, an d. Magistrat v. Gross Berlin Kammerei, Berlin 30.6.1947, p. 2, LA Berlin, Rep 12 Nr. 317. Here one finds the registration of the transaction in the land registers of Berlin-Wedding, vol. 125, p. 2899.

[40]Prof. Dr. Liebenow an den Leiter der Abteilung A im Reichsministerium des Innern, betrifft: Akademie für Jugendmedizin e.V. Berlin 27.1/1947, p. 1, BA Koblenz R–18/3228 (hereafter, Liebenow, Akademie für Jugendmedizin). See also Referent RegRat Pfau, Vermerk, Der Reichsminister des Innern, Berlin 19.2.1945, BA Koblenz R–18/3228. Approval for transferring or for changing the terms of possession of the *Reichsvereinigung*'s assets could be given only with the knowledge and consent of the RHSA, see Adler, *Der verwaltete Mensch, op. cit.*, p. 642.

[41]Liebenow, Akademie für Jugendmedizin, p. 1. This states explicitly that with the establishment of the hospital for children and young people at the site, the Jews would be moved to an evacuation camp (*Ausweichlager*).

representative of the *Reichsvereinigung*.[42] The end result was that even though the property had changed hands, the Jewish Hospital was neither evacuated nor liquidated and did not cease to function as a Jewish hospital. It was apparently spared the fate of similar Jewish institutions precisely because at the time when it was to be liquidated the community no longer owned the property.

It should be noted that even in the period from 1943 to 1945 the hospital was known in the surrounding business and commercial district as an institution belonging to the Jewish community. This is clear from bills submitted by various suppliers to the "hospital of the Jewish community", even though the community no longer existed. Some of these bills were forwarded to the *Reichsvereinigung* in the hospital.[43]

THE FATE OF THE HOSPITAL'S JEWISH PHYSICIANS

The changes that affected the hospital's medical staff were related to the process of personal and professional isolation of Jewish physicians which took place in stages over five years. These developments occurred in complete isolation from the German medical community, with all that this entailed for research and professional progress. In the first stage, following the *Machtergreifung* in 1933, Jewish physicians were removed from their posts in the general hospitals.[44] Next, the race laws promulgated on 15th September 1935 made conditions unbearable for Jewish physicians in private clinics.[45] Finally came the decree of 25th July 1938 which stripped some 3,000 of their professional licenses, effectively forbidding them from practising medicine.[46] In the aftermath 709 were permitted to practise only as "carers of the sick" (*Krankenbehandler*).[47] The impact of the

---

[42]A circular of the *Reichsfinanzministerium*, dated 30th August 1943, stated that, as the *Reichsvereinigung* was still in existence, the property and capital would remain in its possession and be administered by the Finance Ministry, in contrast to capital acquired by the *Reich*. This did not apply to the business administration of property which had previously belonged to the *Reichsvereinigung*, such as hospitals and welfare facilities. See Walk, *op. cit.*, p. 400, Para. 495. It is, therefore, probable that the business administration of the Jewish Hospital remained in the hands of the *Reichsvereinigung*, headed by Dr. Lustig. On the conflict of interests of various authorities in an effort to seize Jewish property of this kind, see Adler, *Der verwaltete Mensch, op. cit.*, pp. 643, 644.

[43]See Gutschriftsanzeige (Kraft u. Licht) für Krankenhaus der jüdischen Gemeinde Berlin N 65 Iranische Str., 2nd April 1944, BA Potsdam 75C Rel, No. 104, p. 76; see also *ibid.*, p. 1015.

[44]The *Gesetz zur Wiederherstellung des Berufsbeamtentums* (BBG) and relating to Jewish physicians who had not served in the First World War. Effective 7th April 1933, they forfeited the right to treat Aryans. A few days later the ring tightened around those whose parents were not German-born. See Ostrowski, *loc. cit.*, p. 230.

[45]Provision No. 2 of the *Reich* Citizenship Law of 21st December 1938. See Blau, *Ausnahmerecht, op. cit.*, p. 34, No. 88.

[46]Provision No. 4 of the *Reich* Citizenship Law of 25th July 1938. Blau, *Ausnahmerecht, op. cit.*, p. 48, Para. 5, No. 169. This law was amended in a first provision regarding a "carer of the sick" (*Krankenbehandler*) of 28th September 1938, whereby a physician of this category was permitted to treat Jews only or to work with Jewish departments. *Ibid.*, p. 52, No. 176.

[47]Avraham Barkai, 'Der wirtschaftliche Existenzkampf', in *Die Juden im nationalsozialistischen Deutschland/The Jews in Nazi Germany 1933–1943*, herausgegeben von Arnold Paucker mit Sylvia Gilchrist und Barbara Suchy, Tübingen 1986 (Schriftenreihe wissenschaftlicher Abhandlungen des Leo Baeck Instituts 45), p. 155. According to Monika Richarz (ed.), *op. cit.*, p. 24, 5,557 Jewish physicians in June 1933. Slightly different figures appear in a report of 15th January 1939, Jews in Germany at the Beginning of 1939, YVA 08/108, p. 10.

laws was particularly severe in Berlin, home to a large number of Jewish physicians, among them many of renown, who had also taught, held administrative posts and been prominent in the medical associations before the Nazis came to power. The Jewish Hospital endeavoured to hire those physicians who had been dismissed from general medical institutions in the city, as well as newly qualified nurses and doctors whose internships were halted by the anti-Jewish decrees.[48] Physicians came to the Jewish Hospital from well-known hospitals such as Moabit, Hufeland, *Charité*, Friedrichshain and Virchow. Some of them had held senior positions before 1933 and among them were famous specialists including Professor Ludwig Pick, who had headed the Pathological Institute at Friedrichshain; Professor Abraham Buschke, a dermatologist from the Virchow; Professor Martin Jakobi, director of the Chemistry Institute at Moabit; Professor Hans Hirschfeld, a haematologist, who was chairman of the Polyclinic and Department for Histology and Haematology at the Cancer Institute in the *Charité*; and others.[49]

At first the hospital seems to have benefited from the large concentration of specialists who now staffed its wards, joining the other top physicians already there. The hospital made efforts, even in the face of the decrees, to maintain this medical staff.

That the authorities apparently also attached importance to the medical personnel is attested by the fact that the hospital's physicians constituted a separate group, and were not among the authorised doctors assigned by the health authorities on 8th August 1938 to treat Berlin's Jewish population. In consultations held by the *Kassenärztliche Vereinigung Deutschland*, in the presence of the government adviser Dr. Leonardo Conti from the Ministry of Health, and the heads of the *Reichsärztekammer*, it was decided to grant the Jewish Hospital a quota of physicians over and above the 175 who were authorised to treat Jewish patients in Berlin. Twenty-seven physicians in the Jewish Hospital were approved on the basis of names submitted by the *Gemeinde*.[50] Attempts presumably made in contact with the authorities to secure a larger quota of physicians gave them the impression that the community was trying to exploit the permit for physicians in Berlin in order to increase the quota further, contrary to the spirit of the law.[51] To correct this impression, the community cited the need for a binding standard in the medical treatment of its population, in accordance with the community's forecasts of a constantly increasing Jewish population in Berlin as a result of the Nuremberg Laws, the isolation decrees and

---

[48]Ostrowski, *loc. cit.*, p. 314.

[49]*Ibid.*, p. 345; Rosenstein, *op. cit.*, p. 266; Lowenthal, *op. cit.*, pp. 38, 95; Pineas, 'Unsere Schicksale', *loc. cit.*, pp. 432, 441; YVA TR/10 1193; Christian Pross und Rolf Winau, *"Nicht misshandeln"*. *Das Krankenhaus Moabit: 1920–1933 ein Zentrum jüdischer Ärzte in Berlin. 1933–1945 Verfolgung, Widerstand, Zerstörung*, Berlin 1984, p. 178.

[50]Besprechung bei der K.V.D. 8.8.1938, LA Berlin Rep 12, Acc. 1641, No. 250, p. 9.

[51]*Ibid.*, p. 44, Vorstand der Jüdischen Gemeinde zu Berlin an den Oberbürgermeister Reichshauptstadt Berlin, 12.8.1938.

internal migration. It was stressed that all parties had a common interest in preventing a deterioration in the health of the Jewish population, bearing in mind its worsening economic plight and the attendant health risk.[52] Hence also the possibility that more doctors would be needed in the future. Indeed, the health authorities did seek to maintain basic health standards for fear of epidemics that would affect the German population. Objective conditions thus occasionally made the authorities flexible in determining the number of Jewish physicians authorised to treat Jews and in issuing permits for Jewish specialists to treat patients in spheres from which Jews had been barred from practising. For example, the hospital was permitted to carry out bacteriological tests in its laboratory. The alternative, the authorities feared, was that German hospitals would have to treat Jews, and German institutes perform lab tests for them.[53]

In the lists of names submitted to the health authorities the hospital's physicians were placed in different categories, based on their position and the terms of their employment. Category A included heads of departments, specialists and those with the right ("mit dem Recht") to treat patients in the institution which employed them or in private clinics. In Category B were aides and assistant physicians. Doctors engaged in scientific matters who had no direct contact with patients, such as those working in laboratories or in forensics, were in Category D. Their employment was requested on the grounds that they carried out tests for all German Jewry. Category E referred to medical consultancy by acknowledged authorities. They could be called in only in especially difficult cases, and only by the hospital registrar.[54] A request was made for specialists and directors of departments to be permitted to practise outside the hospital also, privately and by contract with health insurance funds, as some of them had a wage agreement based on reimbursement for expenses and others were unpaid volunteers.[55] In this connection, it was argued that specialists might be tempted to emigrate, causing the collapse of medical treatment in the hospital.[56] Indeed the growing difficulties faced by the medical profession led some of its members to leave Germany. Those who remained found themselves in urgent need of work. The hospital was able to take on new physicians largely because of the relatively high turnover of medical staff as a result of increased emigration, particularly after the "*Kristallnacht*". The spring and summer of 1939 was probably the hospital's most difficult period, as attested by the notices placed in the *Jüdisches Nachrichtenblatt*. Month after month, several

---

[52]*Ibid.*, pp. 44, 45.
[53]Reichsärztekammer Berlin an das Hauptgesundheitsamt Herrn Staatsrat Dr. Conti, 27.10.1938, p. 64. Der Oberbürgermeister Berlin, an den Pol. Präsidenten, Abt. V, Berlin, 3.11.38, LA Rep 12, Acc. 1641, No. 250.
[54]Vorstand der Jüdischen Gemeinde zu Berlin an den Oberbürgermeister Reichshauptstadt Berlin, 12.8.38. LA Rep 12, Acc. 1641, No. 250, pp. 45, 47, 51.
[55]*Ibid.*, pp. 32, 37, Vorstand der Jüdischen Gemeinde zu Berlin an die Reichsärztekammer Berlin, 9.8.38.
[56]*Ibid.*, p. 32.

times a month, the hospital advertised openings for department directors, heads of out-patient clinics and medical assistants.[57]

Beginning in the autumn of 1941, when emigration virtually ceased and large-scale transports to the East began, the absorption process in the hospital was reversed. If in the earlier stage the hospital had benefited from being able to employ physicians forced out of their previous positions, from autumn 1941 the medical staff experienced a constant decline in both quantity and quality. Among the leading physicians deported were Professor Hermann Strauss (summer 1941);[58] the haematologist Professor Hans Hirschfeld, at an unknown date in 1941 or 1943; the dermatologist Professor Abraham Buschke, after November 1942; Dr. Oskar Rosenberg, a paediatrician; and Dr. Erich Fischer, head of surgery.[59] It is probable that at first sufficient replacements could be found among the junior staff and among the physicians the authorities wished to leave in Berlin. Generally, physicians with the rank of professor were replaced by junior doctors. Hence the impression that the *Gestapo* was intent on emptying the Jewish community of its most talented people and destroying everything that had been achieved in the area of Jewish life, as Dr. Hermann Pineas says in his notes.[60] Be that as it may, we do not know what caused one doctor to be considered "irreplaceable" while his colleague was deported.[61] The fall-off in the medical staff was slowed owing to concern about medical treatment for the remaining Jewish population – not, as already noted, for humanitarian reasons, but for fear of the spread of infectious diseases.[62] Paradoxically, this policy, which was inconsistent with the policy of permitting authorised Jewish physicians to remain in relation to the size of the population, gradually improved the ratio between the number of physicians and the number of Jews in Berlin. In August 1938 one physician was permitted for every 1,200 Jews or so,[63] but in July

---

[57] *Jüdisches Nachrichtenblatt*, 23rd June 1939, p. 7, carried an advertisement for the position of director of the Surgical/Urological Department. Ostrowski, *loc. cit.*, p. 343, who was substituting for Rosenstein, who had emigrated, notes that he was given advance notice about the appointment by the community's Health Department. The final notice of this kind in *Jüdisches Nachrichtenblatt* appeared on 14th March 1941.

[58] Rosenstein, *op. cit.*, p. 206, on the circumstances of Prof. Strauss's deportation. The date cited in Lowenthal, *op. cit.*, is impossible, because at that date transports to Theresienstadt had not yet begun. The transport in 1942 came in the aftermath of a clash with a soldier in the Berlin subway. Cf. Bruno Blau, *Vierzehn Jahre Not und Schrecken*, ms. in YIVO Institute for Jewish Research, New York, p. 61. In February 1941 his name appeared on the list of lecturers and in August 1944 he is seen in the film made at Theresienstadt. See H. G. Adler, *Die verheimlichte Wahrheit. Theresienstädter Dokumente*, Tübingen 1958, pp. 220, 221, 328.

[59] For information about the deportation of Hirschfeld, about Rosenberg and about Fischer, see Ostrowski, *loc. cit.*, p. 345; and Lowenthal, *op. cit.*, p. 95. On Buschke see Richarz (ed.), *op. cit.*, p. 441, note 10.

[60] Pineas, 'Unsere Schicksale', *loc. cit.*, p. 433.

[61] Bruno Blau, 'The last Days of German Jewry', *YIVO Annual*, VIII (1953), p. 202. See also *idem*, *Vierzehn Jahre*, *op. cit.*, p. 93, where he notes that some personnel who did not have mixed marriages, as well as directorate workers, were not transported because they were "irreplaceable".

[62] In line with the standard set by the Health Ministry in Berlin, German hospitals had one attendant for every four beds, whereas the Jewish Hospital had one attendant for every 5.5 beds. This standard could not be lowered for fear of the spread of contagious diseases. Aktennotiz, 11.4.1942, 3(2), from Kulka and Hildesheimer, *Documents, op. cit.*

[63] Besprechung bei der Kassenärztlichen Vereinigung LA 8.8.1938, LA Rep 12 No. 250, p. 29.

The Jewish Hospital in Berlin

1941 the ratio was 1:319.[64] On 19th November 1942 the numerical ratio stood at 1:200 – 178 Jewish physicians for a Jewish population of 36,500.[65] That month's figures for the hospital were 20 physicians for 600 patients, a ratio of 1:30.[66] Numerically, there was no significant decline in the hospital's medical staff until this period, and in Berlin as a whole the number remained more or less stable. In August 1938 175 physicians were approved, besides those in the hospital, while the list for autumn 1942 totalled 178, hospital physicians included. In the hospital itself the number of physicians was reduced from 27 in the autumn of 1938 to 20 four years later.[67] It is probable that until this period the rate of deportation of "authorised physicians" was more moderate than that for the general Jewish population.

The last quarter of 1942 witnessed the start of an accelerated process of reduction in the medical staff. First came the large transport of 20th October 1942, encompassing all *Gemeinde* and *Reichsvereinigung* employees,[68] followed by operations, beginning in November 1942 with the arrival in Berlin from Vienna of Alois Brunner, to step up the removal of the Jews.[69] The list of physicians which he demanded be given him on 17th November 1942 showed 20 of the 178 remaining physicians in Berlin working at the hospital.[70] Until that date medical activity was still continuing in the following departments: internal medicine, surgery, dermatology, ophthalmology, gynaecology, paediatrics, neurology, pathology and radiology. The name of the department head was noted in every case, with the exception of the internal medicine department. In addition, the departments employed assistant doctors and interns. For seven of the physicians the hospital is also listed as their place of residence, while some had a private practice in their homes. Only two of the physicians were women. A high percentage, 13 of the 20 on the list, were married. It is noteworthy that only four

---

[64] Prochnik Bericht, *loc. cit.*, pp. 4, 28; Aktennotiz, 10.6.42, 2, No. 7, from Kulka and Hildesheimer, *Documents*, *op. cit.*

[65] Statistical table of 31st October 1942. Taking into account the transports to Theresienstadt by that date (there were no transports to the East in this period), some 36,500 Jews still remained. The number of Jewish physicians in Berlin is taken from the 'Liste der in Berlin zugelassenen jüdischen Krankenbehandler' of 19th November 1942. Cf. July 1941, when the number of Jewish physicians reported was 230, for 73,465 Jews, or one physician per 319 residents. Prochnik Bericht, *loc. cit.*, pp. 4, 28.

[66] *Ibid.*, for number of physicians. The number of hospitalised patients is taken from a list of properties and their status dated 13th November 1942, p. 2. The numbers cited denote the hospital population. The number of patients was arrived at by deducting the number of physicians from the total. At 2–4 Iranische Strasse: hospital – 421, home for the disabled – 222, nurses' building – 117. *Ibid.*

[67] LA Rep 12 No. 250, pp. 45–51. In 1938, 27 physicians were proposed for approval. For the number in autumn 1942 see note 65.

[68] *Gemeindeaktion*: a census of all employees of the community and the *Reichsvereinigung* with the purpose of substantially reducing their number.

[69] See Vermerk über das Ergebnis der staatsanwaltschaftlichen Ermittlungen nach dem Stande vom 30.4.1969, in dem Ermittlungsverfahren gegen Friedrich Bosshammer, Richard Hartmann, Otto Hunsche, Fritz Wöhrn, – Js 1/65 RSHA-Teil C, pp. 982–983, YVA TR–10/767 (hereafter Wöhrn Trial). Brunner arrived in Berlin on 14th November 1942 and remained until the end of January 1943. The date on which the number of Jewish employees was reduced still further, 19th November 1942, was dubbed the "Brunner Appell". *Ibid.*

[70] Aktennotiz, 17.11.1942; 19.11.1942, from Kulka and Hildesheimer, *Documents*, *op. cit.*

were in mixed marriages (*Mischehe*), in addition to the hospital director; a far lower proportion than among Jewish physicians in Berlin overall, 80 of whom, or 45 per cent, were partners in a mixed marriage. The list also shows that despite the major deportation already mentioned, the hospital still employed a relatively large number of Jewish physicians who were not protected under the race laws.[71]

In March 1945, not long before the Liberation, the following physicians are known to have been still at the hospital:[72] Dr. Helmuth Cohen, Head of Internal Medicine; Dr. Wolfsohn, in internal medicine; Dr. Hans Elkan, specialist in lung diseases; Dr. Kurt Marcuse, bacteriologist; and Dr. Shepsko, a dental technician. There are no details about other physicians. A comparison of the two lists shows that only two of the physicians on the November 1942 list were still at the hospital: Dr. Cohen, a "full Jew", and Dr. Marcuse, a spouse in a mixed marriage. It is not known when or from where the two physicians who were not on the above-cited list arrived at the hospital. The large disparity between the autumn 1942 list and what is known about the medical staff on the eve of the Liberation is probably accounted for by the deportation of Jewish physicians. The operations we know about took place in March 1943 and were part of the campaign to purge Berlin of its Jews.[73] Fully 50 per cent of the staff was included in the transport of 10th March 1943, the so-called "*Krankenhausaktion*".[74] In addition, physicians were arrested in their homes on 4th March, following which Dr. Pineas, Director of the Psychiatric Department, decided to go into hiding.[75] There may have been other arrests in this period, but there is a dearth of information. Two members of the medical staff opted for an "illegal life" even before the publication of the above list. They were Dr. Else Levy, head of the Ear, Nose and Throat Department, who apparently took this step on 20th October 1942 during Operation "*Gemeindeaktion*", and Dr. Hans Knopp, an assistant in the Surgical Department.[76] Other attempts at escape were also made, some successfully, but the descriptions contained in the existing testimonies are of a general character and do not enable us to identify the doctors involved.[77] Information pertaining to the period between the spring of 1943 and the eve of the Liberation is generally based on Blau's undetailed description.[78] It seems there were some "full Jews" on the remaining medical staff, and that only a few were in "*Mischehe*". Nothing is known about any physicians other than those we have mentioned, or those who survived until the Liberation. Apparently the

---

[71]*Ibid.*, 19.11.1942.
[72]'The Jewish Hospital in Berlin', *loc. cit.*, WLT, PIIIa. No. 202, p. 1. On Cohen see also Pineas, 'Unsere Schicksale', *loc. cit.*, pp. 433, 442, note 15.
[73]For more on this see below, p. 172.
[74]This appellation is noted in the Wöhrn Trial, Part 3, p. 996, YVA TR–10/7/767. In this operation 300 members of the medical staff and their families were finally transported. See also Kahan, *Chronik, op. cit.*, pp. 20, 21.
[75]Pineas, 'Unsere Schicksale', *loc. cit.*, pp. 434, 435.
[76]*Ibid.*, p. 432. According to Dr. Pineas, Else Levy went into the underground a few weeks before he did, but her absence from the list of physicians of 19th November 1942 indicates that she took this step earlier. See also Ostrowski, *loc. cit.*, p. 435. On Dr. Knopp, *ibid.*, p. 351.
[77]Blau, *Vierzehn Jahre, op. cit.*, pp. 83, 109.
[78]*Ibid.*, p. 93.

burden of caring for some 800 patients, who crowded into the hospital at the end of the war, fell on a very small staff.

CHANGES IN ORGANISATIONAL STRUCTURE

The changes that occurred in the hospital's structure and organisation were in general the direct result of the authorities' implementation of the anti-Jewish policy and of military and civilian needs caused by the vicissitudes of war. At the outset of the period under discussion the hospital was still expanding and making building additions. In January 1938 the hospital submitted a request to effect changes in its structure as part of an expanding project, for which approval was granted at the end of March.[79] In the summer of 1938 it was felt that the institution's 400 beds would be insufficient for future needs, and an expansion of 50 to 100 beds was planned, even though this would not be enough in the event of epidemics (such as influenza or diphtheria).[80] Beyond this, the forecasts as to the number of Jews who would need hospital services as a result of the government's race policy compelled the administration to examine additional solutions.[81] The events of the "*Kristallnacht*" necessitated an extra 150 beds in the Surgical Department.[82] The number of departments was increased in October 1942, when for the first time, by order of the authorities, the hospital opened a Psychiatric Department.[83] This 120-bed ward was to replace the *Jacobische Heil- und Pflegeanstalt für Nerven und Geisteskranke*, located at Bendorf-Sayn, near Koblenz, which was closed and then turned into a military hospital. The establishment of a psychiatric section was a departure from the norm in the hospital and contravened the statutes,[84] so that suitable arrangements were not available. The hospital's capacity increased from 400 beds in the summer of 1938 to 585 beds on 28th December 1942.[85] In December 1941, following the start of the large-scale transports in October, a special Examinations Section was opened in the nurses' home to deal with appeals of those slated for deportation.[86]

---

[79]See Ostrowski, *loc. cit.*, pp. 344, 345.
[80]LA Rep 12, Acc 1641, No. 250, p. 31. Vorstand der Jüdischen Gemeinde zu Berlin an die Reichsärztekammer Berlin.
[81]*Ibid.*
[82]Ostrowski, *loc. cit.*, p. 348.
[83]Rd. Erl. d. Mdl. v. 10.11.42. IV g 8794/42 – 51069, BA Koblenz R–18/3768 (hereafter: Interior Ministry Circular). This circular changes the order of 12th December 1940, so that hospitalisation was possible only in the Berlin institution. The operative order of 7th October 1942 gave the hospital two weeks to prepare a ward, as the premises at Sayn had to be evacuated. Aktennotiz, 7.10.1942, from Kulka and Hildesheimer, *Documents, op. cit. Jüdisches Nachrichtenblatt*, 31st December 1942, p. 1, carries an announcement about the closure of the Sayn unit and of the special department for the mentally ill in the hospital at 2 Iranische Strasse. On the arrivals in the summer of 1942 see Pineas, 'Unsere Schicksale', *loc. cit.*, p. 432; and see also Kahan, *Chronik, op. cit.*, p. 10. For details about Sayn see also Richarz (ed.), *op. cit.*, p. 441, note 11.
[84]The *Revisierte Statuten, op. cit.*, Par. 12, note that mental patients were among those who would not be admitted to the hospital.
[85]Abschrift der Polizeipräsident, Berlin, den 28. Dezember 1942, BA Potsdam 75C Rel, No. 759, p. 102.
[86]Hildegard Henschel, Gemeindearbeit und Evakuierung von Berlin 16. Oktober 1941 – 16. Juni 1943, YVA 01/52. p. 4.

When the incidence of suicide increased because of the transports, a special wing was set aside for failed attempts.[87]

Late 1942 saw the start of a process in which the hospital's space was reduced by a series of expropriations. In November 1942 the nursing school building was confiscated for a reserve infirmary for the *Wehrmacht*; the following month the gynaecological block with the surgical theatre and the institute for infectious diseases were added to this. Thus, of the seven buildings which comprised the hospital, three were commandeered by the *Wehrmacht*, forcing their departments to relocate to the main structure together with the internal and surgical/urological departments.[88] The out-patient clinics of the administration building, by then hardly in use, housed an old-age home which had been evacuated from 3 Iranische Strasse. The spring and summer of 1942 also saw other confiscations of Jewish medical institutions for military hospitals, medical projects and civil defence purposes.[89]

The expropriations at the Jewish Hospital in Berlin took a different form from those at other hospitals, where the building was confiscated and the occupants were relocated; two examples are the *Israelitisches Krankenhaus* in Hamburg and the Rothschild Hospital in Vienna.[90] In Berlin, only some of the buildings were confiscated and the Jewish administration remained responsible for the inventory and for maintenance even in the confiscated sections.[91] Probably the hospital's distinctive structure – it was composed of a network of buildings rather than a single large building – enabled it to continue functioning even after some

---

[87] *Ibid.*, p. 8; Pineas, 'Unsere Schicksale', *loc. cit.*, p. 433; Blau, *Vierzehn Jahre*, *op. cit.*, p. 63. The last two named sources say that these cases were hospitalised in the prison that was situated in the hospital.

[88] Kahan, *Chronik*, *op. cit.*, p. 15. A report of 27th March 1943 on the situation of Berlin's Jews in December 1942 states that the Jewish Hospital still existed, although many of its departments had been commandeered by the Nazis for "special needs", cited *ibid*. The three structures that were confiscated were located next to one another. Like all the hospital buildings, they were connected by underground passages.

[89] H. G. Adler cites a letter of December 1942 referring to the possible transfer of certain Jewish institutions – a hospital, an old-age home and children's shelters – to the Nazi authorities for use as *Wehrmacht* hospitals, educational or training facilities etc. See Adler, *Der verwaltete Mensch*, *op. cit.*, p. 641. He notes that hardly any Jewish institutions of the type being sought were then available. Jewish hospitals were also used for the *Lebensborn* programme; see Adler, *Die verheimlichte Wahrheit*, *op. cit.*, p. 15, for a letter from Himmler of 1st May 1942 to the head of the Berlin secret police regarding a request to evacuate to Theresienstadt the 120 patients of the Jewish hospital in Munich so that it could be made into a hospital for the *Lebensborn* programme.

[90] Even before its liquidation in June 1943 the Hamburg hospital was relocated, initially because of its debts and later, in mid-1942, because of its reduced number of patients. The hospital was turned into a reserve infirmary of the *Wehrmacht*, Lindemann, *op. cit.*, pp. 67–69. In Vienna the Rothschild Hospital was obliged to evacuate its premises and its inventory was divided up in a special arrangement with Lowenherz, hospital director Dr. Rashkes and the *Gestapo*. The hospital, now with 120 beds, was moved to a different street and the original building was seized by the SS. See Dr. Emil Tuchmann, Bericht über meine Tätigkeit bei der Wiener Kultusgemeinde in den Jahren des Naziregimes 1938–1945, II Stp. 341/45, Dokumentationsarchiv des österreichischen Widerstandes, Wien.

[91] The inventory remained with the hospital even after the property was sold. As noted by Prüfer in a conversation with the *Gestapo*, the inventory was to be put up for sale only after the property was handed over. Aktennotiz 28.9.1942, in Kulka and Hildesheimer, *Documents*, *op. cit*. See also Curt Radlauer to Dr. Ball-Kaduri, 13th August 1959, YVA 01/254; and see also Kahan, *Chronik*, *op. cit.*, p. 14.

The Jewish Hospital in Berlin

parts were taken over, and this may also have precluded its full evacuation. One example is the pathology building, converted by the *Gestapo* into a collection point in March 1944, in place of the one at 26 Grosse Hamburger Strasse: because it was accessible through the guard hut facing Schulstrasse, it could function as a separate unit.[92] This *Sammellager* was completely separate from the general hospital. Access to the entire area was denied to the service and administration personnel. In the guard hut adjacent to the *Sammellager* the *Gestapo* set up a centre for information and surveillance in Jewish affairs to which data flowed from various sources, particularly about Jews in mixed marriages and their offspring.[93] The connection with the camp was maintained through the hospital directorate and administration in matters relating to payments, supplies and transports. The final year before the Liberation saw constant movement between the hospital and the camp. Those whose fate was sealed were sent to the *Sammellager* for deportation: unclear cases, among them children and couples from mixed marriages, might be moved from the camp to the hospital.[94]

One ward that was eliminated completely was the Psychiatric Department, in the autumn of 1943, when the last of its mental patients were deported. The reduction in the hospital's area was ostensibly accounted for by its decreased population, owing to the transports, but the reality was different. In place of those who left, the authorities moved in a healthy population, as will be shown later. In the final year before the Liberation the hospital had at its disposal three large buildings: the one at the main entrance, housing the administration and the nurses; the central building, divided among the remaining medical departments; and the plant and services building, which housed the hospital staff who had lost their former place of residence, mixed-marriage Jews who were concentrated there from all parts of the *Reich* for forced labour, and those who had been given *Gestapo* protection. Besides this, some of the buildings were damaged in the heavy bombings of Berlin, which intensified towards the end of the war, causing definite overcrowding.[95]

In the final months before the Liberation the *Gestapo* took over one of the large halls to set up a workshop for the production of children's clothing, the workforce

---

[92] *Ibid.*, p. 36. See also Blau, *Vierzehn Jahre, op. cit.*, p. 69. The camp commandant was Dobberke, who had held the same post in the previous camp. He was assisted by two Jewish overseers, one of whom was Max Reschke, a former teacher and headmaster. Reschke survived the war and faced trial, see Heinemann Stern, *Warum hassen sie uns eigentlich?*, Düsseldorf 1970, pp. 155, 238, 345, note 137. The other Jewish overseer, named Blund, was charged with beating prisoners. See also 'The Jewish Hospital in Berlin', *loc. cit.*, WLT, PIIIa, No. 202, p. 4.

[93] Blau, *Vierzehn Jahre, op. cit.*, p. 93. The centre was headed by Mrs. Raphael (a Jew). The information reaching the centre included reports about cases of death, particularly of mixed-marriage "Aryans", following which the Jewish spouse could be transported. The centre also kept statistics about the number and status of Jews remaining in Berlin and throughout the *Reich*. See also Kahan, Interview, 2nd August 1988.

[94] Hans Friedländer an Dr. Lustig, 7th August 1944, BA Potsdam 75C, Rel, No. 7653, p. 5. *Kinderunterkunft*, 1st March 1944–31st August 1944, *ibid.*, p. 306.

[95] Blau, *Vierzehn Jahre, op. cit.*, p. 107. The damage suffered by the Hospital in the heavy bombing raids is described, with dates, in connection with their inability to effect the purchase. The dates listed are: in 1943, 3rd September, 16th, 18th, 23rd November; and in 1944, 28th January, 22nd March, 21st June, Protokoll . . . Akademie für Jugendmedizin, *loc. cit.*, p. 1, BA Koblenz R–18/3228. See also Kahan, *Chronik, op. cit.*, p. 35.

consisting largely of detainees from the *Sammellager*.[96] The crowding of the departments into a single building and the reduction in the medical staff suggests that the organisational structure of the medical departments which had existed at the beginning of the period had fallen apart and that from the autumn of 1943 divisions between the departments were blurred. Much of the same process occurred at the Jewish hospital in Vienna.[97]

THE HOSPITAL AND THE TRANSPORTS FROM BERLIN

The transports of Berlin's Jews began on 18th October 1941, part of the large-scale, systematic deportations from Germany. The first waves, until the spring and summer of 1942, were sent to the Lodz ghetto and the areas of Riga, Minsk, Kovno and Lublin. Transports to the death camps in the Riga areas took place in May–September 1942, and to Auschwitz from October 1942 until January 1945. Deportations to Theresienstadt began in July 1942.[98] A massive operation, called the *Fabrikaktion* because of its roundup of Jewish forced labourers in the war-effort industrial plants, took place from 27th February to 7th March 1943.[99] This operation was supposed to purge Berlin of its Jews. The deportation of Berlin's Jews to the East in 63 transports was executed by the Berlin police who followed a programme prepared by Section IV B 4 in the RHSA.

The hospital had two functions in the mass deportations, both imposed on it by the *Gestapo*. One was to handle appeals on medical grounds of people scheduled for deportation, the other was to proffer medical aid to deportees at the railway stations.

Appeals against deportation on medical grounds were referred to the Jewish community[100] and were handled by the Examinations Section set up in the nurses' ward of the hospital by Dr. Lustig in December 1941. The examinations were carried out by physicians, among them specialists. The medical opinion was forwarded to the *Gestapo* and was supposed to determine the appellant's fate, that is, whether he or she was fit for deportation.[101] The system created for this purpose attests to the Jewish population's intense fear of transports and to their efforts to avoid them. The medical team was comprised of six physicians, six secretaries and six auxiliary nurses. In addition, bedridden cases could avail

---

[96]Blau, *Vierzehn Jahre*, op. cit., p. 71.

[97]Author's interview with Karoline Schwarz, Vienna 15th September 1988. Mrs. Schwarz was a nurse in the Rothschild Hospital – including the time when it was in the Malzgasse – until the Liberation. She says that separate medical departments existed until 1942, then the departments were all mixed together.

[98]Adler, *Der verwaltete Mensch*, op. cit., chap. 8.

[99]When the mass transports began, 18,700 Jews in Berlin were employed in industry, *ibid.*, p. 223.*

*For a detailed study of Jewish forced labour in Berlin see the essay by Konrad Kwiet, 'Forced Labour of German Jews in Nazi Germany', in *LBI Year Book XXXVI* (1991), pp. 389–407 – (Ed.).

[100]Henschel, *loc. cit.*, p. 4. The *Gestapo* dealt with appeals of factory owners who wanted to delay the transport of vital workers, but made the Jewish community responsible for appeals on medical grounds. See also Kahan, *Chronik*, op. cit., p. 8.

[101]*Ibid.* See also Henschel, *loc. cit.*, p. 4.

The Jewish Hospital in Berlin

themselves of housecalls made by two doctors. According to the testimonies, the physicians tried to delay or prevent the deportation of those they examined.[102] The rigorousness of the examinations was necessary both to seek every possible cause to prevent deportation and also to prevent suspicion. In any event, the final decision rested with the *Gestapo*, which received a second opinion from physicians in the government service. Hildegard Henschel, who worked in the hospital's Examinations Section, believes that Dr. Lustig was generally able to induce the *Gestapo* to accept the original medical opinion.[103] This was a notable achievement, if this was still the case in the later stages of the transports, given what was happening elsewhere in Germany.[104] As the deportations accelerated and the Jewish population dwindled, scrutiny of the criteria for exempting Jews from deportations and for hospitalising them became more strict. Acting in his capacity as head of the Berlin community's health services, in September 1942 Lustig issued guidelines for admitting patients to the hospital. These were stringent, apparently owing to the large number of people trying to escape the transports in this way. Hospitalisation was denied to those who decided to undergo surgery only after receiving eviction notices and being notified of the number of the transport in which they were to be deported.[105] Only the most urgent, life-threatening cases, such as cancer patients, were admitted.[106] But even then the deportation was delayed only temporarily. The guidelines, as Dr. Lustig explained in a letter to Dr. Paul Eppstein refuting complaints lodged against him, were intended to ensure that the hospital did not become a shelter for those under threat of deportation, but whose hospitalisation was not essential, at the expense of those who were genuinely in need of urgent treatment.[107] To prevent possible favouritism, three physicians were given charge of selecting the patients, and were held personally responsible for their decisions.[108] At the same time, memoranda issued in Lustig's name to regional physicians in Greater Berlin, who were responsible for granting certificates concerning fitness for transports and for work, instructed them to adhere scrupulously to the guidelines and not to issue unjustified certificates. The warning came following a meeting between Lustig and a *Gestapo* agent, Franz Prüfer, on 21st September 1942, in which the latter complained that the examining physicians were being lenient in granting certificates, a situation

---

[102] *Ibid.*

[103] *Ibid.*, p. 5; Kahan, *Chronik, op. cit.*, p. 9. On illnesses and other medically-based exemptions from transport – infectious and contagious diseases, such as scarlet fever, unsuccessful suicide attempts, advanced pregnancy and the post-natal period – see Adler, *Der verwaltete Mensch, op. cit.*, p. 428.

[104] *Ibid.*, pp. 428, 429, gives an example of the obduracy of *Gestapo* personnel in Stuttgart and an example from Würzburg when a physician's opinion was not accepted in November 1941.

[105] BA Potsdam, 75C Rel, No. 759, p. 111, 2.9.1942.

[106] *Ibid.*, Par. d. The other sections refer to cases in which the development of the disease necessitated immediate medical intervention and hospitalisation.

[107] *Ibid.*, p. 110, Dr. Dr. Lustig an Herrn Dr. Eppstein, 2.9.1942.

[108] *Ibid.*, p. 111, Par. 4.

which Lustig feared could lead to punitive measures.[109] By now the Examinations Section had probably already revised its methods, conducting at least some of the examinations in the neighbourhoods outside the hospital. The testimonies suggest that the section operated for about a year, until autumn 1942, but the calls to private homes ceased earlier, in May 1942, when Jews were denied the use of public transportation, thus preventing the physicians from reaching patients' homes.[110] One reason for the section's closure was that by this time there were fewer Jews in Berlin who could be transported,[111] and very few among those who were "unfit". Hence also the authorities' reduced willingness to exempt Jews on the basis of a medical opinion.[112] The heightened scrutiny was obviously the result of the authorities' dissatisfaction with the pace of the transports, a situation they hoped to remedy by bringing Alois Brunner to Berlin. The feelings of those who worked in the Examinations Section are indicated by Hilde Kahan,[113] who at the time was responsible for recording the medical findings. She and her colleagues felt helpless in not being able to assist even relatives and acquaintances when there was no good reason for them to be exempted. The hospital's second function in the transports involved treatment given by medical and auxiliary staff at the train station to those about to be transported. Everyone had to perform this duty, with the exception of the hospital director.[114] Already during the first transport, on the 18th October 1941, the hospital sent a team to Grunewald station to assist the needy. Hildegard Henschel notes that doctors and nurses were stationed permanently in the *Sammellager* at the old-age home on Grosse Hamburger Strasse to try to alleviate the deportees' suffering.[115] A striking example of this "compulsory service" appears in a description of the *Fabrikaktion* on 27th February 1943, when the *Gestapo* ordered the hospital to place on standby medical and administrative staff for five or six first-aid stations. These teams, suitably equipped, waited on alert in the nurses' building.[116] The testimonies already mentioned show that the medical personnel were forced to become an element in the deportation system, and were not always able to proffer help where it was needed. As mentioned above, each wave of transports produced a surge in the number of cases of suicide

---

[109]*Ibid.*, p. 108, circular from Dr. Lustig to the 14 senior district physicians, 10th October 1942. Personal reminder to the physicians from Lustig, 12th October 1942.
[110]Henschel, *loc. cit.*, p. 5; Kahan, *Chronik, op. cit.*, p. 9; Walk, *op. cit.*, p. 368, Par. 326 (24th March 1942 – on an approval to use public transportation).
[111]In Berlin the number of Jews decreased from 73,153 on 31st August 1941 to 37,082 on 31st October 1942, and to 27,281 on 1st March 1943. From these we have to deduct those doing forced labour in factories until 27th February 1943. See Adler, *Der verwaltete Mensch, op. cit.*, p. 201.
[112]*Ibid.*, p. 396.
[113]Kahan, *Chronik, op. cit.*, pp. 8, 9.
[114]*Ibid.*, p. 10. An example of a request made 2nd March 1942 to the *Gestapo* by Dr. Metz and Dr. Eppstein to receive certificates for doctors assigned to this service, noting the date and number of the transport, appears in Kulka and Hildesheimer, *Documents, op. cit.*
[115]Henschel, *loc. cit.*, pp. 3, 8.
[116]*Ibid.*, p. 9; Kahan, *Chronik, op. cit.*, p. 17.

attempts treated in hospital.[117] They were hospitalised in special wards in the Internal Medicine Department and care of them was entrusted to the medical staff.[118] The idea was to make them fit for the next transport. From the documents we know of two cases from the *Baum Gruppe*, who were admitted to the hospital after trying to take their lives in a *Gestapo* jail and after recovering were tried and executed. The handling of suicide cases shows that the authorities wanted to eradicate the Jews in their own way, without giving them a choice in the matter.[119] The hospital had to cope with suicide attempts from 1938, when the arrests and incarcerations in concentration camps began, with the peak coming in 1942.[120] Treatment of these cases was a severe mental burden for the medical personnel and also confronted them with a harsh ethical dilemma: should they try to revive these people only to have them meet a cruel fate afterwards, or should they respect their decision and let them die in peace?[121] Opinions were divided on this issue.

During this period transports from within the hospital also took place. If in the first years the institution was a haven for Jews, affording a source of employment or a place for hospitalisation, in the period of the destruction of Berlin's Jews it became a trap, its occupants finding themselves at the absolute mercy of the National-Socialist authorities. Three different groups in the hospital faced deportation: (a) the medical staff and other personnel; (b) the patients, including *Gestapo* detainees; and (c) the detainees in the *Sammellager* (beginning in the spring of 1944).

Deportation of the medical staff took two main forms: small numbers of personnel were included in each transport, and large quotas were set in the "special actions". Each transport included a medical team, nurses and at least one doctor, who shared the deportees' fate; a larger team was often assigned to big transports, particularly those bound for Theresienstadt. The purpose of the medical team was on the one hand to give the deportees a sense of security, and on the other to free *Gestapo* agents from the need to deal with unexpected situations. During the journey the medical team served as little more than

---

[117]Konrad Kwiet and Helmut Eschwege, *Selbstbehauptung und Widerstand. Deutsche Juden im Kampf um Existenz und Menschenwürde 1933–1945*, Hamburg 1984, p. 203. The table on p. 340 notes that there were between 3,000 and 4,000 suicides in Berlin. The graph on p. 199 shows a rise in Jewish suicides, becoming steep in 1941 and peaking in early 1943 (in Berlin in late 1942). See also the essay by Konrad Kwiet, 'The Ultimate Refuge. Suicide in the Jewish Community under the Nazis', in *LBI Year Book XXIX* (1984), esp. pp. 148ff. Blau maintains that a quarter of all deaths among Berlin Jews in 1941 and 1942 were suicides, Blau, 'The Last Days of German Jewry', *loc. cit.*, p. 205.

[118]Henschel, *loc. cit.*, p. 8. See also Kahan, *Chronik, op. cit.*, pp. 15, 16. She notes that from 1941 to 1943 suicide cases were recorded in red ink in the hospital admissions' books.

[119]Blau, *Vierzehn Jahre, op. cit.*, cites the case of Felix Heymann from the Baum Group; Charlotte Holzer notes the case of Sala Kochmann, YVA 01/297, p. 4. On Nazi policy in this area see Kwiet and Eschwege, *op. cit.*, p. 196.

[120]Ostrowski, *op. cit.*, p. 347; Martin Riesenburger, *Das Licht verlöschte nicht*, Berlin 1960; Henschel, *loc. cit.*, p. 10; Hermann Samter, Letters from Berlin 1940–1943, YVA 02/30, 22.11.1942, p. 2.

[121]Pineas, 'Unsere Schicksale', *loc. cit.*, p. 433; Kwiet and Eschwege, *op. cit.*, p. 207. See also Irgun Olej Merkas Europa (Hrsg.), *Die letzten Tage des deutschen Judentums. Berlin Ende 1942. Tatsachenbericht eines Augenzeugen*, Tel-Aviv 1943; Mrs. A., Jewish Hospital Berlin, YVA 02/29, p. 5 (hereafter, Nurse A.).

windowdressing.[122] Some of the medical personnel were included in the small groups as punishment for alleged infractions. A case in point is Dr. Carl Windmüller, who was deported with his wife for maintaining ties with a former patient (an Aryan).[123]

Orders to increase the number of medical personnel in transports are known to have been issued in the later stages of the deportations. The pressure intensified in October 1942 with a major action to reduce the staff of Jewish institutions.[124] This operation was a turning point, heralding a constant drop in the number of workers in the institutions, in fairly close correlation with the decline in the Jewish population overall. Hospital staff were included in the "selection" carried out during the census of 20th October 1942, conducted in the Jewish community building on Oranienburger Strasse and encompassing all employees of the community and the *Reichsvereinigung*. Based on lists drawn up by the heads of department, the workers were divided into two categories: those who were vital to the community's functioning, and those slated for deportation. Ninety-one hospital personnel were taken in this operation,[125] a severe blow to the institution which then had 600 beds, all of them occupied. According to one testimony, Dr. Lustig, in his capacity as *Gesundheitsdezernent* and director of the hospital, tried to have personnel who were vital for the hospital's functioning removed from the list.[126] As we have seen, a second such census was conducted on Brunner's arrival in Berlin. The subsequent transport, carried out on the 19th November 1942, was reported in the Wöhrn Trial, but no other information exists. The list of physicians which Brunner demanded suggests the intention of reducing the staff.[127]

The major action, in which the number of hospital workers was slashed by 50 per cent, was connected with the so-called *Krankenhausaktion* carried out at the conclusion of the sweeping operation of 27th February–7th March 1943 to empty Berlin of Jews. On the 10th March *Gestapo* agents arrived with officials of the Criminal Police with the intention of completely evacuating the hospital. That

---

[122]Adler, *Der verwaltete Mensch, op. cit.*, pp. 398, 431, 434; Pineas, *loc. cit.*, p. 430.

[123]Kahan, *Chronik, op. cit.*, pp. 26, 30, 31; Anklageschrift in der Strafsache Fritz Wöhrn u. 11 weitere Angeschuldigte, YVA TR-10/652, p. 32. See also Blau, *Vierzehn Jahre, op. cit.*, p. 73.

[124]Henschel, *loc. cit.*, p. 6; Hermann O. Pineas, 'Meine aktive Verbundenheit mit dem jüdischen Sektor Berlins', in Herbert A. Strauss and Kurt R. Grossmann, *Gegenwart im Rückblick*, Heidelberg 1970, p. 300.

[125]*Ibid.* Pineas and Samter note that the hospital had to provide 91 candidates for transport. Samter adds that the hospital's then administrator, Scheinfeld, submitted a list of 90 names and was himself selected as No. 91. He and his wife then committed suicide. Samter, YVA 02/10, p. 2. On this see also Blau, *Vierzehn Jahre, op. cit.*, p. 64. See also Wöhrn Trial, YVA TR-10/767, p. 990. War Criminals Trial, YVA Tr-1193, p. 50, states that lawyers, Jewish physicians and officeholders in Jewish institutions were left commensurate to the number of Jews still alive.

[126]Henschel, *loc. cit.*, p. 7. The suggestion in the Wöhrn Trial that only 5 doctors and 15 nurses were left in the hospital following this operation is inconsistent with the list of doctors of 19th November 1942, stating that 27 doctors were still working there on that date. See Wöhrn Trial, YVA TR-10/767, p. 983; and cf. list for 19th November 1942 in Kulka and Hildesheimer, *Documents, op. cit.*

[127]*Ibid.*; Wöhrn Trial, YVA TR-10/767, p. 982.

The Jewish Hospital in Berlin

plan was not carried out,[128] but on that day the hospital director was ordered by Wöhrn to draw up a list to include half the staff. Hilde Kahan related that there were 300 people on the list, including families of the staff.[129] That very night the list was dictated to her and to another secretary behind closed doors by the administrative director, Dr. Selmar Neumann, and by Dr. Lustig's assistant, Erich Zwilsky. It is known that at least some of those on the list were sent to Auschwitz.[130] Transport No. 36, which left Berlin for Auschwitz on 12th March 1943, included some 38 hospital personnel. Following this the transports continued, the aim from then on being to reduce as much as possible the number of "full Jews" and replace them with Jews in *Mischehen* and with half-Jews (*Mischlinge*). A similar tactic was employed against the patients. Just as a medical team was dispatched with each transport, so the hospital director was ordered to include patients in each transport. In addition, patients were occasionally picked arbitrarily by *Gestapo* agents and the official in charge of the hospital during routine visits.[131] In contrast to the situation in late 1941, when illness might exempt one from being transported, a report of December 1942 about the situation of Berlin's Jews show that illness was a high-risk factor for transports: "Krankheit ist die grösste Gefahr für Deportation. Es ist wiederholt vorgekommen, dass Krankenhäuser 'ausgeräumt' wurden und transportfähige, wie auch schwerkranke Juden zur Deportation gebracht wurden."[132] On 29th May 1943, 300 bedridden patients were sent from the home for the disabled on Auguststrasse to Theresienstadt.[133] The last major transport of patients commenced on 16th June 1943, when about 200 patients from the Jewish hospital were sent to Theresienstadt, and with them the last of the patients from the home for the disabled and from the home for the chronically ill on Elsasser Strasse. Altogether more than 300 bedridden patients and a large medical staff were included in the transport, about which the hospital administration was apprised eight days in advance, the notification including a list of all the patients involved and details of the illness and treatment of each. The official announcement stated that these patients were being transferred to another hospital in Theresienstadt. To be sent there was considered a stroke of good fortune, and Bruno Blau relates that when the news arrived a party was held with the participation of hospital staff.[134] Nothing illustrates better the success of the Nazis' deception. This transport

---

[128]Hilde Kahan testified that the event recalled a similar action in the Munich hospital, in which all the occupants, medical staff and workers were loaded onto trucks and deported, Wöhrn Trial, YVA TR–10/767, p. 992.

[129]Kahan, *Chronik, op. cit.*, pp. 20, 21.

[130]According to a report from Auschwitz dated the 15th of that month, the "selection" was made from the 964 Jews of that transport, YVA TR–10797, pp. 997, 998.

[131]Kahan, *Chronik, op. cit.*, pp. 21, 22. See also Curt Radlauer to Dr. Ball-Kaduri, YVA 01/254; and Kurt Jacob Ball-Kaduri, 'Berlin Purged of its Jews', in *Yad Vashem Studies*, V, p. 228.

[132]Von der Lage der Juden in Berlin, Dezember 1942, 27.3.1943, Leo Baeck Institute, Jerusalem, G/L, p. 2. On the non-transport of the sick in the initial stages for reasons of convenience, not humanity, see Kahan, *Chronik, op. cit.*, p. 8.

[133]Henschel, *loc. cit.*, p. 12. According to H. G. Sellenthin, *Geschichte der Juden in Berlin*, Berlin 1959, p. 84, on 28th May 1943 327 people were sent in Transport No. 90.

[134]Kahan, *Cronik, op. cit.*, p. 8; Henschel, *loc. cit.*, p. 13; 'The Jewish Hospital in Berlin', *loc. cit.*, WLT, PIIIa, No. 202, p. 2; Blau, *Vierzehn Jahre, op. cit.*, p. 95.

included the last of the Berlin Jewish community's workers. Smaller groups of patients that were deported after this date included mental patients who had been brought from across Germany. On 15th October 1943 19 mental patients were sent to Theresienstadt,[135] and near the end of the year mental patients who were nationals of neutral states were transported in a special operation, escorted by medical staff.[136] Until then foreign citizens had been exempted; their deportation became possible when their governments failed to take steps to protect them by 31st July 1943 (as demanded by Heinrich Müller's ultimatum), after which date they were treated like the rest of Germany's Jews.[137] We have few details about the patients who remained in the hospital after the deportation of the last mental patients. The fragmentary evidence that exists suggests that they were, for the most part, protected in some manner, such as being partners in mixed marriages. From the spring of 1944, when the collection point on Grosse Hamburger Strasse was moved to the hospital's Pathology Department, the transports were generally carried out from there. Detainees who had recovered were sent from there, along with Jews who were betrayed by informers. The transports in this period were characterised by their smaller scale, lesser frequency and their generally haphazard nature.[138]

THE DIRECTORATE AND ITS FUNCTION

Assuming that the revised hospital statutes from 1909 were still valid in the 1930s, the hospital directorate was comprised of a team of senior physicians and an administrative director, accountable to a board of directors possessing powers of control and supervision. The administrative director and the medical management staff were appointed with the community's approval.[139]

Substantively, there was apparently no change in the administrative management of the hospital until Dr. Walter Lustig's appointment as director. We do know of one personnel change in October 1942, when Selmar Neumann was appointed administrative director, replacing Julius Scheinfeld, who committed suicide during the *Gemeindeaktion*.[140] In contrast, substantial changes occurred in medical management. If until the war's outbreak the medical directorate was

---

[135] War Criminals Trial, YVA TR–10/1193, p. 21. The sick were numbered from 33–51. According to Sellenthin, 51 people were sent on Transport No. 97 on that day, Sellenthin, *op. cit.*, p. 84.

[136] In this connection see also Hilde Kahan's comment about a secret order from Wöhrn to Dobberke – which she came across by chance – to murder mental patients around Sachsenhausen, Kahan, *Chronik, op. cit.*, p. 34; see also *idem*, Interview, YVA.

[137] Ruth Zariz, 'Officially Approved Emigration from Germany after 1941. A Case Study', in *Yad Vashem Studies*, XVIII, Jerusalem 1987, p. 278, says that only 89 recognised foreign nationals remained in Germany, 55 of them in Berlin. Thirty mental patients of foreign nationality reached the Hospital, Kahan, *Chronik, op. cit.*, p. 10.

[138] *Ibid.*, p. 43; Sellenthin, *op. cit.*, p. 85.

[139] *Revisierte Statuten, op. cit.*, p. 2, No. 4; p. 3, Nos. 8 and 18.

[140] Blau, *Vierzehn Jahre, op. cit.*, p. 64. On Selmar Neumann see also 'The Jewish Hospital in Berlin', *loc cit.*, WLT, PIIIa, No. 202, p. 1, which states that he had in his possession a certificate for Palestine and that his wife, who was also Jewish, worked in the Hospital kitchen (confirmed by other sources).

comprised of the hospital's senior physicians, the developments following the start of the mass transports led to the concentration of the medical management in the hands of a single individual. Until the summer of 1942 it was apparently Professor Hermann Strauss who held the post,[141] but our information in this matter is insufficient. From December 1941 the name of Dr. Lustig is cited in the various testimonies as ". . . der damalige ärztliche Direktor des Jüdischen Krankenhauses . . ."[142] He is mentioned as being the medical director in the critical years of the mass transports and the eradication of Berlin Jewry, and until the end of the war. In this period the function of the medical director changed significantly, and he became a general overlord. Before assuming his central position in the hospital, Dr. Lustig had a rich professional career, holding a wide variety of posts which had given him considerable administrative and public experience.[143] He held the title of *Oberregierungs- und Obermedizinalrat* and administered the Medical Department of the Berlin *Polizeipräsidium* until he was made to retire in 1933 after the enactment of the *Gesetz zur Wiederherstellung des Berufsbeamtentums*.[144] He had become active in the Jewish community not long before, and we know for certain that in 1931 and in 1932 he was a member of the community's Relief and Welfare Committee.[145] From the middle or end of 1935 he was evidently assigned to the executive of the community's health services, headed by the hygienist Erich Seligmann. His first dealings with the hospital may have come in this capacity, in assigning the replacements for staff who had emigrated.[146] In 1939, following Dr. Seligmann's emigration, he became head of the community's health services executive, in charge of the health system on behalf of the *Reichsvereinigung*.[147] After June 1943 he was appointed by the *Gestapo* to head what remained of the *Reichsvereinigung*, whose offices had been virtually shut down and most of whose employees had been deported. Dr. Lustig was at this stage protected from deportation because his wife was an Aryan.[148] Information about the circumstances and the exact date of his appointment as the hospital's medical director is scant and problematic. The testimony of Hilde Kahan and of Hildegard Henschel, both of whom worked with him, suggests that he took over as director around the time of the establishment of the Examinations Section in December 1941,[149] but no documentary evidence has been found to confirm this. A different impression emerges from testimonies in the Wöhrn Trial, including statements by Wöhrn himself, according to which

---

[141]If this was Prof. Hermann Strauss, he was sent on the "Alters Transport" of 30th July 1942 to an unknown destination. It is known that a transport of the elderly was sent to Theresienstadt and that the phrase "destination unknown" was meant as camouflage. See Walk (ed.), *op. cit.*, p. 369, No. 335, order of 5th April 1942.
[142]Henschel, *loc. cit.*, p. 4.
[143]See Daniel S. Nadav and Manfred Stürzbecher, 'Walter Lustig', in Hartung-von Doetinchem and Winau, *Zerstörte Fortschritte, op. cit.*, pp. 221–226.
[144]*Ibid.*, p. 223. See also Ball-Kaduri, *loc. cit.*, p. 238; Richarz (ed.), *op. cit.*, p. 441.
[145]*Jewish Book of Addresses for Greater Berlin*, 1931, p. 81; Wöhrn Trial (Appeal), YVA TR/695, p. 24.
[146]Nadav and Stürzbecher, *loc. cit.*, p. 223.
[147]Wöhrn Trial (Appeal), YV, TR–10/695, p. 24.
[148]Following the liberation of Berlin, Dr Lustig was seized by the Russians and, according to rumour, was accused of collaboration and executed.
[149]Kahan, *Chronik, op. cit.*, p. 8. See also *Jüdisches Nachrichtenblatt*, 8th August 1941.

Dr. Lustig was appointed director by Rolf Günther, Eichmann's deputy, on 20th October 1942, during the *Gemeindeaktion*. That operation, which was of crucial importance in the vicissitudes that struck the hospital, was accompanied by changes in the hospital directorate and in its supervision: Dr. Lustig's appointment as director, the appointment of a new administrative director, and the appointment of Wöhrn as the hospital's direct supervisor.[150] The implications of Lustig's appointment have a bearing on the hospital's survival until the end of the war, as is explained below. The timing can be explained by the vacuum in the medical management and the suicide of the administrative director in circumstances already noted.[151] The inconsistencies between these accounts may be resolved by the explanation that Lustig had already become part of the hospital's management by the summer of 1941, in his capacity as the official in charge of the health system for the community and the *Reichsvereinigung*. In October 1942 the directorship of the health services and of the hospital were officially united in the hands of a single individual. The manner of Lustig's appointment by Günther did not follow past procedural regulations and signifies the start of the process whereby the community lost its influence over the hospital.[152] Yet, it should be recalled that Dr. Lustig was part of the Jewish establishment; he was not brought in from the outside and his appointment should be seen as being acceptable to the community.[153] Nevertheless, the fact that he drew his powers from the authorities and not from the community points to his commitment to and dependence on the Germans. We find a similar pattern in the Jewish hospital in Vienna, where Dr. Emil Tuchmann, in his capacity as head of the Jewish community's health services, effectively abrogated administrative powers at the Rothschild Hospital, while the official director, Dr. Rashkes, was gradually eased out. Dr. Tuchmann was the institution's acting director and was recognised as such by the authorities, who made their contacts with him. The experiences of Tuchmann and Lustig during the Nazi period are remarkably alike. Both were dismissed from their posts in 1934 following adoption of the race laws. From October 1938 Dr. Tuchmann was chief physician in the Relief and Welfare Services of the Jewish community, and from 1940, like Dr. Lustig, he headed the Jewish public-health services, in which capacity he was responsible for medical institutions. In his appointment as medical adviser of the Rothschild Hospital he too was placed by the *Gestapo* in charge of an institution to which he had not previously belonged, and one of the functions was to decide on "*Transportfähigkeit*".[154] The similar patterns we find here may reflect a *Gestapo* method of appointing, as head of "centres of control" under their supervision,

[150]Wöhrn Trial, YVA TR–10/767, p. 990; and see also YVA TR–10/652, pp. 29, 30.
[151]*Ibid*. Regarding the date of Prof. Strauss's deportation see note 141.
[152]*Revisierte Statuten, op. cit.*, p. 1, Nos. 8, 18. Procedure demanded that the appointment of the administrative director be approved by the Jewish community.
[153]*Jüdisches Nachrichtenblatt*, 8th August 1941, marking Lustig's 50th birthday.
[154]Dokumentationsarchiv des österreichischen Widerstandes, Wien (DÖW), 13.9.1945, Schlussbericht, Stp. IID, 341/45. Wien (hereafter, DÖW 1945). In a report Tuchmann made on his activities during this period, he said his work was to assist the director, Dr. Rashkes, in moving the institution to its new location at Malzgasse 16 in the summer of 1942. Bericht, Dr. Emil Tuchmann, Stp. 341/45.

The Jewish Hospital in Berlin

officials who conformed with their demands. Dr. Lustig represented the hospital in dealings with the authorities, a function entrusted to the board of directors by the statutes. In the course of the changes undergone by the hospital, the medical aspect lost its meaning in terms of the director's responsibilities. In the initial phase of the mass transports medical matters were still central in contacts with the authorities, with the focus on the Examinations Section (approximately December 1941–December 1942), but gradually, medical questions were pushed aside to the point where Lustig virtually ceased to function as a medical director. The contents of their dealings can only be inferred by analysing the events in the hospital and various testimonies; no written documentation remains. Generally, these dealings were a form of bargaining, focusing on the scale of transports from the hospital, selecting those to be sent, removing names from prepared lists or extricating people from the collection camp. The medical director thus effectively became at best a mediator, the lives of the hospital's occupants hanging on his success in countering the liquidation programme. How successful was Dr. Lustig?

His administrative talents were acknowledged even in unflattering testimonies. He is portrayed as a very capable manager and a skilled negotiator. His manipulative ability *vis-à-vis* the authorities is best illustrated in his successful effort to thwart the *Gestapo* attempt to evacuate the entire hospital on 10th March 1943.[155] As mentioned above, *Gestapo* agents and local police turned up at the hospital that day with lorries, their obvious intent being to clear the whole place. Lustig mustered all his knowledge and experience, particularly his intimate knowledge of the German establishment and its weak points. He referred the Germans to the hospital's supervising authority for approval to carry out the mission. That approval was not given (the explanation is missing from the documentation).[156] Information about his years at police headquarters suggests that Lustig was a tough-minded individual, a trait reflected in his uncompromising management of the hospital, his scrupulous adherence to all orders. Any deviation from them was in his view a punishable offence. Thus his repeated warnings to the physicians in charge of granting "certificates of fitness" to follow the *Gestapo*'s guidelines strictly, and his written opinion in favour of punishing physicians who continually made unjustified exemptions. His approach towards questions of principle, ethics and conscience is less explicit. Kurt Jacob Ball-Kaduri notes that ". . . every time his name is mentioned, it was with great reservation and a note of hostility, without any explanation being given for the grounds of this negative attitude".[157] This ambivalent attitude is evident in the testimonies of two women who worked with him. Hildegard Henschel, who was part of the Examinations' Section staff, stated that on the one hand he used his good connections with the *Gestapo* to further the interests of patients chosen for transport, without the *Gestapo* being any the wiser; but on the other hand these connections also produced less commendable conduct, with personal preference

---

[155]Henschel, *loc. cit.*, p. 5; Pineas, 'Unsere Schicksale', *loc. cit.*, p. 433; Kahan, *Chronik, op. cit.*, p. 20.
[156]*Ibid.*
[157]Ball-Kaduri, *loc. cit.*, p. 242. For possible reasons for this attitude see, primarily, Sigbert Kleemann, YVA 01/193; Blau, *Vierzehn Jahre, op. cit.*, p. 66; Kahan, *Chronik, op. cit.*, p. 24.

colouring the choice of candidates for the transports.[158] Hilde Kahan notes the concern he showed for the orphan children who were transferred to the hospital, but also the pressures, including threats of deportation that he exerted on her and on other workers.[159] From late 1942, when the major effort was in the day-to-day struggle for the hospital's survival, it is claimed that Dr. Lustig actively collaborated with the *Gestapo* and was not just a tool in its hands. The crux of the allegations is that hospital staff and patients were transported at his intervention.[160] An examination of these charges should take into account that around this time Dr. Lustig was officially appointed hospital director by Günther, and probably a major reason for the appointment was Lustig's record of subservience to his superiors.[161] Perhaps this is what Bruno Blau had in mind when he spoke about "a person after their own heart", in reference to the new director.[162] Evidence presented at the Wöhrn Trial about Lustig's good relations with Günther,[163] could give rise to questions about how far he could have used those ties on behalf of the hospital and its occupants. What pressure was brought to bear on him, how much room for manoeuvre did he have? At the same time that Lustig was named hospital director, Fritz Wöhrn[164] was made its direct supervisor by Günther. What significance lay in that conjunction of appointments? In the absence of documentation we can only infer the answers to such questions.

The significance of the new situation, from the standpoint of the hospital's place in Jewish institutions overall, was that orders which it had previously received through the *Reichsvereinigung* were now transmitted directly.[165] Wöhrn's supervision in the hospital and the purposes for which he was apparently appointed left Lustig little leeway as regards the transports. Testimonies given in the trial showed that Wöhrn was a stringent overseer, involved in the minutest

---

[158]Henschel, *loc. cit.*, pp. 4, 5.
[159]Kahan, *Chronik, op. cit.*, p. 24.
[160]Blau, *Vierzehn Jahre, op. cit.*, pp. 66, 104; Henschel, *loc. cit.*, pp. 4, 5; and letter in response to Dr. Ball-Kaduri on 6th August 1947, YVA 01/52.
[161]Nadav and Stürzbecher, *loc. cit.*, p. 222.
[162]Blau, *Vierzehn Jahre, op. cit.*, p. 64.
[163]Wöhrn Trial (Appeal), YVA TR–10/695, p. 32, noting that he also got on well with Fritz Wöhrn. It is possible that they knew each other from Berlin police headquarters in the 1920s. In the Wöhrn Trial it was noted that when first arrested Wöhrn had inquired whether Lustig was still alive. It is not clear whether he was concerned that Lustig might incriminate him or hoped that he might help Wöhrn obtain acquittal. *Ibid.*
[164]Fritz Wöhrn, having been in the police force from 1926, was eventually appointed *SS-Obersturmführer* in August 1938. The areas under his supervision in the *Gestapo* were: Jews, freemasons and Jewish emigration and, later, Jewish organisations, associations and bureaus. At the end of November 1940 he moved to the Jewish Affairs section, when this became an independent department in the RSHA. In January 1945 he was transferred to Prague with the rest of the section. Shortly before the Liberation he and his wife, together with friends, moved to Leitmeritz, where he acquired an identity card, in his own name but listing a different profession. From there he moved to the Rhineland and from 1948 until his arrest in 1967 worked for an electronics firm. Wöhrn Trial (Appeal), YVA TR–10/695, pp. 4–6; and YVA TR–10/652, pp. 1–3.
[165]Since after October–November 1942 Hospital affairs were not in the *Aktennotiz*, it may be presumed that direct contact was maintained then between Section IV B 4 and the Hospital. The explanation for the shortcut in issuing orders being that the head of the Jewish health services on behalf of the *Reichsvereinigung* was appointed official director of the Hospital.

The Schwesternwohnheim in the Iranische Straße in the 1930s

By courtesy of Archive of the Jüdisches Krankenhaus, Berlin

Pages from the admissions book of the Jewish Hospital
1942 and 1943
Attempted suicides account for the majority of these patients

By courtesy of Archive of the Jüdisches Krankenhaus, Berlin

details and exceeding even the orders of his superiors. As distinct from his method of supervising the *Reichsvereinigung*, Wöhrn made frequent visits to the hospital, touring the buildings and holding talks in Lustig's office. During these visits, some of which were unannounced, he created an atmosphere of fear and intimidation, looking for opportunities to torment individuals and punish them by including them on the next transport.

The court likened his behaviour to that of a ghetto or concentration-camp commandant.[166] The testimonies refute Wöhrn's claim that he visited the hospital in order to examine how closely the supervising authority's instructions were being followed.[167] His real purpose was apparently to reduce drastically the number of occupants. Wöhrn, who was described as one of the most extreme of the SS officers, laboured mightily to fulfil that purpose. He singled out patients for every transport and inquired into the importance of the various employees for the hospital's functioning, determining their fate accordingly. On occasion he arbitrarily chose hospital inmates for deportation.[168] Lustig could only pursue his efforts to ensure the institution's continued survival in these circumstances and do his best to mitigate the pressure. Still, it is obvious that he could not always avoid drawing up the lists for the transports and carrying out Nazi orders: for example, in the aftermath of the episode, mentioned above, in which the plan to evacuate the whole hospital was foiled. Apparently Wöhrn turned up at the hospital and demanded that half the staff be added to the transport.[169] Dr. Lustig prepared the list; in such cases he was in effect "master of life and death". Lustig's reasoning in these circumstances is not known, but the considerations that may have guided him can be gleaned indirectly from the testimony of others. His considerations were either pragmatic, based on the hospital's needs, or personal.

The practical motive was given expression in the *Gemeindeaktion* on 20th October 1942, when Lustig made efforts to rescue vital staff. Similarly, in March 1943, when the physicians were arrested, his intervention saved both Dr. Pineas, who was essential to the hospital as the head of the Psychiatric Department, and his own secretary, Hilde Kahan, whose efficiency and trustworthiness facilitated his work.[170] In these cases we may assume that his prime concern was the hospital's orderly functioning. As for personal motives, Dr. Lustig seems to have rescued close associates and to have listed staff who violated discipline or who did not follow his orders.[171] The impression is that in cases where he had a

---

[166]Wöhrn Trial, YVA TR–10/652, p. 48. For examples of cases of abuse of Hospital employees, see *ibid.*, p. 32; and see also YVA TR–10/695, pp. 22, 24, 25.

[167]Wöhrn Trial, YVA TR–10/767, p. 990.

[168]*Ibid.*; YVA TR–10/652, p. 30.

[169]Wöhrn gave Lustig the task of preparing the list, Kahan, *Chronik, op. cit.*, p. 20. See also Wöhrn Trial, YVA TR–10/652, p. 31.

[170]Pineas and his wife were extricated from a transport (4th March 1943), thanks to Lustig's intervention, when they were already in the collection camp and their apartment had been sealed. Pineas, 'Unsere Schicksale', *loc. cit.*, p. 434. Lustig was also able to save Kahan and her mother, Kahan, *Chronik, op. cit.*, p. 24. Two nurses who worked in the hospital and were personally close to Dr. Lustig also escaped arrest in this operation, *ibid.*; and see also Kahan, Interview, *loc. cit.*

[171]Charlotte Holzer, YVA 01/298, p. 4. In a conversation with Ball-Kaduri, she states that Lustig turned over to the *Gestapo* a nurse named Ilona, because she had helped conceal Jews.

special interest, he went to great lengths to exempt people from transports; and, as we know from other sources, every exemption meant that someone else was deported instead.[172]

Did he use his position for personal reasons in determining who among the sick and the healthy would be included on the lists? There is little concrete evidence, though the above provides some clues. How far in advance was he apprised of operations and arrests? Did he set himself a barrier not to be crossed, in acceding to the authorities' demands? The problem is that we have neither Lustig's own account nor documentary evidence from the Germans. We can, however, infer that Dr. Lustig was apprised in advance of at least some of the Nazi operations and that he did not pass the information on to the hospital inhabitants. His secretary, Hilde Kahan, recalled that the "boss" occasionally reminded her of the great responsibility she bore in having access to information and that if word of an impending operation got out, she would pay with her life.[173] One reason for witholding the information was fear of extreme reactions which would tarnish the directorate and do harm to the hospital. Thus, successful escape attempts brought in their wake greater pressure by the supervising authorities, a worsening of conditions and closer scrutiny: those suspected of aiding the runaways were sent on the next transport.[174] It is likely that Lustig did not wish to undermine the authorities' evident confidence in him, but by not making known the information in his possession about impending operations did he not effectively made himself a tacit accomplice? In the absence of any source able to shed clear light on his perceptions and his motives, one can only assume that his subjective argument would be that he tried to rescue those who could be rescued, while doing everything he could to keep the hospital functioning normally. One of the gravest accusations against him is that he preferred to consign the sick rather than the healthy to the transports.[175] Had Dr. Lustig been afforded the opportunity to present his case, he would probably have given an explanation identical to that provided by his colleague, Dr. Tuchmann, of the Rothschild Hospital in Vienna. Tuchmann explained that he preferred to send the sick on transports because the healthy stood a better chance of surviving.[176] Yet this argument undermines the very foundation of a medical facility; the contradiction inherent in his choice calls into question the meaning of the institution as a hospital in this period. Did not the hospital, whose purpose was to treat the sick, become instead primarily a place where Jews were concentrated under the watchful eyes of the National-Socialist authorities?

---

[172]Henschel, *loc. cit.*, p. 7; Jacob Jacobson, in Richarz (ed.), *op. cit.*, p. 405.
[173]Kahan, *Chronik, op. cit.*, p. 12; and *idem*, Interview, *loc. cit.*
[174]On escapes from the Hospital see report by Nurse A.; Roskampf, *loc. cit.*, p. 88; and Erich Boehm, *We survived. The Stories of Fourteen of the Hidden and Hunted of Nazi Germany. As Told to Erich Boehm*, New Haven 1949, p. 158.
[175]Ernst Einhorn, YVA 01/258.
[176]Bericht Tuchmann, *loc. cit.* – DÖW, II Stp. 341/45.

The Jewish Hospital in Berlin 185

THE HOSPITAL AS A JEWISH GHETTO

There was no Jewish ghetto in Berlin. The Jews were scattered across the city, although they were more heavily concentrated in certain neighbourhoods. This situation complicated the *Gestapo*'s task of rounding up Jews for deportation. During the first transports (October 1941) Jews were evacuated from their apartments and concentrated in so-called "Jewish houses" (Jüdische Häuser).[177] But this did not cover the entire Jewish population and apparently the National Socialists never intended to create a ghetto in the city. Only in the final stage, from 1943-1945, was anything of this kind created for the remnants of Berlin Jewry in particular and of German Jewry in general. In the spring of 1943, when the Jewish institutions were liquidated, the hospital still remained intact, its occupants representing the vestiges of Germany's Jews.

Hilde Kahan describes the hospital after the spring of 1943 as "the only Jewish home in Germany and the only place where sick Jews could be treated by nurses and doctors".[178] Blau speaks of it as the "Berlin hospital ghetto" ("Berliner Krankenhausghetto"), since nowhere else were so many Jews concentrated; and because in the hospital representative institutions were unified and continued to deal with Jewish affairs for better or for worse.[179] Blau describes this "ghetto" in terms of its two defining traits: a concentration of population and a concentration of institutions. The *Reichsvereinigung* was housed in the hospital and power was concentrated in the hands of a single individual who was also the hospital's director and served, unusually, as the sole chairman of the *Reichsvereinigung*. As for population, three main groups can be distinguished: "Full Jews"; Jews in mixed marriages and half-Jews (*Mischlinge*); and children.

Offically, 285 "full-Jews" remained in Berlin on 30th June 1943 and 162 on 28th February 1945.[180] They may be subdivided as follows:

Medical and administrative staff and labourers who survived for various reasons, not all of which are known.
An unknown number of Jews who arrived in Berlin for various reasons and were confined to the hospital by order of the authorities.
Patients who were *Gestapo* detainees and had not yet been transported owing to their poor health. According to one testimony, this group numbered about twenty people in the autumn of 1942 and increased over time to about eighty.[181]
Mental patients who were nationals of neutral countries and remained in the hospital until autumn 1943.
"Protected Jews"[182] remained in the facility for various reasons, generally

---

[177]Henschel, *loc. cit.*, pp. 1, 8; Kahan, *Chronik, op. cit.*, pp. 10, 11; Jüdische Kultusvereinigung zu Berlin, Rechnungslegung 1941, WLT, W 1b/JUD, p. 34.
[178]Kahan, *Chronik, op. cit.*, p. 35.
[179]Blau, *Vierzehn Jahre, op. cit.*, pp. 107, 110.
[180]Statistics of the Jewish Population in Berlin, YVA E/161–2–6, No. 7811.
[181]Blau, *Vierzehn Jahre, op. cit.*, pp. 63, 91.
[182]Behörden Liste – B Liste: a list of those protected by the authorities. Kahan, *Chronik, op. cit.*; and idem, Interview, *loc. cit.* An example is found in *Aktennotiz*, 18.11.1942, signed by Philipp Kozower. On the suspension of transports of Jewish functionaries, see the order of Section IV B 4, dated 22nd April 1942, signed by Eichmann. Wöhrn Trial, YVA TR–10/767, p. 969.

because they could still be put to some use,[183] though some were held for an exchange of civilians. There were a number of well-known figures in this group.

Jews who were employed in the *Sammellager*: overseers, orderlies (about ten), artisans and others. It is also known that two Jews served as deputies to the head of the *Sammellager*.

Detainees in the collection camp, nearly all of them arrested as "illegals". Their stay in the camp was very brief.[184]

Entrappers and informers (*Greifer und Spitzel*), who aided in the arrest of Jews who were in hiding; the best-known being Stella Kübler, Rolf Isaaksohn, Manfred Gutmann and Fyodor Friedländer. This group of about twenty people had previously lived as "illegals" and when caught went to work for the Gestapo.[185]

Jews in mixed marriages and *Mischlinge* constituted the majority of the hospital's occupants (from 30th June 1943 until February 1945 the number of mixed-marriage Jews and their offspring in Germany stood at approximately 13,000, about half of them in Berlin):[186]

Medical staff and administrative and maintenance workers, some of whom were employed in the hospital as part of the *Gestapo*'s programme to replace the Jewish personnel there.[187]

Patients from Berlin and elsewhere in Germany who were barred from being admitted to general medical institutions.

Jewish spouses who were brought from outside Berlin after being separated from their Aryan partners. This operation consisted of two waves, the first made up of males (from Frankfurt a. Main, Hamburg and other areas), who were pressed into forced labour, including the construction of the bunker at 115/116 Kurfürstenstrasse where Section IV B 4 was located.[188] This *Arbeitseinsatz*, which removed people from their residences, was carried out parallel to efforts to get legislation passed to enable the deportation of mixed couples.[189] The second wave, in the autumn of 1944, comprised some 300 men and women from the Westphalia and Rhine areas who had been found unfit for work in labour camps.[190] The decrees and restrictions applied in this period against this population were designed to concentrate them in one area so that they could be dealt with as soon as the status of mixed-marriage Jews and half-Jews was legally made the same as that of full Jews.[191]

---

[183]Else Hannack, YVA 01/158. See Blau, *Vierzehn Jahre, op. cit.*, p. 69.

[184]One transport once or twice a month, Sellenthin, *op. cit.*, pp. 84, 85.

[185]Blau, *Vierzehn Jahre, op. cit.*, pp. 69, 70. See also Hannack, YVA 01/158, p. 2. In professional jargon the group was called *Jüdischer Fahndungsdienst*. See also 'The Jewish Hospital in Berlin', *loc. cit.*, WLT PIIIa, No. 202, p. 2. On their activity see Cordelia Edvardson, *Gebranntes Kind sucht das Feuer*, München–Wien 1986, pp. 71, 73, 75. See also Leonard Gross, *The Last Jews in Berlin* New York 1982, pp. 214ff. On Stella Kübler see also Nurse A., *loc. cit.*, p. 8.

[186]Statistics on the Jewish Population in Berlin, YVA E/161–2–6, No. 7811.

[187]Curt Radlauer, YVA 01/254. See also Ball-Kaduri, *loc. cit.*, p. 228.

[188]Blau, *Vierzehn Jahre, op. cit.*, p. 90.

[189]Uwe Dietrich Adam, *Judenpolitik im Dritten Reich*, Düsseldorf 1972, p. 329. See also Blau, *Vierzehn Jahre, op. cit.*, p. 98.

[190]*Ibid.*, p. 91; see also Kahan, *Chronik, op. cit.*, p. 39; Nurse A., *loc. cit.*, p. 7.

[191]Adam, *op. cit.*, p. 330. The summer of 1944 witnessed partial success, in that their rights were cut, *ibid.*, pp. 316–333.

Children in the hospital also belonged to one of the categories noted: they might be full Jews, offspring of a mixed marriage, or of unclear racial affiliation. The case of the children in the hospital deserves to be discussed more extensively than is possible here. This was evidently one of the rare instances in which the hospital management initiated efforts to save a group from the transports, even enlisting the aid of lawyers to prove the children's Aryan origins.[192] Lustig apparently spared no efforts in this matter as long as the law was on his side. There were two bases for the children in the hospital, each having evolved at different times according to prevailing circumstances: the *Kinderstation* and the *Kinderunterkunft*.[193] The children in question were offspring and orphans from mixed marriages who could not be placed with Aryan relatives; mixed Jews whose racial identity was the subject of court decisions; and Jewish children who for various reasons had not yet been transported, the majority illegitimate children whose father's identity or origin was not clear.[194] The monthly reports show that their number fluctuated between seventy-seven in June 1943 and ninety-seven in November 1944.[195] From June 1943 until the end of the war the children in both groups were under supervision of the hospital's social aid section, headed by Hans Friedländer.[196] The *Kinderstation*, where it seems the younger children and infants were cared for, was apparently in existence before the *Kinderunterkunft*. The documents show that in the second half of November 1944 it contained 51 out of a total of 94 children.[197]

The *Kinderunterkunft* was set up in several stages. First to arrive, in the autumn of 1942, were children and youngsters from the now-closed homes and institutions for Jewish children.[198] The second stage saw the arrival, on 10th June 1943, of 79 children, aged 4-17, from the shelter in Oranienburger Strasse, when the Jewish community's institutions were shut down and the last of their staff deported. In November 1944 this group comprised 43 of the 94 children in the hospital,[199] the numbers fluctuating as newcomers arrived and others were released.[200] Some of those released were fortunate to be taken in by their Aryan relatives,[201] thanks in part to the hospital directorate's efforts; others were

---

[192] Kahan, *Chronik, op. cit.*, pp. 32, 33; and *idem*, Interview, *loc. cit.*
[193] BA Potsdam, 75C Rel, No 764, p. 168.
[194] Kahan, *Chronik, op. cit.*, p. 33. See also the order re determining the origin of *Mischlinge* ("Abstammungsfeststellung bei jüdischen Mischlingen", 24th May 1941), Walk, *op. cit.*, p. 341, No. 199.
[195] BA Potsdam, 75C Rel, No. 764, p. 208 (24th July 1943); p. 30 (10th November 1944); and additional documents until January 1945.
[196] BA Potsdam, 75C Rel, No. 764. Friedländer is the signatory on various documents and requests in the name of the Hospital's Social Department.
[197] *Ibid.*, No. 763, p. 17, report of 16th–30th November 1944.
[198] Kahan, *Chronik, op. cit.*, p. 32. The arrivals included a group of 60 children, aged 2–18, mainly from the Auerbach Orphanage in Berlin, which was closed down in October 1942; those of its wards who were defined as full Jews were sent on Transport No. 21 to Riga. On this see also, *Wegweiser durch das Jüdische Berlin*, Berlin 1987, p. 270; BA Potsdam 75C Rel, No. 759, p. 62.
[199] On the date – 10th June 1943 – see *ibid.*, No. 763, p. 324. On the numbers in November 1944 see *ibid.*, report of 16th–30th November 1944, p. 17.
[200] *Ibid.*, p. 20 (16th–31st October 1944); No. 764, p. 208 (24th July 1943); p. 30 (10th November 1944); and documents up to January 1945.
[201] *Ibid.*, No. 467, pp. 158, 174.

deported.[202] The category to which they belonged sealed their fate. In an absurd twist, those whose identity was left unresolved remained at the hospital and were not sent on the transports.

This diverse Jewish population was housed in a few buildings on the hospital grounds under the *Gestapo*'s close scrutiny. In what ways did the hospital resemble a ghetto? Raul Hilberg notes three stages in the ghettoisation process in the East: marking (of boundaries), restrictions on movement and the formation of Jewish control machinery. A ghetto, he says, was an enclosed area under the absolute sway of the German authorities.[203] Is this definition applicable to the Jewish Hospital in Berlin in the period from June 1943 to May 1945?

The large complex of buildings that comprised the hospital was bounded by Iranische Strasse and Schul Strasse, with access to the institution available on only two sides, and from this point of view the hospital was an enclosed area and could be used to concentrate the population which was not yet subjected to the "Final Solution". Restrictions on movement applied to both the sick and the healthy. The majority were forbidden to leave the enclosed area.[204] The exceptions being medical staff and maintenance personnel, who still resided in their city apartments, and those working in the service of the *Gestapo*. Workers engaged in forced labour were transported under *Gestapo* supervision to and from work sites, in erstwhile removal vans, which were also used to move Jews slated for transport. The costs of the work transports were covered by the financial department of the *Reichsvereinigung* in the hospital.[205] For many of the hospital's healthy population the facility was little better than a prison. Those who were brought from outside Berlin, and were ostensibly protected from deportation, were locked in and treated like everyone else: they, too, were restricted in sending letters and receiving visitors. Even those who were given freedom of movement outside the hospital grounds were under the *Gestapo*'s unrelenting and absolute supervision. The yellow pass (*Gelber Schein*) they had to carry attested to their constant dependence and constituted part of the supervisory mechanism. Just as the hospital's occupants were under the unceasing watch of the *Gestapo* and could be arrested and transported at any moment, so, too, could those who were allowed some freedom of movement. The *Gestapo*'s long arm is known to have reached these people in their homes even on the eve of the Liberation.[206]

Overall control of the institution was exercised by Section IV B 4 through direct and constant communication with the director, although the hospital's administration was left in his hands. In his capacities as hospital director, head of the health services and chairman of the *Reichsvereinigung*, he was the connecting

---

[202] Edvardson, *op. cit.*, p. 77; BA Potsdam 75C Rel, No. 764, p. 779, personal file for Gita Torigovski; Robert M.W. Kempner, 'Die Ermordung von 35 000 Berliner Juden. Der Judenmordprozess in Berlin schreibt Geschichte', in Strauss and Grossmann, *op. cit.*, p. 187; BA Potsdam 75C Rel. No. 764, p. 6.

[203] Raul Hilberg, *The Destruction of the European Jews* (rev. and definitive edn.), New York 1985, p. 215.

[204] Blau, *Vierzehn Jahre, op. cit.*, p. 91.

[205] Transport Degen (Spedition Möbeltransport), Rechnung an die Gestapo, Sammellager Berlin N 65, Schul Str. BA Potsdam 75C Rel, No. 102, pp. 142–145; W. Grassow (Möbeltransport), *ibid.*, pp. 328, 329.

[206] Kahan, *Chronik, op. cit.*, p. 8; Blau, *Vierzehn Jahre, op. cit.*, p. 99.

link between the authorities and the Jews who remained in the *Altreich*. As such, he effectively constituted the internal supervisory machinery, the connecting arm between the medical institution and Section IV B 4 of the RSHA. The situation in the hospital was such that all the patients, irrespective of their reason for being there, even those who did not belong to the police station, were effectively prisoners and the directorate could not alter the decisions of the supervisory authority regarding their fate. Representatives of that authority made frequent visits to the hospital and carried out sudden arrests, in addition to the hospital's quotas for the transports. In such operations the Nazis drew on the Jewish directorate for assistance, as they drew on the internal Jewish control machinery in the ghettos of the East.

Lustig in his function as head of health, welfare and the *Reichsvereinigung* became the instrument used by the National-Socialist authorities to advance their destruction process. Yet in his role as medical director Lustig continued to fight for life and survival. This duality raises the familiar question about the very possibility of functioning within this kind of paradoxical framework. This same dilemma faced many Jewish leaders in the ghettos. However, while endeavouring to rescue some people to ensure the hospital's continued functioning, Lustig nevertheless sacrificed others, and it would seem that one factor he took into account when compelled to draw up the lists for the transports, was to what extent an individual obeyed orders. He did make some efforts to save children, but there is no evidence that these were prompted by any long-term policy of giving priority to the survival of the young.

As already mentioned, the frequent visits to the hospital by representatives of the supervisory authority kept the hospital's directorate and occupants under constant pressure. Fear and uncertainty were generated by the unexpected actions and reactions of *Gestapo* agents. Exemption from one transport was no guarantee for the future: the transports continued, sweeping up even the supposedly protected eventually.[207] Throughout, right up to the end of the war, the fear was that the entire hospital would be liquidated.[208] The feeling of a ghetto existence was intensified by the crowding of healthy and sick into an ever smaller area. In this stressful atmosphere many hospital staff resorted to drugs to calm their nerves and dull their senses. The general shortage of food and the Jews' more and more reduced rations led personnel to steal food from patients and produced black-marketeering. Theft of the stored personal effects of the deceased, or of items belonging to deportees was not unknown.[209] The medical routine was also broken, as patients tried to remain ill in order to prolong their stay in the hospital. A cure was tantamount to a death sentence. Patients resorted to all manner of stratagems, faking symptoms and using artificial means to keep their temperatures high. Some physicians took a flexible attitude and also employed ruses to prolong the patients' recovery period. In rare cases a few of the nurses helped people to hide or escape. Yet, despite all the pressures and

---

[207]Edvardson, *op. cit.*, p. 75. See also Kahan, *Chronik, op. cit.*, p. 21.

[208]*Ibid.*, p. 39; Blau, *Vierzehn Jahre, op. cit.*, p. 112.

[209]*Ibid.*, pp. 64, 65; Edvardson, *op. cit.*, p. 75.

fears which were the lot of every person in the institution, some preferred that closed facility to the dangers lurking outside.[210]

The hospital was in no way an organised Jewish community; not only because of its character as a medical institution – it was no longer fully functioning as such in this period – but because the inmates were largely composed of part-Jews. Jewish life was alien to at least part of this population, some of whom even blamed the Jews for their fate.[211] No Jewish religious life developed in the institution, beyond the occasional minyan attendance of services on Sabbaths or Holy Days. Even these were held clandestinely, in the apartment of the administrative director, away from the scrutiny of Dr. Lustig, who, quite apart from his strict adherence to *Gestapo* orders, apparently attached no importance to religion.[212]

The assumption which prevailed in late 1938, that the institution would be left to its own devices, was based on a false premise. It was realised only insofar as the hospital was not expropriated or evacuated like others in Germany. Its directorate was Jewish throughout the period, members of its staff were Jewish, including some defined as "Volljuden" and some patients apparently also belonged to this category. In the final stage the hospital represented the remnants of German Jewry. At the same time, the hospital lost something of its worth as a medical foundation. Despite orders from the authorities, efforts were made to keep up the image of a medical facility. There was a conflict between the director's endeavours to safeguard the medical staff and maintain a hospital routine and the invidiousness of the directorate having to implement orders designed to bring about the eventual liquidation of the hospital.

As we have seen, in the early phase, from late 1938 until the start of the transports, the hospital managed to preserve a certain continuity of internal-organisational structure and of personnel, notwithstanding a high turnover as a result of accelerated emigration and organisational changes. Beginning in October 1941, however, the internal structure was affected and shifted under the impact of the change in the situation of Berlin's Jews. The hospital was integrated into the deportation system as an institution of the Jewish community, running first-aid stations at the collection and transport points and setting up an Examinations Section. Again we find contradictions: the tenacious efforts of the physicians in the Examinations Section to diagnose faults and illnesses which would exempt the patient from being transported, set against the first-aid service which facilitated the authorities' work in implementing the transports.

The hospital's central figure was its director, Dr. Walter Lustig. His control of the hospital and his behaviour in this extraordinary difficult period, together with his implementation of the authorities' orders, are consistent with his being a first-rate medical administrator, a well-known public figure with good connec-

---

[210]Blau, *Vierzehn Jahre, op. cit.*, pp. 80, 88, 89, 107.
[211]Nurse A., *loc. cit.*, p. 7.
[212]Blau, *Vierzehn Jahre, op. cit.*, p. 100.

tions. But as regards his judgements and the moral criteria that guided him, opinions are divided and some questions remain open.[213]

There was obviously a diminishing relationship between the hospital and the Jewish community, as the hospital was brought increasingly under the authority of its supervisory body, Section IV B 4, even before the community was stripped of its ownership of the hospital property. Effectively, the Germans' direct control had replaced the Jewish community even earlier, with the appointment of Walter Lustig as director and Fritz Wöhrn as supervisor. The net result was to strengthen administrative powers disproportionately and to nullify professional authority. From being originally a local community institution, the hospital became a countrywide factor. This was most noticeable in its admittance of patients from all over Germany following the closure of Jewish medical institutions. As a result, a population different from that of the past was concentrated in the hospital. Parallel to this, the process of evacuation reduced both the professional staff and the number of patients, with medical departments being pared down. Absurdly, the same authority that sent Jews to their deaths continued to allow sick Jews to be hospitalised. June 1943 saw the start of a new period, as the hospital began to accommodate a healthy population as well, consisting largely of mixed-marriage Jews, half-Jews and Jews who were foreign nationals. From late 1943, with the intensification of the Allied bombing raids, the hospital also became home to the majority of the medical staff.

In the final period the hospital became a quasi-ghetto where the remnants of Germany's Jews were concentrated. The haphazard nature of the transports from the hospital, unlike the virtually continuous transports from the collection camp, nourished the hospital's occupants with the hope that they might escape that fate, even though their hope was tempered by constant dread. Nor was that fear groundless. The process of decimation, of both grounds and occupants, which began in late 1942 and was stepped up in 1943, was a hint that the Germans intended to liquidate the institution (*viz.* the abortive attempt of 10th March), while confiscating its assets, as they had other hospitals.[214] The hospital's inhabitants were ultimately spared this fate, probably owing to the Russians' rapid thrust into Berlin.[215]

Still, the question of why the hospital was left intact throughout the period remains. There is no unequivocal answer. We can only theorise. The "Jewish problem" in Germany was never really resolved absolutely,[216] not even after the large-scale purges of the spring of 1943. In November 1944 there were still 13,000 Jews in the *Altreich*, half of them in Berlin; the majority were spouses in mixed marriages or the offspring of such marriages, who were defined as Jews but

---

[213]Some consider the fact that he was arrested by the Russians as evidence that he collaborated with the *Gestapo*. But as he was killed without a trial the truth cannot be finally established.

[214]See 'The Jewish Hospital in Berlin', *loc. cit.*, WLT PIIIa, No. 202, p. 2.

[215]Blau, *Vierzehn Jahre, op. cit.*, p. 78, says that after Dobberke, the commandant of the *Sammellager*, was imprisoned by the Soviet forces, he confirmed that the *Gestapo* had a plan to eliminate the remaining Jews in the Hospital at the last minute, but this was prevented by the speed of the Red Army's conquest of Berlin.

[216]Richarz (ed.), *op. cit.*, p. 66. In the years 1943 and 1944 some 10,000 Jewish workers were returned to the territory of the *Reich*, owing to the serious shortage of workers in the munitions industry.

whose fate was not yet decided.[217] As long as there were still Jews in Germany, a Jewish institution was required where they could be hospitalised, not for humanitarian reasons but out of concern for the health of the German population. With all the other Jewish hospitals liquidated (with the exception of the Hamburg hospital, which operated in a different format), only in the Jewish Hospital in Berlin could Jews be hospitalised under the watchful eye of Eichmann's office. This theory assumes greater credence in the light of the fact that Section IV B 4 delayed the transfer of the property to its new owners because the hospital was needed to treat sick Jews.

It also bears recalling that from the summer of 1943 the hospital became a place of concentration and temporary accommodation for all Jews for whom no "solution" had yet been found. Cordelia Edvardson's description of the hospital as the "place into which all the remnants of Berlin's Jews were swept",[218] aptly describes the role that the supervisory authority had in mind for the institution.

Another possibility for the hospital's survival credits its director with being able to manoeuvre in his dealings with the *Gestapo*. His skill in negotiating with them stemmed from his former position in the *Polizeipräsidium* and the connections he formed with the *Gestapo* agents are traceable in part to that experience.

A further question is why the hospital was left on its original site and was not relocated, despite the sale of the property and despite the shortage of buildings in Berlin? We know of no actions that were taken with a view to relocating the hospital. Indeed, the protracted delaying tactics taken by Eichmann's office in transferring the property's ownership would seem to indicate an opposite intention. It is difficult to avoid the conjecture that the delaying tactics of Section IV B 4 were prompted by a desire to control and keep the property.

The probability is that the hospital's survival was due to a combination of all the factors just mentioned. It had a seemingly "conditional" existence. It may be deduced that the hospital underwent the same process of liquidation as Berlin Jewry, but more slowly. Final eradication was averted thanks to the Liberation.

---

[217]On 20th June 1943, there were 9,529 Jews of various categories in the *Altreich*, 6,790 of them in Berlin. This proportion changed by November 1944. On 1st November there were 12,930 Jews of various categories, of whom 6,113 were in Berlin. (The categories were: full Jews, Jews in regular and preferential mixed marriages, offspring of mixed marriages who were defined as Jews, *Geltungsjuden* and Jews who were foreign nationals.) In Berlin on 28th February 1945, there were 6,284 Jews of these categories. Statistics of the Jewish Population in Berlin, YVA E/161-2-6, No. 7811. On the Party's efforts to have the offspring of mixed marriages included in the first degree (*Mischlinge I Grades*) for the purposes of the "Final Solution", see Adam, *op. cit.*, pp. 316-333.*

* For three detailed studies of Nazi policy towards Jews in *Mischehe* and *Mischlinge*, see further the essays by John A. S. Grenville, 'Die "Endlösung" und die "Judenmischlinge" im Dritten Reich', in Ursula Büttner (Hrsg.), *Das Unrechtsregime. Internationale Forschung über den Nationalsozialismus*, Bd. 2, Hamburg 1986; Ursula Büttner, 'The Persecution of Christian-Jewish Families in the Third Reich' and Jeremy Noakes, 'The Development of Nazi Policy towards German-Jewish "Mischlinge" 1933-1945', in *LBI Year Book XXXIV* (1989), pp. 267-279 and 291-354 – (Ed.).

[218]Edvardson, *op. cit.*, p. 74.

Walter Gyssling, the Centralverein and the Büro Wilhelmstraße, 1929–1933

BY LEONIDAS E. HILL

Over twenty years ago Arnold Paucker's book provided an admirable description of Jewish defensive efforts against antisemitism and National Socialism in the last years of the Weimar Republic.[1] The chapter devoted to the *Büro Wilhelmstraße* mentioned one of its employees, the Gentile Walter Gyssling, and was partly based on his report, *Propaganda gegen die NSDAP in den Jahren 1929–1933*, written in 1962 for the Leo Baeck Institute in London. Only recently did a published sketch of Gyssling's life become available,[2] and at almost the same time I found a copy of the autobiography of Walter Gyssling amongst 256 others submitted in 1939–1940 for the prize competition 'My Life in Germany before and after Hitler', which is the title of his essay.[3] Gyssling had sent his manuscript from Paris in 1939 and only in 1941 received the news (in Zürich) that he had won a third prize of $100 for it. The manuscript very much deserved the prize, and is worth publication today. It answers many of the questions one might have asked about the background and motives of its intrinsically interesting author, at least for the period until 1933. Further research in archives and Gyssling's journalism has made it possible to sketch his life in Paris from 1933 to 1939, in Zürich during the war, then in Paris and Zürich again from 1945 until his death in 1980. One purpose of this article is a fuller biographical account to throw light on Walter Gyssling's complex character.*

---

[1]Arnold Paucker, *Der jüdische Abwehrkampf gegen Antisemitismus und Nationalsozialismus in den letzten Jahren der Weimarer Republik*, Hamburg ²1969. Although in his book Paucker discusses the role of the *Büro Wilhelmstraße* in detail for the first time, on the basis of his interviews with Hans Reichmann and the Gyssling ms., there is an earlier, though brief account by Reichmann, in *In Zwei Welten. Siegfried Moses zum fünfundsiebzigsten Geburtstag*, herausgegeben von Hans Tramer, Tel-Aviv 1962, p. 566.

[2]Werner Röder and Herbert A. Strauss (eds.), *Biographisches Handbuch der deutschsprachigen Emigration nach 1933*, Band I, *Politik, Wirtschaft, öffentliches Leben*, München–New York–London–Paris 1980, pp. 257–258. This sketch of Gyssling's life up to 1975 was based on a questionnaire filled out by Gyssling himself; the original, with some further details, is on microfilm at the *Institut für Zeitgeschichte* in Munich. I am grateful to Dr. Alfred Cattani of the *Neue Zürcher Zeitung* for finding the date of Gyssling's death and the address of his daughter for me, as well as facilitating my research in Zürich. A celebration of Gyssling's 75th birthday and an obituary in *Der Freidenker. Monatsschrift der Freidenker-Vereinigung der Schweiz*, LXI, No. 3 (March 1978); and LXIII, No. 11 (November 1980), p. 85, add very little to the information in the *Biographisches Handbuch*.

[3]His autobiography is in the 'My Life in Germany' collection in The Houghton Library, Harvard University. I am grateful to the staff there for providing me during a number of visits with all of the collection. I am also grateful to David and Helene Roberts for their hospitality in Cambridge.

*My thanks to the Social Sciences and Humanities Research Council of Canada for research support. My wife Nancy has skilfully produced numerous drafts of this article on the computer.

A second purpose is to elaborate on the *Büro Wilhelmstraße* and Gyssling's work in it. His two manuscripts and information he provided in a questionnaire support claims to his being the author of some publications previously thought to be the work of many hands. He was not only a highly organised and attentive archivist, but also a very productive journalist, working industriously almost until he died.

A third purpose of this paper is to examine aspects of the problem of propaganda and covert as well as public action against the National Socialists in the last years of the Weimar Republic. Arnold Paucker's book relied partly on Gyssling's 1962 manuscript to show how some successes in collaboration with republican parties could be achieved. An article by Dan S. White examined the SPD's partially successful efforts to counter the Nazis without mentioning the *Centralverein* (C.V.) This camouflaged effort by the C.V. has been ignored hitherto in general historical accounts of the period.[4]

I

Walter Gyssling was born in 1903 in Munich and died in Zürich in 1980. His father, a widower when he married his much younger second wife, died the year his son was born. His mother was an opera singer and ended her career when she married. His father had been an engineer, founded an organisation which tested the safety of various means of transportation, such as trams, railways, ships and automobiles. He was also director of an insurance company. His wealth sustained the family until the great inflation of 1923. Thus Walter spent his childhood in reasonably affluent circumstances with an entrée to the best Munich society, and saw much of many artists, particularly musicians, i.a. Anna Pavlova. He proved to be a bright child, teaching himself to read at the age of four, and at an early age showed precocious interest in history and politics. In his teens he came heavily under the influence of the Left-wing psychiatrist and sociologist Franz-Carl Müller-Lyer.[5] Even after Müller-Lyer's death in 1916 Gyssling continued to share his mentor's views and to frequent his house, where he met the pacifist Ludwig Quidde, the sociologist Rudolf Goldscheid and Kurt Eisner, who was later to be *Minister-Präsident* of the Bavarian *Räterepublik*.

The men of his family, uncles and cousins, were professional soldiers; a number of them were killed or wounded in the First World War, which Gyssling followed with avid interest. Having earlier decided he would also become an officer, in the spring of 1917 he entered the Bavarian cadet corps. But the

---

[4]Cf. Dan S. White, 'Outpropagandizing the Nazis. The SPD's "Front Generation"', in Michael B. Barrett (ed.), *Proceedings of the Citadel Symposium on Hitler and the National Socialist Era 24–25 April 1980*, Charleston, S.C. 1982, pp. 124–130; and Gerhard Paul, *Aufstand der Bilder. Die NS-Propaganda vor 1933*, Bonn 1990, which claims that before 1933 NSDAP propaganda was much less successful and less organised than scholars have hitherto believed.

[5]Gyssling commemorated him in 'Franz-Carl Müller-Lyer. Zur 50. Wiederkehr seines Todestages', in *Der Freidenker*, IXL, No. 10 (October 1966), pp. 77–78; 'Zum Gedenken an Franz Müller-Lyer', *ibid.*, LIX, No. 11 (November 1976), p. 91.

subversive effects of his association with Müller-Lyer soured him on many aspects of cadet life, such as the endless drilling, the lack of freedom, the primitiveness of military thinking, the injustice and arbitrariness, the poor food. Soon in trouble for his undisciplined behaviour, he was saved by his talent as a student and by the favour of a few officers, but he no longer had any desire to be an officer. He again became interested in politics, wrote an article on Prussian constitutional reform which was promptly published in a Munich newspaper; read revolutionary literature such as the Communist Manifesto in his spare time; in civilian clothes attended some political assemblies addressed by members of the *Unabhängige Sozialdemokratische Partei Deutschlands* (USPD) and the *Sozialdemokratische Partei Deutschlands* (SPD) and began cautiously to tell some of his comrades that the war was lost.

Suddenly during the November Revolution of 1918 it almost seemed as though the cadets would play a role in their uniforms, but they did not because the much more formidable military, militia and police dominated the scene. However, he tasted revolutionary politics as the elected representative of the cadet corps, and after its dissolution returned to his *Gymnasium* where his schoolmates elected him to the student council. Soon he was chairman of this council, then chairman of the assembly of representatives from all the Munich student councils, finally chairman of a comparable assembly for all Bavaria. This body attempted some reforms in the schools, the counterpart of the reforms being advanced in the workers' and soldiers' councils at the time. They aimed at the democratisation of the entire school system; Gyssling became acquainted with a number of important adult reformers, such as Gustav Wyneken.[6] This was for Gyssling a wonderful period of freedom and innovation, and his studies were of secondary importance. Greatly disappointed by the violent end of the first *Räterepublik*, he was the more encouraged by the emergence of the second *Räterepublik* under the Communists, who were, to his horror, dislodged and murdered by the army in May 1919.

The widow of Müller-Lyer rescued him from despair over these developments by asking him to help her order and edit the papers of her husband. This he did during every spare minute left from school, and connected with this work he read classics of sociology and ethnology by writers as diverse as Herbert Spencer, John Lubbock, James George Frazer and Henry Thomas Buckle. In school he attempted in small ways to thwart the reactionaries, for example when a teacher wanted to hang a picture of Count Arco, the assassin of Eisner, in the classroom. At this time under the influence of another teacher he read not only Shakespeare, Marlowe, Hölderlin, Stifter and Nietzsche but also Heinrich and Thomas Mann, Hermann Kayserling and Ricarda Huch. In 1921 he joined the pacifist

---

[6]Gustav Wyneken (1875–1964), pedagogue and reformer of education; antibourgeois opponent of nationalism, militarism and the churches; atheist; head of a famous school at Wickersdorf, but deposed when accused of paedophilia; after 1920 lived as writer; close to youth movement. See Gyssling's appreciations of Wyneken in *Der Freidenker*, XLVII, No. 4 (April 1964), p 31; XLVIII, No. 1 (January 1965), p. 7; LVIII, No. 5 (May 1975), p. 39.

organisation, the *Deutsche Friedensgesellschaft*.[7] Somewhat later he renewed his acquaintance with Ludwig Quidde, and met leading figures in German pacifism such as Hellmuth von Gerlach, Graf Kessler, Helene Stöcker and Kurt Hiller.[8] Although influenced by them and a member of their organisation, he was not personally or politically a pacifist.

In 1922 he entered university and became deeply engaged in republican student politics. He studied first in Munich and then in Leipzig, where he had a leading role in the republican student organisation. The politics of this organisation were essentially Social Democratic, except that they proposed a more radical transformation of the universities, the economy and the government than the Social Democratic governments of the time attempted. On 18th May 1923 he was fined 450 marks or three days in jail for carrying a forbidden weapon.[9] The circumstances of his arrest are not clear, but Gyssling seems to have been combative, and the police watched or intervened frequently in Left-wing student politics. He studied economics and law for five semesters until 1924, but the inflation, as mentioned earlier, consumed his mother's inherited wealth and made continuation of his university studies impossible.

Consequently he first undertook volunteer work with the *Allgemeine Zeitung*, a (largely Liberal) newspaper in Munich, and during 1922–1923 became acquainted with the NSDAP, whose rallies he sometimes attended. The Nazis recognised him as an opponent and some Nazi youths once attacked him in a narrow street. Red haired, blue eyed, strongly built and pugnacious Gyssling had learned to box so that in these ideal circumstances he felled a few of them and the rest ran off. He was himself wounded and triumphant; even though in subsequent years he frequently engaged in verbal and written exchanges with the Nazis, he was never again attacked. In this period he was a close student, through the newspapers and pamphlets, of the attempted Nazi Putsch in 1923 and of the trial of Hitler and of the Right-wing Nationalist, Paul Nikolaus Cossmann.[10]

In 1926 he travelled around Yugoslavia as a journalist. Then from Munich he went to the *Regensburger Neueste Nachrichten*[11] as associate editor for a year. This newspaper supported the German Democratic Party, which in the next election suffered such a devastating defeat in Bavaria that it could no longer subsidise its

---

[7]See Roger Chickering, *Imperial Germany and a World without War. The Peace Movement and German Society, 1892–1914*, Princeton 1975; Friedrich-Karl Scheer, *Die Deutsche Friedensgesellschaft (1892–1933). Organisation, Ideologie, politische Ziele. Ein Beitrag zur Geschichte des Pazifismus in Deutschland*, Frankfurt a. Main 1982; Karl Holl and Wolfram Wette (eds.), *Pazifismus in der Weimarer Republik*, Paderborn 1981.

[8]For the roles of these four during the Weimar Republic see Holl and Wette, *Pazifismus, op. cit.*

[9]*Ausbürgerungsakte* for Walter Gyssling, Geheime Staatspolizei, 28th December 1937, Signatur R99691, Auswärtiges Amt, Bonn. My thanks to Dr. Gehling for sending me this document.

[10]Paul Nikolaus Cossmann (1869–1942), Right-wing Conservative and founder-editor of the *Süddeutsche Monatshefte* in Munich; a leading propagandist of the *Dolchstoßlegende*, at first he expressed approval of Hitler's nationalism, but soon became his fierce opponent: He was arrested and imprisoned when Hitler came to power. Released after two years he was later re-arrested and died in Theresienstadt.

[11]A short-lived newspaper which is not even listed in the main compilation of German newspapers for this period.

own newspaper. It then came under the control of the Right. He recognised that there was scarcely place for a journalist with his political views in reactionary Bavaria and that he must find permanent work elsewhere. Therefore he moved to Berlin in June 1928, though some of the impetus for this move seems also to have come from the breakdown of a short-lived marriage, from which his daughter was born.[12] In Berlin he witnessed the celebratory beginning of the new Müller *Große Koalition* and reported events as a free-lance journalist. Soon he found steadier employment with the *Verein zur Abwehr des Antisemitismus*, whose general secretary, Dr. Richard Horlacher, had been the lieutenant of his company in the cadet corps. This organisation was non-denominational; despite an important role in the past, by 1928 it was in decline.[13] Within a month of working there Gyssling wrote some studies, based on his previous experience of the National Socialists, about the psychology of the National Socialist movement and the preconditions for a successful struggle against them. The publication attracted little attention, but probably on the basis of it he shifted to the much more successful and important *Centralverein deutscher Staatsbürger Jüdischen Glaubens*.[14] In his portrayal this was *the* organisation of the assimilationist Jewish bourgeoisie. It was closely connected with Jewish academic organisations, had some 60,000 members and the financial support of a number of its wealthy members, especially those who owned the great department stores and banks and were under attack from National Socialists.[15] In this same period, on 21st January 1929, he was fined 100 marks or ten days imprisonment for the distribution of writings unacceptable to the state; no more information than this is given in the Nazi summary of the justifications for the loss of his citizenship in 1938. Presumably he was distributing leaflets attacking them.[16]

The C.V. apparently recognised Gyssling's special knowledge of the Nazis and employed him to expand their *Büro Wilhelmstraße*, which will be examined below. Only a month after his arrival in Berlin he went on commission from the C.V. to Coburg, where he studied the social basis of the NSDAP movement. He returned to Berlin with rich material, some of which he published as articles in the *C.V.-Zeitung*.[17] He also wrote some internal memoranda recommending that the C.V. concentrate its effort on defeating the NSDAP in three voting districts, one in Franken, another in Thuringia and a third in South Saxony. But the C.V. did not want to centralise its efforts in this fashion.

They then sent him to do a short investigation of a wave of antisemitic actions in Helgoland, which were insignificant. In subsequent months he travelled

---

[12]They divorced in 1935. Gyssling's daughter, Mrs. Erika Klein, Munich, who first met her father after the war, has generously given the author permission to attempt to publish her father's autobiography.

[13]For a detailed account of the development of the *Abwehrverein*, see the essays by Barbara Suchy, 'The Verein zur Abwehr des Antisemitismus (I). From its Beginnings to the First World War', in *LBI Year Book XXVIII* (1983), pp. 205–239; and *idem*, 'The Verein zur Abwehr des Antisemitismus (II). From the First World War to its Dissolution in 1933', in *LBI Year Book XXX* (1985), pp. 67–103.

[14]See Paucker, *op. cit.*

[15]*Ibid.*, p. 111.

[16]*Ausbürgerungsakte* for Gyssling.

[17]Paucker, *op. cit.*, p. 242, note 21.

widely in Brandenburg, Poznań-West Prussia, Mecklenburg and Pomerania, later also Schleswig-Holstein, to investigate the social basis of National Socialism in a number of provincial towns.[18]

In 1932 Gyssling was seriously ill for some months and took a long cure in Switzerland, during which time he may have confirmed his hereditary claims to citizenship[19] and have created other ties that facilitated his entry in 1933. After Hitler's appointment Gyssling helped transport the C.V. archives to Bavaria, where they were subsequently destroyed.[20] He returned to Berlin and lodged with a different friend every night so as to evade the police, then fled into exile, or rather to his second homeland, by crossing the border at Basel on 23rd March. By July he had found employment with the *Basler National-Zeitung* as its Paris correspondent. From 1934 to 1941 he also wrote for the *Berner Tagwacht*, a Social Democratic newspaper. He was a member of the Left-wing German exile community, and was particularly friendly with Hellmuth von Gerlach, Hans Venedey,[21] Georg Bernhard,[22] Leopold Schwarzschild,[23] Hilde Walter[24] and Walter Mehring.[25] Occasionally he published sensational reports on the National-Socialist menace, such as in 1936(?) a memorable and widely noted article on Germany's creation of a new nerve gas for the approaching war.[26] In April 1938 the Nazi government revoked his citizenship[27] on the basis of their records concerning his Left-wing activities in the 1920s, as well as knowledge of his work for the C.V., his role in the archives and in writing the *Anti-Nazi*.[28] During his last months in Paris he wrote his autobiography for the Harvard competition, was interned from September 1939 to February 1940, apparently in Le Vernet,[29] was released until internment again for fourteen days, then was one

---

[18] *Ibid.*, p. 126.
[19] *Historisch-biographisches Lexikon der Schweiz*, Neuenburg 1926, vol. III, p. 532, on the Gyssling family's sixteenth-century origins in Zürich.
[20] Paucker, *op. cit.*, p. 126.
[21] For Hans Venedey (1902–1969), see *Biographisches Handbuch, op. cit.*, p. 780.
[22] Georg Bernhard (1875–1944), 1914–1930, editor of the *Vossische Zeitung*; member of the *Reichstag* from 1928–1930; in exile in Paris he founded and edited the *Pariser Tageblatt* and in 1941 he fled to the USA.
[23] Leopold Schwarzschild (1891–1950), founder and editor of several journals, including *Das Tagebuch* after 1927; 1933 fled to Vienna and then Paris; in 1940 he fled to the USA.
[24] Hilde Walter (1895–1976), 1929–1933 she worked on the *Berliner Tageblatt* and *Die Weltbühne*; in 1933 she fled to France and in 1941 to the USA. In 1952 she returned to Germany.
[25] Walter Mehring (1895–1981), writer. In 1933 he fled to France and to the USA in 1941. He returned to Switzerland in 1960.
[26] Information given in a 'Protocol of an interview with Professor Dr. Erwin H. Ackerknecht, Zürich, on 29th March 1971', Institut für Zeitgeschichte, Munich, p. 6.
[27] Michael Hepp (ed.), *Die Ausbürgerung deutscher Staatsangehöriger 1933–1945 nach den im Reichsanzeiger veröffentlichten Listen*, Band I, *Listen in chronologischer Reihenfolge*, Munich–New York–London–Paris 1985, p. 43.
[28] *Der Anti-Nazi. Handbuch im Kampf gegen die NSDAP*, herausgegeben vom Deutschen Volksgemeinschaftdienst, Berlin 1932. (The *Deutscher Volksgemeinschaftdienst* was a fictitious organisation, one of several names used by the C.V. for the *Büro Wilhelmstraße*.) See also *Ausbürgerungsakte* for Walter Gyssling, *op. cit.*
[29] See Karl Hans Bergmann, *Die Bewegung 'Freies Deutschland' in der Schweiz, 1943–1945*, Munich 1974, p. 62.

Walter Gyssling and the Büro Wilhelmstraße 199

of the many foreigners called into the *Prestataire*.[30] He obtained release because of his Swiss citizenship after intervention by the embassy. Various Swiss newspapers employed him during the war, when Zürich became his home, and he was known as a debonair *habitué* of select cafes.[31] He did not reveal even to close acquaintances, however, anything about his role in Berlin before 1933, or Paris from 1933 to 1939. Switzerland was very sensitive to Nazi pressures and the Swiss police were ubiquitous.[32] Towards the end of the war he played a small role in the *Bewegung Freies Deutschland in der Schweiz*.[33] From 1945 to 1958 he was again correspondent in Paris for Swiss newspapers, the *Tages-Anzeiger* and the *Tagwacht*, then returned to Zürich. In that year he published with Karl Hammer a small volume on *Automation and Unions*, in which Gyssling wrote the section on 'The Economic and Social Consequences of Automation'.[34] He also married again, though his wife was to die only six days later.[35] During subsequent years he wrote frequently in newspapers and periodicals about ballet and theatre, not only in Switzerland but also in the Federal Republic of Germany and the German Democratic Republic, both of which he visited regularly. He was also president, later honorary president of the Swiss *Freidenker* (atheist) association.[36]

During the last fifteen years of his life he wrote monthly for their journal, *Der Freidenker*, and on a great range of subjects, which tell us much about his outlook. Most of Gyssling's articles concerned aspects of the history or contemporary problems of Christianity, far more often Catholicism than Protestantism, sometimes as reviews of books. He was very critical of some popes, reporting evidence that Pius IX was insane,[37] and discussing Pius XII, first in connection with Rolf Hochhuth's drama *Der Stellvertreter*, then as exemplary for the historian Friedrich Heer's thesis that Christianity throughout its history had been hostile to the Jews.[38] An article on a book by Paul Rassinier makes clear Gyssling's conviction that the Hitler regime had murdered six million Jews and that deniers of a figure in this range were neo-Nazis.[39]

His articles of this period reflect his view that the power of Christianity was also diminishing because of the directions in which society and the economy were developing, especially through education. This interest in education was surely a continuation of his youthful enthusiasm for reform after the First World War.

---

[30] *Prestataire* was a French labour battalion. They wore uniforms, but were forbidden by the Geneva Convention to carry arms or engage in combat.
[31] Conversation with Dr. Paul Parin, Zürich, July 1991.
[32] Letter from Dr. Paul Parin to the author, 7th January 1992.
[33] Bergmann, *op. cit*. Bergmann deposited the archival materials on which he had based his book in the *Institut für Zeitgeschichte* in Munich and I have examined these carefully for evidence of Gyssling's activities. There are only a few innocuous notes by him in this collection. Later he wrote about his work on the committee in *Neues Deutschland* (East Berlin), but I have not been able to find the article.
[34] Karl Hammer and Walter Gyssling, *Automation und Gewerkschaften*, 1958. Each of the authors wrote half of this work.
[35] From a card registering Gyssling's residency, Stadtarchiv, Zürich.
[36] For background on the movement see Joachim Kahl (ed.), *Freidenker. Geschichte und Gegenwart*, Cologne 1981.
[37] *Der Freidenker*, LXI, No. 2 (February 1978), p. 15.
[38] *Ibid.*, XLIX, No. 5 (May 1966), pp. 1, 42; L, No. 10 (October 1967), p. 90. Gyssling reviewed Heer's *Gottes erste Liebe. 2000 Jahre Judentum und Christentum. Genesis des österreichischen Katholiken Adolf Hitler*.
[39] *Der Freidenker*, XLIX, No. 10 (October 1966), p. 82.

His articles have an attractively old-fashioned rationalistic quality, reflecting his earlier study of sociology and psychology. Later he obviously appreciated the semanticists Alfred Korzybski and S. Hazakawa,[40] as well as the philosopher Bertrand Russell's exemplary freedom and independence, outspokenness, devotion to the most advanced scientific and technical knowledge, and readiness to change his views in accordance with new knowledge and discoveries. Russell had been a pacifist and suffered the consequences in the First World War, but good judgement and wisdom triumphed over doctrine when he supported the war against Hitler.[41] Gyssling recognised the importance of knowledge, but urged even more the development of powers of judgement. Education of the mind was not enough: the body must also be tended and developed. The objective was a non-authoritarian education promoting the fullest possible development of the entire person in a well-ordered society, a political, economic and social democracy.[42] Nowhere in these articles did he even suggest that such a system existed behind the Iron Curtain, even though he reportedly admired some aspects of the system in the German Democratic Republic and was critical of the state and society in the Federal Republic of Germany.

Clearly Gyssling was argumentative and an activist in his later years just as he had been earlier. He remained a guardedly optimistic rationalist; he mixed objectives which he had pursued throughout his adult life with newer ecological concerns. It is obvious that he wanted a role as an educator in print. After 1962 he frequently taught at summer seminars in Sonnenberg in the Harz. To the end he was apparently a remarkably consistent personality. His journalism after the war casts some light on his own description of his life, character and interests until 1933. In 1980 he died after a fall. His personal papers have not survived.[43] It remains to examine his work from 1929 to 1932.

II

Gyssling was employed by the C.V. in what they called the *Büro Wilhelmstraße*,[44] located some distance from the headquarters of the C.V. The separation concealed the connection between the two organisations and made the *Büro*'s work acceptable to clients who otherwise might not have tolerated it. The *Büro* was, however, financed entirely by the C.V. and followed its policies. Thus the *Büro* concentrated on the struggle against the NSDAP and rising antisemitism in Germany, but, like the C.V., was politically neutral.[45] It could not obviously support one of the republican parties more than another and could not propose a political platform with solutions to the broader political, financial, social and economic problems that afflicted Germany after 1929, contributed to the rise of

---

[40]*Ibid.*, LII, No. 7 (July 1969), pp. 62–63; LX, No. 9 (September 1977), p. 71.
[41]*Ibid.*, LIII, No. 3 (March 1970), pp. 18–19; LIX, No. 6 (June 1976), p. 42.
[42]*Ibid.*, LVII, No. 19 (October 1974), pp. 77–78.
[43]Conversation with Mrs. Erika Klein, Munich, June 1991.
[44]See Paucker, *op. cit.*, p. 114.
[45]*Ibid.*, p. 112.

the NSDAP, and accelerated the demise of the Republic. The C.V. was not so well financed that it could spend a large part of its budget on the *Büro*. Consequently the staff was small: a director, Dr. Hans Reichmann; a retired police officer Max Brunzlow, for the administration and accounts; Gyssling as archivist-journalist, the author of much of their material; an assistant archivist; a typist; and a man who filed material in the archive.[46]

The archive was the chief resource of the *Büro*. Gyssling proposed and designed it on the basis of his experience earlier at a *Zentralarchiv für Politik und Wirtschaft* in Munich. By his own account he organised it in a logical fashion in 580 dossiers, many of which had up to 30 subdivisions, so the total was over 800. In these were filed a variety of materials which were cross referenced with slips of paper. Individual files were chronological. By 1933 there were over 500,000 items in the archive[47] and over 100,000 reference slips for other files with related materials.

There were six main divisions to the archive. The first concerned the positions of the NSDAP on all national and international political issues. These files became so detailed that when the Foreign Office sought references in 1932 on the NSDAP's views on German-Lithuanian relations, about which it had nothing, the *Büro* could provide them with 35 clippings from National-Socialist newspapers, pamphlets and books.[48] Division two of the archive contained material on the relationships of the NSDAP to other German parties and organisations. The third part recorded Nazi antisemitic agitation. The fourth had reports about Nazi excesses, destruction of property and gravestones, criminal acts, etc. The fifth and smallest division was a record of the struggle being conducted against the National Socialists. Finally, a sixth and alphabetically-ordered part held records of the leaders and subordinate leaders of the Nazi movement.

Their sources for the archive were the NSDAP newspapers, pamphlets, flyers, posters and books, which constituted a library. They took cuttings from these newspapers; from the principal large distribution non-Nazi newspapers; and from a few provincial newspapers from across the entire political spectrum. Branches of the C.V. throughout Germany sent cuttings, as well as their reports about Nazi actions and politics in their areas. C.V. staff or members attended trials of individual National-Socialist leaders during this period and took detailed notes, which provided important information for the archive.[49] Furthermore, the C.V. dispatched Gyssling and others to report on conditions in various parts of Germany. Their reports were in the archives. Although it may seem that such an archive was a banal idea and that the labour to maintain it was of no great moment, Gyssling's claim for its uniqueness is probably true. No other organisation had such an archive; nowhere else was there such a complete collection relating to the NSDAP, and press-cutting services were not so common

[46] *Ibid.*, p. 114.
[47] These figures are from his autobiography of 1939, p. 57, whereas Paucker, *op. cit.*, p. 115, has followed his *Propaganda gegen die NSDAP*, *op. cit.*
[48] Paucker, *op. cit.*, p. 117. Gyssling provided this example in his autobiography and his *Propaganda gegen die NSDAP*, *op. cit.*
[49] Paucker, *op. cit.*, p. 116.

then as they are today. But the archive endangered everyone who had worked for it and all of those who were named in its files. It is astonishing that this archive, so extensive in size and weight, could have been transported to Bavaria, and a happy circumstance for its creators that it could be destroyed, although the man who initially harboured it became a Nazi.[50]

On the basis of this archive, then, the *Büro* and C.V. staff studied the social structure, organisation, ideology, methods of agitation and positions of the NSDAP on all questions of public life. The *Büro* made this material available to a wider public in a variety of ways. The first of these was press releases to newspapers, politicians and public figures. They also wrote longer articles, some of which grew into essays. Gyssling wrote essays of between five and ten thousand words on the 'NSDAP and Christianity', 'National Socialism and the Position of Women' and 'The Organisation of National Socialist Cells'.[51] Such information was reproduced in a four to five-pages long hectographed weekly newsletter in 200–250 copies, which eventually filled five bound volumes. Gyssling and his colleagues in the *Büro* also contributed some articles to the aggressive and sensationalistic C.V.-funded journal *Alarm*, edited by Arthur Schweriner, which had been first published in October 1929, and became a weekly in October 1931. In some ways it consciously imitated the National Socialist press in its efforts to attract the Nazi readership.[52] One of Gyssling's articles in 1932, based on documents from police files in Vienna that he had seen in 1931, claimed that Hitler had been sought by the police in preliminary proceedings (*Ermittlungsverfahren*) as a procurer (*Zuhälter*), but the National Socialists did not respond to this, presumably because they did not want to give the claim prominence.[53]

In the course of a week, some time before the September 1930 election, Gyssling dictated[54] the first version of the *Anti-Nazi* which was somewhat over 30 pages long.[55] This was printed in an edition of 180,000 copies. The second and third editions were greatly expanded; that of 1932 was 180 pages long. A first section of 49 pages demonstrated that the NSDAP's racial policy was utterly unscientific; that in foreign policy they pretended to claim all Germans, but were prepared to renounce the South Tyrol and even the Polish Corridor; that the Party's internal, economic and cultural policies were equally full of contradictions and absurdities. Throughout the book points were carefully docu-

---

[50]*Ibid.*, p. 126.
[51]*Ibid.*, p. 118 and note 31. Gyssling claimed authorship in his autobiography.
[52]Paucker, *op. cit.*, pp. 120–122.
[53]In *Der Freidenker*, LV, No. 4 (April 1972), p. 31. Gyssling referred to the "Zuhälter Adolf Hitler". An old monist from Munich, who had never been a member of the NSDAP and had nothing good to say about Hitler, nevertheless questioned the use of the word. On behalf of Gyssling his colleague, A. Hellmann, responded to this letter with the information given above and the further point that evasion of this investigation had been the reason for Hitler's departure from Vienna for Munich. *Ibid.*, LV, No. 6 (June 1972), p. 45.
[54]Gyssling dictated quickly, as a secretary of the *Tages-Anzeiger* in Zürich complained in 1954. My thanks to Dr. Urs Reber, *Direktion des Innern des Kantons Zürich*, who sought information for me about Gyssling in Zürich. Letter of 11th July 1991.
[55]See Paucker, *op. cit.*, p. 118, note 32. Gyssling claimed authorship in his autobiography and in the questionnaire he completed for the *Biographisches Handbuch*, *op. cit.*

mented through quotations from a great range of Nazi sources. A second 30-page section concerned the role of the NSDAP in the *Reichstag* and each of the provincial parliaments. A 25-page part on the theory and practice of the NSDAP explained how the Party opposed the emancipation of women and would make them serve their husbands and bear children; that National Socialists had frequently been convicted in the courts of various kinds of treason, but without hesitation labelled their opponents traitors; that only approximately ten per cent of the Nazis had served in the war, and a number of the most prominent of them had not served although they were old enough, yet claimed that their party embodied the experience of the front; that the NSDAP claimed to be a workers' party, but the *Reichstag* delegation contained only seven workers and their leaders frequently spoke contemptuously about workers or, like Hitler, intended to destroy the unions; that many National-Socialist politicians had been convicted of different forms of corruption, but hypocritically condemned their opponents for precisely this vice; that the NSDAP claimed to represent unity and was obviously beset with many forms of divisiveness: Hitler against lower leaders, the Party against the military formations, the SA against the SS, and regions in conflict with one another. A fourth part of 15 pages described their crass and sensational methods of agitation; their murderousness by listing their victims; their lies and hoary myths about Jews; their attacks on cemeteries and synagogues; their hostility to Catholics, indeed to all Christians; their open talk of seizing power and murdering their opponents after they did so; and their theories about blood. A fifth section of 10 pages dealt with the Harzburg Front,[56] agitation against Hindenburg, their condemnation of the bourgeoisie even while they courted them, and the relationship of the swastika to the Soviet star, that is, the way the National Socialists made much of their anti-Bolshevism even while at times admitting similarities of the two systems. Finally, 50 pages provided biographies of 32 leading Nazis to show their criminal or sleazy backgrounds, their mendaciousness and viciousness.[57] This very useful booklet of 1930, expanded into a book in 1932, contained much straightforward information about National Socialist actions and activities as well as quotations from the materials in the archive. In an intensely rational way the pages of the *Anti-Nazi* demonstrated the irrationality, the illegality, the murderousness and cruelty of the Nazis.[58] This material released to newspapers, politicians, public figures, administrators and unions was intended to inform them and the wider public of the menace constituted by the National Socialist movement. Members of the *Büro* and the C.V. informed these people personally as well and Gyssling even participated in union-sponsored mini-courses about the menace of Nazism. This was not all.

Gyssling also described his role and that of a few others in reporting on the Nazis. Most of the members of the C.V. and the *Büro* were Jews and were not allowed by the National Socialists to attend their meetings, but as a Gentile

---

[56]On 11th October 1932 the parties of the Nationalist Right, including the NSDAP, united at Harzburg in the Harz Mountains. This "Front" lasted until February 1933.
[57]See also Paucker, *op. cit.*, p. 119.
[58]*Ibid.*

Gyssling could. Attempts were made to prevent members of the audience from recording what was being said. Nevertheless, Gyssling and another C.V. employee, Feddern, who was a particularly adept and fast stenographer, scribbled notes at these meetings and wrote reports afterwards, so that they sometimes confounded the Nazis with embarrassing quotations.[59]

Having played a role in the student republican movement in his university years Gyssling already had experience as a public speaker – a role he began to play again in various kinds of political assemblies. Sometimes he spoke alone and was attacked verbally by Nazis in the audience; or from the floor Gyssling challenged a Nazi speaker; sometimes a debate between Gyssling and a Nazi was arranged. From his writing it seems he was an accomplished speaker and certainly he knew his subjects, but he discovered that a purely rational response to National Socialist arguments was ineffectual. When the rational response was also witty, he was successful, as in a debate with Gottfried Feder[60] about Nazi economic policy when he referred to "Federgeld", which caught on and was apparently soon used across Germany. This amused the fundamentally hostile Nazi audience, but it did not change their minds. On another occasion when he contradicted a Nazi speaker, an SA squad advanced menacingly, and Gyssling stuck a monocle in his eye, then barked orders in stentorian Prussian officer's tones. The leader of the SA squad automatically obeyed the orders and withdrew. This was an enormous momentary success, but not an enduring one. Once Gyssling spoke even though he had a fever; and was more successful than he had ever been before. He thought this was because he touched levels of banality and emotionalism that he ordinarily did not reach. The crowd repeatedly cheered him. This response was what the republicans sought.

He and a number of others during this time considered how the opponents of National Socialism might be as successful with crowds as the Nazis were. A Russian named Serge Chakotin teaching at Heidelberg collaborated with Carlo Mierendorff[61] and Julius Leber[62] and they published their ideas on the role of propaganda and symbols in some articles; they attempted to unite the SPD, *Reichsbanner*, Iron Front and the unions, and were also particularly active in a few local elections.[63] Gyssling knew them, seems to have learned from them, and perhaps added a few ideas of his own. The leading idea was to "rape" the masses

[59]*Ibid.*, p. 116.
[60]Gottfried Feder (1883–1941), engineer; after 1924 he was a member of the *Reichstag*. From 1933–1934 he was *Staatssekretär* in the Ministry of Economics. He was a Nazi ideologue and author of some volumes of propaganda from the early 1930s.
[61]Carlo Mierendorff (1897–1943), in the 1920s he founded the journal *Das Tribunal* in Darmstadt. In 1933 he was an SPD representative in the *Reichstag*: 1933–1937 in a concentration camp. He was killed in an air-raid on Leipzig.
[62]Julius Leber (1891–1945) A volunteer in the First World War, he was promoted to officer rank. Became a journalist in Lübeck and from 1924–1933 was an SPD representative in the *Reichstag*. Leber was executed following the failure of the Bomb Plot of 20th July 1944.
[63]See the references to these articles in White's essay, *loc. cit.* See also Paucker, *op. cit.*, pp. 122–123; Richard Albrecht, 'Symbolkampf in Deutschland 1932. Sergej Tschachotin und der "Symbolkrieg" der Drei Pfeile gegen den Nationalsozialismus als Episode im Abwehrkampf der Arbeiterbewegung gegen den Faschismus in Deutschland', in *Internationale wissenschaftliche Korrespondenz zur Geschichte der deutschen Arbeiterbewegung*, 22 (1986), pp. 498–533; idem, *Der militante Sozialdemokrat Carlo Mierendorff 1897 bis 1943. Eine Biografie*, Berlin–Bonn 1987.

as the Nazis did, to use the title of the English version of Chakotin's book published in 1940 from a translation of the original French.[64] They realised that their efforts against the Nazis were too rational, too defensive, not emotional and dynamic enough. They appealed to the minds rather than affecting the sensations of audiences. As Gyssling had found in his own experience, a speaker's brave and bold challenges to the Nazis could win the temporary tolerance of a Nazi audience, which amounted to success. But in order to win their audiences they had to do something more. Thus they mustered members of the Iron Front[65] and carefully distributed and placed them in assemblies, where they jeered the National Socialist speakers and were sufficiently menacing to hold the bullies in the audience at bay.[66] This successful administration of some of the Nazi's medicine heightened the *esprit de corps* of the Iron Front, and conveyed to the broader public a sense that the National Socialist movement was not an irresistible tide.

They developed a new assessment of the psychological and symbolic aspects of the highly organised and enthusiastic support that the NSDAP had obtained. They needed not only to demonstrate their opposition through their new role in political meetings but also to exhibit their strength in marches and symbolically. By assembling their manpower, marching in an organised fashion, wearing and carrying their own colours (uniforms, badges, flags), accompanied by a number of automobiles, with bands and music, and asserting themselves with chants and their own symbolic gestures (the extended arm with the clenched fist), they believed they could tap the irrational powers of the "masses". They designed simple, multicoloured leaflets, pamphlets, and posters with aggressive and catchy headlines and carefully designed photographs. All of this appeared to make inroads gradually in the population in the areas where they were active, such as Hesse.[67] They only began to achieve these successes late in 1932 when, for other reasons, time was running out. But the recent book by Gerhard Paul[68] provides a different perspective even on that question of time. We have long known the electoral support for the NSDAP had diminished in the same period, and he shows that the Party propaganda was not then as powerful, well-financed and technologically, organisationally advanced in as many areas, such as newspapers, radio, film, as it became after they seized control in 1933. Their later sophistication, modernity and impressive orchestration has been projected back to the earlier period. The National Socialists' triumph has to be assigned more to other reasons, however: it appears somewhat less inevitable; and the role of their active opponents seems more estimable.

[64]Serge Chakotin, *The Rape of the Masses. The Psychology of Totalitarian Political Propaganda*, New York 1940. There is a much expanded French version, Serge Tchakotine, *Le Viol des Foules par la Propagande politique*, Paris 1952.
[65]An umbrella organisation for the SPD, the Socialist trade unions and the *Reichsbanner Schwarz-Rot-Gold*.
[66]See Paucker, *op. cit.*, p. 124.
[67]Wolfram Pyta, *Gegen Hitler und für die Republik. Auseinandersetzung der deutschen Sozialdemokratie mit der NSDAP in der Weimarer Republik*, Düsseldorf 1989 (Beiträge zur Geschichte des Parlamentarismus und der politischen Parteien 87), pp. 476–479.
[68]Paul, *Aufstand der Bilder, op. cit.*

At a deeper level, because of a number of trips he had made to different areas of Germany on behalf of the C.V., Gyssling realised that there were endemic political and social structural problems that could hardly be overcome by their kind of measures. For example, he noted from his investigatory travels for the C.V. that in the small towns of East Prussia, Pomerania and Mecklenberg, the old order still existed. The dominant people in local society remained the great landowners and after them the wealthier bourgeois who wanted access to the homes of these landowners. The conservative caste of this society was so strong that anyone who violated their canons was virtually isolated, which is what happened to local officials with republican sympathies. It was extremely difficult for republican officials at the centre of power to exercise an abiding republican influence in such towns. Somewhat similarly in Coburg Gyssling found that small town society was orientated towards the *Hof*, the court of the Duke, who retained his magnetic social position and was a National Socialist, which made an enormous difference in the political domain too. The old imperial social order still prevailed and it was decidedly anti-republican.

During his travels he observed that republican officials could hardly function in these small towns and tended to resign their offices and return to private business or professional enterprises. Local customs of respect and subordination were almost impossible to break. Other officials were above all concerned to preserve their jobs and did not want to use their power against the National Socialists unless they were guaranteed protection. Gyssling had the impression over and again that if the law and the police had been used against the Nazis, their rise might have been slowed, if not prevented. On one occasion in Osnabrück Gyssling successfully mobilised the local government, law and police against a quack doctor of NSDAP sympathies, who had almost taken over the town. The officials only acted because Gyssling brought them assurances of support from the Ministry of the Interior under Severing.[69] But this happened all too seldom because of a widespread passivity in the face of the Nazis.

Gyssling noted how badly disunited the parties sympathetic to the republic were. They had no united response to the post-1929 crisis. They offered no hope, no solution, no utopian vision such as the Nazis had, however ludicrous and appalling that vision seemed then to some or does now to all of us. These parties disagreed with one another about solutions and as a consequence collectively and passively tolerated the deflationary policies of the Brüning regime, as well as its other policies that were, as we now know from Brüning's memoirs,[70] consciously destructive of the Weimar Republic.

Even the Social Democratic Party was guilty of passivity and unimaginative political action. Gyssling had long been critical of the SPD, indeed since his years as a student, but he found no other home during the last years of the Weimar Republic. He joined the SPD in order to press for reform from its Left wing, which achieved little. Up and down the hierarchy of the SPD there were too many officials who simply wanted to retain their jobs and would not undertake innovative action. They utterly mistook the menace from the NSDAP because of

---

[69]On the Osnabrück episode see Paucker, *op. cit.*, p. 124.
[70]Heinrich Brüning, *Memoiren, 1918–1934*, Stuttgart 1970.

their lack of imagination. This was especially demonstrated in their acceptance of Papen's 20th July 1932 coup in Prussia.[71] Gyssling condemned not only the Braun-Severing government in Prussia for its failure to present anything more than ineffectual legal opposition, but also criticised the Iron Front, of which he was a member, for its passivity. Despite the rational and persuasive works of some historians, who argue the impossibility of an armed response by the Prussian police and the Iron Front, Gyssling himself later believed that if only the workers had had their arms at home and had been trained in their use, as Swiss citizens were, Papen's coup might have been prevented, and the subsequent National Socialist takeover resisted.[72]

His was an ineffectual position because the *Büro*, dependent in a concealed way on the C.V., had to maintain political neutrality. The *Büro* could not generate a programme, nor with its limited means could it finance a major propaganda campaign, even if that had offered convincing prospects of blocking the National Socialists. Thus the organisational base for a major campaign was missing. At the same time, however, electoral support for the NSDAP diminished at the end of 1932 and the Party was in financial difficulty. Nevertheless, the Weimar Republic failed, and Hitler was appointed, which resulted in the closure of the *Büro Wilhelmstraße* and Gyssling's flight.

III

In conclusion some reflections about the experience of Walter Gyssling, his work for the C.V., and the *Anti-Nazi* are in order. Walter Gyssling's autobiography lifts this attractive, nearly unknown republican into the pages of history; publication of his interesting autobiography, the document he wrote in 1962 for Arnold Paucker of the Leo Baeck Institute in London, and the *Anti-Nazi* would make his experience even more accessible. Reichmann judged him second only to Konrad Heiden in his knowledge of Nazism.[73] Second, we know more about the archive, examined years ago in Arnold Paucker's excellent book, but nowhere since elucidated in such detail or in English. Gyssling's claim for the uniqueness of the archive is useful.[74] It stimulates the reflection that just as it was very intelligent of the C.V. to establish the *Büro Wilhelmstraße* and of Gyssling to organise it on such a grand scale for all possible information on the National Socialists, so today it is important for some institutions to assemble material from a great range of sources about similar groups that menace our society. Third, one cannot help but be struck by the obviousness of the remedial measures that Gyssling and others advocated and carried out; beginning with the effort to bring these matters to the attention of the public, especially through

---

[71] Papen ousted the Braun-Severing government in Prussia, claiming that it could not maintain order. His real reason was to displace the Socialist and Democratic Prussian government in order to establish Nationalist control in Germany.
[72] *Der Freidenker*, LV, No. 4 (April 1972), pp. 30–31.
[73] See Paucker, *op. cit.*, p. 277, note 19, for Hans Reichmann's comments *vis à vis* Konrad Heiden.
[74] See also Paucker, *op. cit.*, p. 128.

the press, continuing with their willingness to confront National Socialists personally and publicly in assemblies, and finally their attempts to tap the enthusiasms of the elusive "masses". Fourth, coupled with this was a modern sociological assessment of the distress of the different sections of the population so that measured governmental responses to their plight might have been devised. Fifth, Gyssling's observations about the government's failure to maintain the law and to use the police should be remembered. The Weimar government should have done more to protect its citizenry, particularly Jews, from the Nazi louts and that, too, could have been part of a larger pattern of preservation of the Republic. Finally, when we consider these concretely observed situations and their human participants in action, we are reminded of the dangers of crowding our accounts with abstractions such as the "masses" and of accepting the inevitability of Hitler's assumption of power. A different range of reflections and judgements on the accomplishments of their C.V. and SPD opponents is also encouraged by Paul's book, in which National Socialist propaganda is asserted to have been less co-ordinated and irresistible than has frequently been claimed and accepted.

Hans Hinkel and German Jewry, 1933–1941

BY ALAN E. STEINWEIS

In early 1960, Hans Hinkel died in Göttingen at the age of 58. The death received little attention in the German press. Several newspapers noted that Hinkel had been an important official in the *Reich* Ministry of Propaganda and Public Enlightenment in the Nazi era, and that he had served as a *Reich* Culture Manager (*Reichskulturwalter*) in the *Reich* Chamber of Culture (*Reichskulturkammer* [RKK]). To one newspaper, however, Hinkel's death possessed a far greater significance. The *Allgemeine Wochenzeitung der Juden in Deutschland* published a detailed obituary, recounting aspects of Hinkel's career that had been curiously omitted by other papers.[1] As the "Aryan" supervisor of the *Jüdischer Kulturbund*, the *Wochenzeitung* pointed out, Hinkel had been the regime's chief overseer of Jewish artistic and cultural life in Germany during the National-Socialist era. The *Wochenzeitung* also deemed it significant that Hinkel had joined the NSDAP in 1921, early enough to receive party number 287.[2] These were hardly trivial details in Hinkel's 24-year career as a National Socialist. The *Wochenzeitung* speculated that the silence over Hinkel's past reflected the dismal failure of German society to come to terms with its history. Even lesser figures of the National-Socialist leadership like Hinkel served as unpleasant reminders of a past most Germans were unwilling to digest fully.

Several recent scholarly and popular treatments of the *Jüdischer Kulturbund* have underscored the importance of Hinkel's role in the Nazi era.[3] They have, however, done little to examine Hinkel's activity as cultural overlord to the Jews within the context of his long career as a National Socialist and antisemite. The motives and personality of a figure who so profoundly influenced the lives of German Jews during the Nazi era require closer examination than they have received.

Hinkel was born into a Protestant family in Worms, in the Rhineland, on 22nd June 1901. The son of a successful businessman, he grew up only a few minutes'

---

[1]'PG 287', in *Allgemeine Wochenzeitung der Juden in Deutschland*, 26th February 1960.
[2]Although after the re-founding of the Nazi Party in 1925 Hinkel received a much higher membership number, he remained quite proud of the original number 287, boasting of it whenever he could. See, e.g., the entry for Hinkel in *Das Deutsche Führerlexikon 1934/1935*, Berlin 1934, p. 197.
[3]See especially Volker Dahm, 'Kulturelles und geistiges Leben', in Wolfgang Benz (ed.), *Die Juden in Deutschland 1933–1945. Leben unter nationalsozialistischer Herrschaft*, Munich 1988, pp. 75–267; and Akademie der Künste (Berlin), *Geschlossene Vorstellung. Der Jüdische Kulturbund in Deutschland 1933–1941*, Berlin 1992.

walk from the old Jewish neighbourhood.[4] Defensive about his middle-class origins, Hinkel preferred to depict his father as the antithesis to the "dizzy, mentally sluggish, effete bourgeois type" that dominated Worms society. Among the "effete" bourgeoisie that the young Hinkel had often encountered in Worms were many Jews. Hinkel later recalled that his Jewish neighbours had treated him politely, albeit with condescension.[5] According to the recollections of Herbert Freeden, a Jewish cultural official who had contact with Hinkel in the 1930s, some of the better students in the young Hinkel's school had been Jewish, and Hinkel had both resented and admired their success. Freeden claims that Hinkel carried forward from his youth a highly ambivalent attitude towards Jews. In the 1930s, Hinkel could indeed exhibit a surprising degree of respect towards individual members of the German-Jewish community.[6] Yet in his memoir (as in hundreds of other places), Hinkel reserved his worst epithets for the Jews. "The Jew", the memoir asserted, is "the eternal parasite and homeless master of lies".[7]

Although too young to have fought in the Great War, Hinkel shared in the bitter disappointment over Germany's defeat in 1918. Like many contemporaries, it was easy for him to conclude that "Jewish internationalist money powers" in cahoots with Marxists, Freemasons and Liberals had stabbed the Fatherland in the back.[8] While pursuing university studies in Munich (which he never completed), the disillusioned 20-year-old fell under the spell of Adolf Hitler and joined the Nazi Party. As a member of the *Bund Oberland Freikorps* unit, Hinkel participated in the ill-fated *Putsch* of 9th November 1923. After the second founding of the Nazi Party in 1925, Hinkel became an effective Nazi organiser and publicist in Southern and Central Germany. In 1927 he collaborated with the Strasser brothers in the founding of the *Kampfverlag*, which quickly emerged as a leading National-Socialist publishing house. In 1930, after Hitler had forced a split between the Strasser brothers and brought about the dissolution of the *Kampfverlag*, Hinkel accepted the position of Press Chief of the Berlin *Gau* of the Nazi Party. The move to Berlin marked the beginning of the association between Hinkel and Joseph Goebbels. In Berlin, Hinkel helped edit *Der Angriff*, the official *Gau* organ, and also served on the editorial staff of the local edition of the Party's national newspaper, the *Völkischer Beobachter*.

In Berlin, Hinkel was active not only in political organising and propaganda, but also in cultural agitation and mobilisation. In 1930, he founded the Berlin branch of the Nazi-affiliated *Kampfbund für deutsche Kultur*. As leader of the local

---

[4]Hans Hinkel, *Einer unter Hunderttausend*, Munich 1938, pp. 11–12. This memoir does not specify the nature of the Hinkel family business in Worms. According to a report of his post-war interrogation by American officials, his father owned a "butcher shop and a vineyard". Washington, National Archives and Records Administration (hereafter NARA), Record Group 238, Collection of War Crimes Records, Report No. SAIC/28, Seventh Army Interrogation Center, 'Hans Heinrich Hinkel', 28th May 1945, p. 1.
[5]Hinkel, *Einer unter Hunderttausend, op. cit.*, pp. 13–16.
[6]Herbert Freeden, *Jüdisches Theater in Nazideutschland*, Tübingen 1964 (Schriftenreihe wissenschaftlicher Abhandlungen des Leo Baeck Instituts 12), pp. 40–41.
[7]Hinkel, *Einer unter Hunderttausend, op. cit.*, p. 33.
[8]*Ibid.*

Kampfbund, and as editor of the *Kampfbund*'s organ, the *Deutsche Kultur-Wacht*, Hinkel established himself as a leading NSDAP spokesman on artistic and cultural matters. Yet he possessed no artistic training or special experience in cultural affairs. Whether he was a "philistine", as one historian has alleged,[9] is a matter of interpretation, but there was certainly little in his experience to qualify him for the decisive role he would be called upon to play in German artistic and cultural life after 30th January 1933.

During the first three months of Nazi rule, two official appointments empowered Hinkel to supervise the artistic-cultural purge in the German state of Prussia. On 30th January 1933 Bernhard Rust, the new Nazi minister of Education and Culture in Prussia, appointed Hinkel special *Staatskommissar* for the *Entjudung* of cultural life. In April 1933, in the wake of the passage of the notorious Civil Service Law (*Gesetz zur Wiederherstellung des Berufsbeamtentums* [BBG]) of 7th April, Hermann Göring named Hinkel head of the Prussian Theatre Commision, a body charged with monitoring personnel policies of theatres, orchestras and opera companies. Aside from these state positions, Hinkel retained his post at the head of the Berlin branch of the *Kampfbund*, whose size and power had been greatly enhanced by the Nazi seizure of power. So influential had Hinkel become in these early months of the Nazi regime, that one Nazi activist observed that Hinkel was the *de facto* Minister of Culture in Prussia.[10]

Hinkel's triple portfolio placed him at the centre of artistic-cultural *Gleichschaltung* in Prussia in early 1933. Numerous cultural associations and interest groups declared their loyalty to the new regime, and placed themselves at the disposal of the *Kampfbund*, which many mistakenly expected would evolve into a permanent institution. By issuing statements of official approval, Hinkel prompted the process by which the boards of directors and executive staffs of such organisations were "purified" of ideologically objectionable persons, be they Jewish or Socialist, and reorganised according to the National Socialist leadership principle.[11]

Even more important was Hinkel's role as co-ordinator of the regime's early purges in Prussia. In February and March 1933, only generally applicable emergency decrees provided legal cover for moves against Jews, Communists, and other "unwanted" persons in the cultural sphere. The BBG, which stipulated the dismissal of most "non-Aryans" from government positions, simplified the assault on Jewish artists employed by state-run cultural institutions. Systematic mechanisms for artistic-cultural censorship and personnel screening were instituted only in the second half of 1933, concentrated mainly in the new *Reich* Ministry of Propaganda and its subordinate mass organisation, the *Reichskulturkammer* (RKK). Consequently, during the key phases of artistic-

[9]Willi Boelcke (ed.), *Kriegspropaganda 1939–1941. Geheime Ministerkonferenzen im Reichspropagandaministerium*, Stuttgart 1966, p. 86.
[10]Berlin Document Centre, Reichskulturkammer Collection, File of Gustav Havemann, 'Auszug aus dem Tatsachenbericht', no date, attached to Seidel to Göring, 6th May 1933.
[11]For example, when the *Deutsche Grammophon-Gesellschaft* decided to declare its loyalty to the new regime, it did so in the form of a letter to Hinkel. Bundesarchiv Koblenz, R561 (Reichskulturkammer-Zentrale), file 66: Wuensch to Hinkel, 27th April 1933.

cultural *Gleichschaltung* in early 1933, activists such as Hinkel had to rely by and large on improvised methods, at times exploiting intimidation provided by National-Socialist thugs.

The cases of the conductors Bruno Walter and Otto Klemperer exemplify both Hinkel's technique as well as the general environment in which the early purges occurred. In a *Frankfurter Zeitung* interview of 6th April 1933, Hinkel attempted to place the new regime's domestic and foreign image in a better light by explaining why Walter and Klemperer had disappeared from the German music scene. He claimed their concerts had not been cancelled by the authorities, but rather by their own producers on account of insufficient security at the concert halls. "German public opinion", Hinkel asserted, had long been provoked by "Jewish artistic bankrupters". The SA and SS, "whom we need for more important things", could not be spared to protect Walter and Klemperer from the "popular mood".[12] This attempt to characterise the measures against Walter and Klemperer as a by-product of a popular uprising, in which the government only passively participated, arose from the absence of a legitimate legal justification. Once the BBG had taken effect, Hinkel no longer needed to fall back on such manipulations, and could turn his attention away from celebrated personalities such as Walter and Klemperer and to the far larger number of more or less anonymous Jewish artists employed by the state in Prussia.

Ironically, Hinkel's extensive powers to purge Jews from artistic-cultural institutions led to his long involvement with the *Jüdischer Kulturbund*, the Nazi regime's organisational ghetto for Jewish cultural life. The *Kulturbund* originated in the spring of 1933 as an initiative of Jewish civic leaders, including Leo Baeck, who sought relief from the economic and spiritual deprivation many Jewish artists felt as a result of the mass dismissals. Their plans envisaged an officially tolerated cultural association that would provide employment for Jewish artists and entertainers, and would serve as a source of cultural enrichment for the Jewish population. In May, Hinkel was approached about the idea by Dr. Kurt Singer, a physician whose interest in music had impelled him to become manager of the Berlin City Opera (which had "released" him in March 1933). After securing Göring's consent, Hinkel approved Singer's plan for a *Kulturbund* in Berlin that would operate one theatre, employ only Jews, and perform before audiences composed exclusively of Jews.

The plan appealed to Hinkel for several reasons. It encouraged Jews who had been dismissed from state cultural institutions to seek employment with the new *Kulturbund* rather than with other private theatres or orchestras, which were not covered by the BBG and, therefore, had not yet been legally closed off to Jews. A Jewish cultural organisation would also provide grist for the German propaganda effort abroad, which needed ammunition to counter allegations about mistreatment of Jews. Finally, Hinkel recognised the plan as an opportunity to expand his own authority. Here, his instinct proved particularly keen. After the experiment of the *Kulturbund* had proved successful in Berlin, many additional local branches began to spring up. In March 1935, the 46 existing local

[12]Comité des Délégations Juives, *Die Lage der Juden in Deutschland 1933. Das Schwarzbuch – Tatsachen und Dokumente*, Paris 1934; reprinted Frankfurt a. Main 1983, pp. 412–415.

organisations were placed under a supervisory umbrella agency, the *Reichsverband der jüdischen Kulturbünde*. By 1937, the organisations supervised by Hinkel had grown to encompass about 50,000 people.

Much of the impetus for the creation of the *Reichsverband* in March 1935 had come from Joseph Goebbels, and the assignment to supervise the organisation opened a new phase in Hinkel's relationship with him. Since the creation of the Propaganda Ministry in March 1933, Goebbels had been steadily consolidating his grip on power over cultural affairs. The creation of the RKK in September 1933 as a subsidiary of the Propaganda Ministry had represented a victory for Goebbels over Robert Ley, who had wanted to organise the artistic-cultural occupations in the *Deutsche Arbeitsfront*. Also, owing to Goebbels's steadily increasing influence, the *Kampfbund für Deutsche Kultur* had been pushed to the margin of German cultural policy by the end of 1933, despite its instrumental role in *Gleichschaltung* earlier in that year. By mid-1935, the numerous Jewish cultural associations throughout Germany stood conspicuously outside Goebbels's empire. Moreover, Goebbels had been growing increasingly frustrated with the existing leadership of the RKK, which, the Minister believed, had been too tolerant of modernism, and had been equivocating on the expulsion of Jewish members.

Goebbels turned to Hinkel, his former employee, for assistance. Hinkel possessed the experience, skills and knowledge needed by Goebbels to stake his claim to jurisdiction over the Jewish cultural organisations, and his dynamic role in the *Gleichschaltung* of cultural organisations in 1933 made him a natural choice to force through organisational and policy reforms in the RKK. In May 1935, Goebbels appointed Hinkel one of the triumvirate of *Reichskulturwalter* in charge of the RKK. Several weeks later, Goebbels added to Hinkel's responsibilities the special task of supervising "non-Aryan" culture. Hinkel received the formidable title of "Special Commissioner for the Supervision and Monitoring of the Cultural and Intellectual Activity of all non-Aryans Living in the Territory of the German Reich".

For this second office, in particular, Goebbels had based his choice not merely on Hinkel's obvious qualifications, but also on the fact that Hinkel had already attained the rank of *Sturmbannführer* in the SS. The *Sicherheitsdienst* (SD) of the SS had recently begun to express close interest in the regime's management of the "Jewish Question". The SD favoured ghettoisation of Jewish cultural-intellectual life, believing it would discourage assimilationist optimism among Jews and thereby promote emigration. Goebbels, a virulent antisemite in his own right, probably had few grounds for ideological disagreement with the Jewish experts in the SD. He probably recognised that co-ordinating policy with them would preclude interference from those quarters.[13]

Hinkel did not wait long to make his presence felt in the Propaganda Minister's empire. In the spring, summer and autumn of 1935, Hinkel implemented a thoroughgoing purge of the RKK bureaucracy, in many cases replacing Conservative-Nationalists with Nazi *Alte Kämpfer* like himself. Simul-

[13]Dahm, *loc. cit.*, p. 108; Uwe Dietrich Adam, *Judenpolitik im Dritten Reich*, Düsseldorf 1972, p. 106.

taneously, he engineered sweeping organisational changes resulting in a far more centralised, authoritarian system in the RKK, essentially ending the professional self-administration that had characterised the Chamber during the first two years of its existence.[14] In addition, Hinkel oversaw the final stages of the mass purge of Jewish members from the RKK, which had begun earlier in 1935. Goebbels was impressed by Hinkel's energetic measures, but reservations about Hinkel's ambition and lack of loyalty persisted. "Hinkel works well, but he is not personally reliable", the Minister recorded in his diary in September 1935.[15] Several days later, Goebbels's patience had worn thin; now Hinkel was a "born intriguer and liar".[16] Although Goebbels's doubts about Hinkel's character would never be calmed, Hinkel stayed on in his important positions, and would even receive several promotions from Goebbels.

Once he had completed the shake-up of the RKK, Hinkel devoted most of his energies to the solution of the "Jewish Question" in the cultural sphere. In the RKK he concerned himself primarily with eliminating Jews, offspring of Jews in mixed marriages (*Mischlinge*) and persons related to Jews (*Versippte*), who had remained in the Chamber with "special dispensations" beyond the great purge of 1935. Hjalmar Schacht, the Finance Minister, had repeatedly intervened with Hitler to prevent the RKK from moving against economically important book, art and antique dealers. Goebbels had little patience for Schacht's financial calculations, and urged Hinkel to press forward with the expulsions as fast as economic circumstances would allow.[17]

Hinkel's supervision of the increasingly ghettoised Jewish cultural life formed a logical complement to his overseeing of the RKK expulsion process; in effect, Jews who were purged from the RKK were transferred from one sphere of Hinkel's jurisdication to another. In the fields of music and theatre, the Hinkel-controlled *Reichsverband* provided the sole refuge; the Jewish press and publishing industry, although not formally incorporated into the *Reichsverband*, also gradually came under the direction of Hinkel's office at the Propaganda Ministry, the so-called *Büro Hinkel*.

Hinkel's office exercised "comprehensive prophylactic control" over the content of Jewish artistic-cultural programming.[18] In practical terms, pre-censorship was carried out by Jewish officers at the *Reichsverband* level; the *Büro Hinkel* exercised a veto power, and made decisions in questionable cases. For the Jews involved, the stamp of approval from *Büro Hinkel* could be used as protection against police officials, the *Gestapo*, and other government and Party agencies that may have wished to prohibit *Reichsverband* functions.

[14]See the author's doctoral dissertation, *The Reich Chamber of Culture and the Regulation of the Culture Professions in Nazi Germany*, University of North Carolina, Chapel Hill 1988, chap. 4.
[15]*Die Tagebücher von Joseph Goebbels. Sämtliche Fragmente. Teil 1: Aufzeichnungen 1924–1941*, ed. by Elke Fröhlich, 4 vols., Munich 1987 (hereafter *Goebbels-Tagebücher*), entry for 8th September 1935.
[16]*Ibid.*, entry for 19th September 1935.
[17]*Goebbels-Tagebücher*, entries for 4th September 1935, 5th October 1935, 2nd July 1936, 11th December 1936, 3rd February 1937, 5th May 1937, 5th June 1937, 21st September 1937, 9th October 1937, 4th November 1937, 24th November 1937, 15th and 17th December 1937, 13th January 1938, 9th February 1938, 18th May 1938, 27th July 1938 and 26th January 1939.
[18]Dahm, *loc. cit.*, p. 112.

The Jüdischer Kulturbund
Above: A concert given in the Oranienburgerstr. synagogue, Berlin, in 1938
Below: Members of the audience at a Kulturbund event,
including Otto Hirsch (right foreground)

From the Archives of the Leo Baeck Institute, New York

WAS DER KULTURBUND BIETET:

3 VERANSTALTUNGEN IM MONAT FÜR RM 2.50

Künstl. Gesamtleitung: Dr. Kurt Singer
Musikal. Leitung: J. Rosenstock
Oberspielleiter: Dr. Fritz Jessner
Dramaturg: Julius Bab
Bühnenbilder: Heinz Condell

THEATER
Schauspiel und Oper
Regie: Jessner, Singer, Baumann u. a.

KONZERT
Orchester-Konzerte, Chor-Konzerte, Kammermusik, Liederabende
Dirigenten: Rosenstock, Taube u. a.

VORTRAG
Nach freier Wahl aus allen Wissensgebieten
Vortragende u. a.:
Bab, Baeck, Eloesser, Hardt, Landau, Osborn, Plaut, Prinz u. a.

Heitere Kinder-Nachmittage, Kunstausstellungen, Aufführungen für Schüler und Erwerbslose

ZUR AUFFÜHRUNG GELANGEN:

Im Januar: „DIE NEUGIERIGEN FRAUEN"
Komische Oper von Wolf-Ferrari

Im Februar: „PARACELSUS"
Schauspiel von Arthur Schnitzler
„SONKIN UND DER HAUPTTREFFER"
Lustspiel von Juschkewitsch

In den kommenden Monaten sind in Aussicht genommen:
„JAACOBS TRAUM" von Beer-Hofmann
„DIE MACHT DER FINSTERNIS" v. Tolstoi
„DIE TROËRINNEN"
Drama von Franz Werfel
„HOFFMANNS ERZÄHLUNGEN"
Von Jacques Offenbach
Eine Operette von Strauß

Mitglied des Ehrenpräsidiums — Bundesvorsitzender und Intendant — Generalmusikdirektor

WAS DER KULTURBUND BISHER GELEISTET HAT:

Er hatte:
am 1. Oktober 1933 über 10 000 Mitglieder
am 1. November 1933 über 16 000 Mitglieder
am 1. Dezember 1933 über 20 000 Mitglieder

Er beschäftigte:
am 1. Juni 1933 . . . . . 3 Mitarbeiter
am 1. September 1933 . . . . . 10 Mitarbeiter
am 1. Oktober 1933 . . . . . 160 Mitarbeiter
am 1. Januar 1934 . . . . . 215 Mitarbeiter

Er veranstaltete: von Oktober bis Dezember 1933:
151 Theater-, Opern- und Konzertaufführungen und Vortragsabende.

Er gibt kostenlos für seine Mitglieder eine eigene Zeitschrift heraus

Promotional leaflet for the Jüdischer Kulturbund c. 1934

From the Archives of the Leo Baeck Institute, New York

The censorship policy of the *Büro Hinkel* towards the *Reichsverband* constituted an effort at enforced artistic-cultural dissimilation, intended to negate the German component of German-Jewish identity. From the very beginning, the repertoire available to the Jewish cultural associations had excluded the works of German romantics such as Wagner, and those of composers particularly valued by the regime, such as Richard Strauss. With the passage of time, Hinkel's office steadily restricted the range of possibilities. The works of Goethe and other classics of German literature were added to the blacklist in 1936; Beethoven's turn came in 1936 as well; Mozart and Händel were added relatively late in 1938. Works by non-German authors and composers were generally tolerated, provided they were not objectionable on political grounds. The *Büro Hinkel* particularly encouraged the Jews to perform pieces by Jewish authors and composers. Thus by the late 1930s, the *Büro Hinkel* was seeking to enhance a stereotyped (hence ahistorical) Jewishness, while systematically eliminating ostensibly purer artistic manifestations of German-ness.

In speeches and publications, Hinkel frequently tried to interpret this progressive ghettoisation as evidence of the regime's enlightenment and magnanimity. In effect, he argued, the Jews had been granted special recognition as a minority, entitled to cultivate their own cultural heritage. "Jewish artists are working for Jews", he pointed out in a speech in 1936.

> "They may work unhindered so long as they restrict themselves to the cultivation of Jewish artistic and cultural life, and so long as they do not attempt, openly, secretly, or deceitfully, to influence our culture."

Furthermore, Hinkel asked, how could foreigners criticise measures that had received the blessing of the Jews who were most directly affected? "The leadership of the *Reichsverband der jüdischen Kulturbünde* has repeatedly assured us", Hinkel claimed, "that the measure we have taken is a humane one", both "for Jewish artists and for the cultivation of Jewish art". At the same time, Hinkel covered himself against accusations of deviationism from Nazi hard-liners: The *Reichsverband*, he emphasised, was a "practical solution to the Jewish Question in National-Socialist cultural policy entirely consistent with the basic principles of National Socialism".[19]

Such propaganda highlights what may well have been one of the most profound consequences of the *Kulturbund*'s existence. Among German Jews as well as "Aryans", the *Jüdischer Kulturbund* served as a mechanism for psychological accommodation to Jewish cultural disenfranchisement. By providing Jewish artists and audiences with an outlet for creative expression, the *Kulturbund* rendered Jewish existence in National-Socialist Germany somewhat less desperate than it otherwise might have been, thereby lulling German Jews into a tragically false sense of security about the future. Similarly, "Aryans" who found the regime's antisemitic measures distasteful could reassure themselves that Jewish artists were at least permitted to remain active in their chosen professions.

Hinkel's own comportment may have contributed to the illusion. In an

---

[19]*Ibid.*, p. 111.

interview in 1960, Hinkel attempted to advance the notion that he had actually been a protector of the Jews, who shielded them from the designs of radically anti-Jewish elements in the regime.[20] Although this contention, when considered in retrospect, is absurd, Hinkel's defence of the *Kulturbund* seems to have won him a measure of reluctant gratitude from the leaders of the Jewish artistic and cultural community. According to Herbert Freeden, for example, German Jews connected with the *Kulturbund* saw Hinkel both as promoter and oppressor, protector and tyrant. On the negative side, Hinkel most directly personified for German Jews their own cultural disenfranchisement. On a less symbolic level, in the late 1930s Hinkel presided over a steady tightening of the artistic restrictions governing Jewish artistic and intellectual activity. On the positive side, however, Freeden recalls Hinkel intervening on behalf of the Jews when police or other local officials attempted to prevent *Kulturbund* productions from taking place. Hinkel also seemed to have had genuine respect for the Jewish officers of the *Kulturbund*, especially Kurt Singer. Freeden describes Hinkel's demeanour in the presence of his Jewish underlings as polite, even considerate.[21] This image of Hinkel as a paternalistic dictator attained wide currency among Jews in Germany after the war; even the obituary in the *Allgemeine Wochenzeitung der Juden in Deutschland*, which otherwise stressed Hinkel's function as an "outspoken Jew hater", felt obliged to mention Hinkel's strange benevolence.[22]

In the wake of the "*Kristallnacht*" in 1938, the Propaganda Ministry ordered Hinkel to close the *Reichsverband* and all Jewish cultural activity with it. But as the foreign policy implications of the brutal pogrom and its attendant repressive measures became clear, the Ministry reversed its decision.[23] On 12th November, only two days after the violence, Hinkel convened a group of Jewish leaders and ordered them to resume their cultural programme. So urgent was this matter that Hinkel had to pull strings to arrange for Jewish performers to be released from the concentration camps to which they had been dragged only a couple of days earlier. Nevertheless, after November 1938 Jewish artistic-cultural life continued on a much narrower basis than had been the case before the "*Kristallnacht*". The mechanism for more intrusive official supervision was set in place in January 1939, when the *Reichsverband*, which had been essentially an umbrella organisation for the local associations, was dissolved and replaced by the *Jüdischer Kulturbund in Deutschland*, a single, centralised organisation.

In general, the "*Kristallnacht*" had spurred a radicalisation of the regime's policy towards the Jews. The opportunistic Hinkel experienced little difficulty in

---

[20]Institut für Zeitgeschichte, Munich, Zeugenschrift Collection, ZS 1878, 'Hans Hinkel Zeugenschrift', February 1960.

[21]Freeden, *op. cit.*, p. 40. Freeden's recollection of Hinkel's polite, respectful demeanour towards Jewish officials is borne out by the surviving minutes of the *Reichsverband*'s founding meeting of April 1935. New York, Leo Baeck Institute Archives, Estate Alfred Hirschberg, Jüdischer Kulturbund, AR 166: 'Protokoll der Tagung der jüdischen Kulturbünde Deutschlands', 27th–28th April 1935.

[22]'PG 287', *loc. cit.*

[23]Dahm attributes the change of mind not to foreign policy considerations, but rather to Goebbels's fear that the SS-SD would seize upon the shut-down of the *Reichsverband* as an opportunity to expand its power over Jewish policy. Dahm's case for this interpretation, however, is circumstantial, providing no supporting documentation. Dahm, *loc. cit.*, p. 224.

adjusting to the new conditions. He had come to be widely acknowledged as one of the Propaganda Ministry's foremost experts on the "Jewish Question". Hinkel seemed to savour this reputation and did much to enhance it. In 1939 he edited and published *Judenviertel Europas*, a collection of essays about "the Jews from the Baltic to the Black Sea".[24] Hinkel's own contribution to the collection, 'Germany and the Jews', contained the familiar vitriol and stereotypes, although it also emphasised the vitality of the cultural life that the Jews had been permitted to pursue in Germany since 1933. Yet, Hinkel claimed, the Jews had exhibited little gratitude for the regime's generosity, as evidenced by the Jewish murder of Ernst vom Rath. Writing as though he had been personally betrayed by his Jewish wards, Hinkel concluded his piece with the observation that "the present struggle of World Jewry against National-Socialist Germany as the heart of Europe is nothing more and nothing less than a struggle against the thousand-year-old culture of the West!"[25]

This post-"*Kristallnacht*" propaganda was designed to accompany and to justify intensified anti-Jewish measures. As the Propaganda Ministry's foremost Jewish expert, Hinkel inevitably became involved in the formulation of these measures. In 1938, Hinkel had emerged as an intermediary between the Propaganda Ministry and the SS–SD. The Propaganda Ministry had been confronted by the threat of the SS-SD's aggressive campaign to monopolise authority over Jewish policy. To protect the Propaganda Ministry's position, Hinkel opened negotiations with the SD's *Referat* II 112, which specialised in Jewish matters, in May 1938.[26] Despite the institutional rivalries, the liaison offered practical advantages to both sides. Hinkel provided the SD with sensitive information about Jews, homosexuals and other ideologically tainted persons still active in the cultural sphere; in return, Hinkel hoped for SD assistance in racial and political investigations of RKK members and applicants. A factor allowing for co-operation between the two rival agencies was that both favoured an accelerated purge of the vestigial Jewish presence in German public and economic life.[27] Hinkel certainly showed little personal resistance to co-operation with the SS; he encouraged his immediate staff to join the SS, and he, himself, met Himmler on several occasions in order to discuss censorship and personnel policy for the RKK.[28] For Hinkel personally, the liaison with the SD may have helped advance his ambitions for promotion within the SS. In September 1940, Himmler approved Hinkel's promotion from *SS-Oberführer* to *SS-Brigadeführer*.[29]

Goebbels had often expressed frustration with what he saw as the slow pace of

---

[24]Hans Hinkel (ed.), *Judenviertel Europas. Die Juden zwischen Ostsee und Schwarzem Meer*, Berlin 1939.
[25]*Ibid.*, p. 16.
[26]See the documentation in Bundesarchiv Koblenz, R58 (Reichssicherheitshauptamt), file 984. On the power rivalry see Dahm, *loc. cit.*, pp. 224–225.
[27]Adam, *op. cit.*, pp. 258–263.
[28]See the correspondence in NARA, Microfilm Publication T–175, *German Records Filmed at Alexandria, Virginia. Records of the Reich Leader of the SS and Chief of the German Police* (hereafter T–175), T–175, roll 42, frames 2553576–2553610.
[29]T–175, roll 42, frame 2553564, Hinkel to Himmler, 16th September 1940.

the *Entjudung* process.[30] The outbreak of war presented new opportunities. In July 1940, bolstered by the recent humiliation of France, Goebbels, who in addition to being Minister of Propaganda and Public Enlightenment was also *Gauleiter* of Berlin, directed his chief assistants at the Propaganda Ministry to expedite planning for the evacuation of the Jews of Berlin to German-occupied Poland. "Within a period of at most eight weeks immediately after the end of the war", Goebbels hoped that "all 62,000 of the Jews still living in Berlin" would have been deported to the East. The report of this meeting goes on to state:

> "Hinkel reported on the evacuation plan already worked out with the police. It should make certain above all else, that Berlin would be first in line to be purified (*gesäubert*), as the Kurfürstendamm will retain its Jewish face . . . until Berlin is really free of Jews. Only after Berlin will the other Jewish cities (Breslau, etc.) receive their turns."[31]

At a meeting of Goebbels's staff on 6th September, Hinkel issued an updated report on evacuation plans for both Berlin and Vienna. He noted that while good progress had already been made in Vienna, there were still 71,800 Jews in Berlin. Hinkel assured those present, however, that 60,000 Jews would be removed from Berlin to the East "within four weeks" of war's end, while the remaining 12,000 "would also disappear within an additional four weeks".[32] Except for the records of these conferences at the Ministry of Propaganda, documentation is lacking on the nature of Hinkel's involvement with these plans. The precise numbers cited in his presentations suggest that his involvement was more than casual.

Hinkel's most thorough briefing for his colleagues at the Ministry (including Goebbels) came at a conference on 17th September 1940. Hinkel supplied a demographic breakdown of the "72,327 Jews still in Berlin", as well as more general statistics on the 4 million Jews living in German-occupied Europe. Hinkel then reported on the so-called "Madagascar Project" (as submitted in detail by the *Reichssicherheitshauptamt* [RHSA]), which envisioned the transfer of "about $3\frac{1}{2}$ million Jews" to the remote island in the Indian ocean.[33] It seems likely then that Hinkel had been assigned the task of maintaining contact between the RSHA and the Propaganda Ministry. Unfortunately, the available documentation tells us little else about Hinkel's role in these events.

In 1940 and 1941, constraints on *Kulturbund* activity intensified considerably. In September 1941, the *Gestapo* dissolved it. With the onset of the mass murder and deportation of the German Jews the *Kulturbund* lost its utility to the regime.

Hinkel's special role in Jewish affairs essentially came to an end. By the time of the *Kulturbund*'s demise, Hinkel had already turned most of his attention to other priorities in German cultural policy. While continuing to preside over the racial and political purge mechanism of the *Reichskulturkammer*, Hinkel undertook a succession of special assignments from Goebbels, the main purpose of which was to prepare and mobilise the German cultural establishment for war. Among Hinkel's responsibilities was the organisation of extensive entertainment pro-

---

[30]See note 17 above.
[31]Boelcke, *op. cit.*, p. 431.
[32]*Ibid.*, p. 492.
[33]Adam, *op. cit.*, pp. 256–257.

grammes for German soldiers. During a tour through Poland in 1942, Hinkel took several of his entertainers on a sightseeing visit through the Warsaw Ghetto. Looking at the dreary scene through the windows of the sealed bus, Hinkel demonstratively voiced his contempt for "God's chosen people".[34] In contrast to his polite demeanour in the presence of *Kulturbund* officials in earlier years, Hinkel now seemed determined to emphasise his antisemitic credentials. The one-time "protector" of the Jews was now viciously ridiculing them on the very eve of their annihilation.

As the supervisor of Jewish cultural life and as a central figure in the *Reichskulturkammer*, Hinkel had become one of the Propaganda Ministry's most powerful and prominent officials. His main responsibilities prior to the outbreak of war underscored the duality of Nazi artistic-cultural policy. On the one hand, Hinkel purged German cultural life of Jews and other "undesirables". On the other, he helped implement a variety of RKK measures that aimed at ameliorating poverty and unemployment in the artistic-cultural occupations. In a very real way, Hinkel had come to occupy a central place in a system designed to address the problems of which he first became conscious during his student days in Munich in the early 1920s. No longer would the German government take its artists for granted; and no longer would it tolerate Jewish domination of artistic-cultural life.

After 1945, Hinkel faded into obscurity, a broken man.[35] Unlike many physicians, jurists, civil servants, and artists, who encountered little difficulty in making the transition from the Nazi era to post-war conditions in West Germany, Hinkel led a fruitless life after the demise of National Socialism. He possessed no technical skills or special talents that made him indispensable. Despite his experience in cultural administration, he had never been anything more than an energetic dilettante. He had known little in life other than National Socialism. Having embarked on his National-Socialist career in the early 1920s, convinced that his generation would save Germany, the end of National Socialism rendered him an anachronism. When Hans Hinkel died in 1960, the national memory had little place for this *Alter Kämpfer*. It is, therefore, with some degree of ironic justice that the rediscovery of Hans Hinkel's role in history comes as the result of recent endeavours to reconstruct and understand the lives of his Jewish victims.

---

[34]Lale Andersen, *Der Himmel hat viele Farben. Leben mit einem Lied*, Stuttgart 1972, p. 251.
[35]'PG 287', *loc. cit.*

A Question of Fundamental Principles
The Church of England and the Jews of Germany 1933–1937

BY ANDREW CHANDLER

I

In recent years much has been written of the responsibility Christianity bore for the Jewish Holocaust. The weight of that responsibility may long be debated.[1] Was Auschwitz the logical and natural conclusion of centuries of Christian antisemitism, or the expression of an evil that was essentially something different? Is it really acceptable to see the "Final Solution" as an aberration, looming suddenly out of the chaos of the unfolding European narrative? Or should we understand it more nearly by recognising that it occurred in the heart of an historic society, once called Christendom, pervaded for generations by the teachings of the Christian Church?[2]

The tenets of Christian antisemitism were simple, and their simplicity no doubt encouraged their popularity. It was held that the Judaism of the Old Testament was rejected and superseded by the "new covenant" of the New Testament. The Jews did not accept the teachings of Jesus. Then they crucified Him. This is what earnest Christians read in the Gospels. They believed that ever after the Jews were to be an abject people, scattered across the nations of the earth, spurned and abused.[3]

The theology of these views was confused. They hardly related at all to other strong strands of Christian thought, which preached that Christ died as an act of self-sacrifice to conquer death and pay for the sins of the world. Furthermore, the historical foundation of Christian antisemitism was inadequate and mistaken.

---

[1]The author would like to thank Professor John Grenville at the University of Birmingham, Professor John Conway of the University of British Columbia, and Dr. David Thompson of Fitzwilliam College, Cambridge for their suggestions and interest. He would also like to acknowledge his particular thanks to Lambeth Palace Library. He would like especially to express his appreciation and gratitude to his friend Richard Gutteridge.

[2]See, for example, Franklin Littell, *The Crucifixion of the Jews*, New York 1975. See too, Hyam Maccoby, *The Sacred Executioner*, New York 1983. For a very brief, but excellent, historical overview, see Marc Saperstein, *Moments of Crisis in Jewish-Christian Relations*, London 1989, pp. 38–50.

[3]See, for example, Charlotte Klein, *Anti Judaism in Christian Theology*, transl. by Edward Quinn, London 1975. See too, Geoffrey Wigoder, *Jewish-Christian Relations since the Second World War*, Manchester 1988, pp. 1–47.

Significantly, it is only since 1945 that its weaknesses have been explored and exposed.[4]

It is perhaps difficult to think that one so utterly secular as Hitler owed his racial ideology to the Christian faith. But the society in which he lived listened to his hatred of the Jews, and found that it struck a chord. It was respectable. Hitler became Chancellor on 30th January 1933 through a combination of popular approval in the first place, and political mismanagement in the second. Once in power his views became policies and his policies were largely uncontested. The churches, which were so great a part of German life, did not stir against him. When his regime was superintending the extermination camps, they still did not.

One striking aspect of religious history is how often men and women of the same faith, but of different denominations and cultures, confronted the same fundamental issues, saw them in quite different lights, and then acted in completely contradictory ways. It is not the purpose of this article to discuss the reasons why the Protestant and Roman Catholic churches of Germany did not defend their Jewish neighbours between 1933 and 1945. It is to suggest that historians and religious thinkers must remember that German Christianity was but one regional member of the broad body of the universal church. If we are to estimate how crucially the integrity of Christianity itself was questioned by the Holocaust we must ask how churches, outside Germany as well as inside, viewed the crisis. Only when we have understood them all, and seen how such contrasts could arise, may we pass some kind of historical judgement on its impact on the Jewish-Christian relationship. It is the purpose of this article to shed a partial light on this question by describing the response to the persecution of one particular European church, the Church of England.

The two Protestant communities of Germany and England were profoundly contrasting. Both had histories as State Churches. The Church of England retained its formal connection with the British State into the twentieth century, while it also sought to affirm its own institutional identity and distinctive moral authority. Some were given to wonder if it was indeed a State church any longer, even though monarchs were splendidly crowned by primates and bishops officially appointed by prime ministers.[5] Certainly it was very unlike the Lutheran Church in Germany which, as the century turned, was something like a department of the State. After the Great War the new German State disestablished the Church. Lutherans were sullen, resentful and suspicious of the

---

[4]See, for example, the survey of Anglo-American authors in Klein, *op. cit.*, pp. 127–156. For a most interesting example of such work see Ellis Rivkin, *What Crucified Jesus?*, London 1986. In recent years the movement to understand Jesus by viewing him within Jewish life and culture has been led by Jewish writers. See Geza Vermes, *Jesus the Jew*, London 1973. For an important recent work on the religious proximity of Judaism and Christianity by a Christian scholar, see James Dunn, *The Parting of the Ways between Christianity and Judaism, and their Significance for the Character of Christianity*, London 1991.

[5]For a concise and opinionated outline, see Herbert Hensley Henson, *The Church of England*, Cambridge 1939.

new political authorities, even though the Weimar Republic did little to threaten it. In fact, the Lutheran Church continued to receive generous state subsidies.[6]

Although their church was "Established", the leaders of the Church of England affirmed a right and duty to judge political issues, independently, in the light of their religious priciples. They would approve of the policies of the State if they appeared just, and condemn them if they did not. By contrast, German Protestantism preached political quietism and simultaneously espoused the cause of authoritarian conservatism.

The same may be said of their reactions and responses to the racialism of the National Socialist movement. In Britain the civil and political disabilities of Jews had been steadily removed during the course of the nineteenth century. Jews were admitted to the House of Commons in 1858, and to the House of Lords in 1885. Jews had been barred from politics and universities not because the State was specifically antisemitic, but, as David Englander has observed, because they were not Anglicans. Their emancipation took place beside the legal recognition of Nonconformist and Roman Catholic Christians: the British establishment had recognised the pluralism of British society, and expanded its regulations to accommodate it. The Church of England had not played a very laudable role in the process; in each of these moves its leaders were liable to see the erosion of the status of their church, and the undermining of the historic Church-State relationship. At large, the public was more readily roused to anti-Catholicism than antisemitism.[7]

Antisemitism in Britain was most apparent in the cities, where Jews were reputed to run businesses, and in the upper classes. But institutional Christianity did not much encourage it. Very possibly hard-line Anglo-Catholics and Evangelicals in the Church of England were more likely to subscribe to a religious antisemitism than other varieties. But the essential character of Anglicanism, in the bishops' palaces and the vicarages, lay in a broad middle ground between these two positions. This is not to say that there were no antisemitic clerics. But it is to suggest that Christian antisemitism was not a recognisable, organised force, and that antisemitism, broadly-speaking, found little sanction or encouragement in the Christian churches. English Judaism, meanwhile, was much influenced by Anglicanism. Englander has remarked that the Chief Rabbi from 1891 to 1911, Hermann Adler, "did a good deal of hobnobbing with the Anglican episcopate" and went so far as to call himself "the Very Reverend".[8] This is very suggestive. During the tsarist pogroms at the turn of the century the Archbishop of Canterbury, Randall Davidson, registered his protest in sympathetic letters to Rabbi Adler, and wrote also to *The Times*.[9] In general, the two communities appeared to coexist harmoniously and respectfully. The conversion of Jews to Christianity was hardly a *cause célèbre* of many

---

[6]See J. R. C. Wright, *'Above Parties'. The Political Attitudes of the German Protestant Church Leadership 1918–1933*, Oxford 1974, pp. 1–31.
[7]See David Englander, 'Anglicized Not Anglicans. Jews and Judaism in Victorian Britain', in Gerald Parsons (ed.), *Religion in Victorian Britain*, vol. I, Manchester 1988, pp. 235–273.
[8]Englander, *loc. cit.*, p. 249.
[9]See G. K. A. Bell, *Randall Davidson. Archbishop of Canterbury*, vol. II, Oxford 1935, pp. 484–486.

English churchpeople. Thirty years into the twentieth century the proselytising Church Mission to the Jews retained an impressive list of nominal patrons, but was a long way down a declining slope, and very much in debt. In any case it gave little appearance of a body which held the Jews responsible for the crucifixion of Christ. Every year a letter from the suffragan Bishop of Fulham and North and Central Europe was printed in the Evangelical Anglican weekly, *The Record*. The work of the Christian Mission to the Jews, wrote Bishop Batty in 1933:

> ". . . enables the Church to repay the Jewish nation the great debt we owe them for our Saviour, born of a Jewish mother, our Church, which is a continuation of the Jewish Church, and our Bible, written by Jews, with the exception of the two Books written by Gentiles, who derived their material from Jewish sources. We are also indebted to the Jewish nation for the Apostles. And it would be possible to extend this list of benefits we have received from them in many directions."[10]

The picture was profoundly different in Germany. Luther had written one tract that was sympathetic to the Jews, and one that was grotesquely venomous and violent.[11] It was the second that received the more attention in later years. In the nineteenth century the dynamic and alarming figure of Adolf Stoecker, Court and Cathedral Preacher in Berlin, began to agitate against the Jews in 1879. Thereafter his influence, though not uncontested, grew rapidly. Adolf von Harnack observed unhappily that it was "a tragic scandal to inscribe antisemitism upon the banner of evangelical Christianity".[12] In later years Stoecker came to be regarded as a forerunner of Hitler himself. His church did not repudiate his views. In fact, it soon discovered that antisemitic diatribes were likely to swell its congregations. After the Great War German Protestantism, for all its claims to be "above parties", endorsed the antisemitic *Deutschnationale Volkspartei* without the slightest compunction.[13]

At the onset of 1933 the theological, historical and cultural differences between the English and German Protestant communities were powerfully exposed. In 1933 German Protestantism embraced the National Socialist movement. Its leaders perceived that Hitler would save the German nation from bolshevistic nihilism, international humiliation, chaos and oblivion. For their part, British Christians regarded the spectacle with anxiety and distaste. German church leaders were inclined to think the antisemitism of the new regime understandable, if not laudable. That such virulent and blatant antisemitism was new to the experience of those who led the Church of England was suggested by its initial reaction to events in Germany. They were surprised by them. They did not understand them. They were offended by them. English bishops found them senseless and incomprehensible, vulgar and violent, and very alien. Many of them reacted with a certain disbelief.

---

[10] *The Record*, 24th February 1933, p. 104d.
[11] *That Jesus Christ was Born a Jew*, 1523; and *On the Jews and Their Lies*, 1543.
[12] Quoted in R. J. C. Gutteridge, *Open Thy Mouth for the Dumb! The German Evangelical Church and the Jews 1879–1950*, Oxford 1976, p. 5. See too, Uriel Tal, *Christians and Jews in Germany. Religion, Politics, and Ideology in the Second Reich, 1870–1914*, transl. by Noah Jonathan Jacobs, Cornell 1975.
[13] Gutteridge, *op. cit.*, pp. 35–36.

The Archbishop of Canterbury naturally felt that this matter was a matter of concern to him, in his capacity as head of the Church of England. It was a humanitarian issue. By Christian lights racial persecution was intolerable and immoral. But Archbishop Lang now found that he knew little of German affairs. He sought to learn more.

II

Basil Staunton Batty was a very large, brilliantly anecdotal, and much admired London bishop. His responsibilities for Fulham on the one hand, and for the church's work across the face of North and Central Europe on the other, cannot have been easy to reconcile. His diocesan colleagues found that he was liable to disappear for several days on end into the middle of the Continent, sitting uncomfortably in the narrow seats of aeroplanes, before turning up surprisingly at assorted diocesan board meetings in London. This must have imparted a gratifying sense of mystery to the agreeable bishop. It is with him that the story begins, for Batty was the first church leader to write to Archbishop Lang of the antisemitism of the new German regime. On 12th March 1933, when Hitler had been Chancellor for six weeks, he wrote to Lambeth Palace:

> "I am leaving home this week for a tour and am rather worried by the reports reaching me of the campaign against the Jewish nation in Germany. I am asking for further information from those I can trust. One of the great difficulties [of] our work amongst the Jews is their recollection of the unworthy part the Christian Church has often played in persecutions of their nation. It may be that the Hitler regime will give us a chance of making some reparation. My object in writing is to suggest that if I can stir up the Church in Germany to protest against any persecution on religious grounds, and this will not be easy as I have to avoid politics, we might make some pronouncement in England which would show that we stood behind them in this matter. The matter will of course require very delicate handling."[14]

Lang's chaplain and secretary, Alan Don, replied that so far the Archbishop had lacked "any really authoritative information" from Germany. He would be very grateful for any.[15]

The Church, even in the midst of a steadily secularising country, was still recognised by the broad, and mostly absent, public as a unique institution with a distinctive moral purpose. It remained, for many, the professional conscience of the nation. Accordingly, on the 16th March 1933 a letter from Cicily Andrews, who published novels under the pen name "Rebecca West", arrived at Lambeth Palace. Unmarried partner for more than a decade of the staunch atheist, H. G. Wells, mother of his son, and a biographer of D. H. Lawrence to boot, some might not have thought her one of the Archbishop's natural correspondents or constituents. But she wrote because she recognised the Archbishop as a man with a moral vision of the world that might make him a sympathiser and an ally. She implored Lang, as a religious leader, to lend his name to a letter of protest, or else take "some private action" on behalf of Germany's Jews.[16]

---

[14]Batty to Lang, 12th March 1933, London, Lambeth Palace Library, *Lang Papers*, vol. 38, fol. 1.
[15]Don to Batty, 13th March 1933, *ibid.*, fol. 2.
[16]Andrews to Lang, 16th March 1933, *ibid.*, fol. 3.

Lang was cautious, always. He had no intention of signing this petition. He had little faith in such gestures. But he needed advice. It was natural to him, as the head of the Established Church, to turn to the guidance of the State, with which he was familiar. His secretary wrote to Sir Robert Vansittart at the Foreign Office. Had representations been made to the German government through diplomatic channels, or were any likely? Might "any good purpose" be served by his signing Andrews's letter?[17]

Vansittart's secretary replied to Lang's secretary: "We have of course no *locus standi* in any country for representations except on behalf of British subjects." That was a crucial point. Might the Archbishop and Sir Robert meet to talk about it all?[18]

They met between 16th and 24th March. The new German government, said Vansittart, was "truculent", sensitive like all heady youths, and very resentful of any interference in their own affairs. Lang's memorandum of the conversation hints, importantly, at how he suggested such a government might be approached and persuaded. He was told: "It was useless to write to them about our own ardent friendship and the like as a basis for the appeals about Jews." Moreover, Vansittart worried about the diplomatic consequences: "the need of keeping them in with Italy, France and Great Britain", presumably against the Soviet Union.[19]

On 24th March Lang met the newly appointed chairman of the Anglo-Jewish Association, Claude Montefiore. Such a meeting, between the respected heads of two religious institutions, was natural to them both. There was, in the tone of the Archbishop's recollections of the conversation, a hint of seniority which rather unsettles. "He was", wrote Lang to Vansittart afterwards, "very sensible and quite accepted the reasons which I gave for regarding any official interventions at the present time as undesirable. If necessary . . . some quiet and tactful remonstrance may be given if the trouble grows. Meanwhile I deprecated with Mr. Montefiore's agreement any attempts to work up at present indignation protests in this country, though I think they are sure in certain quarters to break out." Lang would ask Vansittart simply to "keep an eye on what was happening". Montefiore would tell Lang if "later facts came to his knowledge about really serious and deliberate persecution".[20]

These were significant exchanges. Lang's concern was self-evident, although his timidity may not have struck Montefiore as impressive. However, it was understandable. They knew that protest could only be made on the firm ground of unquestionable facts. In 1933 the Archbishop of Canterbury found Germany a distant country. Generally, he knew little of its affairs. The condemnation of the internal policies of sovereign foreign states was largely uncharted and potentially perilous territory. National governments staffed by professional politicians and

---

[17]Sargent to Vansittart (no date), *ibid.*, fol. 5.
[18]Nordon to Sargent (n.d.), *ibid.*, fol. 9.
[19]Recounted in 'Jews in Germany', a memorandum by Lang of a conversation with Claude Montefiore, 24th March 1933, *ibid.*, fol. 11.
[20]Lang to Vansittart, 24th March 1933, *ibid.*, fol. 10.

experienced civil servants did not venture on to such ground. The Archbishop of Canterbury might very well hesitate.

On the last day of March Bishop Batty dispatched his report, 'Germany and the Jews', to Lambeth Palace. First, asked Batty, how were they to understand this virulent racialism? Antisemitism had long been a pervasive influence in Germany. The "popular mind" held the Jews responsible for the "low standards of the Press", a general malaise in the Arts, and the propagation of Marxism. Hitler was a proven antisemite, blatantly so before power, and moderately so since, in office a sorcerer's apprentice struggling to restrain the powers and passions he had invoked. Göring was "a dangerous fellow", an incendiary influence. In this new Germany Jews were losing their jobs: "I am told that it is useless for a Jewish lawyer or advocate to appear in court before a Nazi judge." Many were already trying to escape to Palestine. The Lutheran Church would not protest. He sensed its intimidation. He found the Senior Superintendent in Berlin, Max Diestel, deprecated the persecution as isolated acts lacking official sanction. He was surprised at Batty's suggestion that the Lutheran Church should intervene. Batty perceived that Hitler's racialism was supported by "a large mass of German opinion". He stressed again, "My own opinion is that a protest should be made by the Lutheran Church and that the Christian Church throughout the world should support it, but I fear the Lutheran Church will not take action through fear of Hitler."[21] The English churches could protest only for themselves.

Diestel's deprecations were hardly persuasive when he made them, but when the German government announced a boycott of all Jewish shops and businesses for 1st April, the bottom dropped out of all talk of revolutionary extremes, sporadic bullying by irregular hoodlums, and "alleged persecution".[22] It was, openly, an official act contrived for an international audience. Its formal justification was that it was an expedient, a response to the malicious protests of the Jewish community abroad. *The Record* noted, however, that "it may be remarked that opposition to the Jews as a race was part of the original Nazi programme".[23] In return it brought from the Church of England its first episcopal pronouncement. It was a modest but firm remonstrance in the House of Lords by the Archbishop of Canterbury, supported by his friends, the High Tory Anglican Viscount Cecil of Chelwood, the Roman Catholic Lord Iddesleigh, and the prominent Jewish peer, Lord Reading. It was an appeal not to the government of Germany, but to their own:

> "I most earnestly trust that His Majesty's Government will be able to give assurances – I know they will – that they are doing whatever seems to them possible to express the concern of the people of this country and of their Christian fellow citizens with regard to the Jewish community, and not least, the concern of those among them who are animated by feelings of sincere friendship for the German people."[24]

[21]'Germany and the Jews', memorandum by Batty, 31st March 1933, *ibid.*, fols. 14–16.
[22]A phrase used by Bishop Bell in a letter to Hermann Kapler, 30th March 1933, London, Lambeth Palace Library, *Bell Papers*, vol. 4, fol. 7.
[23]*The Record*, 7th April 1933, p. 185.
[24]*Parliamentary Debates*, House of Lords, 5th series, vol. 87, col. 225, 30th March 1933.

It was moderate and brief. It was hardly eloquent. But it was the very fact of the Archbishop of Canterbury making a sound at all, and in the Parliament of the British State, which mattered to the world outside. That a leader of the Church had expressed unhappiness, publicly, could severely undermine any moral claim that the boycott, be it ideological or expedient, sought to make. Perhaps it had some effect. The following day Lord Reading wrote warmly to thank Lang for his lead to the Christian world: 'I assure you that your observations have very largely assisted the modification of the original act and the comparatively orderly manner of carrying it out.'[25] Bishop Batty added that the primate's words had given "a dignified expression to our feelings and will do good".[26]

Information continued to arrive at Lambeth Palace. In this increasingly ecumenical age foreign church people thought to send their thoughts and impressions to England. A "private and confidential", and very extensive, document, dated 28th April and "not for publication in any form", was forwarded on 22nd May to Lang by Henry Fox, Honorary Secretary of the British Council of the World Alliance for International Friendship through the Churches. Its author was H. L. Henriod, the General International Secretary of the World Alliance at Geneva. He had visited Germany in April to talk with "well qualified German Christians and a few foreigners". Henriod described a Germany outwardly normal and stable, but seething with disorder and uncertainty underneath. The Germans were congratulating themselves that they could have had a revolution with so little bloodshed. Christians were "deeply moved by the national revival". But, observed Henriod, the new Germany was a police state. Telephones were tapped, correspondence opened, all rights suspended. To the German churches he was sympathetic, but his discussion of their affairs was preceded by two sections on the plight of the Jews. They demonstrated a not uncommon naïvety, retelling blandly that only 0.9 per cent of the population were Jewish, and yet that ninety per cent of the doctors in certain hospitals were Jewish. He recounted the prominence of Socialist and Communist Jews. He described the boycott of 1st April, and listed the exclusions they faced. Christian protest was difficult. Criticism might provoke violence. "The ecclesiastical authorities, deprived of all liberty of expression" had been unable to act publicly on the Jews' behalf. But behind the scenes "personal interventions" were taking place: "The leaders of the Church, conscious of the gravity of the question which confronts the Christian conscience, will take up their position as soon as the Church's situation has become clear." Christians abroad must not judge them too hastily. They must recognise extenuating circumstances, and the dangers of protest. If they wish to speak out themselves they must be sure to see that they protested only against "proved and certain facts".[27] It was hardly an invitation to do so.

Lang's situation was not simple. He stood at the heart of a web of information and advice, from those of his own church, from Christians of other churches, from the Jewish community at home, and from his political friends. Cautious and

---

[25] Reading to Lang, 1st April 1933, *Lang Papers*, vol. 38, fols. 17–18.
[26] 'Germany and the Jews', memorandum by Batty, 31st March 1933, *ibid.*, fol. 16.
[27] Memorandum by H.-L. Henriod, French version dated 28th April 1933, *ibid.*, vol. 37, fols. 5–14.

uncertain, an acute quizzer and careful listener, he was, not unnaturally, inclined to defer to the judgements of his connections. On 3rd April 1933 his secretary, Sargent, reported to Batty, "he has been in communication with a good many leading members of the Jewish community in England and all agree that such things as protest meetings or other strong expressions of indignation would only prejudice the already sufficiently difficult position of the Jews of Germany". A private and personal meeting with the German ambassador, Hoesch, would take place shortly.[28]

Lang liked Hoesch, who was a civil and courteous gentleman, and a diplomat very much of the old order. The relationship between the two men was a pleasant and agreeably conversational one. The Archbishop invited the ambassador to Lambeth on 16th May and questioned him thoroughly and lengthily. Then the two were joined by Lang's chaplain, Alan Don, for tea. That no memorandum was kept of the meeting is perhaps suggestive of the very social and relaxed view the two took of each other. But Alan Don was an assiduous diary writer and recorded how the ambassador told him, "the hatred of the Jews is due to the fact that many of that race have profited by the misfortunes of Germany and have grown rich while Germans starved, flaunting their ill-gotten gains and giving foreigners a false impression of German prosperity – others of a lower sort have corrupted the German youth at nightclubs & [sic] the like". Don added, innocently, "There is no doubt a good deal of truth in this", but concluded firmly, "and yet nothing can really excuse this deliberate fomenting of race hatred".[29]

Whether the Archbishop was at all persuaded is hard to say. One suspects not. On 25th May he met the German theologian Adolf Deissmann at Lambeth. His new German guest very probably anticipated a discussion of the future of the German churches. But certainly he found himself questioned about the Jews. Lang reported, "Deissman [sic] confirmed everything that I had heard from the German ambassador about the reasons why the Jews have become so intensely disliked in Nationalist Germany. He did not defend much that had happened but I could see that he was in a good deal of sympathy with this dislike of the Jews." Why had the German churches made "no kind of remonstrance?" asked Lang. The Press was censored, replied Deissmann, and everything must be done quietly. He said that the April boycott was largely aborted because of the representations of church leaders. Deissmann, remarked Lang straightly, "was rather pathetic in his plea that I should try to help people here to understand things from the point of view of the German people themselves".[30]

Six days later the indefatigable American church leader J. R. Mott went to Lambeth. Lang discussed both the Jews and the churches of Germany, and entitled his memorandum, "Germany and the Jews". Once again, the tone of his language is suggestive. Mott too confirmed earlier reports: "Even the most spiritually minded of the Protestant Churches", recorded his host, "while anxious to do what was possible in a charitable way with individual Jews, did not

---

[28] Sargent to Batty, 3rd April 1933, *ibid.*, vol. 38, fol. 19.
[29] *Journal of Alan C. Don*, M. S. 2862, p. 14, 16th May 1933, London, Lambeth Palace Library.
[30] 'Conditions in Germany', memorandum by Lang of a conversation with Adolf Deissmann on 25th May 1933 (no date), *Lang Papers*, vol. 37, fols. 15–16.

seem disposed to make any kind of public protest". Mott remarked that such protests would be "unavailing and provocative", and "he was bound to admit that he could not but have at least some understanding of the reasons that had made the Jews so unpopular to this new Nationalist generation in Germany".[31]

Here was no encouragement to protest. The German churches said nothing and evidently did nothing. Those who visited Germany found German Christians, if not quite sympathetic to the persecution, sure that the Jews were not wholly undeserving of it. In any case, their obvious sympathy for the National Socialist regime apparently led them to sweep it under the carpet.

This could only make English Christians still more uncertain. But it was perhaps less important to them than their apprehension about the possible consequences of criticism. If it was, in English eyes at least, morally inexcusable to persecute Jews, were Christians bound to say so if that might only antagonise the persecutors and multiply the afflictions of the persecuted? The boycott of 1st April served expressly to plant such a doubt in foreign minds; and there were few foreign church leaders who did not think of the Nazis as fanatical, resentful and perverse.

And yet silence must suggest indifference. The very culture of English Christianity would be betrayed by passivity and acquiescence. And would not the outright silence of opinion abroad encourage the Nazi State to believe that it could persecute with impunity, and so persecute more than ever before?

The answer that the leaders of the Church of England framed was one of sympathetic protest. From the beginning it was evident to most that if criticism was to be effective, and not counter-productive, it must be preceded by expressions of sympathy and goodwill. Outward hostility would not persuade. National Socialists must be flattered. A courteous preamble stressing the "good" side of Hitler's Germany, that a beleaguered nation had recovered its self-respect, that the youth of Germany enjoyed a new sense of purpose, might earn concessions. Nor would it be insincere. If little was known of Germany before 1933, many believed it to have been humiliated by the Versailles Treaty, and harshly treated since. They wanted to see its self-esteem and confidence restored. They believed that Hitler had done this. It would be quite wrong, however, to think that Lang, and most of his bishops, attached great weight to the lauded national revival of the German spirit. It did not outweigh the vices of National Socialism. They acknowledged the "good side" with expediency, passingly, in speeches of protest. They did not lament the ill-treatment of minorities in speeches devoted to praise. The careful Bishop Bell of Chichester remarked to an ecumenical colleague, the American Henry Leiper:

> "I have seen Germans – both German pastors and Jews, and one prominent Jew who has been sent out of the country. The advice that I get is that we should remember the two elements which are really at war for the soul of Germany. There is a real movement of good in the Nazi revolution, and the denial of this deprives one of any influence in modifying the present situation. You simply do not get a hearing if you ignore the good side."[32]

[31]'Germany and the Jews', memorandum by Lang of a conversation with J. R. Mott on 31st May 1933 (no date), *ibid.*, fol. 17.
[32]Bell to Leiper, 27th October 1933, *Bell Papers*, vol. 4, fol. 270.

Anglican Church and Jews in Germany, 1933–1937 231

Lang respected the opinions of ministers and servants of the State, and usually he deferred to them because he genuinely agreed with them, and because he had a complete regard for their authority. But on this occasion he did not heed Sir Robert Vansittart's robust advice. He could not accept that protest, couched even in sympathetic terms, must be futile. It must be made somehow. He could not acquiesce. He would oblige his Christian conscience and try to alleviate the situation without aggravating it.

The Canterbury Convocation met regularly to discuss matters of the moment, usually clerical. The Archbishop's choice to refer to the Jews in Germany in such a forum was significant. But it was also natural to the cautious Lang. Convocation offered an orderly and rather reserved forum. It fell entirely under the control of the Chair. A small number of bishops seated quietly and thoughtfully, and even rather reluctantly, around a long table was not the forum for impassioned and indignant appeals to principle and the rousing exaggerations of rhetoric. This was the place for carefully weighed judgements. It was also assured of publicity. Minutes were taken and then released to the press. Evidence of serious disturbance, if any arose at all, was likely to be omitted beforehand. On 31st May 1933 Archbishop Lang went to Convocation and there he firmly, if rather respectfully, deplored the ongoing persecution. He granted that Germany sought to recover her self-confidence, but wished to "remind the German people that the true strength of a nation, the true ground for its self-respect, and of the respect of other nations for it, is shown by the administration of impartial justice to all who live within its borders".[33]

Convocation was one thing. A public meeting was quite another, and earlier in the year Lang had been invited to address a protest meeting in London. He turned for advice to Dean Tissington Tatlow, chairman of the Student Christian Movement, who was well informed about Germany, and spoke of it at assorted public meetings. He had recently forwarded to Lambeth Palace a memorandum by a secretary of the movement in Geneva, Kotschnig, which Lang had read and found "most interesting".[34] Earlier in the year Lang had signed a request, framed by Jewish leaders and addressed to the Lord Mayor of London, for a public gathering at the Guildhall to protest against the persecution. The Lord Mayor had decided against it. Lang recounted to Tatlow, "to relieve the disappointment of my friends I promised that should another equally representative meeting be arranged" he would speak out from that other platform. But now he hesitated. Would such a meeting be wise? He had thought so then, but how was he to act now that an assembly at the Queen's Hall had been arranged for 27th June, and he had been invited to speak? Now, "I know so much about the real situation in Germany that it will be impossible I fear to speak with the vehemence which the Jews might expect. I know well how sensitive the new German National spirit is and I do not want to offend it. But", he added, "I feel that we owe it to all we call civilisation to make some appeal to it."[35]

[33] *Chronicle of Convocation*, 31st May 1933, London 1933, pp. 22–23.
[34] 'Reflections on a visit to Germany, May 1933', memorandum by Kotschnig, 15th May 1933, *Lang Papers*, vol. 38, fols. 19b–30.
[35] Lang to Tatlow, 7th June 1933, *ibid.*, fol. 31.

Tatlow forwarded the anxious letter to the young James Parkes. He commended Parkes to Lang as "one of the most reliable sources of information today about Jewish affairs on the Continent".[36] A young man completing his doctorate at Oxford on the historical relations of Church and Synagogue, Parkes was a prophet of a new Christian awareness of Judaism in Britain. A friend of the Archbishop of York, William Temple, once a secretary to the Student Christian Movement, he was now a secretary of the International Student Service.

Parkes replied at length and with vigour. He was very sure what the Archbishop should do: "It seems to me, rather, that this is a unique opportunity for a declaration of fundamental Christian principles . . . it lies unanswerably within the competence of the Primate of a great Christian community to affirm as categorically as possible at such a juncture that a better life cannot be founded upon a lie" – the lie of racialism. The Archbishop should appeal to German Christianity to dissociate itself from that lie. "I do not believe the doctrine of racial superiority consistent with the idea of the Fatherhood of God", no Christian could accept the racialist National Socialist idea and the racialist legislation of the Hitler regime which persecuted "absolutely innocent individuals". The German churches were threatened. Parkes did not accept that this justified their silence. That any Christian could countenance the "whole racial conception" of National Socialism was incomprehensible to him. The Papacy had made its peace with the new German government. It too was silent. "The Archbishop of Canterbury can speak with a weight and an authority possessed by no one else. It would be a tragedy for any pronouncement of his to deal with small issues, and with technical judgements . . . If we are to shoulder our responsibility with other nations we can only do it by unflinching proclamation of the truth which is entrusted to us."[37]

Parkes met Alan Don. He disabused him of the ideas of Hoesch; that the German Jews had made fortunes out of economic collapse; that they flooded the professions; that they corrupted the morals of the young: "In relation to all these points the same answer is valid: Attack these abuses whether Jewish or 'Aryan' and you have a right to the sympathy of the world; attribute these abuses to 'The Jews' and you are shirking your own responsibility for them and blaming a section of the people who as a whole detest them as much as you do."[38]

So Lang went to the Queen's Hall on 27th June to protest. It was an impressive gathering. The Jewish community was eager that this should not be viewed as a Jewish meeting. It should be representative of the broad spectrum of British life and opinion. Lord Buckmaster, a senior lawyer, occupied the chair. Lord Cecil spoke from the platform beside two prominent Jews, Lord Reading and Lord Samuel, the Roman Catholic Iddesleigh, and the Moderator of the Free Churches, Scott Lidgett. Archbishop Lang penned the motion and spoke on its behalf. The resolution was, for all Parkes's fine words, a cumbersome creation. It should also be viewed as a defensive gesture, for Lang feared to associate himself

---

[36]Tatlow to Lang, 9th June 1933, *ibid.*, fol. 39.
[37]Parkes to Don, 9th June 1933, *ibid.*, fols. 32–34.
[38]'Notes on the three points raised in our conversation', memorandum of a conversation between Parkes and Don (n.d.), *ibid.*, fols. 36–38.

with words that were not his own and that might not account for his anxieties. Even so, the world outside did not know this, and his authorship could appear a demonstration of his commitment. And that was not untrue, in any case.

However cautious the motion, its mover spoke eloquently on its behalf. Lang's speech was, to date, the lengthiest example of sympathetic criticism to reach the world. He disclaimed the wish to interfere "with the laws of other nations". He wished for the friendship of the two countries. The German revolution was "the upstirring . . . of a long pent-up passion of desire to associate with . . . the nations of the world. Who was there who must not have understanding sympathy with such a movement, and especially with the younger members of the German people." He flattered this "great movement" of the "great German people". But he had come to appeal to them that they were staining their revolution "by the abolition of the principles of justice, tolerance and equity". He revealed a comprehensive understanding of the nature and extent of the racial discrimination in Germany, listing the exclusion of Jews from State services, from medicine and the universities; "they were being driven even from the concert room, where music was once supposed to be the common language of mankind". The speech, fully reported by *The Times*, amply illustrated what a very fine speaker Lang could be, and how effectively he could combine a command of detail with a sense of emotion, engaging both the minds and the sensitivities of his audience:

> "He asked them to think of the families now hiding from the persecution in the streets of Germany and those who were suffering agonies of apprehension and of humiliation. In the schools of Germany children were being segregated and kept apart from other children as though they were something unclean. He asked them to imagine the effect of the segregation upon the children who had borne it upon them [sic] at a tender age that they were not fit to associate with German children. Still more important was its effect on the German children of non-Jewish race who were at the start of their lives being educated in contempt and scorn of their fellow creatures."[39]

On 29th June the Chief Rabbi, J. H. Hertz, wrote of his "warmest gratitude" and "deepfelt appreciation" for such a "notable expression of the noble sentiments of tolerance and humanity".[40] But equally happy, it seemed, was the *Frankfurter Zeitung*. The editor of *The Times* sent to Lambeth a cutting from the German newspaper, clearly based upon *The Times*'s own report. This stated that the Archbishop of Canterbury had conceded that they had no right to interfere in the internal affairs of a foreign state, had stressed how they desired friendly relations with the new Germany, and how it was wrong to treat Germany as a second rank nation, and it declared, "Everybody should appreciate and have sympathy with the new movement in Germany and especially with the youth of Germany." There were no words of protest.[41] Sympathetic criticism had its obvious dangers. An exasperated Alan Don wrote, "It is pathetic to think how little chance the average German has of learning what is going on in his own country, much less what is being said and thought in other countries."[42] "Experience shows how

[39] *The Times*, 28th June 1933, p. 16b.
[40] Hertz to Lang, 29th June 1933, *Lang Papers*, vol. 38, fol. 41.
[41] Cutting sent by the secretary to the editor of *The Times*, John Webb (n.d.), *ibid.*, fol. 41.
[42] Don to Montefiore, 24th July 1933, *ibid.*, fol. 48.

ready these Nazis are to make the most of any words which they can quote as giving approval and to suppress any words of criticism", Lang remarked sourly to Bishop Headlam of Gloucester later in October.[43] Sympathetic or critical or both, there appeared little reason to think the speech a success. On 22nd July Leonard Montefiore wrote to Lambeth Palace, "the persecution shows no sign of abating".[44]

Bishop Bell was also the president of the executive comittee of the ecumenical "Life and Work" movement. On 30th August he wrote to Norman Bentwich of the Joint Foreign Committee of the Board of Deputies and the Anglo-Jewish Association, asking if he might have "half a dozen copies" of the verbatim report of the Queen's Hall meeting. He was shortly to attend the "Life and Work" conference at Novi Sad, and "I am rather anxious to present some to the Germans, that they may know what serious people really feel."[45]

III

The broad body of the Church of England in the twentieth century has bequeathed to the historian a rather fragmented, sporadic and incomplete record of its life and work. But there may be found many illustrations of the concern its leaders and members felt for the Jews of Germany in 1933. The Anglican press was observant from the first. On 3rd March the Anglo-Catholic *Church Times* had predicted a possible "reign of terror" for Jews under the Hitler regime.[46] On the last day of the month it ridiculed the motion that "pure-blooded Teutons" were the "Chosen People": "we doubt whether there are any 'pure-blooded Teutons': we are sure they are not the Chosen People".[47] In its issue of 13th April the columnist "Laicus Ignotus" reported that Hitler himself was half a Slav, his mother having been a Czech.[48] The liberal *Guardian* was less lively, but quite as critical. After Lang had responded to the 1st April boycott by raising the issue gently in the House of Lords, the weekly was quick to repudiate the conventional political wisdom that racialism in Germany was not the business of the international community:

> "It has been announced in both Houses of Parliament that there is nothing in the Covenant [of the League of Nations] which would enable protest to be made at Geneva against the Nazi boycott of the Jews. If there is not there ought to be. Surely we are not calmly invited to believe what used to be possible under the old diplomacy is impossible now. Gladstone not only made the world ring with his denunciation of atrocities but also put all the forces of diplomacy into play when he found, as often he did, any plausible opening for calling the attention of foreign Governments to the wrongs of minorities."[49]

[43] Lang to Headlam, 11th October 1933, *ibid.*, fol. 121.
[44] Montefiore to Don, 22nd July 1933, *ibid.*, fol. 46.
[45] Bell to Bentwich, 30th August 1933, *Bell Papers*, vol. 27, fol. 8.
[46] *Church Times*, 3rd March 1933, p. 251a.
[47] *Ibid.*, 31st March 1933, p. 379b.
[48] *Ibid.*, 13th April 1933, p. 445b.
[49] *The Guardian*, 7th April 1933, pp. 239a–b.

Across the country public meetings were held. It occurred naturally to their organisers to invite church leaders on to their platforms, alongside local politicians and city mayors. There their contributions sometimes lost a little force in striving to be "balanced" and restrained, but they carried humane sentiment and, as they believed, Christian principle to crowds everywhere. George Bell of Chichester would become the most active Anglican bishop on their behalf. On 30th March he had written to the president of the German Protestant *Kirchenbund*, Hermann Kapler, that the calling of the boycott of Jewish businesses had, "without doubt", made a particularly deep impression on his fellow church people.[50] After the boycott Bishop David and Archbishop Downey of Liverpool, Protestant and Roman Catholic together, stood before an "overflowing" rally at the city's Central Hall. It was the duty of the Christian, said David, to try to understand people. But, he confessed, he could not understand the rulers of Germany. How could they complain at one moment that foreign press reports of the persecution were published to arouse hostility against them, and the next turn around to incite still more violence? "I must with great sorrow enter my emphatic protest. I do so with almost equal sorrow for the Germans themselves."[51] In the same month Bishop Batty also voiced his anxiety publicly.[52] At the beginning of May the Anglican newspaper the *Church Times* observed, "there are prayers in most churches, protests on all hands".[53] Later in the same month the Archbishop of York, William Temple, and two bishops of his Northern province, Henson of Durham and Burroughs of Ripon, followed him.[54]

Henson had addressed a meeting at the Victoria Hall in Sunderland on 7th May. Having arrived he surveyed his audience and thought it very largely composed of working-class Jews, Socialists and Nonconformists; people, he glumly reflected, with little affection for a bishop, whatever he may say. Then he noted coldly how they gave "their most ardent plaudits" to a Labour politician and "a Fundamentalist sectary".[55] A sensitive man, he felt awkward and defensive, and even suspected some embarrassment at his presence among the meeting's organisers – quite possibly that was his own invention. None the less, he received vindication of a kind when his words alone were reported by the local press the next day.[56] Antisemitism unsettled Henson. He remarked privately how curiously widespread it was in his own social circles (Henson was a freemason and one who delighted in the argumentative and provocative male company to be found in his clubs). 'To what lengths will partisan bigotry carry even kindly and intelligent people?" he asked in his journal. He was still more disconcerted to find something of it, heavily repressed by a sense of religious principle, lingering in his own breast.[57]

---

[50] Bell to Kapler, 30th March 1933, *Bell Papers*, vol. 4, fol. 7.
[51] *The Record*, 13th April 1933, p. 210c.
[52] *The Times*, 27th April 1933, p. 9b.
[53] *Church Times*, 5th May 1933, p. 525a.
[54] Johan M. Snoek, *The Grey Book*, Assen 1968, pp. 66–67. This work should be used with some caution on account of occasional factual errors.
[55] *Journal of Bishop Henson*, vol. 57, pp. 267–268, 7th May 1933, Durham Cathedral Library.
[56] *Ibid.*, 8th May 1933, vol. 58, p. 2.
[57] *Ibid.*, 17th August 1933, p. 252.

In June a correspondent remarked to Bell, "in all towns in England the Bishops and Clergy of all denominations have most eloquently shown their sympathy and pleaded for justice for the Jews and for all who have suffered by reason of their race and faith".[58] Such a comment should perhaps be treated rather cautiously, but it was not ill founded. In October Temple spoke out again, at a meeting in York.[59]

Henson was stepping wistfully towards retirement and sad decline in 1933. Of a similar age was his friend Arthur Headlam, the Bishop of Gloucester. The two had grown close as students at Oxford, and afterwards had remained staunchly loyal to each other as priests and then bishops. Both were essentially Conservatives whose basic political values owned their debt to an earlier age. But forty years after they had met their long friendship was thrown into difficulty and awkwardness as they confronted the challenges of the National-Socialist era. In the late autumn of 1933 Henson dined at his London club, and there found the Bishop of Gloucester "curiously wrong-headed about the Jews whose treatment in Germany", he added firmly, and perhaps in reply to what his friend had said, "cannot be excused by any objections to their international character, anti-social activities, and general unpopularity".[60] On this issue, in fact, Headlam had already got himself into trouble.

When, in the spring and summer of 1933, many bishops in England were condemning the persecution in Germany, Headlam became its wilful apologist. He thought the criticism of his peers ignorant and ill-judged. He decided to provide some sense of balance by proposing the other side of the argument. He became, in Henson's disgusted words, "the pertinacious apologist" of the new National-Socialist regime.[61] He conceded that it victimised innocent people. He perceived that it was often ugly and excessive. But he believed that the German people had recovered their self-respect, and that most of them enthusiastically supported their new government. Who was to say that they should not?

Headlam had great intellectual power, but his was not a subtle mind; he simplified and characterised, and was unhappily susceptible to prejudice. For him, the Jews were inexorably different, racially, religiously and socially: they enjoyed many international relations and "a capacity for obtaining for themselves wealth and position".[62] He clearly thought them, as a phenomenon, doubtful. In August 1933 he wrote of the persecution in Germany in his diocesan magazine. They all, he remarked, condemned the folly and violence of it. But rather than voicing his sympathy for the suffering, he decided that a word of warning was necessary to those who protested. The violence of Socialist communities, and most especially of the Russian Communists, was often inspired by Jews; they were "not altogether a pleasant element in German, and in particular in Berlin life": "Those of alien nationality who receive the hospitality of other countries ought to recognize that wisdom and gratitude alike

---

[58]Jacobs to Bell, 24th June 1933, *Bell Papers*, vol. 65, fol. 31.
[59]*The Times*, 24th October 1933, p. 9b.
[60]*Journal of Bishop Henson*, vol. 59, p. 79, 14th November 1933.
[61]Herbert Hensley Henson, *Retrospect of an Unimportant Life*, vol. II, Oxford 1943, p. 413.
[62]Bishop's Letter, *Gloucester Diocesan Magazine*, October 1933.

demand that they should become healthy elements in the population." He concluded that, "although we think they are wrong, we have respect for the Jew who faithfully adheres to his religious customs, but many Jews take no interest in their own faith, are free-thinkers, and use their Judaism very largely as a basis for attacking the Christian faith".[63]

Parts of the pastoral letter were reprinted in the *Western Mail* and *The Guardian*. A stir was inevitable. George Bell wrote to Henry Leiper that Headlam had said "some very unfortunate things", and given "great offence".[64] Claude Montefiore wrote to the Bishop of Gloucester of the "pain and astonishment" his remarks had occasioned. The letter, he said was "ill-founded and erroneous". Should a whole community be so treated because of the sins of a few? Was Judaism nothing deeper and greater than a collection of customs? How free-thinking Jews might employ their Judaism to attack the Christian faith was a puzzle to him.[65]

Typically obdurate, Headlam did not learn from this. His natural reaction to a dispute was not to concede, but to dig in his heels. In the subsequent number of the diocesan magazine he returned to the matter, and not apologetically. He remarked that he had been astonished at the number of protesting letters he had received, and at the violence of the attacks upon him. The Jewish community in this country was, "for the most part a wholesome element", but even here there were "most undesirable" circles. Abroad there were more. Clearly, from somebody he had heard that the Jews had degraded the morals of Berlin. He insisted that the conduct of the German government was not to be excused, but Jews worldwide must recognise "the real facts of the case". They enjoyed wealth and influence; they must not flaunt those things, but instead exercise some "self-suppression". Montefiore, he declared, had asked him to print his own protest. He would do nothing of the sort; it was neither necessary nor reasonable, and he might as well print other sympathetic letters which he had received.[66] In the same month Headlam complained to the editor of *The Times* that the Jews, who were "clever and malicious", sought to spread "false or one-sided views" about the new Germany.[67]

Headlam was soon recognised as an unpleasant embarrassment within the church. It is likely that Lambeth Palace heard of these views, but there exists no reference to the controversy in Lang's papers. Nor did Lang rebuke him for his unwholesome sympathies.

As summer faded into autumn the ecumenical movement abroad stirred. In September 1933 the executive committee of the World Alliance, meeting in Sofia, affirmed "the super-racial character of the Gospel", and expressed "our profound emotion at the treatment inflicted in Germany on its citizens who are of Jewish origin or have Jews in their families . . . It is our conviction that this action is altogether in contradiction to the teaching and the spirit of the Gospel of Jesus

---

[63]Bishop's Letter,*ibid.*, August 1933.
[64]Bell to Leiper, 27th October 1933, *Bell Papers*, vol. 4, fol. 269.
[65]Montefiore to Headlam, 9th August 1933, London, Lambeth Palace Library, *Headlam Papers*, M.S. 2643, fols. 1–4.
[66]Bishop's Letter, *Gloucester Diocesan Magazine*, October 1933.
[67]Headlam to Dawson, 27th October 1933, *Headlam Papers*, M.S. 2643, fols. 58–59.

Christ." However, the conference did not think that the movement should interfere in this internal German affair by addressing the swelling refugee crisis. Fox sent a copy of the statement to Lambeth Palace on 2nd October.[68] He had already submitted a report on the refugee crisis to the new Archbishop of Canterbury's Council on Foreign Relations. Lang awaited its discussion there before endorsing its call for a relief fund. On 13th October George Bell wrote to Lang of a church appeal for "Non-Aryan Christians" on the Sunday after Christmas.[69] Lang approved it "gladly".[70] In November Lang lent his name to an appeal by the German Refugees Assistance Fund. It was published in *The Times* on 17th November.[71] In the meantime he awaited instructions from the League of Nations High Commissioner for Refugees, McDonald, to "give the word that the time is ready" to launch a church appeal.[72] The collection for "Non-Aryan Christians", sanctioned by both archbishops, took place in parish church services on the last day of the year. It raised little money. In Durham Bishop Henson thought it "a very astonishing proceeding for (as far as I know) there was no similar appeal made for the Russian refugees, who were fellow Christians".[73]

IV

At Lambeth Palace Archbishop Lang turned increasingly to his gentle and thoughtful, but tenacious, Bishop of Chichester for advice. By the end of 1933 George Bell, with his extensive international ecumenical connections in the "Life and Work" movement, was the most frequently invoked source of authority in the Anglican church. In time the anxious Lang was quite eclipsed by him.

Everything that happened in Germany concerned Bell; the victims of the new state all commanded his sympathy, be they Christians, Jews, pacifists, intellectuals, or political opponents. But as 1933 wore on he found that he could not busy himself with them all. He must choose particular issues with a mind to where he could work with the greatest authority and to the greatest effect. He must work for the most vulnerable and the friendless. He was a Christian bishop. The National-Socialist State, which did not think it proper for Christians to speak out on "political" affairs, was more likely to listen to a bishop abroad who spoke of Church matters in particular than one who, in their eyes, discredited himself with things that lay beyond his rightful jurisdiction. His commitment to the welfare of German Christianity was therefore seemly, and most likely to be influential. For Roman Catholics and Protestants he cared in equal measure, but Bell was a Protestant bishop. He judged that Roman Catholics in Germany could best be defended by the Vatican. The Protestant churches, who lacked

---

[68] Fox to Don, 2nd October 1933, *Lang Papers*, vol. 38, fols. 68–69.
[69] Bell to Lang, 13th October 1933, *ibid.*, fol. 70.
[70] Don to Bell, 28th November 1933, *Bell Papers*, vol. 27, fol. 207.
[71] *The Times*, 17th November 1933, p. 10d.
[72] Don to Bell, 23rd November 1933, *Bell Papers*, vol. 27, fol. 180.
[73] *Journal of Bishop Henson*, vol. 59, p. 120, 8th December 1933.

such support abroad, who participated, however cautiously, in the "Life and Work" movement, and whose leaders he had long known, should naturally engage his attentions.

Bell thought of the Jews. Racial persecution was anathema to him. If the international Roman Catholic Church existed to care for Roman Catholics there was, he thought, also a strong and active international Jewish community to offer "practical help and sympathy" for the Jews of Germany.[74] But Norman Bentwich wrote to him in August that those who now found themselves classified as "non-Aryan" Christians in Germany had nowhere to turn.[75] Bell explained to a correspondent, "these non-Aryans are veritable pariahs and belong to no corporate body which unites them". And, unlike the imprisoned pacifists and Socialists, whose incarceration he abhorred, they had "no political convictions in common". A "non-Aryan" was isolated at home and abroad. He referred to remarks made by Helen Bentwich in support of his thoughts.[76] On 20th November 1933 he wrote to a friend, "At present the Jews are contributing generously to the needs of Jews. But those who are Jews in religion may quite rightly feel that they ought not be expected to look after those who are not Jews in religion, at any rate Church members".[77] Bell adopted the National-Socialist phrase "non-Aryan" unthinkingly. It did not occur to him that to use the term was to concede to Nazi language and ideology more than was proper. It was another of those signs of innocence which were so common in a society struggling to comprehend a situation that appeared so foreign and remote.

But, however busy the Bishop of Chichester might be, it was still the Archbishop of Canterbury who possessed the greater weight. Only the words of the Primate could carry the full weight of the institution. In May 1934 Bell forwarded to Lambeth Palace a particularly disgusting edition of Julius Streicher's paper, *Der Stürmer*. The publication had already acquired an international reputation for the depraved vulgarity of its propaganda, and its officially sanctioned public display in glass cases in German streets presented a disturbing image to decent minds. This number appeared to observers even more offensive than its predecessors. It revived the archaic antisemitic libel of ritual murder, and printed a series of gruesome illustrations. Lang was incensed by it. At once he decided that it could not pass; he must protest publicly. Just then a number of British church leaders were visiting Lambeth to discuss a united statement on the international situation. The Archbishop wrote with their approval. His letter was strikingly forthright. It seemed, he protested, "almost incredible" to him that such a journal, recalling "the worst excesses of Medieval fanaticism", could be permitted in any civilised country, let alone be promoted by one of its rulers. He challenged the German government to disown "this odious incitement to religious bigotry and . . . brutal persecution".[78] There was

---

[74]Bell to Hughes, 7th October 1933, *Bell Papers*, vol. 27, fol. 40.
[75]Cited by P. J. Ludlow in 'The Refugee Problem in the 1930s: the failures and successes of Protestant relief programmes', in *English Historical Review*, vol. XC (1975), p. 572.
[76]Bell to Hughes, 7th October 1933, *Bell Papers*, vol. 27, fol. 40.
[77]Bell to Ehrenberg, 20th November 1933, *ibid.*, fol. 176.
[78]*The Times*, 16th May 1934, p. 17e.

no caution or hesitation whatever in what he wrote. Gone too were the polite professions of sympathy. Alan Don remarked to the Chief Rabbi, "the letter was the immediate and spontaneous expression of a sense of indignation such as His Grace seldom feels".[79] Bell would later remember the letter as an effective riposte. In November 1935 at a meeting of the Anglican Church Assembly, he expressed his belief that the letter had "a very considerable effect at the time". Informed friends told him that *Der Stürmer* had become, for a while, quieter.[80] This could well have been so; the Hitler regime still possessed a certain sensitivity to foreign opinion in 1934.

Totalitarian dictatorships encourage officially sponsored and thoroughly organised tourism. National-Socialist Germany made every effort to sway world opinion in this way. Tours by specially invited "guests of the German Government" were very remarkable affairs. Parties of the English well-to-do, who brought with them on their outward journeys a rather shaky moral vision, were brimful of new and agreeable convictions, put up in stately hotels, spoilt at dinner parties, treated to a Nuremberg rally, introduced to the great men at the top of it all, and then flown home to speak with the irrefutable authority of those who had seen for themselves.

In the late summer of 1934 a Gloucestershire vicar, H. V. Hodson, visited the Third *Reich* as a member of such a party. In the middle of the tour he was introduced to Alfred Rosenberg. Rosenberg had offended Christians everywhere with his extraordinarily odd book, a racialist anti-religious epic called *Der Mythos des 20. Jahrhunderts. Eine Wertung der seelisch-geistigen Gestaltenkämpfe unserer Zeit* ("The Myth of the Twentieth Century"). Hodson talked to him. But he did not speak of Christianity, or of race and religion, or of the harassed churches of Germany. Instead he told him "quite frankly" that "the whole of the Christian civilised world was aghast at the treatment of the Jews" there. Rosenberg tried to reassure him, but Hodson would not be swayed.[81] Perhaps the episode suggests a good deal; perhaps it reveals rather little. Hodson was not eminent; but was he significant? Was his concern unusual, or characteristic of others like him?

After 1933 the records of Anglican concern in England become still more sporadic. This may suggest a decline of interest. It may be due only to broadening gaps in records that are, at best, fragmentary. Most likely it was due to an uncertainty in the Church of England. For, once the speeches and protests had been delivered, the platforms cleared, and the church and town halls emptied, what were they all to do? On 12th June 1934 an informal conference took place in London between members of the Church of England's International Missionary Council, including the eminent and inexhaustible William Paton, and of the Council on Foreign Relations, including Henry Fox. Dr. Conrad Hoffmann, whom the persecution had made something of a centre of attention in the church, attended too.

The purpose of the gathering was "to discuss the present position of the Jews in Germany and to consider what should be done to mitigate it". A memorandum,

[79] Don to Hertz, 17th May 1934, *Lang Papers*, vol. 38, fol. 90.
[80] *Proceedings of the Church Assembly*, vol. XVI, London 1935, 20th November 1935, p. 469.
[81] Cutting from the *Gloucester Echo*, 13th September 1934, in the *Headlam Papers*, M.S. 2643, fol. 127.

"The Position of Jews in Germany", was written by Ruth Pittman.[82] Hoffmann noted the many agencies helping those who had escaped from Germany. But what might be done for those who remained? Perhaps they could ask the Baptists, soon to hold their world conference in Berlin, to raise the issue with German church leaders and government authorities?[83] Henry Fox believed that representations from England, and especially from the Anglican Church, carried "very great weight" in Germany. He doubted the point of resolutions, but thought "if an approach could be made by the right people to the right people there was the possibility of amelioration". Hoffmann suggested that public opinion might be influenced by the clergy of foreign churches in Germany and various Jewish missionary societies there. Fox observed tersely that the German Protestant and Roman Catholic churches were more committed to their own well-being; the plight of the Jews probably "did not occupy their thoughts at all".[84] William Paton, who also kept a record of the conference, confusedly entitled, "Notes on the Conditions of Non-Jewish Non-Aryans in Germany", remarked with asperity, "it appears that the German Church has been silent on this subject. While German Church leaders in the minority have protested against the so-called 'Aryan Clause', in thereby registering their protest against the idea of a racial church, it is difficult to find a single instance of protest against the indignities offered to the Jews or the Jewish Christians simply on the grounds of their birth. It was Dr Hoffman's [sic] experience, as it was recently mine on a visit to Germany, to hear from every quarter the same excuse offered – the Jews were too numerous in the professions, they were responsible for much of the evil in the national life etc., etc."[85]

They all agreed that publicity and financial assistance were important, and so too the creation of "some kind of liaison between the non-Aryan Union in Germany and the foreign missionary societies".[86] The minutes of the meeting, and Paton's own notes, suggest vagueness and a certain demoralisation. Germany was discussed like a hopelessly distant province. Their links with it were slender and weak. The German churches would not provide the foundation they, as Christians abroad, required if they were to act effectively. Nothing, not even a second meeting, appears to have followed. Had demoralisation prevailed?

The silence of the German churches would continue to perplex and embarrass English Christians. Some were openly resentful. In September *The Record* printed an article on 'The Plight of the Hebrew Christians in Germany':

> "It might be reasonably expected that the Lutheran or Evangelical Church in Germany would come to the assistance of these people, but its attitude is extraordinary . . . A pastor was remonstrated with for an anti-semitic article in his periodical. He replied . . . 'I consider the

---

[82]'The Position of Jews in Germany', memorandum by Ruth Pittman, 12th June 1934, London, Lambeth Palace, *Archives of the Archbishop of Canterbury's Council on Foreign Relations*, Box L.R. 3 F 7, "Germany".

[83]For a history of the conference, see Keith Clements, 'A Question of Freedom? British Baptists and the German Church Struggle', in *Baptists in the Twentieth Century*, London 1983, pp. 96–113.

[84]Ruth Pittman memorandum, 12th June 1934.

[85]'Notes on the Conditions of Non-Jewish Non-Aryans in Germany', memorandum by William Paton (n.d.), *Lang Papers*, vol. 38, fols. 95–96.

[86]Ruth Pittman memorandum, 12th June 1934.

Bible as the most antisemitic book in the world.' That is an idea of the Church in Germany and the position of the Jewish Christians in that country. It is an unfortunate fact, therefore, that no help may be expected from that quarter."[87]

V

1935 was a year of profound significance in the unfolding history of National-Socialist antisemitism. The Nuremberg Laws in September framed and legalised discrimination with a pretence of order and moderation. Curiously their inhumanity was successfully disguised behind a vaunted wish to curb irregular violence and intimidation. The law would protect the Jews once it had defined what their status should be. But the acrobatic logic and the affected morality of the Nuremberg Laws made an impression on many minds, at home and abroad. Many were reassured.

George Bell was visiting Germany at the time. As he travelled through Bavaria he saw for himself placards and posters, 'Jews not wanted', outside the public buildings and parks, and the loathsome *Der Stürmer* exhibited in glass cases on town and village streets. And he was deeply troubled by it all. The morning after the new race laws were announced a Dr. Gerl of Hinderlang came to his hotel to assure him that the Jews now enjoyed a security which would "enable them to follow their calling, though not as German citizens yet in peace and without disturbance". Hitler had, Gerl stressed, emphasised that personal "baiting" must cease.[88] On 20th September Bell met Rudolf Hess at his home, "a nice house with a garden" and an SS guard at the gate, in the Harthauserstrasse in Munich. He thought his sallow and anxious face rather suggestive of melancholy. Frau Hess was by contrast friendly and pleasant company. Bell hoped for the best.[89]

The Nuremberg Laws defined a Jew and a "non-Aryan" by "blood", and not by status or confession. A "non-Aryan" might be a Lutheran, but that was neither here nor there. The German churches, who felt they must look after their own, were not drawn even by this new development. In England, however, the significance of these legal definitions was not lost on the *Church Times*:

> "The Nuremberg Laws have outlawed, not only Jews, but also persons suspected of being partly of Jewish descent, and it is certain that the blackmailer is flourishing and that private enmity is successfully parading as public duty. The baptized Jew suffers with the unbaptized. Professional eminence and distinguished service are of no account. The Nazis are sending the Jews, many of them domiciled in Germany for generations, back to the ghetto, and are making the ghetto a place of privation and peril."[90]

Some information about events on the Continent could be provided by embassy chaplains abroad. In 1935 the British chaplain in Vienna was C.H.D. Grimes. On 22nd October Grimes sent a letter to Bell. The plight of the Jews in Germany

---

[87] *The Record*, 14th September 1934, p. 531d.
[88] Bell to Gerl, 11th December 1935, *Bell Papers*, vol. 7, fol. 511.
[89] 'Interview with Rudolf Hess', memorandum by Bell, 20th September 1935, *ibid.*, fols. 361–367.
[90] *Church Times*, 22nd November 1935, p. 575b.

was a constant concern to him. During that summer he had visited Germany and discussed the situation with the Germans themselves. "I may say", he wrote, "that I myself am pro-Jew & [*sic*] have always been so – I found however in Germany that the Jews were universally disliked & usually hated – no doubt this is due to a large extent to the recent propaganda – but it goes much farther back as I knew from earlier visits to Germany." He observed that British businessmen in Germany were antisemitic. "I found however that the great majority of decent Germans are very uncomfortable when one speaks to them about the persecution which is going on. But they do not dare to say anything – so their opinion does not count." The Swiss chaplain, Forell, suggested an ecumenical council to put pressure on the German government. Grimes himself perceived that the regime was "really sensitive to the options of the two great English speaking states . . . I know the German people are . . . That is our strong card." He thought that many members of the German government wished to relieve the hardship of "the very effective" international Jewish boycott of the country. If the churches in Britain and America could issue a clear pronouncement that friendship was possible only if the persecution ceased, the German government might step down. But he feared the consequences of such a project, if it misfired, suggesting that it might only encourage the "wild men", who cried for the "extermination" of hostile Jews abroad.[91]

There is no evidence to suggest that Bell did approach the British government, as Grimes suggested. But he was busy in his own way. His contact, Herr Gerl, a friend of Rudolf Hess, visited London early in November. Bell "impressed upon him the very bad impression made in England by the present policy of the Government with regard to the Jews". Gerl replied that Bell must say these things to Hess and Hitler himself.[92]

Naturally, Bell was eager to meet Hitler. He wrote of the invitation to his friend, the German refugee Kurt Hahn. But Hahn was not sanguine. "No visitor", he said, "even you, will win through unless Berlin senses a current of opinion behind you which it would like to appease". He was to see Archbishop Temple on the 25th November, and visit Lambeth Palace the day after. Ideally, he thought, Lang might write a second letter to *The Times* condemning Streicher.[93]

On 15th November Bell replied to Hahn that he had decided to propose a motion, on the persecution in Germany, to the Assembly of the Church of England. He would welcome advice.[94]

Five days later, on the 20th November 1935, the Assembly met in London. It was, in effect, the national representative body of the Church of England. Created in 1921 it was an expression of the church's spiritual independence from the political establishment, but also a power that submitted to the judgement of parliament. Its members were drawn from all quarters of the institution; bishops, deans, clergy, laity. On this day the Assembly welcomed the Bishop of

---

[91] Grimes to Bell, 22nd October 1935, *Bell Papers*, vol. 27, fols. 428–429.
[92] Bell to Hahn, 12th November 1935, *ibid.*, vol. 28, fol. 26.
[93] Hahn to Bell, 14th November 1935, *ibid.*, fol. 28.
[94] Bell to Hahn, 15th November 1935, *ibid.*, fol. 29.

Chichester's motion on the Jews of Germany by pushing other business to one side to make room for it.

Bell's resolution was, characteristically, over-long and careful. But it was stern enough. It was not hesitant. It may have lacked edge, but it did have weight:

> "That this assembly desires to express its sympathy with the Jewish people and those of Jewish origin in the sufferings which are being endured by many of their number in Germany, and trusts that people in this and other countries will exert their influence to make it plain to the rulers of Germany that the continuance of their present policy will arouse widespread indignation and prove a grave obstacle to the promotion of confidence and goodwill between Germany and other nations."[95]

Archbishop Lang, who disliked chairing Church Assembly debates as much as he disliked meetings of Convocation, remained in the hall long enough to deliver his own thoughts before chasing off to christen the king's grandson. Some thought his priorities wrong. But while he was present he "felt bound most strongly to protest against the persecution– administrative, economic and social – which seemed unhappily to have broken out with a new intensity" in Germany. No longer could it be pleaded that the Nuremberg Laws would protect the Jewish community. He "most earnestly" hoped that "the ultimately responsible" authorities there would, in the interests of justice, restrain the acts of irresponsible individuals and local authorities and seek to restore "the rights, I do not say of citizenship, but of mere humanity".[96]

Bell had written to Hahn that he wished his speech to be a factually accurate, "telling and judicial presentation". Now, on the platform, he was gentle at first. He said that he moved his motion reluctantly. He rather shuffled through the usual appreciations of the "creative" side of National Socialism, made customary allowances, recalled his own visits to Germany and his many friends there, some of whom, he added firmly, were Nazis themselves. There could be no question of the design of such words; his protestations that Germany was a great nation led him to insist that the persecution must be unworthy of it. He used the rhetoric of the National-Socialist state to embarrass it. He stressed that his Christianity, his humanity, compelled him to speak, "because as a Christian I see a wrong offered to that positive Christianity on which National Socialism itself professed to be based". He did not wish for invective, nor even for criticism, but to draw attention to the situation and voice sympathy for the suffering. He lamented the "overwhelming and indiscriminate attack" they had beheld since 1933, that a whole people should be so rejected and defamed from one end of the country to another. Goebbels, "one of the most powerful influences in present-day Germany", had spoken of the Jews as vermin. *Der Stürmer* was more vicious than ever, striving to "train the new generation for the task of solving the Jewish problem unrestrained by scruple or pity". How, Bell asked, might German Jews be protected from such slanders? The answer must be by the Church, in England and in Europe. That was why he had brought his motion before the Assembly.[97]

The Bishop of Southwark, Richard Parsons, seconded Bell. The German Jews,

---

[95] *Proceedings of the Church Assembly, op. cit.*, 20th November 1935, p. 467.
[96] *Ibid.*, p. 466.
[97] *Ibid.*, pp. 467–470.

he said, were now as the helots of ancient Greece had been. He explained, and lucidly, the citizenship argument of the Nuremberg Laws. Legislation, he said, concerned him more than violence, "which was of the moment". It was becoming impossible for the Jews to live in Germany and equally impossible for them to leave, except as paupers. As a bishop of the Church of Christ, and in the name of civilisation, he pleaded with the German government for "a wiser, humane and more truly noble mind".[98]

Bell had wanted little debate, if any at all. What followed was a significant exchange of views which did much to illustrate the anxieties and inhibitions which frequently characterised the Anglican response to National Socialism at large through the pre-war years.

The German Vice-Consul at Plymouth, Mr. Carlisle Davis, opposed the motion outright. He asked, was this not "a political question pure and simple", and a foreign one too? It was not a religious matter; it was not for them. Surely they were not going to deny to Germany the right to deal with their "race question" in their own way? The Nuremberg Laws were not so bad – they had been modified. He talked of moderates and extremists in that country, and how such interfering criticism must hinder the former and encourage the latter. The motion would only be misunderstood; he hoped they would not pass it.[99]

Carlisle Davis was not alone, for he was seconded. But clearly the feeling of the hall was against him. Bishop Henson heard the speech and knew that he must repudiate it. He had not intended to speak, and he was unprepared. His speech struck a note of such authority and passion that he transported his audience and received their rapturous approval.

The issue before them, declared Henson, was of so exceptional a character that a clear pronouncement from this "great representative assembly of Christian men" was absolutely demanded. They must remember and affirm the solidarity of civilisation. They were children of Christendom, inheritors of an order which had its origin in the revelation of God in Christ. After centuries of stuttering progress, "a certain treasure of convictions and precedents had been reached which it was criminal and treason against humanity itself to ignore or violate". Germans must be told that, for all the "fervours and frenzies of their revolution", such conduct carried them beyond those bounds.

In his arguments, if not his tone and language, Henson shared these approaches with Bell and Parsons before him. But now he charged from quite another direction. Diplomatically, Bell had made allowances. He did not say that the root of the persecution lay in the wickedness of National Socialism, but remarked instead upon the former prevalence of Jews in government, medicine, and law. Henson would have none of that. He pronounced to the world that such racialism was lunatic. A virulent and contemptible madness had arisen in Germany; he conceded nothing to it. He bitterly confessed himself filled with "a kind of blind rage". The German people were "hypnotised by a fiction", a nonsense, an hallucination. They must be told so. The Jews were as mixed a race

[98] *Ibid.*, pp. 470–472.
[99] *Ibid.*, pp. 473–474.

as were the Germans themselves, and he knew them to be a gifted, kind and good people.

Henson stressed the great debt owed by the "children of Christendom" to "the ancient people of God"; that Jesus was a Jew and His Apostles also; that the sacred book which they as Christians read was a Jewish book. Religiously, spiritually and morally they owed to the Jews almost everything they valued. Without the slightest reserve or qualification he stood beside the oppressed and afflicted. He thundered his exasperation and anger that, in the words of the Book of Judges, they could not draw the sword and go to the help of the low against the mighty. If they were powerless, they could yet voice their detestation of such criminal cruelty.[100]

This was at once a famous utterance. What is striking is how distinctively Christian the speech appeared to be in its foundation and ideas. It placed Jew and Christian so closely and sympathetically beside each other, embraced both of their traditions and cultures so powerfully, and affirmed so profound a kinship between them, that even today it deserves to be seen as a prophetic statement.

Henson so dominated the day's proceedings that the remainder received little attention. But his was not, in fact, the last word. Sir Raymond Beazley, a distinguished Birmingham historian and a lay member of the assembly, said he sympathised with the motion, of course. But might it do more harm than good? He dwelt upon their reasons for uncertainty and encouraged their temerity. He too had been in Germany when the Nuremberg legislation was passed, and many important people there had pressed its virtues upon him: "It defined what discrimination there should be." Would that there were no discrimination at all, but still it was better than a surrender to mob rule. Like Carlisle Davis, he spoke of moderates and extremists in the National Socialist Party. Extremists were "the curse of every great movement". There were excesses, individual rather than general, and they were being addressed by the proper authorities. The Jews were not ostracised socially; he had seen this for himself. He told them that Schacht, whom he regarded, after Hitler and Göring, as probably the most important figure in the *Reich*, had decreed that there should be no discrimination in the business world. That may be a sign of things to come. The question was too incomplete, too constantly changing, to justify a firm judgement now.[101]

Lord Hugh Cecil, a leading light in the Anglican world and the brother of the Bishop of Exeter, replied that his faith rested in the judgement of the Bishop of Chichester, who was so well informed, and unlikely to mistake his words or his moment. Moreover, "nothing in the world could be more deplorable than that the motion should not be carried . . . It would give the impression that that representative assembly of Christians rather sympathised with the German government than with the persecuted Jews."[102]

After another speaker from Devon had reiterated the arguments of Carlisle Davis and Beazley before him, Bell concluded the debate, repeating firmly that

---

[100] *Ibid.*, pp. 476–477.
[101] *Ibid.*
[102] *Ibid.*, pp. 477–478.

the motion was not an attack, "but an appeal of the deepest and friendliest character to the rulers of Germany".[103]

The motion was carried overwhelmingly. The secular press made the most of it, and of Henson especially. The *Daily Telegraph* and *Yorkshire Post* even printed his photograph. In Germany, Henson soon heard, a newspaper reported his speech and used his quotation from the Book of Judges to suggest that the Bishop of Durham proposed war.[104] Although he received abusive post from British antisemites, he also read grateful letters from as far afield as Vienna, and heard that his speech was spoken of in Palestine.

"Your noble step in the cause of humanity gives us some hope, as it seems hardly possible that your words will fall on deaf ears, words which must resound throughout the whole civilised world", wrote Lord Rothschild to Lang.[105] Leonard Montefiore, who had been sitting in the Church Assembly audience, told Bell that he was "deeply impressed and moved. I am more grateful than I know how to put into words to you." Perhaps a pamphlet of the debate might be published?[106] Some days later he wrote that copies of the *Danziger Echo*, which had carried the resolution on its front page, had been confiscated in Germany.[107] The Chief Rabbi, J. H. Hertz, said that the Assembly's protest would come "as a ray of hope to hundreds of thousands whose annihilation seems to have been decided upon".[108] Neville Laski wrote, "If anything will deflect the rulers of Germany from their course of persecution – and that is doubtful – it is the protest of the Church of England in the name of Christianity."[109] Later Sir Wyndham Deedes wrote that he had been told in Germany that the Church Assembly debate had "a far-reaching effect" on Jews rather than "non-Aryan" Christians; "but all Jews and non-Aryans look to you, my Lord, to espouse their cause!"[110] "How one wishes that the mind of the rulers of Germany could be changed!" remarked Bell to a sympathetic correspondent. "It is a relapse into paganism as you say."[111]

Hermann Maas, a German pastor working in Geneva for Jewish "non-Aryan" refugees with the German secretary of the ecumenical World Alliance, Friedrich Siegmund-Schultze, wrote to Bell to show him how restrictive the Nuremberg Laws were, and to thank him for "your wonderful and very Christian action".[112] His second letter declared, "The crime of Christianity towards the people of the Bible, indeed the people of our Lord, grows enormously day by day, and I feel an awful judgement threatening us."[113] But, privately, Maas was fearful that the dramatic debate might have alienated German churchpeople, and "driven them

---

[103]*Ibid.*, pp. 478–479.
[104]*Journal of Bishop Henson*, vol. 65, p. 210, 29th November 1935.
[105]Rothschild to Lang, 23rd November 1935, *Lang Papers*, vol. 38, fol. 104.
[106]Montefiore to Bell, 20th November 1935, *Bell Papers*, vol. 28, fol. 31.
[107]Montefiore to Bell, 5th December 1935, *ibid.*, fol. 89.
[108]Hertz to Bell, 21st November 1935, *ibid.*, fol. 35.
[109]Laski to Bell, 26th November 1935, *ibid.*, fol. 75.
[110]*Journal of Bishop Henson*, vol. 66, p. 260, 11th June 1936.
[111]Bell to Matthias, 26th November 1935, *Bell Papers*, vol. 28, fol. 70.
[112]Maas to Bell, 28th November 1935, *ibid.*, fol. 78.
[113]Maas to Bell, 12th December 1935, *ibid.*, fol. 103.

back once again into the arms of the [National Socialist] Party", just when they were taking more notice of their government's persecution of racial minorities. He sympathised with the Jews, but regretted that the Church Assembly had not spoken directly of the "non-Aryans".[114] At all events, the Protestant churches in Germany were too preoccupied with their own hectic affairs in the autumn of 1935 to address the plight either of "non-Aryans" or Jews. However, it was still possible that they benefited from the episode. A Canadian woman who was married to a German surgeon, and who lived in Berlin, wrote to an English friend, Dr. Mary Radford, "I know that only the moral pressure of the resolution passed by the English Church Assembly has so far prevented the German Government from carrying out these threats [to prosecute a number of German pastors] & more they are vigorously suppressing any news-leakage to England." The letter was sent to Henson, and he in turn passed it on to Bell.[115]

If the Church Assembly was indeed Henson's "great representative assembly" of Christian opinion, the light it might be seen to throw upon the state of English feelings, clerical and lay, may be strong. Certainly the response of the church press would support this. The Anglican newspapers welcomed the resolution with eager enthusiasm; the *Church Times* was moved to declare that it "rejoiced" at the Bishop of Durham's words – something in fact it rarely did, for the two were old enemies.[116]

Archbishop Temple, on the other hand, appeared to undermine the consensus a little in the following December, when he visited America for a lecture tour. Unfortunately he turned up in New York on board a steamship, the *Bremen*, which was owned by a German company. Many American Jews, Roman Catholics and Protestants already boycotted the line, and in anticipation of robust protests, the *Bremen* had been escorted into the harbour by a fleet of coastguard cutters and greeted there by a number of marine policemen. When he stepped off the Archbishop was confronted by a horde of reporters. In Britain the *Church Times* described the scene coldly:

> "When asked about oppressions of Jews and Christians in Germany, he was very mild indeed. He did not approve of the boycott of the Olympic Games in Berlin, and said, 'there is no reason to refuse to deal with a people merely because you disapprove of certain minor points in their Government policy.'"[117]

It was a curious remark for Temple to make. Within the Church his popularity owed much to his genius for conciliation. But this time he had mistaken the occasion. Privately, in fact, Temple found the Hitler regime almost unspeakable.[118]

---

[114]See Ludlow, *loc. cit.*, p. 584.
[115]Henson to Bell, 12th December 1935, enclosing letter from Mrs. Anne Schultze Fiske to Dr. Mary Radford, *Bell Papers*, vol. 28, fol. 101.
[116]*Church Times*, 22nd November 1935, p. 575b.
[117]*Ibid.*, 27th December 1935, p. 742.
[118]For example, "My antipathy to the Nazi Movement as a whole is so intense that I do not think I have the necessary bonds of sympathy which can alone make criticisms effective." Temple to Headlam, 8th March 1934, *Headlam Papers*, M.S. 2643, fol. 116.

VI

Herbert Hensley Henson always needed great issues to exercise his mind; his journal is a succession of them. After his rather unhappy experience at Sunderland in May 1933 he had said nothing more for over two years. His journal lamented the persecution now and then, but sporadically and briefly. After 20th November 1935 there was a lively change. He wrote letters to the newspapers, spoke to public gatherings, agitated, turned it all over in his mind. Although he remained wary of "cranks", who arrived at his door in consequence of his new celebrity, he now responded to the warmth of the Jewish community generously. His reputation as an eloquent and powerful critic of National-Socialist racialism flourished justly. In February 1936 he was invited to speak at the West London Synagogue. "I had never before encountered such a concourse of non-Christians", he later reflected.[119] While Lang and Bell were cluttered with cautious advice about the benefits of discretion and tact, and even reticence, Henson appeared almost gloriously free of it. But still, after he left the meeting he wrote, a little uncertainly, "I don't think I said anything that can do any harm, though I spoke strongly about the German oppression". The speech was reported briefly by *The Times*, and later published as a pamphlet. Henson remarked, "It reads badly, but I don't think that it will do much harm."[120]

In the same month Henson was asked by that *paterfamilias* of the literary Left, Victor Gollancz, to contribute a foreword for a soon-to-be published history of the persecution: *The Yellow Spot*. The book announced itself as "a collection of facts and documents relating to three years' persecution of German Jews, derived chiefly from National Socialist sources, very carefully assembled by a group of investigators". It is still a distressing publication. There are almost three hundred pages listing the various acts of discrimination and barbarism, extensively reprinting legislation, articles, slogans, verses and obscene cartoons from the pages of *Der Stürmer*. There are photographs, too, of children in uniforms standing around notices in town squares, and of the persecuted themselves, hapless and alone, marched through streets with grotesque placards round their necks, amid eager and hostile crowds. Henson thought it a horrible work, and one that was necessary "to bring home to the public mind the character and extent of the great oppression".[121] He accepted the commission. Interestingly, a few days later Leonard Montefiore suggested that he might set the work aside: its French publishers had connections with Communists; a Communist had assisted the preparation of a German edition. At least one and a half per cent of it was inaccurate or mistranslated. Bell, for whom any protest must be anchored on entirely exact facts and universally respected associations, might well have heeded Montefiore's advice. Henson did not: he had given Gollancz his word. He wrote the foreword at once and posted it off to London that same day. He was in no doubt of the "substantial trustworthiness" of the book: "It is entirely

---
[119] *Journal of Bishop Henson*, vol. 66, p. 79, 6th February 1936.
[120] *Ibid.*
[121] *Ibid.*, p. 145, 11th March 1936.

accordant with what we already know on evidence which cannot be shaken, and which accumulates daily." He continued:

> "We find ourselves looking on a woeful spectacle of oppression – cold, cunning, complete, covering every part of social life, closing every door of escape, pursuing the innocent, the helpless, the humble, the educated, even the illustrious members of the persecuted race with a merciless boycott from the cradle to the grave."

Germany had repudiated "the restraints of traditional Christianity more completely than any other community in Christendom". Christian principles could not be denied and offended with impunity in any country, or they would be threatened everywhere.[122]

Henson also spoke with a certain influence when he protested that, in the name of academic liberty, English universities should not send representatives to the five hundred and fiftieth anniversary of the foundation of Heidelberg University. Once again he was responding to a request, this time from Charles Singer, who had sent him "a bundle of notes" detailing the most disturbing antisemitic discrimination in the university, and from George Bell, who asked, "Is it not a case for a rocket in *The Times* from the Bishop of Durham?"[123]

It is not difficult to perceive why the sending of academic representatives to National-Socialist universities should stir Henson. Freedom of argument and intellectual companionship was everything to him. After the exhilaration of his Oxford days he retained an unshakeable sense of what a university was, and what it should represent. The intrusion of mindless prejudice and brutal vulgarity was scandalous and abhorrent; and that learned men should so demean themselves, peculiarly grotesque. Although he was at first only half-inclined to oblige Bell, he spent the whole of the next morning on an admonitory letter. Dissatisfied, he still sent it. The following morning he found his words prominent on the front page: "It cannot be right that the universities of Great Britain, which we treasure as the very citadels of sound learning, because they are the vigilant guardians of intellectual freedom, should openly fraternize with the avowed and shameless enemies of both." To send delegations would be to condone racial injustice.[124]

The letter provoked a spate of correspondence. He learnt that Eden and Kenyon, whom he took to represent political and academic opinion, both thought well of it; so too Sir Edwyn Bevan, Trevelyan and Rutherford – all men whom Henson admired. The politician, Sir Arnold Wilson replied, "To show our disapproval in the manner advocated by the Bishop of Durham will not help matters; it will certainly make them worse. If his object is to help the Jews in Germany they may well pray to be saved from him." Racial intolerance had a biological as well as an economic origin. It was worse in the United States.[125] General Sir Ian Hamilton of the British Legion was ruder still.[126] But Henson respected neither. On 18th February a letter from Sir Charles Grant Robertson

---

[122] *The Yellow Spot. The outlawing of half a million human beings* ... London 1936, pp. 5–8.
[123] *Journal of Bishop Henson*, vol. 66, p.66, 1st February 1936.
[124] *The Times*, 4th February 1936, p. 13e.
[125] *Ibid.*, 7th February 1936, p. 15e.
[126] *Ibid.*, 13th February 1936, p. 13e.

announced that the University of Birmingham had declined to send a representative to Heidelberg. On 24th February Oxford withdrew from the commemoration. It was followed by Cambridge, four days later. On 3rd March the authorities at Heidelberg withdrew their invitations altogether. In America Henson's letter was published as a pamphlet. When, on 17th September, *The Times* reported that eighteen distinguished American philosophers had written to the Philosophical Association declining to attend a session in Berlin later that month, Henson thought it "heartening".[127] In the same month he broadcast to the United States a talk, 'Universities and Freedom'.[128]

In May 1936, while the fourth most senior bishop in the Anglican hierarchy ruminated on academic liberty, a vicar in Sussex, Basil Eldridge at Crowborough, wrote to Bishop Bell of an influential friend who had just returned from Germany, and whom he had questioned about the plight of the Jews there. Eldridge had learned that it was "perfectly appalling and that something far worse than the Armenian massacres is taking place. Some half million Jews are being literally starved to death in their own homes." He asked, could nothing be done to awaken British public opinion? "If we wait much longer there will be no Jews left." Might Bell himself write to *The Times* on their account, or possibly ask the Archbishop of Canterbury to make representations to the German clergy? "One cannot bear the thought of this great wickedness being perpetrated by a nominally Christian nation."[129] But, as Bell might have observed, letters had already been written to *The Times*, and representations to the German Churches were futile. And as for rousing public opinion, he was making every effort.

VII

Part of the significance of the Church Assembly debate of 20th November 1935 lies in its date. It took place at a time when Christians in England were failing to respond with vigour to the miserable plight of refugees from Germany. James McDonald, appointed the League of Nations High Commissioner for Refugees in April 1933, resigned in frustration the month after the Church Assembly passed its momentous resolution. His accompanying public letter, published on 27th December, was bitter and disillusioned. For three dismal and frustrating years his office had unsuccessfully attempted to co-ordinate its efforts with international Protestant organisations, and watched the refugee crisis escalate inexorably. The weakness and uninterest of the churches inside Germany had proven profoundly undermining, and the evident unconcern of the Christian public outside Germany had impaired any great hopes of international assistance. An ambitious plan to resettle 1,500 refugees in South America had been privately supported by Archbishop Lang, and endorsed by the ecumenical World Alliance in August 1935. In November McDonald's aide, Walter

---
[127] *Journal of Bishop Henson*, vol. 67, p. 239, 17th September 1936.
[128] *Ibid.*, p. 263, 27th September 1936.
[129] Eldridge to Bell, 27th May 1936, *Bell Papers*, vol. 28, fol. 132.

Kotschnig, met Lang and other British churchmen and they agreed to launch an international appeal in support of the project. But it was doomed to founder. The international agencies together lacked the strength and organisation to ensure its success. McDonald's departure only served to make matters worse.[130] In England Leonard Montefiore sent a copy of the withering resignation letter to Henson. The bishop remarked, "It is painful reading, and makes it almost impossible to regard Germany as any longer entitled to be regarded as a civilized country."[131]

On 25th April 1936 *The Times* published a letter from Archbishop Lang to inaugurate a national appeal for German "non-Aryan" Christians. It was part of an international church campaign held simultaneously in the United States, Scandinavia, France and Holland. "It is all to do with human beings", broadcast Bishop Bell, "their feelings, their misery . . . And the mere telling of the tale, if we use our imagination, at once throws up picture after picture of human poverty, suffering, desolation . . . They are outcastes from Germany. They are nobody's children. Germany offers them no future. There is no national home for them in Palestine, as there is for the Jews . . . But – and it ought to be a very big but indeed – they are Christians. Christianity is a bigger thing than race, a bigger thing than nation. And if the Christian Church of our generation is to be true to the spirit of Christ, then Christians of all countries, and of all denominations, must recognize their suffering fellow-Christians as brethren – and come to their rescue, just because they are brethren."[132]

With this emotional appeal to Christian sensitivities Bell set the stage for something momentous. The bishops commended it to their dioceses in their pastoral letters. In April 1936 £2,365 came in. But afterwards the fund appeared to founder. Its organisers had set their sights on a target of £25,000. By the middle of the next year £9,700 had been collected. In fact, as Peter Ludlow has observed, the British appeal was notably more successful than those in America, Sweden, Norway, Holland ("The public is no longer interested in the matter", reported the secretary), and France, which failed even to organise a committee.[133]

If Bell knew of this, it did not much console him. Both to him and to later writers it appeared that English Christians had failed to rise to their responsibilities to their suffering neighbours. Fine words had been spoken, but few pounds given. The Church Assembly debate indicated high and earnest feeling on the issue. But it was neither preceded nor followed by the giving of material help. This clear disparity was difficult to understand, and it was damaging, for what value could be attached to splendid speeches and ringing condemnations, if the victims of National Socialism were left abandoned and miserable on foreign shores?

In his introduction to Charles Singer's important book, *The Christian Approach*

---

[130] See Ludlow, *loc. cit.*, pp. 564–603.
[131] *Journal of Bishop Henson*, vol. 66, p. 3, 2nd January 1936.
[132] 'The Tragedy of the Christian Outcastes', Thursday, 24th September 1936, *Bell Papers*, vol. 28, fols. 161–163.
[133] Ludlow, *loc. cit.*, pp. 590–592.

to the Jews, published in that year, Bell wrote, "It is humiliating, but it is true. The plight of these so-called 'non-Aryan' Christians is grievous in the extreme . . . But the Christian Churches in England and elsewhere have made the minutest response. There have been individual Christians who have been generous. But the Churches as a whole are silent and, it seems, unconcerned."[134] Later Bell would attribute this silence to "ignorance as well as indifference".[135]

A number of answers may be only suggested. To begin with, it is very possible that, for those outside Germany, the drama of the persecution subsided after 1933. It would not be an exaggeration to suggest that the issue, no longer new and sensational, went stale in the public mind. The energy shown by English church leaders in that first year did ebb away. Some have remarked since how curious it was that English Christians should lavish such attention on developments in the German Church struggle, and yet neglect those who faced a greater despair, a ceaseless hostility, destitution and destruction.[136] It is natural, and obvious, to wonder. But, however dismal the picture, perhaps it should not seem particularly surprising. If a great issue is to be held in the public mind it must engage it, constantly change, arrest attention. Events in the German Church passed from one "news-worthy" event to the next: the rise of the *Deutsche Christen* movement and the affronted goodness of Friedrich von Bodelschwingh, the ineptitude and folly of Ludwig Müller, the Aryan Paragraph and the Confessional synods, the advent of a state-encouraged paganism, and, later, the arrest, trial and incarceration of Martin Niemöller. The British press reported all these complicated and difficult episodes at surprising length, arguably because it appeared to present the heartening spectacle of resistance to the Hitler regime. By contrast, the persecution of Jews and "non-Aryans" offered nothing so dramatic. It appeared, until 1938, rather a case of more of the same and worse. The broadsheet newspapers, such as the *Manchester Guardian* and *The Times*, kept abreast of events and offered their comments, but they were busier with other matters. The *Daily Express*, meanwhile, was inclined to regard the reception of refugees as a threat.[137] The crisis itself grew steadily, and was sporadically observed. But, with the possible exception of McDonald's very public resignation in December 1935, there was no jolt, no fresh disaster, at a time when the world witnessed a succession of dramatic horrors of one sort and another. As far as the church press went, the *Church Times* would remind its readers of the refugees now and again, but found nothing particularly new to say about them. It is perhaps understandable if Christian opinion nodded off. For all its strengths, British church culture was too weak in itself to keep the conscience of the Christian community alive on one question. The preoccupations of the average woman or man in the pew were, for most of the week, affected more profoundly by other powerful secular influences and agendas. Poor George Bell, with his few resources, often despaired of drawing a response. "Do Christians

---

[134] Charles Singer, *The Christian Approach to the Jews*, London 1937, p. 8.
[135] *The Record*, 24th June 1938, p. 407d.
[136] See, for example, Adrian Hastings, *A History of English Christianity 1920–1985*, London 1986, p. 344.
[137] See Andrew Sharf, *The British Press and the Jews under Nazi Rule*, Oxford 1964, pp. 155–192.

care?" he would ask bleakly.[138] He saw the very integrity of the international Church at stake. But few clergy and laity viewed it so dramatically. In truth, it was not that Bell found himself shouting in the wilderness, or to people who would not listen, rather that he stood in a crowded world among other people who were shouting more loudly.

Bell's caution, and his wish not to aggravate the Hitler regime itself, may also account for the modest success of his appeals. He purposely detached the refugee crisis from its cause. He sought to mitigate the consequence of National-Socialist racialism without judging the racial policies themselves. The result was blandness and a certain abstraction. The feelings of the British public were evidently stirred by striking protests, be they at the Church Assembly or a London hall. But protest and appeal had been separated. The crisis had been lifted out of context and placed in an unprovocative vacuum.

Possibly the situation was not much helped by the very phrase "non-Aryan", which might have seemed too foreign and remote to strike a popular and human chord. Certainly William Simpson, the Methodist who, with James Parkes, represented a new generation of English Christians specifically concerned with Christian-Jewish relations, wrote to the *Church Times* suggesting that there might be some confusion between "German Jews proper" and "so-called 'Non-Aryans' ".[139] In fact, as late as April 1938 a correspondent to the paper could still ask the editor what a "non-Aryan" was. It would, perhaps, have been wiser to have repudiated the National-Socialist terminology and campaigned broadly for the "Jews". It might also have proven more effective. And although Bell wished only to help the friendless and isolated victims of the National-Socialist state, his appeal may have led susceptible minds to suspect that the "Jews proper" were only looking after their own. This was not at all the case, as he himself knew.

The shortcomings of the international Protestant relief agencies during these years now appear clear, as Peter Ludlow has brilliantly shown. From the start they were hesitant. They worked badly with each other and, most fatally, the German churches did not provide them with a stable foundation inside Germany itself. There were many refugee organisations in Britain, some of them religious, others academic or political. All of them were small and busy. They often sought to co-ordinate their efforts, but rarely possessed an overall cohesion. It is surely true that an important issue can only be well served by unified, coherent and central direction, and the funds to publicise and promote the issue in question. Too many committees, however earnest and vigorous, will only bewilder the broad public, churchgoing or not, and make even the greatest need obscure. In the mid-1930s, when the British people had much on their minds, this was even more true than it would be today. It was perhaps significant that six days after his wrathful explosion at the Church Assembly, Henson wrote to Bell that he had received a piteous call for help from a Jewish correspondent: "but I haven't a notion how to answer it. Can you advise me of any person or organisation which could be of service to the writer?"[140]

[138]*Church Times*, 14th October 1936, p. 408a.
[139]*Ibid.*, 26th June 1936, p. 784b.
[140]Henson to Bell, 26th November 1935, *Bell Papers*, vol. 28, fol. 73.

In the early summer of 1937 Bell wrote to the chairman of the Church Mission to the Jews, the Bishop of Worcester, asking if that organisation might assist relief efforts. Bishop Perowne replied: "a considerable section of our society" had believed that "charity is not our work, and that it would be contrary to our rules to issue such an appeal". The rules had now been inspected, and appeared to permit such activities. But: "The second reason why we have not been as keen as we ought . . . is because we have a very large debt at the moment, and we have only just finished an appeal for wiping out that debt, which has not been altogether successful." Members of the General committee, meanwhile, were perpetually on the brink of "open conflict". Even so, said Perowne, their will to help was not lacking.[141]

In July Bell's own sister-in-law, Laura Livingstone, went to Germany as a representative of the International Christian Committee for German Refugees. Livingstone was an experienced social worker, and she spoke German fluently. Bell had hoped that she might send information out of Germany through the embassy bag in Berlin. But the embassy would not allow this. It did, however, assure her of its assistance.[142]

As the National Appeal foundered in the autumn of 1937 a number of eminent church people, Lord Robert Cecil and Dorothy Buxton among them, began to make a film in which celebrated speakers might describe the refugee crisis to the public and appeal for funds. Ideally they wished for an appearance by Archbishop Temple. Though willing, he was not at liberty to oblige them until after Christmas. They decided not to wait for him. But then a number of the group, including the well informed and much admired public servant, Sir Wyndham Deedes, feared that the film would prove "very unpopular with the German Government". Deedes had been told that a similar production in the United States had antagonised the German authorities and been "used as an excuse . . . for enforcing the full rigour of the 'non-Aryan' laws". At all events, he thought, public speeches would prove more successful: "A film cannot answer questions."[143] This persuaded Bell. Buxton clung doggedly to the idea; upsetting the German government was unavoidable if they were to make any kind of stand. Temple had now sent a letter for the film makers to use. But Bell was no longer sure: "We shall probably all of us say things which would be very much resented by Hitler."[144] "I am, of course, familiar with the argument used by Sir Wyndham Deedes, but there are many good authorities who hold exactly the opposite view, i.e. that nothing *encourages* Hitler so much as the quietness of British public opinion", replied Buxton firmly.[145] But the plan sank soon enough, achieving nothing, but consuming much time and effort. That so crucial a debate was still unresolved so late in the day is notable.

In the same month, October 1937, and four and a half years after Hitler came to power, Bell moved to establish the Church of England Committee for "Non-

---

[141] Perowne to Bell, 2nd June 1937, *ibid.*, fol. 351.
[142] Bell to Salomon, 5th July 1937, *ibid.*, fol. 431.
[143] Deedes to Buxton, 25th October 1937, *ibid.*, vol. 29(2), fol. 180.
[144] Bell to Buxton, 28th October 1937, *ibid.*, fol. 198.
[145] Buxton to Bell, 29th October 1937, *ibid.*, fol. 207.

Aryan" Christians. He outlined its objects to be: the education of Christian children from Germany in English schools; to train and settle young refugees; and to address individual "special cases".[146]

At the end of the year he wrote once again, "If the Christian Churches could only be aroused to the appalling and well nigh catastrophic character of the present situation, it would make all the difference to the possibilities of helping."[147] The tone of the letter suggested that little had changed or improved. As far as the press at large was concerned, the last two years had been quiet and unprovocative. Perhaps it had grown accustomed to refugees, and no longer thought much of them.

Meanwhile Bishop Henson continued to play a notable role in the isolation of German higher education. In May 1937 the senate of Durham University decided to send a delegation to the bicentennial of the University of Göttingen, where antisemitic discrimination was quite as awful as at Heidelberg. The intended visit was, Henson suspected, the design of Durham's Chancellor, Lord Londonderry, an engaging National-Socialist sympathiser with whom Henson enjoyed a cordial and distrustful friendship. Anxiously turned to, the Bishop wrote to both the Chancellor and Vice-chancellor of the university to express, privately, his disapprobation. He threatened that should a delegation go to Göttingen he would make his disdain public and dissociate himself from Durham's own impending anniversary commemoration. Shortly afterwards he heard from his good friend the Bishop of Jarrow that the university senate had reconsidered and overturned its former decision.[148] It is impossible to know how profoundly Henson's letters affected the outcome; it is natural to suspect that they did.

But Henson's contemporary, Headlam, was at the same time involved in an occasional correspondence with no less a National Socialist than Alfred Rosenberg. These polite letters, between an austerely conservative Anglican bishop and the author of the notoriously anti-Christian *Mythus*, present a curious spectacle. Headlam sought to influence Rosenberg for the better. But in doing so he also went a significant way to justify National-Socialist policies. Certainly the correspondence offered an opportunity for Headlam to expound his views of the Jews at further length:

> "The Jews again are only a danger when they are not free. I recognise, however, the difficulties that have arisen through the excessive influence that they have obtained in Berlin, and through their unfortunate activities in village life, and personally I am not inclined to be too severe a judge, but we think that nothing can excuse the anti-semitism of Streicher and his paper. Moreover we believe that the whole Aryan theory is entirely unscientific and baseless, that in all European nations there is a strong non-Aryan element, and we find by experience that a strain of Jewish blood may strengthen the race. At any rate, the policy by which clergymen, for example, of some Jewish descent are turned out of their livings, seems to us equally stupid and cruel."[149]

[146]Bell to Rouse, 28th October 1937, *ibid.*, fol. 200.

[147]Bell to *The Times*, 29th December 1937, *ibid.*, fol. 311. Evidently this letter was not published.

[148]Journal of Bishop Henson, vol. 69, p. 223, 18th May 1937. For a full discussion of the episode see Owen Chadwick, *Hensley Henson. A Study in the Tension between Church and State*, Oxford 1983, pp. 260–261.

[149]Headlam to Rosenberg, 5th February 1937, *Headlam Papers*, M.S. 2643, fol. 155.

Headlam condemned Streicher, but so did everybody. In truth, many who stressed their disapproval of *Der Stürmer* did so to dodge the judgement of antisemitism in its other, less bizarre, forms. Headlam did not do that, he affirmed, with a vague sense of eugenics not untypical of many of his generation, the beneficial qualities of Jewish blood. But while he protested against the dismissals of "non-Aryans", he did not use the opportunity of a letter to Rosenberg to speak on behalf of full Jews. His own suspicions of the Jews ensured that he was far less likely to dwell upon their persecution, and less susceptible to the moral outrage of Henson. While Headlam's debunking of "Aryan" theory was typically robust and laudable, it is the phrase, "personally I am not inclined to be too severe a judge", that hangs in the reader's memory.

VIII

1936 and 1937 appeared to world opinion rather quiet years. The critics of National Socialism were not mollified by the quietness, but those who were less ardent in their opposition sensed that Germany had settled down. The reoccupation of the Rhineland in March 1936 had caused barely a ripple in Britain; too easily could it be explained away as an understandable and excusable act of treaty revision. Besides, the eyes of the world were turned to Abyssinia. National-Socialist sympathisers were at this time at their most confident and cheerful.[150] They were also, to uncommitted minds, as credible as they ever would be. It was, therefore, significant that when hospitable aristocrats were inviting Ribbentrop over to their country houses for the weekend, and a significant number of politicians and public figures felt they could declare that Hitler's Germany had its admirable features, and say so without provoking excessive hostility, only one English bishop did the same. There did now exist an Anglo-German Brotherhood, a group of churchpeople sympathetic to the National-Socialist regime, but it was hardly flourishing, as Richard Griffiths has suggested.[151] Led by one Baron von der Ropp, those bishops who knew of it seemed to regard it as a somewhat remote and vague phenomenon. Its biggest name was that of the secretary to the Archbishop of Canterbury's Council of Foreign Relations, A. J. Macdonald. In general, the critics of 1933 were the critics of 1937, and the initial apologists continued to play their first tunes.

It is broadly true that National Socialism revealed very little sign of racial prejudice in the Church of England. Antisemitism was seen as something disreputable. It contradicted the humane broad principles of the English Christian conscience. National-Socialist antisemitism at once suprised and baffled. The persecution did not square with the assumptions that English church leaders presumed to govern the world in the twentieth century. "Germany had leaped back to the Middle Ages", wrote a perplexed Henson in

---

[150]See Richard Griffiths, *Fellow Travellers of the Right. British Enthusiasts for Nazi Germany 1933–9*, London 1980, pp. 191–288.
[151]*Ibid.*, p. 251–252.

May 1933.[152] Many others reacted with quite the same thought. It is revealing that they could neither understand nor account for it. Henson's friend Ralph Inge, the celebrated "gloomy dean" of St. Paul's Cathedral, was a man who usually found some kind of reason for most things. But he owned in his regular column in London's *Evening Standard*, "I am completely puzzled by this atavistic outbreak in Germany. We can be silly enough ourselves at times, but . . . we have got beyond the baiting of Jews, the burning of witches and the torture of witnesses."[153] They felt it reflected very badly on the German people. *The Guardian* referred cynically to "that strange pseudo-mystical conception of the purity of the Nordic race", and argued that perhaps it attempted to "fill the void left by the decay of religious belief. The German even more than other men cannot live by bread alone. This Aryan business appeals just because it is an 'Ersatz-religion'."[154] Inevitably there were exceptions; a Doncaster clergyman who visited Germany in 1935 and said that the Jews there were "far from happy, and it was their own fault"; a vicar who wrote for the British Fascist journal, *Blackshirt*. As Richard Gutteridge has gently observed, "these are just a few isolated instances, most of which suggest unbalanced eccentricity".[155] Occasional expressions of such sentiments were invariably contested by indignant and disapproving replies. Disapproval often characterises the voices of those who believe they speak for the offended orthodoxy of the majority. For his part, Bishop Headlam was neither obscure nor quite eccentric. But among the bishops he was clearly isolated. To some extent he was misled by A. J. Macdonald, who advised him on German matters at the Council of Foreign Relations, whose meetings Headlam chaired. The Headlam-Macdonald axis was, to say the least, unfortunate. Certainly there is very little reason to think it representative of Anglican opinion. In fact, the airing of their views often served to provoke the embarrassment and indignation of the majority around them and to underline further how very contrary to the mainstream of opinion they were.

If the Church of England was largely a firm critic of the persecution of Jews in Germany before 1938, how much value should the historian attach to the words that were spoken? In 1975 Peter Ludlow wrote, "Although it would be unfair simply to dismiss these protests as 'Belegexemplare für Archive' – their absence would have been noted, had they not been made – there was nothing particularly noteworthy or suprising about them. They were consistent with most of the public comment made in the western press and parliaments and with the liberal outlook on secular problems that had long predominated within the small elite responsible for the running of the major interdenominational organizations at national and international levels."[156] A year later Edward Norman remarked in his provocative study, *Church and Society in England, 1770–1970*: "The clergy [of the Church of England] were not attracted to Fascism for the reason that English-

---

[152] *Journal of Bishop Henson*, vol. 57, p. 267, 7th May 1933.
[153] W. R. Inge, *A Rustic Moralist*, London 1937, p. 243.
[154] *The Guardian*, 30th June 1933, p. 454a–b.
[155] R. J. C. Gutteridge, 'The Churches and the Jews in England, 1933–1945', in Otto Dov Kulka and Paul Mendes-Flohr (eds.), *Judaism and Christianity under the Impact of National Socialism*, Jerusalem 1987, pp. 353–378.
[156] Ludlow, *loc. cit.*, p. 564.

men in general were not. Its methods did not seem to recommend it to the familiar political culture . . . the English clergy were never likely to stomach immoderate political conduct. Everything had to be according to rules they could recognize – the ideas might change, they could be radical or 'socialist': but a wall of resistance went up against anything which went beyond the conventions of their class."[157] These arguments deserve serious attention in the light of the material discussed here.

The protests that English Christians made against the National-Socialist persecution of the Jews were certainly important, both in Britain and in Germany. In their own country they encouraged general awareness of the issue and guided the public debate. Morality is a vital aspect of political discourse, as Hitler himself knew well. It was crucially important to his regime that its policies appeared morally defensible, or at the very least, morally understandable, both to domestic and foreign opinion. The Church of England for the most part contested these claims with a unique authority. The persecution of Jews was a policy without moral reason or integrity. Antisemitism was immoral. It may be said that words come cheaply, but these words were precious. Moreover, when bishops agonised over the painful dilemma of whether protest would improve matters, or make them worse, it would be unfair to argue that their protests came casually and easily. In such circumstances, committed and earnest thought preceded public condemnation.

Norman's suggestion that those who led Church and State in England shared the same social class is, broadly speaking, true. But to suggest that they therefore viewed the world through the same spectacles is not always convincing. Bishop Henson was not alone in remarking how often he heard antisemitic conversations in his clubs. Ralph Inge, whose opinions were often rather wayward, and who was given to suspect that the Jews were influential in the newspaper world he inhabited, remained an acute judge of people. Inge, too, found many of his eminent contemporaries apologists both for National Socialism and for antisemitism. The observations of these two aware men should perhaps invite the historian to be less complacent of the liberal outlook of the English elites and upper classes. In fact, they did not prove consistent and comitted critics of the Hitler regime.

The story of another senior cleric might be cited. Until 1942, when he became Archbishop of York, Cyril Garbett was bishop of Winchester – the fifth highest appointment in the Anglican episcopacy. Adrian Hastings, an acute and sensitive writer on English Christianity, has described Garbett as a most representative churchman of his generation; a gentle and humane man with essentially conservative inclinations and tastes, an earnest piety, an awareness of political and social issues, and a core of solid good sense.[158] Towards the end of his life Garbett recalled how Lord Brocket "once asked me if I would meet Ribbentrop when he next stayed with him at Bramshill. I said yes, provided I

---

[157]E. R. Norman, *Church and Society in England 1770–1970. A Historical Study*, Oxford 1976, pp. 359–360.
[158]Hastings, *op. cit.*, p. 447.

might speak to him plainly about Hitler's treatment of Jews and minorities. Needless to say, I did not get invited."[159]

It is possible that both Norman and Ludlow do underestimate the distinctiveness, integrity and moral vitality of English Christian culture. It was noticeably different from the culture of the nobility, or of the politician or diplomat. How easy it would have been for Garbett to assure himself that social courtesy prohibited the expression of contentious politics. He did not, because certain principles were profoundly important to him as a Christian. English aristocrats in their country houses, or public servants in London clubs, could more readily minimise racial discrimination, intolerance and persecution than English bishops. Perhaps their ethical lights were not so fixed that their liberal outlook on the world could be taken for granted. They could be pragmatic, and they could be expedient. While English social elites were often liberal, their attitudes could not be said to be underlined by a consistent doctrinal foundation, or characterised by firm ethical priorities. In fact, the atmosphere of upper-class life was heavily tinged with antisemitism. Of course, it might be argued that the very fact that Britain never submitted to Fascism is proof of how very alienating such political extremism was to its leading circles. But it is legitimate to wonder quite how staunchly the elites of the country would have defended democratic interests, and protected persecuted minorities, if Mosley's Fascism had become a more powerful popular force in British life.

At all events, it is perhaps not enough to argue that a liberal consensus prevailed throughout the institutions of British life without asking who was responsible for that outlook in the first place, and how was it sustained thereafter? A definitive answer is, of course, impossible. However, the claim by many Anglicans in the twentieth century that the assumptions and principles which informed the life of the British State owed a basic debt to the pervasive historic influence of Christian institutions had a genuine weight. A church that had long addressed political and social matters, and numbered the leading lights of the nation in its congregations, had certainly influenced the political climate perceptibly during the previous half century.

It is clear that the historian cannot write of Christianity as a universal set of ethical values. In the 1930s German and English church leaders reacted to National Socialism in radically different ways. If the culture of German Protestantism led the churches there to welcome the coming of Hitler, and to avoid confrontations with his government on behalf of the Jews, the culture of English Christianity produced the opposite response. When Bishop Batty met Max Diestel in Berlin in March 1933 he had found him surprised at the idea of Christian protest. To Batty himself it appeared the most natural and proper course for a church. In this ecumenical age, when churches across the world were reaching out towards each other in Christian fellowship, they were becoming aware of fundamental disparities. Any assessment of what we now broadly call the "Christian" response to the National-Socialist persecution of the Jews of

---

[159] *M. S. Memoirs of Archbishop Garbett*, vol. VI, coll. 1982/5/A, p. 59, York Minster Library.

Germany must embrace these contrasts, and ask if the German example deserves to be definitive.

Antisemitism offended the theology and values of English Christianity. Henson articulated that outrage most forcefully, but it was only his eloquence that was exceptional. He spoke in the language of his church. The foundations and arguments of his speech to the Church Assembly in 1935 were consciously religious. This was not a speech that the public might expect from a politician, a civil servant or an aristocrat. It was the speech of a Christian bishop. It is all the more important to recognise that Henson's own social instincts were faintly antisemitic. By the ethical lights that he followed he knew them to be unacceptable, and he suppressed them. Confronted by the racialism of National Socialism he became an earnest and passionate defender of the Jewish people.

But National Socialism also highlighted the hesitations and limitations of English Anglican culture. A Church where everybody had a right to their own opinions was surely a laudable institution. But it could not present the world with a conscious sense of corporate vision, and a clear direction. The consensus of its views was generally detectable. But the opinions of an errant bishop like Headlam could only be judged beside the individual opinions of others – even if the others were by far the majority. This could only make him appear more significant and credible than he deserved. The Bishop of Gloucester was not reprimanded formally; the tastes of Anglicanism would not encourage it.

When the Hitler regime persecuted the Jews, the Church of England replied in an earnest, but rather *ad hoc* fashion. Bishops spoke for themselves; their consensus was not framed more systematically. This could only weaken its power. The problem was equally evident, and far more worrying, when the refugee crisis broke. Little committees and sporadic appeals were an insufficient response to an enormous issue and an immense moral responsibility. The philosophy that informed the institutional structure of the Church of England, an hierarchical framework which lent itself admirably to a unified response, could impair its capability as an instrument of a broad and decisive purpose; whether the purpose was to condemn racial persecution abroad, or to assist its victims. If Anglicans were sure that their church must work to influence the world in which they lived, their ideas on how best to do so were as yet too unfocused and vague. Until 1938 this was, perhaps, the lesson that the National-Socialist persecution of the Jews suggested. Over the next seven years the pressure of that crisis on the Church of England would intensify.

The Perfect Deception. The Danish Jews and Theresienstadt 1940–1945

BY HANS SODE-MADSEN

This is the account of the Danish Jews who did not reach freedom in Sweden in October 1943, but spent eighteen months in the so-called "model ghetto" Theresienstadt. Much has been written about the daring operation which rescued some 7,000 Danish Jews and stateless Jews who had found refuge in Denmark. However, of the extraordinary efforts of Danish officials to protect also those Jews who were caught or did not leave, even after their deportation to Theresienstadt, far less is known. What the records reveal is the unique relief work which, during the years of occupation, was organised by the Ministry of Social Affairs under the leadership of Hans Henrik Koch, its head of department. It culminated in the return of Danish and Norwegian concentration camp prisoners from Theresienstadt in Red Cross buses in April and May 1945. The action is associated with the Swedish Count Bernadotte, despite the fact that his role was less constructive and important than is generally thought.[1]

The relief work of the Ministry of Social Affairs was activated by the internment of Danish Communists in the summer of 1941, the action against the Jews in October 1943 and the deportation of the Danish police in September 1944. The behaviour of the Danes exemplifies their lack of prejudice, their skilful manipulation of the situation and the generosity of the Danish people in

---

[1] The archival material consulted is not generally available. There is access to the public records at the Records Office of the State Archives in Copenhagen, but individual rules apply to the privately owned records. Most of the literature is in Danish. English speakers are referred to: Henrik S. Nissen (ed.), *Scandinavia during the Second World War*, Minneapolis 1983 which contains an excellent outline and bibliography. On Theresienstadt and Danes in Theresienstadt, see Leni Yahil, *The Rescue of Danish Jewry. Test of a Democracy*, Philadelphia 1969; Ruth Bondy, *Elder of the Jews. Jakob Edelstein of Theresienstadt*, New York 1989; Lucy Dawidowicz, *The Jewish Presence. Essays on Identity and History*, New York 1978, chap. 17 'Bleaching the Black Lie. The Case of Theresienstadt'; Steven Koblik, ' "No Truck with Himmler". The Politics of Rescue and the Swedish Red Cross Mission, March–May 1945', in *Scandia. Tidsskrift för historisk forskning*, vol. 51, Nos. 1–2 (1985); Monty Noam Penkower, *The Jewish were Expendable. Free World Diplomacy and the Holocaust*, Chicago 1983; Paul Thygesen, Knud Hermann and Rolf Willinger, 'Concentration Camp Survivors in Denmark. Persecution, Disease, Disability and Compensation', in *Danish Medical Bulletin*, vol. 17, Nos. 3–4 (March–April 1970). With the commendable exception of Koblik (a revised and extended version of which has been published in the US: *The Stones Cry Out. Sweden's Response to the Persecution of the Jews 1933–1945*, New York 1988), these accounts are generally characterised by the fact that the authors have had to use insufficient source material translated in English. This article was only possible with the help of Mr. Vagn Dybdahl, the former Keeper of the Public Records. The Carlsberg Foundation enabled me to travel to Yad Vashem, Theresienstadt and Prague. I owe special thanks to Dr. Judith S. Goldstein of "Thanks to Scandanavia" in New York for her very constructive reading of the manuscript.

providing financial aid. However, the relief work could not have taken place without exceptionally good, informal co-operation between a number of state and local authorities, private organisations and individuals, who had hitherto never had to work together so closely. The results were impressive.

Denmark is a small country and before the outbreak of war had done its best to avoid offending its powerful "brown" neighbour.[2] Hitler's offer of a non-aggression pact in May 1939 was a gesture the Danish government believed it could not refuse. In the slim hope of safeguarding Denmark's security, the Danes followed a policy of accommodation with National-Socialist Germany.[3] It might have been expected that this would extend to accepting some measure of discrimination against the Jews, but on this issue the Danish authorities firmly drew the line.

At the outbreak of war in September 1939 there were about 8,000 Jews in Denmark.[4] Of these 3,500 belonged to the old assimilated families, who had primarily emigrated from Germany and Holland during the fifteenth century. They were completely assimilated into the middle classes. Most of them lived in Copenhagen. Following the pogroms in Russia and Poland between 1905 and 1921, a similar number of East European Jews arrived in the country. Unlike the established Jews, they were poor artisans and small shop-keepers, mostly tailors and shoemakers, they had many children and were politically and religiously committed. They maintained Yiddish as an important part of their cultural heritage and were active in the Zionist movement or in the Social Democratic movement, the *Bund*. Members of Copenhagen's Jewish community were none too pleased with these new arrivals, who were regarded as strangely alien. Another group which was not particularly welcomed by established Jewry in Copenhagen consisted of 1,500 refugees from Nazi Germany and, after 1938, from Austria and Czechoslovakia. In his memoirs Marcus Melchior, who later became Chief Rabbi, spoke ironically of the state of affairs, in the period up to the outbreak of war:

> "The Jewish community in Copenhagen in its attitudes regarding the tasks and problems of the time was hopelessly out of touch, provincial and narrow in outlook. Clearly, the predominating sentiment was: The disasters in the outside world are no concern of ours. We are spectators, as we were before when evil occurred . . .
> True, when I first visited the Chief Rabbi [Max Friediger], he had mentioned that the ill fortunes out there in Jewish Europe caused severe disturbances to his nightly sleep. But he had been honest enough to add that Providence had graciously taken him personally under his wing and placed him in this Denmark which enjoyed the time-honoured conceit that her borders were closed to the adversities of the twentieth century."[5]

---

[2] Viggo Sjöqvist, *Danmarks udenrigspolitik 1933–1940*, Copenhagen 1966, p. 42.
[3] See Henrik S. Nissen, 'Udenrigspolitik 1933–1940', in Søren Mørch (ed.), *Danmarks historie*, vol. 7, *Tiden 1914–1945*, Copenhagen 1988, p. 339.
[4] It is almost impossible to produce exact figures. The census of 1921 was the last containing information about religious affiliation. See Leni Yahil, *Et demokrati på prøve. Jøderne i Danmark under Besættelsen*, Copenhagen 1966. English edition: *The Rescue of Danish Jewry*, op. cit., see here pp. 25–26. From a Danish point of view Yahil's book is a somewhat idyllic description, cf. Hans Kirchhoff's review in *Historisk Tidsskrift*, vol. XII, No. 4 (1969–1970), pp. 269–277.
[5] Marcus Melchior, *Darkness over Denmark. A Rabbi Remembers*, London 1973, pp. 104–105.

Generally the Danish Jews kept a low profile. They were under pressure from refugees from Germany, Austria and Czechoslovakia. While the Danish authorities recognised political refugees, i.e. Communists and Social Democrats, albeit reluctantly, there was little appreciation of the fact that people were forced to flee for their lives purely because of their "race" and religion. When the Nordic Social Democrats met in Oslo in May 1938, they committed themselves to approving residence permits for 300 Jewish refugees. Sweden was willing to take fifteen, not including women and children, Norway would take "some", Denmark none. "We have been contacted by hundreds of Jews wanting to get out of Germany more for racial than for political reasons. We do not mind participating in talks on this question, but we have to say, once and for all, that we cannot take any more refugees", was the statement made by the chairman of the Danish Social Democratic Party, Hans Hedtoft-Hansen.[6] (Incidentally, the same man played a most active role in the later escape of Danish Jews to Sweden.) It was possible to obtain an entry permit if family connections to Danish citizens could be proved, and if these relations would guarantee the support of the refugees. It was practically impossible to get a work permit. The authorities tried quite deliberately to get the refugees out of the country as quickly as possible. Between 1933 and 1940, 4,500 Jewish refugees arrived. Of these, 1,500 so-called stateless Jews were still in Denmark on 9th April 1940 – Jews who had had their German citizenship taken away from them. In accepting refugees, Danish policy was no different from that of other countries in its generally negative attitude.

On 9th April 1940 German troops marched into Denmark and established a "peaceful occupation" which, in its mild form, lasted until 29th August 1943 and, in its harsher version, was brought to an end with the liberation on 5th May 1945. The German justification for their "protection" of Denmark contained the significant statement that "Germany has no intention through its conduct, either now or in the future, of violating the territorial integrity or political independence of the Kingdom of Denmark".[7] While not believing these fine words, the Danes attempted to utilise this undertaking to their advantage and based their relationship with the occupying power on this "arrangement of 9th April". Under the terms of the "peaceful occupation", Denmark was considered a sovereign state against whom Germany was not waging war.[8] The Royal family, the government and the *Rigsdag* (Parliament), as well as the civil and military forces of law and order continued their duties with very few reductions. It followed from this that the occupying power did not create its own civil service; all Danish civil servants were subject to the Danish government. When the government resigned in August 1943, the heads of department of the ministries replaced the political ministerial representatives. German laws, including the

---

[6]Krister Wahlbäck and Kersti Bildberg (eds.), *Samråd i Kristid. Protokoll från den Nordiska Arbetarrörelsens Samarbetskommitté 1932–1946*, Stockholm 1986, p. 171.
[7]Henrik S. Nissen, *1940. Studier i Forhandlingspolitikken og Samarbejdspolitikken*, Copenhagen 1973, p. 42.
[8]As a brief and clear summary I recommend Henning Poulsen, 'Die Deutsche Besatzungspolitik in Dänemark', in Robert Bohn *et al.* (eds.), *Neutralität und totalitäre Aggression. Nordeuropa und die Grossmächte im Zweiten Weltkrieg*, Stuttgart 1991.

race classifications of the Nuremberg Laws, were not introduced into Denmark. It was not until Theresienstadt that Danish Jews wore the Yellow Star.

There was an unusual atmosphere of normality in relations between the Danish and German authorities. The people in the Danish ministries dealt with the German officials through much the same channels as before the occupation, except that the occupiers had their own chief representative in Denmark. Major questions were negotiated with the *Auswärtiges Amt* and the Foreign Minister, von Ribbentrop, in Berlin, while more minor matters were negotiated with the German plenipotentiary (*der Bevollmächtigte des Deutschen Reiches*) in Copenhagen, Cecil von Renthe-Fink who was succeeded in 1943 by Werner Best. Only the *Wehrmacht*, the occupying army, was an alien force that could make things a little awkward at times. But jealousy between the diplomatic services and the military was kept under control by daily morning meetings in the German Embassy.

The success of the peaceful occupation was based on an aspect of the Danish political system manifested in the "policy of negotiation". The Social Democratic-Radical government under Thorvald Stauning included the two big opposition parties *Venstre* (the farmers' party) and *Det konservative Folkeparti* (the Conservative Party) who co-operated closely. In effect, they created a form of national coalition government. After the occupation the government remained in power, as was the overwhelming wish of the Danish electorate, but the normal democratic processes were put under pressure in the summer of 1940. While the small Danish Nazi Party tried to gain influence, Conservative Nationalists and others demanded that the politicians should admit "positive" non-political professional ministers to the government. The government gave in to this latter demand on 8th July 1940. One change of great significance for the future course of events in Denmark was that Erik Scavenius replaced Peter Munch as Foreign Minister. In the view of the opposition parties, Munch was the symbol of the defeatist foreign policy which had landed the country with an ignominious occupation. His retirement was the inevitable sacrifice on the altar of the new national co-operation. Erik Scavenius, a career diplomat, had been Foreign Minister during the First World War and had a reputation as a problem solver.

Scavenius favoured a more active approach than Munch. His tactics were to anticipate and meet the expected demands of the Germans, almost before they had been put forward and in so doing to retain the ruling power in Danish and non-Nazi hands. Recognising the unlimited power of Germany was the basis of the policy of negotiation. As long as the country was quiet it would be subject to the *Auswärtiges Amt*. The *Wehrmacht*, however, was already waiting in the wings – and the *Gestapo* a latent threat.

Compared to Norway and Holland, there were no national experiments with National Socialism in Denmark. The local *"Führer"*, Fritz Clausen, was considered so utterly useless by people in general, that it was hard to believe that the Germans would turn to him. Whereas the former observation was valid, the latter proved to be an error of judgement. Neither Hitler nor von Ribbentrop worried much about the personal qualities of Clausen as long as he was a reliable puppet. As a matter of fact, there were serious discussions during the late summers of 1940 and 1942 about a Danish "Quisling Government". Yet Fritz

Danish Jews and Theresienstadt

Clausen and his DNSAP, supported by 20,000 members and 30,000–40,000 votes, based upon the elections of 1939 and 1943,[9] were kept out of all parliamentary influence, because the German civil and military authorities in Denmark much preferred a co-operative government composed of the old parties with broad electoral support. Even after 29th August 1943 when the policy of negotiation broke down, Werner Best did not consider the Danish Nazis a viable alternative to replace the outgoing government. Fritz Clausen drew his own conclusion from this by entering active service on the Russian front as an army surgeon.

During the first years of occupation there were apparently no problems relating to the Jews in Denmark. During the period of the policy of negotiation such questions were more or less ignored. At a cabinet meeting on 22nd December 1941, the government decided that German demands for special actions against Jews were quite out of the question.[10] When in 1942 Renthe-Fink demanded that two allegedly Jewish heads of department had to leave their posts, the answer given was a clear no. Renthe-Fink's demand was typical of the double-dealing contained in playing the game based on the "arrangement of 9th April". It is doubtful whether the German plenipotentiary wanted anything more than to demonstrate that the "Jewish Question" would have to be dealt with sometime. On 15th April 1940 he had, in a report to von Ribbentrop on the progress of the occupation, explained that the government were worried that they "would be required to take action against Jews, émigrés and Left-wing circles and create a special police apparatus for this purpose. If we proceed along this line further than is absolutely necessary it would create a paralysing effect and generate serious disturbances in political and economic life."[11] This conclusion was backed by the *Auswärtiges Amt*. As Denmark was subject to the agreement, von Ribbentrop watched zealously over his area of authority; here in the "model protectorate" order prevailed – Jews or no Jews. Renthe-Fink's successor, Werner Best also shared this view.

In June 1941 the Germans launched Operation Barbarossa. The Danish government was told that all leading Communists were to be interned immediately. This was a flagrant infringement of the Danish constitution, which said that nobody was to be arrested on account of religious or political views. The fact that the *Rigsdag* subsequently "legalised" the constitutional infringement through the so-called Communist Law on 21st August 1941, did not make it any more palatable to Danish democracy. Little comfort was found in the fact that the 300 Communists were held under reasonable conditions in the camp at Horserød in Northern Zealand on Danish territory. Furthermore, Denmark joined the Anti-Comintern Pact in November in response to demands from Germany. The Danes had also confirmed "the arrangement of 9th April".

---

[9] See Henning Poulsen, *Besættelsesmagten og de danske nazister*, Copenhagen 1970, p. 381.

[10] Account given to *Folketinget* by the commission it established under Section 45 of the Danish constitution: *Regering og Rigsdag under Besættelsen* (hereafter *Parliamentary Commission*). Here *Appendix IV*, Copenhagen 1948, p. 456.

[11] *Parliamentary Commission. Appendix XII*, Copenhagen 1951, p. 216.

Officially the Pact was only directed against the USSR, but most politicians feared that it would clear the way for persecution of the Jews and for conscription of Danish troops for the Eastern front.

During the signing of the Pact in Berlin, Göring had drawn Scavenius's attention to the fact that Denmark could not avoid the question of the Jews. To this Scavenius had answered that the Danes did not recognise that there was a "Jewish Question".[12] However, press statements from Berlin talked openly of Denmark fighting against Communism to help create a new Europe. This fight would have to apply to the Jews as well since, according to National-Socialist ideology, the Jews and Communists were engaged together in the world-wide Jewish-Bolshevik conspiracy. Despite this new pressure, the Minister of Ecclesiastical Affairs summoned the Chief Rabbi, Max Friediger, and assured him that the rumours of the introduction of the Nuremberg Laws in Denmark were false. "As long as a Danish government has anything to say in this country, the Jews have nothing to fear", said the Minister, who referred to the cabinet decision following the return of Scavenius from Berlin.[13]

From the first days of the occupation, the Jewish congregation had coordinated its policy with that of the government. Both sides were determined to avoid any steps which might embarrass the Danish government and provoke the Germans into action. The Jewish organisations combatted all attempts to engage in illegal activities and opposed even the most minimal plans for escape. "They were apprehensive not only of German wrath but of Danish indignation at the fact that these Jews, who were willing to live with them in normal times, deserted in the hour of trial."[14] No one in Copenhagen – in the government, Foreign Ministry or in the Jewish congregation – knew that the extermination of the Jews was being planned at the Wannsee Conference in Berlin. According to the record of the Conference it appeared that Denmark was located on the periphery of the plan, but was among the countries where measures against the Jews were to be implemented. As was the case before, the occupying power in Denmark played its own game; the plenipotentiary, as well as the commander-in-chief of the army, agreed to keep the question of the Jews out of active consideration. This was a policy for which von Ribbentrop was willing to take responsibility. At the Wannsee Conference itself, it was noted that the Scandinavian countries were to be kept out of the *Endlösung* until further notice. The numbers of Jews in these countries was, of course, small.[15]

Following German military setbacks and the American entry into the war, by the late autumn of 1942 support for passive resistance on the Danish home front ("the cold shoulder") became more active. Over the BBC, the Danish Conservative politician Christmas Møller encouraged the Danes to carry out sabotage. The reply from the Danish illegal paper *Frit Danmark* (Free Denmark) was: "Yes

---

[12] Erik Scavenius, *Forhandlingspolitiken under Besættelsen*, Copenhagen 1948, p. 142.
[13] Max Friediger, *De Danske Jøder under Besættelsen*, Copenhagen 1945 (Dansk Udsyn XXV), p. 307; see also note 9.
[14] Yahil, *op. cit.*, p. 201.
[15] Yahil, *op. cit.*, p. 57. See also note 3.

Christmas, we're ready". However, resistance did not amount to much at first.[16] On 26th September 1942 King Christian X's insultingly brief answer, "My best thanks", to Hitler's birthday greeting made the latter furious. The military commander-in-chief, Colonel Lüdke, and the plenipotentiary Renthe-Fink were recalled to Berlin and replaced by von Hanneken and Werner Best respectively. Both had a reputation for toughness, but Best soon showed that he, too, approved of the "arrangement of 9th April". A month later, on 30th October, Erik Scavenius met von Ribbentrop and was presented with demands for normalising the Danish-German relationship. Among other things, the Prime Minister's office was to be taken over by Scavenius himself. The government consented and managed once again to maintain the policy of negotiation and keep the Danish Nazis away from all influence.[17]

There were many problems in the relationship between the Danes and the Germans and it would be a misinterpretation of events during the first years of the occupation to claim that the Danish and German authorities were preoccupied with the question of the Jews to any real degree. Antisemitism took up very little space in practical policy. Thus the ideological significance of the "Jewish Question" for the Germans was inversely proportional to the role it actually played in current Danish policy, at least until August 1943.[18]

After the German defeat at Stalingrad in January 1943 quite a number of people confidently counted on a swift victory for the Allies. At the same time there was an increase in the number, quality and popularity of acts of sabotage. These culminated in July and, together with a wave of strikes, triggered off the "August uprising" in 1943. When it seemed as if the situation was getting out of hand, von Hanneken requested that the *Wehrmacht* take over control of Denmark. At the German headquarters it was communicated to Werner Best that the policy of negotiation was failing and he was told to present a series of demands to the Danish government. He acted on 28th August. The demands included declaring a state of emergency, the imposition of a curfew, withdrawing the right of assembly, and the organisation of Danish military courts with the power to issue death sentences for acts of sabotage.

The following day the government rejected the demands. The three-year policy of fruitful negotiation between Germany and Denmark was now in ruins. The *Wehrmacht* and *Gestapo* took control of the Danish as well as the German civil administration. As a result, both the Danish Army and Navy were disarmed and Danish troops were interned in detention camps. In addition, the Danish police cut down on their activity – a fact which was to prove crucial to the outcome of the impending raids against the Jews. Finally, the Germans took a number of hostages and the camp in Horserød, where the Danish Communists had been interned since the summer of 1941, came under the control of the *Wehrmacht*. Werner Best, the undisputed loser as a result of these changes, threw himself into

---

[16]See Kirchhoff's review of Yahil, *loc. cit.*, pp. 247f.
[17]On the so-called telegram crisis, see Hans Kirchhoff, *Kamp eller tilpashning. Politikerne og modstanden 1940–1945*, Copenhagen 1987, pp. 84–94.
[18]As note 14.

an internal power struggle to try and regain his position. The first weapon he used was the question of the Jews.

On 8th September 1943 Werner Best sent a telegram to the German Foreign Minister, von Ribbentrop, in Berlin in which he stated that: "In accordance with the consistent application of the new policy in Denmark, it is my opinion that measures should now be taken toward a solution of the problems of the Jews and the freemasons. The necessary steps should be taken as long as the present state of emergency exists."[19] Why did Best do this? He must have realised that the telegram would shake the foundations of the policy of negotiation. He probably thought action against the Jews was approaching anyway and that by sending the telegram he would have an advantage over von Hanneken and the *Wehrmacht* and keep his power in Denmark.[20] As a high-ranking SS officer he had to be in sympathy with the target itself – a *Judenrein* Denmark – albeit only in the more academic sense of "neat" operation, far removed from the persecution of Jews on the street.[21] He must have welcomed having this question taken care of at a time when the country was under martial law and when, as a result, von Hanneken was technically responsible. This facilitated Best's subsequent negotiations with the Danish authorities. His tactics were to recommend action against the Jews on the one hand and on the other to accompany his recommendations with so many negative aspects that the action could only appear to be most inconvenient. In addition, he immediately started his own counter-offensive.

On 11th September he told his confidant and collaborator, the shipping expert at the German Embassy, Georg Ferdinand Duckwitz, about the notorious telegram. Two days later Best and Duckwitz agreed that the latter should go to Berlin and try to stop the telegram. However, they were too late. On 17th September it was announced that: "The *Führer* has decided that the deportation of the Jews will be carried out". Neither the warnings of Paul Kanstein, the Embassy's commissioner of police activities, and Rudolf Mildner, the newly appointed security police chief, nor the protests of the German Army and Naval Command were to much avail.[22]

On 21st September Duckwitz went to Stockholm and informed the Prime Minister Per Albin Hansson of the impending catastrophe. Shortly after this the Swedes offered to intern the Danish Jews,[23] an offer which was turned down by the Germans. In Denmark, Duckwitz broke all the rules on 28th September by contacting his influential Danish acquaintances: Hans Hedtoft-Hansen, the chairman of the Social Democratic Party, and Frants Hvass, the head of

---

[19]Quoted from Yahil, *op. cit.*, p. 138. Like most others before and since her, Yahil builds upon Jørgen Hæstrup's exposition of the course of events in *Til landets bedste. Hovedtræk af departementschefsstyrets virke 1943–45*, vol. I, Copenhagen 1966, pp. 134–150.

[20]For a thorough but fairly brief exposition of "the telegram of 8th September" and its consequences see Bjørn Rosengreen, *Dr. Werner Best og tysk besættelsespolitik i Danmark 1943–1945*, Odense 1982, pp. 47–55; see also Hans Kirchhoff, *Georg Ferdinand Duckwitz. Skitser til et politisk portræt*, Lyngby-bogen 1978. (Historisk-topografisk Selskab for Lyngby Taarbæk Kommune 1978). G. F. Duckwitz's private records (5344), Record Office, Copenhagen.

[21]The German historian Ulrich Herbert is preparing to publish a thesis on Werner Best. The thesis contains the point of view mentioned here.

[22]See Hæstrup, *Til landets bedste, op. cit.*, pp. 138ff., for this unbelievably intricate course of events.

[23]*Ibid.*, p. 161.

department in the Ministry of Foreign Affairs. Furthermore, Duckwitz persuaded the commanding officer of the German naval forces to look the other way in the case of any escapes across the Sound. This dangerous and drastic initiative took place on the same day that orders arrived from the *Führer* directing the action against the Jews to take place on the night of 2nd October. At this time Adolf Eichmann's agents, led by his second-in-command, *Sturmbannführer* Rolf Günther, arrived to plan and oversee the operation.[24]

As a final example of Best's ambiguous behaviour, it should be mentioned that as early as 17th September Best gave the Jewish community a clear hint of what was to come. He let the German police search the community's office and seize a file of members, although they only took an out-of-date card index. Obviously this step increased the already strong rumours. Among others, the Bishop of Copenhagen, Fuglsang-Damgaard asked Best whether the rumours of the forthcoming persecution of the Jews were true. "Over my dead body", Best replied.[25] The Director of the Ministry of Foreign Affairs, Nils Svenningsen also made enquiries and his mind was sufficiently put at ease for him to be able to inform the chairman of the congregation, C. B. Henriques, that the rumours were only guesswork. However, only three days later, Hans Hedtoft-Hansen saw Henriques privately in Charlottenlund outside Copenhagen and told him agitatedly about his conversation with Duckwitz:

> "'Henriques, there has been a great disaster. The dreaded action against the Jews is coming. On the night between 1st and 2nd October the *Gestapo* will search for all the Jews in their homes and then transport them to ships in the harbour. You must do all that is in your power to warn every single Jew in town immediately. Obviously we are ready to help you in any way.' Today [1952] I can reveal that Henrique's reaction was different from that which I had expected. He said only two words: 'You're lying', and it took me a long time to convince him that what I said was true. 'I don't understand how it can be true', he kept repeating despairingly. 'I've just talked to Director Svenningsen at the Ministry of Foreign Affairs and he put my mind at ease and said that he sincerely believed that nothing will happen'. I answered that Svenningsen's statements were put forward in good faith, he could only repeat what the Germans had said. The following morning, 29th September, there was an early morning service in the Synagogue. This was the day before the Jewish New Year's celebration and here the forthcoming raid was announced to the congregation."[26]

Three troop transports with the capacity to carry 5,000 Jews had been ordered to Copenhagen harbour by the *Sonderkommando Eichmann* ready for the deportation by sea. In Ålborg in North Jutland goods wagons were ready to take 2,000 Jews by rail. Meanwhile Theresienstadt was being prepared for the reception of a large number of Danes.[27]

---

[24]Yad Vashem, Jerusalem, interrogation of Adolf Eichmann 1960, transcript of shorthand notes and tapes in six vols., pp. 253–254 (the Red Cross visit to Theresienstadt June 1944), 1749–1763 (the deportation from Copenhagen) and 2652–2667 (the action itself).
[25]Quoted from Yahil, *op. cit.*, p. 173.
[26]Aage Bertelsen, *Oktober 43. Oplevelser og tilstande under jødeforfølgelserne i Danmark*, Copenhagen 1952. Preface by Hans Hedtoft-Hansen.
[27]Miroslav Kárny, 'Vorgeschichte, Sinn und Folge des 23. Juni 1944 in Theresienstadt', in *Judaica Bohemiae*, vol. XIX, No. 2 (1983), p. 87.

It is well known that the action was a complete failure. Thanks to an incredibly effective effort by many Danes, more than 7,000 Jews escaped to Sweden. However, without the double-dealing of Best – with Duckwitz as an active participant – without an only half-hearted German effort, without a turn in Swedish foreign policy away from a German orientation and without the geographical proximity of Sweden, the Danish rescue operation would not have been possible. When it comes to the German effort, or lack of it, it is necessary to reassess the importance of the legendary "nice German" who looked the other way. In fact, there is good reason to emphasise the role of the Danish coastguard. Its decision to stop patrolling the coastline, immediately after 29th August, was decisive for the failure of the raid. Eivind Larsen, head of department in the Ministry of Justice, clearly notified Paul Kanstein that it was not to be expected that Danes should make "a stand against Danes".[28] The regular German troops in the country were mainly kept in their garrisons and were not used in the raid, whereas the newly arrived police soldiers and *Gestapo* tried their best to catch the escaping Jews. They were, however, too few to perform effectively.[29] This does not, however, alter the fact that several *Wehrmacht* soldiers remained as passive as was possible.

Finally the idea of establishing detention camps in Denmark itself, which was one of a range of hazardous rescue attempts, must be mentioned. The idea was put forward from two completely different sources on the same day. The root of this idea was the detention camp at Horserød where the Communists had been interned since 1941 and its purpose was obviously to keep Danish citizens away from German prisons and concentration camps. The ways the idea was launched were, to put it mildly, very different.

In a telegram sent to the *Auswärtiges Amt* on 29th September, Werner Best reported on a suggestion put to him by the Director of the Danish Red Cross, Helmer Rosting. He suggested a "barter" between the interned Danish soldiers and the Danish Jews. The Jews would replace the soldiers who would be sent home and the Jews would then function as hostages. In the case of sabotage, 50 to 100 Jews would be deported South. An agreement along these lines was to be publicised to the Danish public upon whom it was supposed to have a quietening effect.[30] Best found the suggestion interesting and used the linking of soldiers and Jews in his press statement on 2nd October:

> "After the anti-German incitement of the Jews, their moral and material support for acts of terror and sabotage, which to a considerable degree have contributed to the aggravation of the situation in Denmark, they have, as a result of measures taken by the German authorities, been removed from public life and prevented from continuing to poison the atmosphere. In the next few days, in response to the widespread wish of the Danish population, the release of interned Danish soldiers will begin and take place at a rate determined by the technical possibilities."

---

[28] Hæstrup, *Til landets bedste, op. cit.*, p. 268. Before 29th August 1943 the coastal police were very active and effective. An example of this was the arrest of three escaping parachutists in Skovshoved, December 1942. See Jørgen Hæxstrup, *Kontakt med England*, Copenhagen 1954, pp. 223f.

[29] Hæstrup, *Til landets bedste, op. cit.*, p. 142.

[30] *Parliamentary Commission. Appendix XIII*, Copenhagen 1954, p. 1379.

At a meeting of the heads of department the same day, the question of a Danish internment, including the "provision" of the Jews was debated. In other words, were they to employ the same methods as those used against the Communists in the summer of 1941? The disregard of the principles of law could be excused by the humane nature of the purpose, but only as an absolutely last resort and with no Danish participation in the arrests.[31]

Due to the course of the action against the Jews, the plan lost its relevance. However, Helmer Rostings's initiative implied that the administration had lost confidence in the Danish Red Cross. When help for the Danish prisoners in Germany increased considerably at the end of 1943 beginning of 1944, it took place within the framework of the Ministry of Social Affairs.

Shortly before midnight on 1st October the Director of the Foreign Ministry, Nils Svenningsen, managed to obtain an interview with Werner Best. After having been put off with talk, lies and half lies for so long, Svenningsen wanted to get authentic knowledge about the German plans from the source itself. He got just that. The raid was about to be launched. Able-bodied Jews were to be put to work. The elderly and those unable to work would be sent to Theresienstadt. Svenningsen was told that it was "a town where the Jews were self-governing and lived under appropriate conditions". First thing in the morning they would be taken to Germany. For the first time it was openly declared where the Danish Jews were to be taken and what fate the Germans had in mind for them. The latter was put in worryingly vague terms.[32]

The *Gestapo* managed to catch 202 Jews in Copenhagen, where most of the Jews lived, and 82 in the provinces. These 284 Jews were sent from Copenhagen harbour directly to Theresienstadt on 2nd October, together with 150 Communists who had been interned in the camp at Horserød and who were to be sent to the concentration camps at Stutthof and Ravensbrück.[33] On 5th and 6th October the two first transports arrived in Theresienstadt with 83 and 198 Danes respectively. On their way to Roskilde, south of Copenhagen, three of the prisoners jumped out of the window.[34]

In the following weeks, the *Gestapo* captured another 190 Jews who were attempting to escape to Sweden. They, too, were sent southwards on 13th October and 23rd November. As late as 13th January and 20th April 1944, eight and two Danes arrived in the camp, sent on from Sachsenhausen and Ravensbrück respectively. In this way the total number of Danish Jews (and Jews who were refugees in Denmark) there reached 481. Over the years there have been discrepancies in the numbers of Danish Jews reported as being in Theresienstadt. There are several reasons for this. Apart from the question of separating Jews from non-Jews and Danes from non-Danes, which is not as simple as it may appear, the authorities simply had trouble making accurate

---

[31]Hæstrup, *Til landets bedste, op. cit.*, pp. 158ff.
[32]*Ibid.*, p. 163.
[33]Corrie and Sven Meyer, *Theresienstadt – det iscenesatte bedrag. Erindringer fra nazisternes "model"-ghetto*, ed. by Hans Sode-Madsen, Copenhagen 1991, p. 28.
[34]*Ibid.*, pp. 44ff. and 62ff.

counts. Registration of the population through a national register and the census reports were not reliable. The German bureaucracy was not as meticulous as Danish prejudice would have us believe. The Foreign Ministry did operate with a list of 481 names, though. Officially, the *Gestapo* only accepted 295 persons as "genuine" Danish Jews, but all the 481 persons actually enjoyed the same privileges, including protection from transportation to Auschwitz-Birkenau.

Once in Germany they continued by rail, forty or fifty people in each cattle truck. From the mooring of the ship in Swinemünde until the hatches were opened two and a half days later, the prisoners were only allowed to get out a couple of times and relieve themselves in the fields. The diet consisted of a little dry bread with a bit of jam. Salomon Katz, who was arrested together with his family shortly before midnight on 2nd October described their journey:

> "After this ordeal we were ordered down into the hold. It is arranged as a troop carrier which it probably has been, too. All of a sudden, as we walk around to find a place, we catch sight of father, mother and Anna. There was wailing and moaning, not just from us, but from everybody. Suddenly a yell is heard: there must be silence. It is one of the SS-officers, leading the transportation, who is yelling. Silence prevails for a short while, then the wailing and moaning start over again, now mixed with the crying of small children. Again the yell is heard; if we are not silent we shall pay for it. Now we become quiet and talk in whispers. Shortly afterwards we are ordered to line up in front of the leader of the transport. We have to fill in forms with our names, place of birth, date of birth and other information. Now we sense that the ship is sailing. We wonder if we will leave this ship alive. Such are our thoughts when we see the crew put on their life jackets. But we do leave the ship alive. In Swinemünde we are thrown into cattle trucks and here a journey begins which we shall remember for a long time. Around fifty persons are packed into each truck. The rest is easy to imagine. The nights were the worst, everybody tried to lie down and get a little rest, but nobody could lie down, there was no space to lie on. No, let me skip this journey and go directly to the moment we arrived at Theresienstadt. That was on the night of 5th October at around 10 pm."[35]

The town of Theresienstadt is located approximately 62 km north of Prague where the Elbe and Eger rivers meet and was originally built as a garrison. Until the small ramshackle town was re-shaped into a ghetto towards the end of 1941, it was inhabited by 7,000 Czech residents. Apart from a dozen assimilated Jews there was no Jewish society in the town. The boundary between the German and the Jewish residents was immediately marked with a board partition. The market square, the church, the parks and the two main streets were to be frequented by Aryans only.

As a concentration camp, Theresienstadt was one of the most bizarre phenomenons of the Nazi *Endlösung* projects. At the Wannsee Conference in January 1942 the Nazis planned an "Altersghetto" intended for selected Jews from Germany, Austria, Czechoslovakia and Holland. This would include people above the age of 65 years, whom it was not considered "convenient" to evacuate – in reality, to kill – war cripples and veterans from the First World War who had been decorated with the Iron Cross First Class, prominent Jews, i.e. high-ranking politicians and civil servants, prominent intellectuals, scientists, and artists. Very rarely indeed have so many prominent people been gathered under such strange circumstances as in Theresienstadt. The ghetto was self-

---

[35]Salomon Katz, *Dagbog fra Theresienstadt 1943–45*, Privately owned. The present author is trying to have the diary published. It consists of 925 hand-written pages.

governing through a Council of the Elders who saw to the administrative and economic life of the town.[36]

Viewed from the outside Theresienstadt functioned as a small town. It seemed able to take care of the citizens from birth to death through an orphanage, hospital, police, central kitchens, sports building, electricity- and waterworks, employment office, bank, old people's home. From the inside you saw a strange entity which is best described as a concentration- assembly- and transit camp, a stop on the way to extermination in Auschwitz. It was intended as such and it worked as such.

When the Danes arrived at Theresienstadt 45,000 Jews were crammed together in a space intended for 10,000 inhabitants. From the nearby railway station, they walked three km to the camp, where their first meeting with the immense bureaucracy of the camp was *die Schleuse*, the "sluice". They were signed in as newly arrived citizens and were deprived of all their valuable possessions, including wedding rings. They were only allowed to keep the clothes they were wearing. After this they went to the peculiar reception of the camp commander, *Obersturmbannführer* Karl Rahm and the leader of the Council of the Elders, Paul Eppstein, who in ceremonious terms told them about life in the ghetto. None of the Danes had been able to imagine what everyday life was like in the camp. Totally unprepared, they confronted miserable living conditions in overcrowded, unheated attics with lice, fleas and bed-bugs, unspeakably filthy sanitary conditions, and a daily dread of the future. One did not have to stay long in Theresienstadt to witness a transport to the East and the oppressive hopelessness surrounding these involuntary departures. No wonder that many of the Danes dropped into states of apathy and depression during the first period. This existence was regulated and systematised to the smallest detail. The psychological disintegration of the individual was initiated by separating married couples. Women and children were to live in the Hamburger Barrack and the men in the Hannover Barrack across the street. There was no question of any privacy. A system of House Elders and Room Elders maintained order.

After a brief stay in compulsory quarantine all the able-bodied Danes were put to work. Work teams of up to one hundred people, the so-called *Hundertschaft*, provided for the town's subsistence as well as producing for the war industry: ladies' clothing, leather products, wooden toys, jewellery, fancy goods and artistic prints by the thousands. The Danes in general, were in good physical shape and they were charged with the hard work as pall-bearers, road- and railway workers or, worst of all, assisting in the transportations to Auschwitz.

[36]The most important work on Theresienstadt is definitely H. G. Adler, *Theresienstadt 1941–1945. Das Antlitz einer Zwangsgemeinschaft. Geschichte, Soziologie, Psychologie*, Tübingen 1960. In this connection see *idem*, *Die verheimlichte Wahrheit. Theresienstädter Dokumente*, Tübingen 1958. See also Ruth Bondy, 'The Theresienstadt Ghetto, its Characteristics and Perspective', in *The Nazi Concentration Camps. Proceedings of the Fourth Yad Vashem International Historical Conference*, Jerusalem 1984, pp. 303–313. A short thought-provoking article which, among other things, touches upon the existential problem of whether Theresienstadt was a product of the Jewish "ghetto mentality", which Bruno Bettelheim for one thinks is a distinctive feature of the Central European Jewry.

Many of the women worked in the mica mill where the mica was split for the electrical industry so essential to the war, a job so tiring and monotonous that the women were forced to sing while working.

While all concentration camps were characterised by an incredible coarseness and callousness, Theresienstadt was distinguished by its flourishing cultural life. The first organised recreational activities, the Friendship Evenings, began shortly after the opening of the camp. In the winter of 1942–1943, life was gradually normalised. There were theatres, concerts, cabarets, seminars, courses, libraries and sports. Schooling was prohibited, but took place disguised as a leisure activity for children.[37] The role of Theresienstadt as a model ghetto was enhanced through a substantial effort by the SS. The town was to be exhibited to prominent visitors from humanitarian organisations. The deception, staged by the Germans, was soon turned into an easily understandable self-deception on the part of the Jews. A gruesome atmosphere of destruction brooded over the camp. The prospects were Auschwitz and extermination.

However, until the end of February 1944 when the first parcel from Denmark was received in Theresienstadt, starvation was the one problem which could not be dispelled by "leisure" occupations. The food from the big central kitchens consisted mainly of a grey soup in which floated pieces of potato and barley. Once in a while meat was served. The weekly ration of bread was small indeed. As soon as the inhabitants were permitted to send messages to Denmark saying that they were alive and where they were, they found ways of cheating the censors and telling of the starvation. The first postcards were sent on 5th October 1943, the day of arrival. The style and the content clearly revealed that somebody had ordered the wording which is found on all the postcards (here in *italics*): "We arrived about an hour ago and *considering the circumstances, we are all right*. Miss Bomholt has promised to take care of my things. Until further notice they can be left with you as I don't know yet where I'll live, work, and what I'll need. *We are in a town with Jewish inhabitants only and with Jewish self-government. We are only allowed to write German*, but I hope that father or Erik will be able to read it. Could you send me some food some time? Please write soon."[38] The obligatory wording also included: "we are all in good health" and equally optimistic messages to the anxious world. As the censorship became more sensitive the postcard writers developed a flourishing imagination. Among the many inventions was the reference to Knut Hamsun's main work (*Sult* = "hunger"), and many greetings were sent to the baker and the butcher back home in Copenhagen. The messages were received and understood.

Immediately after the deportation, all efforts were pooled in the central administration to prevent new raids from being launched, to prevent the Jews in

---

[37]Inger Merete Nordentoft and Aage Svendstorp (eds.), *Og hverdagen skiftede. Skolen i de onde år*, Copenhagen 1946. On this see also Sulamith Gutkin's (née Cholewa) description of the teaching of Danish in the school in Theresienstadt: Sulamith Cholewa, 'Dansk skoleundervishning i Theresienstadt', *ibid*.

[38]Quoted from Jørgen Hæstrup, *Dengang i Danmark. Jødisk ungdom på træk 1932–1945*, Odense 1982, p. 249.

Theresienstadt from being deported to camps in Poland, to ensure Danish civil servants access to the camp, and to get permission to send parcels with foodstuffs and clothes to Theresienstadt. Quite soon the Germans responded positively to the wishes of the Danes and even better, the Danes gradually accomplished their aims.[39]

It was part of Werner Best's double-dealing that as early as 5th October he stated in writing that "half Jews and persons with a lower percentage of Jewish blood would not be affected by the measures that applied to pure Jews. The same goes for pure Jews married to non-Jews."[40] At the same time he let it be known that there was no danger of new actions against the Jews. In this way Werner Best introduced the possibility of the return from Theresienstadt of the, according to the statements, erroneously arrested half Jews and Jews in mixed marriages – if these statements were to be believed at all. As a matter of fact five out of twenty possible wrongly arrested Jews were returned in January 1944 after interminable negotiations.[41]

On 2nd November 1943 Adolf Eichmann visited Copenhagen and the following day Werner Best sent a telegram to the *Reichssicherheitshauptamt* in Berlin about the result of the negotiations. On 4th November Best received confirmation. Considering the situation the agreement was astonishing. First, Jews over the age of 60 years were not to be arrested or deported. Second, deported half Jews and Jews living in mixed marriages were to be returned to Denmark. Third, all Jews deported from Denmark – i.e. not only Danish Jews, but also Jews who were refugees in Denmark, the so-called stateless Jews – were to remain in Theresienstadt. Fourth, representatives of the Danish authorities were to visit them in the near future.

The answering telegram elaborated the agreement by mentioning that no parcels with foodstuffs were to be sent, whereas parcels with clothes were permitted, and that the visit to Theresienstadt could not take place before the spring of 1944. The agreement was forwarded to the Foreign Ministry immediately and the framework of future official and semi-official aid to the Jews was marked out. Unfortunately, it took longer for the agreement to come into effect. On 26th November H. H. Koch, the head of department of the Ministry of Social Affairs and the co-ordinator of relief work for the concentration camp prisoners, reminded his colleague Svenningsen about the sending of the parcels – food as well as clothes – to Theresienstadt, now that an arrangement for the Communists in Stutthof had been reached. "As I've understood it, it hasn't so far been possible to obtain permission to send parcels with foodstuffs, but I do believe that this question has to be raised continually in order to reach a result if at all possible. Regarding the sending of clothes I believe that permission has been given for the sending of clothes by relatives residing in this country, although I

---

[39] See Hæstrup, *Til landets bedste, op. cit.*, pp. 383ff., on the conditions behind the incredible achievements of the Foreign Ministry and the Ministry of Social Affairs. Hæstrup builds primarily upon material from the records of the Ministry of Social Affairs, Record Office, Copenhagen, 2.kt., j.nr. 880/1943.

[40] Quoted from Hæstrup, *Til landets bedste, op. cit.*, p. 182.

[41] *Ibid.*, pp. 350f.

don't know much about it as we in the ministry have had no opportunity to see the wishes expressed by those in question in the letters which were sent to Denmark through the German police and were distributed through the Borough of Copenhagen. We, in this office, are willing to participate in a negotiation concerning the question of rationalising and sending of clothes and a possible extension of the arrangement to include parcels with foodstuffs."

About a week later Svenningsen was able to announce the result. They had been granted permission, with the Danish Red Cross as an intermediary, to send parcels with clothes containing personal things as a "once only favour". They had to display the greatest care and discretion in the despatch. No whole car loads were to be shipped off, it was impressed on Svenningsen. However, all the exhortations covered the fact that there was a wide range of possibilities for handling the aid as long as discretion was employed. "Concerning the sending of the parcels with foodstuffs, the Germans have declared that this is absolutely out of the question. It is our impression that the Germans are anxious that overly conspicuous preferential treatment for the Danish Jews will lead to demands from other countries which will be absolutely impossible to meet."[42]

Experience had shown that promises were not dependable, constant or consistent, and refusals were not always immutable. The result was chaos and only a very limited group of civil servants and their collaborators outside the ministry were able to keep track of what was and was not allowed.[43]

For H. H. Koch it was crucial to have the relief work centralised in the Ministry of Social Affairs. During the first months of 1944, information was pieced together about the conditions in Sachsenhausen and Stutthof. Knowledge of conditions in these two concentration camps led Danish officials to establish a process of rational, stable and economically sound relief work. Koch's temperament did not allow him to hand over a matter of this importance to individuals or private institutions, including the Danish Red Cross. They were to be used as assistants or to cover up the more illegal activities of the Ministry. This was a state assignment and he considered the Ministry of Social Affairs to be best suited to take measures against trivial obstacles and concerns, whether they emanated from an actual lack of goods, rigid interpretations of the law, or frightened adherence to regulations. The parcels had to be sent, as many as possible, as often as possible, and with the right contents.[44]

Very soon after the internment the remaining relatives established relief committees, in the daily ministerial jargon usually referred to as the "ladies committees". They were extremely effective and most appreciated. The prime movers in this large-scale relief work for the Jews, outside the walls of the Ministry of Social Affairs, were the nutritionist Richard Ege, his wife Vibeke, and Ruth Bredsdorff. These three, who had all been active in getting the Jews across to Sweden, now spent all their energies organising "spontaneous" and effective aid for the Danish Jews in Theresienstadt. Apart from the Foreign Ministry and the Ministry of Social Affairs, the Ministry of Supply, the

[42] Record Office, Copenhagen, Ministry of Social Affairs, 2.kt., j.nr. 880/1943.
[43] Hæstrup, *Til landets bedste, op. cit.*, pp. 384f.
[44] *Ibid.*, pp. 399ff.

Visit of the International Red Cross
23rd June 1944
Healthy-looking children are chosen to play their part in the charade
Pictures taken by Dr. Maurice Rossel of the IRC,
against the rules, but with the tacit approval of the SS

By courtesy of Public Record Office, Copenhagen

Visit of the International Red Cross
23rd June 1944
Dr. Rossel's photographs of the "hospital" and the fire brigade

By courtesy of Public Record Office, Copenhagen

Idealised sketches of Theresienstadt made under compulsion
by the Dutch artist Jo Spier as a "souvenir" for visitors

By courtesy of Public Record Office, Copenhagen

Terezín/Theresienstadt today

Unofficial Association of Clergymen, and a large number of individuals were involved in this process of assistance. All of them knew the right people. Needless to say everything, including the German acceptance of what was happening – not least the steadily growing involvement of the Ministry of Social Affairs through its financial support and staff – passed off unobtrusively. In a joint effort, they managed to systematise the spontaneous and individual work as much as was required.[45]

As mentioned above, five Jews returned to Copenhagen in January 1944. The Germans released them on condition that they praise Theresienstadt on their return. In spite of discretion on the part of the Ministry of Social Affairs, the news spread that the state of nutrition in particular was deplorable. When the Germans heard about this leak the further negotiations with the *Auswärtiges Amt* about more releases stopped completely. Based upon these first-hand accounts of the conditions in the camp, Richard Ege worked out what a standard food parcel should contain and had the medical industry produce, in all haste, a special vitamin product. Usually the parcel contained 1.5 lb of sugar, 2 lb of cheese, 1 tin of sprats and 1 tin of mackerel, a piece of soap, 0.5 lb of rye biscuits, 0.5 lb of butter, 20 stock cubes, 1 lb of sausage, 0.5 lb of crispbread and 1 tin of pork. The standard parcel was to be sent to other concentration camp prisoners as well, and was composed regardless of Jewish dietary restrictions. The Supply Office produced ration cards for the rationed commodities; a large shipping business, O. Evensen in Copenhagen, managed the despatch.

Problems still remained. The parcels had to look as if they were being sent individually and, as most relatives and friends had fled themselves, "parcel-sponsors" had to be procured. The illegal Unofficial Association of Clergyman took care of this task. Friends and relatives were produced where possible, otherwise the local minister and his flock sent out the parcels.[46] Finally, there was the question of finding somebody to pay for the parcels. The Danish Red Cross did not dare to run the risk at the time. It was only permitted to send parcels with clothes and, based upon the Geneva Convention, only aid to "genuine" prisoners of war was accepted. People who were interned because of race, faith, or illegal activities (saboteurs), were not considered by the Danish Red Cross to be their responsibility. Thus, the 1944 Fund for Social and Humanitarian Purposes was created for the occasion. The money came mainly from the Ministry of Social Affairs, but also from private organisations: apart from clergymen it came from the medical association and the employers' association. The first food parcels were sent on 21st February. In order not to draw attention to the operation, ten parcels were sent every other day for the first week. The following week twenty parcels were sent at a time and then the number of parcels increased gradually to around 700 a month.[47]

---

[45] *Ibid.*, p. 409.

[46] Harald Sandbæk and N. J. Rald (eds.), *Den danske Kirke under Besættelsen*, Copenhagen 1945, pp. 84f. Cf. Record Office, Copenhagen, private record 10.197, Præsternes Uofficielle Forening (Unofficial Association of Clergymen).

[47] A complete collection of despatch lists exists in the Record Office, Copenhagen, private record 10.488, the 1944 Fund. During the thirteen months parcels were sent, 7,525 were sent through O. Evensen and about 6,000 through the Danish Red Cross.

Through his network of contracts, Richard Ege had composed a file on the deported Jews. The parcels were now sent to each individual. Each delivery was confirmed. It was, of course, not certain that the person who confirmed the delivery was the "right" person, but it was necessary to experiment and the chance was taken. Despite a transportation system that was in disrepair, the parcels reached their destination quickly. Considering the situation, the German railways and postal services worked well, and apparently they knew nothing about the *Gestapo*'s ban against parcels with foodstuffs for Theresienstadt. The system proved useful and the parcels arrived, with only a little of the contents missing. Theresienstadt differed from other concentration camps on this point too.

Following the visit by Danish civil servants to the camp in June 1944, the Germans gave permission for two food parcels a month to be sent to each internee and for the establishment of a Danish library of 1,000 books. At a meeting in the Ministry of Social Affairs at the beginning of July the postal services were organised. The Danish Red Cross arranged to send as many as 240 registered parcels a week. Ege's committee supplied the necessary lists of addresses, maintained the file of parcels on the basis of received receipts and decided the content of the parcels. The Unofficial Association of Clergymen and O. Evensen continued to send parcels to about 350 stateless Jews who had arrived in Theresienstadt with the Danes, as the Danish Red Cross decided they could not take responsibility for this. As a matter of fact, the Ministry of Social Affairs had decided to fire the Danish Red Cross and take charge of mailing the parcels. However, enquiries among the Germans produced the answer that an arrangement like this could not take effect until the end of the year.[48]

The *Gestapo* had held out the prospect of letting a Danish commission of civil servants visit Theresienstadt in the spring of 1944. The visit was part of the propaganda campaign that emanated from Eichmann's office at the time. His purpose was to prove to the world that the rumour of the extermination of Jews was pure fabrication. Eichmann manoeuvred deftly in this case between the International Red Cross, the German Red Cross, the Danish Red Cross, the Danish Foreign Ministry, and the Danish Jews in Theresienstadt. Thanks to the parcels, the Danes were nicely dressed and in good physical condition. They were well suited to be shown to the Red Cross. At the end of June 1943, the German Red Cross had spent two days in Theresienstadt and had been deeply shaken by what they had seen. Information about the appalling conditions, the shocking malnutrition and horrible housing conditions, was sent to the headquarters in Geneva. The adjective, *"grauenhaft"* (gruesome) dominated the report.[49] Since this was a German visit, the *Gestapo* had done nothing to mitigate the impression of the actual conditions. But now, a year later, every ounce of energy was put into covering up the conditions.

The visit was put off several times and was not carried out until 23rd June

---

[48]Record Office, Copenhagen, Ministry of Social Affairs, 2.kt. j.nr. 880/1943.
[49]Adler, *Die verheimlichte Wahrheit, op. cit.*, pp. 304ff.

1944. The delays were caused by the extra time it took to give Theresienstadt a façade of quite farcical dimensions. For one thing, nature had to be seen at its best, with blooming flowers and green trees. The Germans did not leave the embellishment to nature alone. It is virtually impossible to imagine the meticulousness that the Germans put into their work. Everything was staged, down to the tiniest detail. First, the board partition between the "Aryan" town and the ghetto was torn down. The market square was turned into a beautiful park with flowers and lawns (imported from Denmark!) and benches on the newly constructed paths. The inhabitants were to keep off the latter until two days before the arrival of the Commission, though. A beautiful pavilion for music was put up in one corner, where an orchestra of thirty to forty men played light music several hours a day under the Danish conductor Peter Deutsch. An old sports hall (*Sokolovna*) which until now had worked as a hospital for infectious diseases was transformed into a cultural centre with halls for theatre, music and speeches. Modern equipment was installed in the hospitals and the old peoples' home and the number of patients reduced by an increase in deportations to Poland. All in all, 17,500 inhabitants were cleared out to reduce the impression of overpopulation. They went as far as scrubbing the streets with soap-suds. The list of tricks is interminable and included, apart from the visual deceptions described above, language deceptions. The word ghetto disappeared and was replaced by "Jewish Neighbourhood", the SS *Kommandantur* became the *Dienststelle*, the "Orders of the Day" usually issued on mean little pieces of paper reappeared as letter-sized, illustrated "Information from the Jewish Self-Government", a competition was launched to find the most beautiful names for the town squares.

At the beginning of June, those of the Danish Jews who were considered the most presentable by the Germans moved to their own living quarters where they were allowed, as an immense privilege, to lead a family life of their own. In the four "Danish houses" the rooms were repaired and arranged with austere furniture, although tables and chairs usually did not exist in the barracks. Paintings, stolen goods from Prague, were put on the walls and green plants were put in the windows. The Danes were allotted the flats on the ground floor facing the streets, while the original inhabitants were relegated to the first floor where everything remained as miserable as before. Finally, the Head of the German Security Police in Denmark, Rudolf Mildner surveyed the embellishment of the town, and found the ghetto too crowded. Still, it was good enough to receive the visitors.

On 22nd June all the Danes were summoned to the dining area. Under the supervision of the Camp Commander, Eppstein, the leader of the Council of the Elders, notified the prisoners about the exact rules of behaviour during the visit of the commission the following day. For one thing the Jews had to appear "well-bred and cultured" and "answer questions put to them sensibly". They were definitely not recommended to criticise conditions in the town. If the visit did not go according to the wishes of the Germans, food parcels would no longer be received and all the Danes would be deported. To safeguard against disturbances in the harmonious picture, supposedly discontented persons were "invited" to watch an entertainment in one of the rooms. They were not allowed to leave the room during the visit.[50]

The Commission arrived in bright sunshine on 23rd June 1944 at 11 am. The head of department of the Foreign Ministry, Frants Hvass, and Eigil Juel Henningsen, the superintendent of the National Health Service, came from Denmark. In addition, the International Red Cross in Geneva and the German Red Cross were represented. The course of events was watched over by the Camp Commander and a number of SS people, one of whom spoke Danish. For the occasion the Germans were dressed as civilians. They kept themselves in the background and let Eppstein take centre stage in the masquerade. Upon their arrival, the visitors were told that this was the first time that strangers had been granted access to visit Theresienstadt. If they – the visitors – found anything to criticise during the visit, they had to keep in mind how living conditions were for many parts of the German urban population at the present time. Considering that the flight to Berlin had been much delayed by violent air raids over the northern parts of Berlin, this was a very shrewd maneouvre. After this the guests went in three cars to the "*Haus der jüdischen Selbstvervaltung*", where Eppstein addressed the visitors beautifully and quite mendaciously on the merits of Theresienstadt. He terminated the speech, which was interlaced with figures and statistics, by saying that life in the camp was normal and the inhabitants filled with courage to face life: "To many, life in Theresienstadt has meant a substantial reorganisation; You will see that they have succeeded. You will see life in a normal town."[51] For almost eight hours the commission was led along the carefully planned route, shown the repaired institutions and works. They talked to the appointed persons who answered in the ways they had been told to answer. Juel Henningsen wrote:

> "Incidentally, the visit took the shape of a tour round the town guided by Dr. Eppstein, during the entire visit we were accompanied by the said gentlemen. We had free access to see everything we passed, and on no occasion did they intervene in our conversations which were guarded by one or more of our German escorts.
>
> During our tour we had the opportunity to talk to representatives of the Danish Jews, Dr. Friediger, the lawyer Mr. Oppenheim, and the engineer Mr. Ove Meyer. They declared to us that they found that conditions had improved tremendously in the town, and that they now lived under favourable conditions, albeit under mental strain due to the separation from their country and relatives. They emphasised the importance of the food parcels they had received and asked us to continue sendng them. In particular they wanted: butter, cheese, sugar, dried milk, dried vegetables and crispbread. Moreover, the Danes wanted access to Danish literature, partly fiction, partly popular science literature.
>
> In addition to that we met several other Danes in their houses or around the institutions, in the post office, in the nursery school etc. Everybody seemed anxious to make us comprehend that they found their living conditions good and at the same time implored us to make sure that the sendings were continued. They had all received parcels regularly and gave expression to their immense gratitude."[52]

---

[50] Max Friediger, *Theresienstadt*, Copenhagen 1946, p. 109.

[51] Cited in Dansk Røde Kors' Krigshjælp. Dr. Eigil Juel Henningsens beretning om besøg i Theresienstadt fredag den 22. (=23.) (Dr. Eigil Juel Henningsen's account of the visit to Theresienstadt Friday 22 [=23] June 1944). Record Office, Copenhagen, Ministry of Social Affairs, 2. kt., j.nr. 880/1943.

[52] *Ibid.*

The more effectively prepared features included the well-trained football players, the happy, sun-tanned, singing young girls on their way to work in the fields, children rehearsing a children's opera preparing for its first performance, and the distribution of bread by a clean-scrubbed staff, wearing neat white cotton gloves! Eppstein's talk was so deftly and effectively composed that even shrewd spectators were deceived. Rossel, the representative of the International Red Cross in Geneva, was quite convinced that "this Jewish town is astonishing" and wondered why the Red Cross had had problems getting permission to visit. He meant well. As appendices to his report he took some snapshots of the outdoor life. The camp leaders were a bit apprehensive; to take photographs in a concentration camp was strictly forbidden even to the staff. But they trusted the power of the illusion.[53] When the visit was over the Germans were satisfied that the arrangements had gone without a hitch.[54]

Upon their return, Hvass and Juel Henningsen wrote a report on the visit. On the whole, Juel Henningsen's account is a repetition of the information given by the guide on the tour. It contains hardly any reflection on anything but the quite external, staged "reality". His style seems deliberately "neutral". A month after his return, Frants Hvass reported to the heads of departments. The note from this is fairly brief, factual in style, and contains the erroneous descriptions of what had been seen. These were errors which illustrate the power of deception. The camp is no transit camp – those who have come to the place remain there. To specific inquiries the German authorities declared that no Danes had been taken to another place. A total piece of misinformation which did, however, disclose knowledge of "another place".[55]

To the Danish civil servants the fates of the Danes were evidently of prime interest, especially because it had never been accepted that Danish Jews were anything but ordinary Danish citizens. Thus, the impression conveyed was predominantly positive and could hardly be anything else, considering the circumstances. After the war, these interpretations were severely criticised for their apparent naivety. This lent subsequent rationalisation to the controversy which, in a moralising vein, did not take the understandable motives into consideration: the mission of Hvass and Henningsen was to provide evidence of the existence of the Danish Jews under circumstances which could, without warning, change into something much worse. The condition of the Danes in Sachsenhausen and in Stutthof was known. And this knowledge more than sufficed to lead to calls for circumspection in communications with the *Gestapo*. The two civil servants probably played the game consciously, with the evident objective of securing and maybe even extending the unique agreement between Werner Best and Adolf Eichmann. The parliamentary commission which, after the war, delved deeply into the works of the State Administration 1940–1945 was told by Frants Hvass:

---

[53] Adler, *Die verheimlichte Wahrheit, op. cit.*, pp. 201 and 312f. Copies of photographs in the Record Office, Copenhagen, private record 6985, Frants Hvass, pk. 3. See illustrations between pp. 278–279.

[54] Adler, *Theresienstadt, op. cit.*, pp. 163–184.

[55] Records Office, Copenhagen, documents of the Foreign Ministry 1909–1945. 84.A.23/1b.

"Chief physician Juel Henningsen and I were, of course, aware that a number of the measures that had been taken in Theresienstadt had been taken for the occasion of our visit. However, what we were more aware of during the visit was the prisoners' state of health, their clothing and their housing and not these measures. We noted that their state of health was better than we had dared expect which, for some of them, must be put down to the fact that, already at an early stage, the sending of the food parcels for the Danish Jews had worked. Their clothing seemed to be fairly satisfactory and their housing in Theresienstadt, although it could be described as harsh, was not to be compared to those of their co-religionists living in the actual concentration camps. They lived under extreme mental pressure. The fact that the great majority of them survived the stay must, apart from the above-mentioned food parcels, be put down to the unique effort of those Jews who made it possible, within the framework of self-government, to create these *relatively* good external conditions and who infused a feeling of courage and strength into their co-religionists in Theresienstadt, enough to make them carry on with life in the hope of a better future."[56]

It is not, in this case, possible to distinguish subsequent rationalisation, superior knowledge, and apology from the immediate "true" impressions and reactions. However, if you let the contemporary results count more than the speculations of posterity it can rightly be claimed that the game was a success. There was now a fixed framework for the vital sending of the parcels and a substantial library was also shipped off. The Danes, including the 130 whom *Gestapo* did not accept as proper Danish citizens, kept their privileges. The arrangement under which ten German *Reichmark* a month were sent to each individual seemed more like a tragic joke. A private individual had suggested that this be done and it was recommended to the Ministry of Social Affairs by Frants Hvass. Hvass felt a little uneasy in sending such big amounts since this might cause inflationary instability (!) in the camp. None the less, the money was faithfully sent – and just as faithfully seized on its arrival. After the commission had left most things returned to their former condition. Before the façade was cleared away a propaganda film was produced: *Theresienstadt. Ein Dokumentarfilm* (usually referred to as *Der Führer schenkt den Juden eine Stadt*). Fragments of this bizarre film can still be seen.[57]

After this visit, mass deportations to the East began. The first ones to disappear were all those who had participated actively in the embellishment charade, except for the Danes. Morale in the camp dropped disastrously. To the Danish Jews the visit to the camp was clearly a disappointment. They simply did not understand that the civil servants had let themselves be deceived. But it all depends on how we look at it. The Jews in the camp saw the erection of the façade prior to the visit and grieved to see the manipulative guided tour and its ostensible effect. But they were prevented from knowing what went on in the administration office following the visit. And here true knowledge about the conditions was not obtained until the prisoners were brought home. Time alone revealed that imagination never bears comparison with reality.

[56] *Parliamentary Commission. Appendix XI*, Copenhagen 1951, pp. 59f.
[57] The fragments which have been found so far have been skilfully pieced together by Yad Vashem in Jerusalem where video copies can be bought. Dr Karel Magry, of the University of Utrecht in the Netherlands, has re-arranged the clips according to the original script and is preparing a dissertation about the film.

From April 1944 onwards, the Ministry of Social Affairs worked systematically to have the Norwegian and Danish prisoners brought home from the German concentration camps and prisons.[58]

The vast number of prisoners throws the scope of this project into perspective: around 11,000 Danes and Norwegians were at this time in one of the thirty concentrations camps and around 2,000 in minor camps. When the Danish-Swedish relief action was terminated in May 1945, almost 20,000 prisoners had been brought back from Germany and the German-occupied territories by way of Neuengamme.

The initiative emanated originally from the Norwegian minister N. Chr. Ditleff through Borghild Hammerich, who was Norwegian and was married to the Danish Resistance leader, Rear-admiral Carl Hammerich. It reached the powerful head of department of the Ministry of Social Affairs, H. H. Koch. In July 1944 Borghild Hammerich and Koch went to Stockholm to plan a Scandinavian relief action prior to the anticipated collapse of the Third *Reich*. Efforts were considerably intensified when almost 2,000 Danish police officers were deported to Buchenwald. The Ministry of Social Affairs worked out a plan of emergency measures involving, among others, the Civil Air Defence, the National Health Service (the Serum Institute), the Danish State Railways, and the Danish Red Cross. The second office of the Ministry of Social Affairs (the Office of Public Welfare) developed into a regular control centre, staffed by H. H. Koch's collaborators, Mogens Kirstein, Svend Hansen and Finn Nielsen. The workings of the transportation system, in particular, were central. They established a Cartage Department of the Ministry of Social Affairs, a euphemism typical of the time, and kept track of and maintained the vehicles which DSB (the Danish State Railways) and other bus companies were able to supply.[59]

Moreover, the Ministry of Foreign Affairs practically camped on the doorstep of the German authorities in its attempt to have the prisoners brought home.

At the beginning of December, the barrier of a mass German refusal was finally broken. A small convoy of four DSB-buses, four ambulances, a lorry and a passenger car brought two hundred police officers and border gendarmes back to Denmark. The operation was not only a moral victory, giving hope for a turn in the attitude of the Nazis. In addition, the prisoners' reports on the ghastly conditions in the camps gave invaluable knowledge about the way in which future relief operations ought to be planned.[60] When the Swedish Red Cross produced men and equipment for the renowned Bernadotte action the preliminary work was done. The Danes were able to contribute plenty of practical knowledge and hard-won experience, but they lacked vehicles. In general the

---

[58]An excellent introduction to the various phases of the relief work is given by Jørgen Barfod in, *Redning fra Ragnarok*, Copenhagen 1983.

[59]Hæstrup, *Til landets bedste, op. cit.*, vol. II, pp. 182f. Erik Pontoppidan Sørensen, *Mine erindringer fra 2. verdenskrig. Del 2. Hjemtransporten af danske og norske fanger fra de tyske KZ-lejre i 1945*, p. 2. Unpubl. manuscript given to the author. Pontoppidan Sørensen offered himself, in his capacity as "traffic policeman", as driver for the transport home where he was one of the invaluable handymen in this corps of tireless and courageous men.

[60]Hæstrup, *Til landets bedste, op. cit.*, vol. II, pp. 169ff. and 185f. See also Record Office, Copenhagen, privatarkiv 6777, Finn Nielsen (2. pk.)

problem was that so many of the vehicles used a particular kind of gas: gas extracted from beechwood which was burnt in special stoves. This gas substantially reduced the speed and traction power of the vehicles. Likewise, drivers and mechanics were faced with almost insurmountable tasks due to the lack of spare parts and tyres, problems which, oddly enough, were almost always solved. It was absolutely vital to go. The Swedish expeditionary force of around 250 men and 75 vehicles was superbly equipped with the best and newest material from the army store. Without this "grant" one dare not think about how the rescue could have taken place.

Of course the rescue plans included the Danish Jews in Theresienstadt as well. However, in early April 1945 the fronts had converged so much that it was possible that American and Soviet troops might meet around Dresden. If this happened the road north from Theresienstadt, leading towards Denmark, would be blocked by military action. Thus, if a rescue operation was to succeed it would have to occur at the eleventh hour. Operating from their headquarters in Friedrichsruh close to Hamburg, the Swedish Red Cross and the Danish Ministry of Social Affairs had, since March, brought Danish and Norwegian prisoners from various concentration camps to Neuengamme. That this was feasible at all was due to an agreement between the head of the SS, Heinrich Himmler and the head of the Swedish Red Cross, Count Folke Bernadotte.[61]

However, it proved impossible to bring the Danish Jews to Neuengamme. Even in this last phase of the Third *Reich* the favour did not extend to bringing Aryans and Jews together in the same concentration camp. Bernadotte on the other hand, was allowed to take the Danish Jews directly to Sweden. Two incidents almost ruined the plans to bring all the prisoners home. The future of the police officers way out East in the Mühlberg camp and of the Jews in Theresienstadt way down South seemed more than uncertain.

At the end of March 1945 around half the Swedish staff left Friedrichsruh to go home. The staff of the Swedish auxiliary corps was in actual fact a regular military department in civilian clothes. The operation was, optimistically, planned to last for three to four weeks. The staff had all volunteered for duty – a large part of which took place in Sweden preparing the operation. That period had run out now, but half of them chose to continue. The mobility and readiness for action of the auxiliary corps was, however, reduced disastrously. The Danes became disappointed and disheartened and through their man on the spot, Frants Hvass, they conveyed the message to the Foreign Ministry in Copenhagen that now was the time to send new personnel and equipment. They did just that. On 1st and 3rd April, two big convoys left: 33 buses, 15 ambulances, 6 lorries and 7 passenger cars. In the days following the force was replenished with a couple of ambulances and lorries. At the evacuation of the camp at Neuengamme 90 additional buses, 8–10 ambulances, 10 lorries, 5–6 passenger cars, and 5–6 motorbikes were sent to Germany. The diesel-driven buses of DSB, from the Copenhagen-Køge route, were brought into action in the demanding shuttle service to the border and back. During April no less than 450 people were

---

[61] Hæstrup, *Til Landets bedste, op. cit.*, vol. II, pp. 266ff.

sent to Germany to staff the auxiliary corps, including 10 doctors and 16 nurses.[62]

On 8th April it was obvious to the Danish participants in the operation that the whole venture was about to fall through. The German administrative system had actually broken down, there were conflicts of authority between the SS and *Gestapo* and Bernadotte was pursuing his own diplomatic game. Lately he had become convinced that his hard-won right to gather the Scandinavian prisoners in Neuengamme and take them to Sweden would be wrecked if he continued to insist that the Red Cross buses were to go to Theresienstadt. The Germans considered this part of the rescue operation "inconvenient" and Bernadotte chose to yield to their position.

The decision stirred up consternation in the Danish camp and in desperation it was decided to carry out the trip as a purely Danish expedition, if necessary. Unfortunately the crucial permission from the *Gestapo* in Berlin was still missing. The medical superintendent Johannes Holm, who was the National Health Service man in Friedrichsruh, and a helpful *Obersturmbannführer* Rennau went to Berlin to try solve the problem on the spot. Thanks to an energetic effort, negotiated through an abundance of food, cigarettes and *snaps*, the necessary papers were conjured up. To the immense relief of the Danes it appeared that whatever Bernadotte and the Swedish Foreign Ministry considered to be wise, it was quite another matter what the action group in Friedrichsruh decided to do. Sven Frykman, the leader of the expeditionary force, noted with understandable pride:

> "At the agreed time the white convoy sailed past Friedrichsruh, just as minister Richert [the Swedish ambassador in Berlin] was having a conversation with the Foreign Ministry in Stockholm. Due to the critical situation it was pointed out that the expeditionary force was not to expose itself to any unnecessary risks. When the minister told them that a trip to Theresienstadt was to be carried out, he was told to do everything in his power to stop it. The minister answered: 'I'm sorry, I can't do anything about this now. From my window I see that the convoy is already on its way southward.' "[63]

As quick as lightning an armada of 23 buses, 6 lorries, a canteen, a repair van, a crane lorry, 3 passenger cars, and 3 motorcycles was equipped on 12th April. The Germans had demanded that the convoy first bring 400 Frenchmen from Neuengamme to Flossenbürg before collecting the Danish Jews. This barter increased the strain and delayed the expedition one precious day, but it was, on the other hand, carried out with Swedish equipment, employing cars with petrol engines and good tyres. Had the Danes carried out their intentions of going with

---

[62] Note in Finn Nielsen's private record, cf. note 48. All the figures are as approximate as the very hectic situation necessitated.

[63] Johannes Holm, *Sandheden om de hvide busser*, Copenhagen 1984; and Sven Frykmann, *Röda Korsexpeditionen till Tyskland*, Stockholm 1945. Frykman's book was recognised as the official account of the expedition. According to the preface it was written at the request of the Foreign Ministry and the Ministry of Social Affairs in Denmark. The quotation is from p. 57. Holm's book is based on accounts dictated shortly after the return to Denmark, cf. the preface of the book. A copy of the Theresienstadt description exists in Finn Nielsen's private record. This is not the place to resume the vehement discussion about the role of Bernadotte in the relief expedition as a whole. To the Danish reader, however, it is striking how little space the Swedish accounts give the Danish-Norwegian initiative.

their own gas buses, the journey would have taken a couple of days more. The result might well have been disastrous.

On the morning of 13th April 1945, Johannes Holm and his attendant Rennau arrived at the *Kommandantur* in Theresienstadt. They brought the appropriately signed and stamped papers from *Gestapo* headquarters in Berlin. The Camp Commandant, Karl Rahm, proved very obliging but would only release the Danes on the condition that the leader of *Zentralamt Prag* (the *Reich* governor) in Prague, *Sturmbannführer* Hans Günther, to whom Theresienstadt was responsible, gave his consent. Chief rabbi Max Friediger, who worked as the leader of the Danish Jews, was sent for and told by Johannes Holm to contact all the Danes immediately and tell them to pack their things instantly and come to "*die Schleuse*" in the "Jäger" barrack. The dumbfounded Friediger was also told that the Danish Foreign Ministry had arranged that all Danish Jews and the so-called stateless Danish Jews, i.e. the refugees, would be transferred to Sweden and that a Swedish convoy would come the following night to get them. Towards evening they were all assembled and waited for the buses to arrive at the camp.

The following day Holm and Rennau went to Prague to obtain the approval of Hans Günther. The next morning, Sunday 15th March, the Danes left Theresienstadt followed by a forest of waving hands and music played by the camp orchestra, which was called out for the occasion. For the remaining Jews the departure of the Danes was proof that the war would soon be over and that they also would be released. At the same time, however, fear of the future increased. Many had regarded the Danes as some kinds of guardian angels, defending the town against extermination.

The journey through the devastated Third *Reich* was very tense. Dresden, still burning, made a deep impression on the travellers. The situation was extremely dangerous and the leaders of the convoy were anxious to find out whether it was possible to pass the front north of Dresden where Potsdam was bombed to pieces. In the last resort they would turn around and go to Switzerland. Only one day late and without any accidents on the way, the convoy crossed the Danish border at Padborg on Tuesday 17th March and continued to Odense and Copenhagen and then on to the Swedish town of Malmö on the ferry the following day. The rescue operation had succeeded far beyond any expectations. It was almost a miracle. In the transport were 293 Danish Jews and 130 Jews, who were not Danish citizens, but who had been deported from Denmark in October 1943. By mistake, one Danish Jew and a stateless Jew had been left behind in the camp.[64]

In Sweden the Danes were quarantined in two camps. Now, having gained freedom, close to Denmark and close to the end of the war a degree of camp psychosis developed. The Danes had, for obvious reasons, had enough of camps and were somewhat dissatisfied with the Swedes' treatment of them. They found it thoughtless that the quay in Malmö was patrolled by soldiers armed with machine-guns and that people, on the whole, would barely touch them without wearing rubber gloves. In the two barrack camps, located on the edge of civilisation, men and women were once again separated, the food was not good

---

[64]Lists in the Record Office, Copenhagen, Ministry of Social Affairs, 2.kt., j.nr. 880/1943.

and the way they were treated was alienating. So it was a great relief for the Danes to be able to return home during the first week of May 1945.

If one consults the Office of Public Welfare file for the year 1943, there is an entry for "The Jews" written, unlike the other entries, only in pencil so that it could be quickly erased. In 1944 this entry was innocuously headed "The Social Service" in ink. The Social Service was yet another euphemism, characteristic of the relief work of the Ministry of Social Affairs between 1941 and 1945. The 1944 Fund for Social and Humanitarian Purposes has been mentioned above, as well as the Cartage Department of the Ministry of Social Affairs. These neutral designations hid the true functions, which were relief measures wholly or partly funded by the Ministry of Social Affairs with the consent of the Ministry of Finance. The head of department, H. H. Koch, said that there had been "an exceptionally good and informal co-operation between a number of different state and local authorities, private organisations and individuals, who had never worked together before". There was, for example, the case of the Copenhagen Welfare Department, which dealt with relief for the Jews, rather than the matter being dealt with by the municipality.[65] The basis for all this was Section 281 of the Public Welfare Act of 1938.

When Germany attacked the Soviet Union in the summer of 1941 the leading Danish Communists were interned at Horserød. There was no provision in the social legislation to provide help for people in this kind of situation, who were no longer able to support their families. As the administration wished to conceal their aid efforts from the occupying power they used Section 281 of the Public Welfare Law. The interned Communists were to be regarded as persons who had been drafted for special military service (!) and therefore had a right to lucrative benefits. Benefits were to be paid out by the local authorities and the Ministry of Social Affairs would refund all the money. Support was given for all overheads, including rent, heating, electricity, insurance and various debts, as well as living expenses. These arrangements were set up by informing the relevant authorities orally in order to avoid alerting the Germans to what was going on.

When the Jews were deported to Theresienstadt, the Section 281 system was already in place and could be used immediately. In the meantime it had been extended to cover a steadily growing account in the budget from which money was channelled out, both legally and illegally, to various relief measures. Legal help included funds for the food parcels. Money was also channelled into the "1943 Relief Fund", a cover organisation which, among other things, contributed money needed to finance the escape to Sweden. Already after the first week in October, the Ministry of Social Affairs in co-operation with the Copenhagen Welfare Department and the police took upon themselves the task of keeping an eye on Jewish property. Keys to apartments and shops were obtained, although if necessary the premises were broken into. They then made inventories of

---

[65]H. H. Koch, Svend Hansen and Finn Nielsen, 'Træk af Social-ministeriets arbejde under Besættelsestiden', in *Den danske centraladministration 1848–1948*, Copenhagen 1948, pp. 63–86; Record Office, Copenhagen, Ministry of Social Affairs, 2.kt. j.nr. 880/1943.

valuables, stored furniture, paid the rent and so on. Where shops or businesses could be kept open, caretakers were appointed.[66] On the whole the system worked satisfactorily, but in cases where agreements had been made in great haste things sometimes went wrong. Occasionally, an apartment was cleared out and inhabited by someone else or a shop got a new owner. After almost two years in Theresienstadt the returned Jews did not always have sufficient strength to fight the Justice Department and the insurance companies. But in the end at least they had survived.

As time went by the Danish Jews reintegrated into the society from which they had been torn. Unlike other groups of concentration camp prisoners, the concern about what had happened to them quickly dissipated. This suited them well. The knowledge that they were the only national group from which none had been transported to the gas chambers in Auschwitz was undoubtedly decisive. Thanks to the food parcels they did not look like human skeletons on their return home, so that some people got the impression that their fate had not been too harsh. In this strange way Nazi propaganda about the "model ghetto" of Theresienstadt was kept alive, at least in Denmark, long past its time.

---

[66] *Københavns Kommune 1940–1955. Udgivet af Københavns Magistrat*, Copenhagen 1955, pp. 253f.

Displaced Persons and Emigrants

American Relief and Jews in Germany, 1945–1960

Diverging Perspectives

BY RONALD WEBSTER

The following researches focus overwhelmingly on the relations between the New York-based American Jewish Joint Distribution Committee ("Joint" or "JDC") and the Jews who still found themselves on German soil at the end of the Second World War. In fact it was left largely to the Joint to undertake the Herculean task after 1945 of providing relief and emigration possibilities, eventually for almost 200,000 Jews.[1] While it was not the only support organisation to do this, the duration of the Joint's effort, the funds and personnel it deployed allow one to focus almost exclusively on its efforts on behalf of the remnant of European Jewry collected in several and finally one German camp: Föhrenwald near Munich.

Thematically, this paper will chiefly emphasise attitudes, since these reveal the author's main thesis that a serious gulf existed between the indisputably humane goals of the Joint and those of the remnant of the Displaced Persons (DPs) in Germany, the so-called "hardcore", which proved so difficult to resettle after 1945.

In analysing this relationship three main perspectives will be given especial attention. Firstly, how did the resettlement and integration policies of the US-based organisation and its Jewish allies affect relations with Jewish DPs? Secondly, how did the Joint and other support groups cope with the entirely unexpected phenomenon of Jewish DPs – the so-called "illegals" – who after 1949 actually returned to Germany, mainly from Israel, and who also, temporarily at least, reversed the process of relocating the DP population dependent on Joint assistance at Föhrenwald? Thirdly, how did the internationally respected American Joint Distribution Committee cope with the embarrassing phenomenon of illegal activities by a minority of the hardcore DPs?

Before these questions are considered, however, a brief statistical overview is necessary. When the killing stopped in 1945 over 300,000 displaced persons still found themselves in the territory of the former German *Reich*. Of these some forty thousand were Jews. Over the twelve years of activity on behalf of the Jewish DP

---

[1]It is important to note that the Joint Distribution Committee, and other Jewish agencies given less treatment here, were mandated to seek countries of refuge for Jewish DPs, but this was not, as was the case with some non-Jewish DPs, with the direct involvement of their leadership groups.

population, support agencies looked after a peak of over 200,000 in 1946–1947, down to 633 in the last full year of operation (1956) now concentrated exclusively in the Föhrenwald camp, with the last twelve persons leaving Föhrenwald on 28th February 1957.[2] What prolonged the closing of the camp for over a decade was, in part, that between 1949 and 1954 some 3,500 Jews returned to Europe and Germany from Israel. In its last years these people eventually were to make up approximately 50% of the Föhrenwald camp's population.[3]

In the summer of 1945 the situation for all DPs was desperate. In their work with Jewish DPs this desperation was intensified by the difficulties support agencies abroad encountered in rushing to their assistance. As Juliane Wetzel has indicated in her study, *Jüdisches Leben in München*, these had initially to do with cutting through the very thick red tape of military bureaucracy in that turbulent summer.[4] Thus it was not until late September 1945 that the American Joint Distribution Committee was able to reach the larger camps and to begin its humanitarian work on behalf of the Jewish survivors.[5] The problems these survivors faced were totally unimaginable. There was no civilian postal service, the camps were hopelessly overcrowded, Jewish survivors there were jammed together with non-Jewish DPs, a number of whom had co-operated with the National Socialists,[6] and Jewish DPs were frequently bereft of religious facilities and essential social contacts.[7]

Since most of the DPs gravitated to the US zone of occupation after the war's end,[8] it was inevitable that the US military would have to deal with them. In the short term this made things even more difficult, for there appears to have been some reluctance on the part of the American military at the time to recognise the special problems of Jewish DPs, indeed preference seems to have been given to other Displaced Persons, even to the Germans themselves.[9] Friends or critics, however, agree that the armed forces were badly prepared and ill-equipped to

---

[2] Of course, after 1957, international Jewish financial support continued to assist the German-Jewish population and Jewish DPs in Germany and other countries. But their work in helping DP Jews either to settle or emigrate ended in 1957.

[3] These figures were taken from various annual country directors' reports filed in the Archives of the American Jewish Joint Distribution Committee, New York (hereafter JDC) and the Archives of the YIVO Institute for Jewish Research, New York (hereafter YIVO). See Yehuda Bauer, 'The Initial Organization of the Holocaust Survivors in Bavaria', in *Yad Vashem Studies VIII* (1970), p. 153. The years 1945, 1953, 1956 and 1957 were selected.

[4] Juliane Wetzel, *Jüdisches Leben in München 1945–1951. Durchgangsstation oder Wiederaufbau?*, München 1987, pp. 70–94, esp. pp. 70–73.

[5] *Ibid.*, p. 71. In the Joint Offices in New York in December 1991, the author met Stanley Abramovitch, the first Joint field-worker to visit Föhrenwald and other Jewish DP centres in 1945. His 1945 report on these early problems, taken from the Joint archives, is in the author's possession.

[6] Wetzel, *op. cit.*, p. 274, speaks of non-Jewish DPs in the early camps who were as antisemitic as the Germans. On this, see also Leonard Dinnerstein, *America and the Survivors of the Holocaust*, New York 1982, p. 49.

[7] Wetzel, *op. cit.*, pp. 71–72.

[8] According to Leonard Dinnerstein, by the summer of 1947 157,000 Jewish DPs found themselves in the US zone, while there were only 15,000 in the British and 10,000 in the French zones; Dinnerstein, *op. cit.*, Appendix A, 'A Statistical Synopsis', Table A.2, p. 278.

[9] Dinnerstein provides trenchant cases of blatant antisemitism among the US military, citing especially General George Patton in this connection. Even Eisenhower at the time appears to have dragged his feet on the Jewish DP problem; *ibid.*, chaps. 1 and 2.

deal with what came to be a mounting problem of Jewish and other DPs who, by 1946, were streaming into the US zone in entirely unanticipated numbers. For example, by December 1946 these amounted to no less than a total of 1.2 million DPs of all kinds.[10]

Nor was this the only problem. A fierce political battle had already broken out in the United States when hostilities stopped in 1945 about increasing or maintaining the existing immigration quotas. Unable at the time to change existing restrictive quotas for DPs, and equally unable to get the British to allow the Jewish DPs to emigrate freely to Palestine, the whole, apparently insoluble, problem fell back into the lap of the armed forces in Germany.

The occupying armies thus found themselves obliged to help these survivors on an *ad hoc* basis and other international relief organisations, especially the United Nations Relief and Rehabilitation Administration (UNRRA), were also at work attempting to deal with the momentous problems of the DPs as a whole. However, given their rapidly increasing numbers, the army could only devote part of its funds and human efforts specifically to the Jewish survivors, while at the same time these pathetic remnants of European Jewry were often the most in need of care.

Admittedly, soon after the National-Socialist capitulation the most basic necessities – food – were looked after expeditiously by the army and UNRRA, but in reality the actual needs of the Jewish survivors were less material and more human. They felt isolated without postal facilities and other basic amenities; they felt the world, and especially international Jewish organisations, was ignoring their plight. Thus, in a fit of desperation over the apparent tardiness of the Joint to help them, one survivor was prompted to write: "if you can't give us things, give us some Yiddish typewriters so we can criticise the JDC to Jews of the world".[11]

Who were these Jewish DPs who found themselves still in the land of their tormentors after hostilities ceased? The greatest percentage were Eastern European Jews, either liberated in Germany in 1945, or subsequent escapees from Poland and other Eastern European states upon the closing of the Iron Curtain. That is to say they were not German Jews but Polish, Russian, Baltic and a few survivors of the once flourishing Balkan Jewish population. This situation created a special difficulty, especially after 1949, because most of these DPs often were unable and just as often unwilling to return to their homelands. Moreover, as they had not been citizens of the former German *Reich* after 1945 they did not enjoy the legal status of their German-Jewish counterparts. And after German sovereignty was restored, at first piecemeal and then more definitively in 1949, problems connected with their alien status were also magnified.

Therefore, the needs of these people would be long-term, the difficulties of resettlement enormous, especially in the years 1945–1948, until at least the formation of the independent state of Israel. And by the middle of 1947 some

[10]*Ibid.*, pp. 57–59, cites 1,243,263 as of 31st December 1946.
[11]Wetzel, *op. cit.*, p. 72.

180,000 Jews had found their way into German and other European DP camps,[12] most of whom were waiting for resettlement in Israel and the United States. In the light of these numbers, their human problems and the cost of resettlement, of other forms of financial and moral support, a major task for the Joint and its ancillary organisations presented itself.

Here, too, one has to recall just what kinds of experiences these Jewish DPs had endured. They were survivors of death camps, some had been forced to clear the gas ovens of Auschwitz, Treblinka and Chelmno, and they represented the remnants of the few ghettos still in existence at the end of the fighting. They had been slave labour in those camps which had industrial connections, especially again those around Auschwitz-Birkenau. Many of them, fortunate to escape the National-Socialist criminals, had endured the hardships of war and Stalinism in the Soviet Union. Most of them had, therefore, suffered serious and often irreparable physical and, even more importantly, mental damage.

There was another, somewhat specialised problem for the Jewish DPs. While the majority of them could draw on the assistance of relief organisations to find a new homeland and to begin a semblance of normalcy again, an important minority of the difficult DP "hardcore" cases found itself unable to follow suit. This hardcore consisted of people who, mainly for health reasons,[13] could not emigrate and who could actually with only the very greatest difficulty be integrated into the German economy. This human problem was to be a major issue for support agencies, for when they had to look after the needs of such Jews the agencies were frequently dealing with persons who would probably never again be able to lead normal lives; whose physical condition alone was so debilitated that they could never work, or at least not at full capacity.

And then there were the Germans themselves. As the years passed, their attitude to the Jewish DPs became more callous. Why? Firstly, because they had their own refugee masses to deal with, some 11 million in all by 1961, and secondly, because the huge task of economic recovery and a re-establishment of the German infrastructure demanded immense financial resources. In the face of their own problems, many average Germans predictably viewed the remaining Jewish DPs as rather privileged parasites, demanding financial compensation from severely limited resources, lodging comfortably in what Germans wrongly perceived to be opulent refugee centres like Föhrenwald.

It is important to interject here, that what could well have led to this misperception was the unique organisation and ambience of Camp Föhrenwald. Formerly a settlement for workers involved in Hitler's war industries, Föhrenwald had never been a concentration camp. After it was made off-limits in 1945 to all except Jewish DPs, it was gradually to have its own kosher kitchens, synagogues, kindergartens, primary schools, retraining centres for young people and adults, and a host of shops and other enterprises run by DPs from the camp itself. It even had its own Jewish police until the Germans took over in 1951. This, indeed, made the camp attractive to the inhabitants, and helps to explain

[12]See above, note 8. Dinnerstein lists 182,000 Jewish DPs by the summer of 1947.
[13]The most serious health cases had to do with tuberculosis. Open cases were almost impossible to send abroad and non-contagious ones, the so-called "post-TBs", only with considerable difficulty.

its popularity among the DPs during its lifetime.[14] Therefore, during its existence the envious Germans saw "Föhrenwälder" living in plenty while they suffered from want; thus they were disposed to exaggerate its luxuries from less than laudable, usually antisemitic, motives.

This antisemitism was further intensified by examples of a small number of DPs who had become deeply involved, like almost everyone else in post-1945 Germany, in black market activities, in prostitution and, especially in the 1950s, in organising illegal re-immigration into Germany.

Thus, after 1945 a formidable task lay before international Jewish agencies, a task exacerbated by the fact that, while their people were for the most part dedicated and competent, they often just could not really fathom the mentality of DPs. The latter saw themselves better looked after in what they perceived to be their warm Föhrenwald nest than opting for the uncertain vistas of a new life even in *Eretz Israel*, not to mention the questionable prospects of integration into a Western Germany, which, by the 1950s, was beginning its first phase of an economic miracle, the preoccupation with which served to induce within the German psyche a state of mass amnesia respecting memories of and responsibilities for the terrible but recent past.

In handling the many-faceted relations and in fulfilling their mandate to help them, the support groups interacted with the Jews in Germany at two important levels: firstly, on the level of the German-Jewish leadership group and the DP committees in Camp Föhrenwald; secondly, on the level of direct involvement with the camp population as a whole.

A. THE JOINT AND THE LEADERSHIP

Six main issues formed the core of differences at the leadership level. Firstly, there was a serious "personality clash" between Joint representatives and both German-Jewish leaders and the camp executive. Secondly, the Joint especially distrusted the Föhrenwald committee's stubborn determination to keep the camp going, as in their view this intentionally encouraged the return of the "illegals", usually as a "staging area" for re-emigration to the United States.[15] Thirdly, Joint representatives and the committees eventually came to differ about the German take-over of Föhrenwald or, failing that, to hinder its eventual closing. Fourthly, both the German Jews and the camp committees disagreed, often vehemently, with the Joint about the amounts of German compensation the Jews were entitled to or had received, especially as the international Claims Conference negotiated a settlement with the Germans in 1952. In particular they disagreed about the recognition of the Föhrenwald committee at the bargaining

---

[14]For a description of Camp Föhrenwald, including some contemporary photographs, see Wetzel, *op. cit.*, pp. 244–262 and *passim*. See also the illustrations between pp. 310–311.

[15]It is important to note that the United States remained the country of choice throughout for the DPs. In 1952, for example, of the 688 persons who secured immigrant visas, 474 went to the US, 128 to Latin American countries and 86 to Israel. JDC, File 398, Charles Passman report of 30th November 1952.

table in 1952. Fifthly, an "iron curtain" of mistrust eventually descended between the Joint officials and the camp committees because of alleged cases of DP criminality and, moreover, because the Joint suspected that the camp leaders wished to avoid litigation over the extra-legal activities of DPs by hiding behind the Joint and other international support agencies. Finally, there existed a wide ideological gap between Joint policy and that of the Jewish leaders in Germany. For the Joint, all roads led either to DP emigration or integration into the German economy. For the DP leaders, the continued existence of a Jewish refugee camp on German soil had advantages, the most important of which was the possibility of remaining outside German jurisdiction while enjoying financial support from refugee grants and from the German welfare system.

Taking up the first point: the low esteem in which the Jewish leadership in Germany was held by Joint officials: this is clearly expressed in a 1952 letter by Samuel Haber, the Joint's director for Germany, to the head of the *"Zentralrat für die Juden in Deutschland"*, Hendrick van Dam. Haber wrote "we have on a number of occasions discussed the leadership in the Zentralrat and Landesverbaende and we both deplore the fact that no really outstanding Jewish personality can be found in Germany today to act as a real leader of the Jewish community here".[16] On this occasion Haber also questioned whether, for the Joint at least, van Dam himself was a worthy representative of German Jewry when he bitterly censured him for having previously agreed to a common policy in a meeting, only to have apparently reneged on it in an article van Dam had just written in the official organ of the German-Jewish community.[17]

A strong supporter of Joint work in Germany, Jakob Altmaier, a German-Jewish parliamentarian, expressed even more vitriolic opinions about Karl Marx, another leading member of the German-Jewish community and van Dam's close associate. Marx was the editor of the leading Jewish journal in Germany, the *Allgemeine Wochenzeitung der Juden in Deutschland*, and appears to have aroused similar emotions in his critics as had his illustrious namesake. Referring to the 1952 dispute about DP compensation claims,[18] Altmaier labelled the intervention of Marx and his friends as "ugly troublemaking", even asserting that if Marx and his supporters had had their way "they would have torpedoed" the negotiations. As to Marx personally, Altmaier was prompted to describe his conduct as "libellous", "questionable" and even "criminal", escalating his vitriolic assessment of the man by saying that Marx was beneath contempt. The parliamentarian, however, consoled himself with the observation that "one has to absorb such . . . refuse (*Abfallprodukte*) of these gruesome events of our times".[19] In somewhat more measured tones, the 1953 'Report on Germany' corroborated Altmaier's negative assessment of the German-Jewish

---

[16]JDC, File 375, Samuel Haber to Hendrick van Dam, 3rd June 1952. Haber was a key player in the Joint's German operations in the 1950s. As its director for Germany, he and Charles Jordan were the mainsprings of DP policy; oral testimony from Theodore (Ted) Feder, Joint Offices, New York, May and December 1991.

[17]See below, p. 304, for further references to this dispute.

[18]See below, Section C, for a more detailed consideration of this issue.

[19]Jakob Altmaier to Robert Weltsch, 27th June 1952, in Robert Weltsch Papers, Leo Baeck Institute Archives (LBIA), New York, File AR 7185, 1948–1977, 'General Correspondence'.

leadership, by asserting that it sadly lacked such [leadership] qualities, calling its compensation claims at the time "spurious and inflated" and complaining generally of its tendency to demand generous support for almost non-existent Jewish *Gemeinden*. Here the report cited the example of Augsburg which, in 1953, had only one Jewish couple, but for whom van Dam and Marx wanted a host of community services left open.[20]

Parallel with this very low regard for the leaders of German-Jewish survivor organisations, the Joint people seemed to hold their Jewish DP camp counterparts responsible for providing an equally formidable barrier to a harmonious working relationship. An example of this was the case of one of Föhrenwald's committee members, Jakob Goldfarb. According to a 1990 conversation this author had with Ted Feder, a Joint field executive at the time, Goldfarb was, for the Joint, among the most unpopular members of the camp committee. As an example of this, Feder related how Goldfarb once informed him that, after his emigration to Norway (arranged with great difficulty by Feder and the Joint field workers), he was going to refuse to accept any work other than sewing hems on rabbinical garments and, since none was needed in Norway, Goldfarb would have thereby conveniently secured the continuation of his idle camp existence.[21]

The Joint's Charles Jordan[22] also wrote with some passion and bitterness about his own experiences with the camp committee personalities. In 1954 he wrote to Moses Beckelman, head of the Paris office, describing the camp leadership as follows: "The committee is unwilling to defend any policy except to give everybody what he asks for and let everybody do as he wants." Thus Jordan came to the unhappy conclusion that the Föhrenwald leadership "is not a committee with which we can do business", calling it, moreover, a "curse for the camp population". He believed that the committee stood in the way of effecting the emigration of the hardcore refugees.[23] Jordan continued by suggesting that the Joint appeal to camp inmates over the heads of their committee, and failing that close the Joint liaison office in Föhrenwald, the Munich office of Joint, and finally repair to Frankfurt. Moreover, Jordan proposed to bring into the fray US Jewish support groups and donors of monies for the DPs, to separate the DPs from their irresponsible leaders. Thus he wrote: "it would be worth our while to publicise our position . . . and pull no punches".[24] Perhaps the following curious episode prompted Jordan to such strong views: Joint officials claimed, in a June

---

[20]JDC, File 381, 'Report on Germany to 1953 Directors Conference', Joint Country Directors Conference, pp. 13–15.
[21]Interview of 13th December 1990 with Ted Feder at the New York Joint Archives.
[22]Of all the Joint executives and field workers, none was more active in the German DP question than Charles Jordan, then in charge of the Joint's Paris office. Jordan had a long and laudable career with the Joint, stretching from the 1930s, when he participated in the tragic and abortive 1939 *St. Louis* refugee ship negotiations in Cuba, to crucial relief work during the Second World War. Jordan's life was to end tragically and mysteriously in August 1967. After being arrested by the secret police, he was said to have suffered a heart attack. His body was, however, found in the river in Prague. For a personal reminiscence about Jordan, see 'The Mysterious Death of Charles Jordan', in *Dangers, Tests and Miracles. The Remarkable Life Story of Chief Rabbi Rosen of Romania, as told to Joseph Finklestone*, London 1990, pp. 215–223.
[23]Report by Charles Jordan, 21st April 1954, JDC, File 397, p. 8.
[24]*Ibid.*, p. 9.

1954 report, that the camp committee was accusing it of Communist espionage and was calling on Senator Joseph McCarthy to investigate such practices![25]

If possible, Jordan was to be outdone in his low estimation of the camp committee by a devastating 1958 report made by Dr. Erich Rosenberg at a Joint executive committee meeting in New York. In it he stated bluntly that "the camp leader is a criminal surrounded by gangsters".[26] Finally, perhaps the exasperated comments of a field worker, Mary Pavlevsky, at the end of the Joint's Föhrenwald work in 1955, may stand as an emblematic summation of its frustrations in working with the camp committees. Leaning heavily on Churchillian rhetoric Pavlevsky wrote: "never have so few people created so much work for so many, for so little".[27]

Adding to the Joint's troubles was the popular election of the camp committees. After UNRRA turned over its duties for DPs to the International Refugee Organisation (IRO), then in 1951 to the Germans, such popular elections merely fortified the bargaining power of the committees, thereby enabling them to block the closure of Camp Föhrenwald, a goal central to the Joint's mandate. As time passed, and the Joint attempted with growing urgency to wind up its responsibilities for the inmates of the camp, its representatives voiced with growing frequency the complaint that the committee was a reason for the extremely slow progress made in placing the remaining inmates elsewhere; indeed that the committee was actually allowing illegal returnees back into the camp at a time when the Joint and the Germans were desperately attempting to liquidate it completely.[28]

As more and more camp inhabitants either emigrated or were integrated into the German economy, the Joint representatives became increasingly apprehensive about new committees that would be elected, since the selection pool now consisted of the representatives of the extreme hardcore cases, of people whom the Joint was not anyway inclined to trust very far.[29] After several years of confrontations, of sit-ins and protests by the committee and inhabitants of Föhrenwald, and especially after the refugee organisations had to deal with the "illegals" and medical hardcores, relations between the support groups and the committees continued to be most strained.

B. THE JOINT AND THE FÖHRENWALD CAMP POPULATION

Relations with the camp inhabitants were also to reveal similar patterns. A perennial issue between the support groups and the people of Föhrenwald was

---

[25] JDC, File 397, report of 14th June 1954.
[26] Dr. Erich Rosenberg's report to the Joint Executive Committee, 4th June 1958, JDC, File 375, p. 15. In a subsequently edited appendage (p. 34), Jordan gives his emphatic approval to Rosenberg's dramatic exposé. According to Ted Feder, Rosenberg's main function in the organisation was as Jordan's personal confidant, sent to Germany by Jordan at the time to survey the DP situation; conversation with Feder, 18th December 1991, Joint Offices, New York.
[27] JDC, File 396, report of 2nd September 1955, Mary Pavlevsky to Charles Jordan.
[28] JDC, File 397, Field Workers Report for 1954, p. 3.
[29] These sentiments were expressed in a report by Leonard Seidenman dated 6th October 1952, JDC, File 397, p. 19.

the very future of the camp itself. At the beginning of their relationship, however, such differences were not inevitable. In fact, in 1951, when the German civilian authorities took over Föhrenwald, the Joint representatives actually expressed both their own concerns and their sympathy for the opposition of the camp community to the transfer. Thus, Sam Haber, the head of the Joint for Germany, expressed such sympathies when, just before the German authorities took over in November 1951, he wrote that he feared they would lack tact in supervising the camp. He promised at the time to do everything to protect and represent the DPs after the change of jurisdiction.[30] To document the fears of camp inhabitants themselves, the Joint files contain a strong letter of complaint about the transfer at the time by Jakob Goldfarb, the same person with whom the Joint was eventually to cross swords when Goldfarb was later elected to the camp committee.[31]

In spite of opposition to the move within the DP camp at Föhrenwald and of Joint reservations, in December 1951 the West Germans took over and, as Haber had previously predicted, it was not long before a serious confrontation ensued. In May 1952 German police virtually stormed it to investigate illegal business activities allegedly emanating from the camp. The Germans brought dogs and were armed. They were greeted by stones and bottles from the inhabitants and, in order to quell the disturbance, the police even had to fire a warning shot. Indeed, Haber described the police methods at this time as "typically German" reminding one "of Nazi *Einsatz* squads".[32] Even the German administrators in the camp declared themselves in total sympathy with the DPs.[33] On this occasion DP letters of protest went out to Chancellor Adenauer, President Heuss, Churchill and President Truman in which the "Föhrenwälder" asserted that the German police had also used abusive antisemitic epithets.[34] Joint representatives intervened in this particular crisis and called a general camp meeting, managing thereby to smooth the ruffled feelings of the DPs.

Despite this expression of support, in the remaining years of Föhrenwald's life the Joint's efforts on the inhabitants' behalf did not succeed in establishing an amicable relationship between them. Leading to these tensions were the very real pressures – indeed the Joint's mandate to close the camp[35] – and its perception that the inhabitants were showing, at best, lukewarm enthusiasm for its agenda. For example, Joint officials became exasperated at perceived DP obstreperousness respecting the Joint's efforts to find them countries of emigration. As evidence of this, the Joint files contain the case of a "post-TB" couple. According to these files, in 1955 the husband was revealing a serious reluctance to emigrate to Israel since he felt his health would not prove up to the rigours of pioneer life

---

[30]Samuel Haber to M. Laub, AJDC, New York, 2nd November 1951, JDC, File 398.
[31]Jakob Goldfarb to the Lagerverwaltung, Föhrenwald, 28th December 1951, JDC, File 398. See also note 21.
[32]Wetzel, *op. cit.*, p. 260, cites a letter of Haber's to Charles Jordan in Paris contained in the JDC files.
[33]*Ibid.*, p. 259.
[34]*Ibid.*, p. 260.
[35]In 1962 a Joint official, Boris Sapir, summed up its policy as follows: "our main efforts were directed towards the liquidation of the Camp Föhrenwald, i.e. resettlement overseas or integration in Germany of the camp residents", JDC, File 396, report of 24th May 1962.

there and Joint representatives suspiciously presumed that he vaguely wished to get an American visa, although they were inclined to believe that what he really preferred was to remain in Germany, "meanwhile projecting his inability to emigrate on JDC's stinginess".[36] In fairness, the Joint people did not make the camp inhabitants solely responsible for the difficulties they found in trying to settle the hardcore abroad, especially in Israel, but rather at various times blamed the government officials for not wanting these people, especially because of their health problems.[37] And, as the following sections will reveal, other equally serious differences were to emerge to plague Joint–Föhrenwald relations, not the least of which was the thorny question of Jewish compensation from the Germans.

C. DISPUTES OVER MATERIAL CLAIMS

The author has treated elsewhere examples of restitution (*Wiedergutmachung*) for returning Jews holding German citizenship.[38] As already indicated in this paper, for DPs the situation was more complicated because they were not German citizens and thus could not claim restitution for lost property and other punitive financial measures taken against Jews of German citizenship in the 1930s, but rather had to focus exclusively on compensation claims. Indeed, it was only when the subject of compensation beyond German Jews arose in the early 1950s that the plight of Jewish DPs was addressed at all.

This happened when DP compensation demands were linked to claims made after 1948 by the Israeli government and international Jewish organisations for compensation for the Nazi crimes, for the surviving DPs and on behalf of those Jewish victims who had not survived the Holocaust and where there were no immediate heirs. Already in 1951 indirect negotiations had begun between the Israelis, the West Germans and a group of Jewish support organisations, all of whom took upon themselves the task of representing the heirless Jewish victims of the Holocaust. These negotiations were protracted, partly because of the obvious and understandable Israeli wish not to deal directly with the Germans, and because of the complications arising from representing claims for family victims all of whose members had disappeared in the Holocaust.[39]

---

[36] Joint report [no author given], 20th January 1955, JDC, File 396.
[37] Several Joint reports confirm this. JDC, File 398, 7th July 1951, p. 4: "post-TBs who had emigrated to Israel wrote back to their friends in Germany that conditions were unfavourable for them to maintain themselves physically there"; or *ibid.*, *marginalium*, p. 5: "The Families are kept in a TB-Gemeinschaft – can't get jobs"; or File 396, 10th February 1955, case of S.S.: "considered a poor candidate for emigration to that country, in view of his bad health conditions on the one hand and because of his limited work capacity on the other".
[38] See Ronald Webster, 'Why They Returned. How They Fared. Jews in Germany After 1945', in *YIVO Annual of Jewish Social Science* (1993).
[39] For a recent interpretation of the negotiations between the Adenauer government, the Claims Conference and the Israelis, see Nani Sagi, 'Die Rolle der jüdischen Organisationen in den USA und die Claims Conference', in Ludolf Herbst and Constantin Goschler (eds.), *Wiedergutmachung in der Bundesrepublik Deutschland*, München 1989, pp. 99–118.

In order to press more effectively the claims for both restitution and compensation in the name of the heirless estates and the DPs, in 1952 the international Jewish agencies set up a Claims Conference and elected the Joint's Moses Leavitt as its delegate for the negotiations with the West Germans,[40] while his colleague, Jacob Blaustein, was elected Claims Conference vice-president. Blaustein had previously headed an American-based claims committee set up the end of the war.[41]

The negotiations conducted in Wassenaar, Holland, resulted in a compromise whereby the Israelis received 3.45 billion DM in goods over a fourteen-year period while the Claims Conference received 450 million DM out of the Israeli share. Moreover, the Germans agreed to introduce a Compensation Bill into the *Bundestag* to cover individual claims not taken care of by the earlier Restitution decrees and bills.[42]

The results of these negotiations had an immediate impact on the attitudes of Jewish DPs still in Germany, as some of them now began to anticipate large sums coming to them out of the 450 million DM the Claims Conference had received. Moreover, these expectations led DPs, whose emigration was now imminent, to postpone their departure from Germany and to hamper the Joint in its strenuous efforts to find suitable host countries for what was by 1952–1953 largely a very hard-to-place group of long-term DPs.

One incident can stand perhaps as illustrative of this, especially of how precipitously Jewish DPs tended to react to rumours about compensation at the time, and of how symptomatic these tendencies were of camp life: whenever possible to act suddenly and *uni sono*. Thus, a Joint field executive recently told the author of a group of 100 post-tubercular DPs, bound by train from Föhrenwald for Sweden in 1953 when the news spread quickly throughout the train that the *Bundestag* was just then debating new DP compensation measures. Suddenly near Heidelberg the DPs told the field worker to stop the train and then they all disembarked, informing the exasperated Joint official that they would not proceed to Sweden until they learned about the new compensation provisions the *Bundestag* was arranging for them. They then remained at a railway siding until, with the greatest difficulty, the field worker persuaded them to get on the train again. The Joint representative's winning argument was that, if they persisted with their "strike", their Swedish visas would expire and all the strenuous Joint efforts to place them in that country would have been in vain.[43] Such actions betray a combination of mistrust and anxieties experienced only by people who have been through what in fact all Jewish DPs had endured in and after the war.

On this subject the Joint was also to experience problems with local German-Jewish organisations which supported both the DPs and other Jews residing in

---

[40]Nahum Goldmann did not lead the delegation, as he wished to keep his hands free to intervene in the event that difficulties arose between the two sides at Wassenaar; Sagi, *loc. cit.*, p. 113.
[41]*Ibid.*, pp. 103, 109.
[42]*Ibid.*, p. 116.
[43]As related to the author by Ted Feder, New York, December 1991. Mr. Feder was the Joint Official who had to deal with this little 1953 crisis.

Germany seeking compensation after 1945. The most important of these organisations, the *Zentralrat* and its leaders, Hendrik van Dam and Karl Marx, have already been briefly alluded to. Van Dam was to annoy the Joint again at this time, since he was himself a participant at the Wassenaar negotiations of 1951–1952 and harboured then and later a more extreme position on compensation claims than the Joint itself.[44] Therefore, in June 1952 during the Wassenaar negotiations, Sam Haber of the Joint severely censured van Dam personally for complaining in Marx's *Allgemeine* of a lukewarm attitude both of the Joint and other international Jewish groups towards the interests of the Jews residing in Germany.[45] Into 1953 Joint officials continued their criticisms of van Dam, the *Zentralrat* and the German-Jewish communities, accusing them of an unwarranted fixation with compensation. "To an abnormally large extent", one Joint representative wrote, "the Zentralrat and the [German-Jewish] communities have centered almost all of their activities on matters of compensation and restitution, ignoring the long range community needs . . ."[46] Their alleged excessive financial demands for synagogues and for Jewish retirement homes were especially singled out as emblematic of their lack of proportion, since the Joint saw the situation in a very different light, its representatives pointing out that, for 30,000 Jews, such opulence was really unnecessary.[47]

Supporting van Dam and Jews in Germany and also calling for more extensive restitution claims was a largely one-man exile organisation, Bruno Weil's Jewish Axis Victims League.[48] Ostensibly devoted to the claims of all victims of National Socialism, in the wake of the Wassenaar negotiations the New York-based League kept up a steady barrage of opposition to the alleged failure of the Joint and the Claims Conference to co-ordinate their efforts and extract even more than the 1952 claims had yielded from the Germans. Weil, a German-Jewish refugee, was able to provide special emphasis to his own criticisms because he entertained personal contacts with highly placed West Germans, foremost among them President Theodor Heuss and Chancellor Adenauer. He attempted to use these German connections to support his League, also van Dam and the German-Jewish leaders, who objected to what they perceived as too moderate Jewish demands *vis-à-vis* the West Germans.[49] While apparently

---

[44]Sagi, *loc. cit.*, p. 113.

[45]JDC, File 375, letter 3rd June 1952, Haber to van Dam. He was reacting to van Dam's article 'Das Erbe des deutschen Judentums', in *Allgemeine Wochenzeitung der Juden in Deutschland*, 9th May 1952.

[46]JDC, File 381, 'Report on Germany to 1953 Country Directors Conference', p. 14.

[47]Haber to van Dam, 2nd June 1952, JDC, File 375.

[48]Bruno Weil (1883–1968); forced to leave Germany in 1935, he went to the USA via France and Argentina. A jurist by training he had earlier established a considerable reputation as a lawyer and publicist by defending the civilians in the Zabern affair in 1913 and in writing a widely-read book on the Dreyfus Affair [1930], from which the 1930 German film of that name was taken. He established the Axis Victims League in New York and, with a few exceptions, was its sole driving force.

[49]Weil corresponded with and met President Heuss. In 1960 Weil was to have had an interview with Adenauer in New York, but the aging Chancellor seems to have decided to detour round him. In the Weil Papers in the LBIA there is a letter from the German Consul-General in New York excusing the Chancellor from the meeting due to "Terminschwierigkeiten", Folder No. 88a, AR C3055 7108, Generalkonsul Federer to Weil, 25th March 1960. In the same year, through his secretary, Heuss was in communication with Weil, *ibid.*, 18th January 1960.

supporting van Dam and Marx, Weil actually believed even they eventually did not go far enough for him, as he repeatedly criticised them for not wanting to "play the same tune" on the compensations subject.[50]

On behalf of the DPs, the Föhrenwald camp committee followed a similar policy to that of the German Jews by attempting to improve their own compensation chances. In 1953 the committee applied to be recognised as an official organisation under the terms of the Claims Conference in the hopes of receiving some of the monies set aside for this purpose. But in a November 1953 memorandum the Joint's Charles Jordan struck out decisively against such a move, asserting that it "will continue to immobilize the situation". Jordan rightly perceived at the time that, if it was officially recognised, Joint efforts to wind up the camp would come to naught, since the committee's new status would give Föhrenwald a new lease of life. Thus Jordan concluded: "I want to go on record *very strongly* to suggest that the Conference throw out the application *right now* on the grounds that it does not come from the kind of organisation which it can recognize."[51] This reveals yet again what has already been said about the low state of relations between the Föhrenwald leaders and the Joint. And Jordan's problems were also complicated at this juncture by the fact that on 1st October 1953 the West German *Bundestag* had finally passed its own compensation law, the *Bundesentschädigungsgesetz*, which merely heightened the expectations of the camp DPs and their desire to stay put until the implications of this new law became apparent.

Jordan was to continue thereafter to do battle, especially with the camp committee, on the subject of compensation. For by 1954 the committee was now taking the position that it could seek funds from the Germans both under the 1953 *Bundestag* law and from the proceeds of the Claims Conference, without these monies being counted – as Joint was bound to do – against welfare payments individual camp inhabitants were receiving.[52] So, in April 1954 Jordan again felt himself called upon to address the compensation issue in yet another strongly-worded letter to Moses Beckelman, this time in the shadow of a further confrontation and DP sit-in in February at the Joint offices in Munich.[53]

In fact, Jordan and the Joint were attempting at this time to pursue a new tactic: avoid the camp committee entirely in dealing with compensation, by arguing that: "We must try to "reach" the people in the camp directly and not through the committee."[54] He viewed the committee's compensation claims as exorbitant, asserting that they even wanted a family of four to have $10,000 to start them off. With heavy irony Jordan concluded: "I think that most people

---

[50]Bruno Weil Papers, LBIA, Weil to Karl Marx, 12th February 1960. On his differences with van Dam and Marx on compensation at this time, Weil wrote: "Aber niemand von Euch hat ja in dieses Horn stossen wollen."
[51]JDC, File 397, Jordan to Moses Beckelman, 1st November 1953. The italics are Jordan's.
[52]Thus in a 1953 report, Joint officials complained that DPs were not revealing all of their compensation income: "A great number . . . are receiving compensation from WGM [*Wiedergutmachung*] of which Joint knows only a part . . .", JDC, File 381, report of 17th May 1953, p. 11.
[53]Jordan to Beckelman, JDC, File 397, 21st April 1954.
[54]*Ibid.*, p. 9.

would agree, but would insist that this kind of social justice be made worldwide."[55]

In the final analysis, conflicting Joint-DP expectations arising from the 1952 agreements between the Adenauer and Ben-Gurion governments, and the subsequent West German compensation law, had serious implications for their relations and for Joint efforts to relocate the DPs. As long as DPs, or at any rate their leaders in Germany, expected to receive a "windfall" from these sources, and as long as they perceived it necessary to remain in the country, especially to process their claims *vis-à-vis* the Germans under the *Bundestag* law, the Joint's efforts to help them begin a new life abroad would be largely frustrated. For it must be recalled, that looming behind all of this was constant German pressure to disperse the DP camp at Föhrenwald and the parallel wish of the Joint and other support groups to end their obligations there and to find new homes and lives for the hardcore remnant of the Jewish DPs still in Germany. This wish was to be frustrated by the following difficulty.

D. THE PROBLEM OF ILLEGAL RETURNEES

The issue of illegal returnees, already briefly alluded to, was to create serious difficulties, certainly because this was never anticipated at any time before it actually began in 1949. For who would have anticipated that the Joint and the German authorities would be faced with returnees to the "verfluchte Erde" from Israel after that country gained its sovereignty in 1948? Yet this is precisely what occurred. Moreover, the continued existence of Föhrenwald acted as a magnet of sorts towards which the Israel returnees particularly gravitated, as they began to do as early as 1949.

The causes of this "re-immigration" were various. Some returnees found life in a pioneer country too difficult to master: or their personal difficulties were exacerbated by the fighting between Jews and Arabs in 1948 and after: or they returned because they feared that their often chronic medical problems could not be handled adequately in Israel.[56] Others were lured by the expectation of an easier job market than that of Israel in the 1950s.[57] Yet others viewed the German DP camp as a sort of "golden bridge", which would finally carry them across troubled bureaucratic waters to their most cherished destination: the United States. Finally the Adenauer–Ben-Gurion restitution negotiations of 1952 aroused hopes in some of personal compensation and they wished to be "on the spot" to arrange restitution for themselves.[58] Whatever the motive, these

---

[55]*Ibid.*, p. 5.

[56]In dramatic fashion, the *Jewish Morning Journal*'s special correspondent in Munich, Melech Chemney, related a number of stories of Jewish veterans of the 1948 war and those with serious medical problems. JDC, File 402, translation of Chemney's report of 4th July 1950, esp. p. 2.

[57]For example, the case of former German citizen, O. A., who returned in 1953 to supervise family restitution proceedings and who found the job situation in Germany more favourable than in Israel. Subsequently, his parents returned from Israel to West Germany and he and his children still live there. Interview with O.A., June 1989.

[58]See Section C above for a discussion of these issues.

returnees were to create unexpected burdens for the support groups and the German authorities.

Initially the Israel returnees found themselves in a state of limbo since there was no regulation to cover them, as the Germans (and Jewish relief organisations abroad) were totally unprepared for this development. Actually, to forestall a return to Germany, after 1948 the Israeli government had stamped the following in the visas of people leaving Israel: "not to be used to enter Germany", yet a surprising number of Jewish DPs did so anyway. Moreover, upon leaving Germany in the first place, emigrants forfeited their papers as stateless displaced persons, papers which had entitled them to support from the various sources during their period of waiting in Germany.[59]

In spite of this situation, after the first isolated Israeli stragglers appeared in Germany in 1949, the support groups admitted that the initial trickle of illegal returnees had in the meantime became a modest but perceptible stream.[60] By the end of 1951, when the German authorities took over supervision of Föhrenwald and other DP camps, it became necessary to address the Israel group seriously. As already indicated, their legal status was extremely complicated. For the Germans, the IRO and the Joint the returnees were Israeli citizens, as they were for the Israeli authorities. But the illegal returnees regarded themselves as stateless DPs and demanded back their rights under this status in order to be afforded financial and legal protection by the IRO, the Joint and the Jewish Agency operating in Germany. The relief groups, unwilling to recognise this DP demand, were then faced in the summer of 1950 with the first of what was to become a recurrence of returnee-staged sit-down strikes; for without legal status this was their only weapon. At this time illegal immigrants simply occupied the offices of the Jewish Agency, which acted as the unofficial Israeli consulate in Munich,[61] and refused to leave until their DP status was restored and financial assistance was given to them.

Newspaper reports at the time gave graphic descriptions of these people and their cases. For example, the *Jewish Morning Journal* (printed in Hebrew) ran a report on the 1950 sit-in strike in its 4th July issue. According to this several hundred DPs occupied the Jewish Agency offices and threatened to occupy the Consulate a couple of floors below. Understandably perplexed by this phenomenon the *Journal*'s correspondent, Melech Chemney, noted that the protesters actually "want to become again camp Jews, DP Jews".[62] Chemney then went on to provide human interest stories about some of the people involved, most of whom had served in the Israeli army during the 1948 war of independence. One of his interviewees, however, was not, strictly speaking, a DP at all, but had lived in Israel for the previous fourteen years. What seems to have motivated such a

---

[59]In order to overcome the Israeli returnees' loss of their stateless status, the Jewish organisation *Brichah* provided illegal infiltrees with papers from Jews who had already reached Palestine. YIVO, MK 488, Joint Staff Conf. Meeting, 17th–18th October 1947. Details of the legal status taken from JDC, File 397, Leonard Seidenman's report to Charles Jordan, 6th October 1952, pp. 12–13.
[60]JDC, File 397, 1954 Report, p. 3.
[61]On the Jewish Agency and its history, see Wetzel, *op. cit.*, pp. 110–117.
[62]Translation of Melech Chemney, 'Jews Returning from Israel Stage a Strike', from *Jewish Morning Journal*, 4th July 1950, JDC, File 402, p. 1.

person to end up in Germany of all places, as well as "real" DPs, were the "great many" of their fellows "going from Germany to America" at this point.[63]

Whatever their motives the protesters were becoming a serious headache for the relief organisations. Nevertheless, Samuel Haber of the Joint took a hand and mediated in the dispute. First of all, he outlined starkly to the returnees the problems they had created for themselves in returning illegally to Germany in the first place; that the Germany of 1950 no longer had a large variety of DP camps, or generous support systems for them. Haber also told them bluntly that they could not get back their DP papers, but, nevertheless, did offer to consider this and actually provided temporary Joint financial aid. His mediation also succeeded in getting the squatters out of the Jewish Agency office.[64]

For its part, the IRO announced during these negotiations that it would not afford these people any of its protection since it considered them Israeli citizens who should therefore be under the jurisdiction of the Israeli consulate in Munich.[65] This rejection can also be taken as a prelude to the IRO decision in 1951 to turn over the care of the Jewish DP camps in Germany entirely to the German authorities and in this fashion to wind up its own responsibility for the DPs.

These acts of mediation did not hinder, however, a second major confrontation between the "illegals" from Israel and the Germans, as well as the international support agencies. For, once the camp had been placed under German jurisdiction in 1951, it was inevitable that both the support agencies and the Germans would be working towards closing the camp to which Israel returnees were magnetically attracted and winding up relief agency affairs in Germany.

This created a new and extremely onerous task for the Joint and other support groups: what to do about the "illegals", especially since they were proving even harder to relocate outside of Germany than the medical hardcore cases. This was to be made very clear by the Joint's Moses Leavitt at the end of 1953 in a letter to an American supporter of the Joint's work in Germany. Leavitt wrote: "virtually all countries which have been accepting even small numbers of Jewish emigrants from Germany and other areas have refused to accept the 'illegals'. The latest country to make this clear is Canada, which indicated that it will accept no applications whatsoever from Israeli returnees."[66] For if it was difficult for Leavitt's agency to convince host countries to accept the hardcore who had never been able to find any homeland, how much more difficult it was going to be to induce potential recipient countries to consider cases of persons who had already found a new refuge, especially since this happened to be *Eretz Israel*, which until 1948 Jews had been risking their lives to reach!

The stage was thus set for yet another and one of the most serious confrontations between DPs and the Joint in the whole period. Moreover, in the

[63]*Ibid.*
[64]'The substance of Haber's negotiations with the protesters is contained in an article by Marion Gide in the English-language periodical *Forward*: 'The Tragic Position of the Jews Who Are Coming Back from Israel to Germany', issue of 24th August 1950, p. 1, JDC, File 402.
[65]*Ibid.*, p. 2.
[66]JDC, File 402, Moses Leavitt to Louis Lieblich, 18th December 1953.

meanwhile the no man's land such Jewish DPs had occupied since the end of the war was closed off in 1953 by a new and draconian German regulation. For, as the numbers of these returnees continued to grow,[67] a new German *Bundestag* law was passed to try to deal with them. This law gave those entering Germany illegally on or before 17th August 1953 until 17th February 1954, a period of exactly six months to leave or otherwise to regulate their status. Such illegal returnees had to register themselves with the German authorities by 17th August; those not doing so, or those who entered Germany after that date would not be eligible to stay and would be deported. At the time 795 returnees registered.[68]

Predictably, those likely to be excluded resorted to measures already tried successfully in 1950: just before the August 1953 decrees came into effect, "illegals" occupied the Joint offices in the Möhlstrasse in Munich, and staged yet another sit-in strike to protest the new German law and to hinder their deportation from Germany. Again the Joint intervened with the Bonn authorities, thereby securing their assurance that immediate deportations would not occur. After two days of posturing the "illegals" finally vacated the Joint offices.[69]

As evidence of how seriously the Bonn government was now viewing this question of returnees from Israel, on 1st September 1953, immediately following this latest sit-in, they had meetings with Jewish groups in which firm decisions were agreed upon to implement the new decrees. Present were representatives from the Joint, other international Jewish support groups, the *Zentralrat*, Bavarian Jewish organisations, and from the Israeli Purchasing Mission. At the meeting the Germans and the Jewish organisations agreed to provide temporary assistance to the returnees until the six months' grace period ended on 17th February 1954, but no new concessions to the original German measure were made at this time.[70]

Therefore, because of the August 1953 decree and the subsequent arrangements, no further returnees from Israel were able to enter Föhrenwald and to enjoy the temporary protection of the new law, so in October some 150 of them gathered, in yet another sit-down action, at a small synagogue in the Möhlstrasse in Munich to protest the closing of the camp to them. And again the Joint intervened and supplied them with food and welfare until they could be relocated abroad.[71]

After this the Joint files are silent on the Israeli returnee phenomenon, and one must presume that the new German law, plus the fact that the Germans set up a police office in the Föhrenwald camp to register all inhabitants,[72] brought about an end to this issue. Also hastening the end of this episode is evidence that the "illegals" were not entirely welcomed by the Föhrenwald DPs. In the 1953 'Report on Germany' the following view on this was expressed: "The attitude of

[67] According to Joint figures some 3,200 to 3,500 people had returned to Germany from abroad since mid-1949, JDC, File 381, '1953 Report on Germany, p. 4.
[68] *Ibid.*, p. 8.
[69] *Ibid.*, pp. 7–8.
[70] *Ibid.*, pp. 8–10.
[71] JDC, File 397, 'The Foehrenwald Story', February 1954, p. 6.
[72] *Ibid.*

the Camp Committee toward these new arrivals was a thoroughly hostile one." The author went on to indicate the reason for this unlikely attitude: that Föhrenwald inhabitants feared thereby the loss of privileges. He even hinted that they were mildly blackmailing the Germans, for the camp leaders in particular hoped to "secure special grants of moneys from the Germans as an inducement to liquidate the camp".[73] In short the "outsiders" were supposedly getting in their way.

Indeed, the intervention of the Bonn authorities, their meetings with the Joint and other support groups document this concern. For the result of the sit-ins and the subsequent negotiations was not to underscore the need to keep the camp going, but to create a sense of urgency about finding ways to dissolve it – hardly what the camp committees and their constituents had originally in mind.

E. THE THORNY ISSUE OF ALLEGED DP CRIMINALITY

Closely tied in with issues such as illegal returnees was the larger and, for the support groups, most embarrassing question of examples of DP criminality. Much friction was created between themselves and the support agencies by those Jewish survivors who became involved in the black market, in operating brothels, especially for Allied military personnel, and in smuggling illegal DP returnees back into Germany. Initially, such extra-legal activity was no doubt facilitated by the special status DPs in Germany enjoyed between 1945 and 1949, for as long as the occupying powers could override local German legal decisions, they could and did overrule sentences passed by local German courts.

In fact concrete evidence exists that DP violations of the law under occupation jurisdiction were not generally handled with the same severity as later. For example, in 1947 General Lucius Clay, US Military Governor for Germany, intervened on behalf of a Jewish DP who had been sentenced in 1946 by a German court to a three-year prison term and a DM 75,000 fine for smuggling across state borders. In February 1947 General Clay overruled the German court and reduced the sentence to one year proclaiming: "I have decided to make a very substantial alteration in the punishment imposed", because of "my sympathy for people who have suffered persecution".[74] Given such high-level examples, initially the support agencies patterned their conduct on the occupying powers, especially before the establishment of German legal sovereignty, so they frequently turned a blind eye to cases of DP contraventions of the law, even using black-market methods themselves. Thus, a field worker reported in 1946 that she was paying DPs employed by the Joint with black-market cigarettes at three packages per week per worker.[75]

However, after the German state achieved legal sovereignty in 1949, and after

---

[73]JDC, File 381, '1953 Report on Germany', p. 5.
[74]Letter from General Lucius Clay to Rabbi Alex Rosenberg, JDC, File 420, 27th February 1947.
[75]Joint report, 15th December 1946, JDC, File 375, p. 6. In a conversation with Ted Feder in December 1991, he confirmed that the Joint tended to take its cue on such matters from the occupying authorities.

Föhrenwald DP Camp
Above: DP Police at the entrance to the Camp
Below: DPs chop their own wood ration

By courtesy of The Wiener Library, London

Föhrenwald DP Camp
Above: The Camp laundry
Below: Lessons for dressmakers

By courtesy of The Wiener Library, London

1951, when the IRO ceased to hold jurisdiction over DPs in Germany, they became directly subject to the federal German legal system. Actually, in some cases the new West German laws benefited the DPs, for example, in April 1951 the *Bundestag* passed a "Federal Stateless Aliens Act" allowing stateless persons residing in the Federal Republic on or before 30th June 1950 to seek employment and to found businesses under the same provisions that existed for all Germans.

But German jurisdiction had another effect, for it made impossible acts such as General Clay's in 1947, and tended on the whole to bring cases of illegality out into the open. This eventually proved both to be an embarrassment for the Jewish support groups in dealing with illegal DP activities, and to provide unwelcome nourishment for German antisemites.

Under these new conditions, Joint representatives in Germany and the United States were prompted to address directly the issue of DP criminality, and they seemed to harbour the growing conviction that its main centre was to be found in Föhrenwald. As already indicated, the popular election of the camp committee also gave its elected leaders a mandate to block Joint attempts to end cases of criminality, thereby leading to constant friction.

Indeed German authorities, in the initial phase of their jurisdiction at least, were themselves to illustrate occasional examples of legal largesse in treating Jewish DP criminality. Thus, in one report about currency smugglers a German official wrote that, while he had serious reservations about pardoning several of them then being tried in Lindau on the Austrian border, he supported this policy, because "of the hard fate of the accused and their families in the concentration camps", whereupon the smugglers were released without paying fines.[76]

But this appears to have remained largely an exceptional example, for soon Joint officials were charging the West German authorities with taking a more intolerant stand than they did themselves on criminality among the hardcore cases now concentrated at Föhrenwald. In the July 1953 meeting with Bonn officials cited above, the Joint's Charles Jordan complained that the German authorities were labelling the remaining Föhrenwald DPs as "undesirable elements", which he rightly viewed as seriously hindering their mutual desire to resettle the hardcore either abroad or within the German economy.[77]

After 1949, however, the Joint officials became very determined to attack the question of DP criminality themselves. An illustration of this was the oft-repeated Joint charge over the years that there were racketeers in the camp and that one had been identified on the camp committees.[78] Other references to criminal elements continued in the Joint correspondence. For example, in the monthly report of May 1951 the following appeared: "We are seriously concerned with the present conditions, especially since we have now very many

---

[76] Letter from M. Laub to Charles Jordan, 14th April 1952, JDC, File 381.
[77] 'Notes on Meeting in Bonn (Germany)', JDC, File 398, 27th July 1953, p. 3.
[78] JDC, File 398, 9th July 1951, depicted one of the committee leaders as "one of a gangster group". In a report of 1st November 1953, Charles Jordan spoke of the camp committee's racketeering, JDC, File 398, report of M. W. Beckelman and Charles H. Jordan.

criminals of all kinds."[79] Such fears were understandable since the Joint's task was to find appropriate countries for the Föhrenwald inmates to go to, as clearly indicated from the following exasperated comment from a July 1951 report, which censured criminal elements in the camp committee who "will have little chance of emigrating to other countries [so] . . . they too will most probably remain in Germany".[80]

This touched at the core of the support group's concerns: to find appropriate countries to take the hardcore. This, of course, also raised for them the problem that, failing to find a country to take these people, the Germans had to be convinced that they should be the ones to accept the "criminal element", which again aroused dormant antisemitism among the Germans, especially once the rumour began to make the rounds that a number of the hardcore cases were not in fact TB cases, but persons with somewhat shady reputations. Thus, in a 1952 report, Leonard Seidenman[81] reported to Charles Jordan on difficulties involved in implementing an elaborate plan to integrate the Föhrenwald hardcore into the German economy by establishing liaisons with German firms, run both by Jews and others, because of hardcore black-market and other illegal activities. Using the example of the Joint's work in the town of Fürth, Seidenman mentioned a particular street which "the DPs have made a center for shady activities".[82]

Joint general sensitivities about DP criminal activities were also to be heightened by a sensational case in the early 1950s: the trial of Dr. Philipp Auerbach. The 1952 trial of Auberach and Rabbi Dr. Aaron Ohrenstein was to be a major embarrassment for the Jewish community as a whole.[83] A survivor of Auschwitz, Gross-Rosen and Buchenwald, Auerbach was placed in charge of Jewish DPs by the British in their zone in 1945, and in 1946 was made state commissar for the racial, religious and politically persecuted in Bavaria; a post he held until the August 1952 trial. In that year he was accused of accepting bribes (*passive Bestechung*), blackmail (*Erpressung*), misuse of his office and illegally using the title of "Dr.". As a consequence of these serious accusations and of his precarious health, Auerbach committed suicide on 16th August 1952.[84] In the Auerbach trial Rabbi Ohrenstein had also been accused of bribing Justice Minister Müller with DM 20,000.[85] Already before his trial in 1952 Auerbach had, in fact, encountered Joint disapproval because, in its view, he had been supporting the illegal returnees from Israel and elsewhere too generously. Thus,

---

[79]Monthly report, JDC, File 398, 6th May 1951.
[80]JDC, File 398, report of 9th July 1951, p. 8.
[81]At this time Seidenman was the Joint representative in the Low Countries, but was eventually to leave the Joint for the HIAS. Oral testimony of Ted Feder, Joint offices, New York, December 1991.
[82]Leonard Seidenman to Charles Jordan, 6th October 1952, JDC, File 397, p. 10.
[83]For a detailed treatment of the case, see Constantin Goschler, 'Der Fall Philipp Auerbach. Wiedergutmachung in Bayern', in Herbst and Goschler (eds.), *op. cit.*, pp. 77–98;* Wetzel, *op. cit.*, pp. 53–62; Christian Pross, *Wiedergutmachung. Der Kleinkrieg gegen die Opfer*, Frankfurt a. Main 1988, pp. 73–77.
* On this see now also the essay by Constantin Goschler, 'The Attitude towards Jews in Bavaria after the Second World War', in *LBI Year Book XXXVI* (1991), pp. 443–458 – (Ed.).
[84]Summary of Auerbach case taken from Wetzel, *op. cit.*, p. 54, note 14.
[85]Samuel Haber, 'Summary of Activities', June-July 1952, JDC, File 381, 5th August 1952, p. 6.

in a 1949 report Samuel Haber wrote rather sarcastically that "6 easy months, DM 80. – per month from Dr. Auerbach and a free bed are strong inducements" to return.[86]

To this day opinion is very much divided on Auerbach's innocence or guilt.[87] When the case first became public the Joint, for example, took the standpoint that Auerbach was the victim of the Bavarian Minister of Justice, Dr. Josef Müller, a known antisemite.[88] At the time, the organisation asserted that "Müller has been and continues to be Auerbach's worst enemy", speaking as well of Müller's "obvious persecution of the man".[89] In the March 1952 monthly report, Auerbach's trial continued to command attention – with Auerbach's case still enjoying Joint sympathy. To underscore this sympathy, at this time its representatives expressed the view that "most of the Germans charged with the prosecution of the case were either SA, SS or Nazi Party members and thus heavily prejudiced against Auerbach".[90]

However, as the case unfolded in the following months, this sympathy for Auerbach and Rabbi Ohrenstein began to erode, although at first rather slowly. Thus in a Joint activities' report for the period April–June 1952, the agency cautiously expressed the more neutral opinion that: "Auerbach . . . is not being tried because he is a Jew, nor is [sic] there any immediate antisemitic overtones."[91] When more evidence came to light and the trial itself commenced, Samuel Haber was now writing, somewhat resignedly, that while he expected both Auerbach and Ohrenstein to be acquitted of the charges against them, this would occur essentially for a lack of evidence. At this point, it had become patently clear that Joint sympathy for the accused was beginning to wane rapidly, although its censure now focused mainly on Rabbi Ohrenstein, who became the open target of some very vitriolic remarks, especially by Sam Haber. On this occasion Haber wrote that the rabbi was actually to blame for the whole mess, as he "was utterly lacking in character" and had had "a hand in every dirty deal in the restitution office". Moreover, Haber continued by escalating his bitter criticisms calling Ohrenstein "thoroughly unscrupulous", even a "gutter type".[92]

These were very strong words indeed, and as the above passage indicates, Joint opinions on the Auerbach-Ohrenstein case had, in fact, come full circle. Moreover, given Auerbach's former position as the "Tsar" of DP administration in Bavaria, and remembering that the Föhrenwald camp was located in that federal state, it was predictable that this scandal would profoundly heighten both Joint sensitivities about the question of criminality and deeply affect its relations

---

[86] Excerpt from December 1949 report from AJDC Welfare Department – Samuel Haber and Abraham Cohen, JDC, File 402, Returnees from Israel to Germany, p. 2.
[87] Bruno Weil and his supporters even established a "Committee on Fair Play for Auerbach" and solicited funds for him from sympathisers. Eventually Weil and his associates dropped this activity, certainly as a result of the growing doubt about Auerbach's and Ohrenstein's innocence. See Bruno Weil Papers, LBIA.
[88] On Müller's antisemitism, see Goschler, 'Der Fall Philipp Auerbach', *loc. cit.*, pp. 90f.
[89] AJDC-Germany, Summary of Activities February 1952, JDC, File 381, p. 5.
[90] AJDC Monthly report, March 1952, JDC, File 381, p. 6.
[91] Activities report for 6th April to 1st June 1952, JDC, File 381, p. 5.
[92] Samuel Haber, 'Summary of Activities', June–July 1952, JDC, File 381, 5th August 1952, p. 6.

with DP Jews in Germany. Beyond this, the language used by Joint representatives during the Auerbach-Ohrenstein episode tended to mirror the epithets used to describe DP criminality in general. The Auerbach case also vitiated the support agency's constant goals and need to portray to the crucial Jewish support organisations and individuals at home the morals of Jews in the camps in the most positive light possible. Indeed, it was to take some time to calm the waves from this particular trial and, as already indicated, the Jewish support groups were not to be spared other, if less spectacular, examples of DP illegality.

Post-1949 West German legislation was also to bring support groups and DPs other legal difficulties, in this case with respect to the illegal returnees. The 1951 West German DP law had applied only to those DPs residing in Germany before 30th June 1950, but in the meantime, as previously indicated, a mere trickle of Jews from Israel back to Germany had grown into a noticeable problem. In fact, their return was being "facilitated" by an active group of Jewish DP smugglers, and an article in the Jewish periodical *Forward* gave a graphic description of how this was done. For example, the journal reported that the Jews would leave Israel for Italy, from there they would enter Austria. "Marco", the code-name for a Polish Jew in charge of the smuggling ring, along with his helpers would usher the returnees across the Austro-German border. They would then promptly appear at Föhrenwald and demand Joint support. The smugglers were paid "Robin Hood" style, taking more for their services from the wealthier Jewish returnees, less from the poorer. They also confiscated the returnees' Israeli documents for, according to a German Law of 1953, without these the Germans could not turn them out because the returnees were again considered stateless, at least until their status was established: this is precisely what they themselves desired.[93]

In this process even Israeli officials were considered culpable. In a 1953 report on why Jews were leaving Israel, Charles Jordan, while as usual excoriating his perennial *bête noire*, the racketeers, expressed the opinion that some returnees were being assisted "perhaps with the subtle help of responsible governmental or semi-governmental officials who think that Israel better rid itself of certain elements".[94] Apparently among such returnees were some *bona fide* undesirables, for in a long annual report for the same year it was reported that: "It is regrettable that the group of new arrivals – those who came during this year particularly – are very well sprinkled with an assortment of flotsam and jetsam, ne'er-do-wells, irresponsibles, and not infrequently gangster types."[95] Apart from the grotesque aspects of these cases: that Holocaust survivors, for example, would actually pay someone to smuggle them back to the *gescholtene Erde* where they had been persecuted, the appearance of the "illegals" caused much trouble, especially with the German population.

Illegal activities and friction with international support groups also spread to more laudable enterprises. For, not only were Jews being assisted to return to

---

[93]See Gide, *loc. cit.*, JDC, File 402, cuttings prepared by the Joint's Irving R. Dickman.
[94]Charles Jordan, 'Memorandum on the Question of People Leaving Israel', JDC, File 402, 16th August 1953.
[95]'Report on Germany to 1953 Country Directors Conference', JDC, File 381, p. 10.

Germany from Israel illegally, but DPs were also being helped to emigrate illegally to countries such as Brazil; on one occasion through the good offices of a Jewish middleman. He bribed Brazilian consular and embassy officials, at the same time demanding payment from Jewish Agency officials to procure visas for that country. He even warned the Joint officials in 1953 that not "a single visa" could be procured for Brazil except through him and at his price.[96] At the end of the year, the Joint annual report felt obliged again to address and condemn such practices by using the German-Yiddish epithet *machers* to label those, like the middleman, who were procuring visas for Brazil illegally.[97] But such cases should not be exaggerated since they affected only a tiny minority of Jewish DPs at the time.

As the above cases of illegal returnees and of questionable emigration brokers indicate, Joint exasperation reflected, of course, a growing sense of urgency about the need to wind up its DP activities in Germany and to respond to growing German pressure to do this as well. As time passed, and as previously set deadlines to close the camp were not met, the exasperation of Joint officials, coupled with the fact that they now faced the most difficult of DPs either to relocate or integrate into the German economy, meant that the language they used predictably tended to become increasingly bitter. Thus, a report for the year 1953, written in the wake of acrimonious August sit-in strikes in Munich by returnees, concluded that: "Föhrenwald is a corrupt and outlaw society. Its method of getting what it wants is organized blackmail."[98]

Such strong views continued to be expressed. In the June 1958 report already alluded to,[99] and at the very end of Joint activity in Germany on behalf of the survivors, Dr. Erich Rosenberg made some impassioned statements on the hardcore situation. Rosenberg set the tone of his talk by saying his recent visit to Germany left him feeling that he had "come from an insane asylum". Moreover, he called the Jewish population in Germany "not balanced". Speaking of the Jews in the Munich area, he even stated that they constituted the "blackest Jewish community", whose "leader is a criminal surrounded by gangsters". Dr. Rosenberg continued: "What has happened, and what is still happening, is so terrible that I am almost ashamed to give you the details. For instance, you have a so-called red light district there, where bars are owned by Jews and visited mainly by the military personnel of the American armed forces." Suddenly, at this point, the speaker broke off his presentation, and indicated to the committee he was reporting to that he would only be able to continue *in camera*, due, presumably, to the seriousness of the charges.[100] Rosenberg's utterances are a graphic illustration of the sincere embarrassment felt within a major Jewish organisation about such dubious practices. There is no reason to doubt his

---

[96]JDC, File 398, 27th July 1953, p. 3. Notes compiled by Charles Jordan on the Bonn meeting are cited in several places in this paper.

[97]'Report on Germany to 1953 Country Directors Conference', JDC, File 381, pp. 33–34.

[98]'Report on Study and Action Team – 1953', JDC, File 397, 22nd February 1954, p. 3. This is also cited, without a source, in Yehuda Bauer, *Out of the Ashes. The Impact of American Jews on Post-Holocaust European Jewry*, Oxford 1989, p. 295.

[99]See above note 26.

[100]Dr. Erich Rosenberg, Report to Executive Committee, JDC, File 375, p. 15.

statements since it would have been in the interest of the Joint to suppress entirely such compromising information – which indeed partially occurred on this occasion, when Rosenberg indicated his unwillingness, in public at least, to elaborate further on the Munich situation.

To conclude, the issue of criminality touched at the core of differences that existed between Joint attitudes on the subject and the perceptions of the DPs themselves. Why raise the subject of Jewish DP criminality at all? Certainly not to discount the crimes committed against the DPs themselves, but essentially to underscore the exceptional circumstances such DPs living in Germany faced after 1945, and the entirely understandable problems relief agencies, such as the Joint, had in comprehending the DP mentality. Moreover, the existence of such criminality merely fortifies the thesis presented here, that Jewish DPs in particular found it necessary on occasion, even preferable, to enter the grey zone of illegality, to flout conventions, to break laws. They were in fact, at least until the 1948 currency reform, merely following a general trend among Germans in the western zones to become heavily involved in black-market and other illegal activities. And, after all, these people had been themselves victims of limitless violations of the rule of law by Hitler and his minions. Thus, clearly with such trauma in mind, a minority of Jewish DPs committed illegal acts; became involved in disreputable undertakings, feeling that they stood outside the laws of a state whose predecessor had systematically violated their most basic human rights. It was also admittedly symptomatic of a personal breakdown of fundamental concepts of law and order among the death camp survivors, which, as regrettable and unacceptable as this may have been, was equally understandable given the unprecedented circumstances of their plight.

For the Joint representatives it was equally understandable that they could not fathom or condone the survivors' motives and practices in violating the law, even though on occasion they ignored cases of DP infractions. Nor could they justify to their patrons in the United States support for survivors who were engaged in such illegal practices. As a preliminary conclusion, suffice it to say here that both sides had good reason for their diverging attitudes.

But for the Joint alleged criminality was to create difficulties in another area of its involvement at the end of its German activity: placing the hardcore within German society.

F. PROSPECTS OF DP SETTLEMENT WITHIN WEST GERMANY

One method of finding an acceptable solution for the hardcore was to enlist German Jews on their behalf, and the Joint's Leonard Seidenman was to be found in the thick of such plans. In extremely vigorous language, Seidenman expressed strong views on the subject in a long and detailed report he wrote in October 1952.[101] He began by suggesting that German-Jewish entrepreneurs take DPs as apprentices, the Joint making up a part of the short-fall in wages

---

[101]Leonard Seidenman to Charles Jordan, 6th October 1952, JDC, File 397.

between those of an apprentice and a fully-fledged worker. But he saw several problems with this. To begin with, he wrote of the prospective Jewish employers that there were "not enough of them" to take in the camp DPs the Joint wished to place.[102]

Seidenman continued his suggestions by asserting that German Jews actually disliked hiring the DPs and harked back to the DP criminality issue as the reason. He repeated perennial criticisms of hardcore DPs, asserting that the German-Jewish community had had "bad experiences... with their DPs, many of whom were involved in the black market". Indeed, drawing on similar work he had done in France, Seidenman concluded that in Germany, too, "I learned from bitter experience... that they are not the most sympathetic group with whom to discuss the problems of Jewish workers". Seidenman even believed that German-Jewish employers "could easily find some other pretext" for not hiring the DPs. Nevertheless, Seidenman remained basically optimistic and, in spite of such reservations and excepting very negative comments made by a member of the Nuremberg Jewish community,[103] concluded that such an apprenticeship was workable. So Joint fieldworkers proceeded to place DPs within the German economy in the coming years, and naturally Joint attempts to find a solution went beyond the handful of extant German-Jewish entrepreneurs who were willing to help.

Because both the German authorities and Joint representatives were vitally interested in finding means to integrate cases apparently impossible to place overseas into the German economy, they attempted to find joint solutions. Thus at the important 1953 meeting, Bonn representatives expressed a great interest in and financial support for housing for such cases. According to Refugee Ministry claims at the time, in 1953 some 2.5 million DM was to be invested by the West Germans to settle five hundred Föhrenwald inmates, and the Bonn officials naturally urged the Joint and other support groups to make a comparable financial effort.[104] After serious hurdles in the scheme had been overcome,[105] these exertions eventually bore fruit, for in a 1955 report a Joint fieldworker described settling hardcore Jews into German housing constructed for that purpose. She praised the local German officials involved in the resettlement, in this case in Stuttgart, including their understanding of the psychological difficulties concentration camp survivors were sure to encounter when "integrated" into settlements inhabited almost exclusively by Germans.[106]

[102]*Ibid.*, p. 10.
[103]While not entirely sure of this Nuremberg Jew's status, Seidenman used him as prime evidence, calling his opposition to the DPs "highly personalised" and quoting him as saying: "If we wanted to try Nuremberg for jobs – 'bitte schon' [*sic*] – but the Gemeinde could not, and would not do anything", *ibid.*, p. 11.
[104]Meeting in Bonn, 27th July 1953, JDC, File 398, pp. 3–4. It was attended by Charles Jordan and Samuel Haber of the Joint, representatives of other Jewish relief agencies, a German Foreign Office official and one from the *Bundesministerium für Vertriebene, Flüchtlinge und Kriegsgeschädigte* (later to come under the aegis of Theodor Oberländer).
[105]In the Leo Schwarz Papers in the YIVO Archives, a detailed account of serious difficulties in settling hardcore refugees into a Jewish *Altersheim* is given. Of 112 DPs scheduled for integration at the time, only five agreed to go. See Leo Schwarz Papers, YIVO, Report of 1953.
[106]Deborah Levy to Mr. James Rice, 28th July 1955, JDC, File 396.

Standing in the way of these endeavours was yet another suprising barrier: welfare benefits from both the Joint and the Germans worked against resettlement. Thus, in the October 1952 Joint report previously cited, Leonard Seidenman outlined the following scenario: Taking the actual example of a young DP with a wife and two children, under existing arrangements Seidenman asserted he could get some DM 220 in welfare from the Germans and the Joint. The DP was actually offered a job with the Joint, but his salary would have been less than the above-mentioned amount, so he turned it down. Thus Seidenman resignedly concluded that: "Finding people who will leave the camp, will, therefore, prove to be the hardest part of the job."[107] In the next year the following was reported: "the camp offers a sort of financial, political and personal security which the people believe they cannot find in the world outside of the camp . . ." This report continues by complaining that, when Föhrenwald inmates "compare their 'income' (welfare) from the Germans and the supplementation from the 'Joint' with their potential income as workers on the open market, [they] find that 'it does not pay to work' ".[108] Such welfare scenarios are all-too familiar today, but one has to keep in mind that their inequities were all the more stark to a generation of Americans unaccustomed to such practices. At all events, as long as they existed it would prove difficult indeed to resettle DPs and to wind up Joint financial and other forms of involvement.

And on the subject of welfare the German-Jewish organisations, given a role in distributing welfare among DPs and other Jews in Germany, were to prove unhelpful too. Joint field workers complained in 1953 that they were "far from satisfied" with the manner in which welfare requests were handled by what they termed derogatorily the "post office" function which German-Jewish agencies had assigned themselves. It was, moreover, Joint opinion that: "The fault lies primarily in the absence of good leadership in the welfare organisations."[109] This was just part of a larger dispute with Hendrick van Dam, Karl Marx and the *Zentralrat*, already alluded to, but it underscores further problems the relief groups were encountering in trying to co-ordinate their efforts to resettle into the Germany economy or elsewhere the very difficult cases among the camp remnants.

In spite of problems connected with welfare, with the lack of German-Jewish support, with integrating Holocaust survivors into the German economy, in the final analysis these efforts to place the hardcore in German communities met with the desired result. This is documented by the closing of the Föhrenwald camp in 1957, with its inhabitants either emigrating or settling in various German centres. The fact that almost 30,000 Jewish DPs, and their descendants still live in Germany today is evidence of the success of this venture.

---

[107]Seidenman to Jordan, 6th October 1952, JDC, File 397, pp. 8–9.
[108]Leo Schwarz Papers, YIVO, Joint Report of 1953, p. 19.
[109]'Report on Germany to 1953 Country Directors Conference', JDC, File 381, p. 17.

G. CONCLUSIONS: A CONFLICT OF PHILOSOPHIES?

By way of a final summation, it is worth evaluating the philosophical positions of the parties concerned. The most significant area both of internal Joint policy disagreement and of philosophical differences with hardcore DP perceptions had to do with the means whereby "Föhrenwälder" were, failing successful emigration, to be resettled into the German economy. As in all large organisations there were both "hawks" and "doves" among the Joint policymakers. As the evidence brought to bear throughout this paper indicates, Sam Haber appears to have been among the former. A recent scholar, otherwise in full sympathy with the camp inmates, has added her support for a tougher policy when she writes that there was only one way for Jewish DPs to regain normalcy: "the swift (*rasch*) dissolution of the camp", and continues "this alone would have forced the inhabitants to choose the one or the other emigration option, or to integrate into German society".[110]

However, Charles Jordan and other members both of the Joint executive and, especially, field-workers, believed that with judicious casework rehabilitation, emigration and integration into the German economy could succeed. Jordan and his caseworkers wished to make an effort at least to deal with specific cases and to reduce the hardcore in this manner, and even to contemplate long-term support for mentally and physically handicapped inmates.[111] Jordan's approach also had other supporters. Leonard Seidenman, in 1952, concurred and admitted that closing Föhrenwald should be a "longterm" objective, continuing: "We should always bear in mind that we have the problems of individuals to solve" and that "[h]asty closing of the camp" might end Joint-German co-operation on finding "individual solutions" to the inmates' real problems.[112]

In the end, however, the hawks appeared to have prevailed. Thus in 1954, at a time when the Joint was confronted with almost exclusively hardcore and illegal returnee cases, Moses W. Beckelman reported to the Joint executive in New York:

> "we take the position that we cannot and should not attempt to create ideal conditions for their post-Foehrenwald life. We believe that a man must and should do things for himself; we believe that the end of Foehrenwald must spell the end for Foehrenwalders of the complete dependence upon income from welfare sources which has completely demoralized most of them to a point where they have lost all incentive and they must become disabused of that notion. It is a hard thing for them to learn and it will destroy some. But it will be good for many of the young ones, particularly those with children."[113]

These views are corroborated, even elaborated, in a Joint study-action team report of the same year. It concluded: "The history of the Foehrenwald inmates has been one of extreme over-protection, ruinous pampering and yielding to pressure by all agencies dealing with the DPs . . ." In what was, by this time, the established Joint position, the writers of the report continued to argue that:

---

[110]Wetzel, *op. cit.*, p. 254.
[111]Jordan to Beckelman, 21st April 1954, JDC, File 397, pp. 2, 6.
[112]Seidenman to Charles Jordan, 6th October 1952, JDC, File 397, p. 19.
[113]M. W. Beckelman report, 21st April 1954, JDC, File 397.

"What is needed to support casework effort is shock therapy: external pressure, tough policies, progressive withdrawal of material benefits, and sharply defined time limits." That the hardliners prevailed, has been mentioned already; and under admittedly very strong German pressure, they proceeded to press the Föhrenwald hardcores to accept integration as their only remaining option. Nevertheless, whatever differences of approach there may have been, there was a united goal: to find what Joint officials perceived to be the best solution for the Jewish DPs.

There is considerable evidence to illustrate that there existed an atmosphere of acrimony between the support agencies and the DPs and German Jews. Why devote so much time, one might plausibly ask, to issues such as criminality, to illegal returnees, and disharmony over compensation from the Germans? – especially since such evidence could easily be misunderstood as an invitation to rekindle never-extinguished antisemitism in Germany and elsewhere. Certainly the reason was not to discount the crimes committed against the DPs themselves, but essentially to underscore the exceptional circumstances such DPs living in Germany faced after 1945, and the entirely understandable problems Joint and other relief agencies had in comprehending the DP mentality.

For at the very heart of their differences of perspective were the death camp and related experiences of the DP survivors, whose war-time experiences were for them seminally traumatic. Many of these people could never really integrate or emigrate; in fact their lives had been largely destroyed between 1939 and 1945. Thus, it seems a shame that, on more than one occasion, the survivors and the support agencies would find themselves literally on opposite sides of the barricades in unseemly struggles over the wishes of hardcore DPs to remain at Föhrenwald, because the former victims of exploitation by the National Socialists aspired to remain in the only world many of them had ever known: communities hermetically sealed off from what they perceived as their unappealing German surroundings, communities which would provide a familiar ambience for the preservation of their already damaged mental and physical equilibrium. For this they needed, and expected, long-term if not indeed permanent financial and social support in a location such as Föhrenwald.

The question therefore arises whether the hardcore and "illegals" should ever have been forced to face up to the need to restart normal lives either abroad or in German society. This was, of course, the ultimate assumption of the Joint and other Jewish support groups, but it is just too simple to presume that this was feasible or advisable for a survivor of Nazi persecution. Moreover, the camp enabled them to remain in contact with fellow-survivors, to avoid the need either to achieve in the conventional sense or to adjust to a world into which they were no longer capable of fitting. To the American Joint leaders the idea that people would never want to pick up the shattered threads of their lives again, would never find the will to follow an admittedly severely modified version of the American dream Joint workers strongly believed in, simply remained outside their range of comprehension.

In fairness to the American-based support groups, their sense of urgency in closing the camps was heightened by the pressure being applied by the German authorities. After all, the Germans took over Camp Föhrenwald in 1951, they kept the pressure on the Joint to accelerate emigration, and they pushed unabatedly for financial incentives – partly out of their own pockets, partly from the Jewish support groups – to bring this chapter to a close. But it also seems fair to say that, with respect to the camp, Bonn and the Joint in particular were on the same wavelength. While the Jewish agencies might show more understanding of the difficulties involved, the tenor of their criticisms of the camp leaders, of the illegals, of camp morale in general cannot be attributed solely to German pressure. For the Joint was under considerable pressure from its own American constituents who donated funds to the United Jewish Appeal, from which the Joint got the lion's share of its monies. Understandably such supporters did not wish to pour large sums of relief into permanent welfare projects for DPs, or to keep a single camp such as Föhrenwald alive with less than 2,000 hardcore inhabitants. So the Joint had to reflect faithfully its benefactors' wishes, which were that one gave assistance in order to help people bridge difficult times, not to have them as a permanent charge on the purse of the agency and its patrons, as the hardcore people and the "illegals" were threatening to become. Thus a wide gulf existed between the problems of the survivors and the solutions the support agencies and their patrons wished to or could implement.

In the end, only time could and did solve these issues. The incidence of black marketeering eventually receded, the trickle of "illegals" dried up, the hardcore was absorbed into the German economy or found refuge in Israel or other countries willing to take it. Looking back from the space of over thirty years, the support agencies themselves see all of this in a more reflective and positive light. In a recent conversation with a long-time Joint field official, the author gained the impression that these old quarrels have now been truly laid to rest, that the Joint in particular can look back today with a justified sense of accomplishment in the face of yet another serious challenge to its formidable organisational and philanthropic skills. And to be entirely fair, one should not assume from the many examples of acrimony given in this paper that the support agencies did not feel a genuine sense of grief and deep sympathy for the terrible fate of the DPs they were called upon to assist. As in all human affairs, it is difficult to be ever conscious of the overwhelming images of the gas chambers in the East. In these circumstances, the temptation must be to succumb instead to the day-to-day preoccupation with cases of smuggling, of illegal returnees, German pressure to close the DP camps, wranglings over compensation monies due to them from the Germans, and the apparently inexplicable obstreperousness of the remnants of the DPs still in Föhrenwald at the end of the relief operation. At the end of the day one must genuinely appreciate the attitudes reflected by both sides.

The Historical Role of the Central European Immigration to Israel

BY YOAV GELBER

THE YISHUV'S FIRST CONFRONTATION WITH THE HOLOCAUST

From 1933 onwards a wave of immigrants from Central Europe (this term is used in this article to denote Germany, Austria and Czechoslovakia) arrived in Palestine.* For the first time the *Yishuv* confronted the plight that befell the Jews of Europe following Hitler's seizure of power. During the first five years of the National-Socialist regime only the German Jews were victims. Then in 1938 Austrian and Czech Jewries, too, were forced to face National Socialism. Veteran members of the *Yishuv* who were natives of these countries naturally evinced great concern for the fate of their compatriots. As early as March 1933 they urged the Zionist leadership to challenge the crisis in Germany. Their approach was pragmatic and considered the need to negotiate with the new German Government. This contradicted the *Yishuv*'s general tendency to adopt the militant line of Jewish response throughout the world, which manifested itself in the anti-German boycott movement. The German Zionists wished to attract as many German Jews as possible to Palestine, not necessarily Zionists. Thus they hoped to utilise the catastrophe in their homeland for the promotion of the *Yishuv* and the Zionist enterprise.

Initally, the German Zionists mobilised the support of several Zionist leaders, such as Weizmann, Arlosoroff, Ben-Gurion and Berl Katznelson. This partnership made possible the consolidation of the organisations through which the Zionist movement approached the situation in Germany: the Central Office for the Settlement of German Jews in Palestine, the Jewish Agency's German Department, the Youth *Aliyah* project, the *Haavara* company and several others. However, this alliance ended during the second half of the 1930s. In the face of the rapid deterioration of conditions in Germany the German Zionist leaders claimed priority for ameliorating the plight of the German Jews through

---

*This article is an English version of the concluding chapter of my book, *A New Homeland – The Immigration from Central Europe and its Absorption in Eretz Israel, 1933–1948* (in Hebrew), Yad Izhak Ben Zvi, Jerusalem 1990. The book is based on source material found in several Israeli archives, such as the Central Zionist Archives (CZA), the archives of the Association of Immigrants from Germany and Austria (HOGOA), various archives of *kibbutzim*, archives of political parties and figures as well as British documents (Foreign and Colonial Offices) in the Public Record Office in London and the Palestine Government's records at the Israeli State Archives. In addition I used unpublished manuscripts, mostly found at the Leo Baeck Institute in Jerusalem, the HOGOA publications, the German Zionist press, the immigrants' newspapers and the general Hebrew press.

emigration. They advocated the provision of any solutions, not necessarily emigration to Palestine. For this they were ready to surrender traditional Zionist stances and to accept compromises with the Mandatory Power and non-Zionist Jewish organisations.[1]

Weizmann, Ben-Gurion and their colleagues in the Zionist Labour movement considered the privations of German Jewry to be of secondary importance to the Zionist struggle for Palestine. In their view, the treatment of the crisis in Germany should be determined by general Zionist principles and policies.[2] The German Zionist leaders, such as Kurt Blumenfeld and Siegfried Moses, were traditionally Weizmann's adherents. After 1935, however, they became disillusioned. They criticised Weizmann's reservations about the *Haavara* and his disinclination to lend his personal weight to the negotiations with the German Government.[3] Weizmann's opposition to a separate political organisation of the German immigrants in Palestine hurt them. They could not comprehend his refusal to appear before the Evian Conference, and Moses complained about Weizmann's ingratitude to the German Zionists despite their historical devotion to his leadership.[4]

From 1933 on, the ever-worsening situation for Jews in Germany became clear to the *Yishuv* when many immigrants, and later refugee illegal immigrants, arrived in the country from the Third *Reich*. The leaders of the German immigrants were among the first to forewarn that the Nazi menace was the paramount problem facing the entire Jewish people, including the *Yishuv*. They argued that the Zionist movement should lead World Jewry's struggle against National Socialism. This attitude, however, was not general in the *Yishuv* until the Second World War, when Nazi persecution expanded to the occupied and satellite countries throughout Western, Central and Eastern Europe. Only then did concern about the fate of the Jews cease to be confined to Central European immigrants and aroused the fears of the entire community.

From the outset leaders of German-Jewish immigrants distinguished between an emotional response to the National-Socialist persecution and a practical one. In the midst of the war they embarked on preparing the claims for the enormous property that the immigrants had left behind them in Germany. This preparatory work paved the way for the negotiations between the Israeli Government, the World Jewish Organisation and the Federal Government of West Germany, which ultimately led to the Reparations agreements of the early 1950s.[5]

Both the Reparations agreement after the war and the Transfer agreement

---

[1]Siegfried Moses's letters to Berl Katznelson and Georg Landauer, 29th May 1935, CZA, S 7/176; S. Adler-Rudel, 'The Evian Conference on the Refugee Question', in *LBI Year Book XIII* (1968), pp. 235–273; Protocol of the Jewish Agency Executive meeting in London on 13th November 1938, CZA.

[2]The most typical expression of this approach was Ben-Gurion's speech at the meeting of the Jewish Agency's Executive, 31st December 1935, CZA.

[3]Moses's minutes of his talks at the Zionist Office in London, 15th March 1935, CZA, S 7/174.

[4]Moses's letter to Gustav Krojanker and Moshe Bilesky, 3rd November 1938, CZA, S 7/699.

[5]Siegfried Moses, *The Compensation Claims of the Jews*, Tel-Aviv 1943; Neima Barzel, *Israel and Germany, 1945–1956 – Development of the Attitude of Israeli Society and State to Germany Following the Holocaust*, Ph.D. thesis submitted to the University of Haifa, 1990, pp. 133ff.

before, disrupted Jewish solidarity over the issue of boycotting Germany. In many respects, the argument regarding reparations in the early 1950s repeated the Transfer controversy of the 1930s. Despite the lapse of time and the decisive events that had meanwhile taken place, many arguments for and against boycott retained their force after the war. The alignments of those who favoured a settlement with Germany and their opponents underwent only a few changes. The leaders of the German immigration, who played a major role in negotiating the *Haavara* agreement and in the preliminary discussions of the Reparations issue were later replaced by the *Yishuv*'s national institutions and the government of Israel.

THE CHANGING SIGNIFICANCE OF THE YISHUV WITHIN WORLD JEWRY

Until the early 1930s Palestine held a primarily symbolic meaning for World Jewry. During the preceding decade pioneering Zionists had developed important projects in the country. They laid an infrastructure that was an essential precondition for the Zionist enterprise's further growth, but the undertaking itself had only local significance. The *Yishuv* remained on the fringe of the main historic tides that concerned most Jews. Five major concerns can be identified: their position in the new states that emerged from the ruins of the pre-war empires; their struggles for individual status and national minority rights; their day-to-day encountering of economic hardships; the emigration from Eastern to Western Europe and to overseas countries; the world revolution and the growing antisemitism. In comparison with all these issues the Zionist programme was no more than an interesting experiment whose prospects were still uncertain. It appeared to bear little relevance to the current problems which preoccupied the general Jewish public. But Hitler's seizure of power and the subsequent persecutions in Germany put the Zionist undertaking at the centre of Jewish public interest. Palestine constituted a practical solution to German Jewry's plight. During the 1930s Zionism developed from a religious and historic symbol and from a pioneering social experiment into a movement representing hope to large numbers of persecuted Jews.

Soon the growing numbers of immigrants and the increased amount of capital imported became evidence of the change Zionism was undergoing. Palestine became the favoured destination for many German-Jewish emigrants. From 1933 to 1937 it admitted more German-Jewish refugees than any other single country, including the United States. The newcomers were not necessarily all idealists and pioneers. Many had no previous allegiance to the Zionist movement or ideology. Nevertheless, they chose Palestine rather than other countries. Others were driven to Palestine only by the force of circumstance. Their absorption proved that the country was capable of receiving large numbers of diverse origins. It showed, moreover, that Palestine could make room for a broad variety of social and vocational backgrounds. The growth of immigration generated a further expansion of the economy, which in turn made possible the reception of more refugees from Germany and elsewhere.[6]

As the Jewish population of Palestine swelled and the *Yishuv* proved its capacity to provide a haven to persecuted Jews, so did Jewish communities in the Western countries display increased readiness to provide the necessary finance for absorbing additional immigrants. During the 1930s German Jewry had priority on funds raised by Jews in the rest of the world. A large share of the mobilised resources was allocated to Palestine both directly, to finance the immigrants' absorption, and indirectly, to subsidise their *Hachscharah* – the vocational and ideological preparation for immigrants.[7]

The World Jewish community rightly believed that Palestine could make a crucial contribution to alleviating the distress of the Diaspora. The Zionist enterprise became a major issue on the agenda of any Jewish conference that met

---

[6] My estimate of the total number of Central European immigrants in the years 1933–1945 is about 90,000, distributed as follows:
(a) German immigrants who registered with the Jewish Agency until the end of 1938 – 40,061.
(b) German immigrants who in 1933 registered only with the Palestine Government's immigration department and were not included in the Jewish Agency's statistics – 3,150.
(c) German immigrants who, according to the Jewish Agency's estimate, entered through Egypt and Lebanon – 1,800.
(d) Tourists from Germany who until the end of 1938 were officially allowed to stay – 3,228.
(e) Austrian immigrants in the years 1933–1937 – 2,338.
(f) Czech immigrants in the years 1933–1938 – 3,383.
(g) Austrian and Czech tourists who were officially allowed to stay – 1,425.
(h) Immigrants from Austria (1938–1939) and Czechoslovakia (1939) who were not citzens of these countries – 5,722.
(i) Immigrants from Germany, Austria and Czechoslovakia who arrived between the outbreak of the war and the end of 1945 – 12,772.
(j) Illegal immigrants from the Third *Reich* in the years 1939–1945 – 8,463.
(k) Total – 82,342.
This calculation does not count Central European Jews who were not citizens of the three countries and who arrived illegally from other countries. It also does not include tourists who stayed illegally in Palestine (the total number of tourists from Germany who registered with the Jewish Agency in the years 1933–1940 was 24,000). However, there may be some overlapping of legal and illegal immigrants during the war years and hence my estimate of 90,000. The data has been taken from the bulletins of the Jewish Agency statistical department in the CZA, and from D. Gurewicz and A. Gerz, *Statistical Handbook of Jewish Palestine*, Jerusalem 1947, and *Immigration, the Yishuv and Natural Movement of Population in Palestine*, Jerusalem 1945 (in Hebrew). For general data about Jewish emigration from Germany, which is inaccurate as far as Palestine is concerned, see Mark Wischnitzer, 'Jewish Emigration from Germany, 1933–1938', in *Jewish Social Studies*, II (1940), pp. 23–44; Werner Rosenstock, 'Exodus 1933–1939', in Robert Weltsch (ed.), *Deutsches Judentum. Aufstieg und Krise. Gestalten, Ideen, Werke*, Stuttgart 1963. Veröffentlichung des Leo Baeck Instituts, pp. 400–404; Herbert A. Strauss, 'Jewish Emigration from Germany – Nazi Policies and Responses (I)', in *LBI Year Book XXV* (1980), pp. 351–358; and *ibid.* (II), in *LBI Year Book XXVI* (1981), pp. 363–409.
[7] Perez Leshem, *Strasse zur Rettung 1933–1945. Aus Deutschland vertrieben – Bereit sich jüdische Jugend auf Palästina vor*, Tel-Aviv 1973; Yehuda Bauer, *My Brother's Keeper. A History of the American Jewish Joint Distribution Committee 1929–1939*, Philadelphia 1974, pp. 153–158; Abraham Margaliot, 'Emigration – Planung und Wirklichkeit', in *Die Juden im Nationalsozialistischen Deutschland/The Jews in Nazi Germany 1933–1943*, herausgegeben von Arnold Paucker mit Sylvia Gilchrist und Barbara Suchy, Tübingen 1986 (Schriftenreihe wissenschaftlicher Abhandlungen des Leo Baeck Instituts 45), pp. 303–316.

to discuss means to solve the plight of German Jewry. This enhanced the *Yishuv*'s status in the Jewish world and bolstered Zionist influence on "general" Jewish policies.

The shift in the *Yishuv*'s position did not occur overnight, but developed gradually. The non-Zionists did not easily acquiesce to Zionist hegemony.[8] The successful absorption of German immigration made it impossible, however, to ignore Palestine's central role *vis-à-vis* the crisis in Europe. Even before his return to the Zionist organisation's chairmanship in 1935, and all the more so afterwards, Weizmann became a dominant figure in any Jewish conference which discussed the situation of German Jewry, the refugees' problems and the Jewish people's response. However, his main objective was to secure Palestine's central role in any international or inter-organisational plan and a due share in any allocation of funds. While this was a reasonable demand in 1933–1935, the change of circumstances both in Germany and in Palestine in the second half of the 1930s made his task ever more difficult.

The Arab Revolt in Palestine during the years from 1936 to 1939 and the restrictions subsequently imposed by the British Government on the immigration quotas seriously hampered Palestine's role as an asylum for the Jews of the Third *Reich*. Yet there was no way to turn the clock back. The territorial solutions advocated by Britain and the United States following the Evian Conference in the summer of 1938 proved illusory. Palestine remained paramount in any discussion of the Jewish situation, despite the indefatigable British efforts to differentiate between the two issues – Palestine and the Jewish plight in Europe – before, during and after the Second World War. The Jewish refugees who had fled from Europe on the eve of the war, the Jewish activists under the yoke of Nazi occupation during the war and the survivors in the Displaced Persons (DP) camps in the years 1945–1948, all looked to Palestine not only as a spiritual symbol but as a concrete goal. Time reinforced this devotion, which had begun with the Nazi seizure of power in 1933 and culminated after the war. In the post-war years it convinced the Jewish communities of the free world and consequently general public opinion, particularly in the United States, that there was no solution for the surviving remnant after the Holocaust but in Palestine.

THE CHANGE IN THE YISHUV'S STATUS WITHIN PALESTINE

The immigration from Germany in essence altered the *Yishuv*'s position in Palestine *vis-à-vis* the Arab majority and the British authorities. According to the Palestine government census of November 1931, the Jewish community numbered 174,000 and constituted one sixth of the entire population. In the spring of 1936 the *Yishuv* was 400,000 strong – one third of the total population. Thus the *Yishuv* became a factor which could no longer be overlooked when the time came

---

[8]Martin Rosenblüth, *Go Forth and Serve. Early Years and Public Life*, New York 1961; Protocols of the London Conference of Jewish Organisations, 29th October to 1st November 1933, Weizmann Archives.

to decide the country's fate. The immigrants from Germany played a significant, though not exclusive, part in this revolution. However, it was not only the demographic balance which determined the *Yishuv*'s status but rather its economic, technological and social accomplishments, to which the German immigration added considerably.

The expansion of land purchases and settlement, which persisted until the early 1940s, provided a periphery to the older regions of Jewish settlement in the coastal plain and the valley of Esdraelon. It extended the boundaries of the settlements to the Western Galilee north of Haifa and penetrated into new districts in the Beisan valley, east of the Sea of Galilee, in the Hule valley as well as in the South. The pioneer component of the Central European immigration participated in the geographic expansion and created a new type of agricultural settlement: the "middle-class villages", established by former lawyers, doctors, engineers and merchants who now became farmers. The other immigrants accelerated processes of urbanisation in the larger agricultural colonies. They played a major role in Tel-Aviv's rapid growth and reinforced the Jewish communities of the mixed Jewish-Arab towns, particularly Haifa.[9]

In the mid-1930s the *Yishuv*, despite making up only one third of the country's population, already produced more than half its GNP. It was the main motivating power behind the speedy modernisation of Palestine. The capital brought in, the enterprise and the varied professional skills of the German immigrants played a decisive role in the *Yishuv*'s economic growth. They contributed to the industrialisation of the economy, developing new branches in industry, commerce, banking and agriculture, and helped to stabilise and improve existing branches of commerce and industry. They stimulated and enriched the capital market and widened the gap between the competing Jewish and Arab societies.[10]

The German immigrants' contribution to the development of the arts and sciences was especially significant. Palestine became a centre of European academic standards in the midst of the Middle East. The professors from Germany who joined the Hebrew University and the Haifa Technion laid the foundations for research and teaching in several new faculties of sciences, the humanities, Jewish studies, social sciences and technology. Because of their participation these institutions acquired international recognition as research centres and places of learning of excellence. Other specialists from Germany initiated and cultivated the first research institutes such as the Sieff (later: Weizmann) Institute for sciences and the centre for agricultural experiments (later: Wulkany Institute).[11]

The numerous German doctors who arrived during the 1930s turned Palestine

[9] HOG, *Ha-Aliyan Ha-Germanit Be Eretz Israel*, Tel-Aviv 1937, p. 3; Ludwig Pinner, *Agricultural Colonization of Middle-Class Immigrants*, unpublished ms., LBI Jerusalem.

[10] HOG, *Ha-Aliyah Mi-Germania Ve-Darka Ba-Aretz*, Tel-Aviv 1939; Aliyah Hadasha, *Esser Shnot Aliyah Hadasha*, Tel-Aviv 1943; Erich Maschke, *The Part Played by the German Immigrants in the Development of Palestine Industry*, 1943, unpublished ms., LBI Jerusalem.

[11] 'Die Hebräische Universität und die deutsche Alija', in *MB* (*Mitteilungsblatt des Irgun Olei Merkas Europa*), 8th November 1940; *Esser Shnot Aliyah Hadasha*, *op. cit.*; Yoav Gelber and Walter Goldstern, *Vertreibung und Emigration deutschsprachiger Ingenieure nach Palästina 1933–1945*, Düsseldorf 1986.

into a regional medical centre for the entire Middle East. German musicians and performers opened the first conservatory in Jerusalem and played a major part in establishing the Palestine Philharmonic Orchestra. Artists of German origin or education revived the Bezalel Academy of Arts in Jerusalem. Thus they promoted cultural creativity in Palestine and made possible the training and upbringing of the next generation of creators.[12]

The socio-economic and professional variety of the German immigration, its familial character, its social ideas and its consumer habits dramatically changed the style of Jewish Palestine. Within a few years they turned it from a pioneering fraternity based on a Spartan elitist ideology into a pluralist and more refined society. This was the first step towards the growth of an abundant society and a modern welfare state into which Israel later developed. Immigrants from Germany taught the *Yishuv* the need for developing welfare services for both immigrants and older settlers. They also initiated and improved the facilities for dealing with the social problems that were typical of future immigrations.

The contribution of the immigrants from Central Europe to the economic, scientific, social and cultural progress of Palestine in the 1930s and 1940s determined to a large extent the *Yishuv*'s Western character and made Israel an island of modern civilisation in the midst of the then still comparatively backward Middle East.

THE IMMIGRANTS ENCOUNTER THE VETERAN YISHUV

This contribution was neither easily accepted nor taken for granted. The Zionist melting pot in Palestine confronted the immigrants from Germany with the established *Yishuv*. The latter consisted mainly of Eastern European and oriental Jews and its leaders came primarily from Russia and Poland. Even when the immigration from Germany reached its peak, most immigrants still came from Eastern European countries. Moreover, one fifth of the immigrants from Germany were themselves natives of Eastern Europe and many more were descendants of *Ostjuden*. However, they usually adopted the Central European patterns of thought and behaviour, and in this problematic meeting they sided with the German Jews.

For several generations the relations between Central and Eastern European Jews in Europe had been ambivalent and tense, due to the different pace of their adjustment to European civilisation. The friction increased during the middle of the nineteenth century, when assimilated German Jews attempted to disseminate their ideas within the traditional Jewish society in Russia with the connivance of the authorities. A few Russian Jews revered and imitated these German *Maskilim* (Enlighteners). The majority, however, regarded them as collaborators with a hostile regime, which was using them to bring about the

---

[12]Doron Niederland, 'Deutsche Ärzte-Emigration und gesundheitspolitische Entwicklungen in Eretz Israel, 1933–1948', in *Medizin Historisches Journal*, XX (1985), pp. 149–185; G. Ofrat, *Bezalel Ha-Chadash, 1935–1955*, Jerusalem 1987; Ida Ivkan, *Leidata Shel Tizmoret*, Tel-Aviv 1969.

disintegration of Jewish society from within and to weaken its resistance to assimilationist reforms. The Jews of Eastern Europe criticised the Western Jews' arrogance, notwithstanding their respect for the German Jews' education, culture and accomplishments.[13]

Jewish emigration from Eastern Europe westwards in the late nineteenth and early twentieth centuries, as well as the occupation of vast areas by the German army in the First World War and the mass flight of refugees during the years of anarchy which followed that war – all these formed the background to a more intensive encounter and increased friction between the Jews of Eastern and Central Europe. This was a meeting between poor emigrants and refugees on the one hand and proud, well-to-do communities on the other. The latter displayed their readiness, initiative and ingenuity in providing material assistance to their destitute brethren. None the less they refrained from social intercourse, emphasising their cultural superiority over their "poor relations" from the East. The indigenous German and Austrian Jews feared an antisemitic reaction to the flood of immigrants. They were particularly anxious to avoid being identified with the newcomers or of being accused of divided loyalty. In certain circles these apprehensions provoked opposition to the immigrants and to further immigration. Combined with feelings of superiority, this opposition resulted in displays of alienation. Usually, immigrants from the East needed one or two generations to be fully incorporated into their new Jewish environment.

In Palestine the situation was exactly the opposite. Here the Eastern European Jews were the older and welcoming element. They held the *Yishuv*'s key positions, moulded its characteristics, established the social order and determined its rules and standards. Their attitude towards the new immigrants from Germany tended to be patronising.

Following their arrival in the country, most immigrants from Germany underwent at least a temporary change for the worse as far as their status and standard of living were concerned. One of the toughest experiences they had to go through was the need to conform with the *Ostjuden*'s domination. This affront to their self esteem was no less annoying than the necessity of learning a new vocation or even of completely changing their way of life in order to make a living. Many of the German Jews were apprehensive that eventually their descendants would assimilate socially and culturally, to say nothing of their own assimilation into an East European society which they found upon their debarkation. To the immigrants from Central Europe, the veteran *Yishuv*'s life seemed provincial and culturally inferior. It reminded them of the East European Jewish neighbourhoods in the large towns of Germany and Austria.

In Eastern Europe Jews considered assimilation a secondary issue. However, within the spiritual and social milieu of the German Jews it had been of paramount significance for several generations. For a long time they had sought means to preserve their identity while integrating into the surrounding civilisation. Their internal differentiation and self definition were to a large extent an outcome of their attitude towards assimilation. Even the German Zionists

[13]Baruch Kurzweil, 'Deyokano Shel Ha-Yehudi Ha-Maaravi Ba-Sifrut Ha-Ivrit', in A. Tarshish and Jochanan Ginat (eds.), *Perakim Mi-Morashta Shel Yahadut Germania*, Jerusalem 1975, pp. 170–189.

considered their Zionism primarily in terms of a reaction to assimilation. Their leader, Kurt Blumenfeld, coined the phrase "post assimilatory Zionism", to distinguish it from the Zionism of the East European Jews, who had not experienced assimilation. Many German immigrants compared the problems of their cultural and social absorption by the *Yishuv* with the hardships they had endured when they had tried to integrate into German society. They were scared of the idea that they would have to acculturate with an environment which was a mixture of Eastern Europe and the Middle East.[14]

The German immigrants could defend themselves against this threat in two ways. One was to declare the *Yishuv* a society still in a process of formation. Hence German Jews should not accept it as something already accomplished. On the contrary, they should endeavour to influence its development, adding a layer based upon their particular historic experience and their unique cultural heritage – "the German-Jewish symbiosis" as Martin Buber had called it. The alternative was to detach themselves from their surroundings, to fortify their self-awareness and to cling to the past. This meant in essence living in cultural and social isolation, protecting the old legacy in the new environment without trying to affect it.

Both patterns were fiercely criticised. The *Yishuv* expected the newcomers to adjust to the existing order. Those who came from Eastern Europe usually fulfilled this expectation, while most immigrants from the German sphere of culture disappointed the veterans. The veterans were prepared to help the immigrants to adapt themselves to the prevailing system, but would not accept them as they were. Many veterans, from the extreme Orthodox to *Hakibbutz Ha'meuchad* suspected from the beginning the *bona fides* of the German immigration. They doubted the readiness of those whom they called *Hitler Zionisten* to reconcile themselves to their new country and its rules. They were even more worried about the innovations which the newcomers might try to introduce.

The *Yishuv* resented the German immigrants' separatism. The existence of a "German" cultural island was incompatible with the prime aim of merging the Diaspora. Such a separatism seemed to obstruct the resurrection of Hebrew as the common language of immigrants from various countries and, furthermore, to upset the role of Hebrew as the language of the revived national culture.

This mutual antagonism was mainly responsible for the political, social and cultural tensions between the German immigrants and the rest of the *Yishuv* which marked the early phase of the former's absorption. Some immigrants' alienation continued even longer. On the one hand this friction was reflected in criticism of various daily phenomena. On the other hand it aroused sharp reactions on the part of the older settlers to the extent of their vilifying the newcomers or ridiculing them.

This initial conflict notwithstanding, most immigrants ultimately succeeded in finding shelter and employment, in providing their children with a good education and in developing an active social life. Many of them volunteered to

[14]See Kurt Blumenfeld's letter to Ludwig Pinner, 21st March 1932, CZA, K 11/303; Gerhard Holdheim, *Die deutsche Alijah*, 1938; and Gustav Krojanker, *Die Beziehungen zwischen den deutschen Juden und dem Yischuw*, 1943, unpublished mss. in the LBI Jerusalem.

assist their fellow Jews whose attempts at absorption had failed. They willingly undertook the general obligations of national service, such as membership of the *Haganah*, serving in the supernumerary police, paying the voluntary communal taxes and in particular fighting National-Socialist Germany during the Second World War.

In the domain of public life the alienation persisted longer. The Palestinian political parties refused to admit the leaders of German Zionism into their higher echelons. The mass of immigrants, absorbed in their problems of adjustment, detached themselves from politics, displaying a reserved attitude towards the existing parties. In the early 1940s their leaders split their association, the *Hitachdut Olej Germania ve-Austria* (HOGOA), into a general, non-political, social welfare organisation, *Irgun Olej Merkas Europa* (IOME) and an immigrants' political party, *Aliyah Hadasha*. The new faction initially attracted thousands of immigrants and triumphed in the election campaign of 1944, emerging second to the dominant *Mapai*. However, its decline during the years of the anti-British struggle was as fast as its rise and in 1948 it vanished through a unification with the "General Zionists A" faction into "The Progressive Party".[15]

At the root of the immigrants' difficulty in integrating into the *Yishuv*'s political life stood some of the more basic differences between Central and Eastern European Jewries. The Jews of Eastern Europe did not identify themselves with the nations among which they lived. They regarded the authorities as inimical and looked on state laws as something designed to discriminate and oppress them; consequently they sought loopholes to circumvent these laws. In their eyes, the Gentile surroundings were hostile and suspect. In contrast, the German Jews had enjoyed three generations of emancipation. They identified with their homeland and were brought up on values such as loyalty to the state and its authorities. They respected the law, which safeguarded their status, and considered its enforcement essential for guaranteeing their rights. Rather than being suspicious of the Gentiles they strove to merge with them and their incorporation into the German society had made much progress before 1933.

The German Jews transferred to their new homeland their adherence to values such as identification with the state, loyalty to authority and respect for the law. Since in Mandatory Palestine the "State" was Great Britain, this loyalty increased the socio-cultural friction between the *Yishuv*'s Eastern and Central European elements. Although the British administration of Palestine was neither tsarist Russia nor Pilsudsky's Poland, yet it was not the Jewish state about which most of the *Yishuv* dreamt. After the promulgation of the White Paper in May 1939, the *Yishuv* regarded the Palestine government as a hostile regime. Its laws were considered repressive and many maintained that they should be openly resisted or clandestinely evaded. The rest of the *Yishuv* disapproved of the German immigrants', or at least their leadership's, loyalty to Britain, their obedience to the government and its rules as well as their reservations about the means to combat the White Paper. In their eyes, all these were dangerous

---

[15] Miriam Getter, 'Ha-Hitargenut Ha-Politit Ha-Nifredet Shel Oley Germania', in *Ha-Zionut*, VII (1981), pp. 240–291.

deviations from the minimal consensus which was essential for the *Yishuv*'s existence as a voluntary community and for the achievement of its national goals.

The German immigrants' attitude to the Arabs, both in daily routine affairs and in the political sphere, aroused similar disaffection. In this matter, too, they transferred concepts of German origin to the different Palestinian reality. Their conciliatory approach to the Arabs was even more incomprehensible to the veterans than their submissiveness to the British.[16] The German immigrants often found it difficult to accommodate to the competitive atmosphere of the national struggle in the country. Their tolerance of the Arabs was more than the *Yishuv* could swallow. A typical example was their misunderstanding of the unofficial protection of "the country's products", which in practice protected Jewish manufacture and agriculture against Arab competition.[17]

Individuals who had social relationships with Arabs, the British or other foreigners were similarly denounced and sometimes provoked more violent reactions. In the eyes of the majority this behaviour amounted to splitting Jewish solidarity in face of the hostile environment. On the political level the immigrants adhered to the legacy of their forefathers' struggle for equality in Germany. They were more sensitive therefore to the issue of minority rights in the Jewish state if and when it were to be established. Most of the *Yishuv* repudiated the political stance of the German immigrants on the Arab question as expressed by their leadership and publications.

These generalisations do some injustice to many immigrants who did not conform to the customary image of the German Jews. Indeed, among the veterans too there were many who treated the immigrants differently. However, for a long time the actual encounter of East Europeans veterans and German newcomers took place under the shadow of stereotypes that had been imported from the Diaspora. Only after several years and under the pressure of new circumstances were the barriers that had initially burdened the immigrants' full intergration into the *Yishuv* removed.

THE GERMAN IMMIGRATION'S MYTHS AND REALITIES

Persecution was the main motivating force behind the immigration from Central Europe. None the less, it initially bore an image of a "welfare immigration": homogeneous, bourgeois, well-educated and family-orientated. This perception began to change in the *Yishuv*'s consciousness only after the *Anschluss* and the "*Kristallnacht*", when many newcomers were penniless refugees.

Since the beginning of this wave of immigration reality was more complex than this crude stereotype. Not all the immigrants from Germany, Austria and Czechoslovakia were natives of those countries. Their composition reflected the patterns of Jewish emigration from the Russian Pale of Settlement westwards

---

[16]'Tevioteinu Min Ha-Kongress', in *Achdut Ha-Am*, 30th June 1939; and ' "Achdut Ha-Am" Mitchara Be- "Brit Shalom" ', in *Ha-Boker*, 25th June 1939.

[17]*Bemerkungen zur wirtschaftlichen Struktur, Mentalität und Politik in Ankunftzeit der fünften Alijah*, unpublished ms., LBI Jerusalem.

early in the twentieth century and following the First World War. About twenty per cent of the immigrants from Germany had been born in Russia and Poland. The proportion of those who had come from Galicia and Bukovina was even higher among the immigrants from Austria. Hence the immigration represented the social composition of East European Jewry no less than it manifested the stratification of the old German and Austrian communities.

The age spectrum among the immigrants was very broad. Besides thousands of single young pioneers, many families arrived with young children on the one hand, and with grandparents on the other. This immigration from Germany created the Youth *Aliyah* project, but it also introduced the first "homes for the aged", which had previously been unknown to the *Yishuv*.[18]

The immigrants' distribution according to pursuits, property and education has disproved the simple image of a well-to-do immigration. Alongside wealthy and academic middle-class immigrants, who within a short time increased the price of land and accommodation, there arrived thousands of poor Jews, carrying a heavy burden of previous wandering and suffering, lacking any vocational skills or training and ill-educated. The immigrants' occupational variety grew wider in the wake of the changes in professions that many of them had to undergo after their arrival. In addition to the imported socio-economic gaps, new disparities were created because of the absorption processes.

Politically and ideologically, too, the Central European immigration was by no means uniform. Although the veteran German Zionist leadership continued for several years to lead the immigrants in Palestine, the number of old Zionists among them was small and proportional to the Zionist movement's weight within German, Austrian and Czech Jewries after the First World War. The number of "new Zionists" was greater. These were Jews, particularly German Jews, who genuinely adopted Zionism as their personal reaction to the rise to power of the National Socialists and the undoing of emancipation. Besides old and new Zionists, many immigrants arrived without any Zionist background. Others had hardly had any connection with Judaism and came to the country because it was the only feasible escape when they left or were expelled from Nazi-dominated Germany and Europe.

The immigrants adhered to a broad variety of creeds. They were atheists, secular, traditional, national religious and Orthodox Jews. They comprised Communists and Social Democrats, Liberals and Conservatives, "General Zionists", Labour Zionists and Revisionists. Nevertheless, their socio-economic and political grouping notwithstanding, the Central European immigrants had a common quality that for many years after their arrival was stronger than their internal differences. The German cultural-linguistic heritage, to which many of them remained loyal subsequent to their arrival, distinguished them from the rest of the *Yishuv*. Even when they were fully incorporated socially and culturally many retained it as an expression of their uniqueness.

This legacy was not only a matter of language and literary, musical, artistic or architectural preference. Its main manifestation was the modern state concept

---

[18]For the immigrants' distribution according to age see the Jewish Agency's statistical department review of the immigration for Germany, February 1939, CZA, S 25/2482.

that they transferred from Central Europe to Palestine. The principal contribution that they strove to stamp upon the *Yishuv*'s life was in the field of political culture: the cultivation of values such as responsibility and loyalty, quality and meticulousness. When the State of Israel was founded in 1948, many German immigrants, particularly lawyers and former civil servants, were incorporated into the newly-built state machinery in various legal and administrative posts which had been closed to them during the "state in the making" period. They helped to establish the Israeli system of law, instituted the office of State Comptroller and contributed to the development of state social, health and education services. They aspired to raise the standards of public services, law and order and social norms to the level which they had recognised in Germany. This aspiration provoked opposition and their success was incomplete. However, it was sufficient to change the character of Jewish society in Palestine and strengthen its Western-modern element.

The younger immigrants, and their descendants who were born in Palestine, were brought up in Hebrew in the *Yishuv*'s school system. They conformed to its norms and values and were gradually detached from the German cultural heritage, to the regret of their parents. The process was especially marked in the linguistic sphere and less apparent in non-verbal fields such as music and aesthetics. A problem common to many families was the linguistic ambivalence of the second generation. The children spoke German within the family circle and Hebrew among their friends. Sometimes this dualism expanded from the field of language to include the whole social code. Children of German families had to follow certain norms of behaviour expected at home and to behave differently away from their homes in order to conform with the surrounding society.

At first, the immigrants from Germany made a unique contribution to the development of the *Yishuv*. This derived from the particular historic legacy of an organised community having distinct attributes. Later, this communal contribution split into a large variety of individual influences on various spheres of life that were not necessarily inter-related to each other.

The best proof of the Central European immigrants' integration into the *Yishuv* is the difficulty of excluding them in order to follow their history after the establishment of Israel. Their separate political framework, *Aliyah Hadasha*, disappeared a few months later and its decline had begun even earlier.[19] As individuals, they retained many of the qualities that had characterised them when they had been newcomers. But the separate and consolidated body that they had formed during the 1930s and 1940s ceased to exist. The patterns of mutual assistance which they had developed since 1933 persisted, however, serving as a model for other immigrants' communities, while the Germans' outward distinctiveness became blurred. It was only seldom that they worked for a common interest, such as when IOME undertook the handling of the claims for compensation from Germany.

It is even more difficult to differentiate the immigrants' second generation,

[19] Getter, *loc. cit.*

whether with the aim of collecting statistical data or in order to follow their development or to try to establish any common characteristics. The varying patterns of absorption in towns, middle-class settlements and kibbutzim, the subsequent inter-marriages and the growing influence of the Israeli surroundings in the schools, the youth movements, the army and the universities have covered almost any sign of origins. The German immigrants' children, to say nothing of their grandchildren, have become an integral part of Israeli society. It is now barely possible to discern their roots.

ABSORPTION IN PALESTINE IN COMPARISION WITH OTHER COUNTRIES

About a quarter of the total number of Jews who had emigrated from the Third *Reich* before the closing of its exits in 1941 found their way to Palestine, either directly or through transit countries. The other three quarters dispersed over the whole world. Their principal concentrations were in the United States and in Britain. In smaller numbers they settled in various European countries, in the British Commonwealth and in Latin America. In all these countries the immigrants from Central Europe had to give up large parts of their heritage, to endure problems of adjustment, to learn the local language and often to change their profession. It appears that except for those individuals who arrived in exotic under-developed countries in the colonial empires, the change from Central Europe to Palestine was the most radical one.

In the United States, in Britain, in the Dominions and even more so in Switzerland or Sweden, the Central European émigrés were integrated into Western cultures and modern economies similar to those they had left behind them. By contrast, in Palestine they had to reconcile their standards with the backward economy of an under-developed country where modernisation had only recently begun. For the time being they had to adapt themselves to a lifestyle that many of them considered primitive. A few willingly entered into the pioneering spirit demanded by the circumstances and some were even sorry not to have been among the founding fathers. For others, the day-to-day hardships were a source of bitterness and complaint. The majority, however, accepted the new realities, aspired to ameliorate their lot and usually, though by no means always, succeeded.

The transformation from one culture to another, too, was more clear-cut in Palestine than in most other destinations. The transference from German to Anglo-Saxon culture was far smoother than adaptation to the reviving Jewish national culture. Many German immigrants, excluding the Orthodox Jews, had long ago detached themselves from traditional Judaism. The modern Hebrew culture that had emerged in Palestine was strange to most of them, including even old Zionists who had learnt Hebrew in their youth. Its East European and Middle Eastern elements had an alienating effect on many, giving them a sense of "retrogression". Of course, this did not make their absorption any easier.

In Palestine, self-help and mutual assistance partially relieved the intensity of the changes caused by emigration. The immigration from Germany was an organised movement of a large community, which co-operated in solving the problems involved in its assimilation in Palestine. In view of the tense relations with the older settlers and the initial lack of official machinery for supervising integration (except for cadres of pioneers and young people) the immigrants had to find their own way in their new country and to take care of themselves.

One of the German immigrants' most significant qualities was their self-reliance. They transferred to Palestine the splendid tradition of the Central European communal organisation. This, and their strong sense of solidarity which was further reinforced through the encounter with the veteran *Yishuv*, generated the establishment of their own organisation. *Hitachdut Olej Germania* (HOG) played a central role both in admitting the immigrants and paving the road for their incorporation, as well as in urging the national institutions to confront the problems of immigration and absorption. It could rely on previous experience that had been acquired in Germany when solving the problems of material, social and cultural intergration of the heterogeneous emigration from Eastern Europe from the end of the nineteenth century.[20] In 1933 this experience had no parallel in Palestine, which hitherto had absorbed mainly pioneer immigrants. It enabled early detection of the likely problems and helped in providing the proper solutions.

HOG, and later HOGOA and IOME were the backbone of the absorption process. Their co-operation with the Zionists in Germany, while Zionist work was still possible under the National-Socialist regime, and with the World Zionist Organisation and the *Yishuv*'s national institutions laid the foundations of the special facilities that were established to deal with the influx of immigrants from Germany and their absorption into Palestine: the United Committee of the *Yishuv*; the Jewish Agency's German department; *Haavara* and *Paltreu* companies; the Youth *Aliyah* project; the Rural and Suburban Settlement Company (RASSCO); *Ha-Lishka Le-Maan Ha-Oleh* (the Bureau for the Immigrant); *Kupat Milwe* (a small loans fund); *Mifaal Ha-Ezra Ha-Hadadit* (Mutual Aid Project); *Ha-Aguda Le-Chinuch Ve-Tarbut* (Association for Education and Culture) and many others. The immigrants were the principal driving force in the establishment of these organisations and their main beneficiaries.

HOG, and later IOME, were directly involved in the following areas: representing the immigrants before the Palestine Government and the *Yishuv*'s national institutions; representing them in the organisations that dealt with the transfer of Jewish property from Germany and its investment in Palestine; instructing and directing the preparation of personal claims for compensation; admitting the immigrants at the ports and seeing to their preliminary arrangements; housing; vocational retraining and finding employment; education of children and adults; agricultural settlement and instruction; provision of legal and economic advice; arranging Hebrew classes; social and cultural activity; direct financial support; establishment of mutal aid associations, such as

[20]Donald L. Niewyk, *The Jews in Weimar Germany*, Baton Rouge–London 1980.

Kupat Milwe and the *Solidaritätswerk*; and caring for the aged or disabled immigrants through a network of special homes.[21]

Except for the General Federation of Workers (*Histadrut*) there was no voluntary body in the *Yishuv* whose activities were so wide-ranging. The machinery for assimilation built by the German immigrants later served as a model in the establishment of a similar general apparatus by the Jewish Agency. Some of the facilities that had initially been created for the immigration from Central Europe were then reshaped to absorb other immigrations.

Besides their central association and its off-shoots, the German immigrants established various voluntary communities in the larger towns and developed patterns of communal life in the middle-class settlements. These communities served as social and cultural frameworks that alleviated their members' problems of integration, strengthened their spirits and supported them in confronting the hardships of adjustment.[22]

The institutional system erected by HOG in 1933 and after, still left ample room for personal efforts, initiative and resourcefulness. None the less, it distinguished the immigration to Palestine from emigration to other countries. True, other emigrants too were helped by Jewish philanthropic organisations in Germany, in transit countries and in their ultimate destinations. Local voluntary committees spontaneously got together to help the newcomers when they arrived in the United States, in Britain and in other countries. But in all these places immigration and integration were first and foremost a matter for the individual. The contribution of Central European Jews to their new countries was essentially personal. They were incorporated into the existing economic and academic systems and enriched them with their knowledge and skills, but did not create anything new or original.

In comparison with other target-countries, Palestine's uniqueness was manifold: the longer survival of this immigration's collective character, both because of its considerable weight within the *Yishuv* and its well-developed self organisation as well as its inhibitions about assimilating into the prevailing system; the collective mark that the German immigration stamped on the *Yishuv*, beyond the aggregate of its members' personal contributions; the scope of the innovations that it brought to an under-developed country and its historical heritage's clear impact on its own integration as well as on society at large.

The immigration from Central Europe was mainly thought of as a "welfare immigration", but simultaneously it was the first "immigration of distress" that the Zionist enterprise had to cope with. Because of its complexity it is worthwhile to compare it with later waves of immigrants: the Surviving Remnant's immigration of the late 1940s, the mass immigration from Middle Eastern and North African countries during the 1950s and early 1960s, the Polish immigrations of 1956/1957 and 1968 and the immigration from Russia in the 1970s

---

[21]HOG, *Ha-Aliya Mi-Germania Ve-Darka Ba-Aretz*, *op. cit.*; Walter Preuss, *The Central European Immigration and the Histadrut*, 1943, unpublished ms., LBI Jerusalem.
[22]*Esser Shnot Aliyah Hadasha*, *op. cit.*, pp. 15–16; Holdheim, *op. cit.*, pp. 27–30.

and currently. The absorption of these distinct groups of immigrants has not yet been thoroughly researched, so a serious comparison is still impossible. However, it appears that the personal hardships of adjustment, such as the initial shock following the meeting with Israel's reality, the decline of personal status and the gaps between adults and youngsters, are common to all the influxes of immigrants. More surprising is the feeling common to most immigrants that they served as "political cannon fodder". The establishment of the political parties has displayed interest in their fate only in anticipation of election campaigns, but has shown little concern about their true incorporation into public life.

The German immigrants of the 1930s were fortunate in arriving with independent means and in the first years they still influenced the distribution of the national resources which had been mobilised for their sake. They also had their own German Zionist leadership, whose authority had been accepted already in Germany. Members of this leadership, such as Felix Rosenblüth (Pinchas Rosen), Georg Landauer, Alfred Landsberg and others had immigrated earlier and had prepared the infra-structure of self-organisation that would prove its vitality in absorbing the later mass immigration of their fellow countrymen. In Palestine this leadership was accepted by many immigrants who had not recognised it in Germany or in Austria. In this sense the Central European immigration differed from later waves of immigrants who arrived without leadership and lacking any resources, and therefore were totally dependent upon their hosts.

It is also true that the immigrants from Germany, more than immigrants from other countries, remained loyal for a longer time to the linguistic, cultural and historic heritage of their homeland and were slow to detach themselves from it. Because of their resistance to being thrown into the *Yishuv*'s melting pot and thus losing their distinctive identity, their merging was slow and gradual, but also complete and thorough. Among those who came from Central Europe, and as far as their descendants are concerned also, there is scarcely any tendency to search for "roots" or take up again the old legacy. Now, Israel is their homeland, and it is not new any more.

Sources on Jewish History

The Cultural and Intellectual History of Ashkenazic Jews 1500–1750

A Selective Bibliography and Essay

BY JOSEPH M. DAVIS

"What line separates the inside from the outside, the rumble of wheels from the howl of wolves?"

Calvino, *Invisible Cities*

I. EARLY MODERN ASHKENAZIC CULTURE

In 1984, Gershon Bacon and Gershon Hundert gave us a magnificent bibliography of the history of Polish and Russian Jewry.[1] Bacon's essay covers the modern period; Hundert's, the period until 1772. Their accomplishment (recently updated in an article in *Modern Judaism*[2]) is very impressive; Hundert's gazetteer of studies of hundreds of local Jewish communities in Poland, for example, is a *tour de force*.

Hundert focuses mostly on topics of social history, such as demography and economic structure. In this, he follows the dominant trend of scholarly study of Ashkenazic Jews, in which social – often Socialist – concerns have been foremost throughout this century. But six generations of scholars, from the *Maskil* Jacob Reifmann (d. 1895) to the present, have studied intellectual history. Their work is only thinly represented in Hundert's bibliography. He fails to list many important studies; for example, the many studies of Jehuda Löw ben Bezalel, called Maharal of Prague (d. 1609), one of the most profound Jewish thinkers of the sixteenth century.[3]

Hundert is hindered by the limits that he imposes on his bibliography, namely the boundaries of the Polish-Lithuanian Commonwealth. Maharal, he might point out, was a rabbi not in Poland but in Bohemia. In the early modern period, however, the borders between German, Bohemian, Polish, and Lithuanian Jews were still fluid. Maharal himself was born in the Polish city of Poznań; he served

---

[1] See Bacon and Hundert (#1) in the 'Selected Bibliography', below. All notes in this essay will refer to the bibliography, below, where full references are given. I wish to thank Professor Chimen Abramsky, London, for sharing his erudition to fill numerous gaps in the bibliography. I would also like to thank the staff of the Washington University libraries in Saint Louis. Thanks are also due to the Memorial Foundation for Jewish Culture, which supported the preliminary work on this essay in 1987–1989.

[2] See Hundert (#4).

[3] On Maharal, see #164–179 in the bibliography, and the other studies listed after #179.

as rabbi in Prague for many years, but he also served for a few years as rabbi in Poznań. Jewish intellectual life crossed national borders. The "cultural history of early modern *Polish* Jews" is a phantom. So, by the same token, is the "cultural history of early modern *German* Jews." The two groups shared the same common culture. The estrangement of the Jews of the two regions during the eighteenth century was a later process of momentous importance.

In sum, a supplement to Hundert's bibliography on the cultural, religious and intellectual history of modern Ashkenazic Jews will be a useful tool for the student.

The bibliography below is necessarily somewhat selective. Recent works have been favoured over older works. Primary texts, even important ones, are not listed. Nor are basic reference tools of Jewish scholarship, such as encyclopedias, indexes, library catalogues and others, unless they bear some specific relation to the topic of this essay. Many lacunae have been left, but a few works at least from many areas of study are detailed.

II. ONE CULTURE AND THREE FIELDS

Studies of Ashkenazic culture may mostly be divided into three categories: rabbinics, Yiddish literature and Jewish thought.

Different groups of scholars have populated each field. The study of rabbinics has been the territory of religious, often Orthodox, Jews. The subject matter is particularly pertinent to them: rabbis of the early modern period are still regarded among the Orthodox as authoritative guides. The study of Yiddish literature, by contrast, has been associated throughout this century with Yiddishism and hence with Jewish secularism. And Jewish thought is the territory of scholars who cannot live with religion or without it (Gershom Scholem is an example).

All three fields are increasingly dominated by university professors. The days of Israel Zinberg (who died in a Stalinist prison camp in 1939 or 1940) are no more: one of the greatest Jewish scholars of his day, he was a chemist by profession. The university setting has led to a certain homogenisation of the three fields, but also to the familiar vice of specialisation. Each field has tended not only towards a distinctive subject matter, but towards a particular methodological approach as well. Research on rabbinics has concentrated on rabbinic authors, rabbinic institutions and social history. Study of Yiddish writing, on the other hand, has focused on its literary history; not so much on authors or institutions, but on the literary characteristics of texts and genres. Students of Jewish thought, in areas such as Jewish philosophy and mysticism, have inclined towards intellectual history in the narrow sense. Abstracting ideas from both literary and social settings, they place them mainly in the context of systems of ideas.

A full appreciation of Ashkenazic thought and culture, it need hardly be said, requires an understanding of all three fields. But a methodological crossfertilisation would be useful as well.

Consider, for example, the literature of sermons. The pilpulistic sermons typical of the early modern period resist the methods of the intellectual historians because such texts usually appear to have, behind their interpretive pyrotechnics, very little speculative content of any kind. Often, they offer equally little to the student of rabbinics, searching for concrete data on individuals and institutions. A literary approach might be more fruitful. The pilpulistic sermon expresses an aesthetic of erudition, connection and surprise that is typical of the Baroque.[4]

Yiddish literature, by contrast, has not yet been sufficiently probed for its religious conceptions. Do these agree with those of contemporary Hebrew texts, or can we speak of a vernacular religion distinct from the high culture of Hebrew writings? This is the work that Chava Weissler has begun, concentrating on the genre of *tkhines*, Yiddish prayers.[5]

In this essay, each of these areas is considered in turn: first rabbinics, then Jewish thought, and Yiddish literature last. We will conclude with a number of general remarks.

III. THE WORLD OF THE TALMUDIST

It is not always appreciated that a large number of early modern Ashkenazic works are available in any standard rabbinic library. Open any rabbinic edition of any Jewish classic – the Bible, the Midrash, legal codes, and so on – an edition that contains multiple commentaries, and like as not, there will be a commentary written by an Ashkenazic rabbi of the early modern period. The standard Vilna edition of the Talmud contains nearly a dozen such commentaries.

Yet in spite of this wealth of easily available material, rabbinic literature, commentary especially, presents a challenge to the student of early modern Jewish culture. The material often seems to concern technical interpretative questions to the exclusion of all else. Discussions move seemingly at random from one topic to another. Works frequently repeat earlier traditions and interpretations verbatim. We can understand why many scholars prefer *responsa*, whose arguments are usually clearer and more original, and always more concrete, than those of other rabbinic texts,[6] or books of *minhagim*, customs, rich in colourful details of everyday life.[7]

And, recognising the difficulties of the material, we can better appreciate the accomplishment of Jacob Katz, who has laid bare in a series of articles and books the social meaning of certain selected *halakhic* issues, such as the laws governing wine made by non-Jews,[8] the setting of hours of prayer,[9] and the employment of

---

[4]Saperstein's recent survey of Jewish sermon literature (#192) may open up the field, and see also #188–193. Cf. #106 and 108.
[5]See Weissler's studies (#187, 282 and 333).
[6]On *responsa*, see #111–124 in the bibliography.
[7]On *minhagim*, see #125–134 in the bibliography.
[8]See in Katz's books, #16 and #381 below.
[9]Below, Katz (#89).

non-Jews on the Sabbath (the "*Shabbes-goy*").[10] Katz establishes contexts in which legal controversies reflect social conflicts, and interpretative innovations reflect social change.

Yet Katz's work, and other work in the same vein, while extremely valuable, does not illuminate the whole world of the talmudist. Many questions about Ashkenazic Talmudism wait to be answered, or even asked.

Rabbinic literature is characterised by its atmosphere of authority. It is a prismatic authority of many texts reflected through many commentaries, but it is political authority none the less. Rabbis, in addition to being text-scholars and educators, were also politicians. One question that students of rabbinic literature must, therefore, face is the question of political theory. A system of balances, a system of rules – some precise, some vague – kept order among many conflicting authorities: rabbis living and dead, lay leaders, texts of different types, communities larger and smaller.

Daniel Elazar, a political scientist who has begun the work of studying traditional Jewish political thought, calls this system a constitution.[11] Like the British constitution, it was for the most part unwritten and implicit. For this reason, it must be sought out not only in *halakhic* texts but also in the historical records of Jewish political activity and the documents produced by communal governments themselves, and by the Council of Four Lands and the other political institutions of Ashkenazic Jewry. Thus, historians, after generations of mining Ashkenazic religious literature for information on social history, are now using archival texts, such as the communal *pinkas* of Poznań, as sources for the study of implicit political and religious beliefs.[12]

Like any constitution, the constitution of the Ashkenazic Jews contained unresolved problems and flaws. There is no work within Ashkenazic rabbinic literature more authoritative than the notes of Moses Isserles (d. 1572) to the *Shulchan Aruch*. Yet, as Chaim Tchernowitz demonstrated in his *Toldot ha-Poskim*, the authority of the *Shulchan Aruch* was not accepted either immediately or in full.[13] Its acceptance encountered considerable opposition, from Solomon Luria (d. 1573), Joel Sirkes (d. 1642), Maharal of Prague and others. Another constitutional flaw, Elazar suggests, was Messianism. The authority of a Messiah such as Sabbatai Zvi (d. 1676) was theoretically unlimited, and had no way of being contained within the political system. Katz points also to the systemic tensions between *Halakhah* and *kabbalah*, tensions that grew into a crisis during the eighteenth-century disputes between the *Hasidim* and the *Mitnagdim*.[14]

The beliefs of Ashkenazic Jews have too often been assumed rather than investigated. Having supposed that we knew what rabbinic Judaism teaches, we needed only to say that sixteenth- or seventeenth-century Ashkenazic rabbis believed in it. But what is "rabbinic Judaism"? What was it in the sixteenth and seventeenth century in Central and Eastern Europe?

[10] Below, Katz (#90).
[11] See Elazar and Cohen (#137) below.
[12] See #139–142 below.
[13] Tchernowitz (#83) below. Cf. #92–97 on codification.
[14] See Katz (#82) below.

The world of a talmudist is a strange world, composed in part of the familiar and the well known, and in part of the near-legendary. The talmudist jumps freely from the Temple in Jerusalem, which he has never seen and never will see, to the prayers that he and all his family and friends say every day, and the stew that he had for dinner. To describe this world, we must therefore be sensitive to the intimate connections between "Jewish Law and Social and Economic Reality", as the title of Edward Fram's recent thesis suggests,[15] but we cannot stop there.

The historian Jacques Le Goff has coined the term "oneiric horizon" for that horizon of dreams that surrounded medieval man: dream-India, the dream-North, the dream-Atlantic West, and so on.[16] Ashkenazic Jews also had an oneiric horizon. The horizon of dreams separated the mundane present from the miracle-filled past and from the messianic future. The land of Israel, land of miracles and magic, lay on that horizon of dreams.[17]

Part of rabbinic literature, not a small part, lies on the far side of this oneiric horizon. In the land of Israel, we learn, fruits grow larger than in other lands. Here is the great Sanhedrin, the archetype of the rabbinic councils of Poland. Here are kings, High Priests, and golems. Rabbinic literature is full of strange imagined creatures and strange warnings. There is a type of bird that grows on trees; it is dangerous to drink olive oil neat. This is a legal literature and it regulated mundane realities, but it is also (and I speak here of *Halakhah*, not only of *aggadah*) a literature of the imagination.[18]

IV. THE PROBLEM OF THE ASHKENAZIC RENAISSANCE 1500–1620

For the last thirty years, scholars of Ashkenazic culture have been divided over the nature – indeed, the existence – of the "Ashkenazic Renaissance" of the sixteenth century. A number of scholars, including very recently Jacob Elbaum in a masterful survey,[19] and earlier Haim Hillel Ben Sasson, one of the leading Israeli historians,[20] have suggested that Ashkenazic culture had a "Renaissance", parallel to the "Northern Renaissance" in England, Germany, Poland and elsewhere. Ashkenazic culture during this period, they argue, was characterised by the increased prominence of philosophical and scientific study and rationalist beliefs, by an expanded range of intellectual interests and pursuits, and by the opening of Ashkenazic thought to cultural influence from outside itself.

Men such as Moses Isserles in Poland, Josel of Rosheim (d. 1554) in Germany, Elijah Levita (or Elijah Bokher; d. 1549) in Italy, and David Gans (d. 1613) in

---

[15]See Fram (#80) below.
[16]Jacques Le Goff, 'The Medieval West and the Indian Ocean. An Oneiric Horizon', in *Time, Work, and Culture in the Middle Ages*, transl. by A. Goldhammer, Chicago 1980, pp. 189–200.
[17]Cf. Zfatman-Biller (#256) below.
[18]Cf. some of the texts discussed in Freehof (#113) and Jacobs (#116).
[19]Elbaum (#12) below.
[20]See Ben Sasson's studies: #10, 135, 136, 375 and 384.

Prague are taken to typify these trends. Does not Isserles refer to Plato on the first page of his interpretation of the book of Esther? In addition to Talmud and Jewish law, he studied Bible, *kabbalah*, philosophy, science, history and magic.[21] Similarly, Josel, the leader of German Jewry during the early sixteenth century, had an interest in history, philosophy and *kabbalah*.[22] Levita, born a German Jew, was the foremost Hebrew grammarian and Bible scholar of his day; he was the teacher of a number of Christian Hebraists, and also the greatest Yiddish poet of his age.[23] Gans, who worked with the great astronomer Tycho Brahe, was the outstanding Ashkenazic student of science in this period, as well as the outstanding Ashkenazic historian of his day.[24] Jiřina Šedinová has detailed Gans's free use of Christian sources.[25] Mordechai Breuer, noting Gans's lack of emphasis on martyrology, contrasts him with earlier Ashkenazic historians, and speaks of his "modernism".[26]

These same trends towards rationalism and openness, it has been argued, can also be seen in other fields. The best Ashkenazic doctors of the period, for example, had degrees in philosophy and medicine from the University of Padua.[27] In Ashkenazic ethical writing of the sixteenth century, Jacob Elbaum has shown, there was an Aristotelian, anti-ascetic tendency.[28] Furthermore, the educational reforms suggested by Maharal and his followers, discussed by the historian Simhah Assaf and others, show a certain tendency towards rationalism and towards an expansion of intellectual interests. Maharal's criticisms were far-reaching, and included matters such as textbooks, teaching practices, and the use of *pilpul* (which Maharal opposed); significantly, Maharal wished to expand the range of subject matter to include Bible, grammar, philosophy and science.[29] (Parallels to the views of early modern Christian educators, such as Comenius and Calvin, have been suggested.[30])

And yet, respond the critics of this line of interpretation, such as Jacob Katz, when all is said and done, philosophy and science were never truly assimilated into Ashkenazic culture. Levita was an Italian Jew. Isserles's understanding of philosophy was superficial. Gans was a unique exception. Doctors with university educations were marginal to Ashkenazic cultural life.[31] The word "Renaissance", Hava Fraenkel-Goldschmidt has argued, cannot legitimately be applied to Josel of Rosheim.[32] Maharal was another unique exception, and his movement for educational reform failed almost completely. Furthermore, his attachment to any sort of rationalism or "Renaissance" is debatable. In 1965,

---

[21] On Isserles, see #38, 92–97 and 145.
[22] On Josel, see #39, 148 and 384.
[23] On Levita, see #40 and #315–317, 320.
[24] On Gans, see Neher (#34) and also #209–213, 224–230.
[25] Šedinová (#228–230) below.
[26] Breuer (#224–226) below.
[27] See Carpi (#217) below.
[28] See Elbaum (#194–195) below.
[29] On Maharal's suggested reforms, see Assaf (#65) below. Cf. Fishman (#67), Kleinberger (#70 and 170), Rappel (#72 and 108) and Reiner (#109).
[30] Comenius – Adini (#63) and Kleinberger (#70); Calvin – Kulka (#171) below.
[31] On both of these points, see Fishman (#207).
[32] See Fraenkel-Goldschmidt (#148) below.

André Neher wrote an article on 'Maharal as Humanist', comparing Maharal to Michelangelo, Dürer and Montaigne.[33] But in 1978, Rivkah Shatz claimed that "no signs of humanism are discernible in the philosophy of the Maharal".[34] Ashkenazic Jews throughout the early modern period, Katz suggests in an article on the literature of the massacres of 1648–1649, were not realists; they lived in an imagined dream-world of liturgy, ascetic piety and martyrology.[35]

Was David Gans typical of early modern Ashkenazic Judaism, or were the martyrologists of 1648?

It is possible that each one was typical of his day; for 1648 was not 1598. The years between 1610 and 1620 mark a watershed in Ashkenazic culture. Here my own thesis, on the philosopher Joseph ben Isaac of Lithuania (fl. 1610) and his student, the talmudist Yom Tov Lipman Heller (d. 1654), should be mentioned.[36] Joseph was one of the boldest of all early modern Ashkenazic philosophical writers. Rationalist leanings can be found in Heller's early writings as well. But in 1613, after the publication of his first book, Joseph was forced to retreat from his earlier Aristotelianism.

The change in the public attitude towards philosophy may also be seen from a *responsum* written in 1618 by Joel Sirkes, rabbi of Joseph ben Isaac's home town of Brest-Litovsk. He wrote:

> "There is no doubt that [a certain man] deserves . . . excommunication . . . for he . . . mocks the words of the wise and slights the wisdom of the *kabbalah*, the very source and essence of the torah . . . Furthermore, this man is drawn after philosophy, which is heresy itself and the evil woman of whom King Solomon warned."[37]

Both the explicit identification of philosophy with heresy and the presentation of philosophy and *kabbalah* as polar opposites were new to Ashkenazic Jews in 1618. They were to become commonplaces later on.

Why did the study of philosophy and science decline among Ashkenazic Jews? Majer Balaban has suggested parallels to the increasing narrowness of seventeenth-century Polish culture.[38] In the seventeenth century, Polish culture turned inwards; it became more devout and less cosmopolitan. Ashkenazic Jewry also turned inwards, towards Jewish kabbalistic piety and away from the temptations of Gentile philosophy.

Already in 1540, the association of philosophy with the Gentiles had troubled Josel of Rosheim. As he copied a work of philosophy by a Spanish Jew (Hava Fraenkel-Goldschmidt points out), Josel left out the names of the Gentile philosophers.[39] But what in a period of cultural openness was attractive, if dangerous, became forbidden in an age of increased tensions and violence.

---

[33] Neher (#173) below.
[34] Shatz (#177).
[35] Katz (#244). Cf. Liebes in Twersky (#162).
[36] Davis (#147). On Heller, see also #78, 99, 243 and 377.
[37] Quoted in Schochet (#36) below.
[38] See Balaban (#8) below.
[39] See Fraenkel-Goldschmidt (#148), pp. 40–49.

V. THE RISE OF KABBALAH AND SABBATIANISM 1600–1700

During the seventeenth century and the early eighteenth century, the influence and prominence of kabbalists and *kabbalah* attained an almost unchallenged position within Ashkenazic life and thought, a position that had not been not theirs before and would not be again.

The *kabbalah* of Safed was decisive in the development of seventeenth-century Ashkenazic kabbalistic beliefs. Scholem emphasised the influence of the teachings of Isaac Luria, called the Ari (d. 1572);[40] more recently, Beracha Sack has placed added stress on the influence of Luria's older colleague, Moses Cordovero.[41] (Independent Ashkenazic kabbalistic thought may be found in the labyrinthine interpretations [252 interpretations of the same verse !] and *gematriyot* of Nathan Spira [d. 1633].)[42]

The influence of Safed *kabbalah* may be seen not only in mystical speculative thought but also, and especially, in other areas. In a wealth of specific studies, the steady increase of kabbalistic influence throughout the seventeenth century has been found in genres such as law, prayer, folktales and especially, as Zeev Gries has shown, in *musar*, ethical writing.[43]

This influence was not unopposed. Yom Tov Lipman Heller, for example, while he did not challenge the essential legitimacy of *kabbalah*, did object to public preaching on kabbalistic topics, to the publication of kabbalistic books, and to the adoption of certain kabbalistic customs. Similarly, two generations later, Yair Hayyim Bacharach (d. 1702), while admitting in principle that *kabbalah* is "the soul of the Torah and the root of faith", suggests that in practice it should hardly be studied at all.[44]

Why did the study of *kabbalah* flourish, in spite of all opposition, throughout the seventeenth century? In the early modern period, *kabbalah* included a powerful ethical theory; the association of *kabbalah* with *musar* and hence with saintliness must be considered one of its strongest selling points. A major apostle of the teachings of Safed among Ashkenazic Jews was Isaiah Horowitz (d. 1630), author of the *musar* work, *Shenei Luhot ha-Berit*. (The book deserves more study than it has received.[45]) The kabbalists' claim of magical abilities also contributed importantly to its spread. The author of the hagiographic work, *Shivhei ha-Ari*, was an Ashkenazic Jew, Solomon Shlemel ben Hayyim (fl. 1607).[46] Finally, the association of *kabbalah* with new liturgical devotions, such as *kabbalat Shabbat*, aided in its spreading popularity.

The rise of *kabbalah* among Ashkenazic Jews was also the rise of a set of ethical doctrines, the rise of a type of wonder-worker, and the rise of a set of prayers and of a new conception of prayer. *Hasidism*, in its wonder-working, its emphasis on

---

[40] Scholem (#422–423) below.
[41] See below Sack in Twersky (#162), and also Idel (#158) and Wolfson (#163).
[42] See Liebes (#409), and cf. Ginzberg (#208).
[43] See Gries (#200), and the other studies listed after #163 below.
[44] See Twersky in #162 below.
[45] See in the meantime Horodetsky (#155), Newman (#160) and Sack in Twersky (#162). Also, Elliot Wolfson's article on Horowitz (#163) will appear shortly.
[46] See Benayahu (#154).

spiritual and ecstatic prayer, and its stress on ethical introspection, must be seen as the culmination of all three of these trends.[47]

Kabbalah may also have functioned as a political ideology. Early modern Ashkenazic communities were not free from conflict. *Kabbalah* served as an ideology of mystic Jewish unity. When the kabbalist speaks of the unity of the *Sefirot*, he refers as well (for the lower world reflects the upper) to the unity of husband and wife, of teacher and student, and of the Jewish community and the Jewish people.

The second half of the seventeenth century has been somewhat neglected by scholars of Jewish thought. Indeed, from the middle of the seventeenth century to the middle of the eighteenth, the Sabbatian movement has been nearly the sole focus of scholarly attention.[48]

The Sabbatian movement, it is well known, was one of the principal focuses of the life's work of Gershom Scholem. He stressed the movement's antinomian theology and its roots in *kabbalah*.[49] The most recent studies of Sabbatianism, however, while building on Scholem's foundations, have tended to reduce the contrast between the Sabbatians and their rabbinic opponents. Mendel Piekarz finds an antinomian trend of thought that he labels "non-Sabbatian religious radicalism"; it is here, and not in the Sabbatian movement itself, that Piekarz locates the roots of the antinomian tendencies of early *Hasidism*.[50] Still more recently, Elisheva Carlebach has gone further and speaks of a "non-Sabbatian Sabbatianism" – that is, a Sabbatianism in which Sabbatai Zvi himself was no longer regarded as important.[51] (*Kabbalah* tends to blur the concept of the individual personality.)

But if neither antinomianism nor a devotion to the person of Sabbatai Zvi reliably distinguishes Sabbatianism from Orthodox rabbinic Judaism, then how indeed will the two be distinguished?

In 1751, seventy-five years after the death of Sabbatai Zvi, the entire Ashkenazic world was shaken when Jacob Emden (d. 1776), a respected talmudist, accused Jonathan Eybeschuetz (d. 1764), the Chief Rabbi of Hamburg and also a highly regarded talmudist and preacher, of being a Sabbatian. Scholem, his students and his opponents have spilt much ink over the question of whether Eybeschuetz was in truth a Sabbatian or, as he claimed, an Orthodox rabbinic Jew.[52] Piekarz's and Carlebach's studies, although they do not address the question directly, raise the disturbing possibility that, at least in his own eyes and those of some of his supporters, Eybeschuetz may have been simultaneously both heretic and Orthodox.

---

[47]See recently Elior (#438).
[48]On Ashkenazic Sabbatianism, see #416–423. For other studies of the late seventeenth century, see e.g. #231–241.
[49]See Scholem (#421–423).
[50]See Piekarz (#203).
[51]See Carlebach (#418).
[52]On Eybeschuetz, see Scholem (#265 and 421), Perlmuter (#419), Raphael (#420) and Bettan (#188); cf. Cohen (#30) and Shohet (#434). On Emden, see the last two and also recently Schachter (#35 and 368) and Liebes (#408).

VI. HEBREW AND YIDDISH

If we study "the Ashkenazic mind" or "Ashkenazic thought", then we must keep in mind that there was not one mind but two, not one consciousness but a split consciousness. Ashkenazic Judaism was a bilingual culture. Hebrew was the higher language, the language of the law and the court, the prayerbook and the synagogue, the sacred language; Yiddish was the spoken language, the language of the street and the home, the wedding song, the lullaby.

It is somewhat surprising, therefore, but it is true none the less, that in the early modern period Yiddish stood in a closer relation to the Bible than did Hebrew. When Ashkenazic rabbis came to comment in Hebrew on the Bible, they commented either on Rashi's commentary (Elbaum lists more than twenty such supercommentaries from the period 1570–1650[53]), or else, like Samuel Edels (Maharsha; d. 1631) and many others, on *aggadah*.[54] Yiddish writers, however, approach the Bible directly: they translate it, rework it and retell its stories.[55]

In one study, Chava Turniansky has examined two sixteenth-century Yiddish versions of the Book of Joshua.[56] The mid-sixteenth century sees the beginning, as we have said, of a classic age of Ashkenazic rabbinic commentators and text-scholars. But it also sees, not incidentally, the decline of Yiddish poetry. Turniansky, contrasting the earlier and the later works, sees the later as a less accomplished work of art, but also as more "idiomatic, vernacular, familiar and . . . even humorous". Yiddish grew to express a cynicism and a warmth which could not be displayed in the more formal and pious Hebrew language. Already in the sixteenth century, it would appear, it was on its way towards that role.

Chone Shmeruk, too, has studied the juxtaposition of Yiddish and Hebrew writings in the early modern period. Comparing two accounts, one Hebrew, one Yiddish, of a martyrdom that took place in 1682, he finds the Hebrew account more pious, the Yiddish more detailed and realistic.[57] The demotion of Jewish historical writing from Hebrew to Yiddish about the middle of the seventeenth century is a shift that bears noticing. It tells equally of the lowered status of history as a genre, and of the increasing reliance on Yiddish as the sole language for realistic description.[58] Significant also is the geographical shift, about the same time, of the centres of Yiddish printing from Northern Italy and Southern Germany to Prague and (surprisingly) Amsterdam, home of the first Yiddish newspaper in 1687.[59]

Yiddish is a language of translations: both from Hebrew and from German. It is a border language. Arnold Paucker and others have studied the transfor-

---

[53] In appendix A of Elbaum (#12).
[54] On commentaries on *aggadah*, see #180–187.
[55] On Yiddish Bible commentary, see #283–292. There are also Yiddish treatments of *aggadah*; see e.g. #186 and 295.
[56] See Turniansky (#291).
[57] See Shmeruk (#236).
[58] On seventeenth-century historical works in Yiddish, see below #231–241.
[59] See Shmeruk (#299), and esp. Zfatman's discussion in #305. On the newspaper, the *Kurantin*, see #233.

mations that German works underwent in being translated into Yiddish.[60] How does the translator seek, for example, to help his readership identify with the Christian hero or heroine of a knightly romance? Here again is an inkling of the Yiddish difference, not merely a difference of alphabets and inflections, but a difference in point of view.

Indeed, the very existence of Yiddish renditions of German works should be recognised as little short of astonishing: for Ashkenazic Jews in the early modern period did not, after all, translate Gentile works of any kind into Hebrew, the sacred tongue. The Hebrew language was kept pure of such mongrels. Not so the Yiddish language, half-Jewish, half-Gentile. The commonness, the profanity and the secularity of Yiddish literature meant that it was allowed to associate with Gentile culture. Or perhaps we should say to the contrary: that the profane status of Yiddish stemmed from the very fact of that association.

Yiddish is also the language of storytelling. And here we return to the oneiric horizon, that invisible line separating what is from what cannot be, separating dreams and reality. On that line are Esther, the Jewish queen of Poland; Saul Wahl, the Jewish king of Poland – for a day; and the Jewish pope. These Janus figures feature in Yiddish stories of the period.[61] Stories of the "she-demon who marries a man" are the subject of a recent study by Sarah Zfatman-Biller.[62] No better image could be chosen of the Yiddish story itself – perhaps even the Yiddish language – in the early modern period, joining the familiar to the foreign, the safe to the dangerous, the commonplace to the grotesque.

In the Ashkenazic Jewish art of this period, by contrast, the grotesque is largely absent: no she-demons here. But it too is a dream-world, a world of lions, towers, crowns, palace gates: the lions of Judah, towers of the humble, the crowns of the crownless, the gates to a palace that is not of this world.[63] For Jewish art is tied closely to the synagogue and the cemetery, and here we are at the gates of yet another world: the world of the angels and the dead.

At the boundary of these worlds, daily commerce is transacted in Yiddish and in Hebrew, in prayers, in inscriptions, on deathbeds, in visions.[64] There is also a literature of Heaven (and Hell), descriptions written to inspire the pious.[65] Are there pious non-Jews beyond those gates, across the border? Opinion differed: see Katz's article.[66] There are pious Jewish women in Heaven, of course, but in which palace? That is the subject of Weissler's recent study.[67]

---

[60] On Yiddish translations of German works, see Paucker (#297–298). Cf. Yassif (#303) and Zfatman-Biller (#308) on the "specific difference" of Yiddish versions of well-known folktales.
[61] See #300, 293 and 294 on Esther, Saul Wahl and the Jewish pope, respectively.
[62] See Zfatman-Biller (#307).
[63] See #357, 362 and 360, on towers, stars and gates respectively. Cf. generally #335–362 on Jewish art.
[64] See #323–334 on prayer. Also, see Goldberg (#198 and 199) on deathbed literature, Muneles (#328) and Künzl (#361) on gravestones, and Kupfer (#407) on visions.
[65] See Goldberg (#198).
[66] See Katz (#380). Cf. Emanuel (#377).
[67] See Weissler (#187).

354   *Joseph M. Davis*

VII. BORDERS

What were the borders of Ashkenazic Jewry in the early modern period? We have already mentioned some: borders in space and time, borders of the spirit and the mind. We have mentioned some frontier territories: the Land of Israel, Northern Italy and Amsterdam; Yiddish language and literature; philosophy and science.

Three groups marked the social boundaries of early modern Ashkenazic Judaism. Within Polish Jewry, there was the Karaite sect. Polish Karaism has been little studied; much material is available here for the trail-blazing student.[68] Within rabbinic Judaism, there were the non-Ashkenazic Jews of the Mediterranean and Middle Eastern lands.[69] The close intellectual ties of Ashkenazic Jews to the Jews of Italy and the Ottoman Empire, especially the land of Israel, are detailed by Jacob Elbaum in his recent study.[70] If the Ashkenazic Jews had a Renaissance, much of their inspiration, he suggests, came from the Jews of Italy and the Spanish Jews of the Ottoman Empire; direct Christian models were not always necessary.

But it is the third border that is the decisive one: that is the line that separates Jews and Gentiles.

The relations of Christians and Jews has indeed been one of the foremost themes of modern Jewish historiography. Many aspects of the question do not concern us here, such as the legal status of the Jews, or the history of antisemitism and anti-Judaism. But two questions bear closely on our topic. Were there intellectual or cultural contacts between Jews and Christians?[71] And how were Christians and Christian culture viewed from within the Jewish community?[72]

In an important exchange of letters in the journal *Tarbiz* in 1959, Jacob Katz clashed with Haim Hillel Ben Sasson on both these questions.[73] Katz argued that early modern Ashkenazic Jews, rabbis especially, had extremely limited contacts with either Christians or Christianity, and held few opinions about it or them, apart from disdain. Ben Sasson argued that the contacts were more substantial, significant and sustained; there was active Jewish polemicising against Christian beliefs, but also a certain openness to non-Jewish thought, at least, as we have said, until the mid-seventeenth century.

At stake in this debate is the image of the ghetto. The scholarship produced by Ben Sasson and other scholars who emphasise the themes of rationalism and

---

[68] On Karaism, see #373–374.
[69] On contact with Mediterranean Jewry, see #363–372 below.
[70] See Elbaum (#366); cf. his discussion in #12.
[71] On Christian influences on Jewish culture, see generally Balaban (#8) and Kupfer and Mark (#367). See Kulka (#171) on Maharal; Neher (#34), Levine (#209) and Šedinová (#228–230) on Gans; Adler (#64), Lewin (#71) and Carpi (#217) on university education among Jews; Rosa (#233) on a Yiddish newspaper; Abramsky (#348) and Heyd (#350) on book illustrations; and Hrushovski (#315) on Yiddish poetry. On contacts between Jews and Christian Hebraists, see #390–399. See also #424–435 on the pre-Enlightenment.
[72] On Jewish attitudes towards Christians, see #375–389.
[73] See Ben Sasson (#11).

openness satisfies their desire to break down in retrospect the ghetto walls of Ashkenazic Jewry. Against this, Katz and his school assert that those barriers were all too real. Katz imagines a closed Jewish universe, whose social and mental walls were intact until the eighteenth century.

Is Ben Sasson merely feeding a vain Enlightenment optimism about the relations of Christians and Jews? American scholars, culturally inclined towards such a happy view, should beware of a quick acquiescence in his claims. But perhaps it is Katz, Shatz and the others who are only expressing their post-Holocaust despair of relations between Jews and non-Jews? Israeli scholars, given their own cultural predispositions, should beware on this score. But we must do more than merely walk the middle line of scholarly balance.

One group stood, as it were, in the precarious centre between Judaism and Christianity: Jewish converts to Christianity. Our vision of Jewish-Christian relations must include this very ambivalent group. One not infrequent Jewish attitude towards Christianity in the early modern period was conversion to it.[74]

It is also necessary to inquire into the active repression of potential Christian influences on Judaism in the early modern period. We must study the methods by which such influence was in fact successfully prevented (Katz touches on this question, noting particularly the insulation of the rabbinate from contact with non-Jews[75]). The methods by which, not having been prevented, such influences were quarantined (for example, restricted to Yiddish texts), denied, or hidden must also be studied. Josel of Rosheim deleted the names of Arab philosophers from a Spanish-Jewish text. What other deletions and erasures, conscious and unconscious, were performed by early modern Ashkenazic Jews?

VIII. THE HISTORIOGRAPHY OF TRADITION AND THE HISTORIOGRAPHY OF CONFLICT

The study of early modern Ashkenazic Jews has been driven not only by the methodologies of the three fields that we have discussed. It has been guided as well by at least two differing, indeed conflicting, scholarly agendas.

There is, first, what may be called the historiography of tradition: history writing in the spirit of *shalshelet ha-kabbalah*, the "chain of tradition", in which the punchline is always the continuity of the past with the present.[76] Often genealogical links are stressed or (especially before the Holocaust) geographical and local links. Thus Reifmann, in the town of Szczebrzeszyn, studied Issachar Baer of Szczebrzeszyn (fl. 1585);[77] and thus today Czech scholars study Maharal and the other rabbis and Jews of Prague.[78]

Since the Holocaust, however, the historiography of tradition has focused

---

[74]On conversation to Christianity, see #400–405.
[75]See Katz (#16).
[76]I am indebted here to Jacob Neusner's studies of recent Jewish historiography.
[77]See Reifmann (#184).
[78]See e.g. Muneles's beautifully produced work, #18, and many studies in the periodical *Judaica Bohemiae*.

primarily on the continuity of Jewish institutions. Early modern Ashkenazic Jews take their place in surveys on topics such as the Jewish family through the ages, Jewish education from the Bible to the present, and three thousand years of Jewish self-government.[79] Such studies in continuity tend to emphasise the unity of Judaism and of Jews, and more particularly the unity of early modern Ashkenazic Jews. (Hundert complains of the tendency "to adopt the rabbinic principle that there is 'no early or late in Torah' . . . telescoping whole centuries and more".[80]) Differences in period and regional differences tend to be erased, and intra-communal conflicts to be played down, all to avoid presenting the reader with a variety of conflicting origins.

There are, however, Jewish movements and groups that are in fact interested in provoking debate and change. Such groups include, for example, the *Maskilim*, the Socialists, or recently the feminists. Their agenda is therefore different; they wish to find, and do find, conflict; they have created a historiography of conflict. (Historians are, of course, attracted to conflict.) Class conflict, gender conflict, the conflict of rationalism and fanaticism – these may be searched out in every historical period, but not least among the early modern Ashkenazic Jews. The lines are drawn in the fight for class justice, the Yiddish language, Torah values, free thought, women's rights.[81]

Seven conflicts within the intellectual life of early modern Ashkenazic Jews have been studied. (Some have been mentioned already.) These are (1) the conflict over the codification of the law in the late sixteenth century, (2) the attacks on the method of *pilpul*, (3) the conflict over the curriculum in general, (4) the attack on the study of philosophy in particular, (5) the conflict over *kabbalah*, (6) the conflict over the place of the Yiddish language within Jewish culture, and (7) the Sabbatian controversies.[82]

Of these, only the last one, the Sabbatian controversies, can really be called a conflict of ideas. The debates over *kabbalah*, for example, stay – as we have seen – almost entirely out of the realm of ideas. Perhaps this is an expression of an essentially practical cast of mind, a deep scepticism in regard to metaphysics and theology. Perhaps it only reflects a conservative culture in which radical ideas (until the advent of Sabbatianism) were almost never expressed, and hence were no threat.

The issues under discussion were rather: may works of certain types – philosophic, kabbalistic, codes, Yiddish, *pilpul* – be written, published, studied, taught publicly, taken as authoritative? These are conflicts over books and publication, over authority, and over genres.[83]

Students of Yiddish literature have long made the following claim (it too may

---

[79]Goldman (#68), Elazar and Cohen (#137), and Kraemer's collection of essays of which Hundert (#201) is one, are works in this vein.

[80]Hundert (#4), p. 266.

[81]For Yiddishist works, see e.g. #276–279. Henry and Taitz (#25), Weissler (#187 and 333), Minkoff and Melamed (#284), and Davis (#309) are feminist.

[82]See respectively (1) codification: #83, 92–97; (2) *pilpul*: #104–110; (3) curriculum: #65–70, 72, 75–77, 170–171; (4) philosophy: #147, 150–153; (5) *kabbalah*: #156–162; (6) Yiddish: #276–279; and (7) Sabbatianism: #416–423.

[83]On Jewish self-censorship, see #43, 46, 48, 51.

serve a Socialist polemic). The boundaries between Hebrew and Yiddish and between Hebrew and Yiddish genres and literature reflect the social boundaries between readers of Hebrew – that is, learned and powerful men – and readers of Yiddish – namely, the powerless, the illiterate and women. Any infringement upon these distinctions of language and genre also threatened the established order of social divisions. Hence the apprehension about the publication of Yiddish works. Books of the Bible might be translated into Yiddish; the *Shulchan Aruch* was not.[84] (Regrettably, it has not been translated into English either.)

Perhaps conflicts over other genres also reflected social divisions. In a forthcoming study, Elhanan Reiner ties the controversy over codification to the opposition to the purchase of rabbinical positions.[85] The rising Jewish *nouveaux riches* in Poland, he suggests, wished to exercise rabbinic prerogatives, and wanted to decide *halakhic* cases on the bases of codified law. Their opponents, men of the established rabbinic aristocracy, insisted on the need for rabbis with full talmudic training. Reiner's hypothesis pushes forward Ben Sasson's earlier study of Ashkenazic social thought, in which Ben Sasson showed that Isserles (the codifier) was the proponent of a religious ideology favouring the rich, while the preacher Ephraim Lenczyc (d. 1619), Maharal's successor, was a critic of the wealthy.[86]

And yet Ashkenazic rabbis and writers of the period cannot be divided neatly into parties, and hardly even into schools of thought. We must press the question of conflict further; we must consider not only social but inner conflict. S. A. Horodetsky, in an essay on Mordechai Jaffe (d. 1612), writes that Jaffe had a dual allegiance to philosophy and *kabbalah*. Such a stance was typical of Ashkenazic rabbis of that generation, Horodetsky adds. But he finds it puzzling. It was, he writes:

> "as if [Jaffe's] mind could hold contradictory opinions at the same time . . . On the one hand, we see in him a dawning of free thought. [Jaffe writes,] 'God, may He be blessed, does everything in the way of nature,' and 'In prophecy there is some degree of fantasy.' And on the other hand, he believed in magic, in demons, and in the [magical] use of Divine names."[87]

In his kabbalistic writings, Lawrence Kaplan has shown recently, Jaffe offers a kabbalistic explanation of God's nature; in his philosophic work, a philosophic explanation.[88] How were such conflicting beliefs reconciled in Jaffe's mind, or in his readers'?

Surely there must have been a set of rules that told Ashkenazic Jews not only what to read, but more importantly how to read it, a set of rules that regulated the relative weight to be given to ideas of different types and to works of different genres, methods by which conflicting texts could be brought into peaceful coexistence. Surely we must have recourse again not only to hermeneutical theory but to political theory, and to Elazar's implicit constitution.

---

[84] Cf. Fuks (#46).
[85] See Reiner (#109).
[86] See Ben Sasson (#10 and 136).
[87] Horodetsky (#26), p. 173.
[88] Kaplan (#149) below.

IX. THE CRISIS OF THE EIGHTEENTH CENTURY

Changes do not come as stragglers, in ones and twos. They come in groups, in large groups. The end of the eighteenth century saw at one time the demise of the Council of Four Lands and the birth of the innovative Talmudism and exegesis of Elijah ben Solomon, the Gaon of Vilna (d. 1797), and his school; it saw also the beginnings of the Frankist movement, the growth of *Hasidism* and the birth of the Jewish Enlightenment, the *Haskalah*. The feud of Emden and Eybeschuetz at midcentury foreshadowed battles that did not end for two hundred years, of the *Hasidim* against the *Mitnagdim*, the *Maskilim* against the traditionalists, Eastern European Jews against German Jews, and later of Yiddishists against Zionists. This is a sea-change; it is no less than the beginning of the modern era of Judaism. To narrate and explain these changes is one of the central tasks of Jewish history.

Scholars have looked for the roots of these movements, and roots of the divisions between them, in the period before 1750. Several of the conflicts that we have discussed may indeed have a bearing on these later divisions. The predominantly anti-rationalist stance of late seventeenth-century Ashkenazic Judaism was the end-product of a century of conflict over philosophy, and bears closely on the antagonistic reception given to the Enlightenment. Some of the roots of the struggle against *Hasidism* and against the Enlightenment lie in the struggle against Sabbatianism; some further back, in the conflict over *kabbalah*. The struggle over the Yiddish language has clear consequences for the subsequent development of, and conflicts over, Yiddish and Hebrew language and literature.

Differing positions have been staked out, once again by the scholars of Jerusalem, on the questions of the roots of *Haskalah* and *Hasidism*. Katz has argued that the *Haskalah* has in essence no Jewish roots: that its roots lie outside of Judaism, or at least outside of normative Ashkenazic Judaism.[89] Azriel Shohet has argued to the contrary that, among German Jewry, the growth of the Enlightenment was a gradual process, which had already gone a substantial distance before Mendelssohn's day.[90] Scholem argued that both the *Haskalah* and *Hasidism* had roots in the Sabbatian heresies.[91] Katz has argued, to the contrary, that *Hasidism* was without important ties to Sabbatianism. (He has conceded, however, that there were ties, albeit limited ones, between Sabbatianism and *Haskalah*.)[92]

At issue in all these questions is how sharp a dividing line can be drawn between traditional and modern Jewish communities. Is modern Judaism to be seen as a continuation of earlier trends, or as a radical departure in Jewish life and thought? And is there a third body that mediates the difference between the traditional and the modern? Scholem (and also Buber and Dinur)[93] suggests that

---

[89] Katz (#16).
[90] Shohet (#434).
[91] Scholem (#432).
[92] Katz (#429).
[93] See Buber (#436) and Dinur in Hundert (#443).

there is: the Sabbatian and *Hasidic* movements. Others have looked at the circle of the Vilna Gaon in much the same terms, as a "pre-Enlightenment", a middle ground.[94] Shohet makes the same claim for German Jewry 1700–1750. Ben Sasson and his followers, we have seen, suggest such a middle position for the Ashkenazic rabbinate itself of the late sixteenth century. Katz and his students reject all of these, insisting quite adamantly and consistently: there was no middle ground between tradition and Enlightenment.

Where is the line between the modern and the traditional? This is, no doubt, a question of definition and periodisation. But it is an existential question as well, for the historian whose personal identity is bound closely to the concept of the "modern Jew". Yosef Yerushalmi ends his study of Jewish historiography (appropriately) with himself.[95] Like Katz, with regret, with anger, and also with relief, he places the intellectual roots of the *Haskalah* and of modern Jewish historiography – that is, his own intellectual roots – outside of Judaism.

Modernity and the Enlightenment took considerably different forms among different nations and communities. As Peter Gay points out, the English Enlightenment was peculiar in its respect for tradition, the French in its anti-clericalism, the German in its political impotence.[96] Modernity for the Jews, I would suggest, was born under the sign of a personality at war with itself.

Consider the story of the Gaon of Vilna and the angel. The Gaon's disciple, Hayyim of Volozhin, tells us that when a *maggid*, an instructing angel, appeared to the Gaon and offered "to deliver to him the mysteries of the Torah, without any . . . effort", Elijah rejected this angelic offer.[97]

Such a rejection has many aspects. It is a rejection of hidden knowledge, and a rejection of any mediation between man and God; it is a rejection, possibly, of miracle-working. But beyond these, the Gaon is also rejecting some part of himself. A man who has a *maggid* does not reject him and escape unscathed. Some part of himself, some part of his past, goes with that *maggid*. The Gaon in his study in Vilna, no less than the young men who left their parents to join the *Hasidim*, or the young Mendelssohn at the gates of Berlin, was leaving some part of himself behind.

The internal act accompanies and perhaps precedes the external acts of intolerance and separation. The Gaon, who rejected his *maggid*, also persecuted the *Hasidim*; the *Hasidim* who left their families also left the community; Mendelssohn's children, as is well known, left Judaism entirely.

When Jews dreamed now, they dreamed of conciliation. In 1794, the *Maskil* Joseph ha-Ephrati of Tropolowicz wrote a drama about King Saul. At the end, he inserts, in defiance of the biblical account, a deathbed reconciliation scene between Saul and David. In another work, he imagines a heavenly reconciliation between Mendelssohn and Ezekiel Landau. But that too remained in the realm of dreams.

---

[94]On the circle of the Vilna Gaon, see Etkes (#426 and 427) and Klausner (#430).
[95]Yerushalmi (#252).
[96]Peter Gay, *The Enlightenment: an Interpretation. The Rise of Modern Paganism*, New York 1977, p. 4.
[97]The story is translated in Louis Jacobs, *Jewish Mystical Testimonies*, New York 1978, p. 172.

Selected Bibliography

This bibliography is divided into the following sections: (a) general (b) rabbinics (c) Jewish thought (d) Yiddish literature (e) borders of the Ashkenazic community (f) movements: Messianism, Sabbatianism, *Haskalah* and *Hasidism*.
An asterisk (*) indicates that the author has not seen the item.

Abbreviations
AJS   Association of Jewish Studies
PAAJR Proceedings of the American Academy of Jewish Research
WCJS World Congress of Jewish Studies

A. GENERAL

I. Bibliography

1) Gershon C. Bacon and Gershon D. Hundert, *The Jews in Poland and Russia. Bibliographical Essays*, Bloomington, Ind. 1984.
2) Yedidyah Denari (or Dinari) [Bibliography], in his *Hakhmei Ashkenaz be-shilhei Yemei ha-Beinayim*, Jerusalem 1984, pp. 336–422 [on Ashkenazic Jews in the late Middle Ages].
3) Jacob Elbaum (or Elboim), 'Bibliyografyah', in *idem, Petihut ve-Histagrut: ha-yezirah ha-ruhanit-ha-sifrutit be-Folin uve-arazot Ashkenaz be-shilhei ha-me'ah ha-Shesh 'Esreh*, Jerusalem 1990, pp. 397–424.
4) Gershon D. Hundert, 'Polish Jewish History', in *Modern Judaism*, 10 (1990), pp. 259–270.
5) Herman Pollack, 'Bibliography', in *idem, Jewish Folkways in Germanic Lands (1648–1806). Studies in Aspects of Daily Life*, Cambridge, Mass. 1971, pp. 341–391.
6) Uriel Weinreich and Beatrice Weinreich, *Yiddish Language and Folklore: a Selective Bibliography for Research*, 's-Gravenhage 1954.
7) Wiener Library, *German Jewry. History, Life, and Culture* (Catalogue Series, No. 3), London 1957, and *German Jewry: Part II* (Catalogue Series, No. 6), London 1978.

Note: Siev (#94), Cohen (#111), Wachstein (#193 and 205), Steinschneider (#215, 249, 254 and 274), Zfatman (#306), Mayer (#338), Faierstein (#440), and Gries (#441) are also bibliographies.

II. General Studies

8) Majer Balaban, 'Umysłowość i moralność żydostwa polskiego XVI wieku', in *Kultura Staropolska*, Cracow 1932, pp. 606–639.
9) Salo Baron, *Social and Religious History of the Jews*, 2nd edn., vol. XIV, *Catholic Restoration and Wars of Religion*, New York 1967, and vol. XVI, *Poland-Lithuania 1500–1650*, New York 1976.

10) Haim Hillel Ben Sasson, *Hagut ve-Hanhagah: hashkefoteihem ha-hevratiyot shel Yehudei Polin be-shilhei Yemei ha-Beinayim*, Jerusalem 1959.
11) *Idem*, 'Musagim u-mezi'ut ba-historyah ha-Yehudit be-shilhei Yemei ha-Beinayim' [review of Jacob Katz, *Masoret u-Mashber*], in *Tarbiz*, 29 (1959), pp. 297–312. Katz's response is: 'Al halakhah u-derush ke-makor histori', in *Tarbiz*, 30 (1960), pp. 62–68, and Ben Sasson answered, 'Teshuvah', pp. 69–72.
12) Jacob Elbaum, *Petihut ve-Histagrut, op. cit.* (#3).
13) Louis Finkelstein (ed.), *The Jews. Their History, Religion, and Civilization*, 4th edn. (and first paperback edn.), New York 1971. Note esp. Israel Hailperin, 'The Jews in Eastern Europe from Ancient Times until the Partitions of Poland', in vol. I, pp. 305–342, Abraham Menes, 'Patterns of Jewish Scholarship in Eastern Europe', in vol. II, pp. 177–227, and Yudel Mark, 'Yiddish Literature', in vol. II, pp. 417–468.
14) Israel Hailperin (or Halpern), *Yehudim ve-Yahadut be-Mizrah Eiropah*, Jerusalem 1969.
15) *Idem* (ed.), *Beit Yisra'el be-Folin: mi-yamim rishonim ve-'ad li-yemot ha-Hurban*, 2 vols., Jerusalem 1948–1954.
16) Jacob Katz, *Masoret u-Mashber: ha-hevrah ha-Yehudit be-moz'ei Yemei ha-Beinayim*, Jerusalem 1958. English transl., *Tradition and Crisis. Jewish Society at the End of the Middle Ages*, New York 1971.
17) Isaac Lewin, *Mi-Boker la-'Erev: kovez ma'amarim*, Jerusalem 1981 [studies in early modern Polish-Jewish history, focusing on rabbinics].
18) Otto Muneles, *The Prague Ghetto in the Renaissance Period*, Prague 1965.
19) Moshe Shulvass, *Jewish Culture in Eastern Europe. The Classical Period*, New York 1975.
20) Meyer Waxman, *A History of Jewish Literature*, 2nd edn., vol. II, *From the Twelfth Century to the Middle of the Eighteenth Century*, New York 1960.
21) Israel Zinberg, *Di Geshikhte fun der Literatur bay Yidn*, 8 vols., Vilna 1927–1935. English transl., *A History of Jewish Literature*, transl. by B. Martin, 12 vols., Cleveland 1972–1978. Note esp. vol. 6, *The German-Polish Cultural Center* and vol. 7, *Old Yiddish Literature until the Haskalah*.

III. Biography

(a) Communal Biography, Prosopography

22) Israel Cohen, 'Rabbis and Scholars', in *idem*, *Vilna*, Philadelphia 1943, pp. 187–203.
23) Hayim Nathan Dembitzer, *Kelilat Yofi: toldot ha-rabanim . . . de-kehilat kodesh Lvov . . . asher nahagu sham . . . be-tor av bet din . . .*, Cracow 1888; repr. New York 1960.
24) Samuel J. Fuenn, *Kiryah Ne'emanah*, Vilna 1915 [on the rabbis of Vilna].
25) Sondra Henry and Emily Taitz, *Written Out of History. A Hidden Legacy of Jewish Women Revealed Through their Writings and Letters*, New York ³1988. Note also A. M. Haberman, 'Nashim Ma'atikot', in Haberman (#47), pp. 351–360.
26) Samuel Abba Horodetsky, *Le-Korot ha-Rabanut*, Warsaw 1911 [biographies of sixteenth- to eighteenth-century Ashkenazic rabbis].
27) Markus Horovitz, *Rabanei Frankfurt. Frankfurter Rabbinen*, rev. edn., by Joseph Unna and Joshua Amir, Jerusalem 1972.
28) Selma Stern, *The Court Jew. A Contribution to the History of the Period of*

Absolutism in Central Europe, transl. by Ralph Weiman, Philadelphia 1950, esp. 'The Personality of the Court Jew', pp. 227–246.
29) J. M. Zunz, *'Ir ha-Zedek: toldot rabanei 'ir Krako*, Lvov 1874.

Note: Tchernowitz (#83) and Rabinowitz (#191) are works of collective biography; and cf. Klausner (#430).

(b) Individual Biography

30) Mortimer J. Cohen, *Jacob Emden. A Man of Controversy*, Philadelphia 1937. But see Scholem's scathing review, in *Kiryat Sefer*, 16 (1939), pp. 320–338.
31) David Kaufmann, *Jair Hayyim Bacharach*, Trier 1894. An English summary appeared earlier in *Jewish Quarterly Review* (old series), 3 (1891), pp. 292–313, 485–536.
32) Abraham Levinson, *Tuvyah ha-Rofe ve-sifro Ma'aseh Tuvyah*, Berlin 1924 [on Dr. Tobias Cohn (d. 1729)].
33) Samuel Mirsky, 'R. Yo'el Sirkes, ba'al ha-BaH', in *Horeb*, 6 (1941), pp. 41–75.
34) André Neher, *David Gans: disciple du Maharal, assistant de Tycho Brahe et de Jean Kepler*, Paris 1974. English transl., *Jewish Thought and the Scientific Revolution of the Sixteenth Century*, transl. by D. Maisel, Oxford 1986.
35) Jacob J. Schachter, *Rabbi Jacob Emden. Life and Major Works*, Ph.D. dissertation, Harvard University 1988.
36) Elijah J. Schochet, *Bach. Rabbi Joel Sirkes. His Life, Works and Times*, New York 1971.
37) Byron L. Sherwin, 'In the Shadows of Greatness. Rabbi Hayyim ben Betsalel of Friedberg', in *Jewish Social Studies*, 37 (1975), pp. 35–61.
38) Asher Siev (Ziv), *Rabeinu Mosheh Isserles (Rema)*, New York 1972.
39) Selma Stern, *Josel von Rosheim. Befehlshaber der Judenschaft im Heiligen Römischen Reich Deutscher Nation*, Stuttgart 1959. Veröffentlichung des Leo Baeck Instituts. English transl., *Josel of Rosheim. Commander of Jewry in the Holy Roman Empire* . . ., transl. by Gertrude Hirschler, Philadelphia 1965.
40) Gérard Weil, *Élie Lévita: humaniste et massorète (1469–1549)*, Leiden 1963.
41) Eric (Yizhak) Zimmer, *R. Hayim b. Bezalel mi-Friedberg: ahi Maharal mi-Prag*, Jerusalem 1987.
42) *Idem*, 'R. David b. Isaac of Fulda. The Trials and Tribulations of a Sixteenth Century German Rabbi', in *Jewish Social Studies*, 45 (1983), pp. 217–232.

Note: Raphael (#56), Schochet (#93), Freudenthal (#100), Shulman (#121), Eidelberg (#126), Newman (#160), Liebes in Twersky (#162), Sherwin (#178), Minkoff (#313 and 317), Barzilay (#365), Schwarzschild (#433), and Scholem (#447) are also biographies. Cf. #309–314, studies of autobiographical memoirs.

IV. Printing, Censorship and Book Ownership

43) Moshe Carmilly-Weinberger, *Censorship and Freedom of Expression in Jewish History*, New York 1977.
44) Bernhard (Hayyim) Friedberg, *Toldot ha-Defus ha-'Ivri ba-'Arim ha-eleh shebe-Eiropah ha-Tikhonah: Augsburg, Offenbach, Ichenhausen, Altona, Berlin* . . . Antwerp 1935.
45) *Idem, Toldot ha-Defus ha-'Ivri be-Folanyah*, rev. edn., Tel-Aviv 1950.
46) Leib Fuks, 'Ha-Reka' ha-hevrati veha-kalkali le-hadpasat shenei targumei Tanakh be-Yidish be-Amsterdam samukh li-shenat 1680', in *Gal-Ed*, 1 (1973), pp. 31–50.

47) A. M. Haberman, *Perakim be-Toldot ha-Madpisim ha-'Ivrim ve-'Inyenei Sefarim*, Jerusalem 1978.
48) Israel Hailperin, 'Va'ad Arba' Arazot veha-Sefer ha-'Ivri', in *idem, Yehudim ve-Yahadut be-Mizrah Eiropah*, Jerusalem 1969, pp. 78–107 [= *Kiryat Sefer*, 9 (1933), pp. 367–378, 393–394; 11 (1934), pp. 105–110, 250–262; 12 (1935), pp. 250–253].
49) Hayim Liberman (Lieberman), *Ohel Rahel*, 2 vols., New York 1980.
50) Salomon Hugo Lieben, 'Der hebräische Buchdruck in Prag im 16. Jahrhundert', in Samuel Steinherz (ed.), *Die Juden in Prag: . . . Festgabe der Loge Praga des Ordens B'nai Brith*, Prague 1927, pp. 88–106.
51) Leopold Löwenstein, *Mafteah ha-Haskamot*, Frankfurt a. Main 1923.
52) Alexander Marx, 'The History of David Oppenheimer's Library', in *idem, Studies in Jewish History and Booklore*, New York 1944, pp. 238–255.
53) Otto Muneles, *Bibliographical Survey of Jewish Prague*, Prague 1952.
54) Joseph Prijs, *Die Basler hebräischen Drucke (1492–1866)*, ed. by B. Prijs, Olten 1964.
55) Raphael Nathan Neta Rabinovitz, *Ma'amar 'al Hadpasat ha-Talmud*, ed. by A. M. Haberman, Jersualem 1952.
56) Yizhak Raphael, 'R. Shabtai Bass, ha-Bibliograf ha-'Ivri ha-Rishon', in *idem, Rishonim ve-Aharonim: perakim be-toldot Yisra'el ve-sifruto*, Tel-Aviv 1957, pp. 171–200.
57) Agnes Romer-Segal, 'Sifrut Yidish u-kehal kor'eha ba-me'ah ha-16: yezirot be-Yidish bi-reshimat ha-'Zikuk' mi-Mantovah 1595', in *Kiryat Sefer*, 53 (1979), pp. 779–790.
58) Moshe Rosenfeld, *Der jüdische Buchdruck in Augsburg in der ersten Hälfte des 16. Jahrhunderts* [= *Jewish Printing in Augsburg during the First Half of the Sixteenth Century*], London 1985.
59) Menahem Schmelzer, 'Hebrew Printing and Publishing in Germany 1650–1750. On Jewish Book Culture and the Emergence of Modern Jewry', in *LBI Year Book XXXIII* (1988), pp. 369–383.
60) Chone Shmeruk, 'Kavim li-demutah shel sifrut Yidish be-Folin uve-Lita 'ad gezerot Tah ve-Tat [=1648–1649]', in *Tarbiz*, 46 (1977), pp. 258–314. Cf. *idem, Sifrut Yidish be-Folin: mehkarim ve-'iyunim historiyim*, Jerusalem 1981, pp. 11–74.
61) Magnus Weinberg, 'Die hebräischen Druckereien in Sulzbach', in *Jahrbuch der jüdisch-literarischen Gesellschaft*, 1 (1903), pp. 19–202; 15 (1923), pp. 125–155; 21 (1930), pp. 319–370.
62) Leopold Zunz, 'Annalen der hebräischen Typographie von Prag vom Jahre 1513 zum Jahre 1657', in *idem, Zur Geschichte und Literatur*, Berlin ²1919, pp. 268–303.

Note: #348–353 all concern book and manuscript illustration.

V. Education

63) Uziel Adini, 'Hinukh el shelemut: be-'ikevot mishnatam ha-hinukhit shel ha-Maharal mi-Prag ve-'Amos Komenius', in *Shevilei ha-Hinukh*, 37 (1974), pp 102–111.
64) Salomon Adler, 'Die Entwicklung des Schulwesens der Juden zu Frankfurt am Main bis zur Emanzipation', in *Jahrbuch der jüdisch-literarischen Gesellschaft*, 18 (1926), pp. 143–174; 19 (1928), pp. 237–278.
65) Simhah Assaf, *Mekorot le-Toldot ha-Hinukh be-Yisra'el*, vol. I, Jerusalem 1954.
66) Mordechai Breuer, 'Tradition and Change in European Yeshivot. Seven-

teenth to Nineteenth Centuries', in Isadore Twersky and Bernard Cooperman (eds.), *Tradition and Crisis Revisited. Jewish Thought and Society on the Threshold of Modernity*, Cambridge, Mass. 1992.
67) Isidore Fishman, *The History of Jewish Education in Central Europe from the End of the Sixteenth Century to the End of the Eighteenth Century*, London 1944.
68) Israel Goldman, *Lifelong Learning in Judaism: from Biblical Times to the Twentieth Century*, New York 1975.
69) Aaron Fritz Kleinberger, 'Ha-Hinukh ha-Yehudi ba-Me'ot ha-16-ha-18 – Merkaz Eiropah u-Mizrahah', in *Enziklopedyah Hinukhit*, Jerusalem 1964, vol. III, cols. 382–405.
70) *Idem*, 'The Didactics of Rabbi Loew of Prague', in *Scripta Hierosolymitana*, 13 (1963), pp. 32–55.
71) Louis Lewin, 'Die jüdischen Studenten an der Universität Frankfurt an der Oder', in *Jahrbuch der jüdisch-literarischen Gesellschaft*, 14 (1921), pp. 217–238; 15 (1923), pp. 59–96; 16 (1924), pp. 43–85.
72) Dov Rappel, *Sheva' ha-Hokhmot: ha-vikuah 'al limudei hol be-sifrut ha-hinukh ha-Yehudit 'ad reshit ha-Haskalah*, Jerusalem 1990.
73) Moshe (Murray) Rosman, 'Dimuyav shel Beit Yisra'el be-Folin ke-merkaz Torah aharei gezerot Tah ve-Tat [1648–1649]', in *Zion*, 51 (1986), pp. 435–448.
74) David Ruderman, 'Three Contemporary Perceptions of a Polish Wunderkind of the Seventeenth Century', in *AJS Review*, 4 (1979), pp. 143–163.
75) Alvin I. Schiff, 'Jewish Teacher Personnel Practices in European Countries: 16th–18th Centuries', in *Jewish Education*, 28 (1958), pp. 26–37 (= Morris Katz [ed.], *The Jacob Dolnitzky Memorial Volume*, Chicago 1982, pp. 172–189).
76) Azriel Shohet, 'Hevrot-limud be-me'ot 17–18 be-Erez Yisra'el, be-Folin, uve-Germanyah', in *Ha-Hinukh*, 28 (1956), pp. 404–418.
77) Isadore Twersky, 'Talmudists, Philosophers, Kabbalists. The Quest for Spirituality in the Sixteenth Century', in Bernard Cooperman (ed.), *Jewish Thought in the Sixteenth Century*, Cambridge, Mass. 1983, pp. 431–487.

Note: Breuer (#104) and all of #105–110, Rappel (#134 and 257), Kleinberger (#170), Kulka (#171), Berz (#206), and Eschelbacher (#425) also concern education.

B. RABBINICS

I. General

78) Joseph Davis, 'Philosophy and the Law in the Writings of R. Yom Tov Lipman Heller', in Isadore Twersky (ed.), *Studies in Medieval Jewish History and Literature*, vol. 3, Cambridge, Mass. 1993.
79) Menahem Elon, *Ha-Mishpat ha-'Ivri*, 3 vols., Jerusalem 1973.
80) Edward Fram, *Jewish Law and Social and Economic Realities*, Ph.D. dissertation, Columbia University 1991 [on Jewish civil cases in sixteenth-century Poland].
81) Solomon Freehof, 'Ceremonial Creativity among the Ashkenazim', in Abraham Neuman and Solomon Zeitlin (eds.), *The 75th Anniversary Volume of the Jewish Quarterly Review*, Philadelphia 1967, pp. 210–224.
82) Jacob Katz, *Halakhah ve-Kabalah: mehkarim be-toldot dat Yisra'el 'al madoreha ve-zikatah ha-hevratit*, Jerusalem 1984.

83) Chaim Tchernowitz, *Toldot ha-Poskim*, New York 1947 [focuses on the tension between codification and opposition to it].

Note: Lewin (#17), Horodetsky (#26), Twersky (#77), Twersky in Twersky (#162) and Barnai (#364) are also studies of rabbinics.

II. Legal History and Topics

84) Philipp Bloch, 'Der Mamran, der jüdisch-polnische Wechselbrief', in Aron Freimann and Meier Hildesheimer (eds.), *Festschrift zum siebzigsten Geburtstage Abraham Berliners*, Frankfurt a. Main 1903, pp. 50–64.
85) Yedidyah Denari, 'Hishtalshelut takanat ha-mi'un', in *Diné Yisrael*, 10–11 (1981–1983), pp. 319–345.
86) Solomon Freehof, 'Hazkarath Neshamot', in *Hebrew Union College Annual*, 36 (1965), pp. 179–189.
87) Abraham Fuss, 'The Eastern European *Shetar Mamran* Reexamined', in *Diné Yisrael*, 4 (1973), English section, pp. 51–68.
88) Jacob Goldberg, 'Die Ehe bei den Juden Polens im 18. Jahrhundert', in *Jahrbücher für Geschichte Osteuropas*, 31 (1983), pp. 481–515.
89) Jacob Katz, 'Ma'ariv bi-zemano veshe-lo bi-zemano: dugma la-zikah bein minhag, halakhah, ve-hevrah', in *Zion*, 35 (1970), pp. 35–60.
90) Idem, *Goi shel Shabat: ha-reka' ha-kalkali-hevrati veha-yesod ha-halakhi le-ha'asakat nokhri be-Shabatot uve-hagei-Yisra'el*, Jerusalem 1984. English transl., *The 'Shabbes Goy'. A Study in Halakhic Flexibility*, Philadelphia 1989.
91) Samuel Lauterbach, 'Tashlik. A Study in Jewish Ceremonies', in *Hebrew Union College Annual*, 11 (1936), pp. 207–340 [also in *idem, Rabbinic Essays*, Cincinnati 1951, pp. 299–436].

Note: Feldman (#98), Emanuel (#112), Kahana (#117), Schochet (#120), Tal (#123), Sadek and Nosek (#143), and Zimmer (#372) also study legal history.

III. Codification and the Shulchan Aruch

92) Yizhak Nissim, 'Hagahot ha-Rema [R. Mosheh Isserles] 'al *Shulhan 'Arukh'*, in Judah Leb Fishman-Maimon (ed.), *Sinai: Sefer Yovel*, Jerusalem 1958, pp. 29–39.
93) Elijah J. Schochet, *"Taz": Rabbi David Halevi*, New York 1979.
94) Asher Siev, 'Ha-Rema: reshimah bibliyografit', in *Talpiot*, 9 (1965), pp. 314–342.
95) Israel Ta Shema, 'Hilkheta ke-Vatra'ei: behinot historiyot shel kelal mishpati', in *Shenaton ha-Mishpat ha-'Ivri*, 6–7 (1980), pp. 405–425.
96) Jacob Toledano, 'Matai uve-eilu mekomot nitkabel ha-Shulhan 'Arukh le-halakhah pesukah', in Yizhak Raphael (ed.), *Rabi Yosef Karo: 'iyunim u-mehkarim*, Jerusalem 1969, pp. 184–189.
97) Isadore Twersky, 'The Shulhan 'Arukh. Enduring Code of Jewish Law', in *Judaism*, 16 (1967), pp. 141–158 [= Judah Goldin (ed.), *The Jewish Expression*, New Haven 1976, pp. 322–343].

Note: Mirsky (#33), Siev (#38), Zimmer (#41), Tchernowitz (#83), Reiner (#109), and Jonah Ben Sasson (#145) also concern codification.

IV. Talmud Commentary

98) David Feldman, 'The Drama of the Literature', in *idem, Marital Relations, Birth Control, and Abortion in Jewish Law*, New York 1974, pp. 194–226.

99) Judah Leb Fishman-Maimon (ed.), *Li-Khevod Yom Tov: ma'amarim u-mehkarim 'ad shelosh me'ot shanah li-fetirato shel Rabeinu Yom Tov Lipman Heller*, Jerusalem 1956. Versions of certain of the essays appeared in *Sinai*, 35 (1954), pp. 414–456.
100) Max Freudenthal, 'R. David Fränckel', in Markus Brann and Ferdinand Rosenthal (eds.), *Gedenkbuch zur Erinnerung an David Kaufmann*, Breslau 1900, pp. 569–598.
101) Louis Ginzberg, from 'Mavo', in *idem*, *Peirushim ve-Hidushim ba-Yerushalmi* . . . vol. I, New York 1941, pp. 119–126.
102) David Weiss Halivni, *Peshat and Derash. Plain and Applied Meaning in Rabbinic Exegesis*, Oxford 1991.
103) Isaac Ron, 'Mahadurat ha-Talmud she-higiha Maharshal', in *Alei Sefer*, 15 (1988), pp. 65–104.

Note: Ben Sasson (#10), Schachter (#35), Emanuel (#377) and Katz (#380) also discuss Talmud commentary.

V. Pilpul

104) Mordechai Breuer, 'Aliyat ha-pilpul veha-hilukim bi-yeshivot Ashkenaz', in Azriel Hildesheimer (ed.), *Sefer ha-Zikaron le-* . . . *Yehiel Ya'akov Weinberg*, Jerusalem 1969, pp. 241–255.
105) Chaim Zalman Dimitrovsky, 'Al derekh ha-Pilpul', in Saul Lieberman (ed.), *Sefer ha-Yovel li-khevod Shalom Baron* (= *Salo Wittmayer Baron Jubilee Volume*, vol. 3), Jerusalem 1975, pp. 111–181.
106) *Idem*, '*Leket Yosef* ve-*Sugyot ha-Talmud*: le-toldot sifrei kelalei ha-derush veha-hilukim', in *Alei Sefer*, 4 (1977), pp. 70–116.
107) Heinrich Ehrentreu, 'Über den "Pilpul" in den alten Jeschiboth', in *Jahrbuch der jüdisch-literarischen Gesellschaft*, 3 (1905), pp. 206–220.
108) Dov Rappel, *Ha-Vikuah 'al ha-Pilpul*, Tel-Aviv 1979.
109) Elhanan Reiner, 'Ha-Misgeret ha-historit shel ha-vikuah 'al ha-pilpul' (forthcoming).
110) Shmuel ha-Kohen Weingarten, 'Darkhei ha-limud shel Nirnberg-Regensburg', in *Sinai*, 37 (1955), pp. 267–276.

Note: Kleinberger (#69 and 170) and Twersky in Twersky (#162) also discuss *pilpul*.

VI. Responsa

111) Boaz Cohen, *Kuntres ha-Teshuvot: mafteah u-bibliyografyah shel sifrut ha-she'elot u-teshuvot mi-tekufat ha-Ge'onim ve-'ad yamenu*, Budapest 1930, reprinted Jerusalem 1970.
112) *Yonah Emanuel, 'Be'ayot sozyaliyot ve-sikhsukhei 'avodah bi-She'elot u-Teshuvot *Havot Ya'ir* [R. Yair Bacharach, Frankfurt 1699]', in *Levav Shalem: le-zekher Shelomoh Bacharach*, Jerusalem 1971, pp. 23–34.
113) Solomon Freehof, *The Responsa Literature*, Philadelphia 1955.
114) Meir Hildesheimer, *Yahadut Ashkenaz ba-me'ah ha-17 'al pi sifrut ha-She'elot u-Teshuvot*, M.A. dissertation, Bar Ilan University 1972.
115) Simon Hurwitz, *Responsa of Solomon Luria*, New York 1938.
116) Louis Jacobs, *Theology in the Responsa*, London 1975.
117) Yizhak Zeev Kahana, *Mehkarim be-Sifrut ha-Teshuvot*, Jerusalem 1973.
118) Mordechai Kosover, 'Di shayles-tshuves fun R. Yo'el Sirkes (der BaH): mekoyrim zu der geshikhte un lebn-shtayger fun Yidn in Poyln in 16–17 yohrhundert', in *Historishe Shriften*, 2 (1937), pp. 223–247.

119) Judah Rosenthal, 'Le-Korot ha-Yehudim be-Folin le-or She'elot u-Teshuvot ha-Maharam mi-Lublin', in *Sinai*, 31 (1952), pp. 311–338.
120) Elijah J. Schochet, *A Responsum of Surrender. Translation and Analysis*, Los Angeles 1973 [study of a *responsum* by Joel Sirkes].
121) Nisson Shulman, *Authority and Community. Polish Jewry in the Sixteenth Century*, New York 1985 [based on the *responsa* of Benjamin Solnik (d. c. 1619)].
122) Asher Siev, 'Mavo', in his edition of *She'elot u-Teshuvot ha-Rema* (by Moses b. Israel Isserles), Jerusalem 1971.
123) Shlomo Tal, 'Ha-Get mi-Wien, [1611]', in *Sinai*, 78 (1976), pp. 157–185.
124) Bernard Dov Weinryb, 'Responsa as a Source for History (Methodological Problems)', in H. J. Zimmels *et al.* (eds.), *Essays presented to Chief Rabbi Israel Brodie* . . . vol. I, London 1967, pp. 399–417.

Note: Sadek and Nosek (#143), Yudlov (#179), Zimmels (#268 and #371) and Fettke (#378) are studies of *responsa*.

VII. Minhagim Literature

125) Israel Abrahams, 'Hahn's Note Book', in *idem*, *By-Paths in Hebraic Bookland*, Philadelphia 1920, pp. 129–135.
126) Shlomo Eidelberg, *R. Juspa, Shammash of Warmaisa (Worms). Jewish Life in Seventeenth-Century Worms* [= *R. Yuzpa Shamash di-kehilat Vermaisa: 'olam Yehudiyah ba-me'ah ha-17*] [full text in English and in Hebrew], Jerusalem 1991.
127) Abraham Epstein, 'Die Wormser Minhagbücher. Literarisches und Culturhistorisches aus denselben', in Brann and Rosenthal (eds.), *op. cit.* (#100), pp. 288–317.
128) Morris Epstein, 'Simon Levi Ginzburg's Illustrated Custumal (Minhagim-Book) of Venice, 1593 and its Travels', in *Fifth WCJS* (1969), vol. 4, pp. 197–213.
129) Benjamin Hamburger and Eric Zimmer (eds.), *Minhagim de-Kehila Kadisha Wermaysa [=Worms] le-Rabi Yuzfa Shammes*, vol. I, Jerusalem 1988.
130) Isaac Holzer, 'Aus dem Leben der alten jüdischen Gemeinde zu Worms: nach dem *Minhagbuch* des Juspa Schammes', in *Zeitschrift für die Geschichte der Juden in Deutschland*, N.F. 5 (1935), pp. 169–181.
131) Jakob Horovitz, 'Aus der Oxforder Handschrift des *Josif Omez*', in Alexander Marx and Herrmann Meyer (eds.), *Festschrift für Aron Freimann* . . . Berlin 1935, pp. 35–50.
132) Jacob Meitlis, 'Dos Minhagim-sefer'el '*Orah Hayim* [Basel 1601]', in *Pinkes far der Forshung fun der Yidisher Literatur un Prese*, 2 (1972), pp. 170–184.
133) Herman Pollack, *Jewish Folkways in Germanic Lands, op. cit.* (#5).
134) Dov Rappel (ed.), *Pirkei Hinukh mi-tokh Yosif Omez*, Tel-Aviv 1976.

Note: Hildesheimer (#114), Goldberg (#199) and Abramsky (#348) also study custumals.

VIII. Social and Political Thought

135) Haim Hillel Ben Sasson, 'Mishnato ha-hevratit shel R. Yohanan Luria', in *Zion*, 27 (1962), pp. 166–198.
136) *Idem*, ''Osher ve-'oni be-mishnato shel ha-mokhiah R. Efrayim ish Lenczyc', in *Zion*, 19 (1954), pp. 142–166.
137) Daniel J. Elazar and Stuart A. Cohen, *The Jewish Polity. Jewish Political Organization from Biblical Times to the Present*, Bloomington, Ind. 1985.
138) Shmuel Ettinger, 'The Hassidic Movement – Reality and Ideals', in *Journal*

of *World History*, 11 (1968), pp. 251–266. [The journal volume was reprinted as H. H. Ben Sasson and S. Ettinger (eds.), *Jewish Society through the Ages*, New York 1971.] Ettinger's article is also in Hundert (below #443).

139) Ephraim Kupfer, 'A Zushtayer zu der frage fun der baziung fun kahal zum Yidishn ba'al-melokhoh, meshares, un oremshaft in amolikn Poyln', in *Bleter far Geshikhte*, 2 (1949), pp. 207–222.

140) *Idem*, 'Zu der frage vegn der shtayern-politik fun kahal in amolikn Poyln', in *Bleter far Geshikhte*, 8 (1955), pp. 51–67.

141) Daniel Nussbaum, *Social Justice and Social Policy in the Jewish Tradition. The Satisfaction of Basic Human Needs in Poznań in the Seventeenth and Eighteenth Centuries*, Ph.D. dissertation, Brandeis University 1977.

142) Israel Oppenheim, 'Halakhei ha-ruah veha-megamot be-'inyanei hevrah ke-vituyam be-'Pinkas Kesherim' shel Kehilat Pozna', in *Gal-Ed*, 3 (1976), pp. 33–56.

143) Vladimir Sadek and Bedřich Nosek, 'Antagonismes sociaux dans les communautés religieuses juives en Moravie, se reflétant dans l'oeuvre de Menahem Mendl Krochmal', in *Judaica Bohemiae*, 13 (1977), pp. 59–73.

144) Vladimir Sadek, 'Social Aspects in the Work of Prague R. Löw (Maharal) 1512–1609', in *Judaica Bohemiae*, 19 (1983), pp. 3–21.

Note: Ben Sasson (#10) is a major study of social thought. Reiner (#109), Emanuel (#112), Sherwin (#178), Turniansky (#321), and Dinur in Hundert (#443) also concern social and political thought.

C. JEWISH THOUGHT

I. Philosophy

145) Jonah Ben Sasson, *Mishnato ha-'Iyunit shel ha-Rema [R. Mosheh Isserles]*, Jerusalem 1984.

146) Herbert Davidson, 'Medieval Jewish Philosophy in the Sixteenth Century', in Cooperman (ed.), *op. cit.* (#11), pp. 106–145.

147) Joseph Davis, *R. Yom Tov Lipman Heller, Joseph b. Isaac ha-Levi, and Rationalism in Ashkenazic Jewish Culture 1550–1650*, Ph.D. dissertation, Harvard University 1990.

148) Hava Fraenkel-Goldschmidt (ed.), *Sefer ha-Miknah* (by Joseph [Josel] b. Gershon of Rosheim), Jerusalem 1970.

149) Lawrence Kaplan, *Rationalism and Rabbinic Culture in Sixteenth Century Eastern Europe. R. Mordecai Jaffe's Levush Pinat Yikrat*, Ph.D. dissertation, Harvard University 1975. Cf. *idem*, 'Rabbi Mordekhai Jaffe and the Evolution of Jewish Culture in Poland in the Sixteenth Century', in Cooperman (ed.), *op. cit.* (#77), pp. 266–282.

150) Ephraim Kupfer, 'Hasagot min hakham ehad 'al divrei he-hakham R. Yosef ha-Lo'azi she-katav ve-kara be-kol gadol neged ha-Rambam', in *Kovez 'al Yad*, 21 (1985), pp. 213–288.

151) Saul Pinhas Rabinowitz, *'Ikevot shel Hofesh De'ot ba-Rabanut shel Polin*, transl. by Y. D. Abramsky, Jerusalem 1959 [on the Poznań controversy of 1559]. The original appeared in Russian, in *Evreiskaya Starina*, 3 (1911), pp. 3–18.

152) Gershom Scholem, 'Yedi'ot hadashot 'al R. Yosef Ashkenazi, ha-Tana mi-Zefat', in *Tarbiz*, 28 (1958), pp. 59–89 and 201–235.

153) Isadore Twersky, 'R. Yosef Ashkenazi ve-Sefer Mishneh Torah le-Rambam', in Lieberman (ed.), *op. cit.* (#105), pp. 183–194.

Note: Stern (#39), Rappel (#72), Twersky (#77), Davis (#78), Burstein (#181), Kupfer and Mark (#367), and esp. Elbaum (#12) discuss aspects of Ashkenazic rationalism.

II. Kabbalah and Mysticism

154) Meir Benayahu, *Sefer Toldot ha-Ari: gilgulei nusha'otav ve-'erko mi-behinah historit*, Jerusalem 1967.
155) Samuel Abba Horodetsky, *Ha-Mistorin be-Yisra'el*, vol. III, Tel-Aviv 1961.
156) Idem, 'Ha-Reshal [= Solomon Luria] veha-Kabalah', in *Ha-Goren*, 1 (1898), pp. 95–99.
157) Idem, 'Ha-Zeramim ha-mistoriyim be-kerev Yehudei Polin 5300–5500 [= 1540–1740]', in *Ha-'Atid*, 5 (1913), pp. 105–131 [in German as *Mystisch-religiöse Strömungen unter den Juden in Polen im 16.–18. Jahrhundert. Inaugural-Dissertation . . . Bern*, Bern 1912, reprinted New York 1980].
158) Moshe Idel, ' "One from a Family, Two from a Clan". The Question of the Diffusion of Lurianic Kabbalah and Sabbatianism: a Reexamination', in Twersky and Cooperman (eds.), *op. cit.* (#66).
159) Yeruham Leiner, 'Ha-Maharshal veha-Kabalah', in *Sinai*, 44 (1959), pp. 224–229.
160) Eugene Newman, *The Life and Teachings of Isaiah Horowitz*, London 1972.
161) Vladimir Sadek, 'Le Système Cosmologique de Shabtaj ben Akiba Horowitz (vers 1565–1619)', in *Judaica Bohemiae*, 3 (1967), pp. 18–25.
162) Isadore Twersky and Bernard Septimus (eds.), *Jewish Thought in the Seventeenth Century*, Cambridge, Mass. 1987. Note esp. Yehudah Liebes, 'Mysticism and Reality. Towards a Portrait of the Martyr and Kabbalist, R. Samson Ostropoler' (pp. 221–256; the Hebrew original appeared in *Tarbiz*, 52 [1982], pp. 83–110, 661–664); Bracha Sack, 'The Influence of Cordovero on Seventeenth-Century Jewish Thought' (pp. 365–380); and Twersky, 'Law and Spirituality in the Seventeenth Century. A Case Study in R. Yair Hayyim Bacharach' (pp. 447–467).
163) *Elliot Wolfson, 'Hashpa'at ha-Ari 'al ha-Shelah', in *Jerusalem Studies in Jewish Thought* (= *Mehkerei Yerushalayim be-Mahshevet Yisra'el*), forthcoming.

Note: Scholem (#422) is a major study of *kabbalah* in Poland. Elior (#438), Idel (#444) and Weiss (#450) discuss *kabbalah* in early Hasidism.
Katz (#82), Sherwin (#178), Burstein (#181), Elbaum (#195), Goldberg (#198), Gries (#200), Pachter (#202), Zfatman (#241 and 267), Nigal (#296), Z. Newman (#329), Liebes (#408 and 409), and Piekarz (#203) study aspects of kabbalistic influence.

III. Maharal (Jehuda Löw ben Bezalel) of Prague

164) Ben Zion Bokser, *From the World of the Cabbalah. The Philosophy of R. Judah Liwa of Prague*, New York 1954.
165) Martin Buber, 'Kefel Yesodot: 'al Maharal mi-Prag', in *idem, Bein 'Am le-Arzo: 'ikarei toldotav shel ra'ayon*, Tel-Aviv 1944, pp. 78–90. English transl.: 'The Beginning of the National Idea: the High Rabbi Liva', in *On Zion. The History of an Idea*, transl. by S. Godman, New York 1973, pp. 77–88.
166) Théodore Dreyfus, *Dieu parle aux hommes: la théologie juive de la révélation selon le Maharal de Prague 1512–1609*, Paris 1969.
167) Abraham Gottesdiener (or Ovadyah), 'Ha-Ari shebe-hakhmei Prag', in *Azkarah*, 4 (1937), pp. 253–443. Published separately as *Ha-Maharal: hayav, tekufato, ve-torato*, Jerusalem 1976.
168) Benjamin Gross, *Le Messianisme Juif. L'Eternité d'Israel du Maharal de Prague*, Paris 1969.

169) *Idem*, 'Ba'ayat ha-Temimut' ('Temimut in Maharal's Teachings'), in *Da'at*, 17 (1986), pp. 103–116.
170) Aaron Fritz Kleinberger, *Mahashavto ha-Pedogogit shel ha-Maharal mi-Prag*, Jerusalem 1962.
171) Otto Dov Kulka, 'Ha-Reka' ha-histori shel mishnato ha-le'umit veha-hinukhit shel ha-Maharal mi-Prag', in *Zion*, 50 (1985), pp. 277–320. Cf. his 'Comenius and Maharal. The Historical Background of the Parallels in their Teaching', in *Judaica Bohemiae*, 27 (1991), pp. 17–30.
172) André Neher, *Le Puits de l'Exil. La Théologie Dialectique du Maharal de Prague (1512–1609)*, Paris 1966.
173) *Idem*, 'Maharal of Prague as Humanist', in *Judaism*, 14 (1965), pp. 290–304.
174) Tamar Ross, 'Ha-Nes ke-meimad nosaf be-hagut ha-Maharal mi-Prag', in *Da'at*, 17 (1986), pp. 81–96.
175) Vladimir Sadek, 'Rabbi Löw und sein Bild des Menschen', in *Judaica Bohemiae*, 26 (1990), pp. 72–83.
176) Bezalel Safran, 'Maharal and Early Hasidism', in *idem* (ed.), *Hasidism. Continuity and Transition*, Cambridge, Mass. 1988, pp. 47–144.
177) Rivkah Shatz, 'Maharal's Conception of Law – Antithesis to Natural Law Theory', in *Jewish Law Annual*, 6 (1987), pp. 109–125 (= 'Ha-Tefisah ha-Mishpatit shel ha-Maharal: antitezah la-hok ha-tiv'i', in *Da'at*, 2–3 [1979], pp. 147–158).
178) Byron L. Sherwin, *Mystical Theology and Social Dissent. The Life and Works of Judah Loew of Prague*, New Jersey 1982.
179) Yizhak Yudlov, 'Teshuvot Maharal mi-Prag', in Yosef Buksboim (ed.), *Sefer Zikaron li-khevodo . . . shel . . . Rabi Ya'akov Bezalel Zholty*, Jerusalem 1987, pp. 264–296.

Note: Neher (#34), Adini (#63), Kleinberger (#70), Sadek (#144), Elbaum (#182), Ish-Shalom (#183), Segal (#185), Elkouby (#196), Fox (#197), Neher (#263), Breuer (#385), and Shatz (#412) are studies of Maharal.

IV. Interpretation of Aggadah

180) David Bonami, *The Theological Ideas in the Hiddushei Aggadot of Maharsha*, D.H.L. dissertation, Jewish Theological Seminary 1976.
181) Dov Burstein, 'Ha-Kabalah veha-pilosofyah ha-datit be-Hidushei Agadot Maharsha', in *Sinai*, 41 (1957), pp. 172–183.
182) Jacob Elbaum, 'R. Judah Loewe's Attitude to Aggadah', in *Scripta Hierosolymitana*, 22 (1971), pp. 28–47.
183) Benjamin Ish-Shalom, 'Tanin, livyatan, ve-nahash: li-fesharo shel motiv agadi', in *Da'at*, 19 (1987), pp. 79–101 [on Maharal's interpretation of the "sea-serpent"].
184) Jacob Reifman, 'Ohel Yissakhar' [on Issachar Baer of Szczebrzeszyn], in *Beit Ozar ha-Sifrut*, 1 (1887), pp. 1–20.
185) Lester A. Segal, 'Aggadic Exegesis. Between Azariah [de' Rossi]'s Critical Analysis and Maharal's Denunciations'; and 'Maharal versus Azariah: the Issue of Ancients and Moderns', in *idem*, *Historical Consciousness and Religious Tradition in Azariah de' Rossi's Me'or Einayim*, Philadelphia 1989, pp. 133–163.
186) Chava Turniansky, 'Ha-Tirgumim ha-rishonim shel *Sefer ha-Yashar* le-Yidish', in *Tarbiz*, 54 (1985), pp. 567–622.
187) Chava Weissler, 'Women in Paradise', in *Tikkun*, 2, No. 2 (1987), pp. 43–46, 117–120.

Note: Wachstein (#239), Meitlis (#295), Zfatman (#304) and Breuer (#385) are also studies of interpretation of *aggadah*.
Jonah Ben Sasson (#145), Kaplan (#149), Ginzberg (#208), Levine (#209), Liebes (#409) and Perlmuter (#419) are studies of Hebrew Bible interpretation. Cf. #283–292 on Yiddish Bible interpretation, #384–389 on anti-Christian polemic, and 'Torah Study in Early Hasidism', in Weiss (#450).

V. Sermons

188) Israel Bettan, *Studies in Jewish Preaching. Middle Ages*, Cincinnati 1939 [= 'The Sermons of Ephraim Luntshitz', in *Hebrew Union College Annual*, 8–9 (1932), pp. 443–480; 'The Sermons of Jonathan Eybeshitz', *ibid.*, 10 (1935), pp. 553–597].
189) Gedaliah Nigal, 'Derashotav shel R. Shmu'el Yehudah Katzenellenbogen', in *Sinai*, 70 (1972), pp. 79–85.
190) Hayim Goren Perelmuter (ed. and transl.), *Shir haMa'alot L'David and Ktav Hitnazzelut L'Darshanim*, by David Darshan [fl. 1570], Cincinnati 1984.
191) Hayyim Reuben Rabinowitz, *Diyukna'ot shel Darshanim*, Jerusalem 1967.
192) Marc Saperstein, *Jewish Preaching 1200–1800. An Anthology*, New Haven 1989.
193) Bernhard Wachstein, *Mafteah ha-Hespeidim ha-nimza'im veha-nizkarim be-sifrei Beit Ozar ha-Sefarim de-kahal Wien* [= *Zur Bibliographie der Gedächtnis- und Trauervorträge in der hebräischen Literatur*], Vienna 1922–1932.

Note: Ben Sasson (#10, 135 and 136), Dimitrovsky (#106), Rappel (#108), Piekarz (#203) and Saperstein (#383) are studies of sermons and preaching.

VI. Musar

194) Jacob Elbaum, *Zeramim u-Megamot be-Sifrut ha-Mahshavah veha-Musar be-Ashkenaz uve-Folin ba-Me'ah ha-16*, Ph.D. dissertation, Hebrew University 1977. Cf. his 'Aspects of Hebrew Ethical Literature in Sixteenth-Century Poland', in Cooperman (ed.), *op. cit.* (#77), pp. 146–166.
195) Idem, 'R. Avraham Horowitz 'al ha-teshuvah', in *Mehkarim be-Kabalah, be-Filosofyah Yehudit uve-Sifrut ha-Musar vehe-Hagut, mugashim le-Yish'ayah Tishbi* . . . Jerusalem 1986, pp. 537–568.
196) Joseph Elkouby, 'Le repentir ou *teshuba* dans l'oeuvre du Maharal', in *Mélanges André Neher*, Paris 1975, pp. 103–112.
197) Marvin Fox, 'The Moral Philosophy of Maharal', in Cooperman (ed.), *op. cit.* (#77), pp. 167–185.
198) Sylvie Anne Goldberg, 'Les lectures mortuaires des Juifs dans les communautés Ashkénazes (XVIIe–XVIIIe siècles)', in *Revue de l'Histoire des Religions*, 204 (1987), pp. 249–278.
199) Idem, *Les deux rives de Yabbok: la maladie et la mort dans le judaïsme ashkénaze. Prague XVIe–XIXe siècle*, Paris 1989.
200) Zeev Gries, ''Izuv sifrut ha-hanhagot ha-'Ivrit be-mifneh ha-me'ah ha-16 uva-me'ah ha-17 u-mashma'uto ha-historit', in *Tarbiz*, 56 (1987), pp. 527–581.
201) Gershon David Hundert, 'Jewish Children and Childhood in Early Modern East Central Europe', in David Kraemer (ed.), *The Jewish Family. Metaphor and Memory*, Oxford 1989, pp. 81–94.
202) Mordechai Pachter, '*Sefer Reshit Hokhmah* le-R. Eliyahu di Vidas ve-Kizurav', in *Kiryat Sefer*, 47 (1972), pp. 686–710.

203) Mendel Piekarz, *Bi-yemei Zemihat ha-Hasidut: megamot ra'ayoniyot be-sifrut derush u-musar*, Jerusalem 1978.
204) Agnes Romer Segal, 'Yiddish Works on Women's Commandments in the Sixteenth Century', in *Studies in Yiddish Literature and Folklore*, Jerusalem 1986, pp. 37–59.
205) Bernhard Wachstein, 'Mafteah ha-Zava'ot', in *Kiryat Sefer*, 11 (1934), pp. 235–244, 372–383; 12 (1935) pp. 98–108 [a listing of ethical wills].

Note: Elbaum (#12), Newman (#160), Gross (#169), Piekarz (#277), Turniansky (#321), Faierstein (#428) and Meitlis (#431) are studies of *musar*.

VII. Science

206) L. Berz, 'Aritmetishe lernbikher in Yidish 1699–1831', in *Yivobleter*, 19 (1942), pp. 59–79. Cf. H. Liberman's notes in *idem*, *Ohel Rahel*, *op. cit.* (#49), pp. 368–370.
207) David Fishman, 'Rabbi Moses Isserles and the Study of Science among Polish Rabbis', in Twersky and Cooperman (eds.), *op. cit.* (#66).
208) Yekutiel Ginzberg, 'Neshamot to'ot: reshimot le-toldot ha-mada'im be-Yisra'el', in *ha-Tekufah*, 25 (1929), pp. 488–497 [on Nathan Spira's use of arithmetic and *gematria*].
209) Hillel Levine, 'Paradise Not Surrendered. Jewish Reactions to Copernicus and the Growth of Modern Science', in R. Cohen and M. Wertofsky (eds.), *Epistemology, Methodology, and the Social Sciences*, Boston 1983, pp. 203–225.
210) André Neher, 'Homer hadash 'al David Gans ke-tokhen', in *Tarbiz*, 45 (1975), pp. 138–147.
211) Idem, 'Copernicus in the Hebraic Literature from the Sixteenth to the Eighteenth Century', in *Journal of the History of Ideas*, 38 (1977), pp. 211–226.
212) Michael Panitz, 'New Heavens and a New Earth. Seventeenth to Nineteenth Century Jewish Responses to the New Astronomy', in *Conservative Judaism*, 40, No. 2 (1988), pp. 28–42.
213) David Ruderman, 'Science, Medicine and Jewish Culture in Early Modern Europe' (Spiegel Lectures in European Jewish History, No. 7), Tel-Aviv 1987.
214) Ignaz Schwarz, 'Ein Wiener Donaubrückenprojekt aus dem XVI. Jahrhundert', in *Jahrbuch für Länderkunde von Niederösterreich*, 12 (1913), pp. 79–100 [on Mendel of Cracow]. Cf. Gelber in *Yivobleter*, 11 (1937), pp. 401–405.
215) Moritz Steinschneider, *Mathematik bei den Juden*, reprinted Hildesheim 1964 [a listing of mathematical and astronomical writings].

Note: Neher (#34), Rappel (#72) and Breuer (#224) are also studies of science and scientists.

VIII. Medicine

216) Mordecai Bernstein, 'Zvay rezepten-bikher in Alt-Yidish fun 1474 un 1509', in *Davke*, 4 (Buenos Aires 1953), pp. 330–361. English transl.: 'Two Remedy Books in Yiddish from 1474 and 1508', in Raphael Patai *et al.*, (eds.), *Studies in Biblical and Jewish Folklore* [Indiana University Folklore Series #13], Bloomington, Ind. 1960, pp. 289–305.
217) Daniel Carpi, 'Yehudim ba'alei to'ar Doktor li-Refu'ah be-Faduah', in Daniel Carpi *et al.* (eds.), *Scritti in Memoria di Nathan Cassuto*, Jerusalem 1986, Hebrew section, pp. 62–91.
218) Max Dienemann, 'Hygiene der Juden im 17. und 18. Jahrhundert', in Max Grunwald (ed.), *Die Hygiene der Juden*, Dresden 1911, pp. 260–270.

219) Maurycy Horn, 'Medycy nadworni władców polsko-litewskich w latach 1506–1572 ze szczególnym uwględnieniem lekarzy i chirurgów żydowskich', in *Biuletyn Żydowskiego Instytutu Historycznego w Polsce*, 149 (1989), pp. 2–23.
220) Adolf Kober, 'Rheinische Judendoktoren, vornehmlich des 17. und 18. Jahrhunderts', in *Festschrift zum 75 Jährigen Bestehen des Jüdisch-Theologischen Seminars Fraenckelscher Stiftung*, Breslau 1929, vol. II, pp. 173–236.
221) Joshua O. Leibowitz, 'Mavo', in Issachar Ber Teller, *Be'er Mayim Hayim 'im Pirkei Hipokrat*, Jerusalem 1968.
222) Louis Lewin, 'Jüdische Ärzte in Grosspolen', in *Jahrbuch der jüdisch-literarischen Gesellschaft*, 9 (1911), pp. 367–420.
223) Jacob Shatzky, '*Sefer ha-Heshek* – a farfalen refu'oh-bukh in Yidish fun 18-ten yorhundert un zayn mehaber', in *Yivobleter*, 4 (1932), pp. 223–235.

Note: Levinson (#32), Goldberg (#199), Ruderman (#213), Zimmels (#268), Balaban (#363), Barzilay (#365), and Kaufmann (#395) are studies of doctors and medicine.

IX. *Historiography*

(a) *Zemah David* by David Gans (1592)

224) Mordechai Breuer, 'Kavim li-demuto shel R. David Gans, ba'al *Zemah David*', in *Bar Ilan*, 11 (1974), pp. 97–118.
225) Idem, 'Modernism and Traditionalism in Sixteenth-Century Jewish Historiography. A Study of David Gans' *Tzemah David*', in Cooperman (ed.), *op. cit.* (#77), pp. 49–88.
226) Idem (ed.), *Zemah David* (by David Gans), Jerusalem 1983.
227) Ben Zion Degani, 'Ha-Mivneh shel ha-historyah ha-'olamit u-ge'ulat Yisra'el be-*Zemah David* le-R. David Gans', in *Zion*, 45 (1980), pp. 173–200.
228) Jiřina Šedinová, 'Non-Jewish Sources in the Chronicle by David Gans, *Tsemach David*', in *Judaica Bohemiae*, 8 (1972), pp. 3–15.
229) Idem, 'Czech History as Reflected in the Historical Work by David Gans', in *Judaica Bohemiae*, 8 (1972), pp. 74–83.
230) Idem, 'Old Czech Legends in the Work of David Gans', in *Judaica Bohemiae*, 14 (1978), pp. 89–112.

Note: Neher (#34) is the major biography of Gans.

(b) *Yiddish Historiography*

231) Renate G. Fuks-Mansfeld, 'Yiddish Historiography in the Time of the Dutch Republic', in *Studia Rosenthalia*, 15 (1981), pp. 9–19.
232) Meir Halévy, 'A Nay-antdekter ksav-yad vegn dem Metzer 'alilas-dam fun 1669', in *Filologishe Shriften*, 3 (1929), pp. 243–281.
233) Jacob da Silva Rosa, 'Di 'Kurantin' 1686–1687: a Yidishe zaytung in Amsterdam in 17-ten yorhundert', in Jacob Shatzky (ed.), *Zamlbukh li-khevod dem Zvay Hundert un Fufziksten Yoyvel fun der Yidisher Prese 1686–1936*, New York 1937, pp. 7–19.
234) Jacob Shatzky, 'Dos Kloglid oyf dem hurben fun Worms', in *Filologishe Shriften*, 3 (1929), pp. 43–56.
235) Zalman Shazar (Rubashov) (ed. and transl.), *Sipur Ma'aseh Shabtai Zevi/ Beshraybung fun Shabtai Zevi* (by Leib ben Ozer), Jerusalem 1978.
236) Chone Shmeruk, 'Ha-Kadosh R. Shakhna, Krako 442/1682: rishum befinkas shel ha-hevra kadisha le-umat shir histori', in *Gal-Ed*, 7–8 (1985), pp. 57–69.

237) Chava Turniansky, 'An Umbakant 'historish' lid vegn geshe'enishn in Frankfurt de-Main (1612–1616)', in *Ninth WCJS* (1986), Division C, Hebrew section, pp. 423–428.
238) *Idem*, 'Yiddish "Historical" Songs as Sources for the History of the Jews in Pre-Partition Poland', in *Polin*, 4 (1989), pp. 42–52.
239) Bernhard Wachstein, 'R. Azariah de Rossi's *Hadrat Zekenim* in Yidisher Iberzetzung', in *Filologishe Shriften*, 3 (1929), pp. 367–377.
240) Max Weinreich, 'A Yidish lid vegn Shabtai Zevi', in *idem*, *Bilder fun der Yidisher Literaturgeshikhte fun di Onhayben biz Mendele Mokher Seforim*, Vilna 1928, pp. 219–252. Cf. 'Zvay Yidishe kinos oyf Khmelnizkis gezeros' (pp. 192–218); 'Zvay zaytungsmesike barikhten fun 17-ten yorhundert' (pp. 253–266).
241) Sara Zfatman-Biller, 'Geirush ruhot bi-Prag ba-me'ah ha-17: li-she'elat mehemnuto ha-historit shel zhaner 'amami', in *Jerusalem Studies in Jewish Folklore*, 3 (1982), pp. 7–34.

Note: Turniansky (#186) and Zfatman (#267) are studies of Yiddish historiography.

(c) Other and General

242) Abraham David (ed.), *Kronikah 'Ivrit mi-Prag me-Reshit ha-Me'ah ha-17*, Jerusalem 1984.
243) Abraham Haberman, 'Piyutav ve-shirav shel R. Yom Tov Lipman Heller', in Fishman-Maimon (ed.), *op. cit.* (#99), pp. 129–145.
244) Jacob Katz, 'Bein Tatnu [1096] le-Tah-Tat [1648–1649]', in Shmuel Ettinger *et al.* (eds.), *Sefer Yovel le-Yitzhak Baer*, Jerusalem 1961, pp. 318–337.
245) Alan Mintz, *Hurban. Responses to Catastrophe in Hebrew Literature*, New York 1984, esp. 'Medieval Consummations', pp. 84–105.
246) Jiřina Šedinová, 'Hebrew Literature as a Source of Information on the Czech History of the First Half of the 17th Century. The Reflection of Events in Contemporary Hebrew Literature', in *Judaica Bohemiae*, 20 (1984), pp. 3–30; 23 (1987), pp. 38–57.
247) *Idem*, 'Literary Structure of the Seventeenth Century Hebrew Lyrico-Epic Poetry', in *Judaica Bohemiae*, 25 (1989), pp. 82–106.
247) *Jacob Shatzky [Introduction], in Nathan Neta Hannover, *Gezeires Tah*, Vilna, 1938.
249) Moritz Steinschneider, *Die Geschichtsliteratur der Juden*, Frankfurt a. Main 1905 [a bibliography].
250) Magnus Weinberg, 'Untersuchen über das Wesen des Memorbuches', in *Jahrbuch der jüdisch-literarischen Gesellschaft*, 16 (1924), pp. 253–320.
251) Bernard Weinryb, 'The Hebrew Chronicles on Bohdan Khmel'nyts'kyi and the Cossack–Polish War', in *Harvard Ukrainian Studies*, 1 (1977), pp. 153–177.
252) Yosef Hayim Yerushalmi, *Zakhor. Jewish History and Jewish Memory*, Seattle 1982.

X. Miscellaneous: travel, grammar, magic

(a) travel

253) Yizhak Ben Zvi (ed. and transl.), *Gelilot Erez Yisra'el* (by Gershon ben Eliezer ha-Levi), Jerusalem 1952.
254) Moritz Steinschneider, *Jüdische Schriften zur Geographie Palästinas*, Jerusalem 1892; reprinted Hildesheim 1971.

255) Zev Vilnay, *ha-Mapah ha-Ivrit shel Erez Yisra'el*, Jerusalem 1968.
256) Sara Zfatman-Biller, 'Igeret be-Yidish mi-sof ha-mc'ah ha-16 be-'inyan 'Aseret Shevatim', in *Kovez 'al Yad*, 20 (1982), pp. 217-252.

(b) Hebrew and Yiddish grammar

257) Dov Rappel, 'Milonim 'Ivriyim ke-sifrei limud', in *Sinai*, 101 (1988), pp. 235-265.
258) Max Weinreich, 'Dos ershte yohrhundert Yidishe shprakhforshung', in *idem, Shtaplen: far etyudn zu der Yidisher shprakhvisnshaft un literaturgeshikhte*, Berlin 1923, pp. 59-139 [also in his *Oysgeklibene Shriften*, Buenos Aires 1974, pp. 95-178].
259) *Idem*, 'Di Yidishe shprakhforshung in 17-ten yohrhundert', in *Zaytshrift*, 2-3 (Minsk 1928), pp. 689-731.
260) Hayim Liberman (Lieberman), 'Rabonishe etimologies fun Yidisher verter', in *idem, Ohel Rahel*, vol. II, *op. cit.* (#49), pp. 332-336.

Note: Weil (#40), Sherwin (#37), Zimmer (#41) and Reif (#330) are studies of grammar and grammarians.

(c) magic

261) Heinrich Flesch, 'Sympathetische Mittel und Rezepte aus dem Buche *Mif'alot Elokim* des Rabbi Naftali Kohen und Rabbi Joel Ba'al Schem', in *Mitteilungen der Gesellschaft für jüdische Volkskunde*, 15 (1912), pp. 41-48.
262) Moshe Idel, *Golem. Jewish Magical and Mystical Traditions on the Artificial Anthropoid*, Albany 1990.
263) André Neher, *Faust et le Maharal de Prague: le mythe et le réel*, Paris 1987.
264) Gershom Scholem, 'The Idea of the Golem', in *idem, On the Kabbalah and Its Symbolism*, transl. by R. Manheim, New York 1965, pp. 158-204.
265) *Idem*, ' 'Al kami'a ehad shel R. Yehonatan Eybeschuetz u-feirusho 'alav', in *Tarbiz*, 13 (1942), pp. 226-242.
266) Joshua Trachtenberg, *Jewish Magic and Superstition. A Study in Folk Religion*, New York 1939.
267) Sara Zfatman-Biller, 'Ma'aseh shel ruah be-kehila kadisha Korez – shelav hadash be-hitpathuto shel zhaner 'amami', in *Jerusalem Studies in Jewish Folklore*, 2 (1982), pp. 17-65.
268) Hirsch Jacob Zimmels, *Magicians, Theologians, and Doctors. Studies in Folk-Medicine and Folk-Lore as Reflected in Rabbinical Responses (12th-19th Centuries)*, London 1952.

Note: Bernstein (#216), Shatzky (#223), Weinreich ('Zvay Zaytungsmesike . . .' in #240), Zfatman (#241), and Nigal (#296) are studies of magic. Note also the collection of amulets in Shachar (#340).

D. YIDDISH LITERATURE AND JEWISH ARTS

Note also the sections on Yiddish historiography and Yiddish grammar above, and the Yiddish works discussed in the sections on *musar*, medicine and travel, among others.

I. General Studies, Yiddishism and Bilingualism

(a) general

269) Max Erik, pseud. (Zalman Merkin), *Di Geshikhte fun der Yidisher Literatur fun di Alteste Zeiten biz Haskoloh-Tekufah*, Warsaw 1928.

270) Meier Schüler, 'Beiträge zur Kenntnis der alten jüdisch-deutschen Profanliteratur', in *Festschrift zum 75jährigen Bestehen der Realschule mit Lyzeum der Isr. Religionsgesellschaft*, Frankfurt a. Main 1928, pp. 79–132.
271) Chone (or Khone) Shmeruk (or Szmeruk), *Sifrut Yidish: perakim le-toldoteha*, Tel-Aviv 1978.
272) Idem, *Perakim fun der Yidisher Literatur-Geshikhte*, Tel-Aviv 1988.
273) Nahum Shtif, 'Ditrikh fun Bern. Yidishkayt un veltlekhkayt in der alter Yidisher literatur,' in *Yidishe Filologie*, I (1924), No. 1, pp. 1–11; Nos. 2–3, pp. 112–122.
274) Moritz Steinschneider, *Jüdisch-Deutsche Literatur (Serapeum, Leipzig, 1848–1849)*, reprinted Jerusalem 1961. A bibliography; the original article was continued in *Serapeum* 1864–1866.
275) Max Weinreich, *Bilder fun der Yidisher Literaturgeshikhte*, op. cit. (#240).

Note: Weinreich (#6), Mark in Finkelstein (#13), Waxman (#20), Zinberg (#21), Romer Segal (#57), and Shmeruk (#60 and 353) are general studies of Yiddish literature.

(b) Yiddishism

276) Shlomo Noble, 'R. Yehiel-Mikhel Epstein – a derzier un kemfer far Yidish in 17-ten yorhundert', in *Yivobleter*, 25 (1951), pp. 121–138. Cf. Liberman's comments in idem, *Ohel Rahel*, vol. II, op. cit. (#49), pp. 201–230.
277) Mendel Piekarz, 'Vegn "Yidishizm" in sof fun 17-ten yorhundert un der ershter helft fun 18-ten yorhundert', in *Di Goldene Kayt*, 49 (1964), pp. 168–180.
278) Jacob Shatzky, 'Der Kamf kegn Purim-shpiln in Preissen in 18-ten yohrhundert', in *Yivobleter*, 15 (1940), pp. 28–38.
279) Israel Zinberg, 'Der Kamf far Yidish in der Alt-Yidisher literatur', in *Filologishe Shriften*, 2 (1928), pp. 69–106.

(c) bilingualism

280) Chava Turniansky, 'Ha-Yezirah ha-du-leshonit be-Ashkenaz: kavim le-ofiyah', in *Sixth WCJS* (1980), vol. 4, pp. 85–99.
281) Uriel Weinreich, 'Nusah ha-sofrim ha-'Ivri-Yidi' ['The Hebrew-Yiddish Language of Scribes'], in *Leshonenu*, 22 (1958), pp. 54–66.
282) Chava Weissler, 'The Religion of Traditional Ashkenazic Women: Some Methodological Issues', in *AJS Review*, 12 (1987), pp. 73–94.

Note: Shmeruk (#236) and Turniansky (#321) are studies of bilingualism.

II. Yiddish Bible Interpretation, Translation and Retelling

283) Nechama Leibowitz, 'Die Übersetzungstechnik der jüdischdeutschen Bibelübersetzungen des XV. und XVI. Jahrhunderts, dargestellt an den Psalmen', in *Beiträge zur Geschichte der deutschen Sprache und Literatur*, 55 (1931), pp. 377–463.
284) Harvey Minkoff and Evelyn B. Melamed, 'Was the First Feminist Bible in Yiddish?' in *Moment*, 16, No. 3 (1991), pp. 28–33, 52.
285) Jacob Shatzky, 'Dray Hundert Yor *Zenah Renah*', in idem, *Shoten fun 'Ovar*, Buenos Aires 1947.
286) *Ignacy (Yizhak, Isaac) Schiper (or Shiper), *Geshikhte fun Yidisher Teaterkunst un Drame fun di Elteste Zayten biz 1750*, 3 vols., Warsaw 1923–1928. Cf. Shatzky's review in *Filologishe Shriften*, 2 (1928), pp. 214–265.

287) Chone Shmeruk, 'Moyshe Rabeinu Beshraybung: an umbavuste drame fun 18-ten yohrhundert', in *Di Goldene Kayt*, 50 (1964), pp. 296–320.
288) *Idem*, 'Ba-Ma'agal ha-Mikra'i', in *idem, Sifrut Yidish: perakim le-toldoteha, op. cit.* (#271), pp. 105–146.
289) *Idem, Mahazot Mikra'iyim be-Yidish 1697–1750*, Jerusalem 1979.
290) Willy Staerk and Albert Leitzmann, *Die Jüdisch-Deutschen Bibelübersetzungen von dem Anfangen bis zum Ausgang des 18. Jahrhunderts*, Frankfurt a. Main 1923.
291) Chava Turniansky, 'Shtei shirot epiyot be-Yidish 'al Sefer Yehoshu'a', in *Tarbiz*, 51 (1982), pp. 589–632.
292) Max Weinreich, 'Zu der geshikhte fun der elterer Ahashverosh-shpiln', in *Filologishe Shriften*, 2 (1928), pp. 425–452.

Note: Fuks (#46), Turniansky (#186) and Shatzky (#278) are also studies of Yiddish Bible interpretation.

III. Prose Fiction

293) Gustav Karpeles, 'A Jewish King in Poland', in *idem, Jewish Literature and Other Essays*, Philadelphia 1895, pp. 272–292.
294) David Levine Lerner, 'The Enduring Legend of the Jewish Pope', in *Judaism*, 40 (1991), pp. 148–170.
295) Jacob Meitlis, *Das Ma'assebuch: seine Entstehung und Quellengeschichte*, Berlin 1933, reprinted Hildesheim 1987.
296) Gedaliah Nigal, *Sipurei 'Dibuk' be-Sifrut Yisra'el*, Jerusalem 1983.
297) Arnold Paucker, 'Yiddish Versions of Early German Prose Novels', in *Journal of Jewish Studies*, 10 (1959) pp. 151–167.
298) *Idem*, 'Das Volksbuch von den Sieben Weisen Meistern in der jiddischen Literatur', in *Zeitschrift für Volkskunde*, 57 (1961), pp. 177–194.
299) Chone Shmeruk, 'Reshitah shel ha-prozah ha-sipurit be-Yidish u-merkazah be-Italyah', in Daniel Carpi *et al.* (eds.), *Scritti in Memoria di Leone Carpi. Saggi sull'Ebraismo Italiano*, Jerusalem 1967, Hebrew section, pp. 119–140.
300) *Idem, The Esterke Story in Yiddish and Polish Literature. A Case Study in the Mutual Relations of Two Cultural Traditions*, Jerusalem 1985.
301) Erika Timm, 'Beria und Simra. Eine jiddische Erzählung des 16. Jahrhunderts', in *Literaturwissenschaftliches Jahrbuch*, 14 (1973), pp. 1–94.
302) *Idem*, 'Zur Jiddischen Fabelliteratur des 16. Jahrhunderts', in *Eighth WCJS* (1981), vol. 3, pp. 159–164.
303) Eli Yassif, 'From Jewish Oicotype to Israeli Oicotype. The Tale of the Man who Never Swore an Oath', in *Fabula*, 27 (1986), pp. 216–236.
304) Sara Zfatman-Biller, 'Maysehbukh: kavim li-demuto shel zhaner be-sifrut Yidish ha-yeshanah', in *ha-Sifrut*, 28 (1979), pp. 126–152.
305) *Idem, Ha-Siporet be-Yidish me-Reshitah 'ad Shivhei ha-Besht (1504–1814)*, Ph.D. dissertation, Hebrew University 1983.
306) *Idem, Ha-Siporet be-Yidish me-Reshitah 'ad Shivhei ha-Besht (1504–1814). Bibliyografyah Mu'eret*, Jerusalem 1985.
307) *Idem, Nisu'ei Adam ve-Shedah: gilgulav shel motiv ba-siporet ha-'amamit shel Yehudei Ashkenaz ba-me'ot ha-17-ha-19*, Jerusalem 1988.
308) *Idem*, 'Ma'aseh be-shiv'at benei Hyrcanus she-hafkhu le-avazim: le-darkhei 'ibudah be-Yidish shel ma'asiyah bein-le'umit (AT 451)', in *Jerusalem Studies in Jewish Folklore*, 10 (1988), pp. 32–94.

Note: Zfatman (#241, 256 and 267) and Shmeruk (#448) are also studies of prose fiction. Note also the section of Eidelberg (#126) on Juspa's collection of stories.

IV. Memoirs

309) *Natalie Zemon Davis [on Glückel of Hameln], in *idem, Women on the Margins* (forthcoming).
310) David Kaufmann, 'Einführendes', in *idem* (ed.), *Die Memoiren von Glückel von Hameln* [= *Zikhronot Marat Glikl Hamil* . . .], Frankfurt a. Main 1896.
311) Alfred Landau, 'Die Sprache der Memoiren Glückels von Hameln', in *Mitteilungen der Gesellschaft für jüdische Volkskunde*, 7 (1901), pp. 20–68. Cf. I. Ysaye, 'Einiges aus den Memoiren der Glückel von Hameln', *ibid.*, pp. 1–19.
312) Salomon Hugo Lieben, 'Megillath Samuel', in *Jahrbuch der Gesellschaft für Geschichte der Juden in der Čechoslovakischen Republik*, 9 (1938), pp. 307–339.
313) *Nahum Baruch Minkoff, *Glikl Hamil*, New York 1952.
314) Solomon Schechter, 'The Memoirs of a Jewess of the Seventeenth Century', in *idem, Studies in Judaism. Second Series*, Philadelphia 1908, pp. 126–147 [on Glückel].

Note: Davis (#147) includes a study of the memoir of R. Yom Tov Lipman Heller.

V. Secular Poetry and Romances

315) Benjamin Hrushovski, 'The Creation of Accentual Iambs in European Poetry and their First Employment in a Yiddish Romance in Italy (1508–09)', in Lucy S. Dawidowicz *et al.* (eds.), *For Max Weinreich on his Seventieth Birthday*, The Hague 1964, pp. 108–146.
316) Judah Joffe, 'Elia Bachur, the Man and the Artist', in *idem* (ed.), *Elyeh Bokher. Poetishe shafungen in Yidish: reproduktsye fun der ershter oysgabe Bovo de-Antona, Isny, 1541* [= *Elia Bachur's Poetical Works* . . .], New York 1949.
317) Nahum Baruch Minkoff, *Elyeh Bokher un zayn Bove-Bukh*, New York 1950.
318) Felix Rosenberg, 'Über eine Sammlung deutscher Volks- und Gesellschaftslieder in hebräischen Lettern', in *Zeitschrift für die Geschichte der Juden in Deutschland*, 2 (1888), pp. 232–296; 3 (1889), pp. 14–28.
319) Chone Shmeruk, '"Velkher Yontif iz der Bester?": a nit-farefentlekht vikuah-lid zvishn Hanukah un di andere yontoyvim', in *Di Goldene Kayt*, 47 (1963), pp. 160–173.
320) Jerry Christopher Smith, *Elia Levita's Bovo-Buch. A Yiddish Romance of the Early 16th Century*, Ph.D. dissertation, Cornell University 1968.
321) Chava Turniansky (ed.), *Sefer Masah u-Merivah* (by R. Alexander Pfaffenhofen), Jerusalem 1985.
322) *Idem*, 'The Evolution of the Poetical Contest in Ashkenaz', in *Studies in Yiddish Literature and Folklore, op. cit.* (#204), pp. 60–98.

VI. Prayer

323) Chimen Abramsky and Bedřich Nosek (eds.), *Grace After Meals. Birkat ha-Mazon. Facsimile of the 1514 Prague Edition* [= *Birkat ha-Mazon: faksimiliya de-hoza'at Prag 1514*], Verona 1984.
324) Hanoch Avenary [= Loewenstein], *The Ashkenazi Tradition of Biblical Chant Between 1500 and 1900. Documentation and Musical Analysis*, Tel-Aviv 1978.
325) Solomon Freehof, 'Devotional Literature in the Vernacular (Judeo-German, prior to the Reform Movement)', in *CCAR* [Central Conference of American Rabbis] *Yearbook*, 33 (1923), pp. 375–424.

326) Geoffrey Goldberg, 'Hazzan and Qahal. Responsive Chant in Minhag Ashkenaz', in *Hebrew Union College Annual*, 61 (1990), pp. 203–217.
327) Nahum Baruch Minkoff, 'An Alte tehinah un ire literarishe formen', in *Pinkes far der Forshung fun der Yidisher Literatur un Prese*, 2 (1972), pp. 185–213.
328) Otto Muneles, *Ketovot mi-Beit ha-'Almin ha-Yehudi ha-'Atik bi-Prag*, Jerusalem 1988.
329) Zelda Kahan Newman, 'Kabbalistic Ideas in the Women's Yiddish Prayer Book, Tkheenes', in Mark Gelber (ed.), *Identity and Ethos. A Festschrift for Sol Liptzin*, New York 1986, pp. 37–48.
330) Stefan Reif, *Shabbethai Sofer and his Prayer Book*, Cambridge 1979.
331) Siegfried Stein, 'Liebliche Tefilloh. A Judaeo-German Prayer-Book Printed in 1709', in *LBI Year Book XV* (1970), pp. 41–72.
332) Chava Turniansky, 'Ha- 'Bentsherl' veha-zemirot be-Yidish', in '*Alei Sefer*, 10 (1982), pp. 51–92.
333) Chava Weissler, 'Prayers in Yiddish and the Religious World of Ashkenazic Women', in Judith R. Baskin (ed.), *Jewish Women in Historical Perspective*, Detroit 1991, pp. 159–181. Cf. Weissler, 'The Traditional Piety of Ashkenazic Women', in Arthur Green (ed.), *Jewish Spirituality. From the Sixteenth Century to the Present*, New York 1987, pp. 245–275.
334) Leopold Zunz, *Literaturgeschichte der Synagogalen Poesie*, Berlin 1865. Cf. idem, *Die Synagogale Poesie des Mittelalters*, Frankfurt a. Main 1920.

Note: Freehof (#81 and 86), Katz (#89), Lauterbach (#91), Weissler (#187 and 282), Shmeruk (#236), Haberman (#243), Šedinová (#246 and 247), and Mieses (#405) are also studies of prayer, and cf. closely all of #335–362.

VII. *Jewish Arts*

(a) general

335) David Altshuler (ed.), *The Precious Legacy. Judaic Treasures from the Czechoslovak State Collections*, New York 1983.
336) Joseph Gutmann (ed.), *Beauty in Holiness. Studies in Jewish Customs and Ceremonial Art*, New York 1970. Note esp. three essays by Franz Landsberger: 'The Origin of European Torah Decorations' (pp. 87–105); 'Old-Time Torah Curtains. A Propos of a New Acquisition of the Jewish Museum in New York' (pp. 125–163); and 'The Origins of the Ritual Implements for the Sabbath' (pp. 167–203). All three articles appeared originally in *Hebrew Union College Annual*, respectively in vol. 24 (1952), vol. 19 (1945) and vol. 27 (1956).
337) Rudolph Hallo, *Jüdische Kunst aus Hessen und Nassau*, Berlin 1933.
338) Leo A. Mayer, *Bibliography of Jewish Art*, ed. by Otto Kurz, Jerusalem 1967.
339) Naftali Schneid, 'Omanut Yehudei Polin', in *Sinai*, 10 (1942), pp. 248–260.
340) Isaiah Shachar, *Jewish Tradition in Art. The Feuchtwanger Collection of Judaica*, transl. by R. Grafman, Jerusalem 1981. Many collection and exhibition catalogues, such as this one, include a wealth of examples of Ashkenazic ceremonial art.

(b) synagogue architecture

341) David Davidovitch (Davidovicz), *Omanut ve-Omanim be-Vatei Keneset shel Polin: mekorot, signonot, hashpa'ot*, Jerusalem 1982.
342) *Idem, Ziyurei-Kir be-Vatei Keneset be-Folin*, Jerusalem 1968. Cf. his *Wand-*

malereien in alten Synagogen. Das Wirken des Malers Elieser Sussman in Deutschland, Hameln–Hannover 1969.

343) Alfred Grotte, *Deutsche, Böhmische, und Polnische Synagogentypen: vom XI. bis Anfang des XIX. Jahrhunderts*, Berlin 1915.

344) Carol Herselle Krinsky, *Synagogues of Europe. Architecture, History, Meaning*, New York 1985. Includes extensive bibliographies.

345) Maria and Kazimierz Piechotka, *Wooden Synagogues*, Warsaw 1959.

346) Hana Volavková, *The Pinkas Synagogue*, Prague 1955.

347) Rachel Wischnitzer-Bernstein, 'Mutual Influences between Eastern and Western Europe in Synagogue Architecture from the 12th to the 18th Century', in *YIVO Annual of Jewish Social Science*, 2–3 (1948), pp. 25–68 [= 'Mizrah-mayrevdike bindungen in der shuln-arkhitektur fun zvelfen bizn akhzenten yohrhundert', in *Yivobleter*, 29 (1947), pp. 3–50].

(c) illuminated manuscripts and book illustrations

348) Chimen Abramsky, 'Some Early Illustrated Passover Haggadahs', in *idem, Two Prague Haggadahs: the 1556 edition on vellum and the 1590–1606 [?] edition on paper* [facsimile edition], Verona 1978.

349) Iris Fishof, 'Yakob *Sofer mi*-Berlin [fl. 1730]. A Portrait of a Jewish Scribe', in *Israel Museum Journal*, 6 (1987), pp. 83–94.

350) Milly Heyd, 'Illustrations of Early Editions of the Tsene-U'rene. Jewish Adaptations of Christian Sources', in *Journal of Jewish Art*, 10 (1984), pp. 64–86.

351) Ernest Naményi, 'The Illumination of Hebrew Manuscripts after the Invention of Printing', in Cecil Roth (ed.), *Jewish Art: an Illustrated History*, rev. edn. by Bezalel Narkiss, New York 1971, pp. 149–162 (originally published as 'La miniature juive au XVIIe et au XVIIIe siècle', in *Revue des Etudes Juives*, 116 [1957], pp. 27–72).

352) Menahem Schmelzer, 'Decorated Hebrew Manuscripts of the Eighteenth Century in the Library of the Jewish Theological Seminary of America', in Robert Dán (ed.), *Occident and Orient. A Tribute to the Memory of Alexander Scheiber*, Budapest 1988, pp. 331–352.

353) Chone Shmeruk, *Ha-Iyurim le-Sifrei Yidish ba-Me'ot ha-16-ha-17: ha-tekstim, ha-temunot, ve-nim'aneihem*, Jerusalem 1986.

(d) ceremonial art

354) Ruth Eis, *Torah Binders of the Judah L. Magnes Museum*, Berkeley 1979. Cf. Florence Guggenheim-Grünberg, *Die Torawickelbänder von Lengnau. Zeugnisse jüdischer Volkskunst*, Zürich 1967.

355) *Bruno Italiener, 'Eine Sederschüssel aus dem 16ten Jahrhundert', in *Minhat Todah. Festschrift zum 60ten Geburtstage von Max Dienemann*, Frankfurt a. Main 1934, pp. 49–55.

356) Ludmila Kybalová, 'Die ältesten Thoramäntel aus der Textiliensammlung des Staatlichen Jüdischen Museums in Prag (1592–1750)', in *Judaica Bohemiae*, 9 (1973), pp. 23–42.

357) Vivian B. Mann, 'The Golden Age of Jewish Ceremonial Art in Frankfurt. Metalwork of the Eighteenth Century', in *LBI Year Book XXXI* (1986), pp. 389–406.

358) Mordechai Narkiss, 'The Origins of the Spice Box', in *Journal of Jewish Art*, 8 (1981), pp. 28–51 [= 'Reshito shel ha-Hadas li-Besamim', in *Eretz-Israel*, 6 (1960), pp. 189–198].

359) Isaiah Shachar, 'Feast and Rejoice in Brotherly Love. Burial Society Glasses and Jugs from Bohemia and Moravia', in *The Israel Museum News*, 9 (1972), pp. 22–51.
360) Hana Volavková, *The Synagogue Treasures of Bohemia and Moravia*, Prague 1949 [on embroidery and fine textiles].

(e) miscellaneous

361) Hannelore Künzl, 'Symbolism in the Art of Jewish Gravestones in Europe', in *Ninth WCJS* (1986), Division D, vol. 2, pp. 53–58.
362) Gershom Scholem, 'The Star of David. History of a Symbol', in *idem*, *The Messianic Idea in Judaism and other Essays in Jewish Spirituality*, New York 1971, pp. 257–281.

Note: Epstein (#128), Muneles (#18 and 328) and Abramsky (#323) are also studies of Jewish art.

E. BORDERS OF THE ASHKENAZIC COMMUNITY

I. Relations with Sephardic, Italian, Oriental Jews

363) Majer Balaban, 'Jüdische Ärzte und Apotheker aus Italien und Spanien in Krakau', in *Heimkehr. Essays Jüdischer Denker*, Czernowitz 1912, pp. 173–186.
364) Jacob Barnai, 'Zikah ve-nituk bein hakhmei Turkiyah le-hakhmei Polin u-Merkaz Eiropah ba-me'ah ha-17', in *Gal-Ed*, 9 (1986), pp. 13–26.
365) Isaac Barzilay, *Yosef Shlomo del Medigo. His Life and Times*, Leiden 1974.
366) Jacob Elbaum, 'Kesharei tarbut bein Yehudei Polin ve-Ashkenaz le-vein Yehudei Italyah ba-me'ah ha-16', in *Gal-Ed*, 7–8 (1985), pp. 11–40.
367) Ephraim Kupfer and Bedřich Mark, 'Der Renesans in Italia un in Poyln un zayn virkung oyf di Yidn', in *Bleter far Geshikhte*, 6, No. 4 (1953), pp. 4–99.
368) Jacob J. Schachter, 'Cultural Receptivity vs. Ethnic Pride in Early Modern Times. "Hakham Zevi" Hirsch Ashkenazi and Rabbi Jacob Emden', in Gertrude Hirschler (ed.), *Ashkenaz. The German Jewish Heritage*, New York 1988, pp. 69–78.
369) Chone Shmeruk, 'Sifrut Yidish me-'ever la-sevivah ha-doveret Germanit', in his *Sifrut Yidish, op. cit.* (#271), pp. 72–104.
370) Moses Shulvass, 'Dos Ashkenazishe Yidntum in Italye', in *Yivobleter*, 34 (1950), pp. 157–181 [= 'Ashkenazic Jewry in Italy', in *YIVO Annual of Jewish Social Science*, 7 (1952), pp. 110–131].
371) Hirsch Jacob Zimmels, *Ashkenazim and Sephardim. Their Relations, Differences, and Problems as Reflected in the Rabbinical Responsa*, Oxford 1958.
372) Eric Zimmer, 'Rabanei Germanyah ba-me'ah ha-16 ve-zikatam la-rabanim bi-tefuzot aherot', in *Ninth WCJS* (1986) Division B, vol. 1, Hebrew section, pp. 127–134.

Note: Elbaum (#12), Weil (#40), Nigal (#189), Carpi (#217), Fuks-Mansfeld (#231), Rosa (#233), Wachstein (#239), and Shmeruk (#299) also concern the relations of Ashkenazic and Mediterranean Jews.

II. Karaism in Poland and Lithuania

373) Majer Balaban, 'Ha-Kara'im be-Folin', in *ha-Tekufah*, 16 (1922), pp. 293–

307; 21 (1924), pp. 226–235; 25 (1929), pp. 450–487 [= 'Karaici w Polsce', in *idem, Studja Historyczne*, Warsaw 1927, pp. 1–92].
374) Jacob Mann, *Texts and Studies in Jewish History and Literature*, vol. II ('Karaitica'), New York 1931, reprinted 1971, esp. pp. 714–745, 1409–1451.

Note: Dán (#386) Friedman (#387) and Waysblum (#389) are studies of the Karaite scholar and polemicist, Isaac of Troki (d. c. 1594).

III. Jewish Attitudes towards Christianity

375) Haim Hillel Ben Sasson, 'The Reformation in Contemporary Jewish Eyes', in *Proceedings of the Israel Academy of Sciences and Humanities*, 4 (1971), pp. 246–249.
376) *Idem*, 'Jews and Christian Sectarians. Existential Similarity and Dialectical Tensions in Sixteenth-Century Moravia and Poland-Lithuania', in *Viator*, 4 (1973), pp. 369–385.
377) Yonah Emanuel, 'Ha-Yahas le-umot ha-'olam ule-hokhmot kelaliyot be-sifrei ba'al ha-Tosafot Yom Tov', in *ha-Ma'ayan . . . Po'alei Agudat Yisra'el*, 4, No. 2 (1964), pp. 50–59.
378) Dieter Fettke, *Juden und Nichtjuden im 16. und 17. Jahrhundert in Polen: soziale und ökonomische Beziehungen in Responsen polnischer Rabbiner*, Frankfurt a. Main 1986.
379) Jerome Friedman, 'The Reformation in Alien Eyes. Jewish Perceptions of Christian Troubles', in *Sixteenth Century Journal*, 14 (1983), pp. 23–40.
380) Jacob Katz, 'Sheloshah mishpatim apologetiyim be-gilguleihem', in *Zion*, 23–24 (1958), pp. 174–193.
381) *Idem, Exclusiveness and Tolerance. Studies in Jewish-Gentile Relations in Medieval and Modern Times*, Oxford 1961 [= *Bein Yehudim la-Goyim*, Jerusalem 1961].
382) Moshe Rosman, 'Jewish Perceptions of Insecurity and Powerlessness in 16th–18th Century Poland', in *Polin*, 1 (1986), pp. 19–27.
383) Marc Saperstein, 'Christians and Jews – Some Positive Images', in *Harvard Theological Review*, 79 (1986), pp. 236–246.

Note: Katz (#16, 90 and 244), Liebes in Twersky (#162), Buber (#165), Degani (#227), Šedinová (#230), Karpeles (#293), Lerner (#294), Paucker (#297), Shmeruk (#300), and Liebes (#409) also study aspects of Jewish attitudes towards Christians and Christianity.

IV. Jewish Anti-Christian Polemic

384) Haim Hillel Ben Sasson, 'Jewish Christian Disputation in the Setting of Humanism and Reformation in the German Empire', in *Harvard Theological Review*, 59 (1966), pp. 369–390.
385) Mordechai Breuer, 'Vikuho shel Maharal mi-Prag 'im ha-Nozrim: mabat hadash 'al *Sefer Be'er ha-Golah*', in *Tarbiz*, 55 (1986), pp. 253–260.
386) Robert Dán, 'Isaac Troky and his "Anti-Trinitarian" Sources', in *idem* (ed.), *Occident and Orient, op. cit.* (#352), pp. 69–82.
387) Jerome Friedman, 'The Reformation and Jewish Anti-Christian Polemics', in *Bibliothèque d'Humanisme et Renaissance*, 41 (1979), pp. 83–97 [on Isaac of Troki].
388) Judah Rosenthal, 'Martin Czechowic and Jacob of Belzyce. Arian-Jewish Encounters in Sixteenth Century Poland', in *PAAJR*, 34 (1966), pp. 77–95. Cf. his 'R. Ya'akov mi-Belzec ve-sifro ha-vikuhi', in *Gal-Ed*, 1 (1973), pp. 13–30.

389) M. Waysblum, 'Isaac b. Abraham of Troki and Christian Controversy in the Sixteenth Century', in *Journal of Jewish Studies*, 3 (1952), pp. 62–77.

Note: Stern (#39), Ben Sasson (#135) and Shazar (#235) also discuss polemics.

V. Christian Hebraism and Christian Kabbalah in Central and Eastern Europe

390) Majer Balaban, 'Hugo Grotius und die Ritualmordprozesse in Lublin 1636', in *Festschrift Simon Dubnow*, Berlin 1930, pp. 87–112.
391) David A. Frick, *Polish Sacred Philology in the Reformation and the Counter-Reformation*, Berkeley 1989 (University of California Publications in Modern Philology, vol. 123).
392) Jerome Friedman, *The Most Ancient Testimony. Sixteenth Century Christian-Hebraica in the Age of Renaissance Nostalgia*, Athens, Ohio 1983.
393) Ludwig Geiger, *Johann Reuchlin, sein Leben und seine Werke*, Leipzig 1871.
394) R. Po-Chia Hsia, 'The Professors and the Jews', in *idem*, *The Myth of Ritual Murder. Jews and Magic in Reformation Germany*, New Haven 1988, pp. 111–135.
395) David Kaufmann, 'Der zweite Corrector der Claudius'schen hebräischen Bibel, Dr. med. Leo Simon, Rabbiner von Mainz', in *Zeitschrift der Deutschen Morgenländischen Gesellschaft*, 45 (1891), pp. 493–504.
396) Heiko Oberman, *Wurzeln des Antisemitismus. Christenangst und Judenplage im Zeitalter von Humanismus und Reformation*, Berlin 1981. [English transl., *The Roots of Antisemitism in the Age of Renaissance and Reformation*, transl. by James Porter, Philadelphia 1984. Cf. Oberman, 'Three Sixteenth-Century Attitudes to Judaism. Reuchlin, Erasmus, Luther', in Cooperman (ed.), *op. cit.* (#77), pp. 326–364.]
397) Joachim Schoeps, *Philosemitismus im Barock*, Tübingen 1952.
398) François Secret, *Les Kabbalistes Chrétiens de la Renaissance*, Paris 1964.
399) Eric Zimmer, 'Jewish and Christian Hebraist Collaboration in Sixteenth Century Germany', in *Jewish Quarterly Review*, 71 (1980), pp. 69–88. For correspondence between Ashkenazic Jews and Christian Hebraists of the seventeenth century, cf. Weinryb in *The Jewish Review*, 2 (1944), pp. 211–214; Schwarz in *Zeitschrift für Hebräische Bibliographie*, 20 (1917), pp. 72–76.

Note: Weil (#40), Prijs (#54), Weinreich (#258 and 259), and Haberman, 'Ha-Madpis Paulus Fagius', in Haberman (#47), pp. 149–166, also concern Christian Hebraism.

VI. Apostates and Conversion

400) Elisheva Carlebach, 'Sabbatianism and the Jewish-Christian Polemic', in *Tenth WCJS* (1990), Division C, vol. 2, English section, pp. 1–8.
401) Hava Fraenkel-Goldschmidt, 'Be-Shulei ha-hevrah ha-Yehudit: mumarim Yehudim be-Germanyah bi-tekufat ha-Reformazyah', in Reuben Bonfil *et al.* (eds.), *Tarbut ve-Hevrah be-Toldot Yisra'el bi-Yemei ha-Beinayim: Kovez ma'amarim le-zikhro shel Hayim Hillel Ben Sasson*, Jerusalem 1989, pp. 623–654.
402) Martin Friedrich, *Zwischen Abwehr und Bekehrung: die Stellung der deutschen evangelischen Theologie zum Judentum im 17. Jahrhundert*, Tübingen 1988 [discusses the self-perception of Jewish converts].
403) Jacob Goldberg, *Ha-Mumarim be-Mamlekhet Polin-Lita* ['Converted Jews in the Polish Commonwealth'], Jerusalem 1985.
404) Hans-Martin Kirn, *Das Bild vom Juden im Deutschland des frühen 16. Jahrhunderts dargestellt an den Schriften Johannes Pfefferkorns*, Tübingen 1989.

405) *Josef Mieses, *Die älteste gedruckte deutsche Übersetzung des jüdischen Gebetbuchs aus dem Jahre 1530 und ihr Autor Antonius Margaritha*, Vienna 1916.

F. MOVEMENTS: MESSIANISM, SABBATIANISM, HASKALAH, HASIDISM

I. Messianism

406) Gerson Cohen, 'Messianic Postures of Ashkenazim and Sefardim (prior to Sabbethai Zevi)', in Max Kreutzberger (ed.), *Studies of the Leo Baeck Institute*, New York 1967, pp. 3–42 (= G. Cohen, *Studies in the Variety of Rabbinic Cultures*, Philadelphia 1991, pp. 271–298].
407) Ephraim Kupfer, 'Hezyonotav shel R. Asher b. Meir ha-mekhuneh Lemlein Reutlingen', in *Kovez 'al Yad*, 18 (1976), pp. 385–423.
408) Yehudah Liebes, 'Meshihiyuto shel R. Ya'akov Emden ve-yahaso le-Shabta'ut', in *Tarbiz*, 49 (1980), pp. 122–165; cf. 52 (1982), p. 359.
409) *Idem*, 'Yonah ben Amitai ke-Mashiah ben Yosef', in *Jerusalem Studies in Jewish Thought* [= *Mehkerei Yerushalayim be-Mahshevet Yisra'el*], 3 (1984), pp. 274–311.
410) Shalom Rosenberg, 'Exile and Redemption in Jewish Thought in the Sixteenth Century. Contending Conceptions', in Cooperman (ed.), *op. cit.* (#77), pp. 399–430.
411) Gershom Scholem, 'The Neutralization of the Messianic Element in Early Hasidism', in *idem*, *The Messianic Idea in Judaism, op. cit.* (#362), pp. 176–202.
412) Rivkah Shatz, 'Torat ha-Maharal: bein ekhzistenzyah le-eskhatologiyah', in Zevi Baras (ed.), *Meshihiyut ve-Eskhatologiyah: kovez ma'amarim*, Jerusalem 1984, pp. 301–322.
413) Abba Hillel Silver, *A History of Messianic Speculation in Israel*, New York 1927.
414) David Tamar, 'Hishuvei ha-kez ba-hibur *Hag Pesah* [R. Jacob Kitzingen, Cracow 1597]', in *Sinai*, 100 (1987), pp. 131–138.
415) Isaiah Tishby, 'Ha-Re'ayon ha-meshihi veha-megamot ha-meshihiyot bi-zemihat ha-Hasidut', in *Zion*, 32 (1967), pp. 1–45.

Note: Buber (#165), Gross (#168), Degani (#227) and Dinur in Hundert (#443) are also studies of Messianism.

II. Sabbatianism

416) Majer Balaban, *Le-Toldot ha-Tenu'ah ha-Frankit*, 2 vols., Tel-Aviv 1934–1935.
417) Meir Benayahu, 'Ha-Hevrah Kadishah shel Rabi Yehudah Hasid ve-'aliyatah le-Erez Yisra'el', in *Sefunot*, 3–4 (1960), pp. 131–182.
418) Elisheva Carlebach, *The Pursuit of Heresy. Rabbi Moses Hagiz and the Sabbatian Controversies*, New York 1990.
419) Moshe Arye Perlmuter, *R. Yehonatan Eybeschuetz ve-yahaso el ha-Shabta'ut*, Jerusalem 1947.
420) Yizhak Raphael, 'La-Pulmus 'al Rabi Yehonatan Eybeschuetz', in *idem*, *Rishonim ve-Aharonim, op. cit.* (#56), pp. 227–243.
421) Gershom Scholem, *Leket Margaliyot: le-Ha'arakhat ha-Sanigoryah he-Hadashah 'al R. Yonatan Eybeschuetz*, Tel-Aviv 1941.
422) *Idem*, 'Ha-Tenu'ah ha-Shabta'it be-Folin', in Hailperin (ed.), *Beit Yisra'el be-*

Folin, vol. II, *op. cit.* (#14), pp. 36–76 [also in Scholem's *Mehkarim u-Mekorot le-Toldot ha-Shabta'ut*, Jerusalem 1974, pp. 68–140. French transl. 'Le mouvement sabbataïste en Pologne', *Revue de l'Histoire des Religions*, 143 (1953), pp. 30–90, 209–232; 144 (1953), pp. 42–77].
423) *Idem, Sabbatai Sevi. The Mystical Messiah*, Princeton 1973.

Note: Cohen (#30), Schachter (#35), Idel (#158), Shazar (#235), Weinreich (#240), Scholem (#265 and 432), Carlebach (#400), Liebes (#408), Katz (#429), and Tishby (#449) are also studies of Sabbatianism.

III. Pre-Enlightenment and the Origins of the Haskalah

424) Isaac Barzilay (Eisenstein), 'The Italian and Berlin Haskalah: Parallels and Differences', in *PAAJR*, 29 (1961), pp. 17–54.
425) Joseph Eschelbacher, 'Die Anfänge allgemeiner Bildung unter den deutschen Juden vor Mendelssohn', in *Beiträge zur Geschichte der deutschen Juden. Festschrift . . . Martin Philippson*, Leipzig 1916, pp. 168–177.
426) Immanuel Etkes, 'Ha-Gra veha-Haskalah – tadmit u-mezi'ut', in *Perakim le-Toldot ha-Hevrah ha-Yehudit . . . mukdashim le-Prof. Ya'akov Katz*, Jerusalem 1980, pp. 192–217. [= 'The Gaon of Vilna and the Haskalah Movement: Image and Reality', in *Binah*, 2 (1989), pp. 147–176.]
427) *Idem*, 'Li-She'elat Mevasrei ha-Haskalah be-Mizrah Eiropah', in *Tarbiz*, 57 (1988), pp. 95–114.
428) Morris M. Faierstein, 'The Liebes Brief. A Critique of Jewish Society in Germany (1749)', in *LBI Year Book XXVII* (1982), pp. 219–242.
429) Jacob Katz, 'Li-She'elat ha-kesher bein ha-Shabta'ut le-vein ha-Haskalah veha-Reformah', in Siegfried Stein and Raphael Loewe (eds.), *Studies in Jewish Religious and Intellectual History presented to Alexander Altmann . . .* Alabama 1979, Hebrew section, pp. 83–100.
430) *Israel Klausner, *Vilna bi-tekufat ha-Ga'on: ha-milhamah ha-ruhanit veha-hevratit bi-kehilat Vilna bi-tekufat ha-Gera*, Jerusalem 1942.
431) Jacob Meitlis, 'Der Bodleianer ksav-yad 'Libes-Brif': a far-Haskoloh-dike Reform-shrift', in *Yivobleter*, 2 (1931), pp. 308–333.
432) Gershom Scholem, 'Redemption through Sin', in *idem, The Messianic Idea in Judaism, op. cit.* (#362), pp. 78–141 [= 'Holiness through Sin', in *Commentary*, 51 (1971), No. 1, pp. 41–70].
433) Steven and Henry Schwarzschild, 'Two Lives in the Jewish Frühaufklärung. Raphael Levi Hannover and Moses Abraham Wolff', in *LBI Year Book XXIX* (1984), pp. 229–276.
434) Azriel Shohet, *'Im Hilufei Tekufot: Reshit ha-Haskalah be-Yahadut Germanyah*, Jerusalem 1960.
435) David Sorkin, 'Origins of the Haskalah', in *idem, The Transformation of German Jewry 1780–1840*, Oxford 1987, pp. 41–62.

Note: Katz (#16), Stern (#28), Levinson (#32), Schachter (#35), Schmelzer (#59), Adler (#64), and Lewin (#71) are studies of the pre-Enlightenment.

IV. Pre-Hasidism, the Origins of Hasidism and Israel, Baal Shem Tov

436) Martin Buber, *The Origin and Meaning of Hasidism*, transl. and ed. by Maurice Friedman, New York 1988.
437) Yaffa Eliach, 'The Russian Dissenting Sects and their Influence on Israel Baal Shem Tov, Founder of Hasidism', in *PAAJR*, 36 (1968), pp. 57–83.

438) Rachel Elior, 'Ha-Zikah she-bein Kabalah le-Hasidut: rezifut u-temurah', in *Ninth WCJS* (1986), Division C, Hebrew section, pp. 107–114.
439) Idem, ' 'Melo khol ha-arez kevodo' ve-'khol adam': bein tehiyah ruhanit li-temurah hevratit be-reshit ha-Hasidut', in Moshe Hallamish (ed.), *'Alei Shefer: mehkarim be-sifrut ha-hagut ha-'Ivrit mugashim le- . . . Alexander Safran*, Tel-Aviv 1990, pp. 29–40.
440) Morris Faierstein, 'Hasidism. The Last Decade in Research', in *Modern Judaism*, 11 (1991), pp. 111–124.
441) *Ze'ev Gries, 'Hasidism. The Present State of Research and some Desirable Priorities', in *Numen*, 34 (1987), pp. 97–108, 179–213.
442) Ya'akov Hasdai, 'Eved ha-Shem be-doram shel avot ha-Hasidut', in *Zion*, 47 (1982), pp. 253–292.
443) Gershon D. Hundert (ed.), *Essential Papers on Hasidism. Origins to Present*, New York 1991. Collected essays by various authors. Note Ben Zion Dinur, 'The Origins of Hasidism and Its Social and Messianic Foundations' (pp. 86–208). [The Hebrew original appeared in *Zion*, 8–10 (1943–1945), and again in Dinur's *Ba-Mifneh ha-Dorot: mehkarim ve-'iyunim be-reshitam shel ha-zemanim ha-hadashim be-toldot Yisra'el*, Jerusalem 1955, pp. 81–227.] Note also Moshe Rosman, 'Miedzyboz and Rabbi Israel Baal Shem Tov' (pp. 209–225). [The Hebrew original of Rosman's article appeared in *Zion*, 52 (1987), pp. 177–190. Cf. Rosman's essay, 'The Quest for the Historical Baal Shem Tov', in Twersky and Cooperman (eds.), *op. cit.* (#66).]
444) Moshe Idel, *Kabbalah. New Perspectives*, New Haven 1988. Includes material on the kabbalistic roots of *Hasidism*.
445) Mendel Piekarz, *Bi-Yemei Zemihat ha-Hasidut: megamot ra'ayoniyot be-sifrut derush u-musar*, Jerusalem 1978.
446) Avraham Rubenstein, ' 'Al Rabo shel ha-Besht ve-'al ha-ketavim she-mehem lamad ha-Besht', in *Tarbiz*, 48 (1979), pp. 146–158.
447) Gershom Scholem, 'Demuto ha-histori shel R. Yisra'el Ba'al Shem Tov', in *Molad*, 18 (1960), pp. 335–356 [= Scholem, *Devarim be-Go*, Tel-Aviv 1975, pp. 287–324. A French version appeared under the title *'Le Besht hors de sa légende', in *Evidences*, 12 (1960), pp. 15–24].
448) Chone Shmeruk, 'Ha-Sipurim 'al R. Adam Ba'al Shem ve-gilguleihem be-nusha'ot *Sefer Shivhei ha-Besht*', in *Zion*, 28 (1963), pp. 86–105.
449) Isaiah Tishby, 'Bein Shabta'ut la-Hasidut: Shabta'uto shel ha-mekubal R. Ya'akov Kopil Lipshitz mi-Mezeritsh', in *idem*, *Netivei Emunah u-Minut*, Israel 1964, pp. 204–226.
450) Joseph Weiss, *Studies in Eastern European Jewish Mysticism*, ed. by D. Goldstein, Oxford 1985. Studies of *Hasidism*, including several of the Baal Shem Tov.

Note: Safran (#176), Scholem (#411) and Tishby (#415) are also studies of *Beshtian Hasidism*. Cf. Liberman (#49), esp. 'Keizad hokrim Hasidut be-Yisra'el?', in vol. I, pp. 1–50.

Index to Selected Bibliography

Abrahams, Israel, 125
Abramsky, Chimen, 323, 348
Abramsky, Y.D., 151
Adam Baal Shem, 448
Adini, Uziel, 63
Adler, Salomon, 64
Altmann, Alexander, 429
Altshuler, David, 335
Amir, Joshua, 27
Ashkenazi, Joseph, 150–153
Ashkenazi, Zevi Hirsch, 368
Assaf, Simha, 65
Avenary (Loewenstein), Hanoch, 324

Baal Shem Tov, Israel, 437, 443, 446–448, 450
Bacharach, Jair Hayyim, 31, 112, 162
Bacon, Gershon C., 1
Balaban, Majer, 8, 363, 373, 390, 416
Baras, Zevi, 412
Barnai, Jacob, 364
Baron, Salo Wittmayer, 9, 105
Barzilay (Eisenstein), Isaac, 365, 424
Baskin, Judith R., 333
Bass, Shabtai, 56
Ben Sasson, Haim Hillel, 10, 11, 135, 136, 138, 375, 376, 384, 401
Ben Sasson, Jonah, 145
Ben Zvi, Yizhak, 253
Benayahu, Meir, 154, 417
Bernstein, Mordecai, 216
Berz, L., 206
Bettan, Israel, 188
Bloch, Philip, 84
Bokser, Ben Zion, 164
Bonami, David, 180
Bonfil, Reuben, 401
Brann, Markus, 100, 127
Breuer, Mordechai, 66, 104, 224–226, 385
Brodie, Israel, 124
Buber, Martin, 165, 436
Buksboim, Yosef, 179
Burstein, Dov, 181

Carlebach, Elisheva, 400, 418
Carmilly-Weinberger, Moshe, 43
Carpi, Daniel, 217, 299
Cohen, Boaz, 111
Cohen, Gerson, 406
Cohen, Israel, 22
Cohen, Mortimer J., 30
Cohen, R., 209

Cohen, Stuart A., 137
Cohn, Tobias, 32
Comenius, Jan Amos, 63, 171
Cooperman, Bernard, 66, 77, 146, 158, 194, 197, 396, 410, 443
Copernicus, 209, 211
Cordovero, Moses ben Jacob, 162
Czechowic, Martin, 388

Dán, Robert, 352, 386
Darshan, David, 190
David, Abraham, 242
David ben Isaac of Fulda, 42
David ben Samuel ha-Levi, 93
Davidovitch (-wicz), David, 341, 342
Davidson, Herbert, 146
Davis, Joseph, 78, 147
Davis, Natalie Zemon, 309
Dawidowicz, Lucy S., 315
de' Rossi, Azariah, 185, 239
Degani, Ben Zion, 227
del Medigo, Yosef Shlomo, 365
Dembitzer, Hayim Nathan, 23
Denari (Dinari), Yedidyah, 2, 85
Dienemann, Max, 218, 355
di Vidas, Elijah, 202
Dimitrovsky, Chaim Zalman, 105, 106
Dinur, Ben Zion, 443
Dreyfus, Théodore, 166

Edels, Samuel ben Judah, 170, 171
Ehrentreu, Heinrich, 107
Eidelberg, Shlomo, 126
Eis, Ruth, 354
Elazar, Daniel J., 137
Elbaum (Elboim), Jacob, 3, 12, 182, 194, 195, 366
Eliach, Yaffa, 437
Elior, Rachel, 438, 439
Elkouby, Joseph, 196
Elon, Menahem, 79
Emanuel, Yonah, 112, 377
Emden, Jacob, 30, 35, 368, 408
Epstein, Abraham, 127
Epstein, Morris, 128
Epstein, Yehiel-Mikhel, 276
Erasmus, Desiderius, 396
Erik, Max, 269
Eschelbacher, Joseph, 425
Etkes, Immanuel, 426, 427
Ettinger, Shmuel, 138, 244

Eybeshitz, Jonathan, 188, 265, 419–421

Faierstein, Morris M., 428, 440
Feldman, David, 98
Fettke, Dieter, 378
Finkelstein, Louis, 13
Fishman, David, 207
Fishman, Isidore, 67
Fishman-Maimon, Judah Leb, 92, 99, 243
Fishof, Iris, 349
Flesch, Heinrich, 261
Fox, Marvin, 197
Fraenkel-Goldschmidt, Hava, 148, 401
Fram, Edward, 80
Fränckel, David, 100
Freehof, Solomon, 81, 86, 113, 325
Freimann, Aron, 84, 131
Freudenthal, Max, 100
Frick, David, 391
Friedberg, Bernhard (Hayyim), 44, 45
Friedman, Jerome, 379, 387, 392
Friedman, Maurice, 436
Friedrich, Martin, 402
Fuenn, Samuel J., 24
Fuks, Leib, 46
Fuks-Mansfeld, Renate, 231
Fuss, Abraham, 87

Gans, David, 34, 210, 224–230
Gaon of Vilna (Elijah ben Salomon Zalman), 426, 430
Geiger, Ludwig, 393
Gelber, Mark, 329
Gelber, Nathan Michael, 214
Gershon ben Eliezer ha-Levi, 253
Ginzberg, Louis, 101
Ginzberg, Yekutiel, 208
Ginzburg, Simon Levi, 128
Glückel of Hameln, 309–311, 313, 314
Godman, S., 165
Goldberg, Geoffrey, 326
Goldberg, Jacob, 88, 403
Goldberg, Sylvie Anne, 198, 199
Goldin, Judah, 97
Goldman, Israel, 68
Goldstein, D., 450
Gottesdiener (Ovadyah), Abraham, 167
Grafman, R., 340
Green, Arthur, 333
Gries, Zeev, 200, 441
Gross, Benjamin, 168, 169
Grotius, Hugo, 390
Grotte, Alfred, 343
Grunwald, Max, 218
Gutmann, Joseph, 336

Haberman, Abraham M., 25, 47, 55, 243
Hagiz, Moses, 418
Hahn, Joseph Yuzpa, 125, 131, 134
Hailperin (Halpern), Israel, 13, 14, 15, 48

Halévy, Meir, 232
Halivni, David Weiss, 102
Hallamish, Moshe, 439
Hallo, Rudolf, 337
Hamburger, Benjamin, 129
Hannover, Nathan Neta, 248
Hannover, Raphael Levi, 433
Hasdai, Ya'akov, 442
Hayyim ben Bezalel, 37, 41
Heller, Yom Tov Lipman, 78, 99, 147, 243, 377
Henry, Sondra, 25
Heyd, Milly, 350
Hildesheimer, Azriel, 104
Hildesheimer, Meier, 84
Hildesheimer, Meir, 114
Hirschler, Gertrude, 39, 368
Holzer, Isaak, 130
Horn, Maurycy, 219
Horodetsky, Samuel Abba, 26, 155–157
Horovitz, Jakob, 131
Horovitz, Markus, 27
Horowitz, Avraham, 161, 195
Horowitz, Isaiah, 160, 163
Horowitz, Shabtai ben Akiba, 161
Hrushovski, Benjamin, 315
Hsia, R. Po-Chia, 394
Hundert, Gershon David, 1, 4, 201, 443
Hurwitz, Simon, 115

Idel, Moshe, 158, 262, 444
Ish-Shalom, Benjamin, 183
Issachar Baer of Szczebrzeszyn, 184
Isserles, Moses ben Israel, 38, 92–97, 122, 145, 207
Italiener, Bruno, 355

Jacob of Belzyce, 388
Jacobs, Louis, 116
Jaffe, Mordecai, 149
Jehuda Löw ben Bezalel (Maharal of Prague), 63, 70, 144, 164–179, 182, 183, 185, 196, 197, 263, 385, 412
Joel Ba'al Schem, 261
Joffe, Judah, 316
Josel von Rosheim, 39, 148
Joseph ben Isaac ha-Levi, 147

Kahana, Yizhak Zeev, 117
Kaplan, Lawrence, 149
Karo, Joseph, 96
Karpeles, Gustav, 293
Katz, Jacob, 11, 16, 82, 89, 90, 244, 380, 381, 426, 429
Katz, Morris, 75
Katzenellenbogen, Shmu'el Yehudah, 189
Kaufmann, David, 31, 100, 310, 395
Khmel'nyts'kyi, Bohdan, 240, 251
Kirn, Hans-Martin, 404
Kitzingen, Jacob, 414

Index to Selected Bibliography

Klausner, Israel, 430
Kleinberger, Aaron Fritz, 69, 70, 170
Kober, Adolf, 220
Kohen, Naftali, 261
Kosover, Mordechai, 118
Kraemer, David, 201
Kreutzberger, Max, 406
Krinsky, Carol Herselle, 344
Krochmal, Menahem Mendl, 143
Kulka, Otto Dov, 171
Künzl, Hannelore, 361
Kupfer, Ephraim, 139, 140, 150, 367, 407
Kurz, Otto, 338
Kybalová, Ludmila, 356

Landau, Alfred, 311
Landsberger, Franz, 336
Lauterbach, Samuel, 91
Leib ben Ozer, 235
Leibowitz, Joshua O., 221
Leibowitz, Nechama, 283
Leiner, Yeruham, 159
Leitzmann, Albert, 290
Lemlein, Asher ben Meir, 407
Lenczyc, Ephraim, 136, 188
Lerner, David Levine, 294
Levine, Hillel, 209
Lemlein, Asher ben Meir, 407
Levinson, Abraham, 32
Levita (Bachur), Elijah, 40, 315–317, 320
Lewin, Isaac, 17
Lewin, Louis, 71, 222
Libermann (Lieberman), Hayim, 49, 206, 260, 276
Lieben, Salomon Hugo, 50, 312
Lieberman, Saul, 105
Liebes, Yehudah, 162, 408, 409
Lipshitz, Ya'akov Kopil, 449
Loewe, Raphael, 429
Loewenstein, Hanoch, 324
Löwenstein, Leopold, 51
Luria, Isaac, 154, 158, 163
Luria, Solomon, 103, 115, 156, 159
Luria, Yohanan, 135
Luther, Martin, 396

Maimonides (Rambam), 150, 153
Maisel, D., 34
Manheim, R., 264
Mann, Jacob, 374
Mann, Vivian B., 357
Margaritha, Antonius, 405
Mark, Bedřich, 367
Mark, Yudel, 13
Marx, Alexander, 52, 131
Mashiah ben Josef, 409
Mayer, Leo A., 338
Meir of Lublin, 119
Meitlis, Jacob, 132, 295, 431
Melamed, Evelyn B., 284

Mendel of Cracow, 214
Menes, Abraham, 13
Merkin, Zalman, 269
Meyer, Herrmann, 131
Mieses, Josef, 405
Minkoff, Harvey, 284
Minkoff, Nahum Baruch, 313, 317, 327
Mintz, Alan, 245
Mirsky, Samuel, 33
Muneles, Otto, 18, 53, 328

Naményi, Ernest, 351
Narkiss, Bezalel, 351
Narkiss, Mordechai, 358
Neher, André, 34, 172, 173, 196, 210, 211, 263
Neuman, Abraham, 81
Newman, Eugene, 160
Newman, Zelda Kahan, 329
Nigal, Gedaliah, 189, 296
Nissim, Yizhak, 92
Noble, Shlomo, 276
Nosek, Bedřich, 143, 323
Nussbaum, Daniel, 141

Oberman, Heiko, 396
Oppenheim, Israel, 142
Oppenheimer, David, 52
Ostropoler, Samson, 162

Pachter, Mordechai, 202
Panitz, Michael, 212
Patai, Raphael, 216
Paucker, Arnold, 297, 298
Perelmuter, Hayim Goren, 190
Perlmuter, Moshe Arye, 419
Pfaffenhofen, Alexander, 321
Pfefferkorn, Johannes, 404
Piechotka, Maria and Kazimierz, 345
Piekarz, Mendel, 203, 277, 445
Pollack, Herman, 5, 133
Porter, James, 396
Prijs, Joseph, 54

Rabinovitz, Raphael Nathan Neta, 55
Rabinowitz, Hayyim Reuben, 191
Rabinowitz, Saul Pinhas, 151
Raphael, Yizhak, 56, 96, 420
Rappel, Dov, 72, 108, 134, 257
Reif, Stefan, 330
Reifman, Jacob, 184
Reiner, Elhanan, 109
Reuchlin, Johann, 393, 396
Romer-Segal, Agnes, 57, 204
Ron, Isaac, 103
Rosa, Jacob da Silva, 233
Rosenberg, Felix, 318
Rosenberg, Shalom, 410
Rosenfeld, Moshe, 58
Rosenthal, Ferdinand, 100, 127
Rosenthal, Judah, 119, 388

Rosman, Moshe (Murray), 73, 382, 443
Ross, Tamar, 174
Roth, Cecil, 351
Rubenstein, Avraham, 446
Ruderman, David, 74, 213

Sack, Bracha, 162
Sadek, Vladimir, 143, 144, 161, 175
Safran, Bezalel, 176
Saperstein, Marc, 192, 383
Schachter, Jacob J., 35, 368
Schechter, Solomon, 314
Scheiber, Alexander, 352
Schiff, Alvin I., 75
Schiper (Shiper), Ignacy (Yizhak, Isaac), 286
Schmelzer, Menahem, 59, 352
Schneid, Naftali, 339
Schochet, Elijah J., 36, 93, 120
Schoeps, Joachim, 397
Scholem, Gershom, 30, 152, 264, 265, 362, 411, 421–423, 432, 447
Schüler, Meier, 270
Schwarz, Ignaz, 214, 399
Schwarzschild, Steven & Henry, 433
Secret, François, 398
Šedinová, Jiřina, 228–230, 246, 247
Segal, Agnes Romer, 204
Segal, Lester A., 185
Septimus, Bernard, 162
Shabtai Zevi, 235, 240, 406, 423
Shachar, Isaiah, 340, 359
Shakhna of Krakow, 236
Shatz, Rivkah, 177, 412
Shatzky, Jacob, 223, 233, 234, 248, 278, 285, 286
Shazar (Rubashov), Zalman, 235
Sherwin, Byron L., 37, 178
Shmeruk, Chone (Khone Szmeruk), 60, 236, 271, 272, 287–289, 299, 300, 319, 353, 369, 448
Shohet, Azriel, 76, 434
Shtif, Nahum, 273
Shulman, Nisson, 121
Shulvass, Moshe, 19, 370
Siev (Ziv), Asher, 38, 94, 122
Silver, Abba Hillel, 413
Simon, Leo, 395
Sirkes, Joel, 33, 36, 118, 120
Smith, Jerry Christopher, 320
Sofer, Jacob, of Berlin, 349
Sofer, Shabbetai, 330
Solnik, Benjamin, 121
Sorkin, David, 435
Spira, Nathan, 208
Staerk, Willy, 290
Stein, Siegfried, 331, 429
Steinharz, Samuel, 50
Steinschneider, Moritz, 215, 249, 254, 274
Stern, Selma, 28, 39
Sussman, Eliezer, 342

Ta Shema, Israel, 95
Taitz, Emily, 25
Tal, Shlomo, 123
Tamar, David, 414
Tchernowitz, Chaim, 83
Teller, Issachar Ber, 221
Timm, Erika, 301, 302
Tishby, Isaiah, 415, 449
Toledano, Jacob, 96
Trachtenberg, Joshua, 266
Troky, Isaac, 386, 387, 389
Turniansky, Chava, 186, 237, 238, 280, 291, 321, 322, 332
Twersky, Isadore, 66, 77, 78, 97, 153, 158, 162, 443

Unna, Joseph, 27

Vilnay, Zev, 255
Volavková, Hana, 346, 360

Wachstein, Bernhard, 193, 205, 239
Waysblum, M., 389
Waxman, Meyer, 20
Weil, Gérard, 40
Weiman, Ralph, 28
Weinberg, Magnus, 61, 250
Weinreich, Beatrice, 6
Weinreich, Max, 240, 258, 259, 275, 292, 315
Weinreich, Uriel, 6, 281
Weinryb, Bernard Dov, 124, 251, 399
Weiss, Joseph, 450
Weissler, Chava, 187, 282, 333
Wertofsky, M., 209
Wiener Library, 7
Weingarten, Shmuel ha-Kohen, 110
Wischnitzer-Bernstein, Rachel, 347
Wolff, Moses Abraham, 433
Wolfson, Elliot, 163

Yaffa, Eliach, 437
Yassif, Eli, 303
Yehuda Hasid, 417
Yerushalmi, Yosef Hayim, 252
Ysaye, I., 311
Yudlov, Yizhak, 179
Yuzpa Shamash, 126, 129, 130

Zeitlin, Solomon, 81
Zfatman-Biller, Sara, 241, 256, 267, 304–308
Zimmels, Hirsch Jacob, 124, 268, 371
Zimmer, Eric (Yishak), 41, 42, 129, 372, 399
Zinberg, Israel, 21, 279
Zunz, J.M., 29
Zunz, Leopold, 62, 334

Sources for the History of the Jews from the Eighteenth Century to the Twentieth Century in the Archives of the former DDR

BY ELISABETH BRACHMANN-TEUBNER

Before commenting on the sources for the history of the Jews from the eighteenth to the twentieth centuries available in the archives of the former DDR, and to avoid misinterpretations, it is important to point out some aspects regarding the terminology used.[1] Here the term Jewish archive will only be used when reference is made to sources with Jewish provenance, such as records of Jewish communities or organisations.

For clarity's sake, a brief description is first given as to how the archival material of the former DDR – now the five new *Bundesländer* – was organised; this is followed by an account of the sources of Jewish history and how best to use them for research, taking three archives as an example; finally Jewish archival collections deposited in the *Bundesarchiv* Potsdam are listed and described.

I. ARCHIVAL ORGANISATION IN THE DDR

Until 3rd October 1990, the archival material in the DDR was centrally organised. The Ministry of the Interior, with its *Staatliche Archivverwaltung* (StAV), was the supervising department. Its function ceased on 31st December 1990. During the existence of the DDR, to be precise from 1950, many important decisions – political, scientific and administrative – concerning the state archives were taken by the StAV. Some decisions were also made by the political bureau of the SED's Central Committee, via the ministry of the Interior/StAV, and contacts with archive organisations, such as scientific institutions abroad, were handled by the archive administration. Foreigners who wished to use the state archives had to submit their applications to the StAV, not to the directors of state archives. In reaching a decision, the StAV followed the rulings laid down in 1976 governing the use of state archives. The *Zentrales Staatsarchiv* fell within the competence of the *Staatliche Archivverwaltung* and the *Staatsarchive* too, which were responsible for the districts. Archival holdings, including factory and administrative records covering urban and rural areas, fell under the jurisdiction of

---

[1]This article is the revised text of a lecture given in Leipzig on 27th October 1991, at an international meeting of the Leo Baeck Institute concerned with the history of the Jews and their archives in the new *Länder* of the German Federal Republic.

the relevant *Stadt-* and *Kreisarchive*. Less rigorous conditions applied to researchers who required access to the archives housed in scientific institutions, universities and academies. Archives belonging to political parties, to societies involved in community work, to churches and other religious denominations, were all outside the jurisdiction of the *Staatliche Archivverwaltung*.[2]

After the unification of Germany, all the DDR archives were once more integrated into a federal system. The archivists appointed to take charge of them were chosen by the governments of the five *Länder* and attached to the Departments of the Interior or of Education and Science. Every *Land* had its own *Regionalarchiv* – formerly *Staatsarchiv* – : in Mecklenburg-Vorpommern, Brandenburg and Sachsen-Anhalt called *Landeshauptarchiv* (LHA), located in Schwerin, Potsdam and Magdeburg, for Saxony in Dresden, and for Thuringia in Weimar; the latter two called the *Hauptstaatsarchiv* (HStA). There are in individual *Länder*, additional *Staats-* or *Landesarchive*: in Saxony, the *Staatsarchiv* in Leipzig; in Thuringia, the *Staatsarchive* in Meiningen and Rudolstadt; in Mecklenburg-Vorpommern, the *Landesarchiv* in Greifswald.

In addition to a number of *Hauptstaatsarchive* and *Landeshauptarchive*, with branch offices and archive depositories (formerly *Historische Staatsarchive*), there were *Kreisarchive* in over 200 districts. The district councillors at local level were thus involved in the maintenance of these *Kreisarchive*. Of relevance here, however, is that these officials also helped maintain archives in the smaller towns and communities. Increasing changes within communities and the likelihood of future border alterations have left in abeyance a decision as to the continued existence of the *Kreisarchive*.

For research into the history of German Jews from the eighteenth century on, the continuity of the *Stadtarchive* is of the utmost importance. Their holdings, though to some extent – witness the *Stadtarchiv* Erfurt – greatly reduced as a consequence of the last war, certainly show great discrimination in their depth and scope. In city archives one can find what documents are left, such as police registers giving data of birth, marriage and death, tabulated population figures,[3] information about temporary residence of Jews, and of Jews under observation at annual markets and fairs. Also to be found under the heading "Jewish Affairs" are the following: Jewish settlement in the towns, Jewish schools, cultural

---

[2]Law dealing with State Archives, 11th March 1976. GBl. I Nr. 10, p. 165. 1. Implementing regulations – jurisdiction over the State Archives, supplementary holdings, evaluation and *Kassation*. 19th March 1976. GBl. I Nr. 10, p. 169. 2. Implementing regulations – rules on access. 19th March 1976. GBl. I Nr. 10, p. 172; these general rules are reprinted in the journal *Archivmitteilungen*, 4 (1976), pp. 236ff.

[3]Following the ruling on Jews of 17th April 1750, monthly records were maintained by Jewish Elders notifying war departments and the principalities of any changes as regards personal status. These records can be found dispersed in files among the towns of Prussia. It must be noted, however, that in Berlin and in the province of Brandenburg up to 1812 no Jewish personal records were kept by the state institutions. To fill the gap, it is necessary to fall back on records kept by Jewish communities. As for Prussia, the Edict of 11th March 1812 required Jewish registers to be maintained. Accordingly all changes regarding the personal status of Jews had to be reported to the police authorities in towns or to the *Landrat* for Jews residing in the country. From 1847 onwards, the *Amtsgerichte* took over responsibility for these registers, and after 1874 this information may be found in registry offices.

activities, the acquisition of land, the building of synagogues, the planning of funeral plots, elections to the governing boards of synagogues, baptisms, funerals, marriages, the raising and collecting of subscriptions and lists of associations. Additional information is revealed in the official files, as for instance law court records; and for the Holocaust period there is also information available in departments dealing with finance, food and housing. To a certain extent this also applies to records held by territorial state authorities, which exercised their powers and rights of supervision over the Jewish communities. It is essential for all city archives to be thoroughly scrutinised. In this connection it may be useful to refer to the knowledge Manfred Unger gained when doing research in Leipzig's archives.[4] Equally significant are the town archives of Rostock, Chemnitz and Erfurt.

Material on Jewish history can also be found in factory archives, even when factories had changed hands after "Aryanisation". These documents refer to employment and dismissal of Jewish employees and to Jewish forced labour. Since many businesses and state enterprises are on the point of liquidation, or are being privatised, it is uncertain what will happen to their archives. It is as yet unclear whether these archives are to be taken over by state archives or form the core of newly established economic archives. At present there is great uneasiness as regards their final destination. With regard to records of business concerns, I would like to point to documents connected with large banks. Some of these may be found in the State Archives of the former DDR. These sources provide information about the setting up and growth of banks, such as the Dresdner Bank by Eugen Gutmann, Gustav Klemperer and others. They also throw light on the confiscation of Jewish bank accounts.

In a comprehensive survey of relevant sources it is important to include church archives, archives of academies, e.g. the Academy of Sciences, the Academy of Fine Art in Berlin, the Academy of Natural Sciences Leopoldina in Halle and of universities and technical colleges with information about Jewish students, scientists and scholars. In this connection one should mention physicists such as Albert Einstein, Adolf Frank and Lise Meitner. It should also be noted that between 7th April 1933 (the date of the Law for the Restoration of the Civil Service/"Gesetz zur Wiederherstellung des Berufsbeamtentums") and the winter term of 1934/1935, 1,145 lecturers – 14.34% of all the teaching staff at universities and technical colleges – were dismissed.[5]

For the more recent history up to the Holocaust, the archives of political parties and their organisations should be consulted, in particular the *Zentrales Parteiarchiv der PDS*, which, for example, had in its safekeeping a card index of

[4]Manfred Unger, 'Juden in Leipzig. Verfolgung und Selbstbehauptung in archivalischen Quellen 1933–1945', in *Archivmitteilungen*, 5 (1988), pp. 149ff.; Manfred Unger and Hubert Lang, *Juden in Leipzig*, Leipzig 1989.
[5]Helge Pross, *Die deutsche akademische Emigration nach den Vereinigten Staaten 1933–1941*, Berlin 1955, quoted in Bernt Engelmann, *Deutschland ohne Juden. Eine Bilanz*, Berlin 1988, pp. 159f. The decree of 7th April 1933 ("Gesetz zur Wiederherstellung des Berufsbeamtentums" = BBG) resulted in the first wave of dismissals of opponents to the Nazi system and of Jewish civil servants. It was followed by a second wave in 1935 of those previously exempted, and finally in 1937 of those civil servants whose marriages fell foul of the existing laws.

persons and facts relating to anti-Nazi resistance. This index was made use of by the DDR archives after 1983.[6] In addition to these archives I also wish to direct the attention of researchers to the large scientific libraries with their holdings of collections of private papers in their manuscript departments.[7] Of particular value is the German photographic library in Dresden with its pictorial collections,[8] and the museums, such as the *Museum Synagoge Gröbzig*. Such records throw light, at the local level, on the life and fate of Jewish citizens, the contributions they made and the persecution they suffered.

II. PROBLEMS INVOLVING RESEARCH AND THE OPENING UP OF SOURCE MATERIAL

Here we need to be aware that there are two different kinds of sources; those of purely Jewish provenance, which by themselves are insufficient to reconstruct the history of the Jews in Germany, and official sources at state and local level, as well as other non-Jewish material. In establishing a comprehensive archive, such complementary sources have to be taken into account.

In the past various attempts have been made to describe and list archives containing records dealing with Jewish history – the so-called Judaica. With this purpose in mind, the compilation of the *Gesamtarchiv der deutschen Juden* was begun and continued right into the 1930s.[9] With regard to the Middle Ages, it was realised that much of the surviving archival material depended on the fate of specific Jewish communities. Thus the little that has come down from old Jewish community archives or manuscript copies derives from old communities like Worms, Frankfurt a. Main, Fürth. Not until the appearance of new Jewish settlements, towards the end of the seventeenth century, was it possible to collect data allowing a more continuous account of events. The important task that faced the compilers of a general and complete archive (*Gesamtarchiv*) was to compile a *Regestenkatalog*, recording the living conditions of Jews mentioned in the records. Deeds and original documents were to form the basis of such a catalogue. Apart from compiling such material, a further objective was to include files concerning the history of the Jews in Germany, to be found in state and local archives as well as those in the hands of the aristocracy. To facilitate research, excerpts, copies and photocopies were also to be included. The first

---

[6]Heinz Vosske, 'Fünfundzwanzig Jahre Zentrales Parteiarchiv der SED', in *Archivmitteilungen*, 2 (1988), p. 45; and S. Mauksch, I. Pardon and L. Rothe, 'Zur Entwicklung und Arbeit des einheitlichen Parteiarchivwesens der SED', *ibid.*, 4 (1989), p. 142.

[7]*Nachlässe* of scholars and authors in the libraries of the DDR. Part 1. Bequests and collections in the general scientific libraries, Berlin 1959. Part 2. Bequests and collections in scientific institutes and museums, and general libraries, Berlin 1968. Part 3. Additions, supplements, index, Berlin 1971.

[8]The *Deutsche Fotothek* in Dresden holds 70,000 slides, 170,000 enlarged negatives and the relevant picture cards as well as catalogues. See W. May, *Führer durch die Abteilung der Deutschen Fotothek*, Dresden 1985.

[9]Already in 1906, work was started on a catalogue of documents; Eugen Täubler in *Mitteilungen des Gesamtarchivs der deutschen Juden*, 4. Jg. (1913), pp. 1ff., discussed the possibility of compiling a record of the history of the Jews in the Middle Ages.

results, such as the surveys of the Judaica found in the State Archives of Hanover and in the Bavarian *Kreisarchiv* of Oberpfalz in Amberg, were published in *Mitteilungen des Gesamtarchivs der deutschen Juden*.[10]

Towards the end of 1936 the *Reichsinstitut für die Geschichte des neuen Deutschlands* set itself a different aim in its policy vis à vis the Jews. Consultations were held with the *Generaldirektor* of the Prussian State Archives. He instructed the *Geheimes Staatsarchiv* (GStA) and the other Prussian State Archives to compile the Judaica with the help of inventories (*Findbücher*) and to submit the results to the *Reichsinstitut des neuen Deutschlands* under the following headings:

1. For the period 1750 to the present
2. For the period 1500 to 1750
3. For the period prior to 1500[11]

The *Reichsinstitut* did not just confine its search to the Prussian archives, but with the help of Prussian *Ministerpräsidenten* and the *Reich* and Prussian Minister of the Interior collected material from archives outside Prussia.[12]

Records available in the *Bundesarchiv* Potsdam clearly show that a "Gesamtinventar" was never completed. The archives which were requested to cooperate in the compilation of the *Gesamtarchiv* were apparently ambivalent in their efforts: some were eager to assist, some hesitant, some did not bother at all.

During the course of 1937 and with the help of *Findbücher* and similar documents, the following Prussian state archives compiled inventories of their Judaica holdings and submitted these to the *Generaldirektor der preussischen Staatsarchive*: Aurich, Breslau, Düsseldorf, Hanover, Kiel, Koblenz, Königsberg, Magdeburg, Marburg, Münster, Osnabrück, Sigmaringen, Stettin, Wiesbaden and the *Geheimes Staatsarchiv*.

A copy of these inventories was sent to the *Reichsinstitut für die Geschichte des neuen Deutschlands, Forschungsabteilung Judenfrage*, the GStA in Berlin-Dahlem and the *Reichsinnenministerium*.[13] A register of the Judaica ought to be available still in the archives of the departments of the above authorities. To what extent they would meet today's expectations is another matter. Yet they may point to information about sources that are no longer available. In the *Reichssippenamt* in Potsdam only incomplete records have survived. These are reports to the officials responsible to the department for race matters of the Ministry of the Interior about the archives in towns A–F; mainly being information from town archives, occasionally state archives, like the *Staatsarchiv* of Hesse in Darmstadt, the *Staatsarchiv* Düsseldorf, the *Landesarchiv* in Coburg, but also church archives like the *Landeskirchenarchiv der Thüringer Evangelischen Kirche* in Eisenach. The information

---

[10]Mendel Zuckermann, 'Übersicht über den jüdisch-geschichtlichen Inhalt des Königl. Staatsarchivs zu Hannover', in *Mitteilungen des Gesamtarchivs der deutschen Juden*, 2. Jg. (1910), pp. 65–136; Magnus Weinberg, 'Die auf Juden bezüglichen Akten des Kgl. bayerischen Kreisarchivs der Oberpfalz in Amberg', *ibid.*, 3. Jg. (1911/1912), pp. 85–142.
[11]Cf. BA Potsdam, 15.06 Reichsarchiv, Nr. 55, Bl. 21ff.
[12]Cf. *ibid.*, Bl. 22.
[13]The compilation is based on information from GStA, Merseburg, Rep. 178 VII, Nr. 2 E 8, Bd. 1.

given varies considerably, from fully detailed records to summaries of file headings.[14] With the merging of Judaica into the various archives, simultaneous investigations made a start in the compilation of an inventory revealing personal data concerning Jews.

Already in January 1937 Ernst Zipfel, *Generaldirektor* of the Prussian State Archives, issued instructions to archives subordinate to him to make an immediate start with an inventory – if they had not already done so – using state and local authorities; e.g. district presidents (*Landräte*), lawcourts, police, town administrations etc., and to start with the registration of Jewish families using information obtained from the various Jewish community records as well. All this material was to have been placed at a later date under the control of special archival depositories.[15] In August of the same year Zipfel was able to note that considerable progress had already been made with the compilation of personal data.[16]

In their efforts to secure data about Jews for their archives, rivalry between the State Archives and the *Reichsstelle für Sippenforschung* was displayed. From 1938 onwards the latter had written orders to regional courts, mayors and parishes to supply him with information about their registers of Jews, to tell him what these contained and what period of time they covered. Some of this correspondence has survived; in particular requests to authorities located in towns beginning with the letters K to O. In a few instances this correspondence includes replies to questions and statements about registers.[17] Between November 1938 and April 1939, the Director of the *Reichsstelle für Sippenforschung* approached synagogue congregations on the same subject. As far as can be ascertained only correspondence to and from the synagogue congregations of Bavaria, the Palatinate and Swabia has survived.[18]

As we have noted the *Reichsstelle für Sippenforschung* tried to bring together under its control personal registers showing the social status of persons listed, church records and similar documents. A central department was set up for keeping Jewish registers of individuals. In this context attention has to be drawn to Dr. Achim Gercke, who from 1925 had already started to build up the NS-archives of statistics on race and professions, the so-called *Fremdstämmigenkartei* with information about approximately 500,000 Jews.[19] After 1933 Gercke was responsible for race research in the *Reichsministerium des Innern*.[20]

Based on the holdings of the *Deutsches Zentralarchiv* in Merseburg and Potsdam,

---

[14] Cf. BA Potsdam, 15.09 Reichssippenamt, Nr. 158. Fire and water have badly damaged the general file and it has to be restored before it can be used.

[15] *Mitteilungsblatt des Generaldirektors der Staatsarchive*, Nr. 1 (1st January 1937), p. 1.

[16] *Ibid.*, Nr. 9 (16th August 1937), p. 117.

[17] Cf. BA Potsdam, 15.01 Reichssippenamt, Nr. 159; as an example from Lauban illustrating how information is recorded; Birth register 1854–1877, with 38 births. Marriage register 1863–1874, with 16 marriages. Death register 1864–1874, with 10 deaths.

[18] See *ibid.*, Nr. 160.

[19] The discovery of the so-called register for aliens (*Fremdstämmigenkartei*) was only possible with the aid of Thomas Jersch (Berlin), to whom the author is very grateful. The register – its completeness cannot be ascertained at present – was in chaos when it was taken over in 1958 by the then *Zentrales Staatsarchiv*. Because of this it is still unusable.

[20] BA Potsdam, 1501 Reichsministerium des Innern, Personalakte Dr. Achim Gercke.

the *Landeshauptarchiv* in Brandenburg and several, mainly town, archives of Brandenburg, Adelheid Constabel submitted (in 1951/1952) a 'Collection of Sources on the History of German Jews'. Without wishing to comment on the value of this work, the fact that it does not include a great number of the records which were returned by the Soviet Union in the nineteen fifties, much reduces its usefulness. This is particularly noticeable with regard to the *Bundesarchiv* Potsdam, for which only a few records on the *Reichstag*, the *Reichsregierung* and the *Reichskanzler* are noted.

As a rule, in many archives some useful files on Jews can be found. This is a result of the preparations that were made to make available documentary sources on the National-Socialist dictatorship in Germany, to assist research and publication. Some of these files are only fragmentary; their contents are not listed comprehensively. Nevertheless, they are helpful introductions and are a useful guide. The LHA Potsdam[21] makes such help available, yet its records only begin in the year 1812. The *Staatsarchiv* Leipzig,[22] Merseburg and the BA Potsdam are endeavouring to complete their records.

Judaica, the very nature of the history of the Jews in Germany, is represented in the holdings of nearly all the archives. For the period leading to emancipation – for a start – the Jew, as a so-called protected Jew (*Schutzjude*), had to report his presence to the authorities, with the result that a personal dossier was opened in his name. These dossiers are often a useful source for tracing subsequent events which general files do not always reveal. To make the best use of the Judaica holdings it is necessary to know the history of the Jews, and also how the administrative authorities were organised and how they functioned in their individual lands at any given time. The researcher must always bear in mind why and for what reason Jews came to the attention of the authorities and, therefore, why they were placed on record. The archivist, with his special knowledge of how authorities were organised, how archives and records were kept and maintained, can be of great assistance here.

III. DOCUMENTARY SOURCES ON THE HISTORY OF THE JEWS IN INDIVIDUAL ARCHIVES

1. *The Bundesarchiv Potsdam*

Beginning with the *Reichstag* and up to the setting up of the economy, almost all the archives can be expected to have documentary sources for the nineteenth and twentieth centuries on the subject in question. In view of the abundance of available information, only a few examples will be shown: the file headed

---

[21] Cf. Ch. Klose, 'Judenemanzipation und Judenverfolgung. Ein Spezialinventar im Staatsarchiv Potsdam zur Geschichte der jüdischen Bevölkerung in der Provinz Brandenburg und in Berlin', in *Archivmitteilungen*, 5 (1988), pp. 156–159. According to information from LHA Potsdam, this register has been kept up to date since 1988.

[22] Manfred Unger (ed.), *Archivalische Quellennachweise zur Geschichte der Juden im Staatsarchiv Leipzig – Judaicainventar*, revised and expanded for publication in 1990.

Reichstag deals with basic questions regarding the rights of foreigners and their expulsion alongside detailed information such as, for instance, petitions about ritual slaughter. Among the items in the *Reichskanzleramt* File, Judaica can be found in the following groups:

Emigration
Building and land matters
Trade
Police
Taxation
Constitution and administration
Citizenship (granted and removed)

The file *Reichsministerium des Innern* has the following sections with material on Judaica:

Personal status
Religion, religious associations
Unions
Migration
Civil Servants
Welfare
Eugenics

For eugenics see also under *Reichsgesundheitsamt*, racial hygiene and the criminal investigation section of the *Reich* Health Department with its special division on "Race and the Bastard-Biology of the Jews" ("Rassen- und Bastard-Biologie der Juden", 1936–1945).

The files of the *Auswärtiges Amt*, Embassies, Legations, Consulates contain information about Jews in other countries, including German colonies; matters dealing with immigration and emigration; and citizenship; as well as intelligence about Jews residing in annexed, that is occupied, territories.

Records held in the *Reichssippenamt, Reichssicherheitshauptamt*, or the *Reichsvereinigung der Juden in Deutschland* files are obviously the focus of attention for the Holocaust period. One may also point to the records of the *Reichssippenamt* for information extracted from the report of the census of 17th May 1939 about the personal status of Jews. The *Reichssicherheitshauptamt* file contains, in particular, the surviving files handed down to it by *Amt IVB*. Judaica is also contained in files dealing with measures against foreigners and the files on occupied or annexed territories, with their daily reports on the situation, morale and attitude in Austria, the Sudetenland and the protectorate of Bohemia-Moravia. Also to be noted are the files on the surveillance of public opinion and morale, region by region, reporting individual cases of prosecution and police surveillance. These files may unexpectedly yield relevant information. For instance, the file headed "Zusammenarbeit der Sudosteuropa-Gesellschaft e.V. Wien mit dem S.D.", contains material about a confidential cabinet meeting of the Slovak government on 13th April 1942, discussing the "Jewish Question", as well as information about the internment and treatment of Jews in Hungary in January 1942 and about the shooting of Jews in Batschka at the end of January/beginning of February 1942.

By way of example, and without going into detail, attention should be drawn to the holdings of documents from the following authorities: *Reichsjustizministerium, Reichsgericht, Oberreichsanwalt, Volksgerichtshof*. Their holdings have been considerably augmented by documents previously held in the Central Party Archives of the SED and the Ministry of State Security. Furthermore there are archival sources once held by the *Reichswirtschaftsministerium, Statistisches Reichsamt, Reichsarbeitsministerium, Rechnungshof des Deutschen Reichs, Deutsche Reichsbank, Generalbauinspektor für die Reichshauptstadt Berlin, Reichsautobahn-Direktion, Deutsches Auslandswissenschaftliches Institut, Reichsministerien* for *Volksaufklärung und Propaganda* and for *Wissenschaft, Erziehung und Volksbildung*. Also to be included are documents of political parties, associations (*viz. Stahlhelm*) and unions; lastly the private papers of Jews such as Gerson Bleichröder, Walter Jacobson, Hans Natonek etc., and the collections of the papers of non-Jewish politicians, containing correspondence and other material about the "Jewish Question" and Jewish citizens in general.

2. *The Historical State Archive Oranienbaum*

This archive has overall responsibility for Anhalt, including the principalities Anhalt-Dessau, Köthen, Bernburg and Zerbst. It holds considerable archival material for the eighteenth century up to the middle of the nineteenth century, but there is an almost complete gap from the nineteen twenties onwards, since the building which housed the more recent archives was destroyed during the war.

The complete administrative history of the *Land* makes it difficult to exploit its archival sources. Until 1603 a so-called *Gesamtarchiv* for Anhalt was in existence. For the period 1603 to 1848, the principalities Anhalt-Dessau, Köthen, Bernburg and Zerbst share sources, mainly on general matters. For the period from 1848 onwards, the main sources are *Provenienzbestände*, in addition state ministries in every separate part of the land, as well as subordinate departments like those for finance and building, hold archival material. After 1850 material is also to be found in the various districts.

ANHALT-DESSAU

The principality throws light on Jewish affairs in the "correspondence between the Prince and his officials, distinguished citizens of Dessau and Anhalt", in the correspondence with foreign officials, scholars etc.; in laws issued by the Court, decrees, regulations and similar rulings. A great deal of information can also be obtained from archives on general affairs, grouped under the title "Gruppe Innere Landesangelegenheiten, Untergruppe 15, 'Judenschaft'". Here many records for the seventeenth to nineteenth centuries may be found, especially on Jewish communities, e.g. in Bernburg, Harzgerode, Dessau, Wörlitz, Oranienbaum, Jessnitz, Raguhn, Radegast, Gröbzig, Sandersleben, Zerbst, with information on the granting of safe-conduct letters; on confirming the establishment of Jewish associations; on Jewish welfare for the poor; and Jewish educational institutions.

The archival sources of the state ministries for Anhalt-Dessau apply to the period 1848–1945. Records held by the State Ministry Dessau 1 (1848–1853) contain files on school and church affairs, cultural and scientific matters, material on the Jewish schools, the religious community and the emancipation. The records for State Ministry Dessau 2 (1853–1863) are arranged alphabetically, A ("Aufenthaltsgestattungen und Ausweisungen") to Z ("jüdische Kultusgemeinde in Zerbst"). The correct choice of term will facilitate research. For example: under B – *Begräbnisplätze, Beerdigungen, Bekehrung*; under S – *Synagogen, Steuern, Sabbatfeiern*; under W – *jüdische Gemeinde* in Wörlitz, in Wulfen etc.

One's immediate attention is drawn to the ten groups of files held by Dessau 3 (1863–1945), in particular on church and religious affairs, and church and school matters. The index to these documents in the Oranienbaum Archives confirms that during the bombardment of Dessau in the Second World War, the archival material from the nineteenth century on the Jewish communities of the following towns was destroyed: Alsleben, Ballenstedt, Bernburg, Coswig, Dessau, Gernrode, Gröbzig, Gross-Mühlingen, Harzgerode, Hoym, Jessnitz, Köthen, Nienburg, Radegast, Sandersleben, Wörlitz, Wulfen and Zerbst. Information on the rabbinate; on conversion to Judaism; and birth, marriage and death registers were also lost.

ANHALT-ZERBST

The register of the principality's secret chancellery in Zerbst contains documents, papers and books in its 22 sections, starting with building matters in Anhalt-Zerbst, privileges and concessions, mandates and decrees, which may also include some Judaica information. Section 21, which comprises "Akten und Sachen in alphabetischer Ordnung", is of particular interest. Under J, after "Inquisitionskosten", one may find "Acta Juden". In the section "Innungssachen" there are "Gesuche von Juden zur Niederlassung und zur Ausübung von Handelsgeschäften" (Petition of Jews to settle and open businesses); under S, documents dealing with the "Sabaths-Feyer".

The *Facharchiv* Zerbst (1499–1802) has relevant material on finance, customs, escorts, excise orders issued by the Prince, mandates and edicts and related files. Also under this subject there is trade information on factories, guilds, brewing and, under number 18, complaints by the tawers in 1746 about "Jews seen about all over the country". For the period 1769–1793, section 84, with thirteen subsections on Jews, is very important. There we find documents dealing with individual *Schutzjuden*; the edict of 1769, forbidding Jews from being given "herrschaftliches Geld"; documents about foreign Jews and their increased taxation; and complaints made in 1793 by Jews about trade restrictions to which they were subjected in Anhalt-Zerbst. In the *Findbuch* of the *Landes-Administrations-Kollegium* Zerbst (eighteenth century), arranged alphabetically A–Z, are to be found sources under J for "Gesuche der Judenschaft" (petitions by Jews); and under S "Schutzbriefe der Judenschaft" (safe-conduct letters for Jews); and under C, sources on the issuing of trade and other concessions for town and country. The records belonging to the government of Zerbst are, likewise, arranged alphabetically.

ANHALT-BERNBURG

As is the case with Dessau and Köthen, the *Findbuch*, Section (*Abteilung*) Bernburg, vol. IV, under Group C "Innere Landesangelegenheiten, Untergruppe 15, Judenschaft", holds 46 folders with documents covering the middle of the seventeenth century up to the middle of the nineteenth century. These include: safe-conduct letters, records on synagogue construction, burial of rabbis, welfare for the poor; regulations covering all aspects of marriages, Jewish associations and "all sorts of Jewish matters". For the researcher to make full use of this archival material, familiarity with the complex administration and its history, as well as some knowledge of palaeography and languages (Latin, French) would be a prerequisite.

3. *Brandenburgisches Landeshauptarchiv Potsdam*

As mentioned previously, a special inventory for records from 1812 onwards existed, which is divided into the following groups:

1. The development of the legal status of the Jews.
2. Personal records and statistics relating to residence and occupations.
3. Cultural and social matters.
4. Antisemitism up to the time of the National-Socialist seizure of power.
5. Jews during the time of persecution and extermination, 1933–1945.

To research the condition of Jews in the eighteenth century and the beginning of the nineteenth century one has to fall back on records in the *Kurmärkisches Amts* – i.e. the *Kriegs- und Domänenkammer* and (Rep. 2) *Regierung* Potsdam, here above all the "erste und zweite Städteregistratur (Brandenburg, Berlin)" for Jewish affairs, manufacturing and business matters and all general matters, or else Rep. 8, *Stadt* Luckenwalde with "Acta" dealing with synagogue congregations; notification for establishing and closing trades as well as birth, marriages and death registrations. Relevant here also are the holdings of the *Neumärkische Kriegs- und Domänensachen*, in Küstrin (Rep. 3), with its files on Jewish and general matters. Of use also are the records of the *Polizeipräsidium* of Berlin with files on foreign Jews, Jewish communities and clubs, and on the *Polizeidirektion* Potsdam.

4. Records of Jewish Origin Housed in the Bundesarchiv Potsdam

The archives under discussion here refer to the former *Gesamtarchiv* of German Jews. A few words of explanation, even at the risk of repeating what is already known, must be made. The *Gesamtarchiv* was founded in 1905, housed for the time being in rented rooms in the Lützowstrasse, Berlin and since 1910 in the new building of the Berlin Jewish community at Oranienburger Strasse 28. It set itself the following tasks:

a. The collecting of archival material of Jewish communities, societies, associations and private persons. In contrast to the State Archives, their undertaking was not legally enforceable, but depended on purely voluntary co-operation.[23] The larger and more prosperous communities, like the one in Breslau, maintained their own archives and, as in Frankfurt, either housed them themselves or, as in Hamburg, deposited them with a state archive.[24] Many of the smaller communities handed over their archival material to the *Gesamtarchiv*.

b. The making of a survey of the sources on the history of the Jews in state and other archives; an inventory of them; and also the making and obtaining of copies of source material.[25]

In order to augment the archival sources of the *Gesamtarchiv*, Professor Martin Philippson, Chairman of the Board of the *Gesamtarchiv*, and Dr. Eugen Täubler, since October 1906 its Director, sent a communication on the 14th December 1909 to the Director General of the Prussian *Staatsarchive*, Dr. Reinhold Koser (under whom Täubler had earlier obtained his archival training in the *Geheimes Staatsarchiv*), asking for permission to transfer those *Kassationslisten* (lists of discharges) of interest to the history of the Jews in Germany from the Prussian State Archives to the *Gesamtarchiv*.[26] On 5th March 1910 Koser then requested the archives in his charge to separate the *Kassationslisten* on Jewish affairs which were no longer needed and to offer them to the *Gesamtarchiv*.[27]

From the existing holdings of the *Gesamtarchiv* it is apparent that, after ministerial permission had been obtained, only archives that were in the State Archive of Poznań were passed on to the *Gesamtarchiv*. There are files from the district offices of Kolmar in Poznań and Ostrowo, from the magistrates of Pleschen and the government of Bromberg.[28] The subject matter of these files ranges from audits of Jewish corporations and business accounts, budgets and

---

[23]See Eugen Täubler, 'Zur Einführung', in *Mitteilungen des Gesamtarchivs der deutschen Juden*, 1. Heft (1908), p. 2.

[24]The integration of the Berlin Jewish community archive into the *Gesamtarchiv*, where some space for it in the Oranienburger Strasse was made free of charge by the *Gemeinde*, greatly enhanced the reputation of the *Gesamtarchiv*.

[25]See Eugen Täubler's address, given on 28th December 1910 at a ceremony marking the inauguration of the *Gesamtarchiv*, in *Mitteilungen des Gesamtarchivs der deutschen Juden*, 3. Jg. (1911/1912), pp. 68f.

[26]GStA Merseburg, Rep. 178 VII, Nr. 2 E 8, Bd. 1, Bl. 14.

[27]*Ibid.*, Bl. 19.

[28]*Ibid.*, Bl. 24ff.

cash accounts of Jewish corporations to complaints about excessive taxation, the election of representatives, the notices about registration and departure of relatives under protection, regulations applicable to Jews and their way of life, enquiries about naturalised Jews, Jewish clubs, as well as personal documents of Jewish doctors and teachers.

Without exception, these files refer to the first half of the nineteenth century. They were obviously integrated by the *Gesamtarchiv* with the pertinent community holdings.[29] When, in 1932, the head of the *Gesamtarchiv* appealed to the Director General of the Prussian State Archives, Albert Brackmann, for more transfers, reminding him of the directive of 5th March 1910, the response of his successor, Ernst Zipfel, dated 18th January 1937, was unhelpful. Zipfel now claimed that ". . . the directive dated 5th March 1910 . . . has, of course, become null and void".[30] Up to 1927 the *Gesamtarchiv* had integrated the holdings of 344 Jewish community archives by just cataloguing them according to their file headings. A guide to this material unfortunately no longer exists.

With the introduction of the *Gesetz zur Wiederherstellung des Berufsbeamtentums* on 7th April 1933, and the accompanying decrees, the *Gesamtarchiv* took on a new task – namely to obtain documents relating to the status of individual persons (*Personenstandsnachweise*).[31] The *Gesamtarchiv* was, therefore, anxious to obtain the originals or copies of such personal records as birth, marriage or death certificates, *Mohel-* and *Memorbücher* and any other pertinent documents.

Between 1932 and 1935, the archives of 27 communities were taken over and the holdings of six communities – including that of Berlin – were augmented by further acquisitions. Within the same period files belonging to Jewish organisations and institutions, like those of the *Deutsch-Israelitischer Gemeindebund*, the *Centralverein deutscher Staatsbürger jüdischen Glaubens* and the *Gesellschaft zur Verbreitung des Handwerks unter den Juden* were also deposited there. The archive section dealing with family history was enriched by gifts and purchases.[32]

In many places the night of the Pogrom of 9th/10th November 1938 brought with it the destruction and confiscation of archival records.[33] On the 10th November a decree by the *Reichsführer* SS and Chief of Police ordered the seizure

---

[29]Examination of the *Gemeinde* archives of Bromberg, Ostrowo and Pleschen confirms this. The fact that it was not possible to identify all the files from the Poznań State Archives intended for the *Gesamtarchiv* can be explained by the losses that occurred.

[30]*Mitteilungsblatt des Generaldirektors der Staatsarchive*, Nr. 2 (18th January 1937), p. 13.

[31]See the report by the librarian Rosi Regensburger, who worked from 1935 in the *Gesamtarchiv* and was employed in this kind of task, in CAHJP, Jerusalem, M5; see also Ernst G. Lowenthal, 'Rückblick. Das "Gesamtarchiv der deutschen Juden" in Berlin', in *Mitteilungen des Vereins für die Geschichte Berlins*, Heft 1 (1989), pp. 148f.

[32]Cf. report by Dr. Jacob Jacobson about the function of the *Gesamtarchiv der deutschen Juden* between 10th November 1932 and 25th March 1935, a copy of which was kindly put at my disposal by Dr. A. Segall, Director of the CAHJP, Jerusalem. While on a fact-finding visit to Lower Saxony, from 30th November to 7th December 1936, Jacobson opened negotiations that were to lead to the handing over to the *Gesamtarchiv* of archival records belonging to the communities of Wolfenbüttel, Seesen, Holzminden, Osterode, and the former Samson-Schule in Wolfenbüttel. CAHJP, M 5/16.

[33]An undated fragment from the records BA Potsdam, 15.09 Reichssippenamt, Nr. 160, reveals that the registers of the synagogue congregations of Aub, Aschaffenburg, Burgpreppach, Burgsinn, Ermershausen, Ingolstadt, Sandersleben, Völkersleier ". . . were said to have been burnt during the Pogrom of 9th November 1938".

of all Jewish archives. He assigned these confiscated archives to the offices of the State Police. For their evaluation a special department was to be established at the *Reichssicherheitshauptamt*. After a meeting at the Ministry of the Interior on 27th January 1939, it was claimed ". . . the Jewish and Masonic Lodge archives are the daily working tools for the Security Services . . ."[34] For various different reasons the *Reichssicherheitshauptamt*, numerous party agencies and a number of state archives were interested in acquiring these documents; the former for obvious political motives. At this meeting of 27th January, Dr. Winter, the Director of the State Archives, endeavoured to reach a compromise reflecting the interests of the Security Police and those of the Archives. He requested that "though the archives would first be held by the Security Police, their final deposition in the Archives should not be prejudiced". He added the hope that the confiscated archives would be kept together.[35]

On 28th November 1938 Zipfel, in his capacity as Director General of the State Archives, sent a draft of a decree to the *Reich* Ministry of the Interior, whose purpose was "to secure manuscripts and archives of Jews in Germany"; they were to be forfeit, without payment, to the *Reich* and transferred to the relevant state archives. They included: Jewish religious community papers relating to corporations, institutions, charitable foundations, associations, unions, factories; and registers, files, plans, seals and stamps. The existing owners or administrators were, immediately and without further reminder, to notify their local police authorities by 31st January, listing their holdings and, together with three copies, hand them over to the State Archives. This order applied to Austria and the Sudetenland as well. Zipfel assumed that the police authorities would be advised in advance, so that they could enforce the confiscation, notify the archives concerned, and inform them if they themselves needed to keep some records for more than six months for their own investigations.

As for data about individual Jews, a separate ruling was suggested. Zipfel proposed that they should be amalgamated with the *Gesamtarchiv*. He added, "a decision as to who is to administer this *Zentralarchiv* and where it is to be located, has to be made without delay. Its transfer into the *Reichsarchiv* or Prussian *Geheimes Staatsarchiv* is neither possible nor advisable. I suggest that it should be transferred immediately to the *Reichsarchivverwaltung*, where its upkeep would be maintained."[36] Although Zipfel made several written requests to that end, he failed to convince the authorities. The *Reichsstelle für Sippenforschung* forced the *Kultusgemeinde* to concentrate all the documents relating to data about individuals in the *Zentralstelle für jüdische Personenstandsregister*, which they had established for that purpose. It was to be located in the buildings that housed the *Gesamtarchiv* at Oranienburger Strasse 28. The cost of maintenance, cleaning, telephones etc. was to be met by the *Kultusgemeinde*. The archive assistants were confined to two rooms of the library. They were only allowed to issue essential documents; that is authentifications for purely Jewish needs, like identity cards, proof of citizenship

---

[34]BA Potsdam, 15.06 Reichsarchiv, Nr. 7, Bl. 503.
[35]*Ibid.*
[36]*Ibid.*, Bl. 488ff.

and certificates indicating Jewish community membership.[37] Should the former head of the *Gesamtarchiv* require the use of the *Register*, it was possible for him to do so only with a permit. This indicates clearly his loss of authority. The administration of the *Personenstandsregister* and the files to be added for its completion were to be the responsibility of the *Reichsstelle*.[38] An employee of the *Reichsstelle für Sippenforschung*[39] and another who worked for the *Amt für Sippenforschung der NSDAP* were responsible for issuing certificates with proof of ancestry taken from the Jewish *Personenstandsregister*. As time went on, all information about individuals collected from all over Germany, much of it having been confiscated on the night of 9th November 1938, was added to the *Gesamtarchiv* along with Jewish data from baptismal records, law court records, documents of Jewish provenance etc. These *Personenstandsunterlagen* were taken to Schloss Rathsfeld in Kyffhäuser, where they were preserved on film. The originals were most likely lost during the war, but the microfilms are now in the *Bundesarchiv* Potsdam as well as in the archives of the *Altbundesländer*.

After the autumn of 1941 the Director General of the state archives repeatedly tried to take over the documents of the *Gesamtarchiv*, as well as other archives of Jewish origin that up to then had been in the *Reichsstelle für Sippenforschung* in the various towns of the *Reich*. The intention was that this collection would be divided among the various relevant state archives. The *Reichssicherheitshauptamt*, which intended to use these archives for its own archives (the *Judenforschungsinstitut des Sicherheitsdienstes*), opposed Zipfel's plan.[40] After several discussions with representatives of *Amt VII* (Dr. Franz Six) and the office of the Chief of the Security Police and the SD, a compromise was reached. The Jewish material deposited with the *Reichsstelle für Sippenforschung* was to go to the GStA in Berlin-Dahlem, which was to look after it and act as trustee. *Amt IV*, however, was to continue to be the sole authority for all the archives in question.[41] On 11th March 1942, Zipfel informed the *Geheimes Staatsarchiv* of this arrangement and at the same time made a request to take charge of the general archives. In June 1942 preparations were in hand to place archives in about 2,000 cases ready for transfer, but lack of transport facilities caused a further delay. On 22nd July 1942, Zipfel, now promoted *Kommissar für den Archivschutz*, was asked whether the archives were safe from air-raids in their present location. In his reply to the GStA on 29th July, he was unable to give this assurance; his reply seeming to suggest that the archives were kept in a centrally-located building, on the fourth floor near the main telegraph office, which could only refer to Oranienburger Strasse 28 and rooms that housed the *Gesamtarchiv*.[42]

At the end of November 1942 the General Archives and other holdings of the

---

[37]Cf. Bericht des Leiters der Reichsstelle für Sippenforschung, Kurt Mayer an den Reichsminister des Innern vom 31. Marz 1939, *ibid.*, Bl. 561ff.
[38]*Ibid.*, Bl. 562.
[39]Changed on 12th November 1940 to *Reichssippenamt*, which amalgamated with the *Rasse- und Siedlungsamt* of the SS in 1943.
[40]See GStA, Merseburg, Rep. 178 VII, Nr. 2 E 8, Bd. 2, Bl. 120.
[41]*Ibid.*, Bl. 132.
[42]*Ibid.*, Bl. 143.

GStA were stored in Hochwalde.[43] Additional files taken from the *Gesamtarchiv*, which were "of no interest" to the *Reichssippenamt*, were offered by them to the GStA, who in turn suggested combing through the collection to separate the Jewish documents not worth keeping. These were to be taken to Oranienburger Strasse and to remain there until the end of the war. The *Reichssippenamt* was to be responsible for the transport to the GStA. From correspondence it is apparent that up to 21st April 1944 the *Reichssippenamt* made no reply.[44] It must, therefore, be assumed that these archival holdings either remained at Oranienburger Strasse or were lost during the war.

The *Gesamtarchiv* documents, which were deposited elsewhere, were taken over by Soviet troops after the war and then, in 1948, deposited in Merseburg. In June and July 1950 the cantor of the Jewish community in Leipzig, Werner Sander, listed and summarised most of the surviving archives at the request of the Jewish community in the DDR. In the same year they were given to the *Landesverband Berlin*, Oranienburger Strasse 28.

Early in 1958, a representative of the Berlin Jewish community brought to the attention of the *Staatliche Archivverwaltung* the inadequate storage conditions that pertained at Oranienburger Strasse, with the result that in March 1958, at short notice and without formalities, the archives were taken for safekeeping to the ZStA Potsdam. Examination revealed that, having been deposited for years in damp cellars, much of the material had suffered damage;[45] a considerable number of pages and documents had become separated from their files; they were covered in damp, making identification impossible. In 1968, thanks to the efforts of ZStA staff, many of the damaged archives were restored.

The surviving documents could thus be examined and regrouped as follows:

The largest group   75 A *Gemeindearchive* (community archives)
                               75 B *Übergemeindliche Verwaltungsorgane* (administrative bodies responsible for communities)
                               75 C *Vereine, Organisationen* (clubs, organisations)
                               75 D *Nachlässe* (bequests)
                               75 E *Sammlungen* (miscellaneous collections)

In 1985 the ZStA asked the StAV to open up the archival records. After consultations between the Ministry of the Interior and the *Politbüro* of the Central Committee of the SED, permission was granted for the ZStA to start work in 1988 to prepare a carefully worked out plan. In 1988 and 1989 the above archive groups 75 A and 75 B were to be registered, alongside the holdings of the *Reichsvereinigung*; next, in 1989, the archive group 75 C, which contained i.a. many documents of the *Deutsch-israelitischer Gemeindebund* (23 metres long); and finally, in 1990, archives in groups 75 D and 75 E.

---

[43] *Ibid.*, Bl. 148.
[44] *Ibid.*, Bl. 155.
[45] It should be noted that some of the community records were already in poor condition when taken over by the *Gesamtarchiv*. Their storage in various depositories and finally their transport to Berlin was responsible for the considerable deterioration of these archives.

Work on the restoration of the archives was continued by using Japanese silk for protecting documents etc. The *Gemeindebestände* 75 A, with the exception of Berlin, conformed to the classification of the *Gesamtarchiv* and were grouped as follows:

1. Management and organisation of the community
2. Sites and buildings
3. Finance and taxation
4. Religion (*Kultus*) and schools
5. Welfare and subsidies

With the completion of the listing of the archives, and in agreement with the *Stiftung Neue Synagoge Berlin – Centrum Judaicum*, the archives were made available for immediate use, as far as their fragile state allowed. They have become the source of frequent enquiries. The surviving holdings of 376 German-Jewish communities can be found in the Central Archives for the History of the Jewish People (CAHJP) in Jerusalem. About 400 holdings, dealing for the most part with the same *Gemeinde*, are in the BA Potsdam, which like the ZStA before it, regards itself in the light of trustee for the archives. The records are arranged by name of the *Gemeinde* and the *Rabbinatsbezirk*; by their contents and by the period they cover. They are then listed alphabetically and by geographical location. They can be found in Potsdam, Jerusalem, Berlin and Heidelberg. The handwritten indexes are on microfilm; copies were made available to the above archives.[46] The surviving documents from 399 Jewish communities of the former German *Reich* (and seven Polish communities) cover mainly the period from the eighteenth century to the nineteen twenties. They are fragmentary, but nevertheless they are an important source – sometimes the only source – for the history of individual communities as well as for Jewish history as a whole. About two thirds of these documents are mainly from communities located in what was once Prussia, especially provinces like Posen/Poznań, Silesia and West Prussia. Non-Prussian areas are chiefly represented by Bavaria and Hesse.

Comparing the registers listing Jewish communities held by the CAHJP in Jerusalem and those in the BA Potsdam with the register compiled by Sander in 1950, 77 communities appear to be missing. The loss may have come about between 1950 and 1958. There is hope that this missing information will come to light one day. The researcher needs to use both BA Potsdam and the CAHJP Jerusalem and, as regards the holdings for individual Jewish communities, it may well prove worthwhile to check a number of local archives. Thus, for example, in Schwerin, when it was not possible to find suitable accommodation for confiscated archival records in the State Security building, it was decided to hand them over to the State Archives. That is why documents pertaining to the *Israelitischer Oberrat*, rabbis and Jewish communities of Mecklenburg-Strelitz and

---

[46]Meanwhile, a descriptive list has been produced as an aid to researchers.

Mecklenburg-Schwerin can be found in the State Archives of Schwerin to this day. Documents on Jewish communities in Silesia (Breslau, Gleiwitz) and the province of Posen/Poznań (Graudenz) are housed in the *Jüdisches Institut für Geschichte* in Warsaw.

Bibliographical Essay: Recent Publications and Primary Sources on Austrian Antisemitism in the Nineteenth and Twentieth Centuries

BY BRUCE F. PAULEY

If it did nothing else, the revelations about Kurt Waldheim's military career in the Balkan Peninsula transformed the Austrian Presidential campaign of 1986 into a debate about the country's role in the Second World War along with its history of antisemitism. Nevertheless, relatively few books and articles have been published devoted exclusively to Austrian antisemitism, especially during the inter-war years.[*]

This omission is all the more regrettable considering Vienna's former status as the city with Europe's third largest Jewish population (201,000 in 1923), coming after only Warsaw and Budapest. Moreover, over 65,000 Austrian Jews lost their lives during the Holocaust, an event in which, according to Simon Wiesenthal, roughly half of the major perpetrators and three quarters of the commandants of extermination camps were Austrians, even though Austrians made up only about 8.5 per cent of the population of Hitler's Greater German *Reich*.[1] This is not to suggest, however, that there has been any dearth of publications in recent years about the Jews of Austria. On the contrary, there has been a veritable flood of such works, both scholarly and popular and most contain at least some information on antisemitism.

RECENT BOOKS IN ENGLISH

English-speaking historians of Austrian-Jewish history during the past decade have usually written on comparatively broad subjects dealing either with the Jews of the whole Habsburg Monarchy or else the Jews of Vienna; studies of Jews and antisemitism in the federal states are entirely absent and books covering the inter-war years are rare.

---

[*]This article makes no claim to being fully comprehensive. Rather it concentrates on sources which are devoted exclusively, or at least to a significant degree, to Austrian antisemitism, especially those published since 1970. For a much more exhaustive (26-page), albeit unannotated, bibliography, the reader should consult the author's recently published book *From Prejudice to Persecution. A History of Austrian Anti-Semitism*, Chapel Hill, NC 1992, xxix, 426 pp., or its slightly expanded German translation, *Von Vorurteil zur Vernichtung. Die Geschichte des österreichischen Antisemitismus*, Vienna 1993.

[1]*Washington Post*, 20th December 1987, p. A10; Elfriede Schmidt (ed.), *1938 . . . and the Consequences. Questions and Responses*, Riverside, CA 1992, interview with Simon Wiesenthal, p. 301.

409

A superb introduction to the history of Austrian Jewry, published in 1989, is *A History of Habsburg Jews, 1670–1918* by William O. McCagg, Jr.[2] Drawing on unpublished sources found in Jerusalem, Vienna, Munich and New York, as well as hundreds of secondary sources listed in his twenty-page bibliography, the author is especially concerned with Jewish modernisation, and, therefore, concentrates on political, economic, social and demographic history while largely ignoring cultural and intellectual subjects. Although he by no means underestimates the strength of Austrian antisemitism, McCagg also notes that Joseph II's emancipation of Austrian Jews in the 1780s unintentionally marked the first general attack in modern European history against restrictions which had burdened Jews since the Middle Ages. *Kaiser* Franz I treated Viennese Jews abysmally, but the French Revolutionary and Napoleonic Wars facilitated their integration into the new Viennese upper middle class, so that by 1848 they were able to play a prominent role in the mid-century revolutions and regain their legal freedom. The rise of nationalism in the second half of the nineteenth century saw Habsburg Jewry identifying with the dominant German, Magyar and Polish nationalities. These new Jewish loyalties in turn brought on them the wrath of the lesser nationalities without, however, gaining them the gratitude of the German-Austrians or Polish-Galicians. Nevertheless, McCagg concludes that by 1900 Habsburg Jews, "especially in Vienna, were living as modern people in the modern world".[3] Moreover, "nowhere else in the world [did a] large scale transformation of eastern Jewry take place so relatively peacefully" as in the Habsburg Monarchy.[4]

Another work on Habsburg Jews which does not limit itself to those who lived in Vienna is Hillel J. Kieval's book, *The Making of Czech Jewry. National Conflict and Jewish Society in Bohemia, 1870–1918*.[5] Kieval's striking, but not universally accepted, thesis is that Bohemian Jews were not all supporters of German culture; many of them had assimilated into the Czech nationality or, because of the antisemitism of both Bohemian Germans and Czechs, had become Zionist by 1918.[6]

Somewhat narrower in geographical scope than the books by McCagg and Kieval, but even more impressive in detail and scholarship is *The Jews of Vienna in the Age of Franz Joseph* by the British-trained Israeli historian, Robert S. Wistrich.[7] Wistrich's title is unnecessarily modest both geographically and chronologically. Although the book's focus is certainly on Vienna, which was a magnet for Austria-Hungary's most talented Jews, Jews in the rest of the Monarchy are by no means ignored. Likewise, the author provides a generous

---

[2]William O. McCagg Jr., *A History of Habsburg Jews, 1670–1918*, Bloomington 1989, 289 pp.
[3]*Ibid*., p. 200.
[4]*Ibid*., p. 225.
[5]Hillel J. Kieval, *The Making of Czech Jewry. National Conflict and Jewish Society in Bohemia, 1870–1918*, Oxford–New York 1988, 279 pp.
[6]Marsha Rozenblit, in a review article, concedes that antisemitism drove many Bohemian Jews to become Zionists, but seriously doubts that large numbers of Jews moved away from German culture prior to the break-up of the Monarchy. See her 'Jews of the Dual Monarchy', in *Austrian History Yearbook*, XXIII (1992), pp. 160–180, esp. pp. 164–169.
[7]Robert S. Wistrich, *The Jews of Vienna in the Age of Franz Joseph*, Oxford 1989, 696 pp.

introduction into the history of Austrian Jewry before the reign of Emperor-King Franz Joseph. On the other hand, Wistrich has not attempted to be absolutely comprehensive in his coverage of Austrian-Jewish history between 1848 and 1914. Topically rather than chronologically organised, *The Jews of Vienna* concentrates on political, intellectual and cultural trends and especially on the question of Jewish identity among the cultural elite in a rapidly changing world.

For students of antisemitism, the most interesting section is Part II on "Self Defence against Anti-Semitism", in which the author describes what he calls "the most successful modern political movement based on anti-Semitism to emerge anywhere in nineteenth-century Europe",[8] by which he means the racial antisemitism of Georg von Schönerer and especially the religious, cultural and economic antisemitism of the Viennese mayor, Karl Lueger. Most of the nearly 150-page section, however, is devoted to the reaction to this new phenomenon by Adolf Jellinek and the Liberal Party, to the rabbi and journalist, Joseph Samuel Bloch, and to the *Österreichisch-Israelitische Union* (ÖIU), the self-defence organisation which Bloch helped to found in 1886.

Covering almost the same time frame as Wistrich, but concentrating on substantially different subject matter and using very different research methodology is *The Jews of Vienna, 1867–1914. Assimilation and Identity* by Marsha L. Rozenblit.[9] Relying heavily on quantitative sources such as population, birth, marriage and employment statistics (to the near exclusion of narrative sources) the author seeks to prove that the Jews of Vienna retained a distinctive identity on the eve of the First World War – despite a high degree of cultural assimilation – by virtue of their concentration in certain Viennese neighbourhoods, in Viennese secondary schools (*Gymnasien*), in certain occupations, in their continuing tradition of intermarriage, and also because of their involvement in an incredibly large number of Jewish organisations. She also quite rightly points out that their eager adoption of Viennese culture did nothing to prevent their rejection by antisemites. Unfortunately, however, she tells us little about the origins of this rejection or the picture of Jews held by non-Jews prior to 1914.

Concentrating on the same period, but having a very different focus is Steven Beller's *Vienna and the Jews, 1867–1938. A Cultural History*.[10] As the subtitle indicates, the book is devoted primarily to the astonishing cultural contributions of the Viennese Jews. On the other hand, the main title is misleading, because the book virtually ignores the period after 1914. Beller uses the broadest possible definition of who was a Viennese Jew by including both those who had converted to Christianity and those with only a minority of Jewish ancestors. His contention that antisemites themselves used such a definition[11] fails to make any distinction between moderate Catholic and Socialist antisemites and the much more vicious racial antisemitic followers of Georg von Schönerer and Adolf Hitler. However, he is right in maintaining that antisemitism was the political glue holding together Mayor Karl Lueger's Christian Social Party.

[8]*Ibid.*, p. 205.
[9]Marsha L. Rozenblit, *The Jews of Vienna, 1867–1914. Assimiliation and Identity*, Albany 1983, 284 pp.
[10]Steven Beller, *Vienna and the Jews, 1867–1938. A Cultural History*, Cambridge 1989, x, 271 pp.
[11]*Ibid.*, pp. 12, 205.

Another, earlier, cultural history of Vienna around the turn of the century is Carl E. Schorske's celebrated *Fin-de-Siècle Vienna. Politics and Culture*.[12] Although the book's focus is literature, painting, music, architecture and urban development, considerable space is devoted to antisemitism in the chapter 'Politics in a New Key. An Austrian Trio'. Schorske compares the unprincipled, manipulative tactics of Lueger with the uncompromising racial antisemitism of the pan-German, Georg von Schönerer and then shows how Theodor Herzl's Zionism responded to the antisemitic challenge.

> "Of the two leaders, Schönerer was the more ruthless and the stronger pioneer in unleashing destructive instincts. He breached the walls with his powerful anti-Semitic appeal, but Lueger organized the troops to win the victory and the spoils."[13]

Herzl's reaction was caused both by antisemitism he encountered in Vienna and that which he observed in Paris while covering the trial of Alfred Dreyfus. Ironically, however, Herzl "himself regarded the Jews as a whole with distaste, as physically and mentally malformed by the ghetto".[14]

A better source for studying the influence of antisemitism on the rise of the Christian Social Party is John W. Boyer's detailed and richly documented book, *Political Radicalism in Late Imperial Vienna. Origins of the Christian Social Movement, 1848–1897*.[15] Lueger's goal, according to Boyer, was to reunify "the fragmented bourgeoisie into a more imposing, effective political party which would cope both with the demands of Mittelstand extremism and the challenge of Austrian Social Democracy". In accomplishing these goals Lueger resorted to utilising "political antisemitism and political clericalism to disarm and destroy Viennese Liberalism", although in doing so he did not repudiate the idea of a Liberal *Rechtsstaat*. However, his party "presented and instilled models of political behavior which in other hands and in a different time period could destroy the Liberal State . . ."[16]

A book which has the rare attribute of covering Viennese Jewry from the late Monarchy through the First Republic to the present time is *Vienna and its Jews* by George E. Berkley.[17] His entertaining, chronologically-organised narrative of events undoubtedly has considerable appeal to the general, non-scholarly reader of Jewish history. Containing far more information on antisemitism than the books mentioned above, Berkley's theses, that Austrian antisemitism has been a persistent feature of Austrian political and private life for the last hundred years

---

[12]Carl E. Schorske, *Fin-de-Siècle Vienna. Politics and Culture*, New York 1980, 378 pp.

[13]*Ibid.*, p. 145. By far the best biography of von Schönerer is Andrew G. Whiteside, *The Socialism of Fools. Georg Ritter von Schönerer and Austrian Pan-Germanism*, Berkeley 1975, 404 pp. which stresses Schönerer's belief in extremism, the necessity of violence and the rejection of civility in politics.

[14]Schorske, *op. cit.*, p. 151.

[15]John W. Boyer, *Political Radicalism in Late Imperial Vienna. Origins of the Christian Social Movement, 1848–1897*, Chicago 1981, xx, 577 pp.

[16]*Ibid.*, p. 411. Another recent work on Karl Lueger is the thoroughly researched book by Richard S. Geehr, *Karl Lueger. Mayor of Fin de Siècle Vienna*, Detroit 1989. Geehr emphasises that Lueger's antisemitism did not cease once he attained power in 1897. He continued to denounce Jews in his speeches, although no antisemitic legislation was passed during his time in office. The book is rich in detail, but, unfortunately, the author does not offer any conclusions of his own.

[17]George E. Berkley, *Vienna and its Jews. The Tragedy of Success, 1880–1980s*, Lanham, MD 1988, xxi, 422 pp.

and more and that it has been even more extreme than the German variety are surely valid. Equally probable, although undocumented, is Berkley's contention that Austrian Jews harboured illusions about the dangers inherent in Nazi antisemitism because the antisemitism of Karl Lueger proved to be mostly verbal.

In other respects, however, *Vienna and Its Jews* all too obviously bears the marks of having been written rapidly in the heat of the Waldheim controversy. It relies too heavily on the faded memories of eye witnesses and far too little on documentary and especially newspaper sources, not to mention many important secondary works. Above all it ignores comparisons with Polish, Hungarian, French and even American antisemitism as well as Austrian efforts to combat antisemitism both before and after the Second World War. Scholars will also be irritated by the near absence of footnotes. In short, *Vienna and Its Jews* is colourful, albeit unreliable, anecdotal history.

Equally comprehensive, but more scholarly is the anthology, published a year earlier, entitled *Jews, Antisemitism and Culture in Vienna* and edited by Ivar Oxaal, Michael Pollak and Gerhard Botz.[18] Although most chapters deal with Jewish identity, culture and internal politics, three contributions are devoted to antisemitism. Antisemitism among the political parties, paramilitary formations and private organisations during the inter-war years is covered by the present author; Bernd Marin demonstrates how antisemitism has survived in post-Second World War Austria even though the country's Jewish population is now minuscule. A third chapter by Robert S. Wistrich deals with the ambivalent attitude towards Jews and antisemitism held by the Social Democratic Party of Austria both before and after the First World War. "Far from favouring 'Jewish' interests or identifying themselves with other Jews, whether in ethnic, religious or class terms, the so-called 'Jewish' leadership of the Austrian Social Democracy bent over backwards to *dissociate* themselves from their former co-religionists" in order to avoid the charge of forming a "*Judenschutztruppe*".[19]

Internal Jewish politics have been explored by the Israeli historian Jacob Toury and the American historians, Walter R. Weitzmann and Harriet Pass Freidenreich. Toury has written two important articles on the founding and development of the Liberal ÖIU as well as a book on the Jewish press in the Habsburg Monarchy.[20] According to Toury, the Union was founded in 1886 as

---

[18]Ivar Oxaal, Michael Pollak and Gerhard Botz (eds.), *Jews, Antisemitism and Culture in Vienna*, London–New York 1987, 300 pp. The book has also appeared in an expanded Austrian edition called *Eine zerstörte Kultur. Jüdisches Leben und Antisemitismus in Wien seit dem 19. Jahrhundert*, Buchloe 1990, 426 pp.

[19]Robert S. Wistrich, 'Social Democracy, Antisemitism and the Jews of Vienna', in Oxaal *et al.* (eds.), *op. cit.*, pp. 117, 120.

[20]Jacob Toury, 'Troubled Beginnings. The Emergence of the Österreichisch-Israelitische Union', in *LBI Year Book XXX* (1985), pp. 457–475; *idem*, 'The Contest of the Österreichisch-Israelitische Union for the Leadership of Austrian Jewry', in *LBI Year Book XXXIII* (1988), pp. 179–199; *idem*, *Die Jüdische Presse im Österreichischen Kaiserreich. Ein Beitrag zur Problematik der Akkulturation 1802–1918*, Tübingen 1983 (Schriftenreihe wissenschaftlicher Abhandlungen des Leo Baeck Instituts 41), 171 pp. In his book, Toury points out that a major task of the Jewish press after about 1882 was fighting antisemitism, a responsibility which was largely ignored by even the mainstream newspapers which had Jewish editors. See *Jüdische Presse, op. cit.*, pp. 150–151.

an ethnic-religious pressure group to fight antisemitism. However, after taking control of the Viennese *Kultusgemeinde* in 1889 the ÖIU lost much of its fighting spirit and became "a rather over-cautious body in order to attract as wide a membership as possible" which came from the "upward-moving strata of the Vienna Jewish middle classes".[21] The task of fighting racial and religious antisemites was largely left to Bloch's *Österreichische Wochenschrift* and his parliamentary activities. On the other hand, the ÖIU did establish a Defence Committee in 1895, whose considerable success in legal and judicial questions is discussed by Toury in a separate article.[22] Walter Weitzmann, in an article on 'The Politics of the Viennese Jewish Community, 1890–1914',[23] stresses the apathy of most Viennese Jews with regard to Jewish identity, internal politics and antisemitism. The Zionists, of course, were the big exception, but their numbers were too small before the First World War to make them a decisive force.

The most recent publication on Austrian Jewry to appear in the United States and the only one to concentrate exclusively on the inter-war period is *Jewish Politics in Vienna, 1918–1938* by Harriet Pass Freidenreich.[24] Although antisemitism is not her principal concern, her detailed description of the factionalism within the Jewish community between Zionists and non-Zionists, observant and non-observant Jews, and also between Westernised Jews and the *Ostjuden* from Galicia, goes a long way towards explaining why the Jewish response to Austrian antisemitism was so divided, weak and ineffective. The Liberals, organised in the *Union österreichischer Juden* (the pre-war Austrian-Israelite Union), were convinced that Zionist nationalism only confirmed the argument of the antisemites that Jews were a distinct ethnic group, whereas the Zionists were equally certain that the Liberals were hopelessly naive in believing that assimilation was possible and that antisemitism would eventually disappear.

A very different kind of book is George Clare's gripping family memoir, *Last Waltz in Vienna. The Rise and Destruction of a Family, 1842–1942*, published more than a decade ago.[25] Clare (whose name was originally spelled Klaar) gives us a firsthand account of what it was like to grow up as a Jewish boy in inter-war Vienna. Especially interesting are his remarks about the persistence of Jewish optimism in the face of the growing Nazi threat in the 1930s and the relatively mild treatment Viennese Jews received in Berlin compared with post-*Anschluß* Vienna.

Finally, mention should be made of two older, but still useful, books. Peter G. J. Pulzer's *The Rise of Political Anti-Semitism in Germany and Austria* remains a standard work on antisemitism as a political movement, just as George L. Mosse

---

[21]Toury, 'Troubled Beginnings', *loc. cit.*, pp. 461, 473, 475.
[22]Jacob Toury, 'Defense Activities of the Österreichisch-Israelitische Union before 1914', in Jehuda Reinharz (ed.), *Living with Antisemitism. Modern Jewish Responses*, Hanover, NH 1987, pp. 167–192.
[23]Walter R. Weitzmann, 'The Politics of the Viennese Jewish Community, 1890–1914', in Oxaal *et al.* (eds.), *op. cit.*, pp. 121–151.
[24]Harriet Pass Freidenreich, *Jewish Politics in Vienna, 1918–1938*, Bloomington 1991, x, 272 pp.
[25]George Clare, *Last Waltz in Vienna. The Rise and Destruction of a Family, 1842–1942*, New York 1980, 272 pp.

predicted in *The American Historical Review*[26] shortly after the book was first published in 1964.[27] Pulzer's theses have proven especially durable: political antisemitism was part of a larger rejection of Liberalism on the part of the lower middle class; thirty years of propaganda preceding the First World War had made antisemitism "respectable", especially in academic circles, although the antisemites had failed to achieve the enactment of anti-Jewish legislation; the decline of the specifically antisemitic parties in the German Empire and Austria-Hungary after 1900 was more than compensated for by the widespread acceptance of antisemitism; and post-war antisemitism in the German-speaking countries differed little from the pre-war variety except for a greater proclivity for violence, especially that which was displayed by the Nazis of both Germany and Austria. However, Pulzer does admit in the introduction to the revised edition that he had previously underestimated that the "tradition of religiously-inspired Jew-hatred – or at least of unfavorable stereotyping – was a necessary condition for the success of anti-Semitic propaganda, even when expressed in non-religious terms and absorbed by those no longer religiously observant."[28]

The other older, but still valuable, study is *The Jews of Vienna. Essays on their Life, History and Destruction* edited by Josef Fraenkel.[29] The first book to be published on Austrian Jewry after 1945, it consists of essays by no fewer than thirty-five Austrian-Jewish exiles. The book covers a wide range of subjects from demography and migrations to Jewish contributions to Austrian culture in addition to regional Jewish history and a long concluding section on the destruction of the Jewish community in Austria.

RECENT BOOKS IN GERMAN

One older book should also be mentioned with regard to books written in German: *Die Juden Wiens. Geschichte – Wirtschaft – Kultur* by Hans Tietze.[30] Although its coverage of the last hundred years is now outdated and incomplete, it still provides a useful survey on general Jewish history and culture in Vienna as well as on antisemitism from the founding of the Jewish community in Vienna in the early tenth century to the First World War. Moreover, unlike most earlier histories of Viennese Jews, Tietze is careful to integrate the history of Viennese Jews with broader developments in Austrian history. Although intended for a popular audience it includes a bibliography, index, chronology and numerous rare and interesting illustrations.

With the near total destruction of the Jewish community in Vienna, the

---

[26] *The American Historical Review*, vol. 70, No. 3 (April 1965), pp. 772–773.
[27] Peter G. J. Pulzer, *The Rise of Political Anti-Semitism in Germany and Austria*, New York 1964, 364 pp. The book was reprinted in 1988, but remains unchanged except for an updated bibliography and a new 20-page preface in which Pulzer responds to the criticisms made of the first edition.
[28] Peter Pulzer, *op. cit.*, ²1988, p. xxii.
[29] Josef Fraenkel (ed.), *The Jews of Vienna. Essays on their Life, History and Destruction*, London 1967, 585 pp.
[30] Hans Tietze, *Die Juden Wiens. Geschichte – Wirtschaft – Kultur*, Vienna 1933, 304 pp.

writing of Austrian-Jewish history anywhere in the world also came to an end until the publication of Fraenkel's book in 1967. In fact, Austrian antisemitism as well as National Socialism became taboo subjects for the general public prior to the Waldheim affair, but not for Austrian scholars. For example, as early as 1974 Anna Drabek and four other Austrian historians published a comprehensive study of the history of Austrian Jewry entitled *Das österreichische Judentum. Voraussetzungen und Geschichte*.[31] Even broader than the title would indicate, the book traces the history of European Jews from Antiquity to the present day and covers religious, social and economic issues, as well as politics and antisemitism. One lengthy chapter by Karl Stuhlpfarrer is devoted to 'Antisemitism, Racial Politics and the Persecution of Austrian Jews after the First World War'.

Another comprehensive anthology of the history of the Austrian Jews was published in 1982 as a catalogue for the special exhibition in the Jewish Museum in Eisenstadt, Burgenland, on the *1000 Jahre österreichisches Judentum*, edited by Klaus Lohrmann.[32] Topics covered in the book include the foundations of the first Jewish settlements in Austria; histories of the Jewish communal organisations in Vienna, Graz and Klagenfurt; Hebrew literature in Austria in the first half of the nineteenth century; Jewish contributions to medicine, sports and literature; and finally a twenty-page chapter by Jonny Moser on Austrian antisemitism and the Holocaust.

The most recent anthology is *Voll Leben und voll Tod ist diese Erde. Bilder aus der Geschichte der Jüdischen Österreicher (1190 bis 1945)*, edited by Wolfgang Plat.[33] The wide-ranging articles cover everything from the origins of medieval Jew-hatred to the emancipation of the Jews during the Revolutions of 1848 and the catastrophic near-end of Jewish life in Austria after the *Anschluß*. Other chapters are devoted to Jewish contributions to Austrian medicine and general culture, Jews in sport, and the lives of several famous Austrian Jews. For students of modern Austrian antisemitism, the most useful chapter is 'Das Janusgesicht des christlichen Ständestaat' by Isabella Ackerl.[34] Ackerl emphasises that the older generation of Jews was more likely than younger Jews to endorse the corporative state of Chancellors Engelbert Dollfuss and Kurt von Schuschnigg, but that virtually all Jews were united in their support of Austrian independence as being the only alternative to incorporation into the Third *Reich*. Unfortunately, their very support tended to arouse antisemitism among enemies of the *Ständestaat*.

In contrast to most English-speaking historians, the majority of whom are Jews interested in the question of Jewish identity, several contemporary Austrian scholars have concentrated on antisemitism as a separate issue and not just for Vienna, but for the federal states as well. Among these scholars are John Bunzl and Bernd Marin, the authors of *Antisemitismus in Österreich. Sozialhistorische und*

---

[31] Anna Drabek, Wolfgang Häusler, Kurt Schubert, Karl Stuhlpfarrer and Nikolaus Vielmetti, *Das österreichische Judentum. Voraussetzungen und Geschichte*, Wien–München 1974, 342 pp.
[32] Klaus Lohrmann (ed.), *1000 Jahre österreichisches Judentum*, Eisenstadt 1982, 471 pp.
[33] Wolfgang Plat (ed.), *Voll Leben und voll Tod ist diese Erde. Bilder aus der Geschichte der Jüdischen Österreicher (1190 bis 1945)*, Vienna 1988, 342 pp.
[34] Isabella Ackerl, 'Das Janusgesicht des christlichen Ständestaat', *ibid.*, pp. 209–217.

soziologische Studien.[35] Bunzl's eighty-page section traces the three primary streams of political antisemitism – the Liberal, the German Nationalist and the Christian Social – from their origins in the late Monarchy to the *Anschluß*; he also includes a chapter on antisemitism in the Second Republic. Heavily infused with a Marxist perspective, Bunzl sees antisemitism as primarily a disguised form of bourgeois anti-Marxism, although he admits that even the Austrian proletariat was not entirely immune from the prejudice. Moreover, the Social Democrats were too easily persuaded that antisemitism would automatically disappear along with the bourgeoisie. Although there is much truth in his interpretation, it fails to take into account the continuing strength of traditional religious antisemitism. The other four sections by Bernd Marin deal with the strange phenomenon of antisemitism in the Second Republic existing in the near absence of either Jews or people who openly admit to being antisemites. Marin also summarises the results of a number of public opinion polls conducted between 1946 and 1983, which reveal antisemitism to be strongest outside Vienna and among the older generation.

Antisemitism in late nineteenth-century Austria is the topic of Isak A. Hellwing's book, *Der konfessionelle Antisemitismus im 19. Jahrhundert in Österreich.*[36] Hellwing actually retraces many of the same paths covered a few years earlier by Peter Pulzer, in discussing at length the charges of ritual murder made by the biblical "scholar" at the University of Prague, August Rohling, and the devastating rebuttals made by Rabbi Joseph Samuel Bloch. The author largely ignores Karl Lueger's antisemitism; on the other hand he devotes a major section to the populist Viennese priest, Father Josef Deckert and his fiery sermons which revived the entire spectrum of medieval allegations made against Jews. Hellwing's book, in sharp contrast to Pulzer's, is almost entirely devoid of analysis, but does at least have the virtue of quoting at length from the writings, speeches and sermons of his subjects.

Two much more specialised but nevertheless useful books on the Jewish experience in Austria are *Juden in der k. (u.) k. Armee 1788–1918* by Erwin Schmidl[37] and *Erotik und Hakenkreuz auf der Anklagebank. Der Fall Bettauer* by Murray Hall.[38] Schmidl shows that the Austro-Hungarian Army was actually relatively free of the prejudice; no other army in the world, prior to the founding of the Israeli Defence Force, had so many Jewish officers.[39] By contrast, Hall's book, an examination of the murder of the popular Jewish-born author of *Die Stadt ohne Juden*, Hugo Bettauer, in March 1925, and the subsequent trial of his assassin, shows that the whole affair, far from being an isolated incident, demonstrated the relative intensity of antisemitism in the First Republic as compared to the late Monarchy. Bettauer's erotic publications, rather than his murderer, were put on

---

[35]John Bunzl and Bernd Marin, *Antisemitismus in Österreich. Sozialhistorische und soziologische Studien.* Foreword by Anton Pelinka, Innsbruck 1983, 226 pp.

[36]Isak A. Hellwing, *Der konfessionelle Antisemitismus im 19. Jahrhundert in Österreich*, Vienna 1972, 311 pp.

[37]Erwin A. Schmidl, *Juden in der K. (u.) K. Armee 1788–1918/Jews in the Habsburg Armed Forces*, Studia Judaica Austriaca, 11, Eisenstadt 1989, 233 pp.

[38]Murray Hall, *Erotik und Hakenkreuz auf der Anklagebank. Der Fall Bettauer*, Vienna 1978, 219 pp.

[39]The same assertions are made by Istvan Deak in his new book, *Beyond Nationalism. A Social and Political History of the Habsburg Officer Corps, 1848–1918*, New York 1990, xiii, 273 pp.

trial and the killer was given the ridiculously light sentence of two-and-a-half years' imprisonment in a mental institution.

Although antisemitism in the whole of Austria during the democratic era between 1918 and 1934 has been especially neglected by both English and German-language authors, Günter Fellner's *Antisemitismus in Salzburg 1918–1938*[40] is an excellent treatment of a single Austrian state during the First Republic. He demonstrates that it was perfectly possible already at that time to have antisemitism where there were virtually no Jews. He is especially good at describing the little known but fanatically antisemitic umbrella organisation called the *Antisemitenbund* and the vicious diatribes of its journalistic organ, *Der eiserne Besen*.

Another regional study which touches on antisemitism is *Die Juden in Kärnten und das Dritte Reich* by August Walzl.[41] Although incredibly specialised – the book has more pages than the largest number of Jews ever to have lived in Carinthia – it does at least cover a broader period than promised in the title. The entire history of the Carinthian Jews is traced from their settlements in the nineteenth century to the return of small numbers to the federal state following the Holocaust. The book, however, makes few attempts to compare the status of the Carinthian Jews to that of their co-religionists in Vienna or elsewhere. On the other hand, it does show that the Jewish population in Carinthia declined even more rapidly between the wars than in the nation's capital, that its population was more economically and socially homogeneous, and that antisemitism could flourish where practically no Jews lived, although it tended to be overshadowed by anti-Slovene feelings. *Die Juden in Kärnten* is thoroughly documented, but has only an index of names, not subjects, and is in desperate need of a summary and conclusion.

Jewish life and antisemitism in the highly pan-German federal state of Styria is covered in *Judentum in einer Antisemitischen Umwelt. Am Beispiel der Stadt Graz 1918–1938* by Dieter A. Binder, Gudrun Reitter and Herbert Rutgen.[42] Although well researched and containing numerous statistics about the Jewish community in Graz – the second largest in Austria – the book devotes only a few pages to antisemitism and adds little to our understanding of the phenomenon.

The tiny Jewish community in the very Catholic state of Tyrol can be studied in 'Tirol und die Juden' by Gretl Köfler.[43] A more important study, however, is the massive new book entitled *Studenten und Politik. Der Kampf um die Vorherrschaft an der Universität Innsbruck 1918–1938*, by Michael Gehler.[44] This first book-length

---

[40]Günter Fellner, *Antisemitismus in Salzburg 1918–1938*, Vienna 1979, vi, 266 pp.

[41]August Walzl, *Die Juden in Kärnten und das Dritte Reich*, Klagenfurt 1987, 376 pp.

[42]Dieter A. Binder, Gudrun Reitter and Herbert Rutgen, *Judentum in einer Antisemitischen Umwelt. Am Beispiel der Stadt Graz 1918–1938*, Graz 1988, 204 pp.

[43]Gretl Köfler, 'Tirol und die Juden', in Thomas Albrich, Klaus Eisterer and Rolf Steininger (eds.), *Tirol und der Anschluß. Vorausetzungen, Entwicklungen, Rahmenbedingungen 1918–1938*, Innsbruck 1988, pp. 169–182.

[44]Michael Gehler, *Studenten und Politik. Der Kampf um die Vorherrschaft an der Universität Innsbruck 1918–1938*, Innsbruck 1990, 591 pp.*

*For a detailed case-study of the events of the November Pogrom in Innsbruck, see now *idem*, 'Murder on Command. The Anti-Jewish Pogrom in Innsbruck, 9th–10th November 1938' in this volume of the Year Book – (Ed.).

investigation of an Austrian university's role in the rise of Austrian National Socialism demonstrates that antisemitism was more important among students than political issues like the Paris Peace Settlement, the *Anschluß* question and the loss of the South Tyrol, even though Jews never made up much more than one per cent of the enrolment of the University of Innsbruck in the inter-war period.[45]

Antisemitism in the corporative state of Engelbert Dollfuss and Kurt von Schuschnigg is covered by Sylvia Maderegger in *Die Juden im Österreichischen Ständestaat 1934–1938*.[46] Maderegger emphasises the pervasiveness of antisemitism in Austrian society during the authoritarian period: the Catholic and Protestant churches, schools and universities, professional societies and newspapers all exhibited various manifestations of the prejudice. In the face of this massive hostility the Jews could agree only on the need to preserve an independent Austria.

The brutal treatment of Viennese Jews by the city's Gentile population in the months following the *Anschluß* has recently been scrutinised in *Der Novemberpogrom. Die "Reichskristallnacht" in Wien*,[47] which was prepared for a special exhibition commemorating the 50th anniversary of the Pogrom. An anthology by twelve Austrian and foreign scholars, the book proves conclusively that the action was not an isolated incident organised exclusively by German Nazis, but was rooted in Austrian tradition and enjoyed widespread local support. Equally revealing of the active participation in the persecution of Viennese Jews by the general population throughout the whole of 1938 is *Und Keiner War Dabei. Dokumente des alltäglichen Antisemitismus in Wien 1938* edited by Hans Safrian and Hans Witek.[48]

The fate of Austria's Jews in the Holocaust has been thoroughly researched by the Austrian-Jewish exile, Herbert Rosenkranz, who now lives in Israel, in *Verfolgung und Selbstbehauptung. Die Juden in Österreich*,[49] and in a number of more recent articles and chapters in books.[50] Rosenkranz is especially adept at showing how Adolf Eichmann created a veritable conveyer belt system in Vienna for depriving Jews of their property and speeding up their deportation, a system which was later imitated in the *Altreich*. Many of the same topics are also covered by the Viennese-Jewish scholar, Jonny Moser, especially in his long chapter, 'Die

---

[45]For an excellent review of Gehler's book by Robert Wegs, see *The American Historical Review*, vol. 97, No. 1 (April 1992), pp. 243–244.
[46]Sylvia Maderegger, *Die Juden im österreichischen Ständestaat 1934–1938*, Vienna 1973, 284 pp.
[47]*Der Novemberpogrom. Die "Reichskristallnacht" in Wien*, Vienna 1988, 175 pp.
[48]Hans Safrian and Hans Witek (eds.), *Und Keiner War Dabei. Dokumente des alltäglichen Antisemitismus in Wien 1938*, Vienna 1988, 207 pp.
[49]Herbert Rosenkranz, *Verfolgung und Selbstbehauptung. Die Juden in Österreich*, Vienna 1978, 399 pp.
[50]His most recent publications are: 'Entrechtung, Verfolgung und Selbsthilfe der Juden in Österreich, März bis Oktober 1938', in Gerald Stourzh and Birgitta Zaar (eds.), *Österreich, Deutschland und die Mächte. Internationale und österreichische Aspekte des "Anschlusses" vom März 1938*, Vienna 1990; and *Der Novemberpogrom 1938 in Wien*, Vienna 1988.

Katastrophe der Juden in Österreich 1938–1945 – ihre Voraussetzungen und ihre Überwindung'.[51]

Gerhard Botz of the University of Salzburg has argued in a number of works, especially his thoroughly researched *Wohnungspolitik und Judendeportation in Wien 1938 bis 1945*,[52] that it was not just antisemitic ideology, but also pure greed and envy which added a sense of urgency to the Aryanisation of Jewish housing in Vienna after the *Anschluß*. Unfortunately, the usefulness of this book to scholars is again limited by the absence of an index.

Erika Weinzierl, the head of the *Institut für Zeitgeschichte* in Vienna, has also devoted most of her career to studying Austrian antisemitism especially during the Second World War. She is best known for her book, *Zu wenig Gerechte. Österreicher und Judenverfolgung 1938–1945*,[53] in which she blames the unwillingness of all but a few Austrians to aid the Jews during the Holocaust on the country's centuries-old tradition of antisemitism. However, because Weinzierl tries to do so much in relatively little space, the reader is still left wondering why there were so few righteous Austrians and also why there were as many as there were.[54]

The relatively unknown period in Jewish history immediately following the Holocaust is described by Thomas Albrich in his recent book, *Exodus durch Österreich. Die jüdischen Flüchtlinge 1945–1948*,[55] in which he describes the hostility aroused among the Austrian population by Jewish refugees who were merely passing through the country on their way to Palestine or other countries. The number of refugees had been greatly enlarged by post-war pogroms in Poland. Consequently, existing camp facilities, located near traditionally antisemitic small towns and villages, were swamped. Meanwhile, underfed Austrians were convinced that food allotments were being taken from them to feed the refugees. The endlessly drawn-out negotiations over restitution and reparations for Austrian-Jewish victims of Nazi persecution has been explored by the English historian, Robert Knight in *"Ich bin dafür, die Sache in die Länge zu ziehen." Die Wortprotokolle der österreichischen Bundesregierung von 1945 bis 1952 über die Entschädigung der Juden*.[56]

How Jews and non-Jews remember the *Anschluß* and its immediate aftermath fifty years later can be observed in *1938 . . . und was dann?* (translated into English as *1938 . . . and the Consequences?*) interviews which were conducted and edited by Elfriede Schmidt.[57] Although little startlingly new information is revealed in these interviews they do provide a sense of immediacy. No reader of this book can

---

[51] Jonny Moser, 'Die Katastrophe der Juden in Österreich 1938–1945 – ihre Voraussetzungen und ihre Überwindung', in *Studia Judaica Austriaca*, vol. V, *Der gelbe Stern in Österreich*, Eisenstadt 1977, pp. 67–134.
[52] Gerhard Botz, *Wohnungspolitik und Judendeportation in Wien 1938 bis 1945*, Graz ²1985, 208 pp.
[53] Erika Weinzierl, *Zu wenig Gerechte. Österreicher und Judenverfolgung 1938–1945*, Vienna 1975, 200 pp.
[54] Cf. W. Robert Houston, in *Austrian History Yearbook*, VIII (1972), pp. 348–349.
[55] Thomas Albrich, *Exodus durch Österreich. Die jüdischen Flüchtlinge 1945–1948*, Innsbruck 1987, 265 pp.
[56] Robert Knight (ed.), *"Ich bin dafür, die Sache in die Länge zu ziehen." Wortprotokolle der österreichischen Bundesregierung von 1945 bis 1952 über die Entschädigung der Juden*, Frankfurt a. Main 1988, 287 pp.*
 * See also Robert Knight, 'Restitution and Legitimacy in Post-War Austria 1945–1953', in *LBI Year Book XXXVI* (1991), pp. 413–441 – (Ed.).
[57] Elfriede Schmidt (ed.), *1938 . . . und was dann?*, Vienna 1988 (American edn.: *1938 . . . and the Consequences?*, op. cit.).

pretend that Austrian Jews were not the frequent victims of homegrown Austrian antisemitism. Just as interesting as these historical revelations, if not indeed more so, are comments about the Waldheim affair and evaluations of the state of antisemitism in present-day Austria. These assessments vary sharply from those of Teddy Kollek, the Mayor of Jerusalem, who thinks that "nothing has improved"[58] to Simon Wiesenthal – whose interview is by far the most interesting in the book – who says that "thanks to Cardinal König . . . many prejudices have disappeared".[59]

NEWSPAPERS AND DOCUMENTS

Contemporary newspapers are probably the best source for an original study of almost any aspect of Austrian antisemitism. The inter-war years in particular can be considered a golden age of Austrian and especially Viennese journalism, both as to quality and to quantity. Well over thirty weekly and daily newspapers existed in Vienna alone during the period between the two world wars. Every political faction of any consequence, both Jewish and Gentile, had its own newspaper organ. But the researcher need not confine him- or herself to Austrian newspapers. *The New York Times*, for example, had its own reporter in Vienna, G.E.R. Gedye, who wrote many of the more than sixty articles about antisemitic violence, especially at the University of Vienna, which appeared in *The New York Times* between 1918 and the Anschluß. More than fifty years after its publication, his book, *Fallen Bastions. The Central European Tragedy*,[60] still provides useful information on the fate of Austria's Jews, in the period immediately following the Anschluß. The *Times* is actually an especially expeditious way to begin primary research, because, unlike the Austrian newspapers, it is indexed. The newspaper cuttings collection of the *Kammer für Arbeiter und Angestellte* in Vienna does have a number of folders on various aspects of Austrian Jewry and antisemitism, but is by no means complete. In particular, it has no cuttings from Jewish newspapers.

Jewish newspapers, that is to say newspapers which were written by and exclusively for other Jews, are an excellent and until now largely ignored source for Jewish history in Austria. Josef Bloch's personal mouthpiece, *Dr. Blochs Österreichische Wochenschrift* was, from its founding in 1884 until his retirement in 1920, a world forum for discussing the "Jewish Question" and an organ for the refutation of hostile criticism of Jewry. It remains an indispensable source for the history of Viennese Jewry during its golden age. *Die Wahrheit*, the weekly organ of the liberal and assimilationist *Union österreichischer Israeliten* (formerly ÖIU), was especially alert to acts of antisemitism. On the other hand, Zionist newspapers such as the daily *Wiener Morgenzeitung*, or its weekly successor after 1928, *Die Stimme*, are considerably less helpful on antisemitism, because they concentrated on internal Jewish politics and culture as well as on developments in Palestine.

---

[58]*Ibid.* (US edn.), p. 138.
[59]*Ibid.*, p. 311.
[60]G.E.R. Gedye, *Fallen Bastions. The Central European Tragedy*, London 1939, 519 pp.

The Orthodox *Jüdische Presse* also ignored all but the most overt acts of antisemitism. Another extremely valuable contemporary Jewish source is to be found in the reports of the Viennese community organisation (*Bericht der Israelitischen Kultusgemeinde Wien über die Tätigkeit in der Periode 1929–1932, 1933–1936*).[61]

Antisemitic Austrian newspapers and journals are almost too numerous to list, but mention must at least be made of the *Reichspost*, the official organ of the Christian Social Party; *Schönere Zukunft*, a weekly magazine which was filled with articles of traditional Catholic anti-Judaism; and the National-Socialist newspapers, *Deutsche Arbeiter-Presse, Die Volksstimme, Der Kampfruf*, and the *Deutschösterreichische Tages-Zeitung*. Probably the most viciously antisemitic newspaper in Austria up to 1934 was *Der eiserne Besen*, the mouthpiece of the *Antisemitenbund*. The *Neue Freie Presse*, although edited mostly by Jews, was typical of liberal, Jewish-owned and edited newspapers in showing little interest in purely Jewish affairs, but was good at reporting antisemitic riots and demonstrations. *Gerechtigkeit*, a weekly newspaper edited by Irene Harand between 1934 and 1938, was unique among non-Jewish Austrian newspapers, in being outspokenly philosemitic.

There is no single documentary collection exclusively devoted to Austrian antisemitism, but useful information can be found at the *Allgemeines Verwaltungsarchiv* (AVA) in Vienna, especially the fascinating minutes of a special committee of "experts" established by the *Grossdeutsche Volkspartei* (GDVP) to make recommendations to the party on its Jewish policy. The minutes clearly reveal that antisemitism, at least for the GDVP, was not pure demagoguery. The committee genuinely believed in a Jewish world conspiracy with its centre in New York. The AVA also holds the files of *Gau* Wien of the Nazi Party which include cuttings from Nazi newspapers and guidelines for speakers dealing with racial questions. The Archives of Vienna's *Kultusgemeinde* are now located in the Central Archive for the History of the Jewish People (CAHJP) in Jerusalem. Although they contain nuggets of interesting information on Austrian antisemitism they are far more useful for Jewish internal politics. The same can be said for the documents related to Austria at the Central Zionist Archives (CZA) in Jerusalem. Not to be overlooked are the *Papers Related to the Foreign Relations of the United States* (FRUS)[62] which are especially useful in revealing the success American diplomats had in pressing Chancellor Dollfuss to crack down on Nazi violence at the University of Vienna.

The antisemitic developments in Austria following the *Anschluß* are still recent enough to make the interviewing of survivors another significant primary source of information. As with any other type of oral history, however, the researcher must employ great caution. The memories of refugees are influenced not only by

---

[61] *Bericht der Israelitischen Kultusgemeinde Wien über die Tätigkeit in der Periode 1929–1932*, Vienna 1932; . . . *1933–1936*, Vienna 1936.

[62] *Papers Related to the Foreign Relations of the United States*, Washington (US Government Printing Office). Considerable information from British diplomatic sources related to Austrian antisemitism, especially in universities, can be found in F. L. Carsten, *The First Austrian Republic, 1918–1939. A Study Based on British and Austrian Documents*, Aldershot 1986, 309 pp.

the passage of more than half a century, but also by the social class to which they belonged in Vienna or the federal states, the neighbourhood in which they lived, and especially by the date they left Austria. Those Jews who lived in well integrated middle-class neighbourhoods outside Leopoldstadt and who left before the *"Kristallnacht"* are likely to have far happier recollections than Jews who fall into the opposite categories.

Despite the plethora of the new books on Austrian antisemitism and closely related subjects many topics remain comparatively unexplored. Above all, a close look needs to be taken at the *Hochburg* of antisemitism in late imperial Austria and the First Republic, the country's universities, especially the University of Vienna. John Haag has already explored this subject in a number of excellent articles,[63] which, however, only whet our appetite for a promised book on the subject. More work could also be done on antisemitism in some of the Austrian *Bundesländer*, especially Upper Austria and the Burgenland prior to the *Anschluß*. Antisemitism in private organisations also deserves more attention than it has so far received.[64] An even less explored question is the reaction to Austrian antisemitism by Jewish organisations abroad, especially in the United States and Great Britain. All in all, much work remains to be done despite the progress of the last decade or two.

---

[63]See, for example, John Haag, 'Blood on the Ringstrasse. Vienna's Students 1918–1933', in *The Wiener Library Bulletin*, vol. XXIX (1976), New Series Nos. 39/40, pp. 29–34; *idem*, 'Students at the University of Vienna in the First World War', in *Central European History*, XVII, No. 4 (December 1984), pp. 299–309; and *idem*, 'A Woman's Struggle Against Nazism. Irene Harand and Gerechtigkeit, 1933–1938', in *The Wiener Library Bulletin*, vol. XXXIV (1981), New Series Nos. 53/54, pp. 64–72. The one book already published on academic antisemitism in Austria as a whole is Robert Hein, *Studentischer Antisemitismus in Österreich*, Vienna 1984, 169 pp.

[64]See, for example, Reinhard Krammer, 'Die Turn- und Sportbewegung', in Erika Weinzierl and Kurt Skalnik (eds.), *Österreich 1918–1938*, Graz 1983, pp. 731–741; Friedrich Kubl, 'Geschichte der jüdischen Advokaten und Rechtsgelehrten in Österreich', in Hugo Gold (ed.), *Geschichte der Juden in Österreich*, Tel-Aviv 1971, pp. 117–126; and Andreas Wachter, *Antisemitismus im österreichischen Vereinswesen für Leibesübungen 1918–1938 am Beispiel ausgewählter Vereine*, Ph.D. diss., University of Vienna 1983, 250 pp.

Post-War Publications on German-speaking Jewry

A Selected Bibliography of Books and Articles 1992

Compiled by

BARBARA SUCHY and ANNETTE PRINGLE

Leo Baeck Institute
4 Devonshire Street
London W1N 2BH

CONTENTS

		Page
I.	HISTORY	
	A. General	427
	Linguistics/Western Yiddish	432
	B. Communal and Regional History	433
	1. Germany	433
	1a. Alsace	443
	2. Austria	443
	3. Central Europe	444
	4. Switzerland	446
	C. German-speaking Jews in Various Countries	446
II.	RESEARCH AND BIBLIOGRAPHY	
	A. Libraries and Institutes	447
	B. Bibliographies, Catalogues and Reference Books	448
III.	THE NAZI PERIOD	
	A. General	449
	B. Jewish Resistance	467
IV.	POST WAR	
	A. General	468
	B. Education and Teaching. Memorials	470
V.	JUDAISM	
	A. Jewish Learning and Scholars	472
	B. The Jewish Problem	476
	C. Jewish Life and Organisations	477
	D. Jewish Art and Music	479
VI.	ZIONISM AND ISRAEL	479
VII.	PARTICIPATION IN CULTURAL AND PUBLIC LIFE	
	A. General	480
	B. Individual	484
VIII.	AUTOBIOGRAPHY, MEMOIRS, LETTERS, GENEALOGY	494
IX.	GERMAN-JEWISH RELATIONS	
	A. General	498
	B. German-Israeli Relations	500
	C. Church and Synagogue	500
	D. Antisemitism	501
	E. Noted Germans and Jews	504
X.	FICTION AND POETRY	506
	INDEX	509

BIBLIOGRAPHY 1992

I. HISTORY

A. General

28988 AWERBUCH, MARIANNE: *Das Ende und das Fortleben des Judentums in Deutschland*. Hrsg. vom Hessischen Ministerium für Umwelt, Energie und Bundesangelegenheiten. Bonn: Hessische Landesvertretung, 1992. Pp. 4–18. [Also in this publication: CILLY KUGELMANN: Zur Situation der jüdischen Überlebenden 1945 bis 1950. Pp. 19–32.]

28989 BACKHAUSEN, MANFRED: *Hilfe zur Aufarbeitung jüdischer Schicksale im Rahmen von genealogischen Arbeiten*. [In]: Mitteilungen der westdeutschen Gesellschaft für Familienkunde, Jg. 79 und 80, Bd. 35, Neustadt/Aisch, 1991–1992. Pp. 177–178, notes, list of names.

28990 BASKIN, JUDITH R., ed.: *Jewish women in historical perspective*. Detroit: Wayne State Univ. Press, 1991. 300 pp., bibl., index. [Incl.: Introd.[&] Jewish women in the middle ages (Judith R. Baskin, 15–24 [and] 94–114). Prayers in Yiddish and the religious world of Ashkenazic women (Chava Weissler, 159–181). Emancipation through intermarriage in Old Berlin (Deborah Hertz, 182–201). Tradition and Transition: Jewish women in Imperial Germany (Marion A. Kaplan, 202–221). Gender and the immigrant Jewish experience in the United States (Paula E. Hyman, 222–242). Women and the Holocaust: a reconsideration of research (Joan Ringelheim, 243–264).]

—— BATTENBERG, FRIEDRICH: *Das Reichskammergericht und die Juden im Heiligen Römischen Reich*. [See No. 29120.]

28991 BAUMANN, ZYGMUNT: *Assimilation and enlightenment (in reference to the Jewish experience in Germany)*. [In]: Society, Vol. 27, No. 6, New Brunswick, NJ, 1990. Pp. 71 ff.

—— *Bild und Selbstbild der Juden Berlins zwischen Aufklärung und Romantik*. [See No. 29083.]

28992 BIRKHAN, HELMUT, ed.: *Die Juden in ihrer mittelalterlichen Umwelt*. Protokolle einer Ring-Vorlesung gehalten im Sommersemester 1989 an der Universität Wien. Bern; New York [et al.]: Lang, 1992. 296 pp., illus., footnotes. (Wiener Arbeiten zur Germanischen Altertumskunde und Philologie, Bd. 33). [Cont. the following contributions: Vorwort (H.B., VII–XI). Möglichkeiten und Grenzen des christlich-jüdischen Gesprächs (Kurt Schubert, 3–24). Juden und Christen in der spätantiken Umwelt (Günter Stemberger, 25–36). Juden und Christen im Frühmittelalter (37–56). Die Stellung der Juden im Hochmittelalter außerhalb des Reiches (57–78). Die Juden als Mittler II: Petrus Alfonsi als Vermittler zwischen Judentum und Christentum und Übermittler orientalisch-arabischer Weisheit (Kurt Smolak, 79–96). Arabische, jüdische und europäische Wissenschaft (Heinrich Simon, 97–108). Fest- und Alltagsbräuche der Juden im Mittelalter – Ursachen von Antijudaismus? (Magdalena Schultz, 109–142). Die Juden in der deutschen Literatur des Mittelalters (Helmut Birkhan, 143–178). Die Sprache der Juden im Mittelalter und ihre Literatur (Bettina Simon, 179–196). Zu den jüdisch-deutschen Texten des Mittelalters (Ulrike Hirhager/Helmut Birkhan, 197–206). Die Juden in den romanischen Literaturen des Mittelalters (Fritz Peter Kirsch, 207–224). Projektion versus Realität: Der Ritualmord (Magdalena Schultz, 225–248). Magisch-theurgische Überlieferungen im mittelalterlichen Judentum. Beobachtungen zu 'Terafim' und 'Golem' (Johann Maier, 249–287).]

28993 BORUT, JACOB: *'A new spirit among our brethren in Ashkenaz'. German Jewry in the face of economic, social and political change in the Reich at the end of the 19th century*. [In Hebrew, with English summary]. Jerusalem: Hebrew Univ., Diss., June 1991. XXXI, 466 pp.

28994 BORUT, JACOB: *The Jewish press in Germany in the late 19th century as a source of historical information*. [In Hebrew, with English summary]. [In]: Qesher, No. 11, Tel-Aviv, May 1992. Pp. 27–34.

28995 BRENNER, MICHAEL: *Zurück ins Ghetto. Jüdische Autonomievorstellungen in der Weimarer Republik*. [In]: Trumah, 3, Wiesbaden, 1992. Pp. 101–127.

28996 BREUER, MORDECHAI: *Modernity within tradition: the social history of orthodox Jewry in Imperial Germany*. Transl. by Elizabeth Petuchowski. New York: Columbia Univ. Press, 1992. XX,

514 pp., frontis., notes, bibl., index. [For original LBI publication in German and further details see No. 22901/YB XXXII.]

28997 BREUER, MORDECHAI: *Orthodox Judaism in Eastern and Western Europe*. [In]: Comparative studies on government and non-dominant ethnic groups in Europe, 1850–1940. Vol. 2. Ed. by Donald A. Kerr. New York: New York Univ. Press, 1992. Pp. 79–93, notes, bibl.

28998 DIEBOLD, RUTH: *Die Chronologie der Judengesetzgebung in den zum Deutschen Bund gehörenden süd- und mittelwestdeutschen Staaten Baden, Württemberg, Bayern, Hessen-Darmstadt, Frankfurt und Sachsen-Weimar-Eisenach im 19. Jahrhundert bis zur Revolution von 1848/49*. Tübingen: Univ. Tübingen, Diss., 1991. 254 pp.

28999 EISSING, UWE: *Zur Reform der Rechtsverhältnisse der Juden im Königreich Hannover (1815–1842)*. [In]: Niedersächsisches Jahrbuch für Landesgeschichte. Bd. 64. Hannover, 1992. Pp. 287–340, footnotes.

29000 FEINER, SHMUEL: *Did the French Revolution influence the development of the 'Berlin Enlightenment'?* [In Hebrew]. [In]: Zion, Vol. 57, No. 1, Jerusalem, 1992. Pp. 89–92. [A response to the article by Reuven Michael in 'Zion' 56, 3 (1991), contesting his conclusions (see No. 28009/XXXVII).]

29001 *Four centuries of Jewish women's spirituality: a source book*. Ed. by Ellen M. Umansky and Dianne Ashton. Boston: Beacon Press, 1992. XVIII, 350 pp., bibl. (335–340). [A collection mainly of letters, incl. by Rebecca Graetz, Gertrud Kolmar, Bertha Pappenheim, a.o.; also excerpts from the memoirs of Glückel von Hameln.]

29002 FRIEDLANDER, JUDITH: *Zur Geschichte und Kultur des polnischen Judentums*. [In]: Nach Osten. Verdeckte Spuren nationalsozialistischer Verbrechen [see No. 29485]. Pp. 45–70. [On the medieval migration of Jews to Poland and the emergence of a national Jewish culture in the course of the nineteenth century; also on the Bund.]

29003 GAFNI, ISAIAH M./RAVITZKY, AVIEZER, eds.: *Sanctity of life and martyrdom: studies in memory of Amir Yekutiel*. [In Hebrew]. Jerusalem: Zalman Shazar Center for Jewish History, 1992. 312 pp. [Incl. articles in Hebrew, titles transl.: The roots of the sanctification of God's name in early Ashkenaz (Avraham Grossman, 99–130; deals especially with the First Crusade and the Jewish suicides in Worms and Mainz). The sanctification of God's name in Ashkenaz and the story of Rabbi Amnon of Mainz (Ivan G. Marcus, 131–148; compares the story of the Ten Martyrs, the 1096 massacres, and the story of R. Amnon, contending that the latter was a fiction).]

29004 GAY, RUTH: *The Jews of Germany: a historical portrait*. With an introd. by Peter Gay. New Haven, CT: Yale Univ. Press, 1992. XIII, 297 pp., illus., facsims., ports. [An overview of the 1500-year history of the Jews in Germany using texts, pictures, and contemporary accounts.]

29005 *Genizah – Hidden legacies of the German village Jews. Genisa – Verborgenes Erbe der deutschen Landjuden*. [Hrsg.:] Falk Wiesemann. Mit Beiträgen von Fritz Armbruster, Hans-Peter Baum und Leonhard Scherg. Wien: Wiener Verlag, 1992. 224 pp., illus., bibl. (222–224). [Catalogue of an exhibition, organised by the Hidden Legacy Foundation, London (Dir.: Evelyn Friedlander) and held in London in autumn 1992. All contributions in English and German. Incl.: Geleitworte/Prefaces (Elie Wiesel, Hans Zehetmair, Hermann Freiherr von Richthofen, Paul-Werner Scheele, 7–10). Vorwort/Foreword (Evelyn Friedlander, 11–14). 'Verborgene Zeugnisse' der deutschen Landjuden. Eine Einführung in die Ausstellung (Falk Wiesemann, 15–32). Jüdisches Leben in Franken (Hans-Peter Baum, 33–50). Urspringen. Eine jüdische Gemeinde, eine Synagoge und eine Genisa (Leonhard Scherg, 51–57). Ichenhausen. Was war, was blieb: Steine, Papiere – Erinnerung (Fritz Armbruster, 58–65).]

29006 GOLDIN, SIMCHA: *The relationship between the individual and the Jewish community in the Middle Ages in northern France and Germany (1100–1300)*. [In Hebrew, with English summary]. Tel-Aviv: Tel-Aviv Univ., Diss., March 1991. 2 vols., notes, bibl.

29007 GRAETZ, MICHAEL: *From corporate community to ethnic-religious minority, 1750–1830*. [In]: LBI Year Book XXXVII, London. Pp. 71–82, footnotes.

29008 GRAETZ, MICHAEL: *Jüdische Geschichtsschreibung hundert Jahre nach Heinrich Graetz*. Wiesbaden: Reichert, 1992. 18 pp., footnotes. Veröffentlichungen der Hochschule für Jüdische Studien Heidelberg, Nr. 4.)

29009 GREIVE, HERMANN: *Die Juden. Grundzüge ihrer Geschichte im mittelalterlichen und neuzeitlichen Europa*. Mit einem Nachwort von Johannes Wachten. 4., durch ein Nachwort ergänzte,

Aufl. Darmstadt: Wissenschaftl. Buchgesellschaft, 1992. 246 pp. (WB-Forum, Bd. 74.) [First edn., publ. 1980, see No. 16904/YB XXVI.]

29010 GUGGENHEIMER, HEINRICH WALTER/GUGGENHEIMER, EVA H.: *Jewish family names and their origins: an etymological dictionary*. Hoboken, NJ: Ktav, 1992. XLII, 882 pp.

29011 HAVERKAMP, ALFRED/ZIWES, FRANZ-JOSEF: *Juden in der christlichen Umwelt während des späten Mittelalters*. Zeitschrift für Historische Forschung. Beiheft 13. Berlin, 1992. 102 pp.

29012 HERZIG, ARNO: *The process of emancipation from the Congress of Vienna to the Revolution of 1848/1849*. [In]: LBI Year Book XXXVII, London. Pp. 61–69, footnotes.

29013 *Die Juden in der europäischen Geschichte*. Sieben Vorlesungen von Saul Friedländer, Amos Funkenstein, Eberhard Jäckel, Michael A. Meyer, Jehuda Reinharz, David Sorkin, Shulamit Volkov. Mit einer Einleitung von Christian Beck. Hrsg. von Wolfgang Beck. München: Beck, 1992. 154 pp., notes. [Cont.the following essays (titles partly abbr.): Der Mord an den europäischen Juden (Eberhard Jäckel, 20–32). Juden, Christen und Muslime: religiöse Polemik im Mittelalter (Amos Funkenstein, 33–49). Juden und Aufklärung: religiöse Quellen der Toleranz (David Sorkin, 50–66). Die jüdische Reformbewegung in Deutschland in jüdischer und christlicher Sicht (Michael A. Meyer, 67–85). Juden und Judentum im Zeitalter der Emanzipation. Einheit und Vielfalt (Shulamit Volkov, 86–108). Jüdische Identität in Zentraleuropa vor dem Zweiten Weltkrieg (Jehuda Reinharz, 109–135). Trauma, Erinnerung und Übertragung in der historischen Darstellung des Nationalsozialismus und des Holocaust (Saul Friedländer, 136–151).]

29014 *Juden und deutsche Arbeiterbewegung bis 1933. Soziale Utopien und religiös-kulturelle Traditionen*. Hrsg. von Ludger Heid und Arnold Paucker. Tübingen: Mohr (Paul Siebeck), 1992. X, 246 pp., footnotes, index (persons). (Eine Veröffentlichung des Salomon Ludwig Steinheim-Instituts für deutsch-jüdische Geschichte, Duisburg und des Leo Baeck Instituts, London; Schriftenreihe wissenschaftlicher Abhandlungen des Leo Baeck Instituts, 49.) [Cont.(titles partly abbr.): Vorwort (Ludger Heid/Arnold Paucker, VII–IX). Judenhaß und Antisemitismus bei den Unterschichten und in der frühen Arbeiterbewegung (Arno Herzig, 1–18). Stephan Born. Organisator der deutschen Arbeiterschaft in der Revolution von 1848 (Walter Grab, 19–34). Antisemitismus im Frühsozialismus und Anarchismus (Micha Brumlik, 35–42). Die Judenfrage als Frage des Antisemitismus und des jüdischen Nationalismus in der klassischen Sozialdemokratie (Shlomo Na'aman, 43–58). Sozialdemokratie und Antisemitismus zur Zeit der Dreyfus-Affäre (Kurt Koszyk, 59–78). Eduard Bernsteins Einstellung zur Judenfrage (Robert S. Wistrich, 79–90). Sozialismus und Zionismus in Deutschland 1897–1933 (Mario Kessler, 91–102). Paul Singer, soziale Utopie, Judentum und Arbeiterbewegung (Laurenz Demps, 103–114). Sozialismus, Deutschtum, Judentum im Briefwechsel Gustav Landauers und Fritz Mauthners (Hanna Delf, 115–132). Gustav Mayer als Historiker der deutschen Arbeiterbewegung (Gottfried Niedhart, 133–146). Rosa Luxemburg und Luise Kautsky (Susanne Miller, 147–153). Die Beispiele Käte Frankenthal, Berta Jourdan, Adele Schreiber-Krieger, Toni Sender und Hedwig Wachenheim (Christl Wickert, 155–165). Rosi Wolfstein-Frölich (Klaus-Dieter Vinschen, 165–176). Sozialisten zur Ostjudenfrage (Ludger Heid, 177–191). Der Sklarek-Skandal 1929 und die sozialdemokratische Reaktion (Donna Harsch, 193–213). Die Judenfrage in der Entstehungsphase des Reichsbanners Schwarz-Rot-Gold (Jacob Toury, 215–235).]

29015 KANARFOGL, EPHRAIM: *Unanimity, majority, and communal government in Ashkenaz during the High Middle Ages: a reassessment*. [In]: American Academy for Jewish Research. Proceedings, Vol. 58, Jerusalem, New York, 1992. Pp. 79–106.

29016 KATZ, JACOB: *Halacha in straits; obstacles to Orthodoxy at its inception*. [In Hebrew]. Jerusalem: Magnes Press; Hebrew Univ., 1992. 287 pp. [Particularly on 19th-century Germany.]

29017 KOCHAN, LIONEL: *The Jewish renaissance and some of its discontents*. Manchester; New York: Manchester Univ. Press, 1992. 125 pp., notes. [Author compares the recent (post-war) renaissance in Jewish history with earlier periods, e.g. the Moses Mendelssohn era. He warns against seeing modern-day Jewish history only in the context of the Holocaust.]

29018 *Landjudentum im süddeutschen und Bodenseeraum*. Wissenschaftliche Tagung zur Eröffnung des Jüdischen Museum Hohenems vom 9. bis 11. April 1991. Veranstaltet vom Vorarlberger Landesarchiv. Dornbirn: Vorarlberger Verlagsanstalt, 1992. 234 pp. [Incl.: Die Entdeckung der Landjuden. Stand und Probleme ihrer Erforschung am Beispiel Südwestdeutschlands (Monika Richarz, 11–21). Landjudentum und Emanzipation 1831–1850: ein Gegensatz? (Uri Kaufmann, 102–113). 'Erhebend für den Freund des Fortschritts' (Harald

Walser, 124–138). Alltagsleben auf dem Land (Klaus Guth, 190–196). Further contributions are listed according to subject.]

29019 LOTTER, FRIEDRICH: *Zur Geschichte der christlich-jüdischen Beziehungen im Mittelalter, Bericht über neuere Literatur*. [In]: Aschkenas, Jg. 2, Wien, 1992. Pp. 259–272.

29020 LOTTER, FRIEDRICH: *Ist Hermann von Schedas Opusculum De conversione sua eine Fälschung?* [In]: Aschkenas, Jg. 2, Wien, 1992. Pp. 207–218. [On the autobiography of Jehuda ben David ha-Levi, who converted to Christianity in the 12th cent.]

29021 LOTTER, FRIEDRICH: *Talmudisches Recht in den Judenprivilegien Heinrichs IV.? Zu Ausbildung und Entwicklung des Marktschutzrechts im frühen und hohen Mittelalter*. [In]: Archiv für Kulturgeschichte, Bd. 72, H. 1, Köln, 1990. Pp. 24–61, footnotes.

29022 LOWENSTEIN, STEVEN MARK: *The mechanics of change: essays in the social history of German Jewry*. Atlanta, GA: Scholars Press, 1992. IX, 234 pp., maps, tabs. (Brown Judaic studies, 246).

29023 MARCUS, IVAN: *A pious community and doubt: quiddush ha-shem in Ashkenaz and the story of R. Amnon of Mainz*. [In]: Studien zur jüdischen Geschichte und Soziologie. Festschrift Julius Carlebach [see No. 29561]. Pp. 97–114.

29024 MAURER, TRUDE: *Die Entwicklung der jüdischen Minderheit in Deutschland (1780–1933). Neuere Forschungen und offene Fragen*. 4. Sonderheft. Tübingen: Niemeyer, 1992. 195 pp., footnotes, bibl. (181–190), index (persons and authors; places, 191–195). (Internationales Archiv für Sozialgeschichte der deutschen Literatur, 4). [Historiographical analysis of books and articles publ. between 1981 and 1991, arranged under the sections: Religiöse Entwicklung (13–27). Bildung – Akkulturation – Selbstbesinnung (28–59). Bevölkerungsentwicklung und Siedlungsweise (60–69). Landjudentum (70–84). Wirtschaftliche Entwicklung und Sozialstruktur (85–100). Die Juden im politischen Leben (101–112). Politische Organisationen der Juden (113–142). Die jüdische Frau und die jüdische Familie (143–156). Teilintegration und Ausbildung einer deutsch-jüdischen Subkultur (157–166). Die jüdische Minderheit: Akkulturation und Selbstbewahrung (167–179).]

29025 *'Mein Vater war portugiesischer Jude...'. Die sefardische Einwanderung nach Norddeutschland um 1600 und ihre Auswirkungen auf unsere Kultur*. Hrsg. von Sabine Kruse und Bernt Engelmann. Göttingen: Steidl, 1992. 224 pp., illus., ports., facsims. [Exhibition catalogue of an exhibition held in Lübeck in Dec. 1992. Incl. texts by Bernt Engelmann and Sabine Kruse on Sephardic Jews as well as on Jews presumed to have a sephardic family background, incl. Baruch Spinoza, Uriel da Costa, Joseph Salomo Delmedigo, Rodrigo de Castro, Jacob Sasportas, the Texeira and the Hinrichsen families, Johann Friedrich Struensee, Henriette and Marcus Herz, Heinrich Heine, Johann Jacoby, Leopold Ullstein, James Israel, Albert Ballin, Max M. Warburg, Rosa Luxemburg. Further contributions are: Vier sefardische Schriftsteller zwischen Glückstadt und Hamburg (Michael Studemund-Halévy, 97–104). Die heimlichen Spinozisten in Altona (Stefan Winkle, 121–138). 'Sehr viel von meiner mütterlichen Familie' (H. Heine) (Joseph A. Kruse, 162–173). Das medizinische Werk James Israels (Fritz Schulze-Seemann, 197–200).]

29026 MEYER, MICHAEL A.: *Jüdische Identität in der Moderne*. Aus dem Amerikan. von Anne Ruth Frank-Strauss. Erw. Ausg. Frankfurt am Main: Jüdischer Verlag, 1992. 135 pp. [For orig. American edn., publ. in 1990, see No. 27526/YB XXXVI.] [Cf.: Mutter Zion: Michael A. Meyer über jüdische Identität im Horizont neuzeitlich bewegter Geschichte (Manfred Seidler) [in]: Frankfurter Allgemeine Zeitung, Nr. 63, Frankfurt am Main, 16. März 1993, p. 15.]

29027 MEYER, MICHAEL A.: *The German Jews: some perspective on their history*. Syracuse University: The B.G. Rudolph lectures in Judaic Studies, No. 28, 1991. 16 pp.

29028 MEYER, MICHAEL A.: *Tzmichat ha-yehudi ha-moderni: zehut yehudit ve-tarbut Europat be-Germania, 1749–1824*. Jerusalem: Carmel, 1990. 297 pp. [A Hebrew transl. of The origins of the modern Jew: Jewish identity and European culture in Germany, 1749–1824; for American orig. edn., publ. in 1967, see No. 6416/YB XIII.]

29029 MOSSE, WERNER E.: *Integration and identity in Imperial Germany: towards a typology*. [In]: LBI Year Book XXXVII, London. Pp. 83–93, footnotes. [On the Wallich, the Salomonsohn, the Tietz families, the Hirsch family of Halberstadt and on Paul Singer.]

29030 MOSSE, WERNER E./POHL, HANS, Hrsg.: *Jüdische Unternehmer in Deutschland im 19. und 20. Jahrhundert*. Zeitschrift für Unternehmensgeschichte. Beiheft 64. Stuttgart: Franz Steiner, 1992. 375 pp., footnotes, tabs. [Papers presented at a conference organised by the Friedrich-Naumann-Stiftung and the Leo Baeck Institute in Königswinter, April 2–4, 1989.] [Cont.: Vorwort (Werner E. Mosse/Hans Pohl, 7–8); contrib. are arranged under the following sections: I. Jüdische Unternehmer im internationalen Vergleich: Einführung (Jürgen Kocka, 9–10). Entrepreneurship of religious and ethnic minorities (Nachum T. Gross, 11– 23.) Jewish entrepreneurs in England, c. 1850–c. 1950 (Youssef Cassis, 24–35). Jüdische Unternehmer und Prozess der Verbürgerlichung in der Habsburger Monarchie (19.-20. Jahrhundert) (Viktor Karady, 36–53). Jewish entrepreneurship in Germany 1820–1935 (Werner E.Mosse, 54–66). II. Jüdische Unternehmer in ausgewählten Wirtschaftsbereichen. Einführung (Hans Pohl, 67–77). Jüdische Bankiers in Deutschland bis 1932 (Rolf Walter, 78–99). Jüdische Unternehmer in der deutschen Schwerindustrie 1850–1933 (Toni Pierenkemper, 100–118). Jüdische Unternehmer und die deutschen Eisenbahnen (1835– 1933) (Hans Jaeger, 119–131). Jüdische Unternehmer in der deutschen Textilindustrie (Rolf Walter, 132–152). Jüdische Unternehmer in der deutschen chemischen und elektrotechnischen Industrie 1850–1933 (Harm G. Schröter, 153–176). Jüdische Unternehmer im deutschen Groß- und Einzelhandel dargestellt an ausgewählten Beispielen (Konrad Fuchs, 177–195). Der jüdische Beitrag zum deutschen Presse- und Verlagswesen (Kurt Koszyk, 196–218). III. Die soziale Stellung jüdischer Unternehmer im regionalen Vergleich. Einführung (Wolfram Fischer, 219–224). Die soziale Stellung der jüdischen Wirtschaftselite im wilhelminischen Berlin (Dolores L. Augustine, 225–246). Soziales Verhalten jüdischer Unternehmer in Frankfurt und Köln zwischen 1860 und 1933 (Hansjoachim Henning, 247–270). Die soziale Stellung der jüdischen Händler auf dem Lande am Beispiel Südwestdeutschlands (Monika Richarz, 271–283). Jüdisches Mäzenatentum für die Wissenschaft in Deutschland (Wilhelm Treue, 284–308). IV. Jüdisches Unternehmertum in der deutschen Politik. Einführung (Werner E. Mosse, 309–312). Politische Einstellung und politisches Engagement jüdischer Unternehmer (Peter Pulzer, 313–331). Jüdische Unternehmer zwischen wirtschaftsliberalem Laissez-faire, sozialliberalem Emanzipationsdenken und industriekonservativer Sammlungsbewegung (Hans Dieter Hellige, 332–355). Rathenau: ein liberaler Unternehmer? (Hartmut Pogge von Strandmann, 356–365). Walther Rathenaus Entwicklung vom Neokonservatismus zum 'corporate collectivism'. Entgegnung auf den Beitrag Pogge von Strandmanns (Hans Dieter Hellige, 366–370). Stellungnahme zu H.D. Helliges Replik (Hartmut Pogge von Strandmann, 371– 372). Überblick über einige Hauptaspekte der Diskussion (Hans Pohl, 373–375).]

—— *Neues Lexikon des Judentums.* Hrsg. von Julius H. Schoeps. [See No. 29266.]

29031 PERTSCH, DIETMAR: *Jüdische Lebenswelten in Spielfilmen und Fernsehspielen. Filme zur Geschichte der Juden von ihren Anfängen bis zur Emanzipation 1871.* Tübingen: Niemeyer, 1992. 272 pp., illus., footnotes, tabs., bibl. (238–266), index (of films and television productions, 267–272). (Medien in Forschung + Unterricht: Ser. A, Bd. 35). [Incl. the sections: 3.Luther ohne Juden. 4. Die Legende vom Golem in Literatur und Film. 5. Dreimal 'Jud Süß': Die filmische Verwertung der Literatur über den Hoffaktor Joseph Süß Oppenheimer. 6. Spielfilme und Fernsehspiele zur jüdischen Emanzipation im 18. und 19. Jahrhundert. 7. Begegnung mit Tewjes Welt im Spiegel jiddischer Filme.]

29032 PULZER, PETER: *New books on German-Jewish history.* Review article. [In]: Central European History, Vol. 24, Nos. 2&3, Atlanta, GA, 1991. Pp. 176–186, footnotes.

29033 PULZER, PETER: *Jews and the German State. The political history of a minority, 1848–1933.* Oxford: Blackwell, 1992. 370 pp. [Cf.: Different, ignoble and alien (James J. Sheehan) [in]: Times Literary Supplement, London, July 31, 1992, p. 8.]

29034 RAPHAEL, CHAIM: *Minyan: 10 Jewish lives in 20 centuries of history.* Malibu, CA: Joseph Simon/Pangloss Press, 1992. 127 pp., illus. [One is Glückel von Hameln.]

29035 RICHARZ, MONIKA: *In Familie, Handel und Salon. Jüdische Frauen vor und nach der Emanzipation der deutschen Juden.* [In]: Frauengeschichte – Geschlechtergeschichte. Hrsg.: Karin Hausen/Heide Wunder. Frankfurt am Main; New York: Campus, 1992. Pp. 57– 66, notes. (Reihe Geschichte und Geschlechter, hrsg. von Gisela Bock, Karin Hausen und Heide Wunder, Bd.1.)

29036 SCHUMANN, PETER: *Jüdische Deutsche im Kaiserreich und in der Weimarer Republik.* [In]: Geschichte in Wissenschaft und Unterricht, Jg. 43, Stuttgart. Pp. 32–40, footnotes. [Cf.: Kaiserreich und Weimarer Republik – Horte innigster deutsch-jüdischer Symbiose? (Stefan Rohrbacher) [In]: Geschichte in Wissenschaft und Unterricht, Jg. 43, Stuttgart. Pp. 681– 687, footnotes. This critical review is followed by the author's reply: Erwiderung (688–693 =2 pp., wrong paging).]

29037 *Second Chance. Two centuries of German-speaking Jews in the United Kingdom.* Eds.: Werner E. Mosse (Co-ordinating ed.), Julius Carlebach, Gerhard Hirschfeld, Aubrey Newman,

Arnold Paucker, Peter Pulzer. Preface by Claus Moser. Tübingen: Mohr, 1991. XII, 654 pp., footnotes, index of names. (Schriftenreihe wissenschaftlicher Abhandlungen des Leo Baeck Instituts 48.) [For full listing of contributions see No. 27975/YB XXXVII; reviews (cont.): Jüdische Emigration in Großbritannien (Horst R. Sassin) [in]: liberal, Jg. 34, H. 3, Bonn, Aug. 1992, pp. 104–106. Heimisch in der Fremde (Rüdiger Görner) [in]: 'NZZ', Nr. 189, Zürich, 17 Aug. 1992, p. 25.]

29038 SORKIN, DAVID: *Jewish emancipation in Central and Western Europe in the eighteenth and nineteenth centuries.* [In]: The Jewish Enigma. An enduring people. Ed.: David Englander. London: Peter Halban, 1992. Pp. 81–110. [Publ. for the Open University et al.]

29039 SORKIN, DAVID: *Jews, the enlightenment and religious toleration. Some reflections.* [In]: LBI Year Book XXXVII, London. Pp. 3–16, footnotes.

29040 SORKIN, DAVID: *The transformation of German Jewry, 1780–1840.* Oxford; New York: Oxford Univ. Press, 1992. 262 pp., notes, bibl. (Studies in Jewish history.) [For orig. 1987 hardback edn. and further details see No. 23906/YB XXXIII.]

29041 STEINBACH, PETER: *Zur deutsch-jüdischen Beziehungsgeschichte im 19. und 20. Jahrhundert.* [In]: Das Parlament, Jg. 42, Bonn, 3. Jan. 1992. Pp. 3–13.

29042 STRAUSS, HERBERT A.: *Emancipation history – limits of revisionism in the post-Holocaust period.* Comments on the papers by Arno Herzig, Michael Graetz, Werner E. Mosse and Wolfgang Benz. [In]: LBI Year Book XXXVII, London. Pp. 103–108, footnotes. [The papers to which these comments refer were presented at the 38th Versammlung Deutscher Historiker in Bochum on 27th September 1990; see Nos. 29007, 29012, 29029, 29926.]

29043 TA-SCHMA, ISRAEL M.: *Handelsbeziehungen zwischen Juden und Christen an Sonntagen im mittelalterlichen Deutschland und in der Provence.* [In]: Hebräische Beiträge zur Wissenschaft des Judentums Deutsch Angezeigt, Jg. VI, Heidelberg, 1990. P.1.

29044 TA-SHMA, ISRAEL M.: *The attitude to aliya to Eretz Israel in medieval German Jewry.* [In Hebrew]. [In]: Shalem; Studies in the History of the Jews in Eretz Israel, Vol. 6, Jerusalem, 1992. Pp. 315–318.

29045 TA-SHMA, ISRAEL M.: *Early Franco-German ritual and custom.* [In Hebrew]. Jerusalem: Magnes Press; The Hebrew Univ., 1992. 359 pp.

29046 TURA, PEREZ: *'Nomen est omen'. Anmerkungen zu jüdischen Vor- und Familiennamen.* [In]: Tribüne, Jg. 31, H. 121, Frankfurt am Main, 1992. Pp. 176–181.

29047 VERMAN, MARK: *The books of contemplation: medieval Jewish mystical sources.* Albany: State Univ. of New York Press, 1992. 270 pp., bibl. (249–252). [Incl. chaps.: Scholem's studies of early Cabbala; Scholem's historiography and R. Isaac Cohen's legends.]

29048 WEISBERGER, ADAM M.: *Marginality and messianism: German Jews and socialism, 1871–1918.* [In]: Politics and Society, Vol. 20, No. 2, Newbury Park; London, June 1992. Pp. 225–256.

29049 WEISS, NELLY: *Die Herkunft jüdischer Familiennamen: Herkunft, Typen, Geschichte.* Frankfurt am Main; New York: Lang, 1992. 241 pp. [A dictionary of names.]

29050 WIESEMANN, FALK: *Jewish burials in Germany. Between tradition, the enlightenment and the authorities.* [In]: LBI Year Book XXXVII, London. Pp. 17–31, footnotes, illus.

29051 WOLLMERSHÄUSER, FRIEDRICH R.: *Nachsteuer von wegziehenden Juden aus dem Deutschordensgebiet.* [In]: Genealogie, Bd. 20, H. 10, Neustadt (Aisch), 1990. Pp. 342–344. [On documents from the Staatsarchiv Ludwigsburg.]

—— *Zedaka. Jüdische Sozialarbeit im Wandel der Zeit.* 75 Jahre Zentralwohlfahrtsstelle der Juden in Deutschland 1917–1992. [See No. 29647.]

29052 ZIMMERMANN, MOSHE: *German Jews and the emigration from Russia.* [In]: Organizing rescue: national Jewish solidarity in the modern period [see No. 29646]. Pp. 127–140, notes.

Linguistics/Western Yiddish

29053 BAR-EL, JOSEPH: *Sefer Pitronot Rashi.* Tel-Aviv: Publ. House, Tel-Aviv Univ., 1992. 144 pp. [Annotated transcription of the 13th-century Rashi Yiddish manuscript with the editor's introduction.]

29054 DAXELMÜLLER, CHRISTOPH: *Jüdischer Geschicht-Roman von dem grossen König Arturo in Engelland und dem tapffern Helden Wieduwilt.* (Ein schin ma'aße fun kinig artiß hof): Hrsg. von Johann Christoph Wagenseil (1633–1705). Königsberg 1699. [In]: Theodor Brüggemann/Otto Brunken: Handbuch zur Kinder- und Jugendliteratur. Von 1570–1750. Stuttgart: Klett, 1991. Pp. 942–961.

29055 DREESSEN, WULF-OTTO: [Art.] *Schmuelbuch.* [In]: Verfasserlexikon. Die deutsche Literatur des Mittelalters. Bd. 8. Berlin; New York: de Gruyter, 1992. Sp. 769–771.

29056 FUKS-MANSFELD, RENA: *West- en Oost-Jiddisch op het toneel in Amsterdam aan het einde van de achtiende eeuw.* [In]: Studia Rosenthaliana, Vol. 26, Number 1/2, Assen, 1992. Pp. 91–96.

29057 GABEL, GERNOT U.: *The Bibliotheque Medem for Yiddish language and literature in Paris.* [In]: Judaica Librarianship, Vol. 5, No. 2, West Orange, NJ, 1990/1991. Pp. 228–229.

—— HIRHAGER, ULRIKE/BIRKHAN, HELMUT: *Zu den jüdisch-deutschen Texten des Mittelalters.* [See in No. 28992.]

29058 HOWARD, JOHN A.: *Fortunatus. Die Bearbeitung und Umschrift eines spätmittelalterlichen deutschen Prosaromans für jüdisches Publikum.* Würzburg: 1991. 1 vol. (Quellen und Forschungen zur europäischen Ethnologie, 11.)

29059 IWASAKI, EIJIRO/SHICHIJI, YOSHINORI, eds.: *Begegnung mit dem 'Fremden': Grenzen – Traditionen – Vergleiche.* Akten des VII. Kongresses der Internationalen Vereinigung für Germanische Sprach- und Literaturwissenschaft Tokyo 1990. Bd. 11. München, 1991. [Incl. the contributions of the 'Sektion Jiddisch'; those dealing with Western Yiddish are: Das Hiobbild des deutschen Judentums im 16. Jahrhundert (Walter Röll). Das 'ma'asseh-buh': Platz der jiddischen Literatur in der deutschen Umwelt (Astrid Starck). Namen germanischer Herkunft und hebräisches Schriftsystem (Klaus Cuno). Das ältere Jiddisch als Gegenstand sprachpragmatischer Forschung (Erika Timm). Die Bedeutung des Rätoromanischen für die Entstehung der jiddischen Sprache (Paul Wexler).]

29060 *Jiddistik-Mitteilungen: Jiddistik in deutschsprachigen Ländern.* Nr. 7 & 8. Hrsg. von der Jiddistik im Fachbereich Sprach- und Literaturwissenschaften der Universität Trier (Postfach 3825, 5500 Trier). Red.: Gabriele Brünnel. Trier, April & Nov. 1992. 2 issues, notes, bibl.

29061 KATZENELSON, JIZCHAK: *Dos lid funm ojsgehargetin jidischn folk. Das Lied vom letzten Juden in der Nachdichtung von Hermann Adler.* Mit einem Nachwort von Manfred Richter. Berlin: Hentrich, 1992. 168 pp. [First publ. in 1951.]

29062 KIEFER, ULRIKE: *Sprachenpolitik gegenüber fremdsprachigen Minderheiten im 19. Jahrhundert: Jiddisch.* [In]: Das 19. Jahrhundert. Jahrbuch 1990. Berlin, 1991. Pp. 172–177.

29063 *The language and culture atlas of Ashkenazic Jewry.* Volume I: *Historical and theoretical foundations.* Ed.: Yivo Institute for Jewish Research. Prepared and published under the aegis of an Editorial Collegium Vera Baviskar, Marvin Herzog (Editor-in-Chief) [et al.]. Tübingen: Niemeyer, 1992. 136 pp., footnotes, 81 maps (49–131, index), bibl. (132–136). [Incl.: Obits. (Uriel Weinreich; Hebrew transl. at end of book, pp. 1*; Vera Baviskar). Introduction to the language and culture atlas of Ashkenazic Jewry (1–5). Assembly of the data (6–9). The systematic dialectology of Yiddish (15–45). A handbook for the interviewer (in Hebrew, at back of book, pp. *2–*8).] [Also on Western Yiddish.] [Cf.: Besprechung (Erika Timm) [in]: Jiddistik-Mitteilungen, Nr. 8, Trier, Nov. 1992, pp. 19–33.]

29064 RHEIN, VALERIE: *Jiddische Literatur für die jüdische Frau. Handschriften und Drucke aus dem späten Mittelalter und dem frühen 18. Jahrhundert. Eine Übersicht.* Basel, Lizentiatsarbeit 1992. 1 vol.

—— SIMON, BETTINA: *Die Sprache der Juden im Mittelalter und ihre Literatur.* [See in No. 28992.]

29065 THOMMEN, DIETER: *Das Jiddische ('Jüdisch-Deutsche') im Surbtal und im Bodenseekreis.* [In]: Landjudentum im süddeutschen und Bodenseeraum [see No. 29018]. Pp. 87–91.

29066 WARNOCK, ROBERT: *Concordance to the early Yiddish ottava rima epic 'Widiwilst' (Fun kinig Artis hof').* Providence, 1992. [Obtainable from the author or the Jiddistik of the Universität Trier, on paper or on disk.]

—— WEISSLER, CHAVA: *Prayers in Yiddish and the religious world of Ashkenazic women.* [See in No. 28990.]

B. Communal and Regional History

1. Germany

29067 AACHEN. LEPPER, HERBERT: *Von der Emanzipation zum Holocaust 1801–1942. Die Judendokumentation des Stadtarchivs Aachen.* [In]: Der Archivar, Jg. 45, H. 1, Düsseldorf, Feb. 1992. Pp. 52–59.

29068 AHRWEILER. KLEIN, HANS-GEORG: *Die Judengasse zu Ahrweiler.* Heimat-Jahrbuch Kreis

Ahrweiler, Jg. 49, Monschau, 1992. Pp. 50–54, illus, notes. [In same issue: WARNECKE, HANS: *Der Schleier über dem Vorhang. Der Thora-Vorhang in der Ahrweiler Synagoge.* Pp. 82–83, illus. JANTA, LEONHARD: *'Man konnte uns aus der Heimat vertreiben, aber man konnte die Heimat nicht aus uns vertreiben.* Erinnerungen ehemaliger jüdischer Mitbürgerinnen aus Bad Neuenahr und Ahrweiler. Pp. 84–89.]

29069 ALDENHOVEN. DOVERN, WILLI: *Die jüdische Bevölkerung in der Bürgermeisterei Aldenhoven 1799–1935.* Jülich: Verlag des Jülicher Geschichtsvereins, 1990. 163 pp., illus. (Veröffentlichungen des Jülicher Geschichtsvereins, 12.) [Cf.: Besprechung (Dieter Kastner) [in]: Annalen des Historischen Vereins für den Niederrhein, H. 195, Pulheim, 1992, pp. 355–356.]

29070 — PANKOKE, WERNER: *Hinterlassenschaften von Landjuden: Alltagsleben im Spiegel von Nachlassinventaren aus Aldenhoven (Krs. Jülich) 1820–1867.* Siegburg: Rheinlandia-Verlag, 1991. II, 118 pp. (Ortstermine, Bd. 1) [Cf.: Besprechung (Stefan Rohrbacher) [in]: Annalen des Historischen Vereins für den Niederrhein, H. 195, Pulheim, 1992, pp. 354–355.]

29071 — PANKOKE, WERNER: *Zwei Eheverträge Aldenhovener Juden aus den Jahren 1821 und 1850.* [In]: Neue Beiträge zur Jülicher Geschichte, 3/1992. Teil 1. Jülich, 1992. Pp. 162–168, footnotes.

29072 ALTONA. KÜNZL, HANNNELORE: *Zur künstlerischen Gestaltung des portugiesisch-jüdischen Friedhofs in Hamburg Altona.* [In]: Studien zur jüdischen Geschichte und Soziologie. Festschrift Julius Carlebach [see No. 29561]. Pp. 165–174.

29073 — MARWEDEL, GÜNTER: *Juden in Altona zwischen Isolation und Integration.* [In]: Jahrbuch 27. Altonaer Museum in Hamburg. Norddeutsches Landesmuseum. Hamburg, 1992. Pp. 29–56.

29074 AROLSEN. WINKELMANN, MICHAEL: *'Auf einmal sind sie weggemacht'. Lebensbilder Arolser Juden im 20. Jahrundert.* Eine Dokumentation. Unter Mitarbeit von Katrin Burth [et al.]. Kassel: Verlag Gesamthochschul-Bibliothek Kassel, 1992. 428 pp., notes (386–408), illus., facsims., docs., list of names, indexes, bibl. [Refers also to Nazi period.]

29075 BADEN. BERNER, HERBERT: *'Das Hegöw, ein kleines, aber über die Maßen wol erbauen fruchtbar Ländlein' (Sebastian Münster).* Ausgewählte Aufsätze. Festgabe zu seinem 70. Geburtstag. Hrsg.: Franz Götz. Sigmaringen: Thorbecke, 1991. [Incl.: Gailinger Purim – jüdische Fastnacht im Hegau. Ein Beitrag zum jüdischen Gemeindeleben und zur Emanzipation der Juden in Baden. Pp. 470 ff.]

29076 BAIERSDORF. *Aus der jüdischen Gemeinde der Stadt Baiersdorf.* Hrsg.: Trägerverein Jüdisches Regionalmuseum Mittelfranken in Fürth und Schnaittach. Fürth: Jüdisches Regionalmuseum, 1992. 107 pp., port., illus., tabs., glossary, bibl. [Incl.: Hommage an eine ungewöhnliche Frau: Glückel von Hameln und ihre Beziehungen zu Baiersdorf. Hoch hinaus!: Prof. Dr. h.c. Gottfried Merzbacher. Eine erfolgreiche Familie: Die Seligmann. Von der Kleinkinderbewahranstalt zum modernen Kindergarten: Die David und Fanny Seligmann'sche Stiftung. Auflösung und Ende der jüdischen Gemeinde in Baiersdorf (Ilse Sponsel, 9–15; 46–48; 49–55; 56–64; 85–97). Eine emanzipierte Frau? Die Denkwürdigkeiten der Glückel von Hameln (1646/47–1719) (Monika Berthold, 16–21). Rabbiner David ben Joel Dispeck (Adolf Eckstein, 22–25). Ein jüdischer Maler aus Baiersdorf: David Ottensooser (Stephanie Orfali, 26–33). Zum 180. Geburtstag: Lebensspuren des Rabbiners, Bankiers, Numismatikers, Bibliophilen und Mäzens Abraham Merzbacher (1812–1885) (Wolfgang Oppelt, 34–45). Familie Gerngros in Baiersdorf. Ludwig von Gerngros. Wilhelm Ritter von Gerngros. Zur gesellschaftlichen Stellung der Juden in Baiersdorf um die Jahrhundertwende (Horst Gemeinhardt, 65–79). Ein Besuch am 'guten Ort': der Judenfriedhof in Baiersdorf (Günter Reim, 98–102).]

29077 BAMBERG. FUCHS, MARGA/HORN, CHRISTINE: *Die jüdische Minderheit in Bamberg. Schutzjuden. Staatsbürger mosaischen Glaubens. Rassefeinde.* Hrsg. vom Stadtarchiv Bamberg durch Robert Zink [et al.]. Bamberg: Selbstverlag der Stadt Bamberg, 1992. 29 pp., 30 docs., 29 pp.(text), in folder. (Darstellungen und Quellen zur Geschichte Bambergs, 4.) [Deals also with the Nazi period; incl. sample questions for school teachers (pp. 27–29).]

29078 — LOEBL, HERBERT: *Der Kompetenzstreit um den 'Judenschutz' im Fürstbistum Bamberg.* [In]: 128. Bericht des Historischen Vereins Bamberg. Bamberg 1992. Pp. 119–135, docs.

—— BAVARIA. FASSL, PETER: *Geschichte und Kultur der Juden in Schwaben.* [See No. 29174.]

29079 — SCHWIERZ, ISRAEL: *Steinerne Zeugen jüdischen Lebens. Eine Dokumentation.* 2. überarb. Aufl. Hrsg.: Bayerische Landeszentrale für polit. Bildungsarbeit in Zusammenarbeit mit der Bayer. Verlagsanstalt Bamberg. Bamberg: Bayer. Verlagsanstalt, 1992. 368pp., illus., bibl., list of places, of cemeteries, glossary. [On cemeteries and still existing former synagogues,

Jewish schools and houses once owned by Jews, also memorials; incl. Franconia, Schwaben, Oberpfalz.]

29080 — WIESEMANN, FALK: *Zum Religionswesen der Landjuden in Bayern im 19. Jahrhundert.* [In]: Landjudentum im Süddeutschen- und Bodenseeraum [see No. 29018]. Pp. 114–123, notes.

29081 BECHTHOLD-COMFORTY, BEATE: *Spätzle und Tscholent. Aspekte schwäbisch-jüdischer Eßkultur.* [In]: Menora, Bd. 3, München, 1992. Pp.121–143.

29082 BERLICHINGEN. BERLINGER, SIMON: *Synagoge und Herrschaft. Vierhundert Jahre jüdische Landgemeinde Berlichingen.* Sigmaringendorf: regio Verlag Glock und Lutz, 1991. 137 pp., illus., bibl. notes. [Incl.: Zum Geleit (Paul Sauer, 7–8; on the author, b. 1914 in Berlichingen, teacher and cantor, emigr. after the November Pogrom illegally to Palestine via the Netherlands, lives in Haifa. Book deals also with the Nazi period.]

— BERLIN. [See also in No. 29647.]

29083 —*Bild und Selbstbild der Juden Berlins zwischen Aufklärung und Romantik. Beiträge zu einer Tagung.* Hrsg. von Marianne Awerbuch und Stefi Jersch-Wenzel. Berlin: Colloquium, 1992. 246 pp., footnotes. (Einzelveröffentlichungen der Historischen Kommission zu Berlin, Bd. 75.) [Based on a conference organised by the Historische Kommission zu Berlin in autumn 1988; cont. the following contributions (titles partly condensed): Der wirtschaftliche und politische Status der Juden in Brandenburg-Preußen im Zeitalter des Merkantilismus (Wolfgang Ribbe, 1–20). Moses Mendelssohns Judentum (Marianne Awerbuch, 21–42). Die 'natürliche' Toleranz und die unendliche Bemühung der Vernunft, sie zu begründen (Gerhard Bauer, 43–58; on Lessing and Nathan der Weise). Über die bürgerliche Verbesserung der Juden: Christian Wilhelm Dohm und seine Gegner (Horst Möller, 81–106). Soziale Aspekte der Krise des Berliner Judentums 1780 bis 1830 (Steven M. Lowenstein, 81–106). Aufklärung und Schulbildung in Berlin: Friedländers Lesebuch [für jüdische Kinder] (Zohar Shavit, 107–120, bibl.). Emanzipation durch Geselligkeit. Die Salons jüdischer Frauen in Berlin zwischen 1780 und 1830 (Petra Wilhelmy-Dollinger, 121–138). Die Juden im gesellschaftlichen Gefüge Berlins um 1800 (Stefi Jersch-Wenzel, 139–154). Befürworter und Gegner der preußischen Judenemanzipation im Spiegel der Denkschriften und Gesetzgebung (Peter Baumgart, 155–178). Sulamith und Jedidja oder Jeremia Heinemann, der Erstdruck von Mendelssohns Psalmenkommentar in der 'beliebten Zeitschrift Jedidja'. Ein Fund in der Herzog August Bibliothek zu Wolfenbüttel (Friedrich Niewöhner, 179–210). Renaissance des Judentums im 19. Jahrhundert: 'Der Verein für Cultur und Wissenschaft der Juden' 1819 bis 1824 (Michael Graetz, 211–228). The spiritual life of Berlin Jewry following the edict of 1823 (Michael A. Meyer, 229–243).]

29084 — ETZOLD, ALFRED [et al.]: *Die jüdischen Friedhöfe in Berlin.* 4., verbesserte und erweiterte Auflage. Von Alfred Etzold, Joachim Fait, Peter Kirchner, Heinz Knobloch. Berlin: Henschel, 1991. 168 pp., illus., maps, bibl., index (persons). [Cf.: Besprechung (Marina Sassenberg) [in]: Tribüne, Jg. 31, H. 123, Frankfurt am Main, 1992, pp. 228–229.]

29085 — GOTTSCHALK, WOLFGANG: *Die Friedhöfe der Jüdischen Gemeinde zu Berlin.* Berlin: Argon, 1992. 111 pp., index (names), bibl., illus.

29086 — HAHN, BARBARA: *Wanderungen zwischen Osten und Westen – oder: Wo liegt Berlin?* [In]: Nach Osten. Verdeckte Spuren nationalsozialistischer Verbrechen [see No. 29485]. Pp. 71–86. [Deals with Eastern Jews in Berlin.]

— HERTZ, DEBORAH: *Emancipation through intermarriage in Old Berlin.* [See No. 28990.]

29087 — HOLZER, WILLI: *Jüdische Schulen in Berlin: am Beispiel der privaten Volksschule der jüdischen Gemeinde Rykestrasse.* Berlin: Hentrich, 1992. 120 pp., illus. (Reihe deutsche Vergangenheit, Bd. 54. Stätten der Geschichte Berlins.) [Covers also Nazi period.]

29088 — KNOBLAUCH, G./HOLLIN, F., eds.: *Die Neue Synagoge in Berlin.* 1867 (Reprint) Berlin: Hentrich, 1992. Stiftung 'Neue Synagoge Berlin-Centrum Judaicum'. Mit einem Geleitwort von Heinz Galinski sowie einem Beitrag von Hermann Simon. [27]pp., illus., plans [ca. 100 pp.], illus., plans. (Reihe deutsche Vergangenheit, Bd. 70. Stätten der Geschichte Berlins.) [Reprint of the edn., publ. in 1867 by Ernst & Korn, Berlin.]

29089 — KÖHLER, ROSEMARIE/KRATZ-WHAN, ULRICH: *Der jüdische Friedhof Schönhauser Allee.* Berlin: Haude und Spener, 1992. 192 pp., illus.

29090 — LAUSCH, HANS: *Abraham Wolff 'Rechenmeister'. Ein bedeutender Jude der Aufklärungszeit.* [In]: Aschkenas, Jg. 2, Wien, 1992. Pp. 227–238.

— LUCAS, FRANZ D./FRANK, HEIKE: *Michael Sachs – der konservative Mittelweg: Leben und Werk des Berliner Rabbiners zur Zeit der Emanzipation.* [See No. 29597.]

29091 — NACHAMA, ANDREAS/SIMON, HERMANN: *Jüdische Grabstätten und Friedhöfe in Berlin. Eine Dokumentation.* Mit Beiträgen von Alfred Etzold, Heinrich Simon. Berlin: Hentrich, 1992. 194 pp., illus., index (persons). (Reihe Deutsche Vergangenheit. Stätten der Geschichte Berlins, Bd. 67.)

29092 — *Die neue Synagoge Berlin.* Eine Dokumentation zum Wiederaufbau. Textbeitrag: Hermann Simon. Gießen: Alfred Cramer, [1992?]. 20 [16] pp., illus. [On the reconstruction of the Oranienburger Strasse synagogue.]

29093 — PAUL, ARNO: *Die Formierung des jüdischen Theaterpublikums in Berlin im späten 18. Jahrhundert.* [In]: Theatralia Judaica [see No. 30017]. Pp. 64–84.

29094 — SCHEER, REGINA: *Ahawah. Das vergessene Haus. Spurensuche in der Berliner Auguststrasse.* Berlin: Aufbau, 1992. 318 pp., illus. [On the history of a former Berlin Jewish hospital, later children's home and during the Second World War an assembly place for deportees.]

29095 — SIMON, HERMANN: *The New Synagogue, Berlin Past – Present – Future.* Berlin: Hentrich, 1992. 48 pp., illus. [On the reconstruction of the synagogue in the Oranienburger Strasse, which was begun on Nov. 9, 1988.]

29096 — SIMON, HERMANN: *Eine vergessene Synagoge in Berlin.* [In]: Menora, Bd. 3, München, 1992. Pp.256–264, notes. [On a synagogue officially opened in 1908 in the prison of Plötzensee near Berlin.]

29096 — SIMON, HERMANN: *Majestäten in Berliner Synagogen.* [In]: Deutsch-jüdische Geschichte im 19. und 20. Jahrhundert [see No. 29601]. Pp. 175–210.

29098 BOBENHEIM-ROXHEIM. KUKATZKI, BERNHARD/JACOBY, MARIO: *Der jüdische Friedhof in Bobenheim-Roxheim, Landkreis Ludwigshafen.* Schifferstadt (Postfach 1133), 1992. [31] pp. (mimeog.).

29099 BOLLENDORF. COLLJUNG, PAUL: *Die Juden in Bollendorf.* [In]: Beiträge zur jüdischen Geschichte in Rheinland-Pfalz. Jg. 2, H. 1, Bad Kreuznach, 1992. Pp. 29–33.

29100 BOPPARD. BURKARD, KARL-JOSEF: *Geschichte der Bopparder Juden.* [In]: Beiträge zur jüdischen Geschichte in Rheinland-Pfalz. Jg. 2, H. 3, Bad Kreuznach, 1992. Pp. 53–66.

29101 BOVENDEN. BUSCH, RALF: *Zauberkünstler und Musiker aus der jüdischen Familie Basch in Bovenden.* [In]: Plesse-Archiv, H. 27, Göttingen, 1991. Pp. 85–98, illus., ports., facsims.

29102 BRESLAU. REINKE, MARKUS: *Zwischen Tradition, Aufklärung und Assimilation: Die Königliche Wilhelmsschule in Breslau 1791–1848.* [In]: Zeitschrift für Religions- und Geistesgeschichte, Jg. 43, Leiden, 1991. Pp. 193–214, footnotes. [On one of the first and biggest Jewish Gymnasiums.]

29103 CELLE. BAR-GIORA BAMBERGER, NAFTALI: *Der jüdische Friedhof in Celle: Memorbuch.* Heidelberg: Winter, 1992. 231 pp., illus. [Title also in Hebrew; text partly in Hebrew and German; incl. list of the gravestones.]

29104 — BUSCH, RALF: *Zur Problematik von Minderheiten im 18. und frühen 19. Jahrhundert. Sozialgeschichtliche Aspekte der Entwicklung der 'Altenceller Vorstadt' in Celle. Eine Skizze.* [In]: Das Volk als Objekt obrigkeitlichen Handelns. Hrsg. von Rudolf Vierhaus. Tübingen: Niemeyer, 1992. Pp. 51–56. [Refers also to the settlement of Jews in Celle.]

29105 COLOGNE. MAGNUS, SHULAMITH SHARON: *Cologne: Jewish emancipation in a German city, 1798–1871.* 2 vols. Ann Arbor, Mich.: Univ. Microfilms International, 1992. XI, 659 pp., facsims., map, bibl. (602–626). New York: Columbia Univ. Diss., 1988.

29106 — WITTE, MARIA MAGDALENA: *Stationen jüdischen Lebens in Köln.* [In]: Religionsunterricht an Höheren Schulen, Jg. 35, H. 1, Düsseldorf, 1992. Pp. 48 ff.

29107 DARMSTADT. SCHNEIDER, CARLO: *Die Friedhöfe in Darmstadt.* Hrsg. vom Magistrat der Stadt Darmstadt/Kulturamt. Darmstadt: Roether, 1991. 136 pp., illus., map. [Incl.: Der Jüdische Friedhof (112–119) with 8 biographies of persons buried between 1901 and 1980: Heinrich Blumenthal, Julius Goldstein, Sigmund Gundelfinger, Alexander Haas, Herz Hähnle Hachenburger, Ludwig Meidner, Louis Schlösser, Ernst Trier.]

29108 DEUTZ. SCHULTE, KLAUS H.S.: *Familienbuch der Deutzer Juden.* Köln: Böhlau, 1992. 414 pp., notes, illus., maps, index of persons (387–405), of places (405–413).

29109 DÜLMEN. *Der jüdische Friedhof in Dülmen.* 4408 Dülmen: Laumann, 1991. Hrsg.: Stadt Dülmen. Der Stadtdirektor. Kulturamt, Stadtmuseum. Texte: Karina Lehnardt. 168 pp., illus., notes, bibl., indexes (names, places).

29110 EAST FRIESLAND. REYER, HERBERT: *Geschichte der Juden in Ostfriesland.* [In]: Archive in Niedersachsen 1990, Nr. 9, Hannover, 1990. Pp. 27 ff.

29111 ELBING. NEUFELD, SIEGBERT: *Geschichte der jüdischen Gemeinde Elbing.* Hrsg. von Eva Blau [et al.]. Regensburg: CH-Verlag, 1992. 82 pp., footnotes. [Reprint of book, which was written and publ. in 1933 by the last rabbi of Elbing, who emigrated in 1939 to Palestine, returned to Germany in 1951, where he was Landesrabbiner of Württemberg from 1951–1953.]

29112 EMDEN. VALK, WOLF: *Die wir verloren haben: Lebensgeschichten Emder Juden. Mit einer Geschichte der jüdischen Gemeinde Emdens.* Nachwort: Jan Lokers. Hrsg.: Volkshochschule Emden & Ostfriesische Landschaft. Ges. und bearb. von Marianne und Reinhard Claudi. Aurich: Ostfriesische Landschaft, 1991. 607 pp. (Einzelschriften/Ostfriesische Landschaft, Bd. 28.)

—— ENDINGEN. [See No. 29227.]

29113 ERLANGEN. SPONSEL, ILSE: *'Spuren in Stein' – 100 Jahre Israelitischer Friedhof in Erlangen. 30. September 1891–30. September 1991.* Hrsg.: Stadt Erlangen, Bürgermeister und Presseamt. Text: Ilse Sponsel. 68 pp., illus., facsims., lists, docs., maps. (Erlanger Materialien, H.6.) [Incl.: Der jüdische Friedhof – eine Einführung (Nathan Peter Levinson, 5). Die jüdischen Opfer der Stadt Erlangen in der NS-Zeit 1933–1945 (62–63).]

29114 FEUCHTWANGEN. WEISS, DIETRICH: *Aus der Geschichte der jüdischen Gemeinde von Feuchtwangen 1274–1938.* [In]: Bd.3. Feuchtwanger Heimatgeschichte. Schriftenreihe des Arbeitsgemeinschaft für Heimatgeschichte im Verein für Volkskunst und Volkskunde e.V. und des Stadtarchivs Feuchtwangen. 8805 Feuchtwangen, 1991. Pp. 9–107, footnotes, illus., facsims., docs., lists, bibl.

—— FRANCONIA. [See also No. 29005.]

29115 —— DILL, KARL: *Jüdische Friedhöfe in Oberfranken.* [Hrsg. von der Regierung von Oberfranken]. Bayreuth: Regierung von Oberfranken, 1992. 42 pp., illus., map. (Heimatbeilage zum Amtl. Schulanzeiger des Regierungsbezirks Oberfranken, Nr. 187.)

29116 FRANKENAU. BRANDT, HEINZ: *Die Judengemeinde in Frankenau zwischen 1660 und 1940: aus dem Leben jüdischer Landmenschen.* Frankenberg (Eder): Kahm, 1992. 71 pp. (Frankenberger Hefte, 1.)

—— FRANKFURT am Main. [See also in No. 29647.]

—— —— HEIL, JOHANNES: *Dom und Synagoge in Frankfurt 1150–1866.* [See No. 29961.]

—— —— HEUBERGER, RACHEL: *Orthodoxy versus reform. The case of Rabbi Nehemiah Anton Nobel of Frankfurt a. Main.* [See No. 29583.]

29117 —— *Museum Judengasse. Katalog zur Dauerausstellung (Dependance des Jüdischen Museums).* Herausgegeben vom Jüdischen Museum im Auftrag der Stadt Frankfurt am Main. Verantwortlich: Georg Heuberger. Red.: Fritz Backhaus, Heike Drummer. Frankfurt am Main: Magistrat der Stadt Frankfurt am Main, 1992. 103 pp., illus., notes, bibl. [On the reconstructed remains of houses and ritual baths of the former ghetto, today Börneplatz, torn down 1874.]

—— —— *Pinkas Hakehillot: encyclopedia of Jewish communities from their foundation till after the Holocaust.* Germany, part 3: *Hesse, Hesse-Nassau, Frankfurt.* Ed. by Henry Wassermann. [See No. 29137.]

29118 —— SCHLOTZHAUER, INGE: *Erziehung zur Emanzipation. Das Frankfurter Philanthropin in der ersten Hälfte des 19. Jahrhunderts.* [In]: Zeitschrift für Religions- und Geistesgeschichte, Jg. 43, Leiden, 1991. Pp. 233–247, footnotes.

—— —— TREUE, WILHELM: *Eine Frau, drei Männer und eine Kunstfigur. Barocke Lebensläufe.* [See No. 30073.]

29119 FREIBURG i. Br. HAUMANN, HEIKO: *Juden in Freiburg i.Br. von der Mitte des 19. Jahrhunderts bis zur Gegenwart: Assimilation, Antisemitismus, Suche nach Identität.* [In]: Landjudentum im süddeutschen und Bodenseeraum [see No. 29018]. Pp. 155–162.

29120 FÜRTH. BATTENBERG, FRIEDRICH: *Das Reichskammergericht und die Juden des heiligen Römischen Reiches. Geistliche Herrschaft und korporative Verfassung der Judenschaft in Fürth im Widerspruch.* Hrsg.: Gesellschaft für Reichskammergerichtsforschung. Wetzlar, 1992. 46 pp., notes. (Schriftenreihe der Gesellschaft für Reichskammergerichtsforschung, H. 13.)

29121 GAILINGEN. ROMING, GISELA: *Die demographische Entwicklung der jüdischen Gemeinden Gailingen und Randegg zwischen Schutzherrschaft und Emanzipation.* [In]: Landjudentum im süddeutschen und Bodenseeraum [see No. 29018]. Pp. 92–101.

29122 GELDERN. PETEGHEM, PETER VAN: *Geld, Glaube und frühmoderner Staat in den Niederlanden. Die Neuchristen in Antwerpen und die Juden in Geldern: ein Vergleich.* [In]: Aschkenas, Jg. 2, Wien, 1992. Pp. 73–94.

29123 GÖPPINGEN. *Jüdisches Museum Göppingen:* [in der alten Kirche Jebenhausen]. [Inhaltliche Konzeption Karl-Heinz Ruess. Unter Mitarbeit von Gil Hüttenmeister und Kurt Ranger]. Weissenhorn: Konrad, 1992. 147 pp., illus. (Veröff. des Stadtarchivs Göppingen, Bd. 29.)

29124 HALLE. *300 Jahre Juden in Halle. Leben-Leistung-Leiden-Lohn.* Hrsg. von der Jüdischen Gemeinde zu Halle. Halle: Mitteldeutscher Verlag, 1992. 543 pp., illus., lists, docs., index (persons). [Cont.(titles partly abbr.): Von den Anfängen bis zum Jahre 1800 (Volker Dietzel, 9–32). Zur Geschichte der Jüdischen Gemeinde 1800–1933 (Werner Piechocki, 33–82). Zur Geschichte der Juden in Halle 1933–1945 (Clemens Krause/Susanne Meincke, 83–274). Geschichte der Jüdischen Gemeinde nach 1945 (Gudrun Goeseke (275–286). Von 1962 bis zur Gegenwart (Gunther Helbig, 287–292). Die Auswirkungen der antijüdischen Rassenpolitik im Lehrkörper der Universität (Artur Schellbach, 293–312). Jüdische Mediziner in Halle (Wolfram Kaiser/Arina Völer, 313–362). Jüdische Kunstwissenschaftler (Ingrid Schulze, 363–380). Werke jüdischer Künstler im Moritzburg-Museum (Andreas Hüneke, 381–396). Auf Halles Bühnen und Konzertpodien (Margrit Lenk, 397–422). Alfred Wolkenstein (Günter Hartung, 423–440). Der Architekt Alfred Gellhorn in Halle (Ingrid Schulze, 441–452). Der Korrespondenzverlag Martin Feuchtwanger (Ilse Hoppe, 453–472). Edmund Husserl in Halle (1887–1901) (Hans-Martin Gerlach, 473–486). Zum Gedenken an Dr. med. Hermann Jastrowitz (1882–1943) (Wolfram Kaiser/Arina Völker, 487–504). Tagebuchnotizen von Victor Klemperer 1948/49 (Ingrid Schulze, 505–513).]

29125 HAMBURG. BAUCHE, ULRICH, ed.: *Vierhundert Jahre Juden in Hamburg.* Red.: Ulrich Bauche, Reiner Gerckens [et al.]. Hamburg: Dölling und Galitz, 1991. 557 pp., illus. [Catalogue of an exhibition held at the Museum für Hamburgische Geschichte 1991/1992.]

29126 — BÜRGER, FRIEDEGUND [et al.]: *'Der Umgang mit Minderheiten will gelernt sein.' Der jüdische Friedhof in Hamburg-Ottensen – ein Lehrstück für tolerante Tradition und demokratischen Dialog.* [In]: Informationen zur Schleswig-Holsteinischen Zeitgeschichte, 23, Kiel, 1992. Pp. 5–42, illus., notes, bibl.

29127 — JACOBS, BOIKE: *Streit um ein Friedhofsgelände. Die bewegte Geschichte des jüdischen Friedhofs von Hamburg-Ottensen.* [In]: Tribüne, Jg. 31, H. 122, Frankfurt am Main, 1992. Pp. 26–30. [On the controversy see also ULRICH W. SAHM: *Es geht um die Würde der Toten. Rabbinischer Schlichterspruch zur Kontroverse um den jüdischen Friedhof in Hamburg Ottensen. Eine Dokumentation.* [In]: Tribüne, Jg. 31, H. 123, Frankfurt am Main, 1992. Pp. 130–143.]

29128 HANAU. PELES, ISRAEL MORDECHAI: *The yeshiva of Rabbi Raphael ben Yaakov ha-Levi in Hanau;* notes in a manuscript 'Kitzur Mordechai' by R. Shimshon. [In Hebrew, title transl.]. [In]: Tzfunot, Vol. 3, No. 4, Bnei-Beraq, Tammuz 5751 [=June-July 1991]. Pp. 66–68. [Discusses a ms. of the University of Halle, in which a yeshiva in Hanau in 1638 is mentioned.]

29129 HANOVER. SABELLECK, RAINER: *Die Entwicklung jüdischer Religions- und Volksschulen im 19. Jahrhundert. Dargestellt am Beispiel der Verhältnisse in den Landrabbinatsbezirken Hannover und Hildesheim.* [In]: Zeitschrift für Religions- und Geistesgeschichte, Jg. 43, Leiden, 1991. Pp. 215–232, footnotes, tabs.

29130 HEIDELBERG. LÖSLEIN, BARBARA: *Geschichte der Heidelberger Synagogen.* Hrsg. von Peter Anselm Ried. Veröffentlichungen zur Heidelberger Altstadt. H. 26. Heidelberg: Kunsthistorisches Institut der Universität, 1992. 120 pp., illus., facsims., map, plans.

29131 HENNWEILER. ZIEMER, HANS-WERNER: *Nachforschungen zur Geschichte der jüdischen Gemeinde in Hennweiler.* [In]: Beiträge zur jüdischen Geschichte in Rheinland-Pfalz. Jg. 2, H.X , Bad Kreuznach, 1992. Pp. 34–49.

— HESSE. *Bibliographie zur Geschichte der Juden in Hessen.* [See No. 29260.]

29132 — FRIEDEBURG, ROBERT VON: *Social structure and migration: the case of the Schwalm Valley, Hesse, 1840–66.* [In]: German History, Vol. 10, Oxford, 1992. Pp. 131–48.

29133 — FRIEDEBURG, ROBERT VON: *Village strife and the rhetoric of communalism: peasants and parsons, lords and Jews in Hesse, Central Germany, 1646–1672.* [In]: The Seventeenth Century, Vol. VII, No. 2, Durham, 1992. Pp. 201–226, notes.

29134 — GREVE, BARBARA: *Der Ackerbau der Israeliten. Ein Beitrag zu Theorie und Praxis der kurhessischen Judenemanzipation.* [In]: Zeitschrift des Vereins für hessische Geschichte und Landeskunde, Bd. 97, Kassel, 1992. Pp. 107–126, notes.

29135 — HOFFMANN, DIETER: *'. . . wir sind doch Deutsche': zu Geschichte und Schicksal der Landjuden in Rheinhessen.* Hrsg.: Stadt Alzey. Alzey: Verl. der Rheinhessischen Dr.- Werkstätten, 1992. VIII, 409 pp., illus., bibl. (378–399). [Also on the Nazi period.]

29136 — KAUFMANN, URI R.: *Viehhandel und Viehhändler im Umkreis der hessischen Bergstraße 1780–1914.* [In]: Geschichtsblätter Kreis Bergstraße, Bd. 25, Heppenheim, 1992. Pp. 67–83, notes.

29137 — *Pinkas Hakehillot: encyclopedia of Jewish communities from their foundation till after the Holocaust. Germany,* part 3: *Hesse, Hesse-Nassau, Frankfurt.* Ed. by Henry Wassermann. [In Hebrew].

Jerusalem: Yad Vashem, 1992. [12], 725 pp. [For previous vols., see No. 24056/YB XXXIII.]
29138 HEUSENSTAMM. DITTRICH, ALFRED: *Aus der Geschichte der Jüdischen Kultusgemeinde in Heusenstamm:* Dokumentation. Heusenstamm: Magistrat der Stadt/Heimatverein Heusenstamm, 1989. 55 pp., illus. (Heusenstammer Hefte, 2.)
29139 HOFFMANN, DIETER: *Die Pflicht der späten Geburt. Über Nachforschungen zu jüdischen Gemeinden.* [In]: Geschichte in Wissenschaft und Unterricht, Jg. 43, Stuttgart. Pp. 79–92, footnotes.
29140 HOMBURG vor der Höhe. *Geschichte der Juden in Bad Homburg vor der Höhe.* Von Heinz Grosche in Zusammenarbeit mit Klaus Rohde. Mit einem Beitr. von Wolfgang R. Assmann. Hrsg.: Magistrat der Stadt Bad Homburg vor der Höhe. Frankfurt am Main: Kramer, 1991. 122 pp., illus. (Geschichte der Stadt Bad Homburg vor der Höhe, Sonderbd.)
29141 HOYA. HUTH-MALLUS, HEIKE & HUTH, HANS: *Wann wird man je versteh'n. . . .: der Weg der Hoyaer Juden bis 1942.* Mannheim: VWM-Verl. Wagener, 1992. 63 pp., illus. (Jüdische Bibliothek, Bd. 4.)
— ICHENHAUSEN. [See in No. 29005.]
29142 INGELHEIM. MEYER, HANS-GEORG: *Die jüdische Bevölkerungsentwicklung in Ingelheim 1364–1950.* [In]: Beiträge zur jüdischen Geschichte in Rheinland-Pfalz. Jg. 2, H. 3, Bad Kreuznach, 1992. Pp. 37–44.
29143 KARLSRUHE. *Juden in Karlsruhe – Beiträge zu ihrer Geschichte bis zur nationalsozialistischen Machtergreifung.* 2. [erweiterte] Aufl. Karlsruhe: Badenia, 1990. 640 pp. [For first edn. see No. 25064/YB XXXIV.]
29144 — RAMON, ESTHER: *The Homburger family from Karlsruhe: a family study, 1674–1990.* Jerusalem: Posner, 1992. 183 pp., illus., geneal. tabs., ports., bibl.
— KIEL. Dokumentation zur Geschichte der Kieler Synagoge und des Mahnmals an der Goethestrasse 13. [See No. 29537.]
29145 KONSTANZ. BLOCH, ERICH: *Das verlorene Paradies. Ein Leben am Bodensee 1897–1939.* Bearbeitet von Werner Trapp. Sigmaringen: Thorbecke, 1992. 145 pp., illus., indexes (139–144). (Konstanzer Geschichts- und Rechtsquellen, 33.) [Based on interviews made between 1980 and 1981; E.B., b. Aug. 4, 1897 in Konstanz, writer, farmer, ran a training farm for young Jews in Horn near Konstanz from 1933 until the November Pogrom, emigr. to Palestine in 1939.]
29146 LEIPZIG. PLOWINSKI, KERSTIN: *Die jüdische Bevölkerung Leipzigs 1853–1925–1933: sozialgeschichtliche Fallstudien zur Mitgliedschaft einer Grossgemeinde.* Leipzig: Univ., Diss., 1991. [5], XVI, 186 pp.
29147 LÖNINGEN. MEINERS, WERNER: *Bürgerprotest gegen restriktive Gewerbepolitik und Beamtenwillkür im Revolutionsjahr 1848. Der Löninger 'Judenkrawall' vom 10. Dezember 1848 und seine Hintergründe.* [In]: Oldenburger Jahrbuch, Bd. 90, Oldenburg, 1990. Pp. 83–102.
29148 LÜBECK. SCHREIBER, ALBRECHT: *Zwischen Davidstern und Doppeladler. Illustrierte Chronik der Juden in Moisling und Lübeck.* Lübeck: Schmidt-Römhild, 1992. (Kleine Hefte zur Stadtgeschichte. Hrsg.: Archiv der Hansestadt Lübeck, H.8.) [Incl.: Vorwort (Felix F. Carlebach [&] Ulrich Meyenborg, 5–6).]
29149 LÜGDE. WILLEKE, MANFRED: *Die Geschichte der Juden in Lügde.* [In]: Genealogie, Jg. 39., Bd. 20, H. 5, Neustadt/Aisch, 1991. Pp. 129–150, facsims., family trees. [Nachtrag zu: Die Geschichte der Juden in Lügde (by author) [in]: Bd. 20, H. 7, Neustadt/Aisch, 1990. Pp. 220–221.]
29150 MAINZ. GILLESSEN, GÜNTHER, ed.: *Wenn Steine reden könnten. Mainzer Gebäude und ihre Geschichten.* Führungen durch eine Stadtlandschaft. Mainz: von Zabern, 1991. 205 pp., illus., bibl. notes. [Incl. the following chaps.: Zentrum des europäischen Judentums. Die jüdische Gemeinde im Mittelalter (Michael Scheuermann/Rüdiger Jung, 65–72). Emanzipation und Vernichtung. Die jüdische Gemeinde der Neuzeit (Barbara Pörtener, 157–162).]
29151 MANNHEIM. WATZINGER, KARL OTTO: *Der jüdische Anteil an der Entwicklung Mannheims.* [In]: Mannheimer Hefte, Jg. 1992, H.2., Mannheim, 1992. Pp. 121–123. [See also in the same issue: VOLKER KELLER: Das jüdische Altersheim in B7, 3 (pp.124–128).]
29152 MECKLENBURG. *Aus der Geschichte der Juden in den Städten Waren, Röbel, Malchow und Penzlin.* Text: Karl-Heinz Oelke. Hrsg.: Müritz-Sparkasse. [Waren, 1992]. 28 pp., illus. (Bildungshefte Müritzkreis, 1.) [Incl. Nazi period.]
29153 — OELKE, KARL-HEINZ: *Jüdische Geschichte in der Müritz-Region.* Waren: Müritz-Bote, 1991–1992. 23 issues. [A series of 22 articles publ. in the Müritz-Bote between Nov. 11, 1991 and

April 11, 1992 on the history of the Jews in Waren, Röbel, Malchow and Penzlin; incl. Nazi period.]

29154 MEMEL. BENJAMIN, KURT: *Die Geschichte der Juden in Memel*. [In]: 'MB', Jg. 60, Nr. 75, Tel-Aviv, Jan. 1992. Pp. 4–5.

29155 MISTELFELD. DIPPOLD, GÜNTER: '... *auch wohnen viele Juden im Orte'. Die Mistelfelder Juden*. [In]: 850 Jahre Mistelfeld. Im Auftrag der Mistelfelder Vereine herausgegeben von Günter Dippold. 8628 Weismain (Postfach 41): Selbstverlag Vom Main zum Jura, 1992. Pp. 108–126, illus., notes.

29156 MÖNCHENGLADBACH. BECKER, ALBERT/SCHUMACHER, KARL-HEINZ: *Die 'Wickrather Lederfabrik (vormals Z. Spier) Aktiengesellschaft': ein bedeutendes Zeugnis der Orts- und Industriegeschichte in Mönchengladbach*. [In]: Rheydter Jahrbuch 20, Mönchengladbach, 1992. Pp. 37–48. [On a leather goods factory founded in 1855 by Zacharias Spier, 'Aryanised' in 1938.]

29157 ODENBACH. KUKATZKI, BERNARD: *Die Genisa der Synagoge Odenbach*. Schifferstadt, 1992. 46 pp., illus., facsims. (Mimeog.)

29158 OFFENBURG. RUCH, MARTIN: *Familie Cohn. Tagebücher, Gedichte, Briefe einer jüdischen Familie aus Offenburg*. Hrsg. und kommentiert von Martin Ruch. Mit einem Vorwort von Eva Mendelsson. Hrsg.: Stadt Offenburg. 248 pp., illus., notes. Offenburg: Reiff, 1992. (Veröffentlichungen des Kulturamtes, Bd. 17.)

29159 OLDENBURG. SCHECKEL, HARALD: *Die jüdischen Lehrer im Lande Oldenburg*. [In]: Oldenburger Jahrbuch, Bd. 92, Oldenburg, 1992. Pp. 129–140, footnotes, list of names, of places.

29160 OPPENHEIM. KEMP, WOLFGANG: *Dokumentation der Oppenheimer und Niersteiner Juden*. [In]: Beiträge zur jüdischen Geschichte in Rheinland-Pfalz. Jg. 2, H. 1, Bad Kreuznach, 1992. Pp. 4–28.

29161 PALATINATE. GLATZ, JOACHIM: *Synagogen und Denkmalpflege in Rheinland-Pfalz*. [In]: Beiträge zur jüdischen Geschichte in Rheinland-Pfalz. Jg. 2, H. 3, Bad Kreuznach, 1992. Pp. 5–21.

29162 — KUBY, ALFRED, ed.: *Pfälzisches Judentum gestern und heute*. Beiträge zur Regionalgeschichte des 19. und 20. Jahrhunderts. Neustadt a.d. Weinstrasse: Verlag Pfälz. Post, 1992. 443 pp., notes, lists, facsims. [Incl.: Festgabe für Dr. Max Meir Ydit. Lebenslauf, Bibliographie (Bernhard H. Gerlach, 10–16, port.) Danksagung an Rabbiner Dr. Meir Ydit (Michael Deckwerth, 17–20). Rabbiner Dr. Kurt L. Metzger (Bernhard Kukatzki, 21–24). Zu den geistigen Kämpfen unter den pfälzischen Juden: die Position des Bezirksrabbiners Elias Grünebaum (1807–1893) (25–32). Die pfälzischen Juden der napoleonischen Ära (Wilhelm Kreutz, 33–84). Pfälzer Juden und das napoleonische Namensdekret vom 20. Juli 1808 (Dieter Blinn, 85–108). Zur demographischen und sozialen Entwicklung der israelitischen Kultusgemeinde Ludwigshafens (Helga Karch, 151–170). Zum Interesse ländlicher Juden an höherer Schulbildung für ihre Kinder (Alfred H. Kuby, 171–177). Jüdisches Sprachgut in den pfälzischen und südhessischen Mundarten (Rudolf Post, 177–258). Das rituelle Frauenbad in Haßloch (Johannes Theisohn, 259–272). Fundstücke aus den Synagogen Odenbach und Weisenheim am Berg [&] Die Jüdische Kultusgemeinde der Rheinpfalz (Bernhard Kukatzki, 273–286 [&] 387–395). Die 'Judenfrage' im pfälzischen Pfarrerblatt von 1933–1939 (Hans L. Reichrath, 287–320). Kinderemigration 1939 (Sigrun Wipfler-Pohl, 321–386). Erinnerungen an Samuel Kamenetzki (Hannes Ziegler, 396–400). Bibliographie (Bernhard H. Gerlach, 401–440).]

29163 — KUKATZKI, BERNHARD: *Initiative der Grünen im Bezirkstag Pfalz zur Erhaltung jüdischer Kulturdenkmäler*. Eine Dokumentation von Bern. Kukatzki. Schifferstadt 1992. 103 pp., illus., facsims. (Mimeog.) [Obtainable from B. Kukatzki, Postfach 1133, 5707 Schifferstadt.]

29064 — KUKATZKI, BERNHARD/JACOBY, MARIO: *Inventarisierung jüdischer Friedhöfe in der Pfalz*. Ein Projekt. Schifferstadt und Oettingen i. By., 1992. 34 pp., illus., facsims. (Mimeog.)

29165 POMERANIA. KONOW, KARL-OTTO: *Die Judenverfolgung in Pommern im Jahre 1492*. [In]: Baltische Studien, Neue Folge 78, Bd. 124 der Gesamtreihe, Marburg, 1992. Pp. 17–27, footnotes.

29166 REHLINGEN. MÜLLER, GUIDO: *Juden in der Gemeinde Rehlingen-Siersburg*. [In]: Saarländische Familienkunde, Jg. 22, Bd. 6, Saarbrücken, 1989. Pp. 151–160.

29167 RHEINECK. BURMEISTER, KARL HEINZ: *Die jüdische Landgemeinde in Rheineck im 17. Jahrhundert*. [In]: Landjudentum im süddeutschen und Bodenseeraum [see No. 29018]. Pp. 22–37.

29168 RHINELAND. BORMANN, HEIDI und CORNELIUS: *Heimat an der Erft. Die Landjuden in den*

Synagogengemeinden Gymnich, Friesheim und Lechenich. Hrsg.: Stadt Erfstadt-Der Stadtdirektor-Kulturamt. Stadt Erfstadt, 1992. 639 pp., illus., facsims., bibl. (621–626), index (627–639). [Incl.: Biographischer Überblick (names list of Jews living in Gymnich, Friesheim and Lechenich from about 1800, 459–616).]

29169 — *Wegweiser durch das jüdische Rheinland.* Hrsg. von Ludger Heid und Julius H. Schoeps in Verbindung mit Marina Sassenberg. Berlin: Nicolai, 1992. 420 pp., illus., maps, notes, bibl. (397–409), index (persons). (Eine Publikation des Salomon Ludwig Steinheim-Instituts für deutsch-jüdische Geschichte.) [Incl. (titles partly abbr.): Geleitwort (Johannes Rau, 7). Aus zweitausend Jahren. Jüdische Geschichte im Rheinland (Marina Sassenberg, 9–19). Aachen (Werner Ripkens, 20–31). Andernach (Erik Lindner, 32–37). Bonn (Irmgard Schmitz, 38–53). Brühl (Barbara Becker-Jákli, 54–63). Düsseldorf (Barbara Suchy, 64–83). Duisburg (Marina Sassenberg, 84–99). Erftstadt (Cornelius Bormann, 100–105). Essen (Michael Zimmermann, 106–125). Issum, Geldern und das Landjudentum am Niederrhein (Bernhard Keuck 126–141). Kleve (Ruth Benger, 142–147). Köln (Bruno Fischer, 148–175). Krefeld (Rolf Kauffeldt, 176–187). Langenlonsheim (Marina Sassenberg/Karl-Wilhelm Höffler, 188–192). Mönchengladbach (Marion Engbarth/Gerd Lamers, 192–203). Mülheim an der Ruhr (Gerhard Bennertz, 204–213). Neuss (Lisa Nelien, 214–219). Neuwied [and] Oberwesel [and] Trier und Koblenz (Erik Lindner, 220–233; 242–263). Siegburg und Siegkreis (Heinrich Linn, 234–241). Wesseling (Christoph Ehmann, 264–269). Wuppertal (Ulrich Föhse, 270–279). Ostjuden im Rheinland (Ludger Heid, 306–313). Ein demographischer Überblick (Peter Honigmann, 314–323). Synagogen im Rheinland (Hannelore Künzl, 332–337). Jüdische Räuberbanden im Rheinland (Lisa Nelißen, 338–340). Jüdische Presse im Rheinland (Ursula Reuter, 346–354). Incl. also lists of cemeteries, of former synagogues and rabbis. Further essays are listed according to subject.] [Cf.: Besprechung (Bernhard Vogt) [in]: Tribüne, Jg. 31, H. 123, Frankfurt am Main, 1992, pp. 227–228. Besprechung (Stefan Rohrbacher) [in]: Annalen des Historischen Vereins für den Niederrhein, H. 195, Pulheim, 1992, pp. 345–347. Ein populäres Nachschlagewerk für das jüdische Rheinland (Wolfgang Frank) [in]: 'Allgemeine', Jg. 47, Nr. 19, Bonn, 7. Mai, 1992, p. 9.]

29170 — ZÜRN, GABY: *Jüdische Friedhöfe im Rheinland.* Hrsg.: Landesbildstelle Rheinland (Medienstelle des Landschaftsverb. Rheinland). Düsseldorf: Landschaftsverb. Rheinland/Landesbildstelle Rheinland, 1992. 24 Dias & Beiheft (39 pp., illus.).

29171 SAARLAND. MARX, ALBERT: *Die Geschichte der Juden im Saarland vom Ancien Régime bis zum Zweiten Weltkrieg.* Saarbrücken: Die Mitte, 1992. 272 pp., illus.

29172 SCHLESWIG-HOLSTEIN. STOLZ, GERHARD: *Wegweiser zu den jüdischen Stätten in Schleswig-Holstein.* Hrsg. von der Jüdischen Gemeinde in Hamburg. Heide: Boyens, 1992. 96 pp., illus., chronol. tab., lists of rabbis, bibl., map. [Cf.: Besprechung (lz) [in]: 'Allgemeine', Jg. 47, Nr. 41, Bonn, 8. Okt., 1992, p. 10.]

29173 SCHNAITTACH. HILDESHEIMER, MEIR: *Acta communitatis Judaeorum Schnaittach.* Introductione natisque instruxit Meir Hildesheimer. Hierosolymis: Sumptibus Societatis, Mekize Nirdamim, MCMCII. XIV, 401 pp. [=*Pinkas Kehilat Schnaittach*, mit Einleitung und Notizen von Dr. Meir Hildesheimer. Jerusalem: Verlag Mekizei Nirdamim in Zusammenarbeit mit dem Leo Baeck Institut, 1992.] [The original Pinkas Kehila, preserved in the Central Archives for the History of the Jewish People, Jerusalem, has been deciphered and edited by M.H, a descendant of Esriel Hildesheimer.] [Cf.: Besprechung (Benjamin Schlomo Hamburger) [in]: 'MB', Jg. 61, Nr. 86, Tel Aviv, Jan. 1993, pp. 5–6.

29174 SCHWABEN. FASSL, PETER: *Geschichte und Kultur der Juden in Schwaben.* [In]: Aus Schwaben und Altbayern. Festschrift für Pankraz Fried zum 60. Geburtstag. Hrsg. von Peter Fassl, Wilhelm Liebhart und Wolfgang Wüst. Sigmaringen: Thorbecke, 1991. (Augsburger Beiträge zur Landesgeschichte Bayerisch-Schwabens, Bd. 5.) Pp. 21–30, footnotes.

29175 SCHWÄBISCH HALL. TADDEY, GERHARD: *Kein kleines Jerusalem. Geschichte der Juden im Landkreis Schwäbisch Hall.* Hrsg. vom Historischen Verein für Württembergisch Franken, dem Stadtarchiv Schwäbisch Hall und dem Hohenlohe-Zentralarchiv Neuenstein. Sigmaringen: Thorbecke, 1992. 376 pp., illus., tabs., map, family trees, footnotes, bibl., indexes (places, persons, subjects, 348–376). (Forschungen aus Württembergisch Franken, Bd. 36.) [Incl. Nazi period.] [Cf.: Besprechung (Ulrich Brochhagen) [in]: Das Historisch-Politische Buch, Jg. 40, H. 11 und 12, Göttingen, 1992, pp. 521.]

29176 SCHWEICH. *Festschrift zur Eröffnung der ehemaligen Synagoge von Schweich als Kulturstätte.* 3. September 1989. Hrsg.: Stadtverwaltung Schweich, [1989]. 55 pp., illus. [Contributions on the history of the Jews in Schweich by Georg Wagner; incl. also the cemetery.]

29177 SCHWELM. FENNER, WOLFGANG: *Das Museum stellt vor (12): 'Schlehdorn und Rosen' (1891). Ein Gedichtband von Paul Herzsohn.* [In]: Beiträge zur Heimatkunde der Stadt Schwelm und ihrer Umgebung, Neue Folge, H. 42, Schwelm, 1992. Pp. 145–150, notes. [On the son of a Schwelm cattle trader, who became an orientalist and writer; incl. also poems by Herzsohn.]

29178 SILESIA. MASER, PETER/WEISER, ADELHEID: *Juden in Oberschlesien.* Teil 1: Historischer Überblick. Jüdische Gemeinden (I). Berlin: Gebr. Mann, 1992. 228 pp., illus. (Schriften der Stiftung Haus Oberschlesien (Ratingen): Landeskundliche Reihe, Bd. 3.) [Incl. the communities of Beuthen, Bielitz, Gleiwitz, Kattowitz, Königshütte, Kreuzburg, Oberglogau, Oppeln, Sohrau.]

29179 — PIERENKEMPER, TONI: *Jüdische Industrielle in Oberschlesien im 19. Jahrhundert.* [In]: Jahrbuch der Schlesischen Friedrich-Wilhelms-Universität zu Breslau. Sigmaringen: Thorbecke, 1991.

29180 ST. GOAR & OBERWESEL. SPORMANN, DORIS: *Die Synagogengemeinden in St. Goar und Oberwesel im 19. und 20. Jahrhundert* [&] *Wie der Name Gerson in der Familie blieb.* [In]: Beiträge zur jüdischen Geschichte in Rheinland-Pfalz. Jg. 2, H. 3, Bad Kreuznach, 1992. Pp. 22–36.

29181 STADE. BOHMBACH, JÜRGEN: *'Unser Grundsatz war, Israeliten möglichst fernzuhalten': Zur Geschichte der Juden in Stade.* Stade: Stadt Stade. Der Stadtdirektor, 1992. 64 pp., illus. (Veröffentlichungen aus dem Stadtarchiv Stade, Bd. 15.)

—— STEINFURT. GOLDSCHMIDT, EDITH: *Drei Leben: Autobiographie einer deutschen Jüdin.* [See No. 29890.]

29182 STEINHEIM. MENZE, JOSEF: *Judenschule und Synagoge in der Stadt Steinheim während der ersten Hälfte des 19. Jahrhunderts.* Hrsg.: Stadtverwaltung Steinheim, Hauptamt. Steinheim, 1992. 52 pp., illus. (Mitteilungen des Kulturausschusses der Stadt Steinheim. H. 50, 2. Halbjahr 1992).

29183 STUTTGART. HAHN, JOACHIM: *Friedhöfe in Stuttgart. Bd. 3. Pragfriedhof, Israelitischer Teil.* Unter Mitarbeit von Richard Klotz und Hermann Ziegler. Hrsg.: Landeshauptstadt Stuttgart, Stadtarchiv, in Verb. mit dem Presse- und Informationsamt. Stuttgart: Klett-Cotta, 1992. 267 pp., illus., facsims., lists. (Veröffentlichungen des Archivs der Stadt Stuttgart, Bd. 57.)

29184 — SAUER, PAUL: *Die Jüdische Gemeinde Stuttgart in den Jahren der Weimarer Republik.* [In]: Zeitschrift für Württembergische Landesgeschichte, Jg. 51, Stuttgart, 1992. Pp. 321–344, footnotes.

29185 TRIER. HALLER, ANNETTE: *Das Protokollbuch der Jüdischen Gemeinde Trier (1784–1836):* Edition der Handschrift und kommentierte Übertragung ins Deutsche. Frankfurt am Main; New York [et al.]: Lang, 1992. 454 pp. (Judentum und Umwelt, Bd. 34.) (Zugl.: Köln, Univ., Diss.. 1991.)

29186 UNTERSCHWANDORF. *Die Unterschwandorfer Juden: Geschichte einer vergessenen Gemeinde.* [Hrsg.: Otto-Hahn-Gymnasium Nagold. H. 1–7. Text: Manfred Steck, Elisabeth Waldschütz, Biljana Crnogorac.] Nagold: Otto-Hahn-Gymnasium, 1992, [various paging]. [H.1: Unterschwandorf um die Mitte des 19. Jahrhunderts (Manfred Steck, 68 pp., illus., tabs.). H.2: König, Reichsritter und Juden (Elisabeth Waldschütz, 105 pp., illus.). H. 3: Freiherr Gustav von Kechler und Unterschwandorf (Manfred Steck, Elisabeth Waldschütz, 102 pp., tabs.). H.4: Die jüdische Gemeinde. 1.(Manfred Steck, 77 pp., illus., map). H.5: Die jüdische Gemeinde. 2. (Manfred Steck, 117 pp.). H.6: Wohn- und Besitzverhältnisse der Unterschwandorfer Juden (Manfred Steck, 133 pp., map). H. 7: Die Auswanderung nach Amerika (Biljana Crnogorac, Biljana, 94 pp., tabs.).]

29187 — *Der jüdische Friedhof von Unterschwandorf.* Hrsg.: Otto-Hahn-Gymnasium Nagold. Texte: Julia Ettmann [et al.]. Nagold: Otto-Hahn-Gymnasium, 1992. 102 pp., illus., map.

—— URSPRINGEN. [See in No. 29005.]

29188 WEINGARTEN. BÜSING, HAYO: *Die Geschichte der Juden in Weingarten (Baden): von den Anfängen im Mittelalter bis zum Holocaust.* Hrsg.: Bürger- und Heimatverein Weingarten. Weingarten: Bürger- und Heimatverein, 1991. 55 pp., illus. (Weingartener Heimatblätter, 9.)

29189 WESTPHALIA. STEGEMANN, WOLF/EICHMANN, JOHANNA, eds.: *Jüdisches Museum Westfalen.* Dokumentationszentrum und Lehrhaus für jüdische Geschichte und Religion in Dorsten. Ein Beitrag zur Geschichte der Juden in Westfalen – Katalog. Dorsten (Postfach 622): Verein für jüdische Geschichte und Religion, 1992. 1 vol.

29190 WIESBADEN. BEMBENEK, LOTHAR: *Das jüdische Badhaus 'Zum Rebhuhn' in Wiesbaden.* [In]:

Menora, Bd. 3, München, 1992. Pp. 99–120, notes, illus. [On the history of the Jewish bath house (spa) and the attempts to establish a Jewish museum in its old annexe.]

29191 WINDSHEIM. STEINMETZ, HORST/HOFMANN, HELMUT: *Die Juden von Windsheim nach 1871.* Bad Windsheim: Selbstverlag der Autoren, 1992. 472 pp., illus., facsims., plans, ports. [Obtainable at the LBI New York; also covers Nazi period.]

29192 WITTLICH. WEIN-MEHS, MARIA: *Die beiden Kultbauten der Juden in Wittlich: die alte Synagoge und die neue Synagoge.* [Hrsg.: Stadt Wittlich] Wittlich: Stadt Wittlich, 1991. 75 pp., illus.

29193 WORMS. REUTER, FRITZ: *Jüdisches Worms. Raschi-Haus und Judengasse.* Worms: Jüdisches Museum Raschi-Haus (Hintere Judengasse 6, 6520 Worms), 1992. 41 pp., notes, illus., maps. [Extended reprint of an article publ. under the title Das Jüdische Museum Raschi-Haus in Worms in Der Wormsgau. Wissenschaftliche Zeitschrift der Stadt Worms und des Altertumsvereins Worms, Bd.15, 1987/91. This catalogue is also publ. in English (transl. by Ursula Reuter) under the title Jewish Worms. Rashi House and Judengasse.]

29194 WÜRTTEMBERG. JUNG, MARTIN: *Die württembergische Kirche und die Juden in der Zeit des Pietismus (1675–1780).* Berlin: Institut Kirche und Judentum, 1992. 395 pp., notes, tabs., bibl. (307–380), indexes (persons, places, 381–394). (Studien zu Kirche und Israel, Bd. 13. Zugl.: Tübingen, Univ.,Diss., 1990.)

29195 WÜRZBURG. GEHRING-MÜNZEL, URSULA: *Vom Schutzjuden zum Staatsbürger. Die gesellschaftliche Integration der Würzburger Juden 1803–1871.* Würzburg: Ferd. Schöningh, 1992. XV, 599 pp., bibl. (557–578), indexes. (Veröffentlichungen des Stadtarchivs Würzburg, Bd. 6.)

1a. Alsace

29196 *Les Juifs d'Alsace et la Révolution Française.* XIème Colloque de la Société d'Histoire des Israélites d'Alsace et de Lorraine (fév. 1989). Strasbourg, 1990. 1 vol. [Incl.: contributions by Jean Daltroff, Léon Gehler, André-Marc Haarscher, Jean-Claude Richez, Lilian Herisson, Freddy Raphael and Lazare Gehler.]

29197 STRASBOURG. *Strassburg und die Judenverfolgung 1348/49:* historische Dokumentation. Konrad (Cuntze) von Winterthur zum Engel, Stadtmeister von Strassburg. Zusammengestellt und bearb. von Christoph Güntert. Beraten und betreut durch Ludwig Schmugge. Hrsg.: Aytun Altindal. Zürich: Altindal 'Modus Vivendi', 1991. 154 pp., illus.

2. Austria

29198 GENEE, PIERRE: *Die Landsynagogen im Burgenland und Niederösterreich.* Wien: Informationszentrum im Dienste der Christlich-Jüdischen Verständigung (IDCIV), 1991. 31 pp., illus. (IDCIV–Vorträge, Nr. 44.)

29199 GOVRIN, NURIT: *From image to picture: Kaiser Franz Joseph I in Hebrew literature.* [In Hebrew, title transl.]. [In]: Mahut: Journal of Jewish literature and art, Vol. 7, Lod, 1990. Pp. 55–90. [On F.J.'s depiction in 19th-20th century Hebrew literature, usually idealised.]

29200 HOHENEMS. *Beit haChaim – Haus des Lebens. Der jüdische Friedhof in Hohenems.* Mit Fotografien von Arno Gisinger. Katalog zur Ausstellung im Jüdischen Museum Hohenems vom 30. April bis 12. Juni 1992. Hohenems: Jüdisches Museum Hohenems, 1992. 64 pp., illus. [Incl.: Zur Geschichte des jüdischen Friedhofs in Hohenems (Eva Grabherr, 7–13).]

29201 — PURIN, BERNHARD: *Das neue jüdische Museum in Hohenems.* [In]: Mitteilungen der Museen Österreichs, N.F., Nr. 34, 1991. P. 13.

29202 — VIELMETTI, NIKOLAUS: *Einwanderung und Wirtschaftstätigkeit von Hohenemser Juden in Orten auf italienischem Boden (vorw. Triest).* [In]: Landjudentum im süddeutschen und Bodenseeraum [see No. 29018]. Pp. 139–144.

29203 — WEILL, ROGER D.: *Jüdisches Museum in Hohenems eröffnet: ein Denkmal für jüdisches Leben im Bodenseeraum.* [In]: Israelitisches Wochenblatt, Jg. 92, Nr. 16, Zürich, 19. April 1991. Pp. 23–27.

29204 *Das Jüdische Echo.* Zeitschrift für Kultur und Politik. Hrsg. von den jüdischen Akademikern Österreichs und der Vereinigung jüdischer Hochschüler Österreichs. Bd. 41, Wien (Stephansplatz 10), Okt. 1992. 252 pp., illus. [Special issue with the title Die Jugend am Wort. Eine Aktion von 'X – Large', ORF, und der Zeitschrift 'Jüdisches Echo'.] [Cont. texts by young people aged between 14 and 26 dealing with racism, xenophobia, nationalism and

444 *Bibliography*

minorities, right-wing radicalism and antisemitism, and the future of Austria; incl. Die notwendige Allianz (Leon Zelman, 6–7) and the sections: Keine jüdische Opferrolle mehr. Judentum und Antisemitismus (119–153). Vom Nationalismus zum Holocaust. Aufsätze von Schülern des jüdischen Gymnasiums in Wien (154–158).]

29205 PATZELT, HERBERT: *Zur Geschichte der Juden in Österreichisch-Schlesien.* [In]: Oberschlesisches Jahrbuch 1992. Bd. 8. Berlin: Mann, 1992. Pp. 25–41, illus., footnotes. [On the history of Jews mainly in the former Duchy of Teschen.]

29206 SCHMIDL, ERWIN A.: *Jüdische Soldaten in Österreich-Ungarn.* [In]: Etudes Danubiennes, Tome 8, No. 2, Strasbourg, 1992. Pp. 133–144, footnotes.

29207 SPITZER, SHLOMO: *A document of rabbinic appointment for Rabbi Jona from the community of Boskowice* [Moravia]. [In Hebrew, title transl.]. [In]: Moriah, Vol. 18, No. 5–6, Jerusalem, Nissan 5752 [= April 1992]. Pp. 102–107. [Gives the text of the document from 1744. Author suggests that Jona did not take up the appointment through fear following Maria Theresia's declaring the expulsion of the Jews of Moravia in 1744 (later rescinded).]

29208 TISIS. BURMEISTER, KARL HEINZ: *Die Juden in Tisis 1135–1640* [Vorarlberg]. [In]: Tisis Dorf- und Kirchengeschichte. Im Auftrag der Rheticus-Gesellschaft und der Pfarre Tisis, hrsg. von Rainer Lins. Feldkrich, 1992. (Schriftenreihe der Rheticus-Gesellschaft, 28.) Pp. 141–147.

29209 VIENNA. BURSTYN, RUTH: *Die Geschichte der türkisch-sephardischen Juden in Wien von ihren Anfängen 1718 bis zum Jahr 1938.* [In]: Kairos, Neue Folge, Jg. 32./33, Salzburg, 1990/1991. Pp. 98–137.

29210 — JOHN, MICHAEL/LICHTBLAU, ALBERT: *Schmelztiegel Wien einst und jetzt. Zur Geschichte und Gegenwart von Zuwanderung und Minderheiten.* Aufsätze, Quellen, Kommentare. Mit einer Einleitung von Erich Zöllner. Wien: Böhlau, 1990. 487 pp., notes, illus., maps, docs., facsims., tabs. [Collection of 560 source materials preceded by introductory essays; based on a joint co-operation project of Austrian schools and universities aimed at deepening the understanding of migration and integration processes with respect to history and to the present. Refers passim to the Jewish population, and in specific sections: Anzahl, Herkunft und Berufstätigkeit der Zuwanderer in Wien. Die Juden (33–48). Die Ursachen der Zuwanderung der jüdischen Bevölkerung nach Wien (114–120). Die räumliche Verteilungsstruktur der Minderheiten im Wiener Stadtgebiet. Die jüdische Minderheit (143–147). Wohnverhältnisse und Migration. Jüdisches Wohnen in Wien (204–211). Familie, Nachbarschaft, Vereine – Die sozialen Beziehungen im näheren Umfeld der Zuwanderer. Die jüdische Familie (238–244). Sport. Jüdische und tschechische Sportvereine in Wien [and] Jüdische und tschechische Fußballspieler (433–439). Also on assimilation, acculturation, racism and antisemitism (341–415).]

29211 — KOLLER-GLÜCK, ELISABETH: *Der alte Judenfriedhof in der Seegasse. Mit besonderer Berücksichtigung seines Schicksals während und nach der Zeit des Nationalsozialismus.* [In]: Wiener Geschichtsblätter, Jg. 47, Wien, 1992. Pp. 22–31.

29212 — LEMBERGER, TIRZA: *Ideologie und Entwicklungen im jüdischen Unterrichtswesen vom Toleranzpatent bis zur Konstituierung der Kultusgemeinde in Wien (1782–1852).* [In]: Kairos, Neue Folge, Jg. 32./33, Salzburg, 1990/1991. Pp. 138–228, notes (219–228).

29213 — VEIGL, HANS, ed.: *Luftmenschen spielen Theater. Jüdisches Kabarett in Wien 1890–1938.* Hrsg. von Hans Veigl. Wien: Kremayr & Scheriau, 1992. 207 pp., notes, bibl., glossary. [Texts by Heinrich Eisenbach, Armin Berg, Josef Armin, Arthur Franzetti, Louis Taufstein, Adolf Bergmann, Alexander Trebisch, Fritz Löhner-Beda [et al.], arranged under the following headings: Die frühen Jahre. Heinrich Eisenbach und die 'Budapester Orpheumsgesellschaft'; Zores im Zentrum. Jargontheater in der Innenstadt: die 'Possenbühne Max und Moritz'; Klingers! Ein Familienidyll von Robert Weil-Homunkulus; Vergnügungsetablissement Abgrund. Zionistisches Kabarett in Wien.]

——— WEINZIERL, ERIKA: *Das österreichische Judentum von den Anfängen bis 1938.* [See in No. 29282.]

3. Central Europe

29214 ABRAMS, BRADLEY F.: *Bookends of Bohemian Jewish identity: Leopold Kompert and Fritz Mauthner.* [In]: Bohemia, Bd. 33, H. 2, München 1992. Pp. 282–298, footnotes. [On the shift in identity from 'Jewish' to 'German Jewish' of the two writers.]

29215 BÁCSKAI, VERA: *Die Pester Grosskaufleute: Stadtbürger, Unternehmer oder Dritter Stand?* [In]:

ERNST BRUCKMÜLLER [et. al.], ed.: Bürgertum in der Habsburger Monarchie. Wien: Böhlau, 1990. Pp. 21–30, notes. [Incl. numerous references to Jewish merchants.]

29216 GALSKY, D.: *Les juifs de Bohème et de Moravie.* [In]: Istina, Vol. 36, No. 3, Paris, 1991. Pp. 308–311.

29217 *Judaica Bohemiae.* Vol. 28. Praha, Státni Zidovské Muzeum, 1992. 111 pp., illus. [Incl.: Systematic collections of memories organized by the Jewish Museum in Prague (Anna Hyndráková/Anna Lorencová, 53–63). Der Vogel auf dem Hüftknochen (Margit Hermannová, 64–66). Dated lace in synagogal textiles (Ludmila Kybalová, 73–79). The borderline between time and eternity. A note on the symbolism of synagogal textiles (Jana Smejkalová, 80–87). Le cimetière juif à Svihov (Vlastimila Hamácková, 88–92). Further articles are listed according to subject.]

29218 LOMNITZ. MCEWAN, DOROTHEA: *Jüdisches Leben im mährischen Ghetto. Eine Skizzierung der Stetl-Geschichte von Lomnitz bis 1848.* [In]: Mitteilungen des Instituts für österreichische Geschichtsforschung. Bd. 99, Wien, 1991. Pp. 83–145, footnotes. [Also on the legislation of Joseph II concerning German names.]

29219 MORAVIA. STEPHAN, VACLAV: *Die gesellschaftliche und rechtliche Stellung der Juden in Mähren in der vorhussitischen Zeit.* [In]: Judaica Bohemiae 28, Praha, 1992. Pp. 3–21.

— PERLMAN, ROBERT: *Bridging three worlds: Hungarian-Jewish Americans, 1848–1914.* [See No. 29239.]

29220 PRAGUE. HOLZ, H.: *Jüdische Kultur in Prag.* [In]: Evangelische Kommentare, Jg. 24, Nr. 11–12, Stuttgart, 1991. Pp. 677–702.

29221 — KUDELA, JIRY: *Prager jüdische Eliten von 1780 bis in die 1. Hälfte des 19. Jahrhunderts.* [In]: Judaica Bohemiae 28, Praha 1992. Pp. 22–34.

29222 RIFF, MICHAEL: *The face of survival: Jewish life in Eastern Europe past and present.* With personal memoirs by Hugo Gryn, Stephen Roth, Ben Helfgott and Hermy Jankel. Epilogue by Rabbi Moses Rosen. London: Vallentine Mitchell, 1992. 224 pp., illus., maps, bibl. notes. [Incl. Foreword (Peter Levy and Israel Weinstock) and chaps. on Czechoslovakia, Hungary, Poland, Romania; also on Eastern European Jews in Germany.]

29223 SILBER, MICHAEL K., ed.: *Jews in the Hungarian economy 1760–1945.* Studies dedicated to Moshe Carmilly-Weinberger on his eightieth birthday. Jerusalem: Magnes Press, the Hebrew University, 1992. 302 pp., port., tabs., index. [Incl.: (titles partly abbr.) An appreciation (Avraham Harman/Jacob Katz, XI–XII). On three continents (Eliyahu Yeshurun, XIII–XXVIII). Bibliography of Moshe Carmilly-Weinberger (Zvi Erényi, XXIXff.). A Jewish minority in an backward economy (Michael K. Silber, 3–22). Jews and the modernization of commerce in Hungary, 1760–1848 (Péter Hanák, 23–39). Jewish wholesale merchants in Pest in the first half of the nineteenth century (Vera Bácskai, 40–52). Jewish wealth in Vienna 1670–1918 (William McCagg, 53–91). The occupational structure of Hungarian Jewry in the eighteenth and twentieth centuries (László Katus, 92–105). Jewish leaseholders in the course of agricultural development in Hungary, 1850–1930 (Julianna Puskás, 106–126). The standard of living of Jews in Austria-Hungary: the anthropometric evidence, 1860–1920 (John Komlos, 127–134). Hidden urbanization: the birth of the bourgeoisie in mid-nineteenth century Hungary (Peter Hidas, 135–161). Religious divisions, socio-economic stratification and the modernization of Hungarian Jewry after the emancipation (Victor Karady, 161–186). Mór Wahrmann: A Jewish banker in Hungarian politics in the era of the Dual Monarchy (Károlyi Vörös, 187–195). Manfréd Weiss: the profile of a munitions king (Lászlo Varga, 196–209). The search for an urban alliance: the politics of the National Association of Hungarian Industrialists (GyOSz) before World War I (George Deak, 210–226). Hungarian banking and business leaders between the wars: education, ethnicity and career patterns (György Lengyel, 227–236). Interwar antisemitism in the professions: The case of the engineers (Mária Kovács, 237–246). Patterns of Jewish economic behavior in Central Europe in the twentieth century (Yehuda Don, 247–273). The occupational structure of Hungarian Jews in the interwar period (György Ránki, 274–286).]

29224 TALMAGE, FRANK: *Angels, anthems, and anathemas: aspects of popular religion in fourteenth-century Bohemian Judaism.* [In]: Jewish History, Vol. 6, Nos. 1–2, Leiden, Haifa Univ. 1992. Pp. 13–20, notes.

4. Switzerland

29225 KAUFMANN, ROBERT URI: *Die Emanzipation der Juden in der Schweiz im europäischen Vergleich.* [In]: Mundo Multa Miracula. Festschrift für Hans Conrad Peyer. Hrsg.: Hans Berger [et al.]. Zürich: Verlag Neue Zürcher Zeitung, 1992. Pp. 199–251, notes.

29226 KAUFMANN, URI: *Der lange Weg zur Gleichberechtigung: aus der Geschichte der Juden in der Schweiz – der Kanton Aargau war ein wichtiger Schauplatz.* [In]: Isr. Wochenblatt, Jg. 92, Nr. 18, Zürich, 3. Mai 1991. Pp. 38–43, illus., port., facsims.

29227 LENGNAU. ARMBRUSTER, THOMAS: *Die jüdischen Dörfer von Lengnau und Endingen.* [In]: Landjudentum im süddeutschen und Bodenseeraum [see No. 29018]. Pp. 38–86.

29228 LÜTHI, URS: *Der Mythos von der Weltverschwörung. Die Hetze der Schweizer Frontisten gegen Juden und Freimaurer am Beispiel des Berner Prozesses um die Protokolle der Weisen von Zion.* Basel: Helbling & Lichtenhahn, 1992. 139 pp.

29229 ST. GALLEN. WOLFFERS, ARTUR [&] DEGGINGER-UNGER, MARIANNE: *Die Geschichte der Juden in St. Gallen.* [&] *Das Archiv der jüdischen Gemeinde in St. Gallen.* [In]: Landjudentum im süddeutschen und Bodenseeraum [see No. 29018]. Pp. 145–148 [&] 149–154.

C. German-Speaking Jews in Various Countries

29230 AVNI, HAIM: *Argentina and the Jews: a history of Jewish immigration.* Transl. from the Hebrew by Gila Brand. Tuscaloosa: Univ. of Alabama Press, 1991. XII, 267 pp., illus. [Incl. immigration and rescue of children from Nazi Germany.]

29231 BOLKOSKY, SIDNEY M.: *Harmony and dissonance: voices of Jewish identity in Detroit. 1914–1967.* Detroit: Wayne State Univ. Press, 1991. 543 pp., illus. [Incl. German-Jewish community in Detroit.]

29232 EXILE. *Dunera News.* A quarterly publication for refugees from Nazi and Fascist persecution (mistakenly shipped to and interned in Australia at Hay and Tatura, many serving later in the 8th AERC, AMF), their relations and friends.: Ed. by Eric Eckstein. Dandenong, Vic. 3175: Hay-Tatura Association (87 Clow Street), 1992. Nos. 23–25, 3 issues [each 23 pp.], illus., facsims. [Incl. documents and personal memoirs relating to the Nazi period, the internment on the Dunera, and life in Australia; also reports on special events.]

29233 EXTON, INEZ P.: *Children of nowhere: an autobiographical biography of an era.* Riverside, CA: Ariadne Press, 1991. I, 199 pp., illus., ports. [Deals with Austrian-Jewish refugee children in the US.]

— GOLVAN, COLIN: *The distant exodus. Australian Jews recall their immigration experiences.* [See No. 29324.]

29234 GOUGH-YATES, KEVIN: *Jews and exiles in British cinema.* [In]: LBI Year Book XXXVII, London. Pp. 517–541, footnotes, illus.

— HYMAN, PAULA E.: *Gender and the Immigrant Jewish experience in the United States.* [See in No. 28990.]

29235 KLINGENSTEIN, SUSANNE: *Jews in the American Academy 1900–1940: the dynamics of intellectual assimilation.* New Haven; London: Yale Univ. Press, 1991. XXII, 248 pp., illus., ports., notes (209–248). [Incl. also personalities of German-Jewish descent, such as Felix Adler, Horace Meyer Kallen, Ludwig Lewisohn, Leo Wiener.]

29236 MARCUS, JACOB RADER: *United States Jewry 1776–1985.* Vol. II: *The Germanic period.* Detroit: Wayne State Univ. Press, 1991. X, 419 pp., illus., maps, notes (355–386). Vol. III: *The Germanic period*, part 2. 1991. 920 pp., illus. [Incl. German and Austrian Jews, from Posen, Prussia, Silesia.]

29237 MORGENTHAU, HENRY III: *Mostly Morgenthaus: a family history.* New York: Ticknow & Fields, 1991. XXI, 501 pp., illus., bibl. [History of four generations of the Morgenthau family who went to the US from Germany in 1866. Author, who is of the fourth generation, also describes the network of German-Jewish families.]

29238 NAGGAR, BETTY: *Jewish peddlars and hawkers 1740–1940.* Camberley: Porphyrogenitus, 1992. 159 pp., illus. [Incl. Jewish traders from Germany.]

29239 PERLMAN, ROBERT: *Bridging three worlds: Hungarian-Jewish Americans, 1848–1914.* Amherst: Univ. of Massachusetts Press, 1991. XII, 302 pp., illus., maps, bibl. [Between 1848 and

1914, approx. 100,000 Jews emigrated from Hungary to the USA; author describes how their experiences differed from those of other Jewish national groups.]

29240 UFFORD, JACK TWISS QUARLES VAN/MERKX, JOEP (JOSEF): *Ich hab' noch einen Koffer in Berlin: German-Jewish identity in Argentina, 1933–1985*. [In]: Jewish Social Studies, Vol. 50, Nos. 1–2, New York, Winter-Spring 1988/1992. Pp. 99–110.

29241 WAHL, ANGELIKA VON: *Zwischen Heimat und Holocaust. Das Deutschlandbild der Nachkommen deutscher Juden in New York*. Frankfurt am Main; New York [et al.]: Lang, 1992. 150 [&] 173 pp. (Reihe XXI Politikwissenschaft, Bd. 210.) [Based on 16 interviews.]

II. RESEARCH AND BIBLIOGRAPHY

A. Libraries and Institutes

29242 GERMANIA JUDAICA, Kölner Bibliothek zur Geschichte des deutschen Judentums, ed.: *Arbeitsinformationen über Studienprojekte auf dem Gebiet der Geschichte des deutschen Judentums und des Antisemitismus*. Ausgabe 15. (Bearb.: Felicitas Hundhausen) Köln (Josef-Haubrich-Hof 1), 1992. 204 pp., indexes (191–204).

29243 HOCHSCHULE FÜR JÜDISCHE STUDIEN, Heidelberg: *Trumah*. 3. Hrsg. von der Hochschule für Jüdische Studien, Heidelberg. Red.: Uri R. Kaufmann, Daniel Krochmalnik. Koordination: Ursula Beitz. Wiesbaden: Reichert, 1992. VIII, 216 pp., notes. [Incl.: Vorwort (Julius Carlebach, VII–VIII). Contributions relevant to German-Jewish history are listed according to subject.]

29244 — *Zeitschriftenverzeichnis*. Hrsg.: Hochschule für Jüdische Studien, Heidelberg. Wiesbaden: Reichert, 1992. 115 pp.

29245 LEO BAECK INSTITUTE. *Bulletin des Leo Baeck Instituts*. Nr. 89–90. Hrsg. von Joseph Walk, Jacov Guggenheim und Itta Shedletzky. Frankfurt am Main: Hain, 1991. 134 pp. [Final issue of the Bulletin: an index vol. of Nos. 50–88 (1974–1991).]

29246 — GRUENEWALD, MAX. *Obits.*: Max Gruenewald, 93, a rabbinical scholar. [In]: New York Times, Dec. 29, 1992. Dr. Max Gruenewald (Arnold Paucker) [in]: AJR Information, Vol. 48, No. 3, London, March, 1993. P. 15.] [M.G., Dec. 4, 1899 Königshütte – Dec. 28, Millburn, NJ, rabbi in Mannheim 1925–1938, from 1944 in Millburn, NJ, co-founder of the Leo Baeck Institute, from 1956 president of the New York LBI, since 1974 International President of the Leo Baeck Institutes.]

29247 — HACKESCHMIDT, H.J.: *Jüdische Geschichte vor 1933 – ein Stiefkind*. Das Leo-Baeck-Institut intensiviert seine Arbeit in Deutschland. [In]: Süddeutsche Zeitung, Nr. 299, München, 1992. P. 10.

29248 — *Jüdischer Almanach 1993 des Leo Baeck Instituts*. Hrsg. von Jakob Hessing. Frankfurt am Main: Jüdischer Verlag, 1992. 175 pp., illus., ports. [This annual, edited by the Jerusalem Leo Baeck Institute, replaces the Bulletin des Leo Baeck Instituts. Incl.: Vorwort (Jehuda Amichai, 7). Zu diesem Almanach (Jakob Hessing, 8–9). Cont. literary essays on Samuel Joseph Agnon, Thomas Mann, Elazar Benyoetz by Gershon Shaked, Christoph Grubitz, a story by Agnon and poems by Manfred Winkler and Benno Fruchtmann. Essays pertaining to the history of German-speaking Jewry are listed according to subject.]

29249 — *Leo Baeck Institute Year Book XXXVII*. Ed.: Arnold Paucker. London: Secker & Warburg, 1992. XXIX, 685 pp., illus., ports., footnotes, bibl. (545–654), general index (661–685). [Cont.: Preface/Introduction (Arnold Paucker, IX–XXIX, footnotes, illus.; incl. obituaries for Erwin Rosenthal, Curt Wormann and Gerson D. Cohen (p. XXVII). Many essays are dedicated to the retiring editor, Arnold Paucker. Essays are arranged under the sections: I. Jewish culture and religion. II. Emancipation re-assessed. III. Jewish identity and antisemitism. IV. History through the book. V. War and resistance. VI. Attitudes to prejudice. Individual contributions are listed according to subject.]

29250 — *LBI Information*: Nachrichten aus dem Leo Baeck Instituten in Jerusalem, London, New York und der Wissenschaftlichen Arbeitsgemeinschaft des LBI in der Bundesrepublik. Hrsg. von den Freunden und Förderern des LBI e.V. in Frankfurt am Main. Red.: Arno Lustiger. Nr. 2. Winter 1991/Frühjahr 1992. Frankfurt am Main (Liebigstraße 24): Freunde und Förderer des LBI e.V., 1992. 44 pp., illus. [Incl.: Das Leo Baeck Institut und das neuvereinigte Deutschland (Michael A. Meyer, 1, 3–5). Neue Perspektiven deutschjüdischer Geschichtsschreibung. Internationale Tagung des Leo Baeck Instituts in Leipzig

(Michael Brenner, 7–9, on the conference, organised by the LBI, Oct. 26–27, 1991). Bestandsaufnahme der Archivalien zur jüdischen Geschichte in den neuen Bundesländern (13–16).]

29251 — *LBI New York. Library & Archives News.* Ed.: Gabrielle Bamberger. No. 31. New York: Leo Baeck Institute, Spring, 1992. [8] pp.

29252 — LUSTIGER, ARNO: *35 Jahre Leo Baeck Institut.* [In]: Deutsche Juden – Juden in Deutschland [see in No. 29504]. P. 137.

29253 SALOMON LUDWIG STEINHEIM-INSTITUT FÜR DEUTSCH-JÜDISCHE GESCHICHTE, Universität Duisburg. BAGEL-BOHLAN, ANJA E.: *Zur Geschichte eines jungen Instituts. Das Salomon Ludwig Steinheim-Institut für deutsch-jüdische Geschichte.* [In]: Ludger Heid/Joachim H. Knoll, eds.: Deutsch-jüdische Geschichte [see No. 29601]. Pp. 25–42.

29254 — *Dialog.* Mitteilungen für die Freunde und Förderer des Salomon Ludwig Steinheim-Instituts für deutsch-jüdische Geschichte e.V. Erlangen, Jg. 6, Nr. 1–4 (Feb.-Nov. 1992). 4 issues (8 pp. each), illus. [No. 3 incl.: obit. Heinz Galinski (Klaus Schütz).]

29255 — *Menora.* Jahrbuch für deutsch-jüdische Geschichte 1992. Bd. 3. Im Auftrag des 'Salomon-Ludwig-Steinheim-Institutes für deutsch-jüdische Geschichte' hrsg. von Julius H. Schoeps in Verbindung mit Arno Herzig und Hans Otto Horch. Red.: Ludger Heid. München: Piper, 1992. 313 pp., notes, index (names). (Serie Piper 1544.) [Cont.: Einführung (eds., 7–12). Individual contributions are listed according to subject.] [Cf.: Besprechung (Barbara von der Lühe) [in]: Tribüne, Jg. 31, H. 122, Frankfurt am Main, 1992, pp. 221–222. Besprechung (Schalom Ben-Chorin) [in]: Tribüne, Jg. 31, H. 123, Frankfurt am Main, 1992, pp. 224–227.]

29256 WIENER LIBRARY, London. *The Wiener Library Newsletter.* Publ. by the Institute of Contemporary History and Wiener Library. Nos. 18 & 19, Summer 1992 & Winter 1992/1993. 2 issues [4 & 8 pp.]. [Reports on Wiener Library events; No. 18 incl.: (Obit.) Bernard Krikler: a tribute (Tony Wells). No. 19 incl.: Retirement of Walter Laqueur (A. Montefiore/E. Fraenkel, 5).]

——— YAD VASHEM. *Proceedings of the Sixth Yad Vashem International Historical Conference,* 1985. [See No. 29509.]

29257 ZENTRUM FÜR ANTISEMITISMUSFORSCHUNG, Berlin. *Jahrbuch für Antisemitismusforschung 1.* Hrsg. von Wolfgang Benz für das Zentrum für Antisemitismusforschung der Technischen Universität Berlin. Frankfurt am Main; New York: Campus, 1992. 345 pp., notes. [Incl.: Vorwort (Wolfgang Benz, 9–12). Individual contributions relevant to antisemitism and history of German-speaking Jewry are listed according to subject.]

29258 — *News Letter,* No. 3 & 4, Berlin, Feb. & Nov. 1992. Red.: Juliane Wetzel. 2 issues [5 & 9 pp.] [Incl. reports on special events, new research projects and recent publications of the Zentrum für Antisemitismusforschung.] [No.4 incl. Antisemitismus in Europa. Ein Konferenzbericht (Daniel Gerson, 1–4), a report on the international conference, organised by the Zentrum für Antisemitismusforschung in co-operation with the Vidal Sassoon International Center for the Study of Antisemitism, Jerusalem, and the Institute of Jewish Affairs, London.]

B. Bibliographies, Catalogues, Reference Books

29259 *Anglo-Jewish bibliography 1971–1990.* Compiled by Ruth P. Goldschmidt-Lehmann. Ed. and augmented by Stephen W. Massil and Peter Shmuel Salinger. London: The Jewish Hist. Society of England, 1992. 377 pp., index (339–377). [Incl. also publications on Jews from Germany.]

29260 *Bibliographie zur Geschichte der Juden in Hessen.* Hrsg.: Kommission für die Geschichte der Juden in Hessen. Bearb. von Ulrich Eisenbach, Hartmut Heinemann und Susanne Walther. Wiesbaden: Kommission f.d. Gesch. d. Juden in Hessen, 1992. XIV, 346 pp.

——— CARLEBACH, JOSEPH. *Bibliographie seiner Schriften.* [See No. 29560.]

29261 COHEN, SUSAN SARAH, ed.: *Antisemitism: an annotated bibliography.* Vol. 2: 1986–1987. [Publ. by] The Vidal Sassoon International Center for the Study of Antisemitism [of] the Hebrew University of Jerusalem. New York; London: Garland, 1991. XXXIV, 559 pp., author index, subject index. [1483 entries of works on antisemitism publ. 1986–1987; for Vol. 1 see No. YB 24162/YB XXXIII.]

29262 ECKERT, BRITA: *Nachschlagewerke zur deutsch-sprachigen Emigration 1933–1945.* [In]: Aus dem Antiquariat, 1, [Beilage zum] Börsenblatt für den Deutschen Buchhandel, Jg. 159, Nr. 9, Frankfurt am Main, 31. Jan. 1992. A 1–A 11. [Review article. Cf.: Deutsch-deutsche Teilung auch in der Exilwissenschaft? (Frank Albrecht) [in]: Aus dem Antiquariat, 4, [Beilage zum] Börsenblatt für den deutschen Buchhandel, Jg. 159, Nr. 35, Frankfurt am Main, 30. April 1992, A 173–A 175.]

29263 GILBOA, MENUCHA: *A lexicon of Hebrew periodicals in the 18th and 19th century.* [In Hebrew]. Jerusalem: Bialik Institute, 1992. 471 pp., indexes of titles, editors, and cities of publication. [Arranged chronologically, dating from 1691–1896, with bibl. details and short history of each periodical; incl. about 70 periodicals publ. in Austria and Germany.]

29264 *Index of articles on Jewish studies (and the study of Eretz Israel).* Vol. 30: 1988; Vol. 31: 1989 [and] Vol. 32: 1990. Comp. and ed. by 'Kiryat Sefer', the Jewish National and Univ. Library. Ed. board: Bitya Ben-Shammai, Susan Sarah Cohen [et al.]. Jerusalem: The Jewish National and Univ. Library, 1990, 1991 [and] 1992. 3 vols. (XLVII, 454 pp.; XLVIII, 381 pp.; LIII, 436 pp.), author and subject indexes. [A selective bibliography, incl. articles on German-speaking Jewry.]

29265 *Jewish film directory: a guide to more than 1200 films of Jewish interest from 32 countries over 85 years.* Ed. by Matthew Stevens. London: Flicks Books; Westport, CT: Greenwood Press, 1992. 298 pp., indexes, bibl. [Among the topics incl. are films about Anne Frank, the Holocaust, Jewish-Gentile relations, Nazi-occupied Europe, Nazi propaganda, post-war German films on Jewish themes, Terezin.]

— *National registry of Jewish Holocaust survivors.* [See No. 29383.]

29266 *Neues Lexikon des Judentums.* Hrsg. von Julius H. Schoeps. Gütersloh: Bertelsmann Lexikon Verlag, 1992. 496 pp., illus., maps, tabs. [Incl. essays; those mainly dealing with German-speaking Jewry and German antisemitism are: Antisemitismus (Robert S. Wistrich, 41–47). Deutsche Judenheit und Demokratie (Walter Grab, 108–109). Zur Geschichte des deutsch-jüdischen Verhältnisses (Julius H. Schoeps, 117–119). Emanzipation und Assimilation (Jacob Toury, 132–134). Emigration und Exil nach 1933 (Will Jasper, 135–137). Gemeindeleben in Deutschland nach 1945 (Cilly Kugelmann, 165–167). Deutsch-jüdischer Journalismus (Harry Pross, 235–239). Judengesetzgebung (Friedrich Battenberg, 240–242). Jüdisches Lernen (Hildegard Feidel-Mertz, 244–246). Deutschlands jüdische Jugendbewegung (Hermann Meier-Cronemeier, 247–249). Kirche und Judentum (Edna Brocke, 261–264). Die deutsch-jüdische Literatur und ihre Geschichte (Hans-Otto Horch/Itta Shedletzky, 291–294). Geschichte der Juden im Mittelalter (Friedrich Lotter, 319–324). Jüdische Musik (Alphons Silbermann, 328–329). Juden und Nationalsozialismus (Nahum Orland, 334–336). Die Juden in der frühen Neuzeit (Arno Herzig, 339–341). NS-Prozesse in Nachkriegsdeutschland (Heiner Lichtenstein, 342–345). Das Ostjudenbild in Deutschland (Ludger Heid, 350–352). Reformjudentum (Michael A. Meyer, 384). Synagogenbau (Hannelore Künzl, 439). Holocaust und Vergangenheitsbewältigung (Micha Brumlik, 465–469). Deutschland, Israel und die 'Wiedergutmachung' (Michael Wolffsohn, 481–483). Juden und Wirtschaftsleben (Werner E. Mosse, 485–487). Wissenschaft des Judentums (Julius Carlebach, 488–490).]

29267 *Post-war publications on German Jewry.* A selected bibliography of books and articles 1991. Compiled by Barbara Suchy and Annette Pringle. [In]: LBI Year Book XXXVII, London. Pp. 545–654, index (629–654).

29268 *The Schocken guide to Jewish books: where to start reading about Jewish history, literature, culture, and religion.* Ed. Barry W. Holtz. New York: Schocken Books, 1992. X, 357 pp., illus. [Incl. as topics the Jews in Europe 1500–1750; German-Jewish history; Israel and Zionism.]

— WEISS, NELLY: *Die Herkunft jüdischer Familiennamen: Herkunft, Typen, Geschichte* [See No. 29049.]

III. THE NAZI PERIOD

A. General

29269 AACHEN. *Fragen, erinnern, Spuren sichern.* Beiträge aus einer Geschichtswerkstatt beim Kolping-Bildungswerk Aachen von Anle Collet, Heinz Gödde [et al.]. Hrsg. von Annemarie

Haase. Aachen: Alano, 1992. 112 pp. [Incl. contributions on the November Pogrom, on the Voss family and personal recollections of other Jews from Aachen.]

29270 ANNAS, GEORGE/GRODIN, MICHAEL: *The Nazi doctors and the Nuremberg code: human rights in human experimentation.* New York: Oxford Univ. Press, 1992. XXII, 371 pp., illus.

29271 ARNOLD, BEN: *Art, music and the Holocaust.* [In]: Holocaust and Genocide Studies, Vol. 6, No. 4, Oxford. 1991. Pp. 335–349, notes. [Incl. the role music played in Terezin and other camps; discusses individual performances.]

29272 ARONSFELD, C.C.: *Leo Baeck und das 'Ende des deutschen Judentums'. Schon 1933 prophezeit oder erst 1945 erkannt?* [In]: Aufbau, Vol. 58, New York, Jan. 3, 1992. Pp. 5–6. [For previous publ. see No. 27917/YB XXXVII.]

29273 AUSCHWITZ. BENZLER, SUSANNE: *Auschwitz als Zivilisationsbruch. Die Organisation der Vernichtung um der Vernichtung willen.* [In]: Tribüne, Jg. 31, H. 124, Frankfurt am Main, 1992. Pp. 109–116, footnotes.

29274 — DISTEL, BARBARA/KRUMME, WERNER: *'Das System an sich konnte ich nicht ändern. Ich konnte es nur im Rahmen meiner Möglichkeiten an einigen Stellen unterhöhlen'. Erinnerung eines Häftlingsfunktionärs im Lager Auschwitz I.* [In]: Dachauer Hefte, Jg. 7, H. 7, Dachau, Nov. 1991. Pp. 118–128.

29275 — HÖSS, RUDOLPH: *Death dealer: the memoirs of the SS Kommandant at Auschwitz.* Ed. by Steven Paskuly. Transl. by Andrew Pollinger. Buffalo, NY: Prometheus Books, 1992. 390 pp., illus., facsims., maps, appendixes, bibl. ([383]-385), name index. [Memoirs written between Oct. 1946 and April 1947.]

29276 — NEUBROCH, HANS/STERNFELD, ALBERT: *Rezensionen und Stellungnahmen zu Richard Foreggers Essay 'Technical analysis of methods to bomb the gas chambers of Auschwitz'.* [In]: Dokumentationsarchiv des österreichischen Widerstandes. Jahrbuch 1992. Wien: Dokumentationsarchiv des österreichischen Widerstandes, 1992. pp. 120–131. [For Foregger's essay see No.28335/YB XXXVII.]

29277 — SHELLEY, LORE: *Schreiberinnen des Todes: Dokumentation.* Übers.: Gerhard Armanski. Bielefeld: AJZ, 1992. 381 pp., illus. [Incl.: Vorwort zur deutschen Ausgabe (Herbert Langbein, 13–15). A collection of memoirs of Jewish women, incl. the author, who were forced to work in the administration of Auschwitz; the original American edn. publ. in New York: Shengold, 1986 under the title Secretaries of death.]

29278 AUSTRIA. *Jüdische Schicksale. Berichte von Verfolgten.* Hrsg.: Dokumentationsarchiv des österreichischen Widerstandes. Auswahl, Redaktion und Bearbeitung: Brigitte Bailer [et al.], unter Mitarbeit von Jonny Moser. Wien: ÖBV, 1992. 730 pp., illus., index (725–730). (Erzählte Geschichte. Berichte von Widerstandskämpfern und Verfolgten, Bd. 3.) [Incl. interviews with Jews and persons of Jewish descent about their experiences during Nazi period and thereafter. Interviews arranged under the headings: II. Diskriminierung und Verfolgung nach dem 'Anschluss'. III. Die Situation der jüdischen Bevölkerung in Wien vom Ausbruch bis zum Ende des Krieges. IV. Zwischen 'Ariern' und 'Nichtariern' – 'Mischlinge ersten Grades'. V. Flucht, Vertreibung und Exil (incl. resistance and military service in the Allied Armies). VI. Deportation, 'Endlösung' und Konzentrationslager. VII. Leben im Verborgenen – Schicksale der 'U-Boote'. VIII. Leben nach dem Holocaust.]

29279 — MOSER, JONNY: *Die Anhalte- und Sammellager für österreichische Juden.* [In]: Dokumentationsarchiv des österreichischen Widerstandes. Jahrbuch 1992. Wien: Dokumentationsarchiv des österreichischen Widerstandes, 1992. Pp. 71–75.

— — *The November-Pogrom 1938; the ordeal of German Jewry.* [In Hebrew]. [See No. 29429.]

29280 — *Österreicher im Exil. Grossbritannien 1938–1945.* Eine Dokumentation. Hrsg.: Dokumentationsarchiv des österreichischen Widerstandes. Einleitung, Auswahl und Bearbeitung: Wolfgang Muchitsch. Mit einem Geleitwort von Herbert Steiner. Wien: Österreichischer Bundesverlag, 1992. XI, 652 pp., docs., index of places, of persons.

29281 — SCHMIDT, ELFRIEDE: *1938 . . . and the consequences: questions and responses.* Interviews. Transl. by Peter J. Lyth. Riverside, CA: Ariadne Press, 1992. 381 pp., ports., bibl. ([371]-375). [Interviews describing the events of the Austrian 'Anschluß' in 1938; incl. Jews who emigrated; also discusses Austrian antisemitism.]

29282 — WEINZIERL, ERIKA/KULKA, OTTO D., eds.: *Vertreibung und Neubeginn. Israelische Bürger österreichischer Herkunft.* Mit einem Vorwort von Ernst L. Ehrlich. In Zusammenarbeit mit Gabriele Anderl [et al.]. Wien: Böhlau, 1992. 560 pp., illus., glossary, index. [The book is dedicated to Teddy Kollek. Cont.: Das österreichische Judentum von den Anfängen bis 1938 (Erika Weinzierl, 17–166; incl. biographies of Austrian émigrés to Palestine).

Emigration und Vertreibung (Gabriele Anderl, 167–338). Die Immigration (Doron Niederland, 339–444). Israelische Bürger österreichischer Herkunft. Eine statistische Analyse der quantitativen Befragung (Christian W. Haerpfer, 445–488). Anhang: Erinnerungen. Teddy Kollek: Jugend in Wien (491–514). Arie Rath: Autobiographie (515–544).]

29283 BADEN-WÜRTTEMBERG. HAUMANN, HEIKO: *'Lieber 'n alter Jud verrecke als e Tröpfle Schnaps verschütte'. Juden im bäuerlichen Milieu des Schwarzwaldes zu Beginn des Nationalsozialismus.* [In]: Menora, Bd. 3, München, 1992. Pp. 143–152, notes.

29284 BARKAI, AVRAHAM: *The Nazi 'Volksgemeinschaft', the 'Aryanization', and the Holocaust.* [In Hebrew, title transl., with English summary]. [In]: Yalkut Moreshet, No. 53, Tel-Aviv, Nov. 1992. Pp. 37–52.

29285 BAUMANN, ARNULF H., ed.: *Ausgegrenzt. Schicksalswege 'nichtarischer' Christen in der Hitlerzeit. Mario Sello – Ursula Basselmann – Werner Steinberg.* Hannover: Lutherisches Verlagshaus, 1992. 157 pp. [Personal recollections of three 'non-Aryan Christians' in Hamburg during the Nazi persecution.]

—— BEISBART, ORTWIN/KREJCI, MICHAEL: *Nazismus und Holocaust in der deutschprachigen Kinder- und Jugendliteratur.* [See in No. 29673.]

29286 BENZ, UTE: *Facetten der Erinnerungsarbeit. Die Suche der Kinder nach dem Leben der Väter.* [In]: Jahrbuch für Antisemitismusforschung 1, Berlin 1992. Pp. 296–306. [Review article of recent autobiographical accounts of children whose fathers were involved with Nazi crimes; incl. a critical review of Inge Hecht's recollections Von der Heilsamkeit des Erinnerns (see No. 28461/YB XXXVII).]

29287 BENZ, WOLFGANG: *Rassenkrieg gegen Kinder in Ghetto und KZ.* [In]: Jahrbuch für Antisemitismusforschung 1, Berlin 1992. Pp. 182–190, notes.

29288 BENZ, WOLFGANG: *Reaktionen auf die Verfolgung der Juden und den Holocaust in Deutschland vor und nach 1945.* [In]: Das Parlament, Jg. 42, Bonn, 3. Jan. 1992. Pp. 24–32, footnotes.

29289 BERLIN. ALTHAUS, MANON: *Zum Verhältnis von Juden und Christen in der Trinitatisgemeinde und in ihrem Umkreis.* [In]: Matthias Manrique, ed.: Trinitatis [Charlottenburg] im Wandel der Zeit 1896–1961. Studie und Dokumentation. Im Spiegel der Konsistorialakten und des Nachlasses Bleier. Berlin: Alektor-Verl., 1992. Pp. 105–113. [Incl.: the sections: Jüdisches Leben im Umkreis der Trinitatisgemeinde. Reaktion der Trinitatsgemeinde auf den Antisemitismus der 30'er und 40'er Jahre.]

29290 —— BUSEMANN, HERTHA LUISE/DAXNER, MICHAEL/FÖLLING, WERNER: *Insel der Geborgenheit. Die Private Waldschule Kaliski Berlin 1932–1939.* Stuttgart: Metzler, 1992. 379 pp., illus., facsims., lists, notes (349–375), bibl. (375–379). [Cont. the sections: Einleitung: Ein himmlisches Ghetto (Michael Daxner, 1–13). 1. Jüdische Familien in Berlin. 2. Bildung und Erziehung an einer jüdischen Schule. 6. Lehrer und Schüler. 7. Überleben, Flucht und Emigration (Werner Fölling). 3. Die Schulgründerin – Lotte Kaliski. 4. Der Schulleiter – Heinrich Selver (Hertha Luise Busemann); incl. also list of pupils (297–311).]

29291 —— ELKIN, RIVKA: *The Jewish hospital in Berlin: last vestige of German Jewry in the period of the Third Reich.* [In Hebrew, title transl., with English summary]. [In]: Yalkut Moreshet, No. 53, Tel-Aviv, Nov. 1992. Pp. 53–91.

29292 —— FROMM, BELLA: *Blood and banquets: a Berlin diary 1930–1938.* Foreword by Judith Rossner. Introd. by Frederick T. Birchall. New York: Touchstone; Simon & Schuster, 1992. XIV, 338 pp., illus., ports. [B.F. (1900–1972) was society reporter for the 'Vossische Zeitung'. She used her social connections to help Jews escape, until she herself fled in 1938. First edn. appeared in 1942.]

29293 —— *Geschlossene Vorstellung. Der Jüdische Kulturbund in Deutschland 1933–1941.* Hrsg.: Akademie der Künste, Berlin. Berlin: Hentrich, 1992. 454 pp., illus., docs., facsims., notes, index (persons, 445–452). (Reihe Deutsche Vergangenheit, Bd. 60.) [Catalogue of an exhibition under the same title held in Berlin Jan. 27, 1992–April 26, 1992. Incl. (titles partly abbr.): Ein Bund im deutschen Ghetto (Walter Jens, 6–8). Der jüdische Kulturbund in Archiv und Ausstellung (Wolfgang Trautwein, 9–12). Sozialgeschichtliche Betrachtungen zur jüdisch-deutschen Akkulturation (Norbert Kampe, 13–24). Schätze in Pappschachteln (Henryk M. Broder, 25–32). Aspekte zur Geschichte des Jüdischen Kulturbunds (Ingrid Schmidt/Helmut Ruppel, 33–54). Jüdischer Kulturbund ohne 'jüdische' Kultur (Herbert Freeden, 55–66). Theater im Jüdischen Kulturbund Berlin (Jörg W. Gronius, 67–94). Gelächter am Abgrund (Volker Kühn, 95–112). Musik unterm Davidsstern (Fred K. Prieberg, 113–126). Die Kulturbund-Vorträge zwischen Tradition und Augenblick (Matthias Harder, 127–134). Jüdische Künstler und die Ghetto-Ausstellungen (Cordula Frowein, 135–154). Die

Verlagsabteilung des Jüdischen Kulturbunds (Bernd Braun, 155–168). Angestellte und Arbeiter im Jüdischen Kulturbund (Ingrid Schmidt, 169–188). Da Capo in Holland (Eike Geisel, 189–214).]

29294 — Riss, Heidelore: *Das Theater des Jüdischen Kulturbundes, Berlin. Zum gegenwärtigen Forschungsstand.* [In]: Theatralia Judaica [see No. 30017]. Pp. 312–338.

29295 — Simon, Hermann: *Die Berliner Juden unter dem Nationalsozialismus.* [In]: Verdrängung und Vernichtung der Juden unter dem Nationalsozialismus [see No. 29366]. Hamburg: Christians, 1992. Pp. 249–266.

29296 — Wörmann, Heinrich-Wilhelm: *Berlin. Widerstand 1933–1945* [Heft 5]: *Widerstand in Charlottenburg.* Hrsg.: Gedenkstätte deutscher Widerstand. Berlin: Gedenkstätte deutscher Widerstand, 1991. 275 pp., illus. (Schriftenreihe über den Widerstand in Berlin von 1933–1945, H. 5.) [Incl. a chap. titled Selbstbehauptung des deutschen Judentums (190–209), dealing with Jewish organisations; also with 'non-Aryan Christians' and the underground 'Chug Chaluzi' youth organisation.]

29297 BERLIN-STEGLITZ. *Arbeitskreis Nationalsozialismus in Steglitz. Steglitz im Dritten Reich. Beiträge zur Geschichte des Nationalsozialismus in Steglitz.* Hrsg. vom Bezirksamt Steglitz von Berlin. 332 pp., illus., facsims., notes. [Incl.: Zum christlich-jüdischen Verhältnis in der Markusgemeinde (Johannes Riedner, 166–179). Die Rassentrennung im Schulwesen ist im allgemeinen bereits durchgeführt. NS-Schulpolitik und jüdischer Religionsunterricht (Dieter Fitterling, 267–310).]

29298 BIELEFELD. Meynert, Joachim: *Die Deportation der Juden aus Bielefeld.* [In]: Verfolgung und Widerstand im Rheinland und in Westfalen 1933–1945 [see No. 29446]. Köln, 1992. Pp. 162–174, notes.

29299 Birger, Trudi (with Jeffrey M. Green): *A daughter's gift of love: a Holocaust memoir.* Philadelphia, PA: Jewish Publication Society, 1992. 218 pp. [For German edn. in 1990 and data see No. 27213/YB XXXVI.]

29300 Birn, Ruth Bettina: *Austrian higher SS and police leaders and their participation in the Holocaust in the Balkans.* [In]: Holocaust and Genocide Studies, Vol. 6, No. 4, Oxford, 1991. Pp. 352–372, notes.

29301 Block, Gay/Drucker, Malka: *Rescuers. Portraits of moral courage in the Holocaust.* Prologue by Cynthia Ozick. Afterword by Rabbi Harold M. Schulweis. New York; London: Holmes & Meier, 1992. 155 pp., ports., bibl. [Incl. an introductory essay (Malka Drucker, 1–18), portraits (Gay Block) and biographical notes of people from the Netherlands, Belgium, France, Germany, Poland, Czechoslovakia, Hungary, Yugoslavia, Bulgaria and Soviet Union/Ukraine, who helped to rescue Jews from Nazi persecution and deportation.]

29302 Blüdnikow, Bent: *Goering's Jewish friend.* [In]: Commentary, Vol. 94, No. 3, New York, Sept. 1992. Pp. 50–53. [Discusses the friendship between Göring and a German Jew, Hugo Rothenberg, a businessman living in Denmark, who met Göring in 1919, when G. worked as a stuntman in Denmark. They met again in 1938, at the instigation of Wilfrid Israel who asked Rothenberg to intervene to protest the events of 'Kristallnacht'. After several more interviews between 1939–1941 the contact ceased.]

29303 Braham, Randolph, ed.: *Studies on the Holocaust in Hungary.* New York: Columbia Univ. Press [distributor]. 1990. VIII, 267 pp. (East European monographs, 301). [Incl.(titles condensed): An interview with Reverend József Eliás (Sándor Szenes, 1–64). Christian support for Jews in Hungary (Uri Asaf, 65–112). The deportation of Jews and Margit Slachta's intervention on their behalf (Tamás Majsai, 113–165).Destruction of Slovakian Jews (Maria Schmidt, 164–174). The forced labor of the Hungarian Jews (Szabolcs Szita, 175–193). The Hessisch-Lichtenau sub-camp of Buchenwald, 1944–45 (Dieter Vaupel, 194–237). The second and third generation Holocaust survivors (Julia Szilágyi [et al.], 238–255). The losses of Hungarian Jewry (László Varga, 256–265).]

29304 BRAUNSCHWEIG. *'Kristallnacht' und Antisemitismus im Braunschweiger Land: drei Vorträge im November 1988.* [Hrsg.: Freundeskreis für Braunschweigischer Kirchen- und Sozialgeschichte]. Von Ernst August Roloff, Bernhild Vögel und Dietrich Kussner. Braunschweig: Freundeskreis für Braunschweiger Kirchen- und Sozialgeschichte, 1988. 69 pp. (Arbeitskreis zur Gesch. der Braunschw. Evangel.- Luth. Landeskirche im 19. und 20. Jahrh., Nr.6.)

29305 Breitman, Richard: *Himmler and the 'terrible secret' among the executioners.* [In]: The impact of Western nationalism [see No. 29803]. Pp. 77–98.

29306 BREMEN. *Es geht tatsächlich nach Minsk:* Texte und Materialien zur Erinnerung an die Deportation von Bremer Juden am 18. 11. 1941 in das Vernichtungslager Minsk. Hrsg.:

Staatsarchiv Bremen. Mit Beiträgen von Manfred Ernst [et al.] und einem Geleitwort von Heinz L. Rosenberg. Zusammengestellt von Andreas Röpcke, Günther Rohdenburg. Bremen: Staatsarchiv, 1992. 170 pp., illus. (Kleine Schriften des Staatsarchivs Bremen, H. 21.)

29307 — [Bremen-Walle]. ECKLER-VON GLEICH, CECILIE: *Juden in Walle: Leben im Stadtteil und Verfolgung während des Nationalsozialismus.* [Unter Mitarbeit von Rosie Kühne.] Bremen: Steintor, 1990. 40 pp., illus. (Reihe Stadtleben.)

29308 BREMERHAVEN. LOWRY, STEPHEN: *Vertreibung oder Vernichtung. Das Schicksal einer jüdischen Familie aus Bremerhaven-Lehe.* [In]: Niedersächsiches Jahrbuch für Landesgeschichte, Bd. 64, Hannover, 1992. Pp. 445–453, footnotes, bibl. [On the Liebenthal family.]

29309 BROWNING, CHRISTOPHER R.: *The path to genocide:* [8] essays on launching the final solution. Cambridge; New York: Cambridge Univ. Press, 1992. XIII, 191 pp., footnotes, index (185–191). [Cont. essays dealing with the development of Nazi policy, recent historiography and a study of minor and middle-rank Nazis.]

29310 BÜTTNER, URSULA, ed.: *Die Deutschen und die Judenverfolgung im Dritten Reich.* Werner Jochmann zum 70. Geburtstag. Hamburg: Christians, 1992. 394 pp. (Hamburger Beiträge zur Sozial- und Zeitgeschichte, Bd. 29.) [Cont.: Die deutsche Gesellschaft und die Judenverfolgung – ein Forschungsproblem (Ursula Büttner, 7–30). Quellen für die Einstellung der deutschen Bevölkerung zur Judenverfolgung. Analyse und Kritik (Heinz Boberach, 31–50). Die Deutschen und die Judenverfolgung. Mentalitätsgeschichtliche Aspekte (Wolfgang Benz, 51–66). Die deutsche Bevölkerung und die Judenverfolgung 1933–1945 (Ursula Büttner, 67–88). Erfahrungen jüdischer Jugendlicher und Kinder mit der nichtjüdischen Umwelt 1933–1945 (Werner T. Angress, 89–104). Bürokratie und Judenverfolgung (Horst Matzerath, 105–130). Terra incognita? – Die Lager für den 'jüdischen Arbeitseinsatz' (1938–1943) und die deutsche Bevölkerung (Wolf Gruner, 131–160). Wehrmacht und Judenverfolgung (Wolfgang Petter, 161–178). Die Beteiligung der Justiz an der nationalsozialistischen Judenverfolgung (Werner Johe, 179–190). Juden, 'Nichtarier' und 'Deutsche Ärzte'. Die Anpassung der Ärzte im Dritten Reich (John A.S. Grenville, 191–206). Die deutschen Unternehmer und die Judenpolitik im 'Dritten Reich' (Avraham Barkai, 207–230). Die Mitwirkenden bei der 'Arisierung'. Dargestellt am Beispiel der rheinisch-westfälischen Industrieregion 1933–1940 (Dirk van Laak, 231–258). Die schweigende Kirche. Katholiken und Judenverfolgung (Bernd Nellessen, 259–271). Die Haltung der deutschen evangelischen Kirchen zur Verfolgung der Juden im Dritten Reich (Martin Greschat, 273–392). Auseinandersetzungen mit einem Stereotyp: die Judenfrage im Leben Martin Niemöllers (Leonore Siegele-Wenschkewitz, 293–320). Die Auseinandersetzung mit der nationalsozialistischen Judenverfolgung in der evangelischen Kirche nach 1945 (Siegfried Hermle, 321–338). Die Auseinandersetzung um die Rückerstattung 'arisierten' jüdischen Eigentums nach 1945 (Constantin Goschler, 339–356). Zwischen Verdrängung und Aufklärung. Die Auseinandersetzung mit dem Holocaust in der frühen Bundesrepublik (Clemens Vollnhals, 357–392).]

29311 BURGER, ADOLF: *Unternehmen Bernhard. Die Geldfälscherwerkstatt im KZ Sachsenhausen. Zum Fälschen gezwungen.* Ein Tatsachenbericht. Berlin: Hentrich, 1992. 244 pp., illus., tabs., facsims., docs., maps. (Reihe deutsche Vergangenheit, Bd. 82.) [Personal recollections of a Slovakian-born Jew, deported in 1942 to Auschwitz, two years later to Sachsenhausen, where he was forced to work, together with other Jewish typographers and graphic artists, counterfeiting large numbers of foreign notes under the orders of SS-Sturmbannführer Bernhard Krüger.]

29312 CAPLAN, ARTHUR L., ed.: *When medicine went mad: bioethics and the Holocaust.* Totowa, NJ: Humana Press, 1992. XII, 359 pp., illus., bibl. (321–330). (Contemporary issues in biomedicine, ethics, and society.) [Papers from a conference of May 17–19, 1989 at the Univ. of Minnesota.]

29313 CHEMNITZ. RICHTER, JÖRN: *Zu einigen Fragen der antijüdischen Politik der Faschisten in Chemnitz nach dem Pogrom vom November 1938.* [In]: Studia nad Faszyzmem i zbrodniami Hitleroskimi XV. Wroclaw, 1992. Pp. 239–252.

29314 COHEN, ASHER/COCHAVI, YEHOYAKIM/GELBER, YOAV, eds.: *Dapim. Studies on the Shoah.* Transl. and English copy ed.: Carl Alpert. New York; Bern [et al.]: Lang, 1992. 278 pp., notes. (Studies on the Shoah) [Essays pertinent to the persecution of German-speaking Jewry incl.: The Holocaust experience at the mercy of human memory (Shlomo Bresnitz, 7–14). The technocrat as murderer: the murderer as technocrat (Steven T. Katz, 15–38). The

Jews of Danzig under Nazi-rule – struggle, rescue and destruction (Eliyahu Stern, 89–130). The Jewish Agency and the distress of German and Austrian Jewry (1938–39) (Arieh Joseph Kochavi, 131–164). The Hebrew press in Palestine on the annihilation of the Jews of Europe (1941–1942) (Yoav Gelber, 165–202).]

29315 COHEN, EUGENE J.: *Rescue. 2,500,000 Jews were liberated by Mossad from Europe, North Africa and Asia – 1932–1990.* 300 stories and photographs. Riverside, CA: Riverside Publ. Company, 1991. 166 pp., illus., index (155–166). [On the Institute for Illegal Immigration (in Hebrew Mossad l'Aliyah Bet or Bricha); also on the rescue of German- and Austrian-Jewish refugees.]

29316 DACHAU. JAHNKE, KARL HEINZ: *Heinz Eschen – Kapo des Judenblocks im Konzentrationslager Dachau bis 1938.* [In]: Dachauer Hefte, Jg. 7, H. 7, Dachau, 1991. Pp. 24–33. [On a young Jew and Communist, imprisoned in Dachau after a demonstration against Hitler in Munich, Feb. 1, 1933; probably murdered by the SS in Jan. 1938.]

29317 DARMSTADT. *Juden-Deportationen aus Darmstadt 1942/43. Die damalige Liebig-Schule als Sammellager 1942.* Red.: Renate Hess, Ingrid Zahedi [et al.]. Hrsg.: Magistrat der Stadt Darmstadt, Amt für Öffentlichkeitsarbeit und Wirtschaftsförderung. Darmstadt, 1992. 63 pp., illus., facsims., lists. [Based on the research carried out by a study group of the Justus-Liebig-Schule.]

29318 DEPORTATIONS. LOZOWICK, YAACOV: *Documentation: 'Judenspediteur': a deportation train.* [In]: Holocaust and Genocide Studies, Vol. 6, No. 3, Oxford, 1991. Pp. 283–292, notes. [Discusses the bureaucratic operational procedures that were adopted for deportation trains. Incl. text of report by police captain Paul Salitter, who commanded the escort unit for a transport from Düsseldorf to Riga.]

29319 DORTMUND. *Widerstand und Verfolgung in Dortmund 1933–1945.* Katalog zur ständigen Ausstellung des Stadtarchivs Dortmund in der Mahn- und Gedenkstätte Steinwache. Hrsg. von Günther Högl. Wissenschaftliche Bearbeitung: Günther Högl, Karl Bilitzky und Dieter Knippschild. 480 pp., illus., facsims., docs., notes, index (persons). (Veröffentlichungen des Stadtarchivs Dortmund, Bd. 8.) [Incl.: Die Judenverfolgung in Dortmund von 1933–1945 (375–425).]

29320 *The Dunera affair. A documentary resource book.* Ed. by Paul R. Bartrop with Gabrielle Eisen. Melbourne: Schwartz & Wilkinson; The Jewish Museum of Australia, 1990. 423 pp., illus., facsims., docs., lists. [Incl.: governmental and bureaucratic documents; numerous personal recollections of former internees, who were shipped to Australia on the Dunera in 1940; also a list of internees (397–416), most of whom were Jews.]

29321 EISENSTEIN, ALBIN: *Die Kunst zu überleben. Erlebnisse und Beobachtungen in sibirischer Verbannung.* Frankfurt am Main: Herchen, 1992. 146 pp. [In 1941, one year after the occupation of North Bukowina by the Red Army, the author, who had studied engineering in Berlin, was deported together with other members of his family from their home town, Czernowitz, to Siberia, where they had to stay for 35 years, before they could return to the West.]

29322 EITINGER, LEO: *Die Jahre danach. Folgen und Spätfolgen der KZ-Haft.* [In]: Dachauer Hefte, Jg. 8, H. 8, Dachau, Nov. 1992. Pp. 3–17.

29323 EMIGRATION. *Drehscheibe Prag. Zur deutschen Emigration in der Tschechoslowakei 1933–1939.* Hrsg. von Peter Becher und Peter Heumos. München: Oldenbourg, 1992. Pp. 75–86. 206 pp, footnotes. [Incl. the following contributions relevant to the emigration of German-speaking Jews: Drehscheibe – Kampfposten – Fluchtstation. Deutsche Emigranten in der Tschechoslowakei (Werner Röder, 15–30). Die ČSR als Asylland. Historisch-politische Voraussetzungen (Kveta Hyrsilová, 31–40). Die Beziehungen zwischen sudetendeutschen Sozialdemokraten und dem deutschen Exil: dialektische Freundschaft (Martin K. Bachstein, 41–52). Kurt R. Grossmann und die Demokratische Flüchtlingshilfe (Peter Becher, 53–64). John Heartfield und der Künstlerverein Mánes (Jan M. Tomes, 65–74). Zuflucht in Grossbritannien: zur Emigration deutsch-sprachiger Prager Wissenschaftler nach 1938 (Gerhard Hirschfeld, 75–86). Prag 1933 – der Prager Kreis und die Emigration (Margarita Pazi, 97–108). Gegner und Opfer des Nationalsozialismus als Emigranten aus den böhmischen Ländern nach Amerika (Fred Hahn, 151–165). Stimmen aus Böhmen. Die deutschsprachige literarische Emigration aus der Tschechoslowakei in Grossbritannien nach 1938: Rudolf Fuchs, Ernst Sommer und Ludwig Winder (Jennifer A. Taylor, 165–180). Soziale Aspekte der Emigration aus der Tschechoslowakei 1938–1945 (Peter Heumos, 181–197).]

29324 — GOLVAN, COLIN: *The distant exodus. Australian Jews recall their immigration experiences.* Crows

Nest NSW: ABC Enterprises, 1990. 115 pp, illus. [About the immigration experiences of Jews between 1939 and 1950.]

29325 — PILGRIM, VOLKER ELIS/LIFFMAN, DORIS & HERBERT, Hrsg.: *Fremde Freiheit. Jüdische Emigration nach Australien. Briefe 1938–1940.* Reinbek: Rowohlt Taschenbuch Verlag, 1992. 256 pp. [Cf.: (Besprechung) Fremde Freiheit (Willi Jasper) [in] Die Zeit, Nr. 20, Hamburg, 8. Mai 1992, p. 12.]

29326 — THALMANN, RITA: *L'évolution de l'émigration du IIIième Reich de 1933 à 1941.* [In]: Sexe et race. Discours du XIXe au XXe siècle. Responsable de la publication: Rita Thalmann. Paris: CERG et Université Paris 7, 1991. Pp. 141–157, notes. [Incl. a section on the specific situation of women.]

29327 EMMERICH. SCHÜÜRMANN, HERBERT: *Auch in Emmerich herrschte die Gewalt. Von der Reichskristallnacht zur Deportation der Juden.* [In]: Kalender für das Klever Land auf das Jahr 1992, Jg. 42, Kleve, 1991. Pp. 85–88, illus.

29328 FABRY, JOSEPH: *The next-to-final solution. A Belgian detention camp for Hitler refugees.* New York; Bern [et al.]: Lang, 1991. 146 pp., illus., facsims., docs. [Incl. list of refugees in the camp of Merxplas. On the author's experiences, based on notes and diaries, of the detention camp of Merxplas, where six hundred refugees from Nazi persecution were interned.] [J.F., formerly Josef Epstein, (pen name Peter Fabrizius) b. Vienna 1909, fled to Belgium after the 'Anschluss', emigr. via the UK to the USA in 1940; jurist, editor, founder of the International Forum of Logotherapy.]

29329 FEINGOLD, HENRY L.: *Rescue and the secular perception: American Jewry and the Holocaust.* [In]: Organizing rescue: national Jewish solidarity in the modern period [see No. 29646]. Pp. 154–166.

29330 *Final letters. From the Yad Vashem Archive.* Selected by Reuven Dafni and Yehudit Kleiman. Foreword by Chaim Herzog. London: Weidenfeld & Nicolson, 1991. 128 pp., illus., facsims. [Incl. letters from German Jews.]

29331 FINAL SOLUTION. BANKIER, DAVID: *The Germans and the Final Solution: public opinion under Nazism.* Oxford; Cambridge, MA: Blackwell, 1992. VII, 206 pp., notes (157–187), bibl. (188–200). [Incl. chaps. Public responses to antisemitism, 1933–1938 (67–88). Awareness of the Holocaust (101–115). Public responses to antisemitism, 1939–1943 (116–138).]

29332 — FRIEDLÄNDER, SAUL: *Die Genese der 'Endlösung'. Zu Philippe Burrins Thesen.* Aus dem Englischen übersetzt von Ute Hoffmann. [In]: Jahrbuch für Antisemitismusforschung 1, Berlin 1992. Pp. 166–181, notes. [Review article of Burrin's book Hitler et les juifs: genèse d'un génocide, Paris 1989; see No. 27275/YB XXXVI.]

29333 — JÄCKEL, EBERHARD: *Die Konferenz am Wannsee. 'Wo Heydrich seine Ermächtigung bekanntgab'. Der Holocaust war längst im Gange.* [In]: Die Zeit, Nr. 4, Hamburg, 17. Jan. 1992. Pp. 33–34, port.

29334 — KARNY, MIROSLAV: *Die Wannsee-Konferenz nach einem halben Jahrhundert.* [In]: Judaica Bohemiae 28, Praha, 1992. Pp. 35–52.

29335 — PÄTZOLD, KURT/SCHWARZ, ERIKA: *Tagesordnung: Judenmord.* Die Wannsee-Konferenz am 20. Januar 1942. Eine Dokumentation zur Organisation der 'Endlösung'. Berlin: Metropol, 1992. 257 pp., docs., notes. (Reihe Dokumente, Texte, Materialien, veröff. vom Zentrum für Antisemitismusforschung der Technischen Universität Berlin, Bd. 3.)

29336 — PÄTZOLD, KURT: *'Die vorbereitenden Arbeiten sind eingeleitet'. Zum 50. Jahrestag der 'Wannsee-Konferenz' vom 20. Januar 1942.* [In]: Das Parlament, 42. Jg., Bonn, 3. Jan. 1992. Pp. 14–23, footnotes.

29337 — RUMMEL, R.J.: *Democide: Nazi genocide and mass murder.* New Brunswick, NJ: Transaction, 1992. 159 pp., illus., facsims., tabs., bibl. (137–152).

— — TUCHEL, JOHANNES: *Am Grossen Wannsee 56–58: von der Villa Minoux zum Haus der Wannsee-Konferenz.* [See No. 29545.]

29338 FINKELGRUEN, PETER: *Haus Deutschland oder die Geschichte eines ungesühnten Mordes.* Berlin: Rowohlt, 1992. 171 pp., illus., docs. [On the author's search for the history of his family and on the fate of the man who murdered his grandfather in Theresienstadt in 1942.] [P.F., b. 1942 in Shanghai, educated in Prague and Haifa, journalist, lives in Cologne.]

29339 FINKIELKRAUT, ALAIN: *Remembering in vain: the Klaus Barbie trial and crimes against humanity.* Introd. by Alice Kaplan. Transl. by Roxanne Lapidus with Sima Godfrey. New York: Columbia Univ. Press, 1992. XXXVI, 102 pp., illus.

29340 FLAM, GILA: *Singing for survival: songs of the Lodz ghetto, 1940–45.* Champaign: Univ. of Illinois Press, 1992. XV, 207 pp., illus., musical scores, glossary, index of songs, bibl. (191–200). [In

1941, Jews from Germany, Austria, and Czechoslovakia were deported to Lodz. Some songs deal specifically with the fate of German Jews.]

29341 FORCED LABOUR. WOLLENBERG, HANS-WERNER: *und (. . .) der Alptraum wurde zum Alltag. Autobiographischer Bericht eines jüdischen Arztes über NS-Zwangsarbeitslager in Schlesien (1942–1945).* Hrsg. mit ausführlichen Erläuterungen und Anmerkungen von Manfred Brusten und einem Beitrag zur Person des Autors von Godfrey Golzen. Pfaffenweiler: Centaurus, 1992. 219 pp., ports., notes, bibl. [H.-W. W., physician, 1891 Königsberg – 1964 Berlin, emigr. to France in 1938. His memoirs, completed in 1947, were rediscovered by the sociologist Manfred Bruster in 1988 in Australia.]

29342 Fox, JOHN P.: *German and Austrian Jews in Britain's Armed Forces and German citizenship policies 1939–1945.* [In]: LBI Year Book XXXVII, London. Pp. 415–457, footnotes.

29343 *France under the German occupation, 1940–1944.* An annotated bibliography, compiled by Donna Evleth. Westport, CT: Greenwood Press, 1991. XII, 233 pp. [Contains entries on the Jews under occupation, incl. German-Jewish refugees.]

29344 FRANK, ANNE. KOLB, EBERHARD: *Anne Frank. Stimme eines Kindes im Holocaust.* Hrsg.: Niedersächsische Landeszentrale für politische Bildung. Red.: Monika Gödecke. Hannover: [Gedenkstätte Bergen-Belsen], 1992. 30 pp., illus.

29345 — PRESSLER, MIRJAM: *Ich sehne mich so. Die Lebensgeschichte der Anne Frank.* Weinheim: Beltz, 1992. 153 pp., illus., notes, bibl.

— FRIEDLÄNDER, SAUL: *Trauma, Erinnerung und Übertragung in der historischen Darstellung des Nationalsozialismus.* [See in No. 29013.]

29346 FRIEDLANDER, ALBERT H.: *A muted protest in war-time Berlin. Writing on the legal position of German Jewry throughout the centuries – Leo Baeck – Leopold Lucas – Hilde Ottenheimer.* [In]: LBI Year Book XXXVII, London. Pp. 363–380, footnotes, appendix, ports. [On two texts by Leo Baeck, excerpts from which are publ. in the appendix.]

29347 GEISEL, EIKE: *Premiere und Pogrom. Der Jüdische Kulturbund 1933–1941.* [In]: Jüdischer Almanach 1993 [see in 29248]. Frankfurt am Main, 1992. Pp. 35–44.

29348 GEISEL, EIKE/BRODER, HENRYK M.: *Premiere und Pogrom. Der Jüdische Kulturbund 1933–1941.* Texte und Bilder. Berlin: Siedler, 1992. 336 pp., illus. [Cf.: Eine merkwürdige Symbiose (Elke Schubert) [in]: Die Zeit, Nr. 4, Hamburg, 22. Jan., 1993, p. 17.]

29349 GERSTENBERGER, KATHARINA/POHLAND, VERA: *Der Wichser. Edgar Hilsenrath – Schreiben über den Holocaust, Identität und Sexualität.* [In] : Der Deutschunterricht, Jg. 44, No. 1, Seelze, 1992. Pp. 74–91.

29350 GLAS-LARSSON, MARGARETA: *I want to speak: the tragedy and banality of survival in Terezin and Auschwitz.* Ed. and annotated by Gerhard Botz. Foreword by Bruno Kreisky. Transl. by Lowell A. Bangerter. Riverside, CA: Ariadne Press, 1991. XXX, 268 pp., illus., maps. (Studies in Austrian literature, culture, and thought.)

29351 GLAZAR, RICHARD: *Die Falle mit dem grünen Zaun. Überleben in Treblinka.* Mit einem Vorwort von Wolfgang Benz. Frankfurt am Main: Fischer Taschenbuch Verlag, 1992. 188 [3] pp., map. (Lebensbilder. Jüdische Erinnerungen und Zeugnisse, Bd. 4.) [Personal memoirs of R.G., born in Prague in 1920; escaped into hiding in 1939, rounded up by the Germans in 1942 and deported via Theresienstadt to Treblinka. As a slave labourer there he witnessed the mass murder of thousands of Jews, took part in the uprising in August 1943 and escaped via Poland to Germany using a false identity. After the liberation returned to Prague; emigr. after the failure of the 'Prague Spring' to Switzerland.]

29352 GÖTTINGEN. SCHÄFER-RICHTER, UTA/KLEIN, JÖRG: *Die jüdischen Bürger im Kreis Göttingen 1933–1945.* Ein Gedenkbuch. Unter Mitarbeit von Peter Aufgebauer und Matthias Manthey. Hrsg.: Karl-Heinz Manegold. Göttingen: Wallstein, 1992. 310 pp., illus.

29353 GOLDSCHMIDT, DIETRICH: *Erinnerungen an das Leben von Eugen und Marie Schiffer nach dem 30. Januar 1933.* [In]: Berlin in Geschichte und Gegenwart. Jahrbuch des Landesarchivs Berlin 1991. Berlin: Siedler, 1991. Pp. 117–146, port., illus. [On the (baptised) jurist, Liberal politician and Weimar Minister of Finance and Justice Eugen Schiffer (1860–1954) and his daughter Marie, and their survival of Nazi persecution in the Jüdisches Krankenhaus, Berlin.]

29354 GORDON, HARRY: *The shadow of death: the Holocaust in Lithuania.* Lexington: The Univ. Press of Kentucky, 1992. XV, 174 pp., illus. [Incl. the participation by non-Germans in the persecution and extermination of the Lithuanian Jews.]

29355 GOSHEN, SEEV: *Nisko – Ein Ausnahmefall unter den Judenlagern der SS.* [In]: Vierteljahrshefte für Zeitgeschichte, Jg. 40, H. 1, München, Jan. 1992. Pp. 95–106. [Based on the author's own experience as an inmate of the Nisko camp in Poland, which was set up in September 1939 and shut down in 1940.]

29356 GOULD, STEPHEN JAY: *The most unkindest cut of all: scientific rationale behind Adolf Eichmann's justification of the Jewish Holocaust.* [In]: Natural History, No. 5, New York, May 1992. Pp. 2–7.

29357 GRAML, HERMANN: *Anti-semitism in the Third Reich.* Transl. by Timothy Kirk. Oxford; Cambridge, MA: Blackwell, 1992. 256 pp., illus., glossary, chronological tabs., appendixes, notes, bibl. [Incl. chaps. on November Pogrom and persecution of Jews from 1933–1945; also documents. For German edn. in 1988 see No. 25424/YB XXXIV.]

29358 GRUNER, WOLF: *Die Berichte über die Jüdische Winterhilfe von 1838/39 bis 1941/42. Dokumente jüdischer Sozialarbeit zwischen Selbstbehauptung und Fremdbestimmung nach dem Novemberpogrom.* [In]: Jahrbuch für Antisemitismusforschung 1, Berlin 1992. Pp. 307–341, notes, docs.

29359 GRUSS, HERIBERT: *Hat Bischof Clemens August Graf von Galen am Passionssonntag 1942 öffentlich für die Nichtarier (Juden) protestiert?* [In]: Theologie und Glaube, Jg. 81, Nr. 3, Paderborn, 1991. Pp. 368–385.

29360 GRYNBERG, ANNE: *Les camps de la honte. Les internés juifs des camps français (1939–1944).* Paris: Editions la Découverte, 1991. 400 pp., illus., footnotes (347–386), maps, index (persons, 387–392). [Deals also with German-Jewish refugees.]

29361 GURS. *Gurs. Deutsche Emigrantinnen im französischen Exil.* Mit einem Vorwort von Gisèle Freund. Hrsg. von Gabriele Mittag. Mit Fotografien von Birgit Kleber. Berlin: Argon, 1991. 71 pp., illus., ports., bibl., chronol. [Incl. (titles partly abbr.): Verlorene Spuren. Vorwort (Gisèle Freund, 7). Exil in Frankreich (Rita Thalmann, 8–14). In Frankreich unerwünscht. Über die französichen Internierungslager – vor und während des Zweiten Weltkrieges (Mechthild Gilzmer, 41–42). Frauen von Gurs. Stationen des Überlebens (Gabriele Mittag, 43–51). Edith Aron erinnert sich (52–53). Herta Liebknecht über ihre Zeit im französischen Exil (54–57). Lou Albert-Lasard. Zeichnungen vom Leben in Gurs (Renate Flagmeier, 58–62). Die letzten Spuren Maria Leitners (Rose Gauger, 63). Biographien (64–67).]

—— HALLE. [See No. 29699.]

29362 HAMBURG. BOTTIN, ANGELA: *Enge Zeit. Spuren Vertriebener und Verfolgter der Hamburger Universität.* Unter Mitarbeit von Rainer Nicolaysen. Hamburg: Dietrich Reimer, 1992. 199 pp., ports., illus., facsims., index (names). (Hamburger Beiträge zur Wissenschaftsgeschichte.) [Catalogue book of an exhibition of the same title in Hamburg from Feb. 2–June 17, 1991.]

—— — DALBERG, VIBEKE/RENTENAAR, ROB: *Spuren der Bibliothek von Agathe Lasch in Dänemark.* [See No. 29804.]

29363 — LORENZ, INA: *Das Leben der Hamburger Juden im Zeichen der 'Endlösung' (1942–1945).* [In]: Verdrängung und Vernichtung der Juden unter dem Nationalsozialismus [see No. 29366]. Hamburg: Christians, 1992. Pp. 207–248.

29364 HARRISON, TED, ed.: *Political police and lawyers in Hitler's Germany.* [In]: German History, Vol. 10, No. 2, Oxford, June 1992. Pp. 226–237. [Review article; covers books dealing with racial policies and the fate of Jewish jurists.]

29365 HEIDE. REHN, MARIE-ELISABETH: *Lose Enden – einige Überlegungen zur NS-Zeit in Heide.* [In]: Informationen zur Schleswig-Holsteinischen Zeitgeschichte, 23, Kiel, Nov. 1992. Pp. 43–53.

29366 HERZIG, ARNO/LORENZ, INA, eds.: *Verdrängung und Vernichtung der Juden unter dem Nationalsozialismus.* In Zusammenarbeit mit Saskia Rohde. Hamburg: Christians, 1992. 360 pp., notes, index (places, persons). (Hamburger Beiträge zur Geschichte der deutschen Juden, Bd. 19.) [Incl.: Historie und Shoah (Arno Herzig, 13–28). Der 'Holocaust' im Widerstreit der Deutungen (Bernd Jürgen Wendt, 29–76). Die Shoah aus jüdischer Sicht (Walter Zwi Bacharach, 75–84). Zur Historiographie des Schicksals der polnischen Juden im Zweiten Weltkrieg (Frank Golczewski, 85–100). Der 'Holocaust' in Lettland. Zur 'postkommunistischen' Aufarbeitung des Themas in Osteuropa (Margers Vestermanis, 101–130). Volksgemeinschaft, 'Arisierung' und der Holocaust (Avraham Barkai, 133–152). Die Zerstörung der Synagogen unter dem Nationalsozialismus (Saskia Rohde,153–172). Absonderung, Strafkommando und spezifischer Terror: Jüdische Gefangene in nationalsozialistischen Konzentrationslagern 1933–1945 (Detlef Garbe, 173–206). Auschwitz und die Deutschen. Die Erinnerung an den Völkermord (Wolfgang Benz, 333–348). Further contributions are listed according to subject.]

29367 HESSE. KAUFMANN, MENACHEM: *Wie man die hessischen Dörfer und Kleinstädte 'judenrein' machte. Vom Alltagsleben der Landjuden in den Jahren von 1933–1938.* [In]: Tribüne, Jg. 31, H. 124, Frankfurt am Main, 1992. Pp. 174–182, facsim.

29368 HILBERG, RAUL: *Perpetrators, victims and bystanders. The Jewish catastrophe 1933–1945.* New York: Harper Collins, 1992. 340 pp., notes (269–332), index. [German edn. publ. under the title: Täter, Opfer, Zuschauer. Die Vernichtung der Juden 1933–1945. Aus dem Amerikanischen von Hans Günter Holl. Frankfurt am Main: S. Fischer, 1992. 367 pp., notes (295–353), index (names, 355–363; places, 365–367).] [Section Perpetrators also incl. non-German governments and volunteers, section Victims deals also with mixed marriages and Christian Jews and section Bystanders incl. the Jewish rescuers, the Allies, the neutral countries and the churches.] [See also interview with author on his book (Jochanan Shelliem) [in]: 'Allgemeine', Jg. 48, Nr. 1, Bonn, 7. Jan. 1993, p. 8, port. Hitlers Mordpläne und die Helfershelfer (Hans Fenske) [in]: [Beilage] Süddeutsche Zeitung, Nr. 226, München, 30. Sept. 1992, p. 28.] [Täter, Opfer, Gaffer: Raul Hilbergs zweites Buch über 'die jüdische Katastrophe'. Wie es geschehen konnte (Eberhard Jäckel) [in]: Die Zeit, Nr. 41, Hamburg, 2. Okt. 1992, p. 27. Täter, Opfer, Zuschauer (Arno Lustiger) [in]: Der Spiegel, Jg. 47, Hamburg, 15 Feb 1993, pp.54–61; critical examination of Hilberg's treatment of Jewish resistance.]

29369 HIRSCH, HELMUT: *Siegfried Thalheimer und die 'Düsseldorfer Lokal-Zeitung'. Eine Emigrations- und Remigrationsstudie.* [In]: Düsseldorfer Jahrbuch, Bd. 63, Düsseldorf, 1991. Pp.167–186, footnotes.

29370 HISTORIOGRAPHY ('HISTORIANS' DEBATE'). BARTOV, OMER: *Time present and time past: the 'Historikerstreit' and German reunification.* [In]: new german critique, No. 55, Ithaca, NY, winter 1992. Pp. 173–190, footnotes.

29371 — DUDEK, PETER: *'Vergangenheitsbewältigung'. Zur Problematik eines umstrittenen Begriffs.* [In]: Das Parlament, Jg. 42, Bonn, 3. Jan. 1992. Pp. 44–53, footnotes.

29372 — FRIEDLAENDER, SAUL: *Trauma, transference and 'working through' in writing the history of the Shoah.* [In]: History & Memory. Studies in Representation of the Past, Vol. 4, No. 1, Bloomington, 1992. Pp. 39–59, notes.

29373 — HERBERT, ULRICH/GROEHLER, OLAF: *Zweierlei Bewältigung. Vier Beiträge über den Umgang mit der NS-Vergangenheit in den beiden deutschen Staaten.* Hamburg: Ergebnisse Verlag, 1992. 88 pp., notes. [Incl.: Zweierlei Bewältigung [&] Der Holocaust in der Geschichtsschreibung der Bundesrepublik Deutschland (Ulrich Herbert, 7–28 [&] 67–86). Antifaschismus – vom Umgang mit einem Begriff [&] Der Holocaust in der Geschichtsschreibung der DDR (Olaf Groehler, 29–66).]

29374 — HOLMES, COLIN: *Death's shadow: reflections on the Holocaust.* [In]: The Jewish Journal of Sociology, Vol. 34, No. 1, London, June 1992. Pp. 43–50, notes. [Review article on recent books on the Holocaust.]

29375 — KREIS, RUDOLF: *Zur Beantwortung der Frage, ob Ernst Nolte oder Nietzsche mit dem Judentum 'in die Irre' ging.* [In]: Aschkenas, Jg. 2, Wien, 1992. Pp. 293–310.

— — LOEWY, HANNO, ed.: *Holocaust: Die Grenzen des Verstehens. Eine Debatte über die Besetzung der Geschichte.* [See No. 29381.]

29376 HITLER, ADOLF. KERSHAW, IAN: *Ideologe und Propagandist. Hitler im Lichte seiner Reden, Schriften und Anordnungen 1925–1928.* [In]: Vierteljahrshefte für Zeitgeschichte, Jg. 40, H.2, München, Apr. 1992. Pp. 263–271, footnotes. [Based on a new edn. of Hitler's early speeches, writings and other documents published in 1992 by the Institut für Zeitgeschichte and the K.G.Saur-Verlag. Refers also to Hitler's antisemitism.]

29377 HOCHHÄUSER, ALEX: *Zufällig überlebt. Als deutscher Jude in der Slowakei.* Berlin: Metropol, 1992. 178 pp. (Reihe Dokumente, Texte, Materialien. Zentrum für Antisemitismusforschung der Technischen Universität Berlin, Bd. 5. [A.H., born 1912 in Breslau, emigr. in 1933 to Czechoslovakia, caught in the deportations of Slovakian Jewry to the camp of Zilina, from which he escaped in 1942, surviving with false identity and joining a group of partisans in 1944.]

29378 HOHENLIMBURG. Zabel, Hermann, ed.: *Verschwiegen, vergessen, verdrängt. Über die Nazi-Zeit reden. Zugleich ein Beitrag zum Problemkreis 'Sprache im Nationalsozialismus'.* Hagen: Padligur, 1990. 396 pp., footnotes, illus., facsims., docs. [First part of book is based on a discussion held in 1988 under the title 50 Jahre Reichspogromnacht – 50 Jahre deutsche Verdrängung. Participants were: Niklas Frank, Günther Bernd Ginzel, Martin Hirsch, Heinz Jaeckel, Reinhard Kühnl, Heiner Lichtenstein, Horst Mahler, Gisela Marx, Jürgen

Müller-Hohagen, Mirjam Ohringer, Leonie Ossowski. Second part deals with the Hohenlimburg Heimatverein, its role during the Nazi period and after the Second World War.]

29379 HOLOCAUST. DUPUY, B.: *La théologie chrétienne après la Shoah.* [In]: Istina, Vol. 36, No. 3, Paris, 1991. Pp. 291–307.

29380 — KRONDORFER, BJÖRN: *Ethos der Erinnerung. Das liberale amerikanische Judentum und der Holocaust.* [In]: Tribüne, Jg. 31, H. 124, Frankfurt am Main, 1992. Pp. 117–124, bibl.

29381 — LOEWY, HANNO, ed.: *Holocaust: Die Grenzen des Verstehens. Eine Debatte über die Besetzung der Geschichte.* Reinbek: Rowohlt Taschenbuch Verlag, 1992. 288 pp., notes. [Contributions were made in Frankfurt am Main at a conference discussing a future German 'Dokumentationszentrum des Holocaust' in October 1991.] [Essays on the historiography and the public perception of the Nazi mass murder of the Jews and the different ways of 'Vergangenheitsbewältigung'. Incl.: Geleitwort (Linda Reisch, 7–8). Einleitung (Hanno Loewy, 9–20). Erinnerungsgebot und Erfahrungsgeschichte. Institutionalisierung mit kollektivem Gedächtnis (Lutz Niethammer, 21–34). Für eine anamnetische Kultur (Johann Baptist Metz, 35–41). Wider das Bewältigungs-Kleinklein (Götz Aly, 42–51). Im Tode sind alle gleich – Sind im Tode alle gleich? (Edna Brocke, 71–82). Rationalität und Irrationalität des Völkermords (Hermann Lübbe, 83–92). Erfahrung, Aufarbeitung und Erinnerung des Holocaust in Deutschland (Hans Mommsen, 93–100). Auschwitz und Holocaust. Begriff und Historiographie (Norbert Frei, 101–109). Erblasten: der Umgang mit dem Holocaust in der DDR (Olaf Groehler, 110–127; see also No. 29373). Negativer Fixpunkt und Suche nach positiver Identität. Der Nationalsozialismus im Kollektiven Gedächtnis der alten Bundesrepublik (Michael Zimmermann, 128–143). Aporetische Erinnerung und historisches Erzählen (Thomas Sandkühler, 144–159). Arbeitsteilige Täterschaft. Kriminologische Perspektiven auf den Holocaust (Herbert Jäger, 160–165). Das Heer als Faktor der arbeitsteiligen Täterschaft (Manfred Messerschmidt, 160–190). Trauerrituale und politische Kultur nach der Shoah in der Bundesrepublik (Micha Brumlik, 191–212). Die Textur der Erinnerung. Holocaust-Gedenkstätten (James Edward Young, 213–232). Ein Foto aus dem Ghetto Lodz oder: wie die Bilder zerrinnen (Detlef Hoffmann, 233–247). Abwehr – Aneignen. Der Holocaust als Lerngegenstand (Volkhard Knigge, 248–259). Gedenkstätten: Orte der Erinnerung und die zunehmende Distanz zum Nationalsozialismus (Detlef Garbe, 260–284).] [Cf.:Fritz Bauer zu Ehren (Otto Köhler) [in]: Die Zeit, Nr. 50, Hamburg, 4. Dez. 1992, p. 61.]

29382 — MORLEY, J.: *Réflexions historiques sur la Shoah.* [In]: Istina, Vol. 36, No. 3, Paris, 1991. Pp. 263–273.

29383 — *National registry of Jewish Holocaust survivors.* American gathering of Jewish Holocaust survivors in cooperation with the United States Holocaust Memorial Council, Washington, DC; New York: American Gathering/Federation of Jewish Holocaust survivors, 1991. 1 Vol. (various pagings), facsims., ports.

29384 — PATTERSON, DAVID: *The shriek of silence: a phenomenology of the Holocaust novel.* Lexington: The Univ. Press of Kentucky, 1992. 208 pp. [Among the authors examined are Ilse Aichinger, Aharon Appelfeld, Anna Langfus, Primo Levi, Elie Wiesel.]

— — RINGELHEIM, JOAN: *Women and the Holocaust: a reconsideration of research.* [See No. 28990.]

29385 — ROSSEL, SEYMOUR: *The Holocaust: the world and the Jews, 1933–1945.* West Orange, NJ: Berman House, 1992. 191 pp., illus., facsims., ports., bibl. (184–187). [First edn. 1981.]

29386 — VIDAL-NAQUET, PIERRE: *Assassins of memory. Essays on the denial of the Holocaust.* Transl. and with a foreword by Jeffrey Mehlmann. New York: Columbia Univ. Press, 1992. 205 pp., notes (143–191), index (persons, places, subjects, 193–205). [Orig. publ. in 1987 under the title *Un Eichmann de papier et autres essais sur le révisionisme.*]

29387 — WIGODER, GEOFFREY: *La pensée Juive après l'Holocaust.* [In]: Istina, Vol. 36, No. 3, Paris, 1991. Pp. 273–290.

29388 — YOUNG, JAMES EDWARD: *Beschreiben des Holocaust. Darstellung und Folgen der Interpretation.* Aus dem Amerikanischen von Christa Schuenke. Frankfurt am Main: Jüdischer Verlag, 1992. 340 pp., notes, bibl., index. [A collection of essays, some publ. previously; the American original edn. was publ. in 1988 under the title: Writing and rewriting the Holocaust. Narrative and the consequences of interpretation.] [Cf.: Ein tiefer Riß. Wie kann Auschwitz dargestellt, wie in der Erinnerung bewahrt werden? (Peter Reichel) [in]: Die Zeit, Nr. 25, Hamburg, 12. Juni 1992, p. 21.]

29389 ISAACSON, JUDITH MAGYAR: *Befreiung in Leipzig. Erinnerungen einer ungarischen Jüdin.* Transl. from the American by Werner Horch. Witzenhausen: Ekopan, 1991. 238 pp., illus. [Author,

b. in Kaposvár, deported to Auschwitz in July 1944, thereafter a slave labourer in Hessisch-Lichtenau.]

— JÄCKEL, EBERHARD: *Der Mord an den europäischen Juden und die Geschichte*. [See in No. 29013.]

— JÄCKEL, EBERHARD: *Der Mord an den europäischen Juden und die Judenfeindschaft*. [See in No. 29982.]

29390 KAHANE, CHARLOTTE: *Untergetaucht. Eine polnische Jüdin überlebt in Deutschland*. [In]: Dachauer Hefte, Jg. 7, H. 7, Dachau, Nov. 1991. Pp. 87–101.

29391 KARNY, MIROSLAV: *La persécution des Juifs en Tchéchoslovaquie*. [In]: Istina, Vol. 36, No. 3, Paris, 1991. Pp. 325–329.

29392 KEILSON, HANS: *Das 'Nachher' der Überlebenden*. [In]: Dachauer Hefte, Jg. 8, H. 8, Dachau, Nov. 1992. Pp. 32–34.

29393 KIRSTEIN, WOLFGANG: *Das Konzentrationslager als Institution totalen Terrors. Das Beispiel des KL Natzweiler*. Paffenweiler: Centaurus, 1992. 153 pp., footnotes, bibl. (Freiburger Arbeiten zur Soziologie der Diktatur, 2) Zugl.: Freiburg (Breisgau), Univ., Diss., 1991. [1% of the inmates were Jews.]

29394 KLEMPERER, KLEMENS VON: *German resistance against Hitler: the search for allies abroad, 1938–1945*. New York: Oxford Univ. Press; Oxford: Clarendon Press, 1992. XVI, 487 pp., illus., ports., bibl. (442–472), index. [Incl. the resistance leaders' attitudes to the Jewish problem.]

29395 KLÜGER, RUTH: *Weiter leben. Eine Jugend*. Göttingen: Wallstein, 1992. 285 pp. [R.K., b. 1931 in Vienna, was deported as a child of twelve to Theresienstadt, later to Auschwitz-Birkenau and Gross-Rosen, where she worked as a slave labourer. Lives as a professor of literature in California.] [Cf.: Die Auschwitznummer nicht verdecken. Ruth Klügers Erinnerungen – eine Einladung zum Streiten (Hans Joachim Kreutzer) [in]: Süddeutsche Zeitung, Nr. 264, München, 14./15. Nov., 1992, p. IV.]

29396 LEIPZIG. KRALOVITZ, ROLF: *Der gelbe Stern in Leipzig*. Köln: Walter Meckauer Kreis, 1992. 32 pp., illus., facsims. [Autobiographical account of the author's life in Leipzig during Nazi period.] [R.K., b. 1925, deported to Buchenwald in 1943, emigrated to the USA after the Second World War, returned to Germany in 1952; lives in Cologne.]

29397 — UNGER, MANFRED: *Die Juden in Leipzig unter der Herrschaft des Nationalsozialismus*. [In]: Verdrängung und Vernichtung der Juden unter dem Nationalsozialismus [see in No. 29366]. Hamburg: Christians, 1992. Pp. 267–290.

29398 *Lessons and legacies: the meaning of the Holocaust in a changing world*. Ed. and with an introd. by Peter Hayes. Foreword by Theodore Zev Weiss. Evanston, IL: Northwestern Univ. Press, 1991. X, 373 pp., notes (341–373). [Incl. the following contributions (titles partly abbr.): The discovery of the Holocaust (Raul Hilberg, 11–22). The 'Final Solution': on the unease in historical interpretation (Saul Friedländer, 23–35). Holocaust and genocide: some comparisons (Yehuda Bauer, 36–46). Ideology, state power, and mass murder/genocide (Steven T. Katz, 47–89). The history of evil and the future of the Holocaust (Berel Lang, 90–105). The use and the misuse of the Holcaust (Michael R. Marrus, 106–119). After the catastrophy: aspects of contemporary Jewry (David Vital, 120–140). The reaction of the German population to the anti-Jewish persecutions (Hans Mommsen, 141–154). Genocide and eugenics (Claudia Koonz, 155–177). Citizen participation and persecution of the Jews in Nazi Germany (Robert Gellately, 178–195). Initiation to mass murder (Christopher R. Browning, 196–209). Helping behavior and rescue (Nechama Tec, 210–226). Redefining heroic behavior (Lawrence Langer, 227–242). Popularization and memory: the case of Anne Frank (Alvin H. Rosenfeld, 243–278). Israel's memorial landscape: Sho'ah, heroism and national redemption (James E. Young, 279–304). The impact of Holocaust narratives (Holocaust Educational Foundation Volunteers, 316–328). Closing remarks (Geoffrey H. Hartman, 329–336).]

29399 LEVIN, ELENA: *Historias de una emigracion (1933–1939): Alemanes Judios en la Argentina*. Buenos Aires: Zago, 1991. 185, [5] pp., illus., ports., facsims., maps, bibl. (183–[187]).

29400 LICHTER, JÖRG: *Die Diskriminierung jüdischer Sportler in der Zeit des Nationalsozialismus*. Köln: Selbstverlag Forschungsinst. f. Sozial- und Wirtschaftsgesch. a. d. Univ. zu Köln, 1992. 75 pp., footnotes, bibl. (Kölner Vorträge und Abhandlungen zur Sozial- und Wirtschaftsgeschichte, H.39.)

29401 LIEBE, ULRICH: *Verehrt, verfolgt, vergessen: Schauspieler als Naziopfer*. Weinheim: Beltz Quadriga, 1992. 278 pp., illus., filmogr. (253–266).

29402 LILIENTHAL, GEORG: *Arier oder Jude. Die Geschichte des erb- und rassenkundlichen Abstammungs-*

gutachtens. [In]: *Wissenschaft auf Irrwegen. Biologismus – Rassenhygiene – Eugenik.* Peter Popping/Heinz Schott, eds. Bonn: Bouvier, 1992. Pp. 66–84, footnotes.

29403 LIPMAN, STEVE: *Laughter in hell: the use of humor during the Holocaust.* Northvale, NJ: Aronson, 1991. XIII, 279 pp., notes. [Incl. German and German-Jewish political satire, as well as humour in the camps.]

29404 LODZ [LITZMANNSTADT]. MOSTOWICZ, ARNOLD: *Der blinde Maks oder Passierschein durch den Styx.* Hrsg. und Vorwort: Andrzej Bodek. Aus dem Poln. von Karin Wolff und Andrzej Bodek. 246 [1] pp. Berlin: Transit, 1992. (Schriftenreihe der Arbeitsstelle zur Vorbereitung des Frankfurter Lern- und Dok.-zentrums des Holocaust, Bd. 3.) [Recollections of a Polish-Jewish physician, who was for four years an inmate of the ghetto of Lodz.]

29405 LORENZ, DAGMAR C.G.: *Verfolgung bis zum Massenmord. Holocaust-Diskurse in deutscher Sprache aus der Sicht der Verfolgten.* New York: Lang, 1992. 451 pp., notes (339–423), index (427–451). (German Life and Civilization, 11.) [Analysis of actual and fictional accounts by Jewish writers on topics connected with antisemitism, persecution and the Holocaust.]

29406 LORENZ, EINHART: *Exil in Norwegen. Lebensbedingungen und Arbeit deutschsprachiger Flüchtlinge 1933–1943.* Mit einem Vorwort von Willy Brandt. Baden-Baden: Nomos, 1992. 402 pp., footnotes, bibl. (369–390), index (names, 393–402). (Nordeuropäische Studien, Bd. 7.) [Incl. short biographies of refugees (343–368), among them many German-speaking Jews.]

29407 LUCKENWALDE. RIEMER, DETLEV: *Dokumente zur Zeitgeschichte.* Luckenwalde, 1992. 30 pp.(mimeogr.), docs. [Obtainable at the LBI London.] [Deals mainly with the November Pogrom.]

29408 LUDWIG, JOHANNES: *Boykott, Enteignung, Mord: die 'Entjudung' der deutschen Wirtschaft.* Überarb. Neuausgabe, München: Piper, 1992. 399 pp., illus., bibl. (379–382). [For first edn. publ. in 1989 see No. 26406/YB XXXV.]

29409 MAGDEBURG/SCHÖNEBECK. KUNTZE, GÜNTER: *Unter aufgehobenen Rechten. Juden unerwünscht.* Magdeburg: Helmuth Block-Verlag, 1992. 123 pp., append. (50 pp.), illus., facsims., docs. [Documentation about, a.o., three Jewish families from Magdeburg and Schönebeck; see also, by same author, on the Jews of Schönebeck No. 28103/YB XXXVII.]

29410 MAINZ. WECKBECKER, MICHAEL: *Schulfrei' zur Reichspogromnacht. Ein Überblick über die Judenverfolgung in Mainz 1933–1945.* [In]: Tribüne, Jg. 31, H. 123, Frankfurt am Main, 1992. Pp. 203–210, footnotes, illus.

29411 MARBURG an der Lahn. HÄNDLER-LACHMANN, BARBARA/SCHÜTT, ULRICH: *'unbekannt verzogen' oder 'weggemacht'. Schicksale der Juden im alten Landkreis Marburg 1933–1945.* Marburg: Hitzeroth, 1992. 245 pp., ports.

29412 — HÄNDLER-LACHMANN, BARBARA/WERTHER, THOMAS: *Vergessene Geschäfte – verlorene Geschichte. Jüdisches Wirtschaftsleben in Marburg und seine Vernichtung im Nationalsozialismus.* Marburg: Hitzeroth, 1992. 297 pp., illus., docs., facsims.

29413 MATTENKLOTT, GERT: *Zur Darstellung der Shoa in deutscher Nachkriegsliteratur.* [In]: Jüdischer Almanach [see No. 29248]. Frankfurt am Main, 1992. Pp. 27–34.

29414 McEWAN, DOROTHEA: *Facing the Anschluß: Jewish memories 50 years on. Jüdische Erinnerungen an den Anschluß vor 50 Jahren.* [In]: Landjudentum im süddeutschen und Bodenseeraum [see No. 29018]. Pp. 208–232.

29415 MECKLENBURG. JAHNKE, KARL HEINZ: *Die Vernichtung der Juden in Mecklenburg.* [In]: Verdrängung und Vernichtung der Juden unter dem Nationalsozialismus [see No. 29366]. Hamburg: Christians, 1992. Pp. 291–310.

29416 MELSON, ROBERT: *Revolution and genocide: on the origins of the Armenian genocide and the Holocaust.* With a foreword by Leo Kuper. Chicago: Univ. of Chicago Press, 1992. XXI, 363 pp. [Author discusses the similarities between the situation of the Armenians in the Ottoman Empire and Jews in Imperial Germany and tries to establish a connection between revolution and genocide.]

29417 MICHAELIS, MEIR: *Axis policies towards the Jews in World War II.* The Fifteenth Annual Rabbi Louis Feinberg Memorial Lecture Series in Judaic Studies. Univ. of Cincinnati: Judaic Studies Program, 1992. 21 pp.

29418 MINDEN. MEYNERT, JOACHIM: *Ausgegrenzt und allein. Jüdische Jugend in Minden-Ravensberg 1933–1938. Ein Beitrag zum Alltag im Nationalsozialismus.* [In]: Mitteilungen des Mindener Geschichtsvereins, Jg. 63, Minden, 1991. Pp. 115–134, illus., notes.

29419 MULLER, ROBERT: *Niemand rettete Muni. Erinnerung an eine verordnete Abwanderung.* [In]: Die Zeit, Nr. 6, Hamburg, 31. Jan. 1992. P. 80, port. [See also, by same author: *Letters that spelt death* [in]: The Times Saturday Review, London, Feb. 8, 1992. Pp. 4–6, port., illus.] [Personal recollections of a Hamburg-born Jewish boy of his grandmother, deported in 1941 to Riga.]

29420 NESS, D.: *Heinz Helmuth Arnold. Das Schicksal eines judenchristlichen evangelischen Pfarrers im Dritten Reich.* [In]: Jahrbuch für Schlesische Kirchengeschichte, Jg. 69, Ulm, 1990. Pp. 55–92.

29421 NEUBRANDENBURG. MAUBACH, PETER/KRÜGER, DIETER: *Geschmäht und verfolgt – Juden in Neubrandenburg.* [In]: Neubrandeburger Mosaik. Heimatgeschichtliches Jahrbuch des Regionalmuseums Neubrandenburg, Nr. 13. Neubrandenburg, 1991. Pp. 36–45, illus.

29422 NEUPERT, JITTA: *'Ich fand den Weg nicht mehr zurück'. Geschichte der Halbjüdin Lola Sinz.* [In]: Dachauer Hefte, Jg. 8, H. 8, Dachau, Nov. 1992. Pp. 181–192.

29423 NEUWIED. DIETZ, WOLFGANG: *NS-Judenverfolgung im Kreis Neuwied. Zum Schicksal jüdischer Ehefrauen aus Mischehen.* [In]: Heimatjahrbuch des Kreises Neuwied, Neuwied, 1992. Pp. 71–75, notes.

29424 NICOSIA, FRANCIS: *The 'Yishuv' and the Holocaust.* [In]: Journal of Modern History, Vol. 64, No. 3, Chicago, Sept. 1992. Pp. 533–540, footnotes. [Review article; discussing the Zionist movement vis à vis the Nazi regime.]

29425 NOVEMBER POGROM. DOMANSKY, ELISABETH: *'Kristallnacht', the Holocaust and German unity: the meaning of November 9 as an anniversary in Germany.* [In]: History & Memory, Vol. 4, No. 1, Bloomington, 1992. Pp. 60–94, notes.

29426 — FAUST, ANSELM: *Der improvisierte Pogrom. Die 'Kristallnacht' 1938.* [In]: Verfolgung und Widerstand im Rheinland und in Westfalen 1933–1945 [see No. 29446]. Köln, 1992. Pp. 152–161, notes.

29427 — JONCA, KAROL: *'The Crystal Night' and the case of Herschel Grynszpan* [in Polish]. Wroclaw: Wydawnictwo Uniwersytetu Wroclawskiego, 1992. 398 pp. (Acta Universitatis Wratislaviensis, No. 1312.)

29428 — KLIBANSKY, RAYMOND: *Zur fünfzigsten Wiederkehr der Pogromnacht.* [In]: Trumah, 3, Wiesbaden, 1992. Pp. 1–13.

—— — LOEWENBERG, PETER: *Die 'Reichskristallnacht' vom 9. zum 10. November 1938 als öffentliches Erniedrigungsritual.* [See No. 29982.]

29429 — *The November-Pogrom 1938: the ordeal of German Jewry = Pra'ot November 1938: miuchan li-yehudei Germania.* [In Hebrew]. Eds.: Yoel Darom, Asher Nathan. Ramat-Efal: Yad Tabenkin, 1992. 141 pp. [Proceedings of a study day held on Nov. 10, 1988, sponsored by five institutions incl. the Leo Baeck Institute, Jerusalem. Chairmen of the four sessions: Jacob Katz, Dan Michman, Haim Seeligmann, Y. Ansbacher.] [Cont.(in Hebrew): Introduction (Haim Seeligmann, 6). Opening remarks (Ya'akov Sack, 7–9). Aspects of Nazi internal and foreign policy in relation to the Kristallnacht pogrom (Haim Shamir, 9–20). The pogrom of November 1938 in Austria (Herbert Rosenkranz, 21–42). Let us not forget the small communities (Michael Cohen, 42–53). Jewish institutions after the November pogrom 1938 (Yehoyakim Cochavi, 54–63). The reaction of Orthodox Jewry to the National Socialist regime (Esriel Hildesheimer, 64–74). Jewish education in Germany as a reaction to the persecutions (Yehuda ben-Avner, 74–79). The youth movement became predominant (Yitzhak ben-Aharon, 80–84). The influence of the pogroms of November 1938 on the activities of the Jewish youth movements in Germany (Ruth Zariz, 84–91). Vienna and Berlin (Hanan Bar-Am, 91–95). The Hachsharot – the path for Aliya and emigration (Max Ziemels, 96–100). Rescue of Halutzim – with the support of the Gestapo (Pino Ginsburg, 100–106). The Zionist movements in Vienna during the years 1938–1939 (Hanna Weiner, 106–115). The last chapter in the history of German Jewry 1938–1943 (Otto Dov Kulka, 116–125). Synagogues in Germany [photographs] (Edina Meyer-Maril, 125–133). Closing remarks (Avraham Barkai, 134–137). Epilogue (Yitzhak Dana, 138–141).]

29430 — PETERS, HARTMUT: *Die 'Reichskristallnacht' in Jever und die Geschichte der Jeverschen Synagoge.* Jever: H.Peters, 2942 Jever (Mariengymnasium, Terrasse 3), 1992. 83 pp., illus., facsims.

29431 — SCHNEIDER, HORST: *Pogromnacht in Dresden.* [In]: Studia nad Faszyzmem i zbrodniami Hitleroskimi XV. Wroclaw, 1992. Pp. 253–258.

29432 ORTMEYER, BENJAMIN: *Arbeiter streikten für die Juden. Die historische Bedeutung des Februar-Streiks 1941 in den Niederlanden.* [In]: Tribüne, Jg. 31, H. 122, Frankfurt am Main, 1992. Pp. 142–154, illus., footnotes. [On the workers' strike against the persecution of the Jews in the Netherlands, incl. ca. 35,000 Jewish refugees from Germany, Austria and Czechoslovakia.]

29433 OZICK, CYNTHIA: *Of Christian heroism.* [In]: Partisan Review, Vol. 59, No. 1, Boston, Winter

1992. Pp. 44–51. [Deals with people who helped Jews during the Nazi period; also discusses what distinguishes 'heroes' from bystanders.]

29434 PENZBERG. RÖSSLER, HANS: *'Es hat sich Unerhörtes ereignet'. Penzberger Kirchenvorsteher verhindern 1938 die Verhaftung von Juden.* [In]: Zeitschrift für bayrische Kirchengeschichte, Jg. 60, Nürnberg, 1991. Pp. 137–142.

29435 PEREL, SALLY: *Ich war Hitlerjunge Salomon.* Aus dem Französ. von Brigitta Restorff. Mit dem Verf. erstellte Neubearb. des Textes. Berlin: Nicolai, 1992. 196 pp. [Autobiographical account of author's survival with false identity; basis for the film 'Europa Europa'.]

29436 PORAT, DINA: *The Allies, Herzl's testament, the Holocaust and limitations of Jewish policies, July 1944.* [In]: Holocaust and Genocide Studies, Vol. 6, No. 3, Oxford, 1991. Pp. 269–282, notes, illus. [Discusses the reasons why David Ben Gurion's speech, given on July 10, 1944 to commemorate the 40th anniversary of Herzl's death, was omitted from the publication of his collected essays. The speech accused the Allies of indifference to the fate of the Jews.]

29437 POSEN (POZNAŃ). KERSHAW, IAN: *Improvised genocide? The emergence of the 'Final solution' in the 'Warthegau'.* [In]: Transactions of the Royal Historical Society, 6th Series, Vol. 2, London, 1992. Pp. 51–78, footnotes. [Incl. deportation of German Jews.]

29438 PRESS, BERNHARD: *Judenmord in Lettland 1941–1945.* Berlin: Metropol, 1992. 178 pp., bibl. (Reihe Dokumente, Texte, Materialien/Zentrum für Antisemitismusforschung der Technischen Universität Berlin, Bd. 4.) [Augmented new edn. of book, publ. privately by the author, in 1988 [see No. 26474/YB XXXV]. Personal recollections of the author, a professor of pathology, b. 1917 in Riga, who was deported to the Ghetto of Riga in 1941. After escaping he survived in hiding. Refers also to the history of the Latvian Jews.]

29439 PRINZ, WOLFGANG: *'Im ganzen Reich der erste Stein'. Die frühen Pogrome gegen die Juden im November 1938 in den Gauen Kurhessen und Magdeburg-Anhalt.* [In]: Studia nad Faszyzmem i zbrodniami Hitleroskimi XV. Wroclaw, 1992. Pp. 227–238.

29440 QUACK, SIBYLLE: *Schmerz und Selbstbehauptung. Deutsche Jüdinnen in New York.* [In]: Forschung. Mitteilungen der DFG, Nr. 1, Weinheim, 1992. Pp. 12–14, illus. [On the experiences of German-Jewish refugee women in New York 1933–1943.]

29441 REFUGEE POLICY. GRYNBERG, ANNE: *1940: L'internment des Juifs étrangers, un 'remède' à la décadence 'française'.* [In]: Sexe et Race. Discours et formes nouvelles d'exclusion du XIXe au XXe siècle. Responsable de la publication: Rita Thalmann. Paris: CERG et Université Paris 7, 1991. Pp. 159–173, notes. [On the indifference and lack of solidarity of the French towards Jewish refugees from Nazi Germany and other Nazi occupied countries.]

29442 — KOCHAVI, ARIEH J.: *Britain and the illegal immigration to Palestine from France following World War II.* [In]: Holocaust and Genocide Studies, Vol. 6, No. 4, Oxford, 1991. Pp. 383–396, notes. [Incl. refugees from Germany; the story of the 'Exodus'.]

29443 — LEVENE, MARK: *War, Jews, and the new Europe: the diplomacy of Lucien Wolf, 1914–1919.* Oxford; New York: Oxford Univ. Press, 1992. XIV, 346 pp., maps. [L.W., son of an exiled German-Jewish businessman, British anti-Zionist diplomat at the time of the Balfour Declaration. He worked in the Foreign Office to influence foreign governments to adopt liberal, emancipationist policies for the Jews. His contacts incl. German-Jewish organisations. Cf.: Dangerous game of diplomacy (David Cesarani) [in]: Jewish Chronicle, London, Oct. 16, 1992, p. 24.]

29444 REFUGEES. MUCHITSCH, WOLFGANG: *Mit Spaten, Waffen und Worten. Die Einbindung österreichischer Flüchtlinge in die britischen Kriegsanstrengungen 1939–1945.* Wien: Europaverlag, 1992. 266 pp. (Ludwig Boltzmann Institut für die Geschichte der Arbeiterbewegung, Materialien zur Arbeiterbewegung Nr. 61.)

29445 — ZUR MÜHLEN, PATRICK VON: *Fluchtweg Spanien – Portugal. Die deutsche Emigration und der Exodus aus Europa 1933–1945.* [Hrsg.: Forschungsinstitut der Friedrich-Ebert-Stiftung] Bonn: Dietz Nachf., 1992. 223 pp. (Reihe: Politik- und Gesellschaftsgeschichte, Bd. 28.) [Cf.: Fremde Freiheit (Willi Jasper) [in] Die Zeit, Nr. 20, Hamburg, 8. Mai, 1992, p. 12. Transit in die Freiheit (Heribert Seifert) [in]: 'NZZ', Nr. 298, Zürich, 22. Dez. 1992, p. 21.]

29446 RHINELAND. FAUST, ANSELM, ed.: *Verfolgung und Widerstand im Rheinland und in Westfalen 1933–1945.* Mit Beiträgen von Michael Zimmermann [et al.]. Hrsg. von der Landeszentrale für politische Bildung Nordrhein-Westfalen. Köln: Kohlhammer, 1992. 254 pp., notes, bibl. (245–252). (Schriften zur politischen Landeskunde Nordrhein-Westfalens, Bd. 7.) [Incl. (titles partly abbr.): Verfolgung und Widerstand im Nationalsozialismus. Ergebnisse und Aufgaben der Geschichtsschreibung (Michael Zimmermann, 11–29). Further contributions are listed according to subject.]

29447 RÖCHER, RUTH: *Die jüdische Schule im nationalsozialistischen Deutschland 1933–1942*. Frankfurt am Main: dipa-Verlag, 1992. 338 pp., notes (233–278), annex (tabs., docs., facsims., 279–308), bibl. (309–332). (Sozialhistorische Untersuchungen zur Reformpädagogik und Erwachsenenbildung, Bd. 14.) [Incl. Vorwort (Michael Brocke, 11–13).]

29448 RÖCHER, RUTH: *Lernen für die Auswanderung. Die jüdische Schule in Deutschland 1933–1942*. [In]: Zeitschrift für Religions- und Geistesgeschichte, Jg. 43, Leiden, 1991. Pp. 266–281, footnotes.

29449 ROSENKRANZ, ZE'EV: *The corporate activities of the National-Jewish and Zionist student associations in Germany*. Jerusalem: Hebrew Univ. M.A. thesis, 1988. [In Hebrew.]

29450 RUBENSTEIN, RICHARD L.: *After Auschwitz: history, theology and contemporary Judaism*. 2nd edn., Baltimore, MD: The Johns Hopkins Univ. Press, 1992. XXII, 358 pp.

29451 RYAN, JUDITH: *Postmodernism as 'Vergangenheitsbewältigung'*. [In]: German Politics and Society, Issue 27, Cambridge, MA, Fall 1992. Pp. 12–24, notes. [Gives examples of the treatment of the Nazi past in modern German writing.]

29452 SACHSENHAUSEN. HRDLICKA, MANUELA R.: *Alltag im KZ: das Lager Sachsenhausen bei Berlin*. Opladen: Leske & Budrich, 1991. 160 pp., illus.

29453 *Die Schatten der Vergangenheit. Impulse zur Historisierung des Nationalsozialismus*. Hrsg. von Uwe Backes, Eckhard Jesse, Rainer Zitelmann. Frankfurt am Main: Ullstein, 1992. 660 pp., notes. Um ein Nachwort erweiterte Ausgabe. (Zeitgeschichte; Ullstein Buch Nr. 33161) [A collection of 24 contributions on the 'Historians Debate', 'Vergangenheitsbewältigung', other related problems of historiography and some aspects of National Socialism; first published in 1990. Incl.: Offene Fragen der Holocaust-Forschung. Das Beispiel des Baltikums (Hans-Heinrich Wilhelm, 403–425, notes). Der lettische Anteil an der 'Endlösung'. Versuch einer Antwort (Margers Vestermanis, 426–449, notes). Keine Massenvergasungen in Auschwitz? Zur Kritik des Leuchter-Gutachtens (Werner Wegner, 450–476, notes). Further contributions are listed according to subject.] [Cf.: Vom Elend der Unterstellungen. Symptome eines neuen Umgangs mit der deutschen Zeitgeschichte (Peter Steinbach) [in]: Tribüne, Jg. 31, H. 122, Frankfurt am Main, 1992, pp. 194–199. See also the review essay: Verfehlte 'Historisierung' des Dritten Reiches. Eine Auseinandersetzung mit fragwürdigen Tendenzen in der neuen deutschen Geschichtsschreibung (Walther Hofer) [in] 'NZZ', Nr. 24, Zürich, 30./31. Jan. 1993. P. 23.]

29454 SCHUBERT, KATHARINA: *Fluchtweg Eifel. Spurensuche an einer kaum beachteten Grenze*. Köln: Middelhauve, 1992. 110 pp., illus. [On making a television documentary on Jewish refugees and people who helped them to cross the border.]

29455 SEGAL, LILLI: *Bereist die schöne freie Schweiz. Der schwierige Weg von Auschwitz in die Freiheit. Bericht einer Flucht*. [In]: Dachauer Hefte, Jg. 8, H. 8, Dachau, Nov. 1992. Pp. 103–149.

29456 SEGEBERG (Bad). MUSSDORF, TORSTEN: *Die Verdrängung jüdischen Lebens in Bad Segeberg im Zuge der Gleichschaltung 1933–1939*. Frankfurt am Main; New York [et al.]: Lang, 1992. 261 pp., illus., facsims., docs., folder with maps, bibl., list of names. (Kieler Werkstücke; Reihe A: Beiträge zur Schleswig-Holsteinischen und skandinavischen Geschichte, 6.) [Also on the pre-Nazi period.]

29457 SHILLONY, BEN-AMI: *The Jews and the Japanese: the successful outsiders*. Rutland, VT; Tokyo: Charles Tuttle, 1992. 252 pp., illus., notes. [Covers also German Jews in Japan and Shanghai; incl. chap. 'Japan saves Jews in World War II', which incl. several German-Jewish scholars.]

29458 SILVER, ERIC: *The book of the just: the silent heroes who saved Jews from Hitler*. London: Weidenfeld & Nicolson, 1992. 175 pp., illus., bibl. [Incl. Germans who saved Jews.]

29459 SIMON, MARIE: *Das Wort Muselmann in der Sprache der deutschen Konzentrationslager*. [In]: Aus zweier Zeugen Mund. Festschrift für Pnina Navé Levinson und Nathan Peter Levinson [see No. 29923]. Pp. 202–211.

29460 SIMPSON, TESS: *Refugee scholars. Conversations with Tess Simpson*. Ed. by R.M. Cooper. Leeds: Moorland Books, 1992. 258 pp., illus., facsims. [In the 1930s T.S helped to found (and later became secretary of) the Society for the Protection of Science and Learning, under whose aegis a great many scholars and scientists were rescued from Nazi Germany, among them Ernst Chain, Hans Krebs, Karl Popper. T.S. was also instrumental in securing the release of many refugee scholars from war-time internment.]

29461 SOBERNHEIM. HENRY, FRANCES: *Nachbarn und Opfer. Erinnerungen an eine Kleinstadt im Nationalsozialismus*. Mit einem Nachwort von Willy Brandt. Hrsg. vom Förderverein Synagoge Sobernheim. Bonn: Dietz Nachf., 1992. 256 pp., illus. [Transl. into German by

Marianne Boussonville.] [For orig. American edn., publ. in 1984, and data see No. 21101/ YB XXX.] [Incl. the essay 'Vergangenheitsbewältigung' in Sobernheim und anderswo. Ein Nachwort (Hans-Eberhard Berkemann/Thomas Hofmann, 241–254).]

29462 SOEST. Köhn, Gerhard: *Die Soester Opfer der Judenverfolgung im Dritten Reich – Zur Erinnerung an die Deportationen vor 50 Jahren.* [In]: Soester Zeitschrift, H. 104, Soest, 1992. Pp. 84–139, illus., facsims. [Incl. list of deportees.]

29463 Sperber, Manes: *The unheeded warning: Nazism in Germany.* [In]: Partisan Review, Vol. 58, No. 1, Boston, Winter 1991. Pp. 9–20. [See also No. 28823/YB XXXVII.]

29464 STADE. Lohmann, Hartmut: *'Hier war doch alles nicht so schlimm'. Der Landkreis Stade in der Zeit des Nationalsozialismus.* Hrsg. vom Landkreis Stade. Stade: Der Oberkreisdirektor, 1992. 585 pp., illus., facsims., docs., notes (439–464), bibl. (465–482), maps. [Deals passim with the persecution and forced labour of Jews. Incl. chap.: Zum Schicksal der Juden im Landkreis Stade (287–315; incl. list of deportees).]

29465 Stein, Joshua: *Our great solicitor: Josiah C. Wedgwood and the Jews.* London; Cranbury, NJ: Associated Univ. Presses, 1992. 170 pp., illus. [Deals also with Wedgwood's intervention on behalf of Jewish refugees from Germany and Austria.]

29466 Stein, Oswald: *Abgebaut. Eine Familie erlebt das Dritte Reich.* Frankfurt am Main: Haag +Herchen, 1992. 131 pp. [Author, b. 1926 in Mayen, teacher, son of a Jewish mother and a Catholic father, moved with his family in 1928 to Frankfurt am Main, was sent to England with a Kindertransport in 1939.]

29467 Steinberg, Jonathan: *Deutsche, Italiener und Juden. Der italienische Widerstand gegen den Holocaust.* Aus dem Englischen von Ilse Strasmann. Göttingen: Steidl, 1992. 373 pp., notes (313–360), chronology [of the Holocaust] (361–366), index (names, places, 367–373). [First publ. in 1990 under the title All or nothing – the Axis and the Holocaust 1941–1943. Refers also to the rescue of German-speaking refugees with the help of Italian diplomats and soldiers.]

29468 Steindling, Dolly: *Meine Jugend.* Ein Bericht. Wien: Finny Steindling, 1990. 223 pp., illus. [For first publ. 1989 (in Hebrew transl.) and data see No. 27392/YB XXXVI.]

29469 Stern, Guy: *In the service of American Intelligence. German-Jewish exiles in the war against Hitler.* [In]: LBI Year Book XXXVII, London. Pp. 461–477, footnotes, appendix: docs.

29470 Stieg, Margaret F.: *Public libraries in Nazi Germany.* Tuscaloosa: Univ. of Alabama Press, 1992. XVI, 347 pp., illus., tabs., notes (267–305), bibl. [Deals also with the removal from shelves of books by Jewish authors; and the book-burning.] [Cf.: Review (Alan E. Steinweis) [in]: Central European History, Vol. 25, Atlantic Highlands, NJ, 1992, pp. 117–119.]. [On the same topic see also: Margaret Stieg: The Second World War and the public libraries of Nazi Germany. [In]: Journal of Contemporary History, Vol. 27, London, 1992. Pp. 23–40, notes.]

29471 Stone, Michael: *Das Blindeninstitut. Bruchstücke einer Jugend.* Berlin: Kupfergraben Verlagsges., 1991. 190 pp. [M.S., formerly Michael Kuh, writer, journalist, 1922 Berlin – 1993 (Frankfurt am Main?), lived in Vienna until he went in 1939 with a Kindertransport to England, fought in the British Army, returned to Berlin in 1962.]

29472 Strauss, Herbert A., ed.: *Jewish immigrants of the Nazi period in the USA.* Vol. 4: *Jewish emigration from Germany 1933–1942.* A documentary history. Part 4/1: Programs and Policies until 1937 [and] Part 4/2: Restrictions on emigration and deportation to Eastern Europe. Ed. by Norbert Kampe. München; New York: Saur, 1992. 2 vols., pp. 1–288 [and] pp. 289–726, docs., bibl. (origin of docs.), cumulative index to docs. and introd. [Cont.: Preface. Introductions to each chap.; chaps. arranged under the following headings (titles condensed): Special laws, emigration, expulsion, and extermination: antisemitic programs 1879–1932. Nazi 'seizure of power' and creation of pressure to emigrate, 1933–1936. The reaction of German Jewry, 1933–1937. The progressive pauperization of German Jewry until 1937. Nazi refugees face a closed world: international activities to solve the problem of asylum and immigration, 1933–1939. Expropriation, forced emigration, and pogrom, 1938–39: from 'orderly emigration' to panic flight. Towards the end of Jewish emigration in Nazi-controlled Europe, 1939–1942.]

29473 *Studia nad Faszyzmem i zbrodniami Hitleroskimi XV.* Wroclaw: Wydawnictwo Uniwersytetu Wroclawskiego, 1992. Pp. 382 pp., footnotes. [Incl.: Three German essays are listed according to subject; contributions in Polish (titles of German summaries): Juden in der nationalsozialistischen Doktrin 1919–1933 (Marek Maciejewski, 5–34). Die Judenfrage in der 'Historischen Zeitschrift' 1936–1943 (Henryk Olszewski, 83–103). Sozialer Struktur-wandel der Juden im Dritten Reich 1933–1945 (Karol Jonca, 105–119). Wirtschaftlicher Boykott der jüdischen Bevölkerung vor der 'Kristallnacht' und seine internationalen Folgen, 1933–1938 (Karol Fiedor, 121–188). Beteiligung der SS und der Polizei an Judenpogromen in Deutschland, 9.–10. November 1938 (Miroslaw Cygański, 189–198). 'Kristallnacht' anhand von Berichten des Sicherheitsdienstes der Schutzstaffeln (Bohdan Koziello-Poklewski, 199–209). Antisemitismus und 'Kristallnacht' in Ostpreussen (Antoni Soloma, 211–226). Die 'Organisation Schmelt' und ihre Arbeitslager für Juden in Schlesien in den Jahren 1940–1944 (Alfred Konieczny, 281–314). Das Lager für Juden in Riebnig bei Brieg [Lower Silesia], 1941–1943 (Tomasz Kruszewski, 315–341). Bemerkungen über die sozialpolitische Lage der Juden in Schlesien in den Jahren 1919–1939 (Maciej Lagiewski, 342–352). Das Bild des Juden in der deutschen Literatur nach 1945. Stereotypen und Charaktere (Norbert Honsza, Wojciech Kunicki, 365–373).]

29474 STUTTGART. *Der jüdische Frisör. Auf Spurensuche: Juden in Stuttgart-Ost.* Hrsg. von der Stuttgarter Osten Lokalzeitung. Stuttgart: Silberburg, 1992. 128 pp., illus.

—— — TAMIR, ARNON: *Eine Reise zurück. Von der Schwierigkeit, Unrecht wiedergutzumachen.* [See No. 29918.]

29475 TENNENBAUM, SILVIA/SPIELMANN, DIANE R.: *A sense of loss and nostalgia: encounters with the German-Jewish past and present.* Cincinnati, OH: American Jewish Archives, 1992. 59 pp., illus., facsims. (Brochure series of American Jewish Archives, XI.) [Essays on children of Holocaust survivors.]

29476 THERESIENSTADT. FRIEDMANN, SAUL S. ed.: *The Terezin diary of Gonda Redlich.* Transl. by Laurence Kutler. With a foreword by Nora Levin. Lexington: The Univ. Press of Kentucky, 1992. XIV, 173 pp., illus. [G.R., a young Zionist, grew up in Moravia, deported to Terezin in 1941, where he was selected to be in charge of the youth welfare department. Died in Auschwitz in 1944. In Terezin he kept and concealed a diary which was found in 1967.]

29477 —— *Musik in Theresienstadt: die Koponisten Pavel Haas, Gideon Klein, Hans Krasa, Viktor Ullmann, Erwin Schulhoff (gestorben im KZ Wülzburg) und ihre Werke.* Referate des Kolloquiums in Dresden am 4. Mai 1991 und ergänzende Studien. Hrsg.: Heidi Tamar Hoffmann und Hans-Günter Klein. Berlin: Musica Reanimata, 1991. 99 pp. (Verdrängte Musik, Bd. 1.)

29478 —— *Theresienstadt in der 'Endlösung der Judenfrage'.* Veröffentl. von der Theresienstädter Initiative, Internat. Theresienstädter Vereinigung. Hrsg. von Miroslav Kárny [et al.]. Prag: Panorama, 1992. 317 pp., illus. [Publ. also in Czech under the title Terezín v konecném resení zidovské otázky. Cont. 32 contr., from an international conference held in Terezín, Nov. 25–28, 1991 on the occasion of the 50th anniversary of the founding of the Theresienstadt ghetto; authors of contributions are: Gabriele Anderl, Wolfgang Benz, David Bloch, Vojtech Blodig, Ruth Bondy, Ludmila Chládková, Avigdor Dagan, Barbara Distel, Jirí Franek, Albert H. Friedlander, Richard Glazar, Alena Hájková, Zdenek Jelínek, Ivan Kamenec, Nili Keren, Miroslav Kryl, Karel Margry, Sybil Milton, Jonny Moser, Kurt Pätzold, Franciszek Piper, Erik Polák, Edith Raim, Czelslaw Rajca, Livia Rothkirchen, Hanus Schimmerling, Margalit Shlain, Hans Sode-Madsen, Hans de Vries.]

29479 WACKER, JEAN-CLAUDE: *Humaner als Bern! Schweizer und Basler Asylpraxis gegenüber den jüdischen Flüchtlingen von 1933 bis 1943 im Vergleich.* Basel: Kommissionsverlag Friedrich Reinhardt, 1992. 218 pp., bibl., index. (Quellen und Forschungen zur Basler Geschichte, 14.)

29480 WALTER, MARIANNE: *The poison seed: a personal history of Nazi Germany.* Lewis, Sussex: The Book Guild, 1992. 260 pp., illus., list of names. [Author grew up in Hamm, where her father was a doctor; recalls her experiences as one of the few Jewish women to study architecture in Berlin during the 1930s; emigrated to England in 1939.]

29481 WEBB, MARGOT: *Shadows at noon.* Pine Mountain Club, CA: Ascendant Publications, 1992. VI, 153 pp. [An autobiographical story of persecution and eventual escape from Nazi Germany.]

29482 WEISS, YFAAT: *Die deutsche Judenheit im Spiegel ihres Erziehungswesens 1933–1938.* [In]: Zeitschrift für Religions- und Geistesgeschichte, Jg. 43, Leiden, 1991. Pp. 248–265, footnotes.

29483 WELLERS, GEORGES: *Der 'Leuchter-Bericht' über die Gaskammern von Auschwitz. Revisionistische Propaganda und Leugnung der Wahrheit.* [In]: Dachauer Hefte, Jg. 7, H. 7, Dachau, Nov. 1991. Pp. 230–241.

29484 WIENER, JAN: *Immer gegen den Strom. Ein jüdisches Überlebensschicksal aus Prag 1939–1950.* Hrsg. von Erhard Roy Wiehn. Konstanz: Hartung-Gorre, 1992. 139 pp., illus., facsims., docs.

29485 WOBBE, THERESA, ed.: *Nach Osten. Verdeckte Spuren nationalsozialistischer Verbrechen*. Frankfurt am Main: Verlag Neue Kritik, 1992. 238 pp., footnotes, bibl. (228–237). [Cont. essays with special emphasis on the role of women as Nazi victims and as perpetrators. Incl.: Das Dilemma der Überlieferung. Zu politischen und theoretischen Kontexten von Gedächtniskonstruktionen über den Nationalsozialismus (Therese Wobbe, 13–44). Sozialwissenschaftliche Ansätze in der Diskussion um Opfer und Überleben (Kira Kosnick, 87–98). Frauen und Geschlechterbeziehungen in der nationalsozialistischen Rassenpolitik (Gisela Bock, 99–134). Verschleppung, Tod und Überleben. Nationalsozialistische Ghetto-Politik gegen jüdischen Frauen und Männer im besetzten Polen (Joan Ringelheim, 135–160; on the ghettos of Lodz, Warsaw and Theresienstadt). Das Konzentrationslager Stutthof (Rita Malcher, 161–174). 'Ich bitte um baldige Arisierung der Wohnung. . .'. Zur Funktion von Frauen im bürokratischen System der Verfolgung (Brigitte Scheiger, 175–196; on the dispossession of Jews). Verdrängte Täterinnen. Frauen im Apparat der SS (1939–1945) (Gudrun Schwarz, 197–223). Further contributions are listed according to subject.]

29486 WOLFF, MARION: *The shrinking circle: memories of Nazi Berlin, 1933–1939*. New York: UAHC Press [Union of American Hebrew Congregations], 1992. IX, 133 pp., illus., ports. [Author's account of her experiences as a Jewish child in Nazi Berlin.]

29487 WYDEN, PETER: *Stella*. New York; London: Simon & Schuster, 1992. 382 pp., illus., ports., footnotes. [Author tells story of his former schoolmate Stella Goldschlag; she went into hiding after forced labour in an ammunition factory, was discovered and tortured by the Gestapo. In order to save her parents from deportation she became a Gestapo informer in war-time Berlin and helped round up hidden Jews for deportations.] [Cf.: Review (Frank Mecklenburg) [in]: Aufbau, Vol. 58, New York, Nov. 6, 1992, p. 8.]

—— *Zedaka. Jüdische Sozialarbeit im Wandel der Zeit. 75 Jahre Zentralwohlfahrtsstelle der Juden in Deutschland 1917–1992.* [See No. 29647.]

29488 ZIMMERMANN, MOSHE: *Die Folgen des Holocaust für die israelische Gesellschaft.* [In]: Das Parlament, Jg. 42, Bonn, 3. Jan. 1992. Pp. 33–43, footnotes. [Deals with the different stages of attitudes towards the Holocaust; examines critically the third 'mythologisation' stage.]

B. Jewish Resistance

29489 DICK, LUTZ VAN, ed.: *Lehreropposition im NS-Staat. Biographische Berichte über den 'aufrechten Gang'*. Mit einem Vorwort von Hans-Jochen Gamm. Frankfurt am Main: Fischer Taschenbuch Verlag, 1990. 246 pp., illus., docs., facsims. [Incl.: Als 'vierteljüdische' Studienrätin an einem großstädtischen Gymnasium (Helene Hedde, 41–49). Als jüdischer Lehrer und Schulleiter an einer jüdischen Großstadtschule und als Jugendleiter im Untergrund (Jizchak Schwersenz, 50–63).]

29490 ERPEL, SIMONE: *Struggle and survival: Jewish women in the anti-fascist resistance in Germany*. [In]: LBI Year Book XXXVII, London. Pp. 397–414, footnotes, ports.

29491 GRIEBEL, REGINA/COBURGER, MARLIES/SCHEEL, HEINRICH: *Erfaßt? Das Gestapo-Album zur Roten Kapelle, eine Fotodokumentation*. Halle/Saale: audioscop, 1992. 372 pp. [Facsim. reprint of a Gestapo album rediscovered more than ten years ago in the archives of the SED. Incl. photos of 108 political prisoners, among them Jews.] [Cf.: Besprechung (Karl-Heinz Janen) [in]: Die Zeit, Nr. 50, Hamburg, 4. Dez. 1992, p. 20.]

29492 LANDAUER, HANS: *Österreichische Spanienkämpfer in deutschen Konzentrationslagern*. [In]: Dachauer Hefte, Jg. 8, H. 8, Dachau, Nov. 1992. Pp. 170–180.

29493 LARGE, DAVID CLAY, ed.: *Contending with Hitler. Varieties of German resistance in the Third Reich*. Cambridge: German Historical Institute, Washington DC & Cambridge Univ. Press, 1991. VII, 197 pp. [Cont. papers orginally presented at a conference organised by the Goethe House New York in April 1988, contr. incl.: Resistance and opposition. the example of the German Jews (Konrad Kwiet, 65–74). The political legacy of the German resistance; a historiographical critique (Hans Mommsen, 151–162); deals also with the Nationalist Conservative attitude to the 'Jewish question'.]

29494 SASSIN, HORST S.: *Liberals of Jewish background in the anti-Nazi resistance*. [In]: LBI Year Book XXXVII, London. Pp. 381–396, footnotes, ports. [On the Robinsohn-Strassmann-Group.]

29495 SCHIEB-SAMIZADEH, BARBARA: *Die Gemeinschaft für Frieden und Aufbau. Eine wenig bekannte Widerstandsgruppe*. [In]: Dachauer Hefte, Jg. 7, Dachau, Nov. 1991. Pp. 174–190. [On the

Berlin resistance group, initiated by Werner Scharff, in which Jews and non-Jews were active.]

29496 SELIGMANN, AVRAHAM: *An illegal way of life in Nazi Germany*. [In]: LBI Year Book XXXVII, London. Pp. 327–361, footnotes., tabs. [Deals with those German Jews who went underground to avoid deportation.]

29497 WERNER, HAROLD: *Fighting back. A memoir of Jewish resistance in World War II*. Ed. by Mark Werner, with a foreword by Martin Gilbert. New York: Columbia Univ. Press, 1992. 1 vol. [H.W., formerly Hershel Zimmermann, b. 1918, survived Nazi persecution in Eastern Poland as a partisan.]

29498 ZADEK, ALICE & GERHARD: *Mit dem letzten Zug nach England: Opposition, Exil, Heimkehr*. Berlin: Dietz, 1992. 284 pp., illus. [Incl. the authors' pre-war activities in the Baum Group.] [Cf.: Not und Hoffnung der 'kleinen Leute' (Miriam Gluikskind) [in]: 'Allgemeine', Jg. 47, Nr. 17, Bonn, 23. April 1992, p. 13.]

IV. POST WAR

A. General

29499 AUSTRIA. REINPRECHT, CHRISTOPH: *Zurückgekehrt. Identität und Bruch in der Biographie österreichischer Juden*. Wien: Braumüller, 1992. 154 pp., bibl., appendix. (sociologica 3.) [Based on 30 interviews with 'remigrés' and children of the first and second post-war generation, focussing on problems of identity, experiences in post-war Austria and antisemitism; incl. questionnaire (Interviewleitfaden, 151–154).]

29500 BERLIN. GAY, RUTH: *Berlin and its counterworlds*. [In]: American Scholar, Vol. 61, No. 4, Washington, DC, Autumn 1992. Pp. 511–527. [Present-day Berlin from the perspective of a visiting (former German) Jew.]

29501 BRENNER, MICHAEL: *Wider den Mythos der 'Stunde Null'. Kontinuitäten im innerjüdischen Bewußtsein und deutsch-jüdischen Verhältnis nach 1945*. [In]: Menora, Bd. 3, München, 1992. Pp. 155–181, notes.

29502 BRUMLIK, MICHA: *The situation of the Jews in today's Germany*. The 1990 Paul Lecture. Bloomington, Ind.: The Jewish Studies Program, 1991. 16 pp.

29503 BURUMA, IAN: *The ways of survival: anti-Semitism and Jewish survival*. [In]: The New York Review of Books, Vol. 39, No. 13, New York, July 16, 1992. P. 11. [Incl. German Jews.]

29504 *Deutsche Juden – Juden in Deutschland*. Hrsg.: Bundeszentrale für politische Bildung, Bonn. Konzeption: Michael Wuliger. Red.: Peter Juling. [1992, no date given] [A collection of articles on the post-war history of Jews in Germany previously publ. in 'Das Parlament', No. 33, Bonn, Aug. 9, 1991. [For full listing see No. 28459/YB XXXVII; book edn. has been augmented by: Dialog zwischen Christen und Juden: Israel und die Wirklichkeit nicht verdrängen (Martin Stöhr, 71–77), Der Koordinierungsrat der Gesellschaften für Christlich-Jüdische Zusammenarbeit (Ansgar Koschel, 78–80). 25 Jahre Deutsch-Israelische Gesellschaft (Hans Koschnick, 87). 35 Jahre Leo Baeck Institut (Arno Lustiger, 137). Judaistik in Deutschland (138–142). The following contributions were not listed in No. 28459/YB XXXVII: Chronik jüdischen Lebens in Deutschland; Grundbegriffe zum Judentum; Berühmte deutschsprachige Juden (Bernhard Voigt, 49–53; 96–103; 120–123). Was und wieviel wir ihnen verdanken. Jüdische Künstler des 20. Jahrhunderts (Hannes Schmidt, 124–128). Nicht nur Objekte und Opfer (Reinhard Rürup, 59–60).]

29505 DINER, DAN: *The future triumphs over the past: Germany, the Jews, and Europe*. [In Hebrew, with English summary]. [In]: Zmanim, No. 37, Tel-Aviv, Spring 1991. Pp. 53–57. [On present-day Germany – the memory of the Holocaust and present-day antisemitism.]

29506 ESCHWEGE, HELMUT: *The churches and the Jews in the German Democratic Republic*. [In]: LBI Year Book XXXVII, London. Pp. 497–513, footnotes, illus. [Obits.: Abschied von einem Freund (Günther Bernd Ginzel) [in]: 'Allgemeine', Jg. 44, Nr. 47, Bonn, 29. Okt. 1992, p. 3, port.] [For recently publ. autobiography by and data on the historian Helmut Eschwege, who died in Dresden Oct. 19, 1992 see No. 28804/YB XXXVII.] [See also: Heimliches Schielen auf den 'Stützpunkt des Gegners'. Als Feind der DDR vierzig Jahre lang im Visier der Stasi bespitzelt und gemaßregelt (Horst Seferenz) [in] 'Allgemeine', Jg. 43, Nr. 43, Bonn, 22. Okt., 1992, p. 15.]

29507 FOSTER, EDITH: *Reunion in Vienna*. Afterword by Heinrich von Weizsäcker. Riverside, CA:

Ariadne Press, 1991. 180 pp. [Book discusses the experiences of an Austrian Jewess on returning for a 50th school reunion and the way her former schoolmates try to deal with the past.]

29508 FRANK, LIA: *Ernüchterung nach Illusionen. Die sowjetischen Juden und ihre Versetzung in eine neue Welt*. [In]: Tribüne, Jg. 31, H. 123, Frankfurt am Main, 1992. Pp. 78–81.

—— GALINSKI, HEINZ. *Heinz Galinski (Nov. 28, 1912–July 19, 1992)*. Obits. [See No. 29632.]

29509 GUTMAN, YISRAEL/DRECHSLER, ADINA, eds.: *She'erit-Hapletah 1944–1948; rehabilitation and political struggle*. Proccedings of the Sixth Yad Vashem International Historical Conference, Jerusalem, October 1985. Jerusalem: Yad Vashem, 1990. 500 pp. [In Hebrew]. [Incl. the following articles in Hebrew, titles transl.: Zionism and the She'erit-hapletah (Zeev Mankowitz, 189–206). Envoys from Eretz Israel to the DP camps in Germany; first steps, August 1945–May 1946 (Irit Keinan, 207–221). Kibbutz Buchenwald (Judith Tydor Baumel, 393–404; relates to a group of Buchenwald survivors who established a Zionist training-farm in June 1945 in Gringshof.]

29510 HEENEN-WOLFF, SUSANN: *Im Haus des Henkers' – Gespräche mit Überlebenden der Shoah, die in Deutschland (West und Ost) geblieben sind*. Frankfurt am Main: Dvorah, 1992. 306 pp. [Based on 18 interviews. Cf.: Besprechung (Ulrike Holler) [in]: Tribüne, Jg. 31, H. 121, Frankfurt am Main, 1992, pp. 183–186. Entwurzelt und heimatlos (Gisela Heitkamp) [in] Die Zeit, Nr. 20, Hamburg, 8. Mai 1992, p. 15.]

29511 HEMPFLING, HELMUT: *Juden in Deutschland – deutsche Juden. Jüdisches Selbstverständnis nach der Vereinigung der beiden deutschen Staaten*. [In]: Tribüne, Jg. 31, H. 123, Frankfurt am Main, 1992. Pp. 70–77. [Also on the immigration of Russian Jews.]

29512 *Jüdische Kulturbühne*. Dr. Moses Rosen Institut für jüdische Geschichte und Kultur in Zusammenarbeit mit dem Dokumentationsarchiv München. Hrsg.: Chaim Frank und Karl W. Schubsky. 8000 München 5 (Hans-Sachs Strasse 6): Dokumentationsarchiv München, 1992. 12 issues [44 pp.]. [Incl.: reports on recent events in the Jewish communities of Germany and other political and cultural matters; historical and biographical sketches and book reviews, excerpts.]

29513 KIESSLING, WOLFGANG: *'Von Geburt her Verbrecherin. . .'. Hannelore Baender – ein jüdisches Schicksal in der ehemaligen DDR*. [In]: Tribüne, Jg. 31, H. 121, Frankfurt am Main, 1992. Pp. 152–168. [Recollections of H.B. née Goldschmidt, b. Sept. 14, 1919 in Leipzig, emigr. via the USA to Bolivia, after the war returned with her husband, Paul Baender, to Germany (East).]

—— KUGELMANN, CILLY: *Zur Situation der jüdischen Überlebenden 1945 bis 1950*. [See No. 28988.]

29514 LICHTENSTEIN, HEINER: *Die Minderheit der 30.000. Juden in der Bundesrepublik*. [In]: Deutsch-jüdische Geschichte im 19. und 20. Jahrhundert [see No. 29601]. Pp. 337–349.

—— MATTENKLOTT, GERT: *Über Juden in Deutschland*. [See No. 29704.]

29515 RABINOWITZ, ELIEZER: *Emissary for UNRRA with Jewish displaced persons, 1946–1948*. [In Hebrew]. Tel-Aviv: Moreshet; Sifriat Poalim, 1990. 240 pp. [Recollections of a post-war emissary from Palestine to the DP camps in Germany, organising the children's hostel in Lindenfels near Frankfurt and later the relief for the passengers of the 'Exodus', who were returned to Germany.]

29516 RABINOWITZ, ELIEZER: *Jewish journalism in the refugee camps in Germany*. [In]: Our Press, No. 7, Tel-Aviv, 1991. Pp. 27–38. [Publ. simultaneously in English, Hebrew, and Yiddish.]

29517 RAPAPORT, LYNN: *The difficulties of being Jewish in Germany today*. [In]: Trumah, 3, Wiesbaden, 1992. Pp. 189–215.

29518 RESTITUTION. GOSCHLER, CONSTANTIN: *Wiedergutmachung. Westdeutschland und die Verfolgten des Nationalsozialismus 1945–1954*. München: Oldenbourg, 1992. 343 pp. (Quellen und Darstellungen zur Zeitgeschichte, Bd. 34.)

29519 RHINELAND. *'Begegnung mit Menschen als Aufgabe'. Die Vereinigung ehemaliger Kölner und Rheinländer in Haifa*. [In]: Wegweiser durch das jüdische Rheinland [see No. 29169]. Berlin: Nicolai, 1992. Pp. 362–365. [Based on an interview with Heinrich Schupler, Haifa, chairman of the Vereinigung ehemaliger Kölner und Rheinländer.]

29520 RUNGE, IRENE: *Vom Kommen und Bleiben: osteuropäische jüdische Einwanderer in Berlin*. Berlin: Die Ausländerbeauftragte des Senats, 1992. 56 pp. (Miteinander leben in Berlin.)

29521 SCHARDT, ANGELIKA: *'Der Rest der Geretteten'. Jüdische Überlebende im DP-Lager Föhrenwald 1945–1957*. [In]: Dachauer Hefte, Jg. 8, H. 8, Dachau, Nov. 1992. Pp. 53–68.

29522 SCHMIDT, JOHN: *Unification unsettling for some German Jews*. [In]: The Christian Century, Vol. 108, No. 16, Chicago, 1992. Pp. 508–510.

29523 SILBERMANN, ALPHONS/SALLEN, HERBERT: *Juden in Westdeutschland. Selbstbild und Fremdbild einer Minorität*. Köln: Verlag Wissenschaft und Politik, 1992. 115 pp., footnotes, tabs. [Incl.: Exkurs zu Vorurteilsforschung und Vergangenheitsbewältigung (Alphons Silbermann, 71–93).] [Cf.: Die Juden sollen sich nicht verstecken (Gisela Dachs) [in]: Die Zeit, Nr. 47, Hamburg, 13. Nov. 1992, p. 2.]

29524 STEINBERG, BERNARD: *Rebuilding Jewish education in Europe after the war*. [In]: The Jewish Journal of Sociology, Vol. 34, No. 1, London, June 1992. Pp. 25–42, notes. [Incl. post-war Germany.]

29525 STERN, ELIJAHU, ed.: *A guide to the archive of the Zionist Socialist youth organisation 'Dror' in Germany 1945–1949*. [In Hebrew, title transl.]. Kibbutz Lochamei Haghetaot: Beit Lochamei Haghetaot, 1992. 51 pp.

29526 TAGLIABUE, JOHN: *New German Jews: land is haunted, shadow of Holocaust remains*. [In]: New York Times, Vol. 141, New York, March 23, 1992. P. A4, col. 1.

— *Zedaka. Jüdische Sozialarbeit im Wandel der Zeit. 75 Jahre Zentralwohlfahrtsstelle der Juden in Deutschland*. [See No. 29647.]

B. Education and Teaching. Memorials

29527 AUSCHWITZ. YOUNG, JAMES E.: *The future of Auschwitz*. [In]: Tikkun, Vol. 7, No. 6, Oakland, CA, Nov./Dec. 1992. Pp. 31–33, 77. [Reports on a meeting in 1990 of a group of Jewish intellectuals to discuss the problems of Auschwitz as a tourist attraction and how to devise a code of behaviour for the future.]

29528 *Brandenburgische Gedenkstätten für die Verfolgten des NS-Regimes. Perspektiven, Kontroversen und internationale Vergleiche*. Hrsg.: Ministerium für Wissenschaft, Forschung und Kultur des Landes Brandenburg in Zusammenarbeit mit der Brandenburgischen Landeszentrale für politische Bildung. Red.: Stefanie Endlich. Berlin: Hentrich, 1992. 270 pp., illus., maps. (Reihe deutsche Vergangenheit, Bd. 81.) [Contributions to an international 'Gedenkstätten-Colloquium' held in Potsdam, March 8–9, 1992; incl. 4 essays on the 'system' of Nazi concentration camps by Andreas Graf, Ulrich Herbert, Boris S. Orlov, Hermann Weber (21–51); further contributions incl.: Antifaschismus und Kalter Krieg – Eine Geschichte von Einengung, Verdrängung und Erstarrung (Annette Leo, 74–80). Nationalsozialistische Verfolgung und Widerstand – Etappen bundesrepublikanischer Erinnerung (Wolfgang Benz, 81–85). Orte des kollektiven Gedächtnisses (Lutz Niethammer, 95–104). Eine angemessene Erinnerung (Sybil Milton, 121–125). Ein Blick auf Brandenburg aus Israel (Michael Yaron, 126–130). Die Gedenkstätte Majdanek – Kontinuität im Wandel (Tomasz Kranz, 131–134). Wie können Erfahrungen des Nationalsozialismus zukünftigen Generationen vermittelt werden (Joke Kniesmeyer, 135–137). 'Vergegenständlichte Erinnerung' (Detlef Hoffmann, 138–140). Überlegungen zur Bildungsarbeit in Gedenkstätten für die Opfer des NS-Regimes (Thomas Lutz, 141–147). Gegen eine Instrumentalisierung der Vergangenheit (Reinhard Rürup, 148–150). Nach-Denken über Gedenkstättenpolitik (Dan Diner, 151–155).]

29529 BREMEN. *Heimatgeschichtlicher Wegweiser zu Stätten des Widerstandes und der Verfolgung 1933–1945*. Band 6. *Bremen. Stadt Bremen, Bremen-Nord, Bremerhaven*. Hrsg. vom Studienkreis Deutscher Widerstand. Mit einem Vorwort [von] Bernhard Baumeister und Günter Spanjer. Autorin: Susanne Engelbertz. Frankfurt am Main: Verlag für Akad. Schriften, VAS, 1992. 135 pp., illus., bibl., maps, street index. [Refers also to persecution of Jews and 'Aryanisation' of their property.]

29530 *The British Journal of Holocaust Education*. Vol. 1, No.1, London: Cass, Summer 1992. VI, 126 pp.

29531 BUCHENWALD. BURUMA, IAN: *Buchenwald*. [In]: Granta 42, London, Winter 1992. Pp. 65–75, illus. [On the author's visit to the Mahn- und Gedenkstätte Buchenwald before and after German reunification.]

— FUCHS, MARGA/HORN, CHRISTINE: *Die jüdische Minderheit in Bamberg. Schutzjuden. Staatsbürger mosaischen Glaubens. Rassefeinde*. [See No. 29077.]

29532 GEHRKE, RALPH: *'Es ist nicht wahr, daß die Geschichte nichts lehren könnte, es fehlen ihr bloß die Schüler . . .'. 'Weilchenfeld': Gert Hofmanns Lehrstück zu Auschwitz und Fremdenhaß und* sein Bezug zur Gegenwart. [In]: Der Deutschunterricht, Jg. 44, H. 3, Seelze, 1992. Pp. 103, footnotes, bibl.

29533 GÖTTINGEN. *Verewigt und Vergessen. Kriegerdenkmäler, Mahnmale und Gedenksteine in Göttingen.* Hrsg. von Carola Gottschalk unter Mitarbeit von Holger Biermann im Auftrag der Geschichtswerkstatt Göttingen. Mit einem Vorwort von Alf Lüdtke. Göttingen: Schmerse, 1992. 157 pp., illus. [Incl. (titles abbr.): Das Mahnmal am Platz der zerstörten Synagoge (Susanne Schurr, 84–93). Die Gedenktafel an die im Nationalsozialismus vertriebenen und entlassenen Professoren und Dozenten der Universität Göttingen (Frauke Lindhoff, 106–113). Das Göttinger 'Judenhaus' Weender Landstraße 26 (Uta Schäfer-Richter, 142–151).]

29534 HEINONEN, R.E.: *Zur Behandlung des Judentums im Religionsunterricht.* [In]: Nordisk Judaistik, Vol. 12, No. 2, Abð, 1991. Pp. 116–124.

29535 HESS, ROBERT: *Die pädagogische Umsetzung des Themas Holocaust als Projektthema an Schulen der DDR.* Greifswald: Univ., Diss., 1991. 163 pp.

29536 HOLOCAUST. *Days of remembrance, April 26–May 3, 1992. Fifty years ago: in the depths of darkness.* Commemoration planning guide. Washington, DC: U.S. Holocaust Memorial Council, 1992. XII, 280 pp., illus., facsims., map, ports., bibl. (199–209).

29537 KIEL. *Dokumentation zur Geschichte der Kieler Synagoge und des Mahnmals an der Goethestrasse 13.* Hrsg. von der Versorgung und Verkehr Kiel (VVK), Pressestelle. Red. und Gestaltung: Walter Niebergall. Kiel, 1992. 63 pp., illus., facsims. [Incl. an essay on the history of the synagogue (Walter Niebergall, 7–32) and several speeches at the dedication of the new memorial on the site of the destroyed synagogue.]

29538 KOLINSKY, EVA: *Geschichte gegen den Strom. Zur Darstellung des Holocaust in neuen Schulgeschichtsbüchern.* [In]: Internationale Schulbuchforschung, Jg. 13, Braunschweig, 1991. Pp. 121–145.

—— LOEWY, HANNO, ed.: Holocaust: *Die Grenzen des Verstehens. Eine Debatte über die Besetzung der Geschichte.* [See No. 29381.]

—— PERTSCH, DIETMAR: *Jüdische Lebenswelten in Spielfilmen und Fernsehspielen. Filme zur Geschichte der Juden von ihren Anfängen bis zur Emanzipation 1871.* [See No. 29031.]

29539 REINPRECHT, CHRISTOPH/WEISS, HILDE: *Antisemitismus – ein Thema in österreichischen Schulbüchern? (Geschichtsunterricht).* [In]: Internationale Schulbuchforschung, Jg. 12, Frankfurt am Main, 1990. pp. 285–305.

29540 RENDSBURG, JÜDISCHES MUSEUM. *Streitfall Kunst-Geschichte Jüdisches Museum Rendsburg.* Red.: Frank Trende. Mit Beiträgen von Franke Dettmer, Bernt Engelmann, Arie Goral, Kurt Hamer, Ole Harck, Jens Christian Jensen, Nathan Peter Levinson, Eva Rühmkorf, Heinz Spielmann, Frank Trende und Johannes Tuchel. Kiel: Neuer Malik Verlag, 1991. 87 pp., illus., bibl. (Veröffentlichung. d. Beirats f. Geschichte d. Arbeiterbewegung und Demokratie, Bd. 8.) [Cont. opening addresses and essays discussing the founding of the Rendsburg Jewish museum opened in 1988. Incl.: Die Entdeckung der Rendsburger Synagoge [and] Jüdische Gemeinde Rendsburg: Verfolgung und Untergang in nationalsozialistischer Zeit (Ole Harck, 13–18). Juden in der Kunst, jüdische Kunst und ein jüdisches Museum (Arie Goral, 63–79).]

29541 SCHEFFER, CHRISTOPH: *Land der Täter und Mitläufer. Der Holocaust als Gegenstand schulischer und außerschulischer Bildung.* [In]: Tribüne, Jg. 31, H. 122, Frankfurt am Main, 1992. Pp. 40–44.

29542 SCHREIER, HELMUT/HEYL, MATTHIAS, eds.: *Das Echo des Holocaust. Pädagogische Aspekte des Erinnerns.* Hamburg: Krämer, 1992. 273 pp., footnotes. [A collection of articles (incl. personal memoirs of Nazi persecution by some of the authors) on the political, psychological and psycho-analytical implications of the Holocaust for politics and education by Ido H.B. Abram, Elie A. Cohen, Ruth Elias, Binjamin Heyl, Matthias Heyl, Emanuel Hurwitz, Dierk Juelich, Hans Keilson, Judith S. Kestenberg, Wolfgang Kraushaar, Johannes Lansen, Ingrid Lohmann, Margit Maronde, Jürgen Müller-Hohagen, Helmut Schreier, Fulbert Steffensky, Martin Wangh.]

29543 SHIMONI, GIDEON, ed.: *The Holocaust in university teaching.* Oxford; New York: Pergamon Press, 1991. XIII, 297 pp.

29544 SILBERMANN, ALPHONS: *Zur Handhabung von Erinnern und Vergessen.* [In]: Menora, Bd. 3, München, 1992. Pp. 13–20.

29545 TUCHEL, JOHANNES: *Am Grossen Wannsee 56–58: von der Villa Minoux zum Haus der Wannsee-Konferenz.* Berlin: Hentrich, 1992. 191 pp., illus. (Publikationen der Gedenkstätte Haus der Wannsee-Konferenz, Bd. 1.) [See also on the the Wannsee Villa: Ein Lehrhaus der Demokratie. Verfluchter Ort wird jetzt endlich zur Erinnerungsstätte (Gerhard Schoenberner) [in] 'Allgemeine', Jg. 47, Nr. 3, Bonn, 16. Jan. 1992, p. 3.]

29546 *Über-Lebens-Mittel. Kunst aus Konzentrationslagern und in Gedenkstätten für die Opfer des Nationalsozialismus.* Hrsg. von Wulff E. Brebeck, Angela Genger [et al.]. Red.: Thomas Lutz, Wulff E. Brebeck [et al.]. Marburg: Jonas, 1992. 173 pp., bibl.

29547 VERGIN, SIEGFRIED: *Der Ort der 'Schreibtischtäter'. 'Haus der Wannseekonferenz': Gedenk- und Bildungsstätte zugleich.* [In]: Tribüne, Jg. 31, H. 122, Frankfurt am Main, 1992. Pp. 35–40.

29548 WANNSEE. SCHOENBERNER, GERHARD: *Der lange Weg nach Wannsee. Von der Gründerzeitvilla zur Gedenkstätte.* [In]: Dachauer Hefte, Jg. 8, H. 8, Dachau, Nov. 1992. Pp. 150–153.

29549 WEBER, B.: *Geschichte und Schicksal jüdischer Schülerinnen und Schüler.* [In]: Religionsunterricht an Höheren Schulen, RHS, Jg. 35, H. 3, Düsseldorf, 1992. Pp. 172–177.

29550 WEGNER, GREGORY P.: *The legacy of Nazism and the history curriculum in the East German secondary schools.* [In]: The History Teacher, Vol. 25, No. 4, Long Beach, CA, 1992. Pp. 471–484, notes. [Refers also to Nazi persecution of Jews and antisemitism.]

29551 WEIGAND, WOLF/SCHMADERER, FRANZ-OTTO: *Exkursionsblätter zur Geschichte und Kultur der Juden in Bayern.* München: Bayerische Staatskanzlei, Haus der Bayerischen Geschichte, 1991. [8] pp.

29552 WOLFFSOHN, MICHAEL/PUSCHNER, UWE: *Geschichte der Juden in Deutschland. Quellen und Kontroversen. Ein Arbeitsbuch für die Oberstufe des Gymnasiums.* München: Bayerischer Schulbuch-Verlag, 1992. 328 pp., chronol., bibl. [Sources arranged under the following headings: Siedlungsmuster; Diskriminierungsmuster; Integrationsmuster; Gemeindeleben; Vergangenheitsbewältigung.]

29553 YOUNG, JAMES E.: *The counter-monument: memory against itself in Germany today.* [In]: Critical Inquiry, Vol. 18, No. 2, Chicago, Winter 1992. Pp. 267–296. [Covers Holocaust memorials and monuments, incl. former synagogues, in present-day Germany.]

—— ZABEL, HERMANN, ed.: *Verschwiegen, vergessen, verdrängt. Über die Nazi-Zeit reden. Zugleich ein Beitrag zum Problemkreis 'Sprache im Nationalsozialismus'.* [See No. 29378.]

V. JUDAISM

A. Jewish Learning and Scholars

29554 ALTMANN, ALEXANDER: *The meaning of Jewish existence: the theological essays, 1930–1939.* Ed. by Alfred L. Ivry. Introd. by Paul Mendes-Flohr. Transl. by Edith Ehrlich and Leonhard H. Ehrlich. Hanover, NH: Univ. Press of New England [for] Brandeis Univ., 1991. 169 pp., bibl. (Tauber Institute for the Study of European Jewry series, 12.) [A collection of 15 essays first published in Germany in the 1930s.]

29555 —— ENGEL-HOLLAND, EVA J.: *Alexander Altmann in Memoriam.* [In]: Mendelssohn Studien, Bd. 7. Berlin: Duncker & Humblot, 1990. Pp. 13–29.

—— BAECK, LEO. ARONSFELD, C.C.: *Leo Baeck und das 'Ende des deutschen Judentums'.* [See No. 29272.]

29556 —— HEITMANN, MARGRET: *'Die Motive seiner Lehre rechtfertigen sich in der Wahrheit seines Lebens'. Jüdische Existenz und deutsche Kultur am Beispiel Leo Baecks.* [In]: Deutsch-jüdische Geschichte im 19. und 20. Jahrhundert [see No. 29601]. Pp. 211–230.

29557 —— KORRENZ, RALF: *Das Judentum als Lerngemeinschaft: die Konzeption einer pädagogischen Religion bei Leo Baeck.* Weinheim: Deutscher Studien-Verl., 1992. 109 pp. (Forum zur Pädagogik und Didaktik der Religion, Bd. 6.) Zugl.: Bonn, Univ., Diss., 1992.

—— BARZILAY, EISIG: *Perez Smolenskin and Moses Hess.* [See No. 29610.]

29558 BERLIN, ISAIAH BEN JUDAH LOEB. ABRAMSON, SHRAGA: *The 'notebooks' in the book 'Hafla'ah she-be-arakhin' by Rabbi Isaiah Berlin.* [In Hebrew, title transl.]. [In]: Sinai, Vol. 110, Jerusalem, Nisan-Iyar 5752 [=April-May 1992]. Pp. 1–28. [I.b.J.L.B., 1725 Eisenstadt – 1799 Breslau, rabbi and author.]

—— BUBER, MARTIN: *The Letters of Martin Buber: a life of dialogue.* [See No. 29874.]

—— —— BROCKE, MICHAEL: *Bible translations of German Jews.* [See No. 29575.]

—— —— LAPIDE, PINCHAS: *Heinrich Heine und Martin Buber: streitbare Gott-Sucher des Judentums.* [See No. 29780.]

29559 —— OLIVEIRA, MANUEL DUARTE DE: *The election of Israel in the thought of Martin Buber.* Jerusalem, Hebrew Univ., Diss., June 1991. 411, [10] pp. [In English, with Hebrew summary.]

29560 CARLEBACH, JOSEPH. GILLIS-CARLEBACH, MIRIAM, comp. & ed.: *Joseph Carlebach. Bibliographie seiner Schriften.* Zusammengestellt und ediert von Miriam Gillis-Carlebach. Ramat-Gan: Joseph Carlebach-Institut/Bar-Ilan Universität, 1992. 28 pp. [Mimeog.]

29561 CARLEBACH, JULIUS. *Studien zur jüdischen Geschichte und Soziologie. Festschrift Julius Carlebach.* Hrsg. von Mitarbeitern der Hochschule für Jüdische Studien. Heidelberg: Carl Winter Univ.-Verl., 1992. XX, 220 pp., frontis., notes. [Incl.: Grußworte (Gisbert Frhr. zu Putlitz, Tom Bottomore, Colin Thompson, IX–XI). Contributions dealing with the history of German-speaking Jewry are listed according to subject.]

29562 DAN, JOSEPH: *Hasidim in medieval Germany.* [In Hebrew]. Tel-Aviv: Ministry of Defence, 1992. 82 pp. [Based on a radio series broadcast on the IDF radio channel 'Galei Zahal'.]

29563 ELDAR, ILAN: *'Mafteah shel dikduk' – a 13th-century Ashkenazic work.* [In Hebrew]. [In]: Balshanut Ivrit [Hebrew Linguistics], No. 33–35, Ramat-Gan, June 1992. Pp. 125–148. [On an anonymous Hebrew grammar, traditionally attributed to a German origin, but Eldar contends it was written in Northern France. Pp. 131–138 contain parts of the text.]

29564 ELIEZER BEN NATHAN of Mainz. HERSCHLER, ALTER YEHUDAH: *A commentary on the Siddur and Machzor, attributed to Rabbi Eliezer ben Nathan of Mainz, the Raban.* Now published for the first time from the Frankfurt ms., with sources and annotations by A.Y. Herschler. [In Hebrew]. [In]: Genuzot, Vol. 3, Jerusalem, 1991. Pp. 1–128. [E.b.N., known as RaBaN, ca. 1090 – ca. 1170, one of 'The Elders of Mainz', and a leading rabbinic authority.]

29565 FINKELSTEIN, NORMAN: *The ritual of new creation: Jewish tradition and contemporary literature.* Albany: State Univ. of New York Press, 1992. 192 pp. (Suny series: modern Jewish literature and culture.) [Among the writers discussed are Gershom Scholem and George Steiner.]

29566 FUNKENSTEIN, AMOS: *Perceptions of Jewish history from antiquity to the present.* [In Hebrew]. Tel-Aviv: Am Oved, 1991. 351 pp. [English title taken from back of title-page; the literal transl. of the Hebrew title is: 'Image and historical consciousness in Judaism and in its cultural environment'. A collection of Hebrew articles, most of them publ. previously, some in languages other than Hebrew. Those dealing with German-speaking Jewry: The attitude of the Jewish 'Haskalah' to medieval Jewish philosophy (189–198). The political theory of Jewish emancipation from Mendelssohn to Herzl (199–216). Also two articles on Franz Rosenzweig (217–227 & 228–231).]

29567 HASIDA, SIMCHA: *A commentary on the poem 'Or le-yom hanef' from the school of the early sages of Ashkenaz (relating to the Omer).* [In Hebrew, title transl.]. [In]: Moriah, Vol. 18, No. 5–6, Jerusalem, Nissan 5752 [=April 1992]. Pp. 3–11. [Presents the text of Ms. Hamburg 152, written in the year 1319.]

29568 HAVATZELET, AVRAHAM/PELES, ISRAEL: *Followers of the Tosaphists – Tosaphot Gornisch.* [In Hebrew, title transl.]. [In]: Moriah, Vol. 18, No. 5–6, Jerusalem, Nissan 5752 [= April 1992]. Pp. 12–15. [Discusses the origins of the halakhic compilation known as 'Tosaphot Gornisch' (exact meaning not known), apparently compiled in the mid-13th century by disciples of the Tosaphists, in Erfurt and surroundings (Eastern Ashkenaz).]

29569 HESCHEL, ABRAHAM JOSHUA. KASIMOW, HAROLD/SHERWIN, BYRON L., eds.: *No religion is an island: Abraham Joshua Heschel and interreligious dialogue.* Maryknoll, NY: Orbis Books, 1991. XXV, 205 pp., bibl.

29570 HESS, MOSES. LUNDGREN, SVANTE: *Moses Hess on religion, Judaism and the Bible.* Abö: Abö Akademis Förlag, 1992. X, 206 pp. [Incl. short biography of Hess.]

29571 HIRSCH, SAMSON RAPHAEL. KURZWEIL, ZWI ERICH: *S.R. Hirschs 'Neunzehn Briefe' im Lichte der Kritik.* [In]: Kairos, Neue Folge, Jg. 32./33, Salzburg, 1990/91. Pp. 229–237, notes. [On the critique of Abraham Geiger, Joseph Wohlgemuth and Friedrich Thieberger.]

29572 KÜNG, HANS: *Judaism: the religious situation of our time.* Transl. from the German by John Bowden. London: SCM Press, 1992. XXII, 753 pp., illus., maps, indexes. [American edn. under the title: *Judaism: between yesterday and tomorrow.* New York: Crossroad Publishing, 1992. German orig. edn.: *Das Judentum. Die religiöse Situation der Zeit.* München: Piper, 1991. 907 pp. Deals also with German Jewry, the Holocaust and the possibility of greater understanding between Jews and Christians.]

29573 KURZWEIL, ZWI ERICH: *Auf der berühmten Jeschiwa von Mir. Erinnerungen und Erkenntnisse eines deutschen Talmud-Studenten.* [In]: Tribüne, Jg. 31, H. 124, Frankfurt am Main, 1992. Pp. 206–220. [The author's recollections of his studies at the Yeshiva in Mir, Poland 1936–1937.]

29574 LAX, RUTH E. *The Golem in history and modern literature.* [In]: Midstream, Vol. 38, No. 4, New York, May 1992. Pp. 23–26. [Incl. Gershom Scholem's writings.]

29575 MEIR BEN BARUCH of Rothenburg. KADDARI, MENAHEM: *Intensifiers in the writing of Rabbi Meir of Rothenburg*. [In Hebrew]. [In]: Balshanut Ivrit (Hebrew Linguistics), No. 33–35, Ramat-Gan, June 1992. Pp. 185–193.

— MENDELSSOHN, MOSES. AWERBUCH, MARIANNE: *Moses Mendelssohns Judentum* [see in No. 29083].

29576 — BROCKE, MICHAEL: *Bible translations of German Jews: between Moses Mendelssohn and Martin Buber and Franz Rosenzweig*. [In Hebrew]. [In]: Proceedings of the 10th World Congress of Jewish Studies, 1989, Division C, Vol. 2: Jewish thought and literature. Jerusalem, 1990. Pp. 35–40.

29577 — GREEN, KENNETH HART: *Moses Mendelssohn's opposition to the Herem: the first step toward denominationalism?* [In]: Modern Judaism, Vol. 12, No. 1, Baltimore, Feb. 1992, Pp. 39–60.

29578 — HONIGMANN, PETER: *Der Einfluß von Moses Mendelssohn auf die Erziehung der Brüder Humboldt*. [In]: Mendelssohn Studien, Bd. 7. Berlin: Duncker & Humblot, 1990. Pp. 39–76.]

29579 — LAUSCH, HANS: *'Der Mathematiker schwimmt in Wollust'. Mathematik bei Moses Mendelssohn – Mathematiker im Familienstammbaum*. [In]: Mendelssohn Studien, Bd. 7. Berlin: Duncker & Humblot, 1990. Pp. 77–106, ports.

29580 — SCHMIDT, JAMES: *What enlightenment was: how Moses Mendelssohn and Immanuel Kant answered the Berlinische Monatsschrift*. [In]: Journal of the History of Philosophy, Vol. 30, No. 1, St. Louis, MO, January 1992, pp. 77–101.

29581 — ZOHAR, NAOMI: *Mendelssohn and the Haskalah of Berlin in S.D. Luzzatto's 'On the cities that have gone astray'*. [In Hebrew]. [In]: Proceedings of the 10th World Congress of Jewish Studies, 1989, Division C, Vol. 2: Jewish thought and literature. Jerusalem, 1990. Pp. 65–72.

29582 MORGAN, MICHAEL L.: *Dilemmas in modern Jewish thought: the dialectics of revelation and history*. Bloomington: Indiana Univ. Press, 1992. 181 pp., notes (157–178), index. [Incl. the chaps.: History and modern Jewish thought: Spinoza and Mendelssohn on the Ritual Law (14–26); Liberalism in Mendelssohn's *Jerusalem* (27–39); The curse of historicity: the role of history in Leo Strauss's Jewish thought (40–54); Leo Strauss and the possibility of Jewish philosophy (55–67); Jewish ethics after the Holocaust (79–95); Philosophy, history, and the Jewish thinker: Jewish thought and philosophy in Emil Fackenheim's *To mend the world* (111–124); Franz Rosenzweig, objectivity, and the New Thinking (125–132).]

29583 NOBEL, NEHEMIAH ANTON. HEUBERGER, RACHEL: *Orthodoxy versus reform: the case of Rabbi Nehemiah Anton Nobel of Frankfurt a. Main*. [In]: LBI Year Book XXXVII, London. Pp. 45–58, footnotes, port.

29584 — HEUBERGER, RACHEL: *Nehemias Anton Nobel – ein orthodoxer Rabbiner zwischen deutschem Patriotismus und religiösem Zionismus*. [In]: Trumah, 3, Wiesbaden, 1992. Pp. 151–174.

29585 OPPENHEIM, ISAAC. PELES, ISRAEL MORDECHAI: *Responsa and halakhic decisions of Rabbi Isaac Oppenheim*. [In Hebrew, title transl.]. [In]: Tzfunot, Vol. 4, No. 4, Bnei-Beraq, Tammuz 5752 [=July 1992]. Pp. 9–13. [Presents ten excerpts from mss. referring to R. Isaac, also citing him as the rabbi of Erfurt, where he apparently resided for a lengthy period.]

29586 PELLI, MOSHE: *The meaning of 'melitza' in early Hebrew Haskalah literature*. [In Hebrew, title transl.]. [In]: Lashon ve-Ivrit (Language and Hebrew), No. 8, Even-Yehuda, June 1991. Pp. 31–48. [Particularly on the works of Isaac Euchel, Naphtali Herz Wessely and Isaac Satanow.]

29587 PLAUT, GUNTHER W.: *German-Jewish bible translations: linguistic theology as a political phenomenon*. Leo Baeck Memorial Lecture 36. New York: Leo Baeck Institute, 1992. 24 pp.

29588 RABINKOW, SALMAN BARUCH. HONIGMANN, PETER: *Jüdische Studenten zwischen Orthodoxie und moderner Wissenschaft. Der Heidelberger Talmudistenkreis um Salman Baruch Rabinkow*. [In]: Menora, Bd. 3, München 1992. Pp. 85–96, notes. [Salman Baruch Rabinkow, talmudic scholar, Sosniza 1882–1941 Wassenaar, lived from 1907 until the Nazi period in Heidelberg.]

29589 ROSENZWEIG, FRANZ: AMIR, YEHOYADA: *'The Star of Redemption' between Judaism and Christianity*. [In Hebrew]. [In]: Daat, No. 29, Ramat-Gan, Summer 1992. Pp. 107–130.

29590 — BIENENSTOCK, MYRIAM: *Myth and revelation in the 'Star of Redemption'*. [In Hebrew]. [In]: Iyyun, Vol. 40, Jerusalem, Oct. 1991. Pp. 363–378.

29591 — BRUMLIK, MICHA: *Trotz der Katastrophe gültig? Zur Aktualität von Franz Rosenzweigs Bildungsphilosophie*. [In]: Aus zweier Zeugen Mund. Festschrift für Pnina Navé Levinson und Nathan Peter Levinson [see No. 29923]. Pp. 177–187.

29592 — FRIEDLANDER, ALBERT H.: *Die messianische Dimension bei Franz Rosenzweig und Leo Baeck*.

[In]: Aus zweier Zeugen Mund. Festschrift für Pnina Navé Levinson und Nathan Peter Levinson [see No. 29923]. Pp. 167–176.

29593 — GIBBS, ROBERT: *Correlations in Rosenzweig and Levinas.* Princeton, NJ: Princeton Univ. Press, 1992. 312 pp.

29594 — HORWITZ, RIVKA: *Franz Rosenzweig and Gershom Scholem on Zionism and the Jewish people.* [In]: Jewish History, Vol. 6, No. 1–2, Haifa, 1992. Pp. 99–111.

29595 — MOSÈS, STÉPHANE: *System and revelation: the philosophy of Franz Rosenzweig.* Transl. by Catherine Tihanyi. Foreword by Emmanuel Levinas. Detroit, MI: Wayne State Univ. Press, 1992. 318 pp., charts.

29596 — MOSÈS, STÉPHANE: *L'Ange de l'histoire: Rosenzweig, Benjamin, Scholem.* Paris: Seuil, 1992. 258 pp. (Couleur des idées.)

29597 SACHS, MICHAEL. LUCAS, FRANZ D./FRANK, HEIKE: *Michael Sachs – der konservative Mittelweg: Leben und Werk des Berliner Rabbiners zur Zeit der Emanzipation.* Tübingen: Mohr, 1992. IV, 161 pp., illus., docs., facsims. [M.S., Sept. 3, 1808 Glogau – Jan. 31, 1864 Berlin, rabbi, charismatic preacher, scholar.]

29598 SATANOW, ISAAC. PELLI, MOSHE: *Utopia in Hebrew Haskalah literature: the image of modern Judaism in the utopian vision of Isaac Satanow.* [In Hebrew, with English summary]. [In]: Medinah, Mimshal ve-Yehassim Beinleumiyin (State, Government and International Relations), No. 35, Jerusalem, Autumn-Winter 1991. Pp. 119–130.

29599 — PELLI, MOSHE: *Utopia as a genre in Haskalah literature: Isaac Satanow's 'Divrei Rivot'.* [In Hebrew]. [In]: Proceedings of the 10th World Congress of Jewish Studies, 1989, Division C, Vol. 2: Jewish thought and literature. Jerusalem, 1990. Pp. 73–80.

29600 SCHOEPS, HANS-JOACHIM. KNOLL, JOACHIM H.: *In memoriam Hans-Joachim Schoeps. Der Mensch, sein Werk und seine Zeit.* [In]: Deutsch-jüdische Geschichte im 19. und 20. Jahrhundert [see No. 29601]. Pp. 231–248.

29601 SCHOEPS, JULIUS H. HEID, LUDGER/KNOLL, JOACHIM H., eds.: *Deutsch-jüdische Geschichte im 19. und 20. Jahrhundert.* Sachsenheim: Burg, 1992. 568 pp., footnotes, port., index (559–568). [A collection of articles dedicated to Julius H. Schoeps on the occasion of his 50th birthday; articles are listed according to subject; incl.: Schriftenverzeichnis Julius H. Schoeps (545–555).]

29602 SCHOLEM, GERSHOM: *Judaica 5. Erlösung durch Sünde.* Hrsg., aus dem Hebr. Übers. und mit einem Nachwort versehen von Michael Brocke. Frankfurt am Main: Suhrkamp, 1992. [First publ. in Hebrew in 1937 under the title Mizwa haba'a ba'awera.]

29603 — FUNKENSTEIN, AMOS: *Gershom Scholem: Charisma, Kairos and the Messianic dialectic.* [In]: History & Memory, Vol. 4, No. 1, Bloomington, 1992. Pp. 123–140, notes.

29604 — HESSING, JAKOB: *Der sündige Erlöser. Gershom Scholems Sabbatai Zwi.* [In]: Jüdischer Almanach 1993 [see No. 29248]. Frankfurt am Main, 1992. Pp. 89–95. [First publ. in 'Frankfurter Allg. Zeitung', April 14, 1992.]

29605 SCHWARZSCHILD, STEVEN S. SAMUELSON, NORBERT: *The Jewish philosophy of Steven Schwarzschild.* [In]: Modern Judaism, Vol. 12, No. 2, Baltimore, May 1992. Pp. 185–201, notes.

29606 — SEESKIN, KENNETH: *The rational theology of Steven S. Schwarzschild.* [In]: Modern Judaism, Vol. 12, No. 3, Baltimore, Oct. 1992. Pp. 277–286, notes.

29607 SHEAR-YASHUV, AHARON: *Religion, philosophy and Judaism.* Vol. 2: Conversion; an autobiography of a rabbi. [In Hebrew, title transl.]. Jerusalem: [the author], 1992. [For Vol. 1 see No. 25651/YB XXXIV.]

29608 SINASON, JACOB H.: *The Gaon of Posen: a portrait of Rabbi Akiva Guens-Eger.* 2nd rev. edn. Jerusalem; New York: Feldheim, 1991. XV, 184 pp., illus., facsims., geneal. tabs., map, ports, bibl. [First edn. 1989.]

29609 SINCLAIR, DANIEL: *Trends in rabbinic policy in relation to insincere conversions in post-emancipation responsa.* [In]: Diné Israel: an annual of Jewish law, Vol. 16, Tel-Aviv, 1992. Pp. 46–70. [Incl. chap.: The conversion policy of German poskim (62–69; refers to the 19th and 20th centuries).]

29610 SMOLENSKIN, PEREZ. BARZILAY, EISIG: *Perez Smolenskin and Moses Hess.* [In Hebrew]. [In]: Bitzaron, No. 49–51, New York, Sept. 1991–June 1992. Pp. 57–79. [On the Jewish Nationalist ideologies of both men.]

29611 — FEINER, SHMUEL: *Smolenskin's confrontation with the Haskalah movement and the roots of Jewish nationalist historiography.* [In Hebrew]. [In]: Zionism, Vol. 16, Tel-Aviv, 1991. Pp. 9–31. [Discusses Smolenskin's attack on the influence of Mendelssohn and the Berlin Haskalah.

P.S., 1842 Monsterschtschina (Gouv. Mohilew) – 1885, Meran, editor of the Hebrew periodical 'Haschachar' in Vienna, co-founder of the National-Jewish student organisation Kadimah (1882) in Vienna.]

29612 STEINHEIM, SALOMON LUDWIG. *Steinheim on revelation and theocracy: selection of Salomon Ludwig Steinheim's works.* Ed. and transl. by Aharon Shear-Yashuv. [In Hebrew]. Jerusalem: Rubin Mass, 1989. 221 pp.

29613 — LEVINGER, YAACOV: *The kingdom of God according to Salomon Ludwig Steinheim.* [In Hebrew]. [In]: Sefer ha-yovel le-rav Mordechai Breuer (Rabbi Mordechai Breuer Festschrift). Vol. 2. Ed.: Moshe Bar-Asher. Jerusalem: Academon Press, 1992. Pp. 833–837.

29614 WESTREICH, ELIMELECH: *Grounds for the relaxation of the Rabbenu Gershom ban during the later middle ages.* [In Hebrew]. [In]: Diné Israel: an Annual of Jewish law, Vol. 16, Tel-Aviv, 1992. Pp. 39–95. [Refers to Germany and Spain.]

29615 WIENER, MAX. SCHINE, ROBERT S.: *Deutsches Judentum' – 'Jüdisches Judentum': der Weg Max Wieners (1882–1950).* [In]: Trumah, 3, Wiesbaden, 1992. Pp. 129–149.

29616 — SCHINE, ROBERT S.: *Jewish thought adrift: Max Wiener (1882–1950).* Atlanta, GA: Scholars Press, 1992. XII, 211 pp., ports., bibl. (195–202). (Brown Judaic studies, 259.) [M.W., Berlin rabbi, historian; book incl.: The writings of Max Wiener (185–194).]

29617 *Wissenschaft des Judentums. Anfänge der Judaistik in Europa.* Hrsg. von Julius Carlebach. Darmstadt: Wiss. Buchges., 1992. 231 pp., notes, bibl.(221–230). [Incl.: Einleitung (Julius Carlebach, VII–XIII). Jüdische Wissenschaft und jüdische Identität (Michael A. Meyer, 3–20). Das Collegio Rabbinico von Padua (Nikolaus Vielmetti, 23–35). Die letzten Jahre der Hochschule (Lehranstalt) für die Wissenschaft des Judentums, Berlin: 1936–1942 (Herbert A. Strauss, 36–58). Das orthodoxe Rabbinerseminar in Berlin. Ziele, Probleme und geschichtliche Bedeutung (Mordechai Eliav, 59–73). Das Budapester Rabbinerseminar. Der Platz des Rabbinerseminars in der jüdischen Wissenschaft (József Schweitzer, 74–85). Vermächtnis als Frage der Zukunft. Die jüdische Kulturarbeit und die Rezeption der Wissenschaft des Judentums in der Schweiz 1919 bis 1961 (Jacques Picard, 86–109). Die Wissenschaft des Judentums in ihrer Beziehung zur allgemeinen Geistesgeschichte im Deutschland des 19. Jahrhunderts (Richard Schaeffler, 113–131). Jüdische Geschichtswissenschaft in Deutschland: 1918–1938 (Christhard Hoffmann, 132–152). Zunz als Begründer der Onomastik im Rahmen der Wissenschaft des Judentums (Marie Simon, 165–179). Die jüdischen wissenschaftlichen Zeitschriften in Deutschland von den Anfängen bis zum Ersten Weltkrieg. Ein Überblick (Barbara Suchy, 180–198). Die Wissenschaft des Judentums und deren Vertreter in Frankreich: 1830–1970 (Maurice R. Hayoun, 199–211). Wissenschaft des Judentums und die jüdische Identität in Italien (Amos Luzzatto, 212–219). Ausgewählte Bibliographie zur Wissenschaft des Judentums (Julius Carlebach und Uri Kaufmann, unter Mitarbeit von Bettina Kaldenberg, 221–230).

29618 YUVAL, ISRAEL JACOB: *Rishonim and Aharonim, antiqui et moderni (periodisation and self-awareness in Ashkenaz).* [In Hebrew, with English summary]. [In]: Zion, Vol. 57, No. 4, Jerusalem, 1992. Pp. 369–394. [On the rabbis in medieval Ashkenaz.]

29619 ZUNZ, LEOPOLD. SCHORSCH, ISMAR: *History as Consolation.* [In]: LBI Year Book XXXVII, London. Pp. 33–43, footnotes. [An analysis of Zunz's *Memorbuch*.]

B. The Jewish Problem

29620 BEN-CHANAN, YAACOV: *Jüdische Identität – heute: drei Essays.* Kassel: Ed. Clavis, 1992. 51 pp.

29621 FISCHER, JENS MALTE: *Identifikation mit dem Aggressor? Zur Problematik des jüdischen Selbsthasses um 1900.* [In]: Menora, Bd. 3, München, 1992. Pp.23–48, notes.

— GRAETZ, MICHAEL: *Renaissance des Judentums im 19. Jahrhundert: 'Der Verein für Cultur und Wissenschaft der Juden' 1819 bis 1824.* [See in No. 29083.]

29622 JACOBS, JACK: *On Socialists and "the Jewish question" after Marx.* New York: New York Univ. Press, 1992. XI, 300 pp., glossary, bibl. [Discusses the attitudes and ideologies of Marxist and Social Democratic intellectuals towards Zionism, antisemitism.]

29623 KIEFER, ANNEGRET: *Das Problem einer 'jüdischen Rasse': Eine Diskussion zwischen Wissenschaft und Ideologie (1870–1930).* Frankfurt am Main; New York [et al.]: Lang, 1991. 209 pp., notes (171–209). (Marburger Schriften zur Medizingeschichte, Bd. 29.) Zugl.: Mainz, Univ., Diss., 1990.

29624 KROCHMALNIK, DANIEL: *Fundamentalismus und Judentum.* [In]: Aus Politik und Zeitgeschichte,

Bonn, 7. Aug. 1992. Pp. 31–43, footnotes. [Refers also to the discussions about assimilation, tradition and identity in Mendelssohn's Germany and in post-war Germany.]

— MISHKINSKI, MOSHE: *A Bundist polemic against Marx's 'On the Jewish question' and its historical context.* [See No. 29816.]

29625 ROHWER, JÖRN: 'Ich möchte Deutschland eine Chance geben'. Jüdische Identität in Deutschland: zwischen sozialer Konvergenz und Separation. 157 pp. (mimeog.). [Obtainable at the LBI London.] [Based on interviews with seven Jews living in Germany.]

29626 SILBERMANN, ALPHONS: *Über die Bilddarstellung im Judentum.* [In]: Deutsch-jüdische Geschichte im 19. und 20. Jahrhundert [see No. 29601]. Pp. 251–260.

29627 WOLFFSOHN, MICHAEL: *Die jüdische Verkettung deutscher Identität.* [In]: Judaica Bohemiae 28, Praha, 1992. Pp. 67–72.

C. Jewish Life and Organisations

— BORUT, JACOB: *The Jewish press in Germany in the late 19th century as a source of historical information.* [See No. 28994.]

29628 BRENNER, MICHAEL: *East and West in Orthodox German-Jewish novels (1912–1934).* [In]: LBI Year Book XXXVII, London. Pp. 309–323, footnotes.

29629 BRÜGGEMANN, THEODOR: *Jüdische Kinder- und Jugendliteratur im nationalsozialistischen Deutschland.* [In]: Aus dem Antiquariat, 10, [Beilage zum] Börsenblatt für den Deutschen Buchhandel, Jg. 159, Nr. 87, Frankfurt am Main, 30. Okt. 1992. A 417–A 428. [Incl. bibliography: Deutschsprachige jüdische Kinderliteratur 1900–1938.]

— BUSEMANN, HERTHA LUISE/DAXNER, MICHAEL/FÖLLING, WERNER: *Insel der Geborgenheit. Die Private Waldschule Kaliski Berlin 1932 bis 1939.* [See No. 29290.]

29630 DAXELMÜLLER, CHRISTOPH: *Jüdische Volkskunde in Mittel- und Osteuropa. Überlegungen zur Wissenschaftsgeschichte einer vergessenen Institution.* [In]: Aschkenas, Jg. 2, Wien, 1992. Pp. 173–206.

29631 DAXELMÜLLER, CHRISTOPH: *Wissenschaft im Ghetto. Jüdische Volkskunde in Deutschland.* [In]: Beiträge zur Geschichte der Volkskunde. Eine Wissenschaft im Widerspruch zwischen Leistung und Versagen. (Wissenschaftliche Zeitschrift der Humboldt-Universität zu Berlin – Geistes- und Sozialwissenschaften, H. 11.) Pp. 93–102.

29632 GALINSKI, HEINZ. *Obituaries.* [In]: 'Allgemeine', Jg. 47, Nr. 30, Bonn, 23. Juli, 1992. [Obits. incl.: Auschwitz – das war der Daseinskompass (Ralph Giordano,1). Die Zeitläufte gestatteten das Schweigen nicht (Karla Müller-Tupath, 2). Die innere Verletzung stets verborgen (Lea Rosh, 4). Er hatte einen außergewöhnlichen Einfluß auf die deutsche Öffentlichkeit (Interview with Klaus Schütz by Karin Adelmann, 6).] [H.G., Nov. 28, 1912 Marienburg (West Prussia) – July 19, 1992, Berlin, during World War II forced labour in Berlin, deported to Auschwitz-Monowitz 1943, later to Dora-Nordhausen and Bergen-Belsen, where he was liberated in April 1945; from 1949 Vorsitzender des Vorstandes der Jüdischen Gemeinde zu Berlin, since 1988 Vorsitzender des Direktoriums des Zentralrats der Juden in Deutschland.]

29633 HABONIM. PELLES, YEDIDA, ed.: *To build and to be built: the 'Habonim' movement in Germany, 1920–1942.* [In Hebrew]. Kibbutz Lochamei Haghetaot; Tel-Aviv: Hakibbutz Hameuchad, 1990. 333 pp. [A collection of excerpts from letters, periodicals, memoranda, guide-books, and personal memoirs, mostly translated from German.]

29634 HERZIG, ARNO: *Das jüdische Armenwesen im ausgehenden Ancien Régime.* [In]: Deutsch-jüdische Geschichte im 19. und 20. Jahrhundert [see No. 29601]. Pp. 45–62.

29635 HEUBERGER, GEORG, ed.: *Mikwe. Geschichte und Architektur jüdischer Ritualbäder in Deutschland.* Mit Beiträgen von Georg Heuberger, Hannelore Künzl, Michael Lenarz, Rabbiner Meir Posen, Linda Reisch. Katalog. Red.: Annerose Baumann, Eva Blum, Michael Lenarz. Übers.: Annerose Baumann, Johannes Wachten. Hrsg. im Auftrag des Dezernats für Kultur und Freizeit, Amt für Wissenschaft und Kunst der Stadt Frankfurt am Main. Frankfurt am Main: Jüdisches Museum, 1992. 184 pp., illus., notes, bibl. [Catalogue of an exhibition held in Frankfurt am Main Sept. 10–Nov. 15, 1992.]

29636 LEIBOWITZ, JOSHUA/URBACH, JOSEPH: *Medical and halakhik aspects of circumcision, from the manuscript notes of an early 19th-century German mohel.* [In Hebrew, with English summary]. [In]: Koroth, Vol. 9, No. 11–12, Jerusalem, 1991. Pp. 345–353. [Journal dated 1991, but publ. in early 1993.] [The hand-written list, found at the back of a book printed in Amsterdam in

1745, of nearly 400 circumcisions performed by the mohel Uri Shraga ben Joseph between 1795–1843.]

29637 LINDNER, ERIK: *Presse und Obrigkeit. Beitrag zur jüdischen Publizistik in den 1820er bis 1840er Jahren unter Einbeziehung archivalischer Quellen der ehemaligen DDR.* [In]: Trumah 3, Heidelberg, 1992. Pp. 175–187, footnotes. [On David Fränkel's *Sulamith*, Ludwig Philippson and the 'Allgemeine Zeitung des Judentums' and other Jewish periodicals.]

29638 LÜTKEMEIER, HILDEGARD: *Hilfen für jüdische Kinder in Not. Zur Jugendwohlfahrt der Juden in der Weimarer Republik.* Freiburg: Lambertus, 1992. 160 pp., illus., notes, bibl.

29639 MEHLITZ, WALTER: *Der jüdische Ritus in Brautstand und Ehe.* Berlin; New York [et.al.]: Lang, 1992. XXIII, 317 pp., bibl. (Europäische Hochschulschriften: Reihe 19, Volkskunde, Ethnologie: Abt. Volkskunde, Bd. 39.)

29640 MENDES-FLOHR, PAUL: *Rosenzweig and the Kameraden: a non-Zionist alliance.* [In]: The impact of Western nationalism [see No. 29803]. Pp. 31–48.

29641 PAÁL, JÁNOS: *Mein Großvater, der Gabbe. Zur Gruppendynamik jüdischen Gemeindelebens.* [In]: Aus zweier Zeugen Mund. Festschrift für Pnina Navé Levinson und Nathan Peter Levinson [see No. 29923]. Pp. 212–216.

—— RÖCHER, RUTH: *Die jüdische Schule im nationalsozialistischen Deutschland 1933–1942.* [See No. 29447.]

29642 ROSENKRANZ, ZE'EV: *'Der Zionismus des Dreinschlagens': die Rituale der nationaljüdischen und zionistischen Studenten im ausgehenden Kaiserreich.* [In]: Menora, Bd. 3, München, 1992. Pp. 63–84, notes.

29643 SCHINDLER, THOMAS: *Aus der Photographiensammlung des Zionistischen Zentralarchivs.* [In]: GDS-Archiv für Hochschul- und Studentengeschichte, Band 1, Schernfeld: SH-Verlag, 1992. Pp. 62–67, footnotes, illus. [On photographs of Jewish student organisations; also in this issue, by same author and F. Golücke: Jüdische Studenten und Korporationen – eine Stichwortsammlung (68–84).]

29644 SEEWANN, HARALD, ed.: *Zirkel und Zionsstern. Bilder und Dokumente aus der versunkenen Welt des jüdisch-nationalen Korporationswesens. Ein Beitrag zur Geschichte des Zionismus auf akademischen Boden.* Bd. 3. Graz: H. Seewald (A 8011 Graz, Postfach 358), 1992. 418 pp., illus., facsims., docs. (Historia Academica Judaica, Folge 1/3.)

—— STERN, ELIJAHU, ed.: *A guide to the archive of the Zionist Socialist youth organisation 'Dror' in Germany 1945–1949.* [In Hebrew. [See No. 29525.]

—— TA-SHMA, ISRAEL M.: *Early Franco-German ritual and custom* [In Hebrew]. [See No. 29045.]:

29645 TOURY, JACOB: *Jewish periodicals in Germany, 1817–1837.* [In]: Qesher, No. 11, Tel-Aviv, May 1992. Pp. 7–19. [Article is publ. in Hebrew, without notes, in this issue.]

29646 TROEN, SELWYN ILAN/PINKUS, BENJAMIN, eds.: *Organizing rescue: National Jewish solidarity in the modern period.* London: Cass, 1992. 424 pp. [A collection of essays dealing with the religious and historical aspects of Jewish solidarity and relief organisations in different countries. Contributions pertaining to German-Jewish relief activities and to the rescue of refugees from Nazi Germany are listed according to subject.]

29647 *Zedaka. Jüdische Sozialarbeit im Wandel der Zeit. 75 Jahre Zentralwohlfahrtsstelle der Juden in Deutschland 1917–1992.* Hrsg. von Georg Heuberger im Auftrag des Dezernats für Kultur und Freizeit, Amt für Wissenschaft und Kunst der Stadt Frankfurt a.M., Jüdisches Museum, und der Zentralwohlfahrtsstelle der Juden in Deutschland e.V. Red.: Frank Kind, Esther Alexander-Ihme. Frankfurt am Main: Jüdisches Museum, 1992. 447 pp., illus., facsims., docs., notes, index, bibl. (432–447). [Catalogue for an exhibition held in Frankfurt am Main, Dec. 3–Feb. 1993. Cont.: Zum Geleit (Andreas von Schoeler, Ignatz Bubis, 7–8). Vorworte (Paul Spiegel, Georg Heuberger, 9–12). Incl.(titles partly abbr.): Wohlstand und Armut: Eine jüdische Analyse (Jonathan Sacks, 14–29). Der Jude als 'der Fremde' in der mittelalterlichen Gesellschaft und Wohltätigkeitspraxis (Aryeh Grabois, 30–43). Armut und Wohltätigkeit in der Kunst der Aschkenasim (Anne Alter, 44–57). Die Tradition jüdischer Wohltätigkeitspflege in Frankfurt am Main vom 15 bis zum 19. Jahrhundert (Patricia Stahl, 58–70). Die Gründung der Zentralwohlfahrtsstelle 1917 (Rachel Heuberger, 71–78). 'Arbeit, nicht Wohltätigkeit' für ostjüdische Proletarier im Ruhrgebiet (Ludger Heid, 79–92). Die Ostjudenfürsorge in Berlin (Rolf Landwehr, 93–113). Die jüdische Winterhilfe im Deutschland des Nationalsozialismus [and] Zur Betreuung jüdischer Reisender auf deutschen Bahnhöfen (Christina Schwarz, 114–123 [&] 124–128). Georg Lubinski. Ein Leben für die Sozialarbeit (Oded Heilbronner, 129–134). Ghetto Theresienstadt: Fürsorge zwischen Leben und Tod. Ein Interview mit Trude Simonsohn und Minka Pradelski (135–

141). Neugründung der Zentralwohlfahrtsstelle der Juden in Deutschland nach 1945 (Bertold Scheller, 142–157). Jüdische Wohlfahrtspflege in der DDR: 1949–1990 (Peter Kirchner, 158–161). Partner der freien Wohlfahrtspflege (Dieter Sengling, 162–172). Ausblick in die neunziger Jahre (Benjamin Bloch, 173–179). Zur Integration jüdischer Zuwanderer aus der ehemaligen Sowjetunion (Dalia Moneta, 212–218).]

D. Jewish Art and Music

29648 BOHLMANN, PHILIP V.: *The World Centre for Jewish Music in Palestine, 1936–1940: Jewish musical life on the eve of World War II.* New York: Oxford Univ. Press; Oxford: Clarendon Press, 1992. XXX, 297 pp., illus., notes, docs., index (287–297). [Incl. selected documents from the correspondence and publications of the WCJMP; examines the history of European Jewish music on the eve of its destruction; gives accounts by musicians and others on the difficulties before and during their exile; the WCJMP was founded mainly by German-speaking exiles from Central Europe; incl. appendix: inventory of the archives housed in the Jewish Music Research Centre of the Jewish National University Library.]

—— GORAL, ARIE: *Juden in der Kunst, jüdische Kunst und ein jüdisches Museum.* [See No. 29540.]

29649 KÜNZL, HANNELORE: *Jüdische Kunst: von der biblischen Zeit bis in die Gegenwart.* München: Beck, 1992. 266 pp., illus., bibl. (228–257).

29650 LEWANDOWSKI, LOUIS. NACHAMA, ANDREAS/STÄHR, SUSANNE: *Die vergessene Revolution. Der lange Weg des Louis Lewandowski.* [In]: Menora, Bd. 3, München, 1992. Pp. 241–255, notes. [L.L., director of music, liturgical composer, April 4, 1821 Wreschen – February 4, 1894 Berlin.]

29651 SULZER, SALOMON. *Salomon Sulzer: cantor, composer, innovator.* An exhibition from the state of Vorarlberg and the Jewish Museum Hohenems (Austria). Idea and concept by Bernhard Purin. Transl. by Paul Lerner and others. Ed. by Neil W. Levin. Bregenz: Land Vorarlberg, 1991. 40 pp. [For German edn. see No. 28591/YB XXXVII.]

VI. ZIONISM AND ISRAEL

29652 CATALAN, T.: *L'emigrazione ebraica in Palestina attraverso il porto di Trieste (1908–1938).* [In]: Qualestoria, Anno 19, No. 2/3, Trieste, Ag.- Dic. 1991. Pp. 57–107. [Covers the emigration of German Jews to Palestine.]

29653 FACKENHEIM, EMIL: *Pillars of Zionism.* [In]: Midstream, Vol. 38, No. 9, New York, Dec. 1992. Pp. 13–14, notes. [Discusses the historic roots of Zionism; Buber's letter to Ghandi; the emergence of German Zionism in response to 'Kristallnacht'.]

—— FEINER, SHMUEL: *Smolenskin's confrontation with the Haskalah movement and the roots of Jewish Nationalist historiography.* [In Hebrew]. [See No. 29611.]

—— HAUSER, MARTIN: *Wege jüdischer Selbstbehauptung. Tagebuchaufzeichnungen 1929–1967.* [See No. 29892.]

29654 HERZL, THEODOR. HAREL, CHAYA: *The image of the leadership in the eyes of Herzl and its realization.* [In Hebrew]. [In]: Irad Malkin/Zeev Tzahor, eds.: Manhiq ve-han haga. Jerusalem: Historical Society of Israel; Zalman Shazar Center for Jewish History, 9, 1992. Pp. 165–185.

—— HORWITZ, RIVKA: *Franz Rosenzweig and Gershom Scholem on Zionism and the Jewish people.* [See No. 29594.]

29655 KAISER, WOLF: *The Zionist project in the Palestine travel writings of German-speaking Jews.* [In]: LBI Year Book XXXVII, London. Pp. 261–286, footnotes.

29656 KATZ, JACOB: *Messianismus und Zionismus.* [In]: Jüdischer Almanach 1993 [see No. 29248]. Frankfurt am Main, 1992. Pp. 11–25.

29657 KEDAR, ARON: *Die Einwanderung aus Deutschland als apolitische Opposition in der Vereinigten Kibbuzbewegung zur Zeit der fünften Aliah.* [In]: Hebräische Beiträge zur Wissenschaft des Judentums deutsch angezeigt, Jg. VI, Heidelberg, 1990. Pp. 63–74.

—— KESSLER, MARIO: *Sozialismus und Zionismus in Deutschland 1897–1933.* [See in No. 29014.]

29658 KOHN, HANS. REUVENI, YAACOV: *National movements in the 20th century and Jewish*

Nationalism: what did Hans Kohn contribute and where did he fail? [In Hebrew]. [In]: Gesher, No. 125, Jerusalem, Summer 1992. Pp. 57–70.

29659 KÜHNTOPF-GENTZ, MICHAEL: 'Israel geht vor Zion'. Nathan Birnbaum und die Palästinafrage. [In]: Zeitschrift für Religions- und Geistesgeschichte, Jg. 43, Leiden, 1991. Pp. 118–139, footnotes.

29660 LAVSKY, HAGIT: Before catastrophe: the distinctive path of German Zionism. [In Hebrew]. Jerusalem: Magnes Press, Hebrew Univ.; Hassifriya Haziyonit, 1990. 292 pp.

29661 MOSSE, GEORGE L.: The Jews and the civic religion of nationalism. [In]: The impact of Western nationalism [see No. 29803]. Pp. 319–330.

29662 MOSSE, GEORGE L.: Max Nordau, liberalism and the New Jew. [In]: Journal of Contemporary History, Vol. 27, London, 1992. Pp. 565–581, notes. [Deals with Nordau's book Degeneration, publ. in 1892.]

—— NICOSIA, FRANCIS R.: Zionism and Palestine in anti-semitic thought in Imperial Germany. [See No. 30010.]

—— NIEDERLAND, DORON: Die Immigration. [In]: Erika Weinzierl/Otto D. Kulka, eds.: Vertreibung und Neubeginn. Israelische Bürger österreichischer Herkunft. [See No. 29282.]

29663 OFER, DALIA: The dilemma of rescue and redemption: mass immigration to Israel in the first year of statehood. [In]: Yivo Annual, Vol. 20, New York, 1991. Pp. 185–210, notes. [Incl. immigration of German Jews.]

29664 REINHARZ, JEHUDA: European Jewry and the consolidation of Zionism. [In]: The impact of Western nationalism [see No. 29803]. Pp. 305–318.

29665 REINHARZ, JEHUDA: German Jewish refugees in Palestine: the early years, 1932–1939. [In]: Organizing rescue: national Jewish solidarity in the modern period [see No. 29646]. Pp. 167–190.

29666 REINHARZ, JEHUDA: Jewish nationalism and Jewish identity in Central Europe. [In]: LBI Year Book XXXVII, London. Pp. 147–167, footnotes. [A comparative study of the emergence of Zionism in Germany, Austria and Bohemia.]

—— SEEWANN, HARALD, ed.: Zirkel und Zionsstern. Bilder und Dokumente aus der versunkenen Welt des jüdisch-nationalen Korporationswesens. [See No. 29644.]

29667 SHAVIT, YAAKOV: The 'glorious century' or the 'cursed century': fin-de-siècle Europe and the emergence of modern Jewish nationalism. [In]: The impact of Western nationalism [see No. 29803]. Pp. 199–220.

—— STERN, ELIJAHU, ed.: A guide to the archive of the Zionist socialist youth organisation 'Dror' in Germany 1945–1949. [In Hebrew]. [See No. 29525.]

—— TAMIR, ARNON: Eine Reise zurück. Von der Schwierigkeit, Unrecht wiedergutzumachen. [See No. 29918]

29668 WALLAS, ARMIN A./LAURITSCH, ANDREA M., eds.: Israel III. A-9500 Villach (Rennsteiner Str. 118): Armin A.Wallas, Dez. 1991. 63 pp. (Mnemosyne, H. 12.) [Last isssue in the special Israel series of Mnemosyne. Cont. prose texts and poems by German- and Austrian-Jewish writers now living in Israel or connected with this subject; incl. also book reviews.]

29669 WASSERMANN, HENRY: Zur Einwanderung mitteleuropäischer Juden in Palästina 1933–1940. [In]: Aschkenas, Jg. 2, Wien, 1992. Pp. 285–292.

VII. PARTICIPATION in CULTURAL and PUBLIC LIFE

A. General

29670 ADUNKA, EVELYN: Prager deutschsprachige jüdische Literatur in österreichisch-jüdischen Zeitschriften. [In]: Aschkenas, Jg. 2, Wien, 1992. Pp. 273–284. [Review article.]

29671 ALBERG, WERNER: 'Die Familie Bendemann' und andere. Zu den jüdischen Künstlern im Rheinland des 19. bis zur Mitte des 20. Jahrhunderts. [In]: Wegweiser durch das jüdische Rheinland [see No. 29169]. Berlin: Nicolai 1992. Pp. 280–299.

29672 BARNER, WILFRIED: Von Rahel Varnhagen bis Friedrich Gundolf. Juden als deutsche Goethe-Verehrer. Göttingen: Wallstein, 1992. 56 pp., ports., illus., facsims., notes. (Kleine Schriften zur Aufklärung. Hrsg. von der Lessing-Akademie Wolfenbüttel, 3.)

—— BOTTIN, ANGELA: Enge Zeit. Spuren Vertriebener und Verfolgter der Hamburger Universität. [See No. 29362.]

29673 BREITBART, ORTWIN/ABRAHAM, ULF, eds.: Einige werden bleiben. Und mit ihnen das Vermächtnis.

Der Beitrag jüdischer Schriftsteller zur deutschsprachigen Literatur des 20. Jahrhunderts. Bamberg: Bayerische Verlagsanstalt, 1992. 186 pp., notes. [Based on a series of lectures held in Bamberg and Nürnberg during the winter semester 1990/1991.] [Incl. the following contributions (titles abbr.): Jakob Wassermann. Sein Weg als Franke und Jude (Wulf Segebrecht, 12–31). Kafka und die Thora (Ulf Abraham, 33–55). Walter Benjamin (Hans Mayer, 56–76). Elias Canetti (Lydia Schieth, 77–104). Paul Celans Sprachsuche nach der Shoah (Jürgen Wertheimer, 105–123). Zur Lyrik Erich Frieds (Heinz Gockel, 124–141). Jurek Becker (Peter Hanenberg, 142–147). Die beliebteste Familiengeschichte (Jurek Becker, 148–163). Nazismus und Holocaust in der deutschsprachigen Kinder- und Jugendliteratur (Ortwin Beisbart, Michael Krejci, 164–185; incl. Kinder- und Jugendliteratur – Bibliographie-Auswahl, 179–185).]

29674 DANCO, ARMIN: *Jüdische Corpsbrüder nach 1933.* [In]: Corpsnachrichten der Heidelberger Schwaben, Jg. 1992, Nr. 1/April 1992 (Red.: Dr. Armin Danco, Flachskampstraße 67, 4000 Düsseldorf 12). Pp. 24–27, port. [Incl.: Obituary (Theo Schroeder) of Max Rothfels, previously publ. by Hannovera in its report of 1935/1936.] [M.R., June 10, 1873 Kassel – Oct. 22, 1935 Kassel, lawyer.]

29675 EFRON, JOHN M.: *The 'Kaftanjude' and the 'Kaffeehausjude': two models of Jewish insanity. A discussion of causes and cures among German-Jewish psychiatrists.* [In]: LBI Year Book XXXVII, London. Pp. 169–188, footnotes.

29676 EISFELD, RAINER: *Ausgebürgert und doch angebräunt. Deutsche Politikwissenschaft 1920–1945.* Baden-Baden: Nomos Verl.-Ges., 1991. 233 pp., notes (171–204), bibl. (205–220), indexes (persons, subjects, 221–232). [Incl. Jewish political scientists.]

29677 EXILE. BOECKL, MATTHIAS: *Begrenzte Möglichkeiten. Vorgeschichte, Vertreibung und weitere Laufbahn österreichischer Architekten der klassischen Moderne in den Vereinigten Staaten 1938–1945.* [In]: Dokumentationsarchiv des österreichischen Widerstandes. Jahrbuch 1992. Wien: Dokumentationsarchiv des österreichischen Widerstandes, 1992. Pp. 132–156.

29678 — *Exilforschung. Ein internationales Jahrbuch.* B.10: Künste im Exil. Hrsg. im Auftrag der Gesellschaft für Exilforschung/Society for Exile Studies von Claus-Dieter Krohn [et al.]. München: Edition Text + Kritik, 1992. 212 pp., notes. [Incl.: Die verfemte Kunst im Exil – Kunsthandel und Nationalsozialismus. Das Schicksal der modernen Kunst am Beispiel der Sammlung Ludwig und Rosy Fischer (Cordula Frowein, 74–83). Julius Posener à L'Architecture d'Aujourd'hui: un regard parisien sur l'architecture allemande des années 30 (Jean-Louis Cohen, 84–99). 'Amerikanische Oper' und antinazistische Propaganda. Aspekte in Kurt Weills Produktion im US-Exil (Hanns-Werner Heister, 152–167). Hollywood – Hölle oder Paradies? Legende und Realität der Lebens- und Arbeitsbedingungen der Exilanten in der amerikanischen Filmindustrie (Helmut G. Asper, 187–200).]

29679 — SKEMER, DON C.: *German emigré publishers in New York. The archives of the Frederick Ungar Publishing Company.* [In]: Publishing History, Vol. 31, Cambridge, 1992. Pp. 77–84, notes. [On the publisher F.U. (1898–1989), founder of the Phaidon Verlag in Vienna (later Phaidon Press, London), and also of Saturn, emigr. in 1938–1939 to the USA via Prague, Zürich and London, where he established the Frederick Ungar Publishing Company.]

29680 — RITCHIE, JAMES M.: *The sciences in exile.* [In]: Austrian Studies, Vol. 3, 1992. Pp. 138–194.

29681 — RITCHIE, JAMES M.: *Exile in New York.* [In]: German Life and Letters, Vol. XLV, No. 2, April 1992. Pp. 178–189.

29682 — SOCIETY FOR EXILE STUDIES=GESELLSCHAFT FÜR EXILFORSCHUNG, ed.: *Nachrichtenbrief=Newsletter.* Nr. 13, Dez, 1991. Bearb. von Barbara Seib unter Mitarb. von Patrick von zur Mühlen. Frankfurt am Main (Postfach 550207): Ernst Loewy, 1991. 260 pp. [Cont.: bibliography of current books, book reviews and articles referring to exile studies and related conferences and events; incl.: Eine wundersame Heimkehr. Das Archiv der deutschsprachigen Exilabteilung des Allert de Lange-Verlags in Amsterdam (Ursula Langkau-Alex, 66–69). Die Herbert und Elsbeth Weichmann Stiftung (Patrick von zur Mühlen, 70–72).]

29683 — STEPHAN, ALEXANDER: *Communazis: Deutsche Exilautoren in den Akten des FBI. Ein vergessenes Kapitel der deutsch-amerikanischen Geschichte nach 1940.* [In]: literatur für leser, 32/3, Frankfurt am Main, 1992. Pp. 151–165, footnotes. [Deals a.o. with Feuchtwanger and other German-Jewish refugees.]

29684 — UHLIG, RALPH, ed.: *Vertriebene Wissenschaftler der Christian-Albrechts-Universität zu Kiel (CAU) nach 1933: zur Geschichte der CAU im Nationalsozialismus. Eine Dokumentation.* Bearb. von Uta Cornelia Schmatzer und Matthias Wieben. Frankfurt am Main; New York [et al.]:

Lang, 1991. 158 pp. (Kieler Werkstücke: Reihe A, Beiträge zur schleswig-holsteinischen und skandinavischen Geschichte, Bd. 2.)

29685 EXILE LITERATURE. *Exil. Forschung, Erkenntnisse, Ergebnisse.* Jg. 12, Nr. 1. Hrsg. von Edita Koch. Frankfurt am Main: E. Koch (Rheinstrasse 20), 1992. 1 issue. [Incl. (titles cond.): Das Jüdische bei Nelly Sachs (Ruth Dinese, 19–29). Max Raphael. Unveröffentlichte Dokumente zu seinem Werk (Hans-Jürgen Heinrichs, 46–57). Die Rezeption der Exilliteratur in der frühen Nachkriegsperiode am Beispiel der Schriftstellerkongresse in Berlin und Frankfurt (Johannes G. Pankau, 58–67). Die Wiederentdeckung eines großen Künstlers: der Maler Hanns Ludwig Katz (Edita Koch, 68–70). Karl Jakob Hirsch: Quintessenz meines Lebens (Gerhard Müller, 71–75).]

29686 — FURTADO KESTLER, IZABELA MARIA: *Die Exilliteratur und das Exil der deutschsprachigen Schriftsteller und Publizisten in Brasilien.* Frankfurt am Main; New York [et al.]: Lang, 1992. 267 pp. (Europäische Hochschulschriften: Reihe 1, Deutsche Sprache und Literatur, Bd. 1344.) Zugl.: Freiburg i. Br., Univ., Diss., 1991.

29687 — RITCHIE, JAMES M.: *Literary exile in Great Britain.* [In]: German writers and politics, 1918–39. Ed. by Richard Dove and Stephen Lamb. London: Macmillan, 1992. pp. 149–162.

29688 — STOOP, PAUL: *Verlegen im Schatten NS-Deutschlands. Aus dem erstmals zugänglichen Archiv des Amsterdamer Verlags Allert de Lange.* [In]: Tribüne, Jg. 31, H. 122, Frankfurt am Main, 1992. Pp. 156–164, footnotes.

29689 — WERNER, KLAUS ULRICH: *Exil im Archiv: das 'deutsche Exilarchiv 1933-1945' der Deutschen Bibliothek.* Herzberg: Bautz, 1991. 126 pp., bibl. (Bibliothemata, Bd. 4.)

29690 *Framing the past: the historiography of German cinema and television.* Ed. by Bruce A. Murray and Christopher J. Wickham. Carbondale: Southern Illinois Univ. Press, 1992. VII, 348 pp., illus., notes. [Incl. the work of Siegfried Kracauer and Ernst Lubitsch; also the Holocaust as a subject.]

29691 *Frauenleben im 18. Jahrhundert.* Hrsg. von Andrea van Dülmen. München: Beck; Leipzig: Kiepenheuer, 1992. 436 pp., index. [Incl. texts by Moses Mendelssohn (56–57), Henriette Herz (61–62; 111–112), Rahel Levin (235–236).]

29692 GARDNER, SHELDON/STEVENS, GWENDOLYN: *Vienna and the golden age of psychology, 1918-1938.* Foreword by Rudolf Ekstein. New York; London: Praeger, 1992. XIV, 285 pp., footnotes, glossary, bibl. (263–278). [Incl. Alfred and Victor Adler, Helene Deutsch, Sigmund and Anna Freud a.o. Also on Austrian antisemitism.]

29693 GELBLUM, AMIRA: *Feminism and Pacifism: the case of Anita Augspurg and Lida Gustava Heymann.* [In]: Tel Aviver Jahrbuch für deutsche Geschichte, Bd. 21, 1992: Neuere Frauengeschichte. Gerlingen: Bleicher, 1992. Pp. 207–225.

29694 GILMAN, SANDER L.: *Inscribing the other.* Lincoln; London: Univ. of Nebraska Press, 1991. XII, 372 pp., notes (317–[360]). [A collection of articles on Yiddish and German literature, a.o. on Freud, Heine, Karl Kraus, Nietzsche, and literature in Germany from 1933–1945; incl. also the essay: Jewish writers in contemporary Germany: the dead author speaks (249–278).]

29695 GOLDSTEIN, BLUMA: *Reinscribing Moses: Heine, Kafka, Freud, and Schoenberg in a European wilderness.* Cambridge, MA; London: Harvard Univ. Press, 1992. 218 pp., notes ([169])-206). [Deals with German-Jewish cultural assimilation.]

29696 GRADENWITZ, PETER: *Literatur und Musik in geselligem Kreise. Geschmacksbildung, Gesprächsstoff und musikalische Unterhaltung in der bürgerlichen Salongesellschaft.* Stuttgart: Steiner, 1991. 284 pp. [Incl. 'salons' and social life of the Jewish bourgeoisie.]

29697 HENZE, WILHELM, ed.: *B. Zimmermann, H. Nohl, K. Hahn. Ein Beitrag zur Reformpädagogik.* Duderstadt: Mecke, 1991. 212 pp., illus., notes. (Schriftenreihe des Niedersächsichen Instituts für Sportgeschichte Hoya, Bd. 9.) [Incl. contributions on Bernhard Zimmermann by Wilhelm Henze, Peter Carpenter, Hajo Bernett and Wolfgang Buss; on Kurt Hahn and the Salem School by Georg Wilhelm Prinz v. Hannover and Peter Carpenter.] [Bernhard Zimmermann, July 10, 1886 Emden – March 28, 1969 Oxford, sports educator, director of the Göttingen Institut für Leibesübungen, promoter of sports science as an academic discipline, dismissed from all his positions in 1937 because of his Jewish wife Eva, née Rosenberg; emigr. to UK in 1938, where he worked in the Gordonstoun School in Scotland together with Kurt Hahn. Kurt Hahn, June 5, 1886 Berlin – Dec. 14, 1974 in Ravensberg nr. Salem, teacher, educator, founder and director of the Landerziehungsheim Schloss Salem on Lake Constance from 1920 until 1933. In 1933 imprisonment and emigration to UK. In 1934 he founded the British Salem Schools. Converted to the Anglican Church in 1945, returned to Hermannsberg nr. Salem in 1953.] [On Kurt Hahn see also: Anja Pielorz & Gilbert A. Gratzel: Liberale Pädagogik und politischer Liberalismus – die Bildungspolitik Kurt Hahns zwischen Wertekontinuität und Wertewandel [in]: liberal, Jg. 34, H. 3, Bonn, Aug. 1992. Pp. 65–71.]

29698 HOMBURG, HEIDRUN: *Warenhausunternehmen und ihre Gründer in Frankreich und Deutschland oder: eine diskrete Elite und mancherlei Mythen*. [In]: Jahrbuch für Wirtschaftsgeschichte, 1992/1, Berlin, 1992. Pp. 183–219, footnotes. [Refers to many German-Jewish founders of department stores.]

29699 KAISER, WOLFRAM: *Die Fakultät wurde 'judenfrei'. Eine Chronologie zum Schicksal jüdischer Mediziner in Halle 1933–1943*. [In]: Tribüne, Jg. 31, H. 124, Frankfurt am Main, 1992. Pp. 153–164, footnotes.

29700 KATER, MICHAEL H.: *Different drummers: Jazz in the culture of Nazi Germany*. Oxford; New York: Oxford Univ. Press, 1992. XIV, 291 pp., illus., notes (213–269), sources. [Deals with the Nazis' attitude to jazz as a degenerate product of Jews and negroes. Incl. Jews as jazz fans, as musicians and impresarios.]

29701 KATER, MICHAEL H.: *The revenge of the fathers: the demise of modern music at the end of the Weimar Republic*. [In]: German Studies Review, Vol. 15, No. 2, Tempe, AZ, May 1992. Pp. 295–315, notes. [Incl. Alban Berg, Arnold Schönberg, Kurt Weill; also discusses how antimodernism often had elements of antisemitism.]

29702 KORFMACHER, NORBERT: *Im Dienst von Recht und Gerechtigkeit. Jüdische Abgeordnete der SPD im Preußischen Abgeordnetenhaus 1919–1933*. [In]: Tribüne, Jg. 31, H. 124, Frankfurt am Main, 1992. Pp. 165–173, footnotes.

29703 LANGENBUCHER, WOLFGANG R., ed.: *Sensationen des Alltags. Meisterwerke des österreichischen Journalismus. Friedrich Austerlitz, Theodor Herzl, Egon Erwin Kisch, Karl Kraus, Anton Kuh, Alfred Polgar, Joseph Roth u.a.* Hrsg. von Wolfgang R. Langenbucher unter Mitarbeit von Hannes Haas [et al.]. Wien: Ueberreuter, 1992. 231 pp. [52 texts, most of them by Austrian-Jewish journalists; incl. an introduction by the editor and short biographies and bibl. notes.]

29704 MATTENKLOTT, GERT: *Über Juden in Deutschland*. Frankfurt am Main: Jüdischer Verlag, 1992. 202 pp. [Revised and augmented new edn. of Jüdische Intelligenz in deutschen Briefen. 1619–1988, publ in 1988 [see No. 25656/YB XXXIV]; incl.: Deutsche Juden – jüdische Deutsche. Gespräche und Interviews (Julius H. Schoeps, Doron Kiesel, Micha Brumlik, Walter Boehlich, Peter Lilienthal).]

29705 MAYER, DIETER: *Die Weltbühne, ein Forum linksbürgerlichen Denkens*. [In]: literatur für leser, H. 2, Frankfurt am Main, 1991. Pp. 100–114.

29706 MENDELSSOHN FAMILY: *Mendelssohn Studien. Beiträge zur neueren deutschen Kultur- und Wirtschaftsgeschichte*. Bd. 7. Berlin: Duncker & Humblot, 1990. 368 pp., footnotes. [Incl. contributions on different members of the Mendelssohn family by Jürgen Böhme, Wolfgang Dinglinger, Klaus Häfner, Hans-Günter Klein, Manfred Kliem, Cécile Lowenthal-Hensel, Ilse Rabien, Ingeborg Stolzenberg; further contributions are listed according to subject.]

29707 SCHÜTZ, HANS J.: *Juden in der deutschen Literatur: eine deutsch-jüdische Literaturgeschichte im Überblick*. München: Piper, 1992. 382 pp. (Serie Piper, Bd. 1520.) [Previously publ. in Börsenblatt für den deutschen Buchhandel, Jg. 158, Jan. 11–Aug. 19, 1991 in 22 pts.; see No. 28671/YB XXXVII.]

29708 SILBERMANN, ALPHONS: *Rheinisch-jüdisches Musikleben in Köln seit dem 15. Jahrhundert*. [In]: Wegweiser durch das jüdische Rheinland [see No. 29169]. Berlin: Nicolai, 1992. Pp. 355–361. [Incl. Jacques Offenbach, Ferdinand Hiller, Walter Braunfels.]

29709 TIMM, ANGELIKA: *Zur Biographie jüdischer Hochschullehrerinnen in Berlin bis 1933. Nach Materialien des Archivs der Humboldt-Universität zu Berlin*. [In]: Tel Aviver Jahrbuch für Geschichte, Bd. 21, Gerlingen, 1992. Pp. 243–258, footnotes. [On Lise Meitner, Charlotte Leubuscher, Mathilde Hertz, Hedwig Hintze, Gertrud Kornfeld, Hilda Pollaczek.]

29710 TOURY, JACOB: *Jewish aspects as contributing factors to the genesis of the Reichsbanner Schwarz-Rot-Gold*. [In]: LBI Year Book XXXVII, London. Pp. 237–257, footnotes.

29711 WESTPHAL, UWE: *Berliner Konfektion und Mode. Die Zerstörung einer Tradition 1836–1939*. Mit einem Vorwort von Rolf Bothe und einem Beitrag zu Lieselotte Friedlaender von Christa Gustavus. 2., erw. Aufl. Berlin: Hentrich, 1992. 264 pp., illus., list [of names & companies]. [First edn. publ. 1986.]

29712 YATES, W.E.: *Schnitzler, Hofmannsthal and the Austrian theatre*. New Haven, CT: Yale Univ. Press, 1992. XVII, 286 pp., illus.

B. Individual

29713 ADLER, MAX. HURWITZ, YAACOV: *The Marxist elements in the political thought of Max Adler.* [In Hebrew, with English summary]. [In]: Ya'ad, No. 9, Givat-Haviva, April 1992. Pp. 62–70. [M.A., data see No. 18374/YB XXVII.]

29714 ADORNO, THEODOR: *Quasi una fantasia: essays on modern music.* Transl. by Rodney Livingstone. London: Verso, 1992. 336 pp. [For orig. German edn. 1963 see No. 3994/YB IX.]

29715 AMÉRY, JEAN. *Jean Améry: Der Grenzgänger. Gespräch mit Ingo Herrmann in der Reihe 'Zeugen des Jahrhunderts'.* Hrsg. von Ingo Herrmann. Red.: Jürgen Voigt. Göttingen: Lamuv, 1992. 153 pp., notes, bibl. (Zeugen des Jahrhunderts.) [Based on an interview in 1978, a few months before Jean Améry committed suicide (Oct. 18, 1978).] [See also: Das Leben vom Tode her. Der Gaskammer entkommen, durch eigene Hand gestorben: Erinnerung an Jean Améry (Hartmut Diessenbacher) [in] Frankfurter Allgemeine Zeitung, Nr. 289, Frankfurt am Main, 12. Dez. 1992 (Beilage).]

—— ARENDT, HANNAH. [See also No. 30036.]

29716 — BUBIS, NOMI: *Die totale Herrschaft des Bösen. Hannah Arendt und der Eichmann-Prozess in Jerusalem.* [In]: Tribüne, Jg. 31, H. 122, Frankfurt am Main, 1992. Pp. 163–172. [On Hannah Arendt's essays, written on the occasion of the Eichmann trial in Jerusalem in 1962 and published under the title Eichmann in Jerusalem, in 1963 [see Nos. 3790–3793/YB IX].

29717 — ISAAC, JEFFREY C.: *Arendt, Camus, and modern rebellion.* New Haven, CT: Yale Univ. Press, 1992. XI, 326 pp.

29718 — WATSON, DAVID: *Arendt.* London: Fontana Press, 1992. 143 pp., notes, bibl. (137–143).

29719 AUERBACH, FRANK. HUGHES, ROBERT: *Frank Auerbach.* London: Thames and Hudson, 1992. 240 pp., illus., ports. [F.A., b. April 29, 1931, German-Jewish artist, emigr. to UK in 1939.]

29720 AUSLÄNDER, ROSE. *'Durch Zeitgeräusch wandern von Stimme zu Stimme. . .'. Die Lyrikerin Rose Ausländer. Ein Porträt in Gedichten.* [In]: German Life and Letters, Vol. 45, No. 4, Oxford; Cambridge, MA, Oct. 1992. pp. 345–357, footnotes. [On the biography of R.A.; examines also the reception and editions of R.A.'s works.]

29721 BADT, HERMANN. ILSAR, YEHIEL: *Im Streit für die Weimarer Republik. Stationen im Leben des Hermann Badt.* Berlin: Transit, 1992. 400 pp., port., notes. [H.B., data see No. 23884/YB XXXIII.]

29722 BEER-HOFMANN, RICHARD. PAZI, MARGARITA: *Zu Richard Beer-Hofmanns 125. Geburtstag (1866 Wien – 1945 New York).* [In]: Menora, Bd. 3, München, 1992. Pp. 49–62.

29723 BEN DAVID, GERSHON. KULKA, OTTO DOV: *Der Dichter Gershon Ben David.* [In]: Jüdischer Almanach [see No. 29248]. Frankfurt am Main, 1992. Pp. 45–54. [Incl. the poem In den Wind werfen. G.b.D., orig. Georg Levkovitz, 1930 Cologne – 1975 Jerusalem, survived with foster parents, went to Israel in 1947 and started, during the fifties, to write in German mainly about the Shoa.]

29724 BENJAMIN, WALTER. DODERER, KLAUS: *Kritik an Kolonialherren der Kinderstuben.* [In]: Börsenblatt für den Deutschen Buchhandel, Jg. 159, Nr. 69, Frankfurt am Main, 28. Aug. 1992. Pp. 204–207, bibl. notes. [On Walter Benjamin as a collector, analyst and writer of children's literature.]

29725 — GROSSMAN, JEFFREY: *The reception of Walter Benjamin in the Anglo-American literary institution.* [In]: The German Quarterly, Vol. 65, Nos. 3–4, Cherry Hill, NJ, Summer/Fall 1992. Pp. 414–428, notes.

29726 — MAYER HANS: *Der Zeitgenosse Walter Benjamin.* Frankfurt am Main: Jüdischer Verlag, 1992. 96 pp. [Cf.: Besprechung (Martin Meyer) [in]: 'NZZ', Nr. 157, Zürich, 10. Juli 1992, p. 33; in the same issue: Von der Kraft des Briefs. Aus Anlaß des 100. Geburtstags von Walter Benjamin (Gert Mattenklott, p.33).]

29727 — MOSÈS, STÉPHANE: *The theological-political model of history in the thought of Walter Benjamin.* [In Hebrew, with English summary]. [In]: Zmanim, No. 38, Tel-Aviv, Summer 1991. Pp. 7–15.

29728 — SCHOLEM, GERSHOM: *Walter Benjamin und sein Engel: vierzehn Aufsätze und kleine Beiträge.* Hrsg. von Rolf Tiedemann. Frankfurt am Main: Suhrkamp, 1992. 223 pp., illus. (Suhrkamp-Taschenbuch, 1967.)

29729 BERLINER, CORA. EXLER, MARGARETE: *Im Dienste der Mitmenschlichkeit.* Vor 50 Jahren fand Frau Prof. Dr. Cora Berliner den Tod in der Gaskammer. [In]: Tribüne, Jg. 31, H. 122, Frankfurt am Main, 1992. Pp. 86–90, port. [C.B., data see No. 28562/YB XXXVII.]

29730 BERNSTEIN, ARON. SCHOEPS, JULIUS H.: *Bürgerliche Aufklärung und liberales Freiheitsdenken. A. Bernstein in seiner Zeit.* Stuttgart: Burg, 1992. 319 pp., illus., footnotes. [Cf.: Ein jüdischer Preuße (Helmut Hirsch) [in]: Frankfurter Allg. Zeitung, Frankfurt am Main, July 23, 1992. Ein Leben für die Emanzipation: der liberale Publizist Aaron Bernstein (Jürgen Frölich) [in]: liberal, Jg. 34, H. 3, Bonn, Aug. 1992, pp. 99–100.]
29731 BERNSTEIN, EDUARD: *Sozialdemokratische Lehrjahre. Entwicklungsgang eines Sozialisten.* Hrsg. und mit einem Nachwort versehen von Manfred Tetzel. Berlin: Dietz, 1991. 248 pp. (Soziales Denken des 19. und 20. Jahrhunderts.)
29732 BEYERCHEN, ALAN: *What we know about Nazism and science.* [In]: Social Research, Vol. 59, No. 3, New York, Fall 1992. Pp. 615–645. [Incl. the dismissal of Jewish scientists and the impact of this on German scientific research.]
29733 BLOCH, ERNST. FEIGE, HANS-UWE: *Willkommen und Abschied. Ernst Bloch in Leipzig (1949–1961).* [In]: Bloch-Almanach, Jg. 11, 1991, Ludwigshafen, 1991. Pp. 159–189, notes.
29734 BLOCHMANN, ELISABETH. KLAFKI, WOLFGANG/MÜLLER, HELMUT-GERHARD: *Elisabeth Blochmann (1892–1972).* Marburg: Universitätsbibliothek Marburg, 1992. 133pp. [E.B., April 14, 1892 Apolda (Thuringia) – Jan. 27, 1972 Marburg/Lahn, educationalist, professor of pedagogy; emigr. 1933 to UK, 1952 returned to Fed. Rep. of Germany.]
29735 BLUMENTHAL-WEISS, ILSE. EICHMANN-LEUTENEGGER, BEATRICE: *'Und pflücke tausend Schmerzen von den Wänden . . .' Die deutsch-jüdische Autorin Ilse Blumenthal-Weiss, 1899–1987.* [In]: NZZ, Nr. 266, Zürich, 14./15. Nov. 1992. P. 67. [I.B.- W., Oct. 14, 1899 Berlin – Aug. 28, 1987, New York, poet, writer, librarian; emigr. with her family to the Netherlands in 1937, in 1943 interned in Westerbork, in 1944 deported to Theresienstadt, from where her husband was deported to Auschwitz and murdered. In 1947 emigr. to the USA, worked from 1962 in the Leo Baeck Institute, New York.]
29736 BOENHEIM, FELIX. RUPRECHT, THOMAS M.: *Felix Boenheim (1890–1960): Humanist, Citoyen und Leibarzt seiner Majestät des Volkes.* [In]: Menora, Bd. 3, München, 1992. Pp. 265–301, notes. [F.B., endocrinologist, Communist politician, medical historian, January 17, 1890 Berlin – February 1, 1960 Leipzig, emigrated in 1933 to France, in 1934 to Palestine, in 1935 via France to the USA, returned to Germany (East) in 1949.]
29737 BÖRNE, LUDWIG. HESS, JONATHAN M.: *Ludwig Börne's visit to the anatomical cabinet: the writing of Jewish emancipation.* [In]: new german critique, No. 55, Ithaca, NY, Winter 1992. Pp. 105–126, footnotes.
29738 — JASPER, WILLI: *'Schreibt, was ihr denkt von euch selbst'. Ludwig Börne und Sigmund Freud. Eine Vorgeschichte der Psychoanalyse.* [In]: Deutsch-jüdische Geschichte im 19. und 20. Jahrhundert [see No. 29601]. Pp. 353–358.
— BORCHARDT, RUDOLF. FISCHER, JENS MALTE: *Identifikation mit dem Aggressor? Zur Problematik des jüdischen Selbsthasses um 1900.* [See No. 29621.]
29739 BROD, MAX. BÄRSCH, CLAUS-EKKEHARD: *Max Brod im Kampf um das Judentum: zum Leben und Werk eines deutsch-jüdischen Dichters aus Prag.* Wien: Passagen-Verl., 1992. 202 pp., bibl. (Max Brod, 185–194), bibl. (194–202). (Passagen-Literatur.)
29740 CAHN, ARNOLD. KLUGE, FRIEDRICH: *Arnold Cahn (1858–1927). Wirken und Schicksal eines deutsch-jüdischen Arztes.* [In]: Zeitschrift für die Geschichte des Oberrheins, Bd. 139 (der neuen Folge Bd. 100), Stuttgart, 1991. Pp. 283–308. [A.C., 1858 Worms – 1927 Homburg, professor of medicine, lived for 40 years in Strassburg.]
29741 CANETTI, ELIAS. DARBY, DAVID: *A literary life: the textuality of Elias Canetti's autobiography.* [In]: Modern Austrian Literature, Vol. 25, No. 2, Riverside, CA, 1992. Pp. 37–49, notes.
29742 COHEN, HERMANN. *Hermann Cohen (1842–1918). Kantinterpret – Begründer der 'Marburger Schule'- jüdischer Religionsphilosoph. Eine Ausstellung in der Universitätsbibliothek Marburg vom 1. Juli bis 14. August 1992.* 204 pp., illus., facsims., docs. (Schriften der Universitätsbibliothek Marburg, 63.)
29743 ORLIK, FRANZ: *'Religion der Vernunft' und Judentum. Hermann Cohens Notizen zur Religionsphilosophie.* [In]: alma mater philippina, Sommersemester 1992, Marburg, 1992. Pp. 20–23, port., facsims.
29744 COURANT, RICHARD. FUCHS, KONRAD: *Der Mathematiker Richard Courant aus Lublinitz (1888–1972).* [In]: Oberschlesisches Jahrbuch 1992. Bd. 8. Berlin: Mann, 1992. Pp. 125–142, port., footnotes. [R.C., Jan. 8, 1888 Lublinitz – Jan. 27, 1972 New York. Mathematician, from 1909 at Göttingen University, from 1920 professor of mathematics, dismissed in 1933, emigr. to USA via Great Britain in 1934. Founder of Inst. of Mathematical Sciences of New York University, which was re-named after him in 1958.]

29745 DÜMLING, ALBRECHT: *Die verweigerte Heimat. Léon Jessel, der Komponist des 'Schwarzwaldmädel'.* Düsseldorf: dkv, der kleine verlag, [1992]. 164 pp., illus., facsims., catalogue of works (145–155), chronol. tab. [Léon Jessel, Jan. 22, 1871 Stettin – Jan. 4, 1942 Berlin, composer of popular songs and operettas.]

29746 EHRENSTEIN, ALBERT. MITTELMANN, HANNI: *Albert Ehrenstein: Judentum und Zionismus.* [In]: Jüdischer Almanach 1993 [see No. 29248]. Frankfurt am Main, 1992. Pp. 76–82. [A.E., Dec. 23, 1886 Vienna – April 8, 1950 New York, emigrated to Switzerland in 1932, to the USA in 1941, writer. Article deals with his essay Menschlichkeit! published in 1919, reprinted on pp. 70–75.]

29747 EINSTEIN, ALBERT. *Albert Einstein/Mileva Maric: the love letters.* Ed. and with an introd. by Jürgen Renn and Robert Schulmann. Transl. by Shawn Smith. Princeton, NJ: Princeton Univ. Press, 1992. 160 pp., illus., bibl.

29748 — BUCKY, PETER A.: *Der private Albert Einstein. Gespräche über Gott, die Menschen und die Bombe.* In Zusammenarbeit mit Allen G. Weakland. Aus dem Amerikanischen von Kurt Simon. Düsseldorf: Econ, 1991. 304 pp., ports., illus. [First publ. in 1990 under the title Conversations with Einstein. Private glimpses of a public life.]

29749 — DAECKE, S.M.: *Naturgesetz und Judentum im Denken Albert Einsteins.* [In]: Evangelische Kommentare, Jg. 24, H. 11–12, Stuttgart, 1991. Pp. 642–645.

29750 EINSTEIN, CARL: *Werke. Bd. 4. Texte aus dem Nachlass.* Hrsg. von Hermann Haarmann und Klaus Siebenhaar. Berlin: Fannei und Walz, 1992. 1 vol. [See also: Das Kunstwerk ist Sache der Willkür. Ein Portrait des Dichters und Kunsthistorikers Carl Einstein (Fritz J. Raddatz) [in]: Die Zeit, Nr. 51, Hamburg, 11. Dez. 1992. P. 58.] [For C.E. data see No. 28700/YB XXXVII.]

29751 ELIAS, NORBERT. MENNELL, STEPHEN: *Norbert Elias: an introduction.* Oxford; Cambridge, MA: Blackwell, 1992. XI, 339 pp. [Paperback edn. with substantial new afterword.]

29752 FELD, HANS. *Obituary.* Hans Feld. [In]: The Times, London, July 29, 1992. [Hans Nathan Feld, July 15, 1902 Berlin – July 15, 1992 London, film critic and film historian, emigr. to Prague in 1933, to London in 1935, founder and Executive Member of the London LBI; see also, on the occasion of H.F.'s 90th birthday Dr. Hans Feld [in]: AJR Information, Vol. 47, No. 7, London, July 1992. P. 15.]

29753 FREUD, SIGMUND: *The diary of Sigmund Freud, 1929–1939: a record of the final decade.* Transl., annotated, with an introd. by Michael Molnar. London: The Hogarth Press; New York: Scribner's, 1992. XXVI, 326 pp., illus. [Cf.: The small couch at Maresfield Gardens (Anita Brookner) [in]: The Observer, London, May 3, 1992, p. 55.]

29754 — ALTER, ROBERT: *Freud's Jewish problem.* [In]: Commentary, Vol. 93, No. 1, New York, Jan. 1992. Pp. 48–51.

29755 — APPIGNANESI, LISA/FORRESTER, JOHN: *Freud's women.* London: Weidenfeld & Nicolson, 1992. 563 pp., illus., notes (477–526), bibl. (527–545), index. [Incl. his famous women patients and disciples, as well as the women in his personal life.] [Cf.: Review (John E. Toews) [in]: Central European History, Vol. 25, Atlantic Highlands, NJ, 1992, pp. 107–108.]

29756 — DECKER, HANNAH S.: *Freud, Dora, and Vienna 1900.* New York: Free Press, 1992. XII, 299 pp., illus., facsims., maps, ports., bibl. (269–284).

29757 — FRIEDEN, KEN: *Teller's first and last visits to Sigmund Freud* [in 1937]. [In]: Proceedings of the 10th World Congress of Jewish Studies, 1989, Division C, Vol. 2: Jewish thought and literature. Jerusalem, 1990. Pp. 85–92.

29758 — GILMAN, SANDER L.: *Freud, race and gender.* [In]: American Imago, Vol. 49, No. 2, Baltimore, Summer 1992. Pp. 155–183, notes. [Incl. Freud's Jewish identity.]

29759 — GOODNICK, BENJAMIN: *A misunderstood marriage certificate.* [In]: Jewish Social Studies, Vol. 50, Nos. 1–2, New York, Winter-Spring 1988/1992. Pp. 37–48, facsim. [On the marriage contract of Freud's father, Jacob.]

29760 — KÄTZEL, HEDI: *Sigmund Freud: ein biographischer Essay. Einführung in sein Leben und Denken.* München: Quintessenz, 1992. 104 pp., illus. (Quintessenz-Studium.)

29761 — PUNER, HELEN WALKER: *Sigmund Freud: his life and mind.* With a new introd. by Paul Roazen. Foreword by Erich Fromm, and an afterword by Samuel P. Puner. New Brunswick, NJ: Transaction, 1992. XX, 269 pp.

29762 FROMM, ERICH: *The art of being.* Ed. by Rainer Funk. New York: Continuum, 1992. XI, 131 pp. [This vol. is an expansion of and supplement to Fromm's To have or to be.]

29763 FULDA, LUDWIG. KÜHN-LUDEWIG, MARIA: *Erfolgreich unter Feinden. Ludwig Fulda in seinem*

Briefwechsel 1882–1939. [In]: Euphorion, Bd. 85, Heidelberg, 1991. Pp. 199–219, footnotes. [L.F., 1862, Frankfurt am Main – March 30, 1939 Berlin (suicide), author, playwright. Article deals with Fulda's life and work on the basis of an edn. of his letters: Briefwechsel 1882–1939. Zeugnisse literarischen Lebens in Deutschland, hrsg. von Bernhard Gajek und Wolfgang von Ungern-Sternberg. T. 1: Mit einem Vorwort von Golo Mann; Briefe; T. 2: Erläuterungen, Bibliographie, Selbstzeugnisse und Dokumente. Frankfurt am Main: Lang, 1988. 1094 pp. (Regensburger Beiträge zur deutschen Sprach- und Literaturwissenschaft, Reihe A, Quellen, Bd. 4.)]

29764 GERRON, KURT. FELSMANN, BARBARA/PRÜMM, KARL: *Kurt Gerron – gefeiert und gejagt. Das Schicksal eines deutschen Unterhaltungskünstlers.* Berlin: Hentrich, 1992. 251 pp., illus., notes (233–238), index. (Reihe Deutsche Vergangenheit, 63.) [K.G., 1897 Berlin – 1944 Auschwitz, entertainer, actor, film director, emigr. in 1933 to the Netherlands, deported in Sept. 1943 to Westerbork, where he played in the revue, deported in Feb. 1944 to Theresienstadt, in Oct. 1944 to Auschwitz.]

29765 GRÜNWALD, ALFRED. *Ein Walzer muß es sein. Alfred Grünwald und die Wiener Operette.* Mit Beiträgen von Henry Grunwald, Georg Markus, Marcel Prawy, Hans Weigel. Wien: Ueberreuter, 1991. 184 pp., illus., bibl., index (persons). [On the life story of A.G., Vienna, Feb. 16, 1886–Feb. 24, 1951, New York; emigr. to the USA in 1938, librettist, author of numerous popular Viennese songs, writer and literary critic.]

29766 HABER, FRITZ. HARRIS, HENRY: *'To serve mankind in peace and the fatherland in war': the case of Fritz Haber.* [In]: German History, Vol. 10, No. 1, Oxford, Feb. 1992. Pp. 24–38, footnotes. [Deals with the implications of Haber's invention of poison-gas in the First World War, also discusses his Jewish background.]

29767 HAMBURGER, KÄTE. ZELLER, BERNHARD: *Gedenken an Käte Hamburger.* [In]: Jahrbuch der Deutschen Schillergesellschaft, 36. Jg., Stuttgart, 1992. Pp. 458–463.

29768 HEARTFIELD, JOHN. *John Heartfield.* Hrsg. von der Akademie der Künste zu Berlin, der Landesregierung Nordrhein-Westfalen und dem Landschaftsverband Rheinland. Konzeption: Peter Pachnicke, Klaus Honnef. Red.: Karin Thomas. Köln: DuMont Buchverl., 1991. 438 pp., illus. [Catalogue of exhibition held in Berlin, Bonn, Tübingen and Hanover from May 1991 to May 1992.; incl. 17 essays on the life and work of J.H.]

29769 HEIMANN, HUGO. RUDISCHHAUSER, SABINE: *Hugo Heimann und die Sozialdemokratische Kommunalpolitik im alten Berlin.* [In]: Jahrbuch für die Geschichte Mittel- und Ostdeutschlands, Bd. 40, Berlin 1991. Pp. 88–118.

29770 HEINE, HEINRICH. BAR-YOSEF, HAMUTAL: *The Heine cult in Hebrew literature of the 1890s and its Russian context.* [In Hebrew, with English summary]. [In]: Dappim le-Mechkar be-Sifrut, Vol. 8, Haifa, 1992. Pp. 319–332.

29771 — FINGERHUT, KARLHEINZ: *Spanische Spiegel. Heinrich Heines Verwendung spanischer Geschichte und Literatur zur Selbstreflexion des Juden und des Dichters.* [In]: Heine Jahrbuch 1992, Jg. 31, Hamburg, 1992. Pp. 106–136, notes.

29772 — GELBER, MARK H., ed.: *The Jewish reception of Heinrich Heine.* Tübingen: Niemeyer, 1992. 234 pp., footnotes, index (persons, 225–234). [Cont. (titles partly abbr.): Introduction (Mark S. Gelber, 1–4). The exhaustion of current Heine studies [and] Jewish reception as the last phase of the American Heine reception (Jeffrey L. Sammons, 5–20 [and] 197–214). Heinrich Heine and Karl Marx (Renate Schlesier, 21–44). Aron Bernstein as a writer and literary critic (Julius H. Schoeps, 45–52). The impact of Heine in nineteenth-century German-Jewish writers (Lothar Kahn/Donald D. Hook, 53–66). Heine and the Yiddish poets (Sol Liptzin, 67–76). Freud reads Heine reads Freud (Sander L. Gilman, 77–94). Sexuality and Jewish identity in Karl Kraus's literary polemics against Heinrich Heine (Leo A. Lensing, 95–112). On Else Lasker-Schüler's relation to Heinrich Heine (Itta Shedletzky, 113–126). The Heine cult in Hebrew literature of the 1890s and its Russian context (Hamutal Bar-Yosef, 127–138). Heinrich Heine's Jewish reception in Croatia (Mirjana Stancic, 153–162). Lion Feuchtwanger's discovery of himself in Heinrich Heine (Wulf Koepke, 163–172). Max Brod's presentation of Heinrich Heine (Margarita Pazi, 173–184). Fritz Heymann's approach to Heine (Joseph A. Kruse, 185–196; see also No. 29790). Appendix (in French with English transl.): Moise, Heine, Celan (Alain Suied, 213–222).]

29773 — GUTLEBEN, BURKHARD: *Heinrich Heine und seine Beziehungen zu Zeitgenossen und Zeitgeschichte.* Frankfurt am Main: R.G.Fischer, 1992. 118 pp., bibl.

29774 — *Heinrich Heines Werk im Urteil seiner Zeitgenossen.* Hrsg. von Eberhard Galley und Alfred Estermann. Hamburg: Hoffmann und Campe, Heinrich-Heine Verl.,1992. (Heine Studien,

Bd. 6. Rezensionen und Notizen zu Heines Werken aus den Jahren Juli 1840–Dezember 1841.)

29775 — HINCK, WALTER: *Die Wunde Deutschland. Heinrich Heines Dichtung im Widerstreit von Nationalidee, Judentum und Antisemitismus* [title from inner title page]. Frankfurt am Main: Insel, 1990. 305 [4] pp., notes, bibl., index.

29776 — HOHENDAHL, PETER UWE/GILMAN, SANDER L., eds.: *Heinrich Heine and the occident: multiple identities, multiple receptions.* Ed.[and introduced] by Peter Uwe Hohendahl and Sander L. Gilman. Lincoln: Univ. of Nebraska Press, 1991. 235 pp., notes, illus. [Incl. the following essays (titles condensed): Heine's legacy to Germans, Jews and liberals (Jost Hermand, 19–41). Heine's reception in France (Michael Werner, 42–62). Heine and the generation of 1898 (Egon Schwarz, 63–86). Heine's reception in Italy (Luciano Zagari, 87–109). Heine in Mexico (Susanne Zantop, 110–138). Heine's image of foreign cultures and peoples (Hartmut Steinecke, 139–162). Heine as a cartoonist (T.J. Reed, 163–186). The diversity of Heine's reception in Western European and American Art (Joseph A. Kruse, 187–198).]

29777 — HOLUB, ROBERT C.: *Heinrich Heine on the slave trade: cultural repression and the persistance of history.* [In]: The German Quarterly, Vol. 65, Nos. 3–4, Cherry Hill, NJ, Summer/Fall 1992. Pp. 328–339, notes.

29778 — KIBA, H.: *Heine und Italien. Zu seinen italienischen Reisebildern.* [In]: Doitsu Bungaku, No. 89, Tokyo, Herbst 1992. Pp. 33–43. [In Japanese with German summary.]

29779 — KRUSE, JOSEPH A.: *'. . . ich bin des freien Rheines noch weit freierer Sohn'. Heinrich Heine (1797–1856).* [In]: Wegweiser durch das jüdische Rheinland (see No. 29169]. Pp. 324–331.

29780 — LAPIDE, PINCHAS: *Heinrich Heine und Martin Buber: streitbare Gott-Sucher des Judentums.* [Vortrag im Wiener Rathaus am 12. Dezember 1990.] Wien: Picus, 1991. 52 pp. (Wiener Vorlesungen im Rathaus, Bd. 12.)

29781 — REGENSTEINER, HENRY: *Heinrich Heine and Karl Marx: a perspective.* [In]: Midstream, Vol. 38, No. 5, New York, June/July 1992. Pp. 18–19. [Discusses the differences between their respective views of the world.]

29782 — REICH-RANICKI, MARCEL: *Heine und die Liebe.* [In]: Vorträge und Ansprachen anläßlich der Verleihung der Ehrendoktorwürde durch die Philosophische Fakultät II der Universität Ausgburg. Hrsg. von Helmut Koopmann und Henning Krauß. München: Vögel, 1992. Pp. 23–39, footnotes. (Schriften der Philosophischen Fakultäten der Universität Augsburg, Nr. 45.) [In the same publ.: Streit und Humanität – Nachdenken über Lessing (Walter Jens, 47–62).]

29783 — *Die Sammlung Gottschalk und weitere Heine-Archivalien.* Hrsg. von der Kulturstiftung der Länder in Verbindung mit dem Heinrich-Heine-Institut, Düsseldorf. Red.: Joseph A. Kruse. Düsseldorf, 1992. 27 pp., illus. [On recent acquisitions of the Heinrich-Heine-Institut; incl. contributions by Joseph A. Kruse, Bernhard R. Appel, Inge Hermstrüwer and Marianne Tilch.]

29784 — SCHANZE, HELMUT: *Heines Geburtsjahre* [In]: Heine Jahrbuch 1992, Jg. 31, Hamburg, 1992. Pp. 192–197, notes.

29785 — SOLL, KARL/KRUSE, JOSEPH A.: *'Lebensverhältnisse des Heinrich Heine'. Zwei Dokumente aus dem Jahre 1835 über Heines Taufe und Geburtsjahr.* [In]: Heine Jahrbuch 1992, Jg. 31, Hamburg, 1992. Pp. 198–202, notes.

29786 — ZEPF, IRMGARD: *Heines dichterische Ironie als Einspruch in die positiven Religionen.* [In]: Aus zweier Zeugen Mund. Festschrift für Pnina Navé Levinson und Nathan Peter Levinson [see No. 29923]. Pp. 217–235.

29787 HENSEL, FANNY [MENDELSSOHN]. *Quellen zur Biographie von Fanny Hensel, geb. Mendelssohn Bartoldy* [In]: Mendelssohn Studien, Bd. 7. Berlin: Duncker & Humblot, 1990. Pp. 171–218. [Incl.: III. Ein Schweizer Reisebrief aus dem Jahr 1822 von Lea und Fanny Mendelssohn Bartholdy an Henriette Mendelssohn, geb. Meyer (Christian Lambour, ed., 171–177). IV. A diary-album for Fanny Mendelssohn Bartholdy (Phyllis Benjamin, 178–218). Autographe und Abschriften von Werken Fanny Hensels im Mendelssohn-Archiv zu Berlin – Verzeichnis der Abschriften und Neuerwerbungen 1976–1990 (Hans-Günter Klein, 343–346.).]

29788 HERTZ, PAUL. ESCHER, FELIX: *Paul Hertz und die Übernahme der Initiative in der Berliner Wirtschaftspolitik der Nachkriegszeit durch die SPD.* [In]: Jahrbuch für die Geschichte Mittel- und Ostdeutschlands, Bd. 40, Berlin 1991. Pp. 119–144.

29789 HEYM, STEFAN. HUTCHINSON, PETER: *Stefan Heym: the perpetual dissident.* Cambridge; New York: Cambridge Univ. Press, 1992. IX, 270 pp. (Cambridge studies in German.)

29790 HEYMANN, FRITZ. KRUSE, JOSEPH A.: *Auf den Spuren von Fritz Heymann (1897–1943). Ein Schriftsteller, Journalist und Heine-Kenner aus Bocholt*. [In]: Unser Bocholt. Zeitschrift für Kultur und Heimatpflege, Jg. 41, H. 4, Bocholt 1990. Pp. 27–32, port., facsims. [Biographical notes on Fritz Heymann incl. personal recollections of the author, director of the Düsseldorf Heine Institut and also born in Bocholt, on how he became involved with Heine and, subsequently, with Heymann.] [See also on Heymann by same author [in]: No. 29772.]

29791 — NUSSBAUM, LAUREEN: *'Tod oder Taufe'. Zur Herausgabe der Marranen-Chronik Fritz Heymanns*. [In]: Zeitschrift für Religions- und Geistesgeschichte, Jg. 44, Leiden, 1992. Pp. 76–81, footnotes. [On the background of Heymann's book, written after a series of lectures organised by the Joodsche Raad in Amsterdam during the Spring 1942; corrects some of the biographical details given by Schoeps.]

29792 HINRICHSEN, HENRI. STACHAU, CHRISTIANE: *Mut für das noch nicht Gehörte. Der Leipziger Musikverleger und Mäzen Henri Hinrichsen*. [In]: Frankfurter Allgemeine Zeitung, Nr. 271, Frankfurt am Main, Nov. 21, 1992, Beilage. [On the former owner of C.F.Peters, Leipzig.]

29793 HOUTERMANS, FRITZ. KHRIPLOVICH, IOSIF B.: *The eventful life of Fritz Houtermans*. [In]: Physics Today, Vol. 45, No. 7, Washington, DC, July 1992. Pp. 29–37. [F.H., Jan. 22, 1903 Zoppot – March 1, 1966 Bern, of Jewish descent, physicist, Communist, fled to UK in 1933, went to Kharkov (Ukraine) in 1935, imprisoned by the NKVD in 1937, extradited to the Gestapo in April 1940, released with the help of Max von Laue, worked in the private laboratory of Manfred von Ardenne in Lichterfeld and at Göttingen University, from 1952 at Bern University.]

29794 JENSEN, FRITZ. BARILICH, EVA: *Arzt an vielen Fronten. Fritz Jensen. Biografische Texte zur Geschichte der österreichischen Arbeiterbewegung*. Wien: Globus, 1991. 188 pp., illus., index. [F.J., formerly Friedrich Albert Jerusalem, Dec. 26, 1903 Prague – April 11, 1955, physician, Communist, fought in the Spanish Civil War, emigr. to China, returned to Austria in 1948, lived in China from 1953.]

29795 KAFKA, FRANZ. GRÖZINGER, KARL ERICH: *Kafka und die Kabbala. Das Jüdische im Werk und Denken von Franz Kafka*. Frankfurt am Main: Eichborn, 1992. 267 pp. [Cf.: Jüdisches in Kafkas Werk? (Hartmut Binder) [in]: 'NZZ', Nr. 43, Zürich, 22. Feb., 1993, pp. 15–16.]

29796 — KARL, FREDERICK ROBERT: *Franz Kafka: representative man*. New York: Ticknor & Fields, 1991. XIX, 810 pp., illus., map, bibl. (761–787). [Incl. also discussion of Kafka's attitude to his Jewish background. Cf.: Smothering Kafka (Gabriel Josipovici) [in]: TLS, London, March 6, 1992.]

29797 KANTOROWICZ, ERNST. GRÜNEWALD, ECKHART: '*. . . und dabei bin ich noch an einer der angenehmsten der Küsten gestrandet*. [In]: Börsenblatt für den Deutschen Buchhandel, Jg. 159, Nr. 43, Frankfurt am Main, 29. Mai 1992. pp. 84–90, port. [On the life and work of the historian E.K.; data see No. 28742/YB XXXVII.]

29798 KATZ, HANNS LUDWIG. *Hanns Ludwig Katz: 1892–1940*. Hrsg.: Jüdisches Museum im Auftr. des Magistrats der Stadt Frankfurt am Main, Dezernat für Kultur und Freizeit, Amt für Wissenschaft und Kunst. Verantw.: Georg Heuberger. Köln: Ed. Wienand, 1992. 222 pp., illus., facsims., docs. [Catalogue of an exhibition held at the Jüdisches Museum, Frankfurt, March 18–June 8, 1992 and the Kunsthalle Emden, Stiftung Henri Nannen, June 21–Aug. 23, 1992.] [Incl.: Hanns Ludwig Katz, Leben und Werk (Karl-Ludwig Hofmann/Helga Krohn, 11–93).] [H.L.K., 1892 Karlsruhe – 1940 Johannesburg, painter, Socialist, emigr. to Johannesburg 1936.] [See also in No. 29685.]

29799 KISSINGER, HENRY. ISAACSON, WALTER: *Kissinger: a biography*. London: Faber & Faber; New York: Simon & Schuster, 1992. 893 pp., illus., ports., bibl.

29800 KOLMAR, GERTRUD. EICHMANN-LEUTENEGGER, BEATRICE: *'Da an die Welten flog ein grosser Schrei. . .'. Gertrud Kolmar (1894–1943)*. [In]: Jüdischer Almanach 1993 [see No. 29248]. Frankfurt am Main, 1992. Pp. 55–62. [G.K., orig. Chodziesner, Dec. 10, 1894 Berlin – 1943 deported (date and place of death not known, presumed murdered in Auschwitz), writer.]

— KOMPERT, LEOPOLD. [See No. 29214.]

29801 KORNFELD, PAUL. PAZI, MARGARITA: *Paul Kornfelds Drama Jud Süß, 1933 und die dramatische Bearbeitung des Feuchtwangerschen Romans in hebräischer Sprache von Avi-Shaul, 1933*. [In]: Theatralia Judaica [see No. 30017]. Pp. 281–298.

29802 KRONBERG, SIMON: *Werke. Gedichte, Prosa, Theaterstücke*. Hrsg. von Armin A. Wallas. München: Klaus-Boer-Verl., 1992. 800 pp. [S.K., 1891 Vienna – 1947 Haifa, odd-jobber, choir director, writer, emigr. in 1934 to Palestine.] [See also 'Über allem faltet sich die Stille bitterlich'. Zum 100. Geburtstag von Simon Kronberg (Armin A. Wallas) [in]: 'NZZ', Nr. 149, Zürich, 1. Juli 1991, p. 19.]

29803 LAQUEUR, WALTER. REINHARZ, JEHUDA/MOSSE, GEORGE L., eds.: *The impact of Western nationalism: essays dedicated to Walter Z. Laqueur on the occasion of his 70th birthday*. London: Sage Publications, 1992. 336 pp., footnotes. [Essays relevant to the history of German-speaking Jewry are listed according to subject.] [Cf.: National concerns (Zev Ben-Schlomo) [in]: Jewish Chronicle, London, Jan. 15, 1993.]

29804 LASCH, AGATHE. DALBERG, VIBEKE/RENTENAAR, ROB: *Spuren der Bibliothek der Agathe Lasch in Dänemark*. [In]: Niederdeutsches Jahrbuch, Jg. 1990. Jahrbuch des Vereins für niederdeutsche Sprachforschung, 113, Neumünster, 1990. Pp. 157–162. [A.L., professor of linguistics at the Univ. of Hamburg from 1923 until 1934, deported in 1942 from Berlin to Auschwitz.]

29805 LASKER-SCHÜLER, ELSE. BĂLEANÚ, AVRAM ANDREI: *Zwei jüdische Dichterinnen im Rheinland: Else Lasker-Schüler und Rose Ausländer*. [In]: Wegweiser durch das jüdische Rheinland [see No. 29169]. Berlin, Nicolai, 1992. Pp. 300–305.

29806 — COLIN, AMY: *Marginalität und Phantasie-Judentum. Else Lasker-Schülers Travestie als postmoderne Kulturkritik*. [In]: Deutsch-jüdische Geschichte im 19. und 20. Jahrhundert [see No. 29601]. Pp. 425–450.

29807 LASSALLE, FERDINAND. HEID, LUDGER: *Rebell, Religionsstifter, Rosenkavalier. Jüdische Aspekte bei Ferdinand Lassalle*. [In]: Deutsch-jüdische Geschichte im 19. und 20. Jahrhundert [see No. 29601]. Pp. 107–130.

29808 LESSING, THEODOR. SPRENGEL, PETER: *Urszene im Café Leopold. Theodor Lessings Satire auf Samuel Lublinski und die jüdische Kontroverse um Assimilation oder Zionismus*. [In]: Germanisch-Romanische Monatsschrift, NF, Jg. 42, Heidelberg, 1992. Pp. 341–347.

— LEVI, PAUL. JENS, WALTER: *Ein Jud aus Hechingen. Requiem für Paul Levi*. [See No. 30060]

29809 LUBITSCH, ERNST. HAKE, SABINE: *Passions and deceptions: the early films of Ernst Lubitsch*. Princeton, NJ: Princeton Univ. Press, 1992. 224 pp., illus. [E.L., (1892–1947), film director, theatre producer.] [See also, on the occasion of the 100th anniversary of E.L.'s birthday: Die Welt als Schaufenster. Über Ernst Lubitsch, den Regisseur des Paradieses (Fritz Göttler) [in]: Die Zeit, Nr. 5, Hamburg, 24. Jan., 1991, p. 53.]

29810 LUDWIG, EMIL: *Für die Weimarer Republik und Europa. Ausgewählte Zeitungs- und Zeitschriftenartikel 1919–1932*. Hrsg. von Franklin C. West. Frankfurt am Main; New York [et al.]: Lang, 1991. 276 pp. (Trouvaillen. Editionen zur Literatur- und Kulturgeschichte, Bd. II.) [Incl.: Nachwort (ed., 243–259; on life and work of E.L.]

29811 LUKACS, GEORG: *German realists in the nineteenth century*. Ed. and with an introd. and notes by Rodney Livingstone. Transl. by Jeremy Gaines and Paul Keast. Cambridge, MA: MIT Press, 1992. 350 pp. [These previously untransl. essays were written between 1936–1950 and incl. an essay on Heine.]

29812 MAHLER, GUSTAV. ADORNO, THEODOR W.: *Mahler: a musical physiognomy*. Chicago: Univ. of Chicago Press, 1992. X, 178 pp. [For German orig. in 1960 see No. 2286/YB VI.]

29813 — DANUSER, HERMANN: *Gustav Mahler und seine Zeit*. Laaber: Laaber-Verl., 1991. 380 pp., illus., music. (Grosse Komponisten und ihre Zeit.)

29814 — SCHORSKE, CARL E.: *Gustav Mahler: formation and transformation*. New York: Leo Baeck Institute, 1991. 24 pp., notes. (The Leo Baeck Memorial Lecture, 35.)

29815 MARX, KARL. MARCUS, MARCEL: *Eine frühe jüdische Rezension von Karl Marx' 'Zur Judenfrage'*. [In]: Studien zur jüdischen Geschichte und Soziologie. Festschrift Julius Carlebach [see No. 29561]. Pp. 175–184.

29816 — MISHKINSKI, MOSHE: *A Bundist polemic against Marx's 'On the Jewish question' and its historical context*. [In]: Shvut, Vol. 15, Tel-Aviv, 1992. Pp. vii–xxxi.

29817 — NA'AMAN, SHLOMO: *Heinrich Marx, Karl Marx and Eleanor Marx: three generations and the challenge of civic equality*. [In Hebrew, with English summary]. [In]: Zion, Vol. 57, No. 4, Jerusalem, 1992. Pp. 395–427.

29818 — PELED, YOAV: *From theology to sociology: Bruno Bauer and Karl Marx on the question of Jewish emancipation*. [In]: History of Political Thought, Vol. 13, No. 3, London, Autumn 1992.

— MAUTHNER, FRITZ. [See No. 29214.]

29819 MENDELSOHN, ERICH. STEPHAN, REGINA: *Studien zu Waren- und Geschäftshäusern Erich Mendelsohns in Deutschland*. München: tuduv-Verlagsges., 1992. 276 [42] pp., illus., notes. (tuduv-Studien. Reihe Kunstgeschichte, Bd. 55.) [E.M., Allenstein March 21, 1887–San Francisco Sept. 15, 1953, architect, emigr. to USA in 1933.]

29820 MENDELSSOHN, PETER DE. STRICKHAUSEN, WALTRAUD: *Exil oder zweite Heimat? Peter de Mendelssohn in London (1936–1970)*. [In]: German Life & Letters, Vol. 45, No. 3, Oxford; Cambridge, MA, 1992. Pp. 254–260.

29821 MEYER, EDUARD. HOFFMANN, CHRISTHARD: *Classical scholarship, modern anti-semitism and the Zionist project: the historian Eduard Meyer in Palestine (1926)*. [In]: Studies in Zionism, Vol. 13, No. 2, Ramat Aviv, 1992. Pp. 133–146, footnotes. [On Meyer's journey to Palestine, financed for him by his students and colleagues as a present on the occasion of his seventieth birthday.]

29822 MÜHSAM, ERICH. *Mühsam-Magazin*. H.2 [&] 3, Jan. 1991 [&] April 1992, Lübeck, 1991 [&] 1992. 2 issues, 70 [&] 87 pp., footnotes. [Cont. contributions on the life and work of Mühsam; incl.: H.2: Zur Freundschaft zwischen Erich Mühsam und Gustav Landauer (Siegbert Wolf, 22–34). H.3: Erich Mühsams jüdische Identität (Lawrence Baron, 47–61).]

29823 OPPENHEIMER, OLGA. REINHARDT, HILDEGARD: *Olga Oppenheimer und die Kölner Sezession*. [In]: Wegweiser durch das jüdische Rheinland [see No. 29169]. Berlin: Nicolai, 1992. Pp. 341–345.

29824 OPPLER, ERNST. *Ernst Oppler 1867–1929*. [In English and Hebrew]. Catalogue: Jochen Bruns. Hebrew transl.: Aya Breuer. Ein Harod: Mishkan Le'omanut – Museum of Art. 98 pp., illus. [E.O., Sept. 19, 1867 Hanover – March 1, 1929 Berlin, impressionist painter and etcher.]

29825 PANOFSKY, ERWIN. WUTTKE, DIETER: *Einstein der Kunstgeschichte. Erwin Panofsky zum hundertsten Geburtstag*. [In]: Wolfenbütteler Renaissance Studien, Jg. 16, H.3, Wiesbaden, Dez. 1992. Pp. 91–99. [See also: Ein Kunsthistoriker mit Weltwirkung. Erwin Panofsky in Leben und Werk (Dieter Wuttke) [in]: 'NZZ', Nr. 68, Zürich, 21./22. März 1992, p.69. Kunst, zu einer schönen Erinnerung geworden. Erwin Panofsky zum 100. Geburtstag (Martin Warnke) [in]: 'NZZ', Nr. 68, Zürich, 21./22. März 1992, p. 68.]

29826 PAPPENHEIM, BERTHA: *Sisyphus: gegen den Mädchenhandel – Galizien*. Bertha Pappenheim, Die Anna O. Auswahl von Reden, Aufsätzen, Schriften zur Bekämpfung des Mädchenhandels. Hrsg. von Helga Heubach. Freiburg i. Br.: Kore, 1992. 315 pp., illus.

29827 PERUTZ, LEO. MANDELARTZ, MICHAEL: *Christliche und jüdische Geschichtstheologie in den historischen Romanen von Leo Perutz*. Tübingen: Niemeyer, 1992. 207 pp., footnotes, bibl. (Conditio Judaica, 2.)

29828 — MÜLLER, HANS-HARALD/SCHERNUS, WILHELM: *Leo Perutz. Eine Bibliographie*. Frankfurt am Main; New York [et al.]: Lang, 1991. 153 pp., index. (Hamburger Beiträge zur Germanistik, Bd. 15.) [Incl. short biography (9–27).]

29829 PHILIPPSON FAMILY. GUTZMER, KARL, Bearb.: *Die Philippsons in Bonn. Deutsch-jüdische Schicksalslinien 1862–1980*. Dokumentation einer Ausstellung in der Universitätsbibliothek Bonn 1989. Bonn: Bouvier, 1991. 169 pp., illus., family tree. [Cf.: Besprechung (Dieter Kastner) [in]: Annalen des Historischen Vereins für den Niederrhein, H. 195, Pulheim, 1992, pp. 355–356.]

29830 PICARD, JACOB. BOSCH, MANFRED: *Ausgewandert und doch stets daheim. Jüdisches Schicksal am Bodensee. Zum 25. Todestag Jacob Picards*. [In]: Tribüne, Jg. 31, H. 123, Frankfurt am Main, 1992. Pp. 211–215, port. [See also No. 28764/YB XXXVII.]

29831 PREUSS, HUGO. LEHNERT, DETLEF: *Hugo Preuss als moderner Klassiker einer kritischen Theorie der 'verfaßten' Politik*. [In]: Politische Vierteljahresschrift, Jg. 33, H. 1, Opladen, 1992. Pp. 33–54, notes.

29832 RATHENAU, WALTHER. GÖHL, WALTER: *Vor 70 Jahren. Der Rathenau-Mord und sein Echo im Birkenfelder Land*. [In]: Mitteilungen des Vereins f. Heimatkunde i. Landkreis Birkenfeld und der Heimatfreunde Oberstein, Jg. 66, Birkenfeld, 1992. Pp. 35–56, port., notes.

29833 — LANGE, ERHARD H.M.: *Ein Spiegelbild der in sich zerrissenen Weimarer Republik*. [In]: Das Parlament, Nr. 27, Bonn, 26. Juni 1992. P. 19.

29834 — ORTH, WILHELM: *Die Partei und der Individualist. Walther Rathenau und die DDP*. [In]: liberal, 34. Jg., H. 3, Bonn, Aug. 1992. pp. 72–78.

29835 — SABROW, MARTIN: *Reichsminister Rathenau ermordet. Hinter dem Mord verbarg sich ein von langer Hand geplantes Komplott zur Auslösung der Gegenrevolution*. [In]: Die Zeit, Nr. 26, Hamburg, 19. Juni 1992. P. 78.

29836 — SCHLÜTER, HENNING: *Zwei Fabeltiere ihrer Zeit. Eine Freundschaft, die in Haß umschlug: Maximilian Harden und Walther Rathenau*. [In]: Frankfurter Allgemeine Zeitung, Nr. 153, Frankfurt am Main, 4. Juli 1992, Beilage: Bilder und Zeiten.

29837 — SCHULIN, ERNST: *Walther Rathenau: Repräsentant, Kritiker, Opfer seiner Zeit*. 2., verb. Aufl.

Göttingen: Muster-Schmidt, 1992. 146 pp., illus. (Persönlichkeit und Geschichte, Bd. 104/ 104a.)

29838 ROSENTHAL, HANS. HORCH, HANS OTTO: *Hans Rosenthal: Gullivers fünfte Reise nach der fabelhaften Insel Palina*. [In]: Deutsch-jüdische Geschichte im 19. und 20. Jahrhundert [see No. 29601]. Pp. 381–424. [H.R., Feb. 6, 1906 Stettin – July 16, 1950 Tel-Aviv, poet, writer, Communist activist, emigr. to Palestine 1935.]

29839 ROSENZWEIG, FRANZ. MOSÈS, STÉPHANE: *Franz Rosenzweig. Stationen eines inneren Weges*. [In]: Jüdischer Almanach 1993 [see No. 29248]. Frankfurt am Main, 1992. Pp. 63–69.

29840 ROTH, JOSEPH: *Werke 1–6*. 6 Bde. Köln: Kiepenheuer & Witsch, 1989–1991. XXIV, 1116 [&] XVI, 1028 [&] XVI, 1078 [&] 1086 [&] 898 [&] 814 pp. Bd. 1 (1989): Das journalistische Werk 1915–1923. Hrsg. von Klaus Westermann. Mit einem Vorwort zur Werkausgabe von Fritz Hackert und Klaus Westermann. Bd. 2 (1990): Das journalistische Werk 1924–1928. Hrsg. und mit einem Nachwort von Klaus Westermann. Bd. 3 (1991): Das journalistische Werk 1929–1939. Hrsg. und mit einem Nachwort von Klaus Westermann. Bd. 4 (1989): Romane und Erzählungen 1916–1929. Hrsg. und mit einem Nachwort von Fritz Hackert. Bd. 5 (1990): Romane und Erzählungen 1930–1936. Hrsg. und mit einem Nachwort von Fritz Hackert. Bd. 6 (1991): Romane und Erzählungen 1936–1940. Hrsg. und mit einem Nachwort von Fritz Hackert. [The definitive edn. of the complete works of J.R.; see also: The empire of Joseph Roth (Nadine Gordimer) [in]: The New York Review of Books, Vol. 38, No. 20, New York, Dec. 5, 1991. pp. 16–21. Der unbehauste Grenzgänger. Zur neuen Joseph-Roth-Werkausgabe (Arthur Zimmermann) [in]: 'NZZ', Nr. 56, Zürich, 7./8. März 1992, p. 69.]

29841 SAHL, HANS: *'Und doch . . .': Essays und Kritiken aus zwei Kontinenten*. Hrsg. von Claus Blanc. Frankfurt am Main: Luchterhand, 1991. 264 pp. (Sammlung Luchterhand, 980.) [See also: Emigration als geistige Haltung. Zum neunzigsten Geburtstag von Hans Sahl (20. Mai) (Charitas Jenny-Ebeling) [in]: 'NZZ', Nr. 116, Zürich, 20. Mai 1992, p. 25.]

29842 — RATHENOW, LUTZ: *Mehr als ein Verweigerer jeglicher Anpassung. Das Exil im Exil: Memoiren eines Moralisten II*. [In]: Germanic Notes and Reviews, Vol. 23, No. 4, Bemidji, MN, 1992. Pp. 53–56.

29843 SCHNITZLER, ARTHUR. LIPTZIN, SOL: *Remembering Arthur Schnitzler*. [In]: Modern Austrian Literature, Vol. 25, No. 1, Riverside, CA, 1992. Pp. 1–6.

29844 SENDER, TONY. *Tony Sender 1888–1964. Rebellin, Demokratin, Weltbürgerin*. Katalog: Jürgen Steen; Wiss. Mitarb.: Gabriele Weiden. Frankfurt: Historisches Museum Frankfurt am Main, 1992. 232 pp., illus., ports., facsims., docs., notes, bibl. (Kleine Schriften des Historischen Museums, Bd. 50.) [Catalogue book of an exhibition held in Frankfurt am Main in Nov. 1992.] [T.S., Dec. 4, 1888 Biebrich – June 26, 1964 New York, Socialist politician, trade unionist, member of the Reichstag (SPD), fled via Czechoslovakia and Belgium in 1935 to the USA, there also politically active, esp. for the UN.]

29845 SIMMEL, GEORG. LOYCKE, ALMUT, ed.: *Der Gast, der bleibt. Dimensionen von Georg Simmels Analyse der Fremdseins*. Frankfurt am Main; New York: Campus; Paris: Ed. de la maison des Sciences, 1992. 124 pp., footnotes. (Edition Pandora, Bd. 9.) [Cont. the following essays: Exkurs über den Fremden (Georg Simmel, 9–18; first publ. in 1908). Das Gastrecht (Julian Pitt-Rivers, 17–41). Fremde (Meyer Fortes, 43–79). Die Nächstenliebe im Talmud (Hermann Cohen, 80–102; first publ. in 1935). Der Gast, der bleibt. Dimensionen von Georg Simmels Analyse des Fremdseins (Almut Loycke, 103–123).] [Cf.: Nah und fern (Andreas Kuhlmann) [in]: Die Zeit, Nr. 47, Hamburg, 13. Nov., 1992, p. 20.]

29846 SPIEL, HILDE. LORENZ, DAGMAR C.G.: *Hilde Spiel: 'Lisas Zimmer'. Frau, Jüdin, Verfolgte*. [In]: Modern Austrian Literature, Vol. 25, No. 2, Riverside, CA, 1992. Pp. 79–95, notes.

29847 STERNBERG, LEO. MAIBACH, HEINZ: *Leo Sternberg. Zum Leben und Werk des jüdischen Dichters, Richters und Kulturhistorikers*. [In]: Nassauische Annalen. Wiesbaden, 1990. Pp. 173–184. [L.St., Oct. 7, 1876 Limburg – Oct. 26, 1937 Hvar [island], Yugoslavia, judge, writer, lyrical poet, converted to Catholicism in 1933.]

29848 STRAUSS, LUDWIG. HORCH, HANS OTTO: *Ungleiche Welten. Ludwig Strauß im Briefwechsel mit Hans Carossa. Zum 100. Geburtstag des deutsch-jüdischen Dichters und Literaturwissenschaftlers am 28. Oktober 1992*. [In]: Jüdischer Almanach 1993 [see No. 29248]. Frankfurt am Main, 1992. Pp. 105–123.

29849 — SHEDLETZKY, ITTA: *'Zum wirklichen Zentrum des Judentums'. Eine Kontroverse zwischen Gerhard (Gershom) Scholem und Ludwig Strauß*. [In]: Jüdischer Almanach 1993 [see No. 29248].

Frankfurt am Main, 1992. Pp. 96–103. [On the correspondence between Scholem and Strauß from August 1917 until July 1920.]

29850 ULLMANN, VIKTOR. KLEIN, HANS-GÜNTER, Hrsg.: *Viktor Ullmann Materialien.* Hamburg: von Bockel, 1992. 118 pp., notes. [Incl. inventory of music (Werkverzeichnis).]

29851 UNGER, ERICH: *Vom Expressionismus zum Mythos des Hebräertums.* Schriften 1909 bis 1931. Hrsg. von Manfred Voigts. Würzburg: Königshausen und Neumann, 1992. 151 pp., index. [E.U., Oct. 25, 1887 Berlin – Nov. 11, 1950, London, philosopher, emigr. 1933 via Paris to London.]

29852 VARNHAGEN, RAHEL. MARON, AVRAHAM: *Rahel Varnhagen's 'salon': the turbulent life of Berlin in the beginning of the 19th century.* [In Hebrew, title transl.]. [In]: Eit-mol, No. 102, Tel-Aviv, April 1992. Pp. 20–21.

29853 — WEISSBERG, LILIANE: *On Rahel Varnhagen's letters.* [In]: In the shadow of Olympus. German women writers around 1800. ed. by Katherine R. Goodman and Edith Waldstein. Albany: State Univ. of New York Press, 1992. 53–70, notes.

29854 — WEISSBERG, LILIANE: *Changing weather: a review essay.* [In]: The Germanic Review, Vol. 67, No. 2, Washington, DC, Spring 1992. Pp. 77–86. [Essay on recent publications on Rahel Varnhagen, incl. German publications.]

29855 VIERTEL, BERTHOLD. JANSEN, IRENE: *Berthold Viertel. Leben und künstlerische Arbeit im Exil.* Frankfurt am Main; New York: Lang, 1992. 243 pp., notes (171–212), bibl. (213–237), index of persons (239–243). [Incl. also letters written in exile.]

29856 WARBURG, ABY M. GOMBRICH, ERNST H.: *Aby Warburg: eine intellektuelle Biographie.* Aus dem Engl. von Matthias Fienbork. Hamburg: Europ. Verl.-Anstalt, 1992. 477 pp., illus., notes, bibl. (451–464). [The author, E.H.G., born Vienna March 30, 1909, emigr. to England in 1936, art historian, former director of the London Warburg Institute; on E.H.G. see also Das Prinzip Gleichgültigkeit. Über Ernst H. Gombrich (Eckhard Nordhofen) [in]: Die Zeit, Nr. 7, Feb. 7, Hamburg, 1992, p. 66.]

29857 WASSERSTEIN, BERNARD. *Herbert Samuel: a political life.* Oxford: Clarendon Press; New York: Oxford Univ. Press, 1991. XVI, 427 pp., illus., ports., bibl. (407–411). [H.S. (1870–1973), British, of German-Jewish background, Liberal politician. Incl. Samuel's efforts on behalf of German Jews during the 1930s.] [Cf. A faithful servant (Martin Gilbert) [in]: Midstream, Vol. 38, No. 9, New York, Dec. 1992, pp. 37–38.]

29858 WEILL, KURT. HINTON, STEPHEN, ed.: *Kurt Weill: The Threepenny Opera.* Cambridge; New York: Cambridge Univ. Press, 1990. XV, 229 pp., illus., musical scores. [Incl. essays by Adorno, Benjamin, and Ernst Bloch on the opera.]

29859 WERFEL, FRANZ. *Modern Austrian Literature.* Journal of the International Arthur Schnitzler Research Association. Special Franz Werfel Issue. Vol. 24, No. 2, Riverside, CA, 1991. 1 Vol. [Incl. letters by Franz Werfel, Alma Mahler Werfel, Ben Huebsch, Stefan Zweig and contributions by Erhard Bahr, Jeffrey B. Berlin, Hartmut Binder, Donald G. Daviau, James C. Davidheiser, Jorun B. Johns, Donald A. Prater, Lionel B. Steiman.]

29860 WITTGENSTEIN, LUDWIG. CHATTERJEE, RANJIT: *Wittgenstein as a Jewish thinker.* [In]: Proceedings of the 10th World Congress of Jewish Studies, 1989, Division C, Vol. 2: Jewish thought and literature. Jerusalem, 1990.

29861 ZWEIG, ARNOLD: *Jüdischer Ausdruckswille. Publizistik. Publizistik aus vier Jahrzehnten.* Auswahl und Nachwort: Detlev Claussen. Berlin: Aufbau Taschenbuch Verlag, 1991. 1 vol.

29862 — HERMAND, JOST: *Das Licht in der Finsternis. Arnold Zweigs 'Ritualmord in Ungarn' als prosemitisches Tendenzstück.* [In]: Deutsch-jüdische Geschichte im 19. und 20. Jahrhundert [see No. 29601]. Pp. 359–380.

29863 — WOLF, ARIA: *Größe und Tragik Arnold Zweigs. Ein deutsch-jüdisches Dichterschicksal in jüdischer Sicht.* London: The World of Books, 1991. 1 vol. [438 ff.]

29864 ZWEIG, MAX. *Erinnerung an Max Zweig.* Zum 100. Geburtstag am 22. Juni 1992 zusammengestellt von Wilhemine Bucherer-Zweig. Jerusalem: W. Bucherer, Rehov Pinsker 7, 92 228 Jerusalem, 1992. (Mimeog.) 70 pp., ports., illus., facsims. [A collection of documents on the life and work of M.Z.] [M.Z., June 22, 1892 – Jan. 5, 1992.]

29865 — *Mnemosyne*, H. 13 [with the issue title]: Max Zweig. Hrsg.: Armin A. Wallas, Andrea M. Lauritsch. A-9500 Villach (Rennsteiner Str. 118): Armin A. Wallas, 1992. 60 pp. [Incl.: Max Zweig an Elazar Benyoetz (4–5). Humanismus nach Auschwitz. Zum 100. Geburtstag des Dramatikers Max Zweig (Armin A. Wallas, 6–9).]

29866 ZWEIG, STEFAN. WEINZIERL, ULRICH, ed.: *Stefan Zweig – Triumph und Tragik.* Aufsätze,

Tagebuchnotizen, Brief. Frankfurt am Main: Fischer Taschenbuch-Verl., 1992. 1 vol. (Originalausgabe).

VIII. AUTOBIOGRAPHIES, MEMOIRS, LETTERS, GENEALOGY

29867 ARENDT, HANNAH/JASPERS, KARL: *Correspondence 1926–1969*. Ed. and with an introd. by Lotte Kohler and Hans Saner. Transl. by Robert and Rita Kimber. New York: Harcourt Brace Jovanovich, 1992. 821 pp., notes (689–800), index of works by H.A. [For orig. German edn. see No. 22767/YB XXXI.]

29868 ARON, WELLESLEY: *Rebel with a cause: a memoir*. Ed. by Helen Silman-Cheong. Foreword by Samuel Lewis and Marcus Sieff. London: Vallentine Mitchell, 1992. XVIII, 206 pp. [W.A. 1901–1988, of German-Jewish descent, founder of the Habonim youth movement in Britain; assistant political secretary to Chaim Weizmann; first Palestinian Jewish major in the British army.]

29869 BAR-MENACHEM, ABRAHAM [formerly Alfred Gutsmuth]: *Bitterer Vergangenheit zum Trotz. Lebenserinnerungen, Reden eines Israelis aus Hessen*. Frankfurt am Main: Insel Verl., 1992. 212 pp., illus.

29870 BEER, FRITZ: *Hast du auf Deutsche geschossen, Grandpa? Fragmente einer Lebensgeschichte*. Berlin: Aufbau, 1992. 576 pp. (Schicksale im 20. Jahrhundert.) [F.B., b. Aug. 25, 1911 in Brünn, journalist, radio broadcaster, writer; functionary of the Czech Communist party, fled to England in 1939, left the Party in 1939, from 1946 until 1975 editor of the BBC German broad-casting programme, from 1988 president of the PEN-Zentrum Deutschsprachiger Autoren im Ausland.]

29871 BELL, SUSAN GLOAG: *Between worlds: in Czechoslovakia, England, and America*. New York: Dutton/Penguin, 1991. 228 pp., illus. [Author grew up in a Jewish family in Troppau, Sudetenland, before World War II. She and her mother fled to England; father died in a concentration camp. Returned to Czechoslovakia, then later to US.]

29872 BODENSTEIN, LEO: *Und plötzlich mußte ich englisch reden . . . Warum ein Kieler Amerikaner wurde*. Hrsg.: Leo Bodenstein, Florida. Sonderdruck für die Landeszentrale für Politische Bildung Schleswig-Holstein. Kiel, 1991. 296 pp., illus. [Memoirs of the author's youth in Kiel, his emigration to the USA and his experiences in post-war Germany, where he lived for twenty years.]

29873 BORCHARDT, RUDOLF/BUBER, MARTIN: *Briefe, Dokumente, Gespräche. 1907–1964*. In Zusammenarbeit mit Karl Neuwirth, hrsg. von Gerhard Schuster. Ebersberg: Rudolf-Borchardt-Ges. München, 1991. 168 pp. (Schriften der Rudolf-Borchardt-Gesellschaft, Bd. 2.)

29874 BUBER, MARTIN: *The letters of Martin Buber: a life of dialogue*. Ed. by Nahum N. Glatzer and Paul Mendes-Flohr. Transl. by Richard and Clara Winston and Harry Zohn. New York: Schocken Books (distr. Pantheon Books), 1992. XIII, 722 pp., illus., ports., bibl. [Seven decades of correspondence, a.o. with Agnon, Einstein, Kafka, Rosenzweig, Scholem, Weizmann.]

29875 CARLEBACH-PREUSS, LOTTE. GILLIS-CARLEBACH, MIRIAM: *Jedes Kind ist mein Einziges. Lotte Carlebach-Preuss. Antlitz einer Mutter und Rabbiner-Frau*. Hamburg: Dolling u. Gallwitz, 1992. 411 [2] pp., illus., family trees, index, bibl. (397–405), glossary (384–396). [Cont. letters of L.C.-P., b. Dec. 16, 1900 in Berlin, daughter of Dr. Julius Preuss, wife of Dr. Joseph Carlebach, deported with him and 4 of their 9 children from Hamburg in 1941 to Riga.] [Cf.: Bericht aus einer heilen und heiteren Familie (Jörg Bremer) [in]: Frankfurter Allgemeine Zeitung, Nr. 47, Frankfurt am Main, 25. Feb. 1993, p. 13.]

29876 CASSIRER HENRY A.: *Und alles kam anders . . . Ein Journalist erinnert sich*. Aus dem Engl. übers. [by the author]. Konstanz: Univ.-Verlag Konstanz, 1992. 346 pp., illus. (Journalismus, N.F., Bd. 30.) [Orig. title of book, publ. in 1989: Seeds in the wind of change. Through education and communication.] [H.A. C., b. Sept. 2, 1911 in Berlin, emigr. 1933 to UK, journalist, lives in France.]

29877 DEUTSCHKRON, INGE: *Unbequem . . . Mein Leben nach dem Überleben*. Köln: Verlag Wissenschaft und Politik, 1992. 248 pp., notes. [Cont. of the author's Ich trug den gelben Stern, first publ. in 1978, see No. 15142/YB XXIV.]

29878 DISPEKER, SIGMUND: *Dp. Sigmund Dispeker 1877–1961. Lebenserinnerungen eines Kasseler Journalisten*. Hrsg.: Stadtarchiv Kassel. Kassel, 1992. 111 pp., illus. (Kasseler Quellen und Studien.

Schriftenreihe des Magistrats der Stadt Kassel, Kleine Reihe 3.) [S.D., Dec. 12, 1877 Cologne – June 28, 1961 Haifa, journalist, emigr. in 1933 to France, 1942 via Spain to Palestine.]

29879 EDSCHMID, ULRIKE: *Verletzte Grenzen. Zwei Frauen, zwei Lebensgeschichten.* Hamburg: Luchterhand, 1992. 219 pp., illus., notes, index. [Biographies, based on interviews, of Lotte Fürnberg, née Wertheimer, the wife of the author Louis Fürnberg, and Monica Huchel, née Rosenthal, the wife of the author Peter Huchel, who both lived after the Second World War in the German Democratic Republic.]

29880 EYCK FAMILY. EYCK, FRANK: *A diarist in fin-de-siècle Berlin and her family. Helene, Joseph and Erich Eyck.* [In]: LBI Year Book XXXVII, London. Pp. 287–307, footnotes, ports. [On the historian Erich Eyck and his family.]

29881 FABER, ELMAR/WURM, CARSTEN, eds.: *Allein mit Lebensmittelkarten ist es nicht auszuhalten: Autoren- und Verlegerbriefe 1945–1949.* Berlin: Aufbau Taschenbuch Verlag, 1991. 412 pp., illus., facsims. [Incl. letters by Ernst Bloch, Lion Feuchtwanger, Wieland Herzfelde, Alfred Kantorowicz, Egon Erwin Kisch, Georg Lukacs, Nelly Sachs, Anna Seghers, Friedrich Wolf, Arnold Zweig.]

29882 FEUCHTWANGER, LION: *Der Teufel in Frankreich. Erlebnisse. Tagebuch 1940. Briefe.* Mit einem ergänzenden Bericht von Marta Feuchtwanger. Nachwort: Hans Dahlke. Anmerkungen und Textredaktion des Tagebuchs: Harold von Hofe. Berlin: Aufbau, 1992. 413 pp. (Schicksale im 20. Jahrhundert.) [First publ. in 1942 under the title Unholdes Frankreich. The author's memoirs on his internment in Les Milles and his later escape to the USA via Spain and Portugal. Incl. also his diary, written during his internment and which seemed to be lost when he wrote his memoirs in 1940/1941; incl. also letters of Marta and Lion Feuchtwanger and Marta Feuchtwanger's recollections of their flight (Die Flucht, 341–353).] [Cf.: Mausefalle Frankreich (Andreas Breitenstein) [in]: 'NZZ', Nr. 218, Zürich, 19./20. Sept. 1992, p. 68. Mein lieber Lion. Feuchtwangers Briefe aus dem Exil und das Lager-Tagebuch von 1940 (Fritz Rudolf Fries) [in]: Süddeutsche Zeitung, Nr. 152, München, 4./5. Juli 1992, p. IV.]

29883 FISCHER-DEFOY, CHRISTINE: *'Mein c'est la vie'-Leben in einer bewegten Zeit. Der Lebensweg der jüdischen Künstlerin. Gespräch über ein langes Leben in einer bewegten Zeit.* Berlin: Arsenal, 1992. 171 pp., illus., facsim., index. [Based on an interview with Paula Salomon-Lindberg, b. 1897 in Berlin, singer, active in the Jüdischer Kulturbund, since 1939 in the Netherlands, deported to Westerbork, escaped and survived with false papers.]

29884 FREUNDLICH, ELISABETH: *Die fahrenden Jahre. Erinnerungen.* Hrsg. und mit einem Nachwort von Susanne Alge. Salzburg: Otto Müller, 1992. 191 pp., illus. [E.F., b. 1906 in Vienna, film director, writer, emigr. 1938 via France, Spain, Portugal to the USA, returned to Austria in 1950; second wife of Günther Anders.] [Cf.: Kein Blick zurück im Zorn (Ulrich Weinzierl) [in]: Frankfurter Allgemeine Zeitung, Nr. 269, Frankfurt am Main, 19. Nov., 1992, p. 34.]

29885 FRIED, ANNE: *Farben des Lebens. Autobiographie.* Leipzig: Kiepenheuer, 1991. 220 pp. [Memoirs were orig. written in Finnish in 1987, transl. is based on an earlier unpubl. English version.] [A.F., b. 1903 in Vienna, social worker, writer, wife of the Hungarian painter Theodor Fried, emigr. from France in 1937 to the USA, lives since 1969 in Finland.] [Cf.: Besprechung (Hannes Stein) [in]: Frankfurter Allgemeine Zeitung, Nr. 109, Frankfurt am Main, 11. Mai, 1992, p.34.]

29886 FRIED, ERICH: *Mitunter sogar lachen: Erinnerungen.* Veränd. Neuausg. Berlin: Wagenbach, 1992. 156 pp., illus.

29887 FRUCHT, KARL: *Verlustanzeige. Ein Überlebensbericht.* Wien: Kremayr & Scheriau, 1992. 288 pp., illus. Vorwort: Brigitte Hamann. [K.F., 1911 Vienna – 1991 Vienna, jurist, publicist, founder (together with Hertha Pauli) of the 'Österreichische Korrespondenz', emigr. to Paris 1938, interned in South France, fled via the Pyrenees and Lisbon to the USA, during and after the war US-Army-Interrogation Officer, after the war technical writer, friend of George Grosz.]

29888 GAERTNER, HANS. SCHEEL, HEINRICH: *Ein jüdischer Lehrer an seinen einstigen Schüler. Briefe Hans Gaertners aus den Jahren 1946–1950.* [In]: Zeitschrift für Religions- und Geistesgeschichte, Jg. 43, Leiden, 1991. Pp. 18–29, footnotes. [H.G. (Jochanan Ginat), 1908 – Jerusalem 1979, teacher, director of the Herzl-Schule in Berlin, 1938 emigr. to Palestine, became Director of Youth Aliyah, from 1970–1978 Director of the LBI Jerusalem.]

29889 GENIN, SALOMEA: *Scheindl und Salomea. Von Lemberg nach Berlin.* Mit einem Nachwort von Wolfgang Benz. Frankfurt am Main: Fischer Taschenbuch Verlag, 1992. 150 pp., illus.

(Lebensbilder. Jüdische Erinnerungen und Zeugnisse, Bd. 3.) [Autobiography of a girl from an Eastern Jewish family from Lemberg, born in Berlin in 1932 and emigr. with her mother and sister to Australia in 1939, returned to Germany (East) after the war.]

29890 GOLDSCHMIDT, EDITH: *Drei Leben. Autobiographie einer deutschen Jüdin.* [Hrsg.: Stadt Steinfurt] Steinfurt: Stadt Steinfurt, 1992. 137 pp. (Steinfurter Schriften, 22.)

29891 GURWITZ, PERCY: *Zähl nicht nur, was bitter war. Eine baltische Chronik von Juden und Deutschen.* Berlin: Verl. Neues Leben, 1992. 356 pp. [P.G., b. 1919, a son of a German-speaking Jewish family from Riga and Göteborg, writer, 1941–1944 internment in ghettos and concentration camps, escaped with the help of Germans; 1950–1954 imprisoned in the GULAG, since 1975 professor in Wladimir, since 1990 Social Democratic city councillor in Wladimir.]

29892 HAUSER, MARTIN: *Wege jüdischer Selbstbehauptung. Tagebuchaufzeichnungen 1929–1967.* 3., erw. Aufl. Hrsg.: Bundeszentrale für politische Bildung, Bonn, 1992. 333 pp., illus., notes. (Schriftenreihe der Bundeszentrale für politische Bildung, Bonn, Bd. 109.) [For first edn., publ. in 1975 under the title Auf dem Heimweg. Aus den Tagebüchern eines deutschen Juden 1929–1945, see No. 12767/YB XXI.] [Author, born in 1921 in Berlin, emigr. in 1933 to Palestine, member of the Haganah, fought in the British army; lives in Ramat Gan nr. Tel-Aviv.]

29893 HAYMAN, EVA: *By the moon and the star.* Auckland, NZ: Random Century, 1992. 131 pp., illus., ports. [Book is based on diaries written during the war. Author left Czechoslovakia for London in 1939, her parents died in concentration camps, she moved to New Zealand in 1957.]

29894 HERZFELD, HANS: *Aus den Lebenserinnerungen.* Hrsg. von Willy Real. Berlin; New York: de Gruyter, 1992. VI, 217 pp., illus. (Veröffentlichungen der Hist. Kommission zu Berlin, Bd. 81.)

29895 HIRSCH, HELMUT & MARIANNE: *Stammte Margarethe Meyer-Schurz aus einer ursprünglich jüdischen Familie? Zur Problematik ihrer ersten Biographie.* [In]: Deutsch-jüdische Geschichte im 19. und 20. Jahrhundert [see No. 29601]. Pp. 85–106, footnotes. [Deals with the wife of Carl Schurz and Hannah Werwath Swart's biography, publ. in 1967, repr. in 1989.]

— HOMBURGER FAMILY. RAMON, ESTHER: *The Homburger family from Karlsruhe: a family study, 1674–1990.* [See No. 29144.]

29896 *Jüdische Familien-Forschung.* Hrsg.: K. Walter Apfelbaum. 4170 Geldern: Arthur Custos Gedächtnis-Archiv, 1992. 252 pp. [7 issues, June-Dec. 1992]. [Incl. mainly facsim. reprints of articles (sometimes without the detailed references) from the Jüdische Familien-Forschung. Mitteilungen der Gesellschaft für jüdische Familienforschung gegr. 1924 von Dr. Arthur Czellitzer. The archives of this periodical, which was publ. from 1924 until 1938, were acquired by the ed., K.W. Apfelbaum in 1980. Issues incl. editorial notes and reports on genealogical and other matters.]

29897 KLEEBERG, JULIUS J.: *Recollections of a medical Doctor in Jerusalem. From Professor Julius J. Kleeberg's notebooks 1930–1988.* Ed. by Philip Gillon. Basel: Karger, 1991. VIII, 174 pp., illus. [J.J. Kleeberg, July 10, 1894 Bösingsfeld/Lippe – April 15, 1988 Haifa, physician, scientist, emigr. to Palestine in 1930.] [Cf.: Besprechung (Eli Rothschild) [in]: 'MB', Jg. 60, Nr. 80, Tel Aviv, Juni 1992, p. 6.]

29898 KLINGER, RUTH: *Die Frau im Kaftan. Lebensbericht einer Schauspielerin.* Hrsg. und eingeleitet von Ludger Heid. Gerlingen: Bleicher, 1992. 368 pp. [Memoirs of R.K., 1906 Prague – 1989 Zürich, actress, emigr., friend and secretary (in Haifa 1943–1947) of Arnold Zweig.] [Cf.: Besprechung (Reuven Assor) [in]: Die Mahnung, Jg. 39, Nr. 9, Berlin, 1. Sept. 1992, p. 4.]

29899 KUCZYNSKI, JÜRGEN: *Kurze Bilanz eines langen Lebens. Große Fehler und kleine Nützlichkeiten.* Berlin: Elefanten Press, 1991. 144 pp.

29900 KUCZYNSKI, JÜRGEN: *Ein linientreuer Dissident. Memoiren 1945–1989.* Berlin: Aufbau, 1992. 436 pp.

29901 KURZWEIL, ZWI ERICH: *Abschied und Neubeginn. Aus dem Leben eines jüdischen Erziehers.* Frankfurt am Main: Waldemar Kramer, 1992. 140 pp., index (persons). [Incl.: Zum Geleit (Linda Reisch/Georg Heuberger, 7–8). Vorwort (Micha Brumlik, 9–10). Zwi Erich Kurzweil zum Geleit (Hans Thiel, 132–133).] [Z.E.K., 1911 Pirnitz (Moravia) – Jan. 4, 1992 Haifa [?], teacher, rabbi, professor of education, emigr. to Great Britain in 1938, lived in Haifa from 1950.]

29902 LAMBERT, ANNA: *Du kannst nicht davonlaufen. Erinnerungen einer auf sich selbst gestellten Frau.* Hrsg. und mit einem Nachwort von Robert Streibel. Aus dem Engl. von Alexander Potyka (Mitarbeit Inge Koleff). Wien: Picus, 1992. 188 pp., illus. [Personal memoirs of A.L. née

Kohn, b. 1906 in Krems; fled 1939 with her sons from Vienna to England without her non-Jewish husband; worked there as a nurse; now lives in Poole.]

29903 LAQUEUR, WALTER: *Thursday's child has far to go. A memoir of the journeying years.* New York: Macmillan, 1992. 418 pp., illus.

29904 LEWALD, FANNY: *Freiheit des Herzens. Lebensgeschichte – Briefe – Erinnerungen.* Hrsg. von Günter de Bruyn und Gerhard Wolf. Mit einem Nachwort von Gerhard Wolf. Frankfurt am Main: Ullstein, 1992. 347 pp., bibl. [of works by F.L.] [First publ. in Berlin (East) in 1987.]

29905 — *The education of Fanny Lewald: an autobiography.* Transl., ed., and annotated by Hanna Ballin Lewis. Albany: State Univ. of New York Press, 1992. XX, 341 pp., bibl. (331–335). (Suny series: women writers in translation). [Transl. of *Meine Lebensgeschichte*. F.L. (1811–1889) German-Jewish writer.]

29906 LIXL–PURCELL, ANDREAS, ed.: *Erinnerungen deutsch-jüdischer Frauen 1900–1990.* Hrsg. und mit einer Einleitung versehen von Andreas Lixl-Purcell. Leipzig: Reclam, 1992. 459 pp., ports., notes, bibl. [Incl. 33 published and unpublished autobiographical texts.]

29907 MARGOLIUS KOVÁLY, HEDA: *Eine Jüdin in Prag. Unter dem Schatten von Hitler und Stalin.* Aus dem Amerikanischen von Hans-H. Harbort. Berlin: Rowohlt, 1992. 256 pp. [Author, deported 1941 with her family from Prague to the ghetto of Lodz and several other concentration camps, fled from Auschwitz to Prague, married after the war Rudolf Margolius, who was one of the 11 Jews sentenced to death and executed in the course of the 'Slánský-Trial' 1952; lives in Brookline, Mass.] [The orginal edn. was publ. in 1986 under the title Under a cruel star. A life in Prague 1941–1968.]

29908 *Mein Elternhaus. Ein österreichisches Familienalbum.* Hrsg. von Georg Markus. Düsseldorf; New York [et al.]: Econ, 1990. 349 pp., ports., biographical notes. [A collection of childhood memoirs, incl. texts by Bruno Kreisky, Georg Kreisler, Simon Wiesenthal, Gottfried Reinhardt (the son of Max Reinhardt).]

29909 MOSSE, GEORGE L. RUNGE, IRENE/STELBRINK, UWE: *George Mosse: 'ich bleibe Emigrant'. Gespräche mit George L. Mosse.* Berlin: Dietz, 1992. 121 pp.

29910 MÜHSAM, PAUL: *Mein Weg zu mir. Aus Tagebüchern.* Hrsg. und kommentiert von Else Levi-Mühsam. Geleitwort von Werner Volke. Konstanz: Hartung-Gorre, 1992. 156 pp., illus. [For orig. edn., publ. in 1978, see 15737/YB XXIV.] [P.M., July 17, 1876 Brandenburg – March 11, 1960 Jerusalem, writer and lawyer, emigr. to Palestine in 1933.]

29911 PETUCHOWSKI, JAKOB J.: *Mein Judesein. Wege und Erfahrungen eines deutschen Rabbiners.* Freiburg: Herder, 1992. 155 pp., notes. [J.J.P., 1925 Berlin – Nov. 12, 1991 Cincinnati, rabbi, professor of Jewish-Christian Studies, went in 1939 with a 'Kindertransport' to Great Britain, student of Leo Baeck in England, later at the Hebrew Union College, Cincinnati.]

29912 SCHNABEL, ARTHUR: *Aus Dir wird nie ein Pianist.* Aus dem Amerikanischen, mit einem Vorwort und Anmerkungen von Hermann J. Metzler. Hofheim: Wolke, 1991. 295 pp., ports., illus., notes, index (289–295). [Orig. publ. under the title My life and music in 1970. A.S., pianist, composer, teacher, Apr. 17, 1882 Lipnik, Galicia – Aug. 15, 1951 Axenstein, Switzerland, emigr. to Italy in 1933, to the USA in 1939.]

29913 SCHUMANN, WILLY: *Being present: growing up in Hitler's Germany.* Kent, OH: Kent State Univ. Press, 1991. XI, 212 pp., illus. [Incl. attitudes to Jews and antisemitism.]

29914 SCHWEITZER, ALBERT/BRESSLAU, HELENE: *Die Jahre vor Lambarene. Briefe 1902–1912.* Hrsg. von Rhena Schweitzer Miller und Gustav Woytt. München: Beck, 1992. 406 pp., illus., notes, bibl., index of names (401–406). [Incl.: Einleitung. Zu Helene Bresslau (Rhena Schweitzer Miller, 16–20; on the author's mother and her family background, especially on her grandfather, the historian Harry Bresslau, who, though he did not convert, raised his three children in the Protestant faith.)] [H.B., born 1879 in Berlin, teacher, nurse, married to Albert Schweitzer in 1912.]

29915 SUSMAN, MARGARETE: *Das Nah- und Fernsein des Fremden.* Essays und Briefe. Hrsg. und mit einem Nachwort versehen von Ingeborg Nordmann. Frankfurt am Main: Jüdischer Verlag, 1992. 275 pp. [Cf.: Judentum und Frauenfrage (Egon Schwarz) [in]: Frankfurter Allgemeine Zeitung, Nr. 157, Frankfurt am Main, 9. Juli 1992, p. 30. Die grundlose Hoffnung (Elsbeth Pulver) [in]: 'NZZ', Nr. 266, Zürich, 14./15. Nov. 1992, pp. 67–68.]

29916 TAL, JOSEF: *Nachtrag zu einer Autobiographie.* [In]: Jüdischer Almanach 1993 [see No. 29248]. Frankfurt am Main, 1992. Pp. 150–154. [For previously publ. autobiography and data see No. 22815/YB XXXI.]

29917 SZONDI, PETER. SPARR, THOMAS: *Zu einem Brief von Peter Szondi.* [In]: Jüdischer Almanach 1993 [see No. 29248]. Frankfurt am Main, 1992. Pp. 83–88. [Incl. letter written to Gershom Scholem in 1970. P.S., 1929 Budapest – October 1971, Berlin (suicide), professor of literary studies.]

29918 TAMIR, ARNON: *Eine Reise zurück. Von den Schwierigkeiten Unrecht wiedergutzumachen.* Aus dem Hebräischen von A.F. Mit einem Nachwort von Klaus Binder. Frankfurt am Main: Fischer Taschenbuch Verlag, 1992. 140 pp. (Lebensbilder. Jüdische Erinnerungen und Zeugnisse, Bd. 5.) [A.T., formerly Arnold Siegfried Fischmann, b. 1917 in Stuttgart, member of Werkleute, deported to Poland in Oct. 1938, from where he emigr. illegally to Palestine, joining Kibbutz Hasorea.]

29919 UHLMAN, FRED: *Erinnerungen eines Stuttgarter Juden.* Aus dem Englischen übersetzt und hrsg. von Manfred Schmid. Stuttgart: Klett, 1992. 201 pp., illus. (Veröffentlichungen des Archivs der Stadt Stuttgart, Bd. 56.) [Autobiography, first publ. in 1960 under the title The making of an Englishman; see No. 2378/YB VI.]

29920 VARON, BENNO WEISER: *Professions of a lucky Jew.* New York: Cornwall Books, 1992. 431 pp., ports. [Author, b. in Czernowitz, grew up in Vienna, emigrated to Ecuador in 1938, where he became a political columnist. Through his work for the Jewish Agency, he became instrumental in 1946 in the campaign to persuade the Latin American countries to support a Jewish state in Palestine. Later he became Israeli ambassador to various Latin American states. He now teaches at Boston University.]

29921 ZINNEMANN, FRED: *A life in the movies. An autobiography.* London: Bloomsbury; New York: Charles Scribner's, 1992. 256 pp., illus. [F.Z., born 1908 in Vienna, film-director, from 1928 in Hollywood ('High Noon', 'From here to eternity').]

IX. GERMAN-JEWISH RELATIONS

A. General

29922 ALTGELD, WOLFGANG: *Katholizismus, Protestantismus, Judentum. Über religiös bedingte Gegensätze und nationalreligiöse Idee in der Geschichte des deutschen Nationalismus.* Mainz: Matthias-Grünewald Verlag, 1992. (Veröffentlichungen der Kommission für Zeitgeschichte: Reihe B, Forschungen, Bd. 59.) Zugl.: Karlsruhe, Univ., Habil.-Schr., 1990. [Deals also with antisemitism and anti-Judaism as constituents of German national movements.]

29923 *Aus zweier Zeugen Mund. Festschrift für Pnina Navé Levinson und Nathan Peter Levinson.* Hrsg. von Julius H. Schoeps. Gerlingen: Bleicher, 1992. 272 pp., footnotes. [A collection of 20 contributions mainly dealing with the theological aspects of Christian-Jewish relations. Incl.: Vorwort (Julius H. Schoeps, 7–9). Grußworte (Helmut Kohl, Lord [Donald] Coggan, Klaus Engelhardt, Klaus Hemmerle, Sir Sigmund Sternberg (13–18). Zwanzig Jahre Weggemeinschaft im Gesprächskreis 'Juden und Christen' beim Zentralkomitee der deutschen Katholiken (Hanspeter Heinz, 21–29). Von der Polemik zur Partnerschaft? Anmerkungen zum aktuellen Stand des jüdisch-christlichen Dialogs (Hildegard Gollinger, 101–113). Menschliche und künstliche Intelligenz. Notizen auch für eine Tagesordnung des jüdisch-christlichen Gespräches (Martin Stöhr, 117–128). Anhang (biographies and bibliographies of publications of P.N. & N.P. Levinson, 249–266). Further contributions relevant to German-Jewish history are listed according to subject.]

29924 BECKER, FRANZISKA/JEGGLE, UTZ: *Im Dorf erzählen – vor Gericht bezeugen. Zur inneren Logik von Sagen und Aussagen über NS-Gewalt gegen Juden.* [In]: Verdrängung und Vernichtung der Juden unter dem Nationalsozialismus [see No. 29366]. Hamburg: Christians, 1992. Pp. 311–332.

29925 BECKER, FRANZISKA: *Das beschwichtigte Gedächtnis oder: Wie man sich in einem schwäbischen Dorf an die Verfolgung der Juden im Nationalsozialismus erinnert.* [In]: Landjudentum im süddeutschen und Bodenseeraum [see No. 29018]. Pp. 197–207.

29926 BENZ, WOLFGANG: *The legend of German-Jewish symbiosis.* [In]: LBI Year Book XXXVII, London. Pp. 95–102, footnotes.

29927 BERGMANN, WERNER: *Die Reaktionen auf den Holocaust in Westdeutschland von 1945 bis 1989.* [In]: Geschichte in Wissenschaft und Unterricht, Jg. 43, Stuttgart. Pp. 327–350, footnotes.

29928 BRAUN, CHRISTINA VON: *'Der Jude' und 'das Weib'. Zwei Stereotypen des 'Anderen' in der Moderne.* [In]: Deutsch-jüdische Geschichte im 19. und 20. Jahrhundert [see No. 29601]. Pp. 289–322.

29929 COHEN, RICHARD I.: *The visual image of the Jew and Judaism in early modern Europe; from symbolism to realism.* [In Hebrew, with English summary]. [In]: Zion, Vol. 57, No. 3, Jerusalem, 1992.

Pp. 275–340. [On Jews depicted in works of art in the 16th-18th centuries in Germany (pp. 283–295; 326–339), Holland, and Italy.]

29930 *Coping with the past: Germany and Austria after 1945.* Ed. by Kathy Harms [et al.]. Madison: Univ. of Wisconsin Press, 1990. IX, 269 pp. [Collection of papers discussing how Austria and Germany have dealt with their Nazi past.]

29931 DAUTZENBERG, GERHARD: *Das christliche-jüdische Gespräch. Geschichte, Themen und Probleme.* [In]: Orientierung, Jg. 56, H. 10, Zürich, 1992. Pp. 121–123.

— *Deutsche Juden – Juden in Deutschland.* [See No. 29504.]

29932 DUBOIS, HORST: *Die Darstellung des Judenhutes im Hochmittelalter.* [In]: Archiv für Kulturgeschichte, Bd. 74, H. 2, Köln, 1992. Pp. 277–301, footnotes.

29933 FRANK, MARGRIT: *Jüdische Namen in deutschsprachiger Dichtung.* [In]: Nordisk Judaistik, Jg. 13, H. 1, Abo, 1992. Pp. 12–22.

29934 FREY, WINFRIED: *Pater noster Pyrenbitz. Zur sprachlichen Gestaltung jüdischer Figuren im deutschen Theater des Mittelalters.* [In]: Aschkenas, Jg. 2, Wien, 1992. Pp. 49–72.

29935 *German-Jewish reconciliation? Facing the past and looking to the future.* A Washington symposium, Dec. 15–17, 1991. A report by Peter Ross Range. Washington, DC: American Institute for Contemporary German Studies, 1991. 20 pp.

29936 GRENVILLE, JOHN: *Die Geschichtsschreibung der Bundesrepublik über die deutschen Juden.* [In]: Studien zur jüdischen Geschichte und Soziologie. Festschrift Julius Carlebach [see No. 29561]. Pp. 195–206.

29937 HEINRICHS, WOLFGANG: *Das Bild vom Juden in der protestantischen Judenmission des Deutschen Kaiserreich. In Umrissen dargestellt an den Äußerungen von 'Saat auf Hoffnung'. Zeitschrift für die Mission der Kirche an Israel.* [In]: Zeitschrift für Religions- und Geistesgeschichte, Jg. 44, Leiden, 1992. Pp. 195–220.

29938 HOFFMANN, CHRISTA: *Die justizielle 'Vergangenheitsbewältigung' in der Bundesrepublik Deutschland. Tatsachen und Legenden.* [In]: Die Schatten der Vergangenheit [see No. 29453]. Pp. 497–521, notes. [On the prosecution of Nazi crimes.]

29939 JESSE, ECKHARD: *Philosemitismus, Antisemitismus und Anti-Antisemitismus. Vergangenheitsbewältigung und Tabus.* [In]: Die Schatten der Vergangenheit [see No. 29453]. Pp. 543–567, notes.

29940 JODICE, DAVID A.: *United Germany and Jewish concerns. Attitudes toward Jews, Israel, and the Holocaust.* New York: The American Jewish Committee, 1991. 43 pp., tabs. (Working Papers on Contemporary Anti-Semitism.)

29941 *Jüdische Begegnungswoche der Stadt Witten vom 1. bis 8. Mai 1991.* Eine Dokumentation. Hrsg.: Stadt Witten. Der Stadtdirektor. Zusammenstellung: Martina Kliner-Lintzen, Siegfried Pape. 111 pp., illus., facsims. [On the visit of former citizens of Witten.]

29942 KANTZENBACH, FRIEDRICH WILHELM: *Exemplarische oder außerordentliche Modellfälle? Pfarrermentalität und Judentum im 19./20. Jahrhundert.* [In]: Deutsch-jüdische Geschichte im 19. und 20. Jahrhundert [see No. 29601]. Pp. 261–272.

29943 KNOCH-MUND, GABY: *Das Judenbild in der erzählenden Literatur des Mittelalters.* [In]: Berliner Theologische Zeitschrift, Jg. 8, Nr. 1, Berlin, 1991. Pp. 31–50.

29944 MAISLINGER, ANDREAS: *'Vergangenheitsbewältigung' in der Bundesrepublik Deutschland, der DDR und Österreich. Psychologisch-pädagogische Maßnahmen im Vergleich.* [In]: Die Schatten der Vergangenheit [see No. 29453]. Pp. 479–496, notes.

29945 NA'AMAN, SHLOMO: *Neues Licht auf das Verständnis der Judenfrage in der frühen sozialistischen Arbeiterbewegung.* [In]: Deutsch-jüdische Geschichte im 19. und 20. Jahrhundert [see No. 29601]. Pp. 131–143.

29946 NEIMAN, SUSAN: *Slow fire: Jewish notes from Berlin.* New York: Schocken Books, 1992. 306 pp. [Author, an American Jew, went to Berlin to study philosophy in 1982 and stayed six years. She discusses her experiences and the way Germans confront their past.]

29947 NOWAK, KURT: *Kulturprotestantismus und Judentum in der Weimarer Republik.* Göttingen: Wallstein, 1991 [also given:1993]. 48 pp., notes. (Kleine Schriften zur Aufklärung, 4.)

29948 ROENBERG, PETER: *Jude – ein Stigma? Die Darstellung der Juden in den religiösen Schauspielen.* [In]: Erziehungskunst, Jg. 54, Nr. 11, Stuttgart, 1990. Pp. 907 ff.

29949 ROSENBAUM, FRED/PICKETT, WINSTON: *Focus on the German question.* [In]: Reform Judaism, Vol. 20, No. 3, New York, Summer 1992. Pp. 19–35, illus, ports. [Several contributions on recent events in Germany, incl. by Emil Fackenheim: 'For visiting only'.]

29950 SCHUCHALTER, J.: *'Mein Eden, lieber Sigismund, öffnet seine Pforten nicht in Amerika': dissenting Jewish images in German popular fiction.* [In]: Nordisk Judaistik, Vol. 12, No. 2, Abo, 1991. Pp. 100–115.

29951 SHAFIR, SHLOMO: *Der Jüdische Weltkongress und sein Verhältnis zu Nachkriegsdeutschland (1945–1967)*. [In]: Menora, Bd. 3, München, 1992. Pp. 210–237, notes.
29952 STERN, FRANK: *The whitewashing of the yellow badge: antisemitism and philosemitism in postwar Germany*. Transl. by William Templer. Oxford; New York: Pergamon Press [for the Vidal Sassoon International Center for the Study of Antisemitism and the Hebrew University], 1992. XXV, 455 pp., bibl. (439–441). [Cf.: Reviews (Arnold Paucker) [in]: German Historical Institute London. Bulletin, Vol. XV, No. 1, London, Feb. 1993, pp. 22–57; (Richard Bosworth) [in]: German History, Vol. 11, No. 2, Oxford, June 1993, pp. 259–260.] [For German edn. publ. in 1991 see No. 28932/YB XXXVII.]
29953 STERN, FRANK: *Wider Antisemitismus – für christlich-jüdische Zusammenarbeit. Aus der Entstehungszeit der Gesellschaften und des Koordinierungsrats*. [In]: Menora, Bd. 3, München, 1992. Pp. 182–209, notes.
29954 WASSERMANN, HENRY: *Das Judentum und die Juden in der bürgerlichen Vorstellungswelt des 19. Jahrhunderts. Die Darstellungen in der Familienzeitschrift Gartenlaube*. [In]: Aschkenas, Jg. 2, Wien, 1992. Pp. 151–172.
29955 WOLFFSOHN, MICHAEL: *Das Bild als Gefahren- und Informationsquelle. Von der 'Judensau' über den 'Nathan' zum 'Stürmer' und zu Nachmann*. [In]: Die Schatten der Vergangenheit [see No. 29453]. Pp. 522–542, notes. [On the distorted and idealised images of Jews and their function in post-war Germany.]

B. German-Israeli Relations

29956 GIORDANO, RALPH, ed.: *Deutschland und Israel: Solidarität in der Bewährung. Bilanz und Perspektive der deutsch-israelischen Beziehungen*. Mit Beiträgen von Inge Deutschkron [et al.]. Gerlingen: Bleicher, 1992. 278 pp. [A collection of 27 essays by German and Israeli journalists, politicians, diplomats and theologians on several aspects and problems of German-Israeli relations. Incl. also a contribution on hostility to Israel and antisemitism in the German Democratic Republic (Konrad Weiss, 73–85).]
29957 JELINEK, YESHAYAHU: *The 'Locarno concept', the Hallstein doctrine and the Ostpolitik: Israel between the two Germanies*. [In]: Studien zur jüdischen Geschichte und Soziologie. Festschrift Julius Carlebach [see No. 29561]. Pp. 185–194.

C. Church and Synagogue

29958 BEN CHORIN, SCHALOM: *Theologia Judaica: gesammelte Aufsätze*. Bd. 2. Hrsg.: Verena Lenzen. Tübingen: Mohr, 1992. 308 pp., indexes (names, subjects, 299–308). [A collection of previously publ. articles and book reviews on the Christian – Jewish dialogue, incl. contributions dealing with Franz Rosenzweig, Gershom Scholem, Edith Stein.]
29959 *Christen und Juden. Voraussetzungen für ein erneuertes Verhältnis*. Hrsg. von Siegfried Schöer. Mit Beiträgen von Edna Brocke, Peter Fiedler, Hubert Frankemölller, Klemens Richter, Herbert Vorgrimler, Erich Ziegler. Altenberge: Oros, 1992. 157 pp.
29960 FALK, GERHARD: *The Jew in Christian theology: Martin Luther's anti-Jewish Vom Schem Hamphoras, previously unpublished in English, and other milestones in church doctrine concerning Judaism*. Jefferson, NC: McFarland, 1992. VIII, 296 pp., bibl. (283–290).
29961 FRANKFURT am Main. HEIL, JOHANNES: *Dom und Synagoge in Frankfurt 1140–1866*. [In]: Archiv für Mittelrheinische Kirchengeschichte, Jg. 43, Speyer, 1991. Pp. 51–78.
— FUNKENSTEIN, AMOS: *Juden, Christen und Muslime. Religiöse Polemik im Mittelalter*. [See in No. 29013.]
29962 HESSE. JASPERT, BERND, ed.: *Kirche und Juden in Hessen 1933–1945*. Dokumentation einer Tagung der Evangelischen Akademie Hofgeismar. Kassel: Verlag Evang. Presseverband, 1992. 99 pp., notes. [Essays on Rudolf Bultmann (Michael Wolter), Hans von Soden (Martin Hein), the Catholic Church (Klaus Wittstadt) and Jewish life in Germany today as a challenge for Christians (Hans Hermann Henrix).]
— JUNG, MARTIN: *Die württembergische Kirche und die Juden in der Zeit des Pietismus (1675–1780)*. [See No. 29194.]
29963 KUSCHEL, KARL-JOSEF: *Die Kirchen und das Judentum. Konsens- und Dissensanalyse auf der Basis neuerer kirchlicher Dokumente*. [In]: Stimmen der Zeit, Bd. 210, Freiburg i Br., 1992. Pp. 147–162, notes.

29964 MASER, PETER: *Synagoge und Ecclesia – Erwägungen zur Frühgeschichte des Kirchenbaus und der christlichen Bildkunst.* [In]: Kairos, Neue Folge, Jg. 32/33, Salzburg, 1990/1991. Pp. 9–26, notes.
29965 MCEWAN, DOROTHEA: *Christen und Judenhaß. Distanzierungsmechanismen der Kirche den Juden gegenüber.* [In]: Landjudentum im süddeutschen und Bodenseeraum [see No. 29018]. Pp. 163–177.
29966 REICHRATH, HANS: *Martin Bucer und die Juden. Die Frage nach der Einheit der 'Kirche'.* [In]: Judaica, Jg. 48, H.3, Basel, 3. Sept. 1992. Pp. 142–153, notes.
29967 *Religionsgespräche im Mittelalter.* Hrsg. von Bernard Lewis und Friedrich Niewöhner. Wiesbaden: Harrassowitz, 1992. 388 pp. (Wolfenbütteler Mittelalter-Studien, Bd.4.) [A collection of essays, also dealing with anti-Jewish Christian and Jewish anti-Christian polemics and disputes.]
— SCHUBERT, KURT: *Möglichkeiten und Grenzen des christlich-jüdischen und des jüdisch-christlichen Gesprächs* [see in No. 28992].
29968 UCKO, HANS: *Christlich-jüdischer Dialog. Diagnose und Prognose.* [In]: Ökumenische Rundschau, Jg. 41, H. 2, Frankfurt am Main, 1992. Pp. 147–159.

D. Antisemitism

29969 ALEXANDER, PHILIP S.: *The origins of religious and racial anti-semitism and the Jewish response.* [In]: The Jewish Enigma. An enduring people. Ed.: David Englander. London: Peter Halban, 1992. Pp. 169–196.
29970 *Der Antisemitismus und die Linke.* Hrsg.: Micha Brumlik, Doron Kiesel, Linda Reisch. Frankfurt am Main: Haag + Herchen, 1991. 97 pp., notes. (Arnoldshainer Texte – Band 72. Schriften aus der Arbeit der Evangelischen Akademie Arnoldshain.) [Incl.: Antisemitismus im Frühsozialismus und Anarchismus (Micha Brumlik, 7–16). Sozialdemokratie und Antisemitismus im deutschen Kaiserreich (Reinhard Rürup, 17–32). Assimilation – Integration – Korporation. Das jüdisch-sozialistische Arbeitsrecht von Weimar als Vehikel gesellschaftlichen Aufstiegs (Otto Ernst Kempen, 33–52). Die ideologische Verblendung – der Allgemeine Deutsche Gewerkschaftsbund angesichts der NS-Ideologie (Nikolaus Simon, 53–72). Täuschungen: Israel, die Linke und das Dilemma der Kritik (73–82). Die antisemitische Erbschaft in der Sowjetgesellschaft (Detlev Claussen, 83–95).]
29971 *Antisemitism world report 1992.* Ed.: Institute of Jewish Affairs. London: Institute of Jewish Affairs, 1992. 127 pp. [Incl. Austria (2–5), Germany (16–22), Switzerland (33–34).]
29972 AUSTRIA. DREIER, WERNER: *Antisemitismus in Vorarlberg: Bemerkungen zu Kontinuität und sozialer Relevanz.* [In]: Landjudentum im süddeutschen und Bodenseeraum [see No. 29018]. Pp. 179–189.
29973 — GREUSSING, KURT: *Die Erzeugung des Antisemitismus in Vorarlberg um 1900.* Bregenz: Vorarlberger Autoren Gesellschaft, 1992. 175 pp., notes, illus., bibl., index.
29974 — HAERPFER, CHRISTIAN: *The structure and extent of antisemitic attitudes in Austria.* [In]: Jewish Social Studies, Vol. 49, Nos. 3–4, New York, 1987 [publ. 1991]. Pp. 217–243, tabs.
29975 — PAULEY, BRUCE F.: *The United States and the Jewish Question in Austria.* [In]: LBI Year Book XXXVII, London. Pp. 481–496, footnotes.
29976 — WODAK, RUTH: *Le discours antijuif dans l'Autriche actuelle. Le langage de ceux qui ne veulent pas être antisemites.* [In]: Sexe et Race: Discours et formes nouvelles d'exclusion du XIXe au XXe siècle. Responsable de la publication: Rita Thalmann. Paris: CERG et Université Paris 7, 1991. Pp. 227–253, bibl., notes.
29977 BAUER, YEHUDA, ed.: *The danger of antisemitism in Central and Eastern Europe in the wake of 1989–1990.* Jerusalem: Institute of Contemporary Jewry, 1991. [Papers presented at a conference held in Jerusalem, Oct. 28–29, 1990.]
29978 BAUER, YEHUDA: *Vom christlichen Judenhaß zum modernen Antisemitismus. Ein Erklärungsversuch.* [In]: Jahrbuch für Antisemitismusforschung 1, Berlin 1992. Pp. 77–90.
29979 BERGMANN, WERNER/ERB, RAINER: *Privates Vorurteil und öffentliche Konflikte. Der Antisemitismus in Westdeutschland nach 1945.* [In]: Jahrbuch für Antisemitismusforschung 1, Berlin 1992. Pp. 13–41, notes.
29980 BERING, DIETZ: *The stigma of names: antisemitism in German daily life, 1812–1933.* Transl. by Neville Plaice. Cambridge: Polity; Ann Arbor: The Univ. of Michigan Press, 1992. 345 pp., illus., chronology, tabs., notes (283–303), index of first names and surnames, bibl. (304–

324). [This English edn. is abridged by one third from the German orig.; see No. 24811/YB XXXIII.]

29981 BESIER, GERHARD: *Anti-Bolshevism and antisemitism: the Catholic Church in Germany and National Socialist ideology 1936–37*. [In]: The Journal of Ecclesiastical History, Vol. 43, No. 3, Cambridge, July 1992. Pp. 447–456, notes.

29982 BOHLEBER, WERNER/KAFKA, JOHN S., eds.: *Antisemitismus*. Bielefeld: Aisthesis, 1992. 208 pp., notes. [Based on a conference of the Breuninger Kolleg on antisemitism held in Stuttgart in April 1991. Cont. the following contributions (each followed by discussions; titles partly condensed): Antisemitismus als Gegenstand interdisziplinärer Erforschung (Werner Bohleber, 11–17). Einleitende Bemerkungen (John S. Kafka, 18–19). Deutschland am Golf (Dan Diner, 20–38). Die 'Reichskristallnacht' als öffentliches Erniedrigungsritual (Peter Loewenberg, 39–64). Der Mord an den europäischen Juden und die Judenfeindschaft (Eberhard Jäckel, 65–74). Vom Gedanken zur Tat (Elisabeth Brainin/Samy Teicher, 75–82). Psychoanalytische Antisemitismustheorien im Vergleich (Hermann Beland, 93–125). Die Reaktion auf Fremde (Peter Neubauer, 126–141). Was ist Judentum ? (Gunnar Heinsohn, 142–162). Die antisemitische Alltagsreligion (Detlev Claussen, 163–173). Antisemitismus in der Bundesrepublik (Frank Stern, 174–196). Persönliche Anmerkungen (Arnost Lustig, 197–205).]

—— BRUMLIK, MICHA: *Antisemitismus im Frühsozialismus und Anarchismus* [see in No. 29014].

29983 CARMICHAEL, JOEL: *The satanizing of the Jews: origin and development of mystical anti-Semitism*. New York: Fromm, 1992. IX, 210 pp., footnotes. [Incl. Luther's and Hitler's antisemitism.]

—— COHEN, SUSAN SARAH, ed.: *Antisemitism: an annotated bibliography*. Vol. 2: 1986–1987. [See No. 29261.]

29984 DITTMAR, PETER: *Die Darstellung der Juden in der populären Kunst zur Zeit der Emanzipation*. Hrsg. vom Zentrum für Antisemitismuforschung der Technischen Universität Berlin. München; London [et.al.]: 1992. 282 pp., illus., notes (451–474), index (persons, 475–477). [Incl. also chapter on pre-Emancipation time.] [Cf.: Besprechung (Ludger Heid) [in]: Das Historisch-Politische Buch, Jg. 40, H. 9 und 10, Göttingen, 1992, p. 435.]

29985 ELSÄSSER, JÜRGEN: *Antisemitismus – das alte Gesicht des neuen Deutschland*. Berlin: Dietz, 1992. 158 pp., footnotes, bibl. [Incl.: Anhang: Antisemitismus und Verharmlosung des Nationalsozialismus in Politik und Öffentlichkeit. Eine Chronologie seit dem 9. November 1989.]

29986 ERB, RAINER, ed.: *Die Legende vom Ritualmord. Zur Geschichte der Blutbeschuldigung gegen Juden*. Berlin: Metropol, 1992. 395 pp.

29987 ERB, RAINER: *Der gekreuzigte Hund. Antijudaismus und Blutaberglaube im fränkischen Alltag des frühen 18. Jahrhundert*. [In]: Aschkenas, Jg. 2, Wien, 1992. Pp. 117–150.

29988 FISCHER, HELMUT, ed.: *Der braune Hass. Das Bilderbuch 'Trau keinem Fuchs auf grüner Heid und keinem Jud bei seinem Eid' von Elvira Bauer*. Essen: Institut für Jugend- und Volksliteratur, Fachbereich 3, Lit.- und Sprachwiss., Universität-Gesamthochschule Essen, 1991. 86 pp., illus., notes.

29989 FRIEDRICH, MARTIN: *Vom christlichen Antijudaismus zum modernen Antisemitismus. Die Auseinandersetzung um Assimilation, Emanzipation und Mission der Juden um die Wende zum 19. Jahrhundert*. [In]: Zeitschrift für Kirchengeschichte, Bd. 102, 1991, Vierte Folge XL, Stuttgart, 1991. Pp. 319–347, footnotes.

29990 GILMAN, SANDER: *The Jew's body*. London; New York: Routledge, 1991. IX, 303 pp., illus. [Incl. antisemitic rhetoric about the Jewish body and mind, also medical and popular depictions of Jewish attributes. Incl. Freud's views on Jews; Jewish self-perception.]

29991 GLAUERT, MARTIN: *Die antisemitischen 'Protokolle der Weisen von Zion'*. [In]: Lutherische Monatshefte, Jg. 31, H. 7, Hamburg, 1992. Pp. 304.

29992 GRIMM, REINHOLD: *The Jew, the playwright, and trash. West Germany's Fassbinder controversy*. [In]: Monatshefte, Vol. 83, No. 1, Madison, WI, Spring 1991. Pp. 17–28, notes. [On the debate triggered by Fassbinder's play *Der Müll, die Stadt und der Tod*; analyses also the antisemitic elements in the play.]

29993 HÄGLER, BRIGITTE: *Die Christen und die 'Judenfrage'. Am Beispiel der Schriften Osianders und Ecks zum Ritualmordvorwurf*. Erlangen: Palm & Enke, 1992. 274 pp., notes (211–251), bibl. (253–274). (Erlanger Studien, Bd. 97.) [On the ritual murder trials in Pösing 1529 and Eichstätt 1540; Andreas Osiander, Protestant pastor in Nuremberg, defended Jews against the polemical attacks of the Catholic theologian Johannes Eck.]

—— HERZIG, ARNO: *Judenhaß und Antisemitismus bei den Unterschichten und in der frühen Arbeiterbewegung* [see in No. 29014].

29994 HOFFMANN, CHRISTHARD: *Neue Studien zur Ideen- und Mentalitätengeschichte des Antisemitismus.* [In]: Jahrbuch für Antisemitismusforschung 1, Berlin 1992. Pp. 274–285, notes. [Review article.]

29995 HOFFMANN, ROBERT: *Gab es ein 'Schönerianisches Milieu'? Versuch einer Kollektivbiographie von Mitgliedern des 'Vereins der Salzburger Studenten in Wien'.* [In]: Bürgertum in der Habsburger Monarchie. Ed. by Ernst Bruchmüller [et al.]. Wien: Böhlau, 1990. Pp. 275–298, tabs., notes. [See also in No. 29215.]

29996 HOLZBACH-LINSENMAIER, HEIDRUN: *Der Sklarek-Skandal, die spektakulärste Korruptionsaffäre der Weimarer Republik, schadete dem Ansehen der jungen Demokratie und beflügelte die Hetzkampagnen der Republikgegner.* [In]: Die Zeit, Nr. 52, Hamburg, 18. Dez. 1992. P. 62.

29997 HORNSHOJ-MOLLER, STIG/CULBERT, DAVID: *'Der ewige Jude' (1940): Joseph Goebbels' unequalled monument to anti-Semitism.* [In]: Historical Journal of Film, Radio and Television, Vol. 12, No. 1, Houston, TX, 1992. Pp. 41–67, illus., ports., notes.

29998 HUSBANDS, CHRISTOPHER: *Neo-Nazis in East Germany: the new danger?* [In]: Patterns of Prejudice, Vol. 25, No. 1, London, Summer 1991. Pp. 1–17, notes. [Incl. antisemitism.]

29999 JÄGER, SIEGFRIED: *Brandsätze. Rassismus im Alltag.* Unter Mitarbeit von Ulrike Busse [et al.]. 2., durchgesehene Aufl. Duisburg: Duisburger Inst. für Sprach- und Sozialforschung (DISS), 1992. 310 pp., footnotes, bibl. [Also on attitudes towards Jews and antisemitism.]

30000 JAKOBOWICZ, RACHEL: *Jews and Gentiles: anti-Semitism and Jewish assimilation in German literary life in the early 19th century.* Bern; New York: Lang, 1992. 164 pp., bibl. (149–164). (Australian and New Zealand studies in German language and literature, 16.)

30001 KATZ, JAKOB: *L'antisémitisme: un point de vue juif.* [In]: Istina, Vol. 36, No. 3, Paris, 1991. Pp. 231–236.

— KOSZYK, KURT: *Sozialdemokratie und Antisemitismus zur Zeit der Dreyfus-Affäre* [see in No. 29014].

30002 KREMERS-SPER, THOMAS: *Antijüdische und antisemitische Momente in protestantischer Kapitalismuskritik: Eine Analyse evangelischer Kirchenzeitungen des Deutschen Kaiserreiches im Jahre 1878.* [In]: Zeitschrift für Religions- und Geistesgeschichte, Jg. 44, Leiden, 1992. Pp. 221–240, footnotes.

30003 KREN, GEORGE M./MORRIS, RODLER F.: *Race and spirituality: Arthur Dinter's theosophical antisemitism.* [In]: Holocaust and Genocide Studies, Vol. 6, No. 3, Oxford, 1991. Pp. 233–252, notes.

30004 KUSHNER, TONY: *The social and cultural roots of contemporary antisemitism.* [In]: Patterns of Prejudice, Vol. 25, No. 1, London, Summer 1991. Pp. 18–31, notes. [Incl. Germany.]

30005 LANGFORD, J.K.: *Germany: special report.* [In]: Connexions, No. 38, Oakland, CA, Winter 1992. Pp. 27–28. [Incl. present-day antisemitism and racism.]

30006 LEWIS, RAND C.: *A Nazi legacy: right-wing extremism in postwar Germany.* New York: Praeger, 1991. XVI, 184 pp.

30007 LINDNER, ERIK: *Houston Stewart Chamberlain: The Abwehrverein and the 'Praeceptor Germaniae', 1914-1918.* [In]: LBI Year Book XXXVII, London. Pp. 213–236, footnotes.

— LÜTHI, URS: *Der Mythos von der Weltverschwörung. Die Hetze der Schweizer Frontisten gegen Juden und Freimaurer am Beispiel des Berner Prozesses um die Protokolle der Weisen von Zion.* [See No. 29228.]

30008 MACINTYRE, BEN: *Forgotten fatherland: the search for Elisabeth Nietzsche.* London: Macmillan, 1992. 256 pp., illus., notes (219–240). [Deals with author's search for survivors of an 'Aryan' colony in Paraguay which was founded by Bernhard Förster and his wife Elisabeth (née Nietzsche) in the late 1880s.] [Cf. Nietzsche's perverted inheritance (R.J. Hollingdale) [in]: Guardian Weekly, London, April 19, 1992. Goosey-Goosey (Geoffrey Hawthorn) [in]: London Review of Books, May 28, 1992. The wicked sister (Malcolm Deas) [in]: TLS, London, April 3, 1992.]

30009 MITTEN, RICHARD: *The politics of antisemitic prejudice: the Waldheim phenomenon in Austria.* Boulder, CO: Oxford: Westview, 1992. IX, 260 pp.

— NA'AMAN, SHLOMO: *Die Judenfrage als Frage des Antisemitismus und des jüdischen Nationalismus in der klassischen Sozialdemokratie* [see in No. 29014].

30010 NICOSIA, FRANCIS R.: *Zionism and Palestine in anti-semitic thought in Imperial Germany.* [In]: Studies in Zionism, Vol. 13, No. 2, Ramat Aviv, 1992. Pp. 115–131.

30011 OCH, GUNNAR: *Alte Märchen von der Grausamkeit der Juden. Zur Rezeption judenfeindlicher Blutschuld-Mythen durch die Romantiker.* [In]: Aurora, Jg. 51, Sigmaringen, 1991. Pp. 81–94.

30012 RITCHIE, JAMES M.: *Artur Dinters antisemitische Trilogie.* [In]: Festschrift für Albert Schneider.

Publications du Centre Universitaire de Luxembourg. Germanistik. Luxembourg: Edn. Saint-Paul, 1992. Pp. 179–194.

30013 ROPER, KATHERINE: *German encounters with modernity: novels of Imperial Berlin*. London: Humanities Press 1991. 269 pp., notes, bibl. (246–259). [Incl. antisemitism and the depictions of Jews in novels; also chap. 'The outsiders: Berlin's Jews'.]

—— SCHULTZ, MAGDALENA: *Projektion versus Realität: der Ritualmord*. [See in No. 28992.]

30014 SIEGELE-WENSCHKEWITZ, LEONORE: *The discussion of anti-Judaism in feminist theology. A new area of Jewish-Christian dialogue*. [In]: Journal of Feminist Studies in Religion, Vol. 7, No. 2, Chico, CA, 1991. Pp. 95–98.

—— SILBERMANN, ALPHONS/SALLEN, HERBERT: *Juden in Westdeutschland. Selbstbild und Fremdbild einer Minorität*. [See No. 29523.]

30015 STERN, FRANK: *Von der Bühne auf die Straße. Der schwierige Umgang mit dem deutschen Antisemitismus in der politischen Kultur 1945 bis 1990. Eine Skizze*. [In]: Jahrbuch für Antisemitismusforschung 1, Berlin, 1992. Pp. 42–76, notes.

30016 STONE, MARLA: *Nationalism and identity in (former) East Germany*. [In]: Tikkun, Vol. 7, No. 6, Oakland, CA, Nov./Dec. 1992. Pp. 41–46. [Incl. neo-Nazism and antisemitism.]

30017 *Theatralia Judaica. Emanzipation und Antisemitismus als Momente der Theatergeschichte. Von der Lessing-Zeit bis zur Shoah*. Tübingen: Niemeyer, 1992. 356 pp., footnotes. (Theatron. Studien zur Geschichte und Theorie der dramatischen Künste, Bd. 7.) [Papers presented at a conference held in Bad Homburg, May 21-25, 1991. Incl. (titles partly condensed): Umrisse und Probleme des Themas (Hans-Peter Bayerdörfer, 1–23). Antijüdische Kontexte des frühen bürgerlichen Lachtheaters (Hans-Joachim Neubauer/Michael Schmidt, 85–114). Fragmente einer Bühnengeschichte Shylocks im deutschen und englischen Theater des 18. und 19. Jahrhunderts (Elmar Goerden, 129–163). Materialien zu Figur und Gestalt des Juden im Puppentheater des 19. Jahrhunderts (Manfred Wegner, 164–183). Auswirkungen antisemitischer Tendenzen in der Kulturpolitik auf das österreichische Theater (Hilde Haider-Pregler, 184–204). Antisemitismus im Musik- und Theaterleben der Weimarer Republik (Jens Malte Fischer, 228–243). Antisemitismus und Judenfiguren in der Dramatik des Dritten Reiches (Barbara Panse, 299–311). Die Auseinandersetzung mit dem Antisemitismus im Drama jüdischer Autoren während der 30er Jahre (Georg-Michael Schulz, 339–356). Further contributions are listed according to subject.]

30018 TREUE, WOLFGANG: *Schlechte und gute Christen. Zur Rolle von Christen in antijüdischen Ritualmord- und Hostienschändungslegenden*. [In]: Aschkenas, Jg. 2, Wien, 1992. Pp. 95–116.

30019 WACKER, MARIE THERES: *Feminist theology and anti-Judaism : the status of the discussion and the context of the problem in the Federal Republic of Germany*. [In]: Journal of Feminist Studies in Religion, Vol. 7, No. 2, Chico, CA, 1991. Pp. 109–116.

30020 WELCH, DAVID: *'Jews out!': Anti-semitic film propaganda in Nazi Germany and the 'Jewish Question'*. [In]: The British Journal of Holocaust Education, Vol. 1, London, Summer 1992. Pp. 55–73.

30021 WISTRICH, ROBERT S.: *The longest hatred*. [In]: Partisan Review, Vol. 59, No. 2, Boston, Spring 1992. Pp. 216–224. [Deals with antisemitism in history.]

30022 WISTRICH, ROBERT S.: *Once again, antisemitism without Jews*. [In]: Commentary, Vol. 94, No. 2, New York, Aug. 1992. Pp. 45–49. [Incl. present-day Germany and Austria.]

30023 WISTRICH, ROBERT S.: *Socialism and Judeophobia – antisemitism in Europe before 1914*. [In]: LBI Year Book XXXVII, London. Pp. 111–145, footnotes.

E. Noted Germans and Jews

30024 ARNIM, BETTINA von. ZIMMERMANN, UWE: *Liberalismus als privater Reflexions- und Kommunikationsprozess. Anmerkungen zum Briefwechsel zwischen Bettina von Arnim und Heinrich Bernhard Oppenheim*. [In]: Jahrbuch zur Liberalismus-Forschung 3, Baden-Baden, 1991. Pp. 157–163.

30025 BLÜHER, HANS. DELF, HANNA: *Als Zeichen der Getrenntheit oder Eine Fensterscheibenangelegenheit. Gustav Landauer und Hans Blüher*. [In]: Deutsch-jüdische Geschichte im 19. und 20. Jahrhundert [see No. 29601]. Pp. 323–336.

30026 BONHOEFFER, DIETRICH. BETHGE, EBERHARD: *Dietrich Bonhoeffer: one of the silent bystanders?* [In]: European Judaism, Vol. 25, No. 1, London, Spring 1992. Pp. 33–40.

[Discusses Bonhoeffer's feelings about the events of the 'Kristallnacht' which he expressed in private to his students and in his diary, although he kept silent in public.]

30027 CALVIN, JOHANNES. ROBINSON, JACK HUGHES: *John Calvin and the Jews*. Frankfurt am Main; New York [et al.]: Lang, 1992. 152 pp., notes, bibl. (126–146), index. (American University Studies, Series VII: Theology and Religion, 123.)

—— CAROSSA, HANS. HORCH, HANS OTTO: *Ungleiche Welten. Ludwig Strauss im Briefwechsel mit Hans Carossa. Zum 100. Geburtstag des deutsch-jüdischen Dichters und Literaturwissenschaftlers am 28. Oktober 1992*. [See No. 29848.]

30028 DOHM, CHRISTIAN WILHELM. BERNARDINI, PAOLO: *La questione ebraica nel tardo illuminismo tedesco. Studi intorno allo 'Über die bürgerliche Verbesserung der Juden' di C.W. Dohm (1781)*. Firenze: Giuntina, 1992. 191 pp.

—— — MÖLLER, HORST: *Über die bürgerliche Verbesserung der Juden: Christian Wilhelm Dohm und seine Gegner* [see in No. 29083].

30029 FICHTE, JOHANN GOTTLIEB. GRAB, WALTER: *Fichtes Judenfeindschaft*. [In]: Zeitschrift für Religions- und Geistesgeschichte, Jg. 44, Leiden, 1992. Pp. 70–75, footnotes.

30030 FRANTZ, CONSTANTIN. DREYER, M.: *Judenhass und Antisemitismus bei Constantin Frantz*. [In]: Historisches Jahrbuch, Jg. 111, Nr. 1, München, 1991. Pp. 137–147.

30031 FREYTAG, GUSTAV. MATONI, JÜRGEN: *Die Juden in Gustav Freytags Werken*. Oberschlesisches Jahrbuch 1992. Bd. 8. Berlin: Mann, 1992. Pp. 107–124, footnotes.

30032 FURTWÄNGLER, WILHELM. SHIRAKAWA, SAM: *The devil's music master: the controversial life and career of Wilhelm Furtwängler*. New York; Oxford: Oxford Univ. Press, 1992. XVI, 506 pp., illus., bibl. [Covers Furtwängler's relationship with Jewish musicians.] [Cf.: Ars longa, spoon longer (Valentine Cunningham) [in]: Observer, London, Oct. 25, 1992.]

30033 GOETHE, JOHANN WOLFGANG. LEVY, ZE'EV: *Between Goethe and Spinoza – the Jewish view*. [In Hebrew, title transl.]. [In]: Tura; Studies in Jewish thought, Vol. 2, Oranim/Tel-Aviv, 1992. Pp. 199–213. [On Goethe's interest in Spinoza and in Judaism.]

30034 GOTTHELF, JEREMIAS. THOMMEN, CHRISTIAN: *Jeremias Gotthelf und die Juden*. Bern; New York [et al.]: Lang, 1991. 227 pp. (Zürcher germanistische Studien, Bd. 27.) Zugl.: Zürich, Univ., Diss., 1991.

30035 HEGEL, GEORG FRIEDRICH. SONNENSCHMIDT, REINHARD: *Zum philosophischen Antisemitismus bei G.W.F.Hegel*. [In]: Zeitschrift für Religions- und Geistesgeschichte, Jg. 44, Leiden, 1992. Pp. 289–301, footnotes.

30036 HEIDEGGER, MARTIN. BARASH, JEFFREY ANDREW: *Martin Heidegger in the perspective of the twentieth century: reflections on the Heidegger Gesamtausgabe*. [In]: Journal of Modern History, Vol. 64, No. 2, Chicago, March 1992. Pp. 52–78, footnotes. [Incl. H.'s relationships with Jews, especially Hannah Arendt.] [See also: Hannah Arendt und Martin Heidegger. Chronik einer Begegnung (Karol Sauerland) [in]: 'NZZ', Nr. 260, Zürich, 7./8.Nov. 1992, p. 66. Der aufgehobene Zweifel. Hannah Arendt und Martin Heidegger (Brigitte Seebacher-Brandt) [in]: Frankfurter Allgemeine Zeitung, Nr. 31, Frankfurt am Main, 6. Feb. 1992, Beilage: Bilder und Zeiten.]

30037 —— — GRANGE, JOSEPH: *Heidegger as Nazi – a postmodern scandal*. [In]: Philosophy East and West, Vol. 41, No. 4, Honolulu, Oct. 1991. Pp. 515–523. [Incl. Heidegger's reply to Victor Farias's book.]

30038 —— — ROCKMORE, TOM: *On Heidegger's Nazism and philosophy*. Berkeley: Univ. of California Press, 1992. XI, 382 pp., bibl.

30039 —— — ROCKMORE, TOM/MARGOLIS, JOSEPH, eds.: *The Heidegger case: on philosophy and politics*. Philadelphia: Temple Univ. Press, 1992. XI, 437 pp. [Heidegger and National Socialism.]

30040 HEISENBERG, WERNER: *Deutsche und jüdische Physik*. Hrsg. von Helmut Rechenberg. München: Piper, 1992. 212 pp. (Serie Piper.) [Refers also to the expulsion of Jewish physicists.]

30041 —— — CASSIDY, DAVID C.: *Uncertainty: the life and science of Werner Heisenberg*. New York: Freeman, 1992. XII, 669 pp., illus., bibl. [Incl. the treatment and dismissal of Jewish scientists and the resulting loss to German physics. Also discusses H.'s failure to oppose this, and his subsequent fight against the establishing of 'German physics'. Also on his later accommodation with the Nazis.] [Cf.: Heisenberg, German science, and the Third Reich (David C. Cassidy) [in]: Social Research, Vol. 59, No. 3, New York, Fall 1992. pp. 643–661, footnotes.]

30042 HESSE, HERMANN. PFEIFER, MARTIN: *Hermann Hesse und das Judentum. Zum 30. Todestag des Dichters und Nobelpreisträgers am 9. August*. [In]: Tribüne, Jg. 31, H. 122, Frankfurt am Main, 1992. Pp. 200–206, illus.

30043 JUNG, CARL GUSTAV. ANCORI, MICHA: *Jung and the Jewish problem.* [In Hebrew]. [In]: Sichot-Dialogue: Israel Journal of Psychotherapy, Vol. 6, No. 2, Ramat Hasharon, March 1992. Pp. 195–197. [A response to 3 articles by Micha Neumann on Jung in 'Sichot' 2,1 (1987), 2,3 (1988), and 5,3 (1991). States that Jung was not an antisemite.]

30044 KAUFMANN, WALTER: *Discovering the mind.* Vol. 2: *Nietzsche, Heidegger, and Buber.* New introd. by Ivan Soll. New Brunswick, NJ: Transaction, 1991. 306 pp. [First publ. in 1980; see No. 18513/YB XXVII, also for preceding and subsequent vols.]

30045 KLEPPER, JOCHEN. NOWOCZIN, HANS GERD: *Leiden und Glauben. Zum 50. Todestag von Jochen Klepper.* [In]: Tribüne, Jg. 31, H. 124, Frankfurt am Main, 1992. Pp. 183–187. [J.K., March 22, 1903 Beuthen – Dec. 11, 1942 Berlin, author, committed suicide with his Jewish wife and her daughter.]

—— LESSING, GOTTHOLD EPHRAIM. BAUER, GERHARD: *Die 'natürliche' Toleranz und die unendliche Bemühung der Vernunft, sie zu begründen* [see in No. 29083].

30046 — ENGEL-HOLLAND, EVA J.: *Lessing, Mendelssohn, Friedrich II. – Das Jahr 1771.* [In]: Mendelssohn Studien, Bd. 7. Berlin: Duncker & Humblot, 1990. Pp. 21–38.

30047 — OCH, GUNNAR: *Lessings Lustspiel 'Die Juden' im 18. Jahrhundert.* [In]: Theatralia Judaica [see No. 30017]. Pp. 42–63.

30048 MAHLER, ALMA. GIROUD, FRANÇOISE: *Alma Mahler: or the art of being loved.* Ed. and transl. by R.M. Stock. New York: Oxford Univ. Press, 1991. 162 pp., illus. [Mainly on A.M.'s marriage to Mahler, but also her relationships and friendships with Canetti, Freud, Hofmannsthal, Kraus, Schönberg, a.o.]

30049 — KEEGAN, SUSANNE: *The bride of the wind: the life and times of Alma Mahler-Werfel.* London: Secker & Warburg, 1991; New York: Viking, 1992. XVI, 346 pp., illus., ports., bibl. (329–331).

30050 NIETZSCHE, FRIEDRICH. ASCHHEIM, STEVEN A.: *Nietzsche and the Nietzschean moment in Jewish life (1890–1939).* [In]: LBI Year Book XXXVII, London. Pp. 189–212, footnotes. [On Jewish champions, purveyors and critics of Nietzsche's philosophy.]

30051 RIEM, ANDREAS. GRAB, WALTER: *Der deutsche Jakobiner Andreas Riem und seine 'Apologie für die unterdrückte Judenschaft in Deutschland'.* [In]: Deutsch-jüdische Geschichte im 19. und 20. Jahrhundert [see No. 29601]. Pp. 63–84.

30052 SCHWEITZER, ALBERT. KICKEL, WALTER: *Albert Schweitzers Bedeutung für den christlich-jüdischen Dialog* [In]: Judaica, 48. Jg., H. 3, Basel, Sept. 1992. Pp. 154–164, notes.

30053 WAGNER, RICHARD. BERGLER, SIEGFRIED: *'Erlösung dem Erlöser': Richard Wagner (1813–1883) zwischen Antisemitismus und Antijudaismus.* [In]: Judaica, Jg. 48, H. 3, Basel, Sept. 1992. Pp. 165–176, notes.

30054 — DOLEV, AHARON: *Why not Wagner.* [In Hebrew]. [In]: Nativ, Vol. 5, No. 5, Tel-Aviv, Sept. 1992. Pp. 36–43. [Describes Wagner's antisemitism and the influence of his ideas on Hitler.]

30055 — ROSE, PAUL LAWRENCE: *Wagner, race and revolution.* London: Faber; New Haven, CT: Yale Univ. Press, 1992. 288 pp., musical scores, appendixes, notes (193–231). [Deals with Wagner's antisemitism and racial themes in his operas.] [Cf.: From sublime to subliminal (Michael Tanner) [in]: TLS, London, July 17, 1992. The food of hate (Hugh Canning) [in]: The Sunday Times, London, July 5, 1992.]

X. FICTION and POETRY

30056 ANDERS, GÜNTHER: *Die molussische Katakombe.* Roman. München: Beck, 1992. 332 pp. [Cf.: Was geht mich meine Hoffnung an (Fritz J. Raddatz) [in]: Die Zeit, Nr. 22, Hamburg, 22. Mai 1992, Lit. Obits.: Freund Hein, Feind Hein (Ludger Lütkehaus) [in]: Die Zeit, Nr. 1, Hamburg, 1. Jan. 1993; Das prophetische Erschrecken (Elisabeth Endres) [in]: Süddeutsche Zeitung, Nr. 293, München, 19./20. Dez., 1992, p.5. See also a selection of previous publ. essays on G.A.: 'Mein Interesse gilt der Welt'. Zum 10. Geburtstag von Günther Anders (Joachim Güntner) [in]: 'NZZ', Nr. 158, Zürich, 10. Juli 1992, p. 19; Der Andersdenkene (Volker Hage) [in]: Die Zeit, Nr. 29, Hamburg, 10. Juli 1992, p. 47; Wir sind schreibende Analphabeten. Laudatio zur Verleihung des Sigmund-Freud-Preises an Günther Anders (Ludger Lütkehaus) [in]: Süddeutsche Zeitung, Nr. 237, München, 14. Okt. 1992, p. 15.] [G.A., July 12, 1902 Breslau – 1992, son of Clara and William Stern, first husband of Hannah Arendt, philosopher, emigr. in 1933 via France to the USA, returned to Austria in 1950.]

30057 APPELFELD, AHARON: *Katerina.* Transl. by Jeffrey M. Green. New York: Random House, 1992. 212 pp.
30058 FRIED, ERICH: *Children and fools.* Transl. by Martin Chalmers. London: Serpent's Tail, 1992. 192 pp. [Short stories, also on the Nazi experience.]
30059 HAMBURGER, MICHAEL: *Roots in the air.* London: Anvil, 1991. 103 pp.
30060 JENS, WALTER: *Ein Jud aus Hechingen. Requiem für Paul Levi.* Stuttgart: Radius, 1991. 58 pp. [Drama; P.L., March 11, 1883 Hechingen – Feb. 10, 1930 Berlin (suicide), lawyer, Socialist politician.]
30061 KOEPPEN, WOLFGANG: *Jakob Littners Aufzeichnungen aus einem Erdloch.* Roman. Frankfurt am Main: Jüdischer Verlag, 1992. 150 pp. [Personal recollections of a Munich stamp dealer, who dictated his story of persecution and survival to the author after the Second World War. The author wrote a novel based on this story, publ. in 1947 with Jakob Littner as the pseudonym.] [Cf.: Literarisches Carepaket. Ein Pseudonym wurde nach 45 Jahren gelüftet (Eberhard Falcke) [in]: Die Zeit, Nr. 20, Hamburg, 8. Mai 1992. 7 Lit.]
30062 MAREK, LIONEL: *Nächstes Jahr in Auschwitz.* Roman. Transl. from the French by Evelyn Roboz. Berlin: Karin Kramer, 1992. 1 vol. [Title of orig. French edn.: L'an prochain à Auschwitz.]
30063 MICHAELIS, MIRIAM: *Ein Brief an Ophira.* Erzählungen. Klagenfurt (Mozartstraße 61/6/19): Mnemosyne, 1992. 77 pp. (Mnemosyne-Schriften, Bd. 4.) [Incl. biographical note by author, b. 1908 in Berlin, who was a co-founder of Kibbutz Dalia, where she has lived since her emigration from Berlin in 1938.]
30064 PERUTZ, LEO: *The Swedish cavalier.* Transl. by John Brownjohn. London: Harvill, 1992. 192 pp. [First publ. in German in 1936.]
30065 PERUTZ, LEO: *Little apple.* Transl. by John Brownjohn. London: Harvill; New York: Arcade. 1992. 199 pp. [First publ. in German in 1928; L.P., 1884–1957, Prague novelist.]
30066 PRAWER, S.S.: *Israel at Vanity Fair. Jews and Judaism in the writings of W.M. Thackeray.* Leiden: Brill, 1992. 439 pp., illus. (Brill's Series in Jewish Studies.) [Incl. characters of German Jews in the work of Thackeray.]
30067 SAHL, HANS: *Der Tod des Akrobaten:* Erzählungen. Hamburg: Luchterhand, 1992. 186 pp. [See also Nos. 29841 and 29842.]
30068 SCHINDEL, ROBERT: *Gebürtig.* Roman. Frankfurt am Main: Suhrkamp, 1992. 358 pp., glossary. [On the awkwardness, prejudices, and complexities of the relationship between Jews and non-Jews in post-war Austria.] [Cf.: Doppellämmer und Tätersöhne (Hubert Winkels) [in]: Die Zeit, Nr. 16, Hamburg, 16. April, 1992, p. 4 Lit.; Unterm Schuldgestirn leben (Gunhild Kübler) [in]: 'NZZ',Nr. 66, Zürich, 19. März 1922, p. 27.]
30069 SCHNITZLER, ARTHUR: *The road to the open.* Transl. from the German by Horace Samuel. Evanston, IL: Northwestern Univ. Press, 1991. XX, 412 pp. [First publ. in 1908.]
30070 SCHULZ, BRUNO: *Gesammelte Werke in zwei Bänden.* 2 vols. Bd. 1: Die Zimtläden und alle anderen Erzählungen. Hrsg. von Mikolaj Dutsch. Aus dem Poln. von Josef Hahn. 384 pp. Bd.2: Die Wirklichkeit ist Schatten des Wortes. Aufsätze und Briefe. Hrsg. von Jerzy Ficowski. Aus dem Poln. von Mikolaj Dutsch und Josef Hahn. 399 pp. München: Hanser, 1992. [B.Sch., July 1892 Drohabycz, Galicia – Nov. 19, 1942 Drohabycz (murdered by the Gestapo).] [See also the catalogue of the exhibition held in Berlin 1 – April 5, 1992 and Munich, April 15–May 31, 1992: Bruno Schulz 1892–1942. Das graphische Werk. Hrsg.: Münchner Stadtmuseum München [et al.]. Katalogred.: M.Wojciech Chmurzynski [et al.]. München: Hanser, 1992. 144 pp., illus., facsims., docs.; incl. biography of B. Sch.] [See also essays on the life and work of B. Sch.: Wenn die Wirklichkeit die Alpträume übertrifft (Ellen Presser) [in] Börsenblatt für den deutschen Buchhandel, Nr. 43, Frankfurt am Main, 29. Mai 1992. A 206–209, port., illus. Die Zaubermühle der Poesie (Andreas Breitenstein) [in]: 'NZZ', Nr. 159, Zürich, 11./12. Juli 1992. P. 54, port. Die zweite Genesis. Zum 100. Geburtstag des Dichters Bruno Schulz (Peter Hamm) [in]: Die Zeit, Nr. 29, Hamburg, 10. Juli 1992, p. 49. Zauberlehrer und Verwandlungskünstler (Wilfried F. Schoeller) [in]: Süddeutsche Zeitung, Nr. 158, München, 11./12. Juli 1992, p. IV.]
30071 SCHUTZ, DAVID: *Gras und Sand.* Aus dem Hebräischen von Judith Brüll-Assan und Ruth Achlama. Hildesheim: Claassen, 1992. 323 pp. [First publ. in Hebrew in 1978 under the title Ha-esev Ve-hahol; autobiographical novel of author, a writer and film producer, b. 1941 in Berlin, who went as an unaccompanied child to Palestine in 1948.]
30072 STERN, CARL: *Gedichte.* Aus dem Nachlaß ausgewählt und mit einem Nachwort versehen von Tilly Boesche-Zacharow. Klagenfurt (Mozartstr. 61/6/19): Mnemosyne, 1992. 53 pp.

(Mnemosyne-Schriften, Bd. 3.) [C.St., Jan. 6, 1918 Troppau – June 26, 1985 Jerusalem, photographer, poet, emigr. to Palestine from Prague in 1938.]

30073 TREUE, WILHELM: *Eine Frau, drei Männer und eine Kunstfigur. Barocke Lebensläufe.* München: Beck, 1992. 284 pp., illus., notes (274–284). [Based on authentic documents, author describes in semi-fictional way the life of 5 people during the seventeenth century. One of these is Salomon Herz Löw Oppenheim (1640–1697) of Frankfurt am Main.] [Cf.: An der Schwelle zur Moderne (Rebekka Habermas) [in]: Die Zeit, Nr. 34, Hamburg, 14. Aug., 1992, p. 18.]

30074 WEIL, JIRI: *Mendelssohn is on the roof.* Transl. from the Czech by Marie Winn. New York: Farrar, Straus & Giroux, 1991. 227 pp. [A novel about Jewish life in Nazi-occupied Prague.]

30075 WEIL, GRETE: *Tramhalte Bethovenstraat.* Zürich: Nagel & Kimche, 1992. 1 vol. [Autobiographical novel on the persecution of Jews in Nazi-occupied Amsterdam, first publ. in 1963.] [Cf.: Die Schreckenstopographie Amsterdams (Beatrice Eichmann-Leutenegger) [in]: 'NZZ', Nr. 137, Zürich, 16. Juni 1992, p. 27.]

Index to Bibliography

Aachen, 29067, 29169, 29269
Aargau, 29226
Abraham, Ulf, 29673
Abram, Ido B.H., 29542
Abrams, Bradley F., 29214
Abramson, Shraga, 29558
Adelmann, Karin, 29632
Adler, Felix, 29235
Adler, Hermann, 29061
Adler, Max, 29713
Adorno, Theodor W., 29714, 29812, 29858
Adunka, Evelyn, 29670
Agnon, Samuel Josef, 29248, 29874
Ahrweiler, 29068
Aichinger, Ilse, 29384
'AJR Information', 29246, 29752
Alberg, Werner, 29671
Albert-Lasard, Lou, 29361
Albrecht, Frank, 29262
Aldenhoven, 29069–29071
Alexander, Philip S., 29969
Alge, Susanne, 29884
'Allgemeine' Jüd. Wochenzeitung, 29169, 29172, 29368, 29498, 29506, 29545
'Allgemeine Zeitung des Judentums', 29637
'Alma Mater Philippina', 29743
Alpert, Carl, 29314
Alsace, 29196
Alter, Anne, 29647
Alter, Robert, 29754
Altgeld, Wolfgang, 29922
Althaus, Manon, 29289
Altmann, Alexander, 29554, 29555
Altona, 29025, 29072, 29073
Aly, Götz, 29381
'American Academy for Jewish Research. Proceedings', 29015
'American Scholar', 29500
Amichai, Jehuda, 29248
Amir, Yehoyada, 29589
Amnon of Mainz, 29023
Amsterdam, 29682, 29791, 30075
Améry, Jean, 29715
Ancori, Micha, 30043
Anderl, Gabriele, 29282, 29478
Andernach, 29169
Anders, Günther, 30056
Angress, Werner T., 29310

'Annalen des Historischen Vereins für den Niederrhein', 29069, 29070, 29169, 29829
Annas, George, 29270
Anschluss, 29278, 29414
Anti-Judaism (see also Antisemitism, Christian), 29922, 29960, 29967, 29987, 29993, 30014, 30019, 30053
Antisemitism (see also Austria), 29014, 29261, 29405, 29623, 29701, 29821, 29922, 29928, 29969–30023, 30029, 30030, 30035, 30053–30055
— Christian (see also Blood Libel), 29960, 29965, 29984, 29986, 29993
— Defence, 29939, 29969, 30007, 30017
— Hungary, 29223
— Imperial Germany, 30002, 30013
— Jewish, 29621
— Middle Ages, 29165
— Nazi, 29310, 29313, 29331, 29356, 29357, 29376, 29473, 29913, 29988, 30017, 30020
— Post War, 29258, 29373, 29501, 29505, 29523, 29939, 29940, 29952, 29956, 29971, 29975, 29977, 29979, 29982, 29985, 29992, 29998, 29999, 30004–30006, 30015, 30016, 30022
— Switzerland, 29228, 29971
— Weimar Republic, 30017
Antwerp, 29122
Apfelbaum, K. Walter, 29896
Appel, Bernard R., 29783
Appelfeld, Aharon, 29384
Appignanesi, Lisa, 29755
Arbeitsinformationen, 29242
'Archiv für Kulturgeschichte', 29021, 29932
'Archiv für Mittelrheinische Kirchengeschichte', 29961
'(Der) Archivar', 29067
'Archive in Niedersachsen', 29110
Arendt, Hannah, 29716–29718, 29867, 30036
Argentina, 29240
— Refugees, 29230, 29399
Armbruster, Fritz, 29005
Armbruster, Thomas, 29227
Armed Forces, Jews in the, 29206, 29342, 29444, 29469
Armenia, 29416
Arnim, Bettina von, 30024
Arnold, Ben, 29271

Arolsen, 29074
Aron, Edith, 29361
Aron, Wellesley, 29868
Aronsfeld, C.C., 29272
Art Historians, 29678, 29825, 29856
Art, Jewish, 29540, 29626, 29647, 29649
Art, Jews in (see also Holocaust, Art), 29671, 29719, 29823, 29824, 29929
Aryanisation, 29310, 29366, 29408, 29412, 29529
Asaf, Uri, 29303
Aschheim, Steven E., 30050
'Aschkenas', 29020, 29090, 29122, 29375, 29630, 29669, 29670, 29934, 29954, 29987, 30018
Ashton, Dianne, 29001
Asper, Helmut G., 29678
Assimilation, Acculturation, 28991, 29029, 29210, 29695, 30000
Assmann, Wolfgang R., 29140
Assor, Reuven, 29898
Auerbach, Frank, 29719
'Aufbau', New York, 29272, 29487
Aufgebauer, Peter, 29352
Augspurg, Anita, 29693
Augustine, Dolores L., 29030
'Aurora', 30011
'Aus dem Antiquariat', 29262, 29629
'Aus Politik und Zeitgeschichte', 29624
Auschwitz, 29273–29277, 29350, 29366, 29389, 29453, 29455, 29483, 29527
Ausländer, Rose, 29720, 29805
Austerlitz, Friedrich, 29703
Australia, Refugees, 29232, 29320, 29325
Austria, 29030, 29198, 29205, 29206, 29208, 29210, 29218, 29280, 29324, 29666, 29670, 29703, 29859, 29908
— Antisemitism, 29210, 29281, 29539, 29692, 29971–29976, 29995, 30009, 30022
— Emigration, 29444
— Nazi Period, 29279, 29281, 29282, 29414, 29429, 29492, 29677
— Post War, 29204, 29499, 29944, 29976, 30009
'Austrian Studies', 29680
Autobiographies, Memoirs, Diaries, Letters, 29001, 29282, 29299, 29321, 29330, 29341, 29351, 29377, 29395, 29396, 29435, 29438, 29466, 29468, 29471, 29476, 29480, 29481, 29484, 29498, 29607, 29747, 29753, 29848, 29867–29921, 30071
Avni, Haim, 29230
Awerbuch, Marianne, 28988, 29083

Bacharach, Walter Zwi, 29366
Bachstein, Martin K., 29323
Backes, Uwe, 29453
Backhaus, Fritz, 29117
Backhausen, Manfred, 28989
Bácskai, Vera, 29215, 29223
Baden, 28998, 29075, 29081

Baden-Württemberg (see also Württemberg), 29283
Badt, Hermann, 29721
Baeck, Leo, 29272, 29346, 29556, 29557, 29592
Baender, Hannelore, 29513
Bärsch, Claus-Ekkehard, 29739
Bagel-Bohlan, Anja E., 29253
Bahr, Erhard, 29859
Baiersdorf, 29076
Bailer, Brigitte, 29278
Baléanu, Avram Andrei, 29805
Ballin Lewis, Hanna, 29905
Ballin, Albert, 29025
'Balshanut Ivrit', 29563, 29575
'Baltische Studien', 29165
Bamberg, 29077, 29078
Bamberger, Gabrielle, 29251
Bankier, David, 29331
Banking, Jews in, 29030, 29223
Bar-am, Hanan, 29429
Bar-el, Joseph, 29053
Bar-giora-Bamberger, Naftali, 29103
Bar-Menachem, Abraham, 29869
Bar-Yosef, Hamutal, 29770, 29772
Barash, Jeffrey Andrew, 30036
Barbie, Klaus, 29339
Barilich, Eva, 29794
Barkai, Avraham, 29284, 29310, 29366, 29429
Barner, Wilfried, 29672
Baron, Lawrence, 29822
Bartov, Omer, 29370
Bartrop, Paul R., 29320
Barzilay, Eisig, 29610
Basch Family, 29101
Baskin, Judith R., 28990
Basselmann, Ursula, 29285
Battenberg, Friedrich, 29120, 29266
Bauche, Ulrich, 29125
Bauer, Bruno, 29818
Bauer, Gerhard, 29083
Bauer, Yehuda, 29398, 29977, 29978
Baum, Hans-Peter, 29005
Baumann, Annerose, 29635
Baumann, Arnulf H., 29285
Baumann, Zygmunt, 28991
Baumgart, Peter, 29083
Bavaria, 28998, 29079, 29080, 29174, 29551
Baviskar, Vera, 29063
Bayerdörfer, Hans-Peter, 30017
Becher, Peter, 29323
Bechtold-Comforty, Beate, 29081
Beck, Wolfgang, 29013
Becker, Albert, 29156
Becker, Franziska, 29924, 29925
Becker, Jurek, 29673
Becker-Jákli, Barbara, 29169
Beer, Fritz, 29870
Beer-Hofmann, Richard, 29722
Beisbart, Ortwin, 29673

Index to Bibliography

'Beiträge z. Heimatkunde d. Stadt Schwelm', 29177
'Beiträge z. Jüd. Geschichte in Rheinland-Pfalz', 29099, 29100, 29131, 29142, 29160, 29161, 29180
Beitz, Ursula, 29243
Beland, Hermann, 29982
Belgium, Nazi Period, 29301, 29328
Bell, Susan Gloag, 29871
Bembenek, Lothar, 29190
Ben David, Gershon, 29723
Ben-Aharon, Yitzhak, 29429
Ben-Avner, Yehuda, 29429
Ben-Chanan, Yaakov, 29620
Ben-Chorin, Schalom, 29255, 29958
Ben-Schlomo, Zev, 29803
Ben-Shammai, Bitya, 29264
Benger, Ruth, 29169
Benjamin, Kurt, 29154
Benjamin, Phyllis, 29787
Benjamin, Walter, 29596, 29673, 29724, 29725–29728, 29858
Bennertz, Gerhard, 29169
Benyoetz, Elazar, 29248, 29865
Benz, Ute, 29286
Benz, Wolfgang, 29257, 29287, 29288, 29310, 29351, 29366, 29478, 29528, 29889, 29926
Benzler, Susanne, 29273
Bergler, Siegfried, 30053
Bergmann, Werner, 29927, 29979
'Bericht d. Hist. Vereins Bamberg', 29078
Bering, Dietz, 29980
Berkemann, Hans-Eberhard, 29461
Berlichingen, 29082
Berlin, 28990, 29000, 29083–29097, 29289–29297, 29353, 29429, 29486, 29487, 29500, 29520, 29597, 29617, 29647, 29650, 29709, 29711, 29788, 29852, 29880, 29889, 30013
— Cemeteries, 29085, 29089
— Charlottenburg, 29289, 29296
— Prenzlauer Berg, 29089
— Steglitz, 29297
'Berlin in Geschichte und Gegenwart', 29353
Berlin, Isaiah Ben Judah Loeb, 29558
Berlin, Jeffrey B., 29859
'Berliner Theologische Zeitschrift', 29943
Berliner, Cora, 29729
Berlinger, Simon, 29082
Bernardini, Paolo, 30028
Berner, Herbert, 29075
Bernett, Hajo, 29697
Bernstein, Aron, 29730, 29772
Bernstein, Eduard, 29014, 29731
Berthold, Monika, 29076
Besier, Gerhard, 29981
Bethge, Eberhard, 30026
Beuthen, 29178
Beyerchen, Alan, 29732
Bible, 29576, 29587

Bibliographies, Catalogues, Inventories, 29162, 29244, 29259–29262, 29264, 29267, 29343, 29648, 29673
Bibliographies, Personal, 29560, 29601, 29828, 29923
Bielefeld, 29298
Bielitz, 29178
Bienenstock, Myriam, 29590
Biermann, Holger, 29533
Bild und Selbstbild der Juden Berlins, 29083
Bilitzky, Karl, 29319
Binder, Hartmut, 29795, 29859
Birchall, Frederick T., 29292
Birger, Trudi, 29299
Birkhan, Helmut, 28992
Birn, Ruth Bettina, 29300
Birnbaum, Nathan, 29659
'Bitzaron', 29610
Blanc, Klaus, 29841
Blinn, Dieter, 29162
Bloch, Benjamin, 29647
Bloch, David, 29478
Bloch, Erich, 29145
Bloch, Ernst, 29733, 29858, 29881
'Bloch-Almanach', 29733
Blochmann, Elisabeth, 29734
Block, Gay, 29301
Blodig, Vojtech, 29478
Blood Libel, 28992, 29986, 29987, 29993, 30011, 30018
Blüdnikow, Bent, 29302
Blüher, Hans, 30025
Blum, Eva, 29635
Blumenthal, Heinrich, 29107
Blumenthal-Weiss, Ilse, 29735
Bobenheim-Roxheim, 29098
Boberach, Heinz, 29310
Bock, Gisela, 29485
Bodek, Andrzej, 29404
Bodenstein, Leo, 29872
Boeckl, Matthias, 29677
Boehlich, Walter, 29704
Böhme, Jürgen, 29706
Boenheim, Felix, 29736
Börne, Ludwig, 29737, 29738
'Börsenblatt f. d. Deutschen Buchhandel', 29724, 29797, 30070
Boesche-Zacharow, Tilly, 30072
Bohemia, 29216, 29224, 29666
'Bohemia', 29214
Bohleber, Werner, 29982
Bohlmann, Philip V., 29648
Bohmbach, Jürgen, 29181
Bolkosky, Sidney M., 29231
Bollendorf, 29099
Bondy, Ruth, 29478
Bonhoeffer, Dietrich, 30026
Bonn, 29169, 29829
Boppard, 29100

Borchardt, Rudolf, 29621, 29873
Bormann, Cornelius, 29168, 29169
Bormann, Heidi, 29168
Born, Stephan, 29014
Borut, Jacob, 28993, 28994
Bosch, Manfred, 29830
Boskowice, 29207
Bosworth, Richard, 29952
Bothe, Rolf, 29711
Bottin, Angela, 29362
Bottomore, Tom, 29561
Botz, Gerhard, 29350
Bovenden, 29101
Braham, Randolph L., 29303
Brainin, Elisabeth, 29982
Brandenburgische Gedenkstätten, 29528
Brandt, Heinz, 29116
Brandt, Willy, 29406
Braun, Bernd, 29293
Braun, Christina von, 29928
Braunfels, Walter, 29708
Braunschweig, 29304
Brazil, Refugees, 29686
Brebeck, Wulff, E., 29546
Breitenstein, Andreas, 29882, 30070
Breitman, Richard, 29305
Bremen, 29306, 29529
Bremen-Walle, 29307
Bremer, Jörg, 29875
Bremerhaven, 29308, 29529
Brenner, Michael, 28995, 29250, 29501, 29628
Breslau, 29102
Bresnitz, Shlomo, 29314
Bresslau, Harry, 29914
Bresslau, Helene, 29914
Breuer, Mordechai, 28996, 28997
Breuer, Mordechai (Festschrift), 29613
'(The) British Journal of Holocaust Education', 29530, 30020
Brochhagen, Ulrich, 29175
Brocke, Edna, 29266, 29381, 29959
Brocke, Michael, 29447, 29576, 29602
Brod, Max, 29739, 29772
Broder, Henryk M., 29293, 29348
Brookner, Anita, 29753
Browning, Christopher R., 29309, 29398
Bruckmüller, Ernst, 29215, 29995
Brüggemann, Theodor, 29629
Brühl, 29169
Brünnel, Gabriele, 29060
Brumlik, Micha, 29014, 29266, 29381, 29502, 29591, 29704, 29901, 29970
Brunner, Karl, 28992
Bruns, Jochen, 29824
Brusten, Manfred, 29341
Buber, Martin, 29559, 29576, 29653, 29780, 29873, 29874, 30044
Bubis, Ignatz, 29647
Bubis, Nomi, 29716

Bucer, Martin, 29966
Buchenwald, 29303, 29396, 29531
Bucherer-Zweig, Wilhelmine, 29864
Bucky, Peter A., 29748
Budapest, 29215, 29617
Bürger, Friedegund, 29126
Büsing, Hayo, 29188
Büttner, Ursula, 29310
Bukowina, 29321
Bulgaria, Nazi Period, 29301
Bultmann, Rudolf, 29962
Burger, Adolf, 29311
Burkard, Karl-Josef, 29100
Burmeister, Karl Heinz, 29167, 29208
Burrin, Philippe, 29332
Burstyn, Ruth, 29209
Burth, Katrin, 29074
Buruma, Ian, 29503, 29531
Busch, Ralf, 29101, 29104
Busemann, Hertha Luise, 29290
Buss, Wolfgang, 29697
Busse, Ulrike, 29999

Cabbala, 28992, 29047
Cahn, Arnold, 29740
Calvin, Johannes, 30027
Canetti, Elias, 29673, 29741, 30048
Canning, Hugh, 30055
Caplan, Arthur, 29312
Caricatures, Jews depicted in, 29984, 29990
Carlebach, Felix F., 29148
Carlebach, Joseph, 29560, 29875
Carlebach, Julius, 29243, 29266, 29617
Carlebach, Julius (Festschrift), 29561, 29023, 29072, 29815, 29936, 29957
Carlebach-Preuss, Lotte, 29875
Carmichael, Joel, 29983
Carmilly-Weinberger, Moshe, 29223
Carossa, Hans, 29848
Carpenter, Peter, 29697
Cassidy, David C., 30041
Cassirer, Henry R., 29876
Cassis, Youssef, 29030
Catalan, T., 29652
Catalogues of Exhibitions, 29005, 29025, 29123, 29125, 29193, 29319, 29635, 29647, 29768, 29798, 29824, 29844, 30070
Cattle Trade, 29136
Celan, Paul, 29673, 29772
Celle, 29103, 29104
Cemeteries, 29050, 29072, 29076, 29079, 29089, 29091, 29098, 29103, 29107, 29109, 29113, 29115, 29126, 29127, 29163, 29164, 29169, 29170, 29176, 29183, 29187, 29200, 29211
'Central European History', 29032, 29470
Cesarani, David, 29443
Chamberlain, Houston Stewart, 30007
Chassidism see Hassidism
Chatterjee, Ranjit, 29860

Index to Bibliography

Chemnitz, 29313
Chládková, Ludmila, 29478
'(The) Christian Century', 29522
Chug Chaluzi, 29296
Church and Synagogue, 28992, 29961, 29964
Church, Christians and Jews, 29194, 29572, 29937, 29942, 29947, 29965, 29967, 30002
— Nazi Period, 29162, 29289, 29297, 29310, 29359, 29368, 29434, 29962, 29981
— Post War, 29506, 29923, 29931, 29953, 29958, 29959, 29963, 29968
Claudi, Marianne & Reinhard, 29112
Claussen, Detlev, 29861, 29970, 29982
Coburger, Marlies, 29491
Cochavi, Yehoyakim, 29314, 29429
Cohen, Asher, 29314
Cohen, Elie A., 29542
Cohen, Eugene J., 29315
Cohen, Gerson D., 29249
Cohen, Hermann, 29742, 29743, 29845
Cohen, Jean-Louis, 29678
Cohen, Michael, 29429
Cohen, Richard I., 29929
Cohen, Susan Sarah, 29261, 29264
Cohn Family, Offenburg, 29158
Colin, Amy, 29806
Collet, Anke, 29269
Colljung, Paul, 29099
Cologne, 29030, 29105, 29106, 29169, 28823
'Commentary', 29302, 29754, 30022
Communal History, 29139; see Name of Country; Region; Town
Communists, 29014, 29316, 29736, 29793, 29794, 29838, 29870, 29900
Concentration and Internment Camps, Ghettos, 29278, 29287, 29306, 29340, 29351, 29355, 29360, 29366, 29393, 29395, 29438, 29452, 29459, 29546 (see also Auschwitz, Buchenwald, Dachau, Gurs, Lodz, Majdanek, Merxplas, Minsk, Nisko, Riga, Sachsenhausen, Theresienstadt, Treblinka)
'Connexions', 30005
Conversion from Judaism, Baptism, 29020, 29609, 29784, 29785, 29937, 29989
— to Judaism, 29607
Cooper, R.M., 29460
Coping with the Past, 29930
Courant, Richard, 29744
'Critical Inquiry', 29553
Crnogorac, Biljana, 29186
Crusades, 29003
Culbert, David, 29997
Cunningham, Valentine, 30032
Cuno, Klaus, 29059
Cyganski, Miroslaw, 29473
Czechoslovakia (see also Bohemia, Moravia, Prague), 29222, 29871, 29907
— Nazi Period, 29301, 29323, 29391, 29484, 29893, 30074

Da Costa, Uriel, 29025
'Daat', 29589
Dachau, 29316
'Dachauer Hefte', 29274, 29316, 29322, 29390, 29392, 29422, 29455, 29483, 29492, 29495, 29521, 29548
Dachs, Gisela, 29523
Daecke, S.M., 29749
Dafni, Reuven, 29330
Dagan, Avigdor, 29478
Dahlke, Hans, 29882
Dalberg, Vibeke, 29804
Daltroff, Jean, 29196
Dan, Joseph, 29562
Dana, Yitzhak, 29429
Danco, Armin, 29674
Danuser, Hermann, 29813
Danzig, 29314
Dapim – Studies on the Shoah, 29314
'Dappim le-Mechkar be-Sifrut', 29770
Darby, David, 29741
Darmstadt, 29107, 29317
Darom, Yoel, 29429
Dautzenberg, Gerhard, 29931
Daviau, Donald G., 29859
Davidheiser, James C., 29859
Daxelmüller, Christoph, 29054, 29630, 29631
Daxner, Michael, 29290
De Castro, Rodrigo, 29025
Deak, George, 29223
Deas, Malcolm, 30008
Decker, Hannah S., 29756
Dechwerth, Michael, 29162
Defence see Antisemitism, Defence
Degginger-Unger, Marianne, 29229
Delf, Hanna, 29014, 30025
Delmedigo, Joseph Salomo, 29025
Demography, Statistics, 29169
Demps, Laurenz, 29014
Department Stores, 29030, 29698
Deportations, 29278, 29279, 29298, 29306, 29317, 29318, 29327, 29419, 29437, 29462, 29472
Detroit, 29231
Dettmer, Frank, 29540
Deutsch-jüdische Geschichte im 19. und 20. Jahrhundert, 29601; 29097, 29253, 29514, 29556, 29600, 29626, 29634, 29738, 29806, 29807, 29838, 29862, 29895, 29928, 29942, 29945, 30025, 30051
Deutsche Juden – Juden in Deutschland, 29252, 29504
(Die) Deutschen und die Judenverfolgung im Dritten Reich, 29310
Deutschkron, Inge, 29877, 29956
'(Der) Deutschunterricht', 29349, 29532
'Dialog', 29254
Dick, Lutz van, 29489
Diebold, Ruth, 28998
Dietz, Wolfgang, 29423

Dietzel, Volker, 29124
Dill, Karl, 29115
Diner, Dan, 29505, 29528, 29982
Dinese, Ruth, 29685
Dinglinger, Wolfgang, 29706
Dinter, Arthur, 30003, 30012
'Diné Israel', 29609, 29614
Dippold, Günter, 29155
Dispeck, David Ben Joel, 29076
Dispeker, Sigmund, 29878
Displaced Persons, 29501, 29509, 29515, 29516, 29521
Distel, Barbara, 29274, 29478
Dittmar, Peter, 29984
Dittrich, Alfred, 29138
Doderer, Klaus, 29724
Dohm, Christian Wilhelm von, 29083, 30028
Dokumentationsarchiv d. österr. Widerstandes, 29278
— 'Jahrbuch', 29276, 29279
Dolev, Aharon, 30054
Domansky, Elisabeth, 29425
Don, Yehuda, 29223
Dorsten, Dokumentationszentrum für Jüd. Geschichte, 29189
Dortmund, 29319
Dovern, Willi, 29069
Drechsler, Adina, 29509
Dreessen, Wulf-Otto, 29055
Dreier, Werner, 29972
Dresden, 29431
Dreyer, M., 30030
Dror (Organis.), 29525
Drucker, Malka, 29301
Drummer, Heike, 29117
Dubois, Horst, 29932
Dudek, Peter, 29371
Dülmen, 29109
Dülmen, Andrea van, 29691
Düsseldorf, 29169, 29318
'Düsseldorfer Jahrbuch', 29369
Duisburg, 29169
Dunera, 29320
'Dunera News', 29232
Dupuy, B., 29379
Dutsch, Mikolaj, 30070

Early Modern Period (Pre-Enlightenment), 29133, 29993, 30073
East Friesland, 29110
East Prussia, 29473
Eastern Jewry, 28997, 29002, 29014, 29086, 29169, 29222, 29501, 29520, 29647, 29889
Eck, Johannes, 29993
Eckert, Brita, 29262
Eckler-von Gleich, Cecilie, 29307
Eckstein, Adolf, 29076
Eckstein, Eric, 29232
Ecuador, 29920

Edschmid, Ulrike, 29879
Education, 29087, 29102, 29118, 29129, 29159, 29162, 29212, 29290, 29447, 29448, 29482, 29489, 29524, 29697, 29888, 29901
Efron, John M., 29675
Eger, Akiva (Rabbi), 29608
Ehmann, Christoph, 29169
Ehrenstein, Albert, 29746
Ehrlich, Ernst Ludwig, 29282
Eichmann, Adolf, 29356, 29716
Eichmann, Johanna S., 29189
Eichmann-Leutenegger, Beatrice, 29735, 29800, 30075
Eifel, 29454
Einstein, Albert, 29747–29749, 29874
Einstein, Carl, 29750
Eisen, Gabrielle, 29320
Eisenbach, Ulrich, 29260
Eisenstein, Albin, 29321
Eisfeld, Rainer, 29676
Eissing, Uwe J., 28999
'Eit-Mol', 29852
Eitinger, Leo, 29322
Elbing, 29111
Eldar, Ilan, 29563
Elias, Norbert, 29751
Elias, Ruth, 29542
Eliav, Mordechai, 29617
Eliezer Ben Nathan of Mainz, 29564
Eliás, József, 29303
Elkin, Rivka, 29291
Elsässer, Jürgen, 29985
Emancipation, 28998, 28999, 29007, 29012, 29013, 29018, 29033, 29035, 29038, 29042, 29083, 29105, 29134, 29225, 29566, 29597, 29645, 29817, 29818, 29853, 29984, 29989
Emden, 29112
Emigration (see also Argentina, Australia, Czechoslovakia, Exile, Great Britain, Netherlands, Refugees, USA), 29324, 29326, 29472
Emmerich, 29327
Endingen, 29227
Endlich, Stefanie, 29528
Endres, Elisabeth, 30056
Engbarth, Marion, 29169
Engel-Holland, Eva J., 29555, 30046
Engelbertz, Susanne, 29529
Engelmann, Bernt, 29025, 29540
Enlightenment (see also Haskalah), 28991, 29000, 29013, 29039, 29040, 29050, 29083, 29093, 29566, 29580, 29598, 29611, 30047
Entrepreneurs (see also Industry, Trade), 29030, 29223
Erb, Rainer, 29979, 29986, 29987
Erényi, Zvi, 29223
Erft, 29168
Erftstadt, 29169
Erfurt, 29585
Erlangen, 29113

Ernst, Manfred, 29306
Erpel, Simone, 29490
'Erziehungskunst', 29948
Eschen, Heinz, 29316
Escher, Felix, 29788
Eschwege, Helmut, 29506
Essen, 29169
Estermann, Alfred, 29774
Ettmann, Julia, 29187
'Études Danubiennes', 29206
Etzold, Alfred, 29084, 29091
Euchel, Isaac, 29586
'Euphorion', 29763
'European Judaism', 30026
'Evangelische Kommentare', 29220, 29749
Evleth, Donna, 29343
Exhibitions see Catalogues
Exil. Forschung, Erkenntnisse, Ergebnisse, 29685
Exile (see also Emigration, Refugees), 29677, 29681
— Journalism, 29870
— Literature and Arts, 29262, 29323, 29648, 29668, 29678, 29679, 29682, 29683, 29685–29689, 29855
— Sciences, 29680, 29684
— Theatre, Film, 29234
'Exilforschung, Int. Jahrbuch', 29678
Exler, Margarete, 29729
Exton, Inez P., 29233
Eyck Family, 29880
Eyck, Erich, 29880
Eyck, Frank, 29880

Faber, Elmar, 29881
Fabry, Joseph (Fabrizius, Peter), 29328
Fackenheim, Emil, 29582, 29653
Fait, Joachim, 29084
Falcke, Eberhard, 30061
Falk, Gerhard, 29960
Fassbinder, Rainer W., 29992
Fassl, Peter, 29174
Faust, Anselm, 29426, 29446
Feidel-Mertz, Hildegard, 29266
Feige, Hans-Uwe, 29733
Feiner, Shmuel, 29000, 29611
Feingold, Henry L., 29329
Feld, Hans, 29752
Felsmann, Barbara, 29764
Fenner, Wolfgang, 29177
Fenske, Hans, 29368
Festschrift see Breuer, Mordechai; Carlebach, Julius; Levinson, Pnina Navé & Nathan Peter
Feuchtwangen, 29114
Feuchtwanger, Lion, 29683, 29772, 29801, 29881, 29882
Feuchtwanger, Marta, 29882
Feuchtwanger, Martin, 29124
Fichte, Johann Gottlieb, 30029
Ficowski, Jerzy, 30070

Fiedler, Peter, 29959
Fiedor, Karol, 29473
Final Letters, 29330
Final Solution (see also Holocaust), 29305, 29309, 29331–29337, 29478, 29545, 29547
Fingerhut, Karlheinz, 29771
Finkelgruen, Peter, 29338
Finkelstein, Norman, 29565
Finkielkraut, Alain, 29339
Fischer, Bruno, 29169
Fischer, Helmut, 29988
Fischer, Jens Malte, 29621, 30017
Fischer, Wolfram, 29030
Fischer-Defoy, Christine, 29883
Fitterling, Dieter, 29297
Flagmeier, Renate, 29361
Flam, Gila, 29340
Föhse, Ulrich, 29169
Fölling, Werner, 29290
Förster, Elisabeth (née Nietzsche), 30008
Forced Labour, 29310, 29341, 29389, 29393, 29473
Foregger, Richard, 29276
Forrester, John, 29755
'Forschung. Mitteilungen d. DFG', 29440
Fortes, Meyer, 29845
Foster, Edith, 29507
Four Centuries of Jewish Women's Spirituality, 29001
Fox, John P., 29342
Fränkel, David, 29637
Framing the Past, 29690
France, 29617
— Nazi Period, 29301, 29339, 29343, 29360, 29442
— Refugees, 29343, 29361, 29441, 29882
Franconia, 29005, 29115, 29175, 29987
Franek, Jiří, 29478
Frank, Anne, 29344, 29345
Frank, Chaim, 29512
Frank, Heike, 29597
Frank, Lia, 29508
Frank, Margrit, 29933
Frank, Niklas, 29378
Frank, Wolfgang, 29169
Frankemölle, Hubert, 29959
Frankenau, 29116
Frankenthal, Käte, 29014
Frankfurt am Main, 28998, 29030, 29466, 29583, 29647, 29961, 30073
— Jüdisches Museum, 29117, 29635, 29647, 29798
— Philanthropin, 29118
'Frankfurter Allg. Zeitung', 29026, 29730, 29792, 29836, 29875, 29884, 29885, 29915, 30036
Frantz, Constantin, 30030
Franz Joseph (Austrian Emperor), 29199
Frederick II [The Great], 30046
Freeden, Herbert, 29293

Frei, Norbert, 29381
Freiburg i.Br., 29119
Freud, Sigmund, 29694, 29695, 29738, 29753–29761, 29772, 29990, 30048
Freund, Florian, 29278
Freund, Gisèle, 29361
Freundlich, Elisabeth, 29884
Frey, Winfried, 29934
Freytag, Gustav, 30031
Fried, Anne, 29885
Fried, Erich, 29673, 29886
Fried, Pankraz (Festschrift), 29174
Friedeburg, Robert von, 29132, 29133
Frieden, Ken, 29757
Friedländer, David, 29083
Friedländer, Saul, 29013, 29332, 29372, 29398
Friedlander, Albert H., 29346, 29478, 29592
Friedlander, Evelyn, 29005
Friedlander, Judith, 29002
Friedman, Saul S., 29476
Friedrich, Martin, 29989
Friedrich-Naumann-Stiftung, 29030
Fries, Fritz Rudolf, 29882
Friesheim, 29168
Frölich, Jürgen, 29730
Fromm, Bella, 29292
Fromm, Erich, 29761, 29762
Frowein, Cordula, 29293, 29678
Frucht, Karl, 29887
Fruchtmann, Benno, 29248
Fuchs, Konrad, 29030, 29744
Fuchs, Marga, 29077
Fuchs, Rudolf, 29323
Fürnberg, Lotte, 29879
Fürth, 29120
— Jüd. Regionalmuseum, 29076
Fuks-Mansfeld, Rena G., 29056
Fulda, Ludwig, 29763
Funk, Rainer, 29762
Funkenstein, Amos, 29013, 29566, 29603
Furtado Kestler, Izabela Maria, 29686
Furtwängler, Wilhelm, 30032

Gabel, Gernot U., 29057
Gaertner, Hans, 29888
Gafni, Isaiah M., 29003
Gailingen, 29075, 29121
Gajek, Bernard, 29763
Galen, Bischof Clemens August Graf von, 29359
Galicia (see also Austria), 30070
Galinski, Heinz, 29088, 29254, 29632
Galley, Eberhard, 29774
Galsky, D., 29216
Gamm, Hans-Jochen, 29489
Garbe, Detlef, 29366, 29381
Gardner, Sheldon, 29692
'Gartenlaube', 29954
Gauger, Rose, 29361

Gay, Peter, 29004
Gay, Ruth, 29004, 29500
'GDS-Archiv', 29643
Gehler, Lazare, 29196
Gehler, Léon, 29196
Gehring-Münzel, Ursula, 29195
Gehrke, Ralph, 29532
Geiger, Abraham, 29571
Geisel, Eike, 29293, 29347, 29348
Gelber, Mark H., 29772
Gelber, Yoav, 29314
Gelblum, Amira, 29693
Geldern, 29122, 29169
Gellately, Robert, 29398
Gellhorn, Alfred, 29124
Gemeinhardt, Horst, 29076
Gemeinschaft für Frieden und Aufbau, 29495
'Genealogie', 29051, 29149
Genealogy, 28989, 29579, 29896
Genee, Pierre, 29198
Genger, Angela, 29546
Genin, Salomea, 29889
Genisa-Genizah, 29005
'Genuzot', 29564
Gerlach, Bernard H., 29162
Gerlach, Hans-Martin, 29124
German Democratic Republic, 29124, 29506, 29513, 29535, 29550, 29647, 29899, 29900, 29944, 30016
'German History', 29132, 29364, 29766, 29952
'German Life & Letters', 29681, 29720, 29820
'German Politics and Society', 29451
'(The) German Quarterly', 29725, 29777
'German Studies Review', 29701
German-Israeli Relations, 29956
Germania Judaica, Köln, 29242
'Germanic Notes and Review', 29842
'Germanic Review', 29854
'Germanisch-Romanische Monatsschrift', 29808
Germany (see also Middle Ages, Early Modern Period, Emancipation, Imperial Germany, Weimar Republic, Nazi Period, German Democratic Republic)
— Immigration, 29052, 29508, 29511, 29520, 29647
— Post War, 29068, 29510, 29511, 29523, 29625, 29632, 29647, 29877, 29944, 29949, 29952, 29953, 29962, 30006
— Reunited, 29940, 29956, 29985
Gerngros Family, 29076
Gerron, Kurt, 29764
Gershom b. Judah me'or ha-Golah (of Mainz), 29614
Gerson, Daniel, 29258
Gerstenberger, Katharina, 29349
'Geschichte in Wissenschaft und Unterricht', 29036, 29139, 29927
'Geschichtsblätter Kreis Bergstrasse', 29136
Geschlossene Vorstellung, 29293

Index to Bibliography

'Gesher', 29658
Gibbs, Robert, 29593
Giessen, 29869
Gilbert, Martin, 29497, 29857
Gilboa, Menucha, 29263
Gillessen, Günther, 29150
Gillis-Carlebach, Miriam, 29560, 29875
Gilman, Sander L., 29694, 29758, 29772, 29776, 29990
Ginat, Jochanan see Gaertner, Hans
Ginsburg, Pino, 29429
Ginzel, Günther Bernd, 29378, 29506
Giordano, Ralph, 29632, 29956
Giroud, Françoise, 30048
Glas-Larsson, Margareta, 29350
Glatz, Joachim, 29161
Glatzer, Nahum N., 29874
Glauert, Martin, 29991
Glazar, Richard, 29351, 29478
Gleiwitz, 29178
Glückel von Hameln, 29001, 29034, 29076
Glückstadt, 29025
Gluikskind, Miriam, 29498
Gockel, Heinz, 29673
Goebbels, Joseph, 29997
Gödde, Heinz, 29269
Göhl, Walter, 29832
Göppingen, Jüd. Museum, 29123
Goerden, Elmar, 30017
Göring, Hermann, 29302
Görner, Rüdiger, 29037
Goeseke, Gudrun, 29124
Goethe, Johann Wolfgang, 29672, 30033
Göttingen, 29352, 29533
Göttler, Fritz, 29809
Golczewski, Frank, 29366
Goldin, Simcha, 29006
Goldmann, Nahum, 29951
Goldschmidt, Dietrich, 29353
Goldschmidt, Edith, 29890
Goldschmidt-Lehmann, Ruth, 29259
Goldstein, Bluma, 29695
Goldstein, Julius, 29107
Golem, 29031
Gollinger, Hildegard, 29923
Golücke, F., 29643
Golvan, Colin, 29324
Golzen, Godfrey, 29341
Gombrich, Ernst, 29856
Goodman, Katherine R., 29853
Goodnick, Benjamin, 29759
Goral, Arie, 29540
Gordimer, Nadine, 29840
Gordon, Harry, 29354
Goschler, Constantin, 29310, 29518
Goshen, Seev, 29355
Gotthelf, Jeremias, 30034
Gottschalk, Carola, 29533
Gottschalk, Wolfgang, 29085

Gough-Yates, Kevin, 29234
Gould, Stephen Jay, 29356
Govrin, Nurit, 29199
Grab, Walter, 29014, 29266, 30029, 30051
Grabherr, Eva, 29200
Grabois, Aryeh, 29647
Gradenwitz, Peter, 29696
Graetz, Heinrich, 29008
Graetz, Michael, 29007, 29008, 29083
Graetz, Rebecca, 29001
Graf, Andreas, 29528
Graml, Hermann, 29357
Grange, Joseph, 30037
'Granta', 29531
Great Britain, 29238, 29259, 29342, 29442
— Refugees, 29234, 29280, 29323, 29444, 29460, 29465, 29871, 29902
Green, Jeffrey M., 29299
Green, Kenneth Hart, 29577
Greive, Hermann, 29009
Grenville, John A.S., 29310, 29936
Greschat, Martin, 29310
Greussing, Kurt, 29973
Greve, Barbara, 29134
Griebel, Regina, 29491
Grimm, Reinhold, 29992
Grodin, Michael, 29270
Groehler, Olaf, 29373, 29381
Grözinger, Karl Erich, 29795
Gronius, Jörg W., 29293
Grosche, Heinz, 29140
Gross, Nachum T., 29030
Grossman, Avraham, 29003
Grossman, Jeffrey, 29725
Grossmann, Kurt R., 29323
Grosz, George, 29887
Grünebaum, Elias, 29162
Grünewald, Eckhart, 29797
Gruenewald, Max, 29246
Grünwald, Alfred, 29765
Gruner, Wolf, 29310, 29358
Grunwald, Henry, 29765
Gruss, Heribert, 29359
Gryn, Hugo, 29222
Grynberg, Anne, 29360, 29441
Grynszpan, Herschel, 29427
'Guardian Weekly', 30008
Güntert, Christoph, 29197
Güntner, Joachim, 30056
Guggenheim, Jacov, 29245
Guggenheimer, Eva H., 29010
Guggenheimer, Heinrich Walter, 29010
Gundelfinger, Sigmund, 29107
Gurs, 29361
Gurwitz, Percy, 29891
Gustavus, Lieselotte, 29711
Guth, Klaus, 29018
Gutleben, Burkhard, 29773
Gutman, Israel (Yisrael), 29509

Gutsmuth, Alfred see Bar-Menachem, Abraham
Gutzmer, Karl, 29829
Gymnich, 29168

Haarmann, Hermann, 29750
Haarscher, André-Marc, 29196
Haas, Alexander, 29107
Haas, Hannes, 29703
Haas, Pavel, 29477
Haber, Fritz, 29766
Habermas, Rebekka, 30073
Habonim, 29633, 29868
Hachenburger, Herz Hähnle, 29107
Hachshara, 29145, 29429
Hackert, Fritz, 29840
Hackeschmidt, H.J., 29247
Häfner, Klaus, 29706
Hägler, Brigitte, 29993
Händler-Lachmann, Barbara, 29411, 29412
Haerpfer, Christian, 29282, 29974
Hage, Volker, 30056
Hahn, Barbara, 29086
Hahn, Fred, 29323
Hahn, Joachim, 29183
Hahn, Josef, 30070
Hahn, Kurt, 29697
Haider-Pregler, Hilde, 30017
Hájková, Alena, 29478
Hake, Sabine, 29809
Halakha, 29016
Halle, 29124, 29699
Haller, Annette, 29185
Hamácková, Vlastimila, 29217
Hamburg, 29125–29127, 29285, 29362, 29363, 29419, 29804
Hamburger, Benjamin Schlomo, 29173
Hamburger, Käte, 29767
Hamburger, Michael, 30059
Hamer, Kurt, 29540
Hamm, 29480
Hamm, Peter, 30070
Hammann, Brigitte, 29887
Hanák, Péter, 29223
Hanau, 29128
Hanenberg, Peter, 29673
Hannover, Georg Wilhelm, Prinz von, 29697
Hanover, 28999, 29129
Harck, Ole, 29540
Harden, Maximilian, 29836
Harder, Matthias, 29293
Harel, Chaya, 29654
Harman, Avraham, 29223
Harms, Kathy, 29930
Harris, Henry, 29766
Harrison, T., 29364
Harsch, Donna, 29014
Hartman, Geoffrey H., 29398
Hartung, Günter, 29124

Hasida, Simcha, 29567
Haskalah, 29566, 29581, 29586, 29598, 29599, 29611
Hassidism, 29562
Haumann, Heiko, 29119, 29283
Hausen, Karin, 29035
Hauser, Martin, 29892
Havatzelet, Avraham, 29568
Haverkamp, Alfred, 29011
Hawthorn, Geoffrey, 30008
Hayes, Peter, 29398
Hayman, Eva, 29893
Hayoun, Maurice R., 29617
Heartfield, John, 29323, 29768
'Hebräische Beiträge z. Wiss. d. Judentums', 29657
Hebrew Literature, 29575, 29586, 29598, 29599, 29611, 29772
Hedde, Helene, 29489
Heenen-Wolff, Susann, 29510
Hegel, Friedrich Wilhelm, 30035
Heid, Ludger, 29014, 29169, 29255, 29266, 29601, 29647, 29807, 29898, 29984
Heide, 29365
Heidegger, Martin, 30036–30039, 30044
Heidelberg, 29130, 29588
Heil, Johannes, 29961
Heilbronner, Oded, 29647
Heimann, Hugo, 29769
'Heimatjahrbuch d. Kreises Neuwied', 29423
— 'Kreis Ahrweiler', 29068
Hein, Martin, 29962
Heine, Heinrich, 29025, 29694, 29695, 29770–29786, 29790, 29811
— 'Heine Jahrbuch', 29771, 29784, 29785
— Heinrich-Heine-Institut, Düsseldorf, 29783
Heinemann, Hartmut, 29260
Heinemann, Jeremia, 29083
Heinonen, R.E., 29534
Heinrichs, Hans-Jürgen, 29685
Heinrichs, Wolfgang, 29937
Heinsohn, Gunnar, 29982
Heinz, Hanspeter, 29923
Heisenberg, Werner, 30040, 30041
Heister, Hanns-Werner, 29678
Heitkamp, Gisela, 29510
Heitmann, Margret, 29556
Helbig, Günter, 29124
Helfgott, Ben, 29222
Hellige, Hans Dieter, 29030
Hempfling, Helmut, 29511
Hennweiler, 29131
Henrix, Hans Hermann, 29962
Henry, Frances, 29461
Hensel, Fanny, 29787
Henze, Wilhelm, 29697
Herbert, Ulrich, 29373
Hermand, Jost, 29776, 29862
Hermann, Ingo, 29715

Hermannová, Margit, 29217
Hermle, Siegfried, 29310
Hermstrüwer, Inge, 29783
Herrison, Lilian, 29196
Herschler, Alter Yehudah, 29564
Hertz, Deborah, 28990
Hertz, Paul, 29788
Herz, Henriette, 29025, 29691
Herz, Marcus, 29025
Herzfeld, Hans, 29894
Herzfelde, Wieland, 29881
Herzig, Arno, 29012, 29014, 29255, 29266, 29366, 29634
Herzl, Theodor, 29436, 29566, 29654, 29703, 29772
Herzog, Marvin, 29063
Herzsohn, Paul, 29177
Heschel, Abraham Joshua, 29569
Hess, Jonathan M., 29737
Hess, Moses, 29570, 29610
Hess, Renate, 29317
Hess, Robert, 29535
Hesse, 28998, 29132–29137, 29260, 29367, 29439, 29962
Hesse, Hermann, 30042
Hessing, Jakob, 29248, 29604
Hessisch-Lichtenau, 29303, 29389
Heubach, Helga, 29826
Heuberger, Georg, 29117, 29635, 29647, 29798
Heuberger, Rachel, 29583, 29584, 29647
Heumos, Peter, 29323
Heusenstamm, 29138
Heydrich, Reinhard, 29333
Heyl, Binjamin, 29542
Heyl, Matthias, 29542
Heym, Stefan, 29789
Heymann, Fritz, 29772, 29790, 29791
Heymann, Lida Gustava, 29693
Hidas, Peter, 29223
Hilberg, Raul, 29368, 29398
Hildesheim, 29129
Hildesheimer, Esriel, 29429
Hildesheimer, Meir, 29173
Hiller, Ferdinand, 29708
Hilsenrath, Edgar, 29349
Himmler, Heinrich, 29305
Hinck, Walter, 29775
Hinrichsen Family, 29025
Hinrichsen, Henri, 29792
Hinton, Stephen, 29858
Hintze, Hedwig, 29709
Hirhager, Ulrike, 28992
Hirsch, Helmut, 29369, 29730
Hirsch, Helmut & Marianne, 29895
Hirsch, Karl Jakob, 29685
Hirsch, Martin, 29378
Hirsch, Samson Raphael, 29571
Hirschfeld, Gerhard, 29323
Historians, 29616, 29797, 29821, 29899, 29900

Historians' Debate, 29366, 29370, 29371, 29375, 29453
'Historical Journal of Film, Radio and Television', 29997
Historiography (see also Historians' Debate), 29008, 29017, 29024, 29032, 29042, 29139, 29242, 29371, 29373, 29374, 29381, 29388, 29617, 29936
— Revisionism, 29453, 29483
'(Das) Historisch-Politische Buch', 29175, 29984
'Historische Zeitschrift', 29473
'Historisches Jahrbuch', 30030
'History & Memory', 29372, 29425
'History of Political Thought', 29818
'The History Teacher', 29550
Hitler, Adolf, 29376, 29983
Hochhäuser, Alex, 29377
Hochschule f. d. Wissenschaft d. Judentums, Berlin, 29617
Hochschule für Jüdische Studien, Heidelberg, 29243, 29244
— Veröffentlichungen, 29008
Höffler, Karl-Wilhelm, 29169
Högl, Günther, 29319
Höss, Rudolph, 29275
Hofe, Harold von, 29882
Hofer, Walther, 29453
Hoffmann, Christa, 29938
Hoffmann, Christhard, 29617, 29821, 29994
Hoffmann, Detlef, 29528
Hoffmann, Dieter, 29135, 29139
Hoffmann, Heidi Tamar, 29477
Hoffmann, Robert, 29995
Hofmann, Gert, 29532
Hofmann, Helmut, 29191
Hofmann, Karl-Ludwig, 29798
Hofmann, Thomas, 29461
Hofmannsthal, Hugo von, 29712, 30048
Hohendahl, Peter Uwe, 29776
Hohenems, 29200, 29202
— Jüd. Museum, 29200, 29201, 29203, 29651
Hohenlimburg, 29378
Holler, Ulrike, 29510
Hollin, F., 29088
Hollingdale, R.J., 30008
Holmes, Colin, 29374
Holocaust (see also Concentration Camps, Final Solution), 29314, 29374, 29398, 29543, 29690
— Art, 29546
— Denial, 29386, 29453, 29483
— Historiography, 29366, 29372, 29382, 29388
— Instrumentalisation, 29017, 29488, 29527, 29528
— in Literature, 29413, 29673, 29723
— Reaction, 28990, 29288, 29331, 29385, 29417, 29488, 29927
— Teaching, 29535, 29538, 29542
— Theological and Philosophical Impact, 29379, 29380, 29387, 29450, 29582

— Trauma, 29013, 29322, 29381, 29392, 29405, 29450, 29475, 29542
Holocaust Educational Foundation Volunteers, 29398
'Holocaust and Genocide Studies', 29271, 29300, 29318, 29436, 29442, 30003
Holub, Robert C., 29777
Holz, H., 29220
Holzbach-Linsenmaier, Heidrun, 29996
Holzer, Willi, 29087
(Bad) Homburg vor der Höhe, 29140
Homburg, Heidrun, 29698
Homburger Family, 29144
Honigmann, Peter, 29169, 29578, 29588
Honnef, Klaus, 29768
Hook, Donald D., 29772
Hoppe, Ilse, 29124
Horch, Hans Otto, 29255, 29266, 29838, 29848
Horn, Christine, 29077
Hornshoj-Moller, Stig, 29997
Horwitz, Rivka, 29594
Houtermans, Fritz, 29793
Howard, John A., 29058
Hoya, 29141
Hrdlicka, Manuela R., 29452
Huchel, Monica, 29879
Huebsch, Ben, 29859
Hüneke, Andreas, 29124
Hüttenmeister, Gil, 29123
Hughes, Robert, 29719
Humboldt, Alexander & Wilhelm von, 29578
Hundhausen, Felicitas, 29242
Hungary, 29215, 29222, 29223, 29239
— Nazi Period, 29301, 29303
Hurwitz, Emanuel, 29542
Hurwitz, Yaacov, 29713
Husbands, Christopher, 29998
Husserl, Edmund, 29124
Hutchinson, Peter, 29789
Huth, Hans, 29141
Hyman, Paula E., 28990
Hyndráková, Anna, 29217
Hyrsilová, Kveta, 29323

Ichenhausen, 29005
Identity, Jewish, 29007, 29026, 29028, 29214, 29231, 29499, 29511, 29617, 29620, 29624, 29625, 29627, 29675, 29758, 29808
Ilsar, Yehiel, 29721
(The) Impact of Western Nationalism, 29803; 29305, 29640, 29661, 29664, 29667
Imperial Germany, 28990, 28993, 28996, 29014, 29033, 29036, 29048, 29052, 29416, 29642, 29937, 29970, 30002, 30007, 30010
Index of Articles on Jewish Studies, 29264
Industry, Jews in, 29030, 29156, 29179
'Informationen zur Schleswig-Holsteinischen Zeitgeschichte', 29126, 29365
Ingelheim, 29142

'Internationale Schulbuchforschung', 29538, 29539
Isaac, Jeffrey C., 29717
Isaacson, Judith Magyar, 29389
Isaacson, Walter, 29799
Israel, 29488, 29509, 29663, 29668, 29892, 29956, 29957, 29970, 30063
— Immigration, 29663
Israel, James, 29025
Israel, Wilfrid, 29302
'Israelitisches Wochenblatt', 29203, 29226
Issum, 29169
'Istina', 29216, 29379, 29382, 29387, 29391
Italy, 29617
— Refugees, 29467
Ivry, Alfred L., 29554
Iwasaki, Eijiro, 29059
'Iyyun', 29590

Jacobs, Boike, 29127
Jacobs, Jack, 29622
Jacoby, Johann, 29025
Jacoby, Mario, 29098, 29164
Jäckel, Eberhard, 29013, 29333, 29368, 29982
Jaeckel, Heinz, 29378
Jäger, Hans, 29030
Jäger, Herbert, 29381
Jäger, Siegfried, 29999
Jahnke, Karl Heinz, 29316, 29415
'Jahrbuch Altonaer Museum', 29073
— d. Deutschen Schillergesellschaft', 29767
— d. Schles. Friedrich-Wilhelms-Univ. zu Breslau', 29179
— für Antisemitismusforschung', 29257; 29286, 29287, 29332, 29358, 29978, 29979, 29994, 30015
— für Schles. Kirchengeschichte', 29420
— für d. Geschichte Mittel- und Ostdeutschlands', 29769, 29788
— für Wirtschaftsgeschichte', 29698
— zur Liberalismusforschung', 30024
Jakobowicz, Rachel, 30000
Jankel, Hermy, 29222
Jansen, Irene, 29855
Janssen, Karl-Heinz, 29491
Janta, Leonhard, 29068
Japan, Refugees, 29457
Jasper, Willi, 29266, 29325, 29445, 29738
Jaspers, Karl, 29867
Jaspert, Bernd, 29962
Jastrowitz, Hermann, 29124
'Jedidja', 29083
Jeggle, Utz, 29924
Jelinek, Yeshayahu, 29957
Jelínek, Zdenek, 29478
Jenny-Ebeling, Charitas, 29841
Jens, Walter, 29293, 29782
Jensen, Fritz, 29794

Jensen, Jens Christian, 29540
Jersch-Wenzel, Stefi, 29083
Jesse, Eckhard, 29453, 29939
Jessel, Léon, 29745
Jever, 29430
'Jewish Chronicle', 29443, 29803
Jewish Enigma, 29038, 29969
Jewish Film Directory, 29265
'Jewish History', 29224, 29594
Jewish Identity see Identity, Jewish, Jewish Problem
'(The) Jewish Journal of Sociology', 29374, 29524
Jewish Life in Germany, 29913
Jewish Problem, 29007, 29517, 29675, 29815, 29816, 29945
'Jewish Social Studies', 29240, 29759, 29974
'Jiddistik-Mitteilungen', 29060; 29063
Jochmann, Werner, 29310
Jodice, David A., 29940
Johe, Werner, 29310
John, Michael, 29210
Johns, Jorun B., 29859
Jonca, Karol, 29427, 29473
Josipovici, Gabriel, 29796
Jourdan, Berta, 29014
'Journal of Contemporary History', 29470, 29662
— of Ecclesiastical History', 29981
— of Feminist Studies in Religion', 30014, 30019
— of Modern History', 29424, 30036
— of the History of Philosophy', 29580
Journalists, 29369, 29471, 29703, 29876, 29878
'Judaica Bohemiae', 29217; 29219, 29221, 29334, 29627
'Judaica Librarianship', 29057
'Judaica', 29966, 30052, 30053
Judaism, 29572, 29573, 29617, 29619
Judaism, Jewish History, Teaching, 29534, 29549
(Die) Juden in der Europäischen Geschichte, 29013
(Die) Juden in ihrer mittelalterlichen Umwelt, 28992
Juden und deutsche Arbeiterbewegung bis 1933, 29014
Judengeleit see Legal History
'(Das) Jüdische Echo', 29204
'Jüdische Familien-Forschung', 29896
'Jüdische Kulturbühne', 29512
Jüdische Schicksale, 29278
Jüdische Unternehmer in Deutschland, 29030
'Jüdischer Almanach', 29248; 29347, 29413, 29604, 29656, 29723, 29746, 29800, 29839, 29848, 29916, 29917
Jüdischer Kulturbund see Kulturbund
Jülich (Kreis), 29070
Juelich, Dierk, 29542
Juling, Peter, 29504
Jung, Carl Gustav, 30043
Jung, Martin, 29194
Jung, Rüdiger, 29150

Kaddari, Menahem, 29575
Kätzel, Hedi, 29760
Kafka, Franz, 29673, 29695, 29795, 29796, 29874
Kafka, John S., 29982
Kahane, Charlotte, 29390
'Kairos', 29209, 29212, 29571, 29964
Kaiser, Wolf, 29655
Kaiser, Wolfram, 29124, 29699
Kaldenberg, Bettina, 29617
'Kalender f. d. Klever Land', 29327
Kaliski, Lotte, 29290
Kamenec, Ivan, 29478
Kamenetzki, Samuel, 29162
Kameraden, Deutsch-Jüdischer Wanderbund, 29640
Kampe, Norbert, 29293, 29472
Kanarfogel, Ephraim, 29015
Kant, Immanuel, 29580
Kantorowicz, Alfred, 29881
Kantorowicz, Ernst H., 29797
Kantzenbach, Friedrich Wilhelm, 29942
Kaplan, Alice, 29339
Kaplan, Marion A., 28990
Karady, Victor, 29030, 29223
Karch, Helga, 29162
Karl, Frederick Robert, 29796
Karlsruhe, 29143, 29144
Kárny, Miroslav, 29334, 29391, 29478
Kasimow, Harold, 29569
Kassel, 29877
Kastner, Dieter, 29069, 29829
Kater, Michael H., 29700, 29701
Kattowitz, 29178
Katus, László, 29223
Katz, Hanns Ludwig, 29685, 29798
Katz, Jacob (Jakob), 29016, 29429, 29223, 29656, 30001
Katz, Steven T., 29314, 29398
Katzenelson, Jizchak, 29061
Kauffeldt, Rolf, 29169
Kaufmann, Menachem, 29367
Kaufmann, Uri (Robert Uri), 29018, 29136, 29225, 29226, 29243, 29617
Kaufmann, Walter, 30044
Kautsky, Luise, 29014
Kedar, Aharon, 29657
Keegan, Susanne, 30049
Keilson, Hans, 29392, 29542
Keller, Volker, 29151
Kemp, Wolfgang, 29160
Kempen, Otto Ernst, 29970
Keren, Nili, 29478
Kershaw, Ian, 29376, 29437
Kessler, Mario, 29014
Kestenberg, Judith, 29542
Keuck, Bernard, 29169
Khriplovich, Iosif B., 29793
Kiba, H., 29778

Kickel, Walter, 30052
Kiefer, Annegret, 29623
Kiefer, Ulrike, 29062, 29063
Kiel, 29537, 29684, 29872
Kiesel, Doron, 29704, 29970
Kiessling, Wolfgang, 29513
Kindertransport, 29162, 29466
Kirchner, Peter, 29084, 29647
Kirsch, Fritz Peter, 28992
Kirstein, Wolfgang, 29393
Kisch, Egon Erwin, 29703, 29881
Kissinger, Henry, 29799
Klafki, Wolfgang, 29734
Klamper, Elisabeth, 29278
Kleber, Birgit, 29361
Kleeberg, Julius J., 29897
Kleiman, Yehudit, 29330
Klein, Hans-Georg, 29068
Klein, Hans-Günter, 29477, 29706, 29787, 29850
Klemperer, Klemens von, 29394
Klemperer, Victor, 29124
Klepper, Jochen, 30045
Kleve, 29169
Klibansky, Raymond, 29428
Kliem, Manfred, 29706
Kliner-Lintzen, Martina, 29941
Klingenstein, Susanne, 29235
Klinger, Ruth, 29898
Klotz, Richard, 29183
Klüger, Ruth, 29395
Kluge, Friedrich, 29740
Kniesmeyer, Joke, 29528
Knigge, Volkhard, 29381
Knippschild, Dieter, 29319
Knoblauch, Gustav, 29088
Knobloch, Heinz, 29084
Knoch-Mund, Gaby, 29943
Knoll, Joachim H., 29600, 29601
Koblenz, 29169
Koch, Edita, 29685
Kochan, Lionel, 29017
Kochavi, Arieh Joseph, 29314, 29442
Kocka, Jürgen, 29030
Köhler, Otto, 29381
Köhler, Rosemarie, 29089
Köhn, Gerhard, 29462
Königshütte, 29178
Koepke, Wulf, 29772
Koeppen, Wolfgang, 30061
Kohler, Lotte, 29867
Kohn, Hans, 29658
Kolb, Eberhard, 29344
Kolinsky, Eva, 29538
Kollek, Teddy, 29282
Koller-Glück, Elisabeth, 29211
Kolmar, Gertrud, 29001, 29800
Komlos, John, 29223
Kompert, Leopold, 29214
Konieczny, Alfred, 29473

Konow, Karl-Otto, 29165
Konstanz, 29145
Koonz, Claudia, 29398
Korfmacher, Norbert, 29702
Kornfeld, Gertrud, 29709
Kornfeld, Paul, 29801
'Koroth', 29636
Korrenz, Ralf, 29557
Koschel, Ansgar, 29504
Koschnick, Hans, 29504
Kosnick, Kira, 29485
Koszyk, Kurt, 29014, 29030
Kovács, Mária, 29223
Koziello-Poklewski, Bohdan, 29473
Kracauer, Siegfried, 29690
Kranz, Tomasz, 29528
Krasa, Hans, 29477
Kratz-Whan, Ulrich, 29089
Kraus, Karl, 29694, 29703, 29772, 30048
Krause, Clemens, 29124
Kraushaar, Wolfgang, 29542
Krefeld, 29169
Kreis, Rudolf, 29375
Kreisky, Bruno, 29350, 29908
Kreisler, Georg, 29908
Krejci, Michael, 29673
Kremers-Sper, Thomas, 30002
Krems, 29902
Kren, George M., 30003
Kreutz, Wilhelm, 29162
Kreutzer, Hans Joachim, 29395
Kreuzburg, 29178
Krikler, Bernard, 29256
Krochmalnik, Daniel, 29243, 29624
Krohn, Claus-Dieter, 29678
Krohn, Helga, 29798
Kronberg, Simon, 29802
Krondorfer, Björn, 29380
Krüger, Bernhard, 29311
Krüger, Dieter, 29421
Krumme, Werner, 29274
Kruse, Joseph A., 29025, 29770, 29772, 29776, 29783, 29785, 29790
Kruse, Sabine, 29025
Kruszewski, Tomasz, 29473
Kuby, Alfred H., 29162
Kuczynski, Jürgen, 29899, 29900
Kudela, Jiri, 29221
Kübler, Gunhild, 30068
Kühn, Volker, 29293
Kühn-Ludewig, Maria, 29763
Kühne, Rosie, 29307
Kühnl, Reinhard, 29378
Kühntopf-Gentz, Michael, 29659
Küng, Hans, 29572
Künzl, Hannelore, 29072, 29169, 29266, 29635, 29649
Kuessner, Dietrich, 29304
Kugelmann, Cilly, 28988, 29266

Index to Bibliography

Kuh, Anton, 29703
Kuhlmann, Andreas, 29845
Kukatzki, Bernard, 29098, 29157, 29162–29164
Kulka, Otto Dov, 29282, 29429, 29723
Kulturbund, Jüdischer, 29293, 29294, 29347, 29348, 29883
Kuntze, Günter, 29409
Kurzweil, Zvi Erich, 29571, 29573, 29901
Kuschel, Karl-Josef, 29963
Kushner, Tony, 30004
Kwiet, Konrad, 29493
Kybalová, Ludmila, 29217

Laak, Dirk van, 29310
Lagiewski, Maciej, 29473
Lambert, Anna, 29902
Lambour, Christian, 29787
Lamers, Gerd, 29169
Landauer, Gustav, 29014, 29822, 30025
Landauer, Hans, 29492
Landen, Johannes, 29542
Landjudentum im Süddeutschen- und Bodenseeraum, 29018; 29065, 29080, 29119, 29121, 29167, 29202, 29227, 29229, 29414, 29925, 29965, 29972
Landwehr, Rolf, 29647
Lang, Berel, 29398
Lange, Erhard H.M., 29833
Langenbucher, Wolfgang R., 29703
Langenlonsheim, 29169
Langer, Lawrence, 29398
Langford, J.K., 30005
Langfus, Anna, 29384
Langkau-Alex, Ursula, 29682
Language and Culture Atlas of Ashkenazic Jewry, 29063
Lapide, Pinchas, 29780
Laqueur, Walter, 29256, 29803, 29903
Large, David Clay, 29493
Lasch, Agathe, 29804
'Lashon ve-Ivrit', 29586
Lasker-Schüler, Else, 29772, 29805, 29806
Lassalle, Ferdinand, 29807
Latvia, 29366
— Nazi Period, 29438
Lauritsch, Andrea M., 29668, 29865
Lausch, Hans, 29090, 29579
Lavsky, Hagit, 29660
Lax, Ruth E., 29574
'LBI Information. Nachrichten aus den Leo Baeck Instituten', 29250
Lechenich, 29168
Legal History, 28992, 28998, 28999, 29021, 29078, 29120, 29219
Legal Professions, Jews in, 29364
Lehnardt, Karina, 29109
Lehnert, Detlef, 29831
Leibowitz, Joshua O., 29636
Leipzig, 29146, 29396, 29397, 29792

Leitner, Maria, 29361
Lemberger, Tirza, 29212
Lenarz, Michael, 29635
Lengnau, 29227
Lengyel, György, 29223
Lenk, Margrit, 29124
Lensing, Leo A., 29772
Leo Baeck Institute, 29030, 29173, 29246, 29247, 29250, 29252, 29504
— 'Bulletin', 29245
— Jerusalem, 29248
— New York, 'Library and Archive News', 29251
— Memorial Lecture, 29587
— 'Year Book', 29249; 29007, 29012, 29039, 29042, 29050, 29234, 29267, 29342, 29346, 29469, 29490, 29494, 29496, 29506, 29583, 29619, 29628, 29655, 29666, 29675, 29710, 29880, 29926, 29975, 30007, 30023, 30050
Leo, Annette, 29528
Lepper, Herbert, 29067
Lessing, Gotthold Ephraim, 29083, 29782, 30046, 30047
Lessing, Theodor, 29808
Lessons and Legacies, 29398
Leubuscher, Charlotte, 29709
Levene, Mark, 29443
Levi, Paul, 30060
Levi, Primo, 29384
Levi-Mühsam, Else, 29910
Levin, Elena, 29399
Levin, Neil W., 29651
Levin, Rahel, see Varnhagen, Rahel
Levinas, Emmanuel, 29593
Levinger, Yaacov, 29613
Levinson, Nathan Peter, 29113, 29540
Levinson, Pnina Navé & Nathan Peter (Festschrift), 29923; 29459, 29591, 29592, 29641, 29786
Levy, Ze'ev, 30033
Lewald, Fanny, 29904, 29905
Lewandowski, Louis, 29650
Lewis, Bernard, 29967
Lewis, Rand C., 30006
Lewisohn, Ludwig, 29235
'liberal', 29037, 29730, 29834
Lichtblau, Albert, 29210
Lichtenstein, Heiner, 29266, 29378, 29514
Lichter, Jörg, 29400
Liebe, Ulrich, 29401
Liebenthal Family, 29308
Liffman, Doris & Herbert, 29325
Lilienthal, Peter, 29704
Lilienthal, Georg, 29402
Lindhoff, Frauke, 29533
Lindner, Erik, 29169, 29637, 30007
Linn, Heinrich, 29169
Lipman, Steve, 29403
Liptzin, Sol, 29772, 29843

Literary Studies, Jews in, 29917
'Literatur für Leser', 29683, 29705
Literature, Hebrew, 29199, 29770
Literature, Jews depicted in, 28992, 29473, 29628, 29673, 29801, 29929, 29933, 29943, 29948, 29950, 29954, 29988, 29992, 30000, 30011, 30013, 30017, 30031, 30066
— Jews in (see also Exile Literature), 29668, 29670, 29673, 29694, 29707, 29722, 29739, 29765, 29770, 29774, 29789, 29800, 29805, 29828, 29830, 29849, 29859
Lithuania, 29154, 29354, 29453
Littel, Franklin H., 29398
Litzmannstadt see Lodz
Livingstone, Rodney, 29811
Lixl-Purcell, Andreas, 29906
Lodz, 29340, 29381, 29404
Loebl, Herbert, 29078
Löningen, 29147
Löslein, Barbara, 29130
Loewenberg, Peter, 29982
Loewy, Hanno, 29381
Lohmann, Hartmut, 29464
Lohmann, Ingrid, 29542
Lokers, Jan, 29112
Lomnitz, 29218
'London Review of Books', 30008
Lorencová, Anna, 29217
Lorenz, Dagmar C.G., 29405, 29846
Lorenz, Ina S., 29363, 29366
Lorenz, Einhart, 29406
Lotter, Friedrich, 29020, 29021, 29266
Lowenstein, Steven M., 29022, 29083
Lowenthal-Hensel, Cécile, 29706
Lowry, Stephen, 29308
Loycke, Almut, 29845
Lozowick, Yaacov, 29318
Lubarsch, Otto, 29621
Lubinski, Georg, 29647
Lubitsch, Ernst, 29690, 29809
Lublinitz, 29744
Lucas, Franz D., 29597
Lucas, Leopold, 29346
Luckenwalde, 29407
Ludwig, Emil, 29810
Ludwig, Johannes, 29408
Ludwigshafen, 29098, 29162
Lübbe, Hermann, 29381
Lübeck, 29148
Lüdtke, Alf, 29533
Lügde, 29149
Lühe, Barbara von der, 29255
Lüthi, Urs, 29228
Lütkehaus, Ludger, 30056
Lütkemeier, Hildegard, 29638
Lukacs, Georg, 29811, 29881
Lundgren, Svante, 29570
Lustig, Arnost, 29982
Lustiger, Arno, 29250, 29252, 29368

Luther, Martin, 29031, 29960, 29983
'Lutherische Monatshefte', 29991
Lutz, Thomas, 29528, 29546
Luxemburg, Rosa, 29014, 29025
Luzzatto, Amos, 29617
Luzzatto, Samuel David, 29581

Maciejewski, Marek, 29473
Madajczyk, Czeslaw, 29473
Magdeburg, 29409
Magdeburg-Anhalt, 29439
Magic, 28992
Magnus, Shulamith Sharon, 29105
Mahler, Gustav, 29812–29814
Mahler, Horst, 29378
Mahler-Werfel, Alma, 29859, 30048, 30049
'(Die) Mahnung', 29898
Maibach, Heinz, 29847
Maier, Johann, 28992
Mainz, 29003, 29023, 29150, 29410
Maislinger, Andreas, 29944
Majdanek, 29528
Majsai, Tamás, 29303
Malcher, Rita, 29485
Malchow, 29152, 29153
Malkin, Irad, 29654
Mallus-Huth, Heike, 29141
Mandelartz, Michael, 29827
Manegold, Karl-Heinz, 29352
Mann, Golo, 29763
Mannheim, 29151
'Mannheimer Hefte', 29151
Manrique, Matthias, 29289
Manthey, Matthias, 29352
Marburg an der Lahn, 29411, 29412
Marcus, Ivan G., 29003, 29023
Marcus, Jacob Rader, 29236
Marcus, Marcel, 29815
Marek, Lionel, 30062
Margolis, Joseph, 30039
Margolius Kovaly, Heda, 29907
Maric, Mileva, 29747
Markus, Georg, 29765, 29908
Maron, Avraham, 29852
Maronde, Margit, 29542
Marrus, Michael R., 29398
Marwedel, Günter, 29073
Marx, Albert, 29171
Marx, Eleanor, 29817
Marx, Gisela, 29378
Marx, Heinrich, 29817
Marx, Karl, 29772, 29781, 29815–29818
Maser, Peter, 29178, 29964
Matoni, Jürgen, 30031
Mattenklott, Gert, 29413, 29704, 29726
Matzerath, Horst, 29310
Maubach, Peter, 29421
Maurer, Trude, 29024

Index to Bibliography

Mauthner, Fritz, 29014, 29214
Mayer, Dieter, 29705
Mayer, Gustav, 29014
Mayer, Hans, 29673, 29726
'MB' Mitteilungsblatt des Irgun Olei Merkas Europa, 29154, 29173, 29897
McCagg, William, 29223
McEwan, Dorothea, 29218, 29414, 29965
Mecklenburg, 29152, 29153, 29415
Mecklenburg, Frank, 29487
Medicine, Jews in, 29291, 29699, 29736, 29740, 29897
— Nazi, 29270, 29312
'Medinah', 29598
Mehlitz, Walter, 29639
Mehlmann, Jeffrey, 29386
Meidner, Ludwig, 29107
Meier, Christian, 29003
Meier-Cronemeier, Hermann, 29266
Meincke, Susanne, 29124
Meiners, Werner, 29147
Meir Ben Baruch of Rothenburg, 29575
Meitner, Lise, 29709
Melson, Robert, 29416
Memel, 29154
Memorials, 29079, 29381, 29528, 29531, 29533, 29536, 29537, 29540, 29541, 29544, 29548, 29553
Mendelsohn, Erich, 29819
Mendelssohn Family, 29706
Mendelssohn, Moses, 29083, 29576–29582, 29611, 29691, 29865
Mendelssohn, Peter de, 29820
Mendelssohn Studien, 29706; 29555, 29578, 29579, 29787, 30046
Mendelsson, Eva, 29158
Mendes-Flohr, Paul, 29640, 29874
Menell, Stephen, 29751
'Menora', 29255; 29081, 29190, 29283, 29501, 29544, 29588, 29621, 29642, 29650, 29722, 29736, 29951, 29953
Menze, Josef, 29182
Merkx, Joep (Jozef), 29240
Merxplas, 29328
Merzbacher, Abraham, 29076
Merzbacher, Gottfried, 29076
Messerschmidt, Manfred, 29381
Messianism, 29592, 29604, 29656
Metz, Johann Baptist, 29381
Metzger, Kurt L., 29162
Metzler, Hermann J., 29912
Meyer Kallen, Horace, 29235
Meyer, Eduard, 29821
Meyer, Hans-Georg, 29142
Meyer, Martin, 29726
Meyer, Michael A., 29013, 29026–29028, 29083, 29250, 29266, 29617
Meyer-Maril, Edina, 29429
Meyer-Schurz, Margarethe, 29895

Meynert, Joachim, 29298, 29418
Michaelis, Meir, 29417
Michaelis, Miriam, 30063
Middle Ages, 28990, 28992, 29003, 29006, 29011, 29013, 29015, 29020, 29021, 29023, 29043–29045, 29053, 29150, 29165, 29197, 29224, 29562–29564, 29567, 29575, 29614, 29618, 29647, 29932, 29934, 29943, 29964, 29967, 29987, 30018
'Midstream', 29574, 29653, 29781, 29857
Migration, 29210
Mikwe, 29635
Miller, Susanne, 29014
Milton, Sybil, 29528
Minden, 29418
Minsk, 29306
Mishkinski, Moshe, 29816
Mistelfeld, 29155
Mittag, Gabriele, 29361
'Mitteilungen d. Inst. f. österr. Geschichts- forschung', 29218
— d. Mindener Geschichtsvereins', 29418
— d. Museen Österreichs', 29201
— d. Vereins f. Heimatkunde, Birkenfeld', 29832
— d. Westdeutschen Ges. f. Familienkunde', 28989
Mittelmann, Hanni, 29746
Mitten, Richard, 30009
Mixed Marriages, 29368, 29423
— Children of, 29278, 29285, 29422, 29466
'Mnemosyne', 29668, 29865
'Mnemosyne-Schriften', 30063, 30072
'Modern Austrian Literature', 29741, 29843, 29846, 29859
'Modern Judaism', 29577, 29605, 29606
Möller, Horst, 29083
Mönchengladbach, 29156, 29169
Mohel, 29636
Moisling, 29148
Molnar, Michael, 29753
Mommsen, Hans, 29381, 29398, 29493
'Monatshefte', 29992
Moneta, Dalia, 29647
Moravia, 29207, 29216, 29218, 29219
Morgan, Michael L., 29582
Morgenthau Family, 29237
Morgenthau, Henry, 29237
'Moriah', 29207, 29567, 29568
Morley, J., 29382
Morris, Rodler F., 30003
Moser, Jonny, 29278, 29279
Mosès, Stéphane, 29595, 29596, 29727, 29839
Moslowicz, Arnold, 29404
Mossad, 29315
Mosse, George L., 29661, 29662, 29803, 29909
Mosse, Werner E., 29029, 29030, 29037, 29266
Muchitsch, Wolfgang, 29280, 29444
Mühsam, Erich, 29822

Mühsam-Magazin, 29822
Mühsam, Paul, 29910
Mülheim, 29169
Müller, Gerhard, 29685
Müller, Guido, 29166
Müller, Hans-Harald, 29828
Müller, Helmut-Gerhard, 29734
Müller-Hohagen, Jürgen, 29378, 29542
Müller-Tupath, Karla, 29632
'Müritz-Bote', 29153
Muller, Robert, 29419
Murray, Bruce A., 29690
Museums, 29189, 29190, 29540
Music, 29340
— Jewish, 29648, 29650, 29651
— Jews in, 29271, 29678, 29708, 29912
Musicians, Composers, 29477, 29648, 29651, 29700, 29701, 29787, 29812, 29814, 29850, 29916
Mussdorf, Torsten, 29456

Na'aman, Shlomo, 29014, 29817, 29945
Nach Osten, 29485; 29002, 29086
Nachama, Andreas, 29091, 29650
Nachmann, Werner, 29955
Naggar, Betty, 29238
Names, Change of, 29218, 29980
— Jewish, 29010, 29046, 29049, 29933, 29980
'Nassauische Annalen', 29847
Nathan, Asher, 29429
Nationalism, 29610, 29661, 29667, 29922
'Nativ', 30054
'Natural History', 29356
Natzweiler, 29393
Nazi Crimes, 29305, 29354, 29368
— Prosecution of, 29338, 29339, 29938
Nazi Period (see also individual countries), 29013, 29371, 29453
— Dispossessions, 29408
— Foreign Reaction, 29472
— in Film, Radio, Theatre, 29454
— German Intellectuals, 30032
— Jewish Life in Germany, 29294, 29295, 29310, 29347, 29363, 29397, 29418, 29473, 29496, 29629, 29647
— Jewish Youth, 29087, 29310, 29448, 29482, 29629
— Survival in Hiding, 29278, 29496
— False Identity, 29377, 29435
— Teaching, 29371, 29381, 29541, 29550, 29944
— Universities, 29684
Nazi Politics and Propaganda, 29402, 29429, 30020
Neiman, Susan, 29946
Nelissen, Lisa, 29169
Nellessen, Bernd, 29310
Neo Nazism (see also Historiography, Revisionism), 29998

Ness, D., 29420
Netherlands, 29122
— Nazi Period, 29301, 29432, 30075
— Refugees, 29688, 29791
Neubauer, Hans-Joachim, 30017
Neubauer, Hermann, 29982
Neubrandenburg, 29421
'Neubrandenburger Mosaik', 29421
Neubroch, Hans, 29276
'Neue Beiträge zur Jülicher Geschichte', 29071
Neues Lexikon des Judentums, 29266
Neufeld, Siegbert, 29111
Neugebauer, Wolfgang, 29278
Neumann, Micha, 30043
Neumann, Robert, 29063
'(Das) Neunzehnte Jahrhundert', 29062
Neupert, Jutta, 29422
Neuss, 29169
Neuwied, 29169, 29423
Neuwirth, Karl, 29873
'new german critique', 29370, 29737
'(The) New York Review of Books', 29503, 29840
'New York Times', 29246, 29526
Nicosia, Francis R., 29424, 30010
Niebergall, Walter, 29537
'Niederdeutsches Jahrbuch', 29804
Niederland, Doron, 29282
'Niedersächsisches Jahrbuch f. Landesgeschichte', 28999, 29308
Niedhart, Gottfried, 29014
Niemöller, Martin, 29310
Nierstein, 29160
Niethammer, Lutz, 29381, 29528
Nietzsche, Elisabeth see Förster, Elisabeth
Nietzsche, Friedrich, 29375, 29694, 30044, 30050
Niewöhner, Friedrich, 29083, 29967
Nisko, 29355
Nobel, Nehemiah Anton, 29584
Nohl, Herman, 29697
Nolte, Ernst, 29375
'Non Aryan' Christians, 29285, 29296, 29310, 29353, 29359, 29368, 29420
Nordau, Max, 29662, 29772
Nordhofen, Eckhard, 29856
'Nordisk Judaistik', 29534, 29933, 29950
Nordmann, Ingeborg, 29915
Norway, Nazi Period, 29406
November Pogrom, 29304, 29327, 29357, 29366, 29378, 29407, 29425–29431, 29434, 29439, 29473, 29982, 30026
Nowak, Kurt, 29947
Nowoczin, Hans Gerd, 30045
Nussbaum, Laureen, 29791
'NZZ' (Neue Zürcher Zeitung), 29445, 29453, 29726, 29735, 29795, 29802, 29825, 29840, 29841, 29882, 29915, 30036, 30068, 30070, 30075

Index to Bibliography

Oberglogau, 29178
'Oberschlesisches Jahrbuch', 29205, 29744, 30031
Oberwesel, 29169, 29180
'(The) Observer', 29753, 30032
Och, Gunnar, 30011, 30047
Odenbach, 29157, 29162
'Ökumenische Rundschau', 29968
Oelke, Karl-Heinz, 29152, 29153
Österreicher im Exil, 29280
Ofer, Dalia, 29663
Offenbach, Jacques, 29708
Offenburg, 29158
Ohringer, Mirjam, 29378
Oldenburg, 29159
'Oldenburger Jahrbuch', 29147, 29159
Oliveira, Manuel Duarte de, 29559
Olszewski, Henryk, 29473
Onomastics, 29617
Oppeln, 29178
Oppelt, Wolfgang, 29076
Oppenheim, 29160
Oppenheim, Heinrich Bernard, 30024
Oppenheim, Isaac (Rabbi), 29585
Oppenheim, Salomon Herz Löw, 30073
Oppenheimer, Joseph Süss, 29031
Oppenheimer, Olga, 29823
Oppler, Ernst, 29824
Orfali, Stephanie, 29076
Organisations, 29296, 29449, 29633, 29638, 29640, 29642–29644, 29646, 29647, 29666, 29710, 29868, 30007
— Nazi Period, 29358, 29418
— Post War, 29519, 29525, 29951, 29953
Organizing Rescue, 29646; 29052, 29329, 29665
'Orientierung', 29931
Orland, Nahum, 29266
Orlik, Franz, 29743
Orlov, Boris S., 29528
Orth, Wilhelm, 29834
Orthodoxy, 28996, 28997, 29016, 29429, 29571, 29573, 29583, 29584, 29588, 29617, 29628
Ortmeyer, Benjamin, 29432
Osiander, Andreas, 29993
Ossowski, Leonie, 29378
Ottenheimer, Hilde, 29346
Ottensooser, David, 29076
'Our Press', 29516
Ozick, Cynthia, 29301, 29433

Paal, Janos, 29641
Pachnicke, Peter, 29768
Padua, 29617
Pätzold, Kurt, 29335, 29336, 29478
Palatinate, 29161–29164
Palestine, 29314, 29655, 29659, 29821, 29868, 29892
— Immigration, 29044, 29282, 29315, 29442, 29652, 29657, 29669

— Refugees, 29665
Palme, Rudolf, 28992
Pankau, Johannes G., 29685
Pankoke, Werner, 29070, 29071
Panofsky, Erwin, 29825
Panse, Barbara, 30017
Pappenheim, Bertha, 29001, 29826
'(Das) Parlament', 29041, 29288, 29336, 29371, 29488, 29504, 29833
'Partisan Review', 29433, 29463, 30021
Paskuly, Steven, 29275
'Patterns of Prejudice', 29998, 30004
Patterson, David, 29384
Patzelt, Herbert, 29205
Paucker, Arnold, 29014, 29037, 29246, 29249
Paul, Arno, 29093
Pauley, Bruce F., 29975
Pazi, Margarita, 29323, 29722, 29772, 29801
Peled, Yoav, 29818
Peles, Israel Mordechai, 29128, 29585
Pelles, Yedida, 29633
Pelli, Moshe, 29586, 29598, 29599
Penzberg, 29434
Penzlin, 29152, 29153
Perel, Sally, 29435
Perlman, Robert, 29239
Pertsch, Dietmar, 29031
Perutz, Leo, 29827, 29828, 30064, 30065
Pest see Budapest
Peteghem, Paul van, 29122
Peters, Hartmut, 29430
Petter, Wolfgang, 29310
Petuchowski, Elizabeth, 28996
Petuchowski, Jakob J., 29911
Peyer, Hans Conrad (Festschrift), 29225
'Pfälzisches Judentum Gestern und Heute', 29162
Pfeifer, Martin, 30042
Philippson Family, 29829
Philippson, Ludwig, 29637
Philosemitism, 29939, 29952
'Philosophy East and West', 30037
Philosophy and Learning, Jews in, 29713, 29717, 29743, 30056
Philosophy, Jewish, 28992, 29566, 29582
'Physics Today', 29793
Picard, Jacob, 29830
Picard, Jacques, 29617
Pickett, Winston, 29949
Piechocki, Werner, 29124
Pierenkemper, Toni, 29030, 29179
Pilgrim, Volker Elis, 29325
Pinkas HaKehillot, 29137
Pinkus, Benjamin, 29646
Piper, Franciszek, 29478
Pitt-Rivers, Julian, 29845
Plaut, W. Gunther, 29587
'Plesse-Archiv', 29101
Plowinski, Kerstin, 29146

Pörtener, Barbara, 29150
Pogge v. Strandmann, Hartmut, 29030
Pohl, Hans, 29030
Pohland, Vera, 29349
Poland, 29222
— Nazi Period, 29301, 29366
Polgar, Alfred, 29703
'Politics and Society', 29048
Politics, Jews in, 29030, 29702, 29769, 29788, 29831, 29844, 29920
'Politische Vierteljahresschrift', 29831
Pollaczek, Hilda, 29709
Polák, Erik, 29478
Pomerania, 29165
Popping, Peter, 29402
Porat, Dina, 29436
Portugal, Nazi Period, 29445
Posen, 29437
Posen, Meir, 29635
Posener, Julius, 29678
Post, Rudolf, 29162
Pradelski, Trude, 29647
Prague, 29214, 29217, 29220, 29221, 29323, 29484, 29670, 29870, 30074
— Jewish Museum, 29217
Prater, Donald A., 29859
Prawer, S.S., 30066
Prawy, Marcel, 29765
Press, Bernhard, 29438
Press, Jewish, 28994, 29169, 29516, 29637, 29645, 29670
Presser, Ellen, 30070
Pressler, Mirjam, 29345
Preuss, Hugo, 29831
Prieberg, Fred K., 29293
Pringle, Annette, 29267
Prinz, Wolfgang, 29439
'Proceedings of the 10th World Congress of Jew. Studies', 29576, 29581, 29599, 29757, 29860
Pross, Harry, 29266
Prümm, Karl, 29764
Prussia, 29083
Psychoanalysts, Psychologists, 29675, 29692, 29755, 29756, 29758, 29761, 29762
Publicists, Journalists, 29686
Publishers, Printers, 29679, 29682, 29792
Pulver, Elsbeth, 29915
Pulzer, Peter, 29030, 29032, 29033
Puner, Helen Walker, 29761
Puner, Samuel P., 29761
Purin, Bernhard, 29201, 29651
Puschner, Uwe, 29552
Puskás, Julianna, 29223
Putschke, Wolfgang, 29063
Putzlitz, Gisbert, Frhr. zu, 29561

'Qesher', 28994, 29645
Quack, Sybille, 29440
'Qualestoria', 29652

Rabbis, 29169, 29207, 29246, 29558, 29564, 29575, 29583–29585, 29588, 29607, 29608, 29616, 29618, 29875, 29911
Rabien, Ilse, 29706
Rabinowitz, Eliezer, 29515, 29516
Racism, 29204, 29210, 29402, 29623, 30055
Raddatz, Fritz J., 29750, 30056
Raim, Edith, 29478
Rajca, Czeslaw, 29478
Ramon, Esther, 29144
Randegg, 29121
Ranger, Kurt, 29123
Ránki, György, 29223
Rapaport, Lynn, 29517
Raphael, Chaim, 29034
Raphael, Freddy, 29196
Rashi, 29053
Rath, Arie, 29282
Rathenau, Walther, 29030, 29832–29837
Rathenow, Lutz, 29842
Rau, Johannes, 29169
Ravitzky, Aviezer, 29003
Real, Willy, 29894
Rechenberg, Helmut, 30040
Redlich, Gonda, 29476
Reed, T.J., 29776
Reform Judaism, 29013, 29650, 29949
Refugee Policy, 29342, 29406, 29417, 29441–29443, 29472, 29479
Refugees (see also individual countries), 29230, 29445, 29454, 29469
— Children of, 29233
Regensteiner, Henry, 29781
Rehlingen, 29166
Rehn, Marie-Elisabeth, 29365
Reich-Ranicki, Marcel, 29782
Reichel, Peter, 29388
Reichrath, Hans, 29966
Reichrath, Hans L., 29162
Reim, Günter, 29076
Reinhardt, Gottfried, 29908
Reinhardt, Hildegard, 29823
Reinharz, Jehuda, 29013, 29664–29666, 29803
Reinke, Andreas, 29102
Reinprecht, Christoph, 29499, 29539
Reisch, Linda, 29381, 29635, 29970
'Religionsunterricht an Höh. Schulen (RHS)', 29106, 29549
Rendsburg, 29540
— Jüd. Museum, 29540
Renn, Jürgen, 29747
Rentenaar, Rob, 29804
Resistance, 29278, 29296, 29316, 29493, 29528
— Jewish, 29489–29491, 29494–29496, 29498
— Non-Jewish, 29394, 29433, 29458, 29467
Restitution, 29310, 29518
Reuter, Fritz, 29193
Reuter, Ursula, 29193
Reuveni, Yaacov, 29658

Index to Bibliography

Reyer, Herbert, 29110
Rhein, Valérie, 29064
Rheineck, 29167
'Rheydter Jahrbuch', 29156
Rhineland, 29170, 29426, 29446, 29671, 29805
Ribbe, Wolfgang, 29083
Richarz, Monika, 29018, 29030, 29035
Richez, Jean-Claude, 29196
Richter, Jörn, 29313
Richter, Klemens, 29959
Richter, Manfred, 29061
Ried, Peter Anselm, 29130
Riedner, Johannes, 29297
Riem, Andreas, 30051
Riemer, Detlev, 29407
Riff, Michael A., 29222
Riga, 29318, 29438, 29891
Ringelheim, Joan, 28990, 29485
Ripkens, Werner, 29169
Riss, Heidelore, 29294
Ritchie, James M., 29680, 29681, 29687, 30012
Rites and Ceremonies, 28992, 29005, 29045, 29050, 29075, 29080, 29631, 29636, 29639
Ritual Bath, 29162, 29635
Ritual Murder see Blood Libel
Roazen, Paul, 29761
Robinsohn, Hans, 29494
Robinson, Jack Hughes, 30027
Rockmore, Tom, 30038, 30039
Röbel, 29152, 29153
Röcher, Ruth, 29447, 29448
Röder, Werner, 29323
Röll, Walter, 29059
Roenpage, Peter, 29948
Röpcke, Andreas, 29306
Rössler, Hans, 29434
Rohde, Klaus, 29140
Rohde, Saskia, 29366
Rohdenburg, Günther, 29306
Rohrbacher, Stefan, 29036, 29070, 29169
Rohwer, Jörn, 29625
Roloff, Ernst August, 29304
Romania, 29222
Roming, Gisela, 29121
Roper, Katherine, 30013
Rose, Paul Lawrence, 30055
Rosen, Moses, 29222
Rosenbaum, Fred, 29949
Rosenberg, Heinz L., 29306
Rosenfeld, Alvin H., 29398
Rosenkranz, Herbert, 29429
Rosenkranz, Ze'ev, 29449, 29642
Rosenthal, Erwin, 29249
Rosenthal, Hans, 29838
Rosenzweig, Franz, 29566, 29576, 29582, 29589–29596, 29640, 29839, 29874, 29958
Rosh, Lea, 29632
Ross Range, Peter, 29935
Rossel, Seymour, 29385

Rossner, Judith, 29292
Rote Kapelle, 29491
Roth, Joseph, 29703, 29840
Roth, Stephen, 29222
Rothfels, Max, 29674
Rothkirchen, Livia, 29478
Rothschild, Eli, 29897
Rubenstein, Richard, 29450
Ruch, Martin, 29158
Rudischhauser, Sabine, 29769
Rühmkorf, Eva, 29540
Rürup, Reinhard, 29504, 29528, 29970
Ruess, Karl-Heinz, 29123
Rummel, R.J., 29337
Runge, Irene, 29520, 29909
Ruppel, Helmut, 29293
Ruprecht, Thomas M., 29736
Rural Jewry, 29005, 29018, 29030, 29070, 29080, 29082, 29116, 29121, 29132–29136, 29162, 29168, 29175, 29227, 29283, 29367
Russia, 29052
Ryan, Judith, 29451

Saar, 29166
'Saarländische Familienkunde', 29166
Saarland, 29171
'Saat auf Hoffnung', 29937
Sabelleck, Rainer, 29129
Sabrow, Martin, 29835
Sachs, Michael, 29597
Sachs, Nelly, 29685, 29881
Sachsenhausen, 29311, 29452
Sacks, Jonathan, 29647
Sahl, Hans, 29841, 29842, 30067
Sahm, Ulrich W., 29127
Salem, 29697
Sallen, Herbert, 29523
Saloma, Antoni, 29473
Salomon-Lindberg, Paula, 29883
Salomonsohn Family, 29029
Salons, 29083, 29696, 29852
Sammons, Jeffrey L., 29772
Samuel, Herbert, 29857
Samuel, Horace, 30069
Samuelson, Norbert, 29605
Sandkühler, Thomas, 29381
Saner, Hans, 29867
Sasportas, Jacob, 29025
Sassenberg, Marina, 29084, 29169
Sassin, Horst R., 29037, 29494
Satanow, Isaac, 29586, 29598, 29599
Sauer, Paul, 29082, 29184
Sauerland, Karol, 30036
Saxony, 28998
Schäfer-Richter, Uta, 29352, 29533
Schaeffler, Richard, 29617
Schanze, Helmut, 29784
Schardt, Angelika, 29521
Scharff, Werner, 29495

(Die) Schatten der Vergangenheit, 29453; 29938, 29939, 29944, 29955
Scheckel, Harald, 29159
Scheel, Heinrich, 29491, 29888
Scheer, Regina, 29094
Scheffer, Christoph, 29541
Scheiger, Brigitte, 29485
Schellbach, Artur, 29124
Scheller, Bertold, 29647
Scherg, Leonhard, 29005
Schernus, Wilhelm, 29828
Scheuermann, Michael, 29150
Schieb-Samizadeh, Barbara, 29495
Schieth, Lydia, 29673
Schiffer, Eugen, 29353
Schimmerling, Hanus, 29478
Schindel, Robert, 30068
Schindler, Thomas, 29643
Schine, Robert S., 29615, 29616
Schlesier, Renate, 29772
Schleswig-Holstein, 29172
Schlösser, Louis, 29107
Schlotzhauer, Inge, 29118
Schlüter, Henning, 29836
Schmaderer, Franz-Otto, 29551
Schmatzer, Uta Cornelia, 29684
Schmidl, Erwin A., 29206
Schmidt, Elfriede, 29281
Schmidt, Hannes, 29504
Schmidt, Ingrid, 29293
Schmidt, James, 29580
Schmidt, John, 29522
Schmidt, Maria, 29303
Schmidt, Michael, 30017
Schmitz, Irmgard, 29169
Schmugge, Ludwig, 29197
Schnabel, Arthur, 29912
Schnaittach, 29173
Schneider, Albert (Festschrift), 30012
Schneider, Carlo, 29107
Schneider, Horst, 29431
Schnitzler, Arthur, 29712, 29843, 30069
(The) Schocken Guide to Jewish Books, 29268
Schöer, Siegfried, 29959
Schoeler, Andreas von, 29647
Schoeller, Wilfried F., 30070
Schönberg, Arnold, 29695, 30048
Schoenberner, Gerhard, 29545, 29548
Schönebeck, 29409
Schönerer, Georg Ritter von, 29995
Schoeps, Hans-Joachim, 29600, 29791
Schoeps, Julius H., 29255, 29266, 29601, 29704, 29730, 29772
Scholem, Gershom, 29047, 29565, 29594, 29596, 29602–29604, 29728, 29849, 29874, 29917, 29958
Schools see Education
Schorsch, Ismar, 29619
Schorske, Carl E., 29814

Schott, Heinz, 29402
Schreiber, Albrecht, 29148
Schreiber-Krieger, Adele, 29014
Schreier, Helmut, 29542
Schröter, Harm G., 29030
Schubert, Elke, 29348
Schubert, Katharina, 29454
Schubert, Kurt, 28992
Schubsky, Karl W., 29512
Schuchalter, J., 29950
Schütt, Ulrich, 29411
Schütz, Hans J., 29707
Schütz, Klaus, 29254, 29632
Schüürmann, Herbert, 29327
Schulhoff, Erwin, 29477
Schulin, Ernst, 29837
Schulmann, Robert, 29747
Schulte, Klaus H.S., 29108
Schultz, Magdalena, 28992
Schulweis, Harold M., 29301
Schulz, Bruno, 30070
Schulz, Georg-Michael, 30017
Schulze, Ingrid, 29124
Schumacher, Karl-Heinz, 29156
Schumann, Peter, 29036
Schumann, Willy, 29913
Schupler, Heinrich, 29519
Schurr, Susanne, 29533
Schurz, Carl, 29895
Schuster, Gerhard, 29873
Schutz, David, 30071
Schwaben, 29174, 29925
Schwäbisch Hall, 29175
Schwarz, Christina, 29647
Schwarz, Egon, 29776, 29915
Schwarz, Erika, 29335
Schwarz, Gudrun, 29485
Schwarzschild, Steven S., 29605, 29606
Schweich, 29176
Schweitzer, Albert, 29914, 30052
Schweitzer, József, 29617
Schweitzer Miller, Rhena, 29914
Schwelm, 29177
Schwersenz, Jizchak, 29489
Schwierz, Israel, 29079
Science of Judaism see Wissenschaft des Judentums
Sciences and Mathematics, Jews in, 29090, 29460, 29732, 29744, 29747, 29748, 29793, 30041
Second Chance. Two Centuries of German-Speaking Jews in the United Kingdom, 29037
Seebacher-Brandt, Brigitte, 30036
Seeskin, Kenneth, 29606
Seewann, Harald, 29644
Seferens, Horst, 29506
Segal, Lilli, 29455
(Bad) Segeberg, 29456
Segebrecht, Wulf, 29673

Index to Bibliography

Seghers, Anna, 29881
Seib, Barbara, 29682
Seidler, Manfred, 29026
Seifert, Heribert, 29445
Seligmann, Avraham, 29496
Seligmann, David & Fanny, 29076
Sello, Mario, 29285
Selver, Heinrich, 29290
Sender, Tony (Toni), 29014, 29844
Sengling, Dieter, 29647
Sephardi Communities, 29072, 29122, 29209
Sephardim, 29025
'(The) Seventeenth Century', 29133
Shafir, Shlomo, 29951
Shaked, Gershon, 29248
'Shalem', 29044
Shamir, Haim, 29429
Shanghai, Refugees, 29457
Shavit, Yaakov, 29667
Shavit, Zohar, 29083
She'erit-Hapletah 1944–1948, 29509
Shear-Yashuv, Aharon, 29607, 29612
Shedletzky, Itta, 29245, 29266, 29772, 29849
Sheehan, James J., 29033
Shelley, Lore, 29277
Sherwin, Byron L., 29569
Shichiji, Yoshinori, 29059
Shillony, Ben-Ami, 29457
Shimoni, Gideon, 29543
Shirakawa, Sam, 30032
Shlain, Margalit, 29478
'Shvut', 29816
'Sichot – Dialogue', 30043
Siebenhaar, Klaus, 29750
Siegburg, 29169
Siegele-Wenschkewitz, Leonore, 29310, 30014
Siersburg, 29166
Silber, Michael K., 29223
Silbermann, Alphons, 29266, 29523, 29544, 29626, 29708
Silesia, 29178, 29179, 29205, 29473
Silman-Cheong, Helen, 29868
Silver, Eric, 29458
Simmel, Georg, 29845
Simon, Bettina, 28992
Simon, Heinrich, 28992, 29091, 29617
Simon, Hermann, 29088, 29091, 29092, 29095–29097, 29295
Simon, Marie, 29459, 29617
Simon, Nikolaus, 29970
Simonsohn, Trude, 29647
Simpson, Tess, 29460
'Sinai', 29558
Sinason, Jacob H., 29608
Sinclair, Danile, 29609
Singer, Paul, 29014, 29029
Sinz, Lola, 29422
Skemer, Don C., 29679
Sklarek, Max, Leo and Willy, 29014, 29996

Slansky Trial, 29907
Slovakia, Nazi Period, 29377
Smejkalová, Jana, 29217
Smolak, Kurt, 28992
Smolenskin, Perez, 29610, 29611
Sobernheim, 29461
Social and Economic Development, 29022
'Social Research', 29732, 30041
Social Sciences, Jews in, 29676, 29729, 29751, 29845
Social Welfare, 29358, 29634, 29638, 29647, 29729
Socialists, Social Democrats, 29014, 29048, 29702, 29721, 29731, 29736, 29844
Society for Exile Studies/Gesellschaft für Exilforschung, 'Nachrichtenbrief', 29682
'Society', 28991
Sode-Madsen, Hans, 29478
Soden, Hans von, 29962
Soest, 29462
'Soester Zeitschrift', 29462
Sohrau, 29178
Soll, Karl, 29785
Sommer, Ernst, 29323
Sonnenschmidt, Reinhard, 30035
Sorkin, David, 29013, 29038–29040
Soviet Union, Nazi Period, 29301, 29321, 29793
Spain, Nazi Period, 29445, 29492
Sparr, Thomas, 29917
Sperber, Manès, 29463
'(Der) Spiegel', 29368
Spiegel, Paul, 29647
Spiel, Hilde, 29846
Spielmann, Diane R., 29475
Spielmann, Heinz, 29540
Spinoza, Baruch, 29025, 29582, 30033
Spitzer, Shlomo, 29207
Sponsel, Ilse, 29076, 29113
Spormann, Doris, 29180
Sports, Jews in, 29400
Sprengel, Peter, 29808
St. Gallen, 29229
St. Goar, 29180
Stachau, Christine, 29792
Stade, 29181, 29464
Stähr, Susanne, 29650
Stahl, Patricia, 29647
Stancic, Mirjana, 29772
Starck, Astrid, 29059
Steck, Manfred, 29186
Steffensky, Fulbert, 29542
Stegemann, Wolf, 29189
Steglitz, 29297
Steiman, Lionel B., 29859
Stein, Edith, 29958
Stein, Joshua, 29465
Steinbach, Peter, 29041, 29453
Steinberg, Bernard, 29524
Steinberg, Jonathan, 29467

Index to Bibliography

Steinberg, Werner, 29285
Steindling, Dolly, 29468
Steinecke, Hartmut, 29776
Steiner, George, 29565
Steinfurt, 29890
Steinheim, 29182
Steinheim, Salomon Ludwig, 29612, 29613
Steinheim-Institut, 29253–29255
Steinmetz, Horst, 29191
Steinweis, Alan E., 29470
Stelbrink, Uwe, 29909
Stemberger, Günter, 28992
Stephan, Alexander, 29683
Stephan, Regina, 29819
Stephan, Vaclav, 29219
Stern, Carl, 30072
Stern, Elijahu, 29525
Stern, Eliyahu, 29314
Stern, Frank, 29952, 29953, 29982, 30015
Stern, Guy, 29469
Sternberg, Leo, 29847
Sternfeld, Albert, 29276
Stevens, Gwendolyn, 29692
Stevens, Matthew, 29265
Stieg, Margaret F., 29470
'Stimmen der Zeit', 29963
Stöhr, Martin, 29504, 29923
Stolz, Gerhard, 29172
Stolzenberg, Ingeborg, 29706
Stone, Marla, 30016
Stone, Michael, 29471
Stoop, Paul, 29688
Strassburg, 29197
Strassmann, Ernst, 29494
Strauss, Herbert A., 29042, 29472, 29617
Strauss, Leo, 29582
Strauss, Ludwig, 29848, 29849
Strickhausen, Waltraut, 29820
Studemund-Halévy, Michael, 29025
'Studia nad Fasczymen i zbrod niami Hitlerowskimi', 29473; 29431, 29439
'Studia Rosenthaliana', 29056
'Studies in Zionism', 29821, 30010
Stuttgart, 29183, 29184, 29474, 29919
Suchy, Barbara, 29169, 29267, 29617
'Süddeutsche Zeitung', 29247, 29368, 29395, 29882, 30056, 30070
Suied, Alain, 29772
'Sulamith', 29083, 29637
Sulzer, Salomon, 29651
'(The) Sunday Times', 30055
Sunshine, Andrew, 29063
Susman, Margarete, 29915
Switzerland, 29225, 29226, 29228, 29617
— Refugees, 29479
Synagogues, 29068, 29079, 29088, 29092, 29095–29097, 29130, 29157, 29161, 29169, 29176, 29192, 29198, 29366, 29429, 29430
Szenes, Sándor, 29303

Szilágyi, Julia, 29303
Szita, Szabolcs, 29303
Szondi, Peter, 29917

Ta-Shma, Israel M., 29043–29045
Taddey, Gerhard, 29175
Tagliabue, John, 29526
Tal, Josef, 29916
Talmage, Frank, 29224
Tamir, Arnon, 29918
Tanner, Michael, 30055
Taylor, Jennifer A., 29323
Teachers see Education
Tec, Nechama, 29398
Teicher, Samy, 29982
'Tel Aviver Jahrbuch f. deutsche Geschichte', 29693, 29709
Tennenbaum, Silvia, 29475
Teschen, 29205
Tetzel, Manfred, 29731
Texeira Family, 29025
Thackeray, W.M., 30066
Thalheimer, Siegfried, 29369
Thalmann, Rita, 29326, 29361, 29441, 29976
Theatralia Judaica, 30017; 29093, 29294, 29801, 30047
Theatre, Cabaret, Cinema, Jews in, 29213, 29401, 29678, 29690, 29712, 29764, 29809, 29921
Theatre, Film, Jews depicted in, 29031, 29934
Theisohn, Johannes, 29162
'Theologie und Glaube', 29359
Theresienstadt, 29338, 29350, 29476–29478, 29647
Thieberger, Friedrich, 29571
Thiel, Hans, 29901
Thommen, Christian, 30034
Thommen, Dieter, 29065
Thompson, Colin, 29561
Tiedemann, Rolf, 29728
Tietz Family, 29029
'Tikkun', 29527, 30016
Tilch, Marianne, 29783
'(The) Times', 29752
'(The) Times Saturday Review', 29419
Timm, Angelika, 29709
Timm, Erika, 29059, 29063
Tisis (Vorarlberg), 29208
'TLS' (Times Literary Supplement), 29033, 29796, 30008
Tomes, Jan M., 29323
Tosaphot Gornisch, 29568
Toury, Jacob, 29014, 29266, 29645, 29710
Trade, Jews in, 29030, 29215, 29223, 29238, 29711
'Transactions of the Royal Hist. Society', 29437
Trapp, Werner, 29145
Trautwein, Wolfgang, 29293
Treblinka, 29351

Index to Bibliography

Trende, Frank, 29540
Treue, Wilhelm, 29030, 30073
Treue, Wolfgang, 30018
'Tribüne', 29046, 29084, 29127, 29169, 29255, 29273, 29367, 29380, 29410, 29432, 29453, 29508, 29510, 29511, 29513, 29541, 29547, 29573, 29688, 29702, 29716, 29729, 29830, 30042, 30045
Trier, 29169, 29185
Trier, Ernst, 29107
Trieste, 29202
Troen, Selwyn Ilan, 29646
'Trumah', 29243; 28995, 29428, 29517, 29584, 29615, 29637
Tuchel, Johannes, 29540, 29545
'Tura', 30033
Tura, Perez, 29046
Tzahor, Zeev, 29654
'Tzfunot: Tora Quarterly', 29128, 29585

Ucko, Hans, 29968
Ufford, Jack Twiss Quarles van, 29240
Uhlig, Ralph, 29684
Uhlman, Fred, 29919
Ukraine, Nazi Period, 29301
Ullmann, Viktor, 29477, 29850
Ullstein Family, 29025
Umansky, Ellen M., 29001
Ungar, Frederick, 29679
Ungar, Gerhard, 29278
Ungar-Klein, Brigitte, 29278
Unger, Erich, 29851
Unger, Manfred, 29397
Ungern-Sternberg, Wolfgang von, 29763
United States Holocaust Memorial Council, 29383
Universities and Jews, 29124, 29362, 29533, 29588, 29642–29644, 29674, 29684, 29709, 29804
'Unser Bocholt', 29790
Unterschwandorf, 29186, 29187
Urbach, Joseph, 29636
Urspringen, 29005
USA, 29235, 29895
— Holocaust, Reaction, 29329
— Immigration, 28990, 29231, 29233, 29236, 29237, 29239, 29871
— WWII, 29469
— Refugees, 29241, 29323, 29440, 29677, 29678, 29681

Valk, Wolf, 29112
Varga, László, 29223, 29303
Varnhagen, Rahel, 29691, 29852–29854
Varon, Benno Weiser, 29920
Vaupel, Dieter, 29303
Veigl, Hans, 29213
Verdrängung und Vernichtung der Juden unter dem Nationalsozialismus, 29366; 29295, 29363, 29397, 29415
Verein für Cultur und Wissenschaft der Juden, 29083
Vereinigung ehemaliger Kölner und Rheinländer, 29519
Verfolgung und Widerstand im Rheinland und in Westfalen, 29446; 29298, 29426
Vergangenheitsbewältigung, 29371, 29373, 29381, 29451, 29461, 29505, 29523, 29544, 29925, 29939, 29946, 29955, 30068
Vergin, Siegfried, 29547
Verman, Mark, 29047
Vertreibung und Neubeginn, 29282
Vestermanis, Margers, 29366, 29453
Vidal-Naquet, Pierre, 29386
Vielmetti, Nikolaus, 29202, 29617
Vienna, 29209–29213, 29223, 29429, 29507, 29692, 29756, 29765, 29902
Vierhaus, Rudolf, 29104
Viertel, Berthold, 29855
'Vierteljahrshefte für Zeitgeschichte', 29355, 29376
Vinschen, Klaus-Dieter, 29014
Vital, David, 29398
Vögel, Bernhild, 29304
Völker, Arina, 29124
Vörös, Károlyi, 29223
Vogt, Bernhard, 29169
Voigt, Bernhard, 29504
Voigt, Jürgen, 29715
Voigts, Manfred, 29851
Volkov, Shulamit, 29013
Vollnhals, Clemens, 29310
Vorarlberg, 29972, 29973
Vorgrimler, Herbert, 29959
Vries, Hans de, 29478

Wachenheim, Hedwig, 29014
Wachten, Johannes, 29009, 29635
Wacker, Jean-Claude, 29479
Wacker, Marie-Theres, 30019
Wagenseil, Johann Christoph, 29054
Wagner, Georg, 29176
Wagner, Richard, 30053–30055
Wahl, Angelika von, 29241
Waldheim Affair, 29975, 30009
Waldschütz, Elisabeth, 29186
Waldstein, Edith, 29853
Walk, Joseph, 29245
Wallas, Armin A., 29668, 29802, 29865
Wallich Family, 29029
Walser, Harald, 29018
Walter, Marianne, 29480
Walter, Rolf, 29030
Walther, Susanne, 29260
Wangh, Martin, 29542
Wannsee Conference, 29334, 29336

Wannsee-Konferenz, Haus der (Gedenkstätte), 29545, 29548
Warburg Institute, 29856
Warburg, Aby M., 29856
Warburg, Max M., 29025
Waren, 29152, 29153
Warnecke, Hans, 29068
Warnke, Martin, 29825
Warnock, Robert, 29066
Washington, Holocaust Memorial Museum, 29536
Wassermann, Henry, 29137, 29669, 29954
Wassermann, Jakob, 29673
Wasserstein, Bernard, 29857
Watson, David, 29718
Watzinger, Karl-Otto, 29151
Webb, Margot, 29481
Weber, B., 29549
Weber, Hermann, 29528
Weckbecker, Michael, 29410
Wedgwood, Josiah C., 29465
Wegner, Gregory P., 29550
Wegner, Manfred, 30017
Wegner, Werner, 29453
Wegweiser durch das jüdische Rheinland, 29169; 29519, 29671, 29708, 29770, 29805, 29823
Weichmann, Herbert & Elsbeth, 29682
Weigand, Wolf, 29551
Weigel, Hans, 29765
Weil, Grete, 30075
Weil, Jiri, 30074
Weill, Kurt, 29678, 29858
Weill, Roger D., 29203
Weimar Republic (see also Antisemitism, Weimar), 28995, 29033, 29036, 29184, 29638, 29702, 29710, 29721, 29819, 29833, 29947, 29970, 29996
Wein-Mehs, Maria, 29192
Weiner, Hanna, 29429
Weingarten (Baden), 29188
Weinreich, Uriel, 29063
Weinzierl, Erika, 29282
Weinzierl, Ulrich, 29866, 29884
Weisberger, Adam M., 29048
Weisenheim am Berg, 29162
Weiser, Adelheid, 29178
Weiss, Dietrich, 29114
Weiss, Hilde, 29539
Weiss, Nelly, 29049
Weiss, Theodore Zev, 29398
Weiss, Yfaat, 29482
Weissberg, Liliane, 29854
Weissler, Chava, 28990
Weizsäcker, Heinrich von, 29507
Welch, David, 30020
Wellers, Georges, 29483
Wells, Tony, 29256
'Weltbühne', 29705
Wendt, Bernd Jürgen, 29366
Werfel, Franz, 29859
Werkleute (org.), 29918
Werner, Harold, 29497
Werner, Klaus Ulrich, 29689
Werner, Mark, 29497
Werner, Michael, 29776
Werner-Birkenbach, Sabine, 29720
Wertheimer, Jürgen, 29673
Werther, Thomas, 29412
Wesseling, 29169
Wessely, Naphtaly Herz, 29586
West, Franklin C., 29810
Westermann, Klaus, 29840
Westphal, Uwe, 29711
Westphalia, 29446
— Jüd. Museum, 29189
Westreich, Elimelech, 29614
Wetzel, Juliane, 29258
Wetzlar, 29120
Wexler, Paul, 29059
Wickert, Christl, 29014
Wickham, Christopher J., 29690
Wieben, Matthias, 29684
Wiehn, Erhard Roy, 29484
'Wiener Geschichtsblätter', 29211
'(The) Wiener Library Newsletter', 29256
Wiener, Jan, 29484
Wiener, Leo, 29235
Wiener, Max, 29615, 29616
Wiesbaden, 29190
Wiesel, Elie, 29384
Wiesemann, Falk, 29005, 29050, 29080
Wiesenthal, Simon, 29908
Wigoder, Geoffrey, 29387
Wilhelm, Hans-Heinrich, 29453
Wilhelminian Germany see Imperial Germany
Wilhelmy-Dollinger, Petra, 29083
Willeke, Manfred, 29149
Winder, Ludwig, 29323
Windsheim, 29191
Winkelmann, Michael, 29074
Winkels, Hubert, 30068
Winkle, Stefan, 29025
Winkler, Manfred, 29248
Winterhilfe, 29647
Wipfler-Pohl, Sigrun, 29162
Wissenschaft des Judentums, 29617
Wistrich, Robert S., 29014, 29266, 30021–30023
Witte, Maria Magdalena, 29106
Witten, 29941
Wittgenstein, Ludwig, 29860
Wittlich, 29192
Wittstadt, Klaus, 29962
Wobbe, Theresa, 29485
Wodak, Ruth, 29976
Wörmann, Heinrich-Wilhelm, 29296
Wohlgemuth, Joseph, 29571
Wolf, Arie, 29863
Wolf, Friedrich, 29881

Index to Bibliography

Wolf, Lucien, 29443
Wolf, Siegbert, 29822
'Wolfenbütteler Renaissance Mitteilungen', 29825
Wolff, Abraham, 29090
Wolff, Marion, 29486
Wolffers, Artur, 29229
Wolffsohn, Michael, 29266, 29552, 29627, 29955
Wolfstein-Frölich, Rosi, 29014
Wolkenstein, Alfred, 29124
Wollenberg, Hans-Werner, 29341
Wollmershäuser, Friedrich A., 29051
Wolter, Michael, 29962
Women, 28990, 29001, 29014, 29035, 29064, 29083, 29277, 29326, 29361, 29440, 29480, 29485, 29490, 29691, 29693, 29709, 29755, 29787, 29804, 29826, 29844, 29846, 29852, 29904–29906, 29928
World Centre for Jewish Music, 29648
World Jewish Congress, 29951
Wormann, Curt, 29249
Worms, 29003, 29193
Woytt, Gustav, 29914
Württemberg, 28998, 29081, 29175, 29194
Würzburg, 29195
Wuliger, Michael, 29504
Wuppertal, 29169
Wurm, Carsten, 29881
Wuttke, Dieter, 29825
Wyden, Peter, 29487

'Ya'ad', 29713
Yad Vashem, 29330, 29509
'Yalkut Moreshet', 29284, 29291
Yaron, Michael, 29528
Yates, W.E., 29712
Ydit, Max Meir, 29162
Yekutiel, Amir (Festschrift), 29003
Yeshurun, Eliyahu, 29223
Yiddish, 28990, 28992, 29053–29066
'Yivo Annual', 29663
Young, James E., 29381, 29388, 29398, 29527, 29553
Youth Movement (see also Nazi Period, Jewish Youth), 29633
Yugoslavia, Nazi Period, 29301
Yuval, Israel Jacob, 29618

Zabel, Hermann, 29378
Zadek, Alice & Gerhard, 29498
Zagari, Luciano, 29776
Zahedi, Ingrid, 29317
Zantop, Susanne, 29776
Zariz, Ruth, 29429
Zedaka, 29647
'(Die) Zeit', 29325, 29333, 29348, 29368, 29381, 29388, 29419, 29445, 29491, 29510, 29523, 29750, 29809, 29835, 29845, 29856, 29996, 30056, 30061, 30068, 30070, 30073
'Zeitschrift d. Vereins für Hessische Gesch. u. Landeskunde', 29134
— für Bayer. Kirchengeschichte', 29434
— für d. Gesch. d. Oberrheins', 29740
— für Historische Forschung', 29011
— für Kirchengeschichte', 29989
— für Religions- und Geistesgeschichte', 29102, 29118, 29129, 29448, 29482, 29659, 29791, 29888, 29937, 30002, 30029, 30035
— für Württembergische Landesgeschichte', 29184
Zeller, Bernhard, 29767
Zelman, Leon, 29204
Zenger, Erich, 29959
Zentralwohlfahrtstelle d. Deutschen Juden (d. Juden in Deutschland), 29647
Zentrum für Antisemitismusforschung, 'Newsletter', 29258
Zepf, Irmgard, 29786
Ziegler, Hannes, 29162
Ziegler, Hermann, 29183
Ziemels, Max, 29429
Ziemer, Hans-Werner, 29131
Zimmermann, Arthur, 29840
Zimmermann, Bernhard, 29697
Zimmermann, Michael, 29169, 29381, 29446
Zimmermann, Moshe, 29052, 29488
Zimmermann, Uwe, 30024
Zinnemann, Fred, 29921
'Zion', 29000, 29618, 29817, 29929
Zionism, 29014, 29424, 29449, 29525, 29584, 29644, 29653, 29655, 29656, 29659, 29661, 29662, 29664, 29666, 29667, 29746, 29772, 29821, 30010
'Zionism', 29611
Zitelmann, Rainer, 29453
Ziwes, Franz-Josef, 29011
'Zmanim', 29505, 29727
Zohar, Naomi, 29581
Zürn, Gaby, 29170
Zunz, Leopold, 29617, 29619
Zur Mühlen, Patrick von, 29445, 29682
Zweig, Arnold, 29861–29863, 29881
Zweig, Max, 29864, 29865
Zweig, Stefan, 29859, 29866

List of Contributors

BRACHMANN-TEUBNER, Elisabeth, Dr. phil., b. 1935 in Tuhanzel, Czech Republic. Archivist at the Bundesarchiv, Potsdam. Editor and author of numerous articles in professional journals for archivists and historians.

CHANDLER, Andrew, Ph.D., b. 1965 in England. Lecturer in history, University of Birmingham. Author of i.a. 'Munich and Morality. The Bishops of the Church of England and Appeasement', in *Twentieth Century British History* (1993); 'The Church of England and the Obliteration Bombing of Germany', in *English Historical Review* (1993).

CLARK, Christopher M., Ph.D., b. 1960 in Sydney. Official Fellow and College Lecturer in Modern European History, St. Catherine's College, Cambridge. Author of i.a. 'The Politics of Revival. Pietists, Aristocrats and the State Church in early 19th-century Prussia', in I. Retallack and L. E. Jones (eds.), *Between Restoration Reaction and Reform* (1993); 'The Frederick Williams of 19th-Century Prussia', in *Bulletin of the German Historical Institute* (1993).

DAVIS, Joseph M., Ph.D., b. 1960 in Washington D.C. Visiting Assistant Professor of Jewish Studies, Washington University, St. Louis. Author of i.a. 'Philosophy and the Law in the Writings of R. Yom Tov Lipman Heller', in *Studies in Medieval Jewish History and Literature*, vol. III (1993); currently working on *The Ten Questions of Eliezer Eulenburg*.

EFRON, John M., Ph.D., b. 1957 in Melbourne. Assistant Professor of Jewish History, Indiana University. Author of *Defining the Jewish Race. The Self-Perception of Jewish Scientists in Europe, 1882–1933* (forthcoming). (Contributor to Year Book XXXVII.)

ELKIN, Rivka, M.A., b. 1935 in Haifa. Formerly a teacher, now a research student at the Institute of Contemporary Jewry, Hebrew University, Jerusalem. Author of *"Das Jüdische Krankenhaus muss erhalten bleiben". Berlin 1938–1945. Das Krankenhaus der Jüdischen Gemeinde zu Berlin* (1992). Currently writing a dissertation on "The Social Work and Welfare Activities of the German Jews under the Nazi Regime".

GEHLER, Michael, Dr. phil., b. 1962 in Innsbruck. Research fellow, Institut für Zeitgeschichte and lecturer, University of Innsbruck. Author of *Studenten und Politik. Der Kampf um die Vorherrschaft an der Universität Innsbruck 1918–1938* (1988); and of numerous articles on modern Austrian history and foreign policy.

GELBER, Yoav, Ph.D., b. 1943 in Israel. Head of the Herzl Institute for Research and Study of Zionism and the Strachlitz Institute for Research and Study of the Holocaust, University of Haifa. Author of i.a. *Why the Palmach was Disbanded* (1986); *Massada. The Defence of Palestine in World War II* (1990); *A New Homeland. The Immigration and Absorption of Central European Jews in Erez-Israel* (1990); *Growing a Fleur-de-Lys. The Yishuv's Intelligence Service, 1918–1947* (1992). (Contributor to Year Book XXXV.)

GRUBER, Helmut, Ph.D., b. 1928 in Austria. Charles S. Baylis Professor, Polytechnic University, New York. Author of i.a. *Red Vienna. Experiment in Working-Class Culture, 1919–1934* (1991) which won the Austrian History Book Prize (US), 1991 and the Victor-Adler-Stateprize (Austria), 1992; and numerous books and articles on European Socialism and social movements. Awarded the *Ehrenkreuz für Wissenschaft und Kunst* by the Republic of Austria for scholarly accomplishments.

HILL, Leonidas E., Ph.D., b. 1934 in Aberdeen, WA. Professor of History at the University of British Columbia. Editor of *Die Weizsäcker Papiere 1900–1932* (1982) and *1933–1950* (1974). Author of i.a. 'The Trial of Ernst Zundel. Revisionism and the Law in Canada', in *Simon Wiesenthal Center Annual* (1989); 'Holocaust und "Historikerstreit" ', in Helmut Donat and Lothar Wieland (eds.), *"Auschwitz erst möglich gemacht?"* (1991).

LEVI, Franz, b. 1920 in Berlin. Emigrated to Palestine in 1936 and finished his schooling at Ben Shemen. Formerly an architectural material scientist. Author of numerous contributions to professional architectural journals.

PAULEY, Bruce F., Ph.D., b. 1937 in Lincoln, Nebraska. Professor of History, University of Central Florida. Author of i.a. *Hahnenschwanz und Hakenkreuz. Steirischer Heimatschutz und österreichischer Nationalsozialismus* (1972); *The Habsburg Legacy, 1867–1939* (1972); *Hitler and the Forgotten Nazis. A History of Austrian National Socialism* (1981); *From Prejudice to Persecution. A History of Austrian Anti-Semitism* (1992). (Contributor to Year Book XXXVII.)

PENSLAR, Derek J., Ph.D., b. 1958 in Los Angeles. Assistant Professor of History and Jewish Studies, Indiana University. Author of i.a. *Zionism and Technocracy. The Engineering of Jewish Settlement in Palestine, 1870–1918* (1991).

SAPERSTEIN, Marc, Ph.D., b. 1944 in New York. Gloria M. Goldstein Professor of Jewish History and Thought, Washington University, St. Louis. Author of i.a. *Jewish Preaching 1200–1800* (1989); *Moments of Crisis in Jewish Christian Relations* (1989); *Essential Papers on Messianic Movements and Personalities in Jewish History* (1992).

SODE-MADSEN, Hans, cand. mag., b. 1942 in Copenhagen. Archivist at the State Archives, Copenhagen. Author of i.a. *Theresienstadt og de danske jöder 1940–45*

(1991); *Corrie og Sven Meyers erindringer fra Theresienstadt – det iscenesalte bedrag* (1991). Currently working on a book on the relief work of the Danish Social Affairs Ministry, 1941–1945.

STEINWEIS, Alan E., Ph.D., b. 1957 in New York. Assistant Professor of History, Florida State University. Author of i.a. *Art, Ideology, and Economics in Nazi Germany. The Reich Chambers of Music, Theater, and the Visual Arts* (1993).

WEBSTER, Ronald D.E., Ph.D., b. 1935 in Stouffville, Canada. Assistant Professor in the Department of History, York University, Toronto. Author of 'Why They Returned, How They Fared. Jewish Returnees to Germany after 1945', in *YIVO Annual* (1992). Translator of Bernd Wegner, *Hitlers Politische Soldaten* (1989).

Abstracts of articles in this Year Book are included in *Historical Abstracts* and *America: History and Life*.

General Index to Year Book XXXVIII of the Leo Baeck Institute

Abel, Karl (gynaecologist, director, Jewish Hospital, Berlin), 158
Abramovitch, Stanley, 294n
Abramsky, Chimen, 343n
Abwehrverein *see* Verein zur Abwehr des Antisemitismus
Academics, Jewish, 63, 69, 328
Acculturation *see* Assimilation
Ackerl, Isabella, 416
Adenauer, Konrad (German statesman), 301, 304, 306
Adermann, Max (SA-Scharführer), 130
Adler, Alfred (psychologist), 105
Adler, Cyrus (statistician), 71
Adler, Hans Günther (historian), 170n
Adler, Hermann (British Chief Rabbi), 90n, 223
Adler, Josef (engineer, Zionist, murder victim), 122, 150
Adler, Marcus (factory owner), 62, 63, 64
Adler, Victor (Austrian Socialist politician), 112, 115n
Agriculture, Jews and, 64, 65–68, 69–70, 328
Ahlem (agricultural school), 62, 65–66
Aichinger, Hans (SS-Hauptsturmführer), 126, 127–129, 131–132, 134, 135, 136, 137, 138, 140, 146, 148, 150
Aid to the persecuted, 143, 420; from outside Germany, 221–261, 263–290; prisoners' parcels, 276–280, 284, 290; refugee organisations, 238, 241, 254–255; escape to Sweden, 265, 270, 272, 289
Akademie für Jugendmedizin, 161, 162
'Alarm' (anti-Nazi paper), 202
Albeck, Hanokh (writer), 3n
Albrich, Thomas, 420
Alexander I (Tsar of Russia), 12
Aliyah Hadasha (immigrants' political party), 332, 335
Alldeutscher Verband, 101, 105n, 106, 107, 108, 109, 112, 113, 412, 418
'Allgemeine Wochenzeitung für die Juden in Deutschland' ('Jüdische Wochenzeitung'), 209, 216, 298, 304
'Allgemeine Zeitung', 196
'Allgemeine Zeitung des Judenthums', 41, 53
Alliance Israélite Universelle, 72
Altmaier, Jakob (German-Jewish politician), 298

'[The] American Historical Review', 415
American Jewish Joint Distribution Committee, 293–321
Amsterdam Jewish community, 85n, 95, 352, 354
Ancillon, Johann Peter Friedrich (Prussian minister), 34
Andreaus, Gottfried (of SS, later of Resistance), 127, 128, 132, 135, 136, 147, 150
Andree, Richard (geographer), 78n, 80
Anglo-German Brotherhood, 257
Anglo-Jewish Association, 226, 234
'[Der] Angriff', 210
Anhalt: Jewish archives, 399–401
Anthropology, 75–96
Anti-Jewish laws, 145, 146, 158, 159, 232, 255, 415; Aryan Paragraph, 241, 253; Gesetz zur Wiederherstellung des Berufsbeamtentums (BBG), 179, 211, 212, 393, 403; Nuremberg Laws, 164, 242, 244, 245, 246, 247, 266, 268, 270
Antisemitenbund (Austria), 418, 422
Antisemitism, 36, 51, 60, 65, 68–69, 81–82, 91, 92, 201, 227, 229; academic, 415, 419, 422, 423; Alldeutscher Verband, 107; anthropologists, 81–82; anti-Christian, 47; anti-Rabbinism, 81, 92; Antisemitenbund, 418, 422; Austrian, 99–118, 144, 152, 409–423; in Britain, 223, 235, 243, 247, 250, 258, 259–261; Catholic, 99–112 *passim*, 422; Christians and, 46–50, 99–117, 199, 221–222, 223, 224–225, 235–237, 257–261: Christlich-Soziale Partei, 99, 417, 422; Conservative, 108–109, 112; Danneberg, 113n; de le Roi, 47, 49; Deckert, 417; Denmark and, 269; towards DPs, 294n; Ecker, 47; Eisenmenger, 49; 'Der eiserne Besen', 418, 422; Fritsch, 48; post-WWII Germany, 296–297, 301, 311, 312, 313, 320; Glagau, 47, 51; Grossdeutsche Volkspartei, 422; guilds, 27, 69; Headlam, 236–237; at Heidelberg, 250; in Heligoland, 197: Herzl and, 412; Hinteregger, 113n; Hofer, 152; Innsbruck, 419. *See also* Pogroms; Jewish defence, 91–93, 193–208, 414, 417, 421. *See also* Centralverein; "Judensozi", 100, 106, 107; Kunschak, 108; Landbund für Österreich, 107; Liberals, 44, 417; Lueger, 99, 107, 109, 411, 412, 413, 417; Luther, 226; Maria Ther-

541

General Index

esa, 8; Marr, 47; medieval, 416, 417; missionaries and, 44, 46–51; J. Müller, 315; Patton, 294n; post-WWII, 413, 417, 420, 421; Protestants and, 221–261; Rebbert, 47; 'Reichspost', 108, 422; Rohling, 47–48, 417; in Salzburg, 418; 'Schönere Zukunft', 422; Schönerer, 411, 412; Seipel, 107–108, 109, 110, 113; Socialists/Social Democrats and, 100, 106–118 *passim*, 413, 417; Sozialistische Arbeiterjugend, 117; students, 133, 419; US military, 294n; Vienna, 99–118 *passim*, 154, 419; 'Wiener Stimmen', 108; workers, 68, 70. *See also* Anti-Jewish laws, November Pogrom, Numerus clausus, "Ritual murder".
Antisemitism: defence, 47–48, 422; Socialist, 100, 105–106, 113–114, 194. *See also* Walter Gyssling, Verein zur Abwehr des Antisemitismus.
Anton Ulrich, Herzog von Sachsen-Meiningen, 17
Arabs, 306, 327, 328, 333
'[Die] Arbeiter-Zeitung', 113
Archaeology, 90–91
Arco, Anton Graf von (assassin of Eisner), 195
Aring, Paul Gerhard (theologian), 36
Arlosoroff, Chaim Victor (Zionist Labour leader), 323
Armenkommission Berlin, 59
Art, Jewish, 329, 353, 379–381; architecture, 75, 379–380; ceremonial art, 380
Artisans, Jewish, 65, 68, 70
Aschenhausen Jewish community, 25
Ashkenazim: bibliography, 343–390; and Sephardim, 3–4, 16, 70–96
Assaf, Simhah (historian), 348
Assimilation, 73, 80, 82, 85–86, 90, 91, 93, 99, 329, 330–331; assimilationism, 90, 144, 197, 213; in Austria, 104–105, 411, 414, 421
Auerbach, Benjamin (director of Jewish Hospital, Cologne), 56
Auerbach, Elias (physician), 89–90
Auerbach, Philipp (Jewish functionary), 312–314
Augsburg Jewish community, 15
Auschwitz extermination camp, 172, 177, 221, 274, 275, 276, 290, 296, 312
Austerlitz, Friedrich (Austrian Socialist, editor), 106
Austrian Jewry, 5, 99–153, 334; Anschluß and, 333, 416, 420–421, 422; emigration, 120, 145–146, 151, 264–265, 323, 326n, 333; expulsion, 120, 145–146; political allegiance, 106, 116
Auswärtiges Amt, 266, 267, 272, 279, 398
Axis Victims League, 304
Axmann, Artur (Nazi youth leader), 161n

Baal-Shem-Tov (Israel ben Eliezer) (founder of Hasidism), 385–386
Bach, David Joseph (Austrian Socialist), 106
Bacharach, Yair Hayyim (Yair Haim Bakhrakh) (talmudist), 84n, 350
Bacon, Gershon C., 343
Baden Jewry, 31, 32, 72
Baeck, Leo (rabbi, scholar, Reichsvertretung President), 212
Baer, Issachar (of Szczebrzeszyn), 355
Baer, Yitzhak (Fritz) (historian), 75n
Balaban, Majer (historian), 349
Ball, Johannes (convert missionary), 39
Ball-Kaduri, Kurt Jacob, 181, 183n
Bamberg Jewish community, 154
Bankers, Jewish, 23, 51, 113, 114, 197
Barfod, Jørgen, 285n
'Basler National-Zeitung', 198
Battenheimer family, 16
Batty, Basil Staunton (Bishop of Fulham), 224, 225, 227, 228, 229, 235, 260
Bauer & Schwarz (department store), 122
Bauer, Bruno (historian), 44
Bauer, Edith (wife of Wilhelm B.), 127, 128, 139
Bauer, Flora (Pogrom victim), 150
Bauer, Karl (department store owner), 121, 122, 124n, 127, 134, 142, 148, 150
Bauer, Otto (Austrian Socialist leader), 101, 106, 110–111, 113, 116, 117
Bauer, Wilhelm (merchant, murder victim), 121–122, 124n, 127–128, 131, 136, 137, 138, 139, 140, 144, 150
Bauerbach Jewish community, 15, 28
Baum Group, 175
Bavaria: Räterepublik, 194, 195
Bavarian Jewry, 15, 31, 309; archives, 395, 396
Bayer, Hans (Pogrom criminal), 150
Beazley, Raymond (historian), 246
Beckelman, Moses (Joint official), 299, 305, 319
Beer, Jacob Herz (banker), 37
Beethoven, Ludwig van (composer), 215
Bell, George Kennedy Allen (Bishop of Chichester), 227n, 230, 234, 235, 236, 237, 238–240, 242–245, 246–248, 249, 251, 252–256
Beller, Steven, 411
Bellson (missionary), 42
Ben Sasson, Haim Hillel (historian), 347, 354–355, 357, 359
Ben-Gurion, David (Israeli statesman), 306, 323, 324
Bendorf-Sayn Jewish community, 169
Benson (Berger), Frederik Richard, 139n, 149
Bentwich, Helen, 239
Bentwich, Norman de Mattos (barrister, writer), 234, 239
Benz, Wolfgang, 119
Berger, Richard (Innsbruck Jewish leader), 121, 125, 129, 133, 137, 139, 149, 150
Bergmann, Karl Hans (historian), 199n
Berkach Jewish community, 6, 15, 16, 17, 20, 28, 60
Berkley, George E., 412–413

Berlin Jewish community, 5, 7, 8, 9, 11, 33–50, 157–192, 218, 402n, 403; Auerbach orphanage, 187n; Jüdische Kultusvereinigung zu Berlin, 161n. See also Jüdisches Krankenhaus Berlin.
'Berliner Tageblatt', 198n
Bernadotte, (Count) Folke (Swedish diplomat), 263, 285, 286, 287
'Berner Tagwacht', 198
Bernhard Erich Freund (son of Georg I of Sachsen-Meiningen), 32
Bernhard I, Herzog von Sachsen-Meiningen, 17
Bernhard II, Herzog von Sachsen-Meiningen, 23
Bernhard, Georg (editor), 198
Best, [Karl Rudolf] Werner (Gauleiter, Nazi plenipotentiary in Denmark), 266, 267, 269–273, 277, 283
Bettauer, Hugo (Austrian novelist), 116n, 417
Bettelheim, Bruno, (psychotherapist), 275n
Bevan, [Sir] Edwyn, 250
Bezalel Academy of Arts, 329
Bible, 345, 352, 357, 376–377
Bibra Jewish community, 15
Bieling, Richard (theological writer), 36
Bielohlawek, Hermann (Austrian politician), 107
Bilesky, Moshe (lawyer, Zionist politician), 324n
Binder, Dieter A., 418
Bisjak, Benno (SS officer), 127, 128
'Blackshirt' (British Fascist paper), 258
'Blätter für Israels Gegenwart und Zukunft' (missionary journal), 42
Blau, Bruno (economist), 168, 177, 182, 185
Blaustein, Jacob (Claims Conference vice-president), 303
Blechmann, Bernhard (anthropologist), 80
Bleichröder, Gerson (banker), 399
Bliem, Maria (housekeeper), 144
Bloch, Ernst (philosopher), 50
Bloch, Joseph Samuel (rabbi, politician, editor), 411, 414, 417, 421
Bludenz Jewish community, 146
Blum, Alphonse (B'nai B'rith leader in Baden), 70, 72
Blum, Léon (French Socialist politician), 111
Blumenfeld, Kurt (German Zionist leader), 324, 331
Blund (Jewish Sammellager overseer), 171n
Board of Deputies of British Jews, 234
Bodelschwingh, Friedrich von (pastor), 253
Bodenheimer, Max Isidor (German Zionist leader), 66–67
Bohemian Jewry, 13, 343, 410. See also Prague, Czechoslovakia.
Bornstein, Aharon, 54n
Botz, Gerhard, 413, 420
Bouillon, Godfrey de (crusader), 45

Boycott: anti-Jewish, 227, 228, 229, 230, 234, 235; anti-Nazi, 243, 248, 323, 325
Boyer, John W., 109, 412
Brackmann, Albert (director of Prussian State Archives), 403
Brahe, Tycho (astronomer), 348
Brandenburgisches Landeshauptarchiv Potsdam, 392, 397, 401
Braun, Otto (Socialist politician), 207
Braunthal, Julius (Socialist historian), 106
Brazil, illegal emigrants, 315
Bredsdorff, Ruth (worker for Jewish relief), 278
Breitner, Hugo (Austrian Socialist), 106, 110, 111
"Bremen" (ship), 248
Brenn, Luis (physician), 121, 143
Breslau Jewish community, 57, 158
Breuer, Mordechai, 348
Britain, British Jewry, 5, 38, 45, 61, 223, 237; Ashkenazim/Sephardim, 6, 83n, 85; Fascism, 258, 260. See also Church of England.
British Academy, IX
Broch, Hermann (novelist), 105
Brocket, Arthur Ronald Nall-Cain, 2nd Baron, 259
Bruch, Rüdiger vom, 52
Brüll family, 121n, 130, 150
Brüning, Heinrich (German chancellor), 206
Brunner, Alois (Nazi official), 167, 174, 176
Brunngräber, G. (judge), 21
Brunzlow, Max (of Büro Wilhelmstraße), 201
Buber, Martin (philosopher), 331, 358
Buchenwald concentration camp, 285, 312
Buckle, Henry Thomas (historian), 195
Buckmaster, Stanley Owen (Viscount), 232
Büro Wilhelmstraße see Centralverein . . .
Bukovinian Jewry, 334
Bund (Jewish Socialist movement), 264
Bund der Opfer des politischen Freiheitskampfes (Tyrol), 147n
Bund jüdischer Frontsoldaten (Austria), 122
Bundesarchiv Potsdam, 391, 395, 397–399, 402–409
Bunzl, John, 116n, 416–417
Burg, Meno (Jewish Prussian officer), 35
Burroughs, Edward Arthur (Bishop of Ripon), 235
Buschke, Abraham (dermatologist), 164, 166
Buttinger, Joseph (Austrian politician), 116
Buxton, Dorothy F. (economist), 255

'C.V.-Zeitung', 197
Calvin, John (Protestant theologian), 348
Canada, emigrants to, 308
Capitalism and Jews, 48, 112, 114
Carinthian Jewry, 418
Caritas (Catholic charity), 52
Carlebach, Elisheva, 351

Castiglioni, Camillo (banker), 104
Catholic Church: in Austria, 99–100, 103, 104, 106, 110–117 *passim*, 422; Catholic Action, 110; in Germany, 222, 232, 238–239, 241, 251, 254; Nazis and, 203, 232
Cattle traders, Jewish, 17, 19, 22–23, 28
Cecil, [Edgar Algernon] Robert Gascoyne, (Viscount), 227, 232, 255
Cecil, [Lord] Hugh, 246
Censorship, 214–215, 217, 229, 247, 362–363
Central Archives for the History of the Jewish People (CAHJP), 407, 422
Central Office for the Settlement of German Jews in Palestine, 323
Central Zionist Archives (CZA), 422
Centralverein deutscher Staatsbürger jüdischen Glaubens (C.V.), 64, 72, 193–208, 403; archives, 198, 201–202, 207; Büro Wilhelmstraße, 197, 200–208
Chakotin, Serge (anti-Nazi propagandist), 204–205
Chamberlain, Houston Stewart (racist writer), 91n
Charles Edward (former Herzog von Sachsen-Coburg-Gotha, National Socialist), 206
Charlotte Amalie, Herzogin von Sachsen-Meiningen, 17
Chelmno death camp, 296
Chemney, Melech (journalist), 306n, 307
Children, Jewish, 40, 55, 233, 276, 283; in Jüdisches Krankenhaus, 182, 185, 187–188, 189
Chlan, Ernst (of Sicherheitsdienst), 120
Christian X (King of Denmark), 269
Christians and Jews, 99–118 *passim*, 141, 224, 232, 354–355, 382–383; Anti-Christian Jews, 382–383; in Britain, 232, 246, 249, 252–253; Christian Hebraists, 348, 383; Christian Kabbalah, 383; "Christian State", 34, 36, 45, 46, 49; Protestant missions, 33–50. *See also* Antisemitism, Catholic, Church of England, Protestant.
Christlich-Sozialer Arbeiterverein, 108
Christlich-Soziale Partei, 99, 100, 101, 104–113 *passim*, 411, 412, 422
Church Mission to the Jews, 224, 255
Church of England, 221–261; Anglican Church Assembly, 240, 243–248, 251, 252, 254, 261; Archbishop of Canterbury's Council on Foreign Relations, 238, 240, 257, 258; Canterbury Convocation, 231; International Missionary Council, 240; and "non-Aryan Christians", 252–256, 257; Queen's Hall meeting, 231, 232–233, 234
'Church Times', 234, 235, 242, 248, 253, 254
Churchill, Winston Leonard Spencer (British statesman), 301
Civil servants, Jewish, 69, 335
Clare, George (Georg Klaar), 414

Clausen, Fritz (Danish Nazi, head of DNSAP), 266–267
Clay, Lucius (US general, Military Governor for Germany), 310, 311
Cohen, Arthur (economist), 72
Cohen, Helmuth (physician), 168
Cologne Jewish community, 67, 158, 160
Comenius, Jan Amos (Komensky) (Czech humanist), 348
Communists, 105n, 195, 249, 263, 265, 268
Concentration camps, 148, 151, 159, 175, 204n, 216, 222, 285; Austrian commandants, 409; psychology of survivors, 303, 317, 320, 321. *See also* individual camps.
Conservatives: in Austria, 99, 100, 107–117 *passim*; in Prussia, 34–36, 38
Constabel, Adelheid (archivist), 397
Conti, Leonardo (physician, Nazi official), 161n, 164, 165n
Conversion, 33–50, 105, 113, 115n, 357, 383–384; in Britain, 223–224
Conway, John, 221n
Cordovero, Moses ben Jacob (kabbalist), 350
Cossmann, Paul Nikolaus (editor), 196
Council of Four Lands, 346, 358
Czechoslovakian Jewry, 334, 410; emigration, 264–265, 323, 333

Da'ud, Abraham ibn (medieval philosopher), 9n
Dachau: concentration camp, 145; SS training camp, 132
Dahm, Volker, 209n, 216n
'Daily Express', 253
'Daily Telegraph', 247
Dalman, Gustav (theological writer), 36
Danish Jewry, 263–290; deportation, 270–274, 277, 289; escape to Sweden, 265, 272, 273, 289
Danish National Socialist Workers' Party (DNSAP), 266, 267, 269
Danneberg, Robert (Austrian Socialist, antisemite), 106, 111, 113n
'Danziger Echo', 247
David, Albert Augustus (Bishop of Liverpool), 235
Davidson, Randall (Archbishop of Canterbury), 223
Davis, Carlisle (German vice-consul), 245, 246
de le Roi, Johannes (antisemitic theologian), 36, 47, 48, 49
Deak, Istvan, 417n
Deckert, Joseph (priest, antisemite), 417
Deedes, Wyndham Henry (of Council for German Jewry), 247, 255
Deissmann, Adolf (theologian), 229
del Banco, Asser (London Sephardi), 83n
Delitzsch, Franz (theologian), 47
Denmark, Occupied, 263–290; in Anti-Comintern Pact, 267, 268; deportation of police, 263, 285; Gestapo in, 266, 269, 271, 272, 273, 274,

General Index

283, 284; hostages, 269, 272; internment of citizens, 267, 269, 272, 273, 277, 289; and Nuremberg Laws, 266, 268; Resistance, 268–269, 272, 285; Wehrmacht in, 269, 270, 271, 272
Department stores, 69, 122, 197
Deportation, 15, 166–168, 169, 171, 172–184, 187–191, 218; of Danish Jews, 270–274, 277, 289; of Danish police, 263, 285; Gemeindeaktion, 178, 180, 183; Dr. Lustig and, 178–184; of physicians, 166–168, 175–176, 179n; from Theresienstadt, 275, 276, 277, 281, 284, 290
Deutsch, Julius (Austrian Socialist), 106, 116
Deutsch, Peter (Danish conductor), 281
Deutsch-Israelitischer Gemeindebund (DIGB), 54–72 *passim*, 403, 406
'Deutsche Arbeiter-Presse', 422
Deutsche Arbeitsfront, 213
Deutsche Christen, 253
Deutsche Demokratische Partei (DDP), 196
Deutsche Fortschrittspartei, 64
Deutsche Fotothek Dresden, 394n
Deutsche Friedensgesellschaft, 196
Deutsche Grammaphon-Gesellschaft, 211n
'Deutsche Kultur-Wacht', 211
Deutsche Turnerschaft, 132, 133, 134
Deutsche Zentralstelle für Jüdische Wanderarmenfürsorge, 54
Deutscher evangelischer Kirchenbund, 235
Deutscher und Österrreichischer Alpenverein, 132, 133
Deutscher Verein für Armenpflege und Wohltätigkeit, 53
Deutscher Volksgemeinschaftdienst, 198n
Deutsches Zentralarchiv, 396, 397
Deutschnationale Volkspartei (DNVP), 224
'Deutschösterreichische Tages-Zeitung', 422
'Dibre Emeth' (missionary journal), 42
Diestel, Max (Lutheran leader), 227, 260
Dietrich, Richard (SA-man), 130, 150
Dimand (Diamant), Mindel and Ephraim (Pogrom victims), 130, 150
Dinglestedt, Franz von (Liberal emancipationist), 44
Dinur, Ben Zion, 358
Disabilities, Jewish, 5, 19, 34–35, 410; marriage, 23–25, 31; special laws, 5, 82n, 400; taxes, 5, 8, 18, 28–31, 401; trading, 18, 19, 23, 24–25, 401
Displaced Persons (DPs), 293–321, 327; black marketeering, 297, 310, 312, 316, 317; criminality, 298, 300, 301, 310–316, 320, 321; German authorities and, 296, 297, 300, 301, 302–306, 309–314, 315, 317–318, 320–321; illegal re-emigration, 293, 297, 300, 306–310, 312, 314–315, 319, 320, 321; integration into West Germany, 298, 300, 302, 316–318, 319; non-Jewish, 294; resist emigration, 298, 299, 301–302, 303. *See also* Germany (post-WWII, Jews of).
Ditleff, N. Chr. (Norwegian minister), 285
Dobberke (Sammellager commandant), 171n, 178n, 191n
Dobringer, Franz, (SS officer), 127, 128
Dollfuss, Engelbert (Austrian Chancellor), 101, 116, 416, 419, 422
Don, Alan (chaplain), 225, 229, 232, 233, 238n, 240
Downey, Richard (Archbishop of Liverpool), 235
Drabek, Anna, 416
Dreissigacker Jewish community, 15, 28
Dreyfus, Alfred (French colonel), 412
Dubnow, Simon (historian), 89
Dubsky family (Pogrom victims), 150
Duckwitz, Georg Ferdinand (German Embassy official), 270–271, 272
Dühring (Karl) Eugen (racist philosopher), 82n
Düsseldorf Jewish community, 65, 68
Dunn, James, 222n
Durham University, 256
Duxneuner, Hermann (Austrian Nazi official), 120, 124, 126
Duy, Robert (SS officer), 129, 150

Eastern European Jewry, 51, 55, 59, 60–61, 62, 66, 70, 80–93 *passim*, 264, 295, 414; and Germans, 329–333, 358
Ebner, Josef (Pogrom criminal), 150
Ecker, Jakob (antisemite), 47
Edels, Samuel Eliezer (Maharsha) (Polish talmudist), 352
Eden, Anthony (Earl of Avon) (British statesman), 250
Eder, Wilhelm (SA-Scharführer), 130
Education, Jewish, 18–22, 27, 55, 60, 85n, 104, 363–364; missionary schools, 33, 40; in Theresienstadt, 276; vocational, 19, 27, 51–73 *passim*
Edvardson, Cordelia, 192
Efron, John, 72
Ege, Richard (nutritionist), 278–279, 280
Ege, Vibeke (helped Danish Jews), 278
Egerth, Kurt (of Austrian Resistance), 136
Ehrenberg, Hans (pastor, corres. of Bishop Bell), 239n
Ehrlich, Hermann (teacher), 21
Ehrwald Jewish community, 123
Eichhorn, Johann Albrecht Friedrich (Prussian statesman), 41
Eichmann, Adolf (Nazi war criminal), 120, 271, 277, 280, 283, 419; and Jewish Hospital Berlin, 159, 160, 161, 162, 180, 185n, 192; Sonderkommando Eichmann, 271
Eidlitz, Zerah (Prague preacher), 8
Einstein, Albert (physicist), 393
Eisenhower, Dwight David (US President), 294n

Eisenmenger, Johann Andreas (orientalist, antisemite), 48
'[Der] eiserne Besen', 418, 422
Eiserne Front, 204, 205, 207
Eisner, Kurt (Socialist politician), 194, 195
Eisterer, Klaus, 131n
Elazar, Daniel, 346, 357
Elbaum, Jacob, 347, 348, 352, 354
Eldridge, Basil (Anglican vicar), 251
Eleazar ben Jehuda ben Kalonymus (kabbalist), 15
Elijah ben Solomon Zalman (talmudist, Gaon of Vilna), 358, 359
Elkan, Hans (physician), 168
Emancipation, 5, 11, 15–32 *passim*, 35, 38, 85n, 223; Christians and, 36, 44–46, 223
Emden, Jacob Israel (Altona rabbi, talmudist), 351, 358
Emigration: from Austria, 120, 145–146, 151, 264–265, 323, 326n, 333; to Britain & Commonwealth, 336, 338; from Eastern Europe, 264–265, 329–339 *passim*; forced, 120, 145–146; from Nazi Germany, X, 159, 165, 166, 182n, 227, 251, 264–265, 323–339; to Latin America, 251, 297n, 315, 336; from Middle East/N. Africa, 338; to Palestine/Israel, 227, 295, 296n, 308, 323–339; to Scandinavia, 264–265, 299, 303, 336; to Switzerland, 336; to USA, 24, 86, 93, 295, 297n, 302, 308, 336, 338; post-WWII, 293–321 *passim*, 338–339. *See also* individual countries.
Endelman, Todd, 61
Englander, David, 223
Enlightenment (Aufklärung), 17, 359
Eppstein, Paul (sociologist, headed Theresienstadt Ältestenrat), 173, 174n, 275, 281, 282–283
Erfurt Jewish community, 15
Evangelisch-Sozialer Kongreß, 52
'Evangelische Kirchenzeitung', 34, 43
'Evening Standard', 258
[O.] Evensen (Danish shippers), 279, 280
Evian Conference, 324
Exner, Rudolf (SS officer), 127
Eybeschütz [Eibenschütz], Jonathan (rabbi, kabbalist), 9–10, 351, 358

Fast, Gustav (SS officer), 124, 138n
Feddern (C.V. employee), 204
Feder, Gottfried (Nazi ideologue), 204
Feder, Theodore (Ted), 298n, 299, 300n, 303n, 310n
Fei[u]erberg, Mordecai Zeev (author), 10
Feil, Hanns von (SS-Oberführer), 124, 126, 127, 132–133, 136, 139
Feld, Hans (editor, film critic), X-XI
Feld, Käthe, XI
Fellner, Günter, 418

'Film Kurier', X
Fischer, Erich (surgeon), 166
Fishberg, Maurice (ethnologist), 87, 93–94, 96
Fiske, Anne Schultze (Canadian wife of German surgeon), 248
Fleckeles, Eliezer (Prague rabbi), 10
Fleiss, Erwin (SS-Standartenführer), 126, 129, 133, 138, 140
Flöck, Carmela (of Resistance), 143n
Flossenbürg concentration camp, 287
Föhrenwald DP camp, 293–321; camp committee, 297, 299–300, 301, 305, 310, 311; closure attempts, 294, 300, 301, 308, 310, 315, 318, 319, 321
Forced labour, 171, 172, 174n, 186, 188, 191n, 296; Fabrikaktion, 172, 174
Forell, (Swiss chaplain in Vienna), 243
'Forward', 314
Fox, Henry (ecumenicalist), 228, 240, 241
Fraenkel, David (Dessau rabbi), 7
Fraenkel, Josef (editor), 415, 416
Fraenkel-Goldschmidt, Hava, 348, 349
Fram, Edward, 347
France, French Jewry, 5
Franconian Jewry, 31
Frank, Adolf (physicist), 393
Frankfurt a. Main Jewish community, 31, 57, 186, 394
'Frankfurter Zeitung', 212, 233
Frankists, 358
Franz I (Emperor of Austria), 12, 410
Franz Joseph (Emperor of Austria), 411
Franzelin, Adolf (SS-Unterstumführer, of Innsbruck police), 124, 137, 138
Frazer, James George (ethnologist), 195
Freeden, Herbert, 210, 216
Freemasons, 182n, 210, 235, 270, 404
'[Der] Freidenker' (Swiss paper), 199
Freidenreich, Harriet Pass, 413, 414
Freie Israelitische Vereinigung, 67
Freies Deutschland (in Switzerland), 199
Freikorps: Bund Oberland, 210
Freud, Sigmund (founder of psychoanalysis), 105
'[Der] Freund Israels', 37
'Friedensbote' (missionary journal), 47
Friediger, Max (Danish Chief Rabbi), 264, 268, 282, 288
Friedländer, Fyodor (Gestapo informer), 186
Friedländer, Hans (almoner, Jewish Hospital, Berlin), 171n, 187
Friedrich II ("the Great", of Prussia), 5, 7, 8
Friedrich Wilhelm III (of Prussia), 12, 33–34, 35, 38
Friedrich Wilhelm IV (of Prussia), 34, 41
Frisch, Ephraim (social historian), 59n
'Frit Danmark' (illegal paper), 268
Fritsch, Theodor (antisemite), 48
Frykman, Sven (headed rescue convoy), 287

General Index

Fuchs, Gottlieb, Jutta and Eduard (Pogrom victims), 130, 150
Fürst, Julius (orientalist), 41, 47
Fürth Jewish community, 394
Fuglsang-Damgaard (Bishop of Copenhagen), 271

Galician Jewry, 334
Gans, David ben Salomo (scientist, historian), 347–348, 349, 373
Garbett, Cyril Forster (Archbishop of York), 259
Gay, Peter, 359
Gedye, G.E.R. (journalist), 421
Geehr, Richard S., 412n
Geheimes Staatsarchiv (GStA) (Prussia), 395, 404, 405–406
Gehler, Michael, 418–419
Gelb, Karl (SS-Obersturmführer, SS chief in Tyrol), 123, 124
'General-Anzeiger für die gesamten Interessen des Judentums', 64
Georg I, Herzog von Sachsen-Meiningen, 18, 32
George II (King of England), 7
Gercke, Achim (archivist), 396
'Gerechtigkeit', 422
Gerl [Dr.] (of Hinderlang), 242, 243
Gerlach, Ernst Ludwig von (jurist, politician), 35, 44
Gerlach, Hellmuth Georg von (politician, pacifist), 196, 198
Gerlach, Leopold von (Prussian general, brother of Ernst L.v.G.), 34
Gerlach, Otto von (GBCJ committee member), 44
German Jewry, 344; immigrants to Palestine/Israel, 323, 327–339; post-WWII, 298–299, 304, 312–314, 316–318. See also Displaced Persons; studies/sources in former DDR, X, 391–408. See also Bavaria, Prussia, Sachsen . . . and other regions, Berlin and other towns.
German language, 7, 8, 11, 22, 33; in liturgy, 37; in Palestine, 334, 335
German Refugees' Assistance Fund, 238
Germany: former DDR: archives, 391–408; Staatliche Archivverwaltung (StAV), 391, 406; Zentrales Staatsarchiv (ZStA), 391, 406, 407
Gesamtarchiv der deutschen Juden, 394, 402–407; 'Mitteilungen . . .', 395
Gesellschaft für Soziale Reform, 71
Gesellschaft zur Beförderung des Christenthums unter den Juden zu Berlin (GBCJ), 33–50 *passim*
Gesellschaft zur Verbreitung der Handwerke und des Ackerbaues unter den Juden im Preußischen Staate, 65, 403
Gestapo, 33, 161, 162n, 166, 170n-192 *passim*, 214, 218, 280, 287, 288; in Austria, 120, 124, 125, 129, 135, 136, 137, 138–140, 142–143, 144; Sammellager (attached to hospital), 171, 172, 174, 175, 178, 186. See also Denmark (Occupied).
Gföllner, Johannes (bishop), 112
Girardi, Josef (Pogrom criminal), 150
Glagau, Otto (antisemite), 47, 51
Gleicherwiesen Jewish community, 15
Gnesetti, Alfred (SA-man), 130, 150
Goebbels, Joseph (Nazi leader), 121, 125, 152, 210, 213–214, 216n, 217–218, 244
Göring, Hermann (Nazi leader), 140, 211, 212, 227, 246, 268
Goethe, Johann Wolfgang von (poet), 20, 215
Göttingen, University of, 256
Goldfarb, Jakob (of Föhrenwald committee), 299, 301
Goldmann, Nahum (Zionist statesman), 303n
Goldscheid, Rudolf (sociologist), 194
Gollancz, Victor (publisher), 249
Graetz, Heinrich (historian), 84, 96
Graubart, Alfred (engineer, brother of Richard G.), 121, 122, 124, 130, 132
Graubart, Margarete (Grete) (wife of Richard G.), 121, 127, 128, 139, 142, 143
Graubart, Maria (wife of Alfred G.), 122, 142
Graubart, Richard (engineer, murder victim), 121–122, 127–128, 131, 136–137, 138–140, 142, 143, 145, 150
Graz Jewish community, 416, 418
Greece, Jews of, 86–87
Grenville, John, 221n
Grierson, John (film director), X
Gries, Zeev, 350
Griffiths, Richard, 257
Grimes, C.H.D. (chaplain), 242–243
Gröben, Karl von der (general), 34
Gröbzig Jewish community, 394
Gross-Rosen concentration camp, 312
Grossdeutsche Volkspartei (GDVP), 422
Gruenewald, Max (rabbi, scholar, International President, Leo Baeck Institute), X
Grynszpan, Herschel (assassin of vom Rath), 121, 142
'[The] Guardian' (Anglican weekly), 234, 237, 258
Günther, Hans (head of Zentralamt Prag), 288
Günther, Rolf (deputy to Eichmann), 180, 182, 271
Guilds, 19, 27, 30, 32, 69
Gutmann, Eugen (founder of Dresdner Bank), 393
Gutmann, Manfred (informer), 186
Gutteridge, Richard, 221n, 258
Gyssling family, 194, 198n
Gyssling, Walter (journalist, organiser of anti-Nazi defence), 193–208

Ha-Lishka Le-Maan Ha-Oleh (Bureau for the Immigrant), 337

General Index

Haag, John, 423
Haavara, 323, 324–325, 337
Haber, Samuel (Joint director, Germany), 298, 301, 304, 308, 313, 317n, 319
Händel, Georg Friedrich (composer), 215
Händes, Friedrich (missionary), 39, 40
Hæstrup, Jørgen, 270n, 277n
Haganah, 332
Hahn, Kurt (educationalist), 243, 244
Hakibbutz Hameuchad, 331
Hall, Murray, 417
Haller, Theodor (Pogrom criminal), 150
Hamburg Jewish community, 56, 57, 67, 95, 186; Israelitisches Krankenhaus, 158, 170, 192
'Hame'asef', 11
Hamilton, Ian (general), 250
Hammer, Karl (writer), 199
Hammerich, Borghild (relief worker), 285
Hammerich, Carl (admiral, Danish Resistance leader), 285
Handl, Karl (Pogrom criminal), 150
Hanneken, Hermann von (German commander in Denmark), 269, 270
Hansson, Per Albin (Danish politician), 270
Harand, Irene (anti-Nazi editor), 422
Harnack, Adolf von (theologian), 224
Harster, Wilhelm (Gestapo chief in Tyrol and The Hague), 138–139, 143, 146
Hartmann von Erffa, Gottlieb Friedrich (Sachsen-Meiningen Master of Horse), 32
Hasidism, 4, 346, 350–351, 358, 359, 385–386; Mitnagdim, 346, 358, 367
Haskalah (Jewish Enlightenment), 11, 36, 51, 64, 358, 359, 385
Hastings, Adrian, 259
Haupt, Anton (SA-man), 130, 150
Hayyim ben Isaac of Volozhin (educator), 359
Hazakawa, S. (semanticist), 200
Headlam, Arthur C. (Bishop of Gloucester), 234, 236–237, 256–257, 258, 261
Hebrew language and literature, 8, 11, 22, 33, 348, 375, 416; Christian Hebraists, 348, 383; in Palestine/Israel, 331, 335, 336, 337; and Yiddish, 345, 352–353, 357, 358, 359, 360–365 *passim*, 375
Hebrew University, 328
Hedtoft-Hansen, Hans (Danish Social Democrat), 265, 270, 271
Heer, Friedrich (historian), 199
Hegel, Georg Wilhelm Friedrich (philosopher), 43
Heidelberg, University of, 250–251, 256
Heiden, Konrad (political writer), 207
Heim, Johann Ludwig (Sachsen-Meiningen minister), 32
Heimwehr, 111n
Hein, Robert, 423n
Heine, Heinrich (poet), 35

Heller, Yom Tov Lipman (talmudist), 349, 350
Hellman, A. (colleague of W. Gyssling), 202n
Hellwing, Isak A., 417
Helmer, Oskar (Austrian politician), 116
Hengstenberg, Ernst (editor), 34, 43
Henningsen, Eigil Juel (physician), 282, 283, 284
Henriod, H.-L. (ecumenicalist), 228
Henriques, Carl Bertil (Danish Jewish leader), 271
Henschel, Hildegard (medical assistant), 173, 179, 181
Hensen, Svend (Danish official), 285
Henson, Herbert Hensley (Bishop of Durham), 235, 236, 238, 245–252 *passim*, 254, 256, 257–258, 259, 261
Hentze, Otto (antisemite), 47
Herbert, Ulrich, 270n
Hertz, Friedrich (writer on race), 91n
Hertz, Joseph Herman (British Chief Rabbi), 233, 240, 247
Herwegh, Georg (poet), 44
Herzl, Theodor (founder of Zionist movement), 99, 412
Hess, Rudolf (Nazi leader), 242, 243
Hesse: Jewry, 31, 72; Nazis, 205
Heß, Ulrich (archivist), 19n, 23
Heuss, Theodor (BRD President), 301, 304
Heydrich, Reinhard (Nazi leader), 124
Heymann, Felix (of Baum Group), 175n
Hilberg, Raul, 188
Hilfsverein der deutschen Juden, 54, 60, 72
Hiller, Kurt (writer, pacifist), 196
Hilliges, Werner (Austrian Gestapo officer), 120, 137, 139–140, 145, 147
Himmler, Heinrich (Nazi leader), 126, 132, 170n, 217, 286, 403–404
Hinkel, Hans (Nazi Reichskulturwalter), 209–219; Büro Hinkel, 214–215
Hinteregger, Christoph (antisemite), 113n
Hirschfeld, Hans (physician), 164, 166
Histadrut (Palestine General Federation of Jewish Labour), 338
Historiography, 343–423; of Austrian antisemitism, 409–423; revisionist, 199; Yiddish, 373–374, 375
Hitachdut Olej Germania (HOG), 337–338
Hitachdut Olej Germania ve-Austria (HOGOA), 332, 337
Hitler, Adolf, 99, 125, 131, 132, 141, 196, 198, 199, 200, 202, 203, 207, 208, 210, 214, 222, 224, 225, 227, 230, 232, 234, 240, 242, 243, 246, 248, 253, 254, 255, 257, 259, 260, 261, 264, 266, 269, 270, 271, 296, 316, 323, 325, 409, 411. *See also* Nazism.
Hitler-Jugend, 134, 146, 161n
Hochhuth, Rolf, 199
Hochrainer, Alois (Pogrom criminal), 150
Hodson, H. V. (Anglican vicar), 240

General Index

Hölderlin, Friedrich (poet), 195
Hörhager, August (Pogrom criminal), 150
Hoesch, Leopold von (German Ambassador to Britain), 229, 232
Hofer, Franz (Gauleiter of Tyrol), 123, 124–126, 146, 152
Hoffmann, Conrad (attended Anglican conference), 240–241
Hofmannsthal, Hugo von (poet), 105
Holländer family, 16
Holm, Johannes (medical superintendant), 287, 288
Holzer, Charlotte (née Abraham, of Baum Group), 175n, 183n
Homosexuality, 217
Hopfgartner, Walter (SS-Untersturmführer), 129, 133–134, 135, 136–137, 140, 148, 149–150, 151
Horlacher, Richard (general secretary, Abwehrverein), 197
Horodetsky, Samuel Abba (writer), 357
Horowitz, Isaiah (kabbalist), 350
Horserød detention camp, 267, 269, 272, 273, 289
Horwitz, Isaiah Halevi (talmudist), 84n
Hosp, Karl (caretaker), 139, 142
Huber, Heinrich (Pogrom criminal), 150
Huch, Ricarda (writer), 195
Hundert, Gershon D., 343, 344, 356
Hungarian Jewry, 399
Huttig, Robert (SS officer), 127, 150
Hvass, Frants (Danish official), 270–271, 282, 283–284, 286

Iberian Peninsula, Jews of, 3, 9, 75n, 77, 78, 80, 82, 83, 84, 86–96 *passim*
Iddesleigh, Henry Stafford Northcote, 3rd Earl of, 227, 232
Ilona (nurse), 183n
Inge, Ralph (Dean of St. Paul's), 258, 259
Innere Mission (Protestant charity), 52
Innerebner family (Pogrom victims), 123
Innsbruck Jewish community, 119–153, 419
'Innsbrucker Nachrichten', 141
Institut für Zeitgeschichte (Vienna), 420
Institutum judaicum, Berlin, 48
Intermarriage, 83, 90, 92; between Sephardim and Ashkenazim, 83, 95. *See also* "Protected Jews".
International Christian Committee for German Refugees, 255
International Refugee Organisation (IRO), 300, 307, 308, 311
International Student Service, 232
Irgun Olej Merkas Europa (IOME), 332, 335, 337
Isaaksohn, Rolf (Gestapo informer), 186
Israel Meir Ha-Kohen (Hafetz Hayyim), 10n
Israel *see* Palestine/Israel

Israeli Purchasing Mission, 309
'Israelitische Wochenschrift', 61
Isserles, Moses (Rema) (Polish rabbi, codifier), 346, 347–348
Italian Jewry, 3, 84, 352, 354, 381

Jacob ben Moses Halevi Moelln (rabbi), 3
Jacobs, Jack, 113n, 117n
Jacobs, Joseph (Anglo-Jewish social scientist), 71, 85–86, 90n, 91n
Jacobson, Israel (Court Jew), 37
Jacobson, Jacob (historian, archivist), 403n
Jacobson, Walter, 399
Jaffe, Mordechai ben Abraham (talmudist, codifier), 357
Jakobi, Martin (medical chemist), 164
Jehudah Löw ben Bezalel (the Maharal of Prague), 84n, 343–344, 346, 348–349, 355, 357, 369–370
Jellinek, Adolf (Vienna Chief Rabbi), 411
'Jeschurun' (missionary journal), 43
Jewish Agency, 307, 308, 323, 326n, 337
Jewish Encyclopaedia, 86, 87
Jewish Hospital, Berlin *see* Jüdisches Krankenhaus Berlin
Jewish Mission (London), 45
'Jewish Morning Journal' (Hebrew paper), 306n, 307
Jewish Theological Seminary of America, X
Joint Foreign Committee *see* Board of Deputies
"Joint" *see* American Jewish Joint Distribution Committee
Jordan, Charles (Joint official), 298n, 299–300, 305–306, 311, 312, 314, 316n, 317n, 318n, 319
Josel of Rosheim (German communal leader), 347, 348, 349, 355
Joseph ben Isaac (philosopher), 349
Joseph ha-Ephrati of Tropolowicz (maskil), 359
Joseph II (of Austria), 11–12, 410
Journalists, Jewish, 105
Judaism, 190, 343–390; liturgical language, 4, 7, 8, 11, 37; liturgy, 38, 75, 349, 350; prayer, 345, 378–379; ritual, 3, 5, 11, 345–346. *See also* Rabbinics, Sermons.
Judt, I. M. (anthropologist), 90–91, 92
Jüdischer Fahndungsdienst, 186n
Jüdischer Kulturbund *see* Kulturbund deutscher Juden, Reichsverband jüdischer Kulturbünde
Jüdisches Institut für Geschichte (Warsaw), 408
Jüdisches Krankenhaus Berlin, 157–192; compared to ghetto, 185–190
Jüdisches Museum Eisenstadt, 416
'Jüdisches Nachrichtenblatt', 165
Jurists, Jewish, 63, 104, 176n, 227, 335

Kabbalism *see* Mysticism (Jewish)
Kahan, Hilde, 160n, 174, 177, 179, 182, 183, 184, 185

General Index

Kahn, Arthur (physician, philanthropist), 62, 64, 65
Kahn, Bernhard (Hilfsverein Secretary-General), 55n
Kahn, Fritz (gynaecologist), 91–92
Kammer für Arbeiter und Angestellte (Austria), 421
Kampe, Norbert, 69
Kampfbund für deutsche Kultur, 210–211, 213
'[Der] Kampfruf', 422
Kampfverlag (Nazi publishers), 210
Kanitz, Otto Felix (Austrian Socialist), 106
Kanstein, Paul (Embassy official), 270, 272
Kant, Immanuel (philosopher), 20, 42–43
Kaplan, Lawrence, 357
Kaplan, Marion, 57
Kapler, Hermann (German Protestant leader), 227n, 235
Karaites, 354, 381–382
Karl Philipp, Fürst zu Schwarzenberg (field-marshal), 13
Karpeles, Gustav (literary historian), 63n
Kassenärtzliche Vereinigung Deutschland, 164
Kattowitz Jewish community, 68
Katz, Jacob, 345–346, 348–349, 353, 354–355, 358, 359
Katz, Salomon (Danish deportee), 274
Katznelson, Berl (Zionist Labour leader), 323, 324n
Kayserling, Hermann (writer), 195
Kayserling, Meyer (historian, Budapest rabbi), 86–87, 96
Kelsen, Hans (jurist), 105
Kenyon, Frederic G. (academic), 250
Keren Kayemet le-Israel (Jewish National Fund), 67
Kessler, Harry Graf (writer, pacifist), 196
Ketteler, Wilhelm (Catholic bishop), 52
Khazars, 79
Kieval, Hillel J., 410
Kirstein, Mogens (Danish official), 285
Kish, Abraham (publisher), 11n
Klagenfurt Jewish community, 416
Klein, Erika, 197n
Klemperer, Gustav (banker), 393
Klemperer, Klemens, 109
Klemperer, Otto (conductor), 212
Knight, Robert, 420
Knopp, Hans (surgeon, lived "underground"), 168
Koblik, Steven, 263n
Koch, Hans Henrik (Danish Minister), 263, 277, 278, 285, 289
Kochmann, Sala (née Rosenbaum, of Baum Group), 175n
Köfler, Gretl, 418
König, (Cardinal) Franz, 421
Könitz, Christian Ferdinand von (Sachsen-Meiningen minister), 32

Kohl, Helmut, X
Kollek, Teddy, 421
Kollmann, Julius (anatomist), 81
Konrad, Helmut, 115n
[Det] Konservative Folkeparti, 266
Korzybski, Alfred (semanticist), 200
Koser, Reinhold (archivist), 402
Kotschnig, Walter (aide to J. McDonald), 231, 251–252
Kovno region, 172
Kozower, Philipp, 185n
Krammer, Reinhard, 423n
Kranz, Jacob (Maggid of Dubno), 4
Kristeller, Samuel (physician), 62, 63
Krojanker, Gustav (Zionist writer, editor), 324n, 331n
Kubl, Friedrich, 423n
Kübler, Stella (Gestapo informer), 186
Künßberg, Karl Konstantin von (Vice-Chancellor of Sachsen-Meiningen), 20, 28n, 30, 32
Kulturbund deutscher Juden, 209, 212, 215–216, 218, 219. *See also* Reichsverband der jüdischen Kulturbünde.
Kunschak, Leopold (Austrian politician, antisemite), 108, 109
Kupat Milwe (loan fund), 337, 338
Kurhessen Jewry, 121
Kurrein, Adolf (Bohemian rabbi), 53
Kurz, Ferdinand (Austrian SS-man), 127

Ladino, 87, 96
Landau, Ezekiel ben Judah (Prague rabbi), 7–8, 11–12, 13, 359
Landau, Samuel (Prague rabbi), 12–13
Landauer, Georg (Zionist politician), 324n, 339
Landbund für Österreich, 107
Landeskirchenarchiv der Thüringer Evangelischen Kirche, 395
Landsberg, Alfred (Zionist leader), 339
Lang, Cosmo (Archbishop of Canterbury), 225–234, 237, 238, 239–240, 243, 244, 247, 249, 251–252
Larsen, Eivind (Danish official), 272
Laski, Neville (British judge), 247
Laub, M. (German official), 311n
Lausegger, Gerhard (lawyer, SS-man), 129, 133, 149
Lazarus, Moritz (Moses) (philosopher), 63n
Le Goff, Jacques, 347
Le Vernet (internment camp), 198
League of Nations, 234, 238, 251
Leavitt, Moses (Joint official), 303, 308
Lebensborn, 161n, 170n
Leber, Julius (Socialist politician, in Resistance), 204
Lehmann, Emil (Dresden lawyer), 62
Leichter, Otto (Austrian Socialist), 106
Leiper, Henry (church leader), 230, 237
Lenczyc, Ephraim (preacher), 357

Leo Baeck Institute, IX-XI, 207
Lessing, Theodor (philosopher), 63
Levi, Isaak (founded school), 21
Levi, Leo (president, American B'nai B'rith), 56n
Levin, Hirschel (Hart Lyon) (London rabbi), 6–7
Levita (Bokher), Elijah (Hebraist, Yiddishist), 347, 348
Levy, Deborah (Joint field-worker), 317
Levy, Else (physician, lived "underground"), 168
Ley, Robert (Nazi leader), 213
Liberalism, 44, 105n, 210, 411, 412, 413, 415, 421
Lichtenstein family, 16
Lichtfreunde (Enlightenment group), 44
Lidgett, Scott (church leader), 232
Liebenow (Hitler Youth physician), 161n, 162n
Liebmann, R. (official), 25
Linser, Walter (SS officer), 128
Lißner family, 16
Lithuanian Jewry, 343, 381–382
Livingstone, Laura (social worker), 255
Łódź ghetto, 172
Löw, Leopold (Hungarian rabbi, scholar, editor), 42n
Löw-Hofmann, Isaak (great-grandfather of H. von Hofmannsthal), 105
Löwensohn family (Pogrom victims), 150
Lohrmann, Klaus, 416
London Society for Promoting Christianity among the Jews (LSPCJ), 33, 34, 45
London, Jews of, 6, 8, 9, 95
Londonderry, Charles S. H. V.-T.-Stewart, 7th Marquess of (Nazi sympathiser), 256
Lowenherz (of Rothschild Hospital, Vienna), 170n
Lubbock, John (British naturalist), 195
Lublin region, 172
Ludlow, Peter, 252, 254, 258, 260
Lüdke (German commander in Denmark), 269
Lueger, Karl (Mayor of Vienna), 99, 107, 109, 411, 412, 413, 417
Lugger, Alois, 153n
Luise Eleonore, Herzogin von Sachsen-Meiningen, 18, 19, 23, 29, 30, 32
Luria, Isaac ben Salomon (Ari) (16th-century Safed kabbalist), 350
Luria, Solomon (Jewish scholar), 346
Lustig, Walter (director of Jüdisches Krankenhaus Berlin), 160n, 162, 163n, 171n, 172–174, 176, 177, 178–184, 187, 188–191, 192
Luther, Martin (religious reformer), 38, 224; Lutheran Church, 222–225, 227

Maas, Hermann (German pastor), 247–248
McDonald, James G. (League of Nations High Commissioner for Refugees), 238, 251–252, 253
Macdonald, A.J. (of [Anglican] Council of Foreign Relations), 257, 258
Madagascar Project, 218
Maderegger, Sylvia, 419
Magdeburg-Anhalt Jewry, 121
Magry, Karel, 284n
Mahler, Gustav (composer), 105
Mahnert, Klaus (Kitzbühel Kreisleiter), 123
Maimann, Helene, 117n
Maimon, Salomon (philosopher), 84n
Maimonides, Moses (Rambam) (medieval codifier, philosopher), 59
'Manchester Guardian', 253
Mann, Heinrich (novelist), 195
Mann, Thomas (writer), 195
Mannheim Jewish community, X
Mannheimer family, 16
Mannlicher, Herbert (of Austrian criminal police), 138–139
Mapai, 332
Marco, (pseud.) (DP smuggler), 314
Marcuse, Kurt (bacteriologist), 168
Maretzki, Louis (physician), 56, 57, 58, 59–60, 63, 69, 72
Maria Theresa (Empress of Austria), 5, 7–8, 11
Marin, Bernd T., 116n, 413, 416, 417
Marisfeld Jewish community, 15
Marlowe, Christopher (poet), 195
Marr, Wilhelm (antisemite), 47
Marx, Karl (post-WWII German-Jewish editor), 298–299, 304, 305, 318
Marxism, Marxists, 210; Austro-Marxism, 101, 105, 117
Maskilim, 51, 87, 329, 343, 356, 358, 359. See also Haskalah.
Mathoi, Johann (of SA), 129–130, 150
Maurer, Friedrich (anthropologist), 79
Mayer, Adolf (B'nai B'rith activist), 57
Mayer, Heinz, 147n, 153n
Mayer, Kurt (head of Reichsstelle für Sippenforschung), 405n
Mayr family (Pogrom victims), 123
Mayr, Georg von (statistician), 72
McCagg, William O., jr, 410
McCarthy, Joseph (US Senator), 300
Mecklenburg archives: M.-Schwerin, 408; M.-Strelitz, 407; M.-Vorpommern, 392
Medicine see Physicians
Medieval Jewry, 3, 4, 9, 15, 84, 90, 394
Mehring, Walter (poet, Dadaist), 198
Meisel family (Pogrom victims), 150
Meitner, Lise (physicist), 393
Melchior, Marcus (Danish Chief Rabbi), 264
Menasseh ben Israel (Dutch rabbi), 86
Mendelssohn, Moses (philosopher), 7, 13–14, 358, 359
Metz Jewry, 10

General Index

Metz (physician), 174n
Meyer, Ove (engineer), 282
Middle Eastern Jewry, 338. *See also* Turkey/Ottoman Empire.
Mierendorff, Carl (Socialist politician), 204
Mifaal Ha-Ezra Ha-Hadadit (Mutual Aid Project), 337
Mildner, Rudolf (German police chief in Denmark), 270, 281
Milestone, Lewis (film director), 110
Military service, Jews in, 6, 9–11, 13, 35, 149, 332, 417; dispensation from, 5, 27, 29
Minsk region, 172
"Mischlinge" *see* Persecuted groups
Mises, Ludwig von (economist), 105
Mösinger, Josef (of Austrian Gestapo), 120
Mohr, Otto (Pogrom criminal), 150
Møller, Christmas (Danish politician), 268–269
Moneylenders, 22; "usurers", 17, 47
Montefiore, Claude (British Jewish leader), 226, 237
Montefiore, Leonard (AJA president), 234, 247, 249, 252
Moser, Hermann (Pogrom criminal), 150
Moser, Jonny, 416, 419
Moses, Julius (physician, Socialist editor), 62, 64, 72
Moses, Siegfried (President, Leo Baeck Institute, Zionist politician), 324
Mosessohn, Aaron (Chief Rabbi of Berlin), 13
Mosley, Oswald (British Fascist), 260
Mosse, George L., 414
Mott, J. R. (US church leader), 229–230
Mozart, Wolfgang Amadeus, 215
Müller (Prussian cabinet secretary), 41
Müller, Hans (SS-Oberscharführer), 127
Müller, Heinrich (head of Gestapo), 178
Müller, Hermann (German Chancellor), 197
Müller, Josef ("Ochsen-Sepp") (Bavarian politician), 312–313
Müller, Ludwig (Deutsche Christen leader), 253
Müller-Lyer, Franz-Carl (psychiatrist, sociologist), 194, 195
Muhlberg concentration camp, 286
Munch, Peter (Danish Minister), 266
Muneles, Otto, 355n
Munich Jewish community, 170n, 177n, 309, 315–316
Musar (ethical writing), 10, 350, 371–372
Musicians, Jewish, 329
Mysticism, Jewish, 10, 15, 346, 348, 349, 350–351, 356, 357, 369; Christian Kabbalah, 383; magic, 350, 375

Names, Jewish, 16
Napoleon Bonaparte (Emperor of the French), 12–13, 31, 32; Napoleonic era, 35, 37, 410
'Nathanael' (missionary journal), 48
Nationalsozialistische Deutsche Arbeiterpartei (in Austria), 106, 108, 109, 112, 113, 120–153 *passim*, 422; illegal period, 131–134, 148, 150, 152
Nationalsozialistische Deutsche Arbeiterpartei (NSDAP), 117, 139; before 1933, 194, 200–208, 209; 1923 Putsch, 123, 125, 196, 210; propaganda against, 194, 202–208; propaganda by, 194n, 202, 203, 205, 208, 210–211; sociology, 197–198, 205
Nationalsozialistischer Deutscher Studentenbund (NSDStB), 133
Nationalsozialistisches Kraftfahrerkorps (NSKK), 129, 138, 142
Natonek, Hans, 399
Nazi regime, 323, 325; foreign views, 240, 256, 257, 258, 259. *See also* Church of England; foreigners under, 178, 185, 191, 192n; Machtergreifung, 158, 163, 203, 209, 210, 222, 260.
Nazi regime, Jews under, 157–192, 209–290, 323–339; archives on Jews, 395–399, 403–406; in Austria, 119–153; Church of England and, 221–261; cultural control, 209–219; Danish Jewry, 263–290; Fremdstämmigenkartei, 396; informers, 178, 186; Jüdisches Krankenhaus Berlin, 157–192; statistics, 167, 185, 186, 192n, 218; underground life, 168, 186; Zentralstelle für jüdische Personenstandsregister, 404–405. *See also* Emigration, Persecuted Groups, Persecution, "Protected Jews".
Neher, André (social historian), 349
Neo-Nazism, 199
Netherlands Jewry, 3
Neubauer, Adolf (Bodleian librarian), 83–85, 96
'Neue Freie Presse', 422
Neuengamme concentration camp, 285, 286, 287
'Neues Deutschland' (DDR paper), 199n
'Neueste Nachrichten', 37
Neumann, Selmar (administrator, Jewish Hospital, Berlin), 177, 178
Neusner, Jacob, 355n
'[The] New York Times', 421
Niedersachsen: Jewish archives, 403n
Nielsen, Finn (Danish official), 285, 287n
Niemöller, Martin (pastor), 253
Nietzsche, Friedrich Wilhelm (philosopher), 195
1943 Relief Fund (Danish), 289
1944 Fund for Social and Humanitarian Purposes (Denmark), 279, 289
Nipperdey, Thomas (historian), 52
Nogaret (French Consul), 130–131
"Non-Aryan Christians" *see* Persecuted groups
Norddeutscher Bund, Jews of, 44, 59
Nordheim Jewish community, 16
Nordheimer family, 16
Nordic Social Democrats, 265
Nordrach (Baden) Jewish community, 161n
Norman, Edward, 258–259, 260
Norway, emigrants to, 299

General Index

Norwegian prisoners, 263, 285, 286
Nossig, Alfred (statistician), 71–72
Nowakowski, Friedrich (Austrian jurist), 149
Numerus clausus, 88, 109n
Nuremberg Jewish community, 15, 317
Nuremberg Laws *see* Anti-Jewish laws
Nurses, Jewish, 57, 69. *See also* Jüdisches Krankenhaus.

Österreichisch-Israelitische Union (ÖIU) (later Union österreichischer Israeliten), 411, 413–414, 421
'[Dr. Blochs] Österreichische Wochenschrift', 414, 421
Ohrenstein, Aaron (Bavarian rabbi), 312–314
Olympic Games, 248
Oppenheim (Danish lawyer), 282
Oppenheimer, Franz (Socialist economist, sociologist), 67
Oranienburg concentration camp, 159
'[Der] Orient', 41, 42
Orthodox Jewry, 37, 44, 54n, 64, 331, 336, 344, 351, 422
Ortweiler family, 16
Osnabrück: Nazis in, 206
Ostrowski, Siegfried (of the Jewish Hospital, Berlin), 158n, 166n
Oxaal, Ivar, 413

Pacifism, pacifists, 194, 195–196, 200, 238, 239
Palatinate Jewry, 396
Palestine Philharmonic Orchestra, 329
Palestine/Israel, 3, 323–339, 356; political parties, 332; Arabs in, 306, 327, 328, 333; British Mandate, 324, 327, 332; cultural life, 328–329, 334–335; illegal immigrants, 324, 326n; land purchase in, 328; Palestine/Israel, emigrants to, 227, 295, 296n, 323–339; State of Israel, 302–303, 306–307, 308, 324, 335; and the Yishuv, 323–336, 337, 339. *See also* Displaced Persons (illegal return).
Paltreu, 337
Pan-Germanism *see* Alldeutscher Verband
Papen, Franz von (German Chancellor), 207
Parin, Paul, 199n
'Pariser Tageblatt', 198n
Parkes, James (promoted Christian-Jewish relations), 232, 254
Parsons, Richard Godfrey (Anglican bishop), 244–245
Pasch (Jewish textile firm), 137
Pasch, Julius (Jewish leader in Innsbruck), 146
Paton, William (of International Missionary Council), 240, 241
Patriotism, Jewish, 3–14
Patton, George (US general), 294n
Paucker, Arnold, IX, 193, 194, 207, 352
Paul, Gerhard, 205, 208
Pauley, Bruce F., 109

Paulus-Bund, Vereinigung nichtarischer Christen, 241
Paumgarten, Karl (antisemitic journalist), 110n
Pavlevsky, Mary (of Joint), 300
Peasant Party (Austrian), 101
Pedlars *see* Traders
Pelinka, Anton, 112n
Perowne, A.W.T. (Bishop of Worcester), 255
Persecuted groups: "Mischlinge", 177, 185–187, 190, 191, 192n, 214, 242, 277; "Non-Aryan Christians", 238, 239, 241–242, 247, 252–254; "Versippte", 214. *See also* "Protected Jews".
Persecution and extermination, 218; in Austria, 409, 416, 419–420; Church of England and, 221–261; dismissals, 163–164, 179, 180, 227, 233, 257; economic persecution, 393, 420; public opinion, 143–144, 152–153, 215, 243; Wannsee Conference, 268, 274; "The Yellow Spot", 249. *See also* Deportation, Pogroms.
Pfefferkorn, Josef (SS officer), 126
Philanthropy, Jewish, 51–73
Philippson, Ludwig (editor), 41, 53
Philippson, Martin (head of Gesamtarchiv der deutschen Juden), 402
Philosophical Association, 251
Physicians, Jewish, 63, 105, 157–192 *passim*, 228, 328–329, 348, 372–373; deportation of, 164–168; dismissal, 163–164, 179, 180
Pick, Ludwig (pathologist), 164
Piekarz, Mendel, 351
Pietism, 9, 48; neo-Pietism, 35, 36, 37, 40, 44, 45, 46
Piffl, Friedrich Gustav (Cardinal), 110
Pineas, Hermann O. (psychiatrist, lived "underground"), 166, 168, 183
Pittman, Ruth, 241
Pius IX (Pope), 199
Pius XII (Pope), 199
Plat, Wolfgang, 416
Plattner, Franz (of Austrian Resistance), 136
Plotke, Julius (Frankfurt a. Main jurist), 56
Pogrom (November 1938), 159, 165, 169, 216, 333, 403: in Innsbruck, 119–153; murders during, 121–122, 126–134, 142; official reaction, 137–141, 143; Party Court proceedings, 140–141, 143; post-war trials, 147–151; synagogue destruction, 123, 128, 142, 144, 146: in Vienna, 419
Pogroms: in Eastern Europe, 223, 264, 420: medieval, 15
Poliakov, Léon (historian), 95
Polish Jewry, 3, 4, 68–69, 84–85, 343, 344, 357, 381–382; archives, 407, 408; expulsion, 121, 146. *See also* Ashkenasim, Emigration, Karaites.
Polla[c]k family, 16, 111
Pollak, Michael, 413
Pollak, Oskar (Austrian Socialist), 106
Polte (of Sicherheitsdienst), 141n, 145

Popp, Fritz (SS driver), 124n
Popper family (Pogrom victims), 122–123, 131n, 143, 150
Poznań Jewry, 33, 40, 70, 72, 343–344, 346
Praesternes Uofficielle Forening (Unofficial Association of Clergymen, illegal Danish body), 279, 280
Prague Jewry, 4, 5, 7–9, 10, 11, 12, 344, 352, 355. *See also* Jehudah Löw ben Bezalel.
Predazzo (Waffen-SS training camp), 134
Prestataire (French labour battalion), 199
Preußische Theaterkommission, 211
Printing, 352, 362–363
Progressive Party (Israel), 332
"Protected Jews": Behörden Liste (B Liste), 185n; Gelber Schein, 188; "protected mixed marriage", 146, 166n, 168, 171, 177, 178, 179, 185, 186, 187, 191, 192n, 277
Protestants, 251; in Britain, 221–261; in Germany, 222–223, 224, 227, 229, 232, 235, 241–242, 248, 251, 253, 254, 260
Prüfer, Franz Wilhelm (Gestapo official), 162n, 170n, 173
Prussian Jewry, 5, 13n, 33–50
Pulzer, Peter J. G., 414–415, 417

Quidde, Ludwig (pacifist), 194, 196
Quirsfeld, Eberhard (of SS), 124n

Rabbinics, 344–359 *passim*, 364–368; Rabbinism, 92
Radford, Mary (assoc. of A.S. Fiske), 248
Rahm, Karl (Theresienstadt commandant), 275, 288
Rahmer, ?Moritz (of Deutsch-Israelitischer Gemeindebund), 56n
Raiffeisen, Friedrich Wilhelm (founder of agricultural cooperatives), 23
Ramersdorfer, Sepp (Pogrom criminal), 150
Rashi (Solomon Yitzhak) (medieval scholar), 352
Rashkes, [Dr.] (director of Rothschild Hospital, Vienna), 170n, 180
"Rassenschande", 140
Rassinier, Paul (writer), 199
Rath, Ernst vom (German diplomat), 121, 124, 125, 126, 129, 130, 142, 217
Rathenau, Walther (German statesman), 63
Ravensbrück concentration camp, 273
Reading, Rufus Daniel Isaacs, Marquess of (British jurist), 227, 228, 232
Rebbert, Joseph (antisemite), 47
'[The] Record' (Anglican paper), 224, 227, 241–242
Red Cross: Danish, 273, 278, 279, 280, 285; German, 280, 282; International, 280, 282, 283; prisoners' rescue convoy, 263, 285–289;
Swedish, 285, 286; Theresienstadt visit, 280–284
Reform Judaism, 37–38, 41–44, 81n, 95
'Regensburger Neueste Nachrichten', 196
Regensburger, Rosi (librarian), 403n
Reichmann, Hans (lawyer, C.V. Syndikus), 193n, 201, 207
Reichsärztekammer, 164
Reichsbanner Schwarz-Rot-Gold, 204, 205n
Reichsinstitut für die Geschichte des neuen Deutschlands, 395
Reichskulturkammer (RKK), 209, 211, 213–214, 217, 218, 219
'Reichspost', 108, 109, 110n, 422
Reichssicherheitshauptamt (RSHA), 137, 140, 141n, 159, 160–162, 182n, 218, 277, 398–399, 404, 405; Judenforschungsinstitut des Sicherheitsdienstes, 405; Sect. IV B, 4, 160, 162, 172, 182n, 185n, 186, 188–189, 191, 192, 398
Reichssippenamt, 395, 398, 406
Reichsstelle für Sippenforschung, 396, 404–405
Reichsverband der jüdischen Kulturbünde (later Jüdischer Kulturbund in Deutschland), 213, 214–215, 216
Reichsvereinigung der Juden in Deutschland, 160, 161–163, 167, 179, 180, 182–183, 185, 188, 189, 398, 406
Reichsvertretung der deutschen Juden (der Juden in Deutschland), X
Reifmann, Jacob (Maskil), 343, 355
Reiner, Elhanan, 357
Reinhardt, Max (theatre director), 105
Reinharz, Jehuda, 63
Reitter, Gudrun, 418
Rendl, Herbert (SS officer), 127
Rennau (Obersturmbannführer), 287, 288
Renthe-Fink, Cecil von (Nazi plenipotentiary in Denmark), 266, 267, 269
Republikanischer Schutzbund (Austria), 106
Reschke, Max (teacher), 171n
Resistance to Nazism: Jews and, 268, 330; by SS-men, 132, 135, 136. *See also* Aid to the persecuted, Denmark.
Restitution, 147, 297, 304–306, 324–325, 420; Claims Conference, 297, 303, 304, 305
Retzius, Andreas (Swedish anatomist), 78
Revolutionäre Sozialisten (Austrian underground party), 116
Revolutions: French, 18, 410; 1848, 45, 51, 416; Germany (1918–1919), 195
Rhineland Jewry, 186
Ribbentrop, Joachim von (Nazi Foreign Minister), 257, 259–260, 266, 267, 268, 269, 270
Rickert (Swedish ambassador), 287
Riedl, Alois (janitor), 142
Riga region, 172, 187n
Rimalt, Elimelech S. (rabbi), 144, 146
"Ritual murder", 47, 239, 417
Rivkin, Ellis, 222n

Robertson, Charles Grant (historian), 250
Rohling, August (antisemitic theologian), 47–48, 417
Romberg (Court Purveyor to Sachsen-Meiningen), 23
Ropp, Freiherr von der (head of Anglo-German Brotherhood), 257
Rose, George (British diplomat), 34, 36
Rosenbaum (SA-Hauptscharführer), 130
Rosenberg, Alfred (Nazi ideologue), 240, 256–257
Rosenberg, Erich (Joint official), 300, 315–316
Rosenberg, Oskar (paediatrician), 166
Rosenblüth, Felix (Pinchas Rosen) (Zionist leader), 339
Rosenkranz, Herbert, 419
Rosenstein, Paul (surgeon, director of Jewish Hospital, Berlin), 158, 166n
Rossel, Maurice (of International Red Cross), 283
Rosting, Helmer (Director of Danish Red Cross), 272, 273
Roth, Joseph (novelist), 105
Rothschild, Lionel Walter, 2nd baron, 247
Rothschild, Louis (Viennese banker), 104
Rozenblit, Marsha L., 104n, 410n, 411
Rüdiger, Ernst (of Austrian Gestapo), 120
Ruedl, Hans (Pogrom criminal), 150
Rügheimer family, 16
Ruge, Arnold (writer), 35, 44
Ruppin, Arthur (sociologist, Zionist leader), 63, 66, 67, 72, 90n
Rural and Suburban Settlement Company (RASSCO), 337
Rural Jewry, 15–28 *passim*, 66, 256. *See also* Agriculture.
Russell, Bertrand Arthur William, 3rd Earl (philosopher), 200
Russian Jewry, 13n, 80, 82, 88, 223, 264, 343, 344. *See also* Emigration.
Rust, Bernhard (Nazi minister), 211
Rutgen, Herbert, 418
Rutherford, Ernest, 1st baron (physicist), 250

SA, 125, 203, 206, 212; in Austria, 119, 124, 125, 129–130, 134, 138, 140
'Saat auf Hoffnung' (missionary journal), 47
Sabbatai Zvi, 346, 351: Sabbatianism, 350–351, 356, 358, 359, 384–385
Sachsen: archives, 392, 397
Sachsen-Meiningen Jewry: Edict of 1811, 15–32; Decree of 1822, 23; Jews' Law of 1856, 25; Decree of 1862, 23; status, 18, 25–26
Sachsen-Weimar Jewry, 25
Sachsenhausen concentration camp, 159, 178n, 273, 278, 283
Sack, Beracha, 350
Safrian, Hans, 419
"St. Louis" (ship), 299n

Salomon, Gotthold (preacher), 81n
Samter, Hermann (eye-witness from Jewish Hospital, Berlin), 176n
Samuel the Nagid (medieval Jewish general), 9
Samuel, Herbert Louis, 1st Viscount (Palestine High Commissioner), 232
Sander, Werner (cantor), 406, 407
Sapir, Boris (Joint official), 301n
Saurwein, Walter (SS-Scharführer), 127
Scandinavia, emigrants to, 264–265
Scavenius, Erik (Danish Foreign Minister), 266, 268, 269
Schacht, Hjalmar Horace Greeley (Reichsbank president), 214, 246
Schärf, Adolf (Austrian politician), 116
Scheinfeld, Julius (administrator, Jewish Hospital, Berlin), 176n, 178
Schenkel family (Pogrom victims), 150
Schiller, Friedrich von (poet), 20
Schindler family (Pogrom victims), 150
Schintlholzer, Alois (SS officer), 122n, 127, 134, 138, 148, 150
Schlesinger family, 16
Schmidl, Erwin, 417
Schmidt, Elfriede, 420
Schneidmadl, Heinrich (Austrian politician), 116
Schnitzler, Arthur (writer), 105, 110
Schönberg, Arnold (composer), 105
'Schönere Zukunft', 422
Schönerer, Georg von (antisemitic Austrian politician), 411, 412
Schöpf, Johann (Pogrom criminal), 150
Scholem, Gershom [Gerhard] (authority on Jewish mysticism), 344, 351, 358
Schorsch, Ismar, 75
Schorske, Carl E., 412
Schulz, Stefan (missionary), 49
Schulze (antisemitic pastor), 46–47
Schuschnigg, Kurt von (Austrian politician), 416, 419
Schutzbund (in Austria), 117
"Schutzhaft", 145
"Schutzjuden", 15, 17, 397, 400, 401
Schwarz family (Pogrom victims), 150
Schwarz, Karoline (nurse), 172n
Schwarz, Rudolf (SS officer), 127, 150
Schwarzkopf (manufacturer), 147n
Schwarzschild, Leopold (editor), 198
Schwendler, Friedrich August (Sachsen-Meiningen official), 27, 29, 30, 31–32
Schweriner, Arthur (editor), 202
Scientists, Jewish, 372
Scult, Mel, 38
Šedinová, Jiřina, 348
Seesen Jewish community, 37
"Sefer Hasidim", 9–10
Seidenman, Leonard (Joint official), 300n, 307n, 312, 316–317, 318, 319

Seipel, Ignaz (Austrian Chancellor), 107–108, 109, 110, 111n, 113
Seipt, Alois (Pogrom criminal), 150
Seitz, Karl "Pollaksohn" (Mayor of Vienna), 111, 113, 116
Self-perception, Jewish, 51–73 *passim*; and antisemitism, 61–63, 68–69; identity, 73, 105, 107; self-hatred, 63
Seligmann, Erich (hygienist), 179
Senfft-Pilsach, Ernst von (Conservative politician), 34
Sepharad (Sardis, Sfard), 95–96
Sephardim: and Ashkenasim, 3–4, 16, 70–96
Sermons, 3–14, 39, 345, 371; humour, 4
Seven Years' War, 5, 6–7, 13, 17
Severing, Carl (Socialist politician, minister), 206, 207
Shakespeare, William, 195
Shatz, Rivkah, 349, 355
Shepsko (dentist), 168
Shmeruk, Chone, 352
Shohet, Azriel, 358, 359
Shulchan Aruch, 346, 357, 365
Sieff Institute *see* Weizmann Institute
Siegmund-Schultze, Friedrich Wilhelm (theologian, social politician), 247
Silberstein (educationalist), 57
Silesian Jewry, 33, 69, 70, 408
Simmershausen Jewish community, 21
Simpson, William (promoted Christian-Jewish relations), 254
Singer, Charles (writer), 250, 252
Singer, Kurt (neurologist, opera-house director), 212, 216
"Sippen" *see* Reichssippenamt, Reichsstelle . . .
Sirkes, Joel (rabbi), 346, 349
Six, Franz (economist, in Sicherheitsdienst), 405
Social democracy, 196, 198, 200, 264; in Denmark, 265, 266, 270. *See also* Nordic, Sozialdemokratische . . .
Social science, Jewish, 71–73
Socialists, 239, 356, 357; in Austria, 101–120; Jews as, 236
Solidaritätswerk, 338
Solomon Shlemel ben Hayyim (kabbalist), 350
Sørensen, Erik Pontoppidan (convoy driver), 285n
Sorkin, David, 57
South America, emigrants to, 251
Sozialdemokratische Arbeiterpartei (SDAP) (Austria), 99–118, 412, 413; Sozialistische Arbeiterjugend, 115
Sozialdemokratische Partei Deutschlands (SPD), 106, 114, 194, 195, 204, 205n, 206–207, 208
Sozialistische Einheitspartei Deutschlands (SED), 391, 399, 406
Spanish Jewry, 354, 381; Marranos, 86. *See also* Iberian Peninsula

Spann (SS officer, in Innsbruck Gestapo), 124
Spencer, Herbert (philosopher), 195
Spener, Philipp Jakob (Pietist, historian), 48
Spindel family (Pogrom victims), 150
Spira, Nathan (kabbalist), 350
SS, 183, 203, 212, 213, 242, 270, 274, 276, 281, 282, 287; in Austria, 119–153; Sicherheitsdienst (SD), 120, 122–125, 131, 137, 141, 142, 144, 145, 213, 216n, 217; Studentensturm, 129, 133; Waffen-SS, 132–133, 134, 136
Stahl, Friedrich Julius (jurist, Conservative politician), 34, 46
'[Der] Standard', 117n
Stanzl (SA-Obersturmführer), 130
Starhemberg, Ernst Rüdiger (leader of Austrian Heimwehr), 111n
Statistics, Jewish, 71–72; Fremdstämmigenkartei, 396; immigrants to Palestine, 324n
Stauning, Thorvald (Danish politician), 266
Stecher (Austrian detective and Gestapo man), 135–136
Stecher, Irmgard (wife of detective), 135, 136
[von] Stein family, 16, 20
Stieda, Ludwig (anatomist), 81
Stifter, Adalbert (Austrian writer), 195
Stiftung Neue Synagoge Berlin – Centrum Judaicum, 407
'[Die] Stimme' 421
Stoecker, Adolf (antisemite, Court preacher, Berlin), 224
Stöcker, Helene (pacifist), 196
Stoiber, Hubert (SA officer), 130
Stolberg, Anton von (revivalist), 35–36
Strack, Hermann Leberecht (theologian), 48
Strasser, Gregor and Otto (Nazi politicians), 210
Strauss, Hermann (director, Jewish Hospital, Berlin), 158, 166, 179
Strauss, Richard (composer), 215
Streicher, Julius (Nazi leader, editor 'Der Stürmer'), 239, 243, 256–257
Student Christian Movement, 231, 232
Studentensturm (SS student body), 129, 133
Students, 105: fraternities, 129, 133, 149
'[Der] Stürmer', 239–240, 242, 244, 249, 256–257
Stuhlpfarrer, Karl, 416
Stutthof concentration camp, 273, 277, 278, 283
Styrian Jewry, 418
'Süddeutsche Monatshefte', 196n
Suevia (fraternity), 129, 133, 149
Suicide, 63, 174–175, 176n, 178, 180
Svenningsen, Nils (Danish official), 271, 273, 277–278
Swabian Jewry, 31, 396
Sweden: and Jews, 265, 270, 272, 289
Switzerland, emigrants to, 198–199

Täubler, Eugen (historian), 394n, 402
'[Das] Tagebuch', 198n
'Tages-Anzeiger' (Swiss paper), 199, 202n

General Index 557

'Tagwacht' (Swiss paper), 199
Talmud, talmudists, 43, 58–59, 84–85n, 345–347, 349, 351, 358, 365–366
Tandler, Julius (Austrian Socialist, anatomist), 106, 111n
Tapavicza, Theodor (physician, SA-Obersturmführer), 130
'Tarbiz', 354
Tatlow, Tissington (Anglican Dean), 231
Tchernowitz, Chaim (talmudist), 346
Teachers, Jewish, 21–22, 105, 393
Technion (Israel Institute of Technology), Haifa, 328
Teichler (missionary), 39–40
Temple, William (Archbishop of York, later of Canterbury), 232, 235, 236, 243, 248, 255
Textile workers, Jewish, 27–28
Thadden, Adolf von (revivalist), 34, 45
Theilhaber, Felix A. (sociologist, Zionist), 63, 72, 90n
Theremin, Franz (Court Chaplain), 34
Theresienstadt ghetto, 166n, 167n, 170n, 172, 175, 177, 178, 179n, 196, 274–290; conditions, 275–276, 279, 280–284, 290; "cultural life", 276, 281, 283, 288; Danes and, 263–290; Nazi film, 284; Red Cross visit, 280–284; rescue of prisoners, 263, 285–289. *See also* Deportation.
Thile, Ludwig Gustav von (general, Prussian minister), 45
Tholuck, Friedrich August (theologian, Orientalist), 34, 37–38, 44
Thompson, David, 221n
Thuringian Jewry, 15
Tietze, Hans (historian), 415
'[The] Times', 223, 233, 237, 243, 249, 250, 251, 252, 253
Toury, Jacob, 25, 413–414
Trade unions, 103, 203, 204, 205n
Traders, Jewish, 22, 23, 24, 27, 62, 64
Treblinka extermination camp, 296
'[Das] Tribunal', 204n
Truman, Harry S. (US President), 301
Tuch, Ernst (son of Gustav T.), 65
Tuch, Gustav (economist, social worker), 56, 57, 65, 67
Tuchmann, Emil (head of Jewish health service, Vienna), 180, 184
Turkey/Ottoman Empire, Jews in, 3, 86–87, 354, 381
Turniansky, Chava, 352
Tyrolean Jewry, 120, 122, 123, 125, 145, 146, 148, 151, 153, 154, 418. *See also* Innsbruck.

Ullmann, Alfons (Pogrom criminal), 150
Unabhängige Sozialdemokratische Partei Deutschlands (USPD), 195
Unger, David (Jewish mathematician), 35
Unger, Manfred, 393
Union österreichischer Juden, 414

United Committee of the Yishuv, 337
United Jewish Appeal (UJA), 321
United Nations Relief and Rehabilitation Administration (UNRRA), 295, 300
United States, emigration to, 24, 86, 93, 198n, 297n, 308
Universities, British, 250–251, 256

van Dam, Hendrick George (Secretary-General, Zentralrat), 298, 399, 304–305, 318
Vansittart, Robert Gilbert, 1st baron (British diplomat), 226, 231
Venedey, Hans (exile in Switzerland), 198
Venstre (Danish farmers' party), 266
Verein für Jüdische Statistik, 71, 72
Verein für Sozialpolitik, 69, 71
Verein zur Abwehr des Antisemitismus (Abwehrverein), 197
Verein zur Förderung der Bodenkultur unter den Juden Deutschlands (VFB), 62, 65, 66, 67
Verein zur Verbreitung und Förderung der Handwerke unter den Juden, 65, 68
Vienna: Allgemeines Verwaltungsarchiv, 422; University, 422, 423
Viennese Jewish community, 5, 99–118, 180, 218, 409–423 *passim*; Rothschild Hospital, 170, 172, 180, 184
[Rudolf] Virchow Stiftung, 88
Vocational training, 19, 27, 51, 54–55, 57, 60, 61–62, 64–71, 73, 326, 337
Völkisch ideas, 66, 89–90n, 100, 132, 258; "Aryans", 82, 86, 100, 112, 123, 256–257
'Völkischer Beobachter', 210
Vogt, Carl (naturalist, physician), 78–79
'[Die] Volksstimme', 422
Vorarlberg Jewry, 122, 125, 148, 153, 154
'Vossische Zeitung', 198n
'Vrij Nederland', 117n

Wachter, Andreas, 423n
Wagner, Richard (composer), 215
'[Die] Wahrheit', 421
Waidacher, Vinzenz (SA officer, Innsbruck police chief), 124, 129, 130
Waldheim, Kurt, 99, 116n, 409, 413, 416, 421
Walldorf Jewish community, 15, 16, 28
Wallnöfer, Eduard, 153n
Walter, Bruno (conductor), 212
Walter, Hilde (journalist), 198
Walzl, August, 418
War Crimes Trials, 128, 147–151, 176, 179, 182
Warburg, Otto (botanist, Zionist leader), 66n, 67
Warsaw Ghetto, 219
Wassermann, Henry, 57
Way, Lewis (emancipationist), 45
Weber (antisemitic pastor), 47
Weil, Bruno (jurist, C.V. leader), 304–305, 313n
Weimar Germany, Jews in, 114, 193–208

Weininger, Otto (philosopher), 63
Weintraut, Georg (Pogrom criminal), 150
Weinzierl, Erika, 420
Weisbach, Augustin (physician), 79–80
Weissenberg, Samuel (ethnologist), 79n, 88–89
Weissensee work colony, 54–55, 61–62
Weissler, Chava, 345, 353
Weitzmann, Walter R., 413, 414
Weizmann, Chaim (chemist, first President of Israel), 323, 324, 327; Weizmann Institute, 328
'[Die] Weltbühne', 198n
Weltsch, Robert (editor 'Jüdische Rundschau', Zionist, founder-editor LBI Year Book), IX, 298n
Werfel, Franz (poet, dramatist), 105
West, Rebecca (Cicily Andrews) (writer), 225–226
'Western Mail', 237
Westphalian Jewry, 19, 37, 186
Wetzel, Juliane, 294, 319
Wetzlar, Isaac (merchant, Yiddishist), 85n
White, Dan S., 194
Whiteside, Andrew K., 412n
Wichern, Johann (Lutheran minister), 52
'Wiener Morgenzeitung' (later 'Die Stimme'), 421
'Wiener Stimmen' (formerly 'Spätnachmittagszeitung für Nichtjuden'), 108
Wiesenthal, Simon, 409, 421
Wilson, Arnold (Right-wing British politician), 250
Windmüller, Carl (physician), 176
Winter (director, Reichsarchiv), 404
Wissenschaft des Judentums, 75, 84, 85n, 95
Wistrich, Robert Solomon, 410–411, 413
Witek, Hans, 419
Wittgenstein, Ludwig (philosopher), 105
Witzleben, Job von (general), 33–34
Wöhrn, Fritz (Nazi supervisor of the Jewish Hospital, Berlin), 160, 176, 177, 178n, 179–180, 182–183, 191
Wolfsohn (physician), 168
Woltmann, Ludwig (writer on race, physician), 92n

Women, Jewish, 56–57, 69, 93–94, 167, 353, 356, 357
World Alliance for International Friendship through the Churches, 228, 237, 247, 251; British Council, 230
'World Film News', X
World Jewish Organisation, 324
World Zionist Organisation (WZO), 66, 67, 337
Worms Jewish community, 210, 394
Würzburg Jewish community, 15
Wulkany Institute, 328
Wyneken, Gustav (educationalist), 195

Yahil, Leni (historian), 270n
Yellow Star, 266
Yerushalmi, Yosef, 359
Yiddish, 4, 22, 33, 87, 96, 264, 295, 352–353, 354, 356, 358, 375; historiography, 344, 373; literature, 85n, 344–345, 348, 352–353, 354, 356–357, 375–379
'Yorkshire Post', 247
Young Workers of Austria, 133
Youth Aliyah, 323, 334, 337

'Zeitschrift für Demographie und Statistik der Juden', 72
Zentrales Parteiarchiv der PDS, 393
Zentralrat für die Juden in Deutschland, 298, 304, 309, 318
Zentralstelle für jüdische Auswanderung, 145
Zfatman-Biller, Sarah, 353
Zinberg, Israel (chemist), 344
Zionism, Zionists, 63, 66–67, 72–73, 77, 89, 96, 104, 105, 109, 122, 129, 144, 264, 323–339 *passim*, 410, 412, 414, 421: German Zionists in Palestine, 323–324, 330–339 *passim*; writers on race, 89–90, 92n; and Yiddishists, 358
Zionistische Vereinigung für Deutschland (ZVfD), 67
Zipfel, Ernst (director of Prussian State Archives), 396, 403, 404, 405
Zollschan, Ignaz (anthropologist), 91n, 92
Zunz, Leopold (Berlin scholar, headmaster), 3
Zweig, Stefan (writer), 105
Zwilsky, Erich (Lustig's assistant), 177

JEWISH STUDIES

There is a Place on Earth *A Woman in Birkenau*
GIULIANA TEDESCHI (Translated by Tim Parks)

'...instantly joins the ranks of the classics...Deeply harrowing, but with unexpected flashes of optimism, this beautifully written book...is essential reading' *Cosmopolitan*

1993   0 413 45711 7   £9.99   Paperback

Perpetrators Victims Bystanders *The Jewish Catastrophe 1933-45*
RAUL HILBERG

A work of ineradicable impact by one of the most widely respected historians of the Holocaust. This is the grave and compelling story of the people who caused, carried out, experienced, survived and witnessed the Holocaust.

1993   0 413 45741 9   £20   Hardback

Piety and Power *The World of Jewish Fundamentalism*
DAVID LANDAU

The definitive book on the world of the ultra-orthodox Jews. David Landau describes life in the *haredi* ghettos in London, New York and Jerusalem, where hassidic rabbis reign supreme and strict rules govern every aspect of *haredi* belief.

1993   0 436 24156 0   £20   Hardback

Secker & Warburg

methuen

AVAILABLE FROM ALL GOOD BOOKSHOPS

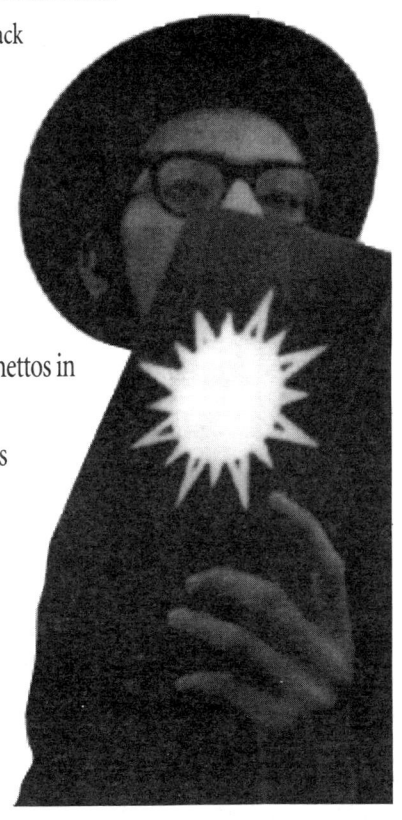

RECENT PUBLICATIONS OF THE LEO BAECK INSTITUTE

Juden und deutsche Arbeiterbewegung bis 1933
Soziale Utopien und religiös-kulturelle Traditionen

Editors: Ludger Heid & Arnold Paucker

This new symposium volume on Jews and the German labour movement contains the enlarged papers and additional contributions of a conference sponsored by the Steinheim Institute, Duisburg, and the London LBI in Mülheim in December 1990.

Schriftenreihe wissenschaftlicher Abhandlungen des Leo Baeck Instituts 49

J. C. B. Mohr (Paul Siebeck), Tübingen, 1992

Hardback, X, 246 pp.

Second Chance
Two Centuries of German-speaking Jews in the United Kingdom

Co-ordinating Editor: Werner E. Mosse
Editors: Julius Carlebach, Gerhard Hirschfeld, Aubrey Newman, Arnold Paucker, Peter Pulzer

Emigration and Reception   Social and Cultural Impact
     Paths to Acceptance   (37 Contributions)

Schriftenreihe wissenschaftlicher Abhandlungen des Leo Baeck Instituts 48

J. C. B. Mohr (Paul Siebeck), Tübingen, 1991.

Hardback, XIV, 658 pp., illus.

BOOKS FROM MOHR: Jewish Life and Fate throughout the Ages

Hanne Trautner-Kromann
Shield and Sword
Jewish Polemics against Christianity and the Christians in France and Spain 1100 – 1500

The description and interpretation of Jewish polemical texts is the first attempt to give an overall account of the reasons for the Jewish polemics in France and Spain in a Christian environment and in a period decisive of the history of European Jewry in the subsequent centuries.
1993. 284 pages (est.) (Texts and Studies in Medieval and Early Modern Judaism).
ISBN 3-16-145995-4 cloth
DM 160.00 (est.) – May

Franz D. Lucas/Heike Frank
Michael Sachs – Der konservative Mittelweg
Leben und Werk des Berliner Rabbiners zur Zeit der Emanzipation

Michael Sachs, charismatic preacher, thorough humanist, acclaimed translator, accomplished poet is symtomatic for German Jewry in the time of Emancipation which set the pace for its greatest glory and ultimate total destruction. Sachs struggled for the unity of Judaism, between the Reform on the left and the Orthodoxy on the right and for a conservative unified structure and philosophy.
1992. V, 161 pages. ISBN 3-16-145888-5 cloth DM 98.00

Second Chance
Two Centuries of German-speaking Jews in the United Kingdom
Edited by Werner E. Mosse with Julius Carlebach, Gerhard Hirschfeld, Aubrey Newman, Arnold Paucker, Peter Pulzer

The first systematic attempt to evaluate the German-Jewish experience in Britain, a comprehensive review of a remarkable chapter in German-Jewish and English history.
1991. XII, 654 pages (Schriftenreihe wissenschaftlicher Abhandlungen des Leo Baeck Instituts 48). ISBN 3-16-145741-2 cloth
DM 128.00

**J.C.B. MOHR
(PAUL SIEBECK)
TÜBINGEN**

The Language and Culture Atlas of Ashkenazic Jewry

Prepared and published under the aegis of an Editorial Collegium: Marvin Herzog (editor-in-chief), Vera Baviskar ל״ת, Ulrike Kiefer, Robert Neumann, Wolfgang Putschke, Andrew Sunshine, and Uriel Weinreich ל״ת

Vol. 1: Historical and Theoretical Foundations
1992. XIV, 136, *8–*1, *IV–*I pages. Cloth DM 216.–. ISBN 3-484-73003-x

Vol. 2: Research Tools
Ca. 180 pages. Cloth DM 242.–. ISBN 3-484-73004-8
Size: 34 x 25 cms. ISBN for complete edition (10 vols.) 3-484-73013-7.

»... what is familiar in one year may be thrust to the brink of oblivion in the next ... What was too obvious for study only yesterday has suddenly become precious. ... what we do not collect in the coming decade or so will be lost forwever« (Uriel Weinreich).

European Jewry was largely destroyed during World War II, and its survivors were displaced by emigration and internal migration. It was a matter of greatest urgency to reconstruct the geography of Ashkenazic folk culture and of European Yiddish while reliable testimony could still be gathered from emigrant informants.
»The Language and Culture Atlas of Ashkenazic Jewry« (LCAAJ), designed towards this end by Uriel Weinreich, is based on an investigation conducted among emigrant informants. Since Weinreich's death in 1967, the investigation has been directed by Marvin Herzog, assisted by Vera Baviskar until her death in 1987. Its ›design‹ reflects the diversity of Weinreich's contributions to Yiddish studies and to the theories of bilingual dialectology, structural dialectology, and the study of language and culture ›at-a-distance‹

Volume 1 of the atlas, the first in a series of ten volumes (five volumes with subvolumes), includes an annotated version of Weinreich's »Outlines of Yiddish Dialectology«, a formulation of some of the linguistic problems underlying the investigations as a whole, accompanied by a set of 80 composite maps which illustrate phonological variation in Yiddish of Central and Eastern Europe before World War II. Volume 2 contains the methodological tools employed during the investigation: the stabilized master questionnaire, its regional abridgements, the westerm questionnaire and ethnographic supplement, indexes to the questionnaires, to the linguistic questions underlying the investigation, to the geographic locations, and to the respondents who were interviewed. Together, the ten volumes will portray the regionalization of the Yiddish language and its associated folk culture, permitting its comparison with the geographic make-up of the languages and cultures of the coterritorial non-Jewish societies in Central and Eastern Europe, and shedding important light on the interplay of areal communication conditions with other causes of cultural variation.

Max Niemeyer Verlag
P.O. Box 2140 · D-72011 Tübingen

RECENT PUBLICATIONS

PRODUCED IN CONJUNCTION WITH THE LONDON LEO BAECK INSTITUTE

Zur Geschichte der jüdischen Frau in Deutschland

Editor: Julius Carlebach

Conference papers of a seminar held in Heidelberg, March 1991, sponsored jointly by the Hochschule für Jüdische Studien, Heidelberg, and the London LBI.

Articles in both English and German.

Metropol-Verlag, Berlin, 1993

Paperback, 272 pp., illus.

Jüdische Unternehmer in Deutschland im 19. und 20. Jahrhundert

Editors: Werner E. Mosse & Hans Pohl

Conference papers of a seminar held in Königswinter, April 1989, sponsored jointly by the Friedrich Naumann Stiftung and the London LBI, and additional contributions

Articles in both English and German.

Zeitschrift für Unternehmensgeschichte - Beiheft 64
Franz Steiner Verlag, Stuttgart, 1992

Paperback, 376 pp.